W9-AYF-270

# Fodor's

# THE COMPLETE GUIDE TO EUROPEAN CRUISES

Where to Stay and Eat
for All Budgets

Must-See Sights
and Local Secrets

Ratings You Can Trust

## FODOR'S THE COMPLETE GUIDE TO EUROPEAN CRUISES

**Editorial Contributors:** Lola Akinmade-Åkerström, Alexia Amvrazi, Lindsay Bennett, Linda Coffman, David Dunne, Jane Foster, Mike Gonzalez, Liz Humphreys, Jennifer Ladonne, Bruce Leimsidor, Giulia Pines, Anne-Sophie Redisch, Ellin Stein, Jessica Steinberg, Paul Sullivan, Joanna Styles, Gelu Sulugiuc, Victoria Tang, Adrian Vrettos, Dorota Wąsik

**Editors:** Douglas Stallings (lead editor), Alexis Kelly, John Rambow

**Production Editor:** Carrie Parker

**Maps & Illustrations:** David Lindroth, *cartographer;* Rebecca Baer, *map editor;* William Wu, *information graphics*

**Design:** Fabrizio La Rocca, *creative director*; Tina Malaney, Chie Ushio, Jessica Ramirez, *designers*; Melanie Marin, *associate director of photography;* Jennifer Romains, *photo research*

**Cover Photo:** Front cover: Peter Adams/awl-images [Description: Santorini, Cyclades Islands, Greece] Back cover (from left to right): Plotnikov | Dreamstime.com; atm2003/ Shutterstock; Britta Kasholm-Tengve/iStockphoto. Spine: Rechitan Sorin/Shutterstock.

**Production Manager:** Angela L. McLean

## COPYRIGHT

Copyright © 2013 by Fodor's Travel, a division of Random House, Inc.

Fodor's is a registered trademark of Random House, Inc.

All rights reserved. Published in the United States by Fodor's Travel, a division of Random House, Inc., and in Canada by Random House of Canada, Limited, Toronto. Distributed by Random House, Inc., New York.

No maps, illustrations, or other portions of this book may be reproduced in any form without written permission from the publisher.

3rd Edition

ISBN 978–0–89141–930–3

ISSN 1939–9936

## SPECIAL SALES

This book is available at special discounts for bulk purchases for sales promotions or premiums. Special editions, including personalized covers, excerpts of existing books, and corporate imprints, can be created in large quantities for special needs. For more information, write to Special Markets/Premium Sales, 1745 Broadway, MD 3-1, New York, NY 10019, or e-mail specialmarkets@randomhouse.com.

## AN IMPORTANT TIP & AN INVITATION

Although all prices, opening times, and other details in this book are based on information supplied to us at press time, changes occur all the time in the travel world, and Fodor's cannot accept responsibility for facts that become outdated or for inadvertent errors or omissions. So **always confirm information when it matters,** especially if you're making a detour to visit a specific place. Your experiences—positive and negative— matter to us. If we have missed or misstated something, **please write to us.** Share your opinion instantly through our online feedback center at fodors.com/contact-us.

PRINTED IN THE UNITED STATES OF AMERICA

10 9 8 7 6 5 4 3 2

# CONTENTS

# ABOUT THIS BOOK

## Fodor's Ratings

Everything in this guide is worth doing—we don't cover what isn't—but exceptional sights, hotels, and restaurants are recognized with additional accolades. Fodor's Choice★ indicates our top recommendations; ★ highlights places we deem highly recommended. Care to nominate a new place? Visit Fodors.com/contact-us.

## Trip Costs

We list prices wherever possible to help you budget well. Hotel and restaurant price categories from $ to $$$$ are noted alongside each recommendation. For hotels, we include the lowest cost of a standard double room in high season. For restaurants, we cite the average price of a main course at dinner or, if dinner isn't served, at lunch. For attractions, we always list adult admission fees; discounts are usually available for children, students, and senior citizens.

## Hotels

Our local writers vet every hotel to recommend the best overnights in each price category, from budget to expensive. Unless otherwise specified, you can expect private bath, phone, and TV in your room. For expanded hotel reviews, facilities, and deals visit Fodors.com.

## Restaurants

Unless we state otherwise, restaurants are open for lunch and dinner daily. We mention dress code only when there's a specific requirement and reservations only when they're essential or not accepted. To make restaurant reservations, visit Fodors.com.

## Credit Cards

The hotels and restaurants in this guide typically accept credit cards. If not, we'll say so.

| Listings | | Hotels & Restaurants | Outdoors |
|---|---|---|---|
| ★ Fodor's Choice | ✉ E-mail | 🏨 Hotel | 🏌 Golf |
| ★ Highly recommended | ✇ Admission fee | ⤵ Number of rooms | ⛺ Camping |
| ⊠ Physical address | ☉ Open/closed times | ⌂ Facilities | **Other** |
| ✛ Directions or Map coordinates | Ⓜ Metro stations | ⦿ Meal plans | ☕ Family-friendly |
| ⌖ Mailing address | ⊟ No credit cards | ✕ Restaurant | ⇨ See also |
| ☎ Telephone | | ⌲ Reservations | ⊠ Branch address |
| ⎙ Fax | | 👔 Dress code | ☞ Take note |
| ⊕ On the Web | | ↘ Smoking | |

# BEST BETS

## Best Cruise Line: Mainstream

■ **Lindblad Expeditions.** A multifaceted strategic partnership with the National Geographic Society enables Lindblad travelers to remain engaged, active explorers who care about the planet.

■ **Norwegian Cruise Line.** Noted for their family-friendly accommodations, specialty dining, and outstanding entertainment, the line gets high marks from passengers of all ages.

■ **Royal Caribbean International.** The line appeals to families with its high-energy entertainment, extensive sports facilities, youth programs, and even nurseries for toddlers and babies.

## Best Cruise Line: Premium

■ **AmaWaterways.** A leader in its niche, this specialty 15-vessel cruise line is all the rage with exceptional staterooms and itineraries that showcase not only Europe, but also Vietnam and Zambezi.

■ **Holland America Line.** Traditional cruise enthusiasts find that HAL hits the right note with gracious, art-filled ships that also include all the latest high-tech gadgets.

■ **Celebrity Cruises.** For sheer beauty and excellent cuisine, Celebrity ships deliver a quality experience in modern surroundings.

■ **Sea Cloud Cruises.** Hamburg-based Sea Cloud Cruises offers a four-masted barque, magnificent windjammers, and a self-proclaimed five-star floating hotel for cruises on the Rhine, Main, Danube, and Black Sea to spectacular destinations.

## Best Cruise Line: Luxury

■ **Compagnie du Ponant.** Expect an exceptional, intimate experience aboard luxurious, all-inclusive yacht cruises to inaccessible worldwide locations and remote ports of call.

■ **Hebridean Island Cruises.** Since 1986, this niche company has been offering guests the highest standards of service with a price tag to match, all in the British Isles and Ireland.

■ **Seabourn Cruise Line.** Divine dining options and posh suite accommodations set theses ships apart.

■ **Silversea Cruises.** Butlers assigned to every suite add an extra level of pampering on luxuriously appointed vessels.

■ **Regent Seven Seas Cruises.** In the luxury segment Regent offers the most all-inclusive cruises, even including all shore excursions in the fare.

■ **Tauck World Discovery.** Among river cruise lines, Tauck stands out for its exceptionally choreographed itineraries focused on culture and destination.

■ **Uniworld Boutique Cruises.** Uniworld commissioned its Red Carnation Hotels partner to provide passengers a five-star experience in five new ships. Expect sumptuous bedding and décor.

## Best Cruise Ship: Large

■ ***Crystal Serenity,* Crystal Cruises.** With overnight calls in many ports and some of the best enrichment programs at sea, *Crystal Serenity* offers an upscale experience on a larger scale than other luxury lines.

■ ***Celebrity Reflection,* Celebrity Cruises.** *Celebrity Reflection* offers a dozen places to dine, with half of them included in the fare, and a serene atmosphere for total relaxation.

■ ***MSC Divina,* MSC Cruises.** *MSC Divina* offers a thoroughly international cruise that appeals to a wide range of passengers, both American and European.

## Best Cruise Ship: Medium

■ **Azamara Journey, Azamara Club Cruises.** Destination-oriented and totally refurbished in 2012, *Azamara Journey* is noteworthy for offering fine dining and a complimentary destination event on every sailing.

■ **MS Fram, Hurtigruten.** The MS *Fram* makes summer expeditions to Greenland as well as a 67-day longitudinal world cruise in the fall with destination-intense itineraries to explore nature.

■ **Oceania Riviera, Oceania Cruises.** The newest ship in the fleet, *Riviera* is the choice of foodies and destination collectors.

■ **Seven Seas Voyager, Regent Seven Seas Cruises.** With its all-suite, all-balcony accommodations and gourmet specialty restaurants, *Seven Seas Voyager* is a stylish choice for discerning travelers.

■ **Seabourn Sojourn, Seabourn Cruise Line.** The 450-passenger ship evokes a club-like atmosphere, scoring high points for impeccable service, elegant suites, and excellent recreational facilities.

■ **MS Aegean Odyssey, Voyages to Antiquity.** With meticulously planned itineraries, celebrated guest speakers, and shore excursions, the 550-passenger ship offers the best of cultural travel to Voyages to Antiquity cruisers.

## Best Cruise Ship: Small

■ **Le Ponant, Compagnie du Ponant.** The 64-passenger, 3-masted cruiser feels like a private sailing yacht and guarantees a unique experience with all the personalized service and attention to detail expected from a luxury operator.

■ **Hebridean Princess, Hebridean Island Cruises.** The line's flagship carries only 50 passengers and has an enviable reputation for fine food, wine, and dedicated crew of 38 with thirty beautifully decorated cabins, 10 of which are suited for single travelers.

■ **Silver Spirit, Silversea Cruises.** The largest ship in the Silversea fleet has more space for high-end specialty restaurants, expansive decks and lounges, and a theater for superior entertainment.

■ **Wind Surf, Windstar Cruises.** Newly upgraded in 2012, the ship offers fine dining in elegant surroundings, comfortable accommodations, and an appealing unstructured atmosphere.

■ **SeaDream I, SeaDream Yacht Club.** *SeaDream I* offers casual luxury on a truly yacht-like vessel with superb food and service.

## Best River Cruise Ships

■ **AmaCerto, AmaWaterways.** The newest ship of the outstanding river cruise operator has a pool with swim-up bar and sofa-laden sundeck worthy of a hip beachfront lounge.

■ **Amaryllis, Afloat in France.** The *péniche-hôtel* decorated with Louis XVI antiques meanders the Saône River through Burgundy for an unforgettable private experience.

■ **MS Amadeus Silver, Lueftner Cruises.** Built in 2013, the upscale contemporary 78-cabin vessel resembles a five-star luxury hotel and has technologically-advanced drop-down panoramic windows, creating a balcony in the room itself.

■ **MS Treasures, Tauck World Discovery.** Accommodating only 118 guests, the newest vessel in Tauck's fleet wins accolades for its club-like atmosphere, luxurious cabins, exceptional attention to detail, culinary menus, and overall quality to ensure comfort and exclusivity.

■ **SS Antoinette,** Uniworld. Awards have showered down for the opulent *SS Antoinette,* where 18th-century French design meets 21st-century technology including electronic balcony windows, Wi-Fi, underwater music, a movie theater, and a heated swimming pool.

## Best Regular Outside Cabins

■ **Costa Deliziosa,** Costa Cruises. Consistently spacious and with plenty of storage space, Costa's standard cabins are ideal for two and surprisingly roomy for families.

■ **Noordam,** Holland America Line. Comfort is key, and all cabins have DVD players, flat-screen televisions, lighted magnifying makeup mirrors, and comfortable bedding.

■ **Wind Surf,** Windstar Cruises. The nautical feel and nautical efficiency of Windstar cabins get our nod for "ship-y" and ultimately ship-shape quarters.

## Best Inside Cabins

■ **Nieuw Amsterdam,** Holland American Line. The large inside cabin category measures in at a whopping 284 square feet—some of the largest inside accommodations at sea.

■ **Norwegian Epic,** Norwegian Cruise Line. Studio cabins for solo travelers aboard *Norwegian Epic* are the ideal accommodations for singles who don't have to pay a supplement to sail.

■ **Disney Magic,** Disney Cruise Line. Designed with families in mind, *Disney Magic's* inside cabins have all the space needed for a comfortable cruise.

## Best Suites

■ **Queen Mary 2,** Cunard Line. Two Grand Duplex apartments with butler service each cover 2,250 square feet on two levels connected by a gently curving staircase.

■ **Norwegian Epic,** Norwegian Cruise Line. High atop *Norwegian Epic,* suites in The Haven are idyllic retreats with an entire private deck, restaurant, and lounge.

■ **Riviera,** Oceania Cruises. Spanning the width of the ship, Owner's Suites are decorated in furnishings by Ralph Lauren Home and have a private fitness room and two whirlpool tubs to relax in.

■ **Silver Spirit,** Silversea Cruises. Owner's Suites are the largest on board and have an ideal midship location, stylish furnishings, and plenty of room to entertain guests.

■ **Viking Idun,** Viking River Cruises. The generous suites aboard Viking's new longships are impressively large and luxurious. The Explorer suite even has a wraparound veranda.

## Best Beds

■ **Holland America Line.** The Mariner's Dream bed on every Holland America ship is a Sealy nine-inch innerspring mattress with a pillow top and additional plush-foam comfort layers.

■ **Oceania Cruises.** Oceania has outfitted its entire fleet with high-quality Euro-top mattresses, 350-thread-count Egyptian cotton linens, silk-cut duvets, and goosedown pillows.

■ **Royal Caribbean Line.** A 9-inch spring mattress with pillow top sets the stage for 220-thread-count cotton blend sheets and cushy microfiber pillows on most ships in the fleet.

## Best Bathrooms

■ **Regent Seven Seas Cruises.** The marble bathrooms with separate shower and full-size tub on *Seven Seas Voyager* are totally pampering.

■ **Seabourn Cruises.** Seabourn's bath amenities are ultradeluxe. Just ask, and

your attendant will draw your bath using luxury products of your choice.

- **Silversea Cruises.** Double vanities, marble-clad showers, separate tubs, and fluffy, oversized towels are luxurious appointments, even in standard suites. Top suites add whirlpool tubs.

## Best Regular Dining Room Cuisine

- **Holland America Line.** Under the leadership of Master Chef Rudi Sodamin, the culinary staff of Holland America Line creates dishes high in quality and taste.

- **Regent Seven Seas Cruises.** Creative dishes and wines chosen to complement all menus are a hallmark of Regent Seven Seas. Service is attentive, but not hovering or intrusive.

- **SeaDream Yacht Club.** A true gourmet meal is hard to come by on land, let alone at sea, but SeaDream chefs accomplish just such a feat. With only 112 passengers on board, every meal is individually prepared.

## Best Specialty Restaurants

- **Lawn Club Grill, Celebrity Cruises.** Celebrity's newest ships house six specialty restaurants and cafés, including the interactive Lawn Club Grill where you can prepare your own pizza or grilled steak under the chef's watchful eye.

- **Silk Road, Crystal Cruises.** Silk Road receives consistently rave reviews for the beautifully prepared dishes, including ultrafresh sushi. Presentation is as beautiful as the food.

- **Todd English, Cunard Line.** Aboard *Queen Mary 2*, cuisine in Todd English Restaurant, named for the award-winning chef and restaurateur, is as otherworldly as the exotic Moroccan surroundings in which it is served.

## Best Ships for Romantics

- ***Seven Seas Mariner,* Regent Seven Seas Cruises.** Every single suite has its own private veranda. The Cordon Bleu restaurant is elegant and the cuisine sublime—perfect for a quiet dinner for two.

- ***SeaDream II,* SeaDream Yacht Club.** Luxurious, intimate settings include snug alcoves for private dining alfresco and suite bathrooms have a to-die-for shower large enough for two with multijet massaging showerheads.

- ***Wind Surf,* Windstar Cruises.** For sheer enchantment, you can't beat billowing white sails overhead and the thrill of skimming across the sea. Cozy and inviting, with warm, unobtrusive service, the ship has a coed sauna.

## Best Ships for Families

- ***Norwegian Epic,* Norwegian Cruise Line.** Facilities for teens and tots have to be seen to be believed. Pools, playrooms, and discos are elaborate, and even picky kids should find the active programs enticing.

- ***Independence of the Seas,* Royal Caribbean International.** Well-conceived areas for children and teens, plus sports facilities that invite family members to play together, are bonuses for parents who want to spend quality family time with the kids.

- ***Disney Magic,* Disney Cruise Line.** Designed from the keel up with family fun in mind, Disney Magic delivers all the entertainment and age-appropriate activities and facilities.

## Best Ships for Spa Lovers

- ***Celebrity Reflection,* Celebrity Cruise Line.** Attractive, tranquil decor and a full complement of wraps, massages, and deluxe treatments are features of the AquaSpa. The expansive Persian Garden thermal suite includes cold and hot rooms as well as a Turkish hammam.

■ *Norwegian Epic,* **Norwegian Cruise Line.** Massages and facials take a backseat to the elaborate pleasures of a soothing whirlpool and indoor relaxation areas worthy of a fine European spa resort.

■ *Queen Mary 2,* **Cunard Line.** Canyon Ranch operates the utterly decadent spa on this ship. In addition to offering a wide range of massages and spa treatments, the Aqua Therapy Center facilities are the finest afloat.

## Best Ships for Fitness Fanatics

■ *MSC Divina,* **MSC Cruises.** Gyms afford a view of the sea from nearly every stairstepper, treadmill, and exercise cycle.

■ *Ruby Princess,* **Princess Cruises.** Stationary bicycles, treadmills, and other machines are positioned for wide-open views of sea and sky. Laps in the swim-against-the-current pool also provide a stimulating workout.

■ *Independence of the Seas,* **Royal Caribbean.** Huge and well-equipped gyms and exercise classes almost take a backseat to full-size outdoor basketball courts, rock-climbing walls, and the unique experience of ice-skating at sea.

## Best Ships for Entertainment

■ *Norwegian Epic,* **Norwegian Cruise Line.** NCL's largest ship offers some of the most elaborate and unique entertainment afloat, including Blue Man Group, a dueling-piano bar, and a Cirque du Soleil–style dinner show.

■ *Independence of the Seas,* **Royal Caribbean Cruise Line.** In addition to lavish production shows and guest entertainers, Royal Caribbean's megasize ship offers ice-skating performances.

## Best Ships for Travelers with Disabilities

■ *Celebrity Reflection,* **Celebrity Cruises.** Although accommodations designed for accessibility are some of the best at sea, equally as desirable are the line's "easy" shore excursion options.

■ *Nieuw Amsterdam,* **Holland America Line.** At the forefront of accessible cruise travel, the ship has a variety of services for passengers with mobility, sight, and breathing impairments. All shore tenders are equipped with wheelchair-accessible platforms.

■ *Ruby Princess,* **Princess Cruises.** Not only are accessible staterooms and suites available in a wide range of categories but there is also shore-side wheelchair access to appropriate tours on vehicles equipped with lifts.

## Best Ships for Shoppers

■ *Celebrity Silhouette,* **Celebrity Cruises.** With more than a dozen shops and boutiques to browse, *Celebrity Silhouette* provides the most extensive retail therapy at sea. There's little you won't find.

■ *Crystal Symphony,* **Crystal Cruises.** Signature apparel, sportswear, formal wear, and luxury cosmetics are all available in thousands of square feet of exclusive boutiques.

■ *Ruby Princess,* **Princess Cruise Line.** Should your luggage be lost or delayed, you're in luck. These shipboard boutiques are stocked with nearly everything you need to carry on in style.

## Best Ships for Service

■ *Eurodam,* **Holland America Line.** Holland America Line's Filipino and Indonesian stewards and servers go out of their way to provide gracious service with a sincere smile and genuine warmth.

■ **SeaDream I, SeaDream Yacht Club.** A Corona with no lime, extra juice in your rum punch: whatever your preference, it will be remembered by all servers on board. They seem to network behind the scenes to ensure perfection.

■ **Seven Seas Mariner, Regent Seven Seas Cruises.** Staff efforts almost go unnoticed, yet even out-of-the-ordinary requests are handled with ease. Butlers provide personalized service to guests in the top-category suites.

■ **Silver Spirit, Silversea Cruises.** The mostly European staff don't seem to understand the word no. Every attempt is made to satisfy even the most unusual request by butlers assigned to every suite.

## Best Enrichment Programs

■ **Crystal Cruises.** Discover your inner artist by learning to play piano in the Creative Learning Institute. Expert instruction and lectures can be found in the areas of arts and entertainment, business and technology, lifestyle, wellness, and wine and food.

■ **Cunard Line.** After a trip through the heavens in the only planetarium at sea, on board *Queen Mary 2* you can attend lectures presented by guest speakers on wide ranging topics, delve into classes ranging from computer instruction to wine appreciation.

■ **Holland America Line.** Guest lecturers cover a wide range of topics and the Culinary Arts Center offers hands-on cooking classes, gourmet food presentations, and tasting events.

## Best Ports for Strolling

■ **Amsterdam, The Netherlands.** Stroll along the canals and have coffee at a sidewalk café. You can easily jump on a tram if your feet are weary, but the real pleasure of Amsterdam is streetside.

■ **Dubrovnik, Croatia.** Dubrovnik's structures have been lovingly restored and the city is surrounded by medieval ramparts. Explore the city center (the Placa), cobbled side streets, and the pathway atop the Old Town's walls the old-fashioned way—by walking.

■ **Ephesus, Kusadasi, Turkey.** The only way to see this spectacular archaeological site is on foot. Walk along the marble road that Mark Antony's chariot once passed over to reach the Great Theater, where gladiatorial contests entertained up to 24,000 spectators.

■ **Oslo, Norway.** A perfect walking city, stroll the historic center, visit the National Gallery, Munch Museum and Viking Ship Museum, or simply enjoy strolling the verdant parks and streets.

## Best Daylong Excursions

■ **The Alhambra, Granada, Spain.** If your ship calls at Málaga, this is one excursion you should consider carefully. The oldest and best-preserved of the 14th-century Moorish palaces, the Alhambra is a feast for the senses, with intricate tile mosaics, carved-wood ceilings, elaborate pools, and lush gardens.

■ **D-Day Beaches, France.** There's little to see in Le Havre itself, but while you could make the two-plus-hour trip into Paris, your time ashore might be better spent exploring a bit of Normandy and the historic (and sobering) D-Day beaches, which are much closer.

■ **Rome, Italy.** Ships dock in Civitavecchia, about a 90-minute drive to Rome. It's impossible to see *everything* in a day ashore, but a comprehensive tour that includes stops at the city's highlights, with

some free time for independent sightseeing or shopping, is a good bet for the first-time visitor.

## Best Ports for Shoppers

■ **Istanbul, Turkey.** Istanbul's Grand Bazaar can't be beat for bargains on a dazzling array of goods. Bartering is expected and merchants often offer a cup of apple tea to sweeten the deal.

■ **Barcelona, Spain.** In Barcelona, fashionable designer shops line Passeig de Gràcia and the local branch of the largest and most glamorous department store in Spain, El Corte Inglés, is located on the Plaça de Catalunya.

■ **Gibraltar.** Since taxes in Gibraltar are lower than in most of Europe, prices here on most goods are cheaper than any others you're likely to find along the way.

## Best Ports for Art Lovers

■ **Paris, France.** Traveling to Paris from Le Havre or Honfleur is time-consuming, but along with the Louvre, Musée d'Orsay, Grand Palais, Petit Palais, there are over 70 museums and monuments to visit, including sculpture parks, public gardens, and historic squares.

■ **Florence, Italy.** Take the trip in from Livorno, and don't miss Michelangelo's David at the Galleria dell'Accademia, Galleria degli Uffizi, the Piazza del Duomo and Basilica, and romantic Ponte Vecchio bridge. An overwhelming amount of awe-inspiring art will humble the most creative.

■ **St. Petersburg, Russia.** St Petersburg is the home of The Hermitage, one of the world's oldest museums. Founded in 1764 by Catherine the Great, it houses the largest collection of paintings in the world.

## Best Ports for Beach Lovers

■ **Ajaccio, Corsica.** In southern Corsica, marine reserves and more than 10 miles of crystalline turquoise waters and white-powder beaches set against lush limestone hills make this region one of the most popular summer destinations for many Europeans and international jetsetters.

■ **Cannes, France.** Known for its famous film festival, Cannes is also a favorite of beachgoers on the French Riviera. While many are private, Plage de la Bocca and the Plage du Mouré Rouge are among the most popular free public beaches

■ **Korčula, Croatia.** The Croatian island measuring only 30 miles long and 5 miles wide can be found on the central Dalmatian coast. Head to the southeast for romantic beaches—hidden coves and unspoiled sands are ideal for swimming and diving.

■ **Poltu Quatu, Sardinia.** Sardinia's gateway to Costa Smeralda (Emerald Coast) is one of the world's best destinations for sun worshippers and sea lovers. Pristine beaches with enchanting blue waters are exclusive and a mecca for windsurfers, divers, and Jet Skiers.

## Best Ports for Active Excursions

■ **Athens, Greece.** Climb to the Parthenon, the temple on top of the Athenian Acropolis, dedicated to the goddess Athena—whom the people of Athens considered their patron—for an incredible view of the city.

■ **Copenhagen, Denmark.** World famous for its biking culture, the city bike—the world's first free-bicycle scheme was launched in Copenhagen in 1995. Best seen from two wheels, bicycle rentals are readily available.

■ **Reykjavík, Iceland.** Whether you want to climb a glacier, soak in a mineral-rich volcanic pool, or hike among the wildflowers, you'll have many opportunities from Icleand's capital.

## Best Ports for Food Lovers

■ **Naples, Italy.** While touring Naples, stop for cappuccino or gelato at one of the many sidewalk cafés—you can't go wrong at most of them. But Naples is most famous for its delicious pizzas, and there are numerous places to stop for pie.

■ **Athens, Greece.** Athens is within easy reach of a cruise stop in Piraeus, and the Plaka alone is filled with inviting restaurants where you can enjoy typically delicious Greek cuisine.

■ **Seville, Spain.** From Cádiz, it's just two hours by train to Seville, where thousands of tapas bars line the streets, perfect for curious palates. The bite-size delectables served on small dishes are best accompanied by an Andalusian wine.

## Best Ports for Wine Lovers

■ **Bordeaux, France.** Whether you love Pauillac, Margaux, or Médoc, the famous French wine region is one of the best to explore some of the world's most renowned vintners and vineyards including Pomerol and Sauternes.

■ **Livorno, Italy.** The cascading hills of Tuscany beckon oenophiles to explore the region's exceptional red wines like Chianti, Vino Nobile di Montepulciano, and Bolgheri. Numerous varieties available here justify the area's nickname of "Little Bordeaux."

■ **Santorini, Greece.** Whether you want a simple glass of piney-tasting retsina or something more luxe, Santorini offers many opportunities for wine tasting and winery visits, including lunches organized by ships.

## Best Ports for Budget Cruisers

■ **Split, Croatia.** Once a major Roman port, Split is a beacon for those interested in history and culture without the high price tag. Enjoy the World Heritage Site by walking through stunning Diocletian's Palace. Scenic bars and restaurants are inexpensive, showcasing local talent and cuisine.

■ **Gdańsk, Poland.** The prices are mild in this large Baltic port, which was once called Danzig and was part of Prussia.

■ **Talinn, Estonia.** The Old Town is a gem, and prices haven't climbed into the stratosphere in this inviting Baltic capital.

## Best Ports for an Overnight

■ **Alexandria, Egypt.** While you may not want to spend your overnight in Alexandria, the extra time gives you the opportunity to spend the night in Cairo and enjoy more time in the Pyramids in the early morning, before the heat is too intense rather than doing a rushed day trip.

■ **Ibiza, Spain.** The relatively small island and its cities are famous for their club scene, which can only be experienced at night.

■ **Mykonos, Greece.** Nightlife rules in this Greek island, where things don't really get going until the wee hours, so a late-night departure is best, an overnight even better.

■ **Venice, Italy.** A gondola ride and a stop at the historic Harry's Bar for a Bellini cocktail—a mixture of prosecco sparkling wine and peach purée—are best enjoyed at night in Venice.

# Planning a European Cruise

Canal in Amsterdam

## WORD OF MOUTH

"My wife and I (late 60s) went on three different cruises 15 or so years ago. . . . We are planning on going on a Caribbean cruise for about nine days in the next month or two. How has cruising changed over those 15 years? What differences can we expect? Thanks in advance."

—Gerhardt

By Linda
Coffman

With a wealth of art, architecture, and culture drawing them, it's easy to understand why Europe is the world's second-most-popular cruising region (only the Caribbean surpasses it). On a single cruise it's possible to visit a different country each day and explore a variety of important destinations, either right alongside the sea or not far from port.

The allure of a sea cruise is its ability to appeal to a wide range of vacationers as a safe and convenient way to travel. This is particularly true in Europe, where differences in language and culture can appear as insurmountable hurdles to the first-time visitor. And on a cruise, meals and accommodations are paid for in advance, so there's no worry about fluctuating euros to spoil your budget. And, although your ship follows the same sea routes as early mariners and traders, you don't have to hassle with transportation from country to country.

Major cruise lines that are familiar to most North Americans position some of their most exciting ships in Europe on a seasonal basis. Passengers are primarily Americans, the U.S. dollar prevails on board, and English is the dominant language. On cruise lines based in the United Kingdom, English is also the primary language, but you'll pay for onboard purchases in British pounds, which can be a distinct disadvantage to Americans with currency fluctuations. The option of European-based cruise lines is also available. On those, you will find a more international flavor, multiple languages are spoken, and the currency is the euro.

## CHOOSING YOUR CRUISE

Are you intrigued by the glory that is Rome or the antiquities of Greece? Do you want to venture behind the former Iron Curtain and unlock the mysteries of Russia? Unlike the "if it's Tuesday, this must be St. Thomas" nature of predictable Caribbean sailings, European itineraries come in shapes and sizes to suit a variety of interests. One voyage might emphasize the highlights of Baltic capital cities, while another focuses on classic Mediterranean cultures and cuisine. Equally rewarding, they nonetheless offer different experiences. Where to go to satisfy your inner explorer is a highly personal decision, and one of the first you must make.

After giving some thought to your itinerary and where in Europe you might wish to go, the ship you select is the most vital factor in your cruise vacation. Big ships offer stability and a huge variety of activities and facilities. Small ships feel more intimate—more like a private club. For every big-ship fan there is someone who would never set foot aboard a "floating resort." Examine your lifestyle to see which kind of ship best meets your needs. But realize also that the size of your ship will also impact which ports you visit as well as how you see them.

Big ships visit major ports of call such as Barcelona, Civitavecchia (for Rome), Amsterdam, and Venice; when they call at smaller, shallower ports, passengers must disembark aboard shore tenders (small boats that ferry dozens of passengers to shore at a time). Or they may skip these smaller ports entirely. Small and midsize ships can visit smaller ports, such as Monte Carlo, Monaco, more easily; passengers are often able to disembark directly onto the pier without having to wait for tenders to bring them ashore.

## ITINERARIES

Ship size and cruise length have the greatest impact on the number of ports you can visit, but the itinerary type and embarkation port will also determine the number and variety of ports. **One-way cruises** are much more prevalent in European sailings than in the Caribbean, and will allow you to visit a wider variety of ports and travel farther from your port of embarkation. **Loop cruises** begin and end at the same point, and often visit ports in relatively close proximity to one another. After deciding where to go, take a hard look at the number of hours your preferred itinerary spends in individual ports. You don't want to be frustrated by a lack of time ashore to do what you've come so far to accomplish. A late departure or overnight stay may be attractive if you wish to enjoy the local nightlife in a particular port.

### NORTHERN EUROPE AND BALTIC ITINERARIES

Typical one-week to 12-night cruises include a day or two at sea, but ships on these itineraries spend as much time as possible docked in Baltic capitals and major cities. Departing from such ports as Dover (U.K.), Amsterdam, Copenhagen, or Stockholm, highlights of Baltic itineraries may include Amsterdam, Oslo, Helsinki, Tallin (Estonia), and St. Petersburg (Russia); ships calling on St. Petersburg often dock for two or three nights there. Some itineraries may focus on a theme or specific region, such as cruises around the British Isles or Norwegian fjords and North Cape.

### WESTERN MEDITERRANEAN ITINERARIES

Some of the most popular Mediterranean itineraries, especially for first-time cruisers to Europe, are one-week sailings that embark in Barcelona and stop in southern European ports that range from Nice to Civitavecchia (Rome), and may include more exotic off-the-beaten-path destinations like Malta and Corsica. A sea day might include a cruise through the narrow Strait of Messina or sailing past the volcanic island of Stromboli. Longer, one-way itineraries can even start in Lisbon and end as far away as Venice, while possibly calling at not only Gibraltar, the French Riviera, and Sicily, but Dubrovnik (Croatia) as well.

### EASTERN MEDITERRANEAN, ADRIATIC, AND GREEK ISLES ITINERARIES

The most exotic and port-intensive cruises are those embarking in Venice, Athens, and Istanbul. Often one-way voyages, these cruises visit coastal centers of antiquity such as Kusadasi (Ephesus) in Turkey and Katakolon (Olympia) in Greece, but also the Roman outposts of Dubrovnik and Korèula, Croatia. For a transit through Greece's historic

Corinth Canal, you'll have to select an itinerary on one of the high-end, small cruise ships, such as Seabourn or SeaDream cruise lines' yacht-size vessels. A sea day might be spent cruising past the grandeur of Mount Athos after leaving Istanbul or along the coastline in the Adriatic Sea. Best explored by small ship—preferably one with sails that add to the allure—Greek Island itineraries that include Santorini, Corfu, Rhodes, and Mykonos are popular with honeymooners and couples for the romantic ambience of sun-splashed beaches and leisurely alfresco meals accompanied by local wines and breathtaking sea views, but these ports are also visited by the larger ships, which must usually tender their passengers ashore.

### EUROPEAN CRUISE SHIPS AND ITINERARIES

| CRUISE LINE | SHIP NAME | ITINERARY/REGION |
|---|---|---|
| Azamara Club Cruises | Azamara Journey | W or E Med., Greek Isles |
| | Azamara Quest | E Med., Baltic |
| Carnival Cruise Lines | Carnival Legend | W or E Med., Baltic, British Isles |
| | Carnival Sunshine | W or E Med. |
| Celebrity Cruises | Celebrity Constellation | W or E Med., Greek Isles |
| | Celebrity Eclipse | W Med., Baltic, British Isles, Norway |
| | Celebrity Equinox | W or E Med., Greek Isles |
| | Celebrity Infinity | Norway, British Isles |
| | Celebrity Reflection | E Med. |
| | Celebrity Silhouette | E Med. |
| Compagnie du Ponant | L'Austral | W or E Med. |
| | Le Boréal | W Med., North Sea |
| | Le Ponant | W Med. |
| | Le Soléal | W Med. |
| Costa Cruises | Costa Atlantica | E Med. |
| | Costa Classica | W or E Med. |
| | Costa Deliziosa | W or E Med., Baltic |
| | Costa Fascinosa | W or E Med. |
| | Costa Favolosa | W or E Med. |
| | Costa Fortuna | W Med., Baltic |
| | Costa Luminosa | W Med., Baltic |
| | Costa Magica | W or E Med. |
| | Costa Mediterranea | W Med. |
| | Costa neoRomantica | W Med., Baltic |
| | Costa Pacifica | W or E Med., Baltic |
| | Costa Serena | W Med. |

## EUROPEAN CRUISE SHIPS AND ITINERARIES

| CRUISE LINE | SHIP NAME | ITINERARY/REGION |
|---|---|---|
| Crystal Cruises | Crystal Serenity | W or E Med., Baltic, British Isles, Norway |
| | Crystal Symphony | W or E Med., Baltic |
| Cunard Line | Queen Elizabeth | W or E Med., Baltic, British Isles, Norway |
| | Queen Mary 2 | Baltic, Norway |
| | Queen Victoria | W or E Med., Baltic, British Isles, Norway |
| Disney Cruise Line | Disney Magic | W Med. |
| Holland America Line | Eurodam | W or E Med., Baltic |
| | Nieuw Amsterdam | W or E Med. |
| | Noordam | W or E Med. |
| | Prinsendam | W or E Med., Baltic, British Isles, Norway |
| | Rotterdam | W or E Med., Baltic, Norway |
| | Ryndam | W or E Med., Baltic, Norwegian Coast |
| Hurtigruten | Finnmarken | Norway |
| | Kong Harald | Norway |
| | Midnastol | Norway |
| | Nordkapp | Norway |
| | Nordnorge | Norway |
| | Nordlys | Norway |
| | Polarlys | Norway |
| | Richard With | Norway |
| | Trollfjord | Norway |
| Lindblad Expeditions | National Geographic Explorer | W Med., Baltic |
| | Lord of the Glens | British Isles, Scotland |
| | Sea Cloud | W or E Med. |
| Louis Cruises | Coral | E Med., Greek Isles |
| | Louis Cristal | E Med., Greek Isles |
| | Louis Olympia | E Med., Greek Isles |
| | Orient Queen | E Med., Greek Isles |
| MSC Cruises | MSC Armonia | W or E Med., Greek Isles |
| | MSC Divina | E Med., Greek Isles |
| | MSC Fantasia | W or E Med. |
| | MSC Lirica | Baltic |
| | MSC Magnifica | Baltic |
| | MSC Melody | W or E Med. |

EUROPEAN CRUISE SHIPS AND ITINERARIES

| CRUISE LINE | SHIP NAME | ITINERARY/REGION |
|---|---|---|
|  | *MSC Musica* | Baltic |
|  | *MSC Opera* | Baltic |
|  | *MSC Orchestra* | W Med. |
|  | *MSC Poesia* | Baltic |
|  | *MSC Preziosa* | W Med. |
|  | *MSC Sinfonia* | W Med. |
|  | *MSC Splendida* | W Med. |
| Norwegian Cruise Line | *Norwegian Epic* | W Med. |
|  | *Norwegian Jade* | W or E Med., Greek Isles |
|  | *Norwegian Spirit* | W or E Med. |
|  | *Norwegian Star* | Baltic |
| Oceania Cruises | *Marina* | W or E Med., Baltic, British Isles |
|  | *Nautica* | W or E Med., Greek Isles, Baltic |
|  | *Regatta* | E Med. |
|  | *Riviera* | W or E Med. |
| Paul Gauguin Cruises | *Tere Moana* | W or E Med. |
| Princess Cruises | *Crown Princess* | Baltic, British Isles, Norway, W Med., Greek Isles |
|  | *Caribbean Princess* | British Isles, Norway |
|  | *Emerald Princess* | Baltic |
|  | *Grand Princess* | W Med., British Isles, Norway |
|  | *Ocean Princess* | W Med., Baltic, British Isles, Norway |
|  | *Pacific Princess* | W or E Med. |
|  | *Ruby Princess* | W or E Med., Greek Isles |
| Regent Seven Seas Cruises | *Seven Seas Mariner* | W or E Med. |
|  | *Seven Seas Voyager* | W or E Med., Baltic, British Isles |
| Royal Caribbean International | *Adventure of the Seas* | W Med., Baltic, Norway |
|  | *Brilliance of the Seas* | Baltic, Norway |
|  | *Independence of the Seas* | W Med., British Isles, Norway |
|  | *Legend of the Seas* | W Med., Greek Isles |
|  | *Liberty of the Seas* | W Med. |
|  | *Navigator of the Seas* | W or E Med. |
|  | *Serenade of the Seas* | W or E Med., Greek Isles |
|  | *Splendour of the Seas* | W or E Med., Greek Isles |

EUROPEAN CRUISE SHIPS AND ITINERARIES

| CRUISE LINE | SHIP NAME | ITINERARY/REGION |
|---|---|---|
|  | Vision of the Seas | Baltic, Norway |
| Seabourn Cruise Line | Seabourn Legend | W or E Med. |
|  | Seabourn Odyssey | E Med., Greek Isles |
|  | Seabourn Pride | W or E Med., Baltic, British Isles |
|  | Seabourn Quest | W or E Med., Greek Isles |
|  | Seabourn Sojourn | W Med., Baltic, Norway |
|  | Seabourn Spirit | W or E Med. |
| SeaDream Yacht Club | SeaDream I | W or E Med. |
|  | SeaDream II | W or E Med. |
| Silversea Cruises | Silver Explorer | British Isles |
|  | Silver Cloud | W or E Med. |
|  | Silver Spirit | W or E Med., Greek Isles |
|  | Silver Whisper | Baltic |
|  | Silver Wind | W or E Med. |
| Star Clippers | Royal Clipper | W Med. |
|  | Star Clipper | E Med., Greek Isles |
|  | Star Flyer | W Med. |
| Windstar Cruises | Wind Spirit | W or E Med., Greek Isles |
|  | Wind Star | W or E Med. |
|  | Wind Surf | W Med., Baltic |

# WHEN TO GO

Baltic cruises are scheduled from May through September, with mid-summer being high season, when the weather is predictably more pleasant. Temperatures throughout the Baltic are somewhat unpredictable, but can range from balmy mid- to high-70sF on sunny days to chilly 50sF in the evening, even if the sun doesn't set until well into the night. Mediterranean cruises are available year-round, with high season from late April through October when temperatures range from the upper 70s to mid-90sF, depending on your ports of call. Early spring and late fall aren't the best times to cruise in the Mediterranean if your plans include spending time on the beaches, yet the cooler temperatures are ideal for touring. Weather can be unpredictable and damp in fall and winter, but days often warm up when the sun is shining.

## TYPES OF SHIPS

Just as cruise ships differ by size and style, so do the cruise lines themselves, and finding a cruise line that matches your personality is as important as finding the right ship. Some cruise lines cater to families, others to couples, active singles, and even food and wine aficionados. Selecting the right one can mean the difference between struggling with unmet expectations and enjoying the vacation of a lifetime. Although some of the differences are subtle, most of today's cruise lines still fall into three basic categories: Mainstream, Premium, and Luxury.

### MAINSTREAM LINES

**What you'll find.** Mainstream cruise lines usually have a little something for everyone: Ships tend to be the big, bigger, and biggest at sea, carrying the highest number of passengers per available space. Cabins can be basic or fancy since most mainstream lines also offer more upscale accommodations categories, including suites. Some mainstream lines still offer traditional dining, with two assigned seatings in the main restaurant for dinner. But increasingly, most mainstream cruise lines have introduced variations of open seating dining and alternative restaurant options that allow passengers to dine when and with whom they please, though almost all alternative restaurants carry an extra charge.

**What won't you find?** As a rule, sodas and bottled water are not complimentary, tipping is not included, and there are many extra charges once you board the ship.

**Who's on board?** First-timers, repeat passengers, young and old alike. Mainstream cruise lines are ideal for anyone who is looking for a fun and exhilarating vacation.

### PREMIUM LINES

**What you'll find.** Premium lines usually offer a more subdued atmosphere and refined style: Ships tend to be newer midsize to large vessels that carry fewer passengers than mainstream ships and have a more spacious feel. Staterooms still range from more basic to more upscale, but even the basic accommodations tend to have more style and space. Cuisine on these ships tends to be a bit better, and most of these ships have à la carte options for more upscale dining for an extra charge, often higher than those on mainstream lines. There are still extra charges on the ship.

**What won't you find?** The cruise staff won't bombard you with noise—announcements are kept to a minimum.

**Who's on board?** First-timers and experienced passengers who enjoy a more upscale experience in lower-key surroundings. Premium lines attract families, singles, and groups; however, expect the passengers to be older on average, particularly on sailings longer than 7 to 10 days.

### LUXURY LINES

**What you'll find.** The air on these deluxe vessels is as rarified as the champagne and caviar: Ships range from megayachts for only a hundred or so privileged guests to midsize vessels, which are considered large for this category. Space is so abundant that you might wonder where the other passengers are hiding. Spacious staterooms are frequently all suites; at the least, they are the equivalent to higher-grade accommodations on mainstream and premium ships. Open seating is the norm, and guests dine where and with whom they please during dinner hours. There are relatively few extra charges on these ships, except for wines by the bottle, spa services, and excursions, but some lines even include excursions and airfare in their prices. A handful still charge for liquor.

**What won't you find?** No one will be groveling for gratuities. If they're not already included in the fare, they are oh-so-discreetly suggested.

**Who's on board?** Well-off couples and singles accustomed to the best travel accommodations and service. Small groups and families gravitate to the larger vessels in this category. Traveling in style to collect exotic destinations is highly desirable to luxury-minded passengers.

## CRUISE COSTS

Average cruise fares vary considerably by itinerary and season, as well as by the category of accommodations you select. Published rates are highest for the most unusual and desirable itineraries, as well as for cruises during peak summer months, when most North Americans plan for vacations in Europe. Europeans are known to prefer late-summer holidays, with August being the busiest month. Typical daily per diems on a luxury line such as Silversea or Seabourn can be as much as three times or more the cost of a cruise on a mainstream line such as Royal Caribbean or even a premium Celebrity Cruises ship. It goes without saying that longer cruises are naturally more expensive.

Solo travelers should be aware that single cabins have virtually disappeared from cruise ships, although they are available on Norwegian Cruise Line's *Norwegian Epic* (in a particularly successful format), and a few older vessels. Taking a double cabin can cost up to twice the advertised per-person rates (which are based on double occupancy). Some cruise lines will find same-sex roommates for singles; each then pays the per-person, double-occupancy rate.

Although the overall price you pay for your cruise is always a consideration, don't think of the bottom line in terms of the fare alone. You also have to figure in the cost of other shipboard charges beyond the basic fare. However, the ultimate cost isn't computed only in dollars spent; it is in what you get for your money. The real bottom line is value. Many cruise passengers don't mind spending a bit more to get the vacation they really want.

## TIPS

One of the most delicate—yet frequently debated—topics of conversation among cruise passengers involves the matter of tipping. Who do you tip? How much? What's "customary" and "recommended?" Should parents tip the full amount for children or is just half adequate? Why do you have to tip at all?

When transfers to and from your ship are a part of your air-and-sea program, gratuities are generally included for luggage handling. In that

**CLOSE UP**

# New Ships in 2013 and Beyond

European-bound ships scheduled for launch in 2013 and beyond include some of the most feature-rich vessels ever to float in new classes, as well as one older vessel that is being entirely rebuilt. We offer an advance preview here of those ships coming over the horizon.

### CARNIVAL SUNSHINE

Launched in 1996, *Carnival Destiny*—Carnival Cruise Lines' first mega-ship weighing in at over 100,000 tons—will be reborn as *Carnival Sunshine* after a 49-day dry dock in early 2013. The ship will emerge from a $155-million makeover that incorporates all of the line's "Fun Ship 2.0" dining, bar, and entertainment features, as well as a variety of innovations unique to the vessel. The refit will include a reconfigured layout, the addition of a partial deck, and the expansion of two other decks within the forward section of the ship. All accommodations will be revamped and 182 cabins will be added, increasing her capacity to 3,006 passengers in double occupancy.

### NORWEGIAN BREAKAWAY AND NORWEGIAN GETAWAY

In an entirely new class, *Norwegian Breakaway* will launch in 2013 with 4,000 passenger berths—a sister ship, *Norwegian Getaway*, is expected in April 2014. A new concept, the ship will have an oceanfront boardwalk lined with shops, restaurants, and bars, combined with three expansive, decks for entertainment and gaming. *Norwegian Breakaway*'s top decks will feature an Aqua Park with five full-size waterslides and a three-story sports complex that includes a ropes course, a nine-hole miniature golf course, basketball court, and rock-climbing wall. The ship will have a mix of traditional staterooms as well as The Haven, comprised of 42 suites at the top of the ship. The innovative Studios, designed for solo travelers, will carry over from *Norwegian Epic*. And there will be spa-category staterooms. Passengers will dine at 15 restaurants (most with cover charge), a buffet, and a pub. On the entertainment side, *Rock of Ages* will be featured on *Norwegian Breakaway* along with two other Broadway-style shows and a new dinner show from the Cirque Dreams group. Also appearing on the ship are comedy troupe The Second City and a Howl at the Moon.

### ROYAL PRINCESS AND REGAL PRINCESS

Set to debut in spring 2013, the new 141,000-ton, 3,600-passenger *Royal Princess* is the first of two new-generation ships for Princess—with sister ship *Regal Princess* following in 2014. New on board are a greatly enlarged atrium; a dramatic overwater SeaWalk, which stretches over 28 feet beyond the edge of the vessel; plush private poolside cabanas; a new *Princess Live!* TV studio with audience seating; a pastry shop; the special Chef's Table private-dining experience that surrounds diners in a curtain of light; and balconies on all outside staterooms. Expanded are the adults-only Sanctuary and the poolside theater that offers high-definition viewing, as well as the spa that includes private Couples Villas. The Enclave—a huge thermal suite—features the line's first hydrotherapy pool. In addition to a portable batting cage for baseball fans and a driving-range facility for golfers, a simulated laser shooting range is a new activity.

case, do not worry about the interim tipping. However, if you take a taxi to the pier and hand over your bags to a stevedore, be sure to tip him. Treat him with respect and pass along the equivalent of at least $5.

During your cruise, room-service waiters generally receive a cash tip of $1 to $3 per delivery. A 15% to 18% gratuity will automatically be added to each bar bill during the cruise. If you use salon and spa services, a similar percentage might be added to the bills there as well. If you dine in a specialty restaurant, you may be asked to provide a one-time gratuity for the service staff.

There will be a "disembarkation talk" on the last day of the cruise that explains tipping procedures. If you are expected to tip in cash, small white "tip" envelopes will appear in your stateroom that day. If you tip in cash, you usually give the tip envelope directly to each person on the last night of the cruise. Tips generally add up to about $11.50 to $14 per person per day. You tip the same amount for each person who shares the cabin, including children, unless otherwise indicated.

Most cruise lines now either automatically add gratuities to passengers' onboard charge accounts or offer the option. If that suits you, then do nothing further. However, you are certainly free to adjust the amounts up or down to more appropriate levels or ask that the charge be removed altogether if you prefer distributing cash gratuities.

### EXTRAS

In addition to the cost of your cruise, there are further expenses to consider, such as airfare to the port city. These days virtually all cruise lines offer air add-ons, which are sometimes—but not always—less expensive than the lowest available airline fare. Airfares to Europe can be considerably more expensive from May through September than during the rest of year.

Shore excursions can also be a substantial expense; the best shore excursions are not cheap. But if you skimp too much on your excursion budget you'll deprive yourself of an important part of the European cruising experience. European shore excursions can be as simple as a stroll through Copenhagen's fanciful Tivoli Gardens or as splendid as tours through the imperial residences of the czars in St. Petersburg. You can inspect the architecture of Gaudí in Barcelona, take an all-day guided tour of Rome with a stop at Vatican City, and climb to the top of the Acropolis in Athens. One of the most popular excursions is from the port of Kusadasi (Turkey) to the ancient excavated city of Ephesus. You will walk along the marble road that Mark Antony's and Cleopatra's chariots once passed over to reach the Great Theater, where gladiatorial contests entertained up to 24,000 spectators and where St. Paul addressed the Ephesians. If you want to take a ship-sponsored shore excursion, prebooking is highly recommended, as they can sell out weeks before you reach the ship.

But you don't necessarily have to take the tour offered by your ship. Although there's a distinct advantage these days to having your shore excursions priced in dollars rather than euros, you can still have a high-quality (though perhaps not cheaper) experience by banding together with a group of like-minded travelers to arrange a private

## CLOSE UP

# Recommended Gratuities by Cruise Line

Each cruise line has a different tipping policy. Some allow you to add tips to your shipboard account, others expect you to dole out the dollars in cash on the last night of the cruise. Here are the suggested tipping amounts for each line covered in this book. Gratuity recommendations are often higher if you're staying in a suite with extra services, such as a butler. *The individual ship profiles give you the details:*

Azamara Club Cruises: No tipping expected

Carnival Cruise Line: $11.50 per person per day

Celebrity Cruises: $11.50 per person per day

Compagnie du Ponant: No tipping expected

Costa Cruises: €6–€7 per person per day, depending on cruise length

Crystal Cruises: No tipping expected

Cunard Line: $11–$13 per person per day

Disney Cruise Line: $36 per person for 3-night cruises; $48 per person for 4-night cruises; $84 per person for 7-night cruises

Holland American Line: $11.50 per person per day

Hurtigruten: Tipping allowed but not expected

Lindblad Expeditions: $12–$15 per person per day

Louis Cruises: €8 per person per day

MSC Cruises: €6–€7 per person per day

Norwegian Cruise Line: $12 per person per day

Oceania Cruises: $14.50 per person per day

Paul Gauguin Cruises: No tipping expected

Princess Cruises: $11.50 per person per day

Regent Seven Seas Cruises: No tipping expected

Royal Caribbean International: $12–$14.25 per person per day

Seabourn Cruises: No tipping expected

SeaDream Yacht Club: No tipping expected

Silversea Cruises: No tipping expected

Star Clippers: €8 per person per day

Windstar Cruises: $12 per person per day

---

tour rather than relying on the ship's big-bus experience. Or if you are more intrepid, you can simply hop in a taxi or onto public transportation and do some independent exploring. Whether you choose to take ship-sponsored tours or go it alone, you do need to budget for off-ship touring because that's the reason you came to Europe in the first place.

Finally, there will be many extras added to your shipboard account during the cruise, including drinks (both alcoholic and nonalcoholic), activity fees (you pay to use that golf simulator), dining in specialty restaurants, spa services, gratuities, and even cappuccino and espresso on most ships.

# CABINS

In years gone by, cabins were almost an afterthought. The general attitude of both passengers and the cruise lines used to be that a cabin is a cabin and is used only for changing clothes and sleeping. That's why the cabins on most older cruise ships are skimpy in size and short on amenities.

Until you actually get on board, you may not realize that nearly every cabin on your ship is identical. These days cruise ships are built in sections and, except for some luxury suites, the cabins are prefabricated and dropped into place with everything all ready to hook up, even the plumbing. There are some variations in size, but the main difference between cabins in the myriad price categories is location: higher or lower decks, forward or aft, inside or outside.

Cabins high on the ship with a commanding view fetch higher fares. But you should know that they are also more susceptible to side-to-side movement; in rough seas you could find yourself tossed right out of bed. On lower decks, you'll pay less and find more stability, particularly in the middle of the ship, but even upper-level cabins in the middle of the ship are more steady than others.

Forward cabins have a tendency to be oddly shaped, as they follow the contour of the bow. They are also likely to be noisy; when the ship's anchor drops, you won't need a wake-up call. In rough seas you can feel the ship's pitch (its upward and downward motion) more in the front.

Should you go for the stern location instead? You're more likely to hear engine and machinery noise there, but you may also feel the pitch and possibly some vibration. However, many passengers feel the view of the ship's wake (the ripples it leaves behind as its massive engines move it forward) is worth any noise or vibration they might encounter there.

Above all, don't be confused by all the categories listed in cruise line brochures—the categories more accurately reflect price levels based on location than any physical differences in the cabins themselves (keep repeating: prefabricated). Shipboard accommodations fall into four basic configurations: inside cabins, outside cabins, balcony cabins, and suites.

## INSIDE CABINS

An inside cabin has no window or porthole. These are always the least expensive cabins and are ideal for passengers who would rather spend their vacation funds on excursions or other incidentals than on upgraded accommodations. Inside cabins are generally just as spacious as outside cabins, and decor and amenities are similar. Many ships locate triple and quad cabins (accommodating three or more passengers) on the inside. Essentially, they look just like a standard double cabin but have bunk beds that either fold down from the wall or disappear into the ceiling. Parents sometimes book an inside cabin for their older children and teens, while their own cabin is an outside across the hall with a window or balcony.

## Saving Money on Your Cruise Fare

You can save on your cruise fare in several ways. Obviously, you should shop around. Some travel agents will discount cruise prices, though this is becoming a thing of the past. One thing never changes—do not ever, under any circumstances, pay brochure rate. You can do better, often as much as half off published fares. These are a few simple strategies you can follow:

■ **Book early:** Cruise lines discount their cruises if you book early, particularly during the annual "Wave" season between January and March.

■ **Cruise during the off-season:** Take your cruise during the very early spring or late fall (especially in March, October, and November).

■ **Book late:** Sometimes you can book a last-minute cruise at substantial savings if the ship hasn't filled all its cabins.

■ **Choose accommodations with care:** Cabins are usually standardized, and location determines the fare. Selecting a lower category can result in savings while giving up nothing in terms of cabin size and features.

■ **Book a "guarantee":** You won't be able to select your own cabin, because the cruise line will assign you one in the category you book, but a "guarantee" fare can be substantially lower than a regular fare.

■ **Cruise with friends and family:** Book a minimum number of cabins, and your group can generally receive a special discounted fare.

■ **Reveal your age and affiliations:** Fare savings may be available for seniors and members of certain organizations, and for cruise-line stockholders.

■ **Cruise often:** Frequent cruisers usually get discounts from their preferred cruise lines.

### OUTSIDE CABINS

A standard outside cabin has either a picture window or porthole. To give the illusion of more space, these cabins might also rely on the generous use of mirrors for an even airier feeling. In addition to the usual amenities, outside staterooms often have a small refrigerator and a sitting area. Two twin beds can be joined together to create one large bed. Going one step further, standard and larger outside staterooms on modern ships are often outfitted with a small sofa or loveseat with a cocktail table or small side table. Floor-to-ceiling curtains that can be drawn from wall to wall to create a private sleeping space are a nice touch in some outside cabins with sitting areas. Some larger cabins may have a combination bathtub–shower instead of just a shower.

### BALCONY CABINS

A balcony—or veranda—cabin is an outside cabin with floor-to-ceiling glass doors that open onto a private deck. Although the cabin may have large expanses of glass, the balcony is sometimes cut out of the cabin's square footage (depending on the ship). Balconies are usually furnished with two chairs and a table for lounging and casual dining outdoors. However, you should be aware that balconies are not always completely private; sometimes your balcony is visible both from balconies next door and also from balconies above, particularly when you are in an aft-facing cabin on the back of a ship with tiered balconies. The furnishings and amenities of balcony cabins are otherwise much like those in standard outside cabins.

## SUITES

Suites are the most lavish accommodations afloat, and although suites are always larger than regular cabins, they do not always have separate rooms for sleeping. Some luxury ships designate all accommodations as suites. The most expansive (and expensive) have large living rooms and separate bedrooms, and may also have huge private outdoor sundecks equipped with hot tubs and dining areas. Even smaller suites (often termed minisuites) and penthouses are generous in size.

Suites almost always have amenities that standard cabins do not have. True suites have separate living and sleeping areas, but these areas are still occasionally separated only by a curtain. Depending on the cruise line, you may find a small refrigerator or minibar stocked with complimentary soft drinks, bottled water, and the alcoholic beverages of your choice. Top suites on some ships include the luxurious touch of complimentary laundry service, in-cabin Internet connections, and complex entertainment centers with large flat-screen TVs, DVD players, and CD stereo systems. An added bonus to the suite life is the extra level of services many ships offer. Little extras might include afternoon tea and evening canapés delivered to you and served by a white-gloved butler.

Although minisuites on most contemporary ships have separate sitting areas with a sofa, chair, and a cocktail table, don't let the marketing skill of the cruise lines fool you: so-called minisuites are usually little more than slightly larger versions of standard balcony cabins and seldom include the extra services and elaborate amenities you can get in regular suites. They're still generally a good value for the price if space matters.

## ACCESSIBILITY ISSUES

As recently as the early 1990s, "accessibility" on a cruise ship meant little more than a few inside staterooms set aside for passengers with mobility issues. Most public restrooms and nearly all en-suite bathrooms had a "step-over" threshold. Newer ships are more sensitive to the needs of passengers with disabilities, but many older ships still have physical barriers in both cabins and public rooms. And once you get off the ship—particularly in ports with cobblestone streets—your problems will be compounded.

All cruise lines offer a limited number of staterooms designed to be wheelchair- and scooter-accessible. Booking a newer vessel will generally assure more choices. On newer ships, public rooms are generally more accessible, and more facilities have been planned with wheelchair users in mind. Auxiliary aids, such as flashers for the hearing impaired and buzzers for visually impaired passengers, as well as lifts for swimming pools and hot tubs, are available. However, more than the usual amount of preplanning is necessary for smooth sailing if you have special needs.

# DECIPHER YOUR DECK PLAN

## LIDO DECK

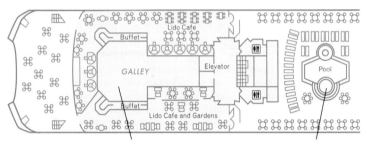

The Lido Deck is a potential source of noise—deck chairs are set out early in the morning and put away late at night; the sound of chairs scraping on the floor of the Lido buffet can be an annoyance.

Music performances by poolside bands can often be heard on upper-deck balconies located immediately below.

## UPPER DECK AFT

Take note of where lifeboats are located—views from some outside cabins can be partially, or entirely, obstructed by the boats.

Upper-deck cabins, as well as those far forward and far aft, are usually more susceptible to motion than those in the middle of the ship on a low deck.

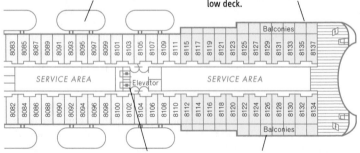

Cabins near elevators or stairs are a double-edged sword. Being close by is a convenience; however, although the elevators aren't necessarily noisy, the traffic they attract can be.

Balcony cabins are indicated by a rectangle split into two sections. The small box is the balcony.

1

## MAIN PUBLIC DECK

Cabins immediately below restaurants and dining rooms can be noisy. Late sleepers might be bothered by early breakfast noise, early sleepers by late diners.

Theaters and dining rooms are often located on middle or lower decks.

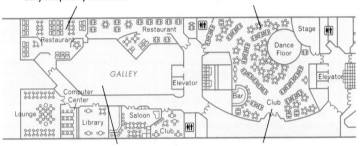

The ship's galley isn't usually labeled on deck plans, but you can figure out where it is by locating a large blank space near the dining room. Cabins beneath it can be very noisy.

Locate the ship's show lounge, disco, children's playroom, and teen center and avoid booking a cabin directly above or below them for obvious reasons.

## LOWER DECK AFT

Cabins designated for passengers with disabilities are often situated near elevators.

Interior cabins have no windows and are the least expensive on board.

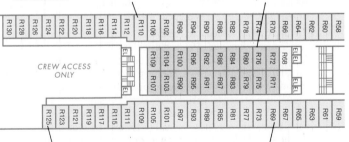

Lower-deck cabins, particularly those far aft, can be plagued by mechanical noises and vibration.

Ocean-view cabins are generally located on lower decks.

For example, when a ship is unable to dock—as is the case in Villefranche or Santorini—passengers are taken ashore on tenders that are sometimes problematic even for the able-bodied to negotiate under adverse conditions. Some people with limited mobility may find it difficult to embark or disembark the ship when docked due to the steep angle of gangways during high or low tide at certain times of day. In some situations, crew members may offer assistance that involves carrying guests, but if the sea is choppy when tendering is a necessity, that might not be an option.

Passengers who require continuous oxygen or have service animals have further hurdles to overcome. You can bring both aboard a cruise ship, but your service animal may not be allowed to go ashore with you if the port has strict laws regarding animal quarantines.

# BOOKING YOUR CRUISE

Charting your cruising course doesn't have to be difficult, but it isn't as simple as booking airplane seats or reserving a hotel room. Even after you've settled on a cruise line and cruise ship that's right for you, there will still be many questions to answer and details to get right. First-time cruisers looking for additional insight and advice may wish to stick to a traditional travel agent who is close at hand. Of course, if you've taken numerous cruises and are more concerned with the price—and if you're willing to go to bat for yourself if something goes wrong—a Web-based agency might be the way to go.

## USING A TRAVEL AGENT

Whether it is your first or 50th sailing, your best friend in booking a cruise is a knowledgeable travel agent. The last thing you want when considering a costly cruise vacation is an agent who has never been on a cruise, calls a cruise ship "the boat," or—worse still—quotes brochure rates. The most important steps in cruise-travel planning are research, research, and more research; your partner in this process is an experienced travel agent. Booking a cruise is a complex process, and it's seldom wise to try to go it alone, particularly the first time. But how do you find a cruise travel agent you can trust?

The most experienced and reliable agent will be certified as an Accredited Cruise Counselor (ACC), Master Cruise Counselor (MCC), or Elite Cruise Counselor (ECC) by CLIA (the Cruise Lines International Association). These agents have completed demanding training programs, including touring or sailing on a specific number of ships. Your agent should also belong to a professional trade organization. In North America, membership in the American Society of Travel Agents (ASTA) indicates that an agency has pledged to follow the code of ethics set forth by the world's largest association for travel professionals. In the best of all worlds, your travel agent is affiliated with both ASTA and CLIA.

Some agencies have preferred-supplier relationships with specific cruise lines and prominently display only their products. If you have done your homework and know what cruise line sounds most appealing to you, be alert if an agent tries to change your mind without specific reasons.

## 10 Questions to Answer Before Visiting a Travel Agent

If you've decided to use a travel agent, congratulations. You'll have someone on your side to make your booking and to intercede if something goes wrong. Ask yourself these 10 simple questions, and you'll be better prepared to help the agent do his or her job:

1. Who will be going on the cruise?

2. What can you afford to spend for the entire trip?

3. Where would you like to go?

4. How much vacation time do you have?

5. When can you get away?

6. What are your interests?

7. Do you prefer a casual or structured vacation?

8. What kind of accommodations do you want?

9. What are your dining preferences?

10. How will you get to the embarkation port?

---

When you've found a jewel of an agent, then what? Ask many questions. Above all else, be honest about your expectations and budget. Seldom can a travel agent who doesn't know you well guess what your interests are and how much you can afford to spend. Don't be shy. If you have champagne taste and a beer budget, say so. Do not hesitate to interview prospective agents and be wary if they do not interview you right back.

Contrary to what conventional wisdom might suggest, cutting out the travel agent and booking directly with a cruise line won't necessarily get you the lowest price. Approximately 90% of all cruise bookings are still handled through travel agents. In fact, cruise-line reservation systems simply are not capable of dealing with tens of thousands of direct calls from potential passengers. Without an agent working on your behalf, you're on your own. Do not rely solely on Internet message boards for authoritative responses to your questions—that is a service more accurately provided by your travel agent.

**Travel Agent Professional Organization American Society of Travel Agents** (ASTA ☎ 703/739–2782, 800/965–2782 24-hr hotline 🖶 703/684–8319 ⊕ www.travelsense.org).

**Cruise Line Organizations Cruise Lines International Association** (CLIA ☎ 754/224–2200 ⊕ www.cruising.org).

**Recommended Travel Agents AAA** (☎ 800/222–6953 ⊕ www.aaa.com) isn't just for car travel. The company has a searchable database to locate member agencies by zip code.

**American Express Travel** (☎ 800/297–5627 ⊕ travel.americanexpress.com) offers options for online booking and a searchable database of local American Express travel offices.

**Cruise Brothers** (☎ 800/827–7779 or 401/941–3999 ⊕ www.cruisebrothers.com), in business since the mid-1970s, is one of the largest family-owned, cruises-only agencies in the United States.

**Cruise Connections Canada** (☎ 800/661–9283 ⊕ www.cruise-connections.com) is Canada's leading cruise retailer, and one of the largest cruise retailers in North America.

**Cruise Master Travel** (☎ 800/603–5755 ⊕ www.cruisemaster.com) specializes in groups and honeymoons.

**Cruise One** (⊕ www.cruiseone.com) is affiliated with Boston-based NLG, the world's largest cruise retailer, and offers a satisfaction guarantee. The company has more than 400 member agencies nationwide, and its website has a searchable database of member cruise specialists.

**Cruise Planners, Inc.** (☎ 800/683–0206 ⊕ www.cruiseplanners.com) is a network of home-based agent franchises. The website offers a searchable database to locate member agencies.

**Cruises Inc.** (☎ 888/218–4228 or 800/854–0500 ⊕ www.cruisesinc.com) is an affiliate of Boston-based NLG, the world's largest cruise retailer. The company has more than 450 member agencies nationwide, and its website has a searchable database of member cruise specialists.

**Cruises Only** (☎ 800/278–4737 ⊕ www.cruisesonly.com) is affiliated with NLG, the world's largest cruise retailer, and offers a lowest-price guarantee as well as a money-back satisfaction guarantee. Agents are available to assist clients around the clock.

**Ensemble Travel** (☎ 866/350–7460 ⊕ www.ensembletravel.com) is an international network of 1,100 expert travel agencies. Call to be connected to the nearest member agency.

**Hartford Holidays** (☎ 800/828–4813 or 516/746–6670 ⊕ www.hartfordholidays.com) has been family-owned and -operated for 30 years.

**Lighthouse Travel** (☎ 800/719–9917 or 805/566–3905 ⊕ www.lighthousetravel.com) specializes in cruises.

**Northstar Cruises** (☎ 800/249–9360 or 973/228–5005 ⊕ www.northstarcruises.com) is a top booker for most major cruise lines.

**Skyscraper Tours, Inc.** (☎ 888/278–9648 ⊕ www.skyscrapertours.com) offers several annual hosted group cruises.

**Uniglobe International** (☎ 604/718-2600 ⊕ www.uniglobetravel.com) has more than 700 franchise locations worldwide; the website has a searchable database of member cruise agencies.

**Vacation.com** (☎ 800/843–0733 ⊕ www.vacation.com) is a network of more than 5,700 travel-agency locations across the United States and Canada.

**Virtuoso** (☎ 866/401-7974 or 817/870-0300 ⊕ www.virtuoso.com) is the world's most exclusive association of upscale travel agencies. Call to locate members specializing in cruises.

## BOOKING YOUR CRUISE ONLINE

In addition to local travel agencies, there are many hard-working, dedicated travel professionals working for websites. Both big-name travel sellers and mom-and-pop agencies compete for the attention of cyber-savvy clients, and it never hurts to compare prices from a variety of these sources. Some cruise lines even allow you to book directly with them through their websites.

As a rule, Web-based and toll-free brokers will do a decent job for you. They often offer discounted fares, though not always the lowest, so it pays to check around. If you know precisely what you want and how much you should pay to get a real bargain—and you don't mind dealing with an anonymous voice on the phone—by all means make your reservations when the price is right. Just don't expect the personal service you get from an agent you know. Also, be prepared to spend a lot of time and effort on the phone if something goes wrong.

**Online Agencies 7 Blue Seas** (⊕ www.7blueseas.com ☎ 800/242–1781) offers a comprehensive online cruise information website; bookings are made through the toll-free call center.

**Cruise.com** (⊕ www.cruise.com ☎ 888/333–3116) lays claim to being one of the largest websites specializing in discounted cruises on the Internet, and offers a lowest-price guarantee.

**Cruise Compete** (⊕ www.cruisecompete.com ☎ 800/764–4410) allows you to get competing bids from top travel agencies, who respond to your request for bids with their best rates for your trip.

**Cruise Direct** (⊕ www.cruisedirect.com ☎ 888/407–2784) allows customers to book their own travel arrangements through the website and a toll-free number.

**Cruise411.com** (⊕ www.cruise411.com ☎ 800/553–7090) has a booking engine online that allows you to book directly or temporarily hold most cruise reservations without deposit or payment if you prefer to call in your booking.

**Expedia** (⊕ www.expedia.com ☎ 800/397–3342) is a full-service online travel seller that books cruises, too.

**iCruise.com** (⊕ www.icruise.com ☎ 866/389–9219) has a good search engine and service but charges a hefty cancellation fee, so be sure you know what you want before using their booking engine.

**jetBlue** (⊕ www.jetblue.com ☎ 800/538–2583) now allows you to book cruises on its website.

**Moment's Notice** (⊕ www.moments-notice.com ☎ 888/241–3366) offers a searchable database for last-minute deals; call toll-free for reservations.

**Orbitz** (⊕ www.orbitz.com ☎ 888/656–4546) is a full-service online travel seller that books cruises.

**Travelocity** (⊕ www.travelocity.com ☎ 877/815–5446) is a full-service online travel seller with a 24-hour help desk for service issues.

# BEFORE YOU GO

To expedite your preboarding paperwork, some cruise lines have convenient forms on their websites. As long as you have your reservation number, you can provide the required immigration information (usually your citizenship information and passport number), prereserve shore excursions, and even indicate any special requests from the comfort of your home. Less-wired cruise lines might mail preboarding paperwork to you or your travel agent for completion after you make your final payment and request that you return the forms by mail or fax. No matter how you submit them, be sure to make hard copies of any forms you fill out and bring them with you to the pier to smooth the embarkation process.

## DOCUMENTS

It is every passenger's responsibility to have proper identification. If you arrive at the airport without it, you will not be allowed to board your plane. Should that happen, the cruise line will not issue a fare refund. Most travel agents know the requirements and can guide you to the proper agency to obtain what you need if you don't have it.

Everyone must have a valid passport to travel to Europe. Additionally, some countries to which cruise ships call require visas, though it's also true that tourist visas are sometimes not required for cruise passengers, even if they are generally required to visit a particular country. For instance, a visa is not necessary in Russia if you book all your shore excursions through your cruise line or through a private tour company that is licensed to participate in the visa-waiver program (in both cases you must sleep on board your ship), but a visa is required if you tour independently without any kind of tour company. If your itinerary requires a visa of *all* passengers prior to boarding, you should receive an information letter from your cruise line with instructions and, possibly, application forms. It is your responsibility to obtain all necessary visas. Visa information and applications may also be obtained through the local embassy or consulate of the country you will be visiting. Although you can obtain visas yourself, a more hassle-free route is to use a visa service, such as Visa Central or Travisa, that specializes in the process. ■ TIP→ **If you arrive at the pier without a required visa, you will not be allowed to board your ship, and the cruise line will not issue a fare refund.**

**Contacts Travisa** (⊕ *www.travisa.com*). **Visa Central** (⊕ *www.visacentral.com*).

Children under the age of 18—when they are not traveling with *both* parents—almost always require a letter of permission from the absent parent(s). Airlines, cruise lines, and immigration agents can deny children initial boarding or entry to foreign countries without proper proof of identification and citizenship *and* a notarized permission letter from absent or noncustodial parents. Your travel agent or cruise line can help with the wording of such a letter.

## GETTING OR RENEWING A PASSPORT

In light of changing government regulations, you should apply for a passport as far in advance of your cruise as possible. In normal times, the process usually takes at least six weeks, but it can take as long as 12 weeks during busy periods. You can expedite your passport application if you are traveling within two weeks by paying an additional fee of $60 (in addition to the regular passport fee) and appearing in person at a regional passport office. Also, several passport expediting services will handle your application for you (for a hefty fee, of course) and can get you a passport in as few as 48 hours. If you are a U.S. citizen, you can read all about the passport application process at the website of the U.S. Department of State; a passport costs $140 if you are 16 or older and is valid for 10 years, $110 if you are under 16, when it is only valid for five years.

If you have left your passport renewal to the last minute, you can call on a company like A. Briggs Passport & Visa Expeditors to help you get a renewal, sometimes in as little as 48 hours. Most visa expeditors can also help you expedite a passport renewal.

**Contacts A. Briggs Passport & Visa Expeditors** (☎ *800/806–0581 or 202/464–3000* ⊕ *www.abriggs.com*). **U.S. Department of State** (⊕ *travel.state.gov/passport*).

## MONEY

On board your ship you won't have any worries about money, but you will need cash while ashore. If you have not arranged for transfers from the airport to the ship, you will need taxi fare in the local currency, which is the euro for most embarkation cities and the British pound in Great Britain. The Scandinavian countries Denmark, Norway, and Sweden also have their own currencies.

Currency exchange is almost always more costly in your home country than at your foreign destination, but many banks, as well as the American Automobile Association (AAA), American Express, and Travelex bureaus offer the service. In addition, you may find a currency exchange booth in the international terminal at your departure airport. However, the simplest, and usually least expensive, method of obtaining local currency is from an ATM. Visa and MasterCard debit and credit cards are widely accepted at ATMs throughout the world; however, some banks impose a fee for international withdrawals. Before leaving home, make sure you have a PIN (personal identification number) for your card and understand any fees associated with its use. Also, notify the credit card company that you will be using your card overseas so they don't refuse your charges when they notice its repeated use in foreign locales.

For days in port you will also want some cash on hand for beverages, snacks, and small souvenir purchases. Your cruise ship may offer a foreign currency exchange service on board, but, like hotels, the exchange rate is not always the most favorable. We suggest that instead of carrying large amounts of cash when ashore, use a credit card for major purchases.

## SAMPLE PERMISSION LETTER

Here's the text you might use for a typical letter of permission. You should type this up yourself, putting in all the specific details of your trip in place of the blanks.

CONSENT FOR MINOR CHILDREN TO TRAVEL

Date: _____

I (we): _____

authorize my/our minor child(ren): _____

to travel to:_____ on _____

aboard Airline/Flight Number: _____

and/or Cruise Ship: _____

with _____.

Their expected date of return is: _____.

   In addition, I (we) authorize:_____ to consent to any necessary routine or emergency medical treatment during the aforementioned trip.

Signed: _____(Parent)

Signed: _____(Parent)

Address: _____

_____

_____

Telephone:_____

Sworn to and signed before me, a Notary Public,

this _____ day of _____, 20_____

_____

Notary Public Signature and Seal

Before You Go What to Pack   **> 41**

# Taking Your Toddler to Sea

Cruise ships are wonderful places for family vacations, but you must understand the rules before promising your littlest sailors unlimited playtime, either in the kids' program or the swimming pool. Nothing is sadder than the face of a toddler who isn't allowed in the ship's pool—even the kiddy pool—because he/she isn't potty-trained. Even swim diapers won't pass muster in most cases.

Cruise ships must comply with the Center for Disease Control's (CDC) Vessel Sanitation Program (VSP) regulations. Charged with the prevention of pool contamination and the resulting spread of bacteria that can cause illness after "accidents" in pools and water parks at sea, the VSP provides health and safety requirements to cruise lines, including the ban on *any* diapers in the pools.

The straight poop is that swim diapers are not completely leak-proof. They can prevent solids from escaping, but cannot contain urine or diarrhea completely, nor do they stop seepage of infection-causing germs.

However, not all cruise ships entirely ban water play for youngsters who are not potty-trained. Special wading pools approved by VSP standards have their own separate water and disinfection systems and heavy-duty filtration units that can be "flushed out" when diaper accidents occur. Such splash zones are found on Disney Cruise Line's *Disney Wonder* and *Disney Magic* and on Royal Caribbean's *Freedom of the Seas, Liberty of the Seas,* and *Independence of the Seas.*

About those kids' programs: check the Cruise Line Profiles for age limits—some are as low as two years of age, but most will accept only children three and older. While being toilet trained isn't always a prerequisite for participation, only the counselors on Disney Cruise Line, Carnival Cruise Lines, and certain Royal Caribbean International ships will change diapers.

**Contacts American Automobile Association** (*AAA* ☎ *315/797–5000* ⊕ *www.aaa.com*). **American Express** (☎ *888/412–6945 in U.S., 801/945–9450 collect outside of U.S. to add value or speak to customer service* ⊕ *www.americanexpress.com*). **Travelex** (⊕ *www.travelex.com*).

## WHAT TO PACK

As far as clothing goes, cruise wear falls into three categories: casual, informal, and formal. Cruise documents should include information indicating how many evenings fall into each category. You will know when to wear what by reading your ship's daily newsletter—each evening's dress code will be prominently announced.

For days on board, you'll need **casual** wear. When your ship has a covered swimming pool or is sailing to warm-weather Mediterranean cruises, you'll typically need swimwear, a cover-up, and sandals for the pool. Time spent ashore touring and shopping calls for comfortable clothing and good walking shoes. At some point, you'll be confronted with cobblestones. Although locals seem to navigate them with ease, even in Italian designer shoes, they can be tricky and even slippery.

Conservative is a rule to dress by in Europe, and mix-and-match will save room in your suitcase. Keep in mind that respectful attire is required when visiting cathedrals, mosques, synagogues, and even some museums. Shorts, and even short skirts, are frowned on or banned outright, and women's arms are expected to be covered. On the other hand, beach resorts in the Mediterranean are more relaxed and resort clothing is entirely appropriate; in fact, be prepared to see topless and even nude sun-worshippers on some of the more permissive beaches along the French Riviera. Leave clothing adorned with slogans or logos and clunky white athletic shoes on the ship unless you want to stand out as an American tourist.

Back aboard your ship, evening casual means khakis and nice polo or sport shirts for men. Ladies' outfits are dresses, skirts and tops, or pants outfits. By sticking to two or three complementary colors and a few accessories, you can mix up tops and bottoms for a different look every night.

**Informal** attire, which has been dropped by many cruise lines, is a little trickier. It applies only to evening wear and can mean different things depending on the cruise line. Informal for women is a dressier dress or pants outfit; for men it almost always includes a dress shirt, sport coat, and sometimes a tie. Check your documents carefully—they may specify country-club or smart casual, which are essentially informal without the sport coat and tie.

**Formal** night means dressing up, but these days even that is a relative notion. You will see women in everything from simple cocktail dresses to elaborate glittering gowns. A tuxedo (either all black or with white dinner jacket) or dark suit is required for men. If you have been a mother-of-the-bride lately, chances are your outfit for the wedding is just perfect for formal night. For children, Sunday best is entirely appropriate.

Men can often rent their formal attire from the cruise line, and if they do so, it will be waiting when they board. Be sure to make these arrangements in advance; your travel agent can get the details from the cruise line. But if you are renting a tux, buy your own studs: a surefire way to spot a rented tuxedo is by the inexpensive studs that come with it. Also, many men with a little girth consider a vest more comfortable than a cummerbund.

## OTHER ESSENTIALS

An absolute essential for women is a shawl or light sweater. Aggressive air-conditioning can make public rooms uncomfortable, particularly if you are sunburned from a day at the beach. Put things you can't do without—such as prescription medication, spare eyeglasses, toiletries, cosmetics, a swimsuit, and change of clothes for the first day—in your carry-on. Most cruise ships provide soap, shampoo, and sometimes conditioner, so you probably won't need those. And plan carefully. In fact, we'd strongly advise you to make a list so you don't forget anything.

## LUGGAGE

You know the days of massive steamer trunks are history, but is there a maximum amount of luggage that you can bring on a cruise ship? Yes, there really is a limit of sorts. Although some cruise lines state that each passenger is allowed 200 pounds of personal luggage, you're unlikely to see anyone's bags actually being weighed. However, it's not the cruise-line restrictions that passengers need to worry about.

Cruisers arriving at their embarkation port by air should be aware of airline baggage restrictions. Most major airlines charge a fee for a second checked suitcase on European flights and stringently enforce luggage size and weight policies, resulting in a rude (and expensive) surprise to some travelers with large, heavy suitcases. In the United States, you will almost always be charged extra for checked bags weighing more than 50 pounds. But some European airlines will not accept check bags over 70 pounds and add significant surcharges if the total weight is more than 20 kilos (44 pounds). Also some intra-Europe flights allow fewer and smaller carry-on items.

Although most airlines and airports require that you check your luggage onto your flight at least 30 minutes before scheduled departure time, some now require 45 minutes or more. Check-in time for international flights can be at least an hour before departure (and often longer). Check with your air carrier for the latest guidelines and restrictions.

If your luggage goes astray, make sure that you leave all the information regarding your ship's itinerary with the airline baggage desk before you leave the airport, and make sure the cruise line's representative knows as well. Ask about any compensation you may be entitled to; in some cases, the airline will give you cash to purchase your immediate necessities. If you booked an air-and-sea package with your cruise line, the cruise line may give you an onboard credit to purchase necessary items if your bags are delayed. With luck, your bags will catch up to you before your ship departs; if that doesn't happen, they will be forwarded to the next port of call by your airline. In the interim, you will have to borrow or purchase clothing and personal items; you may be offered laundry assistance or the use of formal wear by the cruise line. Save the receipts for all purchases to request reimbursement by the airline, or your insurance company, if you have baggage delay coverage.

## INSURANCE

It's a good idea to purchase travel insurance, which covers a variety of possible hazards and mishaps, when you book a cruise. One important concern for cruise passengers is being delayed en route to the port of embarkation and missing the ship. Another major consideration is lost luggage (*for more information on lost luggage, see ⇨ Luggage, above*)—or even the delay of luggage. Both of these possibilities should be covered by your policy. You may miss the first day or two of your cruise, but all will not be lost financially. A travel policy will ensure that you can replace delayed necessities secure in the knowledge that

CLOSE UP

## Duct Tape—the Essential Travel Tool

So, your bags are packed and you're ready to cruise? Not quite yet if you skipped the duct tape. Don't leave your home port without one of a traveler's handiest necessities. Duct tape no longer belongs only in the garage. Some of its more mundane uses are luggage repair (fix a broken hinge with ease) and security (baggage handlers won't tamper with duct tape, it's too much trouble). Wrapped in duct tape, your luggage is easy to spot in terminals as well. For individuality, duct tape comes in colors, as well as the traditional silver. For even higher suitcase visibility, there are snazzy neon colors. It's water resistant (an important feature for ocean travelers) and can serve as an indestructible luggage tag as well as a strap—just write your name and address on the tape. Best of all, duct tape is easy to tear by hand and you don't need scissors to cut it.

There are literally thousands of uses for duct tape. Every homeowner knows that when something is supposed to stick together and it doesn't, nothing holds like duct tape. What about at sea? Is the bottom ready to fall out of your cabin's vanity drawer? Tape it until the carpenter arrives. You're a late sleeper and the drapes don't quite close? Keep the sun at bay by taping them together. Everyone has had the stitching in a hem unravel at the last minute. Duct tape to the rescue! There are bottle lids to secure, rattles to silence, drawers that won't stay shut when the ship is rolling, and other little things that happen when you least expect them.

---

you will be reimbursed for those unexpected expenditures. Save your receipts for all out-of-pocket expenses to file your claim and be sure to get an incident report from the airline at fault.

No one wants his or her cruise vacation spoiled by a broken arm, heart attack, or worse, but if one of life's tragedies occurs, you want to be covered. The medical insurance program you depend on at home might not extend coverage beyond the borders of the United States. Medicare assuredly will not cover you if you are hurt or sick while abroad. It is worth noting that all ships of foreign registry are considered to be "outside the United States" by Medicare. If there is any question in your mind, check your cruise-ship's registry—with very few exceptions, it will *not* be the United States. Without basic coverage, travelers should be prepared to pay for any care they require, either by credit card or wire transfer of funds to the provider.

Some independent insurers such as Travel Guard, Allianz Travel Protection (formerly Access America), or CSA offer comprehensive policies at attractive rates. Nearly all cruise lines offer their own line of insurance. Compare the coverage and rates to determine which is best for you. Keep in mind that insurance purchased from an independent carrier is more likely to include coverage if the cruise line goes out of business before or during your cruise. Although it is a rare and unlikely occurrence, you do want to be insured in the event that it happens.

U.S. Travel Insurers **Allianz Travel Insurance** (☎ 800/284–8300 ⊕ www.allianztravelinsurance.com). **CSA Travel Protection** (☎ 800/711–1197 ⊕ www.csatravelprotection.com). **HTH Worldwide** (☎ 610/254–8700 or 888/243–2358 ⊕ www.hthworldwide.com). **Travelex Insurance** (☎ 800/228–9792 ⊕ www.travelex-insurance.com). **Travel Guard International** (☎ 715/345–0505 or 800/826–4919 ⊕ www.travelguard.com). **Travel Insured International** (☎ 800/243–3174 ⊕ www.travelinsured.com).

---

# ARRIVING AND EMBARKING

Most cruise-ship passengers fly to the port of embarkation, even if their cruise is a transatlantic crossing to Europe. If you book your cruise far enough in advance, you'll be given the opportunity to purchase an air-and-sea package, which may—or may not—save you money on your flight. You might get a lower fare by booking your air independently, so it's a good idea to check for the best fare available. Independent air arrangements might save you enough to cover the cost of a hotel room in your embarkation port so you can arrive early. It's not a bad idea to arrive a day early to overcome inevitable jet lag and avoid the possibility of delayed flights.

If you buy an air-and-sea package from your cruise line, a uniformed cruise line agent will meet you at baggage claim to smooth your way from airport to pier. You will need to claim your own bags and give them to the transfer driver so they can be loaded on the bus. On arrival at the pier, luggage is automatically transferred to the ship for delivery to your cabin. The cruise-line ground transfer system can also be available to independent fliers. However, be sure to ask your travel agent how much it costs; you may find that a taxi or shuttle service is less expensive and more convenient.

---

## BOARDING

Once the planning, packing, and anticipation are behind them, veteran cruise passengers sometimes view embarkation day as anticlimactic. However, for first-time cruise travelers, embarking their first ship can be more than exhilarating—it can be downright intimidating. What exactly can you expect?

Once inside the cruise terminal, you'll see a check-in line. Actual boarding time is often scheduled for noon or later, but some cruise lines will begin processing early arrivals and then direct them to a holding area. During check-in, you will be asked to produce your documents and any forms you were sent to complete ahead of time, plus your passport and a credit card (to cover onboard charges). If you completed the documentation process online, bring along copies of those forms. You are issued a boarding card that often also doubles as your stateroom key card and shipboard charge card. At some point—usually before you enter the check-in area—you and your hand luggage will pass through a security procedure similar to that performed at airports.

# FOREIGN-LANGUAGE CRUISE LINES

Not every cruise line sailing in Europe caters to North Americans, nor is English the universal language of cruising on these ships. Cruise travel has gained favor with European vacationers in recent years, and lines have launched to provide them with the experiences they prefer. For instance, Italians aren't overly fond of casino gaming, but they love to dance, so their ships have spaces where even ballroom champs have the room to show off their moves. Germans like to sunbathe in the buff and have a late-night bite, so there are often places to bare it all and nosh on a midnight *wurst*. And Spaniards don't typically start their evening meal until 9 pm at the earliest, so late seating doesn't end until close to midnight. While Americans can and do sail on some of these ships, booking can pose its own problems as the lines often don't have North American operations, and travel agents in the United States aren't knowledgeable about their policies.

## AIDA CRUISES
Germany's largest cruise line traces its history back to East Germany in the 1960s, but it wasn't until 1994 that the company built its first brand-new ship. Now a member brand of Carnival Corporation, AIDA Cruises operates a fleet of modern vessels ranging in size from 38,000 to 71,000 tons. On board the experience focuses on an active, ultra-casual lifestyle. The emphasis by day is on wellness and fitness activities in the large AIDA Spa and fitness center and poolside on expansive open decks. Meals are generally buffet style, and after dinner there's lively entertainment in the show lounge and a festive, easygoing atmosphere in bars and lounges. ⊕ *www.aida.de*.

## CDF CROISIÈRES DE FRANCE
Founded in 2007 as a subsidiary of Royal Caribbean Cruises Ltd., CDF launched service in 2008 with one ship, the *Bleu de France*, which has since been sold. The line now offers its cruises on the 47,427-ton *L'Horizon* (formerly *Celebrity Horizon*). In addition to accommodations and meals, the cruise fare includes all drinks and gratuities. French is the only language spoken on board. ⊕ *www.cdfcroisieresdefrance.fr*.

## HAPAG-LLOYD CRUISES
Probably best known as a cargo shipping company Hapag-Lloyd nevertheless operates a passenger fleet that includes one of the world's finest cruise ships, the high-end 28,890-ton *Europa* and the new *Europa 2*. Other vessels in the fleet include two expedition ships, *Hanseatic* and *Bremen*, as well as the globe-trotting *Columbus 2*. German is the language spoken on board, although there are occasional bilingual cruises scheduled for English-speaking guests. However, the only concessions made to non-German speakers are menus and daily programs in English. All shore tours and onboard activities and enrichment programs are still only presented in German—even the safety drill is conducted strictly in German. ⊕ *www.hl-cruises.com*.

## IBERO CRUCEROS
Founded in 2007 and based in Madrid, Ibero Cruceros is a subsidiary of Carnival Corporation that operates under the control of Carnival Corporation's European

division, the Costa Cruises Group. The line caters to the Spanish- and Portuguese-speaking markets with its small fleet of former Carnival Cruise Lines ships—*Grand Celebration*, formerly *Carnival Celebration*, and *Grand Holiday*, formerly *Carnival Holiday*—and a chartered vessel *Grand Mistral*. All offer a traditional cruise experience with only Spanish and Portuguese spoken.
⊕ *www.iberocruceros.com.*

### PETER DEILMANN
After closing the German company's riverboat cruising operation and the passing of its founder, the ocean-cruising Peter Dielmann line is still operated as a family company with one ship, the MS *Deutschland*. The high-end 22,400-ton ship's unique interior décor recalls the great German ocean liners of the early 20th century and is recognized as the setting for the television show *Das Traumschiff*—"The Dream Ship"—Germany's version of "The Love Boat." Built in 1998, the luxury ship is quite grand and has an extensive spa and wellness program but is showing her age with accommodations on the small side and only two with balconies.
⊕ *www.deilmann-kreuzfahrten.de.*

### PULLMANTUR CRUISES
In the late 1990s, Pullmantur Cruises was founded as a subsidiary of the Madrid-based travel agency Pullmantur and purchased by Royal Caribbean Cruises Ltd. in 2006. Although Pullmantur markets mainly in Spain and other Spanish-speaking countries, it makes other international passengers welcome with bilingual printed materials in English. The fleet now consists of ships that originally sailed for Royal Caribbean International (now MS *Empress*, MS *Sovereign*, and MS *Monarch*) and Celebrity Cruises (MV *Zenith*), offering a traditional cruise experience with Spanish flair. Most cruises operate on an "all-inclusive" basis where all beverages, including alcohol, are included in the fare.
⊕ *www.pullmantur.es.*

### TUI CRUISES
Another cruise travel option for German speakers began operations in 2009. TUI Cruises is a joint venture of the German tourist company TUI and Royal Caribbean Cruises Ltd. based in Hamburg. Positioned somewhat between the contemporary AIDA Cruises and luxury Hapag-Lloyd Cruises products, the service-oriented, premium line is customized to German tastes. German is the main language spoken on board, and sailings are marketed primarily to residents of Germany, Switzerland, and Austria. The current fleet, consisting of *Mein Schiff 1* and *Mein Schiff 2*, is composed of ships from Celebrity Cruises—the former *Celebrity Galaxy* and *Celebrity Mercury*. TUI is expected to introduce a brand-new ship in 2014.
⊕ *tuicruises.com.*

Don't be alarmed if your passport is retained at check-in. The purser holds passports to expedite the process of "clearing" the ship when entering each country for the first time. To clear the ship, immigration officials board and check the ship's manifest and passengers'—as well as crewmembers'—passports before anyone can go ashore. However, you may find that some banks and currency exchanges in ports of call require identification to exchange money and, for that purpose, it's a good idea to make a color copy of your passport's photo page to carry ashore in lieu of the actual passport itself. Should you be required to carry your actual passport ashore—when visiting Russia, for instance—it will be returned to you for the day.

Check-in lines can be long, particularly at peak times. If check-in starts at noon but continues to 4 pm, you can expect lines to trail off as the boarding deadline approaches. Everyone is anxious to get on board and begin a vacation, so if you arrive at one of the busy periods, keep in mind that this is not the time to get cranky if you have to wait.

Once boarding begins, you will inevitably have your first experience with the ship's photographer, and be asked to pose for an embarkation picture. It only takes a second, so smile. You are under no obligation to purchase any photos taken of you during the cruise, but they are nice souvenirs. Further procedures vary somewhat once you are greeted by staff members lined up just inside the ship's hull; however, you'll have to produce your boarding card and, possibly, a picture ID for the security officer. At some point, either at the check-in desk or when boarding the ship for the first time, you may be photographed for security purposes—your image will display when your boarding card is swiped into a computer as you leave and reboard the ship in ports of call. Depending on the cruise line, you will be directed to your cabin, or a steward will relieve you of your carry-on luggage and accompany you. Stewards on high-end cruise lines not only show you the way, but hand you a glass of champagne as a welcome-aboard gesture. However, if you board early, don't be surprised if you are told cabins are not ready for occupancy—passageways to accommodations may even be roped off. In that case you can explore the ship, sample the luncheon buffet, or simply relax until an announcement is made that you can go to your cabin.

## ON BOARD

Check out your cabin to make sure that everything is in order. Try the plumbing and set the thermostat to the temperature you prefer. Your cabin may feel warm while docked but will cool off when the ship is underway. You should find a copy of the ship's daily schedule in the cabin. Take a few moments to look it over—you will want to know what time the lifeboat (or muster) drill takes place (a placard on the back of your cabin door will indicate directions to your emergency station), as well as meal hours and the schedule for various activities and entertainments.

Rented tuxedoes are either hanging in the closet or will be delivered sometime during the afternoon; bon voyage gifts sent by your friends or travel agent should appear as well. Be patient if you are expecting deliveries, particularly on megaships. Cabin stewards participate in the ship's turnaround and are extremely busy, although yours will no doubt introduce himself at the first available opportunity. It will also be a while before your checked luggage arrives, so your initial order of business is usually the buffet, if you haven't already had lunch. Bring along the daily schedule to check over while you eat.

While making your way to the Lido buffet, no doubt you'll notice bar waiters offering trays of colorful bon voyage drinks, often in souvenir glasses that you can keep. Beware—they are not complimentary! If you choose one, you will be asked to sign for it. Again, like the photos, you are under no obligation to purchase.

Do your plans for the cruise include booking shore excursions and indulging in spa treatments? The most popular tours sometimes sell out, and spas can be busy during sea days, so your next stops should be the Shore Excursion Desk to book tours and the spa to make appointments if you didn't already book your spa visits and excursions in advance.

Dining room seating arrangements are another matter for consideration. If you aren't happy with your assigned dinner seating, speak to the maitre d'. The daily schedule will indicate where and when to meet with him. If you plan to dine in the ship's specialty restaurant, make those reservations as soon as possible to avoid disappointment.

## PAYING FOR THINGS ON BOARD

Let's step back a moment and take a look at what happened when you checked in at the pier. Because a cashless society prevails on cruise ships, an imprint was made of your credit card, or you had to place a cash deposit for use against your onboard charges. Then you were issued a charge card that usually doubles as your stateroom key card. Most onboard expenditures are charged to your shipboard account with your signature as verification, with the possible exception of casino gaming—even so, you can often get cash withdrawals from your account from the casino cashier.

An itemized bill is provided at the end of the voyage listing your purchases. In order to avoid surprises, it is a good idea to set aside your charge slips and request an interim printout of your bill from the purser to ensure accuracy. Should you change your mind about charging onboard purchases, you can always inform the purser and pay in cash or traveler's checks instead. If your cash deposit was more than you spent, you will receive a refund.

## DINING

All food, all the time? Not quite, but it is possible to literally eat away the day and most of the night on a cruise. A popular cruise directors' joke is, "You came on as passengers, and you will be leaving as cargo." Although it is meant in fun, it does contain a ring of truth. Food—tasty and plentiful—is available 24 hours a day on most cruise ships, and the dining experience at sea has reached almost mythic proportions. Perhaps it has something to do with legendary midnight buffets and the absence of menu prices, or maybe it's the vast selection and availability.

## RESTAURANTS

Every ship has at least one main restaurant and a Lido, or casual buffet alternative. Increasingly important are specialty restaurants. Meals in the primary and buffet restaurants are included in the cruise fare, as are round-the-clock room service, midday tea and snacks, and late-night buffets. Most mainstream cruise lines levy a surcharge for dining in alternative restaurants that may also include a gratuity, although there generally is no additional charge on luxury cruise lines.

You may also find a pizzeria or a specialty coffee bar on your ship—increasingly popular favorites cropping up on ships old and new. Although pizza is complimentary, expect an additional charge for specialty coffees at the coffee bar and, quite likely, in the dining room as well. You will also likely be charged for sodas and drinks other than iced tea, regular coffee, tap water, and fruit juice during meals.

There is often a direct relationship between the cost of a cruise and the quality of its cuisine. The food is sophisticated on some (mostly expensive) lines, among them Crystal, Cunard, Regent Seven Seas, Seabourn, SeaDream, and Silversea. In the more moderate price range, Celebrity Cruises has always been known for its fine cuisine. The trend toward featuring specialty dishes and even entire menus designed by acclaimed chefs has spread throughout the cruise industry; however, on most mainstream cruise lines the food is the quality that you would find in any good hotel banquet—perfectly acceptable but certainly not great.

## DINNER SEATINGS

If your cruise ship has traditional seatings for dinner, the one decision that may set the tone for your entire cruise is your dinner seating. Which is best? Early dinner seating is generally scheduled between 6 and 6:30 pm, while late seating can begin from 8:15 to 8:45 pm. European cruise lines generally adhere to the custom of dining later and schedule restaurant hours accordingly. Even cruise lines that cater to Americans may adjust dining hours to begin a bit later when in Europe. So the "best" seating depends on you, your lifestyle, and your personal preference.

Families with young children and older passengers often choose an early seating. Early-seating diners are encouraged not to linger too long over dessert and coffee, because the dining room has to be readied for late seating. Late seating is viewed by some passengers as more romantic and less rushed.

Cruise lines understand that strict schedules no longer satisfy the desires of all modern cruise passengers. Most cruise lines now include alternatives to the set schedules in the dining room, including casual dinner menus in their buffet facilities where more flexibility is allowed in dress and mealtimes. Open seating is primarily associated with more upscale lines; it allows passengers the flexibility to dine any time during restaurant hours and be seated with whomever they please.

However, led by Norwegian Cruise Line and Princess Cruises, more contemporary and premium cruise lines offer adaptations of open seating to offer variety and a more personalized experience for their passengers.

## SPECIALTY RESTAURANTS ON MAJOR CRUISE LINES

| CRUISE LINE | SHIP | CUISINE TYPE | CHARGE (PER PERSON) |
|---|---|---|---|
| Azamara Club Cruises | Azamara Journey and Quest | Steak house | $25 (comp. for suite occupants) |
| | | Mediterranean | $25 (comp. for suite occupants) |
| Carnival | Spirit-class, Conquest-class, and Dream-class | Steaks and seafood | $35 |
| | Carnival Magic and Carnival Breeze | Italian | $12 dinner, lunch no charge |
| | Carnival Breeze | Asian | à la carte |
| | All ships | International with champagne reception | $75 |
| Celebrity | Solstice-class, Millennium-class | Continental | $40 |
| | Solstice-class and Constellation | Italian | $30 |
| | Solstice- and Millennium-class | Creperie | $5 |
| | Solstice and Equinox | Asian | $25 |
| | Eclipse, Infinity, Silhouette, Reflection, Millennium, and Summit | American | $40 |
| | Silhouette and Reflection | Grill | $40 |
| Costa | All ships | Italian | à la carte (comp. dinner for two for suite occupants) |
| Crystal | All ships | Italian, Asian, Sushi | No charge |
| | All ships | International with wine pairings | $210 |
| Cunard | Queen Mary 2, Queen Victoria | Mediterranean | à la carte lunch or dinner |
| | Queen Elizabeth | French | à la carte or $35 Tasting Menu |
| | All ships | Mexican, Asian, or South American themed | $10 |
| Disney | All ships | Northern Italian | $20 dinner, $20 brunch |
| | Disney Dream, Disney Fantasy | French | $75 |
| Holland America | All ships | Steaks and seafood | $25 dinner, $10 lunch |
| | All ships, except Prinsendam | Italian | $10 |

## SPECIALTY RESTAURANTS ON MAJOR CRUISE LINES

| CRUISE LINE | SHIP | CUISINE TYPE | CHARGE (PER PERSON) |
|---|---|---|---|
| | Signature-class | Asian | $15 dinner, lunch no charge |
| | All ships | International | $39 dinner; $59 with wine pairings |
| Norwegian | All ships | French | $20 |
| | All ships | Steak house | $25 |
| | All ships | Italian | $10 |
| | All ships, except *Sky* | Sushi | à la carte |
| | All ships, except *Sky* | Teppanyaki | $25 |
| | All ships, except *Sky* and *Sun* | Asian | $15 |
| | *Norwegian Jade* | Mexican | $10 |
| | *Norwegian Epic* | Chinese | à la carte |
| | All ships except *Norwegian Sky* and *Spirit* | Brazilian Churrascaria | $20 |
| Oceania | All ships | Italian | No charge |
| | All ships | Steak house | No charge |
| | *Marina* and *Riviera* | French | No charge |
| | *Marina* and *Riviera* | Asian | No charge |
| Princess | Sun-class | Steak house | $20 adults; $10 children under 13; no charge children under 2 |
| | Coral-class, Grand-class, *Pacific*, and *Ocean Princess* | Steak house | $20 adults; $10 children under 13; no charge children under 2 |
| | Coral-class, Grand-class, *Pacific*, *Ocean Princess*, *Caribbean*, *Crown*, *Emerald*, and *Ruby Princess* | Italian | $20 adults; $10 children under 13; no charge children under 2 |
| | *Caribbean*, *Crown*, *Emerald*, and *Ruby Princess* | Steaks and seafood | $25 adults; $12.50 children under 13; no charge children under 2 |
| | All ships | International with wine pairings | $95 |
| Regent Seven Seas | All ships | Steaks and seafood | No charge |
| | *Mariner*, *Voyager* | French | No charge |
| Royal Caribbean | *Oasis-*, *Freedom-*, *Radiance-*, *Vision-class* and *Enchantment*, *Mariner*, and *Navigator of the Seas* | Steak house | $30 |

## SPECIALTY RESTAURANTS ON MAJOR CRUISE LINES

| CRUISE LINE | SHIP | CUISINE TYPE | CHARGE (PER PERSON) |
|---|---|---|---|
| | *Oasis-, Freedom-, Voyager-, Radiance-class, Rhapsody,* and *Grandeur of the Seas* | Italian | $15 lunch, $20 dinner |
| | All ships except Vision- and Radiance-class | Johnny Rockets diner | $4.95 |
| | Oasis-class | American | $40 |
| | *Radiance of the Seas* | Brazilian Churrascaria | $25 |
| | Oasis-class | Spa cuisine | $20 dinner, lunch no charge |
| | Oasis-class and *Radiance of the Seas* | Seafood (Oasis), Mexican (Allure and Radiance) | à la carte |
| | All ships except *Majesty* and *Enchantment of the Seas* | Asian | à la carte |
| | All ships except *Majesty of the Seas* | International with wine pairings | $95 |
| Seabourn | All ships | International | No charge |
| Silversea | All ships | International | $30 |
| | All ships | International with wine pairings | $30, plus cost of wines |
| | All ships | Italian | No charge |
| | *Silver Spirit* | Asian | $30 |
| Windstar | *Wind Surf* | International and steak house | No charge |

### SPECIALTY RESTAURANTS

A growing trend in shipboard dining is the emergence of sophisticated specialty restaurants that require reservations and frequently charge a fee. From as little as $25 per person for a complete steak dinner to $200 per person for an elaborate gourmet meal including vintage wines paired with each course, specialty restaurants offer a refined dining option that cannot be duplicated in your ship's main restaurants. If you anticipate dining in your ship's intimate specialty restaurant, make reservations as soon as possible to avoid disappointment.

### SPECIAL DIETS

Cruise lines make every possible attempt to ensure dining satisfaction. If you have special dietary considerations—such as low-salt, kosher, or food allergies—be sure to indicate them well ahead of time and check to be certain your needs are known by your waiter once on board. In addition to the usual menu items, so-called "spa," low-calorie, low-carbohydrate, or low-fat selections, as well as children's menus, are

CLOSE UP

## Drinking and Gambling Ages

Many underage passengers have learned to their chagrin that the rules that apply on land are also adhered to at sea. On most mainstream cruise ships you must be 21 to imbibe alcoholic beverages. There are exceptions—for instance, on cruises departing from countries where the legal drinking age is typically lower than 21 or, on some cruise lines, a parent who is sailing with his or her son(s) and/or daughter(s) who is between the ages of 18 to 20, may sign a waiver allowing the 18- to 20-year old to consume alcoholic beverages, generally limited to beer and wine. However, by and large, if you haven't achieved the magic age of 21, your shipboard charge card will be coded as booze-free, and bartenders won't risk their jobs to sell you alcohol.

Gambling is a bit looser, and 18-year-olds can try their luck on cruise lines such as Carnival, Celebrity, Holland America, Silversea, Norwegian, and Royal Caribbean; most other cruise lines adhere to the age-21 minimum. Casinos are trickier to patrol than bars, though, and minors who look old enough may get away with dropping a few coins in an out-of-the-way slot machine before being spotted on a hidden security camera. If you hit a big jackpot, you may have a lot of explaining to do to your parents.

usually available. Requests for dishes not featured on the menu can often be granted if you ask in advance.

### ALCOHOL

On all but the most upscale lines, you pay for alcohol aboard the ship, including wine with dinner. Wine typically costs about what you would expect to pay at a nice lounge or restaurant in a resort or in a major city. Wine by the bottle is a more economical choice at dinner than ordering it by the glass. Any wine you don't finish will be kept for you and served the next night. Gifts of wine or champagne ordered from the cruise line (either by you, a friend, or your travel agent) can be taken to the dining room. Wine from any other source will incur a corkage fee of approximately $10 to $25 per bottle. Some (though not all) lines will allow you to carry wine aboard when you embark for the first time; almost no line allows you to carry other alcohol on board.

## ENTERTAINMENT

It's hard to imagine, but in the early years of cruise travel shipboard entertainment consisted of little more than poetry readings and passenger talent shows. Those days are long gone. These days, seven-night cruises usually include two original production shows. One of these might be a Las Vegas–style extravaganza and the other a best-of-Broadway show featuring old and new favorites from the Great White Way. Other shows highlight the talents of individual singers, dancers, magicians, comedians, and even acrobats.

Real treats are the folkloric shows or other entertainments arranged to take place while cruise ships are in port. Local performers come aboard, usually shortly before the ship sails, to present their country's songs and dances. It's an excellent way to get a glimpse of their performing arts.

Most ships also have movie nights, in-cabin movies, or you may be able to rent or borrow movies to watch on your in-cabin DVD player, if you have one. The latest twist in video programming can be found on some Princess, Costa, MSC, and Carnival ships—huge outdoor LED screens where movies, music-video concerts, news channels, and even the ship's activities are broadcast for passengers lounging poolside.

Enrichment programs have also become a popular pastime at sea. It may come as a surprise that port lecturers on many large contemporary cruise ships offer more information on shore tours and shopping than insight into the ports of call. If more cerebral presentations are important to you, consider a cruise on a line that features stimulating enrichment programs and seminars at sea. Speakers can include destination-oriented historians, popular authors, business leaders, radio or television personalities, and even movie stars.

### LOUNGES AND NIGHTCLUBS

You'll often find live entertainment in the ship lounges after dinner (and even sometimes before dinner). If you want to unleash your inner–American Idol, look for karaoke. Singing along in a lively piano bar is another shipboard favorite for would-be crooners.

Other lounges might feature easy-listening or jazz performances or live music for pre- and post-dinner social dancing. Later in the evening, lounges pick up the pace with music from the 1950s and '60s; clubs aimed at a younger crowd usually have more contemporary dance music during the late-night hours.

### CASINOS

On most ships lavish casinos pulsate with activity. On ships that feature them, the rationale for locating casinos where most passengers must pass either through or alongside them is obvious—the unspoken allure of winning. In addition to slot machines in a variety of denominations, cruise-ship casinos usually have table games. Casino hours vary based on the itinerary or location of the ship; most are required to close while in port, while others may be able to offer 24-hour slot machines and simply close table games. Every casino has a cashier, and you may be able to charge a cash advance to your onboard account, for a fee.

## SPORTS AND FITNESS

Onboard sports facilities might include a court for basketball, volleyball, tennis—or all three—a jogging track, or even an in-line skating track. Some ships are even offering innovative and unexpected features, such as rock-climbing walls, bungee trampolines, and surfing pools on some Royal Caribbean ships. For the less adventurous, there's always table tennis and shuffleboard. Golf is a perennial seagoing favorite of players who want to take their games to the next level and include Europe's most challenging courses on their scorecards. Shipboard programs can include clinics, use of full-motion golf cages, and even individual instruction from resident pros using state-of-the-art computer analysis. Golf excursions will take you shoreside.

Naturally, you will find at least one swimming pool and, possibly, several. Cruise-ship pools are generally on the small side—more appropriate for cooling off than doing laps—and the majority contain filtered saltwater. But some are elaborate affairs, with waterslides and interactive water play areas for family fun. Princess Grand–class ships have challenging, freshwater "swim against the current" pools for swimming enthusiasts who want to get their low-impact exercise while on board.

Shipboard fitness centers have become ever more elaborate, offering state-of-the-art exercise machines, treadmills, and stair steppers, not to mention weights and weight machines. As a bonus, many fitness centers with floor-to-ceiling windows have the world's most inspiring sea views. Most ships also offer complimentary fitness classes, but you might also find classes in Pilates, spinning, or yoga (usually for a fee). Personal trainers are usually on board to get you off on the right foot, also for a fee.

## SPAS

With all the usual pampering and service in luxurious surroundings, simply being on a cruise can be a stress-reducing experience. Add to that the menu of spa and salon services at your fingertips and you have a recipe for total sensory pleasure. Spas have also become among the most popular of shipboard areas. Steiner Leisure is the largest spa and salon operator at sea (the company also operates the Mandara and the Greenhouse spa brands), with facilities on more than 100 cruise ships worldwide.

In addition to facials, manicures, pedicures, massages, and sensual body treatments, other hallmarks of Steiner Leisure are salon services and products for hair and skin. Founded in 1901 by Henry Steiner of London, a single salon prospered when Steiner's son joined the business in 1926 and was granted a Royal Warrant as hairdresser to Her Majesty Queen Mary in 1937. In 1956 Steiner won its first cruise-ship contract to operate the salon on board the ships of the Cunard Line. By the mid-1990s Steiner Leisure began taking an active role in creating shipboard spas offering a wide variety of wellness therapies and beauty programs for both women and men.

## OTHER SHIPBOARD SERVICES

### COMMUNICATIONS

Just because you are out to sea does not mean you have to be out of touch. However, ship-to-shore telephone calls can cost $5 to $15 a minute, so it makes more economic sense to use email to remain in contact with your home or office. Most ships have basic computer systems, while some newer vessels offer more high-tech connectivity—even in-cabin hookups or wireless connections for either your own laptop computer or one you can rent on board. Expect charges in the 75¢- to

## Safety at Sea

Safety begins with you, the passenger. Once settled into your cabin, locate your life vests if they are stored there and review the posted emergency instructions. Make sure the vests are in good condition and learn how to secure them properly. Make certain the ship's purser knows if you have a physical infirmity that may hamper a speedy exit from your cabin, so that in an emergency he or she can quickly dispatch a crew member to assist you. If you're traveling with children, be sure that child-size life jackets are placed in your cabin.

Before your ship leaves the embarkation port, you'll be required to attend a mandatory lifeboat drill. Do so and listen carefully. If you're unsure about how to use your vest, now is the time to ask. Some cruise lines no longer require you to bring your vest to the muster drill and instead store

them near the muster station, but crewmembers are more than willing to assist if you have questions. Only in the most extreme circumstances will you need to abandon ship—but it has happened. The time you spend learning the procedure may serve you well in a mishap.

In actuality, the greatest danger facing cruise-ship passengers is fire. All cruise lines must meet international standards for fire safety, which require sprinkler systems, smoke detectors, and other safety features. Fires on cruise ships are not common, but they do happen, and these rules have made ships much safer. You can do your part by *not* using an iron in your cabin and taking care to properly extinguish smoking materials. Never throw a lit cigarette overboard—it could be blown back into an opening in the ship and start a fire.

$1-per-minute range for the use of these Internet services. Ships usually offer some kind of package so that you get a reduced per-minute price if you pay a fee up front.

The ability to use your own mobile phone for calls from the high seas is an alternative that is gaining in popularity. It's usually cheaper than using a cabin phone if your ship offers the service; however, it can still cost from $2.50 to $5 a minute. A rather ingenious concept, the ship acts as a cell "tower" in international waters—you use your own cell phone and your own number when roaming at sea and you can even send and receive text messages and email with some smart phones (albeit with a surcharge in addition to any roaming fees). Before leaving home, ask your cell-phone service provider to activate international roaming on your account. When in port, depending on the type of cell phone you own and the agreements your mobile service provider has established, you may be able to connect to local networks. Most GSM phones that use SIM cards are also usable in Europe. Rates for using the maritime service, as well as any roaming charges from European ports, are established by your mobile service carrier and are worth checking into before your trip.

CLOSE UP

## Crime on Ships

Crime aboard cruise ships has occasionally become headline news, thanks in large part to a few well-publicized cases. Most people never have any type of problem, but you should exercise the same precautions aboard ship that you would at home. Keep your valuables out of sight—on big ships virtually every cabin has a small safe. Don't carry too much cash ashore, use your credit card whenever possible, and keep your money in a secure place, such as a front pocket that's harder to pick. Single women traveling with friends should stick together, especially when returning to their cabins late at night. When assaults occur, it often comes to light that excessive drinking of alcohol is a factor. Be careful about whom you befriend, as you would anywhere, whether it's a fellow passenger or a member of the crew. Don't be paranoid, but do be prudent.

Your cruise is a wonderful opportunity to leave everyday responsibilities behind, but don't neglect to pack your common sense. After a few drinks it might seem like a good idea to sit on a railing or lean over the rail to get a better view of the ship's wake. Passengers have been known to fall. "Man overboard" is more likely to be the result of carelessness than criminal intent.

### LAUNDRY AND DRY-CLEANING

Most cruise ships offer valet laundry and pressing (and some also offer dry-cleaning) service. Expenses can add up fast, especially for laundry, since charges are per item and the rates are similar to those charged in hotels, unless your ship offers a fixed-price laundry deal (all you can stuff into a bag they provide for a single fee). If doing laundry is important to you and you do not want to send it out to be done, many cruise ships have a self-service laundry room (which usually features an iron and ironing board in addition to washer and dryer). If you book one of the top-dollar suites, laundry service may be included for no additional cost. Upscale ships, such as those in the Regent Seven Seas Cruises, Silversea Cruises, and Seabourn fleets have complimentary self-service launderettes. On other cruise lines, such as Princess Cruises, Oceania Cruises, Carnival Cruise Lines, and Holland America Line (except Vista-class and Signature-class ships), you can do your own laundry for about $3 or less per load. None of the vessels in the Norwegian, Royal Caribbean, or Celebrity Cruises fleets has self-service laundry facilities.

# DISEMBARKATION

All cruises come to an end eventually, and the disembarkation process actually begins the day before you arrive at your ship's final port. During that day your cabin steward delivers special luggage tags to your stateroom, along with customs forms and instructions on some itineraries.

The night before you disembark, you'll need to set aside clothing to wear the next morning when you leave the ship. Many people dress in whatever casual outfits they wear for the final dinner on board, or change into travel clothes after dinner. Also, do not forget to put your passport or other proof of citizenship, airline tickets, and medications in your hand luggage. The luggage tags go onto your larger bags, which are placed outside your stateroom door for pick-up during the hours indicated.

A statement itemizing your onboard charges is delivered before you arise on disembarkation morning. Plan to get up early enough to check it over for accuracy, finish packing your personal belongings, and vacate your stateroom by the appointed hour. Any discrepancies in your onboard account should be taken care of before leaving the ship, usually at the purser's desk. Breakfast is served in the main restaurant as well as the buffet on the last morning, but room service usually isn't available. Disembarkation procedures vary by cruise line, but you'll probably have to wait in a lounge or on deck for your tag color or number to be called.

Then you take a taxi, bus, or other transportation to your post-cruise hotel or to the airport for your flight home. If you are flying out the day your cruise ends, leave plenty of time to go through the usual check-in, passport control/immigration, and security procedures at the airport. You may also want to do some duty-free shopping at the airport; some airports, particularly Amsterdam's Schiphol Airport, are bursting with last-minute opportunities for retail therapy. However, you need to be aware the EU does not allow you to do any duty-free shopping in an airport unless that airport is your last stop in the EU zone. Thus, if you leave from Athens but connect in Paris, you'll have to do your shopping in Paris rather than Athens. Unless you are flying from a non-EU country to an EU country, you probably won't go through Immigration or Customs until you reenter the United States, always at your first point of reentry; if you are continuing on a U.S. domestic flight to your final destination, you have to recheck your bags as you leave Customs.

## CUSTOMS AND DUTIES

### TAXES

If you make any purchases while in Europe, you should ask for a V.A.T. refund form and find out whether the merchant gives refunds—not all stores do, nor are they required to. Have the form stamped like any customs form by customs officials when you leave the country or, if you're visiting several European Union countries, when you leave the EU. This has to be done at the airport on the day you are flying home. After you're through passport control, take the form to a refund-service counter for an on-the-spot refund (which is usually the quickest and easiest option), or mail it to the address on the form (or the envelope with it) after you arrive home. You receive the total refund stated on the form, but the processing time can be long, especially if you request a credit-card adjustment.

Global Blue (formerly known as Global Refund) is a Europe-wide service with 225,000 affiliated stores and more than 700 refund counters at major airports and border crossings. Its refund form, called a Tax Free Check, is the most common across the European continent. The service issues refunds in the form of cash, check, or credit-card adjustment.

**V.A.T. Refunds Global Blue** (☎ *800/566–9828* ⊕ *www.global-blue.com*).

# FODOR'S CRUISE PREPARATION TIME LINE

### 3 TO 4 MONTHS BEFORE SAILING

■ Check with your travel agent or the State Department for the identification required for your cruise.

■ Gather the necessary identification you need. If you need to replace a lost birth certificate, apply for a new passport, or renew one that's about to expire, start the paperwork now. Doing it at the last minute is stressful and often costly.

### 60 TO 75 DAYS BEFORE SAILING

■ Make the final payment on your cruise fare. Though the dates vary, your travel agent should remind you when the payment date draws near. Failure to submit the balance on time can result in the cancellation of your reservation.

■ Make a packing list for each person you'll be packing for.

■ Begin your wardrobe planning now. Try things on to make sure they fit and are in good repair (it's amazing how stains can magically appear months after something has been dry cleaned). Set things aside.

■ If you need to shop, get started so you have time to find just the right thing (and perhaps to return or exchange just the right thing). You may also need to allow time for alterations.

■ Make kennel reservations for your pets. (If you're traveling during a holiday period, you may need to do this even earlier.)

■ Arrange for a house sitter.

■ If you're cruising, but your kids are staying home:

■ Make child care arrangements.

■ Go over children's schedules to make sure they'll have everything they need while you're gone (gift for a birthday party, supplies for a school project, permission slip for a field trip).

■ If you have small children, you may want to put together a small bag of treats for them to open while you're gone—make a tape of yourself reading a favorite bedtime story or singing a lullaby (as long as it's you, it will sound fantastic to them).

### 30 DAYS BEFORE SAILING

■ If you purchased an Air & Sea package, call your travel agent for the details of your airline schedule. Request seat assignments.

■ If your children are sailing with you, check their wardrobes now (do it too early and the really little kids may actually grow out of garments).

■ Make appointments for any personal services you wish to have prior to your cruise (for example, a haircut or manicure).

■ Get out your luggage and check the locks and zippers. Check for anything that might have spilled inside on a previous trip.

■ If you need new luggage or want an extra piece to bring home souvenirs, purchase it now.

### 2 TO 4 WEEKS BEFORE SAILING

■ Receive your cruise documents through the travel agent or print them from the cruise lines' website.

■ Examine the documents for accuracy (correct cabin number, sailing date, and dining arrangements); make sure names are spelled correctly. If there's something you do not understand, ask now.

■ Read all the literature in your document package for suggestions specific to your cruise. Most cruise lines include helpful information.

■ Pay any routine bills that may be due while you're gone.

■ Go over your personalized packing list again. Finish shopping.

### 1 WEEK BEFORE SAILING

■ Finalize your packing list and continue organizing everything in one area.

■ Buy film or digital media and check the batteries in your camera.

■ Refill prescription medications with an adequate supply.

■ Make two photocopies of your passport or ID and credit cards. Leave one copy with a friend and carry the other copy separately from the originals.

■ Get cash and/or traveler's checks at the bank. If you use traveler's checks, keep a separate record of the serial numbers. Get a supply of one-dollar bills for tipping baggage handlers (at the airport, hotel, pier, etc.).

■ You may also want to put valuables and jewelry that you won't be taking with you in the safety deposit box while you're at the bank.

■ Arrange to have your mail held at the post office or ask a neighbor to pick it up.

■ Stop newspaper delivery or ask a neighbor to bring it in for you.

■ Arrange for lawn and houseplant care or snow removal during your absence (if necessary).

■ Leave your itinerary, the ship's telephone number (plus the name of your ship and your stateroom number), and a house key with a relative or friend.

■ If traveling with young children, purchase small games or toys to keep them occupied while en route to your embarkation port.

### 3 DAYS BEFORE SAILING

■ Confirm your airline flights; departure times are sometimes subject to change.

■ Put a card with your name, address, telephone number, and itinerary inside each suitcase.

■ Fill out the luggage tags that came with your document packet and follow the instructions regarding when and how to attach them.

■ Complete any other paperwork that the cruise line included with your documents (foreign customs and immigration forms, onboard charge application, etc.). Do not wait until you're standing in the pier check-in line to fill them in!

■ Do last-minute laundry and tidy up the house.

■ Pull out the luggage and begin packing.

### THE DAY BEFORE SAILING

■ Take pets to the kennel.

■ Water houseplants and lawn (if necessary).

■ Dispose of any perishable food in the refrigerator.

■ Mail any last-minute bills.

■ Set timers for indoor lights.

■ Reorganize your wallet. Remove anything you will not need (local affinity cards, department store or gas credit cards, etc.), put them in an envelope.

■ Finish packing and lock your suitcases.

### DEPARTURE DAY

■ Adjust the thermostat and double-check the door locks.

■ Turn off the water if there's danger of frozen pipes while you're away.

■ Arrange to be at the airport a minimum of two hours before your departure time (follow the airline's instructions).

■ Have photo ID and/or passport ready for airport check-in.

■ Slip your car keys, parking claim checks, and airline tickets in your carry-on luggage. Never pack these items in checked luggage.

## U.S. CUSTOMS

Each individual or family returning to the United States must fill out a customs declaration form, which will be provided before your plane lands. If you owe any duties, you will have to pay them directly to the customs inspector, with cash or check. Be sure to keep receipts for all purchases; and you may be asked to show officials what you've bought. If your cruise is a transatlantic crossing, U.S. Customs clears ships sailing into arrival ports. After showing your passport to immigration officials, you must collect your luggage from the dock, then stand in line to pass through the inspection point. This can take up to an hour.

ALLOWANCES You're always allowed to bring goods of a certain value back home without having to pay any duty or import tax. But there's a limit on the amount of tobacco and liquor you can bring back duty-free. The values of so-called "duty-free" goods are included in these amounts. When you shop abroad, save all your receipts, as customs inspectors may ask to see them as well as the items you purchased. If the total value of your goods is more than the duty-free limit, you'll have to pay a tax (most often a flat percentage) on the value of everything beyond that limit. For U.S. citizens who have been in Europe for at least 48 hours, the duty-free exemption is $800. But the duty-free exemption includes only 200 cigarettes, 100 cigars, and 1 liter of alcohol (this includes wine); above these limits, you have to pay duties, even if you didn't spend more than the $800 limit.

**U.S. Information U.S. Customs and Border Protection** (⊕ *www.cbp.gov*).

SENDING PACKAGES HOME Although you probably won't want to spend your time looking for a post office, you can send packages home duty-free, with a limit of one parcel per addressee per day (except alcohol or tobacco products or perfume worth more than $5). You can mail up to $200 worth of goods to yourself, or $100 worth of goods to a friend or relative; label the package "personal use" or "unsolicited gift" (depending on which is the case) and attach a list of the contents and their retail value. If the package contains your used personal belongings, mark it "personal goods returned" to avoid paying duty on your laundry. You do not need to declare items that were sent home on your declaration forms for U.S. Customs.

# Cruise Lines and Cruise Ships

*Costa Classica*

**WORD OF MOUTH**

"For first-time cruisers, the variety of cruise lines can be confusing. . . . Which cruise line is more appropriate for the 35–55 age group? Which one has the most relaxed atmosphere (no formal nights)? Looking for fun, relaxation, casual elegance, not stuffy and country-clubby, some activities and a casino but nothing over the top? Also, what's your favorite itinerary on these cruise lines?"

—bosco

By Linda
Coffman

Second only to the Caribbean in popularity with cruise passengers, Europe has it all—beautifully preserved castles, romantic gardens, fabulous art treasures, antiquities, and some of the world's most breathtaking scenery. Great cities flourished along all the coasts of the continent, which makes it possible to explore many of Europe's richest treasures by ship.

Every year major North American cruise lines satisfy the seasonal demand for what amounts to an old-fashioned Grand Tour afloat by repositioning a large portion of their Caribbean fleets to Europe. They join European-based ships that are ported in the Baltic for the summer and the Mediterranean year-round. The largest vessels generally stick to predictable routes that include major cities along the coasts such as Amsterdam, Venice, Barcelona, and Athens, or those, like Rome, close enough to visit during a port call. Small to midsize ships offer the advantage of visiting ports off the beaten path of the large ships and can call at intriguing destinations like the less-visited Greek Isles and jet-set favorite Ibiza without the necessity of tendering passengers ashore.

## CRUISE LINES

Seated in an airplane after a week of enjoying an exceptionally nice cruise, I overheard the couple behind me discussing their "dreadful" cruise vacation. What a surprise when they mentioned the ship's name. It was the one I'd just spent a glorious week on. I never missed a meal. They hated the food. My cabin was comfortable and cheery, if not large. Their identical accommodations resembled a "cave." One size definitely does not fit all in cruising. What's appealing to one passenger may be unacceptable to another. Ultimately, most cruise complaints arise from passengers whose expectations were not met. The couple I eavesdropped on were on the wrong cruise line and ship for them.

I enjoy cruises. Some have suited me better than others, but I've never sailed on a cruise that was completely without merit. Make no mistake about it: Cruise lines have distinct personalities. Lines appeal to different demographics and offer different levels of comfort and service. We have divided the cruise lines in this book into three main categories: Mainstream, Premium, and Luxury, but some defy easy categorization. And when you are cruising in Europe, there are also the European cruise lines to consider. Although they cater to a more international mix of travelers, they also offer the more European experience favored by many Americans when traveling abroad. Just as cruise lines differ, the ships of the line may also differ, although they will share many basic similarities. Most lines try to standardize the overall experience throughout their fleets, which is why you'll find a waterslide on every Carnival ship. But you won't find an ice-skating rink on any but the largest Royal Caribbean ships.

So, which cruise line is best? Only you can determine which is best for you. You won't find ratings by Fodor's—either quality stars or value scores. Why? Think of those people seated behind me on the airplane. They assuredly would rate their experience differently than I did. Instead of rating and ranking lines and ships based on the reviewer's opinion, we've tried to give more objective overviews. Your responsibility is to select the right cruise for you—no one knows your expectations better than you do yourself. The short wait for a table might not bother you because you would prefer a casual atmosphere with open seating; however, some people want the security of a set time at an assigned table served by a waiter who gets to know their preferences. You know what you are willing to trade off in order to get what you want.

## MAINSTREAM CRUISE LINES

The mainstream lines are the ones most often associated with modern cruising. They offer the advantage of something for everyone and nearly every available sports facility imaginable. Some ships even have ice-skating rinks, 18-hole miniature golf courses, bowling alleys, Flow-Riders (for surfing), and rock-climbing walls.

Generally speaking, the mainstream lines have two basic ship sizes—large cruise ships and megaships—in their fleets. These vessels have plentiful outdoor deck space, and many have a wraparound outdoor promenade deck that allows you to stroll or jog the ship's perimeter. In the newest vessels, traditional meets trendy. You'll find atrium lobbies and expansive sun and sports decks, picture windows instead of portholes, and cabins that open onto private verandas. For all their resort-style innovations, they still feature cruise-ship classics—afternoon tea, complimentary room service, and lavish pampering. The smallest ships carry 1,000 passengers or fewer, while the largest accommodate more than 3,000 passengers and are filled with diversions.

These ships tend to be big and boxy. Picture windows are standard equipment, and cabins in the top categories have private verandas. From their casinos and discos to their fitness centers, everything is bigger and more extravagant than on other ships. You'll pay for many extras on the mainstream ships, from drinks at the bar, to that cup of cappuccino, to spa treatments, to a game of bowling, to dinner in a specialty restaurant. You may want to rethink a cruise aboard one of these ships if you want a little downtime, because you'll be joined by 1,500 to 3,000 fellow passengers.

## PREMIUM CRUISE LINES

Premium cruise lines have much in common with the mainstream cruise lines, but with a little more of everything. The atmosphere is more refined, surroundings more gracious, and service more polished and attentive. There are still activities like pool games, although they aren't quite the high jinks typical of mainstream ships. In addition to traditional cruise activities, onboard lectures are common. Production shows are somewhat more sophisticated than on mainstream lines.

Ships tend to be newer midsize to large vessels that carry fewer passengers than mainstream ships and have a more spacious feel. Decor is usually more glamorous and subtle, with toned-down colors and extensive original art. Staterooms range from inside cabins for three or four to outside cabins with or without balconies to suites with numerous amenities, including butlers on some lines.

Most premium ships offer traditional assigned seatings for dinner. High marks are afforded the quality cuisine and presentation. Many ships have upscale bistros or specialty restaurants, which usually require reservations and command an additional charge. Although premium lines usually have as many extra charges as mainstream lines, the overall quality of what you receive is higher.

## LUXURY CRUISE LINES

Comprising only 5% of the market, the exclusive luxury cruise lines, such as Crystal, Cunard, Paul Gauguin Cruises, Regent Seven Seas, Seabourn, SeaDream, and Silversea offer high staff-to-guest ratios for personal service, superior cuisine in a single open seating (except Crystal, which retains two assigned seatings along with an open seating option, and Cunard, with dual-class dining assignments), and a highly inclusive product with few onboard charges. These small and midsize ships offer much more space per passenger than you will find on the mainstream lines' vessels. Lines differ in what they emphasize, with some touting luxurious accommodations and entertainment and others focusing on exotic destinations and onboard enrichment.

If you consider travel a necessity rather than a luxury and frequent posh resorts, then you will appreciate the extra attention and the higher level of comfort that luxury cruise lines offer. Itineraries on these ships often include the marquee ports, but luxury ships also visit some of the more uncommon destinations. With an intimate size, the smaller luxury ships can visit such ports as Bordeaux, France, and Korčula, Croatia.

## OTHER CRUISE LINES

A few small cruise lines sail through Europe and offer boutique to nearly bed-and-breakfast experiences. Notably, Star Clippers appeals to passengers who eschew mainstream cruises. Most of these niche vessels accommodate 200 or fewer passengers, and their focus is on soft adventure. Cruising between nearby ports and anchoring out so passengers can swim and snorkel directly from the ship, as offered by Star Clippers, they have itineraries that usually leave plenty of time for exploring and other activities on- or offshore. Many of these cruises schedule casual enrichment talks that often continue on decks, at meals, and during trips ashore.

## EUROPEAN CRUISE LINES

With more similarities to American-owned cruise lines than differences, these European-owned and -operated cruise lines compare favorably to the mainstream cruise lines of a decade ago. Although some lines have embarked upon shipbuilding programs that rival the most ambitious in the cruise industry, other European fleets consist of older, yet well-maintained vessels. Although they cater to Europeans—announcements may be broadcast in as many as five languages—and Americans are generally in the minority, English is widely spoken. *For more reviews of British cruise lines visit Fodors.com.*

**RIVER CRUISES**

Riverboats and barges present an entirely different perspective on European cruising. Smaller than even the smallest ocean cruise ships, they offer a convenient alternative to bus tours—you only unpack once—while navigating the rivers and canals to reach legendary inland cities. Just as on cruise ships, accommodations and meals are included. Some shore excursions might be part of the package as well. *These cruises are covered in "River and Specialty Cruises."*

# ABOUT THESE REVIEWS

The following Cruise Line Profiles offer a general idea of what you can expect in terms of overall experience, quality, and service. For each cruise line described, we list the ships (grouped by class or similar configurations) that regularly cruise in Europe. We've excluded entirely those that have no regular itineraries in Europe as of this writing. Thus, not all ships owned by the cruise lines we cover are described.

When two or more ships belong to the same class—or are substantially similar—they are listed together in the subhead under the name of the class; the year each was introduced is also given in the same order in the statistics section. Passenger-capacity figures are given on the basis of two people sharing a cabin; however, many of the larger ships have three- and four-berth cabins, which can increase the total number of passengers tremendously when all berths are occupied. When total occupancy figures differ from double occupancy, we give them in parentheses.

Because cruise ships can float off to far-flung (and not always warm) regions, many are designed with an eye to less-than-perfect weather. For that reason, you're likely to find indoor swimming pools featured on their deck plans. Except in rare cases, these are usually dual-purpose pools that can be covered when necessary by a sliding roof or magrodome to create an indoor swimming environment. Our reviews indicate the total number of swimming pools found on each ship, with permanently and/or temporarily covered pools included in the total and also noted as "# indoors" in parentheses. We also indicate whether there is a dedicated children's pool.

Unlike other guidebooks, we describe not only the features, but also the cabin dimensions for each accommodation category available on the ships reviewed. Dimensions should be considered approximate and used for comparison purposes only, as they sometimes vary depending on location. For instance, although staterooms are largely prefabricated in the same size and design with all electrical and plumbing fixtures preinstalled, those at the front of some ships may be oddly curved to conform to the shape of the bow.

But when you're armed with all the right information, we're sure you'll be able to find one that not only fits your style, but also offers you the service and value you expect.

# AZAMARA CLUB CRUISES

In a surprise move parent company Royal Caribbean International announced the formation of an all-new, deluxe cruise line in 2007. Two vessels originally slated for service in the Celebrity Cruises fleet, which were built for now-defunct Renaissance Cruises

*Azamara Journey* at sea

and acquired with the purchase of the Spanish cruise line Pullmantur, were the basis for the new line, Azamara Club Cruises. Designed to offer exotic destination-driven itineraries, Azamara Club Cruises presents a more intimate onboard experience while allowing access to the less traveled ports of call experienced travelers want to visit.

☎ *877/999–9553*
⊕ *www.azamaraclub-cruises.com* ☞ *Cruise Style: Premium.*

When a cruise line sets a course to break the mold in an industry where the product falls into traditional categories—mainstream, premium, luxury—it's an exciting opportunity for experienced travelers who may want more than what a traditional cruise can deliver. More interested in traveling than cruising, they may still prefer the comfort and convenience that only a cruise ship can deliver in some exotic locales. Azamara Club Cruises gives this underserved group of travelers what they want—a cruise experience that's a bit different. Not quite luxury but more than premium, Azamara offers a deluxe cruise with concierge-style amenities for which you'd have to upgrade to a suite on other cruise lines.

In addition, since its launch Azamara Club Cruises has added a number of more inclusive amenities to passengers' fares, with no charge for a specific brand of bottled water, specialty coffees and teas; shuttle bus service to/from port communities, where available; standard spirits, wines, and international beers throughout the ships during bar hours; and complimentary self-service laundry.

Extensive overhauls of two ships that formerly sailed for the now-defunct Renaissance Cruises have resulted in interiors that are brighter with the addition of light, neutral carpeting throughout, and splashes of bold color in the upholstery and drapes. Areas that once appeared stuffy are now welcoming, with contemporary artwork further enhancing the decor. Each vessel weighs in at 30,277 tons and carries only 694 passengers. While the size affords a high level of intimacy and makes the ships easy to navigate, there is no skimping on features normally abundant on larger ships, such as private balconies and alternative dining. Cruisers may feel that they've checked into an upscale boutique hotel that just happens to float.

## Food

Expect dinner favorites to have an upscale twist, such as gulf shrimp with cognac and garlic, or a filet mignon with black truffle sauce. Azamara chefs bring a fresh approach to contemporary and lighter cuisine—a reflection of what's happening all over the United States. Even though the menus list some trendier items, there will always be classic dishes available. Prime rib and other favorites will continue to be featured on the menu.

Specialty restaurants include the Mediterranean-influenced Aqualina and the stylish steak-and-seafood restaurant Prime C. Passengers in Club suite accommodations may dine in the specialty restaurants every night of the cruise at no charge; all other passengers pay a cover charge. Reservations are offered on a space-available basis. Daily in-cabin afternoon tea service and delivery of canapés is available to all passengers.

## Entertainment

One distinguishing feature of Azamara is a wide range of enrichment programs to accompany the destination-rich itineraries. Popular programs include guest speakers who are experts on a wide variety of topics, including destinations, technology, cultural explorations, art, music, and design. Lectures might include how to get the best photos from your digital camera or the proper way to pair wine and food, as taught by resident sommeliers. An onboard "excursion expert" can not only help you select shore excursions based on your personal interests but also will serve as a destination guide, offering information about the culture and history of each port of call, not just shopping suggestions. Entertainment, on the other hand, leans toward cabaret-size production shows and variety entertainers in the main lounge. Diverse musical offerings throughout the ships range from upbeat dance bands to intimate piano bar entertainers.

## KNOWN FOR

■ **More Time in Port:** Azamara ships often spend longer days and overnights in popular and exotic ports of call and offer a complimentary evening event ashore on each voyage.

■ **Service:** Friendly but not obtrusive service, delivered with attention to detail.

■ **Wine:** Extensive wine cellars that hold limited production, small label, and rare vintage wines, along with knowledgeable sommeliers.

■ **No Smoking:** A virtually smoke-free environment; smokers on Azamara ships are restricted to a small section of the pool deck.

2

AZAMARA CLUB CRUISES

Top: Grand Lobby on *Azamara Journey*
Bottom: Chairs grouped on deck allow for quiet conversation

### Fitness and Recreation

In addition to a well-equipped gym and an outdoor jogging track, features of Azamara's fitness program include yoga at sunset, Pilates, and access to an onboard wellness consultant. Both ships offer a full menu of spa treatments, and an aesthetics suite featuring acupuncture, laser hair removal, and microdermabrasion. An outdoor spa relaxation lounge with saltwater therapy pool is complimentary for suite guests and those receiving spa treatments. Passes for other guests are available for $19 per day or $99 per cruise.

### Your Shipmates

Azamara is designed to appeal to discerning travelers, primarily American couples of any age who appreciate a high level of service in an unstructured atmosphere.

### Dress Code

Although passengers who choose to wear formal attire are certainly welcome to do so, there are no scheduled formal nights. The nightly dress code is simply "sophisticated" casual—a jacket and tie are never required, but you may see that many men who are accustomed to wearing them will do so anyway.

### Junior Cruisers

Azamara Club Cruises is adult-oriented and not a good choice for families who depend on the availability of childcare. The ships have no facilities or programs for children; older teenagers, however, might appreciate the diverse itineraries and well-stocked library.

### Service

Gracious and polished service throughout the ships is extended to every guest. Suite accommodations are served by a butler, who will assist with unpacking/packing; delivery of room service, plus afternoon tea, evening hors d'oeuvres, and complimentary cappuccino and espresso; shoe-shine service; and booking assistance with spa, shore excursions, and specialty dining. Stateroom attendants work in teams, and routine stateroom cleaning is done by an assistant steward, much as on other cruise lines.

**CHOOSE THIS LINE IF ...**

Your taste leans toward luxury, but your budget doesn't.

You prefer leisurely open seating dining in casual attire to the stiffness of assigned tablemates and waiters.

The manner in which you "get there" is as important to you as your destination.

## Tipping

Housekeeping, dining, and bar staff gratuities are included in the fare.

## Past Passengers

Once you've sailed with Azamara Club Cruises for the first time, you will automatically become a member of Azamara's loyalty program, "Le Club Voyage," and receive benefits commensurate with the number of cruises you've taken, including such things as onboard bookings savings for future cruises and free Internet minutes. Adventurer members have been on at least one Azamara Club Cruises cruise. Explorer members have sailed five to nine cruises and get more perks, including an invitation to a senior officer's cocktail party, and a complimentary bag of laundry washed, dried, and pressed per week. After 10 cruises, you become a Discoverer member and can take advantage of expanded Internet minutes and other perks. Azamara Club Cruises also offers Reunion Cruises that feature exclusive members-only benefits, activities, and a private, complimentary excursion during the sailings.

## HELPFUL HINTS

Azamara doesn't quite hit the luxury mark, but it is a high-end product at a more affordable price.

In addition to complimentary wine and beer served with meals, standard alcoholic beverages are also included in the fare.

The line is beginning to add more shorter cruises of less than 10 nights, but they are still the minority of sailings.

The best place to relax is the covered patio area near the pool, furnished with comfortable, oversized loungers and other seating.

When Azamara acquired its ships, it converted 48 standard staterooms into spacious Sky suites with more amenities for lower fares than those on true luxury lines.

## DON'T CHOOSE THIS LINE IF ...

You want glitzy, high-energy evening entertainment.

You require the services of a butler; only suites have them.

You insist on smoking whenever and wherever you want to.

# AZAMARA JOURNEY, AZAMARA QUEST

| | |
|---|---|
| Crew Members | 390 |
| Entered Service | 2000, 2001 |
| Gross Tons | 30,277 |
| Length | 593 feet |
| Number of Cabins | 347 |
| Passenger Capacity | 694 |
| Width | 95 feet |

700 ft.

500 ft.

300 ft.

At 30,277 tons, *Azamara Quest* and *Azamara Journey* are medium-size ships and well suited to the somewhat more exotic itineraries for which they are deployed, whether in the Caribbean, Europe, Asia, or South America. The ships initially entered service for Renaissance Cruises and served in Spain under the Pullmantur flag until 2007. With their entry into the Azamara Club Cruises fleet, a new option is available to passengers who prefer the boutique-hotel atmosphere of a smaller ship without the luxury-class price tag.

Each ship has a variety of signature features, including the Martini Bar in Casino Luxe, a casual sidewalk café–style coffee bar, and the distinctive Astral Spa with an acupuncture suite and expansive relaxation deck with therapy pool. Each ship has two specialty restaurants. The exclusive experience includes butler service in suites and concierge-style amenities in all categories of accommodations.

## Cabins

**Layout:** Designed for lengthy cruises, all staterooms have ample closet and storage space, and even standard cabins have at least a small seating area, although bathrooms in lower categories are somewhat tight. Wood cabinetry adds warmth to the decor. In keeping with the trend for more balconies, 73% of all outside cabins and suites have them.

**Amenities:** Amenities include plush beds and Egyptian-cotton bedding. Bath toiletries, a hair dryer, TV, refrigerator, personal safe, and robes for use during the cruise are all included, but you must move up to a suite to have a bathtub, as lower-category cabins have showers only.

**Suites:** Club World Owner's and Club Ocean suites are particularly luxurious, with living–dining rooms, entertainment centers, two TVs, separate bedrooms, whirlpool bathtubs, guest powder rooms, and very large balconies overlooking either the bow or stern. Thirty-two Club Continent suites on each ship have a queen-size bed, television, bathtub, personal safe, and hair dryer. All suites have a welcoming bottle of sparkling wine, minibars with two bottles of spirits, and butler service.

**Accessibility:** Six staterooms are designated as wheel-chair accessible.

Top: Open seating dining
Bottom: Balcony stateroom

## Restaurants

The formal Discoveries restaurant has a single open seating for breakfast, lunch, and dinner. Evening meals feature classic favorites with a twist, such as filet mignon with black truffle sauce. Supplementing the main restaurant is the casual Windows Café, where you can dine indoors or alfresco with a view over the ship's stern. Two upscale alternative restaurants—Aqualina and Prime C—require reservations and carry a cover charge for most guests. A poolside grill offers hamburgers, salads, pasta, and other favorites for lunch and dinner, a pizzeria dishes up a variety of pies by the slice, and patisseries serve specialty coffee drinks and pastries; 24-hour room service augments dining choices.

## Spas

Operated by Steiner Leisure, each ship's spa offers a full menu of massages, facials, and other treatments; and an aesthetics suite featuring acupuncture, laser hair removal, teeth whitening, and microdermabrasion. The relaxation deck with its huge therapy pool is available to guests who book a spa treatment or purchase a day pass.

## Bars and Entertainment

Bars tend to be on the quiet side, suitable for socializing and conversation; however, the Looking Glass observation lounge can be lively when the entertainment staff takes over and the band plays dance music. Entertainment is also sedate, with cabaret-style shows by night and enrichment lectures by day.

## Pros and Cons

**Pros:** one staff member for every two passengers ensures unparalleled service; bartenders in the Martini Bar are willing to follow your instructions to mix your favorite variation; the quiet sounds of a grand piano add to the ambience of the Drawing Room.

**Cons:** aft-facing Sunset Verandas on decks 6 and 7 are simply standard balcony cabins with larger balconies; there are no children's programs or facilities; upscale amenities don't quite make up for the lack of bathroom space in standard staterooms.

| Cabin Type | Size (sq. ft.) |
|---|---|
| Club World Owner's Suite | 560 |
| Club Ocean Suites | 440–501 |
| Club Continental Suites | 266 |
| Sunset Veranda | 175 |
| Ocean-view Balcony | 175 |
| Ocean View | 170–175 |
| Inside | 158 |

## FAST FACTS

- 9 passenger decks
- 2 specialty restaurants, dining room, buffet, pizzeria
- Wi-Fi, safe, refrigerator, DVD (some)
- 1 pool
- Fitness classes, gym, hot tubs, spa, steam room
- 8 bars, casino, dance club, library, show room
- Dry-cleaning, laundry facilities, laundry service
- Internet terminal
- No-smoking cabins

Casual dining

# CARNIVAL CRUISE LINES

The world's largest cruise line originated the Fun Ship concept in 1972 with the relaunch of an aging ocean liner, which got stuck on a sandbar during its maiden voyage. In true entrepreneurial spirit, founder Ted Arison shrugged off an inauspicious

Lobby Bar on board *Carnival Fantasy*

beginning to introduce superliners a decade later. Sporting red-white-and-blue flared funnels, which are easily recognized from afar, new ships are continuously added to the fleet and rarely deviate from a successful pattern. If you find something you like on one vessel, you're likely to find something similar on another.

☎ *305/599–2600*
*or 800/227–6482*
⊕ *www.carnival.com*
☞ *Cruise Style:*
*Mainstream.*

Each vessel features themed public rooms, ranging from ancient Egypt to futuristic motifs, although many of those elements are being replaced with a more tropical decor as older ships are upgraded. Carnival is also introducing features either branded by the line itself, such as the poolside Blue Iguana Tequila Bar with an adjacent burrito cantina and the Red Frog Rum Bar that also serves Carnival's own brand of Thirsty Frog Red beer, or in partnership with well known brands, such as EA SPORTS to create EA SPORTS Bars at sea and Guy's Burger Joint, in partnership with Food Network star Guy Fieri. Implementation of the new features is scheduled for completion in 2015.

### Food

Carnival ships have both flexible dining options as well as casual alternative restaurants. Although the tradition of two set mealtimes for dinner prevails on Carnival ships, the line's open seating concept—Your Time Dining—is available fleet-wide.

Choices are numerous, and the skill of Carnival's chefs has elevated the line's menus to an unexpected level. Although the waiters still sing and dance, the good-to-excellent dining room food appeals to American tastes.

Upscale steak houses on certain ships serve cuisine comparable to the best midrange steak houses ashore.

Carnival serves the best food of the mainstream cruise lines. In addition to the regular menu, vegetarian, low-calorie, low-carbohydrate, low-salt, and no-sugar selections are available. A children's menu includes such favorites as macaroni and cheese, chicken fingers, and peanut butter-and-jelly sandwiches. If you don't feel like dressing up for dinner, the Lido buffet serves full meals, including sandwiches, a salad bar, rotisserie chicken, Asian stir-fry, and excellent pizza.

## Entertainment

More high-energy than cerebral, the entertainment consists of lavish Las Vegas–style revues presented in main show lounges by a company of singers and dancers. Other performers might include magicians, jugglers, acrobats, passengers performing in the talent show, or karaoke. Live bands play a wide range of musical styles for dancing and every ship has a nightclub, piano bar, and a comedy club. Adult activities, particularly the competitive ones, tend to be silly and hilarious and play to full houses. With Carnival's new branding initiative, look for the introduction of Hasbro, The Game Show, and performances created by Playlist Productions.

## Fitness and Recreation

Manned by staff members trained to keep passengers in shipshape form, Carnival's trademark spas and fitness centers are some of the largest and best equipped at sea. Spas and salons are operated by Steiner Leisure, and treatments include a variety of massages, body wraps, and facials; salons offer hair and nail services and even tooth whitening. Fitness centers have state-of-the-art cardio and strength-training equipment, a jogging track, and basic exercise classes at no charge. There's a fee for personal training, body composition analysis, and specialized classes such as yoga and Pilates.

## Your Shipmates

Carnival's passengers are predominantly active Americans, mostly couples in their mid-thirties to mid-fifties. Many families enjoy Carnival cruises in the Caribbean year-round. Holidays and school vacation periods are very popular with families, and you'll see a lot of kids in summer. More than 710,000 children sailed on Carnival ships in 2012—a six-fold increase in just 12 years.

## Dress Code

Two "cruise elegant" nights are standard on seven-night cruises; one is the norm on shorter sailings.

## KNOWN FOR

■ **Fun:** Not surprisingly, the fleet delivers a high-energy cruise vacation for passengers of all ages.

■ **Kid's Stuff:** Each Carnival ship has a water-park area and children's facilities and programs designed to appeal to the pickiest youngsters as well as their parents.

■ **Lack of Hierarchy:** Every Carnival passenger enjoys the same service and attention, including nightly turndown service, room service, and 24-hour pizzerias.

■ **Quieter Zones:** For adults only, each ship has a Serenity Deck dedicated to kid-free relaxation.

■ **Diversions:** Casinos, spas, and fitness centers are some of the most extensive at sea.

Top: *Carnival Victory* dining room
Bottom: *Carnival Legend* waterslide

Top: *Carnival Elation* at sea
Middle: *Carnival Triumph*
walking and jogging track
Bottom: Entertainment on
*Carnival Victory*

Although men should feel free to wear tuxedos, dark suits (or sport coats) and ties are more prevalent. All other evenings are "cruise casual," with jeans and dress shorts permitted in the dining rooms. All ships request that no short-shorts or cutoffs be worn after 6 pm, but that policy is often ignored.

### Junior Cruisers

Camp Carnival, run year-round by professionals, earns high marks for keeping young cruisers busy and content. Dedicated children's areas include great playrooms with separate splash pools. Toddlers from two to five years are treated to puppet shows, sponge painting, face painting, coloring, drawing, and crafts. As long as diapers and supplies are provided, staff will change toddlers. Activities for ages six to eight include arts and crafts, pizza parties, computer time, T-shirt painting, a talent show, and fitness programs. Nine- to eleven-year-olds can play Ping-Pong, take dance lessons, play video games, and participate in swim parties, scavenger hunts, and sports. Tweens ages 12 to 14 appreciate the social events, parties, contests, and sports in Circle C. Every night they have access to the ships' discos, followed by late-night movies, karaoke, or pizza.

Club O2 is geared toward teens 15 to 17. Program directors play host at the spacious teen clubs, where kicking back is the order of the day between scheduled activities. The fleetwide Y-Spa program for older teens offers a high level of pampering. Staff members also accompany teens on shore excursions designed just for them.

Daytime group babysitting for infants two and under allows parents the freedom to explore ports of call without the kids until noon. Parents can also pursue leisurely adults-only evenings from 10 pm to 3 am, when slumber party–style group babysitting is available for children from ages 6 months to 11 years. Babysitting is available for a fee.

### Service

Service on Carnival ships is friendly but not polished. Stateroom attendants are not only recognized for their attention to cleanliness but also for their expertise in creating towel animals—cute critters fashioned from

---

### CHOOSE THIS LINE IF ...

You want an action-packed casino with a choice of table games and rows upon rows of clanging slot machines.

You don't mind standing in line—these are big ships with a lot of passengers, and lines are not uncommon.

You don't mind hearing announcements over the public-address system reminding you of what's next on the schedule.

bath towels that appear during nightly turndown service. They've become so popular that Carnival publishes an instruction book on how to create them yourself.

## Tipping

A gratuity of $11.50 per passenger per day is automatically added to passenger accounts, and gratuities are distributed to stewards and waitstaff. Passengers may adjust the amount based on the level of service experienced. All beverage tabs at bars get an automatic 15% addition.

## Past Passengers

After sailing on one Carnival cruise, you'll receive a complimentary subscription to the company email magazine, and access to your past sailing history on the Carnival website. You are recognized on subsequent cruises with color-coded key cards determined by points or the number of days you've sailed—Red (starting on your 2nd cruise), Gold (when you've accumulated 25–74 points); Platinum (75–199 points); and Diamond (200+ points)—which serve as your entrée to a by-invitation-only cocktail reception. Platinum and Diamond members are eligible for benefits including priority embarkation and debarkation, priority dining assignments, supper club and spa reservations, a logo item gift, and limited complimentary laundry service.

**2**

**CARNIVAL CRUISE LINES**

## HELPFUL HINTS

The line's "Fun Ship 2.0" improvements are toning down the noisy, brash style in lieu of something more relaxed and tropical.

New features introduced in partnership with recognized brands (Hasbro, The Game Show, a diner crafted by Guy Fieri) have stepped up the complimentary elements of the onboard experience.

Casinos are good, and you can use your onboard charge card for casino play.

Carnival's great online planning tool (⊕ *www.carnivalconnections.com*) offers planning tips, cruise reviews, and a message board.

Most activities for children are free, but fees attached to their late-night party program can add up, in addition to the charges for video games.

## DON'T CHOOSE THIS LINE IF ...

You want an intimate, sedate atmosphere. Carnival's ships are big and bold.

You want elaborate accommodations. Carnival suites are spacious but not as feature-filled as the term *suite* may suggest.

You're turned off by men in tank tops. Casual on these ships means casual indeed.

# SPIRIT-CLASS
*Carnival Spirit, Pride, Legend, Miracle*

| | |
|---|---|
| Crew Members | 930 |
| Entered Service | 2001, 2001, 2002, 2004 |
| Gross Tons | 88,500 |
| Length | 960 feet |
| Number of Cabins | 1,062 |
| Passenger Capacity | 2,124 (2,667 max) |
| Width | 105.7 feet |

700 ft.

500 ft.

300 ft.

Spirit-class vessels may seem to be a throwback in size, but these sleek ships have the advantage of fitting through the Panama Canal and, with their additional length, include all the trademark characteristics of their larger fleet mates. They're also racehorses with the speed to reach far-flung destinations. *Carnival Spirit*—for which the class is named—makes its home port in Australia, primarily serving the Australian and New Zealand markets.

A rosy red skylight in the front bulkhead of the funnel—which houses the reservations-only upscale steak house—caps a soaring, 11-deck atrium. Lovely chapels are available for weddings, either upon embarkation or while in a port of call, and are also used for occasional shipboard religious services.

The upper and lower interior promenade decks are unhampered by a mid-ship restaurant or galley, which means that passenger flow throughout the ships is much improved over earlier, and even subsequent, designs.

## Cabins

**Cabins:** Cabins on Carnival ships are spacious, and these are no exception. Nearly 80% have an ocean view and, of those, more than 80% have balconies. Suites and some ocean-view cabins have private balconies outfitted with chairs and tables; some cabins have balconies at least 50% larger than average. Every cabin has adequate closet and drawer–shelf storage, as well as bathroom shelves. High-thread-count linens and plush pillows and duvets are a luxurious touch in all accommodations. Suites also have a whirlpool tub and walk-in closet. Decks 5, 6, and 7 each have a pair of balcony staterooms that connect to adjoining interior staterooms that are ideal for families because of their close proximity to children and teen areas.

**Decor:** Light-wood cabinetry, soft pastels, mirrored accents, a small refrigerator, a personal safe, a hair dryer, and a seating area with sofa, chair, and table are typical for ocean-view cabins and suites. Inside cabins have ample room but no seating area.

**Bathrooms:** Extras include shampoo and bath gel provided in shower-mounted dispensers and an array of sample toiletries, as well as fluffy tow-

Top: *Carnival Legend* at sea
Bottom: Spirit-class balcony stateroom

els and a wall-mounted magnifying mirror. Bathrobes for use during the cruise are provided for all.

**Accessibility:** Sixteen staterooms are designed for wheelchair accessibility.

## Restaurants

One formal restaurant serves open seating breakfast and lunch; it also serves dinner in two traditional assigned evening seatings or an open seating option. The casual Lido buffet with stations offers a variety of food choices (including a deli, salad bar, dessert station, and different daily regional cuisines); at night it becomes the Seaview Bistro for casual dinners. There's also an upscale steak house that requires reservations and an additional charge, a pizzeria, poolside outdoor grills for burgers, hot dogs, and the trimmings, a specialty coffee bar and patisserie, a complimentary sushi bar, and 24-hour room service with a limited menu of breakfast selections, sandwiches, and snacks.

## Spas

Steiner Leisure operates the 14,500 square-foot spas that offer an indoor therapy pool as well as such indulgences as a variety of massages, body wraps, and facials for adults and teens. Complimentary steam rooms and saunas in men's and women's changing rooms feature glass walls for sea views. Salons offer tooth whitening in addition to hair and nail services.

## Bars/Entertainment

*Pride* and *Legend* are scheduled to receive newly branded bars and comedy club features in 2013; All have high-energy shows by resident singers and dancers or guest performers in the main show room, spirited piano bars, and nightclubs featuring music for dancing and listening. Comedy clubs, karaoke, and deck parties add to the fun of nighttime activities.

## Pros and Cons

**Pros:** the enclosed space located forward on the promenade deck is quiet and good for reading; for relaxation, his-and-hers saunas and steam rooms have glass walls and sea views; complimentary self-serve ice-cream dispensers are on the Lido deck.

**Cons:** these are long ships, and some cabins are quite far from elevators; connecting staterooms are relatively scarce; the video arcade is almost hidden at the forward end of the ship.

| Cabin Type | Size (sq. ft.) |
| --- | --- |
| Penthouse Suites | 370 (average) |
| Suite | 275 |
| Ocean View | 185 |
| Interior | 185 |

## FAST FACTS

- 12 passenger decks
- Specialty restaurant, dining room, buffet, ice cream parlor, pizzeria
- Wi-Fi, safe, refrigerator
- 3 pools (1 indoor), children's pool
- Fitness classes, gym, hot tubs, sauna, spa, steam room
- 7 bars, casino, 2 dance clubs, library, show room, video game room
- Children's programs
- Laundry facilities, laundry service
- Internet terminal
- No-smoking cabins

**2**

**CARNIVAL CRUISE LINES**

*Carnival Miracle* Gatsby's Garden

# DESTINY-CLASS
*Carnival Triumph, Victory*

| | |
|---|---|
| Crew Members | 1,100 |
| Entered Service | 1999, 2000 |
| Gross Tons | 102,000 |
| Length | 893 feet |
| Number of Cabins | 1,379 |
| Passenger Capacity | 2,758 (3,470 max) |
| Width | 116 feet |

700 ft.

500 ft.

300 ft.

The first class of Carnival megaships weighing in at more than 100,000 tons, everything on these vessels is in keeping with their size—bold interiors highlighted by nine-deck atriums, 200-foot corkscrew waterslides on the Lido deck, and public areas that often span multiple decks. *Carnival Triumph* and *Carnival Victory* are bigger and have more cabins and crew than the original *Carnival Destiny,* for which the class was named and which was totally refurbished and renamed *Carnival Sunshine* in 2013.

The variety of indoor and outdoor spaces ranges from relatively small lounges with a nightclub atmosphere to huge show rooms where lavish production shows are staged. Most public rooms open off wide indoor promenades that branch fore and aft from the spectacular atrium.

Expansive pools and sport decks have plenty of room to spread out for sunning and more active pursuits; both ships have been retrofitted with massive poolside 270-square-foot LED screens.

## Cabins
**Cabins:** As on all Carnival ships, cabins are spacious and comfortable. More than half have an ocean view, and of those, 60% have balconies. For suites and ocean-view cabins that have them, private balconies are outfitted with chairs and tables, adding living space. Every cabin has adequate closet and drawer–shelf storage, as well as bathroom shelves. High-thread-count linens and plump pillows and duvets are a luxurious touch. Suites also have a whirlpool tub and walk-in closet. Numerous ocean-view and inside stateroom categories have connecting doors and are suitable for families.

**Decor:** Light-wood cabinetry, soft pastels, mirrored accents, a small refrigerator, a personal safe, a hair dryer, and a seating area with sofa, chair, and table are typical for ocean-view cabins and suites. Inside cabins do not have a seating area.

**Bathrooms:** Shampoo and bath gel dispensers are mounted on shower walls; an array of toiletry samples is stocked, as well as fluffy towels. Bathrobes for use during the cruise are provided for all.

**Accessibility:** Twenty-five staterooms are designed for wheelchair accessibility.

Top: *Carnival Victory* in Miami
Bottom: *Carnival Triumph* atrium

| Cabin Type | Size (sq. ft.) |
| --- | --- |
| Penthouse Suite | 345 |
| Suite | 275 |
| Ocean View | 185 |
| Interior | 185 |

**2**

**CARNIVAL CRUISE LINES**

## Restaurants

Two restaurants, each spanning two decks, serve open seating breakfast and lunch. Dinner is served in two traditional assigned evening seatings with an open seating option. Formal dining is supplemented by a casual Lido buffet, offering a variety of food choices (including a deli, salad bar, dessert station, and regional cuisines that change daily); the buffet restaurant becomes the Seaview Bistro by night for casual dining in a relaxed atmosphere. There are also a pizzeria, coffee bar/patisserie, poolside outdoor grill for burgers, hot dogs, and the trimmings, a specialty coffee bar/patisserie, a complimentary sushi bar, and 24-hour room service with a limited menu of breakfast selections, sandwiches, and snacks.

## Spas

Operated by Steiner Leisure, expansive spa facilities offer a full menu of treatments, such as a variety of massages, body wraps, and facials for adults and teens; complimentary steam rooms and saunas are located in men's and women's changing rooms. Hair and nail services and teeth whitening are also on the salon menu.

## Bars/Entertainment

*Triumph* and *Victory* are scheduled to receive newly branded bars and other features in 2013 and 2014 respectively. Both have lively piano bars and nightclubs featuring music for dancing and listening. High-energy production shows, comedy clubs, karaoke, and deck parties are signature nighttime activities.

## Pros and Cons

**Pros:** tiered sunning decks above the Lido pools offer a good view of the jumbo-size LED screens; the upper-level seating area in the Lido restaurant almost always has tables available; the lobby bar is a surprisingly off-the-beaten-path space with a lot of visual impact.

**Cons:** there is no steak house on either ship; private balconies on high decks in the middle of the ship may be noisy when there are activities on the Lido deck above; lines at the buffet can be seemingly endless at peak meal times.

### FAST FACTS

- 13 passenger decks
- 2 dining rooms, buffet, ice cream parlor, pizzeria
- Wi-Fi, safe, refrigerator
- 3 pools (1 indoor), children's pool
- Fitness classes, gym, hot tubs, sauna, spa, steam room
- 7 bars, casino, 3 dance clubs, library, show room, video game room
- Children's programs
- Laundry facilities, laundry service
- Internet terminal
- No-smoking cabins

*Carnival Triumph*

# CELEBRITY CRUISES

The Chandris Group, owners of budget Fantasy Cruises, founded Celebrity in 1989. Initially utilizing an unlovely, refurbished former ocean liner from the Fantasy fleet, Celebrity gained a reputation for professional service and fine food despite the shabby-chic

*Celebrity Century* at anchor

vessel on which it was elegantly served. The cruise line eventually built premium sophisticated cruise ships. Signature amenities followed, including large standard staterooms with generous storage, fully equipped spas, and butler service. Valuable art collections grace the fleet.

☎ *800/647–2251*
⊕ *www.celebritycruis-es.com* ☞ *Cruise Style: Premium.*

Although spacious accommodations in every category are a Celebrity standard, Concierge-class, an upscale element on all ships, makes certain premium ocean-view and balcony staterooms almost the equivalent of suites in terms of service. A Concierge-class stateroom includes numerous extras, such as chilled champagne, fresh fruit, and flowers upon arrival, exclusive room-service menus, evening canapés, luxury bedding, pillows, and linens, upgraded balcony furnishings, priority boarding and luggage service, and other VIP perks. At the touch of a single telephone button, a Concierge-class desk representative is at hand to offer assistance. Suites are still the ultimate, though, and include the services of a butler to assist with unpacking, booking spa services and dining reservations, shining shoes, and even replacing a popped button.

## Food

Aside from the sophisticated ambience of its restaurants, the cuisine has always been a highlight of a Celebrity cruise. Happily, every ship in the fleet has a highly experienced team headed by executive chefs and food and beverage managers who have developed their skills in some of the world's finest restaurants and hotels.

Alternative restaurants throughout the fleet offer fine dining and a variety of international cuisines in splendid surroundings. A less formal evening alternative is offered in Lido restaurants, where you'll find made-to-order sushi, stir-fry, pasta, pizza, and curry stations, as well as a carving station, an array of vegetables, "loaded" baked potatoes, and desserts. The AquaSpa Cafés serve light and healthy cuisine from breakfast until evening. Cafés serve a variety of coffees, teas, and pastries that carry an additional charge. Late-night treats served by white-gloved waiters in public rooms throughout the ships can include mini–beef Wellingtons and crispy tempura.

To further complement the food, in 2004 Celebrity introduced a proprietary Cellarmaster Selection of wines, formulated specifically for Celebrity passengers.

## Entertainment

Entertainment has never been a primary focus of Celebrity Cruises, although every ship offers a line-up of lavish production shows. In addition, ships have guest entertainers and music for dancing and listening, and you'll find guest lecturers on every Celebrity cruise. Presentations may range from financial strategies, astronomy, wine appreciation, photography tips, and politics to the food, history, and culture of ports of call. Culinary demonstrations, bingo, and art auctions are additional diversions throughout the fleet. There are plenty of activities outlined in the daily program of events. There are no public address announcements for bingo or hawking of gold-by-the-inch sales. You can still play and buy, but you won't be reminded repeatedly.

## Fitness and Recreation

Celebrity's AquaSpa by Elemis and fitness centers are some of the most tranquil and nicely equipped at sea, with complimentary access to thalassotherapy pools on Millennium-class ships. Spa services are operated by Steiner Leisure, and treatments include a variety of massages, body wraps, and facials. Trendy and traditional hair and nail services are offered in the salons.

State-of-the-art exercise equipment, a jogging track, and basic fitness classes are available at no charge. There's a fee for personal training, body composition analysis, and specialized classes such as yoga and Pilates. Golf pros offer hands-on instruction, and game simulators allow passengers to play world-famous courses. Each ship also has an Acupuncture at Sea treatment area staffed by licensed practitioners of Oriental medicine.

### KNOWN FOR

■ **Art:** Celebrity's contemporary style is complemented by stunning modern art collections.

■ **Service:** With a high ratio of staff to guests, Celebrity offers personal and intuitive, yet unobtrusive service.

■ **AquaSpa:** The AquaSpa facilities on Celebrity ships are considered some of the finest at sea.

■ **Food:** Sophisticated cuisine and menu options make Celebrity's dining experience outstanding at this level of cruising.

Top: The *Millennium* AquaSpa
Bottom: Millennium-class cinema and conference center

2

CELEBRITY CRUISES

### Your Shipmates

Celebrity caters to American cruise passengers, primarily couples from their mid-thirties to mid-fifties. Many families enjoy cruising on Celebrity's fleet during summer months and holiday periods, particularly in the Caribbean. Lengthier cruises and exotic itineraries attract passengers in the over-sixty age group.

### Dress Code

Two formal nights are standard on seven-night cruises. Men are encouraged to wear tuxedos, but dark suits or sport coats and ties are more prevalent. Other evenings are designated "smart casual and above." Although jeans are discouraged in formal restaurants, they are appropriate for casual dining venues after 6 pm. The line requests that no shorts be worn in public areas after 6 pm, and most people observe the dress code of the evening, unlike on some other cruise lines.

### Junior Cruisers

Each Celebrity vessel has a dedicated playroom and offers a four-tier program of age-appropriate games and activities designed for children ages 3 to 5, 6 to 8, and 9 to 11. Younger children must be toilet trained to participate in the programs and use the facilities; however, families are welcome to borrow toys for their non–toilet-trained kids. A fee may be assessed for participation in children's dinner parties, the Late-Night Slumber Party, and Afternoon Get-Togethers while parents are ashore in ports of call. Evening in-cabin babysitting can be arranged for a fee. All ships have teen centers, where tweens and teenagers (ages 12 to 17) can hang out and attend mock-tail and pizza parties.

### Service

Service on Celebrity ships is unobtrusive and polished. Concierge-class adds an unexpected level of service and amenities that are usually reserved for luxury ships or passengers in top-category suites on other premium cruise lines.

Top: *Century* Rendezvous Lounge
Middle: Lunch on deck
Bottom: Lounging on deck

---

**CHOOSE THIS LINE IF ...**

You want an upscale atmosphere at a really reasonable fare.

You want piping-hot late-night pizza delivered to your cabin in pizzeria fashion.

You want to dine amid elegant surroundings in some of the best restaurants at sea.

## Tipping

Gratuities are automatically added daily to onboard accounts in the following amounts (which may be adjusted at your discretion): $11.50 per person per day for passengers in stateroom categories; $12 per person per day for Concierge-class and Aqua-class staterooms; and $15 per person per day for suites. An automatic gratuity of 15% is added to all beverage tabs.

## Past Passengers

Once you've sailed with Celebrity, you become a member of the Captain's Club and receive benefits commensurate with the number of cruises you've taken, including free upgrades, the chance to make dining reservations before sailing, and other benefits. Classic members have been on at least one Celebrity cruise. Select members have sailed at least six cruises and get more perks, including an invitation to a senior officer's cocktail party. After 10 cruises you become an Elite member and can take advantage of a private departure lounge. Royal Caribbean International, the parent company of Celebrity Cruises, also extends the corresponding levels of their Crown & Anchor program to Celebrity Captain's Club members.

## HELPFUL HINTS

Wine/dining packages are a comparative bargain since fees for specialty restaurants are so high, but they are only offered in limited numbers; book them early.

The line offers stateroom bar se-ups and flat-rate beverage packages to help you avoid per-drink charges.

Ship's photographers will cover individual special events if asked.

Service animals are welcome on board all ships, including those sailing to the United Kingdom if they are in compliance with DEFRA regulations.

Celebrity's private shore excursions (in 50 ports) offer personalized travel in the comfort of a private car or van.

## DON'T CHOOSE THIS LINE IF ...

You need to be reminded of when activities are scheduled. Announcements are kept to a minimum.

You look forward to boisterous pool games and wacky contests. These cruises are fairly quiet and sophisticated.

You think funky avant-garde art is weird. Abstract modernism abounds in the art collections.

# SOLSTICE-CLASS
*Solstice, Equinox, Eclipse, Silhouette, Reflection*

| | |
|---|---|
| **Crew Members** | 1,253 |
| **Entered Service** | 2008, 2009, 2010, 2011, 2012 |
| **Gross Tons** | 122,000/126,000 (*Reflection*) |
| **Length** | 1,033/1,047 feet (*Reflection*) |
| **Number of Cabins** | 1,425/1,515 (*Reflection*) |
| **Passenger Capacity** | 2,850/3,046 (*Reflection*) |
| **Width** | 121 feet/123 feet (*Reflection*) |

Solstice-class ships are the largest in the Celebrity fleet. While the ships are contemporary in design—even a bit edgy for Celebrity—the line included enough spaces with old-world ambience to satisfy traditionalists. The atmosphere is not unlike a hip boutique hotel yet filled with grand spaces, as well as intimate nooks and crannies. *Celebrity Reflection* adds an additional deck for more high-end suite accommodations.

The Lawn Club, a half acre of real grass on deck 15, is where you can play genteel games of croquet, practice golf putting, indulge in lawn games and picnics, or simply take barefoot strolls. In a nearby open-air "theater" on *Solstice, Eclipse,* and *Equinox,* artisans demonstrate glassmaking in the Hot Glass Show. A similar space on *Silhouette* and *Reflection* houses an outdoor grill restaurant, and those ships also have private cabanas in the Lawn Club (for a fee). These ships have a lot to offer families, with a family pool and the most extensive children's facilities in the Celebrity fleet.

## Cabins

**Layout:** Although cabins are larger than those on other Celebrity ships, closet and drawer storage is barely adequate. On the other hand, bathrooms are generous and have plentiful storage space. An impressive 85% of all outside accommodations have balconies. With sofa–trundle beds, many categories are capable of accommodating third and fourth occupants. Connecting staterooms are also available. Family staterooms have a second bedroom with bunk beds.

**Amenities:** A refrigerator, TV, personal safe, hair dryer, seating area with sofa and table, bathroom toiletries (shampoo, soaps, and lotion), and bathrobes for use during the cruise are standard.

**Suites:** Most suites have a whirlpool tub, DVD, and walk-in closet, while all have butler service, personalized stationery, and a logo tote bag. Penthouse suites have guest powder rooms; Penthouse and Royal suites have whirlpool tubs on the balconies. *Celebrity Reflection* introduces several additional suite categories.

**Accessibility:** Thirty staterooms are designed for wheelchair accessibility.

Top: Blu, the AquaClass
specialty restaurant
Bottom: Lawn bowling

## Restaurants

The main restaurant serves open seating breakfast and lunch; dinner is served in two traditional assigned seatings or an open seating option. A second dining room, reserved for Aqua-class passengers, serves lighter cuisine. There are also a casual Lido buffet, pizza, sushi bar, the AquaSpa Café with healthy selections, a luncheon grill, a café that offers crêpes (cover charge), and specialty coffee, tea, and gelato bar (extra charge). Three upscale alternative restaurants require dinner reservations and charge extra for contemporary French, Asian fusion, and Italian. *Eclipse, Silhouette,* and *Reflection* replaced the Asian restaurant with one serving modern American food. Additionally, *Silhouette,* and *Reflection* feature the Lawn Club Grill for evening alfresco dining (cover charge) and The Porch for light fare. Available 24 hours, room service rounds out the dining choices.

## Spas

The AquaSpa by Elemis is one of the most tranquil at sea with spa services operated by Steiner Leisure. In addition to treatments that include a variety of massages, body wraps, and facials, each ship also has an acupuncture treatment area and Medi-Spa Cosmetic services. A relaxation room and thermal suite with dry and aromatherapy steam rooms and a hot Turkish bath are available to Aqua-class passengers and those who have booked a treatment or purchased a pass. Changing rooms for men and women have complimentary saunas.

## Bars/Entertainment

Production companies and guest entertainers perform in the show lounges. Bars and lounges are designed as unique destinations on board with drink menus offering not only a selection of classics, but also "signature" and trendier cocktails. Some drinks are a reflection of the regions you are visiting. Live bands or DJs provide music for listening and dancing.

## Pros and Cons

**Pros:** an interactive TV system allows you to book shore excursions and order room service; Aqua-class has its own staircase direct to the spa; a Hospitality Director oversees restaurant reservations.

**Cons:** closet space is skimpy in standard cabins; there are no self-service laundries; dining choices are plentiful, but pricey.

| Cabin Type | Size (sq. ft.) |
| --- | --- |
| Penthouse/ Refection Suite | 1,291/ 1,636 |
| Royal Suites | 590 |
| Celebrity/ Signature Suites | 394/441 |
| Sky/Aqua-class Suites | 300 |
| Family Ocean-view Balcony | 575 |
| Ocean-view Balcony | 194 |
| Sunset Veranda | 194 |
| Ocean View | 177 |
| Inside | 183–200 |

### FAST FACTS

- 13 passenger decks (14 *Celebrity Reflection*)
- 4 specialty restaurants (5 *Celebrity Reflection*), 3 dining rooms, buffet, ice cream parlor, pizzeria
- Wi-Fi, safe, refrigerator, DVD (some)
- 3 pools (1 indoor)
- Fitness classes, gym, hot tubs, sauna, spa
- 11 bars, casino, dance club, library, show room, video game room
- Children's programs
- Dry-cleaning, laundry service
- Internet terminal
- No-smoking cabins

2

CELEBRITY CRUISES

The solarium on *Solstice*

# MILLENNIUM-CLASS
*Millennium, Summit, Infinity, Constellation*

| | |
|---|---|
| Crew Members | 999 |
| Entered Service | 2000, 2001, 2001, 2002 |
| Gross Tons | 91,000 |
| Length | 965 feet |
| Number of Cabins | 975 |
| Passenger Capacity | 1,950 (2,450) |
| Width | 105 feet |

700 ft.

500 ft.

300 ft.

Millennium-class ships are among the largest and most feature-filled in the Celebrity fleet. Innovations include show lounges reminiscent of splendid opera houses, and an alternative restaurant with a classic ocean liner theme. The spas are immense, and while they offer just about any treatment you can think of—and some you probably haven't—they also house a complimentary hydrotherapy pool and café. These ships have a lot to offer families, with some of the most expansive children's facilities in the Celebrity fleet.

Rich fabrics in jewel tones mix elegantly with the abundant use of marble and wood accents throughout public areas. The atmosphere is not unlike a luxurious European hotel filled with grand spaces that flow nicely from one to the other.

## Cabins

**Cabins:** As on most Celebrity ships, cabins are thoughtfully designed, with ample closet and drawer/shelf storage, as well as bathroom shelves. Some ocean-view cabins and suites have balconies. Penthouse suites also have guest powder rooms. Most staterooms and suites have convertible sofa beds, and many can accommodate third and fourth occupants. Connecting staterooms are also widely available. Family staterooms have huge balconies, and some have two sofa beds. Aqua-class accommodations with direct spa access are a relatively new addition.

**Amenities:** A small refrigerator, personal safe, hair dryer, and a seating area with sofa, chair, and table are typical standard amenities. Extras include bathroom toiletries (shampoo, soaps, and lotion) and bathrobes. Suite luxuries vary, but most include a whirlpool tub, a DVD, an Internet-connected computer, and a walk-in closet, while all have butler service, personalized stationery, and a logo tote bag. Penthouse and Royal suites have outdoor whirlpool tubs on the balconies.

**Accessibility:** Twenty-six staterooms are designed for wheelchair accessibility.

## Restaurants

The formal two-deck restaurant serves open seating breakfast and lunch; while dinner is served in two assigned seatings or open seating. The casual Lido buffet offers breakfast and lunch. For dinner, it has

Top: *Millennium* Café al Bacio
Bottom: *Millennium*
Ocean Grill

made-to-order entrées, a carving station, and an array of side dishes. A poolside grill offers fast food, while a spa café serves lighter fare. Each ship has an upscale alternative restaurant that specializes in tableside food preparation; each also has a demonstration kitchen and wine cellar (reservation and cover charge). Each also has a café that offers crepes and other light items (cover charge), and an extra-charge specialty coffee, tea, and gelato bar. All ships feature a second specialty restaurant serving modern American food except *Constellation*, which has an Italian specialty restaurant. Pizza delivery and 24-hour room service augment dining choices.

## Spas

The AquaSpa by Elemis is one of the most nicely equipped at sea with spa services operated by Steiner Leisure. In addition to treatments that include a variety of massages, body wraps, and facials, each ship also has an acupuncture treatment area and offers Medi-Spa Cosmetic services. A relaxation room and thermal suite with a dry sauna, aromatherapy steam room, and a Turkish bath are available to Aqua-class passengers and those who have booked a treatment or purchased a pass. Changing rooms for men and women have complimentary saunas, and a large hydrotherapy pool is available to all adults at no charge.

## Bars/Entertainment

Production companies and guest entertainers perform in the show lounges. Bars and lounges are designed as unique destinations on board with drink menus offering not only a selection of classics, but also "signature" and trendier cocktails. Some drinks are a reflection of the regions you are visiting. Live bands or DJs provide music for listening and dancing.

## Pros and Cons

**Pros:** stylishly appointed Grand Foyers have sweeping staircases; there's no charge for use of the thalassotherapy pool in the Solarium; the AquaSpa Café serves complimentary light and healthy selections.

**Cons:** these ships just have too many passengers to offer truly personal service; wines in the specialty restaurants are pricey; there are no self-service laundries.

| Cabin Type | Size (sq. ft.) |
|---|---|
| Penthouse Suite | 1,432 |
| Royal Suite | 538 |
| Celebrity Suite | 467 |
| Sky Suite | 251 |
| Family Ocean View | 271 |
| Concierge-class | 191 |
| Ocean View/ Interior | 170 |

### FAST FACTS

- 11 passenger decks
- 3 specialty restaurants, dining room, buffet, ice cream parlor, pizzeria
- Internet (*Constellation*), Wi-Fi, safe, refrigerator, DVD (some)
- 3 pools (1 indoor), children's pool
- Fitness classes, gym, hot tubs, sauna, spa, steam room
- 7 bars, casino, dance club, library, show room, video game room
- Children's programs
- Dry-cleaning, laundry service
- Internet terminal
- No-smoking cabins

**2**

**CELEBRITY CRUISES**

# COMPAGNIE DU PONANT

Compagnie du Ponant operates three designer ships for all-season premium yet unpretentious yacht cruising in places inaccessible to larger cruise ships. At this writing, a fourth ship was expected for delivery in July 2013. With distinctively French flair, the cruise

Le Boréal at sea

company strikes an appealing balance between destination choice and price point on luxuriously refurbished modern sailing vessels that feature French gastronomy, elegant styling, and unique voyages with all-inclusive packages. Travel is privileged yet unpretentious aboard a small majestic three-masted sailing yacht or larger megayacht.

☎ *888/400–1082 (toll-free in the U.S. and Canada) or (033) 4/88–66–64–00 in France ⊕ www.ponant. com ☞ Cruise Style: Luxury.*

### Food

Gastronomy is taken pretty seriously on Compagnie du Ponant ships. Buttery croissants and artisanal baguettes with confiture, fruit, yogurts, coffee, and juices are available for breakfast; eggs and specialty dishes can be ordered à la carte. International buffets for lunch and dinner lay out a high-quality spread of cold and hot appetizers, entrées, salads, and desserts. Fresh ingredients and skilled preparation by resident French chefs and bakers keep culinary standards at an outstanding level for grilled and roasted meat, fish, vegetarian meals, and desserts. In more formal dining areas, most dinner menus offer a choice between two soups, three appetizers/salads, two main courses, a cheese tray, and a couple of sumptuous desserts. While oenophiles may be disappointed with the free table wine served for lunch and dinner, premium bottles can be ordered for a supplementary cost. Back by popular demand, the Food & Wine Cruise pleases passenger palates with Flavors of the Riviera. All lunches and dinners include complimentary mineral water, tea, coffee, and wines. Twenty-four-hour room service is available.

## Entertainment

Special events including the Captain's cocktail party and farewell dinner spice up the rather unimaginative entertainment program that does not promise to be grandiose and theatrical. Instead, most passengers simply relax while watching small groups of performers and dancers. Guest speakers lecture on geography, conservation, and wildlife in the cabaret-style theater on larger ships, which is also used for evening shows. On smaller vessels, piano bars and chic lounges offer opportunities to make new friends from around the world.

## Fitness and Recreation

Passengers burn off calories in a fully equipped gym, outdoor heated swimming pool, or spa equipped with sauna and steam rooms. Plenty of lounges, sundecks, panoramic promenades, bars, reading rooms, library, casino, and shops satisfy early birds and night owls. Shore excursions upon landing perhaps constitute the most fun activity. Some of these include spectacular terrain hikes and Zodiac cruises across frozen vistas, turquoise horizons, or historic coastlines. Themed cruises offer comprehensive activities, including demonstrations, classes, performances, and well-planned excursions. On larger ships, Wi-Fi stations offer gaming consoles. All vessels have Internet rooms and Wi-Fi—which costs €5 per half hour.

## Your Shipmates

Compagnie du Ponant cruisers are a sophisticated group consisting of affluent adventurers and sportive globetrotters. Families with kids are not uncommon on the larger vessels, but the general age ranges between 40 and 70. A multicultural blend of primarily French, Australians, and North Americans comprise the passenger list. The common language heard on board is French, although English is widely spoken and understood by the experienced crew and most of the well-traveled guests.

## Dress Code

There is no strict dress code, and ships are relatively informal. During the day, smart leisurewear is recommended. For excursions and shore leaves, bring practical clothes and comfortable shoes. Expeditions to the Arctic and Antartica using Zodiacs require waterproof parkas (provided on board), flexible trousers, boots, gloves, and fleece hats. Sunglasses are highly advised. Evening attire is at your discretion, but men are required to wear a jacket.

## KNOWN FOR

■ **Exotic Locales:** Compagnie du Ponant provides yacht cruises to inaccessible worldwide locations and remote ports of call.

■ **Luxurious Comforts:** Ultracomfortable cabins, excellent food, and facilities with designer furnishings and elegant French atmosphere are the norm.

■ **Intimacy:** Ships have limited passenger capacity, ranging between 64 and 226 guests.

■ **Special-Interest Cruising:** Themed cruises (culinary, golf, classical music, jazz, bridge, wellness) featuring expert lecturers and special venues on board and ashore are common.

■ **Eco-friendly:** "Green label" ships are outfitted with the latest technology to protect the oceans and marine life.

Top: *L'Austral* at sea
Bottom: Cabin aboard *L'Austral*

Top: The main lobby aboard
*L'Austral*
Middle: Dining al fresco aboard
*Le Ponant*
Bottom: A spacious cabin
aboard *Le Boréal*

### Junior Cruisers

Children over the age of 8 are allowed on board. The good life begins early for young sailors privileged to tag along on Compagnie du Ponant yachts. Outfitted with facilities and amenities catering to both young and old, the four vessels offer flexible "communicating" cabins, children's menus, tea parties, games, and piano and cooking lessons, Wii game consoles, Internet stations, reading areas, and the Ponant Kid's Club on deck 5 (free for one child, age 8–12, sharing a cabin with two adults) that has a carpeted area with sofas, assorted toys, TV, and play zone. Themed family cruises are sometimes offered, and these provide a more child-friendly atmosphere and babysitting service.

### Service

Building a strong reputation for personalized, friendly service, the four cruise ships have multilingual crew and staff that understand the demands and expectations of an international traveler. Attention to detail with food service, cabin maintenance and cleanliness, overall ship hygiene, spa services, and special requests is handled with discretion and satisfactory efficiency. Announcements are made in both French and English.

### Tipping

The cruise line changed its tipping policy in 2012. All gratuities are now included for restaurant, hotel, and ship staffs as well as local guides and drivers.

### Past Passengers

The Ponant Yacht Club loyalty program has Major, Admiral, and Grand Admiral levels. As members, cruisers benefit from exclusive services and amenities on board. They are also eligible for exclusive offers in the shop, wine cellar, or open-bar package depending on membership level.

### Ships of the Line

***L'Austral.*** International dining and destinations stand out on this newer yachting vessel, amenity-wise identical twin to *Le Boréal*. Child-friendly cabins, a knowledgeable crew, friendly staff, and excellent food and service are hallmarks of this ship. Having earned the international "green ship" label (like *Le*

---

### CHOOSE THIS LINE IF ...

You've always dreamt of sailing on your own private yacht.

Destinations in remote ports of call and inaccessible landscapes are a priority.

You appreciate open-air cruising (large sundecks, terraces, sea-level platforms, and cabins with private balconies) and discreet elegance.

*Boréal*), *L'Austral* consistently receives rave reviews from demanding, experienced voyagers for its first-class accommodations and service. The majority of the 132 cabins and suites measure a comfortable 200 square feet and have a small, private balcony.

**Le Boréal.** A unique megayacht carrying 264 passengers, *Le Boréal* boasts a history of fine design by Jean-Philippe Nuel with superb exterior and interior detailing. The ship's sleek silhouette and large arched windows, not to mention the interior, ooze elegance. The ship has 132 spacious staterooms (many have private balconies) with personal safe, hair dryer, and Wi-Fi. Dance floors, live music, library, and large terraces extending toward the sea or overlooking the outdoor heated swimming pool create an upbeat ambience. Leisure facilities include a well-equipped fitness center, full-service salon, hammam and balneo room, and two massage and relaxation rooms.

**Le Ponant.** In the nautical tradition of the three-masted sailing yacht, *Le Ponant* is the ideal vessel on which to embark for a special, intimate voyage of discovery. Carrying only 64 passengers and a 32-member crew, the 288-foot stylishly designed ship offers a luxurious experience with personalized service and modern amenities. Open-air sophistication is shared and savored on four passenger decks with 32 cabins of approximately 150 square feet. For the ultimate indulgence, rent the entire yacht (crew included) for a private charter.

**Le Soléal.** The flagship 264-passenger *Le Soléal* debuts in July 2013, duplicating the elegant contours of her sister ships. Designer chic, the 132 staterooms and suites are decorated in shades of grey, white, and brown. Enjoy a spa, theater, and multiple lounges. Original 4- to 22-day itineraries cruise perennially through the Mediterranean, Norway, Iceland, Greenland, Russia, and the Arctic.

■TIP→ **Two older vessels Le Levant and Le Diamant were put out of commission in Fall 2012.**

## HELPFUL HINTS

In summer 2012, Compagnie du Ponant announced a new all-inclusive pricing structure that includes meals, drinks, minibars, tips, and port charges.

Select itineraries offer air-inclusive pricing.

Open dining allows you to eat meals when you want and with whom you want, though you can still expect group settings for special occasions and lunchtime sightseeing excursions.

Select itineraries allow kids 8 to 18 to sail for free when they stay with their parents in a Superior cabin or Prestige suite.

With direct access to the sea from an open deck, ships offer the chance to swim in the surrounding crystalline waters.

## DON'T CHOOSE THIS LINE IF ...

You seek a no-frills holiday with loud parties and prefer sandwiches for dinner.

You like to dress up in ostentatious glitz and glamorous eveningwear.

Luxury travel with refined French elegance, sophistication, and language just isn't your cup of tea.

# COSTA CRUISES

Europe's number-one cruise line combines a Continental experience, enticing itineraries, and Italy's classical design and style with relaxing days and romantic nights at sea. Genoa-based Costa Crociere, parent company of Costa Cruise Lines, had been

Dining alfresco

in the shipping business for more than 100 years and in the passenger business for almost 50 years when it was bought by Airtours and Carnival Corporation in 1997. In 2000 Carnival completed a buyout of the Costa line and began expanding the fleet with larger and more dynamic ships.

☎ 954/266–5600
or 800/462–6782
⊕ www.costacruise.
com ☞ Cruise Style:
Mainstream.

An ongoing shipbuilding program has brought Costa ships into the 21st century with innovative large-ship designs that reflect their Italian heritage and style without overlooking the amenities expected by modern cruisers. Acknowledging changing habits (even among Europeans), Costa Cruises has eliminated smoking entirely in dining rooms and show lounges. However, smokers are permitted to light up in designated areas in other public rooms, as well as on the pool deck.

### Food

Costa is noted for themed dinner menus that convey the evening's mood. Dining features regional Italian cuisines: a variety of pastas, chicken, beef, and seafood dishes, as well as authentic pizza. European chefs and culinary school graduates, who are members of Chaîne des Rôtisseurs, provide a dining experience that's notable for a delicious, properly prepared pasta course, if not exactly living up to gourmet standards. Vegetarian and healthy diet choices are also offered, as are selections for children. Alternative dining is by reservation only in the upscale supper clubs, which serve traditional Italian cuisine.

While specialty restaurants usually have a separate à la carte charge for each menu item, suite passengers receive one complimentary dinner for two.

Costa ships also retain the tradition of lavish nightly midnight buffets, a feature that is beginning to disappear on other mainstream lines. Room service is available 24 hours from a limited menu.

## Entertainment

Italian-style cruising is a mixture of Mediterranean flair and American comfort, beginning with a *buon viaggio* celebration. The supercharged social staff works overtime to get everyone in the mood during the line's signature nighttime parties and encourages everyone to be a part of the action.

Shipboard activities include games of bocce, dancing the tarantella, and tossing pizza dough during the Festa Italiana, an Italian street festival at sea. Other nights are themed as well—a welcome-aboard celebration (*Benvenuto A Bordo*), hosted by the captain on the first formal night, and *Notte Tropical,* a tropical deck party with a Mediterranean twist that culminates with the presentation of an alfresco midnight buffet. When it is time to say goodbye, Costa throws a Roman Bacchanal.

There's also a nod to the traditional cruise ship entertainment expected by North American passengers. Pool games, trivia, bingo, and sophisticated production shows blend nicely with classical concerts in lounges, where a wide range of musical styles invite dancing or listening. Italian language, arts and crafts, and cooking classes are extremely popular.

## Fitness and Recreation

Taking a cue from the ancient Romans, Costa places continuing emphasis on wellness and sensual pleasures. Spas and salons are operated by Steiner Leisure, and treatments include a variety of massages, body wraps, and facials that can be scheduled à la carte or combined in packages to enjoy during one afternoon or throughout the entire cruise. Hair and nail services are available in the salons.

State-of-the-art exercise equipment in the gym, a jogging track, and basic fitness classes for all levels of ability are available. Costa ships offer a Golf Academy at Sea, with PGA clinics on the ship and golf excursions in some ports.

### KNOWN FOR

■ **Diversity:** Costa is one of Europe's most popular cruise lines, so passengers are often a diverse mix of nationalities.

■ **Italian cuisine:** The line celebrates its Italian heritage in the design of its ships' interiors and with the best of Italy's regional dishes on the menu.

■ **Crowds:** Costa's large ships are spacious but carry so many people that they can feel crowded.

■ **Theme Nights:** Costa still has several theme nights on every cruise.

Top: Showtime on Costa
Bottom: Casino action

Top: Costa chefs
Middle: Jogging on deck
Bottom: Las Vegas–style
entertainment

## Your Shipmates

Couples in the 35- to 55-year-old range are attracted to Costa Cruises; on most itineraries, up to 80% of passengers are European, and many of them are of Italian descent. An international air prevails on board, and announcements are often made in a variety of languages. The vibe on Costa's newest megaships is most likely to appeal to American tastes and expectations.

## Dress Code

Two formal nights are standard on seven-night cruises. Men are encouraged to wear tuxedos, but dark suits or sport coats and ties are appropriate and more common than black tie. All other evenings are resort casual, although jeans are discouraged in restaurants. It's requested that no shorts be worn in public areas after 6 pm.

## Junior Cruisers

All sailings feature age-specific youth programs that include such daily activities as costume parties, board games, junior aerobics, and even Italian-language lessons for children in four age groups: 3 (toilet trained) to 6; 7 to 11; junior teens 12 to 14; and teens 15 to 17. The actual age groupings may be influenced by the number of children on board. Special counselors oversee activities, and specific rooms are designed for children and teens, depending on the ship. Children under three years old can use the playroom facilities if accompanied and supervised by their parents.

Organized sessions for all children between the ages of 3 and 17 are available every day, even when in port, from 9 to noon and 3 to 6, as well as from 9 to 11:30 in the evening. Parents can enjoy at least a couple of evenings alone by taking advantage of two complimentary Parents Nights Out while their children dine at a supervised buffet or pizza party and take part in evening and nighttime activities. Nighttime group babysitting for children ages 3 to 11 is complimentary in the children's area until 1:30 am. Unfortunately, no late-night babysitting service is offered for children under three, nor is there in-cabin babysitting.

## CHOOSE THIS LINE IF ...

You're a satisfied Carnival past passenger and want a similar experience with an Italian flavor.

You want pizza hot out of the oven whenever you get a craving for it.

You're a joiner: there are many opportunities to be in the center of the action.

## Service

Service in dining areas can be spotty and rushed, but is adequate, if not always overly friendly.

## Tipping

A standard gratuity of €7 per adult per day for cruises up to eight nights or €6 per adult per day on longer cruises is automatically added to shipboard accounts and distributed to cabin stewards and dining-room staff. The applicable charge for teens between the ages of 14 and 17 is 50% of those amounts; there is no charge for children under the age of 14. Passengers may adjust the amount based on the level of service experienced. An automatic 15% gratuity is added to all beverage tabs, as well as to checks for spa treatments and salon services.

## Past Passengers

The Costa Club has three levels of membership: Aquamarine (2,000 points), Coral (2,001 to 5,000 points), and Pearl (5,001 or more points). Points are assigned for the number of cruising days (100 points per day) and the amount of money spent aboard (40 points for 52 euros).

Membership privileges vary, and can include discounts on selected cruises, fruit baskets, and bottles of Spumante delivered to your cabin, discounts on boutique merchandise and beauty treatments, or a complimentary dinner in a specialty restaurant.

### HELPFUL HINTS

The currency for on board purchases while sailing in Europe is the euro.

Costa places an emphasis on its ships' furnishings and fittings, and they can be extravagant and beautiful.

All-inclusive drinks packages are available for adults 18 and over; soft drinks packages are available for kids.

Personalized guided excursions tailored to your interests can be arranged for you to tour independently without the restriction of traveling in a group.

Should you wish to don a toga to participate in the Roman Bacchanal, cabin stewards are happy to provide extra sheets.

**2**

**COSTA CRUISES**

### DON'T CHOOSE THIS LINE IF ...

You find announcements in a variety of languages annoying.

You want an authentic Italian cruise. The crew has grown more international than Italian as the line has expanded.

You prefer sedate splendor in a formal atmosphere; many of the ships are almost Fellini-esque in style.

# COSTA FORTUNA, COSTA MAGICA

| | |
|---|---|
| **Crew Members** | 1,027 |
| **Entered Service** | 2003, 2004 |
| **Gross Tons** | 103,000 |
| **Length** | 890 feet |
| **Number of Cabins** | 1,358 |
| **Passenger Capacity** | 2,716 (3,470 max) |
| **Width** | 124/118 feet |

With a bit of interior alteration, *Costa Fortuna* and *Costa Magica* are essentially Euro-clones of parent company Carnival Cruise Line's *Carnival Triumph* and *Carnival Victory*. The mix and size of public rooms was determined to appeal to European as well as North American passengers sailing on itineraries that include the Mediterranean Sea.

Like Carnival ships designed by Joe Farcus, these Costa beauties have a theme running throughout—*Costa Fortuna's* decor is inspired by the grand Italian steamships of the past. Incorporated into the design of the ship, scale models of historic liners grace nearly every public area. A "fleet" of 26 former ships of the Costa fleet boldly "sail" upside down across the ceiling of the atrium. Ceilings in the formal, two-deck dining rooms are also decorated; aboard *Costa Fortuna*, Michelangelo Restaurant features reproductions of the master's frescoes, while Raffaello Restaurant displays its namesake's Vatican artwork. Art deco touches add grace to all the public spaces.

## Cabins

**Layout:** Cabins generally follow the outline of their Carnival counterparts, with the notable addition of a Grand suite category. More than 60% of accommodations have an ocean view and, of those, 60% have balconies. Balconies have chairs and tables, and dividers can be unlocked to connect some cabins. Every cabin has adequate closet and drawer/shelf storage, as well as bathroom shelves. Suites have a generous walk-in closet. Well-designed lifeboat placement ensures unobstructed sea views from all outside cabin windows.

**Amenities:** Light-wood cabinetry, soft pastel decor, mirrored accents, Murano-glass lighting fixtures, a small refrigerator, a personal safe, a hair dryer, and a seating area with a sofa, chair, and table are typical for ocean-view cabins and suites. Inside cabins have ample room, but seating areas consist only of a small table and chairs. Suite passengers also enjoy DVD players and an enhanced room-service menu.

**Bathrooms:** Bathroom extras include shampoo and bath gel in shower-mounted dispensers; suite bathrooms include a whirlpool tub and two sinks.

Top: Romantic dinner
Bottom: *Costa Magica*
Grand suite

**Accessibility:** Twenty-seven staterooms are designed for passengers with disabilities.

## Restaurants

Two main restaurants, each spanning two decks, serve open seating breakfast and lunch; dinner is served in two traditional assigned seatings. The upscale reservations-required alternative restaurant features Italian specialties—while there is a charge, it's well worth it for the intimate atmosphere and interesting menu selection. Casual meals for breakfast, lunch, and dinner and pizza are available in the Lido buffet. The pasta station is always a top choice for lunch or dinner. Costa is one of the few cruise lines to continue the seagoing tradition of midnight buffets. Room service is available 24 hours from a limited menu.

## Spas

The Saturnia spa is quite spacious but has no thermal suite. A complete menu of treatments includes facials, body wraps, and massages. Men's and women's changing rooms have complimentary saunas and steam rooms.

## Bars/Entertainment

The main show lounge takes center stage most nights with performances by the resident production singers and dancers as well as guest entertainers. The large secondary show lounges feature singers and musicians and are the venues for Costa's signature parties, during which the entertainment staff goes into overdrive to encourage passenger participation. There is a quieter and intimate piano bar as well as a disco where the action continues late into the night.

## Pros and Cons

**Pros:** with floor-to-ceiling glass walls, saunas and steam rooms are bright and cheery; dance floors in the main "grand" lounges are large enough for real ballroom dancing; there is a dedicated lounge for cigar smokers.

**Cons:** the library doesn't have many books and is staffed daily at limited times; open decks feel pretty crowded on fully booked sailings; Wi-Fi is often slow, and the computer center can be noisy.

| Cabin Type | Size (sq. ft.) |
| --- | --- |
| Grand Suites | 650 |
| Suites | 360 |
| Minisuites | 300 |
| Ocean View | 185 |
| Interior | 160 |

## FAST FACTS

- 13 passenger decks
- Specialty restaurant, 2 dining rooms, buffet, pizzeria
- Wi-Fi, safe, refrigerator, DVD (some)
- 3 pools (1 indoor), children's pool
- Fitness classes, gym, hot tubs, sauna, spa, steam room
- 7 bars, casino, 2 dance clubs, library, 2 show rooms, video game room
- Children's programs
- Laundry facilities, laundry service
- Internet terminal, WI-Fi

**2**

**COSTA CRUISES**

Deck games

# COSTA ATLANTICA/MEDITERRANEA

| | |
|---|---|
| Crew Members | 920 |
| Entered Service | 2000, 2003 |
| Gross Tons | 86,000 |
| Length | 960 feet |
| Number of Cabins | 1,057 |
| Passenger Capacity | 2,114 (2,682 max) |
| Width | 106 feet |

The basic layout of these contemporary ships is nearly identical to parent Carnival Cruise Line's Spirit-class vessels. Interiors were designed by Carnival's ship architect Joe Farcus, whose abundant use of marble reflects Costa's Italian heritage. Artwork commissioned specifically for each ship was created by contemporary artists and includes intricate sculptures in silver and glass. Don't overlook the lighting fixtures, which were created especially for the ship, most of them crafted by the artisans in Venice's Murano-glass factories.

The nice flow between public lounges is broken only by piazzas, where you can practice the Italian custom of *passeggiata* (strolling to see and be seen). And there's plenty to see; these are visually stimulating interiors, with vivid colors and decor elements to arouse a sense of discovery. One of the most elegant spaces on board *Costa Atlantica* is Café Florian—inspired by the original in Venice's St. Mark's Square.

## Cabins

**Cabins:** Cabins generally follow the outline of their Carnival counterparts, with the distinctive addition of a Grand suite category. Nearly 80% of the suites and staterooms have an ocean view, and of those more than 80% have balconies. Every cabin has adequate closet and drawer/shelf storage, as well as bathroom shelves; suites have a walk-in closet. Although connecting staterooms are somewhat scarce throughout the ships, balcony dividers can be unlocked to provide connecting access in upper-category staterooms.

**Amenities:** Light-wood cabinetry, pastel decor, Murano-glass lighting fixtures, mirrored accents, a small refrigerator, a personal safe, a hair dryer, and a seating area with sofa, chair, and table are typical for ocean-view cabins and suites. Inside cabins have somewhat smaller seating areas for lounging. Suites have DVD players.

**Bathrooms:** Extras include shampoo and bath gel in shower-mounted dispensers; suites have a whirlpool bathtub.

**Accessibility:** Eight staterooms are designed for wheelchair accessibility.

Top: *Costa Mediterranea* at sea
Bottom: European service

| Cabin Type | Size (sq. ft.) |
|---|---|
| Grand Suites | 650 |
| Suites | 360 |
| Ocean View* | 185 |
| Interior | 160 |

*Extended balcony cabins have balconies at least 50% larger than average.

## FAST FACTS

- 12 passenger decks
- Specialty restaurant, dining room, buffet, pizzeria
- Wi-Fi, safe, refrigerator, DVD (some)
- 3 pools (1 indoor), children's pool
- Fitness classes, gym, hot tubs, sauna, spa, steam room
- 6 bars, casino, 2 dance clubs, 2 show rooms, video game room
- Children's programs
- Laundry facilities, laundry service
- Internet terminal

### Restaurants

A single two-deck-high formal restaurant serves open seating breakfast and lunch, while the Italian-accented cuisine is served in two traditional assigned dinner seatings. An upscale, reservations-only alternative restaurant features Italian specialties—while there is a charge, it's well worth it for the intimate, candlelit atmosphere and interesting menu selection. Reserved for guests occupying Wellness cabins and suites, a Wellness Restaurant on each ship serves lighter fare at lunch and dinner. Coffee shops serve delightful, authentic Italian specialty coffees and treats. The casual Lido buffet, pizzeria, and 24-hour room service are alternatives to dining room meals. Costa is one of the few cruise lines to continue the seagoing tradition of lavish midnight buffets. Room service is available 24 hours from a limited menu.

### Spas

The Ischia spa has a hydrotherapy pool and complimentary saunas and steam rooms in men's and women's changing rooms, but it has no thermal suite. A complete menu of spa treatments includes facials, body wraps, and massages.

### Bars/Entertainment

After dinner and a coffee in the coffee bar, on most nights there are performances by the resident production singers and dancers as well as guest entertainers in the main theater. The secondary show lounges feature singers and musicians and are the venues for Costa's signature parties, during which the entertainment staff encourages passenger participation. There is a quieter and intimate piano bar as well as other lounges with music for dancing and listening as well as a disco.

### Pros and Cons

**Pros:** if earlier Costa ships were Armani (cool and serene), then these are Versace (sexy and slightly outrageous); duty-free boutiques offer enough Italian designer items to satisfy most shopaholics; forward on the outdoor promenade decks are serene retreats in the form of enclosed terraces.

**Cons:** Italians consider cappuccino a breakfast beverage, so ordering it in the dining room following dinner is frowned upon; frequent announcements are annoying; coffee is available at numerous bars, but there is a charge.

Workout with a sea view

# COSTA LUMINOSA/DELIZIOSA

| | |
|---|---|
| Crew Members | 921/1,050 |
| Entered Service | 2009, 2010 |
| Gross Tons | 92,600 |
| Length | 965 feet |
| Number of Cabins | 1,130 |
| Passenger Capacity | 2,260 |
| Width | 106 feet |

These thoroughly Italian beauties are a hybrid class of ship based on Carnival Cruise Lines' Spirit-class and Holland America Line's Vista-class. Sister ships *Costa Luminosa* and *Costa Deliziosa* are considered the Costa fleet's "flagships" and, therefore, share the most exclusive and innovative elements in the fleet, designed for Costa's most discerning passengers. *Costa Luminosa* has a contemporary design in a distinctive avant-garde style, including interiors decorated with premium materials. Twenty different types of marble, wood, mother-of-pearl, and granite are incorporated, as are 120 Murano-glass lamps and chandeliers and the use of LED lights. The ship's collection includes 288 original works of art and more than 4,700 reproductions throughout.

*Costa Deliziosa* design is also avant-garde in style and is done up in premium materials similar to those used on its sister ship, including stucco applied by spatula using the technique known as "spatolato veneziano." Other decorative interior finishes including "parchment scroll" lamé, refined Zebrano wood, Wenge timbers, and stylish polished and glazed steel.

The most innovative features on both ships are the multisensory experience of the "4-D" cinema (traditional 3-D plus other sensory elements). There are also golf and Grand Prix racing simulators.

## Cabins

**Cabins:** With the largest percentage of balcony cabins on any Costa ship (772 of 1,130 total), accommodations generally follow the outline of recently introduced fleet mates. Every cabin has adequate closet and drawer/shelf storage, as well as bathroom shelves; suites have generous walk-in closets and come with a pillow menu and robe and slippers to use during the cruise. Connecting staterooms are somewhat scarce, but can be found in ocean-view categories. Light-wood cabinetry, soft pastel decor, mirrored accents, Murano-glass lighting fixtures, and a small seating area are typical in all categories; all accommodations have a small refrigerator, personal safe, and hair dryer. Samsara Spa accommodations (52 cabins and 4 suites) have direct access to the spa via private elevator and stairway.

*Costa Luminosa* anchored in port

**Bathrooms:** Bathroom extras include shampoo and bath gel in shower-mounted dispensers. Suites and Grand suites have whirlpool bathtubs and upgraded toiletries.

**Accessibility:** Twenty-three staterooms are designed for wheelchair accessibility.

### Restaurants

A single, two-deck restaurant serves open seating breakfast and lunch; dinner is in two assigned seatings. The Samsara specialty restaurant is complimentary for passengers in Samsara Spa cabins and suites and requires reservations and a service charge for all other passengers on a very limited space-available basis. An upscale second alternative, reservations-only restaurant carries à la carte charges—a perk for suite passengers is a complimentary dinner for two there. The Lido buffet, pizzeria, and 24-hour room service are alternatives. Costa ships retain the tradition of lavish midnight buffets.

### Spas

The serene Samsara Spa is one of the largest at sea with a thermal suite and hydrotherapy pool available at no charge for occupants of Samsara accommodations and for a fee to all other passengers. A complete menu of treatments includes facials, body wraps, and massages.

### Bars/Entertainment

Performances by the resident production singers and dancers as well as guest entertainers are scheduled most nights in the main theater. Secondary show lounges feature singers and musicians and are the venues for Costa's signature parties, during which the entertainment staff encourages passenger participation. There is a quieter and intimate piano bar as well as other lounges with music for dancing and listening as well as a disco.

### Pros and Cons

**Pros:** golf and Grand Prix simulators are huge attractions for men and women; there is a dedicated children's pool; for skaters, there's a nifty roller skating track.

**Cons:** the pizzeria serves a more American than Italian style of pizza; kid's facilities are less elaborate than you might expect on an otherwise family-friendly ship; spa goers may find it confusing that doors must be unlocked to get from one spa area to another.

| Cabin Type | Size (sq. ft.) |
|---|---|
| Grand Suite | 650 |
| Suite/Minisuite | 360/300 |
| Ocean View with Balcony | 210 |
| Ocean View/Interior | 175/160 |

Dimensions for accommodations with balconies include the balcony square footage.

### FAST FACTS

- 12 passenger decks
- 2 specialty restaurants, 1 dining room, buffet, pizzeria
- Wi-Fi, safe, refrigerator, DVD (some)
- 2 pools (1 indoor), children's pool
- Fitness classes, gym, hot tubs, sauna, spa, steam room
- 11 bars, casino, 2 dance clubs, library, show room, video game room
- Children's programs
- Laundry service
- Internet terminal

An outside cabin

# COSTA SERENA/PACIFICA/ FAVOLOSA/FASCINOSA

| | |
|---|---|
| Crew Members | 1,100 |
| Entered Service | 2007, 2009, 2011, 2012 |
| Gross Tons | 114,500 |
| Length | 951 feet |
| Number of Cabins | 1,500 |
| Passenger Capacity | 3,000 |
| Width | 116 feet |

700 ft.
500 ft.
300 ft.

The largest ships built for an Italian cruise line are larger versions of identical sister ships *Costa Magica* and *Costa Fortuna*, which were derived from parent Carnival Cruise Lines' *Carnival Triumph* and *Carnival Conquest*. But Costa has pulled out all the stops with these vessels.

The Samsara Spas are far from ho-hum, both in facilities and amenities. Some of the largest at sea, they span 20,500 square feet. Luxurious, Samsara staterooms and suites are located adjacent to and one deck below the spa itself. A health-conscious Samsara Restaurant is reserved for their dining pleasure on deck 3. Other cool features are not one, but two swimming pools with retractable roofs, a huge outdoor movie screen, and a Grand Prix racing simulator—just like the ones Formula One race car drivers use for training.

## Cabins

**Cabins:** Accommodations generally follow the outline of recently introduced fleet mates. More than 60% of outside staterooms have a balcony with chairs and a table. Every cabin has adequate closet and drawer/shelf storage, as well as bathroom shelves; suites have generous walk-in closets and come with the services of a butler. Connecting staterooms are somewhat scarce, but can be found in ocean-view categories. Light-wood cabinetry, soft pastel decor, mirrored accents, Murano-glass lighting fixtures, and a small seating area are typical in all categories; all accommodations have a small refrigerator, personal safe, and hair dryer. Some outside cabins have only a lower twin bed and a sofa bed. There are 99 of the popular Samsara Spa accommodations on each ship in the class. Passengers who reserve Samsara suites and staterooms adjacent to the spa facility have direct access to the spa and exclusive access to Samsara Restaurant.

**Bathrooms:** Bathroom extras include shampoo and bath gel in shower-mounted dispensers. Additionally, suites feature a whirlpool tub and double sinks.

**Accessibility:** Twenty-seven staterooms are designed for accessibility.

## Restaurants

Two restaurants serve open seating breakfast and lunch; dinner is in two assigned seatings. An upscale alternative, reservations-only restaurant carries à la carte charges—a perk for suite passengers is a complimentary dinner

Top: *Costa Serena* suite balcony
Bottom: *Costa Serena* lido pool

for two there. Reserved for passengers in Samsara Spa accommodations, the Samsara Restaurant serves light fare at lunch and dinner. It is open to all other passengers on a very limited space available basis by reservation and with a surcharge. The Lido buffet, pizzeria, and 24-hour room service are alternatives. Costa ships retain the tradition of lavish nightly midnight buffets.

## Spas

The Asian-inspired Samsara Spa includes a thermal suite with heated loungers, two steam rooms, and a hydrotherapy pool—available at no charge for occupants of Samsara accommodations and for a fee to all other passengers. A complete menu of treatments includes facials, body wraps, and massages. Special treatment options for men and couples are featured. Steam rooms and saunas are complimentary in men's and women's changing rooms.

## Bars/Entertainment

Performances by the resident production singers and dancers as well as guest entertainers are scheduled most nights in the main theater. Secondary show lounges feature singers and musicians and are the venues for Costa's signature parties, during which the entertainment staff encourages passengers to participate. There is a quieter and intimate piano bar as well as other lounges with music for dancing and listening as well as a disco.

## Pros and Cons

**Pros:** channel your inner speed demon and drive like a pro in a Formula One race-car simulator; PlayStation World for kids is equipped exclusively with PlayStation 3 machines; Samsara Spa accommodations have convenient direct access to the spa.

**Cons:** at maximum capacity these ships feel crowded; midnight buffets are sumptuous but are scheduled shortly after late seating end; announcements are frequent and made in several languages.

| Cabin Type | Size (sq. ft.) |
|---|---|
| Grand Suite | 650 |
| Suite | 360 |
| Minisuite | 300 |
| Ocean View with Balcony | 210 |
| Ocean View/ Interior | 175/160 |

Dimensions for accommodations with balconies include the balcony square footage.

## FAST FACTS

- 13 passenger decks
- Specialty restaurant, 3 dining rooms, buffet, pizzeria
- Wi-Fi, safe, refrigerator
- 3 pools (2 indoor), children's pool
- Fitness classes, gym, hot tubs, sauna, spa, steam room
- 13 bars, casino, 2 dance clubs, library, show room, video game room
- Children's programs
- Laundry service
- Internet terminal

Ceres Restaurant, *Costa Serena*

2

COSTA CRUISES

# COSTA CLASSICA/COSTA NEOROMANTICA

| | |
|---|---|
| **Crew Members** | 590, 622 |
| **Entered Service** | 1992, 1993 |
| **Gross Tons** | 53,000/57,130 |
| **Length** | 723/724 feet |
| **Number of Cabins** | 654, 789 |
| **Passenger Capacity** | 1,308, 1,578 |
| **Width** | 102 feet |

These two sister ships were designed to bring the Costa fleet up to speed with other cruise lines in the 1990s, and the effort paid off. Public areas clustered on upper decks are filled with marble and furnished with sleek, contemporary furnishings and modern Italian artworks. The effect is vibrant, chic, and surprisingly restful. Lounges and bars are sweeping and grand; however, the areas set aside for children are skimpy by today's family-friendly standards. The two ships diverged again after *Costa Romantica*'s major transformation in 2012. Neither ship has a true promenade deck, but the Lido areas for sunning and swimming are expansive.

Midsize and intimate, each ship retains a like-new luster from regular refurbishments. Unfortunately, *Costa Classica* lacks the large number of balconies that have become as popular with Europeans as North Americans. Costa *neoRomantica* holds the edge here, with balconies added during her refurbishment.

## Cabins

**Cabins:** Liberally paneled in light cherrywood, cabins are fairly spacious and have ample storage. Ocean-view staterooms feature large porthole-style windows. Suites are generous in size with large seating areas; they also have butler service. Designed when the balcony craze was just taking off, *Costa Classica* has only 10 suites with balconies; six forward-facing suites do not have balconies, and 18 minisuites have the same amenities as the suites but are not as large. *Costa neoRomantica* now has 28 suites, of which 24 have balconies, and 56 Samsara suite cabins, of which six are full suites; 50 of these Samsara cabins have balconies.

All accommodations have soft-color fabrics in a minimalist style and have a personal safe, TV, and hair dryer. The combination desk and dressing table has a large mirror; a small seating area with a table and two chairs are typical furnishings.

**Bathrooms:** Bathrooms are tight in ocean-view and inside cabins, even by modern cruise-ship standards. The usual bath amenities include the basic soap and shampoo. Suites have the added luxury of a whirlpool bathtub and double sinks.

**Accessibility:** Six staterooms are wheelchair accessible on *Costa Classica*; ten on *Costa neoRomantica*.

Top: *Costa neoRomantica lido pool*
Bottom: *Costa neoRomantica balcony suite*

## Restaurants

The single main restaurant on each ship serves open seating breakfast and lunch, with dinner in two assigned seatings. Breakfast and lunch are also available at the Lido buffet, where seating is indoors or out. Dinner buffets are scheduled for certain nights during the cruise, as are traditional midnight buffets. An upscale alternative, reservations-only restaurant on *Costa neoRomantica* carries à la carte charges—a perk for suite passengers is a complimentary dinner for two there. The Samsara specialty restaurant on *Costa neoRomantica* is complimentary for passengers in Samsara Spa cabins and suites and requires reservations and a service charge for all other passengers on a very limited space-available basis. Each ship has both a pizzeria and a patisserie, and 24-hour room service is available.

## Spas

Caracalla Spa on *Costa Classica* and Samsara Spa on *Costa neoRomantica* offer treatment menus including body wraps, massages, and facials. The Samsara Spa holds the edge with its thalassotherapy pool, but both ships have saunas and steam rooms.

## Bars/Entertainment

Performances by the resident production singers and dancers as well as guest entertainers are scheduled most nights in the main theater. Secondary show lounges feature singers and musicians and are the venues for Costa's signature parties, during which the entertainment staff goes into overdrive to encourage passenger participation. There is a quieter and intimate piano bar as well as other lounges with music for dancing and listening as well as a disco.

## Pros and Cons

**Pros:** the layout of these midsized ships makes it easy to learn your way around; duty-free shops have Italian designer goods as well as the usual logo stuff; the observatory has a 360-degree view by day and morphs into a disco at night.

**Cons:** outside cabins on the lowest passenger decks have large portholes instead of picture windows; there are no self-service passenger laundry rooms; with smoking areas in most lounges, the smell of cigarette smoke can be bothersome.

| Cabin Type | Size (sq. ft.) |
| --- | --- |
| Suite | 580 |
| Minisuite* | 340 |
| Ocean View | 200 |
| Interior | 175 |

*Costa neoRomantica only

## FAST FACTS

- 10 passenger decks
- Specialty restaurant (*Costa neo Romantica* only), dining room, buffet, pizzeria
- Wi-Fi, safe, refrigerator (some)
- 2 pools
- Fitness classes, gym, hot tubs, sauna, spa, steam room
- 7 bars, casino, 2 dance clubs, library, show room, video game room
- Children's programs
- Dry-cleaning, laundry service
- Internet terminal

Restaurant Club, *neoRomantica*

2

COSTA CRUISES

# CRYSTAL CRUISES

Winner of accolades and too many hospitality industry awards to count, Crystal Cruises offers a taste of the grandeur of the past along with all the modern touches discerning passengers demand today. Founded in 1990 and owned by Nippon Yusen Kaisha

*Crystal Serenity* wraparound promenade

(NYK) in Japan, Crystal ships, unlike other luxury vessels, are large, carrying upward of 900 passengers. What makes them distinctive are superior service, a variety of dining options, spacious accommodations, and some of the highest ratios of space per passenger of any cruise ship.

☎ *888/799–4625 or 310/785–9300* ⊕ *www.crystalcruises. com* ☞ *Cruise Style: Luxury.*

Beginning with ship designs based on the principles of feng shui, the Eastern art of arranging your surroundings to attract positive energy, no detail is overlooked to provide passengers with the best imaginable experience. Just mention a preference for a certain food or beverage and your waiter will have it available whenever you request it.

Afternoon tea in the Palm Court is a delightful daily ritual. You're greeted by staff members in 18th-century Viennese brocade and velvet costumes for Mozart Tea; traditional scones and clotted cream are served during English Colonial Tea; and American Tea is a summertime classic created by Crystal culinary artists.

The line's Ambassador Host Program brings cultured gentlemen on each cruise to dine, socialize, and dance with unaccompanied ladies who wish to participate.

### Food

The food alone is reason enough to book a Crystal cruise. Dining in the main restaurants is an event starring a Continental-inspired menu of dishes served by European-trained waiters. Off-menu item requests are honored when possible, and special dietary considerations are handled with ease. Full-course vegetarian menus are among the best at sea. Themed to the region you are sailing, lavish luncheon buffets take place on deck on select days at sea. Casual poolside dining beneath the stars is offered on some evenings in a relaxed, no-reservations option. A variety of hot-and-cold hors d'oeuvres are served in bars and lounges every evening before dinner and again during the wee hours in The Bistro.

But the specialty restaurants really shine. Contemporary Asian cuisine is served in Silk Road and the Sushi Bar, featuring the signature dishes of Nobu Matsuhisa. Both ships also have Prego, which serves regional Italian cuisine by Piero Selvaggio, owner of Valentino in Los Angeles and Las Vegas.

Exclusive Wine & Champagne Makers dinners are hosted in the Vintage Room. On select evenings, casual poolside theme dinners are served under the stars.

Crystal has an extensive wine list, including its own proprietary label called C Wines, which are produced in California. Complimentary wines are poured with meals, as is common on other luxury cruise lines. You won't pay extra for any alcoholic beverages, bottled water, soft drinks, and specialty coffees; all are included in your basic fare.

## Entertainment

The complete roster of entertainment and activities includes Broadway-style production shows and bingo, but where Crystal really shines is in the variety of enrichment and educational programs. Passengers can participate in the hands-on Computer University@Sea, interactive Creative Learning Institute classes, or attend lectures featuring top experts in their fields: keyboard lessons with Yamaha, language classes by Berlitz, wellness lectures with the Cleveland Clinic, and an introduction to tai chi with the Tai Chi Cultural Center. Professional ACBL Bridge instructors are on every cruise, and dance instructors offer lessons in contemporary and social dance styles.

## Fitness and Recreation

Large spas offer innovative pampering therapies, body wraps, and exotic Asian-inspired treatments by Steiner Leisure. Feng shui principles were scrupulously adhered to in their creation, to assure the spas and salons remain havens of tranquility.

Fitness centers have a range of exercise and weight-training equipment and workout areas for aerobics classes, plus complimentary yoga and Pilates instruction. In addition, golfers enjoy extensive

## KNOWN FOR

■ **Style in a big package:** Crystal Cruises are large but notably luxurious and stylish.

■ **Service:** Personalized service is a key component.

■ **Itineraries:** Exotic worldwide itineraries and numerous overnight port calls are signature elements of Crystal's voyages.

■ **Food:** The food is a good enough reason to book a cruise with Crystal—it's that exceptional, and the specialty restaurants are complimentary.

■ **Inclusiveness:** Cruise fares now include gratuities, as well as all alcoholic beverages, soft drinks, and specialty coffees.

*Crystal Serenity* fitness center

Top: Spa treatment
Middle: Keyboard lessons
Bottom: *Crystal Symphony*
Crystal Penthouse

shipboard facilities, including a driving range practice cage and putting green. Passengers can leave their bags at home and rent top-quality Taylor-Made clubs for use ashore. The line's resident golf pros offer complimentary lessons and group clinics.

### Your Shipmates

Affluent, well-traveled couples, from their late-thirties and up, are attracted to Crystal's destination-rich itineraries, shipboard enrichment programs, and elegant ambience. The average age of passengers is noticeably higher on longer itineraries.

### Dress Code

Formal attire is required on at least two designated evenings, depending on the length of the cruise. Men are encouraged to wear tuxedos, and many do, although dark suits are also acceptable. Other evenings are informal or resort casual; the number of each is based on the number of sea days. The line requests that dress codes be observed in public areas after 6 pm, and few, if any, passengers disregard the suggestion. Most, in fact, dress up just a notch from guidelines.

### Junior Cruisers

Although these ships are decidedly adult-oriented, Crystal welcomes children but limits the number of children under age three on any given cruise. Children under six months are not allowed without a signed waiver by parents.

Dedicated facilities for children and teens ages 3 to 17 are staffed by counselors during holiday periods, select summer sailings, and when warranted by the number of children booked. The program is three-tiered for 3- to 7-year-olds, 8- to 12-year-olds, and 13- to 17-year-olds. Activities—including games, computer time, scavenger hunts, and arts and crafts—usually have an eye toward the educational. Teenagers can play complimentary video games to their hearts' content in Waves, the arcade dedicated for their use. Babysitting can be arranged with staff members for a fee. Baby food, high chairs, and booster seats are available upon request.

### CHOOSE THIS LINE IF ...

You crave peace and quiet. Announcements are kept to a bare minimum, and the ambience is sedate.

You prefer to plan ahead. You can make spa, restaurant, shore excursion, and class reservations when you book your cruise.

You love sushi and other Asian delights—Crystal ships serve some of the best at sea.

## Service
Crystal's European-trained staff members provide gracious service in an unobtrusive manner.

## Tipping
Housekeeping and dining gratuities are included in the fare. A 15% gratuity is suggested for spa and salon services.

## Past Passengers
You're automatically enrolled in the Crystal Society on completion of your first Crystal cruise and are entitled to special savings and members-only events. Membership benefits increase with each completed Crystal cruise and include such perks as stateroom upgrades, shipboard spending credits, special events, gifts, air upgrades, and even free cruises. Society members also receive Crystal Cruises' complimentary quarterly magazine, which shares up-to-date information on itineraries, destinations, special offers, and society news.

### HELPFUL HINTS

Before sailing, each passenger receives a personal email address.

Ambassador Hosts on Crystal cruises interact with female passengers.

Each ship has complimentary self-service laundry rooms.

Specialty restaurants can fill up quickly; make reservations immediately after booking.

In more than 24 European ports, Crystal's exclusive Local Insights program brings aboard native experts.

**2**

**CRYSTAL CRUISES**

### DON'T CHOOSE THIS LINE IF ...

You don't want to follow the dress code. Everyone does, and you'll stand out—and not in a good way—if you rebel.

You want a smoke-free environment. Smoking is allowed in cabins and in designated areas of public rooms and decks.

You want a less structured cruise. Even with open seating dining, Crystal is a bit more regimented than other luxury lines.

# CRYSTAL SERENITY

| | |
|---|---|
| Crew Members | 655 |
| Entered Service | 2003 |
| Gross Tons | 68,000 |
| Length | 820 feet |
| Number of Cabins | 544 |
| Passenger Capacity | 1,070 |
| Width | 106 feet |

700 ft.

500 ft.

300 ft.

*Crystal Serenity* was introduced in 2003, the line's first new ship since 1995. Although more than a third larger than Crystal's earlier ships, it's similar in layout and follows the successful formula of creating intimate spaces in understated yet sophisticated surroundings. Stylish public rooms, uncrowded and uncluttered, are clubby in the tradition of elegantly proportioned drawing rooms (even the main show lounge is on a single level).

Muted colors and warm woods create a soft atmosphere conducive to socializing in the refined environment. The Palm Court could be mistaken for the kind of British colonial–era lounge you might have seen in Hong Kong or India in the 19th century. A thoughtful touch is an entirely separate room for scrutinizing the art pieces available for auction. The understatement even continues into the casino, although it contains plenty of slot machines and gaming tables.

## Cabins

**Cabins:** *Crystal Serenity* has no inside cabins. Although suites are generous in size, lesser categories are somewhat smaller than industry standard at this level. All accommodations are designed with ample closet and drawer/shelf storage, as well as bathroom shelves and twin sinks. An impressive 85% of all cabins have private balconies furnished with chairs and tables. Most suites and penthouses have walk-in closets. Crystal Penthouse suites have private workout areas, pantries, and guest powder rooms. There are 50 connecting staterooms and 134 staterooms with a third berth for families.

**Amenities:** All cabins have a refrigerator with complimentary water and soft drinks, a personal safe, two hair dryers, broadband connection, a flat-screen TV with a DVD player, Aveda bath products, slippers, Frette bathrobes, and an umbrella. A seating area with sofa, chair, and table are typical standard features of all cabins. Most suites and penthouses also have CD players; all have butler service, personalized stationery, and a complimentary fully stocked minibar upon embarkation.

**Accessibility:** Eight staterooms are designed for wheelchair accessibility.

## Restaurants

The formal restaurant serves open seating breakfast and lunch and offers international cuisine in

Top: *Crystal Serenity* at sea
Bottom: Sushi bar

two traditional early and late assigned dinner seatings; Open Dining by Reservation is also available. There's no additional charge for the intimate Asian- and Italian-specialty restaurants, but reservations are required. Theme luncheons and dinners are sometimes held poolside; special wine dinners are held in the Vintage Room. Tastes, a casual café, serves breakfast, lunch, and dinner; the Lido buffet has breakfast and lunch; a poolside grill serves casual lunch and snacks; The Bistro, a specialty coffee and wine bar also offers snacks; and there's an ice-cream bar. Afternoon tea is served in the Palm Court. Room service is available 24 hours, and during dinner hours selections can be delivered from the formal restaurant menu. Suite passengers also have the option of ordering dinner from the specialty restaurants, to be served by their butlers.

### Spas

Inspired by the principles of feng shui, the Crystal Spa is a tranquil haven where such services as aroma stone therapy, a Japanese silk booster facial, and well-being massage are offered. A private, canopied relaxation area on the spa's aft deck is available before or after a treatment. Facilities for men and women include saunas and changing areas featuring showers with multiple head and side body jets, fiber optic lighting, and a selection of rain and mist functions.

### Bars/Entertainment

With the open-bar policy setting a convivial tone, Crystal's lounges are the ships' social centers. Every lounge has a different atmosphere, ranging from the signature cocktail and piano bar known for its intimate "clubby" feel to the cigar lounge that is ideal for after-dinner drinks and conversation. After a production show or concert in the main show room, dance aficionados can find musical styles that range from big band to contemporary.

### Pros and Cons

**Pros:** alternative restaurants are yours to enjoy at no additional cost; every bathroom has a full-size tub; a wide teak promenade deck encircles the ship.

**Cons:** few staterooms have a third berth for families; reservations for specialty restaurants can be hard to secure; the clubbiness of repeat passengers can be off-putting to people new to Crystal.

| Cabin Type | Size (sq. ft.) |
|---|---|
| Crystal Penthouse | 1,345 |
| Penthouse Suites | 538 |
| Regular Penthouses | 403 |
| Deluxe Ocean View (w/balcony) | 269 |
| Deluxe Ocean View (regular) | 226 |

All dimensions except for regular Deluxe staterooms (the only category that does not have a balcony) include the balcony square footage.

## FAST FACTS

- 9 passenger decks
- 2 specialty restaurants, dining room, buffet, ice cream parlor
- Wi-Fi, safe, refrigerator, DVD
- 2 pools (1 indoor)
- Fitness classes, gym, hot tubs, sauna, spa, steam room
- 6 bars, casino, 2 dance clubs, library, show room, video game room
- Children's programs
- Dry-cleaning, laundry facilities, laundry service
- Internet terminal
- No kids under 6 months

**2**

**CRYSTAL CRUISES**

# CRYSTAL SYMPHONY

| | |
|---|---|
| Crew Members | 545 |
| Entered Service | 1995 |
| Gross Tons | 51,044 |
| Length | 781 feet |
| Number of Cabins | 470 |
| Passenger Capacity | 922 (1,010 max) |
| Width | 99 feet |

700 ft.

500 ft.

300 ft.

Although large, *Crystal Symphony* is noteworthy in the luxury market for creating intimate spaces in understated, yet sophisticated, surroundings. Generous per-passenger space ratios have become a Crystal trademark, along with forward-facing observation decks, a Palm Court lounge, and a wide teak promenade encircling the ship. An extensive refurbishment in 2009 transformed the Crystal Penthouses, Lido Café, and Prego Italian restaurant. The most dramatic change was the removal of the indoor swimming pool and hot tub to expand seating for the Trident Grill. The remaining hot tub was expanded and includes a water feature. Accented by a lovely waterfall, the focal point of the central two-deck atrium is a sculpture of two ballet dancers created especially for the space. Crystal Cove, the lobby lounge, is the spot to meet for cocktails as you make your way to the nearby dining room. Throughout the ship, public rooms shine with low-key contemporary style and flow easily from one to the next.

## Cabins

**Cabins:** There are no inside cabins on *Crystal Symphony,* but staterooms are relatively small, with boutique-hotel-style decor. All cabins have ample closet and drawer/shelf storage, as well as bathroom shelves. Many have private balconies furnished with chairs and tables. Most suites and penthouses have a walk-in closet. Crystal Penthouse suites have guest powder rooms.

**Amenities:** A small refrigerator with complimentary bottled water and soft drinks, a safe, two hair dryers, a flat-screen TV with DVD player, and a seating area with sofa, chair, and table are typical standard features in all cabins. Suite and penthouse extras vary, but all have a DVD/CD player, butler service, personalized stationery, and fully stocked minibar.

**Bathrooms:** Every bathroom has oval glass sinks, granite counters, a full-size tub, Aveda toiletries, plush towels, and bathrobes for use during the cruise. Many suites and penthouses have a whirlpool tub and separate shower.

**Accessibility:** Five staterooms are wheelchair accessible.

Top: Casino gaming
Bottom: University@Sea

## Restaurants

The formal restaurant serves open seating breakfast and lunch and dinner in two assigned seatings, or an open seating option. Although there's no additional charge for the intimate Asian- and Italian-specialty restaurants, reservations are required. On select days and evenings, theme luncheons and dinners are held poolside; special wine dinners are held in the Vintage Room. Other dining choices include the Lido buffet for breakfast and lunch; a poolside grill for casual lunch and snacks; The Bistro, a specialty coffee and wine bar offering snacks all day and evening; and an ice cream bar. Afternoon tea is served in the Palm Court. Room service, with an extensive menu, is available 24 hours, and during dinner hours selections can be delivered from the formal restaurant menu. Suite passengers can also order from the specialty restaurants, to be served by their butlers.

## Spas

The Crystal Spa is a tranquil haven where such services as aroma stone therapy, Japanese silk booster facial, and well-being massage are offered. A private, canopied relaxation area on the spa's aft deck is available before or after a treatment. Changing areas have elaborate showers with fiber optic lighting and a selection of rain and mist functions as well as saunas.

## Bars/Entertainment

With the open bar policy setting a convivial tone, Crystal's lounges are the ship's social hubs. Lounges feature unique styles ranging from the signature cocktail and piano bar known for its intimate "clubby" atmosphere to the club-like cigar lounge, ideal for after-dinner drinks and conversation. After a production show or concert in the main show room, dance aficionados can find musical styles that range from classic to contemporary.

## Pros and Cons

**Pros:** the professionalism of the ships staff sets them apart; the large theater has ample seating and free popcorn; casual dining areas have more than enough seating indoors and outside.

**Cons:** few staterooms can accommodate families; while large, the solitary pool and hot tub can feel crowded at times; lower-category staterooms can feel cramped for a luxury ship.

| Cabin Type | Size (sq. ft.) |
|---|---|
| Crystal Penthouse | 982 |
| Penthouse Suites | 491 |
| Regular Penthouses | 367 |
| Deluxe Ocean View (w/balcony) | 246 |
| Deluxe Ocean View (regular) | 202 |

All dimensions except for regular Deluxe staterooms (the only category that does not have a balcony) include the balcony square footage.

## FAST FACTS

- 8 passenger decks
- 2 specialty restaurants, dining room, buffet, ice cream parlor
- Wi-Fi, safe, refrigerator, DVD
- 1 pool
- Fitness classes, gym, hot tub, sauna, spa, steam room
- 5 bars, casino, dance club, library, show room, video game room
- Children's programs
- Dry-cleaning, laundry facilities, laundry service
- Internet terminal
- No kids under 6 months

**2**

**CRYSTAL CRUISES**

# CUNARD LINE

One of the world's most distinguished names in ocean travel since 1840, the Cunard Line has a long history of deluxe transatlantic crossings and worldwide cruising. The line's ships are legendary for their comfortable accommodations, excellent cui-

Romantic sunset at sea

sine, and personal service. After a series of owners tried with little success to revive the company's flagging passenger shipping business, Carnival Corporation offered an infusion of ready cash and the know-how to turn the line around in 1998. Exciting new ships have followed.

☎ 661/753–1000 or
800/728–6273
⊕ www.cunard.com
☞ Cruise Style:
Luxury.

Delightful daily events include afternoon tea and the maritime tradition of sounding the ship's bell at noon. The line offers North Atlantic crossings and seasonal shorter cruises, including Northern European and Mediterranean itineraries.

### Food

Dining aboard a Cunard ship is by class, so dining-room assignments are made according to the accommodation category booked. You can get as much luxury as you are willing to pay for on Cunard liners, where passengers in Junior suites are assigned to the single-seating Princess Grill; the posh Queen's Grill serves passengers booked in duplex apartments and the most lavish suites. All other passengers are assigned to one of two seatings in the dramatic, multideck-high Britannia Restaurant or Britannia Club Restaurant on *Queen Elizabeth*.

Although fare in Britannia is reasonably traditional and often outstanding, off-menu requests by Grill passengers are commonly granted—provided the galley has the ingredients. Menus also include vegetarian and low-calorie selections.

The most coveted table reservations are those on *Queen Mary 2* and *Queen Victoria* in the restaurants named for Todd English, the celebrity American chef and restaurateur noted for his innovative Mediterranean cuisine and sumptuous desserts. Both dinner ($30 per-person cover charge) and lunch ($20 per person) are offered in the intimate restaurant.

Aboard *Queen Mary 2,* the Chef's Galley is a small reservations-required restaurant, where diners look on as their food is prepared in an open galley setting; the only charge here is for wine. The King's Court buffet is transformed each evening into three no-charge casual alternative dining spots: the Carvery specializes in carved meats; La Piazza is dedicated to pasta, pizza, and Italian dishes; and Lotus offers Asian regional specialties.

### Entertainment

Entertainment has a decidedly English flavor, with nightly production shows or cabaret-style performances and even plays. An authentic pub gives the liners an even more British air, while music for dancing and listening is played in other bars and lounges. In *Queen Mary 2's* first-ever shipboard planetarium, high-tech presentations and virtual-reality shows offer a virtual ride through space.

Cunard's fine enrichment programs include lectures by experts in their fields, including top designers, master chefs, and artists. Even seamanship and navigation courses are offered to novice mariners. Passengers can plan their activities prior to departure by consulting the syllabus of courses available online at Cunard Line's website.

### Fitness and Recreation

Swimming pools, golf driving ranges, table tennis, paddle tennis court, shuffleboard, and jogging tracks barely scratch the surface of shipboard facilities dedicated to recreation. Top-quality fitness centers offer high-tech workout equipment, a separate weight room, and classes ranging from aerobics to healthy living workshops.

*Queen Mary 2's* Canyon Ranch Spa Club is a one-of-a-kind facility at sea offering salon services for women and men, including the famous land-based spa's signature 80-minute Canyon Stone Massage. A huge 30- by 15-foot thalassotherapy pool offers a deluge waterfall, air tub, neck fountains, and massage-jet benches and recliner lounges located in the pool. The thermal suite has an herbal sauna, Finnish sauna, aromatic steam room, and reflexology basins. Use of these special features is complimentary with a massage or body treatment; otherwise, there's a per-day charge.

**2**

**CUNARD LINE**

## KNOWN FOR

- **Class divisions:** Adherence to classes for dining seatings and admittance to certain semipublic spaces.

- **Dress Codes:** Dress codes are strictly adhered to and strictly enforced on this line, though long dresses aren't required for ladies on formal nights.

- **Itineraries:** One of the most traditional passenger lines, Cunard offers worldwide itineraries.

- **British-ness:** The atmosphere aboard Cunard's liners is unabashedly British.

- **Crossings:** Transatlantic crossings, which are available on a regularly scheduled basis only on Cunard.

Top: Cunard White Star service
Bottom: Illuminations planetarium

The daily SpaClub Passport includes use of the fitness center, thermal suite, aquatherapy center, locker rooms, and a choice of fitness classes. Robes, sandals, and beverages are also available for spa goers and SpaClub Passport holders in the relaxation lounge. Steiner Leisure operates the more pedestrian spas on the rest of the fleet.

### Your Shipmates

Discerning, well-traveled American and British couples from their late-thirties to retirees are drawn to Cunard's traditional style and the notion of a cruise aboard an ocean liner. The availability of spacious accommodations and complimentary self-service laundry facilities makes Cunard liners a good option for families, although there may be fewer children on board than on similar size ships.

### Dress Code

Glamorous evenings are typical of Cunard cruises, and specified attire includes formal, informal, and casual. Although resort casual clothing prevails throughout the day, Cunard vessels are ocean liners at heart and, as expected, are dressier than most cruise ships at night. To maintain their high standards, the cruise line requests passengers to dress as they would for dining in fine restaurants.

### Junior Cruisers

The Kid Zone has a dedicated play area and a splash pool for children ages one to six. Separate programs are reserved for older children ages 7 to 12 and teens up to age 17. Toys and activities range from simple games to more educational computer classes. Children can practice their social graces when they're served their own afternoon teatime goodies. Toddlers are supervised by English nannies. Facilities are operated only until midnight; group babysitting is complimentary. Infants under one year are not allowed; children ages one to two sail free (except for government fees).

### Service

Although most crew members are international rather than British, service is formal and sophisticated.

Top: Fine dining
Middle: Royal Court Theater
Bottom: Junior suite

## CHOOSE THIS LINE IF ...

You want to boast that you have sailed on the world's largest ocean liner, though larger cruise ships are already plying the waves.

You enjoy a brisk walk. *Queen Mary 2* is massive, and you'll find yourself walking a great deal.

A posh English pub is your idea of the perfect place to hang out.

**2**

**CUNARD LINE**

## Tipping

Suggested gratuities of $13 per person per day (for Grill Restaurant accommodations) or $11 per person per day (all other accommodations) are automatically charged to shipboard accounts for distribution to stewards and waitstaff. An automatic 15% gratuity is added to beverage tabs for bar service. Passengers can still tip individual crew members directly in cash for any special services.

## Past Passengers

After one sailing aboard a Cunard liner, passengers are automatically enrolled as members of Cunard World Club; they are accorded Silver status on their second cruise. Silver-level members receive discounts of up to 50% off Early Booking Savings on all sailings, access to the shipboard World Club Representative and World Club Desk, and a quarterly newsletter, *The Cunarder*.

After completing two Cunard cruises or 20 days on board, members are accorded Gold status and are additionally invited to shipboard World Club cocktail receptions, two hours of Internet service, and receive a Gold Cunarder pin. Passengers who complete seven sailings or sail for 48 consecutive days or more achieve the Platinum status. Additional benefits to Platinum members include a shipboard World Club cocktail reception, priority check-in and boarding in certain embarkation ports, an invitation to the Senior Officers' party, four hours of Internet service, and a Platinum Cunarder pin.

Diamond membership is for guests who have completed 15 voyages or 150 days on board. In addition to the above, they receive priority luggage delivery, complimentary lunch in Todd English, eight hours of Internet service, and a Diamond Cunarder pin.

### HELPFUL HINTS

Weddings can't be performed on the spur of the moment, but captains on board all Cunard Line ships can marry couples at sea.

The currency on board is the United States dollar, even for cruises in Europe.

Seasickness pills are available in the medical center or at the reception desk, but they are not free.

Cunard provides gentlemen hosts to dance with unaccompanied ladies.

Men may wish to pack their little-used tuxedos for this ship; on formal nights they are in wide use.

### DON'T CHOOSE THIS LINE IF ...

You prefer informality. Cunard ships are traditional formal liners.

You want real luxury with no add-on costs.

Your sense of direction is really bad. Nearly everyone gets lost on board QM2 at least once.

# QUEEN ELIZABETH

| | |
|---|---|
| Crew Members | 1,005 |
| Entered Service | 2010 |
| Gross Tons | 92,000 |
| Length | 965 feet |
| Number of Cabins | 1,034 |
| Passenger Capacity | 2,068 |
| Width | 106 feet |

700 ft.

500 ft.

300 ft.

Although the deck plans for *Queen Elizabeth* appear to be nearly identical to her fleet mate *Queen Victoria*, make no mistake—this queen bears her own regal trappings. A successor to her namesake, the original *Queen Elizabeth*, which entered service in 1940, Cunard's latest liner boasts touches of art deco that recall a time when the first queen ruled the waves. The newest Cunard ship to bear the name also recalls the *QE2* via artwork and memorabilia and has its own nautically themed Yacht Club, named after the lively aft lounge on *QE2*.

Curved staircases, geometric patterns, and spectacular artwork grace the soaring Grand Lobby, which is overlooked by the two-tier Library—a calm, wood-paneled haven bathed in natural reading light and crowned with a leaded glass ceiling. As on her fleet mates, double- and triple-height spaces play a large part in defining the grand interiors; however, there's still the warmth of an authentic British pub, a clubby cigar room, and lounges with intimate seating areas where you might feel you've stumbled into a high society event of the 1930s or 1940s.

## Cabins

**Cabins:** With more than two-dozen stateroom and suite categories to choose from, cabins really fall into eight basic configurations. At the top are the luxurious Queens Grill suites, which have the most luxurious amenities; next are Princess Grill suites; next are the Britannia Club AA balcony staterooms, standard staterooms (many with a balcony), and inside cabins, all of whose passengers dine in the Britannia Restaurant. The majority of the cabins fall into the standard categories. More than 86% of the staterooms on the ship are outside and 76% have private balconies. All are designed with adequate closet and storage space, and even the least expensive outside categories have a small seating area. Private balconies are furnished with a table and chairs, and some have loungers.

**Amenities:** All passengers are greeted on embarkation with sparkling wine or champagne and will find a refrigerator, safe, hair dryer, fresh fruit basket, bath toiletries, slippers, and a bathrobe for use during the cruise. Butlers are on hand to attend to Queens Grill occupants, whose bars are stocked with spirits, wine, and soft drinks.

Top: A curved staircase in the Grand Lobby
Bottom: *Queen Elizabeth* in a calm harbor

**Accessibility:** Twenty cabins are wheelchair accessible.

### Restaurants

The Britannia Restaurant serves dinner in two assigned seatings for most passengers, while those in Britannia Club, Princess- and Queens Grill–classes dine in a single open seating at an assigned table. The Verandah (reservations, fee), the alternative restaurant, serves French cuisine. In the evenings, one of three regional cuisines—such as Asian, Mexican, and South American—is highlighted, and waiter table service becomes available in the Lido restaurant for a small charge. In addition, the Lido buffet and Golden Lion Pub offer relaxed dining options, while specialty teas, coffees, and pastries are featured in Café Carinthia. A proper English tea is served daily and room service is always available.

### Spas

Operated by Steiner Leisure, the spa offers a wide range of exotic and contemporary treatments. Chakra rasul and herbal steam chambers are designed for couples to indulge in ancient Eastern rituals. A relaxation room, hydrotherapy pool, and thermal suite with three steam and sauna rooms are available for the use of spa clients who've booked a treatment and others who've purchased a pass. Complimentary saunas are found in men's and women's changing rooms.

### Bars/Entertainment

Evening entertainments can include production shows and concerts and Cunard's traditional themed formal balls in the Queen's Lounge ballroom. Other options are as diverse as the clubby Midships Bar with its pianist, an authentic English Pub, or the Yacht Club, an intimate venue for dancing until the small hours with the resident DJ.

### Pros and Cons

**Pros:** professional dance instructors are on board to help you with your technique; dance hosts are available to women looking for a partner; the library's shelves contain 6,000 books so there's no need to pack your own.

**Cons:** *Queen Elizabeth* is more cruise ship than ocean liner but still provides a formal and traditional experience; service is certainly white-glove, but it's more international than British; if you aren't an Anglophile, you might not appreciate the Britishness of a Cunard ship.

| Cabin Type | Size (sq. ft.) |
|---|---|
| Grand Suite/ Master Suite | 1,375–1,493/ 1,100 |
| Penthouse Suite/ Queens Suite/ Princess Suite | 551–615/ 484–671/ 335–513 |
| Ocean View with Balcony | 242–472 |
| Ocean View/ Interior | 180–201/152–243 |

All dimensions include the square footage for balconies.

## FAST FACTS

- 12 passenger decks
- Specialty restaurant, 3 dining rooms, buffet, café, ice cream parlor, pizzeria
- Wi-Fi, safe, refrigerator, DVD (some)
- 2 pools
- Fitness classes, gym, hot tubs, sauna, spa, steam room
- 10 bars, casino, 2 dance clubs, library, show room
- Children's programs
- Dry-cleaning, laundry facilities, laundry service
- Internet terminal
- No-smoking cabins

Britannia Restaurant

2

CUNARD LINE

# QUEEN MARY 2

| | |
|---|---|
| Crew Members | 1,253 |
| Entered Service | 2004 |
| Gross Tons | 151,400 |
| Length | 1,132 feet |
| Number of Cabins | 1,310 |
| Passenger Capacity | 2,620 (3,090 max) |
| Width | 135 feet |

700 ft. 500 ft. 300 ft.

With the clever use of design elements, *Queen Mary 2,* one of the largest passenger liners ever built, bears a striking external resemblance to Cunard's former flagship, the smaller, older *Queen Elizabeth 2,* which was retired from service in 2008. The world's grandest and most expensive liner is a transitional ship, incorporating classic ocean-liner features—sweeping staircases, soaring public rooms, a 360-degree promenade deck, and a grand ballroom—all comfortably within a hull that also includes a trendy Canyon Ranch Spa and a full-scale planetarium.

Interior spaces blend the traditional style of early-20th-century liners with all the conveniences 21st-century passengers expect. Public rooms are mainly located on two decks low in the ship—remember, this is a liner designed for North Atlantic crossings. The grand lobby is palatial, and the wide passageways lead to a variety of lounges, shops, a casino, show room, and planetarium. The Queen's Room is especially regal

## Cabins

**Cabins:** An impressive 78% of accommodations are outside cabins, and more than 86% of these have private balconies. There are fewer than 300 inside cabins, including a few with an atrium view. All are designed with ample closet, drawer/shelf storage, and bathroom shelves. Private balconies are furnished with chairs, loungers, and tables. Duplex apartment and suite luxuries vary, but most have a whirlpool tub, dressing area, entertainment center, and dining area, and all have private balconies. In addition, duplex apartments and most suites feature guest powder rooms and whirlpool tubs; some have his-and-hers dressing rooms.

**Amenities:** A small refrigerator, personal safe, hair dryer, broadband hookup, interactive TV, and seating area with sofa or chairs and dual-height table are standard amenities. Toiletries, slippers, and bathrobes for use during the cruise are also standard.

**Accessibility:** Thirty cabins are wheelchair accessible.

## Restaurants

Dining is assigned by your accommodation category. The Britannia Restaurant serves open seating breakfast and lunch and dinner in two seatings to most passengers; those in AA Britannia Club Balcony Cabins

Top: Intimate lounges
Bottom: Grand Duplex suite

dine in the single-seating Britannia Club Dining Room; those in Junior suites and above dine in the single-seating Queens and Princess Grill restaurants. The Todd English specialty restaurant serves lunch and dinner (by reservation). The Chef's Galley is a small reservations-required restaurant, where diners watch as their food is prepared in an open galley; the only charge is for wine. The King's Court buffet serves breakfast and lunch, and is transformed each evening into three no-charge casual alternative dining spots: the Carvery specializes in carved meats; La Piazza is dedicated to pizza and Italian food; and Lotus offers Asian cuisine. During the day you can opt for a pub lunch, snacks in Sir Samuel's, afternoon tea, and 24-hour room service.

### Spas

The Canyon Ranch Spa Club is a one-of-a-kind facility at sea offering services for women and men, including the famous land-based spa's signature Canyon Stone Massage. A huge thalassotherapy pool offers a deluge waterfall, air tub, neck fountains, and massage-jet benches and recliner lounges located in the pool. The thermal suite has an herbal sauna, Finnish sauna, aromatic steam room, and reflexology basins. Use of these is complimentary with a massage or body treatment; otherwise, there's a per-day charge.

### Bars/Entertainment

Evenings boast another of Cunard's finest traditions as guests take to the floor to enjoy elegant ballroom dancing or groove to more contemporary sounds offered up by the resident DJ. After the theater or a concert, the entertainment options range from a rollicking pub to the more sedate bars and lounges where a pianist plays in the background for easy conversation and socializing.

### Pros and Cons

**Pros:** proper afternoon tea suggests that Britannia still rules the waves; the Queen's Room is a true ballroom, where you can waltz the night away; Todd English restaurant is named for the celebrity chef who designed the menu.

**Cons:** there's no illusion that booking an inside cabin results in the same level of pampering received by occupants of top suites; there is no Lido area buffet; it's very easy to get lost.

| Cabin Type | Size (sq. ft.) |
|---|---|
| Grand Duplex | 2,249 |
| Duplex | 1,194 |
| Royal Suite | 796 |
| Penthouse | 758 |
| Suite | 506 |
| Junior Suite | 381 |
| Deluxe | 248 |
| Premium Balcony | 249 |
| Standard Ocean View/Inside | 194 |

**2**

**CUNARD LINE**

## FAST FACTS

- 14 passenger decks
- 2 specialty restaurants, 3 dining rooms, buffet, ice cream parlor, pizzeria
- Internet, Wi-Fi, safe, refrigerator, DVD (some)
- 5 pools (2 indoor), 2 children's pools
- Fitness classes, gym, hot tubs, sauna, spa, steam room
- 11 bars, casino, cinema, 2 dance clubs, library, show room, video game room
- Children's programs
- Dry-cleaning, laundry facilities, laundry service
- Internet terminal
- No kids under age 1
- No-smoking cabins

# QUEEN VICTORIA

| | |
|---|---|
| Crew Members | 981 |
| Entered Service | 2007 |
| Gross Tons | 90,000 |
| Length | 965 feet |
| Number of Cabins | 985 |
| Passenger Capacity | 1,990 |
| Width | 106 feet |

700 ft.

500 ft.

300 ft.

Designers drew upon the history of previous Cunard ocean liners to conceive *Queen Victoria's* elegant interiors. From the ship's double- and triple-height spaces—design features of grand liners of the past—to rooms imbued with an elegant yet understated British charm, the overall effect is contemporary and historically classic. The impact of the Grand Lobby's triple-height ceiling, sweeping staircase, and sculpted balconies is immediate and unmistakable.

Queen Victoria herself might well feel at home on entering the double-height Queens Room, a loggia-style venue designed in the manner of the grand ballrooms found in large English country estates, such as Her Majesty's own Osborne House. The ballroom has cantilevered balconies overlooking an inlaid-wood dance floor; the staircase is detailed with classically ornate, curved railings.

In addition to the intimate dining spaces and a lounge reserved for occupants of Queens and Princess Grill accommodations, an outdoor terrace is devoted to their exclusive use. All other public rooms are accessible to everyone on board.

## Cabins

**Cabins:** Although there are more than two dozen stateroom and suite categories from which to choose, cabins really fall into eight configurations. At the top are the Queens Grill suite categories, which have the most luxurious amenities; next are Princess Grill suites; finally come the standard staterooms (some with a balcony) as well as inside cabins, whose passengers dine in the Britannia Restaurant. The majority of the cabins fall into the standard categories. More than 86% of the staterooms on the ship are outside and 76% have private balconies. All are designed with ample closet and storage space, and even the least expensive outside categories have a small seating area. Private balconies are furnished with a table and chairs and some have loungers.

**Amenities:** All passengers are greeted upon embarkation with sparkling wine or champagne and will find a refrigerator, safe, hair dryer, fresh fruit basket, bath toiletries, slippers, and a bathrobe for use during the cruise. Butlers are on hand to attend to Queens Grill occupants, whose bars are stocked with spirits, wine, and soft drinks.

**Accessibility:** Fourteen cabins are wheelchair accessible.

Top: Main pool
Bottom: Queens Grill suite

### Restaurants

The Britannia Restaurant serves dinner in two assigned seatings for most passengers, while those in AA Britannia Club Balcony Cabins dine in the single-seating Britannia Club Dining Room, and those in Princess and Queens Grill-classes also dine in a single seating in their respective restaurants. Todd English, the alternative restaurant, requires reservations and has a fee. The Lido buffet and Golden Lion Pub offer relaxed dining options, while specialty teas, coffees, and pastries are featured in Café Carinthia. A proper English tea is served daily, and room service is always available.

### Spas

Operated by Steiner Leisure, the spa features a wide range of exotic and contemporary treatments. Chakra rasul and herbal steam chambers are designed for couples to indulge in ancient Eastern rituals. A relaxation room, hydrotherapy pool, and thermal suite have three steam and sauna rooms that are available for the use of spa clients who've booked a treatment and others who've purchased a pass. Complimentary saunas are found in men's and women's changing rooms.

### Bars/Entertainment

Evening entertainment can include production shows and concerts and Cunard's traditional themed formal balls in the Queen's Lounge ballroom. Other options are as diverse as the exclusive Champagne Bar, an authentic English Pub, or Hemispheres, the glass-domed lounge for dancing until the small hours to the beat of a big band or with the resident DJ.

### Pros and Cons

**Pros:** the promenade deck that encircles the ship is ideal for casual strolls or jogging; the shops on board are well-stocked; the Winter Garden with a glass roof that opens is a pleasing spot to relax with a cup of tea.

**Cons:** the first Cunardia museum exhibit at sea is disappointingly small; standard accommodations don't have enough drawer space; private box seating for shows in the Royal Court Theater requires a reservation and fee.

| Cabin Type | Size (sq. ft.) |
| --- | --- |
| Grand Suite/ Master Suite | 1,918– 2,131/ 1,100 |
| Penthouse Suite/ Queens Suite/ Princess Suite | 520–707/ 508–771/ 335–513 |
| Ocean View with Balcony | 242–472 |
| Ocean View/ Interior | 180–201/ 152–243 |

All dimensions include the square footage for balconies.

### FAST FACTS

- 12 passenger decks
- Specialty restaurant, 3 dining rooms, buffet, café, ice cream parlor, pizzeria
- Wi-Fi, safe, refrigerator, DVD (some)
- 2 pools
- Fitness classes, gym, hot tubs, sauna, spa, steam room
- 10 bars, casino, 2 dance clubs, library, show room
- Children's programs
- Dry-cleaning, laundry facilities, laundry service
- Internet terminal
- No-smoking cabins

2

CUNARD LINE

Britannia stateroom

# DISNEY CRUISE LINE

With the launch of Disney Cruise Line in 1998, families were offered yet another reason to take a cruise. The magic of a Walt Disney resort vacation plus the romance of a sea voyage are a tempting combination, especially for adults who discovered

Disney ships have a classic style

Disney movies and the Mickey Mouse Club as children. Mixed with traditional shipboard activities, who can resist scheduled opportunities for the young and young-at-heart to interact with their favorite Disney characters?

☎ 407/566–3500
or 888/325–2500
⊕ *www.disneycruise. com* ☞ *Cruise Style: Mainstream.*

Although Disney Cruise Line voyages stuck to tried and true Bahamas and Caribbean itineraries in their formative years, and sailed exclusively from Port Canaveral, Florida, where a terminal was designed especially for Disney ships, the line has branched out to other regions, including Europe.

### Food

Don't expect top chefs and gourmet food. This is Disney, and the fare in each ship's casual restaurants is all-American for the most part. A third restaurant is a bit fancier, with French-inspired dishes on the menus. Naturally, all have children's menus with an array of favorite sandwiches and entrées. Vegetarian and healthy selections are also available in all restaurants. A bonus is complimentary soft drinks, lemonade, and iced tea throughout the sailing. A beverage station in the buffet area is always open; however, there is a charge for soft drinks ordered from the bars and room service.

Palo, the adults-only restaurant serving northern Italian cuisine, requires reservations for a romantic evening of fine dining. Although there's a cover charge for dinner, it's a steal and reservations go fast. A brunch also commands a surcharge. More upscale and pricey, Remy on

*Disney Dream* and *Disney Fantasy* serves French cuisine in an elegant atmosphere.

### Entertainment

Shipboard entertainment leans heavily on popular Disney themes and characters. Parents are actively involved in the audience with their children at production shows, movies, live character meetings, deck parties, and dancing in the family nightclub. Teens have a supervised, no-adults-allowed club space in the forward fake funnel, where they gather for activities and parties. For adults, there are traditional no-kids-allowed bars and lounges with live music, dancing, theme parties, and late-night comedy, as well as daytime wine-tasting sessions, game shows, culinary arts and home entertaining demonstrations, and behind-the-scenes lectures on animation and filmmaking. This is Disney, so there are no casinos.

A giant LED screen is affixed to the forward funnels of both the original ships and their newer fleetmates. Passengers can watch movies and special broadcasts while lounging in the family pool area.

### Fitness and Recreation

Three swimming pool areas are designated for different groups: children (Mickey's Pool, which has a waterslide and requires a parent to be present); families (Goofy Pool); and adults (Quiet Cove). Young children who aren't potty trained can't swim in the pools but are invited to splash about in the fountain play area near Mickey's Pool. Be sure to bring their swim diapers.

The salon and spa feature a complete menu of hair- and nail-care services as well as facials and massages. The Tropical Rainforest is a soothing coed thermal suite with heated tile lounges. It's complimentary for the day if you book a spa treatment or available on a daily or cruise-long basis for a fee. SpaVillas are indoor–outdoor treatment suites that feature a veranda with a hot tub and an open-air shower. In addition to a nicely equipped fitness center and aerobics studio are a jogging track and basketball court.

### Your Shipmates

Disney Cruises appeal to kids of all ages—the young and not so young, singles, couples, and families. Multigeneration family groups are the core audience for these ships, and the facilities are ideal for family gatherings. What you might not have expected are the numerous newly-wed couples celebrating their honeymoons on board.

## KNOWN FOR

- **Entertainment:** Some of the best entertainment at sea for guests of all ages.
- **Kid stuff:** Excellent facilities for children and teens.
- **Character interaction:** Disney characters make frequent appearances.
- **Fireworks:** The only ships that are allowed to host fireworks at sea.
- **Classic ships:** Classic ship design (Disney's are the first passenger ships since the 1950s to have two funnels).

Dining in Palo, the adults-only restaurant

## Dress Code

One-week cruises schedule a semiformal evening and a formal night, during which men are encouraged to wear tuxedos, but dark suits or sport coats and ties are acceptable for both. Resort casual is the evening dress code for dinner in the more laid-back dining rooms. A sport coat is appropriate for the restaurants designated as fancier, as well as the adults-only specialty restaurants; however, you won't be turned away and could probably get by without the sport coat.

## Junior Cruisers

As expected, Disney ships have extensive programs for children and teens, including shore excursions designed for families to enjoy together. Parents are issued a pager for peace of mind while their children are participating in onboard activities and to alert them when their offspring need them. Complimentary age-appropriate activities are scheduled from 9 am to midnight in the Oceaneer Club for ages 3 (toilet training required) to 7, in Oceaneer Lab for ages 8 to 12. Activities include arts projects, contests, computer games, pool parties, interactive lab stations, and opportunities for individual and group play. Ocean Quest on *Disney Magic,* designed for 10- to 14-year-olds, has video games, plasma-screen TVs, and a ship simulator where young mariners learn to steer the ship. The emphasis is on fun over education, but subtle educational themes are certainly there. Coffeehouse-style teen clubs offer music, a dance floor, big-screen TV, and Internet café for the younger set. Scheduled activities include challenging games, photography lessons, sporting contests, beach events, and parties, but they are also great places for teenagers 13 to 17 to just hang out with new friends in an adult-free zone.

An hourly fee is charged for child care in Flounder's Reef Nursery, which is open during select hours for infants as young as three months through three years. Supply your own diapers, and nursery attendants will change them. Private, in-cabin babysitting is not available.

Top: A day ashore
Middle: Making a splash in Mickey's Pool
Bottom: *Disney Magic* and *Disney Wonder* at sea

## CHOOSE THIS LINE IF ...

You want to cruise with the entire family—Mom, Dad, the kids, and grandparents.

You enjoy having kids around. (There are adults-only areas to retreat to when the fun wears off.)

Your family enjoys Disney's theme parks and can't get enough wholesome entertainment.

**2**

## Service

Friendly service is extended to all passengers, with particular importance placed on treating children with the same courtesy extended to adults.

## Tipping

Suggested gratuity amounts are calculated on a per-person per-cruise rather than per-night basis and can be added to onboard accounts or offered in cash on the last night of the cruise. Guidelines include gratuities for your dining-room server, assistant server, head server, and stateroom host/hostess for the following amounts: $36 for three-night cruises, $48 for four-night cruises, and $84 for seven-night cruises. Tips for room-service delivery, spa services, and the dining manager are at the passenger's discretion. An automatic 15% gratuity is added to all bar tabs.

## Past Passengers

Castaway Club membership is automatic after completing a Disney cruise. Benefits include a complimentary gift (such as a tote bag or beach towel), communication about special offers, priority check-in, invitations to shipboard cocktail parties during subsequent cruises, and a special toll-free reservation telephone number (☎ *800/449–3380*) for convenience.

### HELPFUL HINTS

There are hidden Mickeys all over the ships, just as in the theme parks.

Consider buying pins and autograph books at a Disney store before your cruise.

You can reserve many services and make dinner reservations prior to sailing.

Roomier than average standard cabins can easily handle four occupants.

Alcohol may be brought on board but must be hand-carried upon embarkation by an adult, age 21 or older.

### DON'T CHOOSE THIS LINE IF ...

You want to spend a lot of quality time bonding with your kids. Your kids may not want to leave the fun activities.

You want to dine in peace and quiet. The dining rooms and buffet can be boisterous.

You want to gamble. There are no casinos, so you'll have to settle for bingo.

# DISNEY MAGIC, DISNEY WONDER

| | |
|---|---|
| Crew Members | 950 |
| Entered Service | 1998, 1999 |
| Gross Tons | 83,000 |
| Length | 964 feet |
| Number of Cabins | 877 |
| Passenger Capacity | 1,754 (2,400 max) |
| Width | 106 feet |

700 ft.

500 ft.

300 ft.

Reminiscent of classic ocean liners, Disney vessels have two funnels (the forward one is nonfunctional) and high-tech interiors behind their art deco and art nouveau styling. Whimsical design accents cleverly incorporate images of Mickey Mouse and his friends without overpowering the warm and elegant decor. Artwork showcases the creativity of Disney artists and animators. The atmosphere is never stuffy.

More than 15,000 square feet—nearly an entire deck—are devoted to children's activity centers, outdoor activity areas, and swimming pools. Theaters cater to family entertainment with large-scale production shows, movies, dances, lively game shows, and even 3-D movies.

Adults-only hideaways include an avenue of theme bars and lounges tucked into the area just forward of the lobby atrium; the Promenade Lounge, near the aft elevator lobby; and Cove Café, a quiet spot adjacent to the adult pool to relax with coffee or a cocktail, surf the Internet, or read.

## Cabins

**Cabins:** Designed for families, Disney ships have some of the roomiest, most functional staterooms at sea. Natural woods, imported tiles, and a nautical flavor add to the decor, which even includes the touch of Disney-inspired artwork on the walls. Most cabins can accommodate at least three people and have a seating area and unique bath-and-a-half arrangement. Three-quarters of all accommodations are outside cabins, and 44% of those include private balconies with kid-proof door handles and higher-than-usual railings for safety. All cabins have adequate closet and drawer/shelf storage, as well as bathroom shelves.

**Suites:** Suites are truly expansive, with master bedrooms separated from the living areas for privacy. All suites have walk-in closets, a dining table and chairs, a wet bar, a DVD player, and a large balcony.

**Amenities:** Though not luxurious, Disney cabins are comfortably furnished. Each has a flat-screen TV, a small refrigerator, a personal safe, and a hair dryer; bathrobes are provided for use during the cruise in the top-category staterooms. All suites have concierge service.

**Accessibility:** Sixteen cabins are wheelchair accessible.

Top: Friendships are forged on a cruise
Bottom: Dreams come true on a Disney cruise

## Restaurants

In a novel approach to dining, passengers (and their waiters) rotate through the three main dining rooms in assigned seatings—two assigned dinner times on *Disney Wonder* and four on *Disney Magic*. Parrot Cay and Animator's Palate are casual, while Triton's (*Disney Wonder*) and Lumière's (*Disney Magic*) are a bit fancier. Palo is a beautifully appointed northern Italian restaurant for adults only that requires reservations for brunch, dinner, or tea and carries an extra charge. Breakfast and lunch are open seating in dining rooms. Disney characters make an appearance at a character breakfast on seven-night cruises. Breakfast, lunch, and dinner are also offered in the casual pool-deck buffet, while poolside pizzerias, snack bars, grills, and ice-cream bars serve everything from pizza, burgers, and hot dogs to fresh fruit, wraps, and frozen treats during the day. Specialty coffees are available in the adults-only Cove Café for an extra charge. Room service is available around the clock.

## Spas

Spas feature a complete menu of facials and massages. The Tropical Rainforest is a soothing coed thermal suite with heated tile lounges and is complimentary for the day if you book a spa treatment; it's available on a daily or cruise-long basis for a fee. SpaVillas, indoor–outdoor treatment suites, each have a veranda with a hot tub and an open-air shower.

## Bars/Entertainment

After the energetic production shows, deck parties, and activities designed for the entire family, adults can slip off to bars and lounges reserved for them after dark, including a sports bar or nightclub where the entertainment staff offers activities such as karaoke or themed dance parties. For quiet conversation and a drink under the stars, there's a cozy bar alongside the adult pool.

## Pros and Cons

**Pros:** there are plenty of connecting cabins that fit three up to seven; soft drinks at meals and beverage stations are complimentary; for adults, each ship has a piano bar/jazz.

**Cons:** Mickey's Pool splash play area is available for youngsters who wear swim diapers; although a Disney cruise isn't all Disney all the time, it can get tiring if you aren't really into the atmosphere; there's no library on board.

| Cabin Type | Size (sq. ft.) |
|---|---|
| Royal Suites | 1,029 |
| 2-Bedroom Suite | 945 |
| 1-Bedroom Suite | 614 |
| Deluxe Family Balcony | 304 |
| Deluxe Balcony | 268 |
| Ocean View | 226 |
| Deluxe Inside | 214 |
| Standard Inside | 184 |

Dimensions include the square footage for balconies.

## FAST FACTS

- 11 passenger decks
- Specialty restaurant, 3 dining rooms, buffet, ice cream parlor, pizzeria
- Wi-Fi, safe, refrigerator, DVD (some)
- 2 pools, children's pool
- Fitness classes, gym, hot tubs, sauna, spa
- 6 bars, dance club, 2 show rooms, video game room
- Children's programs
- Dry-cleaning, laundry facilities, laundry service
- Internet terminal
- No kids under 12 weeks
- No-smoking cabins

2

DISNEY CRUISE LINE

# HOLLAND AMERICA LINE

Holland America Line has enjoyed a distinguished record of traditional cruises, world exploration, and transatlantic crossings since 1873—all facets of its history that are reflected in the fleet's multimillion-dollar shipboard art and antiques collections. Even the

A day on the Lido deck

ships' names follow a pattern set long ago: all end in the suffix *dam* and are either derived from the names of various dams that cross Holland's rivers, important Dutch landmarks, or points of the compass. The names are even recycled when vessels are retired, and some are in their fifth and sixth generation of use.

☎ *206/281–3535 or 800/577–1728*
⊕ *www.hollandameri-ca.com* ☞ *Cruise Style: Premium.*

Noted for focusing on passenger comfort, Holland America Line cruises are classic in design and style, and with an infusion of younger adults and families on board, they remain refined without being stuffy or stodgy. Following a basic design theme, returning passengers feel as at home on the newest Holland America vessels as they do on older ones.

### Food

Holland America Line chefs, led by Master Chef Rudi Sodamin, utilize more than 500 different food items on a typical weeklong cruise to create the modern Continental cuisine and traditional favorites served to their passengers. Vegetarian options as well as health-conscious cuisine are available, and special dietary requests can be handled with advance notice. But the food quality, taste, and selection have greatly improved in recent years. A case in point is the reservations-required Pinnacle Grill alternative restaurants, where fresh seafood and premium cuts of Sterling Silver beef are used to prepare creative specialty dishes. The $25-per-person charge for dinner would be worth it for the Dungeness crab cakes starter and dessert alone. Other delicious traditions are afternoon tea, a Dutch Chocolate Extravaganza, and Holland America Line's signature bread pudding.

Flexible scheduling allows for early or late seatings in the two-deck, formal restaurants. An open seating option from 5:15 to 9 has been introduced fleetwide.

### Entertainment

Entertainment tends to be more Broadway-stylish than Las Vegas–brash. Colorful revues are presented in main show lounges by the ships' companies of singers and dancers. Other performances might include a range of cabaret acts: comedians, magicians, jugglers, and acrobats. Live bands play a wide range of musical styles for dancing and listening in smaller lounges and piano bars. Movies are shown daily in cinemas that double as the Culinary Arts Centers.

Holland America Line may never be considered cutting-edge, but their innovative Signature of Excellence concept sets it apart from other premium cruise lines. An interactive Culinary Arts Center offers cooking demonstrations and wine-tasting sessions; Explorations Café (powered by the *New York Times*) is a coffeehouse, library, and Internet center; the Explorations Guest Speakers Series is supported by in-cabin televised programming on flat-screen TVs in all cabins; the traditional Crow's Nest observation lounge has a nightclub-disco layout, video wall, and sound-and-light systems; and facilities for children and teens have been greatly expanded.

### Fitness and Recreation

Well-equipped and fully staffed fitness facilities contain state-of-the-art exercise equipment; basic fitness classes are available at no charge. There's a fee for personal training, body composition analysis, and specialized classes such as yoga and Pilates.

Treatments in the Greenhouse Spa include a variety of massages, body wraps, and facials. Hair styling and nail services are offered in the salons. All ships have a jogging track, multiple swimming pools, and sports courts; some have hydrotherapy pools and soothing thermal suites.

### Your Shipmates

No longer just your grandparents' cruise line, today's Holland America sailings attract families and discerning couples, mostly from their late thirties on up. Holidays and summer months are peak periods when you'll find more children in the mix. Comfortable retirees are often still in the majority, particularly on longer cruises. Families cruising together who book five or

KNOWN FOR

■ **Tradition Rules:** Holland America Line is one of the most traditional cruise lines, and the line's history is an important part of the experience.

■ **Comfort:** Ships in the fleet are noted for their cozy and warm atmosphere.

■ **Service:** It's not unusual for crew members to remember passengers' names, even if they haven't seen them for years.

■ **The promenade:** A trademark of each ship is its wraparound promenade deck for walking, jogging, or stretching out in the shade on a padded steamer chair.

■ **Consistency:** From afternoon tea to the chimes that announce dinner, each ship in the fleet delivers the expected experience.

Top: Casino action
Bottom: Stay fit or stay loose

**2**

**HOLLAND AMERICA LINE**

more cabins receive perks such as a fountain-soda package for each family member, a family photo for each stateroom, and complimentary water toys at Half Moon Cay (for Caribbean itineraries that call at the private island). If the group is larger than 10 cabins, the Head-of-Family is recognized with an upgrade from outside stateroom to a veranda cabin. It's the best family deal at sea, and there's no extra charge.

### Dress Code

Evenings on Holland America Line cruises fall into two categories: smart casual and formal. For the two formal nights standard on seven-night cruises, men are encouraged to wear tuxedos, but dark suits or sport coats and ties are acceptable, and you'll certainly see them. On smart-casual nights, expect the type of attire you'd see at a country club or upscale resort. It's requested that no T-shirts, jeans, swimsuits, tank tops, or shorts be worn in public areas after 6 pm.

### Junior Cruisers

Club HAL is Holland America Line's professionally staffed youth and teen program. Age-appropriate activities planned for children ages 3 to 7 include storytelling, arts and crafts, ice-cream or pizza parties, and games; for children ages 8 to 12 there are arcade games, Sony PlayStations, theme parties, on-deck sports events, and scavenger hunts. Club HAL After Hours offers late-night activities from 10 pm until midnight for an hourly fee. Baby food, diapers, cribs, high chairs, and booster seats may be requested in advance of boarding. Private in-cabin babysitting is sometimes available if a staff member is willing.

Teens ages 13 to 17 have their own lounge, with activities including dance contests, arcade games, sports tournaments, movies, and an exclusive sundeck on some ships. Most Caribbean itineraries offer water park–type facilities and kid-friendly shore excursions to Half Moon Cay, Holland America Line's private island in the Bahamas.

Top: Wine tasting
Middle: Production Showtime
Bottom: Spa relaxation

**CHOOSE THIS LINE IF ...**

You crave relaxation. Grab a padded steamer chair on the teak promenade deck and watch the sea pass by.

You like to go to the movies, especially when the popcorn is free.

You want to bring the kids. Areas designed exclusively for children and teens are hot new features on all ships.

2

## Service

Professional, unobtrusive service by the Indonesian and Filipino staff is a fleetwide standard on Holland America Line. Crew members are trained in Indonesia at a custom-built facility called the MS *Nieuw Jakarta,* where employees polish their English-language skills and learn housekeeping in mock cabins.

## Tipping

Gratuities of $11.50 per passenger per day are automatically added to shipboard accounts, and distributed to stewards and waitstaff. Passengers may adjust the amount based on the level of service experienced. Room-service tips are usually given in cash (it's at the passenger's discretion here). Gratuities for spa and salon services can be added to the bill or offered in cash. An automatic 15% gratuity is added to bar-service tabs.

## Past Passengers

All passengers who sail with Holland America Line are automatically enrolled in the Mariner Society and receive special offers on upcoming cruises, as well as insider information concerning new ships and product enhancements. Mariner Society benefits also include preferred pricing on many cruises; Mariner baggage tags and buttons that identify you as a member during embarkation; an invitation to the Mariner Society champagne reception and awards party hosted by the captain; lapel pins and medallions acknowledging your history of Holland America sailings; a special collectible gift delivered to your cabin; and a subscription to *Mariner,* the full-color magazine featuring news and Mariner Society savings.

### HELPFUL HINTS

Charges for specialty dining on Holland America Line ships are some of the most reasonable at sea.

All passengers are presented with a complimentary canvas tote bag imprinted with the line's logo.

Narrated iPod art tours of the ships' art collections can be borrowed from the library on each vessel.

A wide variety of shore excursions that fit lifestyles ranging from easygoing to active adventure can be booked before sailing.

A reservation may be cancelled for any reason whatsoever up to 24 hours prior to departure and a refund of 80% to 90% of eligible amounts will be paid.

### DON'T CHOOSE THIS LINE IF ...

You want to party hard. Most of the action on these ships ends relatively early.

Dressing for dinner isn't your thing. Passengers tend to ramp up the dress code most evenings.

You have an aversion to extending tips. The line's "tipping not required" policy has been dropped.

# SIGNATURE-CLASS
*Eurodam, Nieuw Amsterdam*

| | |
|---|---|
| Crew Members | 929 |
| Entered Service | 2008, 2010 |
| Gross Tons | 86,273/86,700 |
| Length | 936 feet |
| Number of Cabins | 1,052, 1,053 |
| Passenger Capacity | 2,104, 2,106 |
| Width | 106 feet |

700 ft.
500 ft.
300 ft.

Signature-class vessels were so named because they are the first ships in the fleet to be launched with all the so-called Signature of Excellence features fully integrated into them. Larger than the other midsize ships in the fleet, they are pure Holland America, with all the traditional amenities and services plus some added bonuses. You'll find familiar public spaces as well as a second specialty restaurant and adjacent lounge, a new bar that anchors the Explorer's Lounge, and an Italian eatery tucked into a corner of the Lido.

No-smoking Spa staterooms near the Greenhouse Spa feature Asian-inspired decor and spa amenities. Poolside are private, draped cabanas, and one deck up the tented Retreat cabanas are filled with amenities that include the use of handheld fans, an Evian spray mister, iPods with music preloaded, and chilled water. You can look forward to icy refreshments and afternoon champagne. Cabanas are reserved by the day or by the cruise (for an extra fee).

## Cabins

**Cabins:** Warm wood tones, burnished nickel fixtures, and punches of color complement the drapery, carpeting, and bedspreads in all categories. Eighty-five percent have an ocean view, and 79% of outside staterooms and suites offer a private veranda with attractive furnishings.

**Suites:** Penthouse suites are the ultimate in luxury, with separate living-room, dining-room, and bedroom areas. A veranda with hot tub, walk-in closets, bathroom with whirlpool tub, double sinks, separate guest powder room, and butler's pantry complete the features. Offering similar amenities, Deluxe and Superior Verandah suites have large verandas, dressing areas, and generous sitting areas; the bathrooms also have double sinks, a whirlpool tub, and a separate shower. Suite occupants can use the private Neptune Lounge and personal concierge service.

**Amenities:** All categories are outfitted with plush pillow-top mattresses, bathrobes, Egyptian cotton towels, flat-panel TVs, DVD players, lighted makeup mirrors, hair dryers, massaging showerheads, personal safes, refrigerators, and closets configured for hanging and/or drop-down shelves.

Top: *Eurodam* at sea
Bottom: The Retreat on
*Eurodam*, the ultimate getaway

**Accessibility:** Thirty cabins are designed for wheelchair accessibility.

## Restaurants

The formal restaurant offers open seating for breakfast and lunch, with dinner in two traditional assigned dinner seatings or open seating. The Pinnacle Grill (reservation, cover charge) serves lunch and dinner. Tamarind (reservation, cover charge) offers Pan-Asian fare, and lunch is free. For casual dining, the Lido restaurant serves buffet breakfast and lunch; for dinner there is waiter service, and a section becomes Canaletto, serving Italian fare (reservation, cover charge). A poolside grill features items ranging from tacos to hamburgers. The extra-charge Explorations Café offers specialty coffees and pastries. Daily afternoon tea service is offered, hors d'oeuvres are served by waiters before dinner, chocolates are offered after dinner, and a chocolate extravaganza buffet is served one night during every cruise. Room service is available 24 hours.

## Spas

Treatments in the Greenhouse Spa include a variety of massages, body wraps, and facials, as well as acupuncture services and tooth-whitening treatments. A hydrotherapy pool and thermal suite with heated ceramic loungers for relaxation as well as dry saunas and steam rooms can be used for a fee (one-time or for the cruise); it's complimentary for the day when a spa appointment is booked.

## Bars/Entertainment

Popular spots before dinner are the Ocean Club and Explorers Lounge, where servers pass through with appetizers. After dinner and a show or concert, those bars are quiet spots for drinks and conversation. For livelier action, there's the Sports Bar, a Piano Bar, or the Crow's Nest for late night dancing.

## Pros and Cons

**Pros:** spa staterooms and suites can be completely no-smoking; with sea views and intimate seating alcoves, the Silk Den Lounge is one of the prettiest in the fleet; guests love culinary presentations in the state-of-the-art demonstration kitchen.

**Cons:** shelves are okay, but drawer space is inadequate in standard accommodations; some spa staterooms offer unusable Juliet balconies; teens are somewhat slighted here compared to other Holland America ships.

| Cabin Type | Size (sq. ft.) |
| --- | --- |
| Penthouse Suite | 1,318 |
| Deluxe Verandah | 510–700 |
| Superior Verandah | 398 |
| Deluxe Verandah | 254 |
| Ocean View | 185 |
| Inside | 170–200 |

Dimensions include the square footage for balconies.

### FAST FACTS

- 11 passenger decks
- 3 specialty restaurants, dining room, buffet, pizzeria
- Wi-Fi, safe, refrigerator, DVD
- 2 pools
- Fitness classes, gym, hot tubs, spa
- 11 bars, casino, 2 dance clubs, library, show room, video game room
- Children's programs
- Dry-cleaning, laundry service
- Internet terminal
- No-smoking cabins

2

HOLLAND AMERICA LINE

*Eurodam* atrium

# VISTA-CLASS
*Zuiderdam, Oosterdam, Westerdam, Noordam*

| | |
|---|---|
| **Entered Service** | 2002, 2003, 2004, 2006 |
| **Passenger Capacity** | 1,916; 1,916; 1,916; 1,918 |
| **Crew Members** | 817, 817, 817, 820 |
| **Number of Cabins** | 958, 958, 958, 959 |
| **Gross Tons** | 82,305 |
| **Length** | 936 feet |
| **Width** | 106 feet |

700 ft.

500 ft.

300 ft.

Ships for the 21st century, Vista-class vessels integrate new, youthful and family-friendly elements into Holland America Line's classic fleet. Exquisite Waterford-crystal sculptures adorn triple-deck atriums and reflect vivid, almost daring color schemes throughout. Although all the public rooms carry the traditional Holland America names (Ocean Bar, Explorer's Lounge, Crow's Nest) and aren't much different in atmosphere, their louder decor (toned down a bit since the introduction of the *Zuiderdam*) may make them unfamiliar to returning passengers.

Veterans of cruises on older Holland America ships will find the layout of public spaces somewhat different; still, everyone's favorite Crow's Nest lounges continue to offer those commanding views.

## Cabins

**Cabins:** Comfortable and roomy, 85% of all Vista-class accommodations have an ocean view, and almost 80% of those also have the luxury of a private balcony furnished with chairs, loungers, and tables. Every cabin has adequate closet and drawer/shelf storage, as well as bathroom shelves. Some suites have a whirlpool tub, powder room, and walk-in closet.

**Suites:** Suites include duvets on beds and a fully stocked minibar; some also have a whirlpool tub, powder room, and walk-in closet. Penthouse and Deluxe Verandah suites have exclusive use of the private Neptune Lounge, personal concierge service, canapés before dinner, and complimentary laundry, pressing, and dry-cleaning services.

**Amenities:** All staterooms and suites are appointed with pillow-top mattresses, 250-thread-count cotton bed linens, magnifying halogen-lighted makeup mirrors, hair dryers, a fruit basket, flat-panel TVs, and DVD players. Bathroom extras include Egyptian cotton towels, shampoo, body lotion, and bath gel, plus deluxe bathrobes to use during the cruise.

**Accessibility:** Twenty-eight staterooms are wheelchair accessible.

Top: *Oosterdam* Hydropool
Bottom: Vista-class Ocean View stateroom

## Restaurants

The formal dining room offers open seating breakfast and lunch, with a choice at dinner between two assigned seatings or open seating. The Pinnacle Grill (reservation, cover charge) serves lunch and dinner. A casual Lido restaurant serves buffet breakfast and lunch; at dinner the Lido offers waiter service with entrées from both the Lido and main dining room menus, and Italian fare is served in the adjacent Canaletto Restaurant. Poolside lunch at the Terrace Grill includes nachos, hamburgers, and hot dogs with all the trimmings to sandwiches and gourmet sausages. The extra-charge Explorations Café offers specialty coffees and pastries. Daily afternoon tea service is elevated to Royal Dutch High Tea once per cruise. Complimentary hors d'oeuvres are served by waiters during cocktail hour, hand-dipped chocolates are offered after dinner in the Explorer's Lounge, and a late-night buffet and chocolate extravaganza is served in the Lido restaurant during every cruise. Room service is available 24 hours.

## Spas

The Greenhouse Spa treatments include a variety of massages, body wraps, and facials, as well as acupuncture and tooth-whitening services. A hydrotherapy pool and thermal suite with heated ceramic lounges for relaxation and dry sauna and steam rooms are free to use when a spa appointment is booked and available for a fee to all other passengers.

## Bars/Entertainment

Before dinner, the Ocean Club and Explorers Lounge are popular spots where servers pass through with appetizers. After dinner and a show or concert, those bars are quiet spots for drinks and conversation. For livelier action, there's the Sports Bar, a Piano Bar, or the Crow's Nest for late-night dancing.

## Pros and Cons

**Pros:** next to the Crow's Nest, an outdoor seating area is a quiet hideaway; exterior panoramic elevators offer an elevated view of the seascape; you can borrow iPod shipboard art tours.

**Cons:** Vista-class ships do not have self-service laundry rooms; murals in Pinnacle Grill restaurants look out of place alongside priceless art found throughout the rest of the ships; some chairs in Pinnacle Grill are so heavy that they barely budge without effort.

| Cabin Type | Size (sq. ft.) |
|---|---|
| Penthouse Suites | 1,318 |
| Deluxe Verandah Suite | 510–700 |
| Superior Verandah Suite | 398 |
| Deluxe Ocean View | 254 |
| Standard Ocean View | 185 |
| Inside | 170–200 |

Dimensions include the square footage for balconies.

## FAST FACTS

- 11 passenger decks
- Specialty restaurant, dining room, buffet, pizzeria
- Internet, Wi-Fi, safe, refrigerator, DVD
- 2 pools (1 indoor)
- Fitness classes, gym, hot tubs, spa
- 9 bars, casino, 2 dance clubs, library, show room, video game room
- Children's programs
- Dry-cleaning, laundry service
- Internet terminal
- No-smoking cabins

**2**

**HOLLAND AMERICA LINE**

# ROTTERDAM, AMSTERDAM

| | |
|---|---|
| Crew Members | 600, 615 |
| Entered Service | 1997, 2000 |
| Gross Tons | 61,859/62,735 |
| Length | 780 feet |
| Number of Cabins | 702, 690 |
| Passenger Capacity | 1,404, 1,380 |
| Width | 106 feet |

700 ft.

500 ft.

300 ft.

The most traditional ships in the fleet, the interiors of sister ships *Amsterdam* and *Rotterdam* display abundant wood appointments in the public areas on promenade and lower promenade decks and priceless works of art throughout.

The Ocean Bar, Explorer's Lounge, Wajang Theater, and Crow's Nest are familiar lounges to longtime Holland American passengers. Newer additions include the spa's thermal suite, a culinary-arts demonstration center in the theater, Explorations Café, and expansive areas for children and teens. Multimillion-dollar collections of art and artifacts are showcased throughout both vessels. In addition to works commissioned specifically for each ship, Holland America Line celebrates its heritage by featuring antiques and artworks that reflect the theme of worldwide Dutch seafaring history.

## Cabins

**Cabins:** Staterooms are spacious and comfortable, although fewer have private balconies than newer fleetmates. Lanai cabins were added during *Rotterdam*'s latest upgrade. Every cabin has adequate closet and drawer/shelf storage, as well as bathroom shelves. Some suites also have a whirlpool tub, powder room, and walk-in closet. Connecting cabins are available in a range of categories, as well as a number of triple and a few quad cabins.

**Suites:** Extras include duvets on beds, a fully stocked minibar, and personalized stationery. Penthouse and Deluxe Verandah suites have exclusive use of the Neptune Lounge, concierge service, canapés before dinner, binoculars and umbrellas for use during the cruise, an invitation to a VIP party with the captain, and complimentary laundry, pressing, and dry-cleaning services.

**Amenities:** All staterooms and suites are appointed with pillow-top mattresses, 250-thread-count cotton bed linens, magnifying halo-lighted mirrors, hair dryers, a fruit basket, flat-panel TVs, and DVD players. Bathrooms have Egyptian cotton towels, nice toiletries, plus deluxe bathrobes to use during the cruise.

**Accessibility:** Twenty-one staterooms are designed for wheelchair accessibility on *Amsterdam,* 22 on *Rotterdam.*

Top: Pinnacle Grill dining
Bottom: *Rotterdam* at sea

## Restaurants

The formal dining room offers open seating breakfast and lunch, as well as two assigned seatings or open seating for dinner. Pinnacle Grill (reservation, cover charge) serves lunch and dinner. A casual Lido restaurant serves buffet breakfast and lunch; at dinner, the Lido offers waiter service and Italian fare in the adjacent Canaletto Restaurant. Poolside lunch at the Terrace Grill includes fast food and sandwiches. The extra-charge Explorations Café offers specialty coffees and pastries. There's daily afternoon tea service. Complimentary hors d'oeuvres are served by waiters during cocktail hour, hand-dipped chocolates are offered after dinner in the Explorer's Lounge, and a late-night buffet and chocolate extravaganza is served in the Lido restaurant during every cruise. Room service is available 24 hours.

## Spas

Treatments in the Greenhouse Spa include a variety of massages, body wraps, and facials, as well as acupuncture and tooth-whitening services. A thermal suite with heated ceramic lounges for relaxation and dry sauna and steam rooms is available for a fee or complimentary for use when a spa appointment is booked. Changing rooms for men and women have complimentary saunas.

## Bars/Entertainment

Popular spots before dinner are the Ocean Club and Explorers Lounge, where servers pass through with canapés. Later, those bars are quiet spots for drinks and conversation. For livelier action aboard *Amsterdam*, there's a Sports and Piano Bar; on *Rotterdam*, try Mix—where champagne, martinis, ales, and spirits are served near the piano. The late night dance spot on both is the Crow's Nest.

## Pros and Cons

**Pros:** *Rotterdam* has The Retreat, a resort-style pool on the aft Lido deck; as the line's flagships, *Rotterdam* and *Amsterdam* have the fleet's most elegant interior decor; realistic landscapes with surreal touches accent walls in *Amsterdam*'s Pinnacle Grill.

**Cons:** one-way window glass in outside cabins on lower promenade deck does not offer occupants complete privacy; there is little shipboard nightlife more than an hour after dinner; despite excellent facilities designed for kids and teens, family cabins are limited.

| Cabin Type | Size (sq. ft.) |
|---|---|
| Penthouse Suite | 1,159 |
| Deluxe Verandah Suite | 556 |
| Verandah Suite | 292 |
| Lanai | 197 (Rotterdam only) |
| Ocean View | 197 |
| Inside | 182 |

Dimensions include the square footage for balconies.

### FAST FACTS

- 9 passenger decks
- Specialty restaurant, dining room, buffet
- Wi-Fi, safe, refrigerator, DVD
- 2 pools (1 indoor), 2 children's pools
- Fitness classes, gym, 2 hot tubs, sauna, spa
- 6 bars, casino, dance club, library, show room, video game room
- Children's programs
- Dry-cleaning, laundry facilities, laundry service
- Internet terminal
- No-smoking cabins

A brisk walk starts the day.

# STATENDAM-CLASS
*Statendam, Maasdam, Ryndam, Veendam*

| | |
|---|---|
| Crew Members | 580 |
| Entered Service | 1993, 1993, 1994, 1996 |
| Gross Tons | 55,819/55,575/55,819/57,092 |
| Length | 720 feet |
| Number of Cabins | 630/658/630/675 |
| Passenger Capacity | 1,260/1,258/1260/1,350 |
| Width | 101 feet |

700 ft.

500 ft.

300 ft.

The sister ships included in the S- or Statendam-class retain the most classic and traditional characteristics of Holland America Line vessels. Routinely updated with innovative features, including Signature of Excellence upgrades, they combine all the advantages of intimate, midsize vessels with high-tech and stylish details.

At the heart of the ships, triple-deck atriums graced by suspended glass sculptures open onto three so-called promenade decks; the lowest contains staterooms encircled by a wide, teak outdoor deck furnished with padded steamer chairs, while interior, art-filled passageways flow past lounges and public rooms on the two decks above. Either reach the lower dining room floor via the aft elevator, or enter one deck above and make a grand entrance down the sweeping staircase.

## Cabins

**Cabins:** Staterooms are spacious and comfortable, although fewer of them have private balconies than on newer ships. Lanai cabins, with a door that directly accesses the promenade deck, were added during the ships' latest upgrades. Every cabin has adequate closet and drawer/shelf storage, as well as bathroom shelves. Connecting cabins are featured in a range of categories.

**Suites:** Suites have duvets on beds, a fully stocked minibar, and personalized stationery. Penthouse Verandah and Deluxe Verandah suites have exclusive use of the private Neptune Lounge, personal concierge service, canapés before dinner on request, binoculars and umbrellas for use during the cruise, an invitation to a VIP party with the captain, and complimentary laundry, pressing, and dry-cleaning services.

**Amenities:** All staterooms and suites are now appointed with pillow-top mattresses, 250-thread-count cotton bed linens, magnifying lighted mirrors, hair dryers, a fruit basket, flat-panel TVs, and DVD players. Bathroom extras include Egyptian cotton towels, shampoo, body lotion, and bath gel, plus deluxe bathrobes to use during the cruise. Accommodations near the spa on *Ryndam, Statendam,* and *Veendam* offer extras such as a yoga mat and iPod docking station.

**Accessibility:** Nine cabins on each ship are modified with ramps although doors are standard width.

Top: Select from an extensive wine list
Bottom: Deluxe Veranda suite

## Spas

Treatments in the Greenhouse Spa include a variety of massages, body wraps, and facials, as well as acupuncture services and tooth-whitening treatments. A thermal suite with heated ceramic loungers for relaxation as well as dry saunas and steam rooms can be used by anyone for a fee or is complimentary when a spa appointment is booked.

## Restaurants

The formal dining room offers open seating breakfast and lunch, as well as both assigned and open seating dinner. Pinnacle Grill (reservation, cover charge) serves lunch and dinner. A casual Lido restaurant serves buffet breakfast and lunch; at dinner the Lido offers waiter service featuring entrées from the Lido and main dining room menus, and Italian fare is served in the adjacent Canaletto Restaurant. Poolside lunch is served at the Terrace Grill; on *Veendam* the pizzeria is in the aft pool Retreat area. The extra-charge Explorations Café offers specialty coffees and pastries. Daily afternoon tea service is elevated to Royal Dutch High Tea once per cruise. Complimentary hors d'oeuvres are served by waiters during cocktail hour, hand-dipped chocolates are offered after dinner in the Explorer's Lounge, and a late-night buffet and chocolate extravaganza is served in the Lido restaurant during every cruise. Room service is available 24 hours.

## Bars/Entertainment

Popular before-dinner spots are the Ocean Club and Explorers Lounge, where servers pass through with appetizers. After dinner and a show, a movie, or concert, those bars are quiet spots for drinks and conversation. For livelier action, try Mix—where champagne, martinis, ales, and spirits are served near the piano. The late-night dance spot is still the Crow's Nest.

## Pros and Cons

**Pros:** Statendam-class ships have some of the fleet's most trendy bars; the Ocean Bar hits the right balance for socializing with the after-dinner crowd; movie theaters double as culinary arts centers.

**Cons:** railings on the balcony level of the main show lounge obstruct the view of the stage; Club HAL may not be too kid-friendly if your cruise is primarily booked by older passengers; popular—and free—coffee bars were eliminated with the addition of Explorations Café.

| Cabin Type | Size (sq. ft.) |
|---|---|
| Penthouse Suite | 1,159 |
| Deluxe Verandah Suite | 556 |
| Verandah Suite | 292 |
| Lanai | 197 |
| Ocean View | 197 |
| Inside | 182 |

Dimensions include the square footage for balconies.

### FAST FACTS

- 10 passenger decks
- Specialty restaurant, dining room, buffet, pizzeria
- Wi-Fi, safe, refrigerator, DVD
- 2 pools (1 indoor), 2 children's pools
- Fitness classes, gym, hot tubs, spa
- 9 bars, casino, dance club, library, show room, video game room
- Children's programs
- Dry-cleaning, laundry facilities, laundry service
- Internet terminal
- No-smoking cabins

Share a sunset.

**2**

**HOLLAND AMERICA LINE**

# PRINSENDAM

| | |
|---|---|
| Crew Members | 470 |
| Entered Service | 1988 |
| Gross Tons | 37,983 |
| Length | 669 feet |
| Number of Cabins | 419 |
| Passenger Capacity | 835 |
| Width | 106 feet |

700 ft.
500 ft.
300 ft.

Alongside her newer fleetmates, *Prinsendam* appears positively diminutive. Launched in 1988 and originally christened *Royal Viking Sun* for the now-defunct Royal Viking Line, the luxury ship subsequently sailed as Seabourn Cruise Line's *Seabourn Sun* before joining Holland America Line in 2002. Extensive renovations added signature Holland America Line features to the boutique-style *Prinsendam*. Artwork, antiques, and Signature of Excellence elements such as a Culinary Arts Center and upgraded cabin amenities have now made their way on board.

Originally designed for lengthy worldwide cruising, Holland America has dubbed *Prinsendam* the "Elegant Explorer," and filled her interiors with classic and comfortable public rooms. A traditional 360-degree promenade deck floored in teak and lined with cushioned deck chairs encircles Lower promenade deck.

## Cabins

**Cabins:** Staterooms are spacious, but furniture placement and amenities within each category can vary. Only a handful of cabins are inside, but a mere 40% of outside cabins and suites have private balconies. Every stateroom has adequate storage for long cruises, and most have walk-in closets. All staterooms and suites are appointed with pillow-top mattresses, 250-thread-count cotton bed linens, magnifying lighted mirror, hair dryer, fruit basket, flat-panel TV, and DVD player. Balcony cabins have refrigerators. Bathroom extras include Egyptian-cotton towels, shampoo, body lotion, and bath gel, plus bathrobes to use during the cruise. Cabin selection must be made carefully, as some cabins near the bow have portholes instead of large windows. Fortunately, the ship's deck plan is very detailed. One interior and two ocean view staterooms are designated single occupancy.

**Suites:** Suites have a stocked minibar and personalized stationery. Occupants have the use of the private Neptune Lounge, concierge service, predinner canapés, binoculars, and umbrellas for use during the cruise, an invitation to a VIP party, and complimentary laundry, pressing, and dry-cleaning service.

**Accessibility:** Ten staterooms are wheelchair accessible.

Top: Holland America Line's "Elegant Explorer"
Bottom: Yoga

| Cabin Type | Size (sq. ft.) |
|---|---|
| Penthouse Suite | 724 |
| Deluxe Verandah Suite | 488 |
| Superior Verandah Suite | 362 |
| Deluxe Verandah Ocean View | 228–238 |
| Ocean View | 181–191 |
| Interior | 128–138 |

Dimensions include the square footage for balconies.

### Restaurants

The formal dining room has two dinner seatings. Alternatives are Pinnacle Grill, the elegant specialty restaurant, and the casual Lido restaurant with indoor and outdoor seating. The Lido buffet and poolside grill also serve breakfast and lunch, and the dining room offers open seating for those meals. Afternoon tea is a daily event, and room service is available around the clock.

### Spas

The smallest Greenhouse Spa in the fleet nevertheless offers a variety of massages, body wraps, and facials, as well as acupuncture services and tooth-whitening treatments. For relaxation there are complimentary saunas and steam rooms.

### Bars/Entertainment

The nautically appointed Ocean Bar and Explorer's Lounge, where servers pass through with appetizers, are favorite gathering spots for predinner drinks, live music, and dancing. After an evening show, movie, or concert, the Crow's Nest offers music for dancing.

### Pros and Cons

**Pros:** magnifying makeup mirrors and salon-quality hair dryers are in all accommodations; the sports deck has bocce and croquet courts as well as putting greens; with classic styling, *Prinsendam* feels more like a large yacht than a cruise ship.

**Cons:** inside staterooms are small and have two lower beds that cannot be combined; *Prinsendam* is more adult-oriented than other HAL ships and not particularly family-friendly; there's little nightlife after dinner.

## FAST FACTS

- 8 passenger decks
- Specialty restaurant, dining room, buffet
- Wi-Fi, safe, refrigerator (some), DVD
- 2 pools
- Fitness classes, gym, hot tubs, sauna, spa, steam room
- 6 bars, casino, library, show room
- Children's programs
- Dry-cleaning, laundry facilities, laundry service
- Internet terminal
- No-smoking cabins

**2**

**HOLLAND AMERICA LINE**

Formal dining

# HURTIGRUTEN

Originally a communications and travel link between the villages on Norway's western coast, Hurtigruten (formerly known in the United States as Norwegian Coastal Voyage) provides an up-close look at the fascinatingly intricate fjords, mountains, and

Cruising the Fjords of Norway

villages that were once isolated and difficult to navigate. The Hurtigruten itineraries are often described as "the world's most beautiful voyages," as they provide access to some of the most stunning scenery and the unique cultures of Norway, many of them above the Arctic Circle.

☎ 800/323–7436
⊕ *www.hurtigruten.us*
☞ *Cruise Style:*
*Small-ship.*

Nine Hurtigruten ships sail year-round on Norwegian coastal express routes. Options include 6-night northbound, 5-night southbound, or 12-night round-trip sailings, calling at 34 ports in each one-way segment. Others spend part of the year on Antarctic and Chilean Fjord itineraries or take trips to Spitsbergen, an island midway between Norway and the North Pole. The MS *Fram* also makes summer expeditions to Greenland as well as a world cruise. These are also working ships, transferring both cargo and passengers, but the ships have the look and feel of traditional cruise ships. However, Mother Nature is the star of this show. Tour leaders on board all voyages assist with practical, cruise-planning details, but these are not traditional cruises.

### Food

The itinerary is the primary point of emphasis on these cruises, and dining takes a far less prominent role than on cruises for the American market. There are two dinner seatings, and the three-course dinners allow no individual selection—everyone on a given evening will have the same appetizer, entrée, and dessert. While the line does its best to meet special dietary requirements, all requests for special meals must be made well in advance of departure. There is a 24-hour café, but it is not free. Liquor, wine, and beer, priced in Norwegian *kroner*, are expensive.

### Entertainment

Destination-rich itineraries are the star on all Hurtigruten ships. Expect no formal splashy entertainment, casinos, shows, cabarets, or nightclubs. In lieu of traditional programming, cruisers can strike up meaningful conversations with interesting fellow passengers, enjoy the pools and hot tubs on younger ships, or simply look up, out, and beyond to appreciate privileged tranquility and beauty.

### Fitness and Recreation

All ships except MS *Lofoten, Nordstjernen,* and *Vesterålen* have a small fitness center on board. Among the newer ships, *Finnmarken* has a swimming pool; *Midnatsol, Trollfjord,* and *Fram* have hot tubs. There is an Internet café on board all ships except MS *Vesterålen, Lofoten, Nordstjernen,* and *Polar Star.* Internet packages can be purchased from reception.

### Your Shipmates

Europeans make up the larger number of passengers, but often there's a minority of Americans. Travelers who find this kind of cruising attractive tend to be independent—comfortable controlling their vacation experience and perfectly content enjoying spectacular scenery and visiting picturesque communities mostly on their own. Families with small kids are few and far between.

### Dress Code

Hurtigruten ships are truly casual, with no dress-up nights. Pack clothing suitable for the area and season in which you are traveling. During the day and throughout the voyage, weather fluctuations can occur rather quickly. It is recommended you dress in layers to accommodate the changes in temperature. Should you choose to pack light, all ships reviewed here are equipped with self-service laundry facilities, including irons and ironing boards. Detergent is included in the price.

### Junior Cruisers

All contemporary ships and *Finnmarken* have an unstaffed children's playroom but no organized activities for kids.

### Service

Service can be splendid but also subtle, without many flourishes.

KNOWN FOR

■ **Norway Coastal Cruising:** No-frills, nontraditional cruising is the line's hallmark, with year-round departures from Norway.

■ **The Hurtigruten Route:** The line calls at 34 ports of call on any of the 6, 7, 11 or 12-day coastal voyages.

■ **Unique Excursions:** The Northern Lights and remote regions, plus polar circle landings in Greenland, Spitsbergen, and Antarctica are all excursion options.

■ **Simple Transportation:** The line offers 1,000 short port-to-port Norwegian coastal cruise possibilities.

■ **No Frills on Board:** These are not traditional leisure cruises; don't expect big-ship amenities or activities.

Top: Observation Lounge on the *Nordnorge*
Bottom: Majestic scenery awaits

### Tipping

Tipping is neither required nor expected, though it is allowed if you feel you have received particularly good personal service from a crew member.

### Past Passengers

If you have traveled with Hurtigruten within the last three years and will travel within the next three years, you may receive a 10% discount on your next Norwegian Coastal Voyage or 5% off your next Explorer cruise (Antarctica, Greenland, Spitsbergen, or Europe). This offer is combinable with other discounts, such as those offered for early booking and groups, but you must travel within three years in order to receive the discounted fare.

### Ships of the Line

Twelve vessels comprise the Hurtigruten fleet, categorized as three Millennium-class, eight Contemporary and Traditional, and the singular Explorer ship.

**Millennium Ships.** Hurtigruten's three Millennium ships offer 21st-century creature comforts and safe sailing while en route to the dramatic glacial peaks of Antarctica and Greenland. The first Hurtigruten ship to bear the MS *Finnmarken* name was introduced in 1912, and her worthy successor designed in 2002 reflects the elegance of the past. The ship's art nouveau-style interior is complemented by modern panoramic lounges, bars, bistro, conference facilities, and a salon. A swimming pool, fitness room, sauna, solarium and outside hot tub are also on board. The other two Millennium ships include the MS *Midnastol* and MS *Trollfjord* (both 2003).

Top: *Polarlys* underway
Middle: *Nordnorge* regular double cabin
Bottom: Panoramic lounge on the *Polarlys*

## CHOOSE THIS LINE IF ...

You wish to sail past some of the most beautiful scenery in the world, including such remote spots as Antarctica and Greenland.

You don't mind a ship short on activities and big-ship features that goes to the smaller villages with little to offer but their quaint charm.

You are a confident, independent traveler and comfortable controlling your daily activities.

**Contemporary and Traditional Ships.** The eight contemporary and traditional ships in the Hurtigruten fleet represent an armada of historical working vessels that have been refitted and refurbished in a variety of styles. Each ship exudes a particular character and carries between 400 and 700 passengers. While amenities and entertainment are sparse on many ships, comfortable facilities, stylish decor, and modern technology have been added to the newer ships for a more aesthetically pleasing, albeit casual, journey. All vessels are multifunctional, carrying cargo and passengers from port to port daily. The fleet consists of the MS *Nordnorge*, MS *Nordkapp*, MS *Polarys*, MS *Nordlys*, MS *Richard With*, MS *Kong Harald*, and MS Vesterålen. For a real vintage feel, hop aboard the old-time favorite MS *Lofoten*, which was christened in 1964.

**Explorer Ship.** Named after the ship used by famous Norwegian explorer Fridtjof Nansen, MS *Fram* has a glass-enclosed observation lounge and excellent leisure facilities, including a gym, sauna, and two heated outdoor hot tubs. The *Fram* is a purpose-built 12,700-ton vessel that incorporates all the best of both practical and traditional design. Built in 2007, *Fram* has a capacity of 400 passengers.

HELPFUL HINTS

All the ships in the Hurtigruten fleet have elevators and cabins specially equipped for passengers with disabilities.

Although there are no medical facilities or doctors on board, the vessels are regularly in sight of land.

Smoking is not permitted inside all the ships, only outside in designated areas of open decks.

Only alcoholic drinks purchased in the ship's restaurant or bar may be consumed on board; any bottled liquor purchased on land must be stored until your return. (The drinking age on the ships is 18.)

All cabins have a private bathroom with 220-volt outlet. In suites, there is also a 110-volt outlet for shavers. The sockets require two-pin European plug adaptors for dual-voltage U.S. appliances.

HURTIGRUTEN

2

**DON'T CHOOSE THIS LINE IF ...**

You require large-scale entertainment activities found on big cruise ships; you will be happier elsewhere.

You want to work out. Some Hurtigruten ships have compact gyms, but the smaller ones do not.

You can't keep up. Ships call at dozens of villages, and destination-intense activities can be vigorous.

# LINDBLAD EXPEDITIONS

Founded in 1979 as Special Expeditions by Sven-Olof Lindblad, the son of Lars-Eric Lindblad, the company changed its name in 1984 to Lindblad Expeditions. Every cruise is educational, focusing on soft adventure and environmentally conscientious travel. Since

Mont St-Michel, a stop on Lindblad's European family itineraries

2004 the line has partnered with *National Geographic* to enhance the cruise experience by including experts and photographers on board to lead discussions and hold workshops and help balance "must-see" destinations and less-traveled spots.

☎ *212/765–7740 or 800/397–3348*
⊕ *www.expeditions. com ☞ Cruise Style: Small-ship.*

Beginning in 2008, National Geographic Expeditions began working exclusively with Lindblad Expeditions. The multifaceted strategic partnership that Lindblad Expeditions has with the National Geographic Society enables Lindblad travelers to participate in the world of natural and cultural history as engaged, active explorers who care about the planet.

The ships of Lindblad Expeditions spend time looking for wildlife, exploring out-of-the-way inlets, and making Zodiac landings at isolated beaches. Each ship has a fleet of kayaks as well as a video-microphone: a hydrophone (underwater microphone) is combined with an underwater camera so passengers can listen to whale songs and watch live video of what's going on beneath the waves. In the evening the ship's naturalist recaps the day's sights and adventures over cocktails in the lounge. All activities and shore excursions, from guided walks and hikes to museum entrance fees to water activities like kayaking and snorkeling, are included in the cost of every Lindblad Expedition. Guests always have the freedom to pick and choose activities as the day unfolds.

## Food

Appetizers are usually served on deck as you sail from port, while regional specialties are served in the dining room. The galley is headed by European-trained chefs, and local markets are scoured for delicacies and indigenous ingredients to serve on board. Breakfast is buffet-style, although you may order eggs and omelets from the kitchen, and lunch is served family-style. Afternoon tea includes sandwiches and sweets; hors d'oeuvres are served during the nightly cocktail hour. The open seating dinner typically consists of two entrées—meat or fish—as well as several always-available items such as steak and chicken. Special dietary restrictions can be accommodated with advance notice. Room service is restricted to ill passengers confined to cabins.

## Entertainment

Lindblad clientele should not expect shuffleboard and glitzy Broadway shows, but it's more likely they prefer reflective moments gazing at constellations, speaking about maritime navigation with the ship's captain, or watching a video slide show about biodiversity anyway. Expect to have the most fun boarding a Zodiac for remote shore visits, snorkeling, or diving surrounded by spectacular marine wildlife.

## Fitness and Recreation

Ships carry exercise equipment on deck or have a dedicated fitness center and offer a holistic Tonic of Wellness program that might include activities such as kayaking and hiking, fitness activities like yoga and Pilates, or massage therapy and other body treatments. The fitness staff provides expertise in massage therapy and relaxation, water sports and aerobic hikes, stretching classes, and personalized guidance with the fitness equipment.

## Your Shipmates

Lindblad attracts active, adventurous, well-traveled over-forties, and quite a few singles, as the line charges one of the industry's lowest single supplements. But the line is making a push to be more family-friendly by adding cruises aimed specifically at families and children. To that end, staff members have undergone extensive training designed by several of Lindblad's family travel experts with years of experience in childhood and environmental education to tailor activities toward children.

### KNOWN FOR

■ **Exotic Destinations:** Expedition "soft adventure" cruising to destinations like Antarctica, the Arctic, and other inaccessible areas of the world.

■ *National Geographic:* Partnered with *National Geographic,* cruises feature expedition experts, trained naturalists, and guest lecturers in various scientific fields depending on the destination.

■ **Premium Pricing:** Expensive all-inclusive fares include first-class travel accommodations and facilities.

■ **Hands-on Family-Friendly Adventures:** The educational emphasis of these cruises and customizable off-boat excursions are ideal for families with children, particularly cruises to the Galapagos.

■ **Video Galore:** Underwater and land videotaping to chronicle destinations and natural wildlife with regular topical presentations and discussions.

Travelers socialize in the lounge

2

LINDBLAD EXPEDITIONS

Relaxing in a comfortable cabin

## Dress Code

Casual and comfortable attire is always appropriate. Recommendations are based on practicality and the likely weather conditions in the region you're exploring. Good walking shoes are essential.

## Junior Cruisers

Although there are no dedicated children's facilities on board, families are welcome on all Lindblad itineraries. In fact, the number of families traveling with the company has grown substantially, so much so that the line will have dedicated staff on some designed "family" cruises that know how to inspire curiosity in young people of all ages. Lindblad emphasizes shared experiences, and while there are always some activities just for children or adults, most are done together.

## Service

Service is friendly and helpful, if not overly polished.

## Tipping

Although gratuities are at your discretion, tips of $12–$15 per person per day are suggested; these are pooled among the crew at journey's end. Tip the massage therapist individually following a treatment.

## Ships of the Line

Lindblad Expeditions currently sails ten vessels for adventure cruising to spectacular regions throughout the world. Ships are comfortable, outfitted with modern amenities, offer top-notch cuisine, and afford privileged travelers both quiet refuge and social interaction.

**Lord of the Glens.** To tour the British Isles and Scotland in particular, the *Lord of the Glens* is a compact, yacht-like vessel carrying only 48 passengers. Linking many of Scotland's picturesque inland lochs, the ship was built specifically to tour the narrow Caledonian waterways and remote islands of the Inner Hebrides. For its small size, it offers spacious cabins, ample open-air viewing areas, two public lounges, and a main dining room where all meals are served. Isolated villages, dramatic castles, and scenic highlands are featured on this ship's primarily Scottish route.

## CHOOSE THIS LINE IF ...

You want to be an ecologically responsible traveler.

You consider travel a learning experience.

What you see from the ship and landings are more important than the vessel itself.

**National Geographic Explorer.** This is the newest addition to the Lindblad fleet. Following a 2008 rebuild, the ship carries 148 passengers in 81 outside cabins, is fully stabilized, and designated a 1A-rated Ice-class ship, enabling it to navigate polar passages. Creature comforts include a full-service bar, restaurant, state-of-the-art A/V equipment, library, and glass-enclosed fitness center. Outfitted with kayaks and Zodiacs for shore landings, the *Explorer* also distinguishes itself with its team of marine experts who operate sophisticated machinery and camera equipment to capture rare images of underwater life. Other popular itineraries for the vessel include the Arctic, Antarctica, Northern Canada, West Africa, and Patagonia.

**Sea Cloud.** The historic, three-masted sailing ship built in 1931 by financier E. F. Hutton as a private sailing yacht has all the graceful lines, wooden details, and nautical charm of an antique vessel. The atmosphere on board is informal, with an "open bridge" to see how the vessel is sailed. Itineraries include the Mediterranean, Adriatic, Ionian, and Aegean seas. The intimate 58-passenger ship has only 30 updated cabins and two Owner's suites kept in their original state. For a special deal in 2013, bar tabs and all crew tips are covered on any *Sea Cloud* Mediterranean departure with a complimentary night stay at the Electra Palace Hotel in Athens.

## HELPFUL HINTS

Although rather expensive wine and cocktails are not included in the fare, non-alcoholic beverages are.

All shore excursions except flightseeing are included, as are transfers to and from airports.

Extensive pre-trip information, including recommended reading, photography guidelines, and what to pack, will arrive with your documents.

There is no elevator on board nor are there accessible features for the mobility impaired.

Don't expect round-the-clock availability of food; room service is only available if you are sick and confined to your cabin.

## DON'T CHOOSE THIS LINE IF ...

You are mobility-impaired; the ships are not accessible, and Zodiacs are used to reach shore for certain explorations.

Your happiness depends on being entertained; other than enrichment programs, there is no formal entertainment.

You consider TV essential; there are none in the staterooms.

# LOUIS CRUISES

In 1935, what began as a one-man travel agency by Louis Loizou has evolved into Louis PLC, one of the biggest tourism conglomerates in the Eastern Mediterranean region. The cruise line itself was established in 1986, with a fleet of refurbished, well-maintained

*Coral,* Louis Cruises

ships. Disaster struck in 2007 when the MV *Sea Diamond* sank off the coast of Santorini, but the line has rebuilt its reputation for safe maritime travel in the interim. Today, the value-oriented line operates six ships, two of which are chartered by and sail under the Thomson brand.

☎ *(44) 0800/0183883 in the UK; (30) 210/4583400 in Greece* ⊕ *www.louiscruises. com* ☞ *Cruise Style: Mainstream.*

Fastidious planning and design of excursions coupled with standard rooms and facilities one would expect on larger vessels offer passengers memorable journeys. Cruises are organized to optimize visiting the best ports of call during the best conditions for sightseeing, walking, hiking, and exploring.

Louis Cruises began cruising with the now-defunct *Princess Marissa* that embarked from Limassol, Cyprus towards Greek islands, Israel, and Egypt. By the 1990s, the line had added the *Sapphire* and *Emerald* (also now retired) as charters to UK-based Thomson Cruises, beginning its long-time affiliation with the British tour operator. Various ships have gone into and out of the Louis Cruises fleet since its inception, but by the beginning of the new millennium, the current line-up of ships began to take shape. The fleet was expanded in 2000 with the purchase of the *Calypso*, which has been recently retired. Louis also purchased what is now the *Thomson Spirit* from Holland America Line. It's other chartered long-term charter, the *Thomson Destiny*, was purchased from UK-based Sun Cruises. *Louis Olympia* entered service in 2005 (and was further refurbished in 2012). In 2006, the *Orient Queen* and *Sea Diamond* joined the fleet, though *Sea Diamond* sank off Santorini in 2007. The *Louis Cristal* was refurbished for seasonal itineraries to replace *Sea Diamond* in 2007.

Today the Louis fleet is composed of mostly second- or third-hand refurbished vessels, purchased since the early 1990s. The diverse collection ranges from the more basic 968-passenger *Coral* and 1,450-passenger *Olympia* to ships that are larger and somewhat newer. Ships vary in size, age, and available amenities, but all the ships' cabins and facilities are well-maintained and clean.

Lacking luxury appointments and the accompanying prices and pretension, a cruise on any of the four Louis Cruises vessels concentrates more on destination than the actual shipboard experience. Passengers can tailor a three- to eight-day holiday to explore Greek islands off the beaten track or access Turkish ports of call. Some Louis ships may not meet the high expectations of well-heeled globetrotters, but the itineraries can be outstanding.

Proud of its Hellenic heritage, Louis Cruises specializes in short, port-intensive, discount cruises from Athens (Piraeus and Lavrion), Greece; Limassol, Cyprus; and Istanbul, Turkey in a fleet of seven classic midsized ships. Cruises typically explore Greece (both World Heritage Sites and remote Aegean Isles), the Turkish coast, ports in Croatia, and Venice.

## Food

On Louis Cruise sailings, onboard chefs provide a variety of freshly prepared meals with healthier Mediterranean, Italian, and Continental flavors and ingredients, but don't expect haute cuisine. More than two-dozen different types of local breads, rolls, and pastries garnish the menus. All sauces, dressings, soups, terrines, jams, and desserts are made in the ship's galley. Salads, olives, local cheeses, moussaka casseroles, pastas, and fresh fruit show up on menus. Local fresh seafood and grilled meat specials appear daily. Expect main dining rooms to be noisy, with tables sandwiched together. Casual bistro-style dining and self-service food areas offer fast food and pizza. Bars and lounges are open throughout the day and night for coffee, teas, sodas, and alcoholic beverages at additional cost. A small selection of local wines is also available for an additional cost.

### KNOWN FOR

■ **Short Cruises:** Discount "fast-paced" cruising on midsized ships to the Mediterranean and Aegean.

■ **Focus on Eastern Mediterranean:** The line focuses solely on cruises to the Greek islands, Cyprus, Croatia, and Turkey.

■ **Value Pricing:** Promotional discounts and special offers are common.

■ **More Enrichment:** The line has a new enrichment-themed cruise program to Greece and Turkey featuring expert lectures.

■ **Off-the-Beaten-Path Greek Isles:** In 2013, a new itinerary was introduced to highlight the company's Greek heritage and showcase the remote islands of Chios and Symi.

Pool on *Louis Cristal*

### Entertainment

Entertainment would not be the primary reason to take a Louis Cruise; however, each vessel carries a number of musicians, bands, and performers for evening variety shows, piano bar music, and traditional Greek dance catering to an older, conservative crowd. Ships have casinos as well as discos and cinemas, and cruise directors often bring on local suppliers so that passengers can purchase local products and sometimes organize fashion shows. But the focus on these cruises remains the itineraries more than the onboard experience.

### Fitness and Recreation

Indoor/outdoor lounges, card and game rooms, and a library provide calm corners. For more active passengers, heated swimming pools, hot tubs, a jogging track, fitness center, and spa offer other ways to relax. Spa packages are also available that include a variety of treatments.

### Your Shipmates

A wide range of ages and nationalities embark on Louis Cruise voyages. While crew and staff are all local Greeks, Cypriots, and other Eastern Europeans, clientele are usually British, French, German, and a variety of northern Europeans, with a growing number of Americans and Canadians as passengers.

### Dress Code

Casual attire is common by day, and the evening dress code is country club casual, with more formal wear visible during special dinners. Women tend to wear long trousers or cocktail dresses. Men wear a jacket and tie. Greek Night suggests attire in blue and white, the colors of Greece.

Top: The casino on *Orient Queen*
Middle: Spa treatments on *Louis Cristal*
Bottom: A cabin on *Louis Olympia*

## CHOOSE THIS LINE IF …

You want a fast way to explore the Greek Isles and the Mediterranean, Cyprus, and Turkey.

Discount cruising with local staff, language, and cuisine is satisfying.

You are traveling with children or enjoy a basic cruise that focuses more on destination rather than ship experience.

## Junior Cruisers

Bringing small children to the Greek islands may not always feel enriching for everyone involved, but Louis Cruises welcomes kids of all ages and is child-friendly. Cabins and restaurants accommodate families. Discounts and specials aimed at families and children are available throughout the year. A Kids' Corner has a full daily program of games and activities to keep little sailors happy in addition to a kids' pool, outdoor play space, a small video arcade, and even a mini golf course. You won't find elaborate bowling alleys, waterslides, or rock-climbing walls on vessels, which are modest in size and moderate in amenities offered; however, shore excursions into interesting ports of call, village hikes, and donkey rides to archaeological sites usually provide enough stimulation to interest even the most bored toddler or teen.

## Service

A professional, multilingual, mostly Mediterranean staff provides friendly, attentive service.

## Tipping

Tipping is expected. The line will debit shipboard accounts €8 per person per day for adults over 16 and €4 per person per day for children ages 6–16. Amounts can be adjusted by speaking with the staff at reception.

## Past Passengers

Louis Cruises has no formal loyalty program.

### HELPFUL HINTS

Louis ships have few upscale amenities on board; you take one of these cruises primarily to experience the various destinations.

The line sometimes offers special fares that include unlimited alcoholic and nonalcoholic drink packages.

Don't be fooled by brochure photos—cabins are small and feel that way.

Onboard classes, excursions, and announcements may be held in different languages.

Bring your own water bottles. Onboard drink prices, including bottled water, are very steep.

Read the fine print on all documentation. You can opt out of the formalized tipping service.

**2**

**LOUIS CRUISES**

---

### DON'T CHOOSE THIS LINE IF ...

High-end luxury cruising with a five-star hotel feel is a must.

You cannot embark in Athens, Greece; Limassol, Cyprus; or Istanbul, Turkey.

You prefer large, feature-rich, brand-new ships.

# LOUIS CRISTAL

| | |
|---:|---|
| **Crew Members** | |
| 400 | |
| **Entered Service** | |
| 2007 | |
| **Gross Tons** | |
| 25,611 | |
| **Length** | |
| 531 feet | |
| **Number of Cabins** | |
| 476 | |
| **Passenger Capacity** | |
| 1,200 | |
| **Width** | |
| 84 feet | |

700 ft.

500 ft.

300 ft.

Replacing the *Sea Diamond*, which tragically sunk off Santorini in early 2007, the 25,611-ton *Louis Cristal* made its debut in late summer of the same year as a unique yacht-like modern vessel, cruising up to speeds of 18 knots. While not an ultraluxe megayacht with all the bells and whistles, expect a traditional array of ship amenities, including multiple restaurants, panoramic bars, a small casino, nightclub, pool, fitness, and full-service spa. Internet and mini golf will help keep children connected and entertained. While not upscale, cabins are basic but comfortable. Entertainment is a hodgepodge of musical performance, showcasing traditional dance and music in classic Greek style alongside karaoke tunes and numbers from recent Broadway hits. Lacking technologically advanced amenities found on a newer ship, good value for money can be expected with port-intensive itineraries.

Whether you desire to journey to the Turkish shores or circumnavigate the Greek isles, this traditional ship sails from Piraeus toward well-known destinations in the Mediterranean, Eastern Mediterranean, and Aegean Sea, including classic Greek havens Mykonos, Patmos, Crete, Santorini, Heraklion, and the UNESCO World Heritage Site of Rhodes. Open promenades with numerous deck chairs invite passengers to sunbathe or take in the scenery. Public spaces and cabins resemble an upscale three-star hotel with upbeat decor and are designed to accommodate larger groups. Round-trip excursions from Athens are available for three- or four-night journeys. Optional shore excursions are available for additional fees ranging from €35 to €100.

## Cabins

**Cabins:** The 476 spacious staterooms and suites are divided into 313 outside cabins and 163 inside cabins. Decorated in light wood, blue, white, and yellow tones, the rooms are clean and categorized as standard, premium, and deluxe. The largest are the two Imperial Suites on deck 6 with private Jacuzzi and balcony for up to three people. Parties of up to five sleep comfortably in the 126 premium outside cabins. All cabins have a TV, refrigerator, safe, and air-conditioning for warm Mediterranean days and nights.

**Bathrooms:** All cabins are equipped with a shower, toilet, sink, and hair dryer. Two Imperial Suites have jetted tubs.

Top: *Louis Cristal* at sea
Bottom: The casino on
*Louis Cristal*

**Accessibility:** Wheelchair-bound passengers are welcome but must be accompanied. Staterooms and public areas have low or no doorsills for easy mobility. To access decks, use one of four elevators, which are adequate for narrow wheelchairs. Six category-XB cabins on deck 5 are suitable for wheelchair users.

## Restaurants

Five restaurants provide ample choices for breakfast, lunch, and dinner. Head to the buffet at Traviata restaurant, or dine in the more formal Caruso and La Scala, but passengers can opt for buffets at every meal. Sit-down lunches and dinners provide full service from friendly, multilingual waiters. Greek celebrity chef Christoforos Peskias owns and operates the stylish à la carte Thalassa restaurant. His menu features Greek fusion cuisine using fresh, local ingredients. A four-course prix-fixe menu averages about €20. Expect delicious Greek meats and salads, a poolside gyro station, and even a special *mezze* (appetizer) event for dinner, in addition to the familiar pastas and potatoes.

## Spas

The Sana Health Spa has steam rooms and saunas and offers traditional and specialized wellness and beauty treatments, including manicures, pedicures, and rejuvenating facials. Other options include relaxing Balinese massage, reflexology, or a mud bath.

## Bars/Entertainment

Cocktails and beverages are enjoyed at the Riviera pool bar or atmospheric Romeo & Juliet Bar. The Caruso Terrace Bar and Rendezvous lounge are hotspots for making new friends. The All Sports Bar is on deck 8. Head up to deck 10 for a midnight snack or a nightcap in the Stars Lounge & Disco.

## Pros and Cons

**Pros:** family-friendly accommodations and facilities; small size means easy embarkation and debarkation at ports of call; friendly service with local crew and staff.

**Cons:** basic, uninspiring cabins; the ship lacks modern amenities cruise passengers have come to expect; uneven entertainment.

| Cabin Type | Size (sq. ft.) |
|---|---|
| Imperial Suite | 460 |
| Junior Suite | 269 |
| Outside State Room | 118–160 |
| Interior State Room | 108–129 |

### FAST FACTS

- 9 passenger decks
- 2 dining rooms, buffet, pizzeria
- Wi-Fi, TV, safe, refrigerator (some)
- 2 pools
- Fitness classes, gym, hot tubs, sauna, spa, steam room
- 6 bars, casino, dance club, library, show room, video game room
- Children's programs
- Dry-cleaning, laundry facilities, laundry service
- Internet terminal, Wi-Fi

**2**

**LOUIS CRUISES**

A typical cabin

# LOUIS OLYMPIA

| | |
|---|---|
| **Crew Members** | 540 |
| **Entered Service** | 2005 |
| **Gross Tons** | 37, 584 |
| **Length** | 705 feet |
| **Number of Cabins** | 724 |
| **Passenger Capacity** | 1,450 |
| **Width** | 93 feet |

700 ft.

500 ft.

300 ft.

Completely refurbished in 2005 and reintroduced in 2012, the 37, 854-ton *Louis Olympia* is one of the largest ships in the Louis Cruise fleet. Her classic shape is what you'd expect for a ship cruising in the soft ocean breezes around the Greek Isles, with a sleek terraced silhouette providing magnificent views of the islands and Greek coastline. Originally sailing as the *Thomson Destiny,* the renamed *Louis Olympia* is now used as the primary vessel for the line's special niche journeys to remote Greek islands and Turkey.

One of the newer ships in the Louis Cruises fleet, *Olympia* has a modern interior design, but presents a friendly and relaxed environment. Depending on itinerary and season, the *Olympia,* when fully loaded, will feel crowded, especially in dining rooms, public rooms, and limited facilities such as the Internet café and beauty salon. Nevertheless, *Olympia* attracts a mixed range of tourists, families, seniors, and groups looking for standard cruising to take in the sun, sea, shopping, and sights.

## Cabins

**Cabins:** Expect relatively small but well-maintained standard cabins with very little storage space. Larger cabins, which have twin beds that convert to a queen, have more storage and half-size bathtubs. The 724 cabins are comprised of 418 outside cabins and 306 inside. All cabins are equipped with TV, music system, and safe. The largest cabins are suites, furnished with king-size beds and lounge areas with sofa. Some categories have small refrigerators; private balconies are only in the top categories. In larger cabins, twin beds convert to queen for more storage. The most luxurious rooms are the two Grand Suites on deck 9 with private balconies that can accommodate up to three people. Inside cabins located on deck 2 and 3 can accommodate up to four people.

**Bathrooms:** Expect tight quarters for attached bathrooms, which are all equipped with shower, mirror, toilet, and hairdryer.

**Accessibility:** Wheelchair access is acceptable. Facilities for passengers with disabilities are few, but mobility around the ship is fairly easy.

*Louis Olympia* at sea

## Restaurants

The expansive Seven Seas Restaurant is separated into two wings with glass picture windows for brightness and views. It offers a tasty variety of typical local cuisine and homemade desserts with attentive full service for breakfast, lunch, and dinner. Expect the main dining room with two seatings to get crowded and noisy, especially if you travel during high season. As an alternative, self-service buffet dining is available at the Lido café. During the day, head to deck 9 where you can enjoy gyros, pizza, and barbecue at the pool grill. Room service (24-hour) is available.

## Spas

The spa offers beauty treatments and saunas for both men and women. Manicures and salon services are popular and can be booked in advance.

## Bars/Entertainment

The Oklahoma and Can Can cabaret lounges provide evening comedy shows, music, game shows, and dancing. Popular nightspots are the Sky Bar perched on deck 12 and Lido bar on deck 9. Blakes, the Mast Bar, and Clipper Bar are perfect retreats to meet other passengers. Got the gambling bug? The neon lights of the Casino Royale tempt with roulette tables and series of slot machines.

## Pros and Cons

**Pros:** good embarkation/debarkation in ports of call; family-friendly ship; outgoing and knowledgeable local crew and officers.

**Cons:** small cabins and bathrooms have limited storage space; dining rooms and public areas are crowded, especially during high season; sound insulation between cabins very poor.

| Cabin Type | Size (sq. ft.) |
|---|---|
| Grand Penthouse Suite | 450+ |
| Junior Suite | 300–400 |
| Deluxe Ocean View | 164–239 |
| Interior | 111–166 |

### FAST FACTS

- 9 passenger decks
- 1 dining room, buffet
- Wi-Fi, safe, refrigerator (some)
- 2 pools, children's pool
- Fitness classes, gym, hot tubs, sauna, spa, steam room
- 5 bars, casino, dance club, library, show room, video game room
- Children's programs
- Laundry facilities, laundry service
- Internet terminal

**2**

**LOUIS CRUISES**

A twin cabin

# ORIENT QUEEN

| | |
|---|---|
| Crew Members | 329 |
| Entered Service | 1968 |
| Gross Tons | 15,781 |
| Length | 525 feet |
| Number of Cabins | 355 |
| Passenger Capacity | 912 |
| Width | 75 feet |

With its signature helipad at the bow, the 15,781-ton *Orient Queen* is slim by current cruising standards, a positive trait if less crowded decks and facilities are desired. With a total of 355 staterooms, the vessel accommodates 912 passengers in an atmosphere that is more contemporary and casual chic than the larger ships in the Louis Cruise armada. A mostly Greek crew offers knowledgeable and friendly service that feels personalized on eight decks of comfortable restaurants, lounges, and bars. Typical activities and facilities include a mini golf course, shopping boutiques, and fitness/spa center. Expect to recognize faces while leisurely strolling the promenades or enjoying a cocktail in the upper-deck lounges. While not providing the height of individual privacy, the cruise experience is tailored for a more intimate journey.

An excursion on the *Orient Queen* tends to please passengers looking for a good informal voyage with outgoing, attentive service, excellent food, and comfortable cabins. Since the vessel is smaller and older, expect to feel the swells of the sea and hear loud engine drones, despite extensive refurbishment and stabilizers. Buffet meals, conservative entertainment, and a variety of onboard programs provide a full experience. The real highlight will be accessing places such as the Greek isles of Paxos, Naros, and the village of Mytilini as well as the Turkish delights of Istanbul and Kusadasi.

## Cabins

**Cabins:** Small but attractively stylish standard cabins are adequate for short cruises. The 355 staterooms are comprised of 190 outside cabins and 165 indoor. All cabins are equipped with satellite TV, music systems, direct-dial phones, safe, and fridge. Suites have a king-size bed and a lounge area with sofa. Up to four people can fit into a standard or premium inside or outside cabin. Some suites have whirlpool bathtubs.

**Bathrooms:** In larger staterooms, appointments are more upscale, with marble-like tiling for counters and shower. In standard cabins, expect tighter quarters. All bathrooms have a shower, sink, mirrored vanity, toilet, and hairdryer. Storage space is limited.

Top: *Orient Queen* at sea
Bottom: The main pool

**Accessibility:** While wheelchair access is allowed and possible, facilities for passengers with disabilities are nonexistent. There's only one wheelchair-accessible room on the Cedars Deck.

## Restaurants

The Horizon Buffet is open for breakfast, lunch, and dinner. For a sit-down full-service meal typical of an upscale restaurant, head to the more formal Mermaid Restaurant, where a dedicated waiter will serve a five-course dinner consisting of appetizer, salad, soup, entrée, and dessert. Mediterranean, Greek and Turkish flavors are highlighted in traditional dishes. Thai and Chinese entrées are also seen on the international menu. Welcome and Farewell dinners are formal affairs, with items such as lobster and tenderloin on the menu. The pool bar has grilled and fast food items. Late at night, savory midnight snacks are served in lounges.

## Spas

The small spa does not offer mega–cruise pampering; however, passengers can book massage and beauty treatments throughout the day. The beauty salon offers hair styling for both men and women.

## Bars/Entertainment

A program of daytime entertainment consists of classes (including language, dancing, and mixology), games, quizzes, and contests. During the evening, head to the aptly named Merry Deck. Nightly musicians at the Stars Lounge invite passengers of all ages to strut their stuff on stage; there's also dancing in the Reflections Lounge. Expect traditional cabaret-style shows with Broadway musical numbers, and more obscure Greek tunes on the Stars Lounge program.

## Pros and Cons

**Pros:** this smaller vessel carries fewer passengers for a less crowded atmosphere; spacious staterooms are available, particularly in higher categories; outgoing and knowledgeable local crew and officers.

**Cons:** noisy engines can be heard on sundecks; a helipad is visible at bow of ship; standard interior cabins feel cramped and offer little storage space.

| Cabin Type | Size (sq. ft.) |
| --- | --- |
| Suite | 450+ |
| Junior Suite | 350+ |
| Deluxe Ocean View | 180+ |
| Standard Interior | 120+ |

### FAST FACTS

- 8 passenger decks
- 1 restaurant, buffet
- Safe, refrigerator (some)
- 2 pools
- Fitness classes, gym, sauna, spa
- Bars, casino, dance club, library
- Children's programs
- Laundry service
- Internet terminal, Wi-Fi

**2**

**LOUIS CRUISES**

Cabin on *Orient Queen*

# CORAL

| | |
|---:|---|
| Crew Members | 315 |
| Entered Service | 1971; rebuilt in 1976 |
| Gross Tons | 14,194 |
| Length | 479 feet |
| Number of Cabins | 374 |
| Passenger Capacity | 968 |
| Width | 72 feet |

700 ft.

500 ft.

300 ft.

Ideal for couples, families, and groups of friends, the 968-passenger *Coral* weighs in at 14,194 tons and cruises at nearly 19 knots. The ship's itineraries are typically three- to seven-day sailings that include ports in Italy and Turkey. The seven decks named after Greek gods are outfitted with a standard array of dining areas, a bar, lounge, café, and casino. Modern conveniences include an Internet corner and the Olympia Fitness Center and Sauna. All staterooms are air-conditioned with attached showers, although due to the ship's age, there have been reports of malfunctioning plumbing and thermostats. An infirmary is located on the Dionysus Deck. Expect a multilingual passenger list and crew, who are primarily of Greek and European descent. There's an open-air swimming pool at the stern. Buffet meals are geared for large crowds; expect friendly service but a less-than-intimate cruise experience on this value-priced ship.

## Cabins

**Cabins:** Small but attractively stylish standard cabins are adequately spacious and air-conditioned. The 355 staterooms are comprised of 190 outside cabins and 165 inside. All are equipped with satellite TV, music system, direct-dial phone, safe, and mini-refrigerator. Suites have a king-size bed and lounge area with sofa. Up to four people can fit into a standard or premium inside or outside cabin. Some suites have whirlpool bathtubs.

**Bathrooms:** In larger staterooms, appointments are more upscale, with marble-like tiling for counters and shower. In standard cabins, expect tighter quarters. All bathrooms have a shower, sink, mirrored vanity, toilet, and hairdryer. Storage space is limited.

**Accessibility:** While wheelchair access is possible, facilities for disabled passengers are nonexistent. Only one wheelchair-accessible room is on the Cedars Deck.

## Restaurants

The Horizon Buffet is open for breakfast, lunch, and dinner. For a sit-down full-service meal typical of an upscale restaurant, head to the more formal Mermaid Restaurant, where a dedicated waiter will serve a multicourse dinner consisting of appetizer, salad, soup, entrée, and dessert. Mediterranean, Greek and Turkish flavors are highlighted in traditional dishes. Thai

*Coral* at sea

and Chinese entrees are also seen on the international menu. Welcome and Farewell dinners are formal affairs, with such items as lobster and tenderloin on the menu. The pool bar has grilled and fast-food items. Later at night, savory snacks are served in lounges.

## Spas

The small spa does not offer mega-cruise pampering; however, passengers can book basic massage and beauty treatments. The salon offers hair styling for both men and women.

## Bars/Entertainment

A program of daytime entertainment consists of classes (including language, dancing, and mixology), games, quizzes, and contests. At night, entertainment is found on the so-called Merry Deck. Musicians play at the Stars Lounge, and there's dancing at the Reflections Lounge. Expect traditional cabaret-style shows with Broadway-musical numbers, and more obscure Greek tunes on the Stars Lounge program.

## Pros and Cons

**Pros:** fewer crowds than on larger megaships; spacious higher-level category staterooms; short, reasonably priced port-intensive routes.

**Cons:** old ship with noisy engines that can be heard on sundecks; helipad is visible at bow of ship; standard interior cabins are cramped and offer little storage space.

| Cabin Type | Size (sq. ft.) |
| --- | --- |
| Suite | 450+ |
| Junior Suite | 350+ |
| Deluxe Ocean View | 180+ |
| Standard Interior | 120+ |

### FAST FACTS

- 7 passenger decks
- 1 restaurant, buffet
- Safe, refrigerator (some)
- 1 pool
- Fitness classes, gym, sauna, spa
- 5 bars, casino, dance club, library
- Children's program
- Laundry service
- Internet terminal, Wi-Fi

**2**

**LOUIS CRUISES**

*Coral* cabin

# MSC CRUISES

More widely known as one of the world's largest cargo shipping companies, MSC has operated cruises with an eclectic fleet since the late 1980s. When the line introduced two graceful, medium-size ships in 2003 and 2004, it ushered in an era of new ship-

Pool deck after dark

building that has seen the fleet grow faster than any other European cruise line. This line is growing into a major player in both Europe and the Caribbean.

☎ *800/666–9333*
⊕ *www.msccruisesusa. com* ☞ *Cruise Style: Premium.*

MSC blankets the Mediterranean nearly year-round with a dizzying selection of cruise itineraries that allow a lot of time in ports of call and include few if any sea days. In summer months, several ships sail off to northern Europe to ply the Baltic. Itineraries planned for repositioning sailings visit some intriguing, off-the-beaten-track ports of call that other cruise lines bypass.

No glitz, no clutter—just elegant simplicity—is the standard of MSC's seaworthy interior decor. Extensive use of marble, brass, and wood reflects the best of Italian styling and design; clean lines and bold colors set their modern sophisticated tone.

MSC adopts some activities that appeal to American passengers without abandoning those preferred by Europeans; however, regardless of the itinerary, be prepared for an Italian-influenced experience. Also expect to hear announcements in several languages.

### Food
Dinner on MSC ships is a traditional multiple-course event centered on authentic Italian fare. Menus list Mediterranean regional specialties and classic favorites prepared from scratch. Some favorites include

lamb-and-mushroom quiche (a Tuscan dish) and veal scaloppini with tomatoes and mozzarella (a recipe from Sorrento in Campania). Although food is still prepared the Italian way, in a nod to American tastes broiled chicken breast, grilled salmon, and Caesar salad are additions to the dinner menu that are always available. Healthy Choice and vegetarian items are offered as well as tempting sugar-free desserts. A highlight is the bread, freshly baked on board daily. Pizza served in the buffet is some of the best at sea. The nightly midnight buffet is a retro food feast missing from most of today's cruises. Room service is always available, though the options are somewhat limited.

## Entertainment

In addition to the guest lecturers, computer classes, and cooking lessons featured in the enrichment programs, Italian-language classes are a popular option. Nightly shows accentuate the cruise line's Mediterranean heritage; there might be a flamenco show in the main show room and live music for listening and dancing in the smaller lounges, although the disco is a happening late-night spot.

MSC entertainment staff members shine offstage as well as in front of the spotlight. They seek out passengers traveling solo, who might be looking for activity or dance partners, so that they feel fully included in the cruise.

## Fitness and Recreation

Up-to-date exercise equipment, a jogging track, and basic fitness classes for all levels are available in the fitness centers.

Spa treatments include a variety of massages, body wraps, and facials that can be scheduled à la carte or combined in packages to encompass an afternoon or the entire cruise. The hottest hair-styling techniques and nail services are offered in the salons. Unlike most cruise lines, MSC Cruises operates its own spas.

## Your Shipmates

Most passengers are couples in the 35- to 55-year-old range, as well as some family groups who prefer the international atmosphere prevalent on board. Although more than half the passengers on Caribbean itineraries are North Americans, expect a more international mix on European cruises, with North Americans in the minority.

KNOWN FOR

■ **Italian Heritage:** MSC embraces its Italian heritage and style—not to flaunt it, but to share it.

■ **Sophia Loren:** An Italian treasure, the iconic movie actress serves as godmother to MSC's ships.

■ **Affordability:** MSC affords a contemporary cruise experience at favorable price points.

■ **Family-friendliness:** With a kids-sail-free policy, MSC Cruises' ships are ideally suited for family cruise vacations.

■ **Eco-friendliness:** If you're looking for a "green" cruise, MSC Cruises has received many awards for its commitment to safeguarding the environment.

Top: Miniature golf is family fun
Bottom: *MSC Lirica*

2

MSC CRUISES

Top: Thermal suite
Middle: Expansive pool deck
Bottom: *MSC Lirica* suite
with balcony

### Dress Code

Two formal nights are standard on seven-night cruises, and three may be scheduled on longer sailings. Men are encouraged to wear dark suits, but sport coats and ties are appropriate. All other evenings are casual, although jeans are discouraged in restaurants. It's requested that no shorts be worn in public areas after 6 pm.

### Junior Cruisers

Children ages 3 to 17 are welcome to participate in age-appropriate youth programs. The Mini Club is for ages 3 to 8, Junior Club for ages 9 to 12, and Teenage Club for youths 13 years and older. Counselors organize daily group activities such as arts and crafts, painting, treasure hunts, games, a mini-Olympics, and shows. Children under age three may use the playroom if accompanied at all times by an adult. Babysitting can be arranged for a fee once you're on board.

### Service

Service can be inconsistent, yet it's more than acceptable, even if it's not overly gracious. The mainly Italian staff can seem befuddled by American habits and expectations. Ongoing training and improved English proficiency for staff are top priorities for MSC, and these weaknesses are showing improvement.

### Tipping

For cruises of eight nights or less, customary gratuities are added to your shipboard account in the amount of €7 per person per day for adults and half that amount for children; for longer cruises, the customary daily amount is €6. You can always adjust these amounts at the reception desk or even pay in cash, if you prefer. Automatic 15% gratuities are incorporated into all bar purchases. You may also reward staff in the spa and casino for exceptional service.

---

**CHOOSE THIS LINE IF ...**

You appreciate authentic Italian cooking. This is the real thing, not an Olive Garden clone.

You want your ship to look like a ship. MSC's vessels are very nautical in appearance.

You want the Continental flair of a premium cruise at a fair price.

## Past Passengers

After sailing on MSC Cruises once, you are eligible to join the MSC Club by completing the registration form found in your cabin or by writing to the club through the line's website. Membership benefits include discounts on your cruise fare for the best itineraries, travel cancellation insurance, shore excursions, and even onboard purchases. You will also receive *MSC Club News* magazine.

Membership levels are achieved on a point system determined by the number of cruises taken. Classic members have up to 21 points; Silver, between 22 and 42 points; Gold, 43 points and over. Silver and Gold members receive pins to commemorate their status.

HELPFUL HINTS

All-inclusive packages for adults and children may be purchased before boarding, and the packages even include stateroom minibar.

For cruises in Europe, as well as transatlantic cruises departing from Europe, the onboard currency is the euro.

To give young passengers under age 18 a taste of independence without overspending their allowance, parents can purchase a prepaid Teen Card for use on board.

You may gamble up to a maximum of €2,000 per day in the casino if you link your key card to a credit card.

Entertainment is designed with the nationality and preferences of the passengers in mind and shows are introduced by a multilingual host in Italian, English, French, German, and Spanish.

2

MSC CRUISES

DON'T CHOOSE THIS LINE IF ...

Announcements in more than one language get on your nerves.

You aren't able to accept things that are not always done the American way.

You prefer myriad dining choices and casual attire. MSC cruises have assigned seating and observe a dress code.

# FANTASIA-CLASS
MSC Fantasia, Splendida, Divina

| | |
|---|---|
| Crew Members | 1,332 |
| Entered Service | 2008, 2009, 2012 |
| Gross Tons | 137,936/137,936/140,000 |
| Length | 1,093 feet |
| Number of Cabins | 1,637/1,637/1,739 |
| Passenger Capacity | 3,274/3,274/3,502 |
| Width | 124 feet |

700 ft.

500 ft.

300 ft.

MSC Cruises' newest ships are also their largest and include the MSC Yachts Club—luxury suites with their own private library, lounge, swimming pool, restaurant, and sundeck. The spa's well-being center has a thermal cave and therapy pool for relaxation. The children's play area includes a swimming pool with waterslide. To test your driving skills, there are Formula 1 simulators. Unusual for a cruise ship, there is also a squash court. The extensive use of various colored marbles adds a luxurious quality to the traditionally styled public lounges and a hint of Italian style as well as art deco and art nouveau touches.

MSC Cruises has always been sensitive to environmental issues, and Fantasia-class ships are on the cutting edge ecologically. They are equipped with the most innovative technological systems to guarantee savings in energy and protection of the environment, such as the water-processing systems. *MSC Divina* has more cabins and a higher double-occupancy rate and a stunning infinity pool at the back of the ship.

## Cabins

**Cabins:** A whopping 80% of staterooms have an ocean view, and 95% of those have balconies. All accommodations are beautifully decorated and comfortable yet still somewhat smaller than comparable cabins on other lines. All are furnished with two twin beds that can be combined to create a king, a vanity-desk, TV, Ethernet connection for use with laptops, adequate closet and storage space, small refrigerator, and hair dryer.

**Suites:** Yacht Club Suites that have access to a private lounge with complimentary bar and a sundeck with swimming pool, bar, and small buffet. Some suites do not have balconies, but all have access to a concierge and butler service, including laundry, dry-cleaning, and pressing services. Amenities include a Nintendo Wii console, pillow menu, complimentary minibar, Egyptian-cotton sheets, slippers and robe during the cruise, walk-in closets, and marble bathrooms with bathtubs. Standard suites are comparable in size to minisuites on most cruise ships. They feature a combination tub-shower in the bathroom, plenty of storage in a walk-in closet, and a sitting area.

Top: A cabin on *MSC Fantasia*
Bottom: Gambling in the ship's casino

**Amenities:** Bathrooms are supplied with MSC Cruises' own brand of shampoo, bath gel, and soaps, plus a handy sewing repair kit.

**Accessibility:** Forty-three cabins are wheelchair accessible, including two in the MSC Yacht Club.

## Restaurants

The two-deck-high formal restaurant serves an open seating breakfast and lunch; dinner is in two assigned seatings. Two specialty restaurants (reservation, extra charge) serve Italian and Tex-Mex cuisine. The Lido buffet is the casual-dining option for all meals; at night, the buffet restaurant also serves pizza. Coffee bars are a good snack option for times when the buffet is closed, but there is a charge for coffee and pastries. Room service has a limited menu of Continental breakfast and cold sandwiches. Midnight buffets vary nightly, ranging from snacks to a gala affair.

## Spas

The Zen-like, Asian-inspired Aurea Spa offers a full menu of treatments, some of them Asian-inspired as well. The large therapy pool and thermal suite, which has a Turkish bath and sauna, are complimentary for occupants of Yacht Club accommodations and available to all for a daily fee.

## Bars/Entertainment

After dinner, the coffee bars are the main social gathering spots, as is customary on European ships. Elaborate evening entertainment in the show lounges is designed for multilingual audiences and relies on sight and familiarity with musical selections rather than language. Bars and lounges range from sports bars, piano bars, and cigar lounges to high-energy dance spots, with the entertainment staff on hand to get things going. More sedate bars are also available for a quiet nightcap.

## Pros and Cons

**Pros:** the buffet is huge, with several serving areas and plenty of seating; extra-charge ice-cream parlors serve excellent gelato; the ship's atrium is designed as a gorgeous Italian piazza.

**Cons:** the Yacht Club sundeck can sometimes be uncomfortably windy; although there is an outdoor big-screen cinema, it's most often used for cruise line–related messages; currency on board is the euro.

| Cabin Type | Size (sq. ft.) |
| --- | --- |
| Yacht Club Suites | 237–549* |
| Standard Suite with Balcony | 290 |
| Ocean-View Balcony | 194 |
| Ocean View | 183–218 |
| Inside | 172 |

*Some forward-facing Yacht Club Suites do not have balconies.

### FAST FACTS

- 13 passenger decks
- 3 specialty restaurants, 1 dining room, buffet, ice cream parlor, pizzeria
- Internet, Wi-Fi, safe, refrigerator
- 3 pools (1 indoor), children's pool
- Fitness classes, gym, hot tubs, sauna, spa, steam room
- 13 bars, casino, dance club, library, show room, video game room
- Children's programs
- Laundry service
- Internet terminal
- No-smoking cabins

MSC CRUISES

2

Colorful shipboard decor

# MSC LIRICA, OPERA, SINFONIA, ARMONIA

| | |
|---|---|
| Crew Members | 700, 730, 700, 700 |
| Entered Service | 2003, 2004, 2004, 2004 |
| Gross Tons | 59,000/50,000/58,600/58,600 |
| Length | 824 feet |
| Number of Cabins | 780, 856, 777, 777 |
| Passenger Capacity | 1,560/1,712/1,554/1,554 |
| Width | 94 feet |

700 ft.

500 ft.

300 ft.

Though these four sleek, medium-sized ships are almost exactly the same dimensions and differ only slightly in basic layout, *Opera* holds almost 200 more passengers typically and has almost 100 extra cabins. Light and bright by day, intimate and sophisticated by night, the contemporary design may not measure up to the sizzle expected by those North American passengers who don't appreciate more understated European tastes.

Public rooms are spacious and uniformly elegant, with grand touches of marble, brass accents, and lots of wood. The refreshing lack of glitz is more than compensated for by the sparkle of glass and a mixture of primary and neutral colors. With most public areas on the lower two passenger decks, getting acclimated is a breeze. Near the elevator and stairway, lobbies make even vertical movement less challenging.

Space around the Lido pools feels particularly lavish, with two swimming pools and hot tubs.

## Cabins

**Cabins:** There are nearly a dozen stateroom price categories that fall into three basic configurations: suite with balcony, ocean view, and inside. The addition of a fourth category on *MSC Opera* (ocean-view cabin with balcony instead of some of the larger suites) increased the number of balconies available, but the size of these new balcony cabins is identical to that of the ocean-view cabins with windows only. Inside cabins were added to nearly an entire deck on *MSC Opera* as well, which accounts for the higher double-occupancy rate.

**Suites:** Suites (which would be more accurately described as minisuites) have a sitting area and a bathroom with bathtub; all but two forward-facing suites on each ship (which are now designated family-size staterooms) have a balcony as well.

**Amenities:** All cabins are comfortably decorated in primary colors and have a vanity-desk, side chair, TV, small minibar refrigerator, personal safe, and a hair dryer. Bathrooms are supplied with MSC Cruises' own brand of shampoo, bath gel, and soaps, plus a handy sewing repair kit. Suites also have a computer connection.

**Accessibility:** Four interior cabins on *MSC Lirica, Sinfonia,* and *Armonia* and five on *MSC Opera* are wheelchair accessible and measure 226 square feet.

Top: L'Approdo Restaurant
Bottom: *MSC Opera* stateroom with balcony

**2**

**MSC CRUISES**

## Restaurants

Two formal restaurants serve Mediterranean- and Italian-accented cuisine in traditional early and late assigned seatings; one restaurant also offers sit-down breakfast and lunch, both in open seating. The Lido buffet serves casual breakfast, lunch, and dinner during set hours. Although there is no true alternative dining restaurant, a casual dining area adjacent to the Lido buffet has outdoor tables protected from the elements by overhead canvas where meals can be enjoyed. A poolside grill and pizzeria offer additional casual options. Although you'll find croissants available in the morning at the coffee bar, you'll pay extra for coffee there. Room service is limited to a menu that includes a Continental breakfast and cold sandwiches. Midnight buffets vary nightly, ranging from themed snack-type offerings to a gala affair.

## Spas

The Zen-like, Asian-inspired Aurea Spa offers a full menu of treatments, some of them also Asian-inspired. The thermal suite, with aromatherapy infused Turkish bath and sauna, is available to all for a daily fee.

## Bars/Entertainment

After dinner, the coffee bars are the main social gathering spots. Elaborate evening entertainment in the show lounges is designed for multilingual audiences and relies on sight and familiarity with musical selections rather than language. Bars and lounges range from high-energy dance spots, with the entertainment staff on hand to get things going, to more sedate spots for a nightcap.

## Pros and Cons

**Pros:** specialty coffees and alcoholic beverages are reasonably priced; extravagant midnight buffets are worth attending; high above the stern, the disco is a cozy place to sit until the volume and action crank up.

**Cons:** oddly, only the forward and aft elevators and stairwells reach all decks; there are no aft-facing cabins with balconies; meal times are designed according to European tastes and begin late when ships are in the Mediterranean.

| Cabin Type | Size (sq. ft.) |
|---|---|
| Suite with Balcony | 247 |
| Family Staterooms | 236 |
| Ocean View with Balcony | 140 |
| Ocean View/ Interior | 140 |
| Inside | 140 |

## FAST FACTS

- 9 passenger decks
- 2 dining rooms, buffet, pizzeria
- Internet (some), Wi-Fi, safe, minibar
- 2 pools
- Fitness classes, gym, hot tubs, sauna, spa, steam room
- 8 bars, casino, dance club, library, show room, video game room
- Children's programs
- Laundry service
- Internet terminal
- No-smoking cabins

*MSC Lirica* sauna

# MUSICA-CLASS
*MSC Musica, Orchestra, Poesia, Magnifica*

| | |
|---|---|
| **Crew Members** | 987 |
| **Entered Service** | 2006, 2007, 2008, 2010 |
| **Gross Tons** | 92,400 |
| **Length** | 964 feet |
| **Number of Cabins** | 1,275, 1,275, 1,275, 1,259 |
| **Passenger Capacity** | 2,550, 2,550, 2,550, 2,518 |
| **Width** | 106 feet |

700 ft.

500 ft.

300 ft.

MSC Cruises took a giant leap into mainstream cruising with the introduction of this large and entirely new ship class. Highlights of the Musica-class design are a three-deck central foyer, where a piano is suspended on a transparent floor, à la carte restaurants, large-screen outdoor cinemas, and, on *MSC Magnifica,* a covered outdoor pool with retractable roof.

Italian culture prevails throughout, and serves as an important part of the entire cruise experience. Interiors are a blend of art deco and art nouveau themes as well as the authentic Italian designs for which other MSC Cruises ships are known. The extensive use of various colored marbles adds a luxurious quality to public spaces. In addition to its soothing Zen garden and Oriental music, the sushi bar is a bonus to the dining experience.

## Cabins
**Cabins:** A whopping 80% of staterooms have an ocean view, and 65% have balconies. Superior balcony staterooms are considerably roomier than standard staterooms with a balcony. Beautifully decorated in jewel-tone colors, all are comfortable yet somewhat smaller than the average cabins found on the new ships of other cruise lines. All cabins are furnished with two twin beds that can be combined to create a king, a vanity-desk, TV, adequate closet and storage space, small refrigerator, hair dryer, and have a broadband connection for a laptop.

**Suites:** Suites, which compare to minisuites on most cruise ships, feature a combination tub-shower in the bathroom, a walk-in closet, plenty of storage, and a sitting area.

**Amenities:** Bathrooms are supplied with MSC Cruises' own brand of shampoo, bath gel, and soaps, plus a handy sewing repair kit.

**Accessibility:** Seventeen cabins (16 on *MSC Magnifica*) that measure 226 square feet are wheelchair accessible.

## Restaurants
Two formal restaurants serve Mediterranean- and Italian-accented cuisine in traditional early and late assigned seatings; one restaurant also offers sit-down breakfast and lunch in open seating. Two adjoining buffet restaurants, which during the day seem like a single dining area with long serving counters, are casual

*Musica theater*

dining options for breakfast and lunch. At night, the aft buffet restaurant is reserved for seated dining with a steak-house menu and tables set with linens for an extra charge; the forward buffet restaurant serves pizza. The à la carte Asian and sushi specialty restaurants require reservations and also carry an additional charge. Room service is limited to a menu that includes a Continental breakfast and cold sandwiches. Midnight buffets vary nightly, ranging from themed snack-type offerings to a traditional shipboard gala affair.

## Spas

The Zen-like Aurea Spa with its Asian accents offers a full menu of treatments, some of them Asian-inspired as well. The large therapy pool and thermal suite, which has both a Turkish bath and sauna, are available to all for a daily fee.

## Bars/Entertainment

After dinner the coffee bars are the main social gathering spots. Elaborate evening entertainment in the show lounges is designed for multilingual European audiences and relies on sight and familiarity with musical selections rather than language. Bars and lounges range from spots to enjoy jazz or a cigar to high-energy nightclubs, where the entertainment staff is on hand to encourage participation. More sedate bars are ideal for a quiet nightcap.

## Pros and Cons

**Pros:** there's a walking track high atop the ship as well as a covered promenade; private gaming rooms for serious gamblers add a Las Vegas vibe to the casinos; smoking is limited to one lounge and outside deck spaces.

**Cons:** announcements are made in several languages; boat drill instructions, also given in several languages, can seem endless; some in-cabin TV programming might be considered too "adult" for family viewing.

| Cabin Type | Size (sq. ft.) |
|---|---|
| Suites | 269 |
| Superior Ocean-View Balcony | 191 |
| Ocean-View Balcony | 161 |
| Ocean View | 183 |
| Inside | 151 |

## FAST FACTS

- 12 passenger decks
- Specialty restaurant, 2 dining rooms, 2 buffets, ice cream parlor, pizzeria
- Internet, Wi-Fi, safe, refrigerator
- 2 pools (1 indoor, *MSC Magnifica* only), children's pool
- Fitness classes, gym, hot tubs, sauna, spa, steam room
- 9 bars, casino, dance club, library, show room, video game room
- Children's programs
- Laundry service
- Internet terminal
- No-smoking cabins

*Orchestra* at sea

# NORWEGIAN CRUISE LINE

Norwegian Cruise Line (originally known as Norwegian Caribbean Line) set sail in 1966 with
an entirely new concept: regularly
scheduled Caribbean cruises from
the then-obscure port of Miami.
Good food and friendly service
combined with value fares estab-

Cirque du Soleil–style extravaganza on
Norwegian Cruise Line

lished Norwegian as a winner for active adults and families. With the
introduction of the now-retired SS *Norway* in 1979, Norwegian ushered in the era of cruises on megasize ships. Innovative and forward-
looking, Norwegian has been a cruise-industry leader for four
decades, and is as much at home in Europe as it is in the Caribbean.

☎ *305/436–4000*
*or 800/327–7030*
⊕ *www.ncl.com*
☞ *Cruise Style:*
*Mainstream.*

Noted for top-quality, high-energy entertainment and
emphasis on fitness facilities and programs, Norwegian combines action, activities, and a variety of dining
options in a casual, free-flowing atmosphere. Freestyle
cruising signaled an end to rigid dining schedules and
dress codes. Norwegian ships now offer a host of flexible dining options that allow passengers to eat in the
main dining rooms or any of a number of à la carte and
specialty restaurants at any time and with whom they
please. Now co-owned by Genting Hong Kong Limited and Apollo Management, a private equity company, Norwegian continues to be an industry innovator.

From a distance, most cruise ships look so similar
that it's often difficult to tell them apart, but Norwegian's largest, modern ships stand out with their
distinctive use of hull art. Each new ship is distinguished by murals extending from bow to midship.

### Food
Main dining rooms serve what is traditionally deemed
Continental fare, although it's about what you would
expect at a really good hotel banquet. Health-conscious
menu selections are nicely prepared, and vegetarian
choices are always available. Where Norwegian really

shines is the specialty restaurants, especially the French-Mediterranean Le Bistro (on all ships), the pan-Asian restaurants, and steak houses (on the newer ships). As a rule of thumb, the newer the ship, the wider the variety, because new ships were purpose-built with as many as 10 or more places to eat. You may find Spanish tapas, an Italian trattoria, a steak house, a pub, and a pan-Asian restaurant complete with a sushi and sashimi bar and teppanyaki room. Most carry a cover charge or are priced à la carte and require reservations. A Norwegian staple, the late-night Chocoholic Buffet continues to be a favorite event.

## Entertainment

More high jinks than highbrow, entertainment after dark features extravagant Las Vegas–style revues presented in main show lounges by lavishly costumed singers and dancers. Other performers might include comedians, magicians, jugglers, and acrobats. Passengers can get into the act by taking part in talent shows or step up to the karaoke microphone. Live bands play for dancing and listening in smaller lounges, and each ship has a lively dance club. Some ships include shows by Chicago's world-famous Second City improvisational comedy company. With the launch of *Norwegian Epic* in 2010, the Blue Man Group and Cirque Productions (a U.S.-based company somewhat similar in style to Cirque du Soleil) joined Norwegian's talent line-up.

Casinos, bingo sessions, and art auctions are well attended. Adult games, particularly the competitive ones, are fun to participate in and provide laughs for audience members. Goofy pool games are a Norwegian staple, and the ships' bands crank up the volume during afternoon and evening deck parties.

## Fitness and Recreation

Mandara Spa offers exotic spa treatments fleetwide on Norwegian, although facilities vary widely. Spa treatments include a long menu of massages, body wraps, and facials, and current trends in hair and nail services are offered in the salons. The latest addition on board is a medi-spa physician, who can create individualized treatment plans using nonsurgical treatments such as Botox Cosmetic. State-of-the-art exercise equipment, jogging tracks, and basic fitness classes are available at no charge. There's a fee for personal training, body composition analysis, and specialized classes such as yoga and Pilates.

2

NORWEGIAN CRUISE LINE

### KNOWN FOR

■ **Dining Options:** Norwegian Cruise Line is an industry innovator in onboard dining, from open seating dining rooms to specialty restaurants.

■ **Casual Atmosphere:** With no dress code, Norwegian's ships have shed the "stuffy" reputation of cruises in the past.

■ **Entertainment:** Their partnership with widely recognized acts and shows has made Norwegian a leader in entertainment at sea.

■ **Itineraries:** With some exceptions, Norwegian's sailings don't stray far from the tried-and-true one-week length.

■ **Family-friendliness:** Numerous connecting staterooms and suites on Norwegian's ships can be combined to create multicabin accommodations ideal for families.

*Norwegian Jewel* spa relaxation suite

Top: Casino play
Middle: Stay connected
to the Internet.
Bottom: *Norwegian Dream*
Superior Ocean-View stateroom

### Your Shipmates

Norwegian's mostly American cruise passengers are active couples ranging from their mid-thirties to mid-fifties. Many families enjoy cruising on Norwegian ships during holidays and summer months. Longer cruises and more exotic itineraries attract passengers in the over-55 age group.

### Dress Code

Resort casual attire is appropriate at all times; the option of one formal evening is available on all cruises of seven nights and longer. Most passengers actually raise the casual dress code a notch to what could be called casual chic attire.

### Junior Cruisers

For children and teens, each Norwegian vessel offers a Kid's Crew program of supervised entertainment for young cruisers ages 2 to 17. Younger children are split into three groups, ages 2 to 5, 6 to 9, and 10 to 12; activities range from storytelling, games, and arts and crafts to dinner with counselors, pajama parties, and treasure hunts. Certain ships feature Nickelodeon programming, and the presence of favorite characters is a highlight for junior cruisers.

Group Port Play is available in the children's area to accommodate parents booked on shore excursions. Evening babysitting services are available for a fee. Parents whose children are not toilet trained are issued a beeper to alert them when diaper changing is necessary. Reduced fares are charged for third and fourth guests in the same stateroom, including all children. Infants under six months of age cannot travel on Norwegian ships.

For teens ages 13 to 17, options include sports, pool parties, teen disco, movies, and video games. Some ships have their own cool clubs where teens hang out in adult-free zones.

## CHOOSE THIS LINE IF ...

Doing your own thing is your idea of a real vacation. You could almost remove your watch and just go with the flow.

You want to leave your formal dress-up wardrobe at home.

You're competitive. There's always a pickup game in progress on the sports courts.

## Service

Somewhat inconsistent, service is nonetheless congenial. Although crew members tended to be outgoing Caribbean islanders in the past; they have largely been replaced by Asians and Eastern Europeans who are well trained yet are inclined to be more reserved.

## Tipping

A fixed service charge of $12 per person per day is added to shipboard accounts. An automatic 15% gratuity is added to bar tabs. Staff members may also accept cash gratuities. Passengers in suites who have access to concierge and butler services are asked to offer a cash gratuity at their own discretion.

## Past Passengers

Upon completion of your first Norwegian cruise you're automatically enrolled in Latitudes, the club for repeat passengers. Membership benefits accrue based on the number of cruises completed: Bronze (1 through 4), Silver (5 through 8), Gold (9 through 13), and Platinum (14 or more). Everyone receives *Latitudes*, Norwegian's e-magazine, Latitudes pricing, Latitudes check-in at the pier, a ship pin, access to a special customer service desk and liaison on board, and a members-only cocktail party hosted by the captain. Higher tiers receive a welcome basket, an invitation to the captain's cocktail party, and dinner in Le Bistro, and priority for check-in, tender tickets, and disembarkation.

### HELPFUL HINTS

Norwegian's Signature Trio dining package saves you 15% if you book three dinners before sailing.

Popular Nickelodeon characters make regular appearances for photo opportunities on certain Norwegian ships and you don't have to pay for pictures if you use your own camera.

Although Norwegian has one of the newest fleets at sea, the oldest ships just don't have quite the panache or as many Freestyle dining venues as are found on the newer ships.

Children three years old and younger dine free in specialty restaurants, and children ages 4 to 12 can eat from the complimentary kids menu or a specialty kids menu for a reduced cover charge.

While the ships are very family-friendly, the line has removed all its self-service laundries to add more inside staterooms.

### DON'T CHOOSE THIS LINE IF ...

You don't like to pay extra for food on a ship. All the best specialty restaurants have extra charges.

You don't want to stand in line. There are lines for nearly everything.

You don't want to hear announcements. They're frequent on these ships—and loud.

# NORWEGIAN EPIC

| | |
|---|---|
| Crew Members | 1,708 |
| Entered Service | 2010 |
| Gross Tons | 153,000 |
| Length | 1,081 feet |
| Number of Cabins | 2,114 |
| Passenger Capacity | 4,100 |
| Width | 133 feet |

700 ft.

500 ft.

300 ft.

NCL's newest and largest ship is all about the entertainment. While *Norwegian Epic* has a unique new cabin design and more than 20 places to dine, entertainment options include Blue Man Group, Howl at the Moon (a dueling-pianos show), the Second City comedy ensemble, Legends in Concert, and a theatrical dining experience with Cirque du Soleil–style performers. For the kids, there are Nickelodeon characters on board and a character breakfast. The only extra entertainment charges are for the Cirque dinner show and the character breakfast.

Also epic are the numerous bars and lounges. For the coolest drinks at sea, *Norwegian Epic* has an ice bar (for an extra charge). Expansive areas are reserved for children and teens and the aft pool is exclusively for adults during the day. The other pool area has three waterslides and a plethora of lounge chairs. For the best view of the sea, there is a rock-climbing wall.

## Cabins

**Cabins:** *Epic*'s New Wave–style staterooms have curved walls and a unique bathroom with toilet and shower in separate compartments and the sink in the main cabin area. All have a sitting area with sofa and table and exceedingly generous storage. All outside staterooms have a balcony. Several spa-accommodations categories have Zen-like appointments and key card access to the spa facilities.

**Courtyard Villas and Penthouses:** Courtyard Villas and Penthouses and Owner's suites have an exclusive concierge lounge and restaurant in addition to a shared private courtyard with pool, hot tub, sundeck, and small gym.

**Studios:** These small cabins are strictly for solo cruisers. Although each is tiny, it has a private bath and occupants have access to the Studio Lounge, a shared lounge for hanging out.

**Amenities:** A small refrigerator, tea/coffeemaker, safe, Wi-Fi, duvets on beds, a wall-mounted hair dryer, and bathrobes are standard. Showers have a shampoo/bathgel dispenser on the wall. Suites have a whirlpool tub, an entertainment center with a CD/DVD player, and concierge and butler service.

**Accessibility:** Some staterooms interconnect in most categories. Forty-two staterooms are wheelchair accessible.

Top: *Norwegian Epic* casino
Bottom: *Norwegian Epic* Courtyard Penthouse

## Restaurants

Two main dining rooms serve open seating breakfast, lunch, and dinner. Specialty restaurants, including Norwegian's signature French restaurant Le Bistro, Cagney's Steakhouse, a Chinese restaurant, sushi bar, teppanyaki room, a South American churrascaria, and an Italian trattoria–style (reservations, cover charge for all). Screens located throughout the ship display wait times for tables. Casual choices are the Lido buffet for breakfast, lunch, and dinner; O'Sheehan's Pub for soup, sandwiches, and snacks; and the poolside grill for lunch. The Atrium Bar serves specialty coffees for an additional charge. While the 24-hour room-service menu is somewhat limited, made-to-order pizza will be delivered to you anywhere on the ship for a fee.

## Spas

Mandara Spa offers unique and exotic spa treatments, including a long menu of massages, body wraps, facials, and teeth whitening. There is also a medi-spa physician on hand who can create individualized treatment plans using nonsurgical treatments that include Botox. The spa features a thermal suite with multitreatment therapy pool, wet and dry saunas, and relaxation area with heated lounges for which there is a charge.

## Bars/Entertainment

Even though show reservations are required, almost all show options are available for no additional charge (Cirque Dreams & Dinner includes a dining charge). Bars and lounges run the gamut from a blues and jazz club, comedy club, an ice bar, martini bar, a beer and whiskey bar, and lounges with bowling alleys, including a pub. Most feature musicians for listening or dancing, but if you want a quiet getaway, the bar at the adult pool is open late for an alfresco nightcap.

## Pros and Cons

**Pros:** restaurant and show reservations can be made prior to sailing; the ice bar is unique; *Norwegian Epic*'s The Haven of luxury suites features more private amenities than older fleetmates.

**Cons:** with their frosted shower and toilet compartments, privacy can be an issue in standard bathrooms; the necessity of reservations for dining and headline shows eliminates spontaneity; pools are great for cooling off but not adequate for swimming laps.

| Cabin Type | Size (sq. ft.) |
|---|---|
| Owner's Suite/ Courtyard Villa | 852/506 |
| Penthouse | 322 |
| Deluxe Balcony | 245 |
| Ocean View with Balcony | 216 |
| Inside | 128 |
| Studio | 100 |
| Square footage includes balconies | |

## FAST FACTS

- 19 passenger decks
- 8 restaurants, 2 dining rooms, buffet, ice cream parlor, pizzeria
- Internet, Wi-Fi, safe, refrigerator, DVD (some)
- 3 pools, children's pool
- Fitness classes, gym, hot tubs, spa
- 10 bars, casino, dance club, library, 3 show rooms, video game room
- Children's programs
- Dry-cleaning, laundry service
- Internet terminal
- No-smoking cabins

*Norwegian Epic* at sea

**2**

**NORWEGIAN CRUISE LINE**

# DAWN-CLASS
*Norwegian Star, Norwegian Dawn*

| | |
|---|---|
| Crew Members | 1,066, 1,065 |
| Entered Service | 2001, 2002 |
| Gross Tons | 92, 250/91,740 |
| Length | 965 feet |
| Number of Cabins | 1,122, 1,174 |
| Passenger Capacity | 2,244, 2,348 (2,683 max) |
| Width | 105 feet |

700 ft.

500 ft.

300 ft.

Purpose-built for Norwegian's Freestyle cruising concept, *Norwegian Dawn* and *Norwegian Star* each have more than a dozen dining options, a variety of entertainment selections, and expansive facilities for children and teens.

These ships introduced Norwegian's superdeluxe Garden Villa accommodations, English pubs, and 24-hour dining in the Blue Lagoon Restaurant. Interior spaces are bright and cheerful, especially the atrium area adjacent to the outdoor promenade, which is flooded with sunlight through expansive windows. A second smaller garden atrium with a prominent waterfall leads the way to the spa lobby. Near the children's splash pool is a hot tub for parents' enjoyment.

## Cabins

**Cabins:** Norwegian ships are not noted for large staterooms, but all have a small sitting area with sofa, chair, and table. Most bathrooms are compartmentalized with a sink area, shower, and toilet separated by sliding glass doors. Every cabin has adequate closet and drawer/shelf storage, as well as limited bathroom storage. Suites have walk-in closets. Family-friendly staterooms interconnect in most categories, enabling families of nearly any size to find suitable accommodations. Nearly every stateroom has a third or fourth berth, and some can sleep as many as five and six.

**Amenities:** Cherrywood cabinetry, tropical decor, mirrored accents, a small refrigerator, tea/coffeemaker, personal safe, broadband Internet connection, duvets on beds, a wall-mounted hair dryer over the dressing table, and bathrobes for use during the cruise are standard. Bathrooms have a shampoo/bath-gel dispenser mounted on the shower wall as well as a magnifying mirror. Suites have a whirlpool tub, an entertainment center with a CD/DVD player, and concierge and butler service.

**Accessibility:** Twenty-four staterooms on *Norwegian Dawn* and 20 staterooms on *Norwegian Star* are designed for wheelchair accessibility.

Top: Cagney's Steakhouse on
*Norwegian Dawn*
Bottom: Minisuite

## Restaurants

Two complimentary dining rooms serve open seating meals for breakfast, lunch, or dinner. Specialty restaurants, including Norwegian's signature French restaurant Le Bistro, Cagney's Steakhouse, an Asian restaurant, sushi bar, teppanyaki room, Tex-Mex eatery, and Italian restaurant carry varying cover charges and require reservations. Screens located throughout the ship illustrate the status (full, moderately busy, empty) and waiting time you can expect for each restaurant on board. Casual choices are the Lido buffet for breakfast, lunch, and dinner; Blue Lagoon for soup, sandwiches, and snacks around the clock; and the poolside grill for lunch. Java Café serves specialty coffees and pastries for an extra charge. Although the 24-hour room-service menu is somewhat limited, suite occupants may order from any restaurant on the ship.

## Spas

The Mandara Spa treatments include a long menu of massages, body wraps, and facials as well as medi-spa treatment plans. With indoor lap pools, the enormous spas have what might be termed a supersize thermal suite on other ships. In addition, the pools are surrounded by lounge chairs, large whirlpools, saunas, and steam rooms; unfortunately, there is an additional charge to use these spa facilities.

## Bars/Entertainment

After attending a high-energy production show, Second City comedy performance, or a show by a featured entertainer, options for the rest of the evening range from an elegant champagne bar to an authentic English pub. You'll find music for dancing, signature Norwegian parties, and even a cigar lounge. The Star Bar's pianist and views to sea are the perfect backdrop for a quiet nightcap.

## Pros and Cons

**Pros:** show rooms have full proscenium stages for the lavish shows; you can look forward to performances by the improvisational company Second City; three-bedroom Garden Villas are among the largest suites at sea, with private whirlpools and outdoor patios.

**Cons:** Freestyle dining doesn't mean you get to eat precisely when you want; overcrowding can be a problem when the ships are fully booked; there is a charge for the most popular restaurants.

| Cabin Type | Size (sq. ft.) |
|---|---|
| Garden Villa | 5,350 |
| Owner's Suite | 750 |
| Penthouse Suite | 366 |
| Romance Suite | 288 |
| Minisuite | 229 |
| Ocean View with Balcony | 166 |
| Ocean View | 158 |
| Inside | 142 |

### FAST FACTS

- 11 passenger decks
- 7 restaurants, 2 dining rooms, buffet, ice cream parlor, pizzeria
- Internet, Wi-Fi, safe, refrigerator, DVD (some)
- 2 pools (1 indoor), children's pool
- Fitness classes, gym, hot tubs, spa
- 9 bars, casino, 2 dance clubs, library, show room, video game room
- Children's programs
- Dry-cleaning, laundry service
- Internet terminal
- No-smoking cabins

*Norwegian Dawn at sea*

2

NORWEGIAN CRUISE LINE

# JEWEL-CLASS
*Norwegian Jewel, Norwegian Jade, Norwegian Pearl, Norwegian Gem*

| | |
|---|---|
| **Crew Members** | |
| 1,081, 1,075, 1,084, 1,092 | |
| **Entered Service** | |
| 2005, 2006, 2006, 2007 | |
| 700 ft. **Gross Tons** | |
| 93,502/93,558/93,530/93,530 | |
| **Length** | |
| 965 feet | |
| 500 ft. **Number of Cabins** | |
| 1,188, 1,201, 1,197, 1,197 | |
| **Passenger Capacity** | |
| 2,376, 2,402, 2,394, 2,394 | |
| 300 ft. **Width** | |
| 105 feet | |

Jewel-class ships are the next step in the continuing evolution of Freestyle ship design: the interior location of some public rooms and restaurants has been tweaked since the introduction of Freestyle cruising vessels, and new categories of deluxe accommodations have been added.

These ships have more than a dozen dining alternatives, a variety of entertainment options, and expansive areas reserved for children and teens. Pools have waterslides and a plethora of lounge chairs, although when your ship is full, it can be difficult to find one in a prime location. *Norwegian Pearl* and *Norwegian Gem* introduced the line's first rock-climbing walls, as well as Bliss Lounge, which has trendy South Beach decor, and the first full-size 10-pin bowling alleys on modern cruise ships.

## Cabins
**Cabins:** Norwegian ships are not noted for large staterooms, but all have a small sitting area with sofa, chair, and table. Every cabin has adequate closet and drawer/shelf storage, as well as limited bathroom storage. Suites have walk-in closets. Some staterooms interconnect in most categories.

**Garden and Courtyard Villas:** Garden Villas, with three bedrooms, a living-dining room, and private deck garden with a spa tub, are among the largest suites at sea. Courtyard Villas—not as large as Garden Villas—have an exclusive concierge lounge and a shared private courtyard with pool, hot tub, sundeck, and small gym.

**Amenities:** A small refrigerator, tea/coffeemaker, personal safe, broadband Internet connection, duvets on beds, a wall-mounted hair dryer, and bathrobes are standard. Bathrooms have a shampoo/bath-gel dispenser on the shower wall and a magnifying mirror. Suites have a whirlpool tub, an entertainment center with a CD/DVD player, and concierge and butler service.

**Accessibility:** Twenty-seven staterooms are wheelchair accessible.

Top: *Norwegian Jewel's* Azura restaurant
Bottom: Hydropool in the spa

## Restaurants

Two main complimentary dining rooms serve open seating breakfast, lunch, and dinner. Specialty restaurants, including Norwegian's signature French restaurant Le Bistro, Cagney's Steakhouse, an Asian restaurant, sushi bar, teppanyaki room, tapas and salsa eatery, and an Italian trattoria–style restaurant carry varying cover charges and require reservations. Screens located throughout the ship illustrate the status (full, moderately busy, empty) and waiting time you can expect for each restaurant on board. Casual choices are the Lido buffet for breakfast, lunch, and dinner; Blue Lagoon for soup, sandwiches, and snacks around the clock; and the poolside grill for lunch. Java Café serves specialty coffees and pastries for an additional charge. Although the 24-hour room-service menu is somewhat limited, suite occupants may order from any restaurant on the ship.

## Spas

The Mandara Spa's treatments include a long menu of massages, body wraps, and facials and include the services of a medi-spa physician. Spa facilities include an enormous thermal suite with hydrotherapy pool, heated lounges, steam rooms, and saunas for which there is a charge.

## Bars/Entertainment

Your evening might start with a high-energy production show, Second City comedy performance, or a show by a featured entertainer, then continue in the bar complex that includes a beer and whiskey bar, martini bar, and a champagne bar. You'll find music for dancing, signature Norwegian parties, and even a cigar lounge. The perfect spot to end the night is the Star Bar with its pianist and views of the pool deck and the sea.

## Pros and Cons

**Pros:** there are both main-stage and nightclub performances by Second City; the ship's tranquil library offers a quiet escape with a sea view; Courtyard Villa accommodations are like a ship within a ship and have a private pool area.

**Cons:** there is a fee for use of the thermal suites in the spa; Freestyle dining doesn't mean you can get to eat precisely when you want to; for such a large ship, the Internet center is tiny.

| Cabin Type | Size (sq. ft.) |
|---|---|
| Garden Villa | 4,390 |
| Courtyard Villa | 574 |
| Owner's Suites | 823 |
| Deluxe Owner's Suites* | 928* |
| Penthouse Suite | 575 |
| Minisuite | 284 |
| Ocean View with Balcony | 205–243 |
| Ocean View | 161 |
| Inside | 143 |

*Deluxe Owner's Suites on *Norwegian Pearl* and *Norwegian Gem* only.

### FAST FACTS

- 15 passenger decks
- 7 restaurants, 2 dining rooms, buffet, ice cream parlor, pizzeria
- Internet, Wi-Fi, safe, refrigerator, DVD (some)
- 2 pools, children's pool
- Fitness classes, gym, hot tubs, spa
- 9 bars, casino, dance club, library, show room, video game room
- Children's programs
- Dry-cleaning, laundry service
- Internet terminal
- No-smoking cabins

The sports deck

**NORWEGIAN CRUISE LINE**

**2**

# NORWEGIAN SPIRIT

| | |
|---|---|
| Crew Members | 949 |
| Entered Service | 1999 |
| Gross Tons | 75,338 |
| Length | 881 feet |
| Number of Cabins | 1,009 |
| Passenger Capacity | 2,018 (2,475 max) |
| Width | 105 feet |

700 ft.

500 ft.

300 ft.

In a curious East-goes-West journey, *Norwegian Spirit* was originally built for the Freestyle cruising concept and launched as *SuperStar Leo* for Norwegian Cruise Line's Asian parent, Genting Hong Kong Limited (formerly Star Cruises). In winter 2004, Norwegian's fledgling Hawaiian venture nearly sank when a freakish storm filled its flagship with water while it was nearing completion in Germany. With a month's worth of bookings and no new ship, arrangements were made to deploy a substitute in Hawaii and transfer *SuperStar Leo* to fill the gap left in its wake.

Rechristened in spring 2004 and updated to better suit American tastes, *Norwegian Spirit* still retains fine examples of Asian artwork. The casino is huge, and facilities for children and teens are particularly extensive, only rivaled by the Disney Cruise Line ships and Norwegian's own newer vessels.

## Cabins

**Cabins:** More than two-thirds of *Norwegian Spirit*'s cabins are outside with ocean views, and more than two-thirds of those have private balconies. Cabins have adequate space, including a sitting area with sofa, chair, and table. Every cabin has closet and drawer/shelf storage, as well as limited bathroom storage. Most bathrooms are compartmentalized with sink area, shower, and toilet separated by sliding glass doors.

**Suites:** Suites include walk-in closets and such amenities as whirlpool tubs and entertainment centers with DVD players.

**Amenities:** Light-wood cabinetry, mirrored accents, a small refrigerator, a tea/coffeemaker, a personal safe, broadband Internet connection, duvets on beds, a wall-mounted hair dryer over the dressing table, and bathrobes for use during the cruise are typical standard features. Electrical outlets are designed for Asian-style 220 volts and, although there's a 110-volt receptacle, it should be reserved for low-wattage appliances. Plug in a megawatt hair dryer, and you'll likely get to meet a ship's engineer because you blew out the power. Bathrooms have shampoo and bath gel in a shower-mounted dispenser.

**Accessibility:** Four interior staterooms are designed for wheelchair accessibility.

Top: Henry's Rub
Bottom: *Norwegian Spirit* at sea

### Restaurants

Two complimentary dining rooms serve open seating breakfast, lunch, and dinner. Specialty restaurants that carry varying cover charges and require reservations include Norwegian's signature French restaurant Le Bistro, a steak house, an Italian eatery, a Pan-Asian restaurant, a sushi and sashimi bar, and a teppanyaki room. Screens located throughout the ship illustrate the status (full to empty) and waiting time you can expect for each restaurant. Casual choices are the Lido buffet for breakfast, lunch, and dinner; Blue Lagoon for soup, sandwiches, and snacks around the clock; the poolside grill for lunch; a pizzeria; and an ice cream bar. A coffee bar serves specialty coffees and pastries priced by item. Room service is available 24 hours from a somewhat limited menu.

### Spas

While the facilities aren't as extensive as on newer ships, Mandara Spa offers a lengthy menu of massages, body wraps, and facials. A medi-spa physician is on hand to create individualized therapies. A sauna and steam room are available to all at no charge.

### Bars/Entertainment

You'll find a nice selection of bars and lounges where musicians or DJs provide dance tunes and the entertainment staff hosts Norwegian's signature late-night parties after performances by the production company, comedians, or featured entertainers in the show room. A traditional English-style pub features dartboards, big-screen TVs, and complimentary pub snacks.

### Pros and Cons

**Pros:** there is a bridge-viewing gallery in the observatory lounge; you may find solitude in the library or writing room; more than 300 staterooms connect.

**Cons:** facilities for children are more expansive than the spa and fitness center; there are no self-service laundry facilities; some top suites have forward-facing balconies that are too windy for use on sea days.

| Cabin Type | Size (sq. ft.) |
|---|---|
| Owner's Suites | 605 |
| Deluxe Penthouse | 555 |
| Penthouse | 436 |
| Ocean View Balcony | 201 |
| Ocean View | 157 |
| Interior | 149 |

### FAST FACTS

- 10 passenger decks
- 4 specialty restaurants, 2 dining rooms, buffet, ice cream parlor, pizzeria
- Wi-Fi, safe, refrigerator (some), DVD (some)
- 3 pools (2 indoor), children's pool
- Fitness classes, gym, hot tubs, sauna, spa, steam room
- 8 bars, casino, dance club, library, show room, video game room
- Children's programs
- Dry-cleaning, laundry service
- Internet terminal
- No-smoking cabins

Balcony stateroom

# OCEANIA CRUISES

This distinctive cruise line was founded by Frank Del Rio and Joe Watters, cruise-industry veterans with the know-how to satisfy the wants of inquisitive passengers. By offering itineraries to interesting ports of call and upscale touches—all for fares much lower

Oceania's *Regatta*

than you would expect—they are succeeding quite nicely. Oceania Cruises set sail in 2003 to carve a unique, almost boutique niche in the cruise industry by obtaining midsize R-class ships that formerly made up the popular Renaissance Cruises fleet. The line is now owned by Prestige Cruise Holdings.

☎ *305/514–2300*
*or 800/531–5658*
⊕ *www.oceaniacruises.*
*com* ☞ *Cruise Style:*
*Premium.*

Intimate and cozy public spaces reflect the importance of socializing on Oceania ships. Indoor lounges feature numerous conversation areas, and even the pool deck is a social center. The Patio is a shaded slice of deck adjacent to the pool and hot tubs. Defined by billowing drapes and carpeting underfoot, it is furnished with plush sofas and chairs ideal for relaxation.

Thickly padded single and double loungers are arranged around the pool, but if more privacy appeals to you, private cabanas are available for rent. Each one has a double chaise longue with a view of the sea; overhead drapery can be drawn back for sunbathing, and the side panels can be left open or closed. Waiters are on standby to offer chilled towels or serve occupants with beverages or snacks. In addition, you can request a spa service in your cabana.

Varied, destination-rich itineraries are an important characteristic of Oceania Cruises, and most sailings are in the 10- to 12-night range.

### Food

Several top cruise-industry chefs were lured away from other cruise lines to ensure that the artistry of world-renowned master chef Jacques Pépin, who

2

crafted five-star menus for Oceania, is properly carried out. The results are sure to please the most discriminating palate. Oceania simply serves some of the best food at sea, particularly impressive for a cruise line that charges far less than luxury rates. The main restaurant offers trendy, French-Continental cuisine with an always-on-the-menu steak, seafood, or poultry choice and a vegetarian option.

Intimate specialty restaurants require reservations, but there's no additional charge for Toscana, the Italian restaurant, or Polo Grill, the steak house. On *Marina*, passengers have those and more restaurants from which to choose—Jacques, the first restaurant to bear Jacques Pépin's name, serves French cuisine; Red Ginger features contemporary interpretations of Asian classics; Privée hosts private, seven-course menu degustation dinners for a single party of up to ten; and La Reserve serves exclusive wine and food pairings.

A casual dinner option is alfresco dining at the Terrace Café (the daytime Lido deck buffet). Although service is from the buffet, outdoor seating on the aft deck is transformed into a charming Mediterranean courtyard with candleholders and starched linens.

The Terrace Café also serves breakfast and lunch buffet-style, and has a small pizzeria window that operates during the day. At an outdoor poolside grill you can order up burgers, hot dogs, and sandwiches for lunch and then take a seat; waiters are at hand to serve you either at a nearby table or your lounge chair by the pool. Afternoon tea is a decadent spread of finger foods and includes a rolling dessert cart, which has to be seen to be believed.

### Entertainment

Culinary demonstrations by guest presenters and Oceania's own executive chefs are extremely popular. Lectures on varied topics, computer courses, hands-on arts and crafts classes, and wine or champagne seminars round out the popular enrichment series on board. Before arrival in ports of call, lectures are presented on the historical background, culture, and traditions of the destinations.

Evening entertainment leans toward light cabaret, solo artists, music for dancing, and conversation with fellow passengers; however, you'll find lively karaoke sessions on the schedule as well. The sophisticated, adult atmosphere on days at sea is enhanced by a combo performing jazz or easy-listening melodies poolside. Enrichment programs feature guest

## KNOWN FOR

- **Midsize Ships:** Oceania's deluxe ships are quite manageable in size: three have fewer than 850 passengers, the largest fewer than 1,300 passengers.

- **Great Destinations:** Oceania itineraries are destination oriented and offer overnights in many top ports.

- **Cuisine:** Oceania Cruises' chefs are serious about food and serve noteworthy cuisine in all restaurants on board.

- **Surprisingly Affordable:** Cruises on Oceania approach true luxury in style, but not when it comes to fares—they are quite affordable.

- **No Smoking:** Oceania ships are almost entirely smoke-free, with small, designated areas set aside for smokers.

Top: Penthouse suite
Bottom: Toscana Restaurant

lecturers who are experts in such topics as wine appreciation, culinary arts, history, and world events.

### Fitness and Recreation

The Canyon Ranch SpaClub spas and salons and well-equipped fitness centers are adequate for the number of passengers on board. In addition to individual body-toning machines and complimentary exercise classes, there's a walking-jogging track circling the top of the ship. A personal trainer is available for individual instruction for an additional charge.

### Your Shipmates

Oceania Cruises appeal to singles and couples from their late-thirties to well-traveled retirees who have the time for and prefer longer cruises. Most are American couples attracted to the casually sophisticated atmosphere, creative cuisine, and high level of service. Many are past passengers of the now-defunct Renaissance Cruises who are loyal to their favorite ships, which now offer a variety of destination-rich itineraries.

### Dress Code

Leave the formal wear at home—attire on Oceania ships is country-club casual every evening, although some guests can't help dressing up to dine in the beautifully appointed restaurants. A jacket and tie are never required for dinner, but many men wear sport jackets, as they would to dine in an upscale restaurant ashore. Jeans, shorts, T-shirts, and tennis shoes are discouraged after 6 pm in public rooms.

### Junior Cruisers

Oceania Cruises are adult-oriented and not a good choice for families, particularly those traveling with infants and toddlers. No dedicated children's facilities are available, and parents are completely responsible for their behavior and entertainment. Teenagers with sophisticated tastes (and who don't mind the absence of a video arcade) might enjoy the intriguing ports of call.

Top: Cocktails before dinner
Middle: Veranda stateroom
Bottom: Martini bar

## CHOOSE THIS LINE IF ...

Socializing plays a more important role in your lifestyle than boogying the night away.

You love to read. These ships have extensive libraries that are ideal for curling up with a good book.

You have a bad back. You're sure to love the Tranquility Beds.

## Service

Highly personalized service by a mostly European staff is crisp and efficient without being intrusive. Butlers are on hand to fulfill the requests of suite guests and will even assist with packing and unpacking when asked.

## Tipping

Gratuities of $14.50 per person per day are added to shipboard accounts for distribution to stewards and waitstaff; an additional $6 per person per day is added for occupants of suites with butler service. Passengers may adjust the amount based on the level of service experienced. An automatic 18% gratuity is added to all bar tabs for bartenders and drink servers and to all bills for salon and spa services.

## Past Passengers

After you take one Oceania cruise, you'll receive several benefits along with a free subscription to the *Oceania Club Journal*. Shipboard Club parties hosted by the captain and senior officers, complimentary amenities or exclusive privileges on select sailings, an Oceania Club membership recognition pin after 5, 10, 15, and 20 cruises, and special pricing and mailings about upcoming promotions are some of the benefits. Members further qualify for elite-level status based on the number of sailings aboard Oceania Cruises. Starting with your fifth cruise, you begin to accrue credit on every cruise you take, beginning with a $200 shipboard credit per stateroom on cruises five through nine. On your 10th cruise, you receive a $400 shipboard credit per stateroom plus complimentary gratuities on cruises 10 through 14. On your 15th cruise, you receive a $500 shipboard credit per stateroom, plus two complimentary spa treatments and complimentary gratuities on cruises 15 through 19. Once you take your 20th cruise, you get a free cruise as well as complimentary spa treatments, a shore excursion, and gratuities on all future cruises.

HELPFUL HINTS

Many Oceania voyages include airfare in the fare pricing.

Pre- or post-cruise Hotel Collection Packages are available and include private group transfers.

There is never a dining charge on Oceania ships, but cocktail and wine prices are relatively high.

You may bring up to three bottles of wine per stateroom on board from ports of call, but there's a corkage fee of $25 per bottle if you bring wine to the dining room.

Oceania Cruises offers two shore excursion collections that must be reserved prior to sailing and can save a lot of money.

Oceania was the first cruise line to upgrade their bedding to the highest standard, so you can count on a good night's sleep on one of these ships.

## DON'T CHOOSE THIS LINE IF ...

You like the action in a huge casino. Oceania casinos are small, and seats at a poker table can be difficult to get.

You want to bring your children. Most passengers book with Oceania anticipating a kid-free atmosphere.

Glitzy production shows are your thing. Oceania's show rooms are decidedly low-key.

# MARINA, RIVIERA

| | |
|---|---|
| Crew Members | 800 |
| Entered Service | 2011/2012 |
| Gross Tons | 65,000 |
| Length | 774 feet |
| Number of Cabins | 629 |
| Passenger Capacity | 1,258 |
| Width | 105 feet |

*Marina* and *Riviera* are the first brand-new ships built for Oceania Cruises and, although they are an all new design in a larger ship, they include the basic deluxe features found on the smaller fleetmates—specialty dining in intimate restaurants, country-club casual ambience, and enrichment programs. The emphasis is on destination cruising in style and the decor is classic and comfortable. With a larger ship, designers expanded some of the elements, such as the staircase in the grand foyer, which has a landing with two sweeping sets of steps.

Attention to detail is an Oceania hallmark that can be found in Privée—the private dining room that can be reserved for dinner parties—where a custom-made one-of-a-kind Lalique-crystal table is illuminated by a white Venini-glass chandelier, and fanciful Murano-glass chandeliers glitter in the buffet restaurant. A classical string quartet plays softly in the background at afternoon tea in Horizons, the observation lounge with dramatic floor-to-ceiling windows.

## Cabins

**Cabins:** All accommodations have a vanity-desk and a seating area with sofa or chair and a table, generous closet and drawer/shelf storage, marble- and granite-clad bathrooms, hair dryer, robes for use during the cruise, safe, and refrigerator. Inside staterooms have a shower only; all other categories have a separate shower and bathtub. Oceania's Tranquility Beds are dressed in high thread-count linens. Concierge-level stateroom occupants are greeted with a bottle of champagne on ice and have access to a private concierge lounge, a laptop to use during the cruise, complimentary shoeshine and pressing services, priority dining reservations, designer toiletries, and a tote bag.

**Suites:** In addition to the concierge amenities, suites have an entertainment center with a DVD and CD player, a refrigerator, walk-in closet, and marble- and granite-bathrooms with a bathtub and designer toiletries. The top three suite categories have whirlpool tubs and separate showers and a guest powder room. Oceania Suites also have a media room, while Vista and Owner's suites have private workout rooms. Butlers are on hand to coordinate reservations and serve evening canapés and dinner ordered from the ship's restaurants.

Top: Balcony suite
Bottom: Barista's Coffee Bar

**Accessibility:** Six staterooms are designed to be wheelchair-accessible.

### Restaurants

The Grand Dining Room serves open seating breakfast, lunch, and dinner. Specialty restaurants require reservations, but there's no additional charge for Toscana, the Italian restaurant; Polo Grill, the steak house; the French cuisine served in Jacques, the first restaurant to bear Jacques Pépin's name; or Red Ginger, featuring contemporary interpretations of Asian classics. Also requiring reservations are the exclusive Privée, which hosts private seven-course-menu degustation dinners for a single party of up to 10; and La Reserve, where wine and food pairings are featured. The casual buffet restaurant is open for breakfast, lunch, and dinner. In addition, a poolside grill serves hamburgers and a variety of sandwiches and salads at lunchtime, and a pizzeria is in the buffet area. Room service is available 24 hours.

### Spas

Canyon Ranch SpaClub offers a long menu of body wraps, massages with an Eastern influence, conditioning body scrubs, skin care and tanning treatments and acupuncture. Thermal suites include single-sex aromatic steam rooms. A highlight of the tranquil open-air Spa Terrace is a therapy whirlpool. All Concierge-level and suite guests have unlimited complimentary access to the private Spa Terrace; all other guests can purchase passes.

### Bars/Entertainment

Bars and lounges have an intimate quality, from the martini bar where piano music is a played, to the show lounge that offers small-scale entertainment ranging from headline acts and concerts to comedians and magicians. The observation lounge is a late night hot spot with dance music and even karaoke on tap.

### Pros and Cons

**Pros:** Baristas coffee bar is conveniently adjacent to the library; the library is well stocked with more than 2,000 books and periodicals; artists share their expertise during hands-on classes in the enrichment center.

**Cons:** self-serve laundry rooms can be crowded on sea days; there is a fee to use the hot tub adjacent to the spa; there is no charge for food and service in Le Reserve, but wine is a pricey addition.

| Cabin Type | Size (sq. ft.) |
|---|---|
| Owner's Suite/ Vista Suite | 2,000/ 1,200– 1,500 |
| Oceania Suite/ Penthouse Suite | 1,000/420 |
| Ocean View with Balcony | 282 |
| Ocean View/ Interior | 242/174 |

## FAST FACTS

- ■ 11 passenger decks
- ■ 6 specialty restaurants, 1 dining room, buffet, café, pizzeria
- ■ Wi-Fi, safe, refrigerator, DVD (some)
- ■ 1 pool
- ■ Fitness classes, gym, hot tubs, sauna, spa, steam room
- ■ 7 bars, casino, dance club, library
- ■ Dry-cleaning, laundry facilities, laundry service
- ■ Internet terminal, Wi-Fi
- ■ No-smoking cabins

**2**

**OCEANIA CRUISES**

Martinis, *Marina*

# REGATTA, NAUTICA

| | |
|---|---|
| Crew Members | 400 |
| Entered Service | 1998, 2000 |
| Gross Tons | 30,277 |
| Length | 594 feet |
| Number of Cabins | 342 |
| Passenger Capacity | 684 (824 max) |
| Width | 84 feet |

700 ft.

500 ft.

300 ft.

Carefully furnished to impart the atmosphere of a private English country manor, these midsize ships are casual yet elegant, with sweeping central staircases and abundant flower arrangements. Brocade and toile fabrics window coverings, overstuffed sofas, and wing chairs create a warm and intimate feeling throughout. The entire effect is that of a weekend retreat in the English countryside.

Authentic-looking faux fireplaces are adjacent to cozy seating areas in the Grand Bar, near the martini bar's grand piano, and in the beautiful libraries—some of the best at sea, with an enormous selection of best sellers, nonfiction, and travel books. The casinos are quite small and can feel cramped, and smoking is prohibited. Though there may be a wait for a seat at a poker table, there are enough slot machines to go around.

Other than decorative trompe-l'oeil paintings in several public areas, the artwork is unremarkable.

## Cabins

**Cabins:** Private balconies outfitted with chairs and tables add additional living space to nearly 75% of all outside accommodations. All cabins have a vanity-desk and a seating area with sofa, chair, and table. Every cabin has generous closet and drawer/shelf storage and bathroom shelves. Owner's and Vista suites have a separate living-dining room, as well as a separate powder room. Several cabins accommodate third and fourth passengers, but few have connecting doors.

**Suites:** Owner's and Vista suites have an entertainment center with a DVD and CD player, a small refrigerator, and a second TV in the bedroom; the main bathroom has a combination shower-whirlpool tub. Penthouse suites also have refrigerators and bathtubs. Butlers are on hand to coordinate reservations and serve evening canapés and dinner ordered from any of the ship's restaurants.

**Amenities:** Dark-wood cabinetry, soothing blue decor, mirrored accents, safe, Tranquility Beds, 350-thread-count linens, goose-down pillows, and silk-cut duvets are typical stateroom features. Bathrooms have a hair dryer, shampoo, lotion, and bath gel, plus robes.

**Accessibility:** Three staterooms are designed for wheelchair accessibility.

Top: Teatime in Horizons
Bottom: Breakfast in bed

## Restaurants

Oceania passengers enjoy the flexibility of four open seating restaurants. The Grand Dining Room, open for breakfast, lunch, and dinner, serves Continental cuisine. Alternative, reservations-required dinner options are Toscana, which serves gourmet Italian dishes, and Polo Grill, the steak house. Terraces, the buffet restaurant, serves breakfast, lunch, and dinner and is transformed into Tapas on the Terrace after dark for a relaxed atmosphere and alfresco dining. All dining venues have nearby bars, and there's no additional cover charge for dining. In addition, a poolside grill serves hamburgers and a variety of sandwiches and salads at lunchtime, and there is a pizzeria in the buffet area. Afternoon tea is an elaborate affair served in Horizons, the observation lounge. Room service is available 24 hours.

## Spas

The Canyon Ranch SpaClub offers a long menu of body wraps, massages, conditioning body scrubs, skin care and tanning treatments, and acupuncture. Thermal suites include complimentary single-sex aromatic steam rooms. A highlight of the tranquil open-air Spa Terrace is a therapy whirlpool, to which all Concierge-level and suite guests have unlimited complimentary access; all other guests must purchase passes.

## Bars/Entertainment

Bars and lounges have an intimate quality, from the martini bar, where piano music is played, to the show lounge that offers small-scale cabaret-style entertainment ranging from headline acts and concerts to comedians and magicians. The observation lounge is a late-night hot spot with music for dancing and even karaoke led by the entertainment staff.

## Pros and Cons

**Pros:** a relaxed, social atmosphere pervades all areas on board; the lobby staircase is a must-see—it's practically identical to the one in the movie *Titanic*; on board, you'll find some of the most lavish afternoon teas at sea.

**Cons:** shipboard charges can add up fast, because drink prices and even Internet services are on the high side; there is only one self-serve laundry room; the absence of a sauna in the spa is an unfortunate oversight.

| Cabin Type | Size (sq. ft.) |
|---|---|
| Owner's | 962 |
| Vista Suite | 786 |
| Penthouse Suite | 322 |
| Concierge/Ocean View with Balcony | 216 |
| Deluxe Ocean View | 165 |
| Standard Ocean View | 150–165 |
| Inside | 160 |

### FAST FACTS

■ 9 passenger decks

■ 2 specialty restaurants, dining room, buffet, pizzeria

■ Wi-Fi, safe, refrigerator, DVD (some)

■ 1 pool

■ Fitness classes, gym, hot tubs, spa, steam room

■ 4 bars, casino, dance club, library, show room

■ Dry-cleaning, laundry facilities, laundry service

■ Internet terminal

■ No-smoking cabins

**2**

**OCEANIA CRUISES**

*Regatta* at sea

# PAUL GAUGUIN CRUISES

With one ship built specifically to sail the waters of Tahiti, French Polynesia, and the South Pacific and synonymous with luxury and exotic destinations, Paul Gauguin Cruises remains a top choice for discerning travelers and honeymooners. The MS *Paul Gauguin*

*Tere Moana* cruising

has been in service since 1998 and lays claim to being the only luxury ship in history to have offered a single-destination focus and high level of expertise on a year-round basis for such an extended period of time. The line now has a second ship that will sail in Europe and the Caribbean.

☎ 800/848–6172
⊕ *www.pgcruises.com*
☞ *Cruise Style: Luxury*.

The well-loved ship sailed for over a dozen years under the flag of Radisson (later Regent) Seven Seas Cruises until the ship was sold. Paul Gauguin Cruises began in 2010 with the single ship when the *Paul Gauguin* was acquired by Pacific Beachcomber SC, the largest luxury hotel and cruise operator in French Polynesia. In order to offer similarly luxurious cruises in other regions—Europe in summer months and the Caribbean during the winter season—the line introduced a second vessel, MV *Tere Moana* in 2012.

Intimate and luxurious, Paul Gauguin ships offer a cruise experience tailored to the regions in which they sail. On board you can enjoy a dip in the swimming pool or simply relax poolside in a deck chair, with a good book and a beverage from the nearby bar. You won't want to miss the Fare Tahiti art exhibit in front of La Veranda restaurant on *Paul Gauguin*, although you may want to bring your own reading material as the library has only a few shelves of mostly English-language books. Passengers aboard *Tere Moana* fare a bit better with a larger library. A relaxed atmosphere prevails throughout both vessels, but the cruise line definitely has a split personality, with voyages on MS *Paul*

*Gauguin* limited to the South Pacific and those of MV *Tere Moana* as varied as the Caribbean and Europe.

### Food

On each ship, the main dining room, L'Etoile, serves French food with Polynesian flair and is open only for dinner. For breakfast and lunch, you either order off the menu or make your selections from the extensive buffet in La Veranda, which often features fare with an international theme. In the evening, La Veranda is transformed into an elegant, reservation-only dining venue featuring gourmet cuisine. In 2013, the culinary creations of Jean-Pierre Vigato, chef and owner of the Michelin two-star Restaurant Apicius in Paris, made their appearance on Paul Gauguin Cruises vessels—in L'Etoile aboard *Tere Moana* and in La Veranda on the *Paul Gauguin*. *Paul Gauguin* also has Le Grill for a more casual dining experience for all meals; breakfast is a buffet, and lunch includes a choice of grilled favorites, salads, and fresh tropical fruits, while dinner features Polynesian specialties in a relaxed atmosphere.

All beverages, including soft drinks, spirits, beer, wine, and bottled water are included in the fare, and wines chosen to complement the menu are served at lunch and dinner. There is a separate charge for premium wines by the bottle and some other premium alcohol. For those on special diets, three options—vegetarian, light and healthy, and no salt—are available.

### Entertainment

Excellent musicians with extensive play lists perform for listening and dancing from the sail-away party through the last farewell. *Paul Gauguin* features Les Gauguines, a group of talented young Tahitian women, who travel with the ship to teach passengers about French Polynesia, as well as to sing, dance, and share the lore of their homeland. These young ladies add a dimension to the cruise that is not available anywhere else. Entertainment aboard *Tere Moana* is as varied as the destinations she visits, but always reflects the spirit of the region through which she is sailing. Nevertheless, entertainment aboard *Moana* is on a smaller scale, befitting a ship with only 90 passengers. Guest lecturers are popular on both ships. The small casino on *Paul Gauguin* offers gaming tables and slot machines. *Tere Moana* has no casino.

### KNOWN FOR

■ **Casual Luxury.** Cruises on Paul Gauguin ships are luxurious but have a casual vibe.

■ **Small Ships.** The ships' intimate size means guests and staff get to know each other and ships visit smaller ports where large ships cannot go.

■ **Destination-oriented Cruising.** Paul Gauguin's small cruise ships are destination-oriented, visiting interesting ports.

■ **Excellent Service.** Service is a hallmark element of all Paul Gauguin cruises.

■ **All-inclusive Pricing.** Meals, drinks (including most alcohol), and tips are included in the fares; airfare from Los Angeles is included on Paul Gauguin cruises in French Polynesia.

**2**

**PAUL GAUGUIN CRUISES**

Ocean View stateroom

Top: La Veranda
Bottom: The sun deck on
Tere Moana

### Fitness and Recreation

The line's spas and fitness centers are on the small side, as would be expected on ships carrying fewer than 350 guests. Each ship features the high-end Deep Nature Spa by Algotherm, noted for combining the art of gentle pampering with services that are uniquely tailored to each individual. Fitness centers are equipped with Lifecycles, treadmills, elliptical trainers, and weight machines. From the onboard water sports marina, you can go kayaking, windsurfing, or paddle boarding. *Paul Gauguin* features an exclusive, optional PADI scuba-diving program.

### Your Shipmates

Paul Gauguin Cruises attracts passengers of all ages, and on *Paul Gauguin* especially you'll see young honeymooners mingling with mature well-traveled couples. Most enjoy the relaxed atmosphere on board in addition to the exotic ports and unique experiences ashore.

### Dress Code

Elegant resort casual attire is appropriate at all times. Slacks and a golf or sport shirt for men and sporty dresses or skirts or pants with a sweater or blouse for women are suggested for evening. Jackets are not required, but many men bring along a sport coat for the Captain's Welcome Reception.

### Junior Cruisers

There are no dedicated children's facilities or youth programs on board either ship. However, on the MS *Paul Gauguin,* the Ambassadors of the Environment Youth program, created in collaboration with Jean-Michel Cousteau's Ocean Futures Society, is offered on select sailings. The program introduces participants ages 9 to 17 to the ecological wonders of Tahiti and French Polynesia by exploring coral reefs, hiking rain forest trails, and visiting ancient Polynesian temples. Otherwise, not a lot of kids travel on these ships, and there is nothing comparable on the *Moana.*

## CHOOSE THIS LINE IF ...

You have a taste for exploring exotic regions and ports; these ships go to places large cruise ships cannot go.

You enjoy a social atmosphere with low-key entertainment; these are not traditional cruises with lots of nightly options.

You love water sports; both ships have excellent water sports offerings.

## Service

Service is attentive, but not intrusive. Top accommodations categories have butlers to provide an additional level of attention.

## Tipping

Tipping is neither required nor expected, though passengers can contribute to the crew welfare fund.

## Past Passengers

Guests become members of the Paul Gauguin Society upon completion of their first cruise and receive savings of 5% when reserving subsequent voyages.

### HELPFUL HINTS

Some premium liquors, specialty wines, and certain Cognacs incur an additional charge.

Groups of 10 or more travelers get an additional 5% discount off the applicable cruise fares.

Tips are included, but passengers can make a donation at the Purser's Office to the Crew Welfare Fund, which is used for crew parties and events.

The itinerary can be changed if you charter the full ship, provided that embarkation and debarkation ports remain as published.

With Paul Gauguin Personalized Services (PGPS), as a guest of *Tere Moana*, you can book private tours and service arranged and customized for you.

**2**

**PAUL GAUGUIN CRUISES**

---

### DON'T CHOOSE THIS LINE IF ...

You never set sail without a tuxedo; these cruises offer a luxurious atmosphere but with very little formality.

Your preference is for a full schedule of high-energy activities; the focus on these cruises is off the ship.

You use a scooter for mobility. These ships are older and smaller and just can't accommodate them.

# TERE MOANA

| | |
|---|---|
| Crew Members | 57 |
| Entered Service | 1999 |
| Gross Tons | 3,504 |
| Length | 330 feet |
| Number of Cabins | 45 |
| Passenger Capacity | 90 |
| Width | 46 feet |

700 ft.

500 ft.

300 ft.

The second vessel acquired by Paul Gauguin Cruises originally entered service in 1999 for French cruise line Compagnie du Ponant Cruises as *Le Levant*. After an extensive multimillion-dollar, multifaceted renovation, the boutique ship debuted as *Tere Moana* with a luxurious new look—chic and stylish with Polynesian touches similar to her fleetmate *Paul Gauguin*—in late 2012. The extreme makeover of *Tere Moana* included new furniture, upholstery, art, lighting, wall coverings, carpeting, ceiling finishes, window treatments, flooring, floor coverings, and a soft color palette throughout.

More megayacht than cruise ship, *Tere Moana*'s public spaces are small but include a high-end spa, a small fitness center equipped with the latest cardio and weightlifting equipment, and water sports marina from where kayaking and paddle boarding are available in select ports. Although there are two restaurants, there is only one lounge for daytime lectures and nightly entertainment. You will find a generous library space on board but no casino. Deck space, with its pool, bar, chaise longues, and Balinese sun beds, is adequate for the small passenger complement.

### Cabins

**Cabins:** All accommodations are luxuriously appointed with tasteful furnishings and decor in soothing tropical colors. Only eight staterooms have balconies, but all have an ocean view and contain amenities such as bathrobes for use during the cruise, slippers, hair dryer, flat-screen TV, CD/DVD player, safe, and a refrigerator stocked with soft drinks, beer, and bottled water. Queen-size beds dressed with fine linens and feather-down duvets are convertible to twin-bed configurations.

**Bathrooms:** Bathrooms are stocked with toiletries including shampoo, conditioner, moisturizer, and bath gel.

**Accessibility:** None of the accommodations is designed for wheelchair accessibility.

### Restaurants

Top: *Tere Moana*
Bottom: Balcony stateroom, *Tere Moana*

Open seating dinners in the formal restaurant L'Etoile are French-inspired and regionally infused by the destinations on the ship's itinerary, often featuring fresh ingredients from local markets. Open only for dinner, L'Etoile showcases culinary creations by Jean-Pierre Vigato, Chef of Apicius restaurant in Paris. For breakfast and lunch, you either order off the menu or make your selections from the extensive internationally themed buffet in La Veranda. Tea is also served in La Veranda, where seating is available indoors or on the adjacent deck. In the evening, La Veranda is transformed into an elegant, reservation-only dining venue featuring gourmet cuisine for which there is no charge. Complimentary wines chosen to complement the menu are freely poured at lunch and dinner. Room service is available around the clock, and select items from the L'Etoile menu can be ordered during dinner hours.

### Spas

The luxurious Deep Nature Spa by Algotherm is noted for combining the art of gentle pampering with services that are uniquely tailored to each individual. A full menu of treatments includes facials utilizing an AlgoDerm machine, skin care therapies and exfoliation, massage, reflexology, aromatherapy, and body wraps. Unique treatments are the supreme "gold massage," inspired by traditional Russian massage methods, and AlgoSilhouette contouring, toning, and firming techniques. Use of the steam room is complimentary.

### Bars/Entertainment

With only one lounge and a pool bar, organized evening entertainment aboard *Tere Moana* is limited. Le Salon is well suited as a venue for cabaret-sized shows, either performed by the Paul Gauguin staff or a guest troupe from ashore. Live music is featured nightly for listening and dancing.

### Pros and Cons

**Pros:** ship's small size means you'll get to know other passengers; dining is elegant, but the ambience is casual; the water sports marina offers complimentary use of kayaks and paddleboards.

**Cons:** with a limited number of stateroom balconies, you'll have to plan ahead to get one; there are no facilities for children; the ship is not suitable for passengers requiring accessible accommodations.

| Cabin Type | Size (sq. ft.) |
|---|---|
| Ocean View With Balcony | 298* |
| Ocean View | 161–194 |

*Square footage includes balcony.

## FAST FACTS

- 5 passenger decks
- Specialty restaurant, dining room, buffet
- Wi-Fi, safe, DVD
- 1 pool
- Fitness classes, gym, spa, steam room
- 2 bars, show room
- Dry-cleaning, laundry service
- Internet terminal
- No-smoking cabins

**2**

**PAUL GAUGUIN CRUISES**

# PRINCESS CRUISES

Princess Cruises may be best known for introducing cruise travel to millions of viewers, when its flagship became the setting for *The Love Boat* television series in 1977. Since that heady time of small-screen stardom, the Princess fleet has grown both in the num-

Splash around in the family pool.

ber and size of ships. Although most are large in scale, Princess vessels manage to create the illusion of intimacy through the use of color and decor in understated yet lovely public rooms graced by multimillion-dollar art collections.

☎ 661/753–0000
or 800/774–6237
⊕ *www.princess.com*
☞ *Cruise Style:*
*Premium.*

Princess has also become more flexible; Personal Choice Cruising offers alternatives for open seating dining (when you wish and with whom you please) and entertainment options as diverse as those found in resorts ashore.

Lovely chapels or the wide-open decks are equally romantic settings for weddings at sea with the captain officiating.

### Food

Personal choices regarding where and what to eat abound, but because of the number of passengers, unless you opt for traditional assigned seating, you might have to wait for a table in one of the open seating dining rooms. Menus are varied and extensive in the main dining rooms, and the results are good to excellent, considering how much work is going on in the galleys. Vegetarian and healthy lifestyle options are always on the menu, as well as steak, fish, or chicken. A special menu is designed especially for children.

Alternative restaurants are a staple throughout the fleet but vary by ship class. Grand-class ships have upscale steak houses and Sabatini's, an Italian restaurant; both require reservations and carry an extra cover charge. Sun-class ships offer complimentary sit-down dining in the pizzeria and a similar steakhouse option, although it's in a sectioned-off area of the buffet restaurant. On *Caribbean, Crown, Emerald,* and *Ruby Princess,* a casual evening alternative to the dining rooms and usual buffet is Café Caribe—adjacent to the Lido buffet restaurant, it serves cuisine with a Caribbean flair. With a few breaks in service, Lido buffets on all ships are almost always open, and a pizzeria and grill offer casual daytime snack choices. The fleet's patisseries and ice-cream bars charge for specialty coffee, some pastries, and premium ice cream. A daily British-style pub lunch served in the ships' Wheelhouse Bar has been introduced fleetwide, with the exception of the Sun-class and smaller ships.

Ultimate Balcony Dining—either a champagne breakfast or full-course dinner—is a full-service meal served on your cabin's balcony. The Chef's Table allows guests (for a fee) to dine on a special menu with wine pairings. After a meeting with the executive chef in the galley (and some champagne and appetizers), guests sit at a special table in the dining room. The chef joins them for dessert.

## Entertainment

The roster of adult activities still includes standbys like bingo and art auctions, but you'll also find guest lecturers, cooking classes, wine-tasting seminars, pottery workshops, and computer and digital photography classes. Nighttime production shows tend toward Broadway-style revues presented in the main show lounge, and performers might include comedians, magicians, jugglers, and acrobats. Live bands play a wide range of musical styles for dancing and listening, and each ship has a disco. The cruise director's staff leads lively evenings of fun with passenger participation. At the conclusion of the second formal night, champagne trickles down over a champagne waterfall, painstakingly created by the arrangement of champagne glasses in a pyramid shape. Ladies are invited to join the maître d' to assist in the pouring for a great photo op.

## Fitness and Recreation

Spa rituals include a variety of massages, body wraps, and facials; numerous hair and nail services are offered in the salons. Both the salons and spa are operated by Steiner Leisure, and the menu of spa services includes special pampering treatments designed specifically for men and teens as well as couples. For a half-day fee, escape to the Sanctuary—the adults-only haven—which offers a relaxing outdoor spa-inspired setting

### KNOWN FOR

■ **Weddings:** Noted as the "Love Boats," Princess ships were the first at sea to offer captain-officiated weddings, and unlike most cruise lines they still do.

■ **Sophistication:** Princess Cruises' ships range from midsize to megaship, but all have a sophisticated ambience.

■ **Movies under the Stars:** An innovative feature copied by other cruise lines, Princess was the first line to offer movies and other programming on giant poolside LED screens.

■ **Accessibility:** Princess is a top choice for travelers with disabilities since the ships and even shore excursions offer more choices for them.

■ **Relaxation:** Ships in the Princess fleet feature another cruise industry first—the Sanctuary, where adults can get away from it all, has become a signature element, imitated by many other lines.

Disco into the night.

**2**

**PRINCESS CRUISES**

Top: Sunset at sea
Middle: Morning stretch
Bottom: Freshwater Jacuzzi

with signature beverages, light meals, massages, attentive service, and relaxing personal entertainment.

Modern exercise equipment, a jogging track, and basic fitness classes are available at no charge. There's a fee for personal training, body composition analysis, and specialized classes such as yoga and Pilates. Grand-class ships have a resistance pool so you can get your laps in effortlessly.

### Your Shipmates

Princess Cruises attract mostly American passengers, ranging from their midthirties to midfifties. Families enjoy cruising together on the Princess fleet, particularly during holiday seasons and in summer months, when many children are on board. Longer cruises appeal to well-traveled retirees and couples who have the time.

### Dress Code

Two formal nights are standard on seven-night cruises; an additional formal night may be scheduled on longer sailings. Men are encouraged to wear tuxedos, but dark suits are appropriate. All other evenings are casual, although jeans are discouraged, and it's requested that no shorts be worn in public areas after 6 pm.

### Junior Cruisers

For young passengers ages 3 to 17, each Princess vessel (except *Ocean Princess* and *Pacific Princess*) has a playroom, teen center, and programs of supervised activities designed for different age groups: ages 3 to 7, 8 to 12, and 13 to 17. Activities to engage youngsters include arts and crafts, pool games, scavenger hunts, deck parties, backstage and galley tours, games, and videos. Events such as dance parties in their own disco, theme parties, athletic contests, karaoke, pizza parties, and movie fests occupy teenage passengers. With a nod toward science and educational entertainment, children also participate in learning programs focused on the environment and wildlife in areas where the ships sail.

To allow parents independent time ashore, youth centers operate as usual during port days, including lunch with counselors. For an additional charge, group babysitting is available nightly from 10 pm until 1 am. Family-friendly conveniences include self-service

---

### CHOOSE THIS LINE IF ...

You're a traveler with a disability. Princess ships are some of the most accessible at sea.

You like to gamble but hate a smoke-filled casino. Princess casinos are well ventilated and spacious.

You want a balcony. Princess ships feature them in abundance at affordable rates.

laundry facilities and two-way family radios that are available for rent at the Purser's Desk. Infants under six months are not permitted; private in-cabin babysitting is not available on any Princess vessel. Children under age three are welcome in the playrooms if supervised by a parent.

### Service
Professional service by an international staff is efficient and friendly. It's not uncommon to be greeted in passageways by smiling stewards who know your name.

### Tipping
A gratuity of $11.50 per person per day ($12 for passengers in suites and minisuites) is added to shipboard accounts for distribution to stewards and waitstaff. Passengers may adjust the amount based on the level of service experienced. An automatic 15% is added to all bar tabs for bartenders and drink servers; gratuities to other staff members may be extended at passengers' discretion.

### Past Passengers
Membership in the Captain's Circle is automatic following your first Princess cruise. All members receive a free subscription to *Captain's Circle News,* a quarterly newsletter, as well as discounts on selected cruises.

Perks are determined by the number of cruises completed: Gold (2 through 5), Platinum (6 through 15), and Elite (16 and above). Although Gold members receive only the magazine, an invitation to an onboard event, and the services of the Circle Host on the ship, benefits really begin to accrue once you've completed five cruises. Platinum members receive upgraded insurance (when purchasing the standard policy), expedited check-in, a debarkation lounge to wait in on the ship, and, best of all, limited free Internet access during the cruise. Elite benefits are even more lavish, with many complimentary services.

## HELPFUL HINTS

Princess Cruises pioneered the concept of affordable balcony accommodations and continues to lead the industry in that regard.

If you're unsure, select Traditional dining when you reserve your cruise; it can be impossible to change from Personal Choice to Traditional onboard, but it's easy to go the other way.

Princess Cruises is the only contemporary cruise line that offers deluxe Ultimate Balcony Dining—either an intimate breakfast or romantic dinner served by your own dedicated waiters on your stateroom balcony.

A Princess cruise can be enhanced by adding a Cruisetour, a five- to eight-day in-depth land tour, to your voyage to create a land and sea vacation.

## DON'T CHOOSE THIS LINE IF ...

You have a poor sense of direction. Most ships, especially the Grand-class ships, are very large.

You think Princess is still as depicted in *The Love Boat.* That was just a TV show, and it was more than three decades ago.

You're too impatient to stand in line or wait. Debarkation from the large ships can be lengthy.

# CARIBBEAN, CROWN, EMERALD, RUBY PRINCESS

| | |
|---|---|
| Crew Members | 1,200, 1,200, 1,200, 1,225 |
| Entered Service | 2004, 2006, 2007, 2008 |
| Gross Tons | 113,000 |
| Length | 951 feet |
| Number of Cabins | 1,557, 1,532, 1,532, 1540 |
| Passenger Capacity | 3,100, 3,080, 3,080, 3,080 |
| Width | 118 feet |

700 ft.

500 ft.

300 ft.

With dramatic atriums and Skywalker's Disco (the spoiler hovering 150 feet above the stern), *Caribbean Princess* is a supersize version of the older Grand-class vessels with an extra deck of passenger accommodations. Not quite identical to *Caribbean Princess*, the younger ships in the class, *Crown, Emerald,* and *Ruby Princess* have introduced more dining options. Several signature public spaces have been redesigned or relocated on these ships as well—the atrium on *Crown, Emerald,* and *Ruby Princess* resembles an open piazza and sidewalk café; Sabatini's Italian Trattoria is found on a top deck with views on three sides and alfresco dining; and Skywalker's Disco is forward near the funnel (where it's topped with a sports court). Inside spaces on all three vessels are quietly neutral, with touches of glamour in the sweeping staircases and marble-floor atriums. Surprising intimacy is achieved by the number of public rooms and restaurants that swallow up passengers.

## Cabins

**Cabins:** On these ships 80% of the outside staterooms have balconies. The typical stateroom has a seating area with a chair and table; all have ample storage. Minisuites have a separate seating area, a walk-in closet, a combination shower-tub, and a balcony, as well as two TVs. Larger deluxe suites have separate sitting rooms and walk-in closets, some with sofa beds. Two family suites have interconnecting staterooms with a balcony and sleep up to eight (D105/D101 and D106/D102). Some staterooms can accommodate three and four, and some adjacent cabins can be connected through interior doors or balcony dividers.

**Amenities:** Decorated in attractive pastel hues, all cabins have a refrigerator, a hair dryer, a safe, and bathrobes to use during the cruise. Bathrooms have shampoo, lotion, and bath gel.

**Accessibility:** Twenty-five staterooms are designed for wheelchair accessibility.

Top: Movies Under the Stars
Bottom: Broadway-style revue

## Restaurants

Passengers choose between two assigned dinner seatings or open seating; breakfast and lunch are always open seating. Dinner options include reservations-only Sabatini's and Crown Grill (both with cover) and the complimentary Café Caribe, a casual Caribbean buffet with linen-dressed tables and limited waiter service. Lido buffets on all ships are almost always open. A pub lunch is served in the Wheelhouse Bar, and a pizzeria and grill offer casual daytime snack choices. The wine bars, patisseries, and ice-cream bars charge for artisan cheeses, specialty coffee, some pastries, and premium ice cream. Ultimate Balcony Dining and Chef's Table options are available, as are afternoon tea and 24-hour room service.

## Spas

Spas operated by Steiner Leisure offer the standard treatments, including a variety of massages, body wraps, and facials, as well as some designed specifically for men, teens, and couples. Medi-spa treatments are also available. The spas' thermal suites have relaxing aromatic wet and dry saunas and heated loungers that are complimentary for those in suites, but a fee is charged for everyone else. Complimentary to all are saunas and steam rooms adjacent to men's and women's changing rooms.

## Bars/Entertainment

Nighttime production shows tend toward Broadway-style revues presented in the main show lounge, and performers might include comedians, magicians, jugglers, and acrobats. Live bands play a wide range of musical styles for dancing and listening in the lounges and each ship has a disco. The cruise director's staff leads lively evenings of fun with passenger participation. Movies Under the Stars with popcorn and other movie fare are a popular option.

## Pros and Cons

**Pros:** Movies Under the Stars on the huge poolside screen have proven to be a big hit; the Wheelhouse Bar serves complimentary pub lunch at noon; the adults-only Sanctuary is a private deck with posh loungers for a fee.

**Cons:** priority dining reservations are extended only to Elite Captain's Circle members; the terrace overlooking the aft pool is a quiet spot after dark, but the nearest bar often closes early; opt for Personal Choice dining and you may encounter a wait for a table.

| Cabin Type | Size (sq. ft) |
|---|---|
| Grand Suite | 1,279 |
| Other Suites | 461–689 |
| Family Suite | 607 |
| Minisuite | 324 |
| Ocean View Balcony | 233–285 |
| Ocean View | 158–182 |
| Inside | 163 |

All dimensions include the square footage for balconies.

## FAST FACTS

- 15 passenger decks
- 2 specialty restaurants, 3 dining rooms, buffet, ice cream parlor, pizzeria
- Wi-Fi, safe, refrigerator, DVD (some)
- 4 pools (1 indoor), children's pool
- Fitness classes, gym, hot tubs, sauna, spa, steam room
- 9 bars, casino, 2 dance clubs, library, 2 show rooms, video game room
- Children's programs
- Dry-cleaning, laundry facilities, laundry service
- Internet terminal
- No kids under 6 months
- No-smoking cabins

Sailing at sunset

PRINCESS CRUISES

2

# GRAND-CLASS
*Grand Princess, Golden Princess, Star Princess*

| | |
|---|---|
| Crew Members | 1,100, 1,100, 1,200 |
| Entered Service | 1998, 2001, 2002 |
| Gross Tons | 109,000 |
| Length | 951 feet |
| Number of Cabins | 1,300 |
| Passenger Capacity | 2,600 |
| Width | 118 feet |

700 ft.

500 ft.

300 ft.

When *Grand Princess* was introduced as the world's largest cruise ship in 1998, futuristic Skywalker's Disco hovered approximately 150 feet above the waterline, but in a dramatic—and fuel saving—transformation, it was removed from *Grand Princess* in 2011 and replaced with a more conventional nightclub in the heart of the ship. Subsequent ships did not have the same design problem, so there are no plans on the drawing board to remove Skywalker's.

All Grand-class vessels have more than 700 staterooms that included private balconies. Like their predecessors, the interiors of Grand-class ships have splashy glamour in the sweeping staircases and marble-floor atriums. Surprisingly intimate for such large ships, human scale in public lounges is achieved by judicious placement of furniture as unobtrusive room dividers. The 300-square-foot Times Square–style LED screens that hover over the pools show up to seven movies or events daily.

## Cabins

**Cabins:** On these ships, 80% of the outside staterooms have balconies. The typical stateroom has a seating area with a chair and table; even the cheapest categories have ample storage. Minisuites have a separate seating area, a walk-in closet, a combination shower-tub, and a balcony, as well as two TVs. More deluxe suites have even more room, some with sofa beds. Two family suites have interconnecting staterooms with a balcony that can sleep up to eight people (D105/D101 and D106/D102). Staterooms in a variety of categories will accommodate three and four people, and some adjacent cabins can be interconnected through interior doors or by unlocking doors in the balcony dividers.

**Amenities:** Decorated in attractive pastel hues, all cabins have a refrigerator, hair dryer, safe, and bathrobes to use during the cruise. Bathrooms have shampoo, lotion, and bath gel.

**Accessibility:** Twenty-eight staterooms are wheelchair accessible.

## Restaurants

Passengers choose between two assigned dinner seatings or open seating; breakfast and lunch are open seating. Alternative dinner options include the reservations-only Crown Grill and Sabatini's Italian

Top: *Star Princess* at sea
Bottom: *Golden Princess*
grand plaza atrium

restaurants (both with cover). Lido buffets on all ships are open around the clock. A pub lunch is served in the Wheelhouse Bar, and a pizzeria and grill offer casual daytime snack choices. The patisseries and ice-cream bars charge for specialty coffee, some pastries, and premium ice cream. A wine bar serves extra-charge evening snacks and artisan cheeses. Ultimate Balcony Dining and Chef's Table options are available, as is afternoon tea and 24-hour room service.

### Spas

Spas operated by Steiner Leisure offer a menu of massages, body wraps, and facials, as well as treatments specifically designed for men, teens, and couples. Acupuncture is also available. Only Star Princess has a thermal suite (complimentary for those in suites but open to others for a fee), but saunas and steam rooms adjacent to men's and women's changing rooms are complimentary on all three ships. Adults can escape to the Sanctuary, a relaxing outdoor spa-inspired setting for which there is a fee.

### Bars/Entertainment

Nighttime production shows presented in the main show lounge lean toward Broadway-style revues; guest performers might include comedians, magicians, jugglers, and acrobats. Live bands play a wide range of musical styles for dancing and listening in the lounges, and each ship has a disco. The cruise director's staff leads lively evenings of fun with passenger participation. Movies Under the Stars, where popcorn is free, is a popular evening option.

### Pros and Cons

**Pros:** Skywalker's Disco on Golden Princess and Star Princess is virtually deserted during the day, when it's the ideal quiet spot to watch the sea; self-service passenger laundry rooms have ironing stations; the nautical Wheelhouse Bar is a Princess tradition for cocktails and dancing.

**Cons:** sports bars get jam-packed—and stuffy—when big games are on; accommodations aft and above the Vista lounge are noisy when bands crank up the volume; minisuites don't include the perks offered to full suites.

| Cabin Type | Size (sq. ft.) |
|---|---|
| Grand Suite | 730/1,314* |
| Other Suites | 468–591 |
| Family Suite | 607 |
| Minisuite | 323 |
| Ocean-View Balcony | 232–274 |
| Standard | 168 |
| Inside | 160 |

All dimensions include the square footage for balconies. *Grand Princess dimensions followed by Golden and Star Princess.*

## FAST FACTS

■ 14 passenger decks

■ 2 specialty restaurants, 3 dining rooms, buffet, ice cream parlor, pizzeria

■ Wi-Fi, safe, refrigerator

■ 4 pools (1 indoor), children's pool

■ Fitness classes, gym, hot tubs, sauna, spa, steam room

■ 9 bars, casino, 2 dance clubs, library, 2 show rooms, video game room

■ Children's programs

■ Dry-cleaning, laundry facilities, laundry service

■ Internet terminal

■ No kids under 6 months

■ No-smoking cabins

PRINCESS CRUISES

2

# PACIFIC, OCEAN PRINCESS

| | |
|---|---|
| Crew Members | 373 |
| Entered Service | 1999 |
| Gross Tons | 30,277 |
| Length | 592 feet |
| Number of Cabins | 334 |
| Passenger Capacity | 670 |
| Width | 84 feet |

700 ft.

500 ft.

300 ft.

At 30,277 tons, these ships appear positively tiny beside their megaship fleetmates. In reality, they are medium-size ships that entered service for the now-defunct Renaissance Cruises. With their entry into the Princess lineup, real choice is available to Princess passengers— a true alternative for those who prefer the clubby atmosphere of a smaller boutique-style ship but with big-ship features galore.

These sister ships have cozy public spaces, a stunning observation lounge—where the view is visible through floor-to-ceiling windows on three sides— and some of the loveliest libraries at sea, with their domed trompe-l'oeil–painted ceilings, faux fireplaces, comfortable seating areas, and (most important) well-stocked bookshelves. Although the main show room isn't particularly suited for glitzy production-company performances, it is ideal for cabaret shows.

## Cabins

**Cabins:** Designed for longer cruises, all staterooms have ample closet and storage space, although bathrooms in lower-priced categories are somewhat tight. Dark-wood cabinetry adds warmth to the pastel decor. In keeping with the rest of the fleet, 73% of all outside cabins and suites have a balcony, and interiors are similar in size to those you'll find on other Princess ships.

**Suites:** Full suites are particularly nice, with living/ dining rooms, entertainment centers, separate bedrooms, whirlpool bathtubs, a guest powder room, and large balconies overlooking the bow or stern.

**Amenities:** Amenities in standard cabins are a bit spartan compared to other Princess ships, yet all have at least a small seating area. Bath toiletries, a hair dryer, safe, and robes for use during the cruise are all included, but you must move up to a minisuite (only available on *Pacific* and *Ocean Princess*) or suite to have a real bathtub.

**Accessibility:** Five staterooms are wheelchair accessible on *Pacific Princess* and four on *Ocean Princess*.

## Restaurants

The only disappointment in this ship class is the lack of a Personal Choice dining room. Although open seating breakfast and lunch are served in the main dining room, the only dinner option is in one of two assigned seatings. Sabatini's Italian Trattoria and Sterling

*Pacific Princess* Grand Lobby

Steakhouse specialty restaurants are reservations-required and extra-charge dinner alternatives. With a few breaks in service, Lido buffets on all ships are almost always open. There is a pizzeria window in the buffet area and a separate poolside grill for casual lunch and snacks. Ultimate Balcony Dining is available, as is afternoon tea, and 24-hour room service.

### Spas

Spa treatments offered by Steiner Leisure include a variety of massages, body wraps, and facials, including some designed especially for men. All the way forward is a relaxing outdoor spa-inspired setting with loungers and a therapy pool, for which there is a fee for everyone except those in suites. Complimentary to all are steam rooms in men's and women's changing facilities.

### Bars/Entertainment

Nighttime shows in the main lounge, which is on the small side, tend to be cabaret style; guest performers often include comedians and magicians. Live bands play a wide range of musical styles for dancing and listening in the lounges. The entertainment staff leads lively evenings of fun with passenger participation.

### Pros and Cons

**Pros:** Decks 6 and 7 have two aft-facing standard cabins with balconies larger than other similar cabins; the pianist in the Casino Bar drowns out the clanging of slot machines; many of Princess Cruises' trademark features are present even though these ships were built to another cruise line's specifications.

**Cons:** show rooms are all on one level and have low ceilings; there are no dedicated children's facilities; the solitary main dining room offers only assigned seating for dinner.

| Cabin Type | Size (sq. ft.) |
| --- | --- |
| Suites | 786–962 |
| Minisuite | 322 |
| Ocean-View Balcony | 216 |
| Ocean View | 165 |
| Inside | 158 |

Only *Pacific* and *Ocean Princess* have minisuites.

## FAST FACTS

- 9 passenger decks
- 2 specialty restaurants, dining room, buffet, pizzeria
- Wi-Fi, safe, refrigerator (some), DVD (some)
- 1 pool
- Fitness classes, gym, hot tubs, spa, steam room
- 8 bars, casino, dance club, library, show room
- Children's programs
- Dry-cleaning, laundry facilities, laundry service
- Internet terminal
- No kids under 6 months
- No-smoking cabins

*Pacific Princess* card room

# REGENT SEVEN SEAS

The 1994 merger of Radisson Diamond Cruises and Seven Seas Cruise Line launched Radisson Seven Seas Cruises with an eclectic fleet of vessels that offers a nearly all-inclusive cruise experience in sumptuous, contemporary surroundings. The line was

The end of a perfect day

rebranded as Regent Seven Seas Cruises in 2006, and ownership passed to Prestige Cruise Holdings (which also owns Oceania Cruises) in 2008.

☎ 877/505–5370
⊕ *www.rssc.com*
☞ *Cruise Style: Luxury*.

Even more inclusive than in the past, the line has maintained its traditional tried-and-true formula—delightful ships offering exquisite service, generous staterooms with abundant amenities, a variety of dining options, and superior lecture and enrichment programs. Guests are greeted with champagne on boarding and find an all-inclusive beverage policy that offers not only soft drinks and bottled water, but also cocktails and select wines at all bars and restaurants throughout the ships. Some shore excursions are included in the cruise fare.

On board, casinos are more akin to Monaco than Las Vegas. All ships display tasteful and varied art collections, including pieces that are for sale.

### Food

Menus may appear to include the usual beef Wellington and Maine lobster, but in the hands of Regent Seven Seas chefs the results are some of the most outstanding meals at sea. Specialty dining varies within the fleet, but the newest ships, *Seven Seas Voyager* and *Seven Seas Mariner,* have the edge with the sophisticated Signatures, featuring the cuisine of Le Cordon Bleu of Paris. Prime 7, on all three ships, is a contemporary adaptation of the classic American steak house offering fresh, distinctive decor and an innovative menu of the finest prime-aged steak and chops, along with fresh seafood and poultry specialties. In addition, Mediterranean-influenced bistro dinners that need no reservations are served in La Veranda, the venue that is the daytime casual Lido buffet restaurant.

Wine Connoisseurs Dinners are offered occasionally on longer cruises to bring together people with an interest in wine and food. Each course on the degustation menu is complemented by a wine pairing. The cost varies according to the special vintage wines that are included.

Room-service menus are fairly extensive, and you can also order directly from the restaurant menus during regular serving hours.

Although special dietary requirements should be relayed to the cruise line before sailing, general considerations such as vegetarian, low-salt, or low-cholesterol food requests can be satisfied on board the ships simply by speaking with the dining room staff. Wines chosen to complement dinner menus are freely poured each evening.

## Entertainment

Most sailings host guest lecturers, including historians, anthropologists, naturalists, and diplomats, and there are often discussions and workshops. Spotlight cruises center around popular pastimes and themes, such as food and wine, photography, history, archaeology, literature, performing arts, design and cultures, active exploration and wellness, antiques, jewelry and shopping, the environment, and marine life. All passengers have access to these unique experiences on board and on shore.

Activities and entertainment are tailored for each of the line's distinctive ships with the tastes of sophisticated passengers in mind. Don't expect napkin-folding demonstrations or nonstop action. Production revues, cabaret acts, concert-style piano performances, solo performers, and comedians may be featured in show lounges, with combos playing for listening and dancing in lounges and bars throughout the ships.

## Fitness and Recreation

Although gyms and exercise areas are well equipped, these are not large ships, so the facilities also tend to be limited in size. Each ship has a jogging track, and the larger ones feature a variety of sports courts. The spas and salons aboard Regent Seven Seas ships are operated by Canyon Ranch SpaClub, which offers an array of customizable treatments and services.

### KNOWN FOR

■ **All-Inclusive:** Regent Seven Seas Cruises offers the longest list of inclusive features for the money.

■ **Destination Focused:** Regent even includes select shore excursions in the fare—a real bonus when the ships reach ports of call.

■ **Fine Cuisine:** Ships in the Regent fleet have some of the finest specialty restaurants afloat and there is no charge for dining in them.

■ **Great Service:** Exemplary service is a signature feature of Regent's voyages.

■ **Luxurious but Informal:** Socializing is easy-going on Regent's less formal ships.

Top: Sunrise jog
Bottom: *Seven Seas Navigator*

Top: Fitness center
Middle: Pool decks are
never crowded.
Bottom: Pampering in
the Carita of Paris spa

## Your Shipmates

Regent Seven Seas Cruises are inviting to active, affluent, well-traveled couples ranging from their late-thirties to retirees who enjoy the ship's chic ambience and destination-rich itineraries. Longer cruises attract veteran passengers in the over-sixty age group.

## Dress Code

Elegant casual is the dress code for most nights; formal and semiformal attire is optional on sailings of 16 nights or longer, but it's no longer required. It's requested that dress codes be observed in public areas after 6 pm.

## Junior Cruisers

Regent Seven Seas' vessels are adult-oriented and do not have dedicated children's facilities. However, a Club Mariner youth program for children ages 5 to 8, 9 to 12, and 13 to 17 is offered on select sailings, both during summer months and during school holiday periods. Supervised by counselors, the organized, educational activities focus on nature and the heritage of the ship's destinations. Activities, including games, craft projects, movies, and food fun, are organized to ensure that every child has a memorable experience. Teens are encouraged to help counselors select the activities they prefer.

## Service

The efforts of a polished, unobtrusive staff go almost unnoticed, yet special requests are handled with ease. Butlers provide an additional layer of personal service to guests in the top-category suites.

## Tipping

Gratuities are included in the fare, and none are expected. To show their appreciation, passengers may elect to make a contribution to a crew welfare fund that benefits the ship's staff.

### CHOOSE THIS LINE IF ...

You want to learn the secrets of cooking like a Cordon Bleu chef (for a charge, of course).

You don't want the hassle of signing bar tabs or extra expense of shore excursions.

A really high-end spa experience is on your agenda.

## Past Passengers

Membership in the Seven Seas Society is automatic on completion of a Regent Seven Seas cruise. Members receive discounted cruise fare savings on select sailings, exclusive shipboard and shore-side special events on select sailings, a Seven Seas Society recognition cocktail party on every sailing, and *Inspirations* newsletter highlighting special events, sailings, and destination- and travel-related information. The tiered program offers rewards based on the number of nights you have sailed with RSSC. The more you sail, the more you accrue. Bronze benefits are offered to members with 4 to 20 nights. From 21 through 74 nights, Silver members also receive complimentary Internet access on board, free pressing, and an hour of free phone time. From 75 through 199 nights, Gold members are awarded priority disembarkation at some ports, an additional two hours of complimentary phone time, more complimentary pressing, an exclusive Gold & Platinum activity aboard or ashore on every sailing, and priority reservations at restaurants and spas. From 200 through 399, Platinum members can add complimentary air deviation services (one time per sailing), nine hours of complimentary phone use, and unlimited free pressing and laundry services. Titanium members who have sailed 400 or more nights also get free dry-cleaning and free transfers.

## HELPFUL HINTS

Other luxury lines don't always include round-trip air, ground transfers, and unlimited shore excursions in every port of call.

Regent Seven Seas ships offer all-suite accommodations.

Regent Choice Shore Excursions carry a supplement, but they delve much deeper into a region's culture and history.

Multinight pre- and post-cruise land programs are available to extend your cruise vacation.

Regent Seven Seas ships are luxurious but not stuffy, and there's a "block party" on every cruise where passengers are invited to meet their neighbors in adjacent suites.

## DON'T CHOOSE THIS LINE IF ...

Connecting cabins are a must. Very few are available, and only the priciest cabins connect.

You can't imagine a cruise without the hoopla of games in the pool; these ships are much more discreet.

You don't want to dress up for dinner. Most passengers still dress more formally than on other lines.

# SEVEN SEAS MARINER/VOYAGER

| | |
|---|---|
| Crew Members | 445, 447 |
| Entered Service | 2001, 2003 |
| Gross Tons | 50,000, 46,000 |
| Length | 709, 670 feet |
| Number of Cabins | 350 |
| Passenger Capacity | 700 |
| Width | 93, 95 feet |

700 ft.
500 ft.
300 ft.

The world's only all-balcony, all-suite ships continue the Regent Seven Seas tradition of offering posh accommodations on vessels with generous space for every passenger. Lounges are predominantly decorated in soothing neutrals and cool marine blues with splashes of bold color, soft leather, and glass-and-marble accents. Even areas that can accommodate all (or nearly all) passengers at once, including the formal dining room and show lounge, appear intimate. Good design elements don't hint at their size, and indoor spaces seem smaller than they actually are. With so much room, public areas are seldom crowded, and you won't have to hunt for a deck chair by the swimming pool. The two-tiered Constellation Theater is a state-of-the-art show room with a full-size proscenium stage, where cabaret revues, headline entertainers, and Broadway-inspired shows are presented.

## Cabins

**Cabins:** Rich-textured fabrics and warm wood finishes add a touch of coziness to the larger-than-usual suite accommodations in all categories. Every suite has a vanity-desk, walk-in closet, and seating area with sofa, chairs, and table. Marble bathrooms have a separate tub and shower. Most balconies are approximately 50 square feet in size.

**Top-Category Suites:** The top three suite categories feature Bose music systems, an iPad, and an iPod docking station. Butler service is available for passengers in Master, Grand, Navigator, and Penthouse suites. The top-category Master suites have a separate sitting–dining room, two bedrooms (each has its own TV), a powder room, and two full bathrooms (the master bath has dual vanities, a bidet, separate shower, and whirlpool tub). Some of the other high-end suites do not have the powder room or whirlpool tub.

**Amenities:** All suites have an entertainment center with CD/DVD player, stocked refrigerator, stocked bar, safe, hair dryer, and fine linens and duvets on the bed. Passengers in Concierge suites and higher receive 15 minutes of free ship-to-shore phone time and 60 minutes of free Internet access. Bathrooms have robes and toiletries, including shampoo, lotion, and bath gel.

Top: Afternoon tea in Horizon Lounge
Bottom: *Seven Seas Voyager* at sea

**Accessibility:** Four suites are designed for wheelchair accessibility and are equipped with showers only.

## Restaurants

Three restaurants function on an open seating basis with no dining assignments. In addition to Compass Rose, the main dining room, which serves breakfast, lunch, and dinner, evening choices include the French restaurant Signatures (reservations required); Prime 7, offering a classic steak-house menu (reservations required); and La Veranda, the daytime buffet for breakfast and lunch that's converted to an evening bistro serving Mediterranean cuisine. Wines are chosen to complement each night's menu, and there is no charge for any specialty dining. At least once during each cruise, dinner is served alfresco on the pool deck. In addition to the buffet, a choice for casual lunch and snacks is the poolside grill. Afternoon tea is served daily, and room service is available 24 hours. Dinner can be ordered from the main dining room menu during restaurant hours and served en suite, course by course.

## Spas

Operated by Canyon Ranch SpaClub, the spas on these ships offer an array of massages, facials, and body wraps utilizing organic and natural materials that can be individually customized. Guests can also enjoy complimentary aromatic steam rooms infused with pure plant essences or Finnish-style saunas.

## Bars/Entertainment

Dining and socializing are major evening pursuits, and there's music for dancing before and after dinner, as well as deck parties in fine weather and even a late-night disco. Dance Hosts are on hand to lead unaccompanied ladies on the dance floor. The main show lounge features small-scale production shows; guest entertainers range from classical to modern vocalists and musicians.

## Pros and Cons

**Pros:** after an effortless check-in and champagne greeting, you are escorted to your suite; self-service passenger launderettes with ironing stations are complimentary; every stateroom is a suite, and every suite has a balcony.

**Cons:** no youth facilities, and kids' programs take place in unused public rooms; unless you pre-book your specialty dining preferences online, you could find them unavailable after boarding; few organized activities are scheduled, so be prepared to make your own fun.

| Cabin Type | Size (sq. ft.) |
| --- | --- |
| Master Suite | 1,204 (Mariner), 1,152–1,216 (Voyager) |
| Grand Suite | 903 (Mariner), 753 (Voyager) |
| Seven Seas Suite | 441–561 |
| Other Suites | 320–650 |
| Deluxe Suite | 252 (Mariner), 306 (Voyager) |

## FAST FACTS

- 9 passenger decks
- 2 specialty restaurants, dining room, buffet, ice cream parlor, pizzeria
- Wi-Fi, safe, refrigerator, DVD
- Pool
- Fitness classes, gym, hot tubs, sauna, spa, steam room
- 5 bars, casino, dance club, library, show room
- Children's programs
- Dry-cleaning, laundry facilities, laundry service
- Internet terminal
- No-smoking cabins

Attentive butler service

# ROYAL CARIBBEAN INTERNATIONAL

Big, bigger, biggest! In the early 1990s, Royal Caribbean launched Sovereign-class ships, the first of the modern megacruise liners, which continue to be the all-around favorite of passengers who enjoy traditional cruising ambience with a touch of daring

*Adventure of the Seas* solarium

and whimsy. Plunging into the 21st century, each ship in the current fleet carries more passengers than the entire Royal Caribbean fleet of the 1970s, and has amenities—such as new surfing pools—that were unheard of in the past.

☎ *305/539–6000 or 800/327–6700*
⊕ *www.royalcaribbean. com ☞ Cruise Style: Mainstream.*

All Royal Caribbean ships are topped by the company's distinctive signature Viking Crown Lounge, a place to watch the seascape by day and dance at night. Expansive multideck atriums and promenades, as well as the generous use of brass and floor-to-ceiling glass windows, give each vessel a sense of spaciousness and style. The action is nonstop in casinos and dance clubs after dark, while daytime hours are filled with poolside games and traditional cruise activities. Port talks tend to lean heavily on shopping recommendations and the sale of shore excursions.

### Food

Dining is an international experience, with nightly changing themes and cuisines from around the world. Passenger preference for casual attire and a resort-like atmosphere has prompted the cruise line to add laid-back alternatives to the formal dining rooms: the Windjammer Café and, on certain ships, Johnny Rockets Diner; Seaview Café evokes the ambience of an island beachside stand. Royal Caribbean offers you the choice of early or late dinner seating and has introduced an open seating program fleetwide.

Room service is available 24 hours, but for orders between midnight and 5 am there is a $3.95 service charge. There's a limited menu.

Royal Caribbean doesn't place emphasis on celebrity chefs or specialty alternative restaurants, although they have introduced a more upscale and intimate dinner experience in the form of an Italian specialty restaurant and/or a steak house on all ships.

## Entertainment

A variety of lounges and high-energy stage shows draw passengers of all ages out to mingle and dance the night away. Production extravaganzas showcase singers and dancers in lavish costumes. Comedians, acrobats, magicians, jugglers, and solo entertainers fill show lounges on nights when the ships' companies aren't performing. Professional ice shows are a highlight of cruises on Voyager-, Freedom-, and Oasis-class ships—the only ships at sea with ice-skating rinks.

## Fitness and Recreation

Royal Caribbean has pioneered such new and previously unheard of features as rock-climbing walls, ice-skating rinks, bungee trampolines, and even the first self-leveling pool tables on a cruise ship. Interactive water parks, boxing rings, surfing simulators, and cantilevered whirlpools suspended 112 feet above the ocean made their debuts on the Freedom-class ships.

Facilities vary by ship class, but all Royal Caribbean ships have state-of-the-art exercise equipment, jogging tracks, and rock-climbing walls; passengers can work out independently or in classes guaranteed to sweat off extra calories. Most exercise classes are included in the fare, but there's a fee for specialized spin, yoga, and Pilates classes, as well as the services of a personal trainer. Spas and salons are top-notch, with full menus of day spa–style treatments and services for pampering and relaxation for adults and teens.

## Your Shipmates

Royal Caribbean cruises have a broad appeal for active couples and singles, mostly in their thirties to fifties. Families are partial to the newer vessels that have larger staterooms, huge facilities for children and teens, and seemingly endless choices of activities and dining options.

## Dress Code

Two formal nights are standard on seven-night cruises; one formal night is the norm on shorter sailings. Men are encouraged to wear tuxedos, but dark suits or sport coats and ties are more prevalent. All other

### KNOWN FOR

■ **Big Ships:** The Royal Caribbean fleet boasts the world's largest cruise ships.

■ **Something for Everyone:** With activities that appeal to a broad demographic, Royal Caribbean is a top choice for multigenerational cruise vacations.

■ **A Step Above:** Offering the same value as other mainstream lines, Royal Caribbean's ships are more sophisticated than its competitors'.

■ **Extra Charges:** You will have to break out your wallet quite often once on board, as the cruise fare is far from inclusive.

■ **Recreation:** Gym rats and sports and fitness buffs find multiple facilities available to satisfy their active lifestyles while at sea.

Top: Adventure Beach for kids
Bottom: Voyager-class interior stateroom

2

ROYAL CARIBBEAN INTERNATIONAL

evenings are casual, although jeans are discouraged in restaurants. It's requested that no shorts be worn in public areas after 6 pm, although there are passengers who can't wait to change into them after dinner.

## Junior Cruisers

Supervised age-appropriate activities are designed for children ages 3 through 17; babysitting services are available as well. Children are assigned to the Adventure Ocean youth program by age. They must be at least three years old and toilet trained to participate (children who are in diapers and pull-ups or who are not toilet trained are not allowed in swimming pools or whirlpools). Youngsters who wish to join a different age group must participate in one daytime and one night activity session with their proper age group first; the manager will then make the decision based on their maturity level.

In partnership with toymaker Fisher-Price, Royal Caribbean offers interactive 45-minute Aqua Babies and Aqua Tots play sessions for children ages 6 months to 36 months. The playgroup classes, which are hosted by youth staff members, were designed by early childhood development experts for parents and their babies and toddlers, and teach life skills through playtime activities. Nurseries have been added for babies 6 to 36 months old, with drop-off options during the day and evening—and if parents supply diapers, attendants will change them. There is an hourly fee, and only eight babies and toddlers can be accommodated at a time.

A teen center with a disco is an adult-free gathering spot that will satisfy even the pickiest teenagers.

## Service

Service on Royal Caribbean ships is friendly but inconsistent. Assigned meal seatings assure that most passengers get to know the waiters and their assistants, who in turn get to know the passengers' likes and dislikes; however, that can lead to a level of familiarity that is uncomfortable for some people. Some ships have a concierge lounge for the use of suite occupants and top-level past passengers.

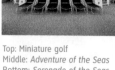

Top: Miniature golf
Middle: *Adventure of the Seas*
Bottom: *Serenade of the Seas* rock-climbing wall

## CHOOSE THIS LINE IF ...

You want to see the sea from atop a rock wall—it's one of the few activities on these ships that's free.

You're active and adventurous. Even if your traveling companion isn't, there's an energetic staff on board to cheer you on.

You want your space. There's plenty of room to roam; quiet nooks and crannies are there if you look.

## Tipping

Tips are added on to shipboard accounts automatically at the end of the cruise. Most passengers pay $12 per day; suite occupants are charged $14.25 per day. A 15% gratuity is automatically added to all bar tabs and spa and salon services.

## Past Passengers

After one cruise, you can enroll in the Crown & Anchor Society. Tiered membership levels are achieved according to a point system. All members receive the *Crown & Anchor* magazine and have access to the member section on the Royal Caribbean website. All members receive an Ultimate Value Booklet and an invitation to a welcome-back party. Platinum members also have the use of a private departure lounge and receive priority check-in (where available), the onboard use of robes during the cruise, an invitation to an exclusive onboard event, and complimentary custom air arrangements. As points are added to your status, the benefits increase to Emerald, Diamond, Diamond Plus, and Pinnacle Club. For instance, Diamond and above receive such perks as access to a private lounge, behind-the-scenes tours, and priority seating for certain events.

## HELPFUL HINTS

Reservations can be made online pre-cruise for specialty restaurants, shore excursions, and spa treatments on all ships, as well as the shows on *Oasis of the Seas*, *Allure of the Seas*, *Freedom of the Seas*, and *Liberty of the Seas*.

The signature Viking Crown Lounge found on every Royal Caribbean ship is a daytime observation lounge and a nightclub after dark.

Popular with children of all ages, the DreamWorks Experience on certain ships offers character meals, meet-and-greet gatherings, and photo ops.

With a multibottle package you can save up to 25% off regular list prices on wine.

A complimentary Coca-Cola souvenir cup is included with the fountain soft drink package.

Bottled water and bottled juice packages of varying quantities can be delivered to your stateroom and will save you up to 25%.

2

ROYAL CARIBBEAN INTERNATIONAL

## DON'T CHOOSE THIS LINE IF ...

Patience is not one of your virtues. Lines are not uncommon.

You want to do your own laundry. There are no self-service facilities on any Royal Caribbean ships.

You don't want to hear announcements. There are a lot on Royal Caribbean ships.

# FREEDOM-CLASS
*Freedom/Liberty/Independence of the Seas*

| | |
|---|---|
| Crew Members | 1,360 |
| Entered Service | 2006, 2007, 2008 |
| Gross Tons | 160,000 |
| Length | 1,112 feet |
| Number of Cabins | 1,817 |
| Passenger Capacity | 3,634 |
| Width | 185 feet |

700 ft.

500 ft.

300 ft.

Although they are no longer the world's largest cruise ships, the Freedom-class vessels live up to Royal Caribbean's reputation for creative thinking that results in features to stir the imagination and provide a resort-like atmosphere at sea. Whether you are hanging 10 in the surf simulator, going a few rounds in the boxing ring, or strolling the Royal Promenade entertainment boulevard, there's almost no reason to go ashore. The layout is more intuitive than you might expect on such a gigantic ship. A mall-like promenade is lined with shops and bistros, an ice-skating rink/theater, numerous lounges, and dining options, but these are not simply enlarged Voyager-class ships. With plenty of room, even the most intimate spaces feel uncrowded. A good fit for extended families, these ships have expansive areas devoted to children and teens and enough adults-only spaces to satisfy everyone.

## Cabins

**Cabins:** Although 60% are outside cabins—and 78% of those have balconies—bargain inside cabins, including some with a bowed window overlooking the promenade, are plentiful. Cabins in every category have adequate closet and drawer–shelf storage, as well as bathroom shelves. Family ocean-view cabins with a window sleep up to six people with two twin beds (convertible to queen size), bunk beds in a separate area, a sitting room with a sofa bed, a vanity area, and a shower-only bathroom. At 1,215 square feet, the Presidential suite sleeps 14 people and has an 810-square-foot veranda with a hot tub and bar.

**Amenities:** Wood cabinetry, a small refrigerator-minibar, broadband Internet connection, a vanity-desk, a flat-panel TV and DVD player, a safe, a hair dryer, and a seating area with sofa, chair, and table are typical features in all categories. Bathrooms have shampoo and bath gel. Premium beds and bedding complete the package.

**Accessibility:** Thirty-two staterooms are wheelchair accessible.

## Restaurants

Triple-deck-high dining rooms serve open seating breakfast and lunch; dinner is served in two assigned seatings or open seating. Two specialty restaurants—Portofino, serving Italian, and Chops Grille, a steak

Top: Dining is fun at Johnny Rockets.
Bottom: Hang 10 on the surf simulator.

house—both charge a supplement and require reservations. The casual Lido buffet offers service nearly around the clock for breakfast, lunch, dinner, and snacks. Jade, a section in the buffet, serves Asian food. Johnny Rockets (cover charge) is a popular option for casual meals. In the promenade are a complimentary pizzeria and a coffee bar serving regular and specialty coffees (also complimentary, unlike on other lines). There's also a Cupcake Cupboard and Ben & Jerry's ice cream, but they charge a fee. A complimentary ice-cream bar is poolside, as is a juice bar, which charges by the item. Room service is available 24 hours; however, there is a delivery charge after midnight.

## Spas

The full-service spa operated by Steiner Leisure offers an extensive treatment menu including facials, teeth whitening, body wraps and scrubs, massages, rasul, acupuncture, and FDA-approved medi-spa treatments performed by trained physicians. Spa rituals also include treatments designed especially for men and teens. While there are no thermal suites, complimentary saunas and steam rooms are located in men's and women's changing rooms.

## Bars/Entertainment

Nightlife runs the gamut from Broadway-style production shows to ice-skating extravaganzas on all three and a real Broadway Show—*Saturday Night Fever*—on *Liberty of the Seas*. Lounges range from a piano bar and a pub to a wine bar, a Latin-themed dance club, and even a disco. You can end the evening with a movie on the outdoor screen overlooking the pool on all three ships or in the 3-D cinema on *Freedom* and *Liberty*.

## Pros and Cons

**Pros:** FlowRider surfing simulator is exciting, even for observers; the H2O Zone is a fun place to beat the heat beneath a waterfall, in the fountain sprays, and along a lazy river; a sports pool accommodates water volleyball, basketball, and golf.

**Cons:** the location of a self-serve frozen-yogurt bar near the kids' pool means that it often ends up messy; hang on to your wallet—the malts in Johnny Rockets diner aren't included in the price; on a ship this large, lines are inevitable, particularly at disembarkation.

| Cabin Type | Size (sq. ft.) |
|---|---|
| Royal Suite | 1,406 |
| Presidential Suite | 1,215 |
| Owner's Suite | 614 |
| Grand Suite | 387 |
| Junior Suite | 287 |
| Family Stateroom | 293 |
| Balcony Stateroom | 177–189 |
| Ocean View | 161–214 |
| Inside | 149–152 |

## FAST FACTS

- 15 passenger decks
- 2 specialty restaurants, dining room, buffet, ice cream parlor, pizzeria
- Internet, Wi-Fi, safe, refrigerator, DVD (some)
- 3 pools, children's pool
- Fitness classes, gym, hot tubs, sauna, spa, steam room
- 14 bars, casino, cinema, 2 dance clubs, library, 3 show rooms, video game room
- Children's programs (ages 3–17)
- Dry-cleaning, laundry service
- Internet terminal
- No-smoking cabins

Climb the wall.

ROYAL CARIBBEAN INTERNATIONAL

2

# VOYAGER-CLASS
*Voyager, Explorer, Adventure, Navigator, Mariner of the Seas*

| | |
|---|---|
| Crew Members | 1,185 |
| Entered Service | 1999, 2000, 2001, 2002, 2003 |
| Gross Tons | 142,000 |
| Length | 1,020 feet |
| Number of Cabins | 1,557 |
| Passenger Capacity | 3,114 (3,835 max) |
| Width | 158 feet |

700 ft.

500 ft.

300 ft.

A truly impressive building program introduced one of these gigantic Voyager-class ships per year over a five-year period. With their rock-climbing walls, ice-skating rinks, in-line skating tracks, miniature golf, and multiple dining venues, they are destinations in their own right. Sports enthusiasts will be thrilled with nonstop daytime action.

The unusual horizontal, multiple-deck promenade-atriums on Voyager-class vessels can stage some of the pageantry for which Royal Caribbean is noted. Fringed with boutiques, bars, and even coffee shops, the mall-like expanses set the stage for evening parades and events, as well as spots to simply kick back for some people-watching.

Other public rooms are equally dramatic. Though it's considered to be three separate dining rooms, the triple-deck height of the single space is stunning. These ships not only carry a lot of people, but carry them well. Space is abundant, and crowding is seldom an issue.

## Cabins

**Cabins:** As on other Royal Caribbean ships, cabins are bright and cheerful. Although more than 60% are outside—and a hefty 75% of those have private verandas—there are still plenty of bargain inside cabins, some with a bowed window for a view overlooking the action-packed promenade. Cabins in every category have adequate closet and drawer/shelf storage and bathroom shelves. Junior suites have a seating area, vanity area, and bathroom with bathtub. Family ocean-view cabins with a window sleep up to six people and can accommodate a roll-away bed and/or crib, have two twin beds (convertible to a queen), and additional bunk beds in a separate area, a separate seating area with a sofa bed, a vanity area, and a private bathroom with shower.

**Amenities:** Wood cabinetry, a small refrigerator-minibar, broadband Internet connection, a vanity-desk, a TV, a safe, a hair dryer, and a seating area with sofa, chair, and table are typical Voyager-class features in all categories. Bathrooms have shampoo and bath gel.

**Accessibility:** Twenty-six staterooms are designed for wheelchair accessibility.

Top: Rock-climbing wall
Bottom: Fitness class

## Restaurants

Triple-deck-high formal dining rooms serve open seating breakfast and lunch; dinner is served in two evening assigned seatings or open seating My Timing Dining. For a more upscale dinner, each ship has an Italian specialty restaurant; *Mariner* and *Navigator* also have a steak house. Both specialty restaurants charge a supplement and require reservations. The casual Lido buffet offers service nearly around the clock for meals and snacks, including dinner; *Mariner* and *Navigator* also serve Asian fare in their Jade section. Johnny Rockets is a popular option for casual meals, though it also has a separate charge. In the promenade are a pizzeria, coffee bar, and Ben & Jerry's ice cream, which charges for frozen treats. All but *Mariner* have Park Café, which serves casual fare. Room service is available 24 hours; however, there is a delivery charge after midnight.

## Spas

The full-service spa operated by Steiner Leisure offers an extensive treatment menu including facials, teeth whitening, body wraps and scrubs, massages, acupuncture, and FDA-approved medi-spa treatments performed by trained physicians. Spa rituals also include treatments designed especially for men and teens. While there are no thermal suites, complimentary saunas and steam rooms are located in men's and women's changing rooms.

## Bars/Entertainment

Nightlife runs the gamut from Broadway-style production shows to bars and lounges that include a piano bar, pub, wine bar, and disco, and on *Mariner* and *Navigator*, a Latin-themed bar. Music abounds for dancing or listening, or you can choose to end the evening with a movie on the outdoor screen overlooking the pool.

## Pros and Cons

**Pros:** Royal Promenade may elicit the biggest "Wow!" on board when a parade is center stage; professional ice-skating performances are staged twice during each cruise; equipment to participate in sports activities is provided at no additional charge.

**Cons:** with the exception of the gym and some fitness classes, nearly everything else on board carries a price tag; although there is no charge to attend, you must get tickets for the ice-skating shows; smokers may be frustrated to find that smoking is prohibited in cabins and in most indoor areas.

| Cabin Type | Size (sq. ft.) |
|---|---|
| Royal Suite | 1,188–1,325 |
| Other Suites* | 277–610 |
| Superior/Deluxe/ Family Ocean View** | 173–328 |
| Large Ocean View | 211 |
| Standard Ocean View | 161–180 |
| Interior | 153–167 |

*Owner's (506–618 sq. ft.), Grand (381–390 sq. ft.), Royal family (512–610 sq. ft.), Junior (277–299 sq. ft). **Superior (202–206 sq. ft.), Deluxe (173–184 sq. ft.), Family (265–328 sq. ft.).

## FAST FACTS

- 14 passenger decks
- 1 specialty restaurant (2 on *Mariner* and *Navigator*), dining room, buffet, ice cream parlor, pizzeria
- Internet, Wi-Fi, safe, refrigerator, DVD (some)
- 3 pools, children's pool (only *Voyager*, *Explorer*, and *Adventure*)
- Fitness classes, gym, hot tubs, sauna, spa, steam room
- 12 bars, casino, 2 dance clubs, library, 3 show rooms, video game room
- Children's programs
- Dry-cleaning, laundry service
- Internet terminal
- No-smoking cabins

# RADIANCE-CLASS
*Radiance, Brilliance, Serenade, Jewel of the Seas*

| | |
|---|---|
| Crew Members | 857 |
| Entered Service | 2001, 2002, 2003, 2004 |
| Gross Tons | 90,090 |
| Length | 962 feet |
| Number of Cabins | 1,056 |
| Passenger Capacity | 2,112 (2,501 max) |
| Width | 106 feet |

700 ft.

500 ft.

300 ft.

Considered by many people to be the most beautiful vessels in the Royal Caribbean fleet, Radiance-class ships are large but sleek and swift, with sun-filled interiors and panoramic elevators that span 10 decks along the ships' exteriors.

High-energy and glamorous spaces are abundant throughout these sister ships. From the rock-climbing wall, children's pool with waterslide, and golf area to the columned dining room, sweeping staircases, and the tropical garden of the solarium, these ships hold appeal for a wide cross section of interests and tastes.

The ships are packed with multiple dining venues, including the casual Windjammer, with its indoor and outdoor seating, and the Latte-Tudes patisserie, offering specialty coffees, pastries, and ice cream treats.

## Cabins

**Cabins:** With the line's highest percentage of outside cabins, standard staterooms are bright and cheery as well as roomy. Nearly three-quarters of the outside cabins have private balconies. Every cabin has adequate closet and drawer/shelf storage, as well as bathroom shelves.

**Suites:** All full suites and family suites have private balconies and include concierge service. Top-category suites have wet bars, separate living–dining areas, multiple bathrooms, entertainment centers with flat-screen TVs, DVD players, and stereos. Some bathrooms have twin sinks, steam showers, and whirlpool tubs. Junior suites have a seating area, vanity area, and bathroom with a tub.

**Amenities:** Light-wood cabinetry, a small refrigerator-minibar, broadband Internet connection, a vanity-desk, a TV, a safe, a hair dryer, and a seating area with sofa, chair, and table are typical Radiance-class features in all categories. Bathroom extras include shampoo and bath gel.

**Accessibility:** Fifteen staterooms are designed for wheelchair accessibility on *Radiance* and *Brilliance*; 19 on *Serenade* and *Jewel*.

## Restaurants

The double-deck-high formal dining room serves open seating breakfast and lunch; dinner is served in two assigned seatings, but open seating is an option. For a more upscale dinner, each ship has an Italian restaurant and a steak house. In addition, *Radiance of*

Top: Pool deck
Bottom: Shared moments on your personal balcony

*the Seas* has a Brazilian-style steak house. All but *Jewel* have an Asian restaurant; *Brilliance* and *Radiance* have Mexican restaurants. There is a supplement charged for specialty dining, and reservations are required. The casual Lido buffet serves nearly around the clock for breakfast, lunch, dinner, and snacks. Seaview Café is open for quick lunches and dinners on *Jewel of the Seas*. A pizzeria in *Serenade*'s Solarium serves slices; the other ships have Park Café for casual fare in that space, and *Radiance* also serves custom hot dogs at Boardwalk Doghouse. The coffee bar features specialty coffees and pastries, for which there is a charge. Room service is available 24 hours; however there is a charge after midnight.

### Spas

The full-service spa operated by Steiner Leisure offers an extensive treatment menu including facials, teeth whitening, body wraps and scrubs. Spa rituals also include treatments designed especially for men and teens. There are thermal suites for a fee as well as complimentary saunas, and steam rooms are located in men's and women's changing rooms.

### Bars/Entertainment

Nightlife options range from Broadway-style productions in the main show lounge to movies in the cinema or on the outdoor screen overlooking the pool. Bars and lounges include a piano bar and wine bar, and most have music for dancing or listening. There's also a pub or sports bar and a lounge for billiards. Look high above for aerial performances in the central atriums on *Brilliance* and *Jewel of the Seas*.

### Pros and Cons

**Pros:** aft on deck 6, four distinct lounges and a billiard room form a clubby adult entertainment center; spacious family ocean-view cabins sleep up to six people; ships offer a wide range of family-friendly activities and games.

**Cons:** upgraded features of the fleet are not consistent throughout this ship class, so check before booking; dining options that charge have replaced some that were previously complimentary; libraries are tiny and poorly stocked for ships this size.

| Cabin Type | Size (sq. ft.) |
|---|---|
| Royal Suite | 1,001 |
| Owner's Suite | 512 |
| Grand Suite | 358–384 |
| Royal Family Suite | 533–586 |
| Junior Suites | 293 |
| Superior Ocean View | 204 |
| Deluxe Ocean View | 179 |
| Large Ocean View | 170 |
| Family Ocean View | 319 |
| Interior | 165 |

### FAST FACTS

- 12 passenger decks
- 2 specialty restaurants, dining room, buffet, pizzeria
- Internet, Wi-Fi, safe, refrigerator, DVD (some)
- 2 pools (1 indoor), children's pool
- Fitness classes, gym, hot tubs, sauna, spa, steam room
- 11 bars, casino, dance club, library, show room, video game room
- Children's programs
- Dry-cleaning, laundry service
- Internet terminal
- No-smoking cabins

Sports courts

# VISION-CLASS
*Legend, Splendour, Grandeur, Rhapsody, Vision of the Seas*

| | |
|---|---|
| **Crew Members** | 726, 762, 760, 765, 742 |
| **Entered Service** | 1995, 1996, 1996, 1997, 1998 |
| **700 ft.**   **Gross Tons** | 69, 130–78, 491 |
| **Length** | 867, 867, 916, 915, 915 feet |
| **500 ft.**   **Number of Cabins** | 902, 915, 996, 1,020, 999 |
| **Passenger Capacity** | 1,800–2,000 (2,076–2,435 max) |
| **300 ft.**   **Width** | 106 feet |

The first Royal Caribbean ships to offer balconies in a number of categories, these Vision-class vessels, named for sister ship *Vision of the Seas*, have acres of glass skylights that allow sunlight to flood in and windows that offer wide sea vistas. The soaring central atrium at the heart of each ship is anchored by a chic bar that fills with music after dark and is the ideal spot for watching the daring aerial performances overhead.

Built in pairs, the ships follow the same general layout but are different in overall size and the total number of passengers on board. Cabin sizes also vary somewhat; as the total size of the ships increased from *Legend* and *Splendour* at 69,130 tons (1,800 passengers) to *Grandeur* at 74,140 tons (1,992 passengers), and finally, *Rhapsody* and *Vision* at 78,491 tons (2,000 passengers), so did the size of the accommodations. In some categories, it's only a matter of a few feet, so don't look for huge—or even noticeable—differences.

## Cabins

**Cabins:** Cabins are airy and comfortable, but the smaller categories are a tight squeeze for more than two adults. Every cabin has adequate closet and drawer/shelf storage.

**Suites:** All full suites and family suites have private balconies and a small minibar; full suites also include concierge service. Royal suites have a living room; wet bar; separate dining area; entertainment center with TV, stereo, and DVD player; separate bedroom; bathroom (twin sinks, whirlpool tub, separate steam shower, bidet); and separate powder room. Owner's suites have a separate living area; minibar; entertainment center with TV, stereo, and DVD player; dinette area; and one bathroom (twin sinks, bathtub, separate shower, bidet). Grand suites have similar amenities on a smaller scale.

**Amenities:** A vanity-desk, a TV, a safe, a hair dryer, and a seating area with sofa, chair, and table are typical Vision-class features in all categories. Bathrooms have shampoo and bath gel.

**Accessibility:** On *Legend* and *Splendour*, 17 cabins are wheelchair accessible; on *Grandeur*, *Vision*, and *Rhapsody*, 14 cabins are wheelchair accessible.

Top: Viking Crown lounge overlooks the pool deck.
Bottom: *Splendour of the Seas* Vision-class Owner's suite

2

## Restaurants

The two-deck formal dining room serves evening meals in two assigned seatings or an open seating; breakfast and lunch in the dining room are always open seating. Windjammer, the casual Lido buffet, serves three meals a day, including a laid-back dinner. As was the norm when these ships were built, dining selections on board are pretty basic; however, specialty-dining options have been added. All ships now have restaurants serving Asian cuisine and a steak house, while Rhapsody and Grandeur also have Italian restaurants. Depending on the ship, Park Café or Solarium Café serves light fare and snacks in the solarium. *Splendour* also has Boardwalk Doghouse serving custom hot dogs. A coffee bar and ice cream bar offer specialty coffees and frozen treats for an additional fee. Room service is available 24 hours a day; however, there is a delivery charge after midnight.

## Spas

The full-service spa operated by Steiner Leisure offers an extensive treatment menu including facials, teeth whitening, body wraps and scrubs, massages, and acupuncture. Spa rituals also include treatments designed especially for men and teens. While there is no thermal suite, complimentary saunas and steam rooms are located in men's and women's changing rooms.

## Bars/Entertainment

Enjoy a Broadway-style production show, performances by guest entertainers, or a movie on the outdoor screen overlooking the pool, but don't forget to look high above the central atrium for dazzling aerial performances. You'll find lounges with music for listening and dancing when the entertainment staff ramps up the fun with themed parties. The Viking Crown Lounge is a great spot for late-night dancing or a nightcap.

## Pros and Cons

**Pros:** open, light-filled public areas offer sea views from almost every angle; each vessel now offers numerous dining options, both free and for a fee; daring aerialists offer a new wow-factor high above the central atrium.

**Cons:** some lounges serve as a thoroughfare and suffer from continuous traffic flow; except for premium suites, accommodations lean toward the small side; there are no self-service laundry rooms.

| Cabin Type | Size (sq. ft.) |
|---|---|
| Royal Suite | 1,074 |
| Owner's Suite | 523 |
| Grand Suite | 355 |
| Royal Family Suite | 512 |
| Junior Suite | 240 |
| Superior Ocean View | 193 |
| Large Ocean View* | 154 |
| Interior | 135–174 |

All cabin sizes are averages of the five ships since cabins vary somewhat in size among the Vision-class ships (all *Legend* and *Splendour* cabins are the same size). *Rhapsody* has family Ocean-View cabins at 237 sq. ft.

## FAST FACTS

- 11 passenger decks
- Dining room, buffet, ice cream parlor, pizzeria
- Wi-Fi, safe, refrigerator (some), DVD (some)
- 2 pools (1 indoor)
- Fitness classes, gym, hot tubs, sauna, spa, steam room
- 6 bars, casino, dance club, library, show room, video game room
- Children's programs
- Dry-cleaning, laundry service
- Internet terminal
- No-smoking cabins

# SEABOURN CRUISE LINE

Seabourn was founded on the principle that dedication to personal service in elegant surroundings would appeal to sophisticated, independent-minded passengers whose lifestyles demand the best. Lovingly maintained since their introduction in 1987—and rou-

Make memories to last a lifetime.

tinely updated with new features—the original megayachts of Seabourn and their new fleetmates have proved to be a smashing success over the years. They remain favorites with people who can take care of themselves but would rather do so aboard a ship that caters to their individual preferences.

☎ *800/929–9391*
⊕ *www.seabourn.com*
☞ *Cruise Style: Luxury.*

Recognized as a leader in small-ship, luxury cruising, Seabourn delivers all the expected extras—complimentary wines and spirits, a stocked minibar in all suites, and elegant amenities. Expect the unexpected as well—from exclusive travel-document portfolios and luggage tags to the pleasure of a complimentary mini-massage while lounging at the pool. If you don't want to lift a finger, Seabourn will even arrange to have your luggage picked up at home and delivered directly to your suite—for a price.

Peace and tranquility reign on these ships, so the daily roster of events is somewhat thin. Wine tastings, lectures, and other quiet pursuits might be scheduled, but most passengers are satisfied to simply do what pleases them. One don't-miss activity is the daily team trivia contest. Prizes are unimportant: it's the bragging rights that most guests seek.

Although the trio of original Seabourn ships has been upgraded over the years, the line launched a newer set of larger, even more luxurious triplets that were introduced in 2009 (*Seabourn Odyssey*), 2010 (*Seabourn Sojourn*), and 2011 (*Seabourn Quest*). Seabourn sold its three original ships to Windstar in 2013, and they will leave service by 2015.

## Food

As expected from a member of Chaîne des Rôtisseurs, Seabourn offers exceptional cuisine prepared *à la minute* and served in open seating dining rooms. Upscale menu offerings include foie gras, quail, fresh seafood, and jasmine crème brûlée. Dishes low in cholesterol, salt, and fat, as well as vegetarian selections, are prepared with the same artful presentation and attention to detail. Wines are chosen to complement each day's luncheon and dinner menus, and caviar is always available. A background of classical music sets the tone for afternoon tea. The weekly Gala Tea features such items as crêpes Suzette.

A casual dinner alternative on the original ships is Restaurant 2, serving innovative cuisine in multiple courses nightly in the Veranda Café, where outdoor tables enhance the romantic atmosphere. Evening attire in the Veranda Café is specified as casual or elegant casual—when men are asked to wear a jacket but no tie. A second and even more laid-back dinner alternative is offered on select occasions in the open-air Sky Bar, where grilled seafood and steaks are served. Sky Grill dinners are scheduled on a couple of nights during each cruise, weather permitting. Both Restaurant 2 and Sky Grill require reservations, but happily there is no additional charge for either. Aboard the new ships, Restaurant 2 has a dedicated space, and the Colonnade indoor-outdoor restaurant is centered on an open kitchen where you can watch chefs prepare your breakfast, lunch, or dinner order. Each evening has a different theme, offering an ever-changing culinary experience.

Room service is always available. Dinner can even be served course by course in your suite during restaurant hours.

## Entertainment

Dining and evening socializing are generally more stimulating to Seabourn passengers than splashy song-and-dance revues. Still, proportionately scaled production shows and cabarets are presented in the main show room and smaller lounges. Movies are shown on the wind-protected sundeck at least one evening on virtually all cruises as long as the weather permits. The library stocks not only books but also DVDs for those who prefer to watch movies in the privacy of their suites—popcorn will naturally be delivered with a call to room service.

## KNOWN FOR

■ **Service:** Service is a premiere element of all Seabourn voyages.

■ **Ever-changing Itineraries:** Seabourn ships seldom repeat port calls from one voyage to the next, nor do ships sail from a single home port.

■ **Formality:** Seabourn cruises are a bit more formal than most other luxury lines, but never stuffy.

■ **Older Clientele:** Fellow passengers on Seabourn's cruises are generally older and more well-traveled than on most cruise lines.

■ **Intimacy:** The line's small luxury ships (even their somewhat larger ones) can sail into the heart of landmark cities as well as visit smaller ports where large ships cannot go.

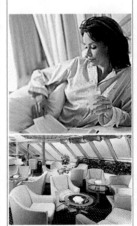

Top: A good book and breakfast in bed
Bottom: The Club

Top: French balcony
Middle: Dining by candlelight
in the Restaurant
Bottom: Relax on deck.

The inspiring enrichment program features guest appearances by luminaries in the arts, literature, politics, and world affairs; during certain culinary-focused sailings you can learn the secrets of the world's most innovative chefs. Due to the size of Seabourn ships, passengers have the opportunity to mingle with presenters and interact one-on-one.

### Fitness and Recreation

A full array of exercise equipment, free weights, and basic fitness classes is available in the small gym, while some specialized fitness sessions are offered for a fee.

Many passengers are drawn to the pampering spa treatments, including a variety of massages, body wraps, and facials. Hair and nail services are offered in the salon. Both spa and salon are operated by Steiner Leisure.

### Your Shipmates

Seabourn's yacht-like vessels appeal to well-traveled, affluent couples of all ages who enjoy destination-intense itineraries, a subdued atmosphere, and exclusive service. Passengers tend to be fifty-plus and retired couples who are accustomed to evening formality.

### Dress Code

At least one formal night is standard on seven-night cruises and three to four nights, depending on the itinerary, on two- to three-week cruises. Men are required to wear tuxedos or dark suits after 6 pm, and the majority prefers black tie. All other evenings are elegant casual, and slacks with a jacket over a sweater or shirt for men and a sundress or skirt or pants with a sweater or blouse for women are suggested.

### Junior Cruisers

Seabourn Cruise Line is adult-oriented and does not accommodate children under six months (or under one year for trans-ocean sailings and voyages of 15 days or longer). A limited number of suites are available for triple occupancy. No dedicated children's facilities are present on these ships, so parents are responsible for the behavior and entertainment of their children.

---

**CHOOSE THIS LINE IF ...**

You consider fine dining the highlight of your vacation.

You own your own tuxedo. These ships are dressy, and most men wear them on formal evenings.

You feel it's annoying to sign drink tabs; everything is included on these ships.

## Service

Personal service and attention by the professional staff are the orders of the day. Your preferences are noted and fulfilled without the necessity of reminders. It's a mystery how nearly every staff member knows your name within hours, if not minutes, after you board.

## Tipping

Tipping is neither required nor expected.

## Past Passengers

Once you have completed your first Seabourn cruise, you are automatically enrolled in the Seabourn Club for past guests. Benefits include discounts on selected cruises (not combinable with Early Booking Savings); the Seabourn Club newsletters and periodic mailings featuring destinations, special programs, and exclusive savings; and an exclusive online email contact point to the club desk through the membership page on the Seabourn website.

On the ships, club members receive a 5% discount on future bookings, special recognition for frequent cruising, and a club party hosted by the captain. As members reach Silver, Gold, Platinum, and Diamond Club levels, the benefits increase. Milestone Awards offer a complimentary cruise of up to seven days when 140 days sailed have been completed, or a complimentary cruise of up to 14 days when 250 days sailed is reached.

### HELPFUL HINTS

Seabourn's shore excursions often include privileged access to historic and cultural sites when they are not open to the general public.

Most warm-weather cruises include a beach picnic (albeit one with champagne and caviar); on itineraries where a beach isn't available, a similar party is held on the ships' water-sports marina.

A Vintage Seabourn pre-purchase wine option offers access to a varied selection of premium wines from the ships' well-stocked cellars at advantageous prices.

Every passenger gets a complimentary canvas logo tote bag.

Ground transfers are included in air and sea packages purchased through Seabourn, but passengers traveling independently are responsible for their own transfer to the ship.

## DON'T CHOOSE THIS LINE IF ...

Dressing down is on your agenda.

You absolutely must have a spacious private balcony. They are limited in number and book fast.

You need to be stimulated by constant activity.

# SEABOURN ODYSSEY, SEABOURN SOJOURN, SEABOURN QUEST

| | |
|---|---|
| Crew Members | 330 |
| Entered Service | 2009, 2010, 2011 |
| Gross Tons | 32,000 |
| Length | 650 |
| Number of Cabins | 225 |
| Passenger Capacity | 450 |
| Width | 84 |

As the first new class of ultraluxurious ships to be introduced in nearly a decade, *Seabourn Odyssey* and her sister ships promise to continue the line's tradition of understated elegance and signature features in a larger setting. With more space, there are more pools, more hot tubs, and a two-deck spa. The specialty dining room gets its own dedicated space, and there's more room to spread out on deck and in gracious public lounges indoors. As on the trio of smaller Seabourn vessels, there is a Club bar for predinner cocktails and an observation lounge affording expansive sea views. New for the larger ships is a spacious show lounge with a proper stage for entertainment. When the water-sports marina is extended, there's even a third swimming option—an enclosed in-sea "pool" with teak deck.

## Cabins

**Cabins:** All suites, 90% with balconies, are located midship to forward; none are aft. Eight categories of roomier accommodations are true suites, with separate bedrooms in all but the least expensive. Even the most modest suites have walk-in closets, a seating area with coffee table that converts to a dining table for meals, a dressing table–desk, and a granite-topped bathroom with double-sink vanities and a separate shower and tub (some with whirlpool tubs).

**Amenities:** Amenities include flat-screen TV with DVD player, safe, hair dryer, fully stocked minibar, fresh fruit and flowers, world atlas, personalized stationery, shampoo, conditioner, designer soap and lotion, Egyptian-cotton towels and robes, slippers, umbrellas, and beds dressed with silky, high-thread-count linens. Top-category suites have a butler's pantry and guest powder room. Wintergarden and Signature suites can be configured with two bedrooms.

**Accessibility:** Seven suites are designed for wheelchair accessibility.

## Restaurants

The formal Restaurant serves breakfast, lunch, and dinner in open seating. In Restaurant 2 (reservations), dishes are prepared individually by the chef in tasting portions. For casual indoor-outdoor dining, The Colonnade serves breakfast, lunch, and dinner from an open

Top: *Seabourn Odyssey* at sea
Bottom: *Seabourn Odyssey* penthouse

kitchen, with à la minute preparation. Breakfast, lunch, and dinner are also offered poolside at the Patio Grill. Espresso and cappuccino are available at the coffee bar. Meals and snacks can be ordered from an extensive room-service menu around the clock. During restaurant hours, dinner can be served course by course en suite.

## Spas

Treatments in the spa operated by Steiner Leisure include massages, facials, and body wraps that incorporate natural ingredients. Along with a treatment, you receive use of the thermal suite, with a large hydrotherapy pool (on *Seabourn Odyssey*) or the Kneipp Walk, a walking pool with hot water on one side and cold water on the other, utilized to stimulate circulation (on *Sojourn* and *Quest*). Heated loungers surround the pools, and a variety of steam and thermal rooms are included. Day passes (for a fee) are available for just the thermal suite, or you can opt for the free sauna in changing rooms.

## Bars/Entertainment

Proportionately scaled production shows, performances by guest artists, and cabarets are presented in the Grand Salon and smaller Club lounge, where dancing is held most nights. A pianist entertains in the Observation Bar. Movies and a deck party with dancing are scheduled on the wind-protected pool deck on most cruises as long as the weather permits.

## Pros and Cons

**Pros:** kayaks, waterskiing, and other complimentary water toys are available at the fold-down marina when the ships are at anchor; the fully equipped gym has a Kinesis Wall, an innovative method of exercise utilizing a pulley-and-cable system; there is never a cover charge for specialty dining.

**Cons:** choose your suite location carefully—not all balconies are equal, even within the same category; although the spa is opulent, it's still operated by Steiner, which operates spas on most cruise ships; past passengers take a proprietary interest in the ships and may seem cliquish to newcomers.

| Cabin Type | Size (sq. ft.) |
|---|---|
| Grand Wintergarden | 1,182 |
| Wintergarden Suites | 914 |
| Grand Signature | 1,135 |
| Signature Suites | 819 |
| Owner's Suites | 611–675 |
| Penthouse Suites | 436–611 |
| Veranda Suite | 269–302 |
| Ocean-View Suite | 295 |

### FAST FACTS

- 8 passenger decks
- Specialty restaurant, dining room, buffet
- Wi-Fi, safe, refrigerator, DVD
- 2 pools
- Fitness classes, gym, hot tubs, sauna, spa
- 5 bars, casino, dance club, library, show room
- Dry-cleaning, laundry facilities, laundry service
- Internet terminal

Standard suite

2

SEABOURN CRUISE LINE

# SEABOURN LEGEND, PRIDE, SPIRIT

| | |
|---:|---:|
| Crew Members | 160 |
| Entered Service | 1992, 1988, 1989 |
| Gross Tons | 10,000 |
| Length | 439 feet |
| Number of Cabins | 104 |
| Passenger Capacity | 208 |
| Width | 63 feet |

700 ft.

500 ft.

300 ft.

The height of absolute luxury, Seabourn's megayachts surround passengers in comfort and understated style punctuated by polished brass accents and etched-glass panels. Public rooms are intimate but not cramped, although predinner cocktail gatherings tend to strain the available room in the popular Club bar.

The relative amount of shipwide space devoted to passengers is among the highest in the cruise industry, and the public areas and deck spaces were designed so that no one aboard feels crowded. Fresh flower arrangements add a gracious touch to the classic decor of every public room.

After ambitious programs of extensive refurbishment, each of Seabourn's yacht-like vessels emerged from dry dock in shipshape.

Seabourn sold all three ships to Windstar in 2013; they will be phased out between April 2014 (*Pride*) through May 2015 (*Legend*).

## Cabins

**Cabins:** All suites are on three midlevel decks and none are aft, which can be noisy on a ship with a water-sports marina. The roomy accommodations are truly of suite proportions, with large walk-in closets, a spacious seating area with coffee table that converts to a dining table for meals, a vanity-desk, and a marble bathroom with a separate shower and tub (in most suites). Owner's, Classic, and Double suites have an actual dining table and chairs; Owner's suites have a guest bathroom. Both Owner's and Classic suites have fully furnished balconies.

**Amenities:** Amenities are also befitting a true luxury suite: a flat-screen TV with DVD player, a Bose Wave CD stereo, a safe, and a hair dryer. Other amenities include a stocked minibar, fresh fruit and flowers, a world atlas, personalized stationery, shampoo, conditioner, designer soap and lotion, Egyptian-cotton towels and robes, slippers, umbrellas, and beds dressed with silky, high-thread-count linens. The only apparent difference between the sister ships is that *Seabourn Spirit* and *Seabourn Pride* have twin sinks in the bathrooms, while *Seabourn Legend* bathrooms have but one.

**Accessibility:** Four suites are designed for wheelchair accessibility.

Top: Sky Bar
Bottom: Balcony suite

## Restaurants

The formal restaurant offers open seating breakfast, lunch, and dinner during scheduled hours. For a more laid-back setting, the Veranda Café has indoor and outdoor seating for breakfast and lunch, plus reservations-required Restaurant 2 serves tasting dinners in a smart-casual atmosphere every evening, including formal nights. The grill serves outdoors when weather permits for lunch and when Sky Grill dinners are scheduled on a couple of nights during each cruise. Tea is served every afternoon, and room service is available 24 hours. While you can order just about anything you want at any time, during scheduled lunch and dinner hours in the formal restaurant, room service is available from the restaurant menu.

## Spas

Treatments that range from massages and facials to body treatments and wraps that incorporate natural ingredients are offered in the Steiner Leisure–operated spa. There is no thermal suite, but complimentary steam rooms and saunas are located in men's and women's changing rooms.

## Bars/Entertainment

Proportionately scaled cabaret shows and performances by guest artists are presented in the Show Lounge and smaller Club Lounge, where the options might be a pianist or a dance party. Movies or dancing are scheduled on the pool deck on most cruises as long as the weather permits. There's little late-night action—most socializing takes place early and is subdued.

## Pros and Cons

**Pros:** as the high crew-to-guest ratio suggests, service is nonstop and the staff seems to anticipate your wishes; for pure indulgence, make a selection from the aromatherapy bath menu before a soak in the tub; complimentary Massage Moments on deck are soothing tension tamers.

**Cons:** a few minibalconies are available in standard suites, but they're simply for fresh air since there's no room to stand outside on them; a single outdoor swimming pool is deep but not long enough for serious laps; art, or the absence of it, is noteworthy on a ship of this style.

| Cabin Type | Size (sq. ft.) |
| --- | --- |
| Owner's Suite | 530–575 |
| Classic Suite | 400 |
| Double Suite | 554 |
| Balcony Suite* | 277 |
| Ocean View Suite | 277 |

*The balcony isn't functional.

### FAST FACTS

- 6 passenger decks
- Specialty restaurant, dining room, buffet
- Wi-Fi, safe, refrigerator, DVD
- Pool
- Fitness classes, gym, hot tubs, sauna, spa, steam room
- 3 bars, casino, dance club, library, show room
- Dry-cleaning, laundry facilities, laundry service
- Internet terminal

Water-sports marina

# SEADREAM YACHT CLUB

SeaDream yachts began sailing in 1984 beneath the Sea Goddess banner, and after a couple of changes of ownership and total renovations, they have evolved into the ultimate boutique ships. A voyage on one of these sleek megayachts is all about personal

*SeaDream I at sea*

choice. Passengers enjoy an unstructured holiday at sea doing what they please, making it easy to imagine the diminutive vessel really is a private yacht. The ambience is refined and elegantly casual.

☎ *305/631–6100 or 800/707–4911*
⊕ *www.seadream. com* ☞ *Cruise Style: Luxury.*

Fine dining and socializing with fellow passengers and the ships' captains and officers are preferred yachting pastimes.

A well-stocked library has books and movies for those who prefer quiet pursuits in the privacy of their staterooms. In addition, MP3 players stocked with all types of music—enough to play for a complete sailing without repeating a selection—are available for personal use at no charge.

The weekly picnic on a private beach is considered by many passengers as their most memorable experience ashore during a SeaDream cruise. It begins with refreshing drinks served during a wet landing from Zodiacs and is followed by SeaDream's signature champagne-and-caviar splash served to passengers from a surfboard bar in the crystal clear water. On voyages where it isn't possible to host the champagne-and-caviar splash ashore, it is celebrated poolside.

SeaDream yachts are often chartered by families, corporations, and other affinity groups, but the company does not charter both ships at the same time. If your chosen sailing is closed to you because of a charter, the other yacht will be available.

2

SEADREAM YACHT CLUB

## Food

Every meal is prepared to order using the freshest seafood and U.S. Prime cuts of beef. Menus include vegetarian alternatives and Asian wellness cuisine for the health-conscious. Cheeses, petits fours, and chocolate truffles are offered after dinner with coffee, and the Grand Marnier soufflé is to die for. A weekly dining event, Le Menu de Degustation, features an interesting medley of dishes planned by the executive chef for their variety and flavor; portions are sensibly sized, enabling diners to enjoy each course.

Weather permitting, daily breakfast, lunch, and special dinners are served alfresco in the canopied Topsider Restaurant. Wines are chosen to complement each luncheon and dinner menu from shipboard cellars that stock 3,500 bottles on each ship. Sommeliers are more than happy to discuss the attributes of each vintage and steam off the labels if you want to search for them at home. Snacks, from caviar to popcorn, are always available and delivered wherever you might be when hunger strikes, although there is a charge for caviar.

Room service is always available, and not just in your suite; you can dine anywhere you wish on deck.

## Entertainment

One of the most important daily events takes place before dinner, either in the Main Salon or poolside for cocktails and a review of the next day's activities. Other than a pianist in the tiny piano bar, a small casino, and movies in the main lounge, there's no roster of activities. The late-night place to be is the Top of the Yacht Bar, where passengers gather to socialize and dance on the teak deck. The captain hosts welcome-aboard and farewell cocktail receptions in the Main Salon each cruise. Otherwise, you're on your own to do as you please.

## Fitness and Recreation

Small gyms on each ship are equipped with treadmills, elliptical machines, recumbent bikes, and free weights. A personal trainer is available for consultation, and tai chi, yoga and aerobics classes are offered on deck as requested by passengers.

The yachts' unique SeaDream Spa facilities are also on the small side, yet offer a full menu of individualized, gentle Asian pampering treatments including massages, facials, and body wraps utilizing Eastern techniques. Hair and nail services are offered in the salon. SeaDream Spa is a member of the Thai Spa Association; products utilized for spa and salon services are among the best available from around the

### KNOWN FOR

■ **Small Size:** SeaDream Yacht Club is as different from big-ship cruising as possible with only 112 passengers on board and 95 crewmembers offering personalized service.

■ **Personal Attention:** The level of attention makes every passenger feel as if they are on a private yacht.

■ **Choices:** There's no pressure; you can be as active or as relaxed as you choose.

■ **Ever-changing Itineraries:** Itineraries are wide-ranging and seldom repeated on a week-to-week basis.

■ **Cuisine:** All food is prepared à la minute, and off-menu requests seldom go unfulfilled.

Top: Relax on a Balinese "dream bed."
Bottom: Fitness classes

Top: Dining at Topside
Restaurant
Middle: SeaDream Spa
Bottom: The Top of the
Yacht Bar

world. Massages are also available in cabanas ashore during the private beach party. Although the spa has regularly scheduled hours, treatments can be arranged outside those hours by special request. It's recommended that passengers schedule time for use of the sauna and steam room, as their size limits the number of people who can comfortably use them at once.

### Your Shipmates

SeaDream yachts attract energetic, affluent travelers of all ages, as well as groups. Passengers tend to be couples in their midforties up to retirees who enjoy the unstructured informality, subdued ambience, and utterly exclusive service.

These ships are not recommended for passengers who use wheelchairs. Although there's one accessible stateroom, public facilities have thresholds and the elevator doesn't reach the uppermost deck. Tide conditions can cause the gangway to be steep when docked, and negotiating shore tenders would be impossible.

### Dress Code

Leave the formal duds at home—every night is yacht casual on SeaDream. Men wear open-collar shirts and slacks; sport coats are preferred but not required. A tie is never necessary. For women, sundresses, dressy casual skirts and sweaters, or pants and tops are the norm.

### Junior Cruisers

SeaDream yachts are adult-oriented. Children under the age of one are not allowed. High chairs and booster seats are available for the youngsters occasionally on board, but no children's facilities or organized activities are available. Parents are responsible for the behavior and entertainment of their children.

---

**CHOOSE THIS LINE IF ...**

You enjoy dining as an event, as courses are presented with a flourish, and wine flows freely.

You don't like to hear the word no.

You have good sea legs. In rough seas, the SeaDream yachts tend to bob up and down.

## Service

Personal service and attention to detail are amazing; everyone will greet you by name within minutes of boarding. Passenger preferences are shared among staff members, who all work hard to assist one another. You seldom, if ever, have to repeat a request. Waiting in line for anything is unthinkable.

## Tipping

Tipping is neither required nor expected.

## Past Passengers

The SeaDream Club was designed to extend appreciation to past passengers, who are automatically enrolled in the club upon completion of one sailing. Members receive the *SeaDreamer* newsletter, which is published three times a year and features news and photos from the SeaDream yachts, profiles of the yachts' captains and other onboard personalities, profiles of various ports of call, news of special sailings, and other information of interest.

Other SeaDream Club benefits include advance notice of new itineraries, an annual club-members cruise, perks for introducing new passengers to SeaDream, a priority wait list on sold-out cruises, the ability to reserve spa appointments and shore excursions online, 5% to 15% savings when booking a future cruise while on board, an onboard club member cocktail party, and 15% onboard savings vouchers, which will be in your stateroom upon embarkation, for use towards onboard wine cellar purchases and treatments in the Asian Spa.

## HELPFUL HINTS

SeaDream Yacht Clubs can be chartered, but the line never charters both ships at once.

If you skip the evening cocktail hour, you may miss hearing about a last-minute decision by the captain to extend a port call or even change the order of ports if there's something of interest going on ashore.

SeaDream gives you the "pillow gift" of logo pajamas, which come in handy if you decide to sleep under the stars on a Balinese dream bed.

Special parties can be arranged on board by the club and activities director.

Even if there is no dinner scheduled on deck, just let the maître d' know at breakfast and your meal will be served outside that evening.

## DON'T CHOOSE THIS LINE IF ...

You like to dress up. Although you could wear a sport coat to dinner, no one ever wears a tie on these ships.

You must have a balcony. There are none on any of Seadream's yacht-like vessels.

You need structured activities. You'll have to plan your own.

# SEADREAM I, SEADREAM II

| | |
|---|---|
| Crew Members | 95 |
| Entered Service | 1984, 1985 |
| Gross Tons | 4,300 |
| Length | 344 feet |
| Number of Cabins | 56 |
| Passenger Capacity | 112 |
| Width | 47 feet |

Although these vessels are not huge, the public rooms are quite spacious; the Main Salon and Dining Salon are large enough to comfortably seat all passengers at once. Decor is elegant in its simplicity and is surprisingly non-nautical. Instead, it's modern and sleek, utilizing the hues of the sea, sky, and sandy beaches. Oriental rugs cover polished teak floors in the reception area and in the large, sun-splashed library, where you'll find more than 1,000 books from which to choose, as well as computers to access the Internet. The library also lends movies to watch on the flat-screen TV/DVD player in your suite. Balinese sun beds are the ideal spot to relax by day, either for sunbathing or reading beneath an umbrella. A telescope mounted at each ship's stern is handy for spotting land and other vessels at sea.

## Cabins

**Cabins:** Although none has a balcony, every stateroom has an ocean view, a seating area, and plenty of drawer space for storage. Bathrooms are marble-clad and have large, glass-enclosed showers with twin showerheads that make up for the tiny bathrooms. The single Owner's suite has a living room, a dining area, a separate bedroom, a bathroom with a sea view (as well as a separate tub and shower), and a guest bathroom. Each ship has an Admiral's suite, which features an open-plan living-dining area, a separate master bedroom, three panoramic windows, a marble bathroom with separate tub and shower, and a guest half-bath. Commodore Club staterooms are basically double staterooms with one side configured as a sitting-dining area room and feature two identical bathrooms with showers.

**Amenities:** All cabins have a large flat-screen TV, CD, and DVD system; broadband Internet connection; personalized stationery; and a wet bar stocked with complimentary beer, soft drinks, and bottled water. A lighted magnifying mirror and hair dryer are at a vanity table. Beds are dressed with Belgian linens and your choice of synthetic or down pillows. Bathrooms are stocked with deluxe Bulgari shampoo, shower gel, soap, and lotion. Turkish cotton bathrobes and slippers are provided for use during the cruise.

**Accessibility:** One stateroom is designed for wheelchair accessibility.

Top: Outdoor table at the Top of the Yacht Bar
Bottom: Casino play

## Restaurants

The formal dining room serves open seating breakfast, lunch, and dinner during scheduled hours. For a more casual setting, the Topside restaurant has outdoor seating for breakfast and lunch—either with table service or from a small buffet—plus scheduled dinners alfresco (the indoor restaurant is also open for those who do not wish to dine outside). Snacks are available at the Top of the Yacht Bar, and you only have to ask to receive anything from popcorn to caviar, although the caviar is no longer complimentary. A beach barbecue is scheduled once during every cruise. Room service is always available, and servers will bring your order to you on deck or in your suite.

## Spas

The Asian-inspired SeaDream Spa features Thai therapies in an extensive menu that includes such treatments as an Asian Blend massage, Javanese Lulur body treatment, and Traditional Thai Massage either in the tiny spa facility or in the open air private massage area (weather permitting). The sauna and steam room are complimentary, but appointments are recommended due to their small size.

## Bars/Entertainment

Passengers gather nightly before dinner for cocktails and a review of the next day's activities. On two evenings during each cruise, the captain hosts welcome aboard and farewell cocktail receptions in the Main Salon. Other than a pianist in the tiny piano bar and perhaps a movie or "disco night" in the Main Salon, there's no formal entertainment. The Top of the Yacht Bar is where most passengers gather to socialize and dance on the teak deck after dinner.

## Pros and Cons

**Pros:** the barbecue held on a deserted stretch of beach would be a highlight even if it didn't include champagne and caviar; the Top of the Yacht Bar is the sociable choice; no smoking is allowed indoors, which is refreshing.

**Cons:** the ships are not appropriate for anyone confined to a wheelchair, as public facilities have thresholds and the elevator doesn't reach the uppermost deck; there's a charge for wines and spirits ordered for your suite; you might miss schedule changes if you skip cocktails before dinner.

| Cabin Type | Size (sq. ft.) |
| --- | --- |
| Owner's Suite | 450 |
| Admiral Suite | 375 |
| Commodore Club | 390 |
| Yacht Club* | 195 |

*Sixteen of the Yacht Club staterooms are convertible to eight Commodore staterooms, giving a variable passenger capacity.

## FAST FACTS

- 5 passenger decks
- Dining room, buffet
- Internet, safe, refrigerator, DVD
- Pool
- Fitness classes, gym, hot tub, sauna, spa, steam room
- 3 bars, casino, library, show room
- Dry-cleaning, laundry service
- Internet terminal
- No-smoking cabins

**2**

**SEADREAM YACHT CLUB**

Pool deck

# SILVERSEA CRUISES

Silversea Cruises was launched in 1994 by the former owners of Sitmar Cruises, the Lefebvre family of Rome, whose concept for the new cruise line was to build and sail the highest-quality luxury ships at sea. Intimate ships, paired with exclusive amenities

The most captivating view on board

and unparalleled hospitality, are the hallmarks of Silversea cruises. All-inclusive air-and-sea fares can be customized to include not just round-trip airfare but all transfers, porterage, and deluxe precruise accommodations as well.

☎ 954/522–2299 or 877/276–6816 ⊕ *www.silversea. com* ☞ *Cruise Style: Luxury.*

Personalization is a Silversea maxim. Their ships offer more activities than other comparably sized luxury vessels. Take part in those that interest you, or opt instead for a good book and any number of quiet spots to read or snooze in the shade. Silversea's third generation of ships introduced even more luxurious features when the 36,000-ton *Silver Spirit* launched late in 2009. Silversea's *Silver Explorer* is the top choice for luxurious soft adventure expedition cruising, and in 2013 Silversea will add a second exploration ship that will sail exclusively in the Galapagos Islands.

### Food

Dishes from the galleys of Silversea's master chefs are complemented by those of La Collection du Monde, created by Silversea's culinary partner, the world-class chefs of Relais & Châteaux. Menus include hot and cold appetizers, at least four entrée selections, a vegetarian alternative, and Cruiselite cuisine (low in cholesterol, sodium, and fat). Special off-menu orders are prepared whenever possible, provided that the ingredients are available on board. In the event that they aren't, you may find after a day in port that a trip to the market was made in order to fulfill your request.

Chef Marco Betti, the owner of Antica Pasta restaurants in Florence, Italy, and Atlanta, Georgia, has designed a new menu for La Terrazza that focuses on one of the most luxurious food trends: the Slow Food movement. The goal of the movement is to preserve the gastronomic traditions of Italy through the use of fresh, traditional foods, and it has spread throughout the world. At La Terrazza (by day, a casual buffet) the menu showcases the finest in Italian cooking, from classic favorites to Tuscan fare. The restaurant carries no surcharge. Seating is limited, so reservations are a must to ensure a table—it's one reservation you'll be glad you took the time to book.

An intimate dining experience aboard each vessel is the wine restaurant by Relais & Châteaux—Le Champagne. Adding a dimension to dining, the exquisite cuisine is designed to celebrate the wines served—a different celebrated vintage is served with each course. Menus and wines are chosen by Relais & Chateaux sommeliers to reflect regions of the world noted for their rich wine heritage.

An evening poolside barbecue is a weekly dinner event, weather permitting. A highlight of every cruise is the Galley Brunch, when passengers are invited into the galley to select from a feast decorated with imaginative ice and vegetable sculptures. Even when meals are served buffet style in La Terrazza, you will seldom have to carry your own plate, as waiters are at hand to assist you to your table. Wines are chosen to complement each day's luncheon and dinner menus.

Grilled foods, sandwiches, and an array of fruits and salads are served daily for lunch at the Poolside Grill. Always available are extensive selections from the room-service menu. The full restaurant menu may be ordered from room service and can be served course by course in your suite during regular dining hours.

### Entertainment

Guest lecturers are featured on nearly every cruise; language, dance, and culinary lessons and excellent wine-appreciation sessions are always on the schedule of events. Silversea also schedules culinary arts cruises and a series of wine-focused voyages that feature award-winning authors, international wine experts, winemakers, and acclaimed chefs from the world's top restaurants. During afternoon tea the ranks of highly competitive trivia teams increase every successive day.

## KNOWN FOR

■ **Varied Destinations:** Silversea's destination-intensive fleet roams the globe, seldom repeating ports from one voyage to the next.

■ **All Suites:** All accommodations on Silversea ships are suites and all come with the service of butlers.

■ **Luxury Chic:** The style of Silversea ships is chic, but not stuffy.

■ **Friendly Crowd:** Unlike on some luxury lines, the well-traveled and well-heeled, sophisticated Silversea passengers are anything but stodgy.

■ **International Clientele:** An international mix of passengers are often found on the luxury line's voyages.

Top: Stylish entertainment
Bottom: La Terrazza alfresco dining

Top: Table tennis
Middle: Caring personal service
Bottom: Veranda suite

After dark, the Bar is a predinner gathering spot and the late-night place for dancing to a live band. A multitiered show lounge is the setting for talented singers and musicians, classical concerts, magic shows, big-screen movies, and folkloric entertainers from ashore. A small casino offers slot machines and gaming tables.

### Fitness and Recreation

The rather small gyms are equipped with cardiovascular and weight-training equipment, and fitness classes on *Silver Whisper* and *Silver Shadow* are held in the mirror-lined, but somewhat confining, exercise room. *Silver Spirit* introduced an expansive 8,300-square-foot spa and more spacious fitness center.

South Pacific–inspired Mandara Spa offers numerous treatments including exotic-sounding massages, facials, and body wraps. Hair and nail services are available in the busy salon. A plus is that appointments for spa and beauty salon treatments can be made online from 60 days until 48 hours prior to sailing.

Golfers can sign up with the pro on board for individual lessons utilizing a high-tech swing analyzer and attend complimentary golf clinics or participate in a putting contest.

### Your Shipmates

Silversea Cruises appeal to sophisticated, affluent couples who enjoy the country-club-like atmosphere, exquisite cuisine, and polished service on board, not to mention the exotic ports and unique experiences ashore.

### Dress Code

Two formal nights are standard on seven-night cruises and three to four nights, depending on the itinerary, on longer sailings. Men are required to wear tuxedos or dark suits after 6 pm. All other evenings are either informal, when a jacket is called for (a tie is optional, but most men wear them), or casual, when slacks with a jacket over an open-collar shirt for men and sporty dresses or skirts or pants with a sweater or blouse for women are suggested.

## CHOOSE THIS LINE IF ...

Your taste leans toward learning and exploration.

You enjoy socializing as well as the option of live entertainment, just not too much of it.

You like to plan ahead. You can reserve shore tours, salon services, and spa treatments online.

## Junior Cruisers

Silversea Cruises is adult-oriented, does not accommodate children less than six months of age, and the cruise line limits the number of children under the age of three on board. The availability of suites for a third passenger is capacity controlled. A youth program staffed by counselors is available on holiday and select sailings. No dedicated children's facilities are available, so parents are responsible for the behavior and entertainment of their children.

## Service

Personalized service is exacting and hospitable yet discreet. The staff strives for perfection and often achieves it. The attitude is decidedly European and begins with a welcome-aboard flute of champagne, then continues throughout as personal preferences are remembered and satisfied. The word *no* doesn't seem to be in the staff vocabulary in any language. Guests in all suites are pampered by butlers.

## Tipping

Tipping is neither required nor expected.

## Past Passengers

Membership in the Venetian Society is automatic on completion of one Silversea cruise, and members begin accruing benefits: Venetian Society cruise days and eligibility for discounts on select voyages, onboard recognition and private parties, milestone rewards; exclusive gifts, the *Venetian Society Newsletter*, ship visitation privileges, complimentary early embarkation or late debarkation at certain milestones, members-only benefits at select Leading Hotels of the World and Relais & Châteaux hotels and resorts, and select offers through Silversea's preferred partners.

Through the Friends of Society programs, members can double their accumulated cruise days and receive a shipboard spending credit by inviting friends or family members to sail on select Venetian Society sailings. Friends or family will enjoy the same Venetian Society savings as members for those cruises, a really nice perk.

## HELPFUL HINTS

Every Silversea voyage includes an exclusive Silversea Experience—a complimentary shoreside event, such as private access to museums after hours.

Silversea offers a customized collection of pre- and post-cruise land programs linking some of Relais & Châteaux's worldwide properties together with Silversea's global itineraries.

For a fee, Silversea will pick up your bags at home and deliver them to the ship, or vice versa.

If adults travel with minors under the age of 18 who are not their children, a signed parental consent guardianship form is required.

Requests must be made in writing no later than 14 days prior to departure if you want to arrange a Bon Voyage Party or have visitors board the ship at your embarkation port.

## DON'T CHOOSE THIS LINE IF ...

You want to dress informally at all times on your cruise. Passengers on these cruises tend to dress up.

You need highly structured activities and have to be reminded of them.

You prefer the glitter and stimulation of Las Vegas to the understated glamour of Monte Carlo.

# SILVER SPIRIT

| | |
|---|---|
| Crew Members | 376 |
| Entered Service | 2010 |
| Gross Tons | 36,000 |
| Length | 642 feet |
| Number of Cabins | 270 |
| Passenger Capacity | 540 |
| Width | 86 feet |

700 ft.
500 ft.
300 ft.

The stylish interiors of *Silver Spirit*'s public rooms reflect a 1930s art deco flavor. Although the decor is warmer and more inviting than previous Silversea ships, you'll still find signature spaces like the Humidor, the Bar, and the indoor–outdoor La Terrazza restaurant.

With one of the most generous space-to-guest ratios in the cruise industry, *Silver Spirit* features an expansive 8,300-square-foot spa with a thermal suite and outdoor whirlpool; a state-of-the-art fitness complex with two aerobics studios; six places to dine; three high-end, duty-free boutiques; and the largest suites in the Silversea fleet. In addition, deck space is expansive, with plenty of teak chaise longues, two whirlpools, and a bar poolside. The resort-style pool is even heated for cooler weather.

## Cabins

**Cabins:** Every suite has an ocean view, and 95% have a private teak-floor balcony. Standard suites have a seating area that can be curtained off from the bed. Marble bathrooms have double sinks and a separate glass-enclosed shower as well as a tub. All suites have generous walk-in closets. Sixteen suites have connecting doors.

**Top Suites:** In addition to much more space, top-category suites have all the standard amenities plus dining areas, separate bedrooms, and CD players. Silver suites and above have whirlpool tubs. All categories have butler service.

**Amenities:** Standard suites have a flat-screen TV and DVD, personalized stationery, cocktail cabinet, safe, and fully stocked refrigerator. A hair dryer is provided at a vanity table. Beds are dressed with high-quality linens, duvets, or blankets, and your choice of synthetic or down pillows. Bathrooms have huge towels and plush terry bathrobes for use during the cruise as well as a choice of designer shampoos, soaps, and lotions.

**Accessibility:** Four suites are designed for wheelchair accessibility.

## Restaurants

The formal restaurant offers open seating breakfast, lunch, and dinner. Le Champagne (reservation, cover charge) offers a gourmet meal and wine pairings; Sieshin Restaurant serves Kobe beef, sushi, and Asian seafood (some items with surcharge). Stars Supper Club offers

Top: *Silver Spirit* at sea
Bottom: Standard suite

trendsetting menus, and La Terrazza serves Italian cuisine. For casual meals, La Terrazza has indoor and outdoor seating for buffet-style breakfast and lunch. The outdoor Grill offers a laid-back lunch option poolside as well as an alfresco dinner, when it is called Black Rock Grill, which allows you to cook meats and seafood to your liking on preheated volcanic stones at your table. Afternoon tea is served daily. Room service arrives with crystal, china, and linens. You may order at any time from the extensive room-service menu, or the full restaurant menu during dining hours.

## Spas

Mandara Spa, a division of Steiner Leisure, offers treatments including exotic massages, facials, and body wraps, teeth whitening, acupuncture, and medi-spa cosmetic treatments. Also available are indoor/outdoor relaxation areas, an outdoor whirlpool, and a thermal suite furnished with heated lounge chairs and a Turkish bath. There's a fee to use the spa's thermal areas, but the men's and ladies' locker rooms have complimentary saunas and steam rooms.

## Bars/Entertainment

A multitiered show lounge is the setting for talented singers and musicians, classical concerts, magic shows, big-screen movies, and folkloric entertainers from ashore. The Bar is a predinner gathering spot and a late-night place for dancing to a live band. A pianist or other entertainers perform in the Panorama Lounge for listening and dancing. When the weather permits, concerts or movies are presented on deck.

## Pros and Cons

**Pros:** onboard atmosphere is sophisticated yet relaxed; chilled champagne welcomes every passenger to his suite; Silver suites are the most popular accommodations on Silversea ships, and *Silver Spirit* has twice as many as her fleetmates.

**Cons:** one accommodations deck doesn't have a passenger laundry room; the addition of a limited children's program could mean more youngsters on board than normal; you could get so spoiled aboard *Silver Spirit* that you'll never want to go home.

| Cabin Type | Size (sq. ft.) |
|---|---|
| Grand Suite | 1,425–1,532 |
| Owner's Suite | 1,292 |
| Royal Suite | 990 |
| Silver Suite | 742 |
| Veranda Suite | 376 |
| Vista Suite | 312 |

## FAST FACTS

- 8 passenger decks
- 4 specialty restaurants, dining room, buffet
- Wi-Fi, safe, refrigerator, DVD
- Pool
- Fitness classes, gym, hot tubs, sauna, spa, steam room
- 3 bars, casino, dance club, library, show room
- Children's program
- Dry-cleaning, laundry facilities, laundry service
- Internet terminal
- No-smoking cabins

The spa at *Silversea*

**2**

**SILVERSEA CRUISES**

# SILVER SHADOW, SILVER WHISPER

| | |
|---|---|
| Crew Members | 295 |
| Entered Service | 2000, 2001 |
| Gross Tons | 28,258 |
| Length | 610 feet |
| Number of Cabins | 191 |
| Passenger Capacity | 382 |
| Width | 82 feet |

700 ft.

500 ft.

300 ft.

The logical layout of these sister ships, with suites in the forward two-thirds of the ship and public rooms aft, makes orientation simple. The clean, modern decor that defines public areas and lounges might seem almost stark, but it places the main emphasis on large expanses of glass for sunshine and sea views as well as passenger comfort.

Silversea ships boast unbeatable libraries stocked with best sellers, travel books, classics, and movies for en suite viewing. Extremely wide passageways in public areas are lined with glass-front display cabinets full of interesting and unusual artifacts from the places the ships visit. The Connoisseur's Corner is a clubby cigar smoking room with overstuffed leather seating and a ventilation system that makes it possible for even non-smokers to appreciate.

## Cabins

**Cabins:** Every suite has an ocean view, and more than 80% have a private teak-floor balcony. Standard suites have a seating area that can be curtained off from the bed. Marble bathrooms have double sinks and a separate glass-enclosed shower as well as a tub. All suites have generous walk-in closets.

**Top Suites:** In addition to much more space, top-category suites have all the standard amenities plus dining areas, separate bedrooms, and CD players. Silver suites and above have whirlpool tubs. The top three categories have espresso makers and separate powder rooms. All are served by butlers.

**Amenities:** Standard suites have a TV and DVD, personalized stationery, cocktail cabinet, safe, and stocked refrigerator. A hair dryer is provided at a vanity table, and you can request a magnifying mirror. Beds are dressed with high-quality linens and your choice of synthetic or down pillows. Bathrooms have huge towels and terry robes for use during the cruise as well as designer shampoo, soaps, and lotion.

**Accessibility:** Two suites are designed for wheelchair accessibility.

Top: The casino
Bottom: *Silver Shadow* at sea

## Restaurants

The Restaurant offers open seating breakfast, lunch, and dinner. Le Champagne (reservation, cover charge) offers a gourmet meal and wine pairings; La Terrazza serves Italian cuisine. For casual meals, La Terrazza has indoor and outdoor seating for buffet-style breakfast and lunch. The outdoor Grill offers a laid-back lunch option with poolside table service. The do-it-yourself Black Rock Grill allows you to cook meats and seafood to your liking on preheated volcanic stones tableside. Elaborate afternoon tea is served daily. An evening poolside barbecue is a weekly dinner event as a galley brunch. Room service is available anytime and arrives with crystal, china, and a linen tablecloth; if desired, service can be course by course.

## Spas

South Pacific–inspired Mandara Spa, a division of Steiner Leisure, offers treatments including exotic-sounding massages, facials, and body wraps, teeth whitening, acupuncture, and medi-spa cosmetic treatments. There is no thermal suite, but complimentary saunas and steam rooms are located in the men's and ladies' locker rooms.

## Bars/Entertainment

The show lounge is the setting for singers and musicians, classical concerts, magic shows, big-screen movies, and folkloric entertainers from ashore. The Bar is the most popular predinner gathering spot and a late-night place for dancing to a live band. A pianist or other entertainers perform in the Panorama Lounge for listening and dancing. Concerts or movies are presented on deck, weather permitting.

## Pros and Cons

**Pros:** champagne flows freely throughout your cruise; sailing on a Silversea ship is like spending time as a guest at a home in the Hamptons where everything is at your fingertips; Silversea is so all-inclusive that you'll seldom use your room card for anything but opening your suite door.

**Cons:** lines can form to use a washing machine in the smallish (yet totally free) laundry rooms; in an odd contrast to the contents of display cases and lovely flower arrangements, artwork on the walls is fairly ho-hum; the spa's complimentary saunas and steam rooms are quite small.

| Cabin Type | Size (sq. ft.) |
|---|---|
| Grand Suite | 1,286–1,435 |
| Royal Suite | 1,312–1,352 |
| Owner's Suite | 1,208 |
| Silver Suite | 701 |
| Medallion Suite | 521 |
| Verandah Suite | 345 |
| Terrace Suite | 287 |
| Vista Suite | 287 |

### FAST FACTS

- 7 passenger decks
- 2 specialty restaurants, dining room, buffet
- Wi-Fi, safe, refrigerator, DVD
- Pool
- Fitness classes, gym, hot tubs, sauna, spa, steam room
- 3 bars, casino, dance club, library, show room
- Dry-cleaning, laundry facilities, laundry service
- Internet terminal
- No-smoking cabins

The Poolside Grill serves lunch and light snacks.

# SILVER CLOUD, SILVER WIND

| | |
|---|---|
| Crew Members | 212 |
| Entered Service | 1994, 1995 |
| Gross Tons | 17,400 |
| Length | 514 feet |
| Number of Cabins | 148 |
| Passenger Capacity | 298 |
| Width | 71 feet |

700 ft.

500 ft.

300 ft.

These two yacht-like gems are all about style, understatement, and personal choice, so if you want to snuggle into a book in the well-stocked library, no one will lift an eyebrow. Although there simply isn't enough square footage on these ships for huge rooms, the public spaces are more than adequate and designed to function well. These ships served as the models for their larger sisters, *Silver Shadow* and *Silver Whisper,* which expanded on the smaller ships' concept of locating all passenger accommodations forward and public rooms aft.

The Restaurant is one of the loveliest dining rooms at sea, with a domed ceiling and musicians to provide dance music between courses. Both the Bar and Panorama Lounge are comfortable spots to socialize, dance, or enjoy cocktails before or after the evening entertainment, which might include a classical concert or smallish production show in the show room or Moonlight Movies, feature films shown outside on the pool deck.

## Cabins

**Cabins:** All accommodations are considered suites; all are outside and have at least an ocean view; 80% also have private balconies. Suite interiors are enhanced with appealing artwork, flowers, seating areas, and bedding topped with plush duvets and choice of pillow style. A writing desk, refrigerator, TV with DVD player, dressing table with lighted mirror and hair dryer, walk-in closet, and safe are all standard. The marble and stone bathrooms have full-size bathtubs. Teak-floor balconies have patio furniture and floor-to-ceiling glass doors. All suites have butler service.

**Amenities:** Champagne on ice awaits the arrival of all passengers, and it is replenished as desired; the beverage cabinet is stocked daily on request with individual selections of wines, spirits, and beverages. A fruit basket is replenished daily. Bathrooms are stocked with plush towels and European toiletries, and slippers and bathrobes are provided for use during the cruise.

**Accessibility:** Two suites are wheelchair accessible.

## Restaurants

The formal restaurant offers open seating breakfast, lunch, and dinner during scheduled hours. Specialty dining is offered by reservation in Le Champagne, where an extra charge applies for the gourmet meal

Top: The Bar
Bottom: Royal suite

and wine pairings, and La Terrazza, which is complimentary and serves Italian cuisine. For casual meals, La Terrazza has indoor and outdoor seating for buffet-style breakfast and lunch. The outdoor Grill offers a laid-back lunch option with poolside table service. An alfresco dinner option on *Silver Cloud* is the Black Rock Grill, which allows you to cook meats and seafood to your liking on preheated volcanic stones right at your table. Elaborate afternoon tea is served daily. An evening poolside barbecue is a weekly dinner event, as is the Galley Brunch, when passengers are invited into the galley to make their selections. Room service arrives with crystal, china, and a linen tablecloth for a complete dining room–style setup en suite. You may order at any time from the extensive room-service menu or the full restaurant menu, which can be served course by course in your suite during regular dining hours.

### Spas

Mandara Spa, operated by Steiner Leisure, offers treatments including exotic massages, facials, and body wraps, teeth whitening, acupuncture, and medi-spa cosmetic treatments. There is no thermal suite, but complimentary saunas and steam rooms are located in the men's and ladies' locker rooms.

### Bars/Entertainment

The show lounge is the setting for singers and musicians, classical concerts, magic shows, big-screen movies, and folkloric entertainers from ashore. The Bar is a predinner gathering spot and a late-night place for dancing to a live band. A pianist or other entertainers perform in the Panorama Lounge for listening and dancing. When the weather permits, concerts or movies are presented on deck.

### Pros and Cons

**Pros:** ambience on board is comfortably upscale, heightened by never having to sign a bar ticket; wine is poured freely at lunch and dinner; every cruise features regionally specific lectures by experts who share insights into areas of the world they know intimately.

**Cons:** minimalist modern decor could be improved; the sophisticated, all-adult atmosphere is sometimes disrupted by bored children who have nothing to do; the slow pace of evening entertainment isn't satisfying if you prefer splashy production revues and Vegas-type shows.

| Cabin Type | Size (sq. ft.) |
|---|---|
| Grand Suite | 1,019–1,314 |
| Royal Suite | 736–1,031 |
| Owner's Suite | 587–827 |
| Silver Suite | 541 |
| Medallion Suite | 470–678 |
| Veranda Suite | 295 |
| Vista Suite | 240 |

Grand, Royal, and Owner's suites available with one or two bedrooms; Medallion suite on deck 7 has no balcony.

## FAST FACTS

- 6 passenger decks
- 2 specialty restaurants, dining room, buffet
- Wi-Fi, safe, refrigerator, DVD
- 1 pool
- Fitness classes, gym, hot tub, sauna, spa, steam room
- 3 bars, casino, dance club, library, show room
- Dry-cleaning, laundry facilities, laundry service
- Internet terminal
- No-smoking cabins

The pool deck

# SILVER EXPLORER

| | |
|---|---|
| Crew Members | 117 |
| Entered Service | 2008 |
| Gross Tons | 6,072 |
| Length | 354 feet |
| Number of Cabins | 66 |
| Passenger Capacity | 132 |
| Width | 52 feet |

700 ft.

500 ft.

300 ft.

In a departure from their usual custom of building new ships, Silversea acquired an older purpose-built expedition ship with an ice-strengthened hull and totally transformed it for soft-adventure expedition cruising in luxurious style. Designed for navigating waters in some of the world's most remote destinations, including both polar regions, passengers on board find not only eight Zodiac boats to whisk them on adventurous excursions, but also many special amenities usually found only on larger ships, including a spacious library with an Internet café, a boutique for shopping, a full-service spa, beauty salon, fitness center, sauna, and two top-deck whirlpools. Unique among expedition vessels, the *Silver Explorer* even features the Connoisseur's Corner, where the finest cigars and cognacs can be enjoyed.

Although there is live evening entertainment, the primary focus aboard is on the destinations and learning about the regions visited. Presentations led by the Expedition Team and guest experts are always well attended.

## Cabins

**Cabins:** All suites and staterooms include champagne upon arrival, refrigerator and bar setup stocked with your preferences, European-designer bath amenities, down duvets, fine bed linens, premium mattresses, a selection from a pillow menu, personalized stationery, TV, hair dryer, and plush robes and slippers. Expedition binoculars and an umbrella are provided for use on board. In addition to daily service and nightly turndown, butler service is available in all accommodations categories. Two hours of complimentary Internet service per day and two hours of international telephone service per voyage, as well as complimentary dry-cleaning and laundry and afternoon canapés, are perks offered to Owner's and Grand suites. Fourteen pairs of suites have interconnecting doors.

**Layout:** When compared to the rest of the luxury fleet, *Silver Explorer*'s accommodations can be disappointing. Only three suite categories—Owner's, Grand, and Medallion—have real balconies. Silver and Veranda suites have French balconies that offer fresh air, but not a seating area.

**Accessibility:** There are no accommodations designed for wheelchair accessibility.

Top: *Silver Explorer* in the harbor
Bottom: Dining on *Silver Explorer*

### Restaurants

The main dining room, simply named the Restaurant, serves breakfast, lunch, and dinner. All meals are open seating, which allows you to dine when and with whom you wish. Menus feature classical and modern cuisine with an international flair. Low-calorie, low-carb, vegetarian, and vegan options are also available. The Outdoor Grill, a casual bar and grill, offers a range of lunch favorites and lighter fare served on the open deck. Room service is available around the clock.

### Spas

The small spa, with a single treatment room, is operated by Steiner Leisure. Despite its size there is a full menu of treatments including exotic-sounding massages, facials, and body wraps, A steam room and sauna are complimentary to all.

### Bars/Entertainment

Adventure- and destination-oriented, the nightlife aboard *Silver Explorer* is amiable and social, but organized entertainment is limited. Passengers gather for drinks and socializing, either in the clubby Connoisseur's Corner where smoking is permitted, or while a pianist or other entertainers perform in the Panorama Lounge for listening and dancing.

### Pros and Cons

**Pros:** a complimentary water-resistant backpack is provided to each passenger; every expedition features complimentary excursions led by the Expedition Team or a guest host; there's no extra charge to send a fax or print something in the Internet café.

**Cons:** special meal requests that are routine on other Silversea ships might not be possible on *Silver Explorer*; children under six are not allowed on Zodiacs (and an adult must remain on board the ship with the child); the ship has 220-volt power with European-style outlets that require a plug adapter or a transformer.

| Cabin Type | Size (sq. ft.) |
|---|---|
| Owners Suite/ Grand Suite | 626/675 |
| Silver/Expedition Suite | 460/460 |
| Medallion Suite | 351 |
| Veranda/Vista/ View Suite | 230/194– 230/230 |
| Explorer/Adventurer Class | 185–275/ 175–184 |

### FAST FACTS

- 5 passenger decks
- Dining room
- Wi-Fi, safe, refrigerator
- Gym, hot tubs, sauna, spa, steam room
- 2 bars, library
- Dry-cleaning, laundry service
- Internet terminal
- No-smoking cabins
- No kids under 1

2

SILVERSEA CRUISES

Veranda Suite

# STAR CLIPPERS

In 1991, Star Clippers unveiled a new tall-ship alternative to sophisticated travelers whose desires include having an adventure at sea but not on board a conventional cruise ship. Star Clippers vessels are four- and five-masted sailing beauties—the world's

Sun yourself on the bow netting.

largest barkentine and full-rigged sailing ships. Filled with modern, high-tech equipment as well as the amenities of private yachts, the ships rely on sail power while at sea unless conditions require the assistance of the engines. Minimal heeling, usually less than 6%, is achieved through judicious control of the sails.

☎ 305/442–0550 or 800/442–0551 ⊕ www.starclippers. com ☞ Cruise Style: Small Ship.

A boyhood dream became a cruise-line reality when Swedish entrepreneur Mikael Krafft launched his fleet of authentic recreations of classic 19th-century clipper ships. The day officially begins when the captain holds an informative daily briefing on deck with a bit of storytelling tossed in.

The lack of rigid scheduling is one of Star Clippers' most appealing attractions. The bridge is always open, and passengers are welcome to peer over the captain's shoulder as he plots the ship's course. Crew members are happy to demonstrate how to splice a line, reef a sail, or tie a proper knot.

As attractive as the ships' interiors are, the focal point of Star Clippers cruises is the outdoors. Plan to spend a lot of time on deck soaking in the sun, sea, and sky. It doesn't get any better than that. Consider also that each ship has at least two swimming pools. Granted, they are tiny, but they are a refreshing feature uncommon on true sailing ships and all but the most lavish yachts.

Although the Star Clippers ships are motorized, their engines are shut down whenever crews unfurl the sails (36,000 square feet on *Star Clipper* and *Star Flyer*, and 56,000 square feet on *Royal Clipper*) to capture the wind. On a typical cruise, the ships rely exclusively on sail power any time favorable conditions prevail. As the haunting strains of Vangelis's symphony "1492: Conquest of Paradise" are piped over the PA system and the first of the sails is unfurled, the only thing you'll hear on deck is the sound of the music and the calls of the line handlers until every sail is in place. While the feeling of the wind powering large ships through the water is spine-tingling, you will miss the wondrous sight of your ship under sail unless the captain can schedule a photo opportunity utilizing one of the tenders. It's one of the most memorable sights you'll see if this opportunity avails itself. However, when necessary, the ships will cruise under motor power to meet the requirements of their itineraries.

## Food

Not noted for gourmet fare, the international cuisine is what you would expect from a trendy shoreside bistro, albeit an elegant one. All meals are open seating in the formal dining room during scheduled hours; breakfast and lunch—an impressive spread of seafood, salads, and grilled items—are served buffet-style, while dinners are leisurely affairs served in the European manner. Hint: If you want your salad *before* your main course, just ask; the French style is to serve it after the main course. Menus, created in consultation with chef Jean Marie Meulien (who has been awarded Michelin stars throughout his career), include appetizers, soups, pasta, a sorbet course, at least three choices of entrées, salad, cheese, and, of course, dessert. Mediterranean-inspired entrées, vegetarian, and light dishes are featured. A maître d' is present at the more formal evening meals to seat passengers, but it isn't uncommon on these small ships for passengers to arrange their own groups of dinner company.

Early risers on each ship find a Continental breakfast offered at the Tropical Bar, and coffee and fresh fruit are always available in the Piano Bar. Should you want to remain in your swimsuit, casual buffets are set up adjacent to the Tropical Bar at noon (the Deck Snack Buffet) and at 5 pm (the Afternoon Snack). Some of the snacks are themed and quite popular—a Neptune seafood luncheon, snacks with waffles or crepes, or a midday taco bar. On select itineraries, an outdoor barbecue is served on shore.

KNOWN FOR

■ **Sailing:** Star Clippers are real sailing vessels that only use their engines to augment the wind and stay on schedule.

■ **Casual:** Totally casual, Star Clipper voyages are unstructured.

■ **Soft Adventure:** Itineraries offer the opportunity to experience adventurous activities ashore and in the water, and most include beach breaks.

■ **Comfort:** Appointments are nautical and cabins a bit small, yet as elegant as a millionaire's yacht.

■ **Unique Destinations:** Star Clippers sailing ships can visit ports where large ships cannot go.

Top: Cooling off in one of the pools
Bottom: *Royal Clipper* Deluxe suite

**2**

**STAR CLIPPERS**

Top: View from the bow
Middle: *Royal Clipper* piano bar
Bottom: *Royal Clipper* spa

With the exception of occupants of Owner's suites and Deluxe suites on *Royal Clipper*, there is no room service unless you are sick and can't make it to the dining room for meals.

### Entertainment

Star Clippers are not cruise ships in the ordinary sense with strict agendas and pages of activities. You're free to do what you please day and night, but many passengers join the crew members topside when the sails are raised or for some of the lighthearted events like crab-racing contests, scavenger hunts, and a talent night. The informality of singing around a piano bar typifies an evening on one of these ships, although in certain ports local performers come aboard to spice up the action with an authentic taste of the local music and arts.

### Fitness and Recreation

Formal exercise sessions take a backseat to water sports, although aerobics classes and swimming are featured on all ships. Only *Royal Clipper* has a marina platform that can be lowered in calm waters to access water sports and diving; however, the smaller ships replicate the experience by using motorized launches to reach reefs for snorkeling. A gym-spa with an array of exercise equipment, free weights, spa treatments, and unisex hair services are also found only on *Royal Clipper*. Despite the lack of a formal fitness center on *Star Flyer* and *Star Clipper*, morning aerobics or yoga classes are usually held on deck for active passengers. Massages, manicures, and pedicures can be arranged as well.

### Your Shipmates

Star Clippers cruises draw active, upscale American and European couples in their thirties and up, who enjoy sailing but in a casually sophisticated atmosphere with modern conveniences. Many sailings are equally divided between North Americans and Europeans, so announcements are made in several languages accordingly.

This is not a cruise line for the physically challenged: there are no elevators or ramps, nor are staterooms or bathrooms wheelchair accessible. Gangways and shore launches can also be difficult to negotiate.

---

### CHOOSE THIS LINE IF ...

You wouldn't consider a vacation on a traditional cruise ship but are a sailing enthusiast.

You love water sports, particularly snorkeling and scuba diving.

You want to anchor in secluded coves and visit islands that are off the beaten path.

## Dress Code

All evenings are elegant casual, so slacks and open-collar shirts are fine for men, and sundresses, skirts, or pants with a sweater or blouse are suggested for women. Coats and ties are never required. Shorts and T-shirts are not allowed in the dining room at dinner.

## Junior Cruisers

Star Clippers ships are adult-oriented. Although children are welcome and may participate in shipboard activities suited to their ability, there are no dedicated youth facilities. Parents are responsible for the behavior and entertainment of their children. Mature teens who can live without video games and the company of other teens are the best young sailors.

## Service

Service is friendly and gracious, similar to what you would find in a boutique hotel or restaurant. You may find that you have to flag down a waiter for a second cup of coffee, though.

## Tipping

Gratuities are not included in the cruise fare and are extended at the sole discretion of passengers. The recommended amount is €8 per person per day. Tips are pooled and shared; individual tipping is discouraged. You can either put cash in the tip envelope provided, and drop it at the Purser's Office, or charge gratuities to your shipboard account. An automatic 15% gratuity is added to each passenger's bar bill.

## Past Passengers

Top Gallant is the loyalty club for past passengers. No specific fare discount is offered to members; however, they receive a newsletter and special offers on fare reductions from time to time. Nearly 60% of all passengers choose to make a repeat voyage on Star Clippers ships.

## HELPFUL HINTS

The currency for all onboard charges is the euro regardless of where you are sailing.

A guaranteed single fare is available at a specific rate depending on the travel season and length of sailing, but passengers sailing as guaranteed singles may not choose their cabin.

Passengers cannot bring alcoholic beverages onboard for consumption on the ship (duty-free liquor is held until the end of the cruise).

Star Clippers aren't handicap accessible. They have no elevators or ramps and access to land is often via the ships' launches.

For pre-cruise planning, detailed port information and shore excursion descriptions are available online at the Star Clippers website.

## DON'T CHOOSE THIS LINE IF ...

You have a preexisting or potentially serious medical condition. There's no physician on board.

You must have a private balcony—there are a few, but only in top accommodation categories.

You can't live without room service. Only *Royal Clipper* has it, and only in a few high-end suites.

# ROYAL CLIPPER

| | |
|---|---|
| Crew Members | 106 |
| Entered Service | 2000 |
| Gross Tons | 5,000 |
| Length | 439 feet |
| Number of Cabins | 114 |
| Passenger Capacity | 227 |
| Width | 54 feet |

700 ft.

500 ft.

300 ft.

*Royal Clipper* is the first five-masted, full-rigged sailing ship built since 1902. As the largest true sailing clipper ship in the world today, she carries 42 sails with a total area of 56,000 square feet. Unusual for a sailing ship, a three-deck atrium graces the heart of the vessel.

Her interior is decorated in Edwardian-era style with abundant gleaming wood, brass fixtures, and nautical touches. Light filters into the piano bar, three-deck-high atrium, and dining room through the glass bottom and portholes of the main swimming pool located overhead.

The rarely used Observation Lounge is forward of the Deluxe suites and affords great sea views. It is also the location of the computer station for all Internet access.

## Cabins

**Cabins:** Think yacht, and the cabin sizes make sense. Although efficiently laid out with tasteful, seagoing appointments and prints of clipper ships and sailing yachts on the walls, cabins are small in comparison to most cruise ships. All have a TV, safe, vanity-desk, small settee, hair dryer, and marble bathroom with standard toiletries. Closet space is compact, and bureau drawers are narrow, but an under-the-bed drawer is a useful nautical touch for extra storage. Cabins have 220-volt electrical outlets and a 110-volt outlet suitable only for electric shavers. For 110-volt appliances, you'll need to bring a transformer; for dual-voltage appliances, pack a plug converter.

**Suites:** Owner's suites, Deluxe suites, and Category 1 cabins have a seating area, minibar, whirlpool tub-shower combination, and bathrobes to use during the cruise. Deluxe suites also feature a private veranda. Category 1 cabins have doors that open onto a semiprivate area on the outside deck. Only the two Owner's suites have connecting doors.

**Accessibility:** None of the staterooms are designed for wheelchair accessibility, nor are there any elevators.

Top: *Royal Clipper* dining room
Bottom: Sighting land

| Cabin Type | Size (sq. ft.) |
|---|---|
| Owner's Suite | 355 |
| Deluxe Suite and Category 1 Ocean View | 204 |
| Standard Ocean View | 150 |
| Category 5 Ocean View | 118 |
| Inside | 107 |

### Restaurants

The multilevel dining room serves a single open seating buffet-style breakfast and lunch. Dinner in the dining room is seated and served European style. For early risers, a Continental breakfast with coffee, fruit, and pastries is set up in the piano bar; specialty coffees are available at the bar for a charge. A buffet lunch is offered most days on deck in the Tropical Bar, as are late-afternoon snacks and predinner canapés. On select itineraries an outdoor luncheon barbecue is prepared one day ashore. Room service is available only to occupants of the Owner's and Deluxe suites and passengers who are ill and unable to make it to the dining room.

### Spas

The tiny spa offers an array of reasonably priced, no-nonsense massages and body treatments, but a large steam room is an unexpected bonus.

### Bars/Entertainment

There is no lavish entertainment, but there are entertaining ways to pass the evenings, starting with the raising of the sails. Performers come aboard in certain ports to provide an authentic taste of local music and arts, but with the exception of live music in the piano bar and for dancing on deck, fun largely takes place outside at the Tropical Bar. Expect crab races, wacky games, and a Talent Night starring crew members and passengers.

### Pros and Cons

**Pros:** the feeling of the wind moving this large vessel through the water is spine-tingling; you won't miss the glorious sight of *Royal Clipper* underway when the captain schedules a photo op via the tenders; the library is a cozy place to read and offers a good selection of books.

**Cons:** in Category 3 cabins near the bow, you'll notice a definite slant to the floor; you may also feel a bit more motion forward than aft, and be aware that creaking sounds are common on sailing ships; tall passengers will find it difficult to use the treadmills in the low-ceilinged gym.

### FAST FACTS

- 5 passenger decks
- Dining room
- Safe, refrigerator, DVD (some)
- 3 pools
- Fitness classes, gym, spa, steam room
- 3 bars, library
- Dry-cleaning, laundry service
- Internet terminal
- No-smoking cabins

*Royal Clipper* under sail

**STAR CLIPPERS**

2

# STAR CLIPPER/STAR FLYER

| | |
|---|---|
| Crew Members | 72 |
| Entered Service | 1992 |
| Gross Tons | 3,000 |
| Length | 360 feet |
| Number of Cabins | 85 |
| Passenger Capacity | 170 |
| Width | 50 feet |

700 ft.
500 ft.
300 ft.

With its bright brass fixtures, teak-and-mahogany paneling and rails, and antique prints and paintings of famous sailing vessels, the interior decor of these ships reflects the heritage of grand sailing vessels.

Porthole-shape skylights create an atrium-like effect in the Piano Bar, which leads to a graceful staircase and the dining room one deck below. The centerpiece of the vaguely Edwardian-style library is a belle époque–period fireplace.

The Piano Bar is intimate and cozy. The Tropical Bar, one of the most popular areas on board, is the center of social activity for predinner cocktails and late-night dancing. It's the covered outdoor lounge adjacent to the open deck space, where local entertainers often perform.

## Cabins

**Cabins:** Traditional, yacht-like, and efficiently designed, cabins are adequate but far from spacious by modern standards. All cabins have a safe, vanity-desk, small settee, hair dryer, TV (except Category 6 inside), and marble bathroom with standard toiletries. As would normally be expected on a sailing vessel, staterooms forward and aft are more susceptible to motion than those midship. There is also a noticeable slant to the floor in cabins near the bow. Unless you are particularly agile, you will want to avoid the inside cabins on Commodore Deck, where beds are strictly upper and lower berths. Some cabins are outfitted with a third pull-down berth, but most passengers will find the space too cramped for three occupants. All cabins are equipped with regular 110-volt electrical outlets and one 110-volt outlet in the bathroom that is suitable for electric shavers only.

**Top-Category Cabins:** The Owner's cabin and Category 1 cabins have a minibar, whirlpool tub-shower combination, and the use of bathrobes during the cruise. Category 1 cabin doors open onto the outside deck, and the Owner's cabin has a sitting room.

**Accessibility:** None of the staterooms are designed for wheelchair accessibility, nor do any staterooms have connecting doors.

Top: Dining on *Star Clipper*
Bottom: Friendly, efficient service

## Restaurants

The mahogany-panel dining room serves a single open seating buffet-style breakfast and lunch. Dinner in the dining room is seated and served European-style. For early risers, a Continental breakfast with coffee, fruit, and pastries is set up in the Piano Bar; specialty coffees are available at the bar for a charge. A buffet lunch is offered most days on deck in the Tropical Bar, as are late-afternoon snacks and predinner canapés. On select itineraries an outdoor luncheon barbecue is prepared one day ashore. Late-night canapés are offered in the Piano Bar. There's no room service unless you're sick and can't make it out to meals.

## Spas

Neither ship has a spa facility.

## Bars/Entertainment

The most entertaining way to start the evening is topside with the raising of the sails. Performers come aboard in certain ports to provide an authentic taste of local music and arts, but with the exception of music in the piano bar and musicians providing accompaniment for dancing on deck, fun takes place outside at the Tropical Bar. Expect crab races, wacky games, and a Talent Night starring crew members and passengers.

## Pros and Cons

**Pros:** the sheer beauty of real sailing combined with the luxury of creature comforts; coffee and tea available around the clock at the piano bar; seating for six to eight in the dining room is designed to maximize socializing.

**Cons:** there are no tables for two in the dining room; designed to conserve water, bathroom taps can be frustrating until you are accustomed to the regulated water flow; on a ship this size there aren't too many spots to get away from fellow passengers.

| Cabin Type | Size (sq. ft.) |
|---|---|
| Owner's Suite | 266 |
| Category 1 Ocean View | 150 |
| Category 2 Ocean View | 129 |
| Standard Ocean View | 118 |
| Inside | 97 |

## FAST FACTS

- 4 passenger decks
- Dining room
- Safe, no TV (some)
- 2 pools
- Fitness classes
- 2 bars, library, laundry service
- Internet terminal
- No-smoking cabins

*Star Clipper* under sail

# WINDSTAR CRUISES

Are they cruise ships with sails or sailing ships designed for cruises? Since 1986, these masted sailing yachts have filled an upscale niche. They often visit ports of call inaccessible to huge, traditional cruise ships and offer a unique perspective of any cruis-

Your Windstar ship at anchor

ing region. Though Windstar ships seldom depend on wind alone to sail, if you're fortunate and conditions are perfect, as they sometimes are, the complete silence of pure sailing is heavenly. Stabilizers and computer-controlled ballast systems ensure no more than a mere few degrees of lean.

☎ 206/292–9606
or 800/258–7245
⊕ www.windstarcruis-es.com ☞ Cruise Style: Luxury.

When you can tear yourself away from the sight of thousands of yards of Dacron sail overhead, it doesn't take long to read the daily schedule of activities on a typical Windstar cruise. Simply put, there are few scheduled activities. Diversions are for the most part social, laid-back, and impromptu. You can choose to take part in the short list of daily activities; borrow a book, game, or DVD from the library; or do nothing at all. There's never pressure to join in or participate if you simply prefer relaxing with a fully loaded iPod, which you can check out on board.

Multimillion-dollar upgrades in 2012 enhanced each ship from stern to stern with chic new decor that mimics the colors of the sky and sandy beaches. The Yacht Club, which replaced the library on *Wind Surf*, is designed to be the social hub of the ship, with computer stations, a coffee bar, and a more expansive feel than the room it replaced. You will be able to join other passengers in comfortable seating around a large flat-screen TV to cheer on your favorite team during sporting events. In addition, all accommodations and bathrooms have been remodeled with updated materials; new weights and televisions were added to the gym;

a couples massage room enhances the *Wind Surf* spa; the casual Veranda was expanded; the decks now have Balinese sun beds; and cooling mist sprayers are near the pools.

## Food

Dining on Windstar ships is as casually elegant as the dress code. There's seldom a wait for a table in open seating dining rooms where tables for two are plentiful. Whether meals are taken in the open and airy top-deck buffet, with its floor-to-ceiling windows and adjacent tables outside, or in the formal dining room, dishes are as creative as the surroundings. Expect traditional entrées but also items that incorporate regional ingredients, such as plantains, for added interest. Save room for petits fours with coffee and a taste of the fine cheeses from the after-dinner cheese cart.

In a nod to healthy dining, low-calorie and low-fat spa cuisine alternatives for breakfast, lunch, and dinner are prepared to American Heart Association guidelines. Additional choices are offered from the vegetarian menu.

A midcruise deck barbecue featuring grilled seafood and other favorites is fine dining in an elegantly casual alfresco setting. Desserts are uniformly delightful, and you'll want to try the bread pudding, a Windstar tradition available at the luncheon buffet. With daily tea and hot and cold hors d'oeuvres served several times during the afternoon and evening, no one goes hungry. Room service is always available, and you can place your order for dinner from the restaurant's menu during scheduled dining hours.

## Entertainment

Evening entertainment is informal, with a small dance combo playing in the main lounges. Compact casinos offer games of chance and slot machines, but don't look for bingo or other organized games. A weekly show by the crew is delightful; attired in the traditional costumes of their homelands, they present music and dance highlighting their cultures. You may find occasional movies in the main lounges, which are outfitted with state-of-the-art video and sound equipment. Most passengers prefer socializing, either in the main lounge or an outdoor bar where Cigars Under the Stars attracts not only cigar aficionados but stargazers as well.

Welcome-aboard and farewell parties are hosted by the captain, and most passengers attend those as well as the nightly informational sessions regarding ports of call and activities that are presented by the staff during predinner cocktails.

## KNOWN FOR

■ **Smaller Ports:** The size of Windstar's motor-sailing ships allows them to call at ports that large ships simply cannot visit.

■ **Not All-Inclusive:** Windstar cruises are luxurious but far less inclusive than other luxury cruise lines.

■ **Fine Dining:** Windstar combines fine cuisine and superb service with a single open seating at dinner.

■ **Just the Right Size:** The graceful sailing ships are large enough to offer a few big ship features, yet small enough to give the feel of a private yacht.

■ **The Romance of the Sea:** With their sails billowing overhead, Windstar ships are among the most romantic at sea.

Top: Dining well on board
Bottom: Compass Rose Bar on *Wind Surf*

2

**WINDSTAR CRUISES**

(top) Backgammon on deck
(middle) Scuba with the dive masters
(bottom) *Wind Surf* stateroom

## Fitness and Recreation

Most of the line's massage and exercise facilities are quite small, as would be expected on a ship that carries fewer than 150 passengers; however, *Wind Surf*'s Wind-Spa and fitness areas are unexpectedly huge. An array of exercise equipment, free weights, and basic fitness classes are available in the gym and Nautilus room. There is an extra charge for Pilates and yoga classes. A wide variety of massages, body wraps, and facial treatments are offered in the spa, while hair and nail services are available for women and men in the salon. Both spa and salon are operated by Steiner Leisure.

Stern-mounted water-sports marinas are popular with active passengers who want to kayak, windsurf, and water-ski. Watery activities are free, including the use of snorkel gear that can be checked out for the entire cruise. The only charge is for diving; PADI-certified instructors offer a two-hour course for noncertified divers who want to try scuba, and are also available to lead experienced certified divers on underwater expeditions. The dive teams take care of everything, even prepping and washing down the gear. If you prefer exploring on solid ground, sports coordinators are often at hand to lead an early-morning guided walk in port.

## Your Shipmates

Windstar Cruises appeal to upscale professional couples in their late-thirties to sixties who enjoy the unpretentious, yet casually sophisticated atmosphere, creative cuisine, and refined service.

Windstar's ships were not designed for accessibility, and are not a good choice for the physically challenged. Although every attempt is made to accommodate passengers with disabilities, *Wind Surf* has only two elevators, and the smaller ships have none. There are no staterooms or bathrooms with wheelchair accessibility, and gangways can be difficult to navigate, depending on the tide and angle of ascent. Service animals are permitted to sail if arrangements are made at the time of booking.

---

### CHOOSE THIS LINE IF ...

You want a high-end experience yet prefer to dress casually every night of your vacation.

You love water sports, particularly scuba diving, kayaking, and windsurfing.

You're a romantic: tables for two are plentiful in the dining rooms.

## Dress Code

All evenings are country-club casual, and slacks with a jacket over a sweater or shirt for men, and sundresses, skirts, or pants with a sweater or blouse for women are suggested. Coats and ties for men are not necessary, but some male passengers prefer to wear a jacket with open-collar shirt to dinner.

## Junior Cruisers

Windstar Cruises' unregimented atmosphere is adult-oriented, and children are not encouraged. Children less than two years of age are not allowed at all; older children traveling as the third passenger in a stateroom with their parents incur the applicable third-person fare. No dedicated children's facilities are available, so parents are responsible for the behavior and entertainment of their children.

## Service

Personal service and attention by the professional staff is the order of the day. Your preferences are noted and fulfilled without the necessity of reminders. Expect to be addressed by name within a short time of embarking.

## Tipping

A service charge of $12 per guest per day (including children) is added to each shipboard account. A 15% service charge is added to all bar bills. All these proceeds are paid directly to the crew.

## Past Passengers

Windstar guests who cruise once with the line are automatically enrolled in the complimentary Foremast Club. Member benefits include savings on many sailings in addition to the Advance Savings Advantage Program discounts, Internet specials, and a free subscription to the *Foremast Club* magazine.

### HELPFUL HINTS

Windstar's luxury sailing ships were completely transformed in late 2012 in a major stem to stern renovation.

Expansive white sails are hoisted on the ships, but they are mostly for show; most sailing is done under engine power.

All nonalcoholic beverages are included in the fare, but there is a charge for beer, wine, and other alcoholic drinks.

Each Windstar ship has a water sports platform with complimentary water sports, including snorkeling, windsailing, paddleboating and even water skiing.

Hotel or hotel and tour packages are available to extend your trip pre- or post-cruise.

Windstar bought three Seabourn ships and may begin phasing them in by 2014.

**2**

**WINDSTAR CRUISES**

### DON'T CHOOSE THIS LINE IF ...

You must have a spacious private balcony. There are none.

You're bored unless surrounded by constant stimulation. Activities are purposely low-key.

You have mobility problems. These ships are simply not very good for passengers in wheelchairs.

# WIND SURF

| | |
|---|---|
| Crew Members | 190 |
| Entered Service | 1990 |
| Gross Tons | 14,745 |
| Length | 617 feet |
| Number of Cabins | 156 |
| Passenger Capacity | 312 |
| Width | 66 feet |

700 ft.

500 ft.

300 ft.

*Wind Surf*'s public areas are designed for comfort and feature wood finishes with sand and marine colors for a casual elegant look and feel. Fresh flower arrangements and sailing-related artwork are lovely touches shipwide. To make finding your way around simple, remember that all dining and entertainment areas are on the top three decks, with restaurants located forward and indoor-outdoor bars facing aft. The main lounge and casino are midship on Main Deck, as is the Yacht Club, which functions as library/Internet café/coffee bar. The fitness center is one deck higher. Most public areas have expansive sea views, although an exception is the spa, which is tucked away aft on Deck 2. Stairways are rather steep, but forward and aft elevators assure that moving about is relatively easy.

## Cabins

**Cabins:** Ocean-view staterooms are a study in efficiency and design. Closets are generous and have a safe; there's also a flat-screen TV, DVD, and Bose SoundDock speakers for an iPod. The combination vanity-desk and bedside table has drawers for ample storage. A few standard cabins have upper fold-down Pullman berths. Special touches are fresh flowers, terry robes and slippers, and toiletries. Teak-floor bathrooms are sensibly laid out and spacious enough for two people to share. All staterooms and suites are equipped with barware, minibar, and hair dryer. All voltage is 220, not 110.

**Suites:** Double the size of standard staterooms, suites were created from two standard cabins and have two bathrooms and a seating area with a sofa bed. A privacy curtain separates the bedroom from the sitting room. New spa suites include plush spa robes, tea service, and credits for certified organic spa services and fitness classes in WindSpa. Two supersize bridge suites have living and dining areas, a bedroom, a walk-in closet, and a bathroom with a whirlpool tub and separate shower.

**Accessibility:** No cabins are wheelchair accessible.

## Restaurants

The formal AmphorA Restaurant serves open seating dinner. For a casual setting, the buffet-style Veranda Café has indoor and outdoor seating for breakfast and lunch. An adjacent grill whips up cooked-to-order breakfast items and serves barbecue selections

Top: Sea views at the rail
Bottom: *Wind Surf* at sea

outdoors. A Continental breakfast spread is offered in the Compass Rose bar. The Yacht Club Sandwich Bar offers a selection of sandwiches and an espresso bar. A French bistro (unnamed at this writing) is the reservations-only, casual alternative for dinner. Other evening choices are Le Marché, an alfresco seafood bar serving fish and shellfish, and Candles, the poolside grill with a steak-and-skewers menu for which there is no charge (although reservations are suggested). Dining service in outdoor areas is subject to weather conditions. Afternoon tea with finger sandwiches and sweets is served daily. Room service is always available, and will serve selections from the dining-room menu during restaurant hours.

### Spas
The Wind Spa, operated by Steiner Leisure, is surprisingly large for a ship this size, with an extensive menu of massages, facials, body wraps, and even teeth whitening. There is a couples massage room, but no thermal suite. However a coed sauna is complimentary.

### Bars/Entertainment
Nightly informational sessions regarding ports of call and activities are presented by the staff before dinner. Evening entertainment is informal and social, with a small dance combo playing in the main lounge and a duo in the Compass Rose. A crew show during each cruise is a delight, showcasing their homeland cultures. You may find occasional movies in the main lounge, which is outfitted with state-of-the-art video and sound equipment.

### Pros and Cons
**Pros:** service is delivered with a smile by staff members who greet you by name virtually from the moment you board; all cabins are outside, and none have obstructed views; teatime, when sweets are served in addition to the finger foods, is an afternoon highlight.

**Cons:** when the caviar spread is served one day during the cruise, you might have to fight fellow passengers to get near it; there are no private balconies on these ships; there are no tables in the standard staterooms, which makes dining from room service trays inelegant at best.

| Cabin Type | Size (sq. ft.) |
|---|---|
| Suite | 376 |
| Ocean View | 188 |
| Bridge Suite | 500 |

### FAST FACTS
- 6 passenger decks
- Specialty restaurant, dining room, buffet
- Wi-Fi, safe, refrigerator, DVD
- 2 pools
- Fitness classes, gym, hot tubs, sauna, spa
- 4 bars, casino, dance club, library
- Laundry service
- Internet terminal
- No-smoking cabins

**WINDSTAR CRUISES**

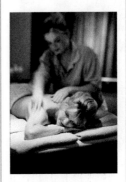
Unwind with a soothing massage.

# WIND SPIRIT, WIND STAR

| | |
|---|---|
| Crew Members | 90 |
| Entered Service | 1988 |
| Gross Tons | 5,350 |
| Length | 440 feet |
| Number of Cabins | 74 |
| Passenger Capacity | 148 |
| Width | 52 feet |

700 ft.

500 ft.

300 ft.

Comfort is the element that ties these ship's interiors together. Blue and cream, echoing hues of the sea and sandy beaches, predominate in the cozy main lounge, where you'll find a tiny casino tucked into a corner. With its large windows and a skylight, the lounge is flooded with natural light during daytime hours.

Public spaces are proportionately small on such a diminutive vessel and feature yacht-like touches of polished wood shipwide, as well as abundant fresh flower arrangements. The library contains books, movies to play in your cabin, and a computer center.

Passenger accommodations and public areas are all found in the aft two-thirds of the ship, with dining and entertainment located on the top two decks.

## Cabins

**Cabins:** The ocean-view staterooms are ingeniously designed for efficiency. Hanging lockers (closets) are generous, and contain shoe racks and shelves for gear. A small, enclosed cabinet conceals a safe, and an entertainment center includes a flat-screen TV, DVD, and Bose SoundDock speaker for an iPod, which you can borrow from reception fully loaded with music. The combination vanity-desk and bedside table has drawers for ample storage. A countertop lifts up to reveal a lighted makeup mirror, a locking security compartment, and a shallow cubby. Special touches in each stateroom are fresh flowers, terry robes and slippers for use during the voyage, and bath toiletries. The teak-floor bathrooms are big enough for two. All staterooms and suites are equipped with barware, a minibar, and hair dryer (voltage is standard 110 AC); portholes have deadheads, which can be closed in high seas. Ten staterooms have adjoining doors on *Wind Spirit* and 12 on *Wind Star,* and a limited number of standard cabins have upper fold-down Pullman berths for a third passenger.

**Suites:** A single Owner's suite, the only premium accommodation on board, has a seating area with a sofa bed to offer a berth for a third passenger.

**Accessibility:** There are no cabins configured for wheelchair accessibility.

Top: Elegant dining in a casual atmosphere
Bottom: A sunny day at the pool

## Restaurants

The formal AmphorA Restaurant offers open seating dinner during scheduled hours and is large enough to serve all passengers at once, so there is seldom a wait for a table. In a more casual setting, the buffet-style Veranda Café has indoor and outdoor seating for breakfast and lunch. A grill whips up cooked-to-order breakfast and lunch choices. Dinner under the stars is available at Candles, the poolside grill with a steak-and-skewers menu (no extra charge, but reservations are suggested). The pool bar has a permanent food station for Continental breakfast, afternoon tea, desserts, and evening canapés. Afternoon tea with finger sandwiches and sweets is served daily. Room service is always available, and will serve selections from the dining-room menu during restaurant hours.

## Spas

The tiny spa consists of only two treatment rooms, but it offers a nice menu of massages and facials. There is a complimentary coed sauna.

## Bars/Entertainment

The captain hosts a reception at least one evening during each cruise, and nightly informational sessions regarding ports of call and activities are presented before dinner. Other evening entertainment is informal and social, perhaps a pianist playing in the main lounge. A crew show, showcasing their homeland cultures, is a delight.

## Pros and Cons

**Pros:** ships have an extensive DVD collection; socializing is effortless on these intimate ships; mist sprayers near the pool offer a refreshing way to keep cool.

**Cons:** the aft pool and hot tub are popular and apt to feel crowded; the water-sports marina can open only when the ship is at anchor; ways to entertain yourself are sparse—the gym and library are tiny, and the casino is small.

| Cabin Type | Size (sq. ft.) |
|---|---|
| Suite | 220 |
| Ocean View | 188 |

### FAST FACTS

- 5 passenger decks
- Dining room, buffet
- Wi-Fi, safe, refrigerator, DVD
- Pool
- Fitness classes, gym, hot tub, sauna
- 2 bars, casino, dance club, library
- Laundry service
- Internet terminal
- No-smoking cabins

**2**

**WINDSTAR CRUISES**

*Wind Spirit* at sea

# River and Specialty Cruises

Canal barging in France

## WORD OF MOUTH

"Some may feel that the river cruises are very expensive. They usually include all the shore excursions, unlike the ocean cruises. There is also always beautiful scenery to watch as you cruise. There are no casinos, not much in the way of entertainment—local groups brought on board are usually very good. There are fewer passengers—an opportunity to really get to know your fellow passengers. We have taken five cruises. . . . They are so relaxing."

—momc

By Victoria
Tang

In 1992 Europe's age-old maritime landscape changed dramatically when the Main–Danube Canal opened, connecting the continent's main arteries—and along with them, all of Europe. The completion of the canal made grand cruise itineraries from Amsterdam to Budapest—and beyond—possible for the first time. An engineering marvel, the 106-mile Main–Danube Canal permits modern-day vessels to travel from the North Sea to the Black Sea, opening up more than 2,200 miles of rivers and exposing today's travelers to life along their banks.

Tributaries and smaller rivers that flow into the Main and Danube rivers provide additional opportunities to reach not only deep into the heart of the continent but also to explore some of its more remote regions. The opening of the canal also meant that no longer would travelers need to sit with their noses pressed against the windows of buses as they moved from one destination to the next. Instead, they can now admire the scenery from the ship's sundeck as they are transported *along with* their accommodations. Nor do travelers have to obligingly put out their luggage by 7 am (or earlier) to be loaded onto the motor coach before it sets off to the next destination. River travelers unpack only once during the course of their cruise as they move from one city to the next.

# THE APPEAL OF RIVER CRUISING

River cruising was an entirely new concept to Europe when it was introduced in the mid-1970s: a floating hotel that journeys between destinations. For many travelers, the slow chug along the river is just the right pace for getting the lay of the land. Sitting on the top deck of a ship under brilliant blue skies, you gaze on fabled landscapes dotted with castles, villages, and vineyards. A flight of stairs down you have all the amenities of a modern hotel—restaurants, bars, lounges, fitness facilities, spas, Internet access, and comfortable staterooms. River cruises offer opportunities to step ashore in fairy-tale towns and major European capitals that can't be reached on a traditional cruise ship.

The onboard ambience spans such a range that there are ships to suit most travel preferences and lifestyles. While some vessels emphasize elegance, others are much more casual. Travelers can find river cruisers that rival Europe's finest boutique hotels at one end of the spectrum, while at the other it's possible to cruise Europe's rivers much like an independent traveler who opts only for basic accommodations and dining.

The main river-cruising season begins in March and continues through the end of December, beginning with "tulip time" cruises in the Benelux countries and ending with "Christmas market" cruises in Hungary, Austria, and Germany. The majority of itineraries are seven nights or longer. Consider cruising from March through May or from September through December, when the crowds are thinner and airfares may be more reasonably priced than during peak periods.

# WHY RIVER CRUISING IS NOT FOR EVERYONE

River cruising is an exceptionally satisfying experience for many people, but it is not for everyone. Nonsmokers, in particular, should beware, because few river ships ban smoking completely. On some vessels smoking is allowed in all public areas or at least a part of the lounge, and sensitive travelers still may be offended by the prevalence of cigarette smoke.

Families with infants or small children may find river cruising to be less than ideal when compared to other forms of cruise travel. While oceangoing ships offer babysitting services and children's programs, river cruisers typically do not. That said, barges are popular options for multigenerational families, as the smaller vessels typically carry family-size loads, from 6 to 24 passengers.

The physically challenged will want to look for vessels with easy access from ship to shore and elevators; not all river vessels have them.

If you're the type who dreads the thought of dining with others each evening, then river cruising may not be for you. Few, if any, river vessels offer room service, and even fewer have alternative dining venues, as is the norm on the big cruise ships. That said, some ships now offer tables for two.

If you're accustomed to ocean cruising and require all of the big-ship trappings, then you may find river cruising a bit boring. River cruisers have fewer facilities. Entertainment is on a much smaller scale, if it exists at all. You won't find expansive gyms and spas with state-of-the-art machines, though they're sometimes offered on the larger ships.

One aspect of river cruising that is not so different from ocean cruising is that single travelers will usually have to pay a hefty supplement if they choose to occupy a double cabin alone. There are few single cabins, just as on regular cruise ships.

# HOW RIVER CRUISES AND BARGE CRUISES DIFFER

The opening of the Main–Danube Canal in 1992 not only spawned river cruising as we know it today but also spawned the contemporary river-cruise vessel. There are more than 100 river cruisers operating on Europe's rivers. A building boom since 2000 has seen the introduction of more than 60 new ships, and even more are due for delivery in the next couple of years. But on a smaller scale, barge cruising has also become more popular. Although large river ships generally offer more bells and whistles, a barge is more intimate and less elaborate. Smaller barges may even be chartered by a small group of friends or family members who prefer to do it themselves.

## WHAT RIVER CRUISES OFFER

Designed specifically to transit the canal's locks, modern river cruisers are long and narrow, as are the locks themselves, which may be 600 feet long but are only about 40 feet wide. These dimensions, particularly the width of the locks, continue to pose challenges for designers of river vessels. Balconies are less common on river cruise ships, but they are becoming more so.

The typical river cruiser has four decks, including an upper sundeck, with two to three decks below it containing a series of staterooms on each side of the ship. Staterooms typically have a queen-size bed that can be reconfigured to two single beds, a TV, storage space, and a small, though generally well-appointed and modern, bathroom with shower and usually no tub. Contrary to an odd yet persistent rumor, toilet paper may be flushed, as opposed to depositing paper in a bin for collection later, on virtually all river cruise ships.

Public rooms typically include a restaurant, lounge, spa, and fitness center. Although other features vary, some ships offer Wi-Fi, complimentary bicycles, a whirlpool tub, and sauna. Several river ships have small pools.

River cruisers are essentially barges with an integrated hotel above, and typically carry 100 or more passengers. Some river cruisers are à la carte, but some are nearly all-inclusive, meaning that wine and beer are served at lunch and dinner, and that some form of shore excursions, such as guided city walks, are included for each port.

Cruises are competitively priced, and you should expect to pay from $200 per person per day to $500 per person per day, depending on the ship, itinerary, and level of accommodations.

## WHAT BARGE CRUISES OFFER

Barges typically are smaller and have fewer frills and amenities than river cruisers. Whereas river cruisers may carry more than 100 passengers, barges range from a few passengers to few dozen. Barges typically have only one deck, smaller staterooms, and a combination dining room and lounge. Barge staterooms almost always have private facilities.

One of the big differences between a river cruise and a barge cruise is the amount of territory you're able to cover. Barge cruises usually span six days and travel fewer than 50 miles of river in a week; river cruisers may travel a few hundred miles. Transiting the locks can be time-consuming, and passengers often prefer to walk or bicycle along the canal's banks (often outpacing the barge).

Barges are usually all-inclusive, including drinks, fine wine and champagne; gourmet cuisine (using fresh, local ingredients and cooked to order); pick-up and drop-off from local airports, train stations, and hotels; shore excursions and all entrance fees. Bicycles are often available for use on shore. Some barges even have a whirlpool tub, pool, and exercise equipment.

Popular barge cruise destinations are France, Belgium, Germany, and Holland. Although you may think of a river ship as a floating hotel, a barge is more reminiscent of a well-appointed houseboat.

Though most barges are staffed, there are self-drive barges. Small groups, such as family or friends, may book the entire barge, or barges may be booked by individuals, preferably like-minded people who don't mind sharing space in a small setting.

Barge cruises are more expensive than river cruises, and can range from $350 per person per day to more than $1,000 per person per day. Rental periods are typically a "week," which actually consists of six-days, because one day is reserved to prepare the barge for the next week's group of passengers. Whole barges can be chartered for $15,000 to more than $60,000.

# WHERE CRUISES GO: EUROPE'S RIVERS

Europe has more navigable rivers than any other region in the world, and arguably more diverse cultures along its riverbanks than almost any other region. Cruising the entire length of the Rhine and Danube rivers alone—made possible thanks to the Main–Danube Canal—exposes travelers to 10 countries in Central and Western Europe. Along the way are charming villages, storied capital cities, fairy-tale castles, vineyards, and more—all accessible from your floating hotel.

The primary European rivers on which cruises operate include Central Europe's Danube; the Rhine, Main, Mosel, Neckar, and Elbe in Germany; and the Seine, Soane, and Rhône rivers in France (which are popular for both river cruising and barging). Although some cruises operate on Italy's longest river, the Po, it is largely unnavigable because of low water levels and sediment. River cruising in Russia is increasing in popularity. Portugal's Douro River has also been added to some cruise plans.

## POPULAR ITINERARIES

### THE DANUBE

The most popular region for river cruising in continental Europe, and a good choice for first-time river cruisers, is the Danube. Immortalized in Strauss's waltz *The Blue Danube,* the river winds from Germany's Black Forest through Austria into the Balkans before flowing into the Black Sea.

Most Danube river cruises span 7 to 10 nights and allow sufficient time to explore the major cities along the river. The Danube flows through six countries and meanders for nearly 2,900 km (1,800 miles). Some of Europe's most fabled cities—**Regensburg, Passau, Linz, Vienna, Bratislava,** and **Budapest**—are on the banks of the Danube. Some vessels operate round-trip from Passau; some operate one way between Regensburg and Budapest; some cruises begin in Amsterdam; and others cruise between Vienna or Budapest to **Nürnberg**, which includes transiting a section of the Main–Danube Canal over Europe's Continental Divide in the Franconian Alps. Cruises that begin on the Main River may begin in **Würzburg**, but more frequently begin or end in Nürnberg, which was virtually destroyed during World War II but has been restored.

To extend the journey, cruises may continue on into Slovakia, Hungary, Serbia, and the border between Romania and Bulgaria.

## THE RHINE, MAIN, MOSEL, AND NECKAR

Romantics, history buffs, wine connoisseurs, and nature lovers will love medieval wine towns, glorious castles, majestic cathedrals, and world-class cities on along Germany's major rivers. Spanning approximately 64 km (40 miles) between **Rüdesheim** and **Koblenz**, Germany's Upper Middle Rhine Valley is a UNESCO World Heritage site. More than 40 castles grace its shores, along with vineyard-terraced landscapes and breathtaking countryside. Take a tour along the Alsatian Wine Road. Indulge in the region's famous Rheingau Rieslings at Castle Vollrads, and view fairy tale Strasbourg as it has appeared for centuries, via a canal cruise.

### THE RHINE

The Rhine, in fact, flows 1,320 km (820 miles) through four countries—Switzerland, France, Germany, and the Netherlands—from the Swiss Alps to the North Sea. Although some cruises operate between Basel, Switzerland, and Amsterdam, in the Netherlands, or Düsseldorf, Germany, the most popular section of the Rhine for cruising is between **Mainz**, at the confluence of the Main and Rhine, and **Cologne**. These cruises might also include **Bonn**. The Rhine has many tributaries, the most important for cruisers being the Main, Mosel, and Neckar rivers.

### THE MAIN

The Main is one of the Rhine's most significant tributaries. It, along with the Main–Danube Canal, connects the North Sea with the Black Sea. The Main has 34 locks and becomes navigable at **Bamberg**, Germany, at the northern end of the Main–Danube Canal. Some river-cruise companies offer itineraries along the Main between **Nürnberg**, which is about midway on the Main–Danube Canal, to **Trier**, on the Mosel, which branches off the Rhine.

### THE MOSEL

The Mosel is regarded as the most beautiful—and perhaps the most romantic—of the navigable European rivers. From its headwaters in the Vogesen Mountains to where it joins the Rhine at Koblenz, the Mosel is only about 175 miles long as the crow flies. But the actual length of the winding river is a little more than 335 miles, making it the Rhine's longest tributary. The Mosel weaves its way through the vertical slopes of the Schiefergebirge Mountains into Luxembourg and northeastern France. Cities and towns along the river are of fairy-tale charm: picturesque **Cochem**, settled by the Celts and later by Romans before being granted a town charter in 1332; **Bernkastel-Kues**, with its castle ruin overlooking the city center of half-timbered buildings and cobblestone streets; and the Romanesque **Trier**, Germany's oldest city and also one that claims to be 1,300 years older than Rome itself.

The Mosel is known for its (mostly) white wines, such as Riesling and Piesporter, and indeed, much of the pleasure of a Mosel cruise can be found in sampling the wines along the way.

## THE NECKAR

This tributary of the Rhine flows 228 miles from the Black Forest through some of Germany's most beautiful countryside. The primary attraction for many travelers is **Heidelberg,** Germany's oldest university town and the cradle of the German Romantic movement.

## RUSSIA AND UKRAINE

Increasingly Western-oriented, Russia is still an exotic experience even for the well-traveled cruiser. But since 2000, new and—mostly—refurbished ships have entered service at a swift pace to cruise on the Volga, Svir, Neva, and Dnieper rivers. River cruising is, in fact, one of the most popular and trouble-free ways to visit Russia.

Still, river cruisers have more work cut out for them than do cruise ship passengers who call in St. Petersburg for up to three days. Ocean-cruise passengers may visit Russia without a visa for up to 72 hours, provided that they are on an organized tour with an operator licensed by Russian authorities. River-cruise passengers will need to apply for visas prior to entry, but river-cruise companies make the process easier than would be the case if you were to apply for a visa on your own. Most cruises between **Moscow** and **St. Petersburg** span 12 to 13 days. Passengers may stay for a couple of days in each of the two cities at the beginning or end of their cruises.

River-cruise vessels operate in both directions, meaning that you could either start your cruise in Moscow and disembark in St. Petersburg, or get on the ship in St. Petersburg and disembark in Moscow. Along the way, you will travel on the Volga, Svir, and Neva rivers and cross four lakes (Lake Rybinsk, the White Lake, Lake Onega, and Lake Ladoga) as you are immersed in Russian language and culture.

Most itineraries include **Uglich,** where in 1591 Ivan the Terrible's son was murdered. The Church of St. Dmitry on the Blood now stands on the place where he was found.

Yaroslavi is also typically on Russian river-cruise itineraries. Considered one of Russia's most beautiful cities, this is where you will find the richly decorated Church of Elijah the Prophet.

After crossing Lake Rybinsk (traveling from Moscow), the village of Goritzy awaits. The renowned Kirillo-Belozersky Monastery is the main point of interest here.

Cross Europe's second-largest lake, Lake Onega, to visit the island village of Kizhi. The town has an open-air museum of architecture that has been proclaimed a UNESCO World Heritage site. The Transfiguration Church there was built in 1714 without the use of one single nail.

Next is the scenic Svir River, leading from Lake Onega to Lake Ladoga (Europe's largest lake). On the way, you typically stop in Mandrogy, a town where the main attraction is the vodka museum.

After crossing Lake Ladoga and traveling along the Neva River, river cruisers arrive in **St. Petersburg.** A city of parks, palaces, and museums, St. Petersburg is a destination worthy of a few days' visit.

For a true immersion in Russian culture and language, some river operators also offer cruises on the Dnieper. Spanning 1,420 miles, the river is Europe's fourth-longest. On its way from Russia (southwest of Moscow) to the Black Sea, the Dnieper flows through Belarus and Ukraine. Cruises on the Dnieper are not as well established as on the Volga. In fact, only one of the better-known river-cruise operators currently offers itineraries. But there are itineraries from Odessa to Kiev (or vice versa), taking in some of the best-known cities and destinations in Ukraine. In addition to the two destinations at the beginning and end of the cruise, some ships call at Sevastopol, Yalta, Kherson, and Dnepropetrovsk.

## THE ELBE

The Elbe runs 1,167 km (725 miles) from the Czech Republic to the North Sea. Most weeklong Elbe itineraries are between Berlin and Prague, and include hotel stays at one or both ends of the cruise. Other ports often include Potsdam, Magdeburg, Wittenberg, Meissen, Dresden, and Königstein.

**Prague,** the capital of the Czech Republic, has a rich architectural heritage extending back more than 1,000 years. Prague's highlight is the Charles Bridge, which crosses the Vltava River. On one side is Prague Castle, dominating the Mala Strana.

**Königstein** and its dramatic fortress, 360 meters (1,180 ft) above the river, provide a scenic backdrop for brief visits, while farther along, **Dresden** is known as "the Florence of the Elbe," for its art treasures.

**Meissen** is known for its porcelain, while **Wittenberg** marks the birthplace of the Protestant Reformation. In 1517 Martin Luther, an Augustine monk and university lecturer, nailed his 95 *Theses* on the door of the Palace Church.

**Magdeburg** is midway on the Elbe. Nearly destroyed during World War II, the rebuilt city is an example of a traditional German town.

Ships usually moor in **Potsdam** (interesting in its own right) for transfers to and from **Berlin** at the beginning or end of each cruise.

## THE DOURO

Portugal is an emerging cruising hotspot. Explore the capital city of **Lisbon** then proceed to **Porto** at the mouth of the Douro River to embark your cruise ship. The river meanders on a winding easterly course between steeply terraced vineyards, stopping at ports of call largely unchanged for centuries with charming town squares, colorful castles, baroque mansions, and historic monasteries. At the Spanish border indulge in a scenic ride into Spain to visit the medieval city of **Salamanca** before the voyage back to Porto. See unspoiled vistas and sample Portuguese specialties like salt cod, hearty soups and stews, and the area's sensational port and wines. Both Viking River Cruises and Uniworld Boutique Cruises offer these itineraries in 2013.

## THE SEINE, RHÔNE, AND SAÔNE

Also popular for barge cruises, the rivers of France course through the vineyard-canopied hillsides of Burgundy to the lavender fields of Provence. Positioned in between is Paris, the City of Light with its illuminated iconic monuments, broad boulevards, charming cafés, and world-renowned museums.

Seine cruises include at least one night in Paris before traveling northwest toward Honfleur and the English Channel. Major stops include **Giverny,** home of the artist Claude Monet and one of France's most-visited destinations; and **Rouen,** known as the "City of 100 Spires" for its many churches and cathedrals. **Paris** is practically synonymous with the Seine; thus it's one of the most important destinations on Seine cruises. The river has been used for sightseeing within Paris since the 19th century.

Coursing 813 km (505 miles), the Rhône is the only major European river flowing south into the Mediterranean. Most river cruises operate from **Lyon** on the Rhône, traveling as far south in Provence as **Arles** and the Côte d'Azur. The same stretch of river is also popular with barge cruises.

Other river cruises combine the Rhône and Saône rivers for itineraries from Chalon-sur-Saône to Avignon. Along the way, passengers enjoy the Papal Palace in **Avignon;** the early Roman ruins in **Vienne** and **Arles;** wine tours of **Beaune,** Burgundy's acclaimed wine capital; the history and beauty of **Lyon** and **Vienne;** and the medieval charm of **Viviers.**

## THE NETHERLANDS AND BELGIUM

One of the most popular springtime cruises include tulip-and-windmill cruises, which take place during April and May in the Netherlands and Belgium. Cruises typically begin and end in **Amsterdam,** overnighting in the Dutch city so that you have time to explore. Leaving Amsterdam, you will cruise past Holland's annual floral splendor surrounded by iconic wooden windmills, still operational today, to visit two of Belgium's most beautifully preserved medieval cities—Brussels and Bruges.

## THE CHRISTMAS MARKETS

Sip *glühwein*, nibble spicy gingerbread, and buy handmade wooden ornaments and nutcrackers at the famous European markets at the end of the year. Although river cruises take place during the spring, summer, and fall, **Nuremberg** hosts the world's largest Christmas market (*Christkindlmarkt* in German), featured on Christmas-market cruises during the months of November and December. Local festivities also take place in major cities like **Frankfurt, Vienna, Budapest, Prague, Amsterdam, Basel, Zurich, Strasbourg,** and **Cologne** (home of four markets). You can start your cruise from a number of embarkation ports. Austrian and German Bavarian markets are hugely popular. During the Christmas season, tastefully decorated ships celebrate against the backdrop of illuminated historic cities and Alpine landscapes to guarantee a magical experience. Book early as demand is high for these annual cruise itineraries.

## SPECIALTY CRUISES IN EUROPE

In cruising, as with many things, small can be beautiful and less can be more—at least if you are looking for authentic experiences that bring you closer to the areas that you visit. General ambience will be more intimate than on larger ships. Expect a much more personal experience and stronger connection to fellow passengers and crew.

### FRENCH CANALS

With more than 8,047 km (5,000 miles) of canals, France is a major barging destination. The country's most popular canals for barging are the Canal de la Marne au Rhin, which links the Rhine with the Marne, and operates between **Strasboug** and **Lagarde**; the Burgundy Canal, which links the Saône and Yonne between **Dijon** and **Migennes**; the Doubs River, which empties into the Saône; Canal Latéral à la Marne, a canal that follows the course of the Marne River, passing through the heart of **Champagne**; and Canal Latéral à la Loire, which follows the course of the upper Loire. (*Latéral* indicates that the waterway parallels the course of the river; some rivers, including the upper Loire, are not navigable, hence the necessity for a latéral.)

Transiting these canals takes lots of time; your barge may take 20 minutes to pass through a single lock. But barge cruising is meant to be relaxing, and if you get bored, just hop on a bike or walk to meet the barge at another lock upstream.

### SWEDISH GÖTA CANAL

The 29-passenger MS *Juno*, which operates on Sweden's Göta Kanal, is believed to be the world's oldest cruise ship still in service. The *Juno* was built in 1874 and has been cruising ever since. Cabins on the *Juno* are similar to train compartments, with one upper and one lower berth. Apart from chaise longues on the bridge deck, the ship has no notable onboard features, although furnishings are of high standards and the vessel itself is well kept. You'll find much the same on *Juno*'s fleetmates, *Wilhelm Tham* (built in 1912) and *Diana* (1931). All are operated by the Göta Canal Steamship Company.

Of course, what persuades guests to cruise on ships like these is the 200-year-old Göta Canal that stretches across Sweden. Passing 58 locks en route from **Gothenburg** on the west coast to **Stockholm** on the east coast (or vice versa), canal cruisers are able to experience Swedish culture and nature up close.

### SCOTTISH CALEDONIAN CANAL

Scotland's Caledonian Canal offers a similar kind of experience to cruising on the Göta Kanal. And the similarities between these canals are more significant than they might seem, in part because both were conceived by the Scottish engineer Thomas Telford. The two canals were built with utilitarian purposes in mind, but the railroad has overtaken their original intended use, freight transportation.

The waterways have been taken over entirely by leisure boats and the occasional cruise ship. On the Caledonian Canal, the Magna Carta Steamship Company operates the 54-passenger *Lord of the Glens*, which offers a similar experience to *Juno*, except the landscape and culture are Scottish rather than Swedish. *Lord of the Glens* cruises the Caledonian Canal between **Inverness** in the northeast to **Fort William,** southwest of Inverness (or vice versa). Along the way, guests experience four lakes: Loch Dochfour, the famous Loch Ness, Loch Oich, and Loch Lochy. The actual canal is only 23 miles long, and connects the four lakes, making it possible to savor the changing scenery of the dramatic Scottish Highlands. *Lord of the Glens* also offers cruises along the rugged Scottish coastline—around the Isle of Skye on the west coast, for example. Some itineraries combine the canal with a coastal voyage.

## NORWEGIAN COASTS

Along the coast of Norway, Hurtigruten offers opportunities to get a glimpse of the daily life of the Norwegians. A dozen vessels, ranging from 400 to 1,000 passengers, cruise the coast of Norway daily year-round. Onboard standards vary noticeably, depending on the ship. The newest offer amenities equal to those of modern cruise ships, while the older ships are lacking many amenities to which cruise-ship passengers have become accustomed.

Hurtigruten was conceived as a part of the infrastructure in Norway, where fjords and high mountains have always posed serious challenges for building roads. Thus, in 1893, the first Hurtigruten ship set out from Trondheim bound for Hammerfest. Today Hurtigruten's ships connect **Bergen** in the south with **Kirkenes** in the north. Typically, 32 ports are visited along the way, with each of those ports receiving at least one call per day year-round. Some of the ports are small, such as Berlevåg (1,060 inhabitants), and may merit only a brief stop of 15 minutes or so; others, such as Trondheim (171,000 inhabitants), are large cities, where Hurtigruten remains docked for eight hours or more. ⇨ *For more information on Hurtigruten, see "Cruise Lines and Cruise Ships."*

# CONTACTS AND RESOURCES

Most of the companies we recommend below operate both river cruisers and barges to navigate a variety of waterways, including smaller canals to larger estuaries.

## MAJOR RIVER CRUISE LINES

**Abercrombie & Kent.** Founded in 1953 as a safari-tour operator, the upscale travel company known as A&K offers canal and river cruising on barges that carry no more than 22 passengers—and some that carry as few as six. Areas of operation in continental Europe include France, Germany, Belgium, Netherlands, Britain, and Ireland. A&K also offers cruises on board the 88-passenger river vessel *River Cloud II,* on the Rhine, Main, and Danube.

Pricing is all-inclusive, from accommodations to three sumptuous meals daily with wine, guided sightseeing, and entry fees. Even transfers and bar drinks are included on most vessels. A&K cruises receive high marks for personalized, friendly service.

A&K cruises have excellent theme voyages suited to particular interests. Oenophiles should board the Wines of Burgundy(Grand Cru) Cruise on *Amaryllis* (from the Orient Express Cruise Collection) and sample the 33 Grand Crus of Burgundy. Passionate about horticulture and gardens? Consider a luxury river cruise on *Magna Carta* in England, passing through lush green countryside and quaint towns along the Thames. ☎ *888/611–4711* ⊕ *www.abercrombiekent.com.*

### Choose If

■ You're traveling alone—more singles are onboard, individual accommodations are readily available, and tour directors provide escorted journeys.

■ Your passions include wine, gastronomy, gardening, and theater—all-inclusive theme cruises are well organized and substantial.

■ Creature comforts are essential—A&K cruises have garnered high praise and loyal customers for providing top-of-the-line amenities and ship cabins to rival a five-star luxury hotel.

### Don't Choose If

■ You're traveling with kids. The slow-moving barges do not offer any programs or facilities for younger ones who will most assuredly get bored.

■ Money is an object. The luxury barge *Amaryllis* Burgundy tour costs a cool $50,000.

■ You prefer standard port-intensive itineraries and megaship activities. This line's focus is on savoring the journey itself, both on board and on shore.

**AmaWaterways.** A leader in its niche, winning eight industry awards for Best River Cruise Line, this specialty 15-vessel cruise line has exceptional staterooms and itineraries that showcase not only Europe, but also Vietnam and Zambezi. Its Austrian founder worked with several of the other major river-cruise companies before launching his own company in 2002. Since then, AmaWaterways has introduced nine new ships in Europe: *Amabella, Amacello, Amadagio, Amadante, Amadolce, Amalegra, Amalyra, Amaverde, and Amavida.* In 2013, the yacht-inspired *Amaprima* and *Amacerto join the fleet.* The refurbished 212-passenger *Amakatarina* cruises between Moscow and St. Petersburg.

AmaWaterways' luxury ships are among the newest of the European river cruisers operating today. Designed exclusively for the English-speaking market, the ships have staterooms equipped with flat-screen TVs and Internet, French balconies on the top two decks, elevator, whirlpool, and free bicycles for exploration ashore. Impressive public rooms use designer fabrics, chic furniture, and subtle lighting for an upscale boutique hotel atmosphere.

They operate a wide range of itineraries in Europe on the Rhine, Main, Danube, and Mosel rivers; and in Russia on the Volga, Svir, and Neva rivers. The company also offers Christmas-market cruises from late November through December. Reserve April to see tulip blossoms cruising Holland and Belgium. ☎ *800/626–0126* ⊕ *www.amawaterways.com.*

### Choose If

■ You enjoy a luxury adventure with few passengers. Weeklong excursions with as few as six passengers snake their way through rural European villages.

■ Your passions include wine, gastronomy, nature, and biking. Popular theme cruises showcase world-famous wine, food, and geographic regions with lectures and land tours.

■ You want good bang for your buck. Excellent itineraries with upgraded accommodations and service are not exorbitantly priced.

### Don't Choose If

■ You want to completely unwind. Certain itineraries are activity-packed with intense touring excursions, leaving little downtime.

■ You don't have a lot of time. A top itinerary takes at least 10 to 15 days. Count on longer durations considering door-to-door travel time.

■ You travel heavy and need storage space. While cabins have drawers and closets, maneuvering in tighter quarters of a smaller ship may cramp fashionistas' styles.

**A-ROSA.** This established German river-cruise company has never reached out before to the English-speaking market, but for the first time in 2013, several itineraries (primarily in the summer months) will be offered to American cruisers.

The two ships on which English itineraries are offered, *A-ROSA Stella* and *A-ROSA Silva,* are luxuriously appointed and offer an all-inclusive pricing structure, even extending to round-trip flights to Europe. Many cabins have balconies, though some are only small Juliet-style. On board, dining is always open seating, and chefs try to locally source ingredients whenever possible. As on other river cruises, shore excursions are included in every port, and the ships carry bicycles that can be borrowed anytime. A real luxury is the small spa, which isn't often found on a river cruise ship. The itineraries offered range from 7 to 14 nights and cover Europe from stem to stern, though they are limited to eight sailings in 2013.

The company is represented in the United States by David Morris International. ☎ 855/552–7672 ⊕ *www.arosacruises.com.*

### Choose If

■ You don't want to pay airfare to Europe. All these cruises include round-trip air from North America.

■ You like balconies. Most cabins on A-ROSA river ships have some kind of balcony, either a "Juliet" balcony or a full balcony.

■ You don't like paying for extras. These cruises really are all-inclusive, including a full open bar and all gratuities to staff.

### Don't Choose If

■ You like a lot of options for itineraries. English-language cruises are only offered on two ships on eight different sailings (for 2013 at least).

■ You want to cruise in the spring. At this writing, itineraries are only offered in the summer months (late June through August) and a couple of holiday cruises.

- You like an international mix of passengers. These sailings are marketed solely to Americans and Canadians.

**Avalon Waterways.** Avalon Waterways operates 11 ships in Europe: *Visionary, Vista, Panorama, Felicity, Luminary, Affinity, Creativity, Scenery, Tranquility, Imagery,* and *Tapestry.* The newest fleet additions in 2013 are *Expression* and *Artistry II.*

Rooms feature big-ship amenities such as hotel-quality beds, satellite TV, floor-to-ceiling sliding glass doors in most staterooms, and even some private balconies. Ships also have Internet and fitness equipment. Cruises operates on the Rhine, Main, Danube, and Mosel rivers in Germany. The company also offers French wine-country excursions on the Saône and Rhône rivers, as well as Christmas-market cruises.

First-class escorted vacations include family-friendly activities and accommodations. Check out faith-based travel theme voyages with escorted in-depth visits to the world's most famous religious sites and destinations. More off-the-beaten-path itineraries appear in 2013 including Friesland in far north Holland and Central European capitals (Vienna, Bratislava, Budapest). Visit iconic Neuschwanstein Castle in Germany on the 13-day magical journey from Munich to Basel, Switzerland. ☎ 877/797–8791 ⊕ *www.avalonwaterways.com.*

### Choose If

- Your passions include wine, gastronomy, sightseeing, and history. As part of the complimentary Culture & Cruise offerings, wine tastings and local delicacies go hand-in-hand with land tours of medieval cities and heritage sites.

- Off-the-beaten-path destinations appeal to you. Excursions take passengers to more obscure yet fascinating places in far northern, central, and eastern Europe.

- You want to stay connected. Vessels are equipped with complimentary Wi-Fi, flat-screen TVs, complimentary use of iPads.

### Don't Choose If

- You prefer a low-key atmosphere at a low price. Everything is premium with fashionable suites, fine dining, fitness center, and on-demand in-room entertainment.

- You expect lavish entertainment. Ambient music from piano lounges and bars replaces loud, glitzy stage performances found on large vessels.

- Anonymity is a priority. Staff and crew keep service personalized and typically get to know you by name, not number.

**Grand Circle Travel.** Grand Circle's 12 privately-owned European and Russian river ships range in capacity from 46 to 216 passengers, with the majority capable of carrying 140 passengers.

In Russia the *Tikhi Don* was completely refurbished before starting operations in 2005. The *Rossia* followed in 2007, also undergoing a complete refurbishment. The 216-passenger *Rossia* and *Tikhi Don* both operate on the Volga, Svir, and Neva rivers between Moscow and St. Petersburg. Ranging in size from 130 to 150 square feet, cabins are equipped with satellite TV.

Designed for the Rhine, Main, and Danube rivers are the 140-passenger *River Harmony, River Melody, River Rhapsody,* and *River Concerto.* Some upper-deck cabins have balconies. Limited primarily to wider sections of the Danube are the 164-passenger *River Aria* and *River Adagio.* On smaller rivers, the company operates the 120-passenger *Bizet.* Smaller still, for cruise programs in France, are the 46-passenger, two-deck *Chardonnay* and *Provence.* Grand Circle's sister company, Overseas Adventure Travel, operates many other small-ship cruises throughout Russia, including some river cruises, on ships that are either owned or leased by the company. ☎ *800/221–2610* ⊕ *www.gct.com.*

### Choose If

■ You enjoy local European cuisine. Regional ingredients are used with above-average preparation and presentation.

■ You are older, have time, and enjoy destination-intense itineraries.

■ Personalized attention is important. Friendly tour directors, crew, and staff have a reputation for making passengers feel at home.

### Don't Choose If

■ You have limited mobility. Accommodations and service are not suitable for disabled or partially disabled passengers.

■ You want to stop and smell the roses. Regimented cruising with tight schedules and excessive port visits can provide an unwelcome sense of urgency.

■ You're traveling with the little ones. Children are not allowed on board.

**Imperial River Cruises.** Partnered with the Russian Orthodox Cruise Company, the largest ship operator in Russia, U.S.-based Imperial River Cruises meander in the waterways of Russia and Ukraine. Its most popular routes are Moscow–St. Petersburg; the Golden Ring cities; the Volga and Dnieper rivers; the Black Sea and Kiev; and Odessa, which includes Yalta, Sevastopol, and Tulcea (Romania). Land tours include the Kremlin, the Hermitage, Catherine's Palace, and Petergoff. Eighteen vessels make their way to UNESCO World Heritage sites, famous monasteries, historic capitals, and rural villages on the banks of spectacular water routes.

Imperial is a member of reputable industry organizations, meeting strict operational, safety, and administrative standards. In recent years the cruise line has handled many corporate travel excursions for American, Canadian, Australian, and European business executives. The company's vast experience enables it to offer land tours in all price categories, from budget to VIP.

For 15 years, Imperial has also provided tours and services specifically for music lovers, orchestras, choirs, and other music organizations, from scholastic to professional. Each spring, culturally savvy passengers can cruise along Russian waters from Volgograd to Moscow with the Russian National Orchestra and have the opportunity to meet and dine with celebrated Russian musicians. Listen to superb classical performances in some of the most beautiful concert halls and on board. The newer ships *Fidelio, Rachmaninoff, Litvinov,* and *Dostoyevsky* are popular, offering casual style with modern amenities equivalent to a two-to three-star hotel. ☎ *888/555–0678* ⊕ *www.imperialrivercruises.com.*

### Choose If

■ You've always dreamt of visiting imperial Russian cities and mysterious Kizhi and Solovki Islands.

■ You can travel between April and September, the only cruising periods available.

■ You're a culture or music buff. Special themed cruises include the classical music journey with the award-winning Russian National Orchestra.

### Don't Choose If

■ You don't prefer a formal atmosphere. Luxury cabins, haute cuisine, and formal wear are required.

■ You don't have at least 11 to 12 days, the minimum duration for most itineraries.

■ You need special meals. Chefs cannot accommodate any dietary requirements.

**Lüftner Cruises.** Lüftner Cruises, headquartered in Austria, ranks among the best-known organizers of river cruises on European waterways. Founded more than 30 years ago by the Lüftner family, the privately owned company currently operates nine first-class ships in its elegant Amadeus fleet. Choose the MS *Amadeus Silver, Brilliant, Elegant, Diamond, Princess, Royal, Symphony, Classic, and Rhapsody* to cruise Dutch and Belgian rivers, the French Rhône, Saône, and up and down the Rhine, Main, Moselle, and Danube. In 2013, the river Seine joins the itinerary.

High standards for the Lüftner fleet afford river cruising with distinction—cruises focus on cultural and environmental awareness, Austrian hospitality, and outstanding service. Exclusive furnishings and decor are personally selected by Mrs. Lüftner to offer elegant and comfortable surroundings with designer touches. Substantial breakfast buffets and table-service menus for lunch and dinner use fresh, regional produce to showcase Austrian gastronomy and fine wine.

The spacious cabins on each vessel are tastefully furnished and give guests the feeling of being in a sleek hotel room with TV, adjustable air-conditioning, telephone, and bathroom with shower and WC. Almost all the cabins have large panoramic windows with French balconies, affording incomparable views of the charming landscapes along the riverbanks. ☎ +33/4–221–30–857 *(international)* ⊕ *www.lueftner-cruises.com.*

### Choose If

■ You want to watch the world go by. Staterooms are private and have large picture windows.

■ You enjoy Austrian culture. From precise itineraries to modestly chic interiors and the German-speaking crew, the taste of Austria permeates all cruises.

■ You support sustainable travel. Partnered with the climate protection group *Atmosfair* and UN's *Green Globe,* the cruise line promotes environment-friendly tourism, voluntary passenger contributions, and matching donations.

### Don't Choose If

■ You don't enjoy Viennese Schrammel folk music. Live musicians play the instantly recognizable accordion and guitar music during meals.

■ You have limited mobility or want to bring your pet. Multilevel vessels do not have elevators or crew availability for physically disabled passengers. No pets are allowed on any ship.

■ You're traveling with kids. Children under 12 cannot be accommodated. The ships—without special facilities or programs for young ones—have a strict policy to allow only a limited number of children under 18, who must be accompanied and share a cabin with parent or legal guardian.

**Tauck World Discovery.** Tauck World Discovery operates four ships in Europe, including the 118-passenger *Swiss Emerald, Swiss Sapphire,* and *Swiss Jewel,* and the MS *Treasure* launched in 2011, the same year the company garnered top awards as the World's Best River Cruise Line by a well-known reader poll.

These well-appointed vessels provide uncommon access to local hot spots for immersive cultural experiences, all-inclusive pricing, and personalized attention. A club-like ambience pervades with only 14 suites measuring 300 square feet with floor-to-ceiling windows (seven Junior suites), walk-in closets, and marble baths with full-size tubs. Wi-Fi access is offered throughout. All cabins have flat-screen TVs, minibar, radio, safe, and aromatic L'Occitane French toiletries.

Ships cruise the Danube, Rhine, Mosel, and Main rivers, as well as the scenic canals of the Netherlands and Belgium in spring. The French waterways cruise is a feast for the senses showcasing local gastronomy and stunning architecture. Signature voyages are the 14-day French Escapade Monte Carlo to Paris cruise and the 24-day Grand European Cruise for those who want to splurge. ☎ *800/788–7885* ⊕ *www.tauck.com.*

### Choose If

■ You want to watch the world go by and stop to smell the roses. Boats move slowly towards well-choreographed excursions on shore.

■ You're traveling alone. Special Solo Traveler discounts are offered.

■ You are looking for a mature crowd. Expect fellow passengers to be around 55-plus, well-traveled, curious, and sociable.

### Don't Choose If

■ You don't have at least 10 days. Ten- to 24-day itineraries are destination-intense and organized on a regimented schedule to optimize port visits.

■ You're an introvert. The small club-like boats are intimate and promote mingling the minute you exit your cabin.

■ Large-scale entertainment is required. The most exciting performers will be the resident pianist, an occasional "step on" performer from the local region, or musicians and dancers at scheduled venues on shore.

**Uniworld Boutique River Cruise Collection.** Founded in 1976, Uniworld Boutique River Cruises is a California-based company offering luxury European river cruises. Operating 13 ships in Europe, Uniworld offers itineraries from 7 to 30 days on the Rhône, Mosel, Danube, Seine, and Saône rivers, as well as in the Netherlands and Belgium. Uniworld is the only North American river-cruise company to tour Portugal and Spain on the Douro River, from Lisbon to Porto. Its 128-passenger *Douro Spirit* was added in 2011. By 2012, awards showered down with the introductioin of the opulent SS *Antoinette*, where 18th-century French design meets 21st-century technology, including electronic balcony windows, Wi-Fi, underwater music, a movie theater, and heated swimming pool. Spending over $100 million in five new ships, Uniworld commissioned partner Red Carnation Hotels to provide passengers a five-star experience. Expect sumptuous bedding and decor in first-class rooms that make you feel like royalty. Joining in 2013, the 118-passenger *Queen Isabel* will also sail Douro routes. Expect equally regal appointments.

On Russia's Volga, Svir, and Neva rivers, the 206-passenger *River Victoria* cruises between Moscow and St. Petersburg. ☎ *800/733–7820* ⊕ *www.uniworld.com.*

### Choose If

■ Money is no object. Uniworld's luxury river cruises are priced on the higher end although fares are all-inclusive, including excursions.

■ You enjoy wine and fine dining. Uniworld is the only river cruise to be recognized as "Top in Dining" in the industry and reader polls; epicurean and oenophile adventure cruises offer tastings, culinary demonstrations, and on-site visits to markets and suppliers.

■ Eclectic interior design appeals to your aesthetic tastes. Every ship has a unique combination of styles and use of colors, fabrics, and textures.

### Don't Choose If

■ You have limited mobility. Ships do not have handicapped or wheelchair-accessible cabins. While there are elevators on five vessels (*Princess, Queen, Empress, Duchess, Countess*), the elevator on River Queen does not reach all decks.

■ You're a party animal. These ships are not traditional party boats with Vegas-style showmanship. Expect intimate, low-key entertainment like small music trios and cocktail parties.

■ You're an Internet addict. Wi-Fi service is available in the lounge and library, but service is inconsistent and inconvenient with an overloaded network and two-hour log-in limit.

**Vantage Deluxe World Travel.** Vantage operates five river cruisers: the 170-passenger *River Odyssey* and the newly refurbished 140-passenger *River Navigator*. Opt for the Owner's Suite on the luxurious *Discovery II*, launched in 2012. Its sister ship, the River Splendor, launches in 2013. The 134-passenger *River Venture* aims to please with a four-to-one crew to guest ratio. All ships are nonsmoking with designated outdoor areas only.

All staterooms have flat-screen TVs, bathroom with shower, and a safe. Junior suites add a French balcony, DVD player, minibar, and tea/coffee-maker. Both *River Odyssey* and *River Explorer* have Wi-Fi throughout. Explore the Rhine, Main, Danube, and Mosel rivers, where Christmas-market cruises are highly popular each season. On the Rhône, Vantage charters the 80-passenger *Rembrandt*. Vantage also charters ships in Portugal (the 48-passenger *Douro Prince*, operating on Portugal's Douro River) and in Russia (the 160-passenger *Tolstoy*, operating between Moscow and St. Petersburg). ☎ *800/322–6677* ⊕ *www.vantagetravel.com*.

### Choose If

■ You like value deals. Popular 11- to 15-day cruises along French, Dutch, or a combo of majestic European waterways cost as little as $190 per day without airfare. Check out special email offers. Lock in discounted fares with the SmartPay discount plan.

■ You enjoy cultural immersion. The cruise line heavily promotes its Learning Discoveries program with special events and opportunities to interact with local culture and language.

■ Good service is a must. Pleasant staff and crew work like a well-oiled machine to accommodate passenger needs.

### Don't Choose If

■ You don't enjoy group outings. Most excursions are traditional format led by a tour director.

■ You need to be online a lot. Wi-Fi, while available, is not reliable.

■ You prefer to meet an international group of passengers. Almost all passengers will hail from North America.

**Viking River Cruises.** In the luxury river cruising niche, Viking is an absolute winner, receiving praise from both the industry and demanding clientele. In 2013, Viking will operate 30 vessels. Nearly half of these were added in the last two years as the new Longship-class of next-generation vessels, inspired by ancient Norse longships and designed with sophisticated elegance by famed Norwegian maritime architects Yran and Storbraaten. All-inclusive fares, superb service, and sleek rooms with exceptional views are showcased. Apart from minor design flaws, river cruising doesn't get any better than this.

Viking's two smallest ships are the intimate 124-passenger *Fontane* and *Schumann*, both built with the shallow Elbe River in mind. Among Viking's other ships, capacity ranges between 150 and 160 guests. These include the *Danube, Europe, Neptune, Pride, Sky, and Spirit.* With capacity for 198 guests, *Helvetia* and *Sun* are larger. The first "green" ship, built in 2009—the 189-passenger *Legend*—features diesel electric hybrid engines. The wow factor is high for newer green vessels *Aegir, Embla, Freya, Idun, Njord,* and *Odin*—all launched in 2012.

Cruises in Europe are offered on the Rhine, Main, Danube, Elbe, Saône, Seine, and Rhône rivers, as well as the canals of the Netherlands and Belgium. Viking also has five ships in Russia and Ukraine. *Kirov, Pakhomov, Peterhof,* and *Surkov* sail on the Volga, while *Lomonosov* meanders the Dnieper. ☎ *800/706–1483* ⊕ *www.vikingrivercruises.com*.

### Choose If

■ You like newer ships with hotel-style appeal. Recent fleet additions offer larger suites, wraparound balconies, and a modern lounge with retractable floor-to-ceiling windows for indoor/outdoor dining.

■ Control is important when dining. Open seating for all meals means you sit where you like, with whom you want.

■ Classic European waterways are on your To-Do list. Included in fares are guided shore excursions at each port of call.

**Don't Choose If**

■ Standing room–only lounges and poor acoustics bother you. At full capacity, there are not enough seats to accommodate all passengers at daily briefings. Dining areas can get noisy.

■ You enjoy sitting on upper outside decks. Some cruises have many low bridges, prohibiting passengers to access the sunny 360-degree panoramic level.

■ You're a die-hard oenophile. While wine is free for lunch and dinner, expect the same red or white to be served at every meal.

## BARGE COMPANIES

**Afloat in France.** Perfect for a group of family or friends, these five spacious Orient Express-style péniche-hôtels accommodate 4 to 12 guests for relaxing, romantic cruises on beautiful French canals and rivers. The individually designed barges can be chartered for customized itineraries. Select the country cottage–style *Alouette*, the Louis XVI-inspired *Amaryllis*, or the grand river cruiser *Napoleon* with three levels and upper-deck whirlpool. Excellent food and dedicated service create a private experience. Discover the majestic Rhône en route to the fragrant fields of Provence. Drift in the tranquil waters of the Canal de Bourgogne and Saône River towards medieval villages and chateaux. Oenophiles, gourmands, or those in search of simply exquisite French charm should hop aboard. The all-inclusive journey with excursions, unlimited bike use, and fine cuisine is *magnifique*. ☎ *800/524–2420* ⊕ *www.afloatinfrance.com.*

**The Barge Company.** Originally Alastair Sawday's Barge Bookers back in 1997, this barge company is, in fact, one of the best independent barge bookers in Europe, providing a comprehensive online resource (in English) for finding and reserving the perfect barge holiday. Under the watchful eye of France-based directors Marie and Mark Gallé, who have long-standing relationships with barge operators, and frequently visit vessels to inspect quality standards, the Barge Company finds special offers, deep discounts, and best excursions throughout the United Kingdom and continental Europe, including the Czech Republic. See undoctored photos of ships on the info-packed website. Check out Barge of the Month for excellent first-account reviews of select vessels. ☎ *800/688–0245* ⊕ *www.thebargecompany.com.*

**The Barge Lady.** Founded in 1986, this Chicago-based booking agency is operated by Ellen Sack, who not only boasts firsthand knowledge of barge vacations but also takes pride in the fact that she always answers the phone herself. In continental Europe the Barge Lady offers barge vacations in France, Holland, Belgium, Germany, Ireland, England, and Scotland. ☎ *800/880–0071* ⊕ *www.bargeladycruises.com.*

**European Waterways.** Based in England, GoBarging/European Waterways works with the English-speaking market worldwide. In continental Europe the company operates 19 luxury barges, ranging in capacity from 4 to 20 people. Countries of operation include France, Belgium, Holland, Germany, Luxembourg, the Czech Republic, and Italy. The company also operates barge cruises in the United Kingdom and Ireland. ☎ 800/394–8630 ⊕ www.gobarging.com.

**French Country Waterways.** For more than 25 years, American-owned and -operated French Country Waterways has cruised the serene canals and rivers of France, offering an insider's perspective of the provincial countryside and inland waterways with six-night excursions. Explore five different regions for a diversity of landscape, each one rich in history and culture. Deluxe refurbished barges include the *Adrienne, Horizon II, Nenuphar*, and *Princess*. All are air-conditioned and offer an open bar, comfortable rooms, and spacious sundecks. Wood paneling, traditional furniture, and friendly service from bilingual staff ooze down-to-earth charm. Departures are every Sunday, April through October. ☎ 800/222–1236 ⊕ www.fcwl.com.

**Le Boat.** Founded in 1979, Le Boat specializes in self-drive barge vacations (the company also markets barges for GoBarging/European Waterways and other operators). Self-drive barges, ranging in capacity from single occupancy to a group of 10, operate in Germany, Belgium, Holland, England, Scotland, Ireland, France, and Italy. ☎ 800/734–5491 ⊕ www.leboat.com.

## SPECIALTY SMALL-SHIP CRUISE LINES

**Club Med Cruises.** Best known for its all-inclusive rates, Club Med Cruises showcases its iconic five-masted *Club Med 2* for eight-night journeys through the Canary Isles and Lisbon, the Iberian Peninsula, and western Italy and Corsica. Perfect for families with children older than eight, the elegant vessel offers a range of facilities, food, and fun activities. Between art programs, organized sports, massage therapies, and cultural tours, there's something for everyone. Sailing through the night, the impressive 637-foot sailing vessel, in the premium category of Club Med's five-trident category, stops each morning in a variety of exotic ports of call. Everything you'd find in a Club Med resort is now at sea, with a huge nautical hall for sports enthusiasts, first-class Carita Spa and Wellness Center, and wide variety of inventive gastronomy. Windsurfing and fitness school are included in cruise fares—perfect to burn excess calories from tempting cocktails, meals, and desserts served throughout the day and night. ☎ 888/932–2582 ⊕ www.clubmed.com.

**Cruise and Maritime Voyages.** UK-based Cruise and Maritime Voyages specializes in adults-only cruises for travelers over 60 who seek a low-key, traditional British experience. Two refurbished 800-passenger ships, *Marco Polo* and *Discovery,* offer classic cruising itineraries from 2-night mini-excursions to 44-night cruises and are designed to maximize time in ports of call. With departure from six UK cities, afternoon tea service, an English-speaking staff, and pounds sterling as onboard currency, the cruise line attracts a predominantly unpretentious, British crowd. ☎ 0845/430–0274 in the UK ⊕ www.cruiseandmaritime.com ☞ Cruise Style: Mainstream

**Fred. Olsen Cruise Lines.** With its Norwegian heritage of seamanship spanning over 150 years, family-owned Fred. Olsen Cruise Lines has built a solid reputation of reliability and comfort for its UK-based fleet of smaller ships. Major refitting and refurbishment of old and recently acquired ships since 2008 have earned the company high industry accolades. Two sister ships from the defunct luxury Royal Viking Line, *Royal Viking Star* and *Royal Viking Sky,* have reunited under the Fred. Olsen house flag and now sail as *Black Watch* and *Boudicca*. The *Balmoral* and *Braemar* complete the four-vessel fleet. ☎ *01473/742–424 in the U.K.* ⊕ *www.fredolsencruises.com* ☞ *Cruise Style: Mainstream.*

**Göta Canal Steamship Company.** Founded in 1869 under the name Motala Ström Steamship Company Ltd., this operator was one of the very first Swedish companies to attract foreign tourists to Sweden through cooperation with the U.K. travel agency Thomas Cook & Co. during the 1880s. Since 2001 the line has been a part of the Strömma Group. Three ships are in operation on the Göta Kanal: *Juno* (29 cabins), *Wilhelm Tham* (25 cabins), and *Diana* (28 cabins). Great Rail Journeys, one of the major tour operators in the United Kingdom, awarded the *Juno* the 2009 Gold Award in the class "Best Food in Scandinavia and the Baltic States." ☎ *(46)31/806315* ⊕ *www.gotacanal.se.*

**Hebridean Island Cruises.** Since 1986, this niche all-inclusive luxury cruising company has been offering guests the highest standards of service with a price tag to match. The flagship *Hebridean Princess* only carries 50 passengers and has an enviable reputation for fine food, wine, and dedicated crew of 38 with 30 beautifully decorated cabins, 10 of which are suited for single travelers. Having reintroduced the Golden Age of Cruising, the vessel sails the dramatic Scottish coast, Western and Northern Isles, and Ireland. In 2012, Hebridean launched the dedicated River Cruises program on board the luxury riverboat *Royal Crown.* Having undergone an extensive renovation in 2010, the luxurious riverboat cruises the Rhine and Danube rivers during spring and autumn with seven-night itineraries. Rub shoulders with expert guest lecturers in art, horticulture, conservation, history, broadcasting, literature, and archaeology. Though cruise prices are steep, some more than $15,000, the wealth of knowledge gained and effortless, five-star experience will be both unique and priceless. ☎ *(44)1756/704–700 in the U.K.* ⊕ *www. hebridean.co.uk.*

**Magna Carta Steamship Company.** Although they are separated by almost 190 years, one could probably draw a straight line between the *Lord of the Glens* and the steam yacht *Gondolier.* In 1822 the *Gondolier* left Inverness for an inaugural passage to Fort William on the brand-new Caledonian Canal. The ship launched by U.K.-based Magna Carta Steamship Company, established in 1999, now carries on the tradition, operating cruises along the same canal as well as along the Scottish coast to view gorgeous lochs and highlands. The company also operates a river-cruise vessel on the Thames. In 2013, the *Spirit of Chartwell* offers seven-day passages along Portugal's Douro River. ☎ *(44)20/7328–1123 in the U.K.* ⊕ *www.magnacarta.bz.*

**P&O Cruises.** P&O Cruises is the oldest cruise in the world and remains Britain's leading cruise line, sailing the UK's largest and most modern fleet. The ships are equipped with every traditional big-ship amenity, including swimming pools, stylish restaurants, spas, bars, casinos, theaters, and showrooms. To offer passengers a variety of choices, P&O has adapted their fleet to match the preferences of their primary markets. Although most of the ships cater to families as well as couples and singles of all ages, *Arcadia, Adonia,* and *Oriana* are adults-only ships. The *Aurora, Azura, Oceana,* and *Ventura* complete the P&O armada and welcome both adults and children. Following customer feedback, P&O announced major refurbishments for the *Ventura, Oceana,* and *Arcadia* in 2013. ☎ *0845/374–0111* ⊕ *www.pocruises.com* ☞ *Cruise Style: Mainstream.*

**Saga Cruises.** Saga Holidays, a UK-based travel and tour company, was founded in 1951 to offer vacation packages to mature travelers. Saga purchased its first ship in 1996, and its itineraries brim with longer sailings to far-flung corners of the globe, making Saga voyages destination oriented. Classic cruisers in every sense of the word, Saga's passengers are travelers who expect inspiring itineraries coupled with traditional onboard amenities and comfortable surroundings. Both ships (*Quest for Adventure* and *Saga Sapphire*) offer numerous accommodations designed for solo cruisers, making Saga Cruises are particularly friendly for senior singles. Especially convenient on lengthy sailings, each ship features complimentary self-service launderettes and ironing facilities. In port, the line offers complimentary shuttle transfers to the town center from the cruise pier. ☎ *0800/096–0079 or (44) 1303/771–111* ⊕ *www.saga.co.uk* ☞ *Cruise Style: Premium.*

**Sea Cloud Cruises.** Since 1979, Hamburg-based Sea Cloud Cruises offers a four-masted barque, magnificent windjammers, and the *River Cloud II*, a self-proclaimed five-star floating hotel for cruises on the Rhine, Main, Danube and Black Sea to spectacular destinations. Light woods, refined fabrics, marble sinks, and golden fixtures recall 1930s elegance. The row of large arched panoramic windows and open upper deck provide space, fresh air, and memorable views. For a private yacht experience, sail the Mediterranean in the glamorous *Sea Cloud.* Her sister windjammer, the *Sea Cloud II*, is the perfect blend of nostalgia and technology. ☎ *(49)40/3095920 in Germany, 888/732–2568 or 201/227–9404 in the U.S.* ⊕ *www.seacloud.com.*

**Swan Hellenic Discovery Cruising.** One hundred percent British in flavor and flair, the first cruise offered in 1954 was the brainchild of the Swan brothers who supplemented visits of legendary Mediterranean sites with eminent guest speakers. A series of mergers and acquisitions through the years by P&O Cruises and Carnival led to the relaunching of summer and winter voyages in Europe, the Middle East and Asia, and South America. In keeping with the guest speaker tradition, passengers can wine, dine, and speak with celebrated scholars, ordained reverends, politicians, authors, musicians, actors, and journalists who lecture, perform or give enrichment workshops. The 350-passenger fully loaded *Minerva* sails as the company's flagship vessel. ☎ *(44)844/8714603 in the U.K.* ⊕ *www.swanhellenic.com.*

# Major European Cruise Ports

3

**Thomson Cruises.** In 1973, the UK-based travel operator Thomson Holidays officially entered the cruising market under the umbrella company Thomson Travel Group, a subsidiary of the larger German enterprise TUI, an international leisure travel corporation having its roots in shipping and maritime industries. *.Thomson Dream, Thomson Majesty, Thomson Celebration,Thomson Spirit.Island EscapeIsland Escape* ☎*(44)870/165–0079 or 0871/230–2800, both in the UK* ⊕*www.thomson.co.uk/cruise* ☞ *Cruise Style: Mainstream.*

**Variety Cruises.** This Greek company is one of the largest operators of small cruise ships worldwide. The 15 vessels in the fleet all vary in size and style. Some of the ships deployed are sailing ships. On board, passengers enjoy locally flavored cuisine and itineraries that blend well-known ports with the hidden gems of the Mediterranean. The company was the result of a merger in 2006 between the two companies Zeus Tours & Yacht Cruises and Hellas Yachts. ☎ *(30)210/6919191 in Greece* ⊕ *www.varietycruises.com.*

**Voyages of Discovery.** A new long-term partnership between two established cruise companies delivers a great value cruise experience. All Leisure Holidays Ltd. has joined forces with Cruise & Maritime Voyages to offer cruises in Northern Europe, the Mediterranean, and the Black Sea. All Leisure Holidays' 700-passenger ship MV *Discovery Sailaway*, which at this writing operates under the Voyages of Discovery banner, will be operated by Cruise & Maritime Voyages under the CMV brand beginning February 2013, following a scheduled extensive dry dock and refurbishment. This joint venture will allow passengers to sail on the much-loved, classic ship, with a wider range of U.K. and Mediterranean cruises. ☎ *+44/844/488–0893 in the U.K.* ⊕ *www.voyagesofdiscovery.co.uk.*

**Voyages to Antiquity.** Combining the comfort of boutique-style cruising with the very best of cultural travel, Voyages to Antiquity offers an opportunity to explore the origins of Western civilization, as well as the rich culture of the East. The meticulously planned itineraries, celebrated guest speakers, and shore excursions bring to life the fascinating history and awe-inspiring sites of the ancient world. The premium, 550-passenger MS *Aegean Odyssey* sails throughout the year. Explore the Byzantine Empire through visits to St. Sophia in Istanbul and San Vitale in Ravenna. Look on the company website for late availability fly-cruise offers if travel dates are flexible. Join the Odyssey Club to be a member of the loyalty program and receive additional savings. ☎ *877/398–1460* ⊕ *www.voyagestoantiquity.com.*

# Western Mediterranean

Gondolas, Venice

## WORD OF MOUTH

"My wife and I are going on a trip of a lifetime next June—12-day Mediterranean/Greece cruise starting [in] Rome and ending in Venice. . . . Probably our biggest dilemma is in Naples. With only one day, do you go to Isle of Capri, try to see Pompeii and Mount Vesuvius, or see the Amalfi Coast?"

—MurrayMartin

If you're a first-time cruiser in Europe and want to stop at some of the most popular European destinations, a Western Mediterranean itinerary might be ideal for you.

Western Mediterranean itineraries often begin in either Barcelona or Civitavecchia (for Rome) and may be one-way or round-trip cruises. More one-week cruises in Europe tend to be one-way cruises than in other cruise regions, while those of 10 days or more are sometimes loop cruises. A few of these itineraries may take you as far as Venice, though that city is a more popular jumping-off point for cruises through the Adriatic and Aegean. Although some of the ports included in this chapter (such as Venice or Bari in Italy) are more likely to be on Eastern Mediterranean itineraries, others (such as Le Havre or Bordeaux in France) may be a part of some Northern European cruise routes. We've kept all the ports in Italy and France together in this chapter to make them easier to find. Larger ships will be limited in the ports at which they can call, but smaller ships may hit some of the lesser-visited spots on the French or Italian Riviera.

## ABOUT THE RESTAURANTS

All the restaurants we recommend serve lunch, and many also serve dinner. If your cruise ship stays late in port, you may choose to dine off the ship. Although the cuisine in Europe is varied, one thing is constant across the continent: Europeans tend to eat a leisurely meal at lunch. In most ports there are quicker and simpler alternatives for those who just want to grab a quick bite before returning to the ship.

# A CORUÑA, SPAIN (FOR SANTIAGO DE COMPOSTELA)

Updated by
Joanna Styles

One of Spain's busiest ports, A Coruña (La Coruña in Castilian) prides itself on being the most progressive city in the region. The weather can be fierce, wet, and windy—hence the glass-enclosed, white-pane galleries on the houses lining the harbor. This is one of two main ports at which cruise ships call so they can offer an overland trek to the pilgrimage city of Santiago de Compostela; the other is Vigo (⇨ *Vigo, below, for information on Santiago de Compostela, including a map*). Though at 57 km (35 miles) to the north, A Coruña is marginally closer. Occasionally, a cruise ship will offer an overland excursion beginning in one port and ending in the other.

## ESSENTIALS

### CURRENCY
The euro.

### HOURS
Museums are generally open from 9 until 7 or 8, many are closed on Monday, and some close in the afternoon. Most stores are open Monday through Saturday 9 to 1:30 and 5 to 8, but tourist shops may open in the afternoon and also on Sunday between May and September.

**PRIVATE TOURS**

SECCHI organizes half- and full-day tours exploring Galician towns, cities, coastline, and countryside.

Contacts **SECCHI.** ☎ *981/554176* ⊕ *www.turismosecchi.com.*

**TELEPHONES**

Most tri- and quad-band GSM phones work in Spain, which has a 3G-compatible network. Public kiosks accept phone cards that support international calls (cards sold in press shops, bars, and telecom shops). Major companies include Vodafone.

**COMING ASHORE**

Ships dock at Liners Quay in the interior of the port. There are few services at the port itself, but from the port entrance you can explore the town on foot.

Bus 1 runs from the port to the main bus station every 15 minutes for €1.20. There is at least one train per hour to Santiago de Compostela. Journey time is 40 minutes, and tickets cost approximately €12 return.

Taxis wait at the port entrance and can be hired by the day for tourist itineraries. Renting a car will allow you to explore Santiago de Compostela plus the rugged countryside of this wild corner of Spain, but prices are expensive. Prices begin at €50 per day for a manual economy vehicle.

## EXPLORING A CORUÑA

**Castillo de San Antón.** At the northeastern tip of the Old Town is the Castillo de San Antón (St. Anthony's Castle), a 16th-century fort. Inside is A Coruña's **Museum of Archaeology**, with remnants of the prehistoric Celtic culture that once thrived in these parts. The collection includes silver artifacts as well as pieces of the Celtic stone forts called *castros.* ⊠ *Paseo do Parrote s/n* ☎ *981/189850* 🎫 *Free* ⊙ *Sept.–June, Tues.–Sat 10–7:30, Sun. 10–2:30; July and Aug., Tues.–Sat. 10–9, Sun. 10–3.*

**Colexiata de Santa María do Campo.** Called "St. Mary of the Field" because the building was once beyond the city's walls, this Romanesque beauty dates to the mid-13th century. The facade depicts the Adoration of the Magi; the celestial figures include St. Peter, holding the keys to heaven. Because of an architectural miscalculation the roof is too heavy for its supports, so the columns inside lean outward and the buttresses outside have been thickened. ⊠ *Pl. de Santa María 1.*

**Iglesia de Santiago.** This 12th-century church, the oldest church in A Coruña, was the first stop on the *camino inglés* (English route) toward Santiago de Compostela. Originally Romanesque, it's now a hodgepodge that includes Gothic arches, a baroque altarpiece, and two 18th-century rose windows. ⊠ *Pl. de la Constitución s/n.*

**Paseo Marítimo.** To see why sailors once nicknamed A Coruña *la ciudad de cristal* (the glass city), stroll the Paseo Marítimo, said to be the longest seaside promenade in Europe. Although the congregation of boats is charming, the real sight is across the street: a long, gracefully curved row of houses. Built by fishermen in the 18th century, they face *away* from the sea—at the end of a long day, these men were tired of looking at the water. Nets were hung from the porches to dry, and fish was sold on the street below. When Galicia's first glass factory opened nearby, someone thought to enclose these porches in glass, like the latticed stern galleries of oceangoing galleons, to keep wind and rain at bay. The resulting **glass galleries** ultimately spread across the harbor and eventually throughout Galicia.

**Plaza de María Pita.** The focal point of the *ciudad vieja* (Old Town), this stirring plaza has a north side that's given over to the neoclassical **Palacio Municipal,** or city hall, built 1908–12 with three Italianate domes. The **monument** in the center, built in 1998, depicts the heroine Maior (María) Pita. When England's Sir Francis Drake arrived to sack A Coruña in 1589, the locals were only half finished building the defensive Castillo de San Antón, and a 13-day battle ensued. When María Pita's husband died, she took up his lance, slew the Briton who tried to plant the Union Jack here, and revived the exhausted Coruñesos, inspiring other women to join the battle.

**Torre de Hércules.** Much of A Coruña sits on a peninsula, on the tip of which is the Torre de Hércules—the oldest still-functioning lighthouse in the world. Originally built during the reign of Trajan, the Roman emperor born in Spain in AD 98, the lighthouse was rebuilt in the 18th century and looks strikingly modern; all that remains from Roman times are inscribed foundation stones. Lining the approach to the lighthouse are sculptures depicting figures from Galician and Celtic legends. At this writing, the interior is closed for renovation, but the park is still worth a visit, whether or not you can get inside the lighthouse. ⊠ *Av. de Navarra s/n* ☎ *981/223730* ⊕ *www.torredeherculesacoruna.com* ⊡ *€3* ☉ *Apr.–June and Sept., daily 10–6:45; July and Aug., Mon.–Thurs. and Sun. 10–8:45, Fri. and Sat. 10–11:45; Oct.–Mar. daily 10–5:45.*

## SHOPPING

**Calle Real** has boutiques with contemporary fashions. A stroll down **Calle San Andrés,** two blocks inland from Calle Real, or **Avenida Juan Flórez,** leading into the newer town, can yield some sartorial treasures.

**José López Rama.** Authentic Galician *zuecos* (hand-painted wooden clogs) are still worn in some villages to navigate mud; the cobbler José López Rama has a workshop 15 minutes south of A Coruña in the village of Carballo. ⊠ *Rúa do Muiño 7, Carballo* ☎ *981/701068.*

**Sastrería Iglesias.** For hats and Galician folk clothing, stop into Sastrería Iglesias —founded in 1864—where artisan José Luis Iglesias Rodrígues sells his textiles. ⊠ *Rúa Rego do Auga 14* ☎ *981/221634.*

## WHERE TO EAT

$    ✕ **Adega O Bebedeiro.** Steps from the ultramodern Domus, this tiny restaurant is beloved by locals for its authentic food. It feels like an old farmhouse, with stone walls and floors, a fireplace, pine tables and stools, and dusty wine bottles (*adega* is Gallego for bodega, or wine cellar). Appetizers such as *pulpo con almejas al ajillo* (octopus with clams in garlic sauce) are followed by fresh fish at market prices and

SPANISH

★

an ever-changing array of delicious desserts. ⑤ *Average main: €15* ✉ *C. Ángel Rebollo 34* ☎ *981/210609* ⊗ *Closed Mon. and first week in Jan. No dinner Sun.*

$ ✕ **La Penela.** The smart, contemporary, bottle-green dining room is the
SEAFOOD  perfect place to feast on fresh fish while sipping Albariño—try at least a
★  few crabs or mussels with béchamel, for which this restaurant is locally famous. If shellfish isn't your speed, the roast veal is also popular. The restaurant occupies a modernist building on a corner of the lively Praza María Pita. Some tables have views of the harbor, or you can eat in a glassed-in terrace on the square. ⑤ *Average main: €15* ✉ *Praza María Pita 12* ☎ *981/209200* ⊗ *Closed Sun. and Jan. 10–25.*

# AJACCIO, CORSICA

Updated by
Victoria Tang

"The best way to know Corsica," according to Napoléon, "is to be born there." Not everyone has had his luck. This vertical chalky granite world of its own, rising in the Mediterranean between Provence and Tuscany, remains France's very own Wild West: a powerful natural setting and, literally, a breath of fresh air. Its strategic location 168 km (105 miles) south of Monaco and 81 km (50 miles) west of Italy made Corsica a prize hotly contested by a succession of Mediterranean powers, notably Genoa, Pisa, and France. Corsica gives an impression of immensity, seeming far larger than its 215 km (133 miles) length and 81 km (50 miles) width, partly because its rugged, mountainous terrain makes for very slow traveling and partly because the landscape and the culture vary greatly from one microregion to another. Much of the terrain of Corsica that is not wooded or cultivated is covered with a dense thicket of undergrowth, which along with chestnut trees makes up the maquis, a variety of wild and aromatic plants including lavender, myrtle, and heather that gave Corsica one of its sobriquets, "the perfumed isle."

## ESSENTIALS

### CURRENCY

The euro.

### HOURS

Stores are generally open Monday through Saturday 9–7, but many close at lunchtime (usually noon–2 or 3) and some will open later and on Sunday during July and August. Museums open 10–5, but most are closed on either Monday or Tuesday.

### TELEPHONES

Tri-band GSM phones work in France. You can buy prepaid phone cards at telecom shops, news vendors, and tobacconists in all towns and cities. Phone cards can be used for local or international calls. Orange, SFR, Bouygues Telecom, and Virgin are leading telecom companies. If you have an unlocked GSM phone, LeFrenchMobile (⊕ *www. lefrenchmobile.com*) offers SIM cards (and micro SIM cards) with support in English, unlimited validity of credits, and prepurchase online.

### COMING ASHORE

Ships dock in Ajaccio port, a short walk from the town of Ajaccio. Cafés and shops can be found immediately outside the port gates.

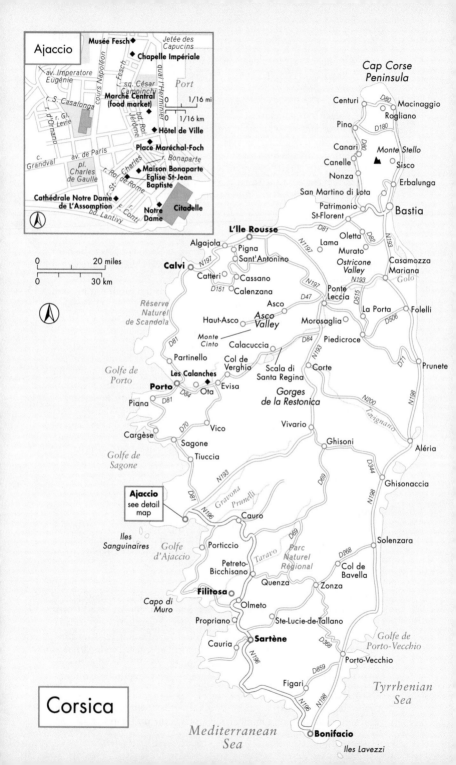

The local bus network, catering to locals (not tourists), operates at least two buses a day to connect all the southern towns with Ajaccio, but timetables may not coincide with your ship's departure time, so check carefully.

Renting a vehicle would allow you to explore several towns and surrounding attractions during your stay on the island; however, be aware that travel times may be longer than map distances suggest, because the mountain roads can be narrow and winding. Vehicle rental costs approximately €60 per day for an economy manual car. Delivery to the port will be an additional charge. Hertz serves the entire island; its 18 offices are at all airports and harbors and in the major towns. Be sure to reserve at least two weeks in advance in July and August.

---

> ### CORSICA BEST BETS
>
> **Bonifacio.** Rising seemingly out of the living rock, this medieval stronghold is now a maze of tourist-friendly cafés and shops.
>
> **The Calanques de Piana.** Russet red inlets of jagged rocks lapped by azure waters, this vista, which you can see if you drive between Ajaccio and Calvi, is truly breathtaking.
>
> **Calvi.** A picture-perfect little town topped by a walled citadel, Calvi also offers some of the finest beaches on the island.

---

## EXPLORING CORSICA

### AJACCIO

Ajaccio, Napoléon's birthplace and Corsica's modern capital, is a busy, French-flavored town with a bustling port and ancient streets. The city has a long history dating back to its founding in 1492, and some of the original buildings can still be seen on rue Roie-de-Rome, near the Musée du Capitellu.

**Cathédrale Notre Dame de L'Assomption.** The 16th-century baroque cathedral where Napoléon was baptized is at the end of rue St-Charles. The interior is covered with trompe-l'oeil frescoes, and the high altar, from a church in Lucca, Italy, was donated by Napoléon's sister Eliza after he made her princess of Tuscany. Eugène Delacroix's *The Triumph of Religion* hangs above the Virgin of the Sacred Heart marble altar from the 17th-century. ⊠ *Rue F.-Conti.* ☎ *04–95–21–41–14* ⊕ *www.ajaccio-tourisme.com/* ⊠ *Free* ☼ *Daily 9–11 am.*

**Chapelle Impériale.** Located on the south wing of the Palais Fesch, the neo-Renaissance-style Imperial Chapel was built in 1857 by Napoléon's nephew, Napoléon III, to accommodate the tombs of the Bonaparte family. The Coptic crucifix over the altar was taken from Egypt during the general's 1798 campaign. Renovated in 2012, the somber chapel officially classified as a historic monument is constructed worth a visit to view its neoclassical cupola and ecclesiastical iconography. ⊠ *50-52 rue Cardinal Fesch* ☎ *04–95–21–48–17* ⊕ *www.ajaccio.fr/La-Chapelle-Imperiale_a353.html* ⊠ *€1.50; children under 15 free* ☼ *Tues.–Sat. 10–12:30 and 3–7.*

**Eglise St-Jean Baptiste.** Wander narrow streets lined with Ajaccio's oldest houses built around 1492, when the city was founded. At the intersection of rue du Roi-de-Rome and rue Saint Charles, you can visit the *confrérie*, or religious brotherhood, of St. Jean Baptiste. On June 24, the patron saint is honored with a solemn mass conducted by the city's bishop and Corsican music concert. Follow the ancestral religious procession from the chapel to the Old Town and Place Charles de Gaulle, where the celebration ends with traditional fire lighting in the evening. ⊠ *rue du Roi-de-Rome* ☎ *04–95–22–27– 38* ⊕ *www.ajaccio.fr/ Confreries-et-pelerinages_a21.html.*

**Hôtel de Ville** (*town hall*). Ajaccio's town hall has an Empire-style grand salon hung with portraits of a long line of Bonapartes. You'll find a fine bust of Letizia, Napoléon's formidable mother; a bronze death mask of the emperor himself; and a frescoed ceiling depicting Napoléon's meteoric rise. ⊠ *Pl. Maréchal-Foch, Avenue Antoine Serafini* ☎ *04–95– 51–52–53* ⊕ *www.ajaccio.fr* 🖼 *€2.30* ☉ *Weekdays 9–noon and 2–6.*

**Fodor's Choice**
★   **Maison Bonaparte** (*Bonaparte House*). One of four national historic museums dedicated to Napoléon, the multilevel house where the emperor was born on August 15, 1769, contains memorabilia and paintings of the extended Bonaparte family. History aficionados can tour bedrooms, dining rooms, and salons where Charles and Letitzia Bonaparte raised their eight children. Period furnishings and antiques in Corsican and Empire styles are scattered about and pay tribute to the family's bourgeoisie upbringing. Head downstairs below the Gallery to see the cellars and granite oil-pressing mill acquired by Napoléon III in 1860. Visit the trapdoor room and find the ground opening located next to the door through which Napoléon allegedly escaped in 1799. The building itself changed hands multiple times through Bonaparte heirs until 1923, when it was donated to the state of France by Prince Victor, elder son of Prince Jérôme Napoleon. ⊠ *Rue St-Charles* ☎ *04–95–21– 43–89* 🖨 *04–95–21–61–32* ⊕ *www.musee-maisonbonaparte.fr* 🖼 *€7 (Apr.–Oct.); €6 (low season); under 26 free* ☉ *Oct.–Mar., Tue.–Sun. 10–noon and 2–4:45; Apr.–Sep., Tue.–Sun. 10:30–12:30 and 1:15–6* ☉ *Last admission 30 min prior to closing.*

★
ℭ   **Marché Central (food market).** For an authentic view of daily Corsican life, tour this wonderful open-air food market brimming with gastronomic delights. There is an array of local cheeses, charcuterie, breads, pastries, olives, condiments, and aromatic meats for sale. Taste samples of chorizo, nougat, liqueur, honeys, and oils from friendly foodstalls managed by original producers and farmers. Everything from artisanal candy to fresh-from-the-field vegetables and fruits, spices, and traditional indulgences like chestnut-infused beignets can be savored in an atmosphere guaranteed to be lively and local. Bring your euros—cash is the preferred method of payment. ⊠ *Square César Campinchi, boulevard du Roi Jérôme* ⊕ *www.ajaccio-tourisme.com* ☉ *Tues.–Sun. 8–1; hours may vary due to weather.*

**Fodor's Choice**
★
ℭ   **Musée des Beaux Arts-Palais Fesch.** Adjacent to the Chapelle Impérial, this internationally recognized museum houses one of the most important collections from the Napoleonic era; it's undoubtedly one of the most

significant displays in France of ancient Italian masterpieces spanning the 14th–20th centuries. The massive treasure trove of objets d'art, sculptures, and paintings is impressive on scale alone—there are nearly 18,000 items, including nearly 16,000 awe-inspiring works from Italian painters. Seek out the dramatic realism of Neapolitan baroque artists Giordano and Giaquinto; view Renaissance masters Botticelli, Titian, Veronese and Fra Bartolomeo—all part of an astounding inventory that belonged to Napoléon's uncle, Cardinal Fesch, archbishop of Lyon and art lover, following the French Revolution. Thanks to his nephew's military conquests, the cardinal was able to amass (steal, some would say) many celebrated old master paintings, the most famous of which are now in Paris's Louvre. The museum's beautiful vaulted corridors, recently renovated for nearly €7 million, also showcase 700 paintings, portraits, still lifes, and sculptures from the First and Second Empire from the French school. ⊠ *50–52 rue Cardinal Fesch* ☎ *04-95-21-48-17* ⊕ *www. musee-fesch.com* ⊠ *€8* ⊙ *Oct.–Apr., Mon., Wed., and Sat. 10–5; Thurs., Fri., and 3rd Sun. of each month noon–5. May–Sept., Mon., Wed. and Sat. 10:30–6; Thur., Fri., and Sun. noon–6* ⊙ *Closed Tues.*

**Place Maréchal-Foch.** Surrounded by a row of stately palm trees, the Place Foch, also called the Place des Palmiers, is the city's magnificent central triangle, easily recognizable with its fountain of four Corsican granite lions encircling the commanding statue of Napoléon, a work by sculptor Jérôme Maglioli. Popular as a spot to people-watch on a sunny day, the place is surrounded by cafés, pharmacies, banks, and opens up to the Ajaccio port. ⊠ *Place Marechal Foch.*

## FILITOSA

★ **Filitosa.** Filitosa is the site of Corsica's largest grouping of megalithic
⟳ menhir statues. The sensorial tour begins with a beautiful stroll down a bucolic tree-lined path with mesmerizing instrumental music emanating from hidden speakers. Discover enigmatic life-size stone figures of ancient warriors that rise up mysteriously from the undulating terrain, many with human faces whose features have been flattened over time by erosion. A small museum on the site houses archaeological finds, including the menhir known as *Scalsa Murta,* whose delicately carved spine and rib cage are surprisingly contemporary for a work dating from some 5,000 years ago. The guidebook in English (€5) by experts Cesari and Acquaviva is supplemented by information in English at each site. After your tour, enjoy a beverage at the small brasserie, where members of the Cesari family proudly discuss the site's historic discoveries on the personal property of Charles-Antoine Cesari in 1946. ⊠ *Centre Préhistorique Filitosa, Petreto-Bicchisano* ⊹ *Route 196 to col de Celaccia; right at Dept 57* ☎ *04-95-74-00-91 for information* ⊕ *www.filitosa. fr* ⊠ *Guided tours in English €5* ⊙ *June–October, daily 8–7.*

## SARTÈNE

*27 km (16 miles) southeast of Filitosa on N196.*

Described as the "most Corsican of all Corsican towns" by French novelist Prosper Mérimée, Sartène, founded in the 16th century, has survived pirate raids and bloody feuding among the town's families. The word *vendetta* is believed to have originated here as the result of a 19th-century family feud so serious that French troops were brought in to serve as a peacekeeping buffer force. Centuries of fighting have left the town with a somewhat eerie and menacing atmosphere. Perhaps adding to this is the annual Good Friday *catenacciu* (enchaining) procession, in which an anonymous penitent, dragging ankle chains, lugs a heavy cross through the village streets.

Surrounded by ancient ramparts, **Vieux Sartène** (Old Sartène) begins at place de la Libération, the main square. To one side is the **Hôtel de Ville** (town hall), in the former Genoese governor's palace. Slip into the Middle Ages through the tunnel under the town hall to place du Maggiu and the ancient **Santa Anna** quarter, a warren of narrow, cobbled streets lined with granite houses. Scarcely 100 yards from the Hôtel de Ville, down a steep and winding street, is a 12th-century *tour de guet* (watchtower). Sartène is a key link to Corsica's prehistory, thanks to its proximity to Pianu de Levie's dolmens and megalithic statues.

★ **Musée Départemental de Préhistoire Corse** (*Regional Museum of Prehis-*
Ⓒ *toric Corsica and Archaeology*). Some of the island's best prehistoric relics are in this renovated museum in what was once the town's prison. Explore this well-maintained depot of more than 250,000 items from Neolithic times to the 15th century. The galleries chronologically catalog the development of crafts, trade, culture, habitats, and demographics of ancient Corsica. ⊠ *Rue Croce* ☎ *04–95–77–01–09* ⊕ *www. prehistoire-corse.org* 🏷 *€4* ۞ *Jun.–Sept., daily 10–6; Oct.–May, weekdays 9–noon and 1:30–5.*

## BONIFACIO
*52 km (31 miles) southeast of Sartène via N196.*

FodorśChoice  The ancient fortress town of Bonifacio occupies a spectacular cliff-top
★  aerie above a harbor carved from limestone cliffs. It's 13 km (8 miles) from Sardinia, and the local speech is heavily influenced by the accent and idiom of that nearby Italian island. Established in the 12th century as Genoa's first Corsican stronghold, Bonifacio remained Genoese through centuries of battles and sieges. As you wander the narrow streets of the **Haute Ville** (Upper Village), inside the walls of the citadel, think of Homer's *Odyssey*. It's here, in the harbor, that scholars place the catastrophic encounter (Chapter X) between Ulysses's fleet and the Laestrygonians, who hurled lethal boulders down from the cliffs.

★ **Bastion de l'Étendard** (*Bastion of the Standard*). From place d'Armes at the city gate, enter the 13th century Bastion de l'Étendard, where you can still see the system of weights and levers used to pull up the drawbridge. The former garrison, the last remaining part of the original fortress, now houses life-size dioramas of Bonifacio's history, which describes the bombardment of the bastion in the 16th century Franco-Turkish war. A visit gives you access to the memorial and Vestiges garden. Climb the steep steps and be rewarded with an incredible panoramic view of the white-chalk cliffs and stunning coastline. ⊠ *Avenue Charles de Gaulle* 🏷 *€2.5* ۞ *Mid-Jun.–mid-Sept., Mon.–Fri. 9–8; Sat.–Sun. 10–7.*

★ **Dragon Grottoes.** From Bonifacio hop on a number of boats that can
Ⓒ  bring you to see the blue Dragon Grottos, a spectacular geological site. Comprehensive tours typically venture to Venus's Bath (the trip

takes one hour on boats that set out every 15 minutes during July and August), sea caves at Sdragonatto and St-Angoine, and the Lavezzi Islands. ⊠ *Boats leave from Bonifacio marina ⊕ www.bonifacio.fr.*

★ **Eglise Sainte Marie Majeure.** The oldest structure in the city, the 12th-century church with buttresses attaching it to surrounding houses is located in the center of the citadel's maze of cobblestone streets. Inside the Pisan-Genoese church, look for the Renaissance baptismal font, carved in bas-relief, and the 3rd-century white-marble Roman sarcophagus. Walk around the back to see the loggia built above a huge cistern that stored water for use in times of siege, as did the circular stone silos seen throughout the town. The 14th-century bell tower rises 82 feet. Relics of the patron Saint Bonifacio reside in the central altar. ⊠ *Rue du Saint Sacrement* ☎ *04–95–73–11–88 ⊕ www.bonifacio.fr.*

## PORTO–LES CALANCHES
*5 km (3 miles) west of Ota, 30 km (19 miles) south of Calvi.*

The flashy resort town of Porto doesn't have much character, but its setting on the crystalline **Golfe de Porto** (Gulf of Porto), surrounded by massive pink-granite mountains, is superb. Activity focuses on the small port, where there is a boardwalk with restaurants and hotels. A short hike from the boardwalk will bring you to a 16th-century Genoese tower that overlooks the bay. Boat excursions leave daily for the **Réserve Naturel de Scandola.**

## CALVI
*92 km (58 miles) north of Piana, 159 km (100 miles) north of Ajaccio.*

Calvi, Corsica's slice of the Riviera, has been described by author Dorothy Carrington as "an oasis of pleasure on an otherwise austere island." Calvi prospered by supplying products to Genoa; its citizens remained loyal supporters of Genoa long after the rest of the island declared independence. Calvi also claims to be the birthplace of Christopher Columbus. During the 18th century the town endured assaults from Corsican nationalists, including celebrated patriot Pasquale Paoli. Today Calvi sees a summertime invasion of tourists, drawn to the 6-km (4-mile) stretch of sandy white beach, the citadel, and the buzzing nightlife.

★ **Citadelle.** The Genoese citadel perched on a rocky promontory at the tip of the bay competes with the beach as a major attraction. An inscription above the drawbridge—*civitas calvi semper fidelis* (the citizens of Calvi always faithful)—reflects the town's unswerving allegiance to Genoa. At the welcome center, just inside the gates, watch the video on the city's history and arrange to take a guided tour given in English (three times a day) or follow the self-guided walking tour. ⊠ *Up hill off Ave. de l'Uruguay* ☎ *04–95–65–36–74 ⊕ www.villedecalvi.fr* ☝ *Guided tour and video show €9 ⊗ Tours Easter–early Oct., daily at 10, 4:30, and 6:30.*

**St-Jean-Baptiste.** The austere façade of the 13th-century church of John the Baptist is worth a visit to see its alabaster Renaissance baptismal font decorated with angel heads and rows of pews where the city's chaste upper-class women used to pray. ⊠ *Pl. d'Armes* ☎ *04–95–65–16–67.*

### L'ILE ROUSSE

*10 km (6 miles) northeast of Algajola, 37 km (22 miles) southwest of St-Florent.*

L'Ile Rousse, famous for its market and named for the island of reddish rock now connected to the town by a causeway, is a favorite for vacationers who come to bask in its Riviera-like mise-en-scène. A small two-car train runs along the coast to Calvi, delivering sun-worshippers to beaches not accessible by road.

## SHOPPING

Traditional handicrafts are found in abundance in the shopping streets of the major towns. Until the mid-20th century most Corsicans had to be relatively self-sufficient, and this has led to all manner of crafts from knives and walking sticks to warm winter sweaters. Look for pottery, for which the island is known. Corsican knives are a specialty item, and the finest examples have exquisite blades and handles. Also look for items carved from wood and bone, some practical, some ornate. Because food had to be put back for the winter, preserved foods became very important parts of the Corsican diet, and are now well known; the charcuterie is excellent—in addition to a range of hams and salamis, you'll find aromatic dried herbs, numerous cheeses, plus fragrant jams and honey. Don't forget to sample a bottle of Corsican wine.

The citadel of Bonifacio has excellent boutiques set in historic stone cottages and cellars. Both Ajaccio and L'Isle Rousse have excellent markets, and in Calvi the major shopping streets are rue Clemenceau and boulevard Wilson.

**Art'Insula.** A large selection of fabrics, leather, and knives crafted by local artisans is available here. Find beautiful jewelry, pottery, and Corsican batik to take home as souvenirs. For the gourmand, select an assortment of confitures, honeys, vinegars, and liqueurs. ⊠ *57 rue Fesch, Ajaccio* ☎ *04–95–50–54–67* ⊕ *www.artisula.com.*

★ **Casa Napoléon.** Belonging to Charles Antona, a native Corsican producer of fine gastronomic goods for more than 30 years, Casa Napoléon is the well-stocked boutique selling organic jams, terrines, traditional dishes, olives oils, wine, sweets and other delicacies straight from his Campestra factory and plantations. A second store is in Porticcio's Espace Commercial La Viva. ⊠ *3 rue Fesch, Ajaccio* ☎ *04–95–21–47– 88* ⊕ *www.charlesantona.com.*

**Paese Nostru.** Spices and Corsican crafts of all kinds are for sale in this tiny souvenir shop. Of special interest is the cutlery, hand-forged with wrought-iron and wooden handles. ⊠ *29 Rue Fesch, Ajaccio* ☎ *04–95– 51–05–07* ☉ *Mon.–Fri., 10–7; Sat. 9–6.*

**U Stazzu.** Look for the big red awning and stone façade of this excellent source for high-quality Corsican charcuterie, cheese, and wine. The award-winning shop offers some of the best hams and saucisson on the island, including the waist-busting Coppa and Lonzu. Ask for tasting samples before purchase. ⊠ *1 rue Bonaparte, Ajaccio* ☎ *04–95–51–10– 80* ⊕ *www.ustazzu.com.*

## ACTIVITIES

The area around Bonifacio is ideal for water sports, including windsurfing and sea kayaking. The island also has several golf courses for those who can't bear to be away from the greens. In summer, sailing is a major pastime, with wealthy French and Italians plying a course to the chic harbors and the secluded rocky coves. Well-being is also taken very seriously, with several excellent spas.

### SPAS

★ **Institut de Thalassothérapie.** Integrated into the Sofitel Hotel, the Institut de Thalassothérapie (Institute of Thalassotherapy) is part of an upscale complex in the luxurious beach resort town about a 30-minute drive from the capital. Notable for its seawater cures, hydrotherapies, and restorative massages and scrubs, the institute is the perfect place to unwind after a long day of sightseeing and sunbathing. ⊠ *Domaine de la Pointe Golfe d'Ajaccio, Porticcio* ☏ *04–95–29–40–00* ⊕ *www.accorthalassa.com.*

### WATER SPORTS

**Club Atoll.** This PADI-endorsed club offers a variety of water sports for beginners or advanced, with equipment rental and training. ⊠ *Rte. de Porto-Vecchio, Cavallo Morto, Bonifacio* ☏ *04–95–73–02–83.*

## BEACHES

There are fine Riviera-like strands north of Calvi reached by a little train service that runs around the bay to L'Isle Rousse. These do get busy between late July and the end of August, but can be delightfully peaceful early or late in the season. In summer there are numerous cafés and restaurants for refreshment. Note that topless sunbathing is acceptable here, and you will find bare breasts at every beach.

**Plage d'Ostriconi.** This long stretch of white-sand beach at the mouth of the Ostriconi River is a popular spot to swim and sunbathe, although strong winds keep waves high. ⊠ *20 km 13 miles north of L'Isle Rousse* ⊕ *www.ot-ile-rousse.fr.*

**Plage Saleccia.** This wild, undeveloped white-sand beach surrounded by rugged maquis and dunes is frequented by nude bathers and was used as a location for the 1960s film *The Longest Day*. No doubt you will be mesmerized by clear turquoise waters along the mile-long shore. ⊠ *St-Florent* ⊕ *www.corsica-saintflorent.com.*

## WHERE TO EAT

**$$$$**
FRENCH
✗ **20123.** Tables are full at this very popular Ajaccio establishment known for its traditional homemade cuisine, fresh daily catches, and, in season, game specials such as *civet de sanglier* (wild boar stew) served in a bubbling earthenware casserole of cheese-infused polenta. The rustic interior invites with a "starry sky" in a mock French village, antique lanterns, music, and stone fountain where guests pour their own water into ceramic jugs. In keeping with the familial style of service and food presentation, cutting boards with fresh-baked loaves of wheat bread are provided to start your copious meal. Three-course fixed menus are

offered in two seatings at 7:30 and 9:30, and include an exquisite cheese platter with homemade fig confiture. $ *Average main: €35* ⊠ *2 rue Roi-de-Rome, Ajaccio* ☎ *04–95–21–50–05* ⊕ *www.20123.fr* ⊘ *Closed Mon. and Jan. 15–Feb. 15. No lunch June 15–Sept. 15.*

**$$$**   ✕ **Le Voilier.** Chef Jean Paul Bartoli and his wife make this casual year-
SEAFOOD   round restaurant at the port a popular dining spot. With warm smiles,
★   chocolate-colored décor, and attentive service, the couple serves care-
fully selected and prepared seafood, along with fine Corsican sausage and traditional cuisine from *soupe corse* to *fiadone* (cheesecake). Try the affordably priced menus. Ordering a three-course meal a la carte will cost about 65€. $ *Average main: €30* ⊠ *81 Quai Comparetti, Bonifacio* ☎ *04–95–73–07–06* ⊕ *n/a* ⊘ *Closed Mon. No dinner Sun.*

# BARCELONA, SPAIN

Updated by
Joanna Styles

Capital of Catalonia, 2,000-year-old Barcelona commanded a vast Mediterranean empire when Madrid was still a dusty Moorish outpost on the Spanish steppe. Relegated to second-city status only in 1561, Barcelona has long rivaled and often surpassed Madrid's supremacy. Catalans jealously guard their language and their culture. Barcelona has long had a frenetically active cultural life. It was the home of architect Antoni Gaudí, and the painters Joan Miró and Salvador Dalí. Pablo Picasso also spent his formative years in Barcelona. Native musicians include cellist Pablo (Pau, in Catalan) Casals, opera singers Montserrat Caballé and José (Josep) Carreras, and early-music master Jordi Savall. One of Europe's most visually stunning cities, Barcelona balances its many elements, from the medieval intimacy of its Gothic Quarter to the grace of the wide boulevards in the moderniste Eixample. In the 21st century innovative structures, such as the Ricardo Bofill *vela* (sail) hotel, demonstrate Barcelona's insatiable appetite for novelty and progress.

## ESSENTIALS

### CURRENCY
The euro.

### HOURS
Museums are generally open from 9 until 7 or 8; many are closed on Monday and some close in the afternoon. Most stores are open Monday through Saturday 9 to 1:30 and 5 to 8, but a few remain open all afternoon. Virtually all close on Sunday.

### SAFETY
Barcelona has a reputation for active pickpocketing and scamming, especially around La Rambla. The risk is much greater at night than during daylight hours, but it always pays to be vigilant to avoid becoming a victim. Keep bags and purses closed, and carry them across the front of your body (this includes backpacks); thieves tend to cut bag straps to steal your belongings. Be aware of any approach by a stranger; it's better to walk away from all such encounters. And certainly don't carry any cash or valuables that you do not need. The best way to avoid being targeted by scams and pickpockets is to act with confidence and don't dress like a tourist. People in Barcelona dress smartly and rarely wear shorts and T-shirts.

**PRIVATE TOURS**

Barcelona Guide Bureau (⊕ *www.barcelonaguidebureau.com*) offers thematic, general, or personalized tours of the city leaving daily from Plaça de Catalunya; personalized tours must be arranged in advance.

**TELEPHONES**

Spain has good land and mobile services. Public kiosks accept phone cards that support international calls (cards sold in press shops, bars, and telecom shops). Mobile services are GSM and 3G compatible. Major companies include Vodafone.

**COMING ASHORE**

Barcelona is one of Europe's busiest cruise ports. Vessels dock at the Port Vell facility, which has seven terminals catering to cruise-ship traffic. All terminals are equipped with duty-free shops, telephones, bar/restaurants, information desks, and currency-exchange booths. The ships docking closest to the terminal entrance are a 10-minute walk from the southern end of Las Ramblas (the Rambla), but those docked at the farthest end require passengers to catch a shuttle bus (the Autobús Azul, a distinctive blue bus) to the port entrance. The shuttle, which runs every 20 minutes, links all terminals with the public square at the bottom of the Rambla. If you walk up Las Ramblas, after about 10 minutes you'll reach Drassanes metro station for onward public transport around the city. The shuttle runs about every 30 minutes A single metro or bus ticket is €2; a day ticket (T-Dia) is €7.

If you intend to explore Barcelona, don't rent a car. Public transportation and taxis are by far the most sensible options. City buses run daily from 5:30 am to 11:30 pm. The FCG (Ferrocarril de la Generalitat) train is a comfortable commuter train that gets you to within walking distance of nearly everything in Barcelona; transfers to the regular city metro are free. The Barcelona Tourist Bus is another excellent way to tour the city. Three routes (Red, Blue, and Green) cover just about every place you might want to visit, and you can hop on and off whenever you want. Buses run from 9 am to 7 pm, and a one-day ticket costs €24; you can buy advance tickets online at ⊕ *www.barcelonabusturistic.cat*.

If you plan to explore the Spanish coast or countryside, a vehicle would be beneficial, but even an economy car (manual transmission) is expensive at approximately €50 per day. Allow for plenty of time to get back to your ship, as Barcelona traffic is always heavy.

**GETTING TO THE AIRPORT**

Barcelona's main airport is El Prat de Llobregat, 14 km (9 miles) south of Barcelona. If you choose not to purchase airport transfers from your cruise line, the simplest way to get from the airport to the cruise port is to take a taxi from the airport to the port (about €30). There are public transport options, but transfers between bus, metro, or rail stations do involve up to 10 minutes of walking, and this may be impractical with many pieces of luggage. If you only have light baggage, this will certainly be a less expensive option.

The RENFE airport train is inexpensive and efficient, but also runs only every 30 minutes. From the airport, the RENFE station is a 10- to 15-minute walk (with moving walkway) from the port gates. Trains

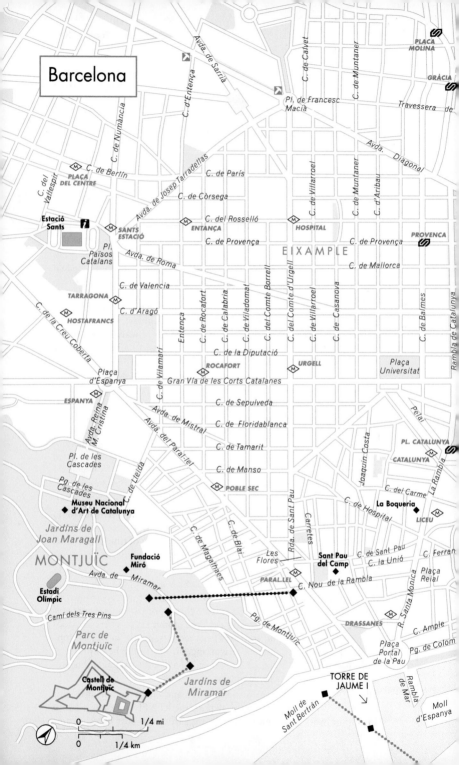

# Barcelona

PLAÇA MOLINA

GRÀCIA

Avda. de Sarrià

C. de Calvet

C. de Muntaner

Pl. de Francesc Macià

Travessera de

C. d'Entença

Avda. Diagonal

C. de Berlín

C. de París

C. de Villarroel

C. de Muntaner

C. d'Aribau

PLAÇA DEL CENTRE

Avda. de Josep Tarradellas

C. de Còrsega

C. del Vallespir

C. de Numància

C. del Rosselló

ENTANÇA

HOSPITAL

PROVENÇA

Estació Sants

SANTS ESTACIÓ

C. de Provença

C. de Provença

EIXAMPLE

Pl. Països Catalans

Avda. de Roma

C. de Mallorca

C. de Balmes

Rambla de Catalunya

C. de Valencia

TARRAGONA

C. de Rocafort

C. de Calàbria

C. de Viladomat

C. del Comte Borrell

C. del Comte d'Urgell

C. de Villarroel

C. de Casanova

HOSTAFRANCS

C. d'Aragó

C. de la Creu Coberta

Entença

C. de la Diputació

ROCAFORT

URGELL

Plaça Universitat

Plaça d'Espanya

C. de Vilamarí

Gran Via de les Corts Catalanes

ESPANYA

Avda. Reina M. Cristina

C. de Sepúlveda

Pelai

Avda. de Mistral

C. de Floridablanca

PL. CATALUNYA

Pl. de les Cascades

Avda. del Paral.lel

C. de Tamarit

Joaquín Costa

CATALUNYA

C. de Lleida

C. de Manso

La Rambla

Pg. de les Cascades

POBLE SEC

C. del Carme

Museu Nacional d'Art de Catalunya

C. de Hospital

LICEU

La Boqueria

Jardíns de Joan Maragall

C. de Magalhaes

C. de Blaí

Rda. de Sant Pau

Carretes

MONTJUÏC

Fundació Miró

Les Flores

Sant Pau del Camp

C. de Sant Pau

C. Ferran

Avda. de Miramar

C. la Unió

Plaça Reial

Estadi Olímpic

PARAL.LEL

C. Nou de la Rambla

R. Santa Monica

Camí dels Tres Pins

DRASSANES

C. Ample

Parc de Montjuïc

Pg. de Montjuïc

Pg. de Colom

Castell de Montjuïc

Jardíns de Miramar

TORRE DE JAUME I

Plaça Portal de la Pau

Rambla de Mar

Moll d'Espanya

0    1/4 mi

0    1/4 km

Moll de Sant Bertrán

Moll de Sant Bertrán

run between 5:30 am and 12:45 am, stopping at the Estació de Sants. The one-way fare is €2.

Barcelona Guide Bureau (☎ 93/2682422 ⊕ *www.barcelonaguidebureau. com*) provides private transfers between El Prat and the cruise port. A round-trip costs around €45 per person.

## EXPLORING BARCELONA

Barcelona's Old City includes **El Barri Gòtic** (the Gothic Quarter). Although this section of the city is being cleaned up, bag snatching is common here, so keep your wits about you, and if at all possible, carry nothing in your hands. Nearby is Sant Pere, which was once Barcelona's old textile neighborhood.

Barcelona's best-known promenade, **La Rambla,** is a constant and colorful flood of humanity with flower stalls, bird vendors, mimes, musicians, and outdoor cafés. Federico García Lorca called this street the only one in the world that he wished would never end; traffic plays second fiddle to the endless *paseo* (stroll) of locals and travelers alike. The whole avenue is referred to as Las Ramblas (Les Rambles, in Catalan) or La Rambla, but each section has its own name: Rambla Santa Monica is at the southeastern, or port, end; Rambla de les Flors is in the middle; and Rambla dels Estudis is at the top, near Plaça de Catalunya.

North of Plaça de Catalunya is the checkerboard known as the **Eixample.** With the dismantling of the city walls in 1860, Barcelona embarked upon an expansion scheme. The street grid was the work of urban planner Ildefons Cerdà; much of the building here was done at the height of Modernisme. The Eixample's principal thoroughfares are Rambla de Catalunya and Passeig de Gràcia, where the city's most elegant shops vie for space among its best art nouveau buildings.

Once Barcelona's pungent fishing port, **Barceloneta** retains much of its maritime flavor. Nearby is **La Ciutadella,** once a fortress but now the city's main downtown park. **Montjuïc,** a hill to the south of town, may have been named for the Jewish cemetery that was once on its slopes.

### WHAT TO SEE

Fodor's Choice **La Boqueria.** Barcelona's most spectacular food market, also known as the
★ Mercat de Sant Josep, is an explosion of life and color sprinkled with delicious little bar-restaurants. A solid polychrome wall of fruits, herbs, wild mushrooms, vegetables, nuts, candied fruits, cheeses, hams, fish, poultry, and provender of every imaginable genus and strain greets you as you turn in from La Rambla and breathe air alive with the aromas of fresh produce and reverberating with the din of commerce. Within this steel hangar the market occupies a neoclassical square built in 1840 by architect Francesc Daniel Molina. Highlights include the sunny greengrocer's market outside (to the right if you've come in from the Rambla), along with **Pinotxo** (Pinocchio), just inside to the right, which has won international acclaim as a food sanctuary. The **Kiosko Universal,** over toward the port side of the market, or **Quim de la Boqueria** offer delicious alternatives. Don't miss the herb- and wild-mushroom stand at the back of the Boqueria. ⊠ *Rambla 91, Rambla* ⊕ *www.boqueria.info* ☉ *Mon.–Sat. 8–8* Ⓜ *Liceu.*

**Fodor's Choice** ★ **Fundació Miró.** The Miró Foundation, a gift from the artist Joan Miró to his native city, is one of Barcelona's most exciting showcases of contemporary art. The airy, white building, with panoramic views north over Barcelona, was designed by Josep Lluís Sert and opened in 1975; an extension was added by Sert's pupil Jaume Freixa in 1988. Miró's playful and colorful style, filled with Mediterranean light and humor, seems a perfect match for its surroundings, and the exhibits and retrospectives that open here tend to be progressive and provocative. Look for Alexander Calder's fountain of moving mercury. Miró himself rests in the cemetery on Montjuïc's southern slopes. During the Franco regime, which he strongly opposed, Miró first lived in self-imposed exile in Paris, then moved to Majorca in 1956. When he died in 1983, the Catalans gave him a send-off amounting to a state funeral. ⊠ *Av. Miramar 71, Montjuïc* ☎ *93/443–9470* ⊕ *www.bcn. fjmiro.es* ⊠ *€8.50* ☉ *Tues., Wed., Fri., and Sat. 10–7, Thurs. 10–9:30, Sun. 10–2:30.*

> **BARCELONA BEST BETS**
>
> **La Sagrada Família.** Gaudí's stalagmites, stalactites, and cylindrical towers add up to the city's most surprising architectural marvel.
>
> **Santa Maria del Mar.** Peerless Mediterranean Gothic style: a sweeping display of form and line. Hearing Renaissance polyphony in this architectural gem is the ultimate.
>
> **Stroll along the Rambla.** This fine avenue is the place to feel Barcelona's heartbeat with milling throngs of cool urbanites, families, and elderly city dwellers all out to see and be seen.

**Fodor's Choice** ★ **Manzana de la Discòrdia.** The name is a pun on the Spanish word *manzana*, which means both apple and city block, alluding to the three-way architectural counterpoint on this block and to the classical myth of the Apple of Discord (which played a part in that legendary tale about the Judgment of Paris and the subsequent Trojan War). The houses here are spectacular, and encompass three monuments of Modernisme—Casa Lleó Morera, Casa Amatller, and Casa Batlló. Of the three competing buildings (four if you count Sagnier i Villavecchia's comparatively tame 1910 Casa Mulleras at No. 37), Casa Batlló is clearly the star attraction, and the only one of the three offering visits to the interior.

**Museu d'Història de Catalunya.** Built into what used to be a port warehouse, this state-of-the-art interactive museum makes you part of Catalonian history from prehistoric times through more than 3,000 years and into the contemporary democratic era. After centuries of "official" Catalan history dictated from Madrid (from 1714 until the mid-19th century Renaixença, and from 1939 to 1975), this is an opportunity to revisit Catalonia's autobiography. Explanations of the exhibits appear in Catalan, Castilian, and English. Guided tours are available on Sunday at noon and 1 pm. The rooftop cafeteria has excellent views over the harbor and is open to the public (whether you visit the museum itself) during museum hours. ⊠ *Pl. Pau Vila 1, Barceloneta* ☎ *93/225–4700* ⊕ *www.mhcat.net* ⊠ *€5; free 1st Sun. of month* ☉ *Tues. and Thurs.– Sat. 10–7, Wed. 10–8, Sun. 10–2:30* Ⓜ *Barceloneta.*

**Fodor's Choice**  **Museu Nacional d'Art de Catalunya** (*MNAC, Catalonian National Museum*
★  *of Art*). Housed in the imposingly domed, towered, frescoed, and columned **Palau Nacional,** built in 1929 as the centerpiece of the International Exposition, this superb museum was renovated in 1995 by Gae
Aulenti, architect of the Musée d'Orsay in Paris. In 2004 the museum's
three collections—Romanesque, Gothic, and the Cambó Collection, an
eclectic trove, including a Goya, donated by Francesc Cambó—were
joined by the 19th- and 20th-century collection of Catalan impressionist
and moderniste painters. Also now on display is the Thyssen-Bornemisza
collection of early masters, with works by Zurbarán, Rubens, Tintoretto,
Velázquez, and others. ⊠ *Mirador del Palau 6, Montjuïc* ☎ *93/622–0360*
⊕ *www.mnac.es* ☑ *€9 (valid for day of purchase and one other day in
same month)* ⊙ *Tues.–Sat. 10–7, Sun. 10–2:30.*

**Fodor's Choice**  **Museu Picasso.** The Picasso Museum is housed in five adjoining pal-
★  aces on Carrer Montcada, a street known for Barcelona's most elegant
medieval palaces. Picasso spent his key formative years in Barcelona
(1895–1904), and this collection, while it does not include a significant
number of the artist's best paintings, is particularly strong on his early
work. The museum was begun in 1962 on the suggestion of Picasso's
crony Jaume Sabartés, and the initial donation was from the Sabartés collection. Later Picasso donated his early works, and in 1981 his
widow, Jaqueline Roque, added 141 pieces. ⊠ *Carrer Montcada 15–19,
Born-Ribera* ☎ *93/319–6310* ⊕ *www.museupicasso.bcn.cat* ☑ *€9.50;
free 1st Sun. of month, free Sun. 3–8* ⊙ *Tues.–Sun. 10–8* Ⓜ *Jaume I.*

★  **Palau de la Música Catalana.** One of the world's most extraordinary music
halls, with facades that are a riot of color and form, the Palau de la
Música (Music Palace) is a landmark of Carrer Amadeus Vives, set
just across Via Laietana, a five-minute walk from Plaça de Catalunya.
From its polychrome ceramic ticket windows on the Carrer de Sant
Pere Més Alt side to its overhead busts of (from left to right) Palestrina,
Bach, Beethoven, and (around the corner on Carrer Amadeus Vives)
Wagner, the Palau is a flamboyant tour de force designed in 1908 by
Lluís Domènech i Montaner. It is today considered the flagship of Bar-
celona's moderniste architecture. The exterior is remarkable in itself.
The Palau's interior is, well, a permanent uproar before the first note of
music is ever heard. ⊠ *Ticket office, Palau de la Musica 4–6 (just off Via
Laietana, around corner from hall), Sant Pere* ☎ *93/295–7200* ⊕ *www.
palaumusica.org* ☑ *Tour €12* ⊙ *Sept.–June, tours daily 10–3:30; July
and Aug., tours daily 10–7* Ⓜ *Urquinaona.*

**Fodor's Choice**  **Santa Maria del Mar.** The most beautiful example of early Catalan Gothic
★  architecture, Santa Maria del Mar is extraordinary for its unbroken
lines and elegance. The lightness of the interior is especially surprising
considering the blocky exterior. Built by a mere stonemason who chose,
fitted, and carved each stone hauled down from the same Montjuïc
quarry that provided the sandstone for the 4th-century Roman walls,
Santa Maria del Mar is breathtakingly and nearly hypnotically symmetrical. The medieval numerological symbol for the Virgin Mary, the
number eight (or multiples thereof) runs through every element of the
basilica: The 16 octagonal pillars are 6.5 feet in diameter and spread
out into rib vaulting arches at a height of 52 feet. The painted keystones

at the apex of the arches are 105 feet from the floor. Furthermore, the central nave is twice as wide as the lateral naves (26 feet each), whose width equals the difference (26 feet) between their height and that of the main nave. The result of all this proportional balance and harmony is a sense of uplift that, especially in baroque and moderniste Barcelona, is both exhilarating and soothing. Set aside at least a half hour to see Santa Maria del Mar. ⊠ *Pl. de Santa Maria, Born-Ribera* ☎ *93/310–2390* ⊘ *Daily 9–1:30 and 4:30–8* Ⓜ *Jaume I.*

**Fodor's**Choice
★
**Temple Expiatori de la Sagrada Família.** Barcelona's most emblematic architectural icon, Antoni Gaudí's Sagrada Família, is still under construction 130 years after it was begun. This striking and surreal creation was conceived as nothing short of a Bible in stone, a gigantic representation of the entire history of Christianity, and it continues to cause responses from surprise to consternation to wonder. No building in Barcelona and few in the world are more deserving of investing anywhere from a few hours to the better part of a day in getting to know it well. In fact, a quick visit can be more tiring than an extended one, as there are too many things to take in at once. However long your visit, it's a good idea to bring binoculars. For a €3 additional charge, you can take an elevator skyward to the top of the **bell towers** for some spectacular views. Back on the ground, visit the **museum**, which displays Gaudí's scale models. The architect is buried to the left of the altar in the **crypt**. ⊠ *Pl. de la Sagrada Família, Eixample* ☎ *93/207–3031* ⊕ *www.sagradafamilia.org* ⊠ *€13, (17 with audioguide) bell-tower elevator €3* ⊘ *Oct.–Mar., daily 9–6; Apr.–Sept., daily 9–8* Ⓜ *Sagrada Família.*

# SHOPPING

Between the surging fashion scene, a host of young clothing designers, clever home furnishings, delicious foodstuffs including wine and olive oil, and ceramics, art, and antiques, Barcelona is the best place in Spain to unload extra ballast from your wallet.

Barcelona's prime shopping districts are the Passeig de Gràcia, Rambla de Catalunya, Plaça de Catalunya, Porta de l'Àngel, and Avinguda Diagonal up to Carrer Ganduxer. For high fashion, browse along Passeig de Gràcia and the Diagonal between Plaça Joan Carles I and Plaça Francesc Macià. There are two-dozen antiques shops in the Gothic Quarter, another 70 shops off Passeig de Gràcia on Bulevard dels Antiquaris, and still more in Gràcia and Sarrià. For old-fashioned Spanish shops, prowl the Gothic Quarter, especially **Carrer Ferran**. The area around the church of Santa Maria del Mar, an artisans' quarter since medieval times, is full of cheerful design stores and art galleries. The area surrounding **Plaça del Pi**, from the Boqueria to Carrer Portaferrissa and Carrer de la Canuda, is thick with boutiques and jewelry and design shops. The **Barri de la Ribera**, around Santa Maria del Mar, especially the Born area, has a cluster of design, fashion, and and food shops. Design, jewelry, and knickknack shops cluster on Carrer Banys Vells and Carrer Flassaders, near Carrer Montcada.

★ **Art Escudellers.** Ceramic pieces from all over Spain converge here at both of these stores across the street from the restaurant Los Caracoles; more than 140 different artisans are represented, with maps showing what part of Spain the work is from. There are wine, cheese, and ham tastings downstairs, and you can even throw a pot yourself in the display workshop. ⊠ *Carrer Escudellers 23–25, Barri Gòtic* ☎ *93/412–6801* ⊕ *www.escudellers-art.com* Ⓜ *Liceu, Drassanes.*

**Galeria Joan Prats.** "La Prats" has been one of the city's top galleries since the 1920s, showing international painters and sculptors from Henry Moore to Antoni Tàpies. Barcelona painter Joan Miró was a prime force in the founding of the gallery when he became friends with Joan Prats. The motifs of bonnets and derbies on the gallery's facade attest to the trade of Prats's father. José Maria Sicilia and Juan Ugalde have shown here, while Perejaume and Eulàlia Valldosera are regulars. ⊠ *Rambla de Catalunya 54, Eixample* ☎ *93/216–0284* ⊕ *www.galeriajoanprats. com* ☉ *Tues.–Sat. 11–8* Ⓜ *Passeig de Gràcia.*

## WHERE TO EAT

**$$**
TAPAS
**Fodor's** Choice
★

✕ **Cal Pep.** Cal Pep, a two-minute walk east from Santa Maria del Mar, is in a permanent feeding frenzy and has been this way for 30 years. Pep has Barcelona's best selection of tapas, cooked and served hot over the counter. For budget reasons, avoid ordering a fish dish (unless you're willing to part with an extra €35–€50), and stick with green peppers, fried artichokes, garbanzos and spinach, baby shrimp, the "trifasic" (mixed tiny fish fry), the nonpareil *tortilla de patatas* (potato omelet), and *botifarra trufada en reducción de Oporto* (truffled sausage in Port wine reduction sauce). The house wines are good, but the Torre la Moreira Albariño white perfectly complements Pep's offerings. Be prepared to wait for 20 minutes for a place at the counter; it's well worth it. ⑤ *Average main: €18* ⊠ *Pl. de les Olles 8, Born-Ribera* ☎ *93/319–6183* ⊕ *www.calpep. com* ☉ *Closed Sun. No lunch Mon. No dinner Sat.* Ⓜ *Jaume I.*

**$$**
ECLECTIC

✕ **Cuines Santa Caterina.** A lovingly restored market designed by the late Enric Miralles and completed by his widow Benedetta Tagliabue provides a spectacular setting for one of the city's most original dining operations. Under the undulating wooden superstructure of the market, the breakfast and tapas bar, open from dawn to midnight, offers a variety of culinary specialties cross-referenced by different cuisines (Mediterranean, Asian, vegetarian) and products (pasta, rice, fish, meat), all served on sleek counters and long wooden tables. ⑤ *Average main: €22* ⊠ *Av. Francesc Cambó 16, Barri Gòtic* ☎ *93/268–9918* ⊕ *www. cuinessantacaterina.com* Ⓜ *Catalunya, Liceu, Jaume I.*

## WHERE TO STAY

**$$$**
HOTEL
**Fodor's** Choice
★

🖼 **Duquesa de Cardona.** Inside a refurbished 16th-century town house, this hotel has contemporary facilities in soothing neutral tones all overlooking the port. **Pros:** great combination of traditional and contemporary; key spot over the port; roof terrace with live music in summer. **Cons:** rooms on the small side; roof terrace tiny; sea views restricted by Maremagnum complex on the port. ⑤ *Rooms from: €185* ⊠ *Passeig de Colom 12, Rambla* ☎ *93/301–2570* ⊕ *www.hduquesadecardona.com* ⇋ *44 rooms* ⑩ *No meals* Ⓜ *Drassanes.*

$$$$  ⌂ **Hotel Neri.** Built into a 17th-century palace over one of the Gothic
HOTEL  Quarter's smallest and most charming squares, Plaça Sant Felip Neri,
**Fodor's**Choice  the Neri marries ancient and avant-garde design. **Pros:** central location;
★  hip design; roof terrace for cocktails and breakfast. **Cons:** noise from the
echo-chamber square can be a problem on summer nights (and winter
morning school days); impractical design details such as the hanging bed
lights. $ *Rooms from: €310* ⌧ *St. Sever 5, Barri Gòtic* ☏ *93/304–0655*
⊕ *www.hotelneri.com* ↻ *22 rooms* ⦿ *No meals* Ⓜ *Liceu, Catalunya.*

$$  ⌂ **Sant Agustí.** In a leafy square just off the Rambla, the Sant Agustí has
HOTEL  long been popular with musicians performing at the Liceu opera house.
**Fodor's**Choice  **Pros:** central location near the Boqueria market, the Rambla, and the
★  opera house; cozy, wood-beam, traditional design. **Cons:** noisy square
usually requiring closed windows; short on amenities and room service.
$ *Rooms from: €150* ⌧ *Pl. Sant Agustí 3, El Raval* ☏ *93/318–2182*
⊕ *www.hotelsa.com* ↻ *77 rooms* ⦿ *No meals* Ⓜ *Liceu.*

# BARI, ITALY

Updated
by Bruce
Leimsidor

Puglia is one of three regions making up the heel and toe of Italy's boot,
and known collectively as the *mezzogiorno*. This is Italy's deep south,
where whitewashed buildings stand silently over the turquoise Mediter-
ranean, castles guard medieval alleyways, and grandmothers dry their
handmade orecchiette pasta in the midafternoon heat. At every turn,
Puglia boasts unspoiled scenery and a wonderful country food tradi-
tion. Beyond the cities, seaside resorts, and the few major sights, there's
a sparsely populated countryside with expanses of silvery olive trees,
vineyards of *primitivo* and *aglianico* grapes, and giant prickly-pear
cacti. Puglia is an increasingly popular tourist destination. Bari is at the
top of the heel of the boot, a lively, varied, and sometimes-seamy port
city on the Adriatic coast.

## ESSENTIALS

### CURRENCY
The euro.

### HOURS
Shops are generally open from 8 am until noon or 1 pm, then again from 3 or
4 until 8, perhaps opening later in summer. Some museums and attractions stay
open throughout the day, while others close in the afternoon; it's best to plan to
visit such attractions in the morning, or check with the local tourist office or the
individual museum or church.

### PRIVATE TOURS
Tour guides may be booked online on Viator, but the site lists only one
tour guide that has certification, Gianluca Guadagnino, who charges
€25 per hour per person for full 8-hour tour. Group tours from the port
can be arranged through the website Get your Guide; a 3-hour walking
tour of the city costs €17 per person and can be prebooked on line. The
company also offers half- and full-day tours to Alberobello and Lecce.

**Contacts Get Your Guide.** ⊕ *getyourguide.com.* **Viator.** ⊕ *viator.com.*

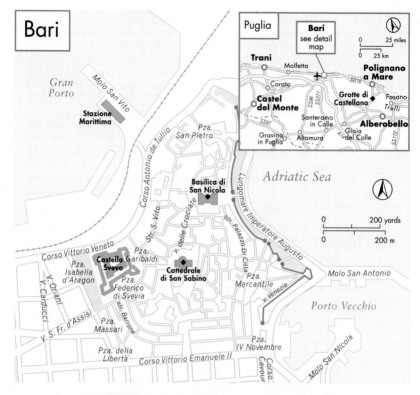

## TELEPHONES

Tri-band GSM phones work in Italy. You can buy prepaid phone cards at telecom shops, news vendors, and tobacconists in all towns and cities. Phone cards can be used for local or international calls.

## COMING ASHORE

Bari is a large port and has a dedicated cruise terminal; ships dock, giving passengers only a short walk to the port entrance. From here, it is a further short walk into the city, where you can explore on foot.

Bari is linked by rail to all the major towns in the region. Trani can be reached in 34 to 40 minutes; there are one or two trains per hour, depending on the time of day, and the single fare ranges from €2.60 to €7.50. Polignano a Mare is less than 30 minutes from Bari by train; there is a train almost hourly, and a single fare costs €2.10. Alberobello is a journey time of 80 to 100 minutes, and tickets cost €4. All train tickets—except those to Alberobello—can be bought online at ⊕ *www. trenilatia.com* and printed out at home, or retrieved from machines in Bari station. Buy tickets for Alberobello from the Ferrovie Sud-Est office at Bari railway station. Renting a vehicle would allow you to explore the Puglia countryside at your own pace. An economy manual vehicle costs from €34 to €75 per day, but delivery to the port may cost more.

# EXPLORING BARI AND PUGLIA

## BARI

Bari is a major port and a transit point for travelers catching ferries across the Adriatic to Greece and Croatia (Dubrovnik and other points along the Dalmatian coast), but it's also an exciting city with one of the most interesting historic centers in the region. Most of Bari is set out in a logical, 19th-century grid, following the designs of Joachim Murat (1767–1815), Napoléon's brother-in-law and King of the Two Sicilies. By day, explore the Old Town's winding alleyways, which offer glimpses into the daily routine of southern Italy—matrons hand-rolling pasta with their grandchildren home from school for the midday meal, and handymen perched on rickety ladders, patching up centuries-old arches and doorways. *Barivecchia*, or the Old City, used to be a "no go" area for tourists because of a high incidence of petty crime. Gentrification has allegedly improved the situation considerably, but caution is still advised.

★ **Basilica di San Nicola.** In the *città vecchia*, overlooking the sea and just off Via Venezia, is the Basilica di San Nicola, built in the 11th century to house the bones of Saint Nicholas, the inspiration for Santa Claus. His remains, buried in the crypt, are said to have been stolen by Bari sailors from Myra, where Saint Nicholas was bishop, in what is now Turkey. The basilica, of solid and powerful construction, was the only building to survive the otherwise wholesale destruction of Bari by the Normans in 1152. ✉ *Piazza San Nicola* ☎ *080/5737111* ⊕ *www.basilicasannicola.it* ⊘ *Daily 7 am–8 pm.*

**Castello Svevo.** Looming over Bari's cathedral is the huge Castello Svevo. The current building dates from the time of Holy Roman Emperor Frederick II (1194–1250), who rebuilt an existing Norman-Byzantine castle to his own exacting specifications. Designed more for power than beauty, it looks out beyond the cathedral to the small Porto Vecchio (Old Port). Inside, a haphazard collection of medieval Puglian art is frequently enlivened by changing exhibitions featuring local, national, and international artists. ✉ *Piazza Federico II di Svevia* ☎ *080/5286262* 🎫 *€2* ⊘ *Thurs.–Tues. 8:30–7:30. Last entrance at 7.*

**Cattedrale di San Sabino.** Bari's 12th-century Cattedrale di San Sabino is the seat of the local bishop and was the scene of many significant political marriages between important families in the Middle Ages. The cathedral's solid architecture reflects the Romanesque style favored by the Normans of that period. ✉ *Piazza dell'Odegitria* ☎ *080/5210605* ⊘ *Mon.–Sat. 8–12:30 and 4–8, Sun. 8–12:30 and 4–10.*

## TRANI

*43 km (27 miles) northwest of Bari.*

Smaller than the other ports along this coast, Trani has a picturesque Old Town with polished stone streets and buildings, medieval churches, and a harbor filled with fishing boats. Trani is also justly famous for its sweet dessert wine, Moscato di Trani.

**Castello.** The boxy, well-preserved Castello was built by Frederick II in 1233. ✉ *Piazza Manfredi 16* ☎ *0883/506603* ⊕ *www.castelloditrani.beniculturali.it* 🎫 *€2* ⊘ *Daily 8:30–7:30.*

**Cattedrale.** The stunning, pinkish-white 11th-century Cattedrale, considered one of the finest in Puglia, is built on a spit of land jutting into the sea. ✉ *Piazza Duomo* ☎ *0883/494210* ⊗ *Daily 9–noon and 3.30–6.*

**Via Sinagoga** (*Synagogue Street*). A Jewish community flourished here in medieval times, and on Via Sinagoga two of the four synagogues still stand. **Santa Maria Scolanova** and **Santa Anna,** both built in the 13th century, are now churches; the latter still bears a Hebrew inscription.

### POLIGNANO A MARE

*40 km (24 miles) southeast of Bari.*

With a well-preserved whitewashed Old Town perched on limestone cliffs overlooking the Adriatic, Polignano a Mare is only a half-hour train ride down the coast from Bari. The town is virtually lifeless all winter, but becomes something of a weekend hot spot for city dwellers in summer.

### CASTEL DEL MONTE

Fodor's Choice ★ **Castel del Monte.** Built by Frederick II in the first half of the 13th century, Castel del Monte is an imposing octagonal castle with eight austere towers on an isolated hill. Little is known about the structure, since virtually no records exist. The ground-floor gift shop (closed in winter months) has many books that explore its mysterious past and posit theories based on its dimensions and Federico II's love of mathematics. It has none of the usual defense features associated with medieval castles, so it probably had little military significance. Some theories suggest it might have been built as a hunting lodge or may have served as an astronomical observatory, or even a stop for pilgrims on their quest for the Holy Grail. Most of the helpful information panels in the castle are translated into English. Note that if coming by car from April to September you have to park in designated areas about a mile away and then get a shuttle bus. ✉ *On signposted minor road 18 km (11 miles) south of Andria* ☎ *0883/569997, 0883/592283 tour reservations* ⊕ *www.casteldelmonte.beniculturali.it* ☐ *€5* ⊗ *Mar.–Sept., daily 10:15–7:15; Oct.–Feb., daily 9–5. Last entrance ½ hr before closing.*

### ALBEROBELLO

*59 km (37 miles) southeast of Bari.*

Although Alberobello is frequently overrun by tourists, the amalgamation of more than 1,000 *trulli* (beehive-shape homes) huddled together along steep, narrow streets is nonetheless an unusual sight (as well as a national monument and a UNESCO World Heritage site). The origins of the beehive-shape trulli go back to the 13th century and maybe further. The trulli, found nowhere else in the world, are built of

---

**BARI BEST BETS**

**Soaking in the atmosphere in Bari's Old Town.** The dramas of life in Italy's deep south are not a show put on for tourists but a fascinating daily performance for lovers of people-watching.

**Exploring Polignano a Mare.** This whitewashed village's roots are well in sync with the Mediterranean heartbeat.

**Touring Trulli country.** These unique humble stone buildings surrounded by vines are one of Italy's most unusual architectural treasures.

local limestone, without mortar, and with a hole in the top for escaping smoke. As one of the most popular tourist destinations in Puglia, Alberobello has spawned some excellent restaurants (and some not-so-excellent trinket shops).

**Trullo Sovrano.** Alberobello's largest trullo, the Trullo Sovrano, is up the hill through the trulli zone (head up Corso Vittorio Emanuele past the obelisk and the basilica). Inside is a fairly conventional domestic dwelling: the real interest is the structure itself.

**Alberobello–Martina Franca road.** The trulli in Alberobello itself are impressive, but the most beautiful concentration of conical trulli is along a stretch of about 15 km (9 miles) on the Alberobello–Martina Franca road. Amid expanses of vineyards, you can see trulli put to all sorts of uses—including as wineries.

## SHOPPING

Puglia is Italy's second most-productive wine region, so taste a few, including the famed dessert wine Moscato di Trani, and buy some bottles of your favorite. Olives are grown in great abundance, too. The virgin olive oil pressed here is of excellent quality. Other souvenirs include ceramics in a range of styles, from practical terra-cotta to beautiful glazed ornaments. Miniature trulli take on many forms, from faithfully finished stone copies to kitsch plastic fridge magnets. Italian styling is very much in evidence in the streets of Bari.

The main shopping streets in Bari are Via Argiro and Via Sparano. Souvenir shops are numerous in the narrow streets of the Old Town. Alberobello has many trulli that have been converted into souvenir shops.

## WHERE TO EAT

$$$$ ✕ **Ristorante al Pescatore.** In the Old Town, opposite the castle and just
SEAFOOD around the corner from the cathedral, stands one of Bari's best seafood restaurants. In summer the fish is grilled outdoors, so you can enjoy the delicious aroma as you sit amid a cheerful clamor of quaffing and dining. Try a whole fish accompanied by a crisp salad and a carafe of invigorating local wine. Reservations are essential in July and August. Beware of bag snatchers if you sit outside. $ *Average main: €45* ✉ *Piazza Federico II di Svevia 6/8, Bari* ☎ *080/5237039* ⊕ *www. ristorantealpescatorebari.com* ☉ *Closed 2 wks mid-Jan.*

# BORDEAUX, FRANCE

Updated
by Jennifer
Ladonne

Bordeaux as a whole, rather than any particular points within it, is what you'll want to visit in order to understand why Victor Hugo described it as Versailles plus Antwerp, and why, when he was exiled from his native Spain, the painter Francisco de Goya chose it as his last home (he died here in 1828). The capital of southwest France and the region's largest city, Bordeaux remains synonymous with the wine trade, and wine shippers have long maintained their headquarters along the banks of the River Garonne at the heart of town. As a whole, Bordeaux is a less exuberant city than many others in France. The profits generated by centuries of fine vintages have been carefully invested in fine yet understated architecture, and an aura of 18th-century elegance permeates the downtown core. Conservative and refined, the city rewards visitors with its museums, shopping, and restaurants.

## ESSENTIALS

**CURRENCY**
The euro.

**HOURS**
Museums are open 10–5, but most close on Monday or Tuesday. Stores are open Monday–Saturday 9–7, but some close for lunch (usually noon–2).

**TELEPHONES**
Tri-band GSM phones work in France. You can buy prepaid phone cards at telecom shops, news vendors, and tobacconists in all towns and cities. Phone cards can be used for local or international calls. Orange, SFR, Bouygues Telecom, and Virgin are leading telecom companies. If you have an unlocked GSM phone, LeFrenchMobile (⊕ *www. lefrenchmobile.com*) offers SIM cards (and micro SIM cards) with support in English, unlimited validity of credits, and prepurchase online.

## COMING ASHORE

Cruise ships sail up the Gironde River and dock directly on the city waterfront within walking distance of all the major city attractions. Because of its proximity to the downtown core, there are no facilities specifically for cruise-ship passengers at the dock site.

Bordeaux is a compact city, and there will be no need to rent a vehicle unless you want to tour the many vineyards in the surrounding countryside independently. Cost of rental is approximately €70 per day for an economy manual vehicle. Taxis are plentiful and can provide tourist itineraries. For single-journey tariffs, rates are €2.30 for pick-up followed by €0.77 per km. There's an hourly rental fee of €29.90 (plus distance covered) if you should choose to take a taxi for a number of hours.

# EXPLORING BORDEAUX

**Cathédrale St-André.** This may not be one of France's finer Gothic cathedrals but the intricate 14th-century chancel makes an interesting contrast with the earlier nave. Excellent stone carvings adorn the facade of this hefty edifice. You can climb the 15th-century, 160-foot **Tour Pey-Berland** for a stunning view of the city; it's open Tuesday–Sunday 10–noon and 2–5. ⊠ *Pl. Pey-Berland* ☎ *05–56–81–26–25* 🖼 *€5.*

★ **Grand Théâtre.** One block south of the Maison du Vin is the city's leading 18th-century monument: the Grand Théâtre, designed by Victor Louis and built between 1773 and 1780. It's the pride of the city, with an elegant exterior ringed by graceful Corinthian columns and a dazzling foyer with a two-winged staircase and a cupola. The theater hall has a frescoed ceiling with a shimmering chandelier composed of 14,000 Bohemian crystals. Contact the Bordeaux tourist office to learn about guided tours. ⊠ *Pl. de la Comédie* ☎ *05–56–00–85–95* ⊕ *www.opera-bordeaux.com* 🖼 *Tours €3.*

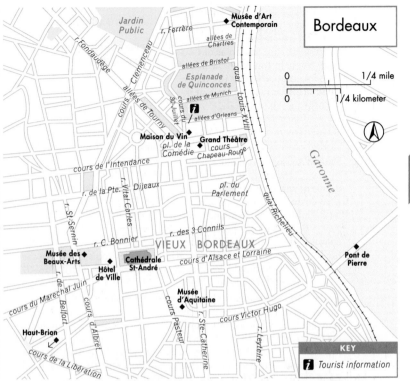

Bordeaux

Jardin Public

r. Ferrère

Musée d'Art Contemporain

allées de Chartres

allées de Bristol

Esplanade de Quinconces

allées de Munich

allées d'Orleans

r. Fondaudège

cours Clemenceau

allées de Tourny

cours du 30 Juillet

quai Louis XVIII

0        1/4 mile
0        1/4 kilometer

Maison du Vin

Grand Théâtre

pl. de la Comédie

cours Chapeau-Rouge

cours de l'Intendance

r. de la Pte. Dijeaux

r. Vital Carles

pl. du Parlement

quai Richelieu

Garonne

4

r. St-Sernin

r. des 3 Connils

r. C. Bonnier

VIEUX BORDEAUX

Musée des Beaux-Arts

Hôtel de Ville

Cathédrale St-André

cours d'Alsace et Lorraine

Pont de Pierre

r. de la Marechal Juin

cours d'Albret

cours Pasteur

Musée d'Aquitaine

r. Ste-Catherine

cours Victor Hugo

r. Leyteire

Haut-Brion

cours du Marechal Juin

cours de Belfort

cours de la Libération

KEY

 *Tourist information*

**Haut-Brion.** One of the region's most famous wine-producing châteaux is actually within the city limits: follow N250 southwest from central Bordeaux for 3 km (2 miles) to the district of Pessac, home to Haut-Brion, producer of the only non-Médoc wine to be ranked a *premier cru* (the most elite wine classification). It's claimed the very buildings surrounding the vineyards create their own microclimate, protecting the precious grapes and allowing them to ripen earlier. The white château looks out over the celebrated pebbly soil. The wines produced at **La Mission–Haut Brion (Domaine Clarence Dillon)**, across the road, are almost as sought-after. ⊠ *135 av. Jean-Jaurès, Pessac* ☎ *05–56–00–29–30* ⊕ *www. haut-brion.com* 🖅 *Free 1-hr visits by appointment, weekdays only, with tasting* ☉ *Closed mid-July–mid-Aug.*

★  **Maison du Vin.** Not far from the banks of the Garonne and the main artery of the Esplanade des Quinconces, tree-lined Cours du 30 Juillet is where you will find the important Maison du Vin (House of Wine), right across the street from the city tourist office. The Maison is run by the CIVB (Conseil Interprofessionnel des Vins de Bordeaux), the headquarters of the Bordeaux wine trade, and before you set out to explore the region's wine country, you should get some tips from the (English-speaking) person at the Tourisme de Viticole desk, who has helpful guides on all the various wine regions. More important, tasting a red (like Pauillac or St-Émilion), a dry white (like an Entre-Deux-Mers, Graves, or Côtes de Blaye), and a sweet white (like Sauternes or Loupiac) will help you decide which of the 57 wine appellations to explore. You can also make purchases at the **Vinothèque** opposite. ⊠ *8 cours du 30 Juillet* ☎ *05–56–52–32–05* ⊕ *www.la-vinotheque.com* 🖃 *Free* ⊙ *Mon.–Sat. 10–7:30.*

★ **Musée d'Aquitaine.** Two blocks south of the Cathédrale St-André, this excellent museum takes you on a trip through Bordeaux's history, with emphases on Roman, medieval, Renaissance, port-harbor, colonial, and 20th-century daily life. The detailed prehistoric section almost saves you a trip to Lascaux II, which is reproduced here in part. ⊠ *20 cours Pasteur* ☎ *05–56–01–51–00* 🖃 *Free* ⊙ *Tues.–Sun. 11–6.*

**Musée d'Art Contemporain** (*Contemporary Art Center*). Just north of the Esplanade des Quinconces, a sprawling square, this two-story museum is imaginatively housed in a converted 19th-century spice warehouse, the Entrepôt Lainé. Many shows here showcase cutting-edge artists who invariably festoon the huge expanse of the place with hanging ropes, ladders, and large video screens. ⊠ *7 rue Ferrère* ☎ *05–56–00–81–50* 🖃 *5€* ⊙ *Tues. and Thurs.–Sun. 11–6, Wed. 11–8.*

**Musée des Beaux-Arts.** Not far from the Cathédrale St-André, this museum adorns tidy gardens behind the ornate Hôtel de Ville (town hall). Inside is a fetching collection of works spanning the 15th to the 21st century, with important paintings by Paolo Veronese (*St. Dorothy*), Camille Corot (*Bath of Diana*), and Odilon Redon (*Apollo's Chariot*), and sculptures by Auguste Rodin. ⊠ *20 cours d'Albret* ☎ *05–56–10–20–56* 🖃 *Free* ⊙ *Wed.–Mon. 11–6.*

**Pont de Pierre.** For a view of the picturesque quayside, stroll across the Garonne on this bridge, built on the orders of Napoléon between 1810 and 1821, and until 1965 the only bridge across the river.

---

## SHOPPING

Between the cathedral and the Grand Théâtre are numerous pedestrian streets where stylish shops and clothing boutiques abound—Bordeaux may favor understatement but there's no lack of elegance. Couture is well in evidence here for both women and men. Wines are of course a must if you haven't bought direct from the château, or indulge in France's other culinary obsession—cheese (perhaps for a picnic lunch).

**Baillardran.** With five stores in Bordeaux alone, Baillardran is going to be hard to walk by without at least looking in its windows at those

---

**BORDEAUX BEST BETS**

**Opening a bottle of a fine wine.** Bordeaux is famed more for its wines than anything else, so indulge your olfactory sense and your taste buds with a vintage from an excellent château.

**Touring the vineyards.** Not only is it wonderful to watch the grapes maturing on the vines, but to tour the historic châteaus and their extensive cellars is to understand the understated essence of this small region of France.

indigenous sweet delights, *Bordelais cannelés!* Much like a Doric column in miniature, these small indented, caramelized cakes, made with vanilla and a dash of rum, are a delicious regional specialty. ⊠ *55 cours de l'Intendance* ☏ *05–56–52–92–64* ⊕ *www.baillardran.com.*

**Jean d'Alos Fromager-Affineur.** For an exceptional selection of cheeses, go to Jean d'Alos Fromager-Affineur. ⊠ *4 rue Montesquieu* ☏ *05–56–44–29–66.*

**Vinothèque.** The Vinothèque sells top-ranked Bordeaux wines. ⊠ *8 cours du 30 Juillet* ☏ *05–56–52–32–05.*

## WHERE TO EAT

$ ✕ **Café Français.** For more than 30 years, Madame Jouhanneau presided
BRASSERIE over this venerable bistro in the heart of the Vieille Ville (Old Town), right by the Cathédrale St-André. Now Madame Mesnard has taken over and renovated the place but has kept the cuisine as it was: solidly based on fresh regional specialties. For solid sustenance at reasonable prices, it's hard to beat. Try for a table on the terrace: the view over Place Pey-Berland is never less than diverting. ⑤ *Average main: €17* ⊠ *5–6 pl. Pey-Berland* ☏ *05–56–52–96–69.*

$ ✕ **l'Oiseau Cabosse.** This straight-up organic restaurant and coffee bar
FRENCH FUSION is a good option for a snack or if you're on a tight budget, and with its warm and welcoming atmosphere and kind and spunky service, it's a welcome find in the city, even if it doesn't really compare with other bistro finds. It's popular for its tasty "homemade food"—not to be confused with "health food"—and options range from duck confit parmentier and lasagna to curry and leek quiche. Fresh baked desserts should not be missed, nor the organic and artisanal cola, lemonade or 100% pure cocoa hot chocolate. There's a nice outside terrace in the bourgeois bohemian *Quartier de la Grosse Cloche* (Big Clock neighborhood). ⑤ *Average main: €12* ⊠ *30 rue Sainte Colombe* ☏ *05–57–14–02–07* ⊘ *Closed Mon., no dinner Tues. or Sun.*

# CÁDIZ, SPAIN (FOR SEVILLE AND JEREZ)

Updated by
Joanna Styles

Gypsies, bulls, flamenco, horses—Andalusia is the Spain of story and song, the one Washington Irving romanticized in the 18th century. Andalusia is, moreover, at once the least and most surprising part of Spain: Least surprising because it lives up to the hype and stereotype that long confused all of Spain with the Andalusian version, and most surprising because it is, at the same time, so much more. All the romantic images of Andalusia, and Spain in general, spring vividly to life in Seville. Spain's fourth-largest city is an olé cliché of matadors, flamenco, tapas bars, gypsies, geraniums, and strolling guitarists. The smaller cities of Cádiz—the Western world's oldest metropolis, founded by Phoenicians more than 3,000 years ago—and Jerez, with its sherry cellars and purebred horses, have much to explore as well.

## ESSENTIALS
### CURRENCY
The euro.

### HOURS

Museums generally open 9 until 7 or 8, many are closed on Monday, and some close in the afternoon. Most stores are open Monday through Saturday 9 to 1:30 and 5 to 8, but a few stay open in the afternoon. Virtually all close on Sunday.

### PRIVATE TOURS

**Sights and Bikes.** The tour company caters specifically to cruise visitors to Cádiz, organizing day trips with a cultural, natural, or sporting theme. ☎ 956/901108 ⊕ *www.sightsandbikes.com.*

### TELEPHONES

Spain has good land and mobile services. Public kiosks accept phone cards that support international calls (cards sold in press shops, bars, and telecom shops). Mobile services support most tri-band GSM phones and are 3G compatible. Major companies include Vodafone.

## COMING ASHORE

Vessels dock at the Alfonso XIII quay in the Cádiz Port, which is in the heart of the city. The passenger terminal has a restaurant, press outlet, phones, and taxi kiosk. From the port, the sights of downtown Cádiz are all within walking distance.

If you wish to travel independently, there is one train per hour from Cádiz to Seville. The journey takes between 1½ and 2 hours. Tickets cost €15 single. Taxi fare from Cádiz to Seville is currently €150 (€168 on weekends) each way—a vehicle takes four people. There is also one train per hour to Jerez. The journey takes 40 minutes, and the ticket price is €5.70 one-way. A car rental would open up much of the region to you, but parking and navigation in the cities is difficult. The price for an economy manual vehicle is approximately €50 per day.

## EXPLORING CÁDIZ, SEVILLE, AND JEREZ DE LA FRONTERA

### CÁDIZ

Founded as Gadir by Phoenician traders in 1100 BC, Cádiz claims to be the oldest continuously inhabited city in the Western world. Hannibal lived in Cádiz for a time, Julius Caesar first held public office here, and Columbus set out from here on his second voyage, after which the city became the home base of the Spanish fleet. During the 18th century Cádiz monopolized New World trade and became the wealthiest port in Western Europe. Most of its buildings—including the cathedral, built in part with gold and silver from the New World—date from this period. Today the Old City is African in appearance and immensely intriguing— a cluster of narrow streets opening onto charming small squares. The golden cupola of the cathedral looms above low white houses, and the whole place has a charming if slightly dilapidated air.

**Ayuntamiento** (*city hall*). The impressive *ayuntamiento* overlooks the Plaza San Juan de Diós, one of Cádiz's liveliest hubs. The building is attractively illuminated at night and open to visits on Saturday mornings. Just ring the bell next to the door. ⊠ *Pl. de San Juan de Dios* ⊙ *Sat. 11–12:45.*

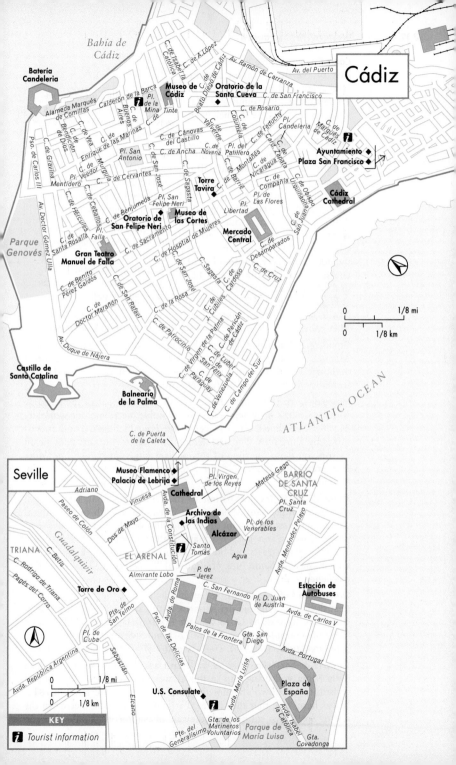

**Cádiz Cathedral.** Five blocks southeast of the Torre Tavira are the gold dome and baroque facade of Cádiz's cathedral, begun in 1722, when the city was at the height of its power. The Cádiz-born composer Manuel de Falla, who died in 1946 at the age of 70, is buried in the **crypt.** The cathedral **museum,** on Calle Acero, displays gold, silver, and jewels from the New World, as well as Enrique de Arfe's processional cross, which is carried in the annual Corpus Christi parades. The entrance price includes the crypt, museum, and church of Santa Cruz. The cathedral is accessible only during mass. ⊠ *Pl. Catedral* ☎ *956/286154* ✆ *€5* ☉ *Museum, crypt and Santa Cruz: Mon.–Sat. 10–6:30, Sun. 1:30–6:30; Cathedral: mass Sun. at noon.*

> **CÁDIZ BEST BETS**
>
> **Explore Seville's Alcázar.** One of Spain's finest historic palaces was built to symbolize victory over the Moors.
>
> **Be awe-inspired by Seville's Cathedral.** The largest Gothic building in the world and the third-largest church, this is a building of superlatives.
>
> **Sip a glass of fine sherry in a sidewalk café accompanied by tasty tapas.** Your tastebuds will tingle, and you can watch the languorous life of southern Spain happen around your table.

**Gran Teatro Manuel de Falla.** Four blocks west of Santa Inés is the Plaza Manuel de Falla, overlooked by this amazing neo-Mudejar redbrick building. The classic interior is impressive as well; try to attend a performance. ⊠ *Pl. Manuel de Falla* ☎ *956/220828.*

**Museo de Cádiz** (*Provincial Museum*). On the east side of the Plaza de Mina is Cadiz's provincial museum. Notable pieces include works by Murillo and Alonso Cano as well as the *Four Evangelists* and a set of saints by Zurbarán. The archaeological section contains Phoenician sarcophagi from the time of this ancient city's birth. ⊠ *Pl. de Mina* ☎ *956/203368* ✆ *€1.50* ☉ *Tues. 2:30–8:30, Wed.–Sat. 9–8:30, Sun. 9–2:30.*

**Museo de las Cortes.** Next door to the Oratorio de San Felipe Neri, the small but pleasant Museo de las Cortes has a 19th-century mural depicting the establishment of the Constitution of 1812. Its real showpiece, however, is a 1779 ivory-and-mahogany model of Cádiz, with all of the city's streets and buildings in minute detail, looking much as they do now. ⊠ *Santa Inés 9* ☎ *956/221788* ✆ *Free* ☉ *Tues.–Fri. 9–6, weekends 9–2.*

**Oratorio de la Santa Cueva.** A few blocks east of the Plaza de Mina, next door to the Iglesia del Rosario, is this oval 18th-century chapel with three frescoes by Goya. ⊠ *Calle Rosario 10* ☎ *956/222262* ✆ *€3* ☉ *Mid-June–mid-Sept., weekdays 11–1 and 5–8, weekends 10–1; mid-Sept.–mid-June, Tues.–Fri. 10–1:30 and 4:30–7:30, weekends 10–1.*

**Oratorio de San Felipe Neri.** A walk up Calle San José from the Plaza de la Mina will bring you to this church, where Spain's first liberal constitution (known affectionately as *La Pepa*) was declared in 1812. It was here, too, that the Cortes (Parliament) of Cádiz met when the rest of Spain was subjected to the rule of Napoléon's brother, Joseph

Bonaparte (more popularly known as Pepe Botella, for his love of the bottle). On the main altar is an *Immaculate Conception* by Murillo, the great Sevillian artist who in 1682 fell to his death from a scaffold while working on his *Mystic Marriage of St. Catherine* in Cádiz's Chapel of Santa Catalina. ⊠ *Calle Santa Inés 38* ☎ *956/229120* 🎫 *€3* ⊗ *Tues.– Sat. 10–1:45 and 5–7:45; Sun. 11–1:45.*

**Plaza San Francisco.** Near the *ayuntamiento* (town hall) is a pretty square surrounded by white-and-yellow houses and filled with orange trees and elegant streetlamps. It's especially lively during the evening *paseo* (promenade).

**Fodor's**Choice
★
☾

**Torre Tavira.** At 150 feet, this is the highest point in the Old City. More than a hundred such watchtowers were used by Cádiz ship owners to spot their arriving fleets. A camera obscura gives a good overview of the city and its monuments; the last show is a half hour before closing time. ⊠ *Calle Marqués del Real Tesoro 10* ☎ *956/212910* 🎫 *€5* ⊗ *Daily 10–6 (to 8 mid-June–mid-Sept.).*

## SEVILLE
*149 km (93 miles) northeast of Cádiz.*

Seville's whitewashed houses bright with bougainvillea, its ocher-color palaces, and its baroque facades have long enchanted both Sevillanos and travelers. Lord Byron's well-known line, "Seville is a pleasant city famous for oranges and women," may be true, but is far too tame. Seville's color and vivacity are legendary but best seen during one of the traditional *fiestas,* when modern dress is swapped for vivid ruffled costume, and the streets come alive with song and dance.

**Fodor's**Choice
★

**Alcázar.** The Plaza del Triunfo forms the entrance to the Mudejar palace built by Pedro I (1350–69) on the site of Seville's former Moorish *alcázar* (fortress). Don't mistake the Alcázar for a genuine Moorish palace like Granada's Alhambra—it may look like one, and it was designed and built by Moorish workers brought in from Granada, but it was commissioned and paid for by a Christian king more than 100 years after the reconquest of Seville. The palace is the official residence of the king and queen when they're in town. ⊠ *Pl. del Triunfo, Santa Cruz* ☎ *954/502324* ⊕ *www.patronato-alcazarsevilla.es* 🎫 *€8.50* ⊗ *Apr.– Sept., daily 9:30–7; Oct.–Mar., daily 9:30–5.*

★ **Cathedral.** Seville's cathedral can be described only in superlatives: it's the largest and highest cathedral in Spain, the largest Gothic building in the world, and the world's third-largest church, after St. Peter's in Rome and St. Paul's in London. After Ferdinand III captured Seville from the Moors in 1248, the great mosque begun by Yusuf II in 1171 was reconsecrated to the Virgin Mary and used as a Christian cathedral. In 1401 the people of Seville decided to erect a new cathedral, one that would equal the glory of their great city. They pulled down the old mosque, leaving only its minaret and outer courtyard, and built the existing building in just over a century—a remarkable feat for the time. ⊠ *Pl. Virgen de los Reyes, Centro* ☎ *954/214971* 🎫 *Cathedral and Giralda €8* ⊗ *July and Aug., Mon.–Sat. 9:30–4:30, Sun. 2:30–6:30; Sept.–June, Mon.–Sat. 11–5:30, Sun. 2:30–6:30.*

Fodor's Choice ★ **Museo del Baile Flamenco.** This private museum in the heart of Santa Cruz (follow the signs) was opened in 2007 by the legendary flamenco dancer Cristina Hoyos and includes audiovisual and multimedia displays explaining the history, culture, and soul of Spanish flamenco. There are also regular classes and shows. ⊠ *Calle Manuel Rojas Marcos 3, Santa Cruz* ☎ *954/340311* ⊕ *www.museoflamenco.com* 🖪*€10* ⊗ *Daily 9:30–7.*

★ **Palacio de la Condesa de Lebrija.** This lovely palace has three ornate patios, including a spectacular courtyard graced by a Roman mosaic taken from the ruins in Itálica, surrounded by Moorish arches and fine azulejos. The side rooms house a collection of archaeological items. The second floor contains the family apartments and visits are by guided tour only. ⊠ *Calle Cuna 8, Centro* ☎ *954/227802* 🖪*€5 first floor only; €8 with second floor tour* ⊗ *July and Aug., weekdays 9–3, Sat. 10–2; Sept.–June, weekdays 10:30–7:30, Sat. 10–2 and 4–6, Sun. 10–2.*

**Torre del Oro** (*Tower of Gold*). Built by the Moors in 1220 to complete the city's ramparts, this 12-sided tower on the banks of the Guadalquivir served to close off the harbor when a chain was stretched across the river from its base to a tower on the opposite bank. In 1248, Admiral Ramón de Bonifaz broke through the barrier, and Ferdinand III captured Seville. The tower houses a small naval museum. ⊠ *Paseo Alcalde Marqués de Contadero s/n, El Arenal* ☎ *954/222419* 🖪*€3; free Mon.* ⊗ *Mon.–Fri. 9:30–6:45, weekends 10:30–6:45.*

## JEREZ DE LA FRONTERA
*52 km (34 miles) northeast of Cádiz.*

Jerez, world headquarters for sherry, is surrounded by vineyards of chalky soil, whose Palomino grapes have funded a host of churches and noble mansions. Names such as González Byass, Domecq, Harvey, and Sandeman are inextricably linked with Jerez. At any given time more than half a million barrels of sherry are maturing in Jerez's vast aboveground wine cellars.

**González Byass.** If you have time for only one bodega, make it this one, home of the famous Tío Pepe. The tour is well organized and includes La Concha, an open-air aging cellar designed by Gustave Eiffel. ⊠ *Calle Manuel María González* ☎ *902/440077* ⊕ *www.bodegastiopepe.com.*

Fodor's Choice ★ ♨ **Real Escuela Andaluza del Arte Ecuestre** (*Royal Andalusian School of Equestrian Art*). This prestigious school operates on the grounds of the Recreo de las Cadenas, a 19th-century palace. The school was masterminded by Alvaro Domecq in the 1970s, and every Thursday (and at various other times throughout the year) the Cartujana horses—a cross between the native Andalusian workhorse and the Arabian—and skilled riders in 18th-century riding costume demonstrate intricate dressage techniques and jumping in the spectacular show "Cómo Bailan los Caballos Andaluces" (roughly, "The Dancing Horses of Andalusia"). Reservations are essential. Admission price depends on how close to the arena you sit; the first two rows are the priciest. At certain other times you can visit the stables and tack room, and watch the horses being schooled. ⊠ *Av. Duque de Abrantes* ☎ *956/319635 information, 956/318008 tickets* ⊕ *www.realescuela.org* 🖪*Shows:*

*€19–€25; stables tour and training sessions: €10 ⊙ Shows: Mar.–mid-Dec., Tues. and Thurs. at noon (also Fri. at noon in Aug.); for Sat. shows check website. Tour and training sessions: Jan.–Feb., Mon. and Tues. 10–2; Mar.–Dec. Weds. and Fri. 10–2.*

## SHOPPING

The region abounds with colorful souvenirs, including fine flamenco costumes, classical guitars, ornate fans traditional to Andalusia. Look out also for copious choices in ceramics, porcelain, and textiles, including beautiful hand-stitched embroidery (be aware that machine-embroidered items have flooded the market). Don't forget a bottle or two of excellent Jerez sherry, or Spanish olives and olive oil to augment your larders back home.

Seville is the region's main shopping area and the place for archetypal Andalusian souvenirs, most of which are sold in the Barrio de Santa Cruz and around the cathedral and Giralda, especially on Calle Alemanes. The main shopping street for Sevillanos themselves is Calle Sierpes, along with its neighboring streets Cuna, Tetuan, Velázquez, Plaza Magdalena, and Plaza Duque—boutiques abound here. The streets of old Cádiz are the place to browse and buy.

**Artesanía Textil.** You can find blankets, shawls, and embroidered table-cloths woven by local artisans at the two shops of Artesanía Textil. ⊠ *Calle García de Vinuesa 33, El Arenal, Seville* ☎ *954/215088* ⊙ *Weekends* ⊠ *Sierpes 70, Centro, Seville* ☎ *954/220125* ⊙ *Weekends.*

## WHERE TO EAT

$ ✕ **Casa Manteca.** Cádiz's most quintessentially Andalusian tavern is in
SPANISH the neighborhood of La Viña (named for the vineyard that once grew
Fodor'sChoice here). *Chacina* (Iberian ham or sausage) served on waxed paper and
★ Manzanilla (sherry from Sanlúcar de Barrameda) are standard fare at this low wooden counter that has served bullfighters and flamenco singers, as well as dignitaries from around the world, since 1953. The walls are covered with colorful posters and other memorabilia from the annual carnival, flamenco shows, and ferias. No hot dishes are available. ⑤ *Average main: €8* ⊠ *Corralón de los Carros 66* ☎ *956/213603* ⊙ *Closed Mon. No lunch Sun.*

$$ ✕ **Enrique Becerra.** Excellent tapas, a lively bar, and an extensive wine
SPANISH list await at this restaurant run by the fifth generation of a family of
★ celebrated restaurateurs (Enrique's brother Jesús owns Becerrita). The menu focuses on traditional, home-cooked Andalusian dishes, such as *pez espada al amontillado* (swordfish cooked in dark sherry) and *cordero a la miel con espinacas y piñones* (honey-glazed lamb stuffed with spinach and pine nuts). Don't miss the fried eggplant stuffed with prawns. If you want a quiet meal, call to reserve a table in one of the small upstairs rooms. ⑤ *Average main: €21* ⊠ *Calle Gamazo 2, El Arenal, Seville* ☎ *954/213049* ⊙ *Closed Sun. and Aug.*

# CANNES, FRANCE (WITH THE ILES DE LÉRINS AND ANTIBES)

Updated by Jennifer Ladonne

A tasteful and expensive stomping ground for the upscale, Cannes is a sybaritic heaven for those who believe that life is short and sin has something to do with the absence of a tan. Backed by gentle hills and flanked to the southwest by the Estérel, warmed by dependable sun but kept bearable in summer by the cool Mediterranean breeze, Cannes is pampered with the luxurious climate that has made it one of the most popular and glamorous resorts in Europe. The cynosure of sun worshippers since the 1860s, it has been further glamorized by the modern success of its film festival. If you're a culture lover into art of the noncelluloid type you should look elsewhere. Come to Cannes for incomparable Continental panache and as a stepping-stone to attractions a little farther afield.

## ESSENTIALS

### CURRENCY
The euro.

### HOURS
Most stores are open Monday–Saturday 9–7, but many close at lunchtime (usually noon–2 or 3) and some will open later and on Sunday during July and August. Museums are open 10–5, but most are closed on either Monday or Tuesday.

### TELEPHONES
Tri-band GSM phones work in France. You can buy prepaid phone cards at telecom shops, news vendors, and tobacconists in all towns and cities. Phone cards can be used for local or international calls. Orange, SFR, Bouygues Telecom, and Virgin are leading telecom companies. If you have an unlocked GSM phone, LeFrenchMobile (⊕ *www.lefrenchmobile.com*) offers SIM cards (and micro SIM cards) with support in English, unlimited validity of credits, and prepurchase online.

## COMING ASHORE
Cruise vessels anchor offshore in Cannes, and passengers are tendered ashore to the Old Port. From there it is walking distance to all the city attractions. Taxis are on hand, and it's a five-minute ride to the train or bus station.

There will be no need to rent a vehicle unless you want to tour the surrounding Provençal countryside. The rental cost is approximately €70 per day for an economy manual vehicle. Taxis are plentiful and can provide tourist itineraries. For single journeys, tariffs are €2.80 at flag fall, then €0.90 per km. If you want to rent by the hour, the daytime tariff is €28 plus the distance covered on the meter.

Local trains are frequent; you can reach Nice in 20 minutes (€7 or €9.50 by faster TGV), Antibes in 10 minutes (€3 or €4 by faster TGV), and almost all other coastal towns can also be reached on a local train in less than an hour. Both RCA and TAM bus lines have frequent service (RCA's 200 bus between Cannes and Antibes runs every 20 minutes).

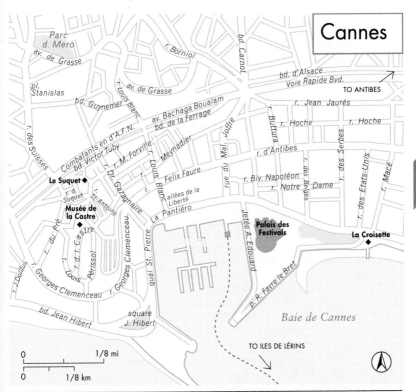

## EXPLORING CANNES

### CANNES

**La Croisette.** Head to the famous mile-long waterfront promenade, La Croisette, which starts at the western end by the Palais des Festivals, and allow the *esprit de Cannes* to take over. This is precisely the sort of place for which the verb *flâner* (to dawdle, saunter) was invented, so stroll among the palm trees and flowers and crowds of poseurs (fur coats in tropical weather, cell phones on Rollerblades, and sunglasses at night). Head east past the broad expanse of private beaches, glamorous shops, and luxurious hotels (among them the wedding-cake Carlton, famed for its see-and-be-seen terrace-level brasserie). The beaches along here are almost all private, though open for a fee—each beach is marked with from one to four little life buoys, rating their quality and expense.

**Le Suquet.** Climb up Rue St-Antoine into the picturesque Vieille Ville neighborhood known as Le Suquet, on the site of the original Roman *castrum*. Shops proffer Provençal goods, and the atmospheric cafés provide a place to catch your breath; the pretty pastel shutters, Gothic stonework, and narrow passageways are lovely distractions.

**Musée de la Castre.** The hill is crowned by the 11th-century château, housing the Musée de la Castre, with its mismatched collection of weaponry, ethnic artifacts, and ceramics amassed by a 19th century aristocrat. The imposing four-sided **Tour du Suquet** (Suquet Tower) was built in 1385 as a lookout against Saracen-led invasions. ⊠ *Pl. de la Castre, Le Suquet* ☎ *04–93–38–55–26* 🖾 *€6* ⊘ *Oct.–Mar., Tues.–Sun. 10–1 and 2–5; Apr.–June and Sept., Tues.–Sun. 10–1 and 2–6; July and Aug., daily 10–7.*

**Palais des Festivals.** Pick up a map at the tourist office in the Palais des Festivals, the scene of the famous Festival International du Film, otherwise known as the Cannes Film Festival. As you leave the information center, follow the Palais to your right to see the red-carpeted stairs where the stars ascend every year. Set into the surrounding pavement, the **Allée des Étoiles** (Stars' Walk) enshrines some 400 autographed imprints of film stars' hands— of Dépardieu, Streep, and Stallone, among others.

**CANNES BEST BETS**

**Stroll along the Croisette.** This seafront promenade is where all the beautiful people go for their walks. Check out the handprints of the stars set in clay on the pavement around the Palais des Festivals.

**Musée Picasso.** The medieval castle in nearly Antibes displays a fascinating array covering the many eras of the artist's long and successful career.

**Wander the streets of Vieux Antibes.** The narrow streets of the Old Town are wonderful for capturing images of life in languorous southern France.

## ÎLES LÉRINS
*15–20 minutes by ferry off the coast of Cannes.*

When you're glutted on glamour, you may want to make a day trip to the peaceful Iles de Lérins (Lérins Islands); boats depart from Cannes's Vieux Port. Allow at least a half day to enjoy either of the islands; you can fit both in only if you get an early start. Access to the ferry is across the large parking in front of the Sofitel hotel, southwest from the Palais des Festivals. You have two ferry options.

**Tour Contacts Compagnie Planaria.** Compagnie Planaria ⊠ *Quai Laubeuf (end of parking lot), port of Cannes, La Croisette, Cannes* ☎ *04–92–98–71–38* ⊕ *www.cannes-ilesdelerins.com.*

**Trans Côte D'Azur.** When it comes to transport to and from Isle St-Margueritte, the Trans Côte D'Azur is the way to go. ⊠ *Quai Laubeuf (end of parking lot), port of Cannes, La Croisette, Cannes* ☎ *04–92–98–71–30* ⊕ *www.trans-cote-azur.com.*

### EXPLORING ILE ST-HONORAT
**Ile St-Honorat.** Ile St-Honorat can be reached in 20 minutes (€13 round-trip) from the Vieux Port. Smaller and wilder than Ste-Marguerite, it's home to an active monastery and the ruins of its 11th-century predecessor. The monks are more famous in the region for their nonreligious activity: manufacturing and selling a rather strong liqueur called Lérina. ⊕ *www.abbayedelerins.com.*

### EXPLORING ILE STE-MARGUERITE

**Ile Ste-Marguerite.** From the Vieux Port it's a 15-minute, €12 round-trip to Ile Ste-Marguerite. Its **Fort Royal,** built by Richelieu and improved by Vauban, offers views over the ramparts to the rocky island coast and the open sea.

**Musée de la Mer** (*Marine Museum*). The complex includes the Musée de la Mer, with a Roman boat dating from the 1st century BC and a collection of amphorae and pottery recovered from ancient shipwrecks. It's more famous, however, for reputedly being the prison of the Man in the Iron Mask. Inside you can see his cell and hear his story, and although the truth of his captivity is not certain, it's true that many Huguenots were confined here during Louis XIV's religious scourges. ⊠ *Fort de l'île Sainte-Marguerite* ☎ *04–93–38–55–26* ☑ €6 ☉ *Oct.–Mar., Tues.–Sun. 10:30–1:15 and 2:15–4:45; Apr.–mid-June, Tues.–Sun. 10:30–1:15 and 2:15–5:45; mid-June–Sept., daily 10:30–5:45.*

### ANTIBES

*11 km (7 miles) northeast of Cannes, 15 km (9 miles) southeast of Nice.*

Fodor's Choice
★

No wonder Picasso once called this home—Antibes (pronounced Awnteeb) is a stunner. With its broad stone ramparts scalloping in and out over the waves and backed by blunt medieval towers and a skew of tile roofs, it remains one of the most romantic Old Towns on the Mediterranean coast. As gateway to the Cap d'Antibes, Antibes's Port Vauban harbor has some of the largest yachts in the world tied up at its berths—their millionaire owners won't find a more dramatic spot to anchor, with the tableau of the snowy Alps looming in the distance and the formidable medieval block towers of the Fort Carré guarding entry to the port. Stroll Promenade Amiral-de-Grasse along the crest of Vauban's seawalls, and you'll understand why the views inspired Picasso to paint on a panoramic scale. Yet a few steps inland you'll enter a souk-like maze of old streets that are relentlessly picturesque and joyously beautiful.

To visit Old Antibes, pass through the **Porte Marine,** an arched gateway in the rampart wall. Follow Rue Aubernon to **Cours Masséna,** where the little sheltered market sells lemons, olives, and hand-stuffed sausages, and the vendors take breaks in the shoebox cafés flanking one side.

Fodor's Choice
★

**Commune Libre du Safranier** (*Free Commune of Safranier*). A few blocks south of the Château Grimaldi is the Commune Libre du Safranier, a magical little neighborhood with a character all its own. Here, not far off the seaside promenade and focused around the Place du Safranier, tiny houses hang heavy with flowers and vines and neighbors carry on conversations from window to window across the stone-stepped Rue du Bas-Castelet. It's said that Place du Safranier was once a tiny fishing port; now it's the scene of festivals.

★ **Eglise de l'Immaculée-Conception.** From Cours Masséna head up to the Eglise de l'Immaculée-Conception, which served as the region's cathedral until the bishopric was transferred to Grasse in 1244. The church's 18th-century facade, a marvelously Latin mix of classical symmetry and fantasy, has been restored in stunning shades of ocher and cream. Its stout medieval watchtower was built in the 11th century with stones "mined" from Roman structures. Inside is a baroque altarpiece painted by the Niçois artist Louis Bréa in 1515. ⊠ *Rue St-Esprit.*

# SHOPPING

Cannes caters to the upmarket crowd with a wealth of designer boutiques such as Chanel and Dior, and high-class jewelers. But if you don't want to max out your credit cards, there's a wealth of choice of less expensive ready-to-wear fashion. Boutiques also sell colorful crafts from the Provence region, including basketwork, bright fabrics, olive-wood items, plus delicious olives, olive oils, honey, dried herbs, and quaffable local wines. Film buffs may also want to stock up on official Cannes Film Festival merchandise.

**Rue d'Antibes,** running parallel with the Croisette but two blocks inland, is Cannes's main high-end shopping street. At its western end is **Rue Meynadier,** packed tight with trendy clothing boutiques and fine food shops. Not far away is the covered **Marché Forville,** the scene of the animated morning food market. The narrow alleyways of **Le Suquet,** are also a great place to browse. Film Festival merchandise can be bought at the **Palais du Festivals,** but the official Film Festival shop is found on La Croisette, close to the Majestic Hotel.

Vieil Antibes has an excellent shopping, though you'll find far fewer designer boutiques than in Cannes. Small shops sell an excellent range of local crafts and foodstuffs and there are several galleries selling work by local artists.

## BEACHES

The pebble beach that fronts the full length of La Croisette has a chic atmosphere in summer. Most sections have been privatized and are owned by hotels and/or restaurants that rent out chaise longues, mats, and umbrellas to the public and hotel guests (who also have to pay). Public beaches are between the color-coordinated private beach umbrellas, and offer simple open showers and basic toilets. The restaurants here are some of the best places for lunch or refreshment, though you do pay extra for the location.

## WHERE TO EAT

$   ✕ **La Pizza.** Sprawling up over two floors in front of the old port, this
PIZZA   busy restaurant (with two sister eateries, La Pizza and Le Quebec in Nice) serves steaks, fish, and salads every day of the year, but come here for gloriously good right-out-of-the-wood-fire-oven pizza in huge portions. ⑤ *Average main: €13* ✉ *3 quai St-Pierre* ☎ *04–93–39–22–56.*

# CIVITAVECCHIA, ITALY (FOR ROME)

Updated
by Bruce
Leimsidor

Rome is a heady blend of artistic and architectural masterpieces, classical ruins, and opulent baroque churches and piazzas. The city's 2,700-year-old history is on display wherever you look; the ancient rubs shoulders with the medieval, the modern runs into the Renaissance, and the result is a bustling open-air museum. Julius Caesar and Nero, the Vandals and the Popes, Raphael and Caravaggio, Napoléon and Mussolini—these and countless other luminaries and villains have left their mark on the city. Today Rome's formidable legacy is kept alive by its people, their history knit into the fabric of their everyday lives. Raphaelesque teenage girls zip through traffic on their *motorini*; priests in flowing robes talking on cell phones stride through medieval piazzas. Modern Rome has one foot in the past, one in the present—a fascinating stance that allows you to tip back an espresso while gazing at a Bernini fountain, then hop on the metro to your next attraction.

## ESSENTIALS
### CURRENCY
The euro.

### HOURS
Stores are generally open from 9 or 9:30 to 1 and from 3:30 or 4 to 8. There's a tendency for shops in central districts to stay open all day. Many places close Sunday, and some also close Monday morning from September to mid-June and Saturday afternoon from mid-June through August.

### PRIVATE TOURS
The most universally acclaimed private tour service in Rome is that offered by When in Rome Tours. The service offers a countless number of tour options. Booking a tour independently for one or two persons can be very expensive (€870 for the Shore excursions Rome option), but many cruise lines arrange group tours with this service, which should cost about €150/person, depending on the size of the group. The Shore Excursion Option includes pick-up at the port, a 3-hour transit to and from, and 7 hours of touring. You can also form your own group with other passengers before you book independently, but these tours must be arranged in advance, so if you are not traveling among a large group of cruise passengers, that can be logistically difficult.

Contacts **When in Rome Tours.** ☎ *(39)06/839–04705 in Rome* ⊕ *www.wheninrometours.com.*

### TELEPHONES
Tri-band GSM phones work in Italy. You can buy prepaid phone cards at telecom shops, news vendors, and tobacconists in all towns and cities. Phone cards can be used for local or international calls.

## COMING ASHORE
Civitavecchia is a large port, and you will be bused from the ship to the terminal area. There are passenger facilities such as cafés and information offices, but these are shared with commercial ferry traffic and can be crowded. A shuttle will take you to the railway station, where you can catch trains to Rome, or you can walk along the harborfront to the station in less than 10 minutes. Taxis charge around €20 for the journey to the train station. Train tickets to Rome cost approximately €5 to €10 one-way, depending on time of travel. If you prebook on the Trenitalia website ⊕ *www.trenitalia.com,* you can print out your tickets at the station. There are two or three trains per hour, and the journey time is 1 hour 15 minutes. The cost for a private car with driver to Rome is approximately €150 one-way.

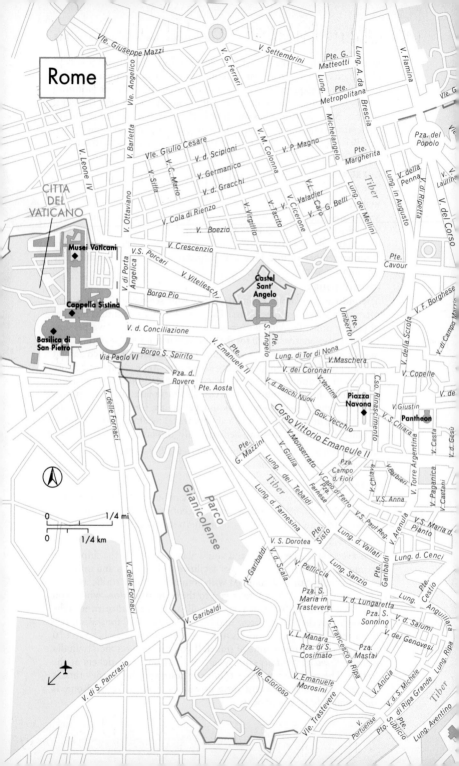

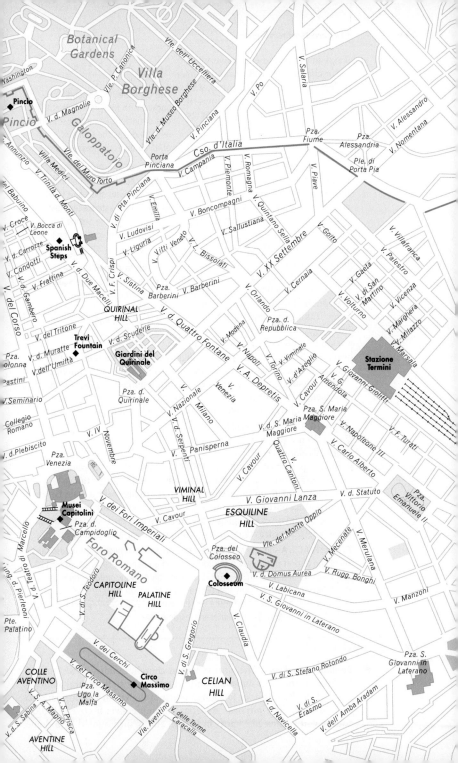

Taxis in Rome are expensive, with extra charges when the taxi travels at less than 20 kph (12 mph), and with surcharges for busier times of the day, for every piece of luggage after the first, to order a taxi by phone, and for travel on holidays. You shouldn't rent a car if you want to explore only Rome, because both traffic and parking are difficult; however, if you want to explore the countryside around Civitavecchia a car would be useful. Rental costs are approximately €50 per day for a compact manual vehicle.

Rome's metro (subway) is somewhat limited, but it's quick if you are headed somewhere that it goes. The public bus and tram system is slow. Taking the compact electric buses of Lines 117 and 119 through the center of Rome can save a lot of walking. A ticket valid for 75 minutes on any combination of buses and trams and one entrance to the metro costs €1. Tickets for the public transit system are sold at tobacconists, newsstands, some coffee bars; you can also buy them in the green machines positioned in metro stations and some bus stops. A BIG ticket, valid for one day on all public transport, costs €4.

> ### ROME BEST BETS
>
> **The Colosseum.** Although jam-packed with tourists, this is still one of ancient Rome's most iconic relics and was the scene of some of its bloodiest contests.
>
> **Basilica di San Pietro.** The mother church for all Catholics is redolent with spirit and filled with artistic masterpieces. Just remember that the Sistine Chapel can only be visited if you go to the Vatican Museums.
>
> **Join the throng at Piazza Navona.** Visit this large square with its three fountains and immerse yourself in the energy that is modern Rome.

### GETTING TO THE AIRPORT

If you do not purchase airport transfers from your cruise line, the most practical option is to take a taxi (with a set price of €120) or private transfer company (which costs around €150) to pick you up at the port and drop you at the airport. The private transfer vehicle will be larger than a taxi and can accommodate up to seven people. You can also take a train between Civitavecchia port railway station and Fiumicino airport (€11 one-way), but the trip involves changing trains in Rome and takes about 2 hours. It is not advised for travelers with lots of luggage (or little patience).

**Contacts ACS.** A somewhat less expensive limousine service in a modest car to Fiumicino airport through ACS (Airport Connection Service) costs €100 to €110 and takes 45 minutes. ☎ (39) 06/3383221 *in Italy* ⊕ *www.airportconnection.it.* **Dock Service.** This company can provide port to airport transfers (or vice versa) as well as guided land tours within Rome. ☎ 239/603–7469 *in the U.S., 338/9139644 in Italy* ⊕ *www.limoservicesrome.net.*

## EXPLORING ROME

★  **Basilica di San Pietro.** The world's largest church, built over the tomb of St. Peter, is the most imposing and breathtaking architectural achievement of the Renaissance (although much of the lavish interior dates to the baroque). The physical statistics are impressive: it covers 18,000 square yards, runs 212 yards in length, and is surmounted by a dome that rises 435 feet and measures 138 feet across its base. Its history is equally impressive. No fewer than five of Italy's greatest artists—Bramante, Raphael, Peruzzi, Antonio Sangallo the Younger, and Michelangelo—died while striving to erect this new St. Peter's.

The history of the original St. Peter's goes back to AD 349, when the emperor Constantine completed a basilica over the site of the tomb of St. Peter, the Church's first pope. The original church stood for more than 1,000 years. The current basilica was completed only in 1626 after more than 100 years of construction.

Under the Pope Pius V monument, the entrance to the sacristy also leads to the **Museo Storico-Artistico e Tesoro** (⊠ *Historical-Artistic Museum and Treasury* 🕾 *06/69881840* 🎟*€10 includes audio guide* ⊙ *Apr.–Sept., daily 8–7; Oct.–Mar., daily 8–6:20*), a small collection of Vatican treasures. Above, the vast sweep of the basilica's dome is the cynosure of all eyes. Proceed to the right side of the Basilica's vestibule; from here, you can either take the elevator or climb the long flight of shallow stairs to the roof (🕾 *06/69883462* 🎟*elevator €7, stairs €5* ⊙ *Apr.–Sept., daily 8–6; Oct.–Mar., daily 8–4; on a Papal Audience Wed., opens after the audience finishes, about noon; closed during ceremonies in piazza*). The entrance to the **Grotte Vaticane** (⊠ *Vatican Grottoes* 🎟*Free* ⊙ *Weekdays and Sat. 9–4; Sun. 1:30–3:30; closed while the papal audience takes place in St. Peter's Square, until about noon on Wed.*) is to the right of the Basilica's main entrance. ⊠ *Piazza di San Pietro, Vatican* ⊙ *Apr.–Sept., daily 7–7; Oct.–Mar., daily 7–6; closed during the papal audience in St. Peter's Square Wed. mornings until about noon* Ⓜ *Ottaviano-San Pietro.*

**Fodor's**Choice **Cappella Sistina** (*Sistine Chapel*). In 1508, the redoubtable Pope Julius
★ II commissioned Michelangelo to fresco the more than 10,000 square feet of the Sistine Chapel's ceiling. (*Sistine*, by the way, is simply the adjective from *Sixtus*, in reference to Pope Sixtus IV, who commissioned the chapel itself.) The task took four years, and it's said that for many years afterward Michelangelo couldn't read anything without holding it over his head. The result, however, was the greatest artwork of the Renaissance. A pair of binoculars helps greatly, as does a small mirror—hold the mirror facing the ceiling and look down to study the reflection. More than 20 years later, Michelangelo was called on again, this time by the Farnese pope Paul III, to add to the chapel's decoration by painting the *Last Judgment* on the wall over the altar. The subject was well suited to the aging and embittered artist, who had been deeply moved by the horrendous Sack of Rome in 1527 and the confusions and disturbances of the Reformation. ⊠ *Vatican Palace; entry only through Musei Vaticani, Vatican.*

**The Colosseum.** The most spectacular extant edifice of ancient Rome, the Colosseo has a history that is half gore, half glory. Here, before 50,000 spectators, gladiators would salute the emperor and cry *Ave, imperator, morituri te salutant* ("Hail, emperor, men soon to die salute thee"). Designed by order of the Flavian emperor Vespasian in AD 72, the Colosseum was inaugurated by Titus eight years later with a program of games lasting 100 days. The arena has a circumference of

573 yards and was faced with travertine from nearby Tivoli. Its construction was a remarkable feat of engineering, for it stands on marshy terrain reclaimed by draining an artificial lake on the grounds of Nero's Domus Aurea. Originally known as the Flavian amphitheater, it came to be called the Colosseo because it stood on the site of the Colossus of Nero, a 115-foot-tall gilded bronze statue of the emperor that once towered here. The newly restored hypogeum, along with the third level of the Colosseum, reopened to much acclaim in fall 2010 (visitable only via a prebooked, guided tour). Since then, however, it's open and shut, depending on the season and recent rains. Check the Pierreci website for its current state.

If you go to the Roman Forum, a couple of hundred yards down Via dei Fori Imperiali on your left, or to the Palatine, down Via di San Gregorio, the €12 ticket you purchase there includes admission to the Colosseum and, even better, lets you jump to the head of the *loooooooong* line. Another way is to buy the Romapass (⊕ *www.romapass.it*) ticket—the Colosseo is covered and you get booted to the front of the line. Or you can book a ticket in advance through ⊕ *www.pierreci.it* (small surcharge)—the main ticket reservation service for many Italian cultural sights. ⊠ *Piazza del Colosseo* ☎ *06/39967700* ⊕ *www.pierreci. it* ✉ *€12 (combined ticket with the Roman Forum, Palatine Hill, and Imperial Forums, if used within 2 days)* ⊘ *Daily 8:30–1 hr before sunset* Ⓜ *Colosseo; Bus 117, 87, 186, 85, 850.*

Fodor'sChoice  **Musei Vaticani** (*Vatican Museums*). Other than the pope and his papal
   ★          court, the occupants of the Vatican are some of the most famous artworks in the world. The museums that contain them are part of the **Vatican Palace**, residence of the popes since 1377. The palace consists of an estimated 1,400 rooms, chapels, and galleries. The pope and his household occupy only a small part of the palace; most of the rest is given over to the Vatican Library and Museums. Beyond the glories of the Sistine Chapel, the collection is so extraordinarily rich you may just wish to skim the surface, but few will want to miss out on the great antique sculptures, Raphael Rooms, and the old master paintings, such as Leonardo da Vinci's *St. Jerome.*

Rivaling the Sistine Chapel for artistic interest—and for the number of visitors—are the **Stanze di Raffaello** (Raphael Rooms). Pope Julius II moved into this suite in 1507, four years after his election. Reluctant to continue living in the Borgia apartments downstairs, with their memories of his ill-famed predecessor Alexander VI, he called in Raphael to decorate his new quarters. Downstairs, enter the recently restored **Borgia apartments**, where some of the Vatican's most fascinating historical figures are depicted on elaborately painted ceilings. Pinturicchio designed the frescoes at the end of the 15th century, though the paintings were greatly retouched in later centuries. It's generally believed that Cesare Borgia murdered his sister Lucrezia's husband, Alphonse of Aragon, in the Room of the Sibyl. Equally celebrated are the works on view in the **Pinacoteca** (Picture Gallery). These often world-famous paintings, almost exclusively of religious subjects, are arranged in chronological order, beginning with works of the 12th and 13th centuries.

To avoid the line into the museums, consider booking your ticket in advance online (⊕ *biglietteriamusei.vatican.va*); there is a €4 surcharge. Guided tours are €31 to €36, including entrance tickets, and can also be booked online. For information on tours, call *06/69883145* or *06/69884676*; visually impaired visitors can arrange tactile tours by calling *06/69884947*. Note: Ushers at the entrance of St. Peter's and sometimes the Vatican Museums will bar entry to people with bare knees or bare shoulders. ⊠ *Viale Vaticano (near intersection with Via Leone IV), Vatican* ⊕ *www.vatican.va* ⊑ *€15; free last Sun. of the month* ⊙ *Mon.–Sat. 9–6 (last entrance at 4), last Sun. of month 9–12:30* ⊙ *Closed Jan. 1 and 6, Feb. 11, Mar. 19, Easter and Easter Monday, May 1, June 29, Aug. 14 and 15, Nov. 1, and Dec. 8, 25, and 26* Ⓜ *Cipro–Musei Vaticani or Ottaviano–San Pietro. Bus 64, 40.*

★ **Trevi Fountain.** Alive with rushing waters commanded by an imperious Oceanus, the Fontana di Trevi (Trevi Fountain) earned full-fledged iconic status in 1954 when it starred in 20th-Century Fox's *Three Coins in the Fountain.* As the first color film in Cinemascope to be produced on location, it caused practically half of America to pack their bags for the Eternal City. The conceit of a fountain emerging full-force from a palace was first envisioned by Bernini and Pietro da Cortona for Pope Urban VIII's plan to rebuild the fountain (which marked the end-point of the ancient Acqua Vergine aqueduct, created in 18 BC by Agrippa). Only three popes later, under Pope Clement XIII, did Nicolo Salvi finally break ground with his winning design. ⊠ *Piazza di Trevi, accessed by Via Tritone, Via Poli, Via delle Muratte, Via del Lavatore, and Via di San Vincenzo, Trevi.*

Fodor'sChoice **Musei Capitolini.** Surpassed in size and richness only by the Musei Vati-
★ cani, this immense collection was the first public museum in the world. A greatest-hits collection of Roman art through the ages, from the ancients to the baroque, it is housed in the twin Museo Capitolino and Palazzo dei Conservatori that bookend Michelangelo's famous piazza. Here, you'll find some of antiquity's most famous sculptures, such as the poignant *Dying Gaul,* the regal *Capitoline Venus,* the *Esquiline Venus* (identified as possibly another Mediterranean beauty, Cleopatra herself), and the *Lupa Capitolina,* the symbol of Rome. Although some pieces in the collection—which was first assembled by Sixtus IV (1414–84), one of the earliest of the Renaissance popes—may excite only archaeologists and art historians, others are unforgettable, including the original bronze statue of Marcus Aurelius whose copy sits in the piazza. ⊠ *Piazza del Campidoglio, Campidoglio* ☎ *06/0608* ⊕ *www. museicapitolini.org* ⊑ *€12; audio guide €5* ⊙ *Tues.–Sun. 9–8* Ⓜ *Bus 44, 63, 64, 81, 95, 85, 492.*

Fodor'sChoice **Pantheon.** One of the wonders of the ancient world, this onetime pagan
★ temple, a marvel of architectural harmony and proportion, is the best-preserved ancient building in Rome. It was entirely rebuilt by the emperor Hadrian around AD 120 on the site of an earlier pantheon (from the Greek *pan,* all, and *theon,* gods) erected in 27 BC by Augustus's general Agrippa. The most striking thing about the Pantheon is not its size, immense though it is (until 1960 the dome was the largest ever built), nor even the phenomenal technical difficulties posed by so

vast a construction; rather, it's the remarkable unity of the building. You don't have to look far to find the reason for this harmony: the diameter described by the dome is exactly equal to its height. It's the use of such simple mathematical balance that gives classical architecture its characteristic sense of proportion and its nobility and why some call it the world's only architecturally perfect building. The great opening at the apex of the dome, the oculus, is nearly 30 feet in diameter and was the temple's only source of light. It was intended to symbolize the "all-seeing eye of heaven." One-hour tours (€8) are run regularly in English; check at the information desk on your right as you enter. ⊠ *Piazza della Rotonda, Navona* ☎ *06/68300230* ⌛ *Free; audio guides €5 suggested donation* ☉ *Mon.–Sat. 8:30–7:30, Sun. 9–6* Ⓜ *Closest bus hub: Argentina (buses 40, 85, 53, 46, 64, 87, 571, tram 8).*

**Piazza Navona.** Here, everything that makes Rome unique is compressed into one beautiful baroque piazza. Always camera-ready, Piazza Navona has Bernini sculptures, three gorgeous fountains, a magnificently baroque church (Sant'Agnese in Agone), and, best of all, the excitement of so many people strolling, admiring the fountains, and enjoying the view. The piazza has been an entertainment venue for Romans ever since being built over Domitian's circus (pieces of the arena are still visible near adjacent Piazza Sant'Apollinare). Although undoubtedly more touristy today, the square still has the carefree air of the days when it was the scene of medieval jousts and 17th-century carnivals. Today, it's the site of a lively Christmas "Befana" fair. At center stage is the Fontana dei Quattro Fiumi, created for Innocent X by Bernini in 1651. Bernini's powerful figures of the four rivers represent the four corners of the world: the Nile; the Ganges; the Danube; and the Plata, with its hand raised. ⊠ *Junction of Via della Cuccagna, Corsia Agonale, Via di Sant'Agnese, and Via Agonale.*

Fodor'sChoice
★
☾ **The Spanish Steps.** That icon of postcard Rome, the Spanish Steps (often called simply *la scalinata*—"the staircase"—by Italians) and the Piazza di Spagna from which they ascend both get their names from the Spanish Embassy to the Vatican on the piazza—even though the staircase was built with French funds in 1723. For centuries, the scalinata and its neighborhood have welcomed tourists, dukes, and writers in search of inspiration—among them Stendhal, Honoré de Balzac, William Makepeace Thackeray, and Byron, along with today's enthusiastic hordes. ⊠ *Junction of Via Condotti, Via del Babuino, and Via Due Macelli, Spagna* Ⓜ *Spagna.*

☾ **Pincio.** The Pincian gardens always have been a favorite spot for strolling. Grand Tourists, and even a pope or two, would head here to see and be seen among the beau monde of Rome. A stretch of ancient walls separates the Pincio from the southwest corner of Villa Borghese. From the balustraded terrace, you can look down at Piazza del Popolo and beyond, surveying much of Rome. Southeast of the Pincian terrace is the **Casina Valadier,** a magnificently decorated neoclassical building that was reopened to the public in 2007 after a decade-long renovation. It remains one of Rome's most historic restaurants (*06/69922090, casinavaladier.it*). ⊠ *Piazzale Napoleone I and Viale dell'Obelisco, Villa Borghese* Ⓜ *Flaminio (Piazza del Popolo).*

## SHOPPING

Italian style is everywhere in Rome, from couture clothing to fashion accessories by all the best names. Specialties of the city include excellent silks, linens, lace, and other fabrics. Edibles include wines, olive oils, pasta, and sweet biscotti, small hard biscuits.

★ The city's most famous shopping district, **Piazza di Spagna,** is a galaxy of boutiques selling gorgeous wares with glamorous labels. **Via del Corso,** a main shopping avenue, has more than a mile of clothing, shoes, leather goods, and home furnishings from classic to cutting-edge. **Via Cola di Rienzo** is block after block of boutiques, shoe stores, department stores, and mid-level chain stores, as well as street stalls and upscale food shops. **Via dei Coronari** has quirky antiques and home furnishings. Via Giulia and other surrounding streets are good bets for decorative arts. Should your gift list include religious souvenirs, shop between Piazza San Pietro and **Borgo Pio.** Liturgical vestments and statues of saints make for good window-shopping on **Via dei Cestari.**

# WHERE TO EAT

$$ ✕ **Da Baffetto.** Down a cobblestone street not far from Piazza Navona,
PIZZA this is Rome's most popular pizzeria and a summer favorite for street-
Fodor'sChoice side dining. The debate is constant whether or not this spot is mas-
★ sively overrated, but as with all the "great" pizzerias in Rome, it's hard to argue with the line that forms outside here on weekends. Happily, outdoor tables (enclosed and heated in winter) provide much-needed additional seating and turnover is fast (and lingering not encouraged). Baffetto 2, at Piazza del Teatro di Pompeo 18, is an extension of the pizzeria with the addition of pasta and *secondi*—and doesn't suffer from the overcrowding of the original location. $ *Average main: €22* ⊠ *Via del Governo Vecchio 114, Navona* ☎ *06/6861617* 🗀 *No credit cards* ☾ *Closed Aug. and Tues. No lunch Mon.–Fri.*

$$$$ ✕ **Dal Bolognese.** The darling of the media, film, and fashion commu-
EMILIAN nities, this classic restaurant on Piazza del Popolo is not only an "in-crowd" dinner destination but makes a convenient shopping-spree lunch spot. As the name promises, the cooking adheres to the hearty tradition of Bologna. Start with a plate of sweet *San Daniele* prosciutto with melon, then move on to the traditional egg pastas of Emilia-Romagna. Second plates include the famous Bolognese *bollito misto,* a steaming tray of an assortment of boiled meats (some recognizable, some inde-cipherable) served with its classic accompaniment, a tangy, herby *salsa verde* (green sauce). During dessert, take in the passing parade of your fellow diners—they love to meet and greet with excessive air kisses. $ *Average main: €75* ⊠ *Piazza del Popolo 1, Spagna* ☎ *06/3611426* ⌕ *Reservations essential* ☾ *Closed Mon. and 3 wks in Aug.*

# WHERE TO STAY

$$ ⌂ **Albergo Santa Chiara.** If you're looking for a good location (right
HOTEL behind the Pantheon) and top-notch service at great prices—not to
Fodor'sChoice mention comfortable beds and a quiet stay—look no further than
★ this historic hotel, run by the same family for some 200 years. **Pros:**

great location in the historical center behind the Pantheon; the staff is both polite and helpful; there is a lovely terrace/sitting area in front of the hotel that overlooks the piazza. **Cons:** the rooms are small and could use some restyling. Some rooms don't have a window. $ *Rooms from: €250* ✉ *Via Santa Chiara 21, Pantheon* ☎ *06/6872979* ✉ *info@ albergosantachiara.com* ⊕ *www.albergosantachiara.com* ➔ *96 rooms, 3 suites, 3 apartments* ⦿ *Breakfast.*

**$$$$**
HOTEL
Fodor'sChoice
★

**Hassler.** When it comes to million-dollar views, this exclusive hotel has the best seats in the house, which is why movie stars like Tom Cruise and Jennifer Lopez, money shakers, and the nouveaux riche are all willing to pay top dollar to stay at this top address of Rome, perched atop the Spanish Steps; they are indeed lucky, for while the Hassler's exterior is bland, the recently restyled guest rooms are among the world's most extravagant and lavishly decorated. **Pros:** charming old-world feel; prime location and panoramic views at the top of the Spanish Steps; just "steps" away from some of the best shopping in the world. **Cons:** VIP prices; many think the staff is too standoffish; the spa facilities are far from 5-star material. $ *Rooms from: €650* ✉ *Piazza Trinità dei Monti 6, Spagna* ☎ *06/69934755, 800/223–6800 Toll-free from the U.S.* ⊕ *www.hotelhasslerroma.com* ➔ *82 rooms, 13 suites* ⦿ *No meals.*

**$$**
B&B/INN
Fodor'sChoice
★

**Scalinata di Spagna.** This tiny hotel's prime location at the top of the Spanish Steps, inconspicuous little entrance, and quiet, sunny charm all add to the character that guests fall in love with over and over again—which explains why it's often booked up for months, even years at a time—but if you're lucky enough to nab a spot here, you'll enjoy stylish rooms accentuated with floral fabrics and Empire-style sofas and the hotel's extravagant rooftop garden: gaze over Rome as you nibble cornetto and sip cappuccino. **Pros:** friendly and helpful concierge; fresh fruit in the rooms; free Wi-Fi throughout. **Cons:** it's a hike up the hill to the hotel; no porter and no elevator; service can be hit-or-miss. $ *Rooms from: €220* ✉ *Piazza Trinità dei Monti 17, Spagna* ☎ *06/6793006* ⊕ *www.hotelscalinata.com* ➔ *16 rooms* ⦿ *Breakfast.*

# GENOA, ITALY

Updated by Bruce Leimsidor

Genoa (Genova, in Italian) claims that it was the birthplace of Christopher Columbus (one of several places that claim the explorer), but the city's proud history predates that explorer by several hundred years. Genoa was already an important trading station by the 3rd century BC, when the Romans conquered Liguria. Known as *La Superba* (The Proud), Genoa was a great maritime power in the 13th century, rivaling Venice and Pisa. But its luster eventually diminished, and the city was outshone by these and other formidable cities. By the 17th century it was no longer a great sea power. It has, however, continued to be a profitable port. Genoa is now a busy, sprawling, but nevertheless elegant city. But with more than two millennia of history under its belt, magnificent palaces and museums, and an elaborate network of ancient hilltop fortresses, Genoa is sure to satisfy your historic and aesthetic interests. Portofino can be visited on a day-trip from Genoa if your ship doesn't call there directly (⇨ *Portofino*).

## ESSENTIALS

### CURRENCY
The euro.

### HOURS
Stores are generally open from 9 or 9:30 to 1 and from 3:30 or 4 to 8. Many shops close Sunday, though this is changing, too, especially in the city center. Many national museums are closed on Monday and may have shorter hours on Sunday.

### PRIVATE TOURS
Benvenuto Tours offers full-day tours out of Genoa to the towns to the east of the city: Portofino, the Cinque Terre, Lerici, and Portovenere. This is a pricey option (€450 per person) but an effortless way to see some dramatic costal scenery and lovely historic villages, including those beloved by the English romantic poets. Most of these places are also served by rail out of Genoa.

**Contacts Benvenuto Tours.** ☎ *(39)081/007–2114 in Genoa* ⊕ *www.benvenutolimos.com.*

### TELEPHONES
Tri-band GSM phones work in Italy. You can buy prepaid phone cards at telecom shops, news vendors, and tobacconists in all towns and cities. Phone cards can be used for local or international calls.

## COMING ASHORE

Genoa is a massive port, and cruise ships usually dock at one of two terminals, the Ponte dei Mille Maritime Station and Ponte Andrea Doria Maritime Station. Ponte dei Mille is an impressive 1930s building (renovated 2001) with good passenger facilities that include shops, restaurants, an information center, and a bank. Neighboring Ponte Andrea Doria was refurbished in 2007 with similar facilities but on a slightly smaller scale. From here it's a few minutes' walk to the port entrance, from which you can also walk into the city; however, the streets around the port are workaday and gritty, so you may want to take a taxi rather than walk into the city proper. There is a "hop on/ hop off" tour bus (from April through October, €15) that starts at Piazza Caricamento, right outside the entry to the cruise port. Buses leave, with a few exceptions, every half-hour, and the complete circuit takes about one hour.

With the occasional assistance of public transportation, the only way to visit Genoa is on foot. Many of the more interesting districts are either entirely closed to traffic, have roads so narrow that no car could fit, or are, even at the best of times, blocked by gridlock. A vehicle might be useful if you want to explore the Ligurian countryside and coastline around Genoa. Rental costs are approximately €35 per day for a compact manual vehicle. The most beautiful scenery is to the east of Genoa, toward the Cinque Terre, but to appreciate it, you will have to take local roads with numerous hairpin turns—not for nervous drivers.

Within Liguria local trains make innumerable stops. Regular service operates from Genoa's two stations: Stazione Principe travel to points

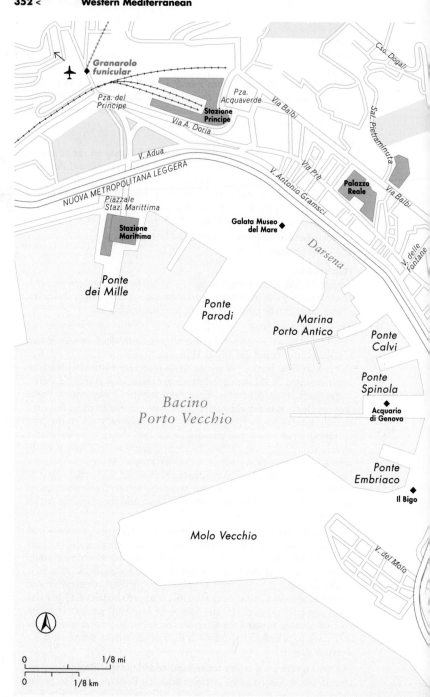

Granarolo funicular

Pza. del Principe

Pza. Acquaverde

Via Balbi

Cso. Dogali

Sal. Pietraminuta

Via A. Doria

Stazione Principe

Via Pre

Via Balbi

V. Adua

Via Antonio Gramsci

Palazzo Reale

NUOVA METROPOLITANA LEGGERA

Piazzale Staz. Marittima

Stazione Marittima

Galata Museo del Mare

Darsena

V. delle Fontane

Ponte dei Mille

Ponte Parodi

Marina Porto Antico

Ponte Calvi

Ponte Spinola

Acquario di Genova

*Bacino Porto Vecchio*

Ponte Embriaco

Il Bigo

*Molo Vecchio*

V. del Molo

0        1/8 mi

0        1/8 km

# Genoa

4

Pza. E. Brignole

Corso Carbonara

Corso Firenze

Corso Carbonara

V. Brig. de Ferrari

Corso Paganini

Corso Paganini

◆ **Zecca-Righi funicular**

Gerolamo

Via Caffaro

Salita S. Maria di Sanità

Via M. Piaggio

Pza. d. Nunziata

Via P. Bensa

◆ **Zecca-Righi funicular**

V. d. S. S.

◆ **Sant'Anna funicular**

Via G. Mameli

V. Cairoli

Gall. Garibaldi

V. del Campo

Lomellini

V. S. Siro

◆ **Palazzo Bianco**

V. Garibaldi

Pza. Portello

Battistine

Gall. Bixio

Piazzale Mazzini

V. Palestro

◆ **Palazzo Rosso**

V. della Maddalena

Pza. Fontane Marose

Via S. Luca

◆ **Galleria Nazionale**

Pza. Corvetto

Pza. Caricamento

Pza. Soziglia

Via Luccoli

NUOVA METROPITIANA LEGGERA

CARUGGI

Chiossone

V. Campetto

V. Roma

Vico degli Indoratori

Pza. San Matteo

V. Ceba

Via 25 Aprile

Viale IV Novembre

Via S. Lorenzo

V. David

**San Lorenzo**

Via F. Turati

V. di Canneto il Curto

V. dei Giustiniani

Pza. G. Matteotti

Salita Pollaioli

Pza. de Ferrari

V. Pia Soprana

V. Dante

E. Vernazza

V. XX Settembre

V. XII Ottobre

Via S. Bernardo

V. S. Donato

Pza. Embriaci

V. Santa Croce

◆ **Santa Maria di Castello**

Strad. di S. Agostino

Vic. d. Fico

Pza. Dante

V. Fieschi

Corso M. Quadrio

Pza. Negri

◆ **Sant'Agostino**

S. Leonardo

Gall. C. Colombo

west and Stazione Brignole to points east and south. All the coastal resorts are on this line. If you buy tickets though Trenitalia's (Italian Railway's) website (⊕ *www.trenitalia.com*), you can print them out at self-service machines in Genoa station.

# EXPLORING GENOA

## THE MEDIEVAL CORE

The medieval center of Genoa, threaded with tiny streets flanked by 11th-century portals, is roughly the area between the port and Piazza de Ferrari. This mazelike pedestrian zone is officially called the Caruggi District, but the Genovese, in their matter-of-fact way, simply refer to the area as the place of the *vicoli* (narrow alleys). In this warren of narrow, cobbled streets extending north from Piazza Caricamento the city's oldest churches sit among tiny shops selling antique furniture, coffee, cheese, rifles, wine, gilt picture frames, camping gear, and even live fish. The 500-year-old apartment buildings lean so precariously that penthouse balconies nearly touch those across the street, blocking what little sunlight would have shone down onto the cobblestones. Wealthy Genovese built their homes in this quarter in the 16th century, and prosperous guilds, such as the goldsmiths for whom Vico degli Indoratori and Via degli Orefici were named, set up shop here.

**Galleria Nazionale.** This gallery, housed in the richly adorned **Palazzo Spinola** north of Piazza Soziglia, contains masterpieces by Luca Giordano and Guido Reni. The *Ecce Homo,* by Antonello da Messina, is a hauntingly beautiful painting, of historical interest because it was the Sicilian da Messina who first brought Flemish oil paints and techniques to Italy from his sojourns in the Low Countries. ⊠ *Piazza Pellicceria 1, Maddalena* ☎ *010/2705300* ⊕ *www.palazzospinola.it* 🎫 *€4, €6.50 with Palazzo Reale* ☉ *Tues.–Sat. 8:30–7:30, Sun. 1:30–7:30.*

**Palazzo Bianco.** It's difficult to miss the splendid white façade of this town palace as you walk down Via Garibaldi, once one of Genoa's most important streets. The building houses a fine collection of 17th-century art, with the Spanish and Flemish schools well represented. ⊠ *Via Garibaldi 11, Maddalena* ☎ *010/2759185* ⊕ *www.museidigenova.it* 🎫 *€8, includes Palazzo Rosso and Palazzo Doria Tursi* ☉ *Tues.–Fri. 9–7, weekends 10–7.*

**Fodor'sChoice** **Palazzo Reale.** Lavish rococo rooms provide sumptuous display space for
★ paintings, sculptures, tapestries, and Asian ceramics. The 17th-century palace—also known as Palazzo Balbi Durazzo—was built by the Balbi family, enormously wealthy Genovese merchants. Its regal pretensions were not lost on the Savoy, who bought the palace and turned it into a royal residence in the early 19th century. The gallery of mirrors and the ballroom on the upper floor are particularly decadent. Look for works by Sir Anthony Van Dyck, who lived in Genoa for six years, beginning in 1621, and painted many portraits of the Genovese nobility. The formal gardens, which you can visit for €1, provide a welcome respite from the bustle of the city beyond the palace walls, as well as great views of the harbor. ⊠ *Via Balbi 10, Pré* ☎ *010/2710236* ⊕ *www.palazzorealegenova.it* 🎫 *€4; €6.50 including Galleria Nazionale* ☉ *Tues. and Wed. 9–1:30, Thurs.–Sun. 9–7.*

**Palazzo Rosso.** This 17th-century baroque palace was named for the red stone used in its construction. It now contains, apart from a number of lavishly frescoed suites, works by Titian, Veronese, Reni, and Van Dyck. ⊠ *Via Garibaldi 18, Maddalena* ☎ *010/2759185* ⊕ *www.museidigenova.it* ☎ *€8 including Palazzo Bianco and Palazzo Doria Tursi* ⊙ *Tues.–Fri. 9–7, weekends 10–7.*

**Zecca-Righi funicular.** This is a seven-stop commuter funicular beginning at Piazza della Nunziata and ending at a high lookout on the fortified gates in the 17th-century city walls. Ringed around the circumference of the city are a number of huge fortresses; this gate was part of the city's system of defenses. From Righi you can undertake scenic all-day hikes from one fortress to the next. ⊠ *Piazza della Nunziata, Pré* ☎ *010/5582414* ⊕ *www.amt.genova.it* ☎ *€2* ⊙ *Daily 6 am–11:45 pm.*

> ### GENOA BEST BETS
>
> **Stroll the warren of narrow alleyways in medieval Genoa.** This is a real slice of daily life, Ligurian style.
>
> **Taking in the views from Il Bigo.** The panorama stretches across the city rooftops and out over the vast expanse of the harbor.
>
> **Visiting San Lorenzo Cathedral.** The architecture is a fine example of the medieval northern Italian style.

## SOUTHERN DISTRICTS AND THE AQUARIUM

Inhabited since the 6th century BC, the oldest section of Genoa lies on a hill to the southwest of the Caruggi District. Today, apart from a section of 9th-century wall near Porta Soprana, there is little to show that an imposing castle once stood here. Though the neighborhood is considerably run-down, some of Genoa's oldest churches make it a worthwhile excursion. No visit to Genoa is complete, however, without at least a stroll along the harborfront. The port was given a complete overhaul during Genoa's preparations for the Columbus quincentennial celebrations of 1992, and additional restorations in 2003 and 2004 have done much to revitalize the waterfront including a prehistoric Biosphere, Il Bigo panoramic lift *(mentioned later in this section)* with towering views over the town and port, and La Citta dei Bambino with over 90 interactive displays aimed especially at children. Combined tickets for these several attractions—marketed as Acquario Village and including entrance to the Aquarium and Galata Museo del Mare *(listed below)*— cost €39, but there are also several packages incorporating two or more of the individual attractions.

★ **Acquario di Genova.** Europe's biggest aquarium, second in the world
☉ only to Osaka's in Japan, is the third-most-visited museum in Italy and a must for children. Fifty tanks of marine species, including sea turtles, dolphins, seals, eels, penguins, and sharks, share space with educational displays and re-creations of marine ecosystems, including a tank of coral from the Red Sea. An entire "Aquarium Village" has been created, which also includes a biosphere, hummingbird forest, and interactive submarine exhibit. If arriving by car, take the Genova Ovest exit from the autostrada. ⊠ *Ponte Spinola, Porto Vecchio* ☎ *0101/2345678* ⊕ *www.acquario.ge.it* ☎ *€19 for adults, €13 for kids ages 4–12, free*

*for children 0–3. Aquarium Village tickets (for entrance to all attractions): €39 for adults, €27 for children 4–12, free for children 0-3.* ⊘ *Mar.–June, weekdays 9–7:30, weekends 8:45–8:30; July and Aug., daily 8:30 am–10 pm; Nov.–Feb., weekdays 9:30–7:30, weekends 9:30–8:30. Entry permitted every ½ hr; last entry 1½ hrs before closing.*

**Galata Museo del Mare.** Devoted entirely to the city's seafaring history, this museum is probably the best way, at least on dry land, to get an idea of the changing shape of Genoa's busy port. Highlighting the displays is a full-size replica of a 17th-century Genovese galleon. ⊠ *Calata de Mari 1, Ponte dei Mille* ☎ *010/2345655* ⊕ *www.galatamuseodelmare.it* ⊠ *€11 for adults, €6 for kids 4–12, free for children 0–3* ⊘ *Mar.–Oct., daily 10–7:30; Nov.–Feb., Tues.–Fri. 10–6, weekends 10–7:30. Last entry 1 hr. before closing.*

↻ **Il Bigo.** This spiderlike white structure, designed by world-renowned architect Renzo Piano, was erected in 1992 to celebrate the Columbus quincentenary. You can take its **Ascensore Panoramico Bigo** (Bigo Panoramic Elevator) up 650 feet for a 360-degree view of the harbor, city, and sea. In winter there's an ice-skating rink next to the elevator, in an area covered by sail-like awnings. ⊠ *Ponte Spinola, Porto Vecchio* ☎ *010/2345278 skating rink* ⊠ *Elevator €4 for adults, €3 for children 4–12 and children under 4 are free; skating rink €8* ⊘ *Elevator: Jan. 7–Feb. and Nov.–Dec. 25, weekends 10–5; Mar.–May, Sept., and Oct., Mon. 2–6, Tues.–Sun. 10–6; June–Aug., Mon. 4–11 pm, Tues.–Sun. 10 am–11 pm; Dec. 26–Jan. 6, daily 10–5. Skating rink: Nov. or Dec.– Mar., weekdays 8 am–9:30 pm, Sat. 10 am–2 am, Sun. 10 am–midnight.*

**San Lorenzo.** Contrasting black slate and white marble, so common in Liguria, embellishes the cathedral at the heart of medieval Genoa— inside and out. Consecrated in 1118, the church honors Saint Lawrence, who passed through the city on his way to Rome in the 3rd century. For hundreds of years the building was used for religious and state purposes such as civic elections. Note the 13th-century Gothic portal, the fascinating twisted barbershop columns, and the 15th- to 17th-century frescoes inside. The last campanile dates from the early 16th century. The **Museo del Tesoro di San Lorenzo** (San Lorenzo Treasury Museum) housed inside has some stunning pieces from medieval goldsmiths and silversmiths, for which medieval Genoa was renowned. ⊠ *Piazza San Lorenzo, Molo* ☎ *010/2471831* ⊠ *Cathedral free, museum €4.50* ⊘ *Cathedral daily 8–12 and 3–7. Museum Mon.–Sat. 9–12 and 3–6, and the first Sunday of the month 3–6.*

**Sant'Agostino.** This 13th-century Gothic church was damaged during World War II, but still has a fine campanile and two well-preserved cloisters that house an excellent museum displaying pieces of medieval architecture and fresco paintings. Highlights of the collection are the enigmatic fragments of a tomb sculpture by Giovanni Pisano (circa 1250–1315). ⊠ *Piazza Sarzano 35/R, Molo* ☎ *010/2511263* ⊕ *www. museidigenova.it* ⊠ *€4* ⊘ *Tues.–Fri. 9–7, weekends 10–7.*

**Santa Maria di Castello.** One of Genoa's most significant religious buildings, an early Christian church, was rebuilt in the 12th century and finally completed in 1513. You can visit the adjacent cloisters and see the fine artwork contained in the museum. Museum hours vary during religious services. ⊠ *Salita di Santa Maria di Castello 15, Molo* ☎ *010/25495-225* ▨ *Free* ☉ *Daily 9–noon and 3:30–6:30.*

## SHOPPING

In addition to the well-known Italian fine leather and haute couture, Liguria is famous for its fine lace, silver-and-gold filigree work, and ceramics. Look also for bargains in velvet, macramé, olive wood, and marble. Genoa is the best spot to find all these specialties. Don't forget the excellent wines, cheeses, dried meats, and olive oils.

In the heart of the medieval quarter, Via Soziglia is lined with shops selling handicrafts and tempting foods. Via XX Settembre is famous for its exclusive shops. High-end shops line Via Luccoli. The best shopping area for trendy but inexpensive Italian clothing is near San Siro, on Via San Luca.

## WHERE TO EAT

**$$$** ✕ **Bakari.** Hip styling and ambient lighting hint at this eatery's creative,
LIGURIAN  even daring, takes on Ligurian classics. Sure bets are the spinach-and-cheese gnocchi, any of several carpaccios, and the delicate beef dishes. Reserve ahead, request a table on the more imaginative ground floor or just stop by for an aperitivo and people-watching. Ⓢ *Average main: €25* ⊠ *Vico del Fieno 16/R, northwest of Piazza San Matteo, Maddalena* ☎ *010/291936* ⊕ *www.bakari.it* ☉ *Sat. lunch and Sun.*

**$$** ✕ **Exultate.** When the weather permits, umbrella-shaded tables spread
LIGURIAN  out from this tiny eatery into the nearby square. Popular with locals, the restaurant's inexpensive daily menu is presented on a chalkboard for all to see; excellent pizza, meal-size salads, and delicious homemade desserts highlight the list. Ⓢ *Average main: €20* ⊠ *Piazza Lavagna 15/R, Maddalena* ☎ *010/2512605* ☉ *Closed Sun.*

# GIBRALTAR

Updated by
Joanna Styles

The tiny British colony of Gibraltar—nicknamed Gib, or simply the Rock—whose impressive silhouette dominates the strait between Spain and Morocco, was one of the two Pillars of Hercules in ancient times, marking the western limits of the known world and in an ace position commanding the narrow pathway between the Mediterranean Sea and the Atlantic Ocean. Today the Rock is like Britain with a suntan. There are double-decker buses, policemen in helmets, and bright red mailboxes. Gibraltar was ceded to Great Britain in 1713 by the Treaty of Utrecht, and Spain has been trying to get it back ever since. Recently, Britain and Spain have been talking about joint Anglo-Spanish sovereignty, much to the ire of the majority of Gibraltarians, who remain fiercely patriotic to the crown. Millions of dollars have been spent in developing the Rock's tourist potential, and Gibraltar's economy is further boosted by its important status as an offshore financial center.

## ESSENTIALS

### CURRENCY

Gibraltar uses the British pound sterling but issues its own notes and coins, which are equivalent in value to British pounds. Euros can also be used in most of the shops, but the exchange rate may be unfavorable; U.S. currency is generally not accepted, but ATMs are common and credit cards are widely accepted.

### HOURS

Shops are open weekdays from 9:30 to 7:30 pm, Saturday from 10 to 1. Some shops open Sunday when a ship is in port. Attractions have varied hours, but these are generally weekdays from 10 to 5, and some may open weekends.

### PRIVATE TOURS

**Gibraltar Rock Tours.** The company offers several different tour options departing from the cruise port that take in the main sights. ☎ *350/5699–9000* ⊕ *www.gibraltartours.org.*

### TELEPHONES

3G services are available on the island. GibTel is the main service provider. Public phones accept phonecards and credit cards.

### VISITOR INFORMATION

**Gibraltar Tourist Office** ✉ *Casement Sq.* ☎ *200/45000.*

## COMING ASHORE

There is a dedicated cruise terminal within Gibraltar's commercial port. The passenger terminal has a range of facilities, including a bar-café, souvenir shop, tourist information center, bank and currency-exchange facilities, and an exhibition area. From here it is an easy walk into Gibraltar itself, where all the sites of town can be accessed on foot (or where you can take a bus to the attractions that are farther afield). You can also take a taxi; fares are £2.40 for pick-up and £0.20 per 200 meters or per minute of travel. On days when a number of cruise ships dock at the same time, taxis may be dfficult to find, and it would be wise to prebook a vehicle.

The town of Gibraltar is compact, and it's easy to walk around. Vehicles rented in Gibraltar can be taken over the border into Spain, so you could explore some of the southern Spanish coastline from here in a day. Vehicles are only rented to people between the ages of 25 and 75. The Official Rock Tour—conducted either by minibus or, at a greater cost, taxi—takes about 90 minutes and includes all the major sights, allowing you to choose which places to come back to and linger at later. Costs are around £18 to £25 per person (six-person max.).

The cable car to the top of the rock costs £8 round-trip.

## EXPLORING GIBRALTAR

The colorful, congested library is where the dignified Regency architecture of Great Britain blends well with the shutters, balconies, and patios of southern Spain. Shops, restaurants, and pubs beckon on busy Main Street; at the Governor's Residence, the ceremonial Changing of the Guard takes place six times a year and the Ceremony of the Keys takes

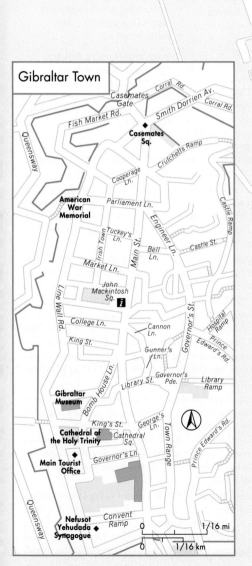

# Gibraltar

## Gibraltar Town

Casemates Gate
Corral Rd.
Fish Market Rd.
Smith Dorrien Av.
Corral Rd.
**Casemates Sq.**
Crutchetts Ramp
Cooperage Ln.
Queensway
Parliament Ln.
**American War Memorial**
Tuckey's Ln.
Irish Town
Main St.
Engineer Ln.
Castle Ramp
Bell Ln.
Castle St.
Market Ln.
**John Mackintosh Sq.** ⓘ
Line Wall Rd.
College Ln.
Cannon Ln.
Hospital Ramp
King St.
Gunner's Ln.
Governor's St.
Prince Edward's Rd.
Library St.
Governor's Pde.
Library Ramp
**Gibraltar Museum**
Bomb House Ln.
King's St.
George's Ln.
Town Range
**Cathedral of the Holy Trinity**
Cathedral Sq.
**Main Tourist Office**
Governor's Ln.
Prince Edward's Rd.
Queensway
**Nefusot Yehudada Synagogue**
Convent Ramp

0 — 1/16 mi
0 — 1/16 km

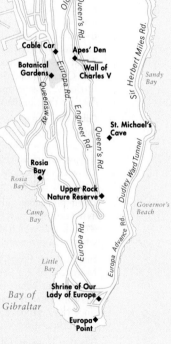

Marina Bay
**Gibraltar Town** see detail map
Devil's Tower Rd.
*Gibraltar Harbor*
**Moorish Castle** ◆
**Great Siege Tunnels** ◆
Queensway
Main St.
Willis's Rd.
Old Queen's Rd.
Queen's Rd.
Catalan Bay Rd.
**Cable Car**
**Apes' Den**
Sir Herbert Miles Rd.
**Botanical Gardens** ◆
**Wall of Charles V**
*Sandy Bay*
Europa Rd.
Queensway
**St. Michael's Cave** ◆
Engineer Rd.
Queen's Rd.
Dudley Ward Tunnel
**Rosia Bay** ◆
*Rosia Bay*
**Upper Rock Nature Reserve** ◆
*Governor's Beach*
*Camp Bay*
Europa Rd.
Europa Advance Rd.
*Little Bay*
**Shrine of Our Lady of Europe** ◆
*Bay of Gibraltar*
**Europa Point** ◆

*Mediterranean Sea*

0 — 1/2 mi
0 — 1/2 km

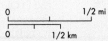

place twice a year. Also, make sure you see the Law Courts, the Anglican Cathedral of the Holy Trinity, and the Catholic Cathedral of St. Mary the Crowned.

**Apes' Den.** The famous Barbary Apes are a breed of cinnamon-color, tailless monkeys (not apes, despite their name) native to Morocco's Atlas Mountains. Legend holds that as long as they remain in Gibraltar, the British will keep the Rock; Winston Churchill went so far as to issue an order for their preservation when their numbers began to dwindle during World War II. They are publicly fed twice daily, at 8 and 4, at Apes' Den, a rocky area down Old Queens Road near the Wall of Carlos V. Among the monkeys' talents are their grabbing of food, purses, and cameras, so be on guard.

> **GIBRALTAR BEST BETS**
>
> **The town of Gibraltar.** Immerse yourself in a little piece of Britain far south of the white cliffs of Dover.
>
> **Take in the panorama from the top of the Rock.** Look south to the northern coast of Africa and north to the southern coastal plains of Spain.
>
> **Make friends with a Barbary ape.** These cheeky primates inhabit the slopes of the Rock. They have a penchant for stealing bags and sunglasses—so you have been warned!

★ **Cable Car.** You can reach St. Michael's Cave—or ride all the way to the top of Gibraltar—on a cable car. The car doesn't go high off the ground, but the views of Spain and Africa from the Rock's pinnacle are superb. It leaves from a station at the southern end of Main Street, which is known as the Grand Parade. ⌧ *Cable car £9 round-trip* ☉ *Apr.–Oct., daily 9:30–6:45; Nov.–Mar., daily 9:30–5:45.*

**Casemates Square.** Gibraltar's social hub is on this pedestrian-only square in the northern part of town, where there are plenty of places to sit with a drink and watch the world go by. The Gibraltar Crystal company, where you can watch the glassblowers at work, is worth a visit.

**Europa Point.** From Europa Point, have a look across the straits to Morocco, 23 km (14 miles) away. You're now standing on one of the two ancient Pillars of Hercules. In front of you is the lighthouse that has dominated the meeting place of the Atlantic and the Mediterranean since 1841; sailors can see its light from a distance of 27 km (17 miles). ⌧ *Continue along coast road to Rock's southern tip.*

**Gibraltar Museum.** Often overlooked by visitors heading to the Upper Rock Reserve, this museum houses a beautiful 14th-century Moorish bathhouse and an 1865 model of the Rock; the displays evoke the Great Siege and the Battle of Trafalgar. There's also a reproduction of the "Gibraltar Woman," the Neanderthal skull discovered here in 1848. ⌧ *Bomb House La.* ☎ *200/74289* ⊕ *www.gibmuseum.gi* ⌧ *£2* ☉ *Weekdays 10–6, Sat. 10–2.*

**Great Siege Tunnels.** These tunnels, formerly known as the Upper Galleries, were carved out during the Great Siege of 1779–82 at the northern end of Old Queen's Road. You can plainly see the openings from which the guns were pointed at the Spanish invaders. They form part of what is arguably the most impressive defense system anywhere in the world.

The nearby and privately managed World War II Tunnels are also open to the public but are less dramatic.

**Moorish Castle.** The castle was built by the descendants of the Moorish general Tariq, who conquered the Rock in 711. The present Tower of Homage dates from 1333, and its besieged walls bear the scars of stones from medieval catapults (and later, cannonballs). Admiral George Rooke hoisted the British flag from its summit when he captured the Rock in 1704, and it has flown here ever since. The castle may be viewed from the outside only.

**Nefusot Yehuda Synagogue.** One of the oldest synagogues on the Iberian Peninsula, Nefusot Yehuda dates back to 1798. Guided tours, which include a short history of the Gibraltar Jewish community, can be reserved by phone. ☎ *200/78804.*

**Rosia Bay.** There are fine views to be had if you drive up above Rosia Bay. The bay was where Nelson's flagship, HMS *Victory,* was towed after the Battle of Trafalgar in 1805. On board were the dead, who were buried in Trafalgar Cemetery on the southern edge of town—except for Admiral Nelson, whose body was returned to England, preserved in a barrel of rum. ⊠ *From Europa Flats, follow Queensway back along Rock's western slopes.*

**Shrine of Our Lady of Europe.** To the north of the lighthouse is the Shrine of Our Lady of Europe, venerated by seafarers since 1462. A former mosque, the small Catholic chapel has a small museum with a 1462 statue of the Virgin and some documents. ⊠ *Just north of Europa Point and lighthouse, along Rock's southern tip* 🖃 *Free* ☉ *Mon.–Thurs. 10–1 and 2:30–6, Fri. 10–1.*

**St. Michael's Cave.** This is the largest of Gibraltar's 150 caves; a visit here is part of the tour of the Upper Rock Nature Preserve. A series of underground chambers full of stalactites and stalagmites, it's an ideal performing-arts venue. The skull of a Neanderthal woman (now in the British Museum) was found at the nearby Forbes Quarry eight years before the world-famous discovery in Germany's Neander Valley in 1856; nobody paid much attention to it at the time, which is why the prehistoric species is called Neanderthal rather than *Homo calpensis* (literally, "Gibraltar Man," after the Romans' name for the Rock, *Calpe*). ⊠ *Queen's Rd..*

**Upper Rock Nature Preserve.** The preserve, accessible from Jews' Gate, includes St. Michael's Cave, the Apes' Den, the Great Siege Tunnels, the Moorish Castle, and the Military Heritage Center, which chronicles the British regiments that have served on the Rock. ⊠ *From Rosia Bay, drive along Queensway and Europa Rd. as far as Casino, above Alameda Gardens. Make a sharp right here, up Engineer Rd. to Jews' Gate, a lookout over docks and Bay of Gibraltar toward Algeciras* 🖃 *£10 for all attractions, plus £2 per vehicle* ☉ *Daily 9–6:15.*

## SHOPPING

The quintessential Britishness of Gibraltar is reflected in its shopping. Many British main-street names can be found here, including Marks and Spencer, so you can stock up on marmalades, biscuits, and Cheddar cheese. Fine English china and glassware also make an appearance along with oodles of Royal memorabilia. Inexpensive items include Union Jack motifs and red double-decker buses printed on everything from T-shirts to coffee mugs. The island is tax-friendly so prices are cheaper than in Spain or the United Kingdom.

## WHERE TO EAT

$    ✕ **Sacarello's.** Right off Main Street, this busy restaurant is as well
BRITISH    known for its excellent coffee and cakes as it is for the rest of its food. There's a varied salad and quiche buffet, as well as filled baked potatoes and daily specials, which could include fresh sole, or stir-fried beef with green beans and chili sauce. Top your meal off with a specialty coffee with cream and vanilla. The restaurant has several warmly decorated rooms with cozy corners, dark-wood furnishings, and low-beamed ceilings, and the whole place has an old-fashioned English feel. ⑤ *Average main: £8* ✉ *57 Irish Town* ☎ *200/70625* ⊕ *www.sacarellosgibraltar. com* ☾ *Closed Sun.*

$    ✕ **Waterfront.** Easily distinguished by its flags and appropriately located
INTERNATIONAL    right at Queensway Quay, this restaurant is a favorite with locals, especially for the Sunday Carvery ($$). Navy and white are the colors that predominate among the cane furniture and the various Mediterranean touches. In addition to the upstairs and downstairs dining inside, there's also a generous terrace and several tables that sit perched on the quay, allowing for views over the marina and to the mountains in Spain. The menu is distinctly international, with specialties including steaks (they're aged on the premises), fish cakes with green curry sauce, and British staples such as bangers and mash (sausages with mashed potatoes in an onion gravy). Service is efficient and comes with a smile. ⑤ *Average main: £15* ✉ *4/5 Ragged Staff* ☎ *200/45666* ⊕ *www.gibwaterfront.com.*

# IBIZA, SPAIN

Updated by
Joanna Styles

Sleepy from November to May, the capital of Ibiza is transformed in summer into Party Central for retro hippies and nonstop clubbers, but the town and the island have so much more to offer. Dalt Vila, the medieval quarter on the hill overlooking Ibiza Town, is a UNESCO World Heritage site with narrow alleyways brimming with atmosphere. Around the coastline the island has 50 sandy beaches. Ibiza was discovered by sun-seeking hippies in the late 1960s, eventually emerging as an icon of counter-culture chic. In the late 1980s and 1990s club culture took over. Young ravers flocked here from all over the world to dance all night and pack the sands of beach resorts all day. That Ibiza is still alive and well, but emblematic of the island's future are its growing numbers of luxury hotels, spas, and gourmet restaurants. Ibiza is toning down and scaling up.

### ESSENTIALS

**CURRENCY**

The euro.

**HOURS**

Museums generally open 9 until 7 or 8, many are closed on Monday, and some close in the afternoon. Most stores are open Monday through Saturday 9 to 1:30 and 5 to 8, but tourist shops may open in the afternoon and also on Sundays between May and September.

**PRIVATE TOURS**

**Ibiza Rutas.** The company offers half-day and full-day trips exploring Ibiza and the neighboring island of Formentera. ☎ 626/633180 ⊕ *www.ibizarutas.com.*

**TELEPHONES**

Tri-band GSM phones should work in Spain, and mobile services are 3G compatible. Public kiosks accept phone cards that support international calls (cards sold in press shops, bars, and telecom shops). Major companies include Vodafone.

### COMING ASHORE

Boats dock on the town pier at the edge of town. From here you can walk into the capital without problem, and for this reason, facilities at the terminal are limited. You won't need transport to enjoy Ibiza Town, however if you rent a car, you can explore much of this small but fascinating island in a day. An economy rental car for one day is €40 (from July through September, you'll really need to book ahead). Buses between Ibiza Town, Sant Rafael, and San Antonio leave every 30 minutes on weekdays (every hour on weekends). There are hourly buses between Ibiza, Sant Jordi, and Salinas. Ibiza and Santa Eulalia are connected by buses every 30 minutes. Fares start at €1.50, and all are under €2.60.

Taxis are also numerous and are metered. They can undertake tourist tours. Fares start at €0.98 per minute (min €3.25) and waiting time of €17.61 per hour. There is a small supplement (€1.65) for port pick-up.

## EXPLORING IBIZA

### IBIZA TOWN (EIVISSA)

Hedonistic and historical, Ibiza (Eivissa, in Catalan) is a city jam-packed with cafés and nightspots and trendy shops; looming over it are the massive stone walls of **Dalt Vila**—the medieval city was declared a UNESCO World Heritage site in 1999—and its Gothic cathedral. Squeezed between the north walls of the Old City and the harbor is **Sa Penya,** a long labyrinth of narrow stone-paved streets that offer the city's best exploring. What would the fishermen who used to live in this quarter have thought seeing so many of their little whitewashed houses transformed into bars and offbeat restaurants and boutiques with names like the Kabul Sutra Tantra Shop, and Good Times Jewelry, and Bitch?

One enters the Dalt Vila via a ramp through the **Portal de ses Taules,** the Old City's main gate. On each side stands a statue, Roman in origin and now headless: Juno on the right, an armless male on the left. Keep going up until you reach the sights.

# Ibiza Island

Cala Xarraca
Caló d'Es Porcs
Portinatx
Sant Vicent
Puerto San Miguel
Cala San Vicente
San Miguel
Sant Joan
Sant Mateo
Balafi
Sant Carles
Santa Agnes
Sant Llorenç
Santa Gertrudis de Fruitera
*Bahía de Sant Antoni*
Santa Eulària des Riu
Sant Antoni
Sant Rafael
**Ibiza Town**
see detail map
Sant Josep
Sant Jordi
Playa d'En Bossa
*Es Vedrà*
Mitjorn
Es Cavallet
Ses Salines

0 — 6 miles
0 — 9 km

*Es Palmador*
*Trucadors*
*Estany Pudent*
Puerto de La Sabina
Es Pujols
Sant Ferran
Sant Francesc Xavier
Cala Sahona
Playa de Mitjorn
El Pilar
*Formentera*
*Cabo de Berbería*

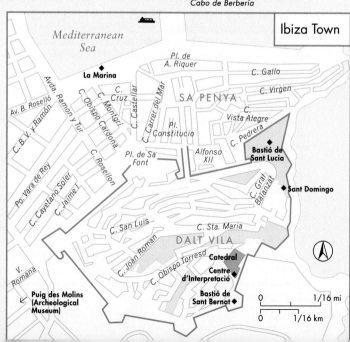

# Ibiza Town

*Mediterranean Sea*

Pl. de A. Riquer
C. Gallo
**La Marina**
C. Virgen
SA PENYA
C. Cruz
C. Castellar
C. Carrer del Mar
C. Montgrí
C. Obispo Cardona
C. Vista Alegre
Pl. Constitucio
C. Pedrera
Avda. Ramon y Tur
Av. B. Rosello
C. B. V. y Ramón
Pl. de Sa Font
Alfonso XII
**Bastió de Sant Lucia**
C. Roselion
**Sant Domingo**
Po. Vara de Rey
C. Cayetano Soler
C. Jaime I
C. Gral. Balanzat
C. San Luis
C. Sta. Maria
DALT VILA
C. Joan Roman
**Catedral**
V. Romana
C. Obispo Torres
**Centre d'Interpretació**
**Puig des Molins (Archeological Museum)**
**Bastió de Sant Bernat**

0 — 1/16 mi
0 — 1/16 km

**Catedral.** On the site of religious structures from each of the cultures that have ruled Ibiza since the Phoenicians, the cathedral was built in the 13th and 14th centuries and renovated in the 18th century. It has a Gothic tower and a baroque nave. ⊠ *Carrer Major s/n* ☎ *971/312774* ⊙ *Weekdays 10–1, Sun. 10:30–noon.*

**Centre d'Interpretació Madina Yabisa.** A few steps from the cathedral, the Centre d'Interpretació Madina Yabisa is a fascinating collection of audiovisual materials and exhibits on the period when the Moors ruled the island. ⊠ *Calle Mayor 2, Eivissa* ☎ *971/392390* 🎟 *€2* ⊙ *Apr.–Jun., Sept. and Oct., Tues.–Sat. 10–3, Sun. 10–1; Jul. and Aug. Tues.–Sat. 10–2 and 6–9, Sun. 10–2; Nov.–Mar., Tues–Sat. 10–3, Sun. 10–2.*

**Sant Domingo.** The roof of the 16th-century church of Sant Domingo is an irregular landscape of tile domes. The nearby *ajuntament* (town hall) is housed in the church's former monastery. ⊠ *Carrer de Balanzat s/n.*

## SANTA EULÀRIA DES RIU
*15 km (9 miles) northeast of Eivissa.*

At the edge of this town on the island's eastern coast, to the right below the road, a Roman bridge crosses what is claimed to be the only permanent river in the Balearics (hence "des Riu," or "of the river"). Ahead, on the hilltop, are the cubes and domes of the church—to reach it, look for a narrow lane to the left, signed "puig de missa," itself so named for the hill where regular mass was once held. A stoutly arched, cryptlike covered area guards the entrance; inside are a fine gold reredos and blue-tile Stations of the Cross. Santa Eulària itself follows the curve of a long sandy beach, a few blocks deep with restaurants, shops, and holiday apartments. From here it's a 10-minute drive to **Sant Carles** and the open-air **hippie market** held there every Saturday morning.

## SANTA GERTRUDIS DE FRUITERA
*15 km (9 miles) north of Eivissa.*

Blink, and you miss it: that's true of most of the small towns in the island's interior—and especially so of Santa Gertrudis, not much more than a bend in the road from Eivissa to the north coast. But don't blink: Santa Gertrudis is strategic, and it's cute. From here you are only a few minutes' drive from some of the island's flat-out best resort hotels and spas. You are minutes from the most beautiful secluded north coves and beaches: **S'Illa des Bosc, Benirràs** (where they have drum circles to salute the setting sun), **S'Illot des Renclí, Portinatx, Caló d'En Serra.** Santa Gertrudis itself has offbeat shops, and laid-back sidewalk cafés, and good food. Artists and expats like it here: they've given it an appeal that now makes for listings of half a million dollars or more for a modest two-bedroom chalet.

---

**IBIZA BEST BETS**

**Explore the narrow alleyways of Sa Penya.** Ibiza Town's most atmospheric quarter is great for browsing and shopping.

**Bring your swimsuit.** Spend an afternoon on one of Ibiza's trendy beaches.

**Stroll uphill in Dalt Vila.** The quarter's architecture has been designated a World Heritage site.

4

## SHOPPING

In the late 1960s and '70s Ibiza built a reputation for extremes of fashion. Little of this phenomenon survives, though the softer designs inspired by Smilja Mihailovich (under the Ad Lib label) still prosper. Clothing and beachwear plus fashion accessories of all kinds are the major buys here, including excellent leather goods, but there is also a community of artists working in glass, ceramics, and bronze. Along Carrer d'Enmig is an eclectic collection of shops and stalls selling fashion and crafts. Although the Sa Penya area of Eivissa still has a few designer boutiques, much of the area is now called the Mercat dels Hippies (hippie market), with more than 80 stalls of overpriced tourist ephemera.

**Ibiza Republic.** For trendy casual gear, sandals, belts, and bags, try Ibiza Republic. ⊠ *Carrer Antoni Mar 15, Eivissa* ☎ *971/314175.*

## BEACHES

Immediately south of Ibiza Town is a long, sandy beach, the nearly 3-km (2-mile) **Playa d'en Bossa**. Farther on, a left turn at Sant Jordi on the way to the airport leads across the salt pans to **Es Cavallet** and **Ses Salines,** two of the best beaches on the island. Topless bathing is accepted all over Ibiza, but Es Cavallet is the official nudist beach. The remaining beaches on this part of the island are accessible from the Ibiza–Sant Josep–Sant Antoni highway, down side roads that often end in rough tracks. North of Sant Antoni there are no easily accessible beaches until you reach **Puerto San Miguel,** an almost rectangular cove with relatively restrained development. Next along the north coast, accessible via San Juan, is Portinatx, a series of small coves with sandy beaches, of which the first and last, **Cala Xarraca** and **Caló d'Es Porcs,** are the best. East of San Juan is the long, curved cove beach of **Cala San Vicente.** Popular with families, it has a more leisurely pace than Ibiza's other resorts. The beaches on the east coast have been developed, but **Santa Eulalia** remains attractive. The resort has a narrow, sloping beach in front of a pedestrian promenade that is much less frenetic than Sant Antoni.

## WHERE TO EAT

$    ✗ **Can Caus.** Ibiza might pride itself on its seafood, but there comes a
SPANISH    time for meat and potatoes. When that time comes, take the 20-minute drive to the outskirts of Santa Gertrudis to this family-style roadside restaurant. Feast on skewers of barbecued *sobrasada* (soft pork sausage), goat chops, lamb kebabs, or grilled sweetbreads with red peppers, onions, and eggplant. Most people eat at the long wooden tables on the terrace. ⑤ *Average main: €16* ⊠ *Ctra. Sant Miquel, Km 3.5* ☎ *971/197516* ⊘ *Closed Mon. Sept.–June.*

$$    ✗ **Mezzanotte.** This charming little port-side restaurant has just 12 tables,
ITALIAN    softly lit with candles and track lighting. In summer, the seating expands to an interior patio and tables on the sidewalk. The kitchen prides itself on hard-to-find fresh ingredients flown in from Italy. The linguine with jumbo shrimp, saffron, and zucchini or with *bottarga* (dried and salted

mullet roe from Sardinia) is wonderful. The prix-fixe menu, served at dinner in summer and lunch in winter, is a bargain. ⑤ *Average main: €18* ⊠ *Paseo de s'Alamera 22, Santa Eulària* ☎ *971/319498* ⊘ *Closed Jan., Feb., and Sun. No lunch June–Aug.*

# LE HAVRE, FRANCE (FOR NORMANDY AND PARIS)

Updated by Jennifer Ladonne

Le Havre, France's second-largest port (after Marseille), was destroyed in World War II. You may find the rebuilt city bleak and uninviting; on the other hand, you may admire Auguste Perret's audacious modern architecture, which earned the city UNESCO World Heritage status in 2005. The city is the perfect starting point for some of the highlights of Normandy, the French region of rolling verdant farmland and long, sandy beaches. Tiny fishing villages dot the coves around the city, a world away from the gritty urban feel of Le Havre itself. Normandy was also the location of the D-Day invasion of Europe by Allied forces during WWII, the largest wartime seaborne invasion of all time. You can visit the beach landing sites and evocative museums about the battle. From Le Havre it's also possible to visit Paris, one of the world's most famous cities.

## ESSENTIALS

### CURRENCY

The euro.

### HOURS

Stores are generally open Monday through Saturday 9–7, but many close at lunchtime (usually noon–2 or 3) and some will open later and on Sunday during July and August. Museums open 10–5, but most are closed on either Monday or Tuesday.

### TELEPHONES

Tri-band GSM phones work in France. You can buy prepaid phone cards at telecom shops, news vendors, and tobacconists in all towns and cities. Phone cards can be used for local or international calls. Orange, SFR, Bouygues Telecom, and Virgin are leading telecom companies. If you have an unlocked GSM phone, LeFrenchMobile (⊕ *www. lefrenchmobile.com*) offers SIM cards (and micro SIM cards) with support in English, unlimited validity of credits, and prepurchase online.

## COMING ASHORE

Le Havre is a large port with vast amounts of freight traffic in addition to cruise ships. Disembarking passengers will find a small welcome center with practical information and multilingual staff, a small shop, plus taxi and tour services, including a shuttle service into the city, which stops at the railway station. If you intend to spend the day in Le Havre, it is only a few minutes' walk from the port entrance to the downtown area.

Le Havre is the main cruise port for visits to Paris (some ships do call in Honfleur); however, the city is a 2- to 2½-hour journey away depending on the service chosen. From the railway station there are hourly trains to Paris terminating at Gare St-Lazare. SNCF (⊕ *www.sncf.com*), the

French railway company, is reliable and efficient. Prices are cheaper if you buy tickets in advance, but a second-class round-trip should be around €66 if purchased on the day of travel.

We would advise against renting a car just to make the trip into Paris (traffic and parking are both very difficult); however, a rental car is an ideal way to explore the rolling countryside of Normandy. An economy manual car costs around €75 per day. Taxis wait outside the port gates and can provide tourist itineraries. For single journeys, fares are €1.80 at pick-up, then €0.89 per km.

Some smaller ships call directly in Honfleur, across the bay from Le Havre (and linked by a modern bridge). It is the most picturesque of the Côte Fleurie's little seaside towns. It was once an important departure point for maritime expeditions, including the first voyages to Canada in the 15th and 16th centuries.

## EXPLORING NORMANDY AND PARIS

### HONFLEUR
*24 km (15 miles) southeast of Le Havre via A131 and the Pont de Normandie.*

**Fodor's** Choice
★
The town of Honfleur, full of half-timber houses and cobbled streets, was once an important departure point for maritime expeditions, including the first voyages to Canada in the 15th and 16th centuries. The 17th-century harbor is fronted on one side by two-story stone houses with low, sloping roofs and on the other by tall, narrow houses whose wooden facades are topped by slate roofs. Note that parking can be a problem, so it's better to come by public transit. Some ships call here directly instead of in Le Havre.

★ **Ste-Catherine.** Soak up the seafaring atmosphere by strolling around the old harbor and paying a visit to the ravishing wooden church of Ste-Catherine, which dominates a tumbling square. The church and the ramshackle belfry across the way—note the many touches of marine engineering in their architecture—were built by townspeople to show their gratitude for the departure of the English at the end of the Hundred Years' War, in 1453. ⊠ *Rue des Logettes* ☎ *02–31–89–11–83.*

### BAYEUX
*10 km (6 miles) southwest of Arromanches via D516, 28 km (17 miles) northwest of Caen.*

Bayeux, the first town to be liberated during the Battle of Normandy, was already steeped in history—as home to a Norman Gothic cathedral and the world's most celebrated piece of needlework: the Bayeux Tapestry.

**Fodor's** Choice
★
**Bayeux Tapestry.** Really a 225-foot-long embroidered scroll stitched in 1067, the Bayeux Tapestry, known in French as the *Tapisserie de la Reine Mathilde* (Queen Matilda's Tapestry), depicts, in 58 comic strip–type scenes, the epic story of William of Normandy's conquest of England in 1066, narrating Will's trials and victory over his cousin Harold, culminating in the Battle of Hastings on October 14, 1066. The tapestry was probably commissioned from Saxon embroiderers by the count of Kent—who was also the bishop of Bayeux—to be displayed in

his newly built cathedral, the Cathédrale Notre-Dame. Despite its age, the tapestry is in remarkably good condition; the extremely detailed, often homey scenes provide an unequaled record of the clothes, weapons, ships, and lifestyles of the day. It's showcased in the **Musée de la Tapisserie** (Tapestry Museum; free audioguides let you to listen to an English commentary about the tapestry). ⊠ *Centre Guillaume-le-Conquérant, 13 bis, rue de Nesmond, Bayeux* ☎ *02–31–51–25–50* ⊕ *www. tapisserie-bayeux.fr* ✉ *€7.80* ⊙ *May–Aug., daily 9–7; Sept.–Apr., daily 9:30–12:30 and 2–6.*

**Cathédrale Notre-Dame.** Bayeux's mightiest edifice, the Cathédrale Notre-Dame, is a harmonious mixture of Norman and Gothic architecture. Note the portal on the south side of the transept that depicts the assassination of English archbishop Thomas à Becket in Canterbury Cathedral in 1170, following his courageous opposition to King Henry II's attempts to control the church. ⊠ *Rue du Bienvenu, Bayeux* ☎ *02–31–92–01–85* ⊙ *Daily 9–6.*

## THE D-DAY BEACHES
*Omaha Beach is 16 km (10 miles) northwest of Bayeux.*

History focused its sights along the coasts of Normandy at 6:30 am on June 6, 1944, as the 135,000 men and 20,000 vehicles of the Allied troops made landfall in their first incursion in Europe in World War II. The entire operation on this "Longest Day" was called Operation Overlord—the code name for the invasion of Normandy.

★ **Omaha Beach.** You won't be disappointed by the rugged terrain and windswept sand of Omaha Beach, 16 km (10 miles) northwest of Bayeux. Here you can find the **Monument du Débarquement** (Monument to the Normandy Landings) and the **Musée-Mémorial d'Omaha Beach,** a large shedlike structure packed with tanks, dioramas, and archival photographs that stand silent witness to "Bloody Omaha." Nearby, in Vierville-sur-Mer, is the **U.S. National Guard Monument.** Throughout June 6, Allied forces battled a hailstorm of German bullets and bombs, but by the end of the day they had taken the Omaha Beach sector, although they had suffered grievous losses. In Colleville-sur-Mer, overlooking Omaha Beach, is the hilltop **American Cemetery and Memorial,** designed by landscape architect Markley Stevenson. You can look out to sea across the landing beach from a platform on the north side of the cemetery. ⊠ *Musée-Mémorial d'Omaha Beach, Les Moulins, Av. de la Libération, Saint-Laurent-sur-Mer* ☎ *02–31–21–97–44* ⊕ *www.musee-memorial-omaha.com* ✉ *€5.90* ⊙ *Daily Feb. 15–Mar. 15, 10–noon and 2:30–6; Mar. 16–May 15, 9:30–6:30; May 16–Sept. 15, 9:30–7; Sept. 16–Nov. 15, 9:30–6:30. Closed mid-Nov. to mid-Feb.*

## PARIS
A day trip to Paris of just a few hours can barely scratch the surface of what one of the world's greatest cities can offer, but that doesn't mean you won't find those few hours really worthwhile. Below are the highlights of the highlights.

**Arc de Triomphe.** Inspired by Rome's Arch of Titus, this colossal, 164-foot triumphal arch was ordered by Napoléon—who liked to consider himself the heir to the Roman emperors—to celebrate his military successes.

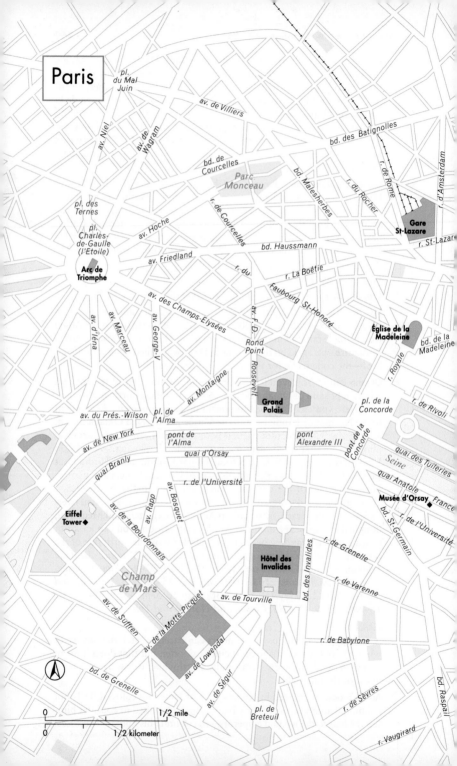

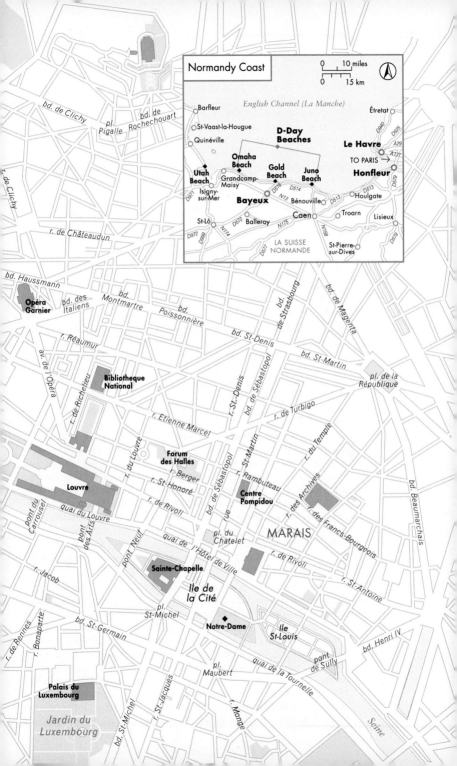

## Normandy Coast

| 0 | 10 miles |
| 0 | 15 km |

English Channel (La Manche)

Barfleur

St-Vaast-la-Hougue

Quinéville

**D-Day Beaches**

Étretat

D940 D925

**Le Havre**

A29 A131

**TO PARIS →**

**Omaha Beach**

**Utah Beach**

Grandcamp-Maisy

**Gold Beach**

**Juno Beach**

**Honfleur**

D579

D911

Isigny-sur-Mer

D518

D514

**Bayeux**

N13

Bénouville

D513

Houlgate

St-Lô

D572

Balleroy

N175

**Caen**

Troarn

Lisieux

D972

D6

N174

D679

N158

St-Pierre-sur-Dives

**LA SUISSE NORMANDE**

D511

---

Paris map (below inset):

bd. de Clichy

pl. Pigalle

bd. de Rochechouart

r. de Clichy

r. de Châteaudun

bd. Haussmann

**Opéra Garnier**

bd. des Italiens

bd. Montmartre

bd. Poissonnière

bd. St-Denis

bd. de Strasbourg

bd. de Magenta

r. Réaumur

av. de l'Opéra

r. de Richelieu

**Bibliothèque National**

r. Etienne Marcel

bd. St-Denis

bd. St-Martin

pl. de la République

r. du Louvre

**Forum des Halles**

r. Berger

bd. de Sébastopol

r. St-Martin

r. de Turbigo

r. du Temple

bd. Beaumarchais

**Louvre**

r. St-Honoré

r. de Rivoli

**Centre Pompidou**

r. Rambuteau

r. des Archives

r. des Francs-Bourgeois

quai du Louvre

pont du Carrousel

pont des Arts

pont Neuf

quai de l'Hôtel de Ville

pl. du Chatelet

**MARAIS**

r. de Rivoli

r. St-Antoine

r. Jacob

**Sainte-Chapelle**

**Ile de la Cité**

r. de Rennes

r. Bonaparte

bd. St-Germain

pl. St-Michel

**Notre-Dame**

**Ile St-Louis**

pont de Sully

bd. Henri IV

Seine

pl. Maubert

quai de la Tournelle

**Palais du Luxembourg**

r. St-Michel

bd. St-Michel

r. St-Jacques

r. Monge

*Jardin du Luxembourg*

Unfortunately, Napoléon's strategic and architectural visions were not entirely on the same plane, and the Arc de Triomphe proved something of an embarrassment: although the emperor wanted the monument completed in time for an 1810 parade in honor of his new bride, Marie-Louise, the arch was still only a few feet high, and a dummy arch of painted canvas was strung up to save face. Empires come and go, but Napoléon's had been gone for more than 20 years before the Arc de Triomphe was finally finished, in 1836. ⊠ *Pl. Charles-de-Gaulle, Champs-Élysées* ☎ *01–55–37–73–77* ⊕ *www.arc-de-triomphe.monuments-nationales.fr/* ⊠ *€9, free under 18* ☉ *Apr.–Sept., daily 10 am–11 pm; Oct.–Mar., daily 10 am–10:30 pm* Ⓜ *Métro or RER: Étoile.*

| LE HAVRE BEST BETS |
| --- |
| **Honfleur.** Wander the tangled knot of cobbled alleyways of the Old Town and enjoy an alfresco lunch in the picturesque harbor. |
| **D-Day Beaches.** The battles that took place on these beaches on June 6, 1944, were the turning point of WWII. |
| **Paris.** The city of romance, Paris is a must-see; it will be a quick tour, but you can see some highlights in a day. |

**Fodor's Choice**
★

**Hôtel des Invalides.** Les Invalides (pronounced *lehz-ahn-vah-leed*), as this baroque complex is known, is the eternal home of Napoléon Bonaparte (1769–1821), or more specifically, the little dictator's tomb, which lies under the towering golden dome. There are two churches here: St-Louis des Invalides Church, built between 1677 and 1706, later subdivided into the Église du Dome and the Église des Soldats (Soldiers' Church). Louis XIV ordered this complex built in 1670 to house-disabled soldiers, and at one time 4,000 military men lived here. Today, a portion of it remains a veterans' residence and hospital. There's also the Musée de l'Armée, an exhaustive collection of military artifacts from antique armor to weapons. The World Wars Department, also housed here, chronicles the great wars that ravaged Europe. ■ TIP➔ **The best entrance to use is at the southern end, on Place Vauban (Avenue de Tourville). The ticket office is here, as is Napoléon's Tomb. There are automatic ticket machines at the main entrance on the Place des Invalides.** ⊠ *Pl. des Invalides, Tour Eiffel* ☎ *01–44–42–38–77* ⊕ *www.invalides.org* ⊠ *€9* ☉ *Église du Dôme and museums Apr.–Sept., daily 10–6; Oct.–Mar., daily 10–5. Closed 1st Mon. of every month Oct–June* Ⓜ *La Tour-Maubourg/Invalides.*

**Fodor's Choice**
★

**The Louvre.** The most recognized symbol of Paris is the Tour Eiffel, but the ultimate traveler's prize is the Louvre. This is the world's greatest art museum—and the largest, with 675,000 square feet of works from almost every civilization on earth. The three most popular pieces of art here are, of course, the *Mona Lisa*, the *Venus de Milo*, and the *Winged Victory*. Beyond these must-sees, your best bet is to focus on whatever highlights interest you the most—and don't despair about getting lost, for you're bound to stumble on something interesting. Pick up an excellent color-coded map at the information desk. There are slick multimedia guides at the entrance to each wing; for €6 you get four self-guided tours and information about 250 works of art, plus a function to help you find your bearings. There are 90-minute guided tours (€9) in English daily at 11 and 2. Thematic leaflets (including some for kids) and Louvre guided tours are available from the front desk. The Louvre is much more than a museum—it is a saga that started centuries ago, as a fortress at the turn of the 13th century, and later a royal residence. It was not until the 16th century, under François I, that today's Louvre began to take shape, and through the years Henry IV, Louis XIII, Louis XV, Napoléon I, and Napoléon III all contributed to its construction. Napoléon Bonaparte's military campaigns at the turn of the 19th century brought a new influx of holdings, as his soldiers carried off treasures from each invaded country. During World War II the most precious artworks were hidden, while the remainder was looted. Most of the stolen pieces were recovered after the liberation of Paris. No large-scale changes were made until François Mitterrand was elected president in 1981, when he kicked off the Grand Louvre project to expand and modernize the museum. ⊠ *Palais du Louvre, Louvre/Tuileries* ☎ *01–40–20–53–17 information* ⊕ *www.louvre.fr* ☑ *€10 (€10.50 projected); €11 for Napoléon Hall exhibitions; ticket allows same-day entry to Musée Eugène Delacroix; free 1st Sun. of month* ⊙ *Mon., Thurs., and weekends 9–6, Wed. and Fri. 9–9:30* Ⓜ *Palais-Royal–Musée du Louvre.*

Fodor's Choice ★ **Musée d'Orsay.** Opened in 1986, this gorgeous renovated Belle Époque train station has a world-famous collection of impressionist and post-impressionist paintings. There are three floors; to visit the exhibits in a roughly chronologic manner, start on the first floor, take the escalators to the top, and end on the second. If you came to see the biggest names on display here, head straight for the top floor and work your way down. Renovations are expected to be completed in 2015, so expect some gallery closings. Galleries off the main alley feature early works by Manet and Cézanne in addition to pieces by masters like Delacroix and Ingres. Impressionism gets going on the top floor, with iconic works by Degas, Pissarro, Sisley, and Renoir. Don't miss Monet's series on the cathedral at Rouen and, of course, samples of his waterlilies. The d'Orsay is closed Monday, unlike the Pompidou and the Louvre, which are closed on Tuesday. English audioguides are available just past the ticket booths; pick up a free color-coded map of the museum here, too. ⊠ *1 rue de la Légion d'Honneur, St-Germain-des-Prés* ☎ *01–40–49–48–14* ⊕ *www.musee-orsay.fr* ☑ *€9.50 (€8 without special exhibit); €7 (€5 without special exhibit) after 4:15 except Thurs. after 6* ⊙ *Tues.–Sun. 9:30–6, Thurs. 9:30 am–9:45 pm* Ⓜ *Solférino; RER: Musée d'Orsay.*

Fodor's Choice ★ **Notre-Dame.** Looming above Place du Parvis on the Ile de la Cité is the Cathédrale de Notre-Dame, the most enduring symbol of Paris. Begun in 1163, completed in 1345, badly damaged during the Revolution, and restored by the architect Eugène Viollet-le-Duc in the 19th century, Notre-Dame may not be France's oldest or largest cathedral, but in beauty and architectural harmony it has few peers—as you can see by studying the facade from the square in front. The most dramatic approach to Notre-Dame is from the Rive Gauche, crossing at the Pont au Double from Quai de Montebello, at the St-Michel métro or RER stop. This bridge will take you to the large square, Place du Parvis, in front of the cathedral. This area is *kilomètre zéro*, the spot from which all distances to and from the city are officially measured. A polished brass circle set in the ground, about 20 yards from the cathedral's main entrance, marks the exact spot.

A separate entrance, to the left of the front facade if you're facing it, leads to the 387 stone steps of the south tower. These steps take you to the bell of Notre-Dame—as tolled by the fictional Quasimodo, in Victor Hugo's 1831 *Notre-Dame de Paris*. ∎TIP→ There are free guided tours in English on Wednesday and Thursday at 2 and Saturday at 2:30. Down the stairs in front of the cathedral is the **Crypte Archéologique**, Notre-Dame's archaeological museum. ⊠ *Pl. du Parvis* ☎ *01–42–34–56–10* ⊕ *www.notredamedeparis.fr* ⊠ *Cathedral free, towers €8,crypt €4, treasury €3* ⊙ *Cathedral daily 7:45–6:45. Towers Apr.–June and Sept., daily 10 am–6:30; July and Aug., weekdays 10–6:30, weekends 10 am–11 pm; Oct.–Mar., daily 10–5:30. Note towers close early when overcrowded. Treasury weekdays 9:30–6 pm, Sat. 9:30–6:30, Sun. 1:30–6:30. Crypt Tues.–Sun. 10–6* Ⓜ *Cité.*

Fodor'sChoice ★ **Sainte-Chapelle.** Built by the obsessively pious Louis IX (1226–70), this Gothic jewel is home to the oldest stained-glass windows in Paris. The chapel was constructed over three years, at phenomenal expense, to house the king's collection of relics acquired from the impoverished emperor of Constantinople. These included Christ's Crown of Thorns, fragments of the Cross, and drops of Christ's blood—though even in Louis's time these were considered of questionable authenticity. Some of the relics have survived and can be seen in the treasury of Notre-Dame, but most were lost during the Revolution.

The upper chapel is where the famed beauty of Sainte-Chapelle comes alive: 6,458 square feet of stained glass is delicately supported by painted stonework that seems to disappear in the colorful light streaming through the windows. The lowest section of the windows was restored in the mid-1800s, and a painstaking five-year renovation should be completed by 2013. The lower chapel is a bit gloomy and plain, but notice the low, vaulted ceiling decorated with fleurs-de-lis and cleverly arranged *L*s for Louis. The dark spiral staircase near the entrance takes you upstairs. Come on a sunny day to appreciate the full effect of the light streaming in through all that beautiful stained glass. Free, guided tours in English are offered most days at 2:30. Call ahead to confirm. ⊠ *4 bd. du Palais* ☎ *01–53–40–60–97* ⊕ *www.sainte-chapelle.monuments-nationaux.fr* ⊠ *€8, joint ticket with Conciergerie €11* ⊙ *Mar.–Oct., daily 9:30–6; Nov.–Feb., daily 9–5* Ⓜ *Cité.*

Fodor'sChoice ★ **Eiffel Tower.** If the Statue of Liberty is emblematic of New York, Big Ben is London, and the Kremlin is Moscow, then the Eiffel Tower is the symbol of Paris. French engineer Gustave Eiffel—already famous for building viaducts and bridges—spent two years working to erect this monument, for the World Exhibition of 1889. You can stride up the stairs as far as the third floor, but if you want to go to the top you'll have to take the elevator. (Be sure to take a close look at the fantastic ironwork.) The view of the flat sweep of Paris at 1,000 feet may not beat the one from the Tour Montparnasse skyscraper, but the setting makes it considerably more romantic, especially if you come in the late evening, after the crowds have dispersed. ■ TIP→ **Beat the crushing lines by reserving your ticket online. You can also book a guided tour.** ⊠ *Quai Branly, Trocadéro/Tour Eiffel* ☎ *01–44–11–23–23* ⊕ *www.tour-eiffel. fr* ⊠ *By elevator: 1st and 2nd levels €8.20, top €13.40. By stairs: 1st and 2nd levels only, €4.50.* ⊘ *June–late Aug., daily 9 am–12:45 am (11:30 pm for summit); late Aug.–June, daily 9:30 am–11 pm. Stairs close at 6 pm in winter* Ⓜ *Bir-Hakeim, Trocadéro, École Militaire; RER: Champ de Mars.*

## SHOPPING

The French practically created ready-to-wear fashion—think Cartier, Chanel, and Lacroix. The French love quality and style—and are willing to pay for it—so prices aren't cheap. The vast department stores **Galeries Lafayette** and **Printemps** on Boulevard Haussmann stock a vast range of clothing. The districts on the Left Bank and the Marais offer excellent boutiques selling one-of-a-kind accessories for the body and the home.

Normandy specialties include heavy cotton sailor's smocks, blue-and-white-stripe T-shirts, and chunky knits; popular choices in this traditional seafaring region. Calvados (distilled apple liqueur) is unique to the area, but other foodstuffs (pure butter and creamy cheeses) aren't really suitable to take home.

Honfleur has a huge choice of art galleries, craft shops, and boutiques with one-of-a-kind items.

## WHERE TO EAT

$   ✕ **La Ferme Opéra.** If your arm aches from flagging down café waiters,
CAFÉ   take a break at this bright, friendly, self-service spot near the Louvre
Ↄ   that specializes in produce from the Ile-de-France region (around Paris). Inventive salads, sandwiches, and pastas are fresh and delicious, and for sweets there are wholesome fruit crumbles, tarts, and cheesecakes. Scones and freshly squeezed juices are served for breakfast every day, and there is brunch on Sunday from 11 am to 4 pm. There's free Wi-Fi in the spacious, barnlike dining room. $ *Average main: €8* ⊠ *55 rue St-Roch, 1er, Opéra/Grands Boulevards* ☎ *01–40–20–12–12* ⊕ *www. restolaferme.com* ⊘ *Open 7 days a week* Ⓜ *Pyramides.*

$$   ✕ **Le Fleur de Sel.** A low-beamed 16th-century fisherman's house provides
MODERN FRENCH   the cozy atmosphere for chef Vincent's Guyon's locally influenced cui-
★   sine, centered on the daily catch. The ambitious menu usually includes at least five different fish dishes—presented with artistic panache— along with plenty of grilled meats, like salt-marsh lamb or pigeon. For starters, the oyster ravioli with a butternut mousse and chestnut foam, draws raves; it might be followed by a delicately crusted salmon with leeks in an almond vinaigrette and fromage blanc. Three fixed-price menus ($$$–$$$$) assure a splendid meal on any budget. Be sure to save room for one of the masterful desserts or an informed cheese course. $ *Average main: €20* ⊠ *17 rue Haute, Honfleur* ☎ *02–31–89– 01–92* ⊕ *www.lafleurdesel-honfleur.com* ⊘ *Closed Tues., Wed., and Jan.*

# LEIXÕES, PORTUGAL (FOR PORTO)

Updated by
Joanna Styles

Lining the river that made it a trading center ever since pre-Roman times, vibrant and cosmopolitan Porto centers itself some 5 km (3 miles) inland from the Atlantic Ocean. The Moors never had the same strong foothold here that they did farther south, nor was the city substantially affected by the great earthquake of 1755; as a result, Porto's architecture shows off a baroque finery little seen in the south of Portugal. Its grandiose granite buildings were financed by the trade that made the city wealthy: wine from the upper valley of the Rio Douro (Douro River, or River of Gold) was transported to Porto, from where it was then exported around the world. Industrious Porto considers itself the north's capital and, more contentiously, the country's economic center. In the shopping centers, the stately stock exchange building, and the affluent port-wine industry, Porto oozes confidence, though the fashionable commercial heart of the city contrasts with the gritty workaday atmosphere in the Old Town.

## ESSENTIALS

### CURRENCY
The euro.

### HOURS
Most shops are open weekdays 9–1 and 3–7 and Saturday 9–1; malls and supermarkets often remain open until at least 10. Some are also open on Sunday. Note that most museums are closed Monday, and that churches generally close for a couple of hours in the middle of the day.

### PRIVATE TOURS
Diana Tours offers guided tours around Porto and day trips into the surrounding countryside and to famous cities such as Coimbra and Braga.

**Contacts Diana Tours.** ☎ *217/998540* ⊕ *www.dianatours.pt.*

### TELEPHONES
Most quad- or tri-band GSM phones work in Portugal, which has a well-organized 3G compatible mobile network. You can buy prepaid phone cards at telecom shops, news vendors and tobacconists in all towns and cities. Phone cards can be used for local or international calls. Major companies include Vodafone and Optimus.

## COMING ASHORE
Vessels dock at the quays of Leixões port, just north of the mouth of the River Douro. It's a two-minute walk or a short shuttle trip to the passenger terminal (depending on the exact quay), which has few facilities, but the restaurants and shops of Leixões town are within walking distance. Taxis wait at the port entrance.

From the port it is another 10-minute walk to the Matosinhos district, where the state-of-the-art metro will transfer you to central Porto in 30 minutes. Single tickets cost between €1.15 and €3.95. The single ticket from the port to downtown is €1.45. A 24-hour card is €13.10 for all zones. From the port to downtown the 24-hour ticket price is €3.80 (but this only entitles you to journey within three zones). Bus 76, which has a stop just outside the port, will also take you into Porto, but the journey time is longer.

If you intend to explore Porto on your day in port, the best option by far is to take the metro into the city. For exploration of the vineyards of the Douro River, a vehicle would be useful. Prices begin at approximately €35 per day for a manual economy car, but they can be very expensive during the high season.

## EXPLORING PORTO

**Avenida dos Aliados.** This imposing boulevard is lined with bright flower beds and grand buildings and is essentially the heart of the central business district. In addition to corporate businesses and banks, you'll find clothing and shoe stores, plus restaurants and coffeehouses. At one end of it is the broad Câmara Municipal (town hall). A tall bell tower sprouts from the roof of this palacelike, early-20th-century building; inside is displayed an impressive Portuguese wall tapestry. Praça da Liberdade—the hub from which Porto radiates—is at the other end of the avenue. Two statues adorn the square: a cast of Dom Pedro IV sitting on a horse and a modern statue of the great 19th-century Portuguese poet and novelist Almeida Garrett.

**Fodor's Choice**
★
**Cais da Ribeira** *(Ribeira Pier).* A string of fish restaurants and *tascas* (taverns) are built into the street-level arcade of timeworn buildings along this pier. In the Praça da Ribeira, people sit and chat around an odd, modern, cubelike sculpture; farther on, steps lead to a walkway above the river that's backed by tall houses. The pier also provides the easiest access to the lower level of the middle bridge across the Douro, the Ponte Dom Luis I. Boats docked at Cais da Ribeira and across the river in Vila Nova da Gaia offer various cruises around the bridges and up the river to Peso da Régua and Pinhão.

**Casa-Museu de Guerra Junqueiro** *(Guerra Junqueiro House and Museum).* This 18th-century white mansion, one of several buildings in Porto attributed by some to a pupil of Nicolau Nasoni and by others to Nicolau himself, was home to the poet Guerra Junqueiro (1850–1923). It's in the picturesque if shabby-in-parts Sé neighborhood, below the cathedral. Although furnishings, sculptures, and paintings are labeled in Portuguese, English, and French (and there are brochures in English), the short, guided tour of the elegant interior is less than enlightening if you don't speak Portuguese. ⊠ *Rua de Dom Hugo 32* ☎ *22/200–3689* 📧 *Tues.–Fri. €2.10, free weekends* ☉ *Tues.–Sat. 10–12:30 and 2–5:30, Sun. 2–5:30.*

**Fodor's Choice**
★
**Estação de São Bento.** This train station was built in the early 20th century (King D. Carlos I laid the first brick himself in 1900) and inaugurated in 1915. It sits precisely where the Convent of S. Bento de Avé-Maria was located, and therefore inherited the convent's name—Saint Bento. The atrium is covered with 20,000 azulejos painted by Jorge Colaço (1916) depicting scenes of Portugal's history as well as ethnographic images. It is one of the most magnificent artistic undertakings of the early 20th century. The building was designed by architect Marques da Silva. ⊠ *Praça Almeida Garret* ☎ *22/205–1714, 808/208208 national call center* ⊕ *www.cp.pt.*

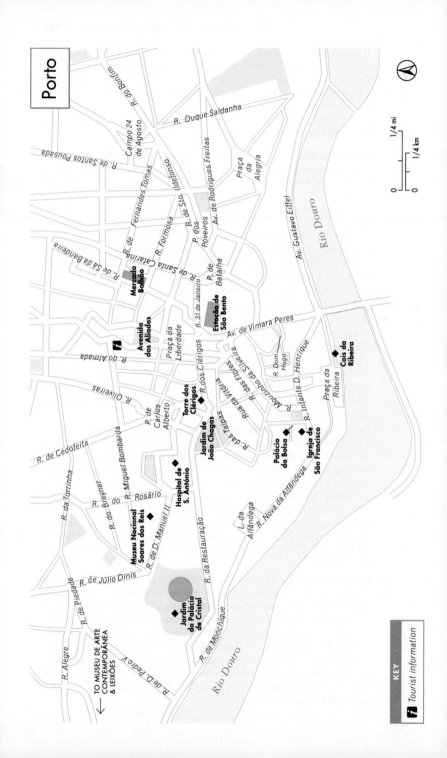

# Porto

**Mercado Bolhão**

**Avenida dos Aliados**

**Estação de São Bento**

R. do Bolhão

R. Duque Saldanha

Campo 24 de Agosto

R. de Santos Pousada

R. de Fernandes Tomas

R. de Sto. Ildefonso

Praça da Alegria

Av. de Rodrigues Freitas

R. de Sá da Bandeira

R. Formosa

R. de Santa Catarina

P. dos Poveiros

P. de Batalha

R. 31 de Janeiro

Av. de Vimara Peres

R. do Almada

Praça da Liberdade

R. Oliveiras

**Torre dos Clérigos**

R. dos Clérigos

**Jardim de João Chagas**

P. de Carlos Alberto

R. de Cedofeita

R. de Miguel Bombarda

R. do Rosário

R. do Breyner

R. da Torrinha

**Museu Nacional Soares dos Reis**

R. de D. Manuel II

**Hospital de S. António**

R. da Restauração

R. de Júlio Dinis

R. de Piedade

R. Alegre

**Jardim do Palácio de Cristal**

TO MUSEU DE ARTE CONTEMPORÂNEA & LEIXÕES

Av. de D. Pedro V

R. de Monchique

Rio Douro

R. das Taipas

R. de Belomonte

Rua das Flores

R. Mouzinho da Silveira

R. Dom Hugo

R. Infante D. Henrique

Av. Gustavo Eiffel

Rio Douro

Praça da Ribeira

**Cais da Ribeira**

**Palácio da Bolsa**

**Igreja de São Francisco**

L. da Alfândega

R. Nova da Alfândega

Rio Douro

0   1/4 mi

0   1/4 km

**KEY**

🛈 Tourist information

**Igreja da Misericórdia** *(Mercy Church).* Today's building represents a compromise between the church first built during the late 16th century and its reconstruction between 1749 and 1755 by painter and architect Nicolau Nasoni. At the church museum next door you can see *Fons Vitae* (Fountain of Life), a vibrant, anonymous, Renaissance painting depicting the founder of the church, Dom Manuel I, his queen, and their eight children kneeling before a crucified Christ. ⊠ *Rua das Flores 5* 🕾 *22/207–4710* ✆ *Church free, museum €1.50* ☉ *Church Tues.– Fri. 8–12:30 and 2–5:30, museum weekdays 9–12:30 and 2–5:30.*

> ### PORTO BEST BETS
>
> **Sip some port.** You can try the country's famous after-dinner wine in the tasting rooms of port producers at Vila Nova de Gaia.
>
> **Climb the Torre dos Clérigos.** The panoramic views across the city are well worth the trip to the top.
>
> **Be dazzled by gold.** The exterior is undistinguished, but acres of gold leaf decorate the interior of Igreja de São Francisco.

**Igreja de São Francisco** *(Church of St. Francis).* During the last days of Porto's siege by the absolutist army (the *miguelistas*) in July 1842, there was gunfire by the nearby São Francisco Convent. These shootings caused a fire that destroyed most parts of the convent, sparing only this church. The church is an undistinguished, late 14th-century Gothic building on the outside, but inside is an astounding interior: gilded carving—added in the mid-18th century—runs up the pillars, over the altar, and across the ceiling. An adjacent museum (Museu de Arte Sacra) houses furnishings from the Franciscan convent. A guided tour (call the day before) includes a visit to the church, museum, and catacombs. Note that the riverside tram ride to Foz starts here. ⊠ *Rua do Infante Dom Henrique 93* 🕾 *22/206–2100* ✆ *€3.50* ☉ *Nov.–Feb., daily 9–5:30; Mar., Apr., and Oct., daily 9–6; May–Sept., daily 9–7.*

**Fodor's Choice**
★ **Museu de Arte Contemporânea.** Designed by Álvaro Siza Vieira, a winner of the Pritzker Prize and Portugal's best-known architect, the Contemporary Art Museum is part of the Serralves Foundation and is surrounded by lovely gardens. It has changing international exhibitions, as well as work from Portuguese painters, sculptors, and designers. Check with the tourist office for the latest information. The original art deco house and its small formal garden is also worth visiting; as well as housing the foundation, it hosts small exhibitions. Various joint tickets are available, including one to the museum and to the Sea Life aquarium in Foz. To get here, take a taxi or catch the metro to Casa da Música and then Bus 201, 203, 502, or 504 from the Rotunda da Boavista; or from downtown take Bus 201 from Avenida dos Aliados—about a 30-minute ride. ⊠ *Rua D. João de Castro 210* 🕾 *22/615–6500 or 808/200–543* ⊕ *www.serralves.pt* ✆ *Museum and garden Tues.–Sat. €7, garden €3; Sun. free to 1 pm* ☉ *Oct.–Mar. museum and house Tues.–Fri. 10–5, weekends 10–8; park Tues.–Sun. 10–7. Apr.–Sept. museum Tues.–Fri. 10–5, weekends 10–8; house Tues.–Fri. 10-5, weekends 10–7; park Tues.–Fri. 10–7, weekends 10–8.*

★ **Museu Nacional Soares dos Reis.** This art museum was the first in Portugal, founded in 1833 by King D. Pedro IV. In 1911 it was renamed after the 19th-century Portuguese sculptor whose works are contained within it. In 1940 it moved to this late-19th-century home, the Palácio dos Carrancas, which was once home to the royal family. The large art collection includes several Portuguese primitive works of the 16th century as well as superb collections of silver, ceramics, glassware, and costumes. ⊠ *Palácio dos Carrancas, Rua de Dom Manuel II* ☎ *22/339–3770* ⊕ *www.ipmuseus.pt* ☜ *Tues.–Sat. €5, free Sun.* ☉ *Tues. 2–6, Wed.–Sun. 10–6.*

**Palácio da Bolsa.** Porto's neoclassical former stock exchange takes up much of the site of the former Franciscan convent at the Igreja de São Francisco. Guided tours (every half hour) are the only way to see the interior of this masterpiece of 19th-century Portuguese architecture. The Arab-style ballroom, in particular, is one of the most admired chambers and was designed by civil engineer Gustavo Adolfo Gonçalves e Sousa. ⊠ *Rua Ferreira Borges* ☎ *22/339–9013* ⊕ *www.palaciodabolsa.pt* ☜ *Tours €6* ☉ *Apr.–Sept., daily 9–6:30; Oct.–Mar., daily 9–12:30 and 2–5:30.*

**Ponte Dom Luís I** *(Luís I Bridge).* Though it was intended to replace the Pênsil Bridge (also called Dona Maria Pia), this two-tier bridge was completed in 1886 at another site. Designed by Teófilo Seyrig with two tiers for both vehicles and pedestrians, it leads directly to the city of Vila Nova de Gaia. Its real glory, however, is the magnificent vistas it affords of downtown Porto. A jumble of red-tile roofs on pastel-color buildings mixes with gray-and-white Gothic and baroque church towers, and all is reflected in the majestic Douro River; if the sun is shining just right, everything appears to be washed in gold. Beside the foot of the bridge on the Porto riverbank is the lower station of the Funicular dos Guindais, the quaintest part of the city's public transportation system, which cranks uphill to the Batalha neighborhood, just to the east of the cathedral.

**Sé do Porto** *(Cathedral).* Originally constructed in the 12th century by the parents of Dom Afonso Henriques (Portugal's first king), Porto's granite cathedral has been rebuilt twice: first in the late 13th century and again in the 18th century, when the architect of the Torre dos Clérigos, Nicolau Nasoni, was among those commissioned to work on its expansion. Despite the renovations, it remains a fortresslike structure—an uncompromising testament to medieval wealth and power. Notice a low relief on the northern tower, depicting a 14th-century vessel and symbolizing the city's nautical vocation. Size is the only exceptional thing about the interior; when you enter the two-story, 14th-century cloisters, however, the building comes to life. Decorated with gleaming azulejos, a staircase added by Nasoni leads to the second level and into a richly furnished chapter house, from which there are fine views through narrow windows. Nasoni also designed the Paço dos Arcebispos (Archbishops' Palace) behind the cathedral. It has been converted to offices, so you can only admire its 197-foot-long facade. ⊠ *Terreiro da Sé* ☎ *22/205–9028* ☜ *Cathedral free; cloisters €3* ☉ *Cathedral Nov.–Mar., Mon.–Sat. 8:45–12:30 and 2:30–6, Sun. 8:30–12:30 and 2:30–6; Apr.–Oct., Mon.–Sat.*

*8:45–12:30 and 2:30–7, Sun. 8:30–12:30 and 2:30–7. Cloisters Nov.–Mar., Mon.–Sat. 9–12:15 and 2:30–5:30, Sun. 2:30–5:30; Apr.–Oct., Mon.–Sat. 9–12:15 and 2:30-6:30, Sun. 2:30–6:30.*

**Solar do Vinho do Porto** *(Port Wine Institute).* On the ground floor of a 19th-century manor house called the Quinta da Macierinha, the institute offers relaxed tastings of Porto's famous wine in much the same fashion as its counterpart in Lisbon—but the wine has only had to travel across the river before being served. As well as 120 ports by the glass (and more by the bottle) table wines from the Douro are on sale, accompanied if you like by fine cheeses and hams. You can also buy crystal glasses and glossy books on local vineyards. There are lovely views of the river from the small formal garden, where chairs are often set out. The Quinta da Macierinha is also home to the **Museu Romântico da Quinta da Macierinha** (Romantic Museum), with displays of period furniture. Don't miss the leafy Palácio de Cristal gardens just uphill, which afford even more stunning river views. ✉ *Quinta da Macierinha, Rua de Entre Quintas 220* ☎ *22/609–4749 Port Wine Institute, 22/605–7000 museum* ⊕ *www.ivp.pt Port Wine Institute* ✉ *dmpc@cm-porto.pt Museum* 💳 *Port Wine Institute free. Museum €2.10 Tues.–Fri., free weekends* ⊙ *Port Wine Institute Mon.–Sat. 4–midnight; museum Tues.–Sun. 10–12:30 and 2–5:30.*

**Torre dos Clérigos.** Designed by Italian architect Nicolau Nasoni and begun in 1754, the tower of the church Igreja dos Clérigos reaches an impressive height of 249 feet. There are 225 steep stone steps to the belfry, and the considerable effort required to climb them is rewarded by stunning views of the Old Town, the river, and beyond to the mouth of the Douro. The church itself, also built by Nasoni, predates the tower and is an elaborate example of Italianate baroque architecture. ✉ *Rua S. Filipe Nery* ☎ *22/200–1729* 💳 *Tower €1.50, church free* ⊙ *Tower Sept.–May, daily 10–noon and 2–5; June and July, daily 9:30–1 and 2:30–7; Aug., daily 10–7. Church 8:45–12:30 and 3:30–7.*

⟳ **Vila Nova de Gaia.** A city across the Rio Douro from central Porto, Vila Nova de Gaia has been the headquarters of the port-wine trade since the late 17th century, when import bans on French wine led British merchants to look for alternative sources. By the 18th century, the British had established companies and a regulatory association in Porto. The wine was transported from vineyards on the upper Douro to port-wine caves at Vila Nova de Gaia, where it was allowed to mature before being exported. Little has changed in the relationship between Porto and the Douro since those days, as wine is still transported to the city, matured in the warehouses, and bottled. Instead of traveling down the river on *barcos rabelos* (flat-bottom boats), however, the wine is now carried by truck. A couple of the traditional boats are moored at the quayside on the Vila Nova de Gaia side.

## SHOPPING

The Portuguese specialize in a range of handicrafts collectively known as *artesanato*. The term includes bright *azulejos* (blue-and-white-glaze tiles), pottery and ceramics, colorful textiles, olive wood, cork items, and basketwork. Gold and plated filigree is also a regional specialty, and the shoe trade is well established. You'll see port on sale throughout the city. But first taste the wine at either the Solar do Vinho do Porto or the caves at Vila Nova de Gaia. You may want to buy a bottle of the more unusual white port, drunk as an aperitif, as it's not commonly sold in North America.

The best shopping streets are those off the Praça da Liberdade, particularly Rua 31 de Janeiro, Rua dos Clérigos, Rua de Santa Catarina, Rua Sá da Bandeira, Rua Cedofeita, and Rua das Flores. Traditionally, Rua das Flores has been the street for silversmiths found along the same street and along Rua de Santa Catarina. On Rua 31 de Janeiro you'll find goldsmiths working.

Fodor's Choice ★ **Livraria Lello e Irmão,** This is one of the most special and important bookshops in Portugal. It opened in 1906, and shelters more than 60,000 books. But it's most famous for its neo-Gothic design and two-story interior with intricate wood-carved details—locals maintain that all this helped inspire J.K. Rowling, who dreamed up Harry Potter while living in Porto. ⊠ *Rua das Carmelitas 144* ☎ *22/200–2880.*

**Via Catarina Shopping.** Unlike most, this mall is in an old restored building. The top floor is occupied by little restaurants that re-create the Ribeira's architecture with small, medieval-style houses. ⊠ *Rua de Santa Catarina 312–350* ☎ *22/207–5600* ⊕ *www.viacatarina.pt.*

## WHERE TO EAT

$ PORTUGUESE Fodor's Choice ★ ✕ **Abadia do Porto.** The cavernous interior, thick tablecloths, and well-heeled clientele tell you this is not just another *tasca*, but the food at this backstreet abbey downtown is ultratraditional. Although the decor has a monastic theme, meals here are far from austere, so come hungry to make the most of the huge servings of *cabrito assado* (roast kid), *rancho* (mixed grill), *bacalhau à Gomes Sá* (codfish with onions, potato, egg, and olives) and Porto *tripas*—tripe with beans, chouriço, and vegetables. It's all great value if you share a dish between two or even three people. The chocolate-flavor *paõ-de-ló* spongecake is divine, too. ⊠ *Rua Ateneu Comercial do Porto 22–24* ☎ *22/200–8757* ⊕ *www. abadiadoporto.com* ☾ *Closed Sun.*

$ PORTUGUESE ✕ **Chez Lapin.** At this Cais da Ribeira restaurant overlooking the river, the service may be slow and the folksy decor may be overdone, but the food is excellent. Grab a table on the attractive outdoor terrace and order generous portions of such traditional Portuguese dishes as bacalhau *à lagareiro* (baked salt cod with potatoes), sardines with rice and beans, and beef medallions with port wine. The restaurant is mainly patronized by foreign visitors, so if you're after authentic Porto cuisine in a less touristy setting, look elsewhere. The family-owned company that owns the restaurant (Douro Acima) offers river excursions on its six traditional boats docked at the quay. ⊠ *Rua dos Canastreiros 40–42* ☎ *22/200–6418* ⊕ *www.issimo.pt* ⚑ *Reservations essential.*

# LISBON, PORTUGAL

Updated by
Joanna Styles

Lisbon bears the mark of an incredible heritage with laid-back pride. Spread over a string of seven hills north of the Rio Tejo (Tagus River) estuary, the city also presents an intriguing variety of faces to those who negotiate its switchback streets. In the oldest neighborhoods stepped alleys are lined with pastel-color houses and crossed by laundry hung out to dry; here and there *miradouros* (vantage points) afford spectacular river or city views. In the grand 18th-century center, black-and-white mosaic cobblestone sidewalks border wide boulevards. *Elétricos* (trams) clank through the streets, and blue-and-white azulejos (painted and glazed ceramic tiles) adorn churches, restaurants, and fountains. Some modernization has improved the city. To prepare for its role as host of the World Exposition in 1998, Lisbon spruced up its public buildings, overhauled its metro system, and completed an impressive bridge across the Rio Tejo, but Lisbon's intrinsic, slightly disorganized, one-of-a-kind charm hasn't vanished in the contemporary mix.

## ESSENTIALS

### CURRENCY

The euro.

### HOURS

Most shops are open weekdays 9–1 and 3–7 and Saturday 9–1; malls and supermarkets often remain open until at least 10. Some are also open on Sunday. Note that most museums are closed Monday, and that churches generally close for a couple of hours in the middle of the day.

### PRIVATE TOURS

Inside Lisbon offers guided walking tours around the city as well as daytrips to some of the most famous sights further afield.

Contacts **Inside Lisbon.** ☎ *968/412612* ⊕ *www.insidelisbon.com.*

### TELEPHONES

You can use most tri- and quad-band GSM phones in Portugal, which has a well-organized 3G-compatible mobile network. You can buy prepaid phone cards at telecom shops, news vendors, and tobacconists in all towns and cities. Phone cards can be used for local or international calls. Major companies include Vodafone and Optimus.

### COMING ASHORE

Facilities for cruise ships in Lisbon are undergoing major expansion at this writing with construction of the Lisbon Cruise Terminal (LCT) adjacent to the Santa Apolinia quay. The LCT will include a new quay, Jardim do Tabaco, able to berth larger ships and expected to be operational in 2013. Meanwhile, vessels dock at one of three quays along the River Tagus in a port area rebuilt for Expo '98 (the 1998 World's Fair). The main cruise port is the Cais de Alcântara, which has a terminal with shops, taxi ranks, and restrooms. Cais da Rocha Conde d'Óbidos also has a terminal with the same facilities. From both these terminals there are public transit routes into the city by bus (Buses 712, 728, 732, 760) or tram (Tram 15E, 18E). A suburban train also runs alongside the cruise terminal, and the Alcântara Mar station is the place to get on; the trip to Lisbon's main railway station takes about 10 minutes.

Fares for all these options are €1.75 per journey (bus) and €2.85 (tram). The walk into town from the cruise port takes around an hour, but is not unpleasant if you have the time. A one-day travel card for bus and metro costs €5.

Some small and midsize ships call at a smaller terminal in Santa Apolónia, which is closer to the center of the city and from where it's possible to walk to Alfalma and central Lisbon.

There are many companies running tours of the city. Don't rent a car if you are staying in Lisbon, where navigation and parking are almost impossible, but if you want to explore the countryside, you'll need one. An economy manual vehicle is about €40 per day.

**AIRPORT TRANSFERS**

Lisbon Airport Transfers offers airport to port transfers from €36 per person.

**Contacts Lisbon Airport Transfers.** ☎ *916/053420* ⊕ *www.lisbon-airport-transfer.com.*

## EXPLORING LISBON

The center of Lisbon stretches north from the spacious Praça do Comércio—one of Europe's largest riverside squares—to the Rossío, a smaller square lined with shops and cafés. The district in between is known as the Baixa (lower town), an attractive grid of parallel streets built after the 1755 earthquake and tidal wave. The Alfama, the old Moorish quarter that survived the earthquake, lies east of the Baixa. In this part of town are the Sé (the city's cathedral) and, on the hill above, the Castelo de São Jorge (St. George's Castle).

West of the Baixa, sprawled across another of Lisbon's hills, is the Bairro Alto (Upper Town), an area of intricate 17th-century streets, peeling houses, and churches. Five kilometers (3 miles) farther west is Belém. A similar distance to the northeast is Lisbon's postmodernist Parque das Nações.

The modern city begins at Praça dos Restauradores, adjacent to the Rossío. From here the main Avenida da Liberdade stretches northwest to the landmark Praça Marquês de Pombal, dominated by a column and a towering statue of the man himself. The praça is bordered by the green expanse of the Parque Eduardo VII, named in honor of King Edward VII of Great Britain, who visited Lisbon in 1902.

**Igreja e Museu de São Roque.** Filippo Terzi, the architect who designed São Vicente on the outskirts of the Alfama, was also responsible for this Renaissance church. He was commissioned by Jesuits and completed the church in 1574. Curb your impatience with its plain facade and venture inside. Its eight-sides chapels have statuary and art dating from the early 17th century. The last chapel on the left before the altar is the extraordinary 18th-century Capela de São João Baptista (Chapel of St. John the Baptist): designed and built in Rome, with rare stones and mosaics that resemble oil paintings, the chapel was taken apart, shipped to Lisbon, and reassembled here in 1747. Adjoining the church, the Museu de São Roque displays a surprisingly engaging collection of clerical

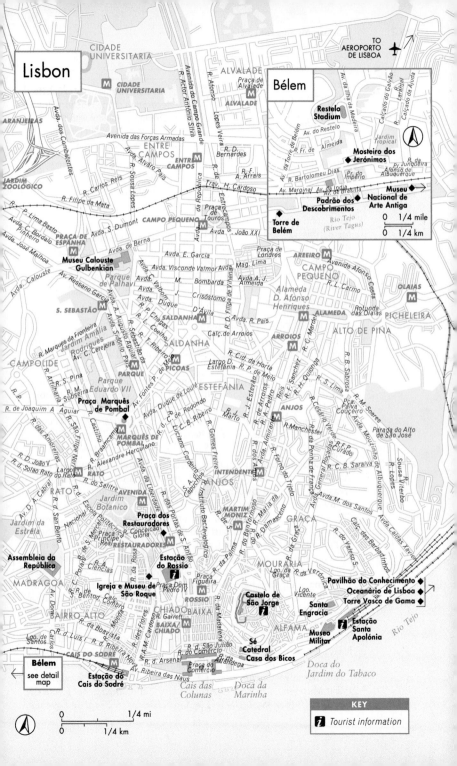

vestments and liturgical objects. ✉ *Largo Trindade Coelho, Bairro Alto* ☎ *21/323–5421* ⊕ *www. museudesaoroque.com* ✉ *Church free; museum €2.50 Mon.–Sat., free Sun.* ◔ *Church Mon. 2–6 pm, Tues., Wed., Fri.– Sun. 9–6, Thurs. 9–9; museum Fri.–Wed. 10–6, Thurs. 2–9* Ⓜ *Baixa-Chiado or Restauradores (then Elevador da Glória).*

**Fodor's Choice** ★ **Mosteiro dos Jerónimos.** Conceived and commissioned by Dom Manuel I, who petitioned the Holy See for permission to build it in 1496, Belém's famous Jerónimos Monastery was financed largely by treasures brought back from Africa, Asia, and South America. Construction began in 1502 under the supervision of Diogo de Boitaca. This UNESCO World Heritage site is a supreme example of the Manueline style of building (named after King Dom Manuel I), which represented a marked departure from the prevailing Gothic. Inside, the spacious interior contrasts with the riot of decoration on the six nave columns and complex latticework ceiling. This is the resting place of both explorer Vasco de Gama and national poet Luís de Camões. ✉ *Praça do Império, Belém* ☎ *21/362–0034* ⊕ *www.mosteirojeronimos.pt* ✉ *Church free, cloister €7, €10 combination ticket includes Torre de Belém, €13 includes Torre and Palacio de Ajuda* ◔ *May–Sept., Tues.–Sun. 10–6; Oct.–Apr., Tues.–Sun. 10–5.*

**Fodor's Choice** ★ **Museu Calouste Gulbenkian.** On its own lush grounds, the museum of the celebrated Calouste Gulbenkian Foundation, a cultural trust, houses treasures collected by Armenian oil magnate Calouste Gulbenkian (1869–1955) and donated to Portugal in return for tax concessions. The collection is split in two: one part is devoted to Egyptian, Greek, Roman, Islamic, and Asian art and the other to European acquisitions. Both holdings are relatively small, but the quality of the pieces is magnificent, and you should aim to spend at least two hours here. In the gardens outside the Fundação Calouste Gulbenkian at **Centro de Arte Moderna**, sculptures hide in every recess. You may want to spend a little time here before following signs to the Modern Art Center—the 20th-century art collection of the Calouste Gulbenkian Foundation, which has at its disposal the finest collection of contemporary and modern Portuguese art, as well as many British works from the same period—a legacy of the foothold the foundation retains in London. ✉ *Av. de Berna 45, Praça de Espanha* ☎ *21/782–3000* ⊕ *www.museu.gulbenkian.pt* ✉ *€4, temporary exhibitions €4–€5, combined ticket €5, combined ticket Museum with Modern Art Center €5, combined ticket for all €7; free Sun.* ◔ *Tues.–Sun. 10–5:45* Ⓜ *São Sebastião or Praça de Espanha.*

---

## LISBON BEST BETS

**Take time to enjoy the exquisite decoration at the Mosteiro dos Jerónimos.** Paid for with the profits from the sale of treasures from New World colonies.

**Enjoy the first-class artifacts on display at Museu Calouste Gulbenkian.** The collection reflects the personal taste of Gulbenkian himself.

**Stroll the avenues of the Biaxa district.** An architectural whole built after the devastating earthquake of 1755 is Lisbon's most attractive neoclassical neighborhood.

FodorśChoice **Museu Nacional de Arte Antiga.** On the route from the center of Lisbon
★ to Belém is the Ancient Art Museum, the only institution in the city to
approach the status of the Gulbenkian. Housed in a 17th-century palace
once owned by the Counts of Alvor and vastly enlarged in 1940 when
it took over the Convent of St. Albert, the museum has a beautifully
displayed collection of Portuguese art—mainly from the 15th through
19th century. The religious works of the Flemish-influenced Portuguese
school stand out, especially Nuno Gonçalves' masterpiece, the *St. Vincent Panels.* Painted between 1467 and 1470, the altarpiece has six
panels believed to show the patron saint of Lisbon receiving the homage
of king, court, and citizens (although there are other theories). Trams 15
and 18 from Praça do Comércio drop you at the foot of a steep flight of
steps below the museum. Otherwise, Buses 727 from Praça Marquês de
Pombal, 60 from Praça Martim Moniz, and 713 from Praça do Comércio run straight to Rua das Janelas Verdes; coming from Belém, you
can pick the 727 up across from the Jerónimos monastery. ⊠ *Rua das
Janelas Verdes, Lapa* ☎ *21/391–2800* ⊕ *www.mnarteantiga-ipmuseus.
pt* ☑ *€5, free Sun. to 2 pm* ☉ *Tues. 2–6, Wed.–Sun. 10–6.*

FodorśChoice **Oceanário de Lisboa.** Europe's largest indoor aquarium wows children
★ and adults alike with a vast saltwater tank featuring an array of fish,
☾ including several types of shark. Along the way you pass through habitats representing the North Atlantic, Pacific, and Indian oceans, where
puffins and penguins dive into the water, sea otters roll and play, and
tropical birds flit past you. You then descend to the bottom of the tank
to watch rays float past gracefully and schools of silvery fish darting this
way and that. ⊠ *Esplanada D. Carlos I (Doca dos Olivais), Parque das
Nações* ☎ *21/891–7002* ⊕ *www.oceanario.pt* ☑ *€12* ☉ *Apr.–Oct., daily
10–8; Nov.–Mar., daily 10–7; last entry 1 hr before closing* Ⓜ *Oriente.*

**Padrão dos Descobrimentos.** The white, monolithic Monument of the Discoveries was erected in 1960 to commemorate the 500th anniversary of
the death of Prince Henry the Navigator. It was built on what was the
departure point for many voyages of discovery, including those of Vasco
da Gama for India and—during Spain's occupation of Portugal—of
the Spanish Armada for England in 1588. Henry is at the prow of the
monument, facing the water; lined up behind him are the Portuguese
explorers of Brazil and Asia, as well as other national heroes, including Luís de Camões the poet, who can be recognized by the book in his
hand. On the ground adjacent to the monument, an inlaid map shows
the extent of the explorations undertaken by the 15th- and 16th-century
Portuguese sailors. Walk inside and take the elevator to the top for river
views. There are also 15- and 30-minute films about Lisbon's history.
⊠ *Av. de Brasília, Belém* ☎ *21/303–1950* ☑ *€2.50; 25-min movie €4,
combined ticket monument and movie €5, €13 includes Torre de Belém*
☉ *Oct.–Apr., Tues.–Sun. 10–6; May–Sept., Tues.–Sun. 10–7.*

☾ **Pavilhão do Conhecimento.** The white, angular, structure designed by
architect Carrilho de Graça for the Expo seems the perfect place to
house the Knowledge Pavilion, or Living Science Centre, as it's also
known. All of the permanent and temporary exhibits here are related
to math, science, and technology; most are also labeled in English (a
manual is available for the few that aren't), and all are interactive.

✉ *Alamada dos Oceanos, Lote 2.10.01, Parque das Nações* ☎ *21/891–9898* ⊕ *www.pavconhecimento.pt/home* 🖃 *€7* ⊗ *Tues.–Fri. 10–6, weekends and holidays 11–7* Ⓜ *Oriente.*

**Praça Marquês de Pombal.** Dominating the center of Marquês de Pombal Square is a statue of the marquis himself, the man responsible for the design of the "new" Lisbon that emerged from the ruins of the 1755 earthquake. On the statue's base are representations of both the earthquake and the tidal wave that engulfed the city; a female figure with outstretched arms signifies the joy at the emergence of the refashioned city.

**Praça dos Restauradores.** This square, which is adjacent to Rossio train station, marks the beginning of modern Lisbon. Here the broad, tree-lined Avenida da Liberdade starts its northwesterly ascent. *Restauradores* means "restoration," and the square commemorates the 1640 uprising against Spanish rule that restored Portuguese independence. An obelisk (raised in 1886) commemorates the event. Note the elegant 18th-century Palácio Foz on the square's west side. Before World War I, it contained a casino; today it houses a national tourist office, the tourist police, and a shop selling reproductions from the country's state museums.

**Torre de Belém.** The openwork balconies and domed turrets of the fanciful Belém Tower make it perhaps the country's purest Manueline structure. It was built between 1514 and 1520 on what was an island in the middle of the Rio Tejo, to defend the port entrance, and dedicated to St. Vincent, the patron saint of Lisbon. Today the chalk-white tower stands near the north bank—evidence of the river's changing course. Cross the wood gangway and walk inside, not so much to see the plain interior but rather to climb the steps to the very top for a bird's-eye view of river and city. ✉ *Av. de Brasília, Belém* ☎ *21/362–0034* 🖃 *€5* ⊗ *Oct.–Apr., Tues.–Sun. 10–5; May–Sept., Tues.–Sun. 10–6.30.*

## SHOPPING

Although fire destroyed much of Chiado, Lisbon's smartest shopping district, in 1988, a good portion of the area has been restored. The neighborhood has a large new shopping complex as well as many small stores with considerable cachet, particularly on and around Rua Garrett. The Baixa's grid of streets from the Rossío to the Rio Tejo have many small shops selling jewelry, shoes, clothing, and foodstuffs. The Bairro Alto is full of little crafts shops with stylish, contemporary goods. Excellent stores continue to open in the residential districts north of the city, at Praça de Londres and Avenida de Roma. Most of Lisbon's antiques shops are in the Rato and Bairro Alto districts along one long street, which changes its name four times as it runs southward from Largo do Rato: Rua Escola Politécnica, Rua Dom Pedro V, Rua da Misericórdia, and Rua do Alecrim.

Handmade goods, such as leather handbags, shoes, gloves, embroidery, ceramics, linens, and basketwork, are sold throughout the city. Apart from top designer fashions and high-end antiques, prices are moderate.

**Antiquália.** This shop is packed with furniture, chandeliers, and porcelain. ✉ *Praça Luís de Camões 37, Chiado* ☎ *21/342–3260.*

**Vista Alegre.** Portugal's most famous porcelain producer, Vista Alegre, established its factory in 1824. A visit to the flagship store is a must even though you can buy perfect reproductions of their original table services and ornaments at dozens of shops. There are also seven other Vista Alegre–owned stores in the city, including those at the Colombo, Amoreiras, and Vasco da Gama malls. ⊠ *Largo do Chiado 20–23, Chiado* ☎ *21/346–1401* ⊕ *www.vistaalegreatlantis.com.*

## WHERE TO EAT

**$$$**
SEAFOOD
**Fodor's**Choice
★

✕ **Aqui Há Peixe.** "There's fish here" is this restaurant's name, and make no mistake: it's one of the most fashionable places in town to eat seafood. Opened in 2009 by the proprietor of a well-known beachside restaurant at Comporta, south of Setúbal, it has a similarly informal vibe. At night it attracts a youngish crowd clearly intent on hitting the Bairro Alto's bars later. Popular dishes here include fish stews and tuna steak sautéed with peppercorns; don't forget to order a light *vinho verde* or a good white wine to wash them down. There are cheaper lunchtime specials, rustled up from whatever was in the market in the morning. ⊠ *Rua da Trindade 18A, Chiado* ☎ *21/343–2154* ⊕ *www.aquihapeixe. pt* ⊗ *Closed Mon. No lunch weekends.*

**$**
PORTUGUESE

✕ **Solar dos Bicos.** This charming restaurant, with its stone arches and beautiful *azulejos* offers typical Portuguese cuisine at very reasonable prices. It's right next to the Casa dos Bicos, which you can marvel at from a large shaded esplanade. Seafood is the main attraction: grilled sole, grouper, sea bass, bream or squid are all good options, or two diners could split a rich *caldeirada* (fish stew) or *arroz de marisco* (a sort of wet seafood risotto). There are plenty of no-nonsense meat dishes, too, such as mixed grill and barbecued pork chops, which come with fries and salad. Then choose between achingly sweet desserts and fresh fruit. ⊠ *Rua dos Bacalhoeiros, 8–A, Alfama* ☎ *21/886–9447* ⊕ *www. solardosbicos.pt* ⊗ *Closed Mon. Closed 2 wks late Dec. or early Jan.*

# LIVORNO, ITALY (FOR FLORENCE AND PISA)

Updated
by Bruce
Leimsidor

One of the biggest and grittiest ports on the northwestern Italian coast, Livorno has little to attract visitors in itself. Nevertheless, the city is one of the most popular cruise ports of call in the western Mediterranean as the gateway to some of Italy's finest attractions, the cities of Florence and Pisa, not to mention the delightful landscapes of Tuscany. Florence gave birth to the Renaissance and changed the way we see the world. For centuries it has captured the imagination of travelers, who have come seeking rooms with views and phenomenal art. Pisa is famous for one of the world's most noted historical attractions: its leaning tower, but this structure is one part of a trio of attractions that offers one of the most dramatic architectural complexes in the country. It's unlikely you'll have time to see everything during this port stop, so plan your time wisely.

## ESSENTIALS

### CURRENCY
The euro.

### HOURS
Shops are generally open 9 to 1 and 3:30 to 8 and are generally closed Sunday. Summer (June to September) hours are usually 9 to 1 and 4 to 8, and some shops close Saturday afternoon.

### PRIVATE TOURS
For tours of Florence or Pisa, you are encouraged not to use the exorbitantly priced and unprofessional tours offered by taxi drivers in Livorno. The best course is to book your tour through a legitimate company based in either Florence or Pisa and travel to those cities by train from Livorno to meet your guide. Undoubtedly the best tours of Florence are offered by Walks Inside Florence (€60/ hour for groups of up to 4 persons), which also offers tours in Pisa and Lucca.

**Contacts Walks Inside Florence.** ☎ *055/488588 in Florence* ⊕ *www.walksinsideflorence.it.*

### TELEPHONES
Tri-band GSM phones work in Italy. You can buy prepaid phone cards at telecom shops, news vendors, and tobacconists in all towns and cities. Phone cards can be used for local or international calls.

## COMING ASHORE
The port of Livorno has good cruise facilities, including car-rental offices, ticket and information offices, a bar, and a garden. It is near the heart of the town, just a few blocks from Livorno's central area. The railway station is 3 km (2 miles) from the port, but there is no good public transport option there. One option is to take a taxi, but the price of about €20 is an exorbitant fare for just 3 km of travel. Better is to take a shuttle into the center of the city (Piazza del Municipio) and then bus #1 or #2 from nearby Piazza Grande (in front of the Cathedral) to the train station; this option costs €1.20. It's only a bit over 1 km to Piazza Grande from the port, so if your cruise line doesn't provide a shuttle, it's not a long walk.

Trains from Livorno to Florence currently run once per hour throughout the day. The journey time is about 90 minutes. Prices are about €14–€20 round-trip depending on time of departure. From Livorno it is just a 15-minute train journey to Pisa, at a price of about €2.90 depending on time of departure; from Pisa Central Station take a train to San Rossore, from where it is a five-minute walk to the Leaning Tower area. If you buy tickets on Trenitalia's (Italian railways') website (⊕ *www.trenitalia.com*), you can print them out at self-service machines in Livorno station.

Taxis are expensive, charging €3.20 initially, then an additional charge per km (½-mile) and a surcharge when traffic moves slowly or when you call for a taxi. Car rental would give you greater flexibility to explore Tuscany, but if you are going only to Florence, then a train will be better, since parking is difficult in Florence. Rentals are approximately €45 per day for a compact manual vehicle.

# EXPLORING FLORENCE AND PISA

## FLORENCE
*95 km (60 miles) east of Livorno, 82 km (51 miles) east of Pisa.*

The heart of Florence, stretching from the Piazza del Duomo south to the Arno, is as dense with artistic treasures as anyplace in the world. The churches, medieval towers, Renaissance palaces, and world-class museums and galleries contain some of the most outstanding aesthetic achievements of Western history.

★ **Bargello.** This building started out as the headquarters for the Capitano del Popolo (captain of the people) during the Middle Ages, and was later used as a prison. The exterior served as a "most wanted" billboard: effigies of notorious criminals and Medici enemies were painted on its walls. Today it houses the **Museo Nazionale,** home to what is probably the finest collection of Renaissance sculpture in Italy. For Renaissance art lovers, the Bargello is to sculpture what the Uffizi is to painting. ⊠ *Via del Proconsolo 4, Bargello* ☎ *055/294883* ⊕ *www.polomuseale. firenze.it* ⊠ *€4* ⊙ *Daily 8:15–1:50; closed 2nd and 4th Mon. of month and 1st, 3rd, and 5th Sun. of month.*

**Battistero** (*Baptistery*). The octagonal Baptistery is one of the supreme monuments of the Italian Romanesque style and one of Florence's oldest structures. Local legend has it that it was once a Roman temple dedicated to Mars; modern excavations, however, suggest that its foundations date from the 1st century AD. The round Romanesque arches on the exterior date from the 11th century. The interior dome mosaics from the beginning of the 14th century are justly renowned, but—glittering beauties though they are—they could never outshine the building's famed bronze Renaissance doors decorated with panels crafted by Lorenzo Ghiberti. The doors—or at least copies of them—on which Ghiberti worked most of his adult life (1403–52) are on the north and east sides of the Baptistery, and the Gothic panels on the south door were designed by Andrea Pisano (circa 1290–1348) in 1330. The original Ghiberti doors were removed to protect them from the effects of pollution and acid rain and have been beautifully restored; they are now on display in the Museo dell'Opera del Duomo. ⊠ *Piazza del Duomo* ☎ *055/2302885* ⊕ *www.operaduomo.firenze.it* ⊠ *€4* ⊙ *Mon.– Sat. 12:15–7; Sun. 8:30–2, 1st Sat. of month 8:30–2.*

**Campanile.** The Gothic bell tower designed by Giotto (circa 1266–1337) is a soaring structure of multicolor marble originally decorated with sculptures by Donatello and reliefs by Giotto, Andrea Pisano, and others (which are now in the Museo dell'Opera del Duomo). A climb of 414 steps rewards you with a close-up of Brunelleschi's cupola on the Duomo next door and a sweeping view of the city. ⊠ *Piazza del Duomo* ☎ *055/2302885* ⊕ *www.operaduomo.firenze.it* ⊠ *€6* ⊙ *Daily 8:30–7:30.*

★ **Cappelle Medicee** (*Medici Chapels*). This magnificent complex includes the **Cappella dei Principi,** the Medici chapel and mausoleum that was begun in 1605 and kept marble workers busy for several hundred years, and the **Sagrestia Nuova** (New Sacristy), designed by Michelangelo and so called to distinguish it from Brunelleschi's Sagrestia Vecchia (Old

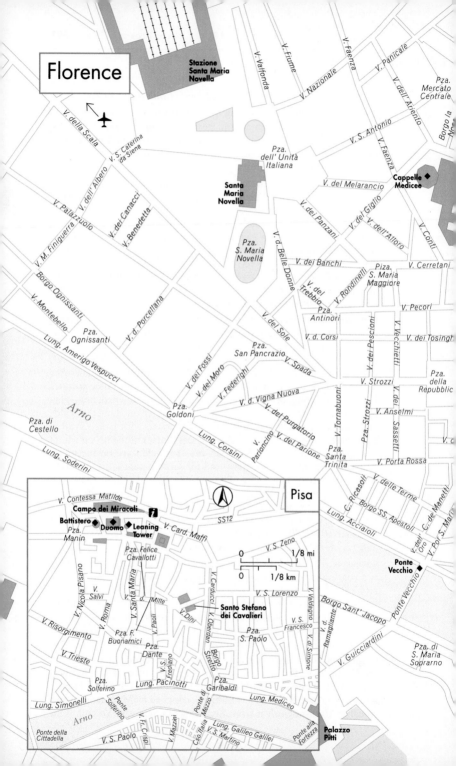

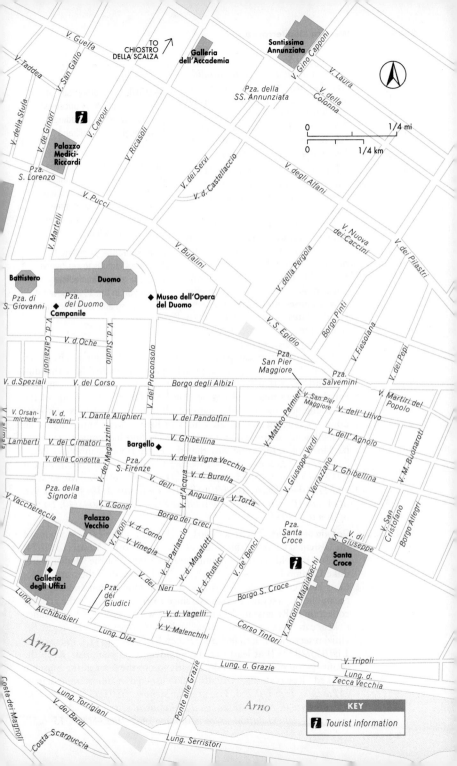

Sacristy) in San Lorenzo. ✉ *Piazza di Madonna degli Aldobrandini, San Lorenzo* ☎ *055/294883 reservations* ☜ *€6; €9 during special exhibits* ☽ *Mar.–Nov., daily 8:15–3:50; Dec.–Feb., daily 8:15–1:50. Closed 1st, 3rd, and 5th Mon. and 2nd and 4th Sun. of month.*

**Fodor's Choice** **Duomo** (*Cattedrale di Santa Maria ★ del Fiore*). In 1296 Arnolfo di Cambio (circa 1245–circa 1310) was commissioned to build "the loftiest, most sumptuous edifice human invention could devise" in the Romanesque style on the site of the old church of Santa Reparata. The immense Duomo was not completed until 1436, the year it was consecrated. The imposing facade dates only from the 19th century; its neo-Gothic style somewhat complements Giotto's genuine Gothic 14th-century campanile. The real glory of the Duomo, however, is Filippo Brunelleschi's dome, presiding over the cathedral with a dignity and grace that few domes to this day can match. Brunelleschi's **cupola** was an ingenious engineering feat. The result was one of the great engineering breakthroughs of all time: most of Europe's later domes, including that of St. Peter's in Rome, were built employing Brunelleschi's methods, and today the Duomo has come to symbolize Florence in the same way that the Eiffel Tower symbolizes Paris. ✉ *Piazza del Duomo* ☎ *055/2302885* ⊕ *www.operaduomo.firenze.it* ☜ *Church free, crypt €3, cupola €8* ☽ *Crypt and Duomo: Mon.–Wed. and Fri 10–5, Thurs. 10–4:30, Sat. 10–4:45, Sun. 1:30–4:45, 1st Sat. of month 10–3:30. Cupola: Weekdays 8:30–7, Sat. 8:30–5:40, 1st Sat. of month 8:30–4.*

**Fodor's Choice** **Galleria degli Uffizi.** The venerable Uffizi Gallery occupies the top floor of ★ the U-shaped **Palazzo degli Uffizi**, designed by Giorgio Vasari (1511–74) in 1560 to hold the *uffizi* (administrative offices) of the Medici grand duke Cosimo I (1519–74). Later, the Medici installed their art collections here, creating what was Europe's first modern museum, open to the public (at first only by request) since 1591. It's probably the greatest collection of Renaissance paintings in the world. For a €4 fee, advance tickets can be reserved by phone, online, or, once in Florence, at the Uffizi reservation booth (*advance tickets* ✉ *Consorzio ITA, Piazza Pitti 1* ☎ *055/294883*) at least one day in advance of your visit. Keep the confirmation number and take it with you to the door at the museum marked "Reservations." Usually you're ushered in almost immediately. ✉ *Piazzale degli Uffizi 6, Piazza della Signoria* ☎ *055/23885* ⊕ *www. uffizi.firenze.it; reservations www.polomuseale.firenze.it* ☜ *€10, €11 during special exhibitions; reservation fee €4* ☽ *Tues.–Sun. 8:15–6:50.*

---

**LIVORNO BEST BETS**

**The Uffizi.** The mother lode of Renaissance art offers priceless examples by artists including Michelangelo, Botticelli, and Raphael.

**Galleria dell'Accademia.** The number one draw in this museum is Michelangelo's *David*, a sculpture that has captured human imagination, but don't miss the rest of the collection.

**Torre Pendente.** Completed in 1173 Pisa's famous tower began to subside almost immediately. Intervention in the 1990s saved it from collapse and stabilized the structure.

★ **Galleria dell'Accademia** (*Accademia Gallery*). The collection of Florentine
☼ paintings, dating from the 13th to the 18th centuries, is largely unremarkable, but the sculptures by Michelangelo are worth the price of
admission. The unfinished *Slaves*, fighting their way out of their marble
prisons, were meant for the tomb of Michelangelo's overly demanding
patron Pope Julius II (1443–1513). But the focal point is the original
*David*, moved here from Piazza della Signoria in 1873. *David* was
commissioned in 1501 by the Opera del Duomo (Cathedral Works
Committee), which gave the 26-year-old sculptor a leftover block of
marble that had been ruined forty years earlier by two other sculptors.
Michelangelo's success with the block was so dramatic that the city
showered him with honors, and the Opera del Duomo voted to build
him a house and a studio in which to live and work. ⊠ *Via Ricasoli 60,
San Marco* ☎ *055/294883 reservations, 055/2388609 gallery* ☑ *€11,
reservation fee €4* ☼ *Tues.–Sun. 8:15–6:50.*

**Museo dell'Opera del Duomo** (*Cathedral Museum*). Ghiberti's original Baptistery door panels (in restoration at press time) and the *cantorie* (choir
loft) reliefs by Donatello and Luca della Robbia (1400–82) keep company
with Donatello's *Mary Magdalene* and Michelangelo's *Pietà* (not to be
confused with his more famous *Pietà* in St. Peter's in Rome). Renaissance sculpture is in part defined by its revolutionary realism, but in its
palpable suffering Donatello's *Magdalene* goes beyond realism. Michelangelo's heart-wrenching *Pietà* was unfinished at his death; the female
figure supporting the body of Christ on the left was added by Tiberio Cal-
cagni (1532–65), and never has the difference between competence and
genius been manifested so clearly. ⊠ *Piazza del Duomo 9* ☎ *055/2302885*
⊕ *www.operaduomo.firenze.it* ☑ *€6* ☼ *Mon.–Sat. 9–7:30, Sun. 9–1:45.*

**Palazzo Vecchio** (*Old Palace*). Florence's forbidding, fortresslike city hall
was begun in 1299, presumably designed by Arnolfo di Cambio, and its
massive bulk and towering campanile dominate Piazza della Signoria. It
was built as a meeting place for the guildsmen governing the city at the
time; today it is still City Hall. The interior courtyard is a good deal less
severe, having been remodeled by Michelozzo (1396–1472) in 1453; a
copy of Verrocchio's bronze *puttino* (cherub), topping the central fountain, softens the space. (The original is upstairs.) The main attraction is on
the second floor: two adjoining rooms that supply one of the most startling
contrasts in Florence. The first is the opulently vast **Sala dei Cinquecento**
(Room of the Five Hundred), named for the 500-member Great Council,
the people's assembly established after the death of Lorenzo the Magnificent, which met here. In comparison, the little **Studiolo**, just off the
Sala dei Cinquecento's entrance, was a private room meant for the duke
and those whom he invited in. Here's where the melancholy Francesco I
(1541–87), son of Cosimo I, stored his priceless treasures and conducted
scientific experiments. Designed by Vasari, it was decorated by him, Giam-
bologna, and many others. ⊠ *Piazza della Signoria* ☎ *055/2768465* ☑ *€6*
☼ *Mon.–Wed. and Fri.–Sun. 9–7, Thurs. 9–2.*

★ **Ponte Vecchio** (*Old Bridge*). This charmingly simple bridge was built in
1345 to replace an earlier bridge swept away by flood. Its shops first
housed butchers, then grocers, blacksmiths, and other merchants. But
in 1593 the Medici grand duke Ferdinand I (1549–1609), whose private

corridor linking the Medici palace (Palazzo Pitti) with the Medici offices (the Uffizi) crossed the bridge atop the shops, decided that all this plebeian commerce under his feet was unseemly. So he threw out the butchers and blacksmiths and installed 41 goldsmiths and eight jewelers. The bridge has been devoted solely to these two trades ever since.

**Fodor's**Choice   **Santa Croce.** Like the Duomo, this church is Gothic, but also like the
★    Duomo, its facade dates from the 19th century. As a burial place, the church probably contains more skeletons of Renaissance celebrities than any other in Italy, including those of Michelangelo, Galileo, Machiavelli, and the composer Rossini, as well as a monument to Dante Alighieri, who is buried in Ravenna. The most famous works are probably the Giotto frescoes in the two chapels immediately to the right of the high altar. ⊠ *Piazza Santa Croce 16* ☎ *055/2466105* 💴 *€5 combined admission to church and museum* ☉ *Mon.–Sat. 9:30–5:30, Sun. 1–5.*

## PISA

*22 km (14 miles) north of Livorno, 82 km (51 miles) west of Florence.*

All of Pisa's treasures date from a short period between the 11th and the 13th centuries, when Pisa was a leading power in the region. The three buildings set on Pisa's grassy Field of Miracles form one of the finest Romanesque ensembles in Italy.

**Battistero.** This lovely Gothic baptistery, which stands across from the Duomo's facade, is best known for the pulpit carved by Nicola Pisano (circa 1220–84; father of Giovanni Pisano) in 1260. Ask one of the ticket takers if he'll sing for you inside; the acoustics are remarkable. ⊠ *Piazza del Duomo* ☎ *050/835011* ⊕ *www.opapisa.it* 💴 *€5, discounts available if bought in combination with tickets for other monuments* ☉ *Nov.–Feb., daily 10–5; Mar., daily 9–6; Apr.–Sept., daily 8–8; Oct., daily 9–7.*

**Duomo.** Pisa's cathedral brilliantly utilizes the horizontal marble-stripe motif (borrowed from Moorish architecture) that became common in Tuscan cathedrals. It is famous for the Romanesque panels on the transept door facing the tower that depict scenes from the life of Christ. The beautifully carved 14th-century pulpit is by Giovanni Pisano (son of Nicola). ⊠ *Piazza del Duomo* ☎ *050835011* ⊕ *www.opapisa.it* 💴 *€5* ☉ *Nov.–Feb., daily 10–12:45 and 2–5; Mar., daily 10–6; Apr.–Sept., daily 10–8; Oct., daily 10–7.*

**Fodor's**Choice   **Leaning Tower (Torre Pendente).** Work on this tower, built as a campa-
★    nile (bell tower) for the Duomo, started in 1173: the lopsided settling began when construction reached the third story. The tower's architects attempted to compensate through such methods as making the remaining floors slightly taller on the leaning side, but the extra weight only made the problem worse. The settling continued, and by the late 20th century it had accelerated to such a point that many feared the tower would simply topple over, despite all efforts to prop it up. The structure has since been firmly anchored to the earth. The final phase to restore the tower to its original tilt of 300 years ago was launched in early 2000 and finished two years later. The last phase removed some 100 tons of earth from beneath the foundation. Reservations, which are essential, can be made online or by calling the Museo dell'Opera del Duomo; it's also possible to arrive at the ticket office and book for the same day.

Note that children under eight years of age are not allowed to climb. ⊠ *Piazza del Duomo* ☎ *050/835011* ⊕ *www.opapisa.it* 🎫 *€17* ⊗ *Dec. and Jan., daily 10–4:30; Nov. and Feb., daily 9:30—5:30; Mar., daily 9–5:30; Apr.–Sept., daily 8:30–8; Oct., daily 9–7.*

## SHOPPING

Window-shopping in Florence is like visiting an enormous contemporary-art gallery. Many of today's greatest Italian artists are fashion designers—Prada, Gucci, Versace, to name but a few—and most keep shops in Florence. Italian leather is famed for its quality and fashioned into clothing, shoes, and accessories. True art also makes a big impact on the souvenir market, with many street artists around the town and smarter galleries in the historic center. Terra-cotta pottery, straw goods, and handmade paper are all traditional handicrafts. Excellent olive oils and wines are also worthwhile buys in Florence.

The fanciest designer shops are mainly on **Via Tornabuoni** and **Via della Vigna Nuova.** The city's largest concentrations of antiques shops are on **Borgo Ognissanti** and the Oltrarno's **Via Maggio.** The **Ponte Vecchio** houses reputable but very expensive jewelry shops, as it has since the 16th century. The area near **Santa Croce** is the heart of the leather merchants' district.

**Sbigoli Terrecotte.** Traditional Tuscan terra-cotta and ceramic vases, pots, and cups and saucers are on offer at this shop in the Santa Croce neighborhood. ⊠ *Via Sant'Egidio 4/r, Santa Croce* ☎ *055/2479713.*

## WHERE TO EAT

**$$$$** ╳**Frescobaldi Wine Bar.** The Frescobaldi family has run a vineyard for
TUSCAN   more than 700 years, and this swanky establishment offers tasty and sumptuous fare to accompany the seriously fine wines. Warm terra-cotta-color walls with trompe-l'oeil tapestries provide a soothing atmosphere. The menu is typically Tuscan, but turned up a notch or two: the *faraona in umido con l'uva* (stewed guinea fowl with grapes) comes with a side of feather-light mashed potatoes. Save room for dessert, as well as one of the dessert wines. A separate, lovely little wine bar called Frescobaldino has a shorter—but equally good—menu and a delightful, multilingual barman called Primo. ⑤ *Average main: €35* ⊠ *Via de' Magazzini 2–4/r, Piazza della Signoria* ☎ *055/284724* ⊗ *Closed Sun. No lunch Mon.*

**$$$$** ╳**Il Latini.** It may be the noisiest, most crowded trattoria in Florence,
TUSCAN   but it's also one of the most fun. The genial host, Torello ("little bull") Latini, presides over his four big dining rooms, and somehow it feels as if you're dining in his home. Ample portions of *ribollita* prepare the palate for the hearty meat dishes that follow. Both Florentines and tourists alike tuck into the *agnello fritto* (fried lamb) with aplomb. There's almost always a wait, even with a reservation. ⑤ *Average main: €32* ⊠ *Via dei Palchetti 6/r, Santa Maria Novella* ☎ *055/210916* ⊗ *Closed Mon. and 15 days at Christmas.*

# MÁLAGA, SPAIN (WITH MARBELLA, NERJA, AND GRANADA)

Updated by
Joanna Styles

The city of Málaga and the surrounding region of eastern Andalusia creates the kind of contrast that makes travel in Spain so tantalizing. A Moorish legacy is a unifying theme and offers some of its most interesting and visually stunning historical attractions. Since the birth of mass tourism, Europeans have flocked here to the Costa del Sol or Sunshine Coast, a 70-km (43-miles) sprawl of hotels, vacation villas, golf courses, marinas, and nightclubs west of Málaga. Since the late 1950s this area has mushroomed from a group of impoverished fishing villages into an overdeveloped seaside playground and retirement haven. Despite the hubbub, you *can* unwind here. Málaga itself is a vibrant Spanish city, virtually untainted by tourism, and inland are quiet whitewashed villages just waiting to be explored.

## ESSENTIALS

### CURRENCY
The euro.

### HOURS
Museums generally open 9 until 7 or 8, many are closed on Monday, and some close in the afternoon. Most stores are open Monday through Saturday 9 to 1:30 and 5 to 8, but a few tourist shops open in the afternoon and on Sunday.

### PRIVATE TOURS
**Julià Travel.** Julià is one of the main companies offering day trips to Córdoba, Granada, Nerja, Seville, and even Tangier from Málaga. ☎ *902/024443* ⊕ *www.juliatravel.com.*

### TELEPHONES
Most tri-band and quad-band GSM phones work in Spain, where mobile services are 3G-compatible. Public kiosks accept phone cards that support international calls (cards sold in press shops, bars, and telecom shops). Major companies include Vodafone.

## COMING ASHORE
The cruise port at Málaga has just completed a major renovation. Along with a new cruise terminal, the port now incorporates shopping and eateries in the area known as Muelle Uno and an aquarium and park with over 400 palms. A spectacular undulating pergola runs the length of the park and provides a fine walkway into the city center. Facilities at the cruise terminals are comprehensive and shuttle buses carry passengers to the terminal areas.

The city of Málaga awaits just beyond the gates of the port, and you can explore the Old Town on foot. Granada is 1½ hours away to the north by road. Bus services to Granada are frequent, and buses are modern and air-conditioned; the fare at this writing is €10.62 for a single leg. The main bus station is next to the railway station in the city. Taking a taxi from the cruise port is the quickest and simplest transfer. Rail travel from Málaga to Granada is a much slower option, at 3 hours, and with few trains each day this is not a realistic option

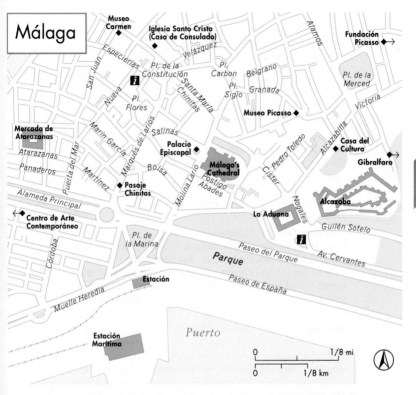

for passengers in town for just a day. Renting a car would allow you to visit Granada or explore some of the resorts or countryside surrounding Málaga. The price for an economy manual vehicle is approximately €30 per day.

## EXPLORING MÁLAGA AND VICINITY

### MÁLAGA

**Alcazaba.** Just beyond the ruins of a Roman theater on Calle Alcazabilla stands Málaga's greatest monument. This fortress was begun in the 8th century, when Málaga was the principal port of the Moorish kingdom, though most of the present structure dates from the 11th century. The inner palace was built between 1057 and 1063, when the Moorish emirs took up residence; Ferdinand and Isabella lived here for a while after conquering the city in 1487. The ruins are dappled with orange trees and bougainvillea and include a small museum; from the highest point you can see over the park and port. ⊠ *Entrance on C. Alcazabilla* 🖾 *€2.20, €3.55 combined entry with Gibralfaro* ☉ *Nov.–Mar., Tues.– Sun. 8:30–7; Apr.–Oct., Tues.–Sun. 9:30–8.*

**Centro de Arte Contemporáneo** (*Contemporary Arts Center*). This museum includes photographic studies and paintings, some of them immense. The 7,900 square feet of bright exhibition hall are used to showcase ultramodern artistic trends—the four exhibitions are used for a changing show from the permanent collection, two temporary shows, and one show dedicated to up-and-coming Spanish artists. The gallery attracts world-class modern artists like the South African William Kentridge or the British Gilbert and George. The Victoria Lounge restaurant, which has a terrace overlooking the river, does a good lunch menu ($). ⊠ *Alemania s/n* ☎ *952/120055* ⊕ *www.cacmalaga.org* ✉ *Free* ⊗ *Sept.–June, Tues.–Sun. 10–8; July–Aug., Tues.–Sun. 10–2 and 5–8.*

> ### MÁLAGA BEST BETS
>
> **Climb the parapets of the Alcazaba.** Málaga's Moorish fortress is the city's greatest monument.
>
> **Take a hike in the Parque Natural del Torcal de Antequera.** Walk through a surreal wind-sculpted landscape of pink granite.
>
> **Strolling through the Alhambra.** The Moorish palace in Granada is about 90 minutes from Málaga and well worth the trip.

**Fundación Picasso.** Málaga's most famous native son, Pablo Picasso, was born here in 1881. Now the Fundación Picasso, the building has been painted and furnished in the style of the era and houses a permanent exhibition of the artist's early sketches and sculptures, as well as memorabilia, including his christening robe and family photos. ⊠ *Pl. de la Merced 15* ☎ *951/926060* ⊕ *www.fundacionpicasso.es* ✉ *€1* ⊗ *Daily 9:30–8.*

**Gibralfaro** (*castle*). Surrounded by magnificent vistas, Málaga's Gibralfaro is floodlit at night. The fortifications were built for Yusuf I in the 14th century; the Moors called them Jebelfaro, from the Arab word for "mount" and the Greek word for "lighthouse," after a beacon that stood here to guide ships into the harbor and warn of pirates. The lighthouse has been succeeded by a small parador (*see Where to Stay*). You can drive here by way of Calle Victoria or take a minibus that leaves 10 times a day, between 11 and 7, roughly every 45 minutes, from the bus stop in the park near the Plaza de la Marina. ⊠ *Gibralfaro Mountain* ✉ *€2.20, €3.55 combined entry with Alcazaba* ⊗ *Nov.–Mar., daily 9–6; Apr.–Oct., daily 9–8.*

**Málaga's Cathedral.** This cathedral, built between 1528 and 1782, is a triumph, although a generally unappreciated one, having been left unfinished when funds ran out. Because it lacks one of its two towers, the building is nicknamed *La Manquita* (the One-Armed Lady). The enclosed choir, which miraculously survived the burnings of the civil war, is the work of 17th-century artist Pedro de Mena, who carved the wood wafer-thin in some places to express the fold of a robe or shape of a finger. The choir also has a pair of massive 18th-century pipe organs, one of which is still used for the occasional concert. Adjoining the cathedral is a small museum of religious art and artifacts. A walk around the cathedral on Calle Cister will take you to the magnificent Gothic Puerta del Sagrario. ⊠ *C. de Molina Larios* ☎ *952/215917* ✉ *€5* ⊗ *Weekdays 10–6, Sat. 10–5.*

**Mercado de Atarazanas.** From the Plaza Felix Saenz, at the southern end of Calle Nueva, turn onto Sagasta to reach the Mercado de Atarazanas.

The typical, 19th-century, iron structure incorporates the original **Puerta de Atarazanas**, the exquisitely crafted 14th-century Moorish gate that once connected the city with the port. Don't miss the magnificent, stained-glass window depicting highlights of this historical port city as you stroll round the stalls, filled with local produce. ☉ *Mon.–Sat. 9–3.*

**Museo Carmen Thyssen Málaga.** Visitors who've been to Madrid are probably familiar with that city's Museo Carmen Thyssen, and in mid-2011 over 200 works from Baroness Thyssen's private collection went on display at Málaga's own branch. Shown in a renovated 16th-century palace, the collection features mainly Spanish paintings from the 19th century and includes some of Spain's greatest artists, like Joaquín Sorolla y Bastida and Francisco de Zurbarán. The museum also hosts regular talks and workshops on art. ⊠ *C. Compañia 10* ☎ *902/303131* ⊕ *www.carmenthyssenmalaga.org* ⌧ *€6 permanent exhibition, €4 temporary exhibition* ☉ *Tues.–Sun. 10–8.*

**Fodor's**Choice **Museo Picasso.** Part of the charm of the Museo Picasso, one of the city's
★  most prestigious museums, is that it's such a family affair. These are the works that Pablo Picasso kept for himself or gave to his family, including the heartfelt *Paulo con gorro blanco* (*Paulo with a White Cap*), a portrait of his firstborn son painted in the early 1920s; and *Olga Kokhlova con mantilla* (*Olga Kokhlova with Mantilla*), a 1917 portrait of his certifiably insane first wife. The holdings were largely donated by two family members—Christine and Bernard Ruiz-Picasso, the artist's daughter-in-law and her son. The works are displayed in chronological order according to the periods that marked Picasso's development as an artist, from Blue and Rose to cubism and beyond. The museum is housed in a former palace where, during restoration work, Roman and Moorish remains were discovered. These are now on display, together with the permanent collection of Picassos and temporary exhibitions. Guided tours in English are held on Wednesdays at 11:30. ⊠ *C. de San Agustín* ☎ *952/127600* ⊕ *www.museopicassomalaga.org* ⌧ *Permanent exhibition €6, combined permanent and temporary exhibition €9, free entry Sun. 6–8* ☉ *Tues.–Thurs. and Sun. 10–8, Fri. and Sat. 10–9.*

**Palacio Episcopal** (*Bishop's Palace*). Facing the cathedral's main entrance, this is a fine 18th-century mansion with one of the most stunning facades in the city, as well as interesting interior details. It's now a venue for temporary art exhibitions. ⊠ *Pl. Obispo 6* ☎ *951/294051* ⌧ *Free* ☉ *Tues. 2.30–8, Wed.–Sat. 10–8, Sun. 10–2.*

**Pasaje Chinitas.** The narrow streets and alleys on each side of Calle Marqués de Larios have charms of their own. Wander the warren of passageways around Pasaje Chinitas, off Plaza de la Constitución, and peep into the dark, vaulted bodegas where old men down glasses of *seco añejo* or *Málaga Virgen,* local wines made from Málaga's muscatel grapes. Silversmiths and vendors of religious books and statues ply their trades in shops that have changed little since the early 1900s. Backtrack across Larios, and, in the streets leading to Calle Nueva, you can see shoeshine boys, lottery-ticket vendors, Gypsy guitarists, and tapas bars serving wine from huge barrels.

## NERJA
*52 km (32 miles) east of Málaga.*

★ Nerja—the name comes from the Moorish word *narixa,* meaning "abundant springs." The village is on a headland above small beaches and rocky coves. In high season, Nerja is packed with tourists, but the rest of the year it's a pleasure to wander the Old Town's narrow streets.

★ **Balcón de Europa.** The highlight of Nerja is the Balcón de Europa, a
Ⓒ tree-lined promenade on a promontory just off the central square, with magnificent views of the mountains and sea. You can gaze far off into the horizon using the strategically placed telescopes, or use this as a starting point for a horse and carriage clip-clop ride around town.

**Cuevas de Nerja** (*Nerja Caves*). The Nerja Caves lie between Almuñécar and Nerja on a road surrounded by giant cliffs and dramatic seascapes. Signs point to the cave entrance above the village of Maro, 4 km (2½ miles) east of Nerja. Its spires and turrets, created by millennia of dripping water, are now floodlit for better views. One suspended pinnacle, 200 feet long, is the world's largest known stalactite. The cave painting of seals discovered here may be the oldest example of art in existence—and the only ones known to have been painted by Neanderthals. The awesome subterranean chambers create an evocative setting for concerts and ballets during the Nerja Festival of Music and Dance, held annually during the second and third weeks of July. There is also a bar-restaurant near the entrance with a spacious dining room that has superb panoramic views. ☎ *952/529520* ⊕ *www.cuevadenerja.com* ✉ *€8.50* ⊙ *Daily 10–7:30.*

## MARBELLA
*52 km (32 miles) west of Málaga.*

Playground of the rich and home of movie stars, rock musicians, and dispossessed royal families, Marbella has attained the top rung on Europe's social ladder. Dip into any Spanish gossip magazine and chances are the glittering parties that fill its pages are set in Marbella. However, much of this action takes place on the fringes—grand hotels and luxury restaurants line the waterfront for 20 km (12 miles) on each side of the town center.

**Old Village.** Marbella's appeal lies in the heart of the old village, which remains surprisingly intact. Here, a block or two back from the main highway, narrow alleys of whitewashed houses cluster around the central **Plaza de los Naranjos** (Orange Square), where colorful, albeit pricey, restaurants vie for space under the orange trees. Climb onto what remains of the old fortifications and stroll along the Calle Virgen de los Dolores to the Plaza de Santo Cristo.

**Puerto Banús.** Marbella's wealth glitters most brightly along the Golden Mile, a tiara of star-studded clubs, restaurants, and hotels west of town and stretching from Marbella to Puerto Banús. A mosque, an Arab bank, and the former residence of Saudi Arabia's late King Fahd betray the influence of oil money in this wealthy enclave. About 7 km (4½ miles) west of central Marbella (between Km 175 and Km 174), a sign indicates the turnoff leading down to Puerto Banús. Though now hemmed in by a belt of high-rises, Marbella's plush marina, with 915 berths, is a gem of ostentatious wealth, a Spanish answer to St. Tropez.

Huge yachts, beautiful people, and countless expensive stores and restaurants make up the glittering parade that marches long into the night. The backdrop is an Andalusian pueblo—built in the 1960s to resemble the fishing villages that once lined this coast.

### GRANADA

*128 km (80 miles) northeast of Málaga.*

Granada rises majestically from a plain onto three hills, dwarfed—on a clear day—by the Sierra Nevada. Atop one of these hills perches the pink-gold Alhambra palace. The stunning view from its mount takes in the sprawling medieval Moorish quarter, the caves of the Sacromonte, and, in the distance, the fertile *vega* (plain), rich in orchards, tobacco fields, and poplar groves. These days much of the Alhambra and Albaicín areas are closed to cars, because of the difficult access, but starting from the Plaza Nueva there are now minibuses—Nos. 30, 31, and 34—that run frequently to these areas.

Fodor'sChoice **Alhambra.** With more than 2.3 million visitors a year, the Alhambra
★ is Spain's most popular attraction. Simply take one of the minibuses, number 30 or 32, up from the Plaza Nueva. They run every few minutes; pay the fare of €1.20 on board. Just past the gate, take the path branching off to the left to the Puerta de la Justicia (Gate of Justice), one of the Alhambra's entrances. Yusuf I built the gate in 1348; its two arches have carvings depicting a key and a hand. The five fingers of the hand represent the five laws of the Koran. The complex has three main parts: the Alcazaba, the Palacios Nazaríes (Nasrid Palaces), and the Generalife, the ancient summer palace.

Construction of the Alhambra was begun in 1238 by Ibn el-Ahmar, the first king of the Nasrids. The great citadel once comprised a complex of houses, schools, baths, barracks, and gardens surrounded by defense towers and seemingly impregnable walls. Today, only the Alcazaba and the Palacios Nazaríes, built chiefly by Yusuf I (1334–54) and his son Mohammed V (1354–91), remain. The palace is an endless, intricate conglomeration of patios, arches, and cupolas made from wood, plaster, and tile; lavishly colored and adorned with marquetry and ceramics in geometric patterns and topped by delicate, frothy profusions of lace-like stucco and *mocárabes* (ornamental stalactites). Built of perishable materials, it was never intended to last but to be forever replenished and replaced by succeeding generations.

Across from the main entrance is the original fortress, the **Alcazaba.** Its ruins are dominated by the Torre de la Vela (Watchtower); from its summit you can see, to the north, the Albayzín; to the northeast, the Sacromonte; and to the west, the cathedral. The tower's great bell was once used, by both the Moors and the Christians, to announce the opening and closing of the irrigation system on Granada's great plain. ⊠ *Cuesta de Gomérez, Alhambra* ⊕ *www.alhambra-patronato.es* ⊠ *Alhambra and Generalife: €13; Generalife and Alcazaba: €7; Fine Arts Museum: €1.50; Museum of the Alhambra and Palace of Carlos V: free* ☉ *Alhambra, Alcazaba, Generalife and Palace of Carlos V: daily 8:30–6 (to 8 pm Mar. 15–Oct. 14); Museum of the Alhambra: Tues.–Sun. 8:30–2; Museum of Fine Arts: Tues. 2:30–8, Wed.–Sat. 9–8, Sun. 9–2:30.*

## SHOPPING

Málaga offers a full range of local specialties made throughout the region. Shoes and leather goods are of high quality. Handmade and mass-produced ceramics are produced in a range of colors and styles. Fans and silk shawls, along with other traditional Spanish clothing, range in price, depending on quality. Olives and olive oil will make gourmets happy, and olive oil is also used for a range of hair and beauty products. Other edibles include dried serrano ham, Manchego cheese, and *turrón* (an almond and honey sweet). *Seco añejo* sweet wine is also produced in the region.

In Málaga the main shopping street is Marqués de Larios, known locally as Larios, a traffic-free boulevard with excellent boutiques.

## BEACHES

Lobster-pink sun worshippers from northern Europe pack these beaches in summer so heavily that there's little towel space on the sand. Beach chairs can be rented for around €5 a day. Beaches range from shingle and pebbles (Almuñecar, Nerja, Málaga) to fine, gritty sand (westward of Málaga). The best are those around Marbella. It's acceptable for women to go topless; if you want to take it *all* off, go to beaches designated *playa naturista*. The most popular nude beach is Maro (near Nerja).

## WHERE TO EAT

$ ✕ **Lo Güeno.** This traditional tapas bar has two dining spaces: the orig-
SPANISH inal well-loved bar, shoehorned into a deceptively small space on a
Fodor's Choice side street near Calle Larios, and a more recent expansion across the
★ street. The original is especially appealing, with its L-shape wooden bar crammed with a choice of more than 75 tantalizing tapas, including many Logueno originals such as grilled oyster mushrooms with garlic, parsley, and goat cheese. There's an excellent selection of Rioja and Ribera wines, and the service is fast and good, despite the lack of elbow room. ⑤ *Average main: €8* ⊠ *Marin Garcia 9* ☎ *952/223048* ⊕ *www.logueno.es.*

$ ✕ **Vino Mio.** This Dutch-owned restaurant is well placed, just off Plaza
ECLECTIC de la Merced, and the menu is diverse and interesting, with dishes like "pasta rasta" (black tagliatelle with king prawns, arugula, and white wine) and the *boda Árabe* (Arab wedding) salad—warm couscous with fresh vegetables and raisins. Save room for the Guinness-and-chocolate cake. Monthly art exhibitions and flamenco music from Monday through Saturday help add to the chic atmosphere. The same menu, along with cocktails served after midnight, are featured at Vino Mio's sister restaurant nearby, at Plaza Jerónimo Cuervo 2. ⑤ *Average main: €12* ⊠ *C. Alamos 11* ☎ *952/609093* ⊕ *www.restaurantevinomio.com.*

# MALLORCA, SPAIN

Updated by
Joanna Styles

More than five times the size of its fellow Balearic Islands, Mallorca is shaped roughly like a saddle. The Sierra de Tramuntana, a dramatic mountain range soaring to nearly 5,000 feet, runs the length of its northwest coast, and a ridge of hills borders the southeast shores; between the two lies a great, flat plain that in early spring becomes a sea of almond blossoms, "the snow of Mallorca." The island draws more than 9 million visitors a year, many of them bound for summer vacation packages in the coastal resorts. The beaches are beautiful, but save time for the charms of the northwest and the interior: caves, bird sanctuaries, monasteries and medieval cities, local museums, outdoor cafés, and village markets.

## ESSENTIALS

### CURRENCY
The euro.

### HOURS
Museums generally open 9 until 7 or 8, many are closed on Monday, and some close in the afternoon. Most stores are open Monday through Saturday 9 to 1:30 and 5 to 8, but tourist shops may open in the afternoon and also on Sunday between May and September.

### PRIVATE TOURS
**Autocares Comas.** The company organizes a year-round program of trips to various locations on the island. ☎ *902/026424* ⊕ *www. autocarescomas.com.*

### TELEPHONES
Most tri-band or quad-band GSM phones will work in Spain, where services are 3G-compatible. Public kiosks accept phone cards that support international calls (cards sold in press shops, bars, and telecom shops). Major companies include Vodafone.

## COMING ASHORE
Vessels dock at the port directly in front of the Old Town of Palma. There is no shuttle, so passengers docking at the farthest berth (south side of the harbor) have a 20-minute walk to the terminal building and the port entrance. From the port entrance you can walk into Palma town. There are few facilities at the cruise terminal or in the port.

If you only want to enjoy Palma, you won't need to worry about transportation; however, Mallorca is a small island, and you can see a great deal of it in a day with a vehicle or on public transportion. Regular and reliable bus services link the major towns, though services are fewer on Sunday. Car rentals cost around €25 per day for an economy manual vehicle (book well in advance, especially in July and August), but it's much cheaper to explore by public transit.

# EXPLORING MALLORCA

## PALMA DE MALLORCA

If you look north of the cathedral (La Seu, or the "seat" of the Bishopric, to Mallorcans) on a map of the city of Palma, you can see the jumble of tiny streets around the Plaça Santa Eulalia that made up the early town. A stroll through these streets will bring you past many interesting neoclassical and moderniste buildings.

**Ajuntament** (*town hall*). Along Carrer Colom is the 17th-century Ajuntament. Stop in to see the collection of *gigantes*—the huge painted and costumed mannequins paraded through the streets during festivals—on display in the lobby. The olive tree on the right side of the square is one of Majorca's so-called *olivos milenarios*—purported to be more than 1,000 years old. ⊠ *Pl. Cort 1.*

**MALLORCA BEST BETS**

**The Cathedral.** Palma's cathedral has a unique circular design as well as decorations by Gaudí.

**Museu d'Es Baluard.** The Museum of Modern and Contemporary Art is an exciting convergence of old and new.

**Sóller.** One of the most beautiful towns on the island, with a large collection of moderniste buildings.

**Castell de Bellver** (*Bellver Castle*). Overlooking the city and the bay from a hillside, the castle was built at the beginning of the 14th century, in Gothic style but with a circular design—the only one of its kind in Spain. It houses an archaeological museum of the history of Majorca, and a small collection of classical sculpture. ⊠ *Camilo José Cela s/n* ☎ *971/730657* ▧ *€3, free Sun.* ☉ *Castle and museum open Oct.–Mar., Mon.–Sat. 8:30–6:45; Apr.–Sept., Mon.–Sat. 8:30–8:30. Museum is closed Sun., but castle is open 10–4:30.*

**Fodor's Choice**
★

**Catedral de Majorca.** Palma's cathedral is an architectural wonder that took almost 400 years to build. Begun in 1230, the wide expanse of the nave is supported by 14 70-foot-tall columns that fan out at the top like palm trees. The nave is dominated by an immense rose window, 40 feet in diameter, from 1370. Over the main altar (consecrated in 1346) is the surrealistic **baldoquí** by Antoni Gaudí, completed in 1912. This enormous canopy, with lamps suspended from it like elements of a mobile, rises to a Crucifixion scene at the top. To the right, in the Chapel of the Santísimo, is an equally remarkable 2007 work by the modern sculptor Miquel Barceló: a painted ceramic tableau covering the walls like a skin. Based on the New Testament account of the miracle of the loaves and fishes, it's a bizarre composition of rolling waves, gaping cracks, protruding fish heads, and human skulls. The **bell tower** above the cathedral's Plaça Almoina door holds nine bells, the largest of which is called N'Eloi, meaning "Praise." The five-ton N'Eloi, cast in 1389, requires six men to ring it and has shattered stained-glass windows with its sound. ■TIP→ **There's an organ concert in the basilica on the first Tuesday of every month, from noon–12:30.** ⊠ *Pl. Almoina s/n* ☎ *971/723130, 902/022445* ⊕ *www.catedraldemallorca.org* ▧ *€6* ☉ *Apr. and May, weekdays 10–5:15, Sat. 10–2:15; June–Sept., weekdays 10–6:15, Sat. 10–2:15; Nov.–Mar., weekdays 10–3:15, Sat. 10–2:15; Sun. year-round for services only, 8:30–1:45 and 6:30–7:45.*

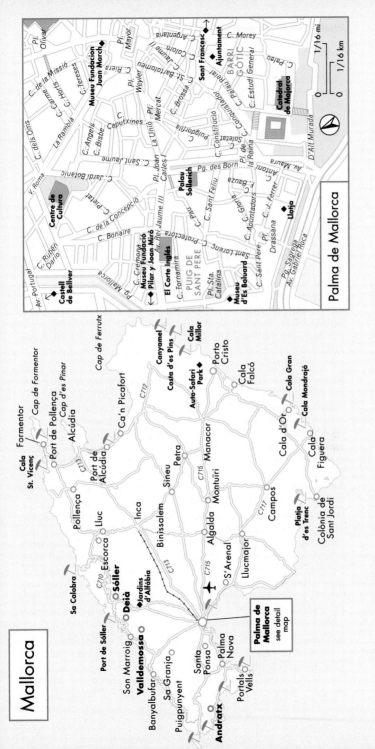

# Mallorca

Cap de Formentor
Formentor
Cap d'es Pinar
Cala St. Vicenç
Port de Pollença
Alcúdia
Cap de Ferrutx
Port de Alcúdia
Sa Calobra
Pollença
Lluc
Canyamel
Escorca
Costa d'es Pins
Port de Sóller
Cala Millor
Sóller
C710
Inca
Binissalem
Sineu
Son Marroig
Jardins d'Alfàbia
Petra
Auto-Safari Park
Deià
C713
Porto Cristo
Valldemossa
Manacor
Cala Falcó
C711
Banyalbufar
Sa Granja
S'Arenal
Algalda
Montuïri
C715
Cala d'Or
Cala Gran
Cala Mondrajó
Puigpunyent
Santa Ponsa
Palma Nova
Llucmajor
Campos
Cala Figuera
Andratx
Portals Vells
Palma de Mallorca
see detail map
Platja d'es Trenc
Colònia de Sant Jordi
C712
C713
C715

0 — 10 miles
0 — 15 km

## Palma de Mallorca

Pl. Olivar
Av. Portugal
C. de la Missió
C. del Oms
C. Rubén Darío
Centre de Cultura
V. Roma
C. Pietat
C. de la Concepció
C. Bonaire
Pg. Mallorca
C. Cremona
Museu Fundació Pilar y Joan Miró
El Corte Inglés
Av. Rei Jaume III
C. de la Concepció
Jardí Botànic
C. Sant Jaume
Pl. Joan Carles I
Pl. de la Unió
Mercat
Pg. des Born
Castell de Bellver
PUIG DE SANT PERE
C. Tornamira
C. Sant Llorenç
C. Protectora
Pl. Sta. Catalina
Museu d'Es Baluard
C. Sant Pere
Drassana
C. Apuntadors
Museu Fundación Juan March
Pl. Mayor
C. Riera
C. Weyler
Pl. Teatre
Pl. Santa Eulalia
La Rambla
C. Angels
C. Bisbe
C. Horts
Carme
La Rambla
Caputxines
C. Teresos
C. Sant Jaume
St. Bartolomeu
C. Jaume II
Colom
Sant Francesc
Ajuntament
C. Morey
C. Palau
Puigdorfila
Pl. Brossa
Constitució
Palau Sollerich
C. Sant Feliu
C. Glòria
F. Bauza
C. J. Ferrer
Llotja
Pg. Sagrera
Av. Gabriel Roca
Antoni
Maura
Av. Maura
C. Soledat
Pl. de la Reina
C. Estudi General
Palau Reial
C. Conquistador
Catedral de Majorca
BARRI GOTIC
D'Alt Murada

0 — 1/16 mi
0 — 1/16 km

**Llotja** (*Exchange*). On the seafront west of the Plaça de la Reina, the Llotja was built in the 15th century and connects via an interior court-yard to the **Consolat de Mar** (Maritime Consulate). With its decorative turrets, pointed battlements, fluted pillars, and Gothic stained-glass windows—part fortress, part church—it attests to the wealth Majorca achieved in its heyday as a Mediterranean trading power. The interior can be visited only during special exhibitions in the Merchants Cham-ber. ⊠ *Pl. de la Llotja 5* ☎ *971/711705* ⊙ *During exhibits, Tues.–Sat. 11–2 and 5–9, Sun. 11–2.*

**Fodor's**Choice  **Museu d'Es Baluard** (*Museum of Modern and Contemporary Art of*
★   *Palma*). At the western end of the city, the Museu d'Es Baluard rises on a long-neglected archaeological site, parts of which date back to the 12th century. The building itself is an outstanding convergence of old and new: the exhibition space uses the surviving 16th-century perimeter walls of the fortified city, including a stone courtyard fac-ing the sea and a promenade along the ramparts. There are three floors of galleries, and the collection includes work by Miró, Picasso, Henri Magritte, Tapiès, Alexander Calder, and other major artists. The courtyard café-terrace Restaurant del Museu (Nov.–May, Tues-day–Sunday 10–8; Jun.–Oct. 10-midnight) affords a fine view of the marina. ⊠ *Pl. Porta de Santa Catalina 10* ☎ *971/908200* ⊕ *www. esbaluard.org* 🎫 *Wed., Thurs. and weekends €6; Tues. €4.50; volun-tary contributions on Fri.; free on some weekends in Feb.* ⊙ *Tues.–Sat. 10–8; Sun. 10–3.*

★   **Museu Fundación Juan March.** A few steps from the north archway of the Plaça Major is the Museu Fundación Juan March. This fine little museum was established to display what had been a private collection of modern Spanish art. The building itself was a sumptuous private home built in the 18th century. The second and third floors were redesigned to accommodate a series of small galleries, with one or two works at most—by Pablo Picasso, Joan Miró, Juan Gris, Salvador Dalí, Antoni Tàpies, and Miquel Barceló, among others—on each wall. ⊠ *Carrer Sant Miguel 11* ☎ *971/713515* ⊕ *www.march.es/museupalma* 🎫 *Free* ⊙ *Weekdays 10–6:30, Sat. 10:30–2.*

**Museu Fundació Pilar y Joan Miró** (*Pilar and Joan Miró Foundation Museum*). The permanent collection in the Museu Fundació Pilar y Joan Miró includes a great many drawings and studies by the Catalan artist, who spent his last years on Majorca, but shows far fewer finished paint-ings and sculptures than the Fundació Miró in Barcelona. Don't miss the adjacent studio, built for Miró by his friend the architect Josep Lluis Sert. The artist did most of his work here from 1957 on. ⊠ *Carrer Joan de Saridakis 29, Cala Major* ☎ *971/701420* ⊕ *miro.palmademallorca.es* 🎫 *€6* ⊙ *Tues.–Sat. 10–6 (to 7 May 16–Sept. 15), Sun. 10–3.*

**Sant Francesc.** The 13th-century monastery church of Sant Francesc was established by Jaume II when his eldest son took monastic orders and gave up rights to the throne. Fra Junípero Serra, the missionary who founded San Francisco, California, was later educated here; his statue stands to the left of the main entrance. The basilica houses the tomb of the eminent 13th-century scholar Ramón Llull. The cloisters are

especially beautiful and peaceful. ⊠ *Pl. Sant Francesc 7, Barrio Antiguo*
📧 *€1.50* ⊘ *Mon.–Sat. 9:30–12:30 and 3:30–6, Sun. 9:30–1.*

## ANDRATX
*16 km (10 miles) west of Palma.*

Andratx is a charming cluster of white-and-ocher hillside houses, rather
like cliff dwellings, with the 3,363-foot Mt. Galatzó behind it. Many of
the towns on Majorca are at some distance from their seafronts; from
Andratx you can take a 4-km (1½-mile) drive through S'Arracó to
Sant Elm and on to the rocky shore opposite Sa Dragonera—an island
shaped indeed like the long-armored back of a dragon. Local history
has it that the tiny island of Pantaleu, just to the west of it, was where
Jaume I chose to disembark in September 1200, on his campaign to
retake Majorca from the Moors.

## VALLDEMOSSA
*18 km (11 miles) north of Palma.*

**Reial Cartuja** (*Royal Carthusian Monastery*). It was founded in 1339,
but when the monks were expelled in 1835, the Reial Cartuja became
apartments for travelers. The most famous lodgers were Frédéric Chopin and his lover, the Baroness Amandine Dupin—a French novelist
who used the pseudonym George Sand. The two spent three difficult
months here in the cold, damp winter of 1838–39.

In the **church,** note the frescoes above the nave—the monk who painted
them was Goya's brother-in-law. The **pharmacy,** made by the monks
in 1723, is almost completely preserved. A long corridor leads to the
apartments occupied by Chopin and Sand, furnished in period style. The
piano is original. Nearby, another set of apartments houses the local
**museum,** with mementos of Archduke Luis Salvador and a collection
of old printing blocks. From here you return to the ornately furnished
**King Sancho's palace,** a group of rooms originally built by King Jaume
II for his son. The tourist office, in Valldemossa's main plaza, sells a
ticket good for all of the monastery's attractions. ⊠ *Pl. de la Cartuja
11* 🕾 *971/612106* ⊕ *www.valldemossa.com* 📧 *€7.50* ⊘ *Dec. and Jan.,
Mon.–Sat. 9:30–3; Feb. and Nov., Mon.–Sat. 9:30–5, Sun. 10–1; Mar.–
Oct., Mon.–Sat. 9:30–5:30, Sun. 10–1.*

## JARDINS D'ALFÀBIA
*17 km (10½ miles) north of Palma, 13 km (8½ miles) south of Sóller.*

**Jardins d'Alfàbia.** Here's a sound you don't often hear in the Majorcan
interior: the rush of falling water. The Moorish viceroy of the island
developed the springs and hidden irrigation systems here sometime in
the 12th century to create this remarkable oasis on the road to Sóller.
Here you'll find 40-odd varieties of trees, climbers, and flowering
shrubs. The 17th-century manor house, furnished with antiques and
painted panels, has a collection of original documents that chronicles
the history of the estate. ⊠ *Ctra. Palma–Sóller, Km 17* 🕾 *971/613123*
⊕ *www.jardinesdealfabia.com* 📧 *€4.50* ⊘ *Nov.–Mar., weekdays 9:30–
5:30, Sat. 9:30–1; Apr.–Oct., Mon.–Sat. 9:30–6:30.*

## SÓLLER

★ *13 km (8 ½ miles) north of Jardins d'Alfàbia, 30 km (19 miles) north of Palma.*

This is one of the most beautiful towns on the island, thick with palatial homes built in the 19th and early 20th centuries by the owners of agricultural estates in the Sierra de Tramuntana, and the merchants who thrived on the export of the region's oranges, lemons, and almonds. Many of the buildings here, like the **Church of Sant Bartomeu** and the **Bank of Sóller**, on the Plaça Constitució, and the nearby **Can Prunera**, are gems of the moderniste style, designed by contemporaries of Antoni Gaudí. The tourist information office in the **town hall**, next to Sant Bartomeu, has a walking tour map of the important sites.

Travel retro to Sóller from Palma on one of the six daily trains (round-trip: €20) from Plaça d'Espanya: a string of wooden coaches with leather-covered seats, dating from 1912.

Visit the Station Building Galleries before you set out on your exploration of the town—and if you're spending the night, book early: Sóller is not overly endowed with hotels.

Return to the station to catch the charming old blue-and-brass trolly (€4) that threads its way through town, down to Port de Sóller. Spend the day at the beach. Better yet: rent a car at the port for the spectacular drive over the Sierra de Tramontana to Deià and Son Marroig, or the Monestary of Lluc.

**Station Building Galleries.** Maintained by the Fundació Tren de l'Art, Sóller's Station Building Galleries have two small but remarkable collections, one of engravings by Miró, the other of ceramics by Picasso. ⊠ *Pl. Espanya 6* ☎ *971/630301* ⊠ *Free* ☾ *Daily 10:30–6:30.*

## DEIÀ

*9 km (5½ miles) southwest of Sóller.*

★ Deià is perhaps best known as the adopted home of the English poet and writer Robert Graves, who lived here off and on from 1929 until his death in 1985. The village is still a favorite haunt of writers and artists, including Graves's son Tomás, author of *Pa amb oli (Bread and Olive Oil),* a guide to Majorcan cooking, and British painter David Templeton. The setting is unbeatable; all around Deià rise the steep cliffs of the Sierra de Tramuntana. On warm afternoons literati gather at the beach bar in the rocky cove at Cala de Deià, 2 km (1 mile) downhill from the village. Walk up the narrow street to the village church; the small **cemetery** behind it affords views of mountains terraced with olive trees and of the coves below. It's a fitting spot for Graves's final resting place, in a quiet corner beneath a simple slab.

**Ca N'Alluny.** The Fundació Robert Graves opened this museum dedicated to Deià's most famous resident in Ca N'Alluny, the house he built in 1932. The seaside house is something of a shrine: Graves's furniture and books, personal effects, and the press he used to print many of his works are all preserved. ⊠ *Ctra. Deià-Sóller s/n* ☎ *971/636185* ⊕ *www.lacasaderobertgraves.com* ⊠ *€7* ☾ *Apr.–Oct., weekdays 10–5, Sat. 10–3; Nov., Feb., and Mar., weekdays 9–4, Sat. 9–2; Dec. and Jan., weekdays 10–3.*

## SHOPPING

Mallorca's specialties are leather shoes and clothing, porcelain, souvenirs carved from olive wood, handblown glass, artificial pearls, and espadrilles. Top-name fashion boutiques line **Avinguda Jaume III** and the nearby Plaça Joan Carles I. You can find several antiques shops on Plaça Almoina. Less-expensive shopping strips are **Carrer Sindicat** and **Carrer Sant Miquel**—both pedestrian streets running north from the Plaça Major—and the small streets south of the Plaça Major. The **Plaça Major** itself has a modest crafts market Monday, Thursday, Friday, and Saturday 10 to 2. In summer the market is open daily 10 to 2; January and February, it's open weekends only.

**Gordiola.** Glassmakers since 1719, visit Gordiola for a variety of original bowls, bottles, plates, and decorative objects. The company's factory is in Alguida, on the Palma–Manacor road, where you can watch the glass being blown and even try your hand at making a piece. ⊠ *Carrera Victoria 8, Centro, Palma* ☎ *971/711541.*

**Las Columnas.** Ceramics from all over the Balearic Islands are sold here. ⊠ *Carrer Sant Domingo 8, San Agustin, Palma* ☎ *971/712221.*

## GOLF

Mallorca has more than a score of 18-hole golf courses, among them PGA championship venues of fiendish difficulty. Cruise passengers who want to play a round while in port should make arrangements through their cruise ship.

## BEACHES

The closer a beach is to Palma, the more crowded it's likely to be. West of the city is **Palma Nova**; behind the lovely, narrow beach rises one of the most densely developed resorts on the island. **Paguera,** with several small beaches, is the only sizable local resort not overshadowed by highrises. **Camp de Mar,** with a good beach of fine white sand, is small and relatively undeveloped, but is sometimes overrun with day-trippers from other resorts. **Sant Elm,** at the end of this coast, has a pretty little bay and a tree-shaded parking lot. East of Palma, a 5-km (3-mile) stretch of sand runs along the main coastal road from C'an Pastilla to Arenal, forming a package-tour nexus also known collectively as **Playa de Palma;** the crowded beach is long with fine white sand.

## WHERE TO EAT

$ ╳ **Café la Lonja.** A great spot for hot chocolate or a unique tea or cof-
TAPAS fee, this classic establishment in the old fishermen's neighborhood has a young vibe that goes well with the style of the place. Both the sunny terrace in front of the Llotja—a privileged dining spot—and the dining room inside are excellent places for drinks and sandwiches. The seasonal menu might include a salad of tomato, avocado, and Manchego cheese; fluffy quiche; and tapas of squid or mushrooms. It's a good

rendezvous point and watering hole. $ *Average main: €12* ⊠ *Carrer Llotja del Mar 2, Palma* ☎ *971/722799* ⊘ *Closed Sun.*

$    ✕ **La Bóveda.** Within hailing distance of the Llotja, this popular restau-
TAPAS    rant serves tapas and inexpensive platters such as chicken or ham croquettes, grilled cod, garlic shrimp, and *revueltos de ajos con morcilla*
(scrambled eggs with garlic and black sausage). The tables in the back
are always at a premium (they're cooler on summer days), but there's
additional seating at the counter or on stools around upended wine
barrels. The huge portions of traditional tapas are nothing fancy but
very good. $ *Average main: €12* ⊠ *Carrer de la Botería 3, La Llotja,
Palma* ☎ *971/714863* ⊘ *Closed Sun.*

# MARSEILLE, FRANCE

Updated
by Jennifer
Ladonne

Marseille may sometimes be given a wide berth by travelers in search of
a Provençal idyll, but it's their loss. Miss it, and you miss one of the most
vibrant, exciting cities in France. With its cubist jumbles of white stone
rising up over a picture-book seaport, bathed in light of blinding clar-
ity and crowned by larger-than-life neo-Byzantine churches, the city's
neighborhoods teem with multiethnic life. Its souk-like African markets
reek deliciously of spices and coffees, and its labyrinthine Vieille Ville
is painted in broad strokes of saffron, cinnamon, and robin's-egg blue.
Feisty and fond of broad gestures, Marseille is a dynamic city, as cosmopolitan now as when the Phoenicians first founded it, and with all the
exoticism of the international shipping port it has been for 2,600 years.
Vital to the Crusades in the Middle Ages and crucial to Louis XIV as
a military port, Marseille flourished as France's market to the world—
and still does today. In 2013 Marseille will be the European Capital of
Culture and will host all manner of special events throughout the year.

## ESSENTIALS

### CURRENCY
The euro.

### HOURS
Stores are open Monday through Saturday 9–7, but many close at
lunchtime (usually noon–2 or 3) and some will open later and on Sunday during July and August. Museums are open 10–5, but most are
closed on either Monday or Tuesday.

### TELEPHONES
Tri-band GSM phones work in France. You can buy prepaid phone
cards at telecom shops, news vendors, and tobacconists in all towns
and cities. Phone cards can be used for local or international calls.
Orange, SFR, Bouygues Telecom, and Virgin are leading telecom companies. If you have an unlocked GSM phone, LeFrenchMobile (⊕ *www.
lefrenchmobile.com*) offers SIM cards (and micro SIM cards) with support in English, unlimited validity of credits, and prepurchase online.

### COMING ASHORE
The Marseille Cruise Terminal is north of the Vieux Port historic area
and has benefited from a €90 million redevelopment. It now offers
three different docking areas depending on the size of the vessel and

a state-of-the-art welcome center with an ATM, shops, bars, and restaurants. Aside from this, the terminal is in an industrial area and is too distant to allow you to walk into the city. Most cruise lines offer shuttle service into town, but you should spring for a taxi if you don't take the shuttle.

A taxi from the cruise terminal into town is approximately €30 and takes around 20 minutes. Once in the Vieux Port area, most of the major attractions are reachable on foot. Taxis are plentiful and can provide tourist itineraries. Single journeys begin at €2.30 and are €0.80 per km thereafter.

Although there is no reason to drive if you're just staying in Marseille, renting a vehicle is the ideal way to explore the beautiful Provençal towns and landscapes around the city. Expect to pay around €75 per day for an economy manual vehicle.

---

### MARSEILLE BEST BETS

**Order bouillabaise.** This aromatic fish stew is one of the world's most famous dishes, and originated here as a way for fishermen to use the leftover catch.

**Stroll around Vieux Port and La Panier.** The Vieux Port bustles with activity, but especially during the morning fish market. Neighboring Le Panier is a maze of narrow streets and picturesque corners with pretty boutiques and good museums.

**Centre de la Vieille Charite.** The museums here have important collections and artifacts from civilizations and societies from around the world.

---

## EXPLORING MARSEILLE

★ **Abbaye St-Victor.** Founded in the fourth century by St. Cassien, who sailed into Marseille full of fresh ideas on monasticism that he acquired in Palestine and Egypt, this church grew to formidable proportions. With a Romanesque design, the structure would be as much at home in the Middle East as its founder was. The **crypt,** St. Cassien's original, is buried under the medieval church, and in the evocative nooks and crannies you can find the fifth-century sarcophagus that allegedly holds the martyr's remains. Upstairs, a reliquary contains what's left of St. Victor, who was ground to death between millstones, probably by Romans. There's also a passage into tiny **catacombs** where Early Christians worshipped St. Lazarus and Mary Magdalene, said to have washed ashore at Stes-Maries-de-la-Mer. The boat in which they landed is reproduced in canoe-shaped cookies called *navettes,* which are sold during the annual procession for Candelmas in February as well as year-round. ⊠ *3 rue de l'Abbaye, Rive Neuve* ☎ *04–96–11–22–60* ⊕ *www.saintvictor.net* ☐ *Crypt €2* ☉ *Daily 9–7.*

**Cathédrale de la Nouvelle Major.** This gargantuan, neo-Byzantine 19th-century fantasy was built under Napoléon III—but not before he'd ordered the partial destruction of the lovely 11th-century original, once a perfect example of the Provençal Romanesque style. You can view the flashy decor—marble and rich red porphyry inlay—in the newer of the two churches; the medieval one is being restored. ⊠ *Pl. de la Major, Le Panier.*

★ **Centre de la Vieille Charité** (*Center of the Old Charity*). At the top of the Panier district you'll find this superb ensemble of 17th- and 18th-century architecture designed as a hospice for the homeless by Marseillais artist-architects Pierre and Jean Puget. Even if you don't enter the museums, walk around the inner court, studying the retreating perspective of triple arcades and admiring the baroque chapel with its novel egg-peaked dome. Of the complex's two museums, the larger is the **Musée d'Archéologie Méditerranéenne** (Museum of Mediterranean Archaeology), with a sizable collection of pottery and statuary from classical Mediterranean civilization, elementally labeled (for example, "pot"). There's also a display on the mysterious Celt-like Ligurians who first peopled the coast, cryptically presented with emphasis on the digs instead of the finds themselves. The best of the lot is the evocatively mounted Egyptian collection, the second largest in France after the Louvre's. There are mummies, hieroglyphs, and gorgeous sarcophagi in a tomblike setting. Upstairs, the **Musée d'Arts Africains, Océaniens, et Amérindiens** (Museum of African, Oceanic, and American Indian Art) creates a theatrical foil for the works' intrinsic drama: the spectacular masks and sculptures are mounted along a pure black wall, lighted indirectly, with labels across the aisle. ✉ *2 rue de la Charité, Le Panier* ☎ *04–91–14–58–80* ✉ *€3 per museum* ⊙ *May–Sept., Tues.–Sun. 10–6.*

★ **Château d'If.** François I, in the 16th century, recognized the strategic advantage of an island fortress surveying the mouth of Marseille's vast harbor and built this imposing edifice. Its effect as a deterrent was so successful that the fortress never saw combat, and was eventually converted into a prison. It was here that Alexandre Dumas locked up his most famous character, the Count of Monte Cristo. Though the count was fictional, the hole through which Dumas had him escape is real enough, on display in the cells. On the other hand, the real-life Man in the Iron Mask, whose cell is also erroneously on display, was not imprisoned here. The IF Frioul Express boat ride (from the Quai des Belges, €10; for information call ☎ *04–91–46–54–65*) and the views from the broad terrace are worth the trip. ☎ *08–26–50–05–00* ⊕ *if.monuments-nationaux.fr/en* ✉ *€5* ⊙ *Mid-May–mid-Sept., daily 9:40–5:40; mid-Sept.–mid-May, daily 9–5:30. Closed Mon. mid-Sept.–Mar.*

Fodor's Choice ★ **Ferry Boat.** This Marseille treasure departs from the Quai below the Hôtel de Ville. For a pittance (although technically free, it is appropriate to tip the crew) you can file onto this little wooden barge and chug across the Vieux Port. ✉ *Pl. des Huiles on Quai de Rive Neuve side and Hôtel de Ville on Quai du Port, Vieux Port* ✉ *Free.*

**Fort St-Nicolas and Fort St-Jean.** These twin forts guard the entrance to the Vieux Port. In order to keep the feisty, rebellious Marseillais under his thumb, Louis XIV had the fortresses built with the guns pointing *toward* the city. The Marseillais, whose identity has always been mixed with a healthy dose of irony, are quite proud of this display of the king's doubts about their allegiance. To view the guns, climb up to the Jardin du Pharo. In spring of 2013 Fort St-Jean will open under the banner of the Musée National des Civilisations de L'Europe et de la Mediterranée (National Museum of the Civilizations of Europe and the Mediterranean), housing in part the folk-art collection of the former Musée

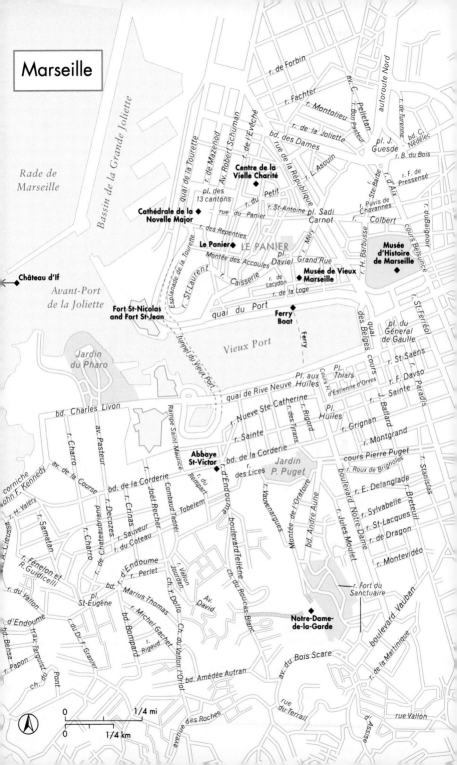

# Marseille

Rade de Marseille

Bassin de la Grande Joliette

Château d'If

Avant-Port de la Joliette

Jardin du Pharo

r. de Forbin
av. C. Pelletan
autoroute Nord
r. de Turenne
r. Fâchter
r. Montolieu
r. Bon pasteur
bd. des Dames
r. de la Joliette
pl. J. Guesde
bd. C. Nédélec
r. B. du Bois
r. L. Astouin
r. Ste-Barbe
r. F. de Pressensé
r. d'Aix
r. de l'Evêché
Av. Robert Schuman
quai de la Tourette
r. de Mazenod
**Centre de la Vielle Charité** ◆
pl. des 13 cantons
r. du Petit
rue du Panier
r. St-Antoine pl. Sadi Carnot
r. Puvis de Chavannes
cours Belsunce
r. du Baignoir
**Cathédrale de la Novelle Major** ◆
r. des Repenties
**Le Panier** ◆
LE PANIER
pl. Daviel
Grand'Rue
r. Méry
r. H. Barbusse
**Musée d'Histoire de Marseille** ◆
Esplanade de la Tourette
Montée des Accoules
r. Caisserie
r. de Lacydon
r. de la Loge
**Musée de Vieux Marseille** ◆
r. St-Laurent
quai des Belges
r. St-Ferréol
**Fort St-Nicolas and Fort St-Jean**
quai du Port
**Ferry Boat** ◆
tunnel du Vieux Port
Ferry
Vieux Port
quai de Rive Neuve
pl. du Général de Gaulle
Pl. aux Huíles
Cours H. d'Estienne d'Orves
Pl. Thiars
r. St-Saëns
r. F. Davso
J. Sainte
bd. Charles Livon
quai de Rive Neuve Huíles
Rampe Saint-Maurice
r. Nueve Ste-Catherine
r. Sainte
r. des Tyrans
r. Rigord
Pl. Huíles
r. Grignan
r. Ballard
r. Montgrand
av. Pasteur
av. de la Course
**Abbaye St-Victor** ◆
bd. de la Corderie
des Lices
Jardin P. Puget
cours Pierre Puget
r. Roux de Brignoles
r. E. Delanglade
r. Sylvabelle
r. St-Lacques
r. de Dragon
r. Montevidéo
r. Charro
bd. de la Corderie
r. Crinas
Joël Recher
Combaud Taddet
r. du Rempart
d'Endoume
Tobelem
boulevard Tellène
Vauvenargues
Montée de l'Oratoire
bd. André Aune
boulevard Notre-Dame
Jules Moulet
Stanislas
Breteuil
corniche John F. Kennedy
r. H. Valéry
av. Liéussa
r. Decozes
r. de Chateaudun
r. Sauveur
r. du Coteau
d'Endoume
r. Perlet
Ch. Vallon Jourdan
Ch. Y. Dolto
du Roucas-Blanc
r. Fort du Sanctuaire
r. Samatan
r. Charro
r. du Vallon
d'Endoume
r. Fénelon et R. Guidicelli
pl. St-Eugène
bd. Marius Thomas
r. Michel Gachet
r. Rigaud
Av. David
Ch. du Vallon l'Oriol
boulevard Vauban
r. de la Martinique
bd. Bensa
r. Papon
trav. Targuist Dr.
du Dr.-F. Granier
bd. Bompard
bd. Amédée Autran
av. du Bois Scare
r. de Assise
rue Vallon
ch. Pont
avenue des Roches
rue du Terrail
**Notre-Dame-de-la-Garde** ◆

0 | 1/4 mi
0 | 1/4 km

des Arts et Traditions Populaires in Paris. ⊠ *Quai du Port, Vieux Port* ☎ *04–96–13–80–90* ⊕ *www.mucem.org.*

★ **Le Panier.** This is the old heart of Marseille, a maze of high-shuttered houses looming over narrow cobbled streets, *montées* (stone stairways), and tiny squares. Long decayed and neglected, the quarter is the principal focus of the city's efforts at urban renewal. Wander this neighborhood at will, making sure to stroll along Rue du Panier, the montée des Accoules, Rue du Petit-Puits, and Rue des Muettes.

★ **Musée d'Histoire de Marseille** (*Marseille Museum of History*). A modern and open space, this museum illuminates Massalia's history with a treasure of archaeological finds and miniature models of the city as it appeared in various stages of history. Best by far is the presentation of Marseille's Classical halcyon days. There's a recovered wreck of a Roman cargo boat, its third-century wood amazingly preserved, and the hull of a Greek boat dating from the fourth century BC. The model of the Greek city should be authentic—it's based on the eyewitness description of Aristotle. The museum is closed for renovation until late 2012. ⊠ *Centre Bourse, entrance on Rue de Bir-Hakeim, Vieux Port* ☎ *04–91–90–42–22* ⊠ *€3 joint ticket with Jardin des Vestiges* ⊙ *June– Sept., Mon.–Sat. noon–7; Oct.–May., Tues.–Sun. 10–5.*

**Notre-Dame-de-la-Garde.** Towering above the city and visible for miles around, this overscaled neo-Byzantine monument was erected in 1853 by Napoléon III. The interior is a Technicolor bonanza of red-and-beige stripes and glittering mosaics, and the gargantuan *Madonna and Child* on the steeple (almost 30 feet high) is covered in real gold leaf. While the panoply of naive ex-votos, mostly thanking the Virgin for deathbed interventions and shipwreck survivals, is a remarkable sight, most impressive are the views of the seaside city at your feet. ⊠ *Off bd. André Aune* ✛ *On foot, climb up Cours Pierre Puget, cross Jardin Pierre Puget, cross bridge to Rue Vauvenargues, and hike up to Pl. Edon. Or catch Bus 60 from Cours Jean-Ballard* ☎ *04–91–13–40–80* ⊙ *May–Sept., daily 7 am–8 pm; Oct.–Apr., daily 7–7.*

## SHOPPING

Marseille offers contrasting shopping opportunities. For lovers of French haute couture there are many boutiques in the new town stocking the major designer labels—Christian Lacroix is a local boy—plus a thriving new fashion scene of young designers selling their own ready-to-wear collections from stylish galleries. Cours Julien is lined with stores, while Rue de la Tour in the Opera district is a center of modern design, known locally as "Fashion Street."

By contrast, the city, particularly Le Panier and rue St-Ferréol, also has numerous shops selling regional crafts and delicacies, including bright fabrics of blue and yellow, pottery, olive-wood items, plus delicious olives, olive oils, honey, tapenade (an olive paste), and dried herbs. **Savon de Marseille** (Marseille soap) is a household standard in France, often sold as a satisfyingly crude and hefty block in odorless olive-oil green. But its chichi offspring are dainty pastel guest soaps in almond, lemon, vanilla, and other scents.

**Four des Navettes.** The famous bakery Four des Navettes, up the street from Notre-Dame-de-la-Garde, makes orange-spice, shuttle-shape *navettes*. These cookies are modeled on the little boat in which it is said that Mary Magdalene and Lazarus washed up onto the nearby shores. ⊠ *136 rue Sainte, Garde Hill* ☎ *04–91–33–32–12* ⊕ *www. fourdesnavettes.com.*

## WHERE TO EAT

$$$$    ✕ **Chez Fonfon.** Tucked into the film-like tiny fishing port Vallon des
SEAFOOD   Auffes, this Marseillais landmark has one of the loveliest settings in greater Marseille. Once presided over by cult chef "Fonfon," it used to be a favorite movie-star hangout. A variety of fresh seafood, impeccably grilled, steamed, or roasted in salt crust are served in two pretty dining rooms with picture windows overlooking the fishing boats that supply your dinner. Try classic bouillabaisse served with all the bells and whistles—broth, hot-chili rouille, and flamboyant table-side filleting. ⑤ *Average main: €50* ⊠ *140 rue du Vallon des Auffes* ☎ *04–91–52–14–38* ⊕ *www.chez-fonfon.com* ⚭ *Reservations essential* ⊘ *Closed Sun. and Mon. in winter; Sun. and Mon. lunch in summer. Closed first 2 wks in Jan.*

$$    ✕ **Étienne.** A historic Le Panier hole-in-the-wall, this small pizzeria is
PIZZA   filled with politicos and young professionals who enjoy the personality of chef Stéphane Cassero, who was once famous for announcing the price of the meal only after he'd had the chance to look you over. Remarkably little has changed over the years, except now there is a posted menu (with prices). Brace yourself for an epic meal, starting with a large anchovy pizza from the wood-burning oven, then fried squid, eggplant gratin, and a slab of rare grilled beef, all served with a background of laughter, rich patois, and abuse from the chef. ⑤ *Average main: €20* ⊠ *43 rue de la Lorette, Le Panier* ▭ *No credit cards.*

# MENORCA, SPAIN (MAHÓN)

Updated by
Joanna Styles

Menorca, the northernmost Balearic Island, is a knobby, cliff-bound plateau with a single central hill—El Toro—from whose 1,100-foot summit you can see the whole island. Prehistoric monuments—*taulas* (huge stone T-shapes), *talayots* (spiral stone cones), and *navetes* (stone structures shaped like overturned boats)—left by the first Neolithic settlers are everywhere on the island, rising up out of a landscape of small, tidy fields bounded by hedgerows and drystone walls. Tourism came late to Menorca, but having sat out the early Balearic boom, Menorca has avoided many of the other islands' industrialization troubles: there are no high-rise hotels, and the herringbone road system, with a single central highway, means that each resort is small and separate.

## ESSENTIALS
### CURRENCY
The euro.

### HOURS

Museums generally open 9 until 7 or 8, many are closed on Monday, and some close in the afternoon. Most stores are open Monday through Saturday 9 to 1:30 and 5 to 8, but a few tourist shops may open in the afternoon and also on Sunday between May and September.

### PRIVATE TOURS

**Rutas Menorca.** The company organizes excursions and hiking trips round the island. ☎ *685/747308* ⊕ *rutasmenorca.com.*

### TELEPHONES

Most tri-band or quad-band GSM phones will work in Spain, where services are 3G-compatible. Public kiosks accept phone cards that support international calls (cards sold in press shops, bars and telecom shops). Major companies include Vodafone.

## COMING ASHORE

Vessels dock at the commercial port in Mahón, which sits directly below the Old Town. From here it is a short but steep walk up to the heart of the Old Town. There are few facilities at the port itself, but a selection of shops and cafés line the shady street outside. Taxis wait outside the port, and drivers can be hired for the day to do tourist itineraries.

Menorca is a small island, and you can travel across it in 40 minutes by vehicle. Public bus services are modern and reliable, but services to the smaller towns may not be frequent. The bus station is at the far side of Mahón and involves a steep climb from the port area. It might be advisable to take a taxi to the station. The journey time from Mahón to Ciutadella is 1 hour. Renting a car is the ideal way to get around; expect to pay as much as €80 per day for an economy manual vehicle (but rates can be much cheaper—from €25—if you pick up a car at the airport).

## EXPLORING MENORCA

### MAHÓN

Established as the island's capital in 1722, when the British began their nearly 80-year occupation, Mahón stills bears the stamp of its former rulers. The streets nearest the port are lined with four-story Georgian town houses in various states of repair; the Mahónese still nurse a craving for Chippendale furniture, and drink gin. You'll notice as you travel around the town and island that Menorcans use both Catalan and Castillian names in signage, Catalon most often by the people themselves. So you may hear Mahón called, simply, Maó by the locals, and will also see this on signs.

**Ajuntament.** From here, walk up Carrer Alfons III and turn right at the Ajuntament to Carrer Isabel II, a street lined with many Georgian homes. ⊠ *Pl. de la Constitució 1* ☎ *971/369800.*

**La Verge del Carme.** This church has a fine painted and gilded altarpiece. Adjoining the church are the cloisters, now a **market,** with stalls selling fresh produce and a variety of local specialties such as cheeses and sausages. The central courtyard is a venue for a variety of cultural events throughout the year. ⊠ *Pl. del Carme* ☎ *971/362402.*

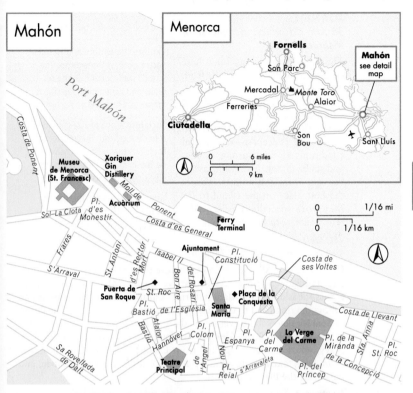

**Plaça de la Conquesta.** Behind the church of Santa María, the Plaça de la Conquesta has a statue of Alfons III of Aragón, who wrested the island from the Moors in 1287.

**Puerta de San Roque.** At the end of Carrer Rector Mort, this massive gate is the only surviving portion of the 14th-century city walls. They were rebuilt in 1587 to protect the city from the pirate Barbarossa (Redbeard).

**Santa María.** Dating from the 13th century, this church was rebuilt during the British occupation and restored after being sacked during the civil war. The church's pride is its 3,200-pipe baroque organ, imported from Austria in 1810. From May or June through September, midday concerts are held here 11:30 to 12:30 every day except Sunday. ⊠ *Pl. de la Constitució* ☎ *971/363949.*

**Teatre Principal.** Built in 1824 as an opera house—the oldest in Spain—the Teatre Principal has five tiers of boxes, red plush seats, and gilded woodwork: a La Scala in miniature. Lovingly restored, it still hosts a brief opera season. If you're visiting in the first week of December or June, buy tickets well in advance. ⊠ *Carrer Costa Deià 40* ☎ *971/355603* ⊕ *www.teatremao.com.*

## FORNELLS

*35 km (21 miles) northwest of Mahón.*

The first fortifications built here to defend the Bay of Fornells from pirates date to 1625. A little village (full-time population: 500) of whitewashed houses with red tile roofs. The bay—Menorca's second largest and its deepest—offers ideal conditions for windsurfing, sailing, and scuba diving. The real draw of Fornells is its restaurants. This is the best place on the island to try Menorca's specialty, *Es Pla caldereta de langosta* (lobster stew).

> ### MENORCA BEST BETS
>
> **Explore the Gothic and Renaissance core of Ciutadella.** The island's old capital was the religious and commercial heartbeat for several hundred years.
>
> **Tuck into a pot of** *Es Pla caldereta de langosta.* This lobster stew is always the most expensive item on the menu, but it's Menorca's pièce de résistance.
>
> **Take to the water.** The bay at Fornells is the perfect place to take up sailing or windsurfing.

## CIUTADELLA

*44 km (27 miles) west of Mahón.*

Ciutadella was Menorca's capital before the British settled in Mahón, and its history is richer. As you arrive via the ME1, the main artery across the island from Mahón, turn left at the second roundabout and follow the ring road to the Passeig Maritim; at the end, near the **Castell de Sant Nicolau** watchtower (visits daily, June–October 10–1 and 5–10) is a **monument to David Glasgow Farragut**, the first admiral of the U.S. Navy, whose father emigrated from Ciutadella to the United States. From here, take Passeig de Sant Nicolau to the **Plaça de s'Esplanada,** and park near the Plaça d'es Born.

**Ajuntament.** From a passage on the left side of Ciutadella's columned and crenellated Ajuntament, on the west side of the Born, steps lead up to the **Mirador d'es Port,** a lookout from which you can survey the harbor. ⊠ *Pl. d'Es Born.*

**Catedral.** Carrer Major leads to the Gothic Catedral, which has some beautifully carved choir stalls. The side chapel has round Moorish arches, remnants of the mosque that once stood on this site; the bell tower is a converted minaret. ⊠ *Pl. de la Catedral at Pl. Píus XII, Ciutadella, Minorca.*

**Convento de Santa Clara.** Carrer del Seminari is lined on the west side with some of the city's most impressive historic buildings. Among them is the 17th-century Convento de Santa Clara, which hosts Ciutadella's summer festival of classical music. ⊠ *Carrer del Seminari at Carrer Obispo Vila.*

**Museu Municipal.** The museum houses artifacts of Minorca's prehistoric, Roman, and medieval past, including records of land grants made by Alfons III to the local nobility after defeating the Moors. It occupies an ancient defense tower, the Bastió de Sa Font (Bastion of the Fountain), at the east end of the harbor. ⊠ *Pl. de Sa Font s/n* ☎ *971/380297* 🖵 *€2.25, free Wed.* ☉ *May–Sept., Tues–Sat. 10–2 and 6–9; Oct.–Apr., Tues.–Sat. 10–2.*

**Palau Salort.** On Carrer Major des Born, this is the only noble home open to the public—though at unpredictable times. The coats of arms on the ceiling are those of the families Salort (*sal* and *ort,* a salt pit and a garden) and Martorell (a marten). ⊠ *Carrer Major des Born* 🎫 €2 🕒 *May–Oct., Mon.–Sat. 10–2.*

**Palau Torresaura.** The blocklong 19th-century Palau Torresaura was built by the Baron of Torresaura, one of the noble families from Aragón and Catalonia that moved to Minorca after it was captured from the Moors in the 13th century. The interesting facade faces the plaza, though the entrance is on the side street. It is not open to the public. ⊠ *Carrer Major del Born 8.*

**Port.** Ciutadella's port is accessible from steps that lead down from Carrer Sant Sebastià. The waterfront here is lined with seafood restaurants, some of which burrow into caverns far under the Born.

4

## SHOPPING

Menorca is known for shoes and leather, cheese, gin (introduced during British rule)—and recently, wine. The fine supple quality of the leather here serves high-class couturiers around the world, the surplus being sold in island factory shops. The streets of the compact center of Mahón are excellent for shopping.

**Jaime Mascaro.** The showroom here, on the main highway from Alaior to Cuitadella, features not only shoes and bags but fine leather coats and belts for men and women. ⊠ *Poligon Industrial s/n, Ferreries* ☎ *971/374500.*

**Marks.** In Mahón, buy leather goods at Marks. ⊠ *Sa Ravaleta 18, Mahón* ☎ *971/362660.*

**Pons Quintana.** In Alaior, this showroom has a full-length window overlooking the factory where its ultrachic women's shoes are made. It's closed weekends. ⊠ *Calle San Antonio 120, Alaior* ☎ *971/371050.*

**Xoriguer.** One gastronomic legacy of the British occupation was gin. Visit the distillery for Xoriguer, on Mahón's quayside near the ferry terminal, where you can take a guided tour, sample various types of gin, and buy some to take home. ⊠ *Anden de Poniente 91, Mahón* ☎ *971/362197.*

## ACTIVITIES

Several miles long and a mile wide, but with a narrow entrance to the sea and virtually no waves, the Bay of Fornells gives the windsurfing and sailing beginner a feeling of security and the expert plenty of excitement.

**Wind Fornells.** Here you can rent boards, dinghies, and catamarans and take lessons. It's open May to October. ⊠ *Carrer Nou 33, Es Mercadal* ☎ *971/188150, 659/577760* ⊕ *www.windfornells.com.*

## WHERE TO EAT

**$$** ✗ **El Jàgaro.** This simple waterfront restaurant, at the east end of the
SEAFOOD   harbor promenade, is a local favorite. The lunchtime crowd comes for
the platter of lightly fried mixed fish with potatoes, while in the evening
you can enjoy grilled *pescado de roca* (rockfish) or *sepia* (cuttlefish).
The *ortigues* (sea anemones) are a house specialty not to be missed. The
menu takes a quantum leap in price for the €75 spiny lobster, a delicacy
in its various forms. The prix-fixe lunch is a good value at €15.50. ⑤ *Average main: €22* ✉ *Moll de Llevant 334–35* ☎ *971/362390* ⊗ *Closed
Mon.; no dinner Sun. Nov.–Mar.*

**$$$** ✗ **Es Moli de Foc.** Originally a flour mill—*de foc* means "of fire," sig-
SPANISH   nifying that the mill was operated by internal combustion—this is the
**Fodor's**Choice   oldest building in the village of Sant Climent, about 4 km (2½ miles)
★   southwest of town. The interior, with paintings by local artists on the
mellow yellow walls, is inviting and the food is exceptional. Don't
miss the prawn carpaccio with cured Mahón cheese and artichoke oil
or the black paella with monkfish and squid. Order off the menu for
the *carrilleras de ternera* (boiled beef cheeks) with potato purée, or ask
for the separate menu of *arrozes* (rice dishes)—the best on the island
and arguably one of the best in Spain. End with Minorcan cheese ice
cream and figs. In summer, book a table on the terrace. With a brewery
now installed on the premises, and visible behind glass, you'll know
what to drink. ⑤ *Average main: €24* ✉ *Carrer Sant Llorenç 65, Sant
Climent* ☎ *971/153222* ⊕ *www.esmolidefoc.es* ⊗ *Closed Jan. and Mon.
Oct.–May. No dinner Sun.*

# MESSINA, ITALY (FOR TAORMINA AND MT. ETNA)

Updated
by Bruce
Leimsidor

Sicily has beckoned seafaring wanderers since the trials of Odysseus
were first sung in Homer's *Odyssey*. Strategically poised between Europe
and Africa, this island has been an important center of every great civilization on the Mediterranean: Greek and Roman; then Arab and Norman; and finally French, Spanish, and Italian. Today Sicily offers the
remains of sackings past: graceful Byzantine mosaics rubbing elbows
with Greek temples, Roman amphitheaters, Byzantine and Romanesque
churches, and baroque flights of fancy. Messina's ancient history lists a
series of disasters, but the city nevertheless managed to develop a fine
university and a thriving cultural environment. On December 28, 1908,
Messina changed from a flourishing metropolis of 120,000 to a heap of
rubble, shaken to pieces by an earthquake that produced a tidal wave
and left 80,000 dead and the city almost completely leveled. For this
reason Messina has few historic treasures, but the town makes a good
jumping-off point for explorations of nearby wonders.

## ESSENTIALS
### CURRENCY
The euro.

### HOURS

Shops are generally open 9 to 1 and 3:30 to 8, and are closed Sunday and Monday morning most of the year. Summer (June to September) hours are usually 9 to 1 and 4 to 8.

### PRIVATE TOURS

Sicily Travel Net offers guided tours to Taormina and Etna from Messina. Prices depend on the number of travelers in the party, the season, and the qualifications and language of the tour guide.

Contacts **Sicily Travel Net.** ☎ *(39)360/397930 in Italy* ⊕ *www.sicilytourguides.net/.*

### TELEPHONES

Tri-band GSM phones work in Italy. You can buy prepaid phone cards at telecom shops, news-vendors, and tobacconists in all towns and cities. Phone cards can be used for local or international calls.

### COMING ASHORE

While some cruise ships do dock directly in Giardini-Naxos, the port far below Taormina, most ships dock in the main port of Messina. Passenger facilities cater to the many commercial ferry passengers who enter Sicily here, and though there are refreshment stands, they are often busy. There is no shuttle service, but it is possible to walk into Messina. Taxis wait at the port entrance, and it's a five-minute transfer to the train station.

It is possible to reach Taormina by train from Messina followed by the cable car from Giardini-Naxos up to Taormina proper. Most services take around an hour and cost €3.50 to €7.50 each way depending on the time of day; note, however, that while trains between Messina and Taormina run frequently in the afternoon and evening, there are no trains between 9:40 am and 12:10 pm. Taxis in Messina charge approximately €3.05 initially, then €0.80 per km with an increment of €0.13 per 140m when the taxi travels at less than 20 kph (12 mph). Mt. Etna is not easy to reach by public transport.

Taormina makes a good departure point for excursions around—but not always to the top of—Mt. Etna, with private companies offering a guiding service. A rental car would allow you to explore much of northern Sicily during your day in port. Rental costs are approximately €60 per day for a compact manual vehicle.

## EXPLORING NORTHEASTERN SICILY

### MESSINA

**Duomo.** The reconstruction of Messina's Norman and Romanesque Duomo, originally built by the Norman king Roger II and consecrated in 1197, has retained much of the original plan—including a handsome crown of Norman battlements, an enormous apse, and a splendid wood-beam ceiling. The adjoining bell tower contains one of the largest and most complex mechanical clocks in the world: constructed in 1933, it has a host of gilded automatons (a roaring lion among them), that spring into action every day at the stroke of noon. ✉ *Piazza del Duomo* ☎ *090/774895* ◷ *Daily 9–1 and 4–7.*

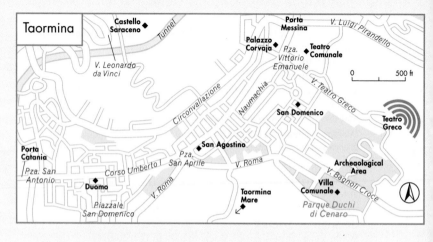

## Taormina

Castello Saraceno

Tunnel

V. Luigi Pirandello

Porta Messina

Palazzo Corvaja

Pza. Vittorio Emanuele

Teatro Comunale

V. Leonardo da Vinci

0    500 ft

Circonvallazione

Naumachia

V. Teatro Greco

San Domenico

Teatro Greco

Porta Catania

Pza. San Antonio

Corso Umberto I

San Agostino

Pza. San Aprile

V. Roma

Archeaological Area

Duomo

V. Roma

V. Roma

Taormina Mare

Villa Comunale

V. Bagnoli Croce

Piazzale San Domenico

Parque Duchi di Cenaro

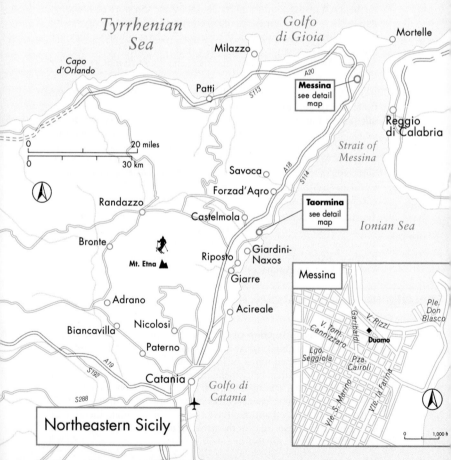

*Tyrrhenian Sea*

*Golfo di Gioia*

Mortelle

Milazzo

Capo d'Orlando

Patti

A20

S113

**Messina** see detail map

Reggio di Calabria

Strait of Messina

0    20 miles

0    30 km

Savoca

A18

S114

Randazzo

Forzad'Aqro

**Taormina** see detail map

*Ionian Sea*

Bronte

Castelmola

Mt. Etna

Riposto

Giardini-Naxos

Adrano

Giarre

Biancavilla

Nicolosi

Acireale

Paterno

S192

A19

Catania

*Golfo di Catania*

S288

## Northeastern Sicily

S114

### Messina

Ple. Don Blasco

V. Tom. Cannizzaro

V. Rizzi

Garibaldi

Duomo

Lgo. Seggiola

Pza. Cairoli

Vle. S. Martino

Vle. la Farina

0    1,000 ft

## TAORMINA

*43 km (27 miles) southwest of Messina.*

The medieval cliff-hanging town of Taormina is overrun with tourists and trinket shops, but its natural beauty is still hard to argue with. The view of the sea and Mt. Etna from its jagged cactus-covered cliffs is as close to perfection as a panorama can get, especially on clear days, when the snow-capped volcano's white puffs of smoke rise against the blue sky. Writers have extolled Taormina's beauty almost since its founding in the 6th century BC by Greeks from Naples; Goethe and D. H. Lawrence were among its more recent well-known enthusiasts. The town's boutique-lined main streets become tiresome pretty quickly, but don't overlook the many hiking paths that wind through the beautiful hills surrounding Taormina. Nor should you miss the trip up to stunning Castelmola—whether on foot or by car.

**Castello Saraceno.** An unrelenting 20-minute walk up the Via Crucis footpath takes you to the church of the Madonna della Rocca, hollowed out of the limestone rock. Above it towers the medieval Castello Saraceno. Though the gate to the castle has been locked for decades, it's worth the climb just for the panoramic views. ⊠ *Monte Tauro.*

**Palazzo Corvaja.** Many of Taormina's 14th- and 15th-century palaces have been carefully preserved. Especially beautiful is the Palazzo Corvaja, with characteristic black-lava and white-limestone inlays. Today it houses the tourist office and the **Museo di Arte e Storia Popolare,** which has a collection of puppets and folk art, carts, and crèches. ⊠ *Largo Santa Caterina* ☎ *0942/23243* 🖼 *Museum €2.60* 🕙 *Museum Tues.–Sun. 9–1 and 4–8.*

**Taormina Mare.** Below the main city of Taormina is Taormina Mare, where summertime beachgoers jostle for space on a pebble beach against the scenic backdrop of the aptly named island of Isolabella.

**Teatro Greco.** The Greeks put a premium on finding impressive locations to stage their dramas, such as Taormina's hillside Teatro Greco. Beyond the columns you can see the town's rooftops spilling down the hillside, the arc of the coastline, and Mount Etna in the distance. The theater was built during the 3rd century BC and rebuilt by the Romans during the 2nd century AD. Its acoustics are exceptional: even today a stage whisper can be heard in the last rows. In summer Taormina hosts an arts festival of music and dance events and a film festival; many performances are held in the Teatro Greco. ⊠ *Via Teatro Greco* ☎ *0942/620198* 🖼 *€6* 🕙 *Daily 9–1 hr before sunset.*

★ **Villa Comunale.** Stroll down Via Bagnoli Croce from the main Corso Umberto to the Villa Comunale. Also known as the Parco Duca di

---

### MESSINA BEST BETS

**Get close up and personal with Mt. Etna.** Europe's only active volcano continues to enchant with its regular fiery plumes.

**Explore Taormina.** This picturesque hilltop village hosts excellent Greek and Roman remains and has many good shops and galleries.

**See the view from Castello Normanno.** The views from the walls of this citadel at Castelmola are spectacular.

**4**

Cesarò, the lovely public gardens were designed by Florence Trevelyan Cacciola, a Scottish lady "invited" to leave England following a romantic liaison with the future Edward VII (1841–1910). Arriving in Taormina in 1889, she married a local professor and devoted herself to the gardens, filling them with native Mediterranean and exotic plants, ornamental pavilions (known as the beehives), and fountains. Stop by the panoramic bar, which has stunning views. ☉ *Daily 9 am–sunset.*

## CASTELMOLA
*5 km (3 miles) west of Taormina.*

You may think that Taormina has spectacular views, but tiny Castelmola, floating 1,800 feet above sea level, takes the word *scenic* to a whole new level. Along the cobblestone streets within the ancient walls, the 360-degree panoramas of mountain, sea, and sky are so ubiquitous that you almost get used to them (but not quite). Collect yourself with a sip of the sweet almond wine (best served cold) made in the local bars, or with lunch at one of the humble pizzerias or panino shops.

A 10-minute drive on a winding but well-paved road leads from Taormina to Castelmola; you must park in one of the public lots on the hillside below and climb a series of staircases to reach the center. On a nice day, hikers are in for a treat if they walk instead of driving. It's a serious uphill climb, but the 1½-km (¾-mile) path is extremely well maintained and not too challenging. You'll begin at Porta Catania in Taormina, with a walk along Via Apollo Arcageta past the Chiesa di San Francesco di Paolo on the left. The Strada Comunale della Chiusa then leads past Piazza Andromaco, revealing good views of the jagged promontory of Cocolanazzo di Mola to the north. Allow 45 minutes on the way up, a half-hour down. There's another, slightly longer—2-km (1-mile)—path that heads up from Porta Messina past the Roman aqueduct, Convento dei Cappuccini, and the northeastern side of Monte Tauro. You could take one path up and the other down.

**Fodor's**Choice  ★   **Castello Normanno.** The best place to savor Castelmola's views is from the ruins of Castello Normanno, reached by a set of steep staircases rising out of the town center. In all of Sicily there may be no spot more scenic than atop it: you can gaze upon two coastlines, smoking Mount Etna, and the town spilling down the mountainside. Come during daylight hours to take full advantage of the vista.

## MT. ETNA
*64 km (40 miles) southwest of Taormina.*

**Fodor's**Choice  ★   Mt. Etna is one of the world's major active volcanoes and is the largest and highest in Europe—the cone of the crater rises to 10,902 feet above sea level. Plato sailed in just to catch a glimpse in 387 BC; in the 9th century AD the oldest gelato of all was shaved off of its snowy slopes; and in the 21st century the volcano still claims annual headlines. Etna has erupted 12 times in the past 30 or so years, most spectacularly in 1971, 1983, 2001, and 2002; many of these eruptions wiped out cable-car stations. There were two eruptions in 2008 and a sizeable one in 2009. The refuge at Sapienza, however, is currently operational. Although each eruption is predictably declared a "tragedy" by the media, owing to the economic losses, Etna almost never threatens human life. Travel in the proximity of the crater depends on Mt. Etna's temperament, but you can walk up and down the enormous lava dunes and wander over its moonlike surface of dead craters. The rings of vegetation change markedly as you rise, with vineyards and pine trees gradually giving way to growths of broom and lichen. Taormina makes a good departure point for excursions around—but not always to the top of—Mt. Etna.

**Circumetnea.** Instead of climbing up Mount Etna, you can circle it on the Circumetnea, which runs near the volcano's base. The private railway almost circles the volcano, running 114 km (71 miles) between Catania and Riposto—the towns are just 30 km (19 miles) apart by the coast road. The line is small, slow, and only single-track, but has some dramatic vistas of the volcano and goes through lava fields. The trip takes about four hours, with about 10 departures a day. After you've made the trip one way, you can get back to where you started from on the much quicker, but less scenic, conventional state railway line between Catania and Riposto. ☒ *Via Caronda 352, Catania* ☎ *095/541250* ⊕ *www.circumetnea.it* 🎫 *€7.25 round-trip* ⊘ *Mon.–Sat. 6 am–9 pm.*

## SHOPPING

Taormina is the place in eastern Sicily for shopping, especially along Corso Umberto I and the surrounding alleyways, where chic boutiques sell lace and linen, including placemats and napkins. The island as a whole is famed for its ceramics, particularly its practical folk pottery from Caltagirone, close by along the north coast. Marble and wrought iron are also fashioned into souvenir pieces, and antique shops are numerous, though prices can be high.

**Pasticceria Etna.** A marzipan devotee should not leave Taormina without trying one of the almond sweets—maybe in the guise of the ubiquitous *fico d'India* (prickly pear) or in more unusual *frutta martorana* varieties—at Pasticceria Etna. A block of almond paste makes a good souvenir—you can bring it home to make an almond latte or granita. It's closed Monday. ☒ *Corso Umberto 112, Taormina* ☎ *0942/24735.*

## ACTIVITIES

Mount Etna is a natural magnet for adventure seekers, but because the volcano is active you should consult experts before tackling the peak. Hiking is certainly a popular choice on the lower slopes, while climbing Mt. Etna proves more challenging.

**Club Alpino Italiano.** Club Alpino Italiano in Catania is a great resource for Mount Etna climbing and hiking guides. If you have some experience and don't like a lot of hand holding, these are the guides for you. ☒ *Via Messina 593/a, Catania* ☎ *095/7153515* ✉ *giorgiopace@ katamail.com* ⊕ *www.caicatania.it.*

**Gruppo Guide Etna Nord.** If you're a beginning climber, call the Gruppo Guide Etna Nord to arrange for a guide. Their service is a little more personalized—and expensive—than others. Reserve ahead. ☒ *Via Roma 93, Linguaglossa* ☎ *095/7774502, 348/0125167* ⊕ *www.guidetnanord.com.*

## WHERE TO EAT

**$$**      ✕ **Al Padrino.** The jovial owner of this stripped-down trattoria keeps
SICILIAN    everything running smoothly. Meat and fish dishes are served with equal
verve in the white-wall dining room. Start with antipasti like eggplant
stuffed with ricotta; then move on to supremely Sicilian dishes such
as pasta with chickpeas or *polpette di alalunga* (albacore croquettes).
⑤ *Average main: €22* ✉ *Via Santa Cecilia 54* ☎ *090/2921000* ⊕ *www.
alpadrino.it* ⊗ *Closed Sun. and Aug. No dinner Sat.*

**$$$$**    ✕ **La Piazzetta.** Sheltered from the city's hustle and bustle, this elegant little
SICILIAN    eatery exudes a mood of relaxed sophistication. Classic dishes such as
risotto *alla marinara* (with seafood) are competently prepared, the grilled
fish is extremely fresh, and the service is informal and friendly. The modest
room has simple white walls—you're not paying for a view. ⑤ *Average
main: €32* ✉ *Vico Francesco Paladini, off Corso Umberto* ☎ *0942/626317*
⊗ *Closed Nov., and 2 weeks in Feb. No lunch Mon.–Thurs., June–Sept.*

# MONTE CARLO, MONACO

Updated       In 1297 the Grimaldi family seized this fortified town and, except for a
by Jennifer   short break under Napoléon, they have ruled here ever since. The Princi-
Ladonne       pality of Monaco covers 473 acres; it would fit comfortably inside New
York's Central Park while its 5,000 citizens would fill only a small frac-
tion of the seats in Yankee Stadium. The Grimaldis made money from
gambling and attracted a well-heeled, monied crowd, but the whole
world watched as Hollywood princess Grace Kelly wed Prince Rainier
ruler of Monaco to put this place on the map. It's the very favorable tax
system, not the gambling, that makes Monaco one of the most sought-
after addresses in the world, and the principality bristles with gleaming
high-rise apartment complexes owned by tax exiles. But at the town's
great 1864 landmark Hôtel de Paris—still a veritable crossroads of the
buffed and befurred Euro-gentry—at the Opéra, or the ballrooms of
the Casino, you'll still be able to conjure up Monaco's belle epoque.

### ESSENTIALS
#### CURRENCY
The euro.

#### HOURS
Most stores open Monday through Saturday from 9 to 7, but many
close at lunchtime (usually noon to 2 or 3), and some will open later
and on Sunday during July and August. Museums are usually open 10
to 5, but most are closed on either Monday or Tuesday.

#### TELEPHONES
Tri-band GSM phones work in France (and Monaco). You can buy
prepaid phone cards at telecom shops, news vendors, and tobacconists
in all towns and cities. Phone cards can be used for local or interna-
tional calls. Orange, SFR, Bouygues Telecom, and Virgin are leading
telecom companies. If you have an unlocked GSM phone, LeFrench-
Mobile (⊕ *www.lefrenchmobile.com*) offers SIM cards (and micro SIM
cards) with support in English, unlimited validity of credits, and pre-
purchase online.

## COMING ASHORE

Cruise ships dock at Port Hercule, just below Monaco-Ville, at a state-of-the-art cruise port within a $200-million breakwater that can accommodate several ships at a time. Even still, on busy days you may be tendered to the landing dock. There are few facilities at the port itself. An elevator about 500 yards away leads up to the town, where the attractions of old Monaco are located. It is approximately 1 mile from the port to the Monte Carlo district; this is a 15- to 30-minute walk depending on your level of fitness. Although the distance is not too great, there are many hills.

If you intend to confine your explorations to the principality, there is no need to hire a car. All the attractions of the Old Town are less than a 10-minute walk apart. Bus services 1 and 2 link Monaco-Ville with Monte Carlo; prices are €2 per journey. If you want to tour the stunning surrounding Provençal countryside, a vehicle would be useful. Expect to pay €85 for an economy manual vehicle for the day. Taxis wait outside the port gates and can provide tourist itineraries. For single journeys, tariffs are €3 initially, then €0.92 per km.

> ### MONTE CARLO BEST BETS
>
> **Watch the Changing of the Guard.** This short ceremony at exactly 11:55 am in the palace square has been taking place for centuries.
>
> **Place your bets.** The Casino de Monte Carlo is surely the most beautiful place in the world to lose your shirt. If you don't want to bet, buy a chip as a souvenir.
>
> **Have an aperitif at the café in the Place du Casino.** This is the place to watch the beautiful and megarich come and go and to enjoy the genteel atmosphere.

# EXPLORING MONTE CARLO

Monte Carlo or Monaco? Many people use the names interchangeably, but officially, the Old Town or Vieille Ville is **Monaco-Ville** (or Le Rocher because it sits on a rocky plateau). This is where the Grimaldis live and the business of government is done. The "new" town, built in the 18th and 19th centuries and expanding upward rapidly even today, is called **Monte Carlo,** while the harbor area, or **La Condamine,** connects the two.

★ **Casino.** Place du Casino is the center of Monte Carlo, and is a must-see, even if you don't bet a sou. Into the gold-leaf splendor of the Casino, the hopeful traipse from tour buses to tempt fate beneath the gilt-edge rococo ceiling (but do remember the fate of Sarah Bernhardt, who lost her last 100,000 francs here). Jacket and tie are required in the back rooms, which open at 3 pm. Bring your passport (under-18s not admitted). Note that there are special admission fees to get into any of the period gaming rooms. ⊠ *Pl. du Casino* ☎ *377/98–06–20–12* ⊕ *www. sbm.mc* ☉ *Daily 2 pm–4 am.*

**Monaco Cathedral.** Follow the flow of crowds down the last remaining streets of medieval Monaco to the 19th-century Cathédrale de l'Immaculée-Conception, which has a magnificent altarpiece, painted

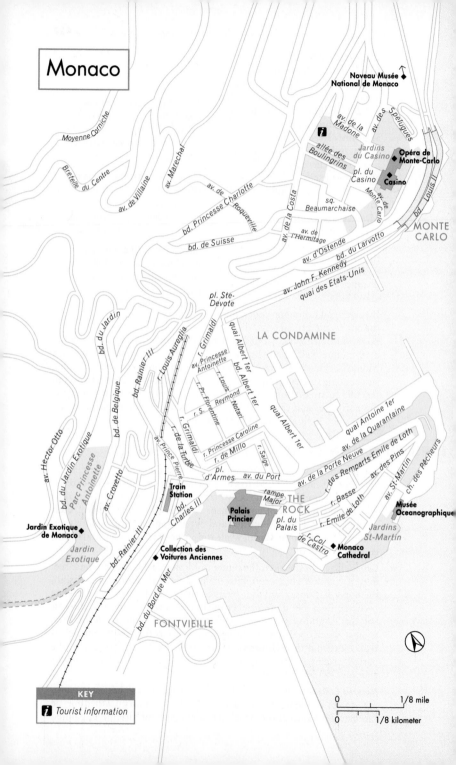

# Monaco

Moyenne Corniche

Bretelle du Centre

av. de Villaine

av. Maréchal

av. de Princesse Charlotte

bd. Princesse Charlotte

bd. de Suisse

av. de la Costa

av. de l'Hermitage

av. d'Ostende

av. de la Madone

allée des Boulingrins

Jardins du Casino

sq. Beaumarchaise

pl. du Casino

Noveau Musée National de Monaco ◆

Opéra de Monte-Carlo ◆

Casino ◆

av. des S.pélugues

bd. Louis II

MONTE CARLO

bd. du Larvotto

av. John F. Kennedy

quai des Etats-Unis

pl. Ste-Devote

LA CONDAMINE

bd. du Jardin

bd. Rainier III

r. Louis Aureglia

r. Grimaldi

av. Princesse Antoinette

quai Albert 1er

bd. Albert 1er

bd. de Belgique

r.Pr. Florentine

r. Louis Notari

r.S. Reymond

r. Grimaldi

r. de la Turbie

av. Prince Pierre

r. Princesse Caroline

r. de Millo

r. Saige

pl. d'Armes

av. du Port

quai Albert 1er

quai Antoine 1er

av. de la Quarantaine

av. de la Porte Neuve

r. des Remparts Emile de Loth

av. des Pins

av. St-Martin

ch. des Pêcheurs

av. Hector Otto

bd. du Jardin Exotique

Parc Princesse Antoinette

av. Crovetto

bd. Rainier III

Train Station

bd. Charles III

Palais Princier

pl. du Palais

rampe Major

THE ROCK

r. Basse

r. Emile de Loth

r.Col de Castro

Jardins St-Martin

Musée Oceanographique ◆

Jardin Exotique de Monaco ◆

Jardin Exotique

Collection des Voitures Anciennes ◆

Monaco Cathedral ◆

bd. du Bord de Mer

FONTVIEILLE

KEY

*i* Tourist information

0      1/8 mile

0      1/8 kilometer

in 1500 by Louis Bréa, and the tomb of Princess Grace. It's best to call ahead to check on the opening hours, which tend to vary. ⊠ *Av. St-Martin* ☎ *377/93–30–87–70.*

♻ **Collection des Voitures Anciennes** (*Collection of Vintage Cars*). In the impressive Collection des Voitures Anciennes, an assemblage of Prince Rainier's vintage cars, you'll find everything from a De Dion Bouton to a Lamborghini Countach. Also on the Terrasses de Fontvieille is the **Jardin Animalier** (Animal Garden), a mini-zoo housing the Grimaldi family's animal collection, an astonishing array of wild beasts that includes monkeys and exotic birds. ⊠ *Terrasses de Fontvieille* ☎ *377/92–05–28–56, 377/93–25–18–31* ⊕ *www.mtcc.mc* ⊡ *€6 Voitures; €4 Animalier* ☉ *Museum: Daily, 10–6; Garden: June–Sept., daily 9–noon and 2–7; Oct.–Feb., daily 10–noon and 2–5; Mar.–May, daily 10–noon and 2–6.*

Fodor's Choice **Jardin Exotique de Monaco** (*Monaco Exotic Garden*). Carved out of the
★ rock face and one of Monte Carlo's most stunning escapes, the gardens are studded with thousands of succulents and cacti, all set along promenades and belvederes over the sea. There are rare plants from Mexico and Africa, and the hillside plot, threaded with bridges and grottoes and studded with faux boulders (actually hollow sculptures), can't be beat for coastal splendor. Prince Albert I established the gardens in the late 19th century. Also on the grounds, or actually under them, are the **Grottes de l'Observatoire**—spectacular grottoes and caves a-drip with stalagmites and spotlighted with fairy lights. The largest cavern is called "La Grande Salle" and looks like a Romanesque rock cathedral. Traces of Cro-Magnon civilization have been found here, so the grottoes now bear the official name of the **Musée d'Anthropologie Préhistorique.** ⊠ *62 bd. du Jardin Exotique* ☎ *377/93–15–29–80* ⊕ *www. jardin-exotique.mc* ⊡ *€7* ☉ *Mid-May–mid-Sept., daily 9–7; mid-Sept.– mid-May, daily 9–6.*

**Nouveau Musée National de Monaco.** Here you'll find a beguiling collection of 18th- and 19th-century dolls and automatons. The museum is housed in Villa Sauber, within a rose garden, in the Larvotto Beach complex—which is artfully created with imported sand. To get here, take the elevator down from Place des Moulins. The Villa Paloma (next door to the Jardin Exotique), recently restored with fabulous stained-glass windows, is also part of NMNM and hosts temporary exhibits. ⊠ *Villa Sauber, 17 av. Princesse Grace* ☎ *377/98–98–91–26* ⊕ *www. nmnm.mc* ⊡ *€6* ☉ *Daily 10–6.*

★ **Musée Océanographique** (*Oceanography Museum*). Perched dramatically
♻ on a cliff, this museum is a splendid Edwardian structure, built under Prince Albert I to house specimens collected on amateur explorations. Jacques Cousteau (1910–97) led the missions from 1957 to 1988. The main floor displays skeletons and taxidermy of enormous sea creatures; early submarines and diving gear dating from the Middle Ages; and a few interactive science displays. The main draw is the famous **aquarium,** a vast complex of backlighted tanks containing every imaginable species of fish, crab, and eel. ⊠ *Av. St-Martin* ☎ *377/93–15–36–00* ⊕ *www. oceano.mc* ⊡ *€14* ☉ *July and Aug., daily 9:30–7:30; Apr.–June and Sept., daily 9:30–7; Oct.–Mar., daily 10–6.*

**Opéra de Monte-Carlo.** This grand theater was designed by Charles Garnier, who also built the Paris Opéra, and is graced with an 18-ton gilt-bronze chandelier and extravagant frescoes. Sarah Bernhardt inaugurated the main auditorium, the Salle Garnier, in 1879. ⊠ *Pl. du Casino* ☎ *377/98–06–28–00* ⊕ *www.opera.mc.*

**Palais Princier.** The famous Rock, crowned by this palace where the royal family resides, stands west of Monte Carlo. An audio guide leading you through this sumptuous chunk of history, first built in the 13th century and expanded and enhanced over the centuries, reveals an extravagance of 16th- and 17th-century frescoes, as well as tapestries, gilt furniture, and paintings on a grand scale. Note that the **Relève de la Garde** (Changing of the Guard) is held outside the front entrance of the palace most days at 11:55 am. ⊠ *Pl. du Palais* ☎ *377/93–25–18–31* ⊕ *www.palais.mc* ▣ *€8 (includes audio guide)* ☉ *Apr.–Oct., daily 10–6.*

## SHOPPING

The wealthy live in Monaco, and the wealthy visit Monaco, so it should not be a surprise that you can buy the finest designer clothing and accessories from very smart boutiques on the streets radiating out from the **Place du Casino. Monaco-Ville,** on the hill, has a range of souvenir emporia with a predominance of Princess Grace memorabilia, from the tacky to the tasteful. **La Condamine** has a range of shopping for those without sky-high credit card limits. Look out also for Formula 1 motor racing souvenirs; this race around the streets takes place in late May and is one of the highlights of the social season.

## BEACHES

Larvotto is the public beach of the principality, but many people choose to buy a temporary membership in a private beach club, which also has facilities such as changing cabins, showers, and restaurants. If you want to spend a day at the beach, that is usually best arranged through your cruise ship.

## WHERE TO EAT

$$$$
BRASSERIE

✕ **Café de Paris.** This landmark Belle Époque "La Brasserie 1900"—better known as Café de Paris—offers the usual classics (shellfish, steak tartare, matchstick frites, and fish boned table-side). Supercilious, super-pro waiters fawn gracefully over titled preeners, jet setters, and tourists alike. Open daily from 8 am, there's good hot food until 2 am. ⑤ *Average main: €32* ⊠ *Pl. du Casino* ☎ *377/98–06–76–23.*

$$$$
FRENCH
Fodor'sChoice
★

✕ **Le Louis XV.** Louis Quinze to the initiated, this extravagantly showy restaurant stuns with neo-baroque details, yet it manages to be upstaged by its product: the superb cuisine of Alain Ducasse, one of Europe's most celebrated chefs. Ducasse leaves the Louis XV kitchen, for the most part, in the more-than-capable hands of chef Franck Cerutti, who draws much of his inspiration from the Cours Saleya market in Nice. Glamorous iced lobster with chestnuts and Alba white truffles slums happily with stockfish (stewed salt cod) and tripe. The decor is magnificent—a surfeit of gilt, mirrors, and chandeliers—and the wait-staff seignorial as they proffer a footstool for madame's handbag. In Ducasse fashion, the baroque clock on the wall is stopped just before 12. Cinderella should have no fears. If your wallet is a chubby one, this is a must. The 400,000 bottles in the wine cellar should offer you enough of a choice. ⑤ *Average main: €100* ✉ *Hôtel de Paris, Pl. du Casino* ☎ *377/98–06–88–64* ⊕ *www.alain-ducasse.com* ⊛ *Reservations essential Jacket required* ⊘ *Closed Dec. (but open for New Year's Eve) and Tues. and Wed. (but open Wed. dinner mid-June–Aug.).*

# NAPLES, ITALY (WITH HERCULANEUM, POMPEII, AND CAPRI)

**4**

Updated by Bruce Leimsidor

Campania is a region of evocative names—Capri, Sorrento, Pompeii, Herculaneum—that conjure up visions of cliff-shaded coves, sun-dappled waters, and mighty ruins. The area's unique geology is responsible for its gorgeous landscape. A languid coastline stretches out along a deep blue sea, punctuated by rocky islands. Heading inland, the hills at first roll gently, then transform into mountains. Campania's complex identity is most intensely felt in its major city, Naples, which sprawls around its bay as though attempting to embrace the island of Capri, while behind it Mt. Vesuvius glowers. It's one of those few cities in the world that is instantly recognizable: lush, chaotic, scary, funny, confounding, intoxicating, and very beautiful. Few who visit remain ambivalent. You needn't participate in the mad whirl of the city, however. The best pastime in Campania is simply finding a spot with a stunning view and indulging in *il dolce far niente* (the sweetness of doing nothing).

## ESSENTIALS

### CURRENCY

The euro.

### HOURS

Shops are open 9:30 until 1, then 4:30 until 8. Most are closed on Sunday and also on Monday morning.

### PRIVATE TOURS

Siteseeings.com offers half-day tours of Naples and Pompeii to small groups in a minibus with an English-speaking guide for €80 per person, exclusive of entry fees. You can reserve and book on the Internet, and you can arrange for a pick-up at the port. This is one of the few services operating out of Naples for a guaranteed fixed price.

**Contacts Sightseeings.com.** ☎ *415/332–7916 in the U.S.* ⊕ *www.siteseeings.it.*

### SAFETY

Naples has a reputation for active pickpocketing and bag snatching, especially in the historic Old Town and on public transportation. It always pays to be vigilant to avoid becoming a victim. Thieves do cut bag straps to steal your belongings. Bag-snatchers often ride on scooters, grabbing your bag on the streetside as they whiz by. The best advice is to do as Neopolitan women do and simply don't carry a bag; keep a wallet with anything essential in an inside pocket. Crowded trams and trains are popular with pickpockets. Certainly never carry any cash or valuables that you don't need.

Generally, you can avoid problems by acting with confidence; thieves are more likely to target travelers who seem confused or lost. And you should try to blend in by dressing smartly. Locals in Naples rarely wear shorts and T-shirts.

### TELEPHONES

Tri-band GSM phones work in Italy. You can buy prepaid phone cards at telecom shops, news vendors, and tobacconists in all towns and cities. Phone cards can be used for local or international calls.

### COMING ASHORE

The Stazione Maritima is on the city's seafront; passenger facilities include a tourist information office, shops, and cafés.

Buses 3S, 152, Sepsa, and CTP run to the train station, Piazza Garibaldi, along with tram routes 1 to 4. By the Circumvesuviana line from Piazza Garibaldi, you can reach Pompeii, Ercolano (Herculanium), and Castellammare (for the funicular to Mount Vesuvius). There are at least three hourly trains, and fares begin at €2.30 to Pompeii (one way, 40 minutes); a single ticket within Naples is €1.20, a day-pass is €3.60 (€3 on weekends).

The EAVBUS route also links central Naples with Vesuvius and Pompeii with Vesuvius. Departing from Piazza Piedigrotta in Naples at 9 am or 10:15. A one-day ticket costs €12.30.

Ferries to Capri depart from the same port where cruise ships disembark; fast ferries leave from the Clata Porta di Massa, and hydrofoils leave from Molo Beverello. Hydrofoils (which are more frequent) make the trip in 40 minutes, other ferries 50 minutes. You can just walk on the ferry after buying a ticket. Fast-ferry prices are €17.80, and hydrofoils are €18.80–€20.20. Once on the island, the funicular railway from the port up to Capri Town is €1.40 round-trip.

Taxis charge approximately €3 initially (more on Sundays and holidays), then €0.05 per 65 meters or 10 seconds of idling. A car rental could be useful if you want to explore the Amalfi coast, but it imperative that you return to Naples with time to spare, because traffic along the coast can be very heavy and slow-moving. Expect to pay €55 per day for a compact manual vehicle.

## EXPLORING NAPLES AND VICINITY

### NAPLES

★ **Castel Nuovo.** Known to locals as Maschio Angioino, in reference to its Angevin builders, this imposing castle is now used more for marital than military purposes—a portion of it serves as a government registry office. Its looming Angevin stonework is upstaged by a white four-tiered triumphal entrance arch, ordered by Alfonso of Aragon after he entered the city in 1443 to seize power from the increasingly beleaguered Angevin Giovanna II. You can visit the Sala dell'Armeria, where a glass floor reveals recent excavations of Roman baths from the Augustan period.

The castle's first floor holds a small gallery that includes a beautiful early Renaissance *Adoration of the Magi* by Marco Cardisco, with the roles of the three Magi played by the three Aragonese kings: Ferrante I, Ferrante II, and Charles V. ✉ *Piazza Municipio, Toledo* ☎ *081/7955877* 🎫 *€5* ⊙ *Mon.–Sat. 9–7* Ⓜ *Montesanto (in construction: Piazza Municipio).*

**Castel Sant'Elmo.** Perched on the Vomero, this massive castle is almost the size of a small town. It was built by the Angevins in the 14th century to dominate the port and the Old City; then remodeled by the Spanish in 1537. The parapets, configured in the form of a six-pointed star, provide fabulous views. Its prison, the Carcere alto di Castel Sant'Elmo, is the site of the **Museo del Novecento Napoli,** which traces Naples's 20th-century artistic output, from the futurist period through the 1980s. You get in the castle free if you have a ticket to the adjoining Certosa di San Martino. ✉ *Largo San Martino, Vomero* ☎ *081/2294401* ⊕ *www. polomusealenapoli.beniculturali.it* 🎫 *€5; Museo del Novecento Napoli, €5* ⊙ *Wed.–Mon. 8:30–7:30; Museo del Novecento Napoli, Wed.–Mon. 9–7* Ⓜ *Vanvitelli.*

**Duomo di San Gennaro.** The Duomo was established in the 1200s, but the building you see was erected a century later and has since undergone radical changes—especially during the baroque period. Inside, 110 ancient columns salvaged from pagan buildings are set into the piers that support the 350-year-old wooden ceiling. Off the left aisle you step down into the 4th-century church of **Santa Restituta,** which was incorporated into the cathedral. Though Santa Restituta was redecorated in the late 1600s in the prevalent baroque style, a few very old mosaics remain in the **Battistero** (Baptistery).

On the right aisle of the cathedral, in the **Cappella di San Gennaro,** are multicolor marbles and frescoes honoring Saint Januarius, the miracle-working patron saint of Naples, whose altar and relics are encased in silver. Three times a year—on September 19 (his feast day); on the Saturday preceding the first Sunday in May, which commemorates the transfer of his relics to Naples; and on December 16—his dried blood, contained in two sealed vials, is believed to liquefy during rites in his honor. On these days large numbers of devout Neapolitans offer up prayers in his memory. The **Museo del Tesoro di San Gennaro** houses a rich collection of treasures associated with the saint. Paintings by Solimena and Luca Giordano hang alongside statues, busts, candelabras, and tabernacles in gold, silver, and marble by Cosimo Fanzago and other 18th-century baroque masters. ✉ *Via Duomo, 149, Spaccanapoli* ☎ *081/449097 Duomo, 081/294764 museum* ⊕ *www. museosangennaro.com* 🎫 *€7, €1.50 for Baptistery* ⊙ *Daily 9–6; Baptistery, 8:30–1, 3:30–6:30.*

**Fodor's Choice**
★ **Museo Archeologico Nazionale** (*National Museum of Archaeology*). Those who know and love this legendary museum—now restyled as MANN (Museo Archeologico Nazionale Napoli)—also know that the museum, which holds one of the world's greatest collections of Greek and Roman antiquities, is undergoing a long-term renovation, the fruits of which are starting to become visible. Some of the "newer" rooms, covering archaeological discoveries in the Greco-Roman settlements and

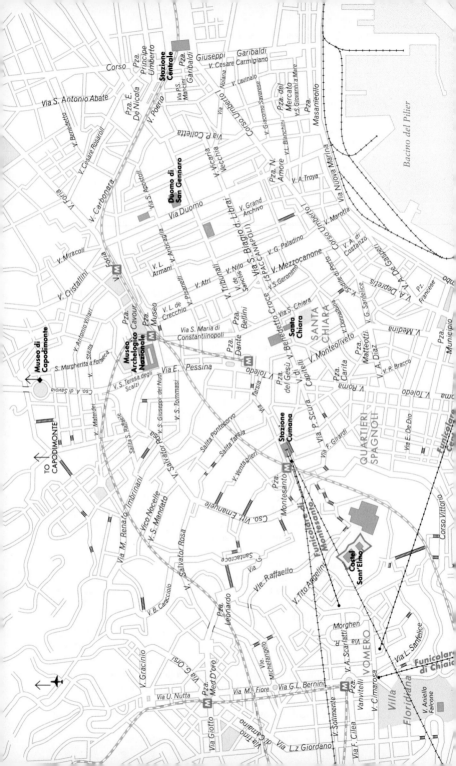

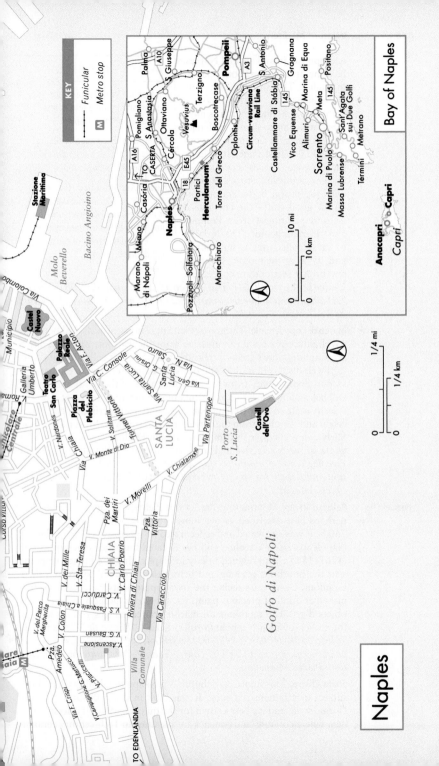

# Naples

## Bay of Naples

**KEY**

- ••••• Funicular
- Ⓜ Metro stop

Golfo di Napoli

Bacino Angioino

Molo Beverello

Porto S. Lucia

necropolises in and around Naples, have helpful informational panels in English. The core of the museum is nucleus of world-renowned archaeological finds that puts most other museums to shame, with over 13,500 items on display (and a further 300,000 in storage). It includes the legendary Farnese collection of ancient sculpture, together with local sculptural finds, and almost all the good stuff—the best mosaics and paintings—from Pompeii and Herculaneum. The quality of these collections is unmatched and, as far as the mosaic, painting, and bronze sections are concerned, unique in the world. ⊠ *Piazza Museo 19, Spaccanapoli* ☎ *081/440166* ⊕ *sbanap.campaniabeniculturali.it* ⊠ *€6.50, more for special exhibits* ⊙ *Wed.–Mon. 9–7* Ⓜ *Museo.*

> **NAPLES BEST BETS**
>
> **Pompeii.** The finest and largest Roman site in the world is less than an hour from Naples.
>
> **Herculaneum.** Pompeii's sibling is smaller, but it's more manageable and better preserved.
>
> **Museo Archeologico Nazionale.** The daily lives of Roman citizens at Pompeii and Herculaneum are brought to life with monumental statues and a wealth of personal and domestic items.

★ **Museo di Capodimonte.** The grandiose 18th-century neoclassical Bourbon royal palace houses an impressive assortment of fine and decorative art. Capodimonte's greatest treasure is the excellent collection of paintings well displayed in the **Galleria Nazionale,** on the palace's first and second floors. Aside from the artworks, part of the royal apartments still has a complement of beautiful antique furniture (most of it on the splashy scale so dear to the Bourbons), and a staggering range of porcelain and majolica from the various royal residences. Most rooms have fairly comprehensive information cards in English, whereas the audio guide is overly selective and somewhat quirky. ⊠ *Via Miano 2, Porta Piccola, Via Capodimonte, Capodimonte* ☎ *199/199100 for information and tickets for special exhibitions* ⊠ *€8* ⊙ *Daily 10–7:30; ticket office closes at 7.*

Fodor's Choice
★ **Palazzo Reale.** Dominating Piazza del Plebiscito, this huge palace—perhaps best described as overblown imperial—dates from the early 1600s. It was renovated and redecorated by successive rulers, including Napoléon's sister Caroline and her ill-fated husband, Joachim Murat (1767–1815), who reigned briefly in Naples after the French emperor sent the Bourbons packing and before they returned to reclaim their kingdom. Don't miss seeing the **royal apartments,** sumptuously furnished and full of precious paintings, tapestries, porcelains, and other objets d'art. The monumental marble staircase gives you an idea of the scale on which Neapolitan rulers lived. ⊠ *Piazza del Plebiscito, 1, Toledo* ☎ *081/400547, 848/800288 schools and guided tours* ⊕ *www.palazzorealenapoli.it* ⊠ *€4* ⊙ *Thurs.–Tues. 9–7* Ⓜ *Dante (in construction: Piazza Municipio).*

**Santa Chiara.** This monastery church is a Neapolitan landmark and the subject of a famous old song. It was built in the 1300s in Provençal Gothic style, and it's best known for the quiet charm of its cloister garden, where columns and benches are sheathed in 18th-century ceramic tiles painted with delicate floral motifs and vivid landscapes. An adjoining museum traces the history of the convent; the entrance is off the courtyard at the left of the church. ⊠ *Piazza Ges³ Nuovo, Spaccanapoli* ☎ *081/7971224* ⊕ *www.monasterodisantachiara.eu* 🖼 *Museum and cloister €5* ☉ *Church: daily 7–13 and 4:30–8. Museum and cloister: Mon.–Sat. 9:30–5, Sun. 10–2* Ⓜ *Dante, Università.*

## HERCULANEUM

★ **Herculaneum Ruins.** About 5,000 people lived here when it was destroyed in AD 79 by the gigantic eruption of Vesuvius (which also destroyed Pompeii). The semiliquid volcanic mass seeped into the crevices and niches of every building, covering household objects, enveloping textiles and wood—and sealing all in a compact, airtight tomb. Today less than half of Herculaneum has been excavated.

Decorations are especially delicate in the **Casa del Nettuno ed Anfitrite** (House of Neptune and Amphitrite), named for the subjects of a still-bright mosaic on the wall of the *nymphaeum* (a recessed grotto with a fountain), and in the **Terme Femminili** (Women's Baths), where several delicate black-and-white mosaics embellished the rooms. Annexed to the former house is a remarkably preserved wineshop, where amphorae still rest on carbonized wood shelves. On the other side of the house is the **Casa del Bel Cortile** (House of the Beautiful Courtyard). One of its inner rooms displays a cast taken of three skeletons found in the store-rooms down at the old seafront, where almost 300 inhabitants sought refuge from the eruption and were ultimately encapsulated for posterity. The **Casa dei Cervi** (House of the Stags), with an elegant garden open to the sea breezes, evokes a lively, luxurious way of life. ⊠ *Corso Resina 6, Ercolano* ☎ *081/8575347* ⊕ *www.pompeiisites.org* 🖼 *€11 for Herculaneum only; €20 for biglietto cumulativo ticket to 5 sites (Pompeii, Herculaneum, Boscoreale, Oplontis, and Stabiae) valid for 3 days* ☉ *Nov.–Mar., daily 8:30–5, ticket office closes at 3:30; Apr.–Oct., daily 8:30–7:30, ticket office closes at 6.*

## POMPEII

★ **Pompeii.** The site of Pompeii, petrified memorial to Vesuvius's eruption on August 24, AD 79, is the largest, most accessible, and probably most famous excavation anywhere. A busy commercial center with a population of 12,000–15,000, ancient Pompeii covered about 160 acres on the seaward end of the fertile Sarno Plain.

As you enter the ruins at Porta Marina, the first buildings to the left after you've gone through the ticket turnstiles are the **Terme Suburbane** (Suburban Baths), built right up against the city walls. These have eyebrow-raising frescoes in the *apodyterium* (changing room) that strongly suggest more than just bathing and massaging went on here. On the walls are scenes of erotic games clients could "play" in the second-floor **Lupanare** (brothel).

Several homes were captured in various states by the eruption of Vesuvius, each representing a different slice of Pompeiian life. The **Casa del Poeta Tragico** (House of the Tragic Poet) is a typical middle-class residence. On the floor is a mosaic of a chained dog and the inscription *cave canem* ("Beware of the dog").

There's no more magnificently memorable evidence of Pompeii's devotion to the pleasures of the flesh than the frescoes on view at the **Villa dei Misteri** (Villa of the Mysteries), a palatial abode built at the far northwestern fringe of Pompeii. Unearthed in 1909 this villa had many rooms, all adorned with frescoes—the finest of which are in the *triclinium*. Painted in the most glowing Pompeiian red, the panels relate the saga of a young bride and her initiation into the mysteries of the cult of Dionysus, who was a god imported to Italy from Greece and then given the Latin name of Bacchus. ☎ *081/8575347* ⊕ *www.pompeiisites.org* 🖅 *€11, tickets are valid for one full day* ⊙ *Apr.–Oct., daily 8:30–7:30 (last admission at 6), and Nov.–Mar., daily 8:30–5 (last admission at 3:30)* Ⓜ *Pompei-Villa dei Misteri.*

## CAPRI
*75 min by boat, 40 min by hydrofoil from Naples.*

Once a pleasure dome to Roman emperors and now Italy's most glamorous seaside getaway, Capri (pronounced with an accent on the first syllable) is a craggy island at the southern end to the bay of Naples.

### CAPRI TOWN
The town is perched some 450 feet above the harbor. Piazza Umberto I, much better known as the Piazzetta, is the island's social hub.

**Certosa di San Giacomo.** You can window-shop in expensive boutiques and browse in souvenir shops along Via Vittorio Emanuele, which leads south toward the many-domed Certosa di San Giacomo. You'll be able to visit the church and cloister of this much-restored monastery and also pause long enough to enjoy the breathtaking sight of Punta Tragara and the Faraglioni, three towering crags, from the viewing point at the edge of the cliff. ⊠ *Via Certosa* ☎ *081/8376218* ⊕ *www.polomusealenapoli. beniculturali.it* 🖅 *Free* ⊙ *Tues.–Sun. 9–2.*

**Giardini di Augusto** (*Gardens of Augustus*). From the terraces of Giardini di Augusto, a beautiful public garden, you can see the village of Marina Piccola below—restaurants, cabanas, and swimming platforms huddle among the shoals—and admire the steep, winding Via Krupp, actually a staircase cut into the rock. Friedrich Krupp, the German arms manufacturer, loved Capri and became one of the island's most generous benefactors. If you find the path too challenging you can reach the beach by taking a bus from the Via Roma terminus down to Marina Piccola. ⊠ *Via Matteotti, beyond monastery of San Giacomo* 🖅 *€1* ⊙ *Daily dawn–dusk.*

### ANACAPRI
A tortuous road leads up to Anacapri, the island's "second city," about 3 km (2 miles) from Capri Town. Crowds are thick down Via Capodimonte leading to Villa San Michele and around the square, Piazza Vittoria, which is the starting point of the chairlift to the top of Monte Solaro. Elsewhere, Anacapri is quietly appealing.

**Monte Solaro.** An impressive limestone formation and the highest point on Capri (1,932 feet), Monte Solaro affords gasp-inducing views toward the bays of both Naples and Salerno. A 12-minute chairlift ride will take you right to the top (refreshments available at the bar), where you can launch out on a number of scenic trails on the western side of the island. Picnickers should note that even in summer it can get windy at this height, and there are few trees to provide shade or refuge. ⊠ *Piazza Vittoria, Anacapri* ☎ *081/8371428* 🎫 *€7.50 one-way, €10 round-trip* ⊙ *Daily 9:30–1 hr before sunset. Closed in adverse weather conditions.*

**San Michele.** In the heart of Anacapri, the octagonal baroque church of San Michele, finished in 1719, is best known for its exquisite majolica pavement designed by Solimena and executed by the *mastro-riggiolaro* (master tiler) Chiaiese from Abruzzo. A walkway skirts the depiction of Adam and a duly contrite Eve being expelled from the Garden of Eden, but you can get a fine overview from the organ loft, reached by a winding staircase near the ticket booth (a privileged perch you have to pay for). Outside the church is the Via Finestrale, which leads to Anacapri's noted **Le Boffe quarter.** This section of town, centered on the Piazza Ficacciate, owes its name to the distinctive domestic architecture prevalent here, which uses vaults and sculpted groins instead of crossbeams. ⊠ *Piazza San Nicola, Anacapri* ☎ *081/8372396* ⊕ *www.chiesa-san-michele.com* 🎫 *€2* ⊙ *Apr.–Oct., daily 9–7; Nov and Mar., daily 10–2.*

**ELSEWHERE ON THE ISLAND**

★ **Grotta Azzurra.** Only when the Grotta Azzurra was "discovered" in 1826 by the Polish poet August Kopisch and Swiss artist Ernest Fries, did Capri become a tourist haven. The water's extraordinary sapphire color is caused by a hidden opening in the rock that refracts the light. At highest illumination the very air inside seems tinted blue. The Grotta Azzurra can be reached from Marina Grande or from the small embarkation point below Anacapri on the northwest side of the island, accessible by bus from Anacapri. ⊠ *Grotta Azzurra* 🎫 *€24.50 from Marina Grande, €12.50 by rowboat from Grotta Azzurra near Anacapri* ⊙ *9–1 hr before sunset closed if sea is even minimally rough.*

## SHOPPING

Leather goods, jewelry, and cameos are some of the best items to buy in Campania. In Naples you'll generally find good deals on handbags, shoes, and clothing. If you want the real thing, make your purchases in shops, but if you don't mind imitations, rummage around at the various street-vendor *bancherelle* (stalls).

In Naples the immediate area around **Piazza dei Martiri,** in the center of Chiaia, has the densest concentration of luxury shopping, with perfume shops, fashion outlets, and antiques on display. **Via dei Mille** and **Via Filangieri,** which lead off Piazza dei Martiri, are home to Bulgari, Mont Blanc, and Hermès stores. The small, pedestrian-only **Via Calabritto,** which leads down from Piazza dei Martiri toward the sea, is where you'll find high-end retailers such as Prada, Gucci, Versace, Vuitton, Cacharel, Damiani, and Cartier. **Via Chiaia** and **Via Toledo** are the two busiest shopping streets for most Neapolitans; there you'll find reasonably priced clothes and shoes. The **Vomero** district yields more shops, especially along Via Scarlatti and Via Luca Giordano. **Via Santa Maria di Costantinopoli,** which runs from Piazza Bellini to the Archaeological Museum, is the street for antiques shops.

**Nel Regno di Pulcinella.** Nel Regno di Pulcinella is the workshop of Lello Esposito, a Neapolitan artist renowned for his renderings of a popular puppet named Pulcinella. ⊠ *Vico San Domenico Maggiore 9, Spaccanapoli* ☎ *081/5514171.*

## WHERE TO EAT

$$$$
SOUTHERN
ITALIAN

✕ **Al Grottino.** This small and friendly family-run restaurant, which is in a 14th-century building handy to the Piazzetta, has arched ceilings and lots of atmosphere; autographed photos of famous customers cover the walls. House specialties are *scialatielli ai fiori di zucchine e gambaretti* (homemade pasta with zucchini flowers and shrimps) and linguine *ai scampi*, but the owner delights in taking his guests through the menu. ⑤ *Average main: €40* ⊠ *Via Longano 27, Capri Town* ☎ *081/8370584* ⊕ *www.ristorantealgrottino.net* ⊗ *Closed Nov.–mid-Mar.*

$
PIZZA
**Fodor's**Choice
★

✕ **Da Michele.** You may recognize this from the movie "Eat, Pray, Love," but for more than 140 years before Julia Roberts arrived this place has been a culinary reference point in Naples. Despite offering only two types of pizza—marinara (with tomato, garlic, and oregano) and *margherita* (with tomato, mozzarella, and basil)—plus a small selection of drinks, it still manages to attract long lines. The prices have something to do with it. But the pizza itself suffers no rivals, so even those waiting in line are good-humored: the boisterous, joyous atmosphere wafts out with the smell of yeast and wood smoke onto the street. Step right up to get a number at the door and then hang outside until it's called. Note: The restaurant is off Corso Umberto, between Piazza Garibaldi and Piazza Nicola Amore. ⑤ *Average main: €7* ⊠ *Via Sersale 1/3, Piazza Garibaldi* ☎ *081/5539204* ⊕ *www.damichele.net* ⊟ *No credit cards* ⊗ *Jun.-Nov. closed Sun. and 2 wks in Aug.*

# NICE, FRANCE

Updated
by Jennifer
Ladonne

The fifth-largest city in France, Nice is also one of the noblest. The city is capped by a dramatic hilltop château, at whose base a bewitching warren of ancient Mediterranean streets unfolds. Although now French to the core, the town was allied with a Latin Duchy until 1860, and this almost 500 years of history adds a rich Italian flavor to the city's culture, architecture, and dialect. In the late 19th century, Nice saw the birth of tourism, as English and Russian aristocrats began to winter in the temperate climate along the famed waterfront, Promenade des Anglais, which is now lined with grand hotels, a part of their legacy. Nowadays Nice strikes an engaging balance between historic Provençal grace, port-town exotica, urban energy, whimsy, and high culture. Its museums—particularly its art collections—are excellent, and the atmosphere is langourous yet urbane.

### ESSENTIALS
**CURRENCY**
The euro.

### HOURS

Most stores open Monday through Saturday from 9 to 7, but many close at lunchtime (usually noon to 2 or 3), and some will open later and on Sunday during July and August. Museums are usually open 10 to 5, but most are closed on either Monday or Tuesday.

### TELEPHONES

Tri-band GSM phones work in France. You can buy prepaid phone cards at telecom shops, news vendors, and tobacconists in all towns and cities. Phone cards can be used for local or international calls. Orange, SFR, Bouygues Telecom, and Virgin are leading telecom companies. If you have an unlocked GSM phone, LeFrenchMobile (⊕ *www. lefrenchmobile.com*) offers SIM cards (and micro SIM cards) with support in English, unlimited validity of credits, and prepurchase online.

### COMING ASHORE

Ships dock at Nice Port, east of the city center and a 30- to 40-minute walk from the city's attractions. The port facilities include a tourist office and currency-exchange desk. There is a free shuttle service into the downtown core in high season, and taxis are also available.

Don't rent a car if you intend to explore in the city, but it is a sensible option if you want to tour the spectacular Provençal countryside. Expect to pay approximately €75 per day for an economy manual vehicle. Taxis are plentiful and can provide tourist itineraries. For single journeys, fares begin at €3 and then €0.90 per km.

Public transport is reliable and comprehensive,, with Ligne d'Azur (⊕ *www.lignedazur.com*) providing services within the city and suburbs. Route 15 heads to Cimiez and offers a free transfer between the Chagall and Matisse museums. Single tickets are €1 at this writing, and allow you to ride for for 74 minutes. A one-day pass is €4. There is fast and reliable train service between Nice and Cannes, Monte Carlo, Antibes, and other coastal towns if you want to explore farther afield without a car.

## EXPLORING NICE

### VIEUX NICE

Framed by the "château"—really a rocky promontory—and Cours Saleya, Nice's Vieille Ville is its strongest drawing point and the best place to capture the city's historic atmosphere. Its grid of narrow streets, darkened by houses five and six stories high with bright splashes of laundry fluttering overhead and jewel-box baroque churches on every other corner, creates a magic that seems utterly removed from the French Riviera fast lane.

**Colline de Château** (*Château Hill*). This hilltop park, acceesible by elevator from the east end of the Promenade des Anglais, commands the site of a once-massive medieval stronghold of which only a few ruins remain. From here take in extraordinary views of the Baie des Anges, the length of the Promenade des Anglais, and the red-ocher roofs of the Vieille Ville. ⊙ *Daily 7–7.*

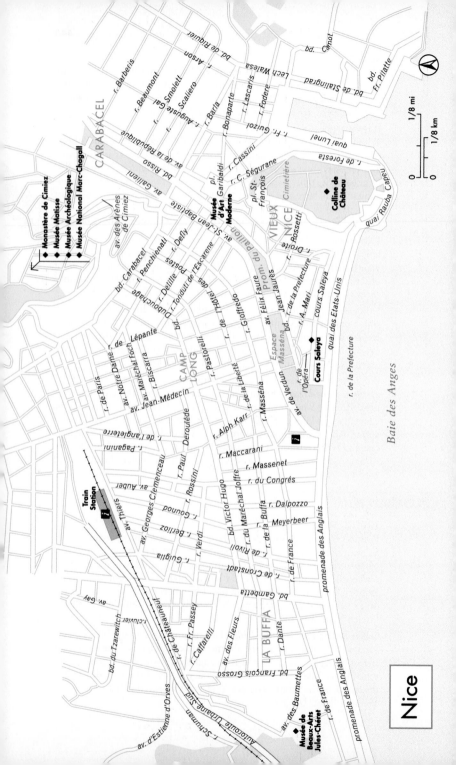

# Nice

**Baie des Anges**

Monastère de Cimiez
Musée Matisse
Musée Archéologique
Musée National Marc-Chagall

CARABACEL

r. Barberis
r. Beaumont
bd. de Riquier
bd. de Carnot
r. Arson
r. Smollett
r. Scaliero
r. Auguste Gal
bd. de Stalingrad
Lech Walesa
bd. Pilatte
bd. fr. Pilatte

av. des Arènes de Cimiez
av. Galliéni
bd. Risso
av. de la République
r. Barla
r. Lascaris
r. Fodéré
r. Cassini
r. Guizot
r. Fr. Guizot
r. Bonaparte
quai Lunel
r. de Foresta
quai Rauba Capeu

bd. Carabacel
r. Penchienati
r. Delille
r. Defly
r. St-Jean Baptiste
bd. J. Fonduti de l'Escarène
r. Tonduti de l'Escarène
pl. Garibaldi
pl. St-François
r. C. Ségurane
Cimetière
Colline de Château

VIEUX NICE

r. Rossetti
r. Droite
r. de la Préfecture

r. de Paris
r. Notre Dame
r. de Lépante
av. Maréchal Foch
r. Biscarra
r. Pastorelli
bd.
r. Dubouchage
CAMP LONG
r. de l'Hôtel
r. Gioffredo
av. Félix Faure
bd. Jean Jaurès
r. A. Mari
Cours Saleya
quai des Etats-Unis

av. Jean-Médecin
r. de la Liberté
r. Masséna
r. Alph. Karr
Espace Masséna
r. de Verdun
r. de l'Opéra

Cours Saleya

r. Paul Deroulède
r. de l'Angleterre
r. Paganini
r. Maccarani
r. Masséna
*i*

av. Georges Clemenceau
av. Auber
r. Rossini
r. Gounod
r. Berlioz
r. Verdi
av. Thiers
Train Station
*i*
r. Victor Hugo
r. du Maréchal Joffre
r. Massenet
r. du Congrès
r. Dalpozzo
r. de la Buffa
r. Meyerbeer

av. Gay
bd. du Tzarewitch
r. Cluvier
r. de Châteauneuf
r. Fr. Passey
r. Caffarelli
r. des Fleurs
r. Dante
LA BUFFA
bd. François Grosso
r. de Rivoli
r. de France
bd. Gambetta
r. Guiglia
r. de Cronstadt

r. Schuman
Autoroute Urbaine Sud
av. d'Estienne d'Orves
av. des Baumettes
Musée de Beaux-Arts Jules-Chéret
promenade des Anglais

Musée d'Art Moderne

0    1/8 mi
0    1/8 km

★ **Cours Saleya.** This long pedestrian thoroughfare, half street, half square, is the nerve center of Old Nice, the heart of the Vieille Ville and the stage set for the daily dramas of marketplace and café life. Framed with 18th-century houses and shaded by plane trees, the long, narrow square bursts into a fireworks-show of color Tuesday through Sunday, when flower-market vendors roll armloads of mimosas, irises, roses, and orange blossoms into *cornets* (paper cones) and thrust them into the arms of shoppers. Cafés and restaurants, all more or less touristy, fill outdoor tables with onlookers who bask in the sun. At the far-eastern end, antiques and *brocantes* (collectibles) draw avid junk-hounds every Monday morning. At this end you can also find Place Félix. Little wonder the great painter Matisse lived (from 1921 to 1938) in the imposing yellow stone building at 1 Place Charles Félix that looms over the square. Indeed, you don't need to visit the city's famous Musée Matisse to understand this great artist: simply stand in the doorway of his former home and study the Place de l'Ancien Senat 10 feet away—the scene is a golden Matisse pumped up to the nth power.

> **NICE BEST BETS**
>
> **Musée Matisse.** Nice, where the artist made his home from 1917 until his death in 1954, has the finest collection of his work.
>
> **Musée National Marc Chagall.** Specially designed galleries house the 17 canvases making up *Message Biblique*, "Biblical Message," one of the postimpressionist's most charismatic works.
>
> **Strolling through the alleyways of Vieux Nice.** The pastel facades of the lively Old Town have inspired generations of artists. Enjoy the cafés, the quaint boutiques, and the flower market on Cours Saleya.

**Musée d'Art Moderne.** The assertive contemporary architecture of the Modern Art Museum makes a bold and emphatic statement regarding Nice's presence in the modern world. The art collection inside focuses intently and thoroughly on contemporary art from the late 1950s onward, but pride of place is given to sculptor Nikki de Saint Phalle's recent donation of more than 170 exceptional pieces. The rooftop terrace, sprinkled with minimalist sculptures, has stunning views over the city. Guided tours are offered Wednesdays at 3 pm. €5 ⊠ *Promenade des Arts, Vieux Nice* ☎ *04-97-13-42-01* ⊕ *www.mamac-nice.org* 🎫 *Free; guide tours €5* ☾ *Tues.–Sun. 10–6.*

★ **Musée des Beaux-Arts Jules-Chéret** (*Jules-Chéret Fine Arts Museum*). Originally built for a member of Nice's Old Russian community, the Princess Kotschoubey, this Italianate mansion is a Belle Époque wedding cake and is replete with one of the grandest staircases on the coast. After the *richissime* American James Thompson took over and the last glittering ball was held here, the villa was bought by the municipality as a museum in the 1920s. Unfortunately, much of the period decor was sold but in its place are paintings by Degas, Boudin, Monet, Sisley, Dufy, and Jules Chéret, whose posters of winking *damselles* distill all the *joie* of the Belle Époque. From the Negresco Hotel area the museum is about a 15-minute walk up a gentle hill. ⊠ *33 av. des Baumettes, Centre Ville* ☎ *04-92-15-28-28* ⊕ *www.musee-beaux-arts-nice.org* 🎫 *Free; guided tours €5* ☾ *Daily 10–6.*

## CIMIEZ

Once the site of the powerful Roman settlement Cemenelum, the hilltop neighborhood of Cimiez—4 km (2½ miles) north of Cours Saleya—is Nice's most luxurious quarter (use Bus 15 from Place Masséna or Avenue Jean-Médecin to visit its sights).

**Monastère de Cimiez.** This fully functioning monastery is worth the pilgrimage. You can find a lovely **garden,** replanted along the lines of the original 16th-century layout; the **Musée Franciscain,** a didactic museum tracing the history of the Franciscan order; and a 15th-century **church** containing three works of remarkable power and elegance by Bréa. ⊠ *Pl. du Monastère, Cimiez* ☎ *04–93–81–00–04* ✉ *Free* ⊘ *Church Thurs.–Tues. 9–6 and Sun. 2:30–8:30. Museum Mon.–Sat. 10–noon and 2–5:30.*

**Musée Archéologique** (*Archaeology Museum*). This museum, next to the Matisse Museum, has a dense and intriguing collection of objects extracted from the digs around the Roman city of Cemenelum, which flourished from the 1st to the 5th century. Among the fascinating ruins are an amphitheatre, frigidarium, gymnasium, baths, and sewage trenches, some dating back to the 3rd century are fascinating; it's best to avoid midday visits on warm days. ⊠ *160 av. des Arènes-de-Cimiez, Cimiez* ☎ *04–93–81–59–57* ⊕ *www.musee-archeologique-nice. org* ✉ *Free; €5 guided tour* ⊘ *Wed.–Mon. 10–6.*

★ **Musée National Marc Chagall** (National Museum *Marc Chagall*). This museum has one of the finest permanent collections of Chagall's (1887–1985) late works. Superbly displayed, 17 vast canvases depict biblical themes, each in emphatic, joyous colors. The museum also hosts chamber music and classical concert series, admission may apply. ⊠ *Av. du Dr-Ménard, head up Av. Thiers, then take left onto Av. Malausséna, cross railway tracks, and take first right up Av. de l'Olivetto, Cimiez* ☎ *04–93–53–87–20* ⊕ *www.musee-chagall.fr* ✉ *€7.50* ⊘ *May–Oct., Wed.–Mon. 10–6; Nov.–Apr., Wed.–Mon. 10–5.*

Fodor'sChoice
★   **Musée Matisse.** In the '60s the city of Nice bought this lovely, light-bathed 17th-century villa, surrounded by the ruins of Roman civilization, and restored it to house a large collection of Henri Matisse's works. Matisse settled along Nice's waterfront in 1917, seeking a sun cure after a bout with pneumonia, and remained here until his death in 1954. During his years on the French Riviera, Matisse maintained intense friendships and artistic liaisons with Renoir, who lived in Cagnes, and with Picasso, who lived in Mougins and Antibes. He eventually moved up to the rarefied isolation of Cimiez and took an apartment in the Hôtel Regina (now an apartment building, just across from the museum), where he lived out the rest of his life. Matisse walked often in the parklands around the Roman remains and was buried in an olive grove outside the Cimiez cemetery. The collection of artworks includes several pieces the artist donated to the city before his death; the rest were donated by his family. In every medium and context—paintings, gouache cutouts, engravings, and book illustrations—the collection represents the evolution of his art, from Cézanne-like still lifes to exuberant dancing paper dolls. Even the furniture and accessories speak of Matisse, from the Chinese

vases to the bold-printed fabrics with which he surrounded himself. A series of black-and-white photographs captures the artist at work, surrounded by personal—and telling—details. ⊠ *164 av. des Arènes-de-Cimiez, Cimiez* ☎ *04–93–81–08–08* ⊕ *www.musee-matisse-nice.org* 🎟 *Free* ☉ *Wed.–Mon. 10–6.*

## BEACHES

Nice's pebble beaches extend all along the Baie des Anges, backed full-length by the Promenade des Anglais. Public stretches alternate with posh private beaches that have restaurants—and bar service, mattresses and parasols, waterskiing, parasailing, windsurfing, and Jet Skiing.

**Beau Rivage.** One of the handiest private beaches is the Beau Rivage, set across from the Opéra and next to the Jardin Albert Ier. The €20 daily rental fee for a lounger is a good investment (book the night before) as it allows access to the toilets and shade of a parasol. The beach restaurant is excellent, but you can bring your own beach bag of goodies. ⊠ *24 rue Saint François de Paule* ☎ *04–92–47–82–82* ⊕ *www. plagenicebeaurivage.com.*

**Florida Beach.** One of the new private beaches making a splash on the Prom, Florida is très hip nd has an excellent restaurant and bar service. ⊠ *71 Promenade des Anglais* ☎ *04–93–44–72–86* ⊕ *www.florida-beach.fr.*

## SHOPPING

As the largest city in Provence, Nice is a trove of regional crafts and delicacies, including basketwork, bright fabrics, perfumes, lavender soaps, olive-wood items, plus delicious olives, olive oils, honey, dried herbs, and quaffable local wines. The city is particularly renowned for its delicious crystallized fruit. The best place to find crafts is in the Old Town, while French couture can be found on the elegant boulevards of the new town.

**Confiserie Florian du Vieux Nice.** A good source for crystallized fruit, a Nice specialty, is the Confiserie Florian du Vieux Nice, on the west side of the port. ⊠ *14 quai Papacino, Vieux Nice* ⊕ *www.confiserieflorian.com.*

**Henri Auer.** The venerable Henri Auer has sold crystallized fruit since 1820. ⊠ *7 rue St-François-de-Paule, Vieux Nice* ⊕ *www.maison-auer.com.*

## WHERE TO EAT

$ ✕ **Chez René Socca.** This back-alley landmark is the most popular dive FRENCH in town for *socca*, the chickpea-pancake snack food unique to Nice. Rustic olive-wood tables line the street, and curt waiters splash down your drink order. Then you get in line, choose your plate, and carry it steaming to the table yourself. It's off Place Garibaldi on the edge of the Vieille Ville, across from the old *Gare Routière* (bus station). $ *Average main: €3* ⊠ *2 rue Miralheti, Vieux Nice* ☎ *04–93–92–05–73* ▤ *No credit cards* ☉ *Closed Mon. and Jan.*

$$$    ✕ **Grand Café de Turin.** Whether you squeeze onto a banquette in the
SEAFOOD    dark, low-ceiling bar or win a coveted table under the arcaded por-
ticoes on Place Garibaldi, this is *the* place to go for shellfish in Nice:
sea snails, clams, plump *fines de claires,* and salty *bleues* oysters, and
urchins by the dozen. It's packed noon and night (and has been since
it opened in 1908), so don't be too put off by the sometimes brusque
reception of the waiters. ⑤ *Average main: €30* ⊠ *5 pl. Garibaldi, Vieux
Nice* ☎ *04–93–62–29–52* ⊕ *www.cafedeturin.fr.*

# PALERMO, ITALY

Updated
by Bruce
Leimsidor

Once the intellectual capital of southern Europe, Palermo has always
been at the crossroads of civilization. Favorably situated on a crescent-
shaped bay at the foot of Monte Pellegrino, it has attracted almost every
culture touching the Mediterranean world. To Palermo's credit, it has
absorbed these diverse cultures into a unique personality that is at once
Arab and Christian, Byzantine and Roman, Norman and Italian. The
city's heritage encompasses all of Sicily's varied ages, but its distinctive
aspect is its Arab-Norman identity, an improbable marriage that, mixed
in with Byzantine and Jewish elements, created some resplendent works
of art. No less noteworthy than the architecture is Palermo's chaotic
vitality, on display at some of Italy's most vibrant outdoor markets,
public squares, street bazaars, and food vendors, and above all in its
grand climax of Italy's most spectacular *passeggiata* (the leisurely social
stroll along the principal thoroughfare).

## ESSENTIALS
### CURRENCY
The euro.

### HOURS
Most shops are open 9 to 1 and 4 or 4:30 to 7:30 or 8 and closed
Sunday; in addition, most food shops close Wednesday afternoon, and
other shops normally close Monday morning. Most museums/attrac-
tions open throughout the day, though some, particularly churches,
close in the afternoon. Because of budget cutbacks and increasing num-
ber of museums have cutback their hours, most often in the afternoon,
so mornings are almost uniformly best for touring.

### PRIVATE TOURS
Siteseeings.com offers half-day tours of Palermo and Monreale to small
groups in a minibus with an English-speaking guide for €35 per person.
You can reserve and book on the Internet. On Thursdays the company
conducts full-day tours in small groups to Agrigento and Piazza Ame-
rina. Tours cost €70 to €80.

Get your guide conducts one day tours of Palermo, Monreale, and
Cefalu with an English-speaking guide, generally on weekends, for €95
per person. Tours should be booked in advance.

**Contacts Get Your Guide.** ☎ *(49)30/540–45944 in Italy* ⊕ *www.getyourguide.com/.*
**Sightseeings.com.** ☎ *415/332–7916 in the U.S.* ⊕ *www.siteseeings.it.*

### TELEPHONES

Tri-band GSM phones work in Italy. You can buy prepaid phone cards at telecom shops, news vendors, and tobacconists in all towns and cities. Phone cards can be used for local or international calls.

### COMING ASHORE

Palermo's cruise port has recently been expanded to accommodate larger vessels. The terminal building has a café and a shop. Just outside the gates are taxis and horse-drawn carriages. It is possible to walk directly from the ship into the city; however, the port area has a reputation for pickpockets and scam artists, so be aware.

Three bus routes (Gialla, Rossa, and Verde) ply the streets of the Old Town, but none links with the port; tickets cost €1. Taxis begin at €3.05, then add €2.25 for the first km and €0.80 per km (½-mile) thereafter, with supplments for slow traffic, luggage, and holidays. Tourists are almost uniform in reporting serious overcharging by taxis in Palermo; it's best to ask at the cruise pier or at a restaurant or shop what the fare should be before you head out. Renting a car would open up much of the island to you, but heavy traffic in Palermo may play havoc with your nerves. Expect to pay about €60 per day for a compact manual vehicle.

## EXPLORING PALERMO

**Catacombe dei Cappuccini.** The spookiest sight in all of Sicily, this 16th-century catacomb houses nearly 9,000 corpses of men, women, and young children—some in tombs but many mummified and preserved—hanging in rows on the walls, divided by social caste, age, or gender. Most wear signs indicating their names and the years they lived. The Capuchins were founders and proprietors of the bizarre establishment (many of the corpses are Capuchin friars) from 1599 to 1911, and it's still under the auspices of the nearby Capuchin church. ⊠ *Piazza Cappuccini 1, off Via Cappuccini, near Palazzo Reale* ☎ *091/212633* 🎫 *€3* 🕙 *Daily 9–12 and 3–5:30.*

★ **Cattedrale.** This church is a lesson in Palermitan eclecticism—originally Norman (1182), then Catalan Gothic (14th to 15th century), then fitted out with a baroque and neoclassical interior (18th century). Its turrets, towers, dome, and arches come together in the kind of meeting of diverse elements that King Roger II (1095–1154), whose tomb is inside along with that of Frederick II, fostered during his reign. The back of the apse is gracefully decorated with interlacing Arab arches inlaid with limestone and black volcanic tufa. ⊠ *Corso Vittorio Emanuele, Capo* ☎ *091/334373* 🎫 *€3* 🕙 *Mar.–Oct., Mon.–Sat. 9:30–5:30; Nov.–Feb., Mon.–Sat. 9:30–1:30.*

**La Martorana.** Distinguished by an elegant Norman campanile, this church was erected in 1143 but had its interior altered considerably during the baroque period. High along the western wall, however, is some of the oldest and best-preserved mosaic artwork of the Norman period. Near the entrance is an interesting mosaic of King Roger II being crowned by Christ. ⊠ *Piazza Bellini 3, Quattro Canti* ☎ *091/6161692* 🕙 *Mon.–Sat. 8:30–1 and 3:30–5:30, Sun. 8:30–1.*

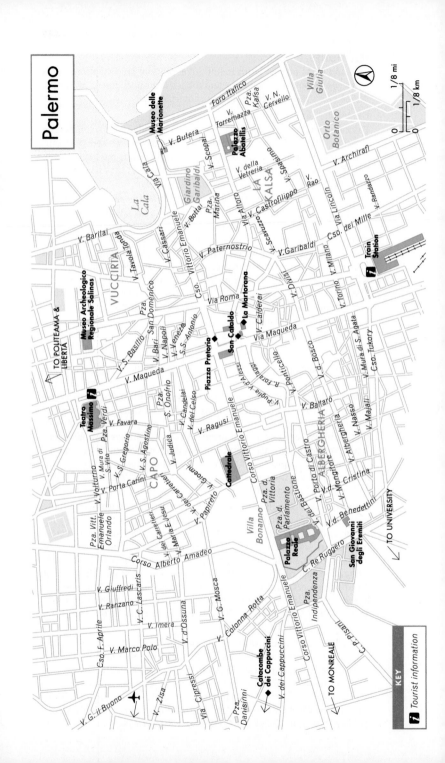

**Museo Archeologico Regionale Salinas** (*Salinas Regional Museum of Archaeology*). Especially interesting pieces in this small but excellent collection are the examples of prehistoric cave drawings and a marvelously reconstructed Doric frieze from the Greek temple at Selinunte, which reveals the high level of artistic culture attained by the Greek colonists in Sicily some 2,500 years ago. (To enter, use the door around the corner on Via Roma.) Extensive renovations at the museum are scheduled to continue through 2012. ⊠ *Piazza Olivella 24, Via Roma, Olivella* ☎ *091/6116806* 🎫 *€4* ⏲ *Tues.–Fri. 8:30–1:30 and 2:30–6:30, weekends 8:30–1; last entry ½ hr before closing.*

---

**PALERMO BEST BETS**

**Marvel at the Duomo in Monreale.** The finest example of Norman fusion architecture in Sicily blends Eastern and Western influences.

**Take a peek at Palazzo Real.** Once home to Bourbon royalty and their particular taste in home decor it now houses the Sicilian Parliament.

**Stroll the Old Town.** A genuine slice of life southern Italian style will play out before your eyes as you kick the dust off your shoes by walking through these streets.

---

**Palazzo Abatellis.** Housed in this late-15th-century Catalan Gothic palace with Renaissance elements is the **Galleria Regionale.** Among its treasures are the *Annunciation* (1474), a painting by Sicily's prominent Renaissance master Antonello da Messina (1430–79), and an arresting fresco by an unknown 15th-century painter, titled *The Triumph of Death,* a macabre depiction of the plague years. Two new rooms were opened in early 2010 after years of work. ⊠ *Via Alloro 4, Kalsa* ☎ *091/6230011* 🎫 *€8* ⏲ *Tues.–Fri. 9–5:30, weekends 9–1.*

**Palazzo Reale** (*Royal Palace*). This historic palace, also called Palazzo dei Normanni (Norman Palace), was the seat of Sicily's semiautonomous rulers for centuries. The building is a fascinating mesh of abutting 10th-century Norman and 17th-century Spanish structures. Because it now houses the Sicilian Parliament, parts of the palace are closed to the public from Tuesday to Thursday when the regional Parliament is sitting. The **Cappella Palatina** (Palatine Chapel) remains open. Built by Roger II in 1132, it's a dazzling example of the harmony of artistic elements produced under the Normans. Here the skill of French and Sicilian masons was brought to bear on the decorative purity of Arab ornamentation and the splendor of 11th-century Greek Byzantine mosaics. The interior is covered with glittering mosaics and capped by a splendid 10th-century Arab honeycomb stalactite wooden ceiling. Biblical stories blend happily with scenes of Arab life—look for one showing a picnic in a harem—and Norman court pageantry.

Upstairs are the royal apartments, including the **Sala di Re Ruggero** (King Roger's Hall), decorated with medieval murals of hunting scenes—an earlier (1120) secular counterpoint to the religious themes seen elsewhere. French, Latin, and Arabic were spoken here, and Arab astronomers and poets exchanged ideas with Latin and Greek scholars in one of the most interesting marriages of culture in the Western world. The Sala is always included with entry to the palace or chapel. ⊠ *Piazza*

*Indipendenza, Albergheria* ☎ *091/6262833* ⊕ *www.federicosecondo. org* ✉ *Palazzo Reale or Cappella Palatina €7, entry to both €8.50* ⊙ *Palazzo Reale: Mon. and Fri. 8:15–5, Sun. 8:15–12:30. Cappella Palatina: Mon.–Sat. 8:15–5, Sun. 8:15–12:30, but closed for Sun. services 9:45–11:15. Last entry ½ hr before closing.*

**Piazza Pretoria.** The square's centerpiece, a lavishly decorated fountain with 500 separate pieces of sculpture and an abundance of nude figures, so shocked some Palermitans when it was unveiled in 1575 that it got the nickname "Fountain of Shame." It's even more of a sight when illuminated at night.

★ **San Cataldo.** Three striking Saracenic scarlet domes mark this church, built in 1154 during the Norman occupation of Palermo. The church now belongs to the Knights of the Holy Sepulchre and has a spare but intense stone interior. If closed, inquire next door at La Martorana. ✉ *Piazza Bellini 3, Kalsa* ☎ *091/7827390* ✉ *€2.50* ⊙ *Daily 9:30–12:30 and 3–6.*

**San Giovanni degli Eremiti.** Distinguished by its five reddish-orange domes and stripped-clean interior, this 12th-century church was built by the Normans on the site of an earlier mosque—one of 200 that once stood in Palermo. The emirs ruled Palermo for nearly two centuries and brought to it their passion for lush gardens and fountains. One is reminded of this while sitting in San Giovanni's delightful cloister of twin half columns, surrounded by palm trees, jasmine, oleander, and citrus trees. ✉ *Via dei Benedettini 14, Albergheria* ☎ *091/6515019* ✉ *€6* ⊙ *Tues.–Sat. 9–7; Mon. and Sun. 9–1:30; last entry ½ hr before closing.*

**Teatro Massimo.** Construction of this formidable neoclassical theater, the largest in Italy, was started in 1875 by Giovanni Battista Basile and completed by his son Ernesto in 1897. A reconstruction project started in 1974 ran into gross delays, and the facility remained closed until just before its centenary in 1997. Its interior is as glorious as ever. *The Godfather: Part III* ended with a famous shooting scene on the theater's steps. Visits, by 25-minute guided tour only, are available in six languages, including English. ✉ *Piazza Verdi 9, at top of Via Maqueda, Olivella* ☎ *091/6053521* ⊕ *www.teatromassimo.it* ✉ *€7* ⊙ *Tues.–Sun. 10–3.*

## MONREALE

*10 km (6 miles) southwest of Palermo.*

**Cloister.** The lovely cloister of the abbey adjacent to the Duomo was built at the same time as the church but enlarged in the 14th century. The beautiful enclosure is surrounded by 216 intricately carved double columns, every other one decorated in a unique glass mosaic pattern. Afterward, don't forget to walk behind the cloister to the belvedere, with stunning panoramic views over the Conca d'Oro (Golden Conch) valley toward Palermo. ✉ *Piazza del Duomo* ☎ *091/6404403* ✉ *€6* ⊙ *Tues.–Sat. 9–6:30; Mon. and Sun. 9–1; last entry ½ hr before closing.*

Fodor's Choice
★ **Duomo.** Monreale's splendid Duomo is lavishly executed with mosaics depicting events from the Old and New Testaments. After the Norman conquest of Sicily the new princes showcased their ambitions through

monumental building projects. William II (1154–89) built the church complex with a cloister and palace between 1174 and 1185, employing Byzantine craftsmen. The result was a glorious fusion of Eastern and Western influences, widely regarded as the finest example of Norman architecture in Sicily.

The major attraction is the 68,220 square feet of glittering gold mosaics decorating the cathedral interior. *Christ Pantocrator* dominates the apse area; the nave contains narratives of the Creation; and scenes from the life of Christ adorn the walls of the aisles and the transept. The painted wooden ceiling dates from 1816–37. The roof commands a great view (a reward for climbing 172 stairs).

Bonnano Pisano's bronze doors, completed in 1186, depict 42 biblical scenes and are considered among the most important of medieval artifacts. Barisano da Trani's 42 panels on the north door, dating from 1179, present saints and evangelists. ⊠ *Piazza del Duomo* ☎ *091/6402424* ☉ *Mar.–Oct., daily 8:30–1 and 3–6:30; Nov.–Feb., daily 8:30–12:45 and 3–5.*

## SHOPPING

Sicilan specialties include lace and linen, including place mats and napkins, and ceramics, particularly its practical folk pottery from Caltagirone, on the north coast. Marble and wrought iron are also fashioned into souvenir pieces and antiques shops are numerous, though prices can be high. Edibles include an excellent range of wines and olive oils, jams, and tasty sweets.

In Palermo, north of Piazza Castelnuovo, **Via della Libertà** and the streets around it represent the luxury end of the shopping scale, with some of Palermo's best-known stores. A second nerve center for shoppers is the pair of parallel streets connecting modern Palermo with the train station, **Via Roma,** and **Via Maqueda,** where boutiques and shoe shops become increasingly upmarket as you move from the Quattro Canti past Teatro Massimo to Via Ruggero Settimo, but are still a serious notch below their counterparts in the Libertà area.

If you're interested in truly connecting with local life while searching for souvenirs, a visit to one of Palermo's many bustling markets is essential. Between Via Roma and Via Maqueda the many *bancherelle (market stalls)* on Via Bandiera sell everything from socks to imitation designer handbags.

**Enoteca Picone.** Enoteca Picone is the best wineshop in town, with a fantastic selection of Sicilian and national wines. Though the service can be curt, you can taste a selection of wines by the glass in the front of the store. There are tables in the back, where meats and cheeses are also served. The branch on Viale Strasburgo offers full meals. Both branches are closed Sunday. ⊠ *Via Marconi 36, Libertà* ☎ *091/331300* ⊕ *www.enotecapicone.it* ⊠ *Viale Strasburgo 235, Resuttana* ☎ *091/6880357.*

## WHERE TO EAT

$   ✕ **Pizzeria Ai Comparucci.** One of Palermo's best pizzerias doubles as a
PIZZA   modern art gallery. The colorful paintings give the place a fun, casual vibe. Better yet are the delicious Neapolitan pizzas coming out of the big oven in the open kitchen—the genius is in the crust, which is seared in a matter of seconds. The owners make their money on a quick turnover (so don't expect a long, leisurely meal). But the pizza is delicious, and the place often serves until midnight—later than almost any other restaurant in the neighborhood. $ *Average main: €12* ⊠ *Via Garzilli 1, Libertà* ☎ *091/6090467* ⊘ *Closed Mon. and lunchtime.*

$$$   ✕ **Trattoria Altri Tempi.** This small and friendly "retro" restaurant is a
SICILIAN   favorite among locals who pine for the rustic dishes served by their
★   ancestors. A meal begins when the server plunks down a carafe of the house red and a superb spread of traditional antipasti on your table. Dishes have old-fashioned names: *fave a cunigghiu* is fava beans prepared with olive oil, garlic, and remarkably flavorful oregano; and *vampaciucia c'anciova* is a lasagna-like dish with a concentrated sauce of tomatoes, anchovies, and grapes. The meal ends well, too, with free house-made herb or fruit liquors and excellent cannoli. $ *Average main: €25* ⊠ *Via Sammartino 65/67, Libertà* ☎ *091/323480* ⊘ *Closed 2 weeks late Aug. and Sun. June–Aug. No dinner Sun.*

# PORTO CERVO, SARDINIA, ITALY

Updated by
Victoria Tang

An uncut jewel of an island, Sardinia remains unique and enigmatic. Would-be conquerors have left their marks, but inland, a proud Sard culture and language flourish. Sardinia has some of Europe's most expensive resort destinations, but it's also home to areas as rugged and undeveloped as anywhere on the continent. Fine sand and clean waters draw sun seekers to beaches that are unquestionably among the best in the Mediterranean. Best known are those along the Costa Smeralda (Emerald Coast), where the superrich have anchored their yachts since the 1960s. But most of the coast is unsettled, a jagged series of wildly beautiful inlets accessible only by sea. And inland, Sardinia remains shepherd's country, silent and stark. Spaghetti Westerns were once filmed here, and it's not hard to imagine why: the desolate mountainous terrain seems the perfect frontier set. Against this landscape are the striking and mysterious stone *nuraghi* (ancient defensive structures), which provide clues to the lifestyles of the island's prehistoric peoples.

### ESSENTIALS

**CURRENCY**

The euro.

**HOURS**

Shops are generally open 9 to 1 and 3:30 to 8 and are generally closed Sunday. Summer (June to September) hours are usually 9 to 1 and 4 to 8, and some shops close Saturday afternoon.

### TELEPHONES

Tri-band GSM phones work in Italy. You can buy prepaid phone cards at telecom shops, news vendors, and tobacconists in all towns and cities. Phone cards can be used for local or international calls.

### COMING ASHORE

Poltu Quatu means "hidden port" in the Sardinian dialect, and it is hidden at the head of a narrow inlet. Small cruise ships can dock at the port, but larger ships dock beyond the mouth of the inlet and tender passengers ashore. The port is one element in an extended tourist "village"; other facilities include a selection of cafés, sports outfitters, and shops. You can rent a boat for the day directly from the harbor to cruise the coast. There is no public transport to the port.

Renting a car gives you a great opportunity to explore the northern half of the island and still have time to relax. Europcar has an office in the port. Other car-rental companies will deliver to the port for an extra charge. Rental prices for a compact manual vehicle start at €80 per day. There is a taxi stand within the resort village. Taxis will meet boats at the port but must be prebooked. Taxi fares are €20 into Puerto Cervo, which is just around the headland.

# EXPLORING NORTHERN SARDINIA

### PORTO CERVO

*35 km (22 miles) southeast of La Maddalena, 30 km (19 miles) north of Olbia.*

★ Sardinia's northeastern coast is fringed with low cliffs, inlets, and small bays. This has become an upscale vacationland, with glossy resorts such as Baia Sardinia and Porto Rotondo just outside the confines of the famed Costa Smeralda, developed by the Aga Khan (born 1936), who in 1965 accidentally discovered the coast's charms—and potential—when his yacht took shelter here from a storm. In the late 1960s and '70s the Costa Smeralda, with its heart in Porto Cervo, was *the* place to summer. The attractions remain geared to those who can measure themselves by the yardstick of Khan's fabled riches. Italy's most expensive hotels are here, and the world's most magnificent yachts anchor in the waters of Porto Cervo. Golf courses, yacht clubs, and numerous alfresco restaurants and bars cater to those who want to see and be seen. All along the coast, carefully tended lush vegetation surrounds vacation villages and discreet villas that have sprung up over the past decade in spurious architectural styles best described as "bogus Mediterranean." The trend has been to keep this an enclave of the very rich. Outside the peak season, however, prices plunge and the majesty of the natural surroundings shines through, justifying all the hype and the Emerald Coast's fame as one of the truly romantic corners of the Mediterranean.

## LA MADDALENA

*30 km (19 miles) east of Santa Teresa di Gallura, 45 km (20 miles) northwest of Olbia.*

From the port of Palau you can visit the archipelago of La Maddalena, seven granite islands embellished with lush green scrub and wind-bent pines that belong to the Olbia-Tempio province. Car ferries make the 3-km (2-mile) trip about every half hour. A handful of sites to see include ancient Roman ruins and squares. Explore the village then head to one of several picture-postcard coves, the perfect spot to pack a picnic and rejuvenate after your journey to the region.

**Tomb of Giuseppe Garibaldi's.** Pilgrims pay homage to the 19th century national hero and military leader who is buried on the grounds of his farm on Isola Caprera. The patriot, who laid the groundwork for the first unification of Italy, lived from 1807 to 1882, and at one point owned half of Isola Caprera. Take the ferry to Isola Maddalena and then the bridge to Isola Caprera. Currently the site is closed to the public. In 2012, upon the request of descendants, authorities are currently exhuming the body and conducting DNA tests to verify the body's authenticity. Garibaldi continues to make history. ⊠ *7 km (4½ miles) east of Isola Maddalena* ☎ *0789/727162* ⊕ *www.compendiogaribaldino.it* ☎ *€4* ⊙ *Oct.–Apr., Tues.–Sun. 9–1:30; May–Sept., Tues.–Sun. 9–6:30.*

## SANTA TERESA DI GALLURA
*55 km (34 miles) west of Porto Cervo.*

At the northern tip of Sardinia, Santa Teresa di Gallura retains the relaxed, carefree air of a former fishing village. Nearby beaches rival those farther down the coast, but manage not to seem overcrowded with tourists.

## GOLFO ARANCI
*47 km (29 miles) southeast of Puerto Cervo.*

At the mouth of the Gulf of Olbia, Golfo Aranci is a small-scale resort and major arrival point for ferries from the mainland. Tour the village to relax on an outdoor terrace or shop in one of many quaint shops. There is a large selection of restaurants, cafés, and bars. On August 15, the annual fish festival promises excellent seafood. The craggy headland west of town has been left undeveloped as a nature reserve. Drive a few miles along the panoramic road to Olbia. You will reach the enchanting waters of Cala Moresca, Cala Greca, Cala Sabina, and White Beach, perfect for swimming, diving, and any other water sport imaginable.

> ### SARDINIA BEST BETS
>
> **Take an espresso in the harbor at Porto Cervo.** Most of Europe's royalty spends at least some time here every summer, as does a sprinkling of celebrities. This is a prime place for people-watching.
>
> **Take a dip on the Costa Smeralda.** The setting of golden sand, russet rocks, and limpid waters is sublime.
>
> **Take a stroll around Alghero.** Built by the Spanish as their capital in medievel times, Alghero is still a little piece of Spain in modern Italy.

## OLBIA
*30 km (19 miles) south of Porto Cervo, 19 km (12 miles) southwest of Golfo Aranci, 65 km (41 miles) southeast of Santa Teresa di Gallura.*

Amid the resorts of Sardinia's northeastern coast, Olbia, a town of about 60,000, is a lively little seaport and port of call for mainland ferries at the head of a long, wide bay.

★ **San Simplicio.** The little Catholic basilica, a short walk behind the main Corso Umberto and past the train station, is worth searching out if you have any spare time in Olbia. The simple granite structure dates from the 11th century, part of the great Pisan church-building program, using pillars and columns recycled from Roman buildings. Playing an important role in the island's evangelical progress, the basilica has three naves separated by a series of arches. ⊠ *Via San Simplicio* ☎ *0789/23358* ⊕ *www.monumentiaperti.com* ⊗ *Sat. and Sun. 9–1 and 3–6.*

## SASSARI
*100 km (62 miles) southwest of Santa Teresa di Gallura.*

The island's second largest city and relatively chaotic with cars, Sassari is an important university town and administrative center, notable for its history of intellectualism and bohemian student culture, an ornate old cathedral, and a good archaeological museum. Look for downtown vendors of *fainè*, a pizzalike chickpea-flour pancake glistening with olive oil, which is a Genoese and Sassarese specialty. Sassari is the hub of several highways and secondary roads leading to various coastal resorts, among them Stintino and Castelsardo.

**Duomo.** A must-see in Sassari, the elegant stone structure of the city's Duomo dedicated to Saint Nicolas of Bari took just under 600 years to build. The foundations were laid in the 12th century and the facade, in Spanish colonial style, was finished in the 18th. Of particular interest in the interior are the ribbed Gothic vaults, the 14th-century painting of the Maddona del Bosco on the high alter, and the early-19th-century tomb of Placido Benedetto di Savoia, the uncle of united Italy's first king. ⊠ *Piazza Duomo 3* ☎ *079/233185* ⊕ *www.ilportalesardo.it* ⊠ *Free* ☉ *Apr.–Oct., daily 9–noon and 5–7; Nov.–Mar., daily 9–12:30 and 4–6.*

🜊 **Museo Sanna.** Sassari's excellent cultural museum has the best archaeological collection outside Cagliari, spanning nuraghic, Carthaginian, and Roman histories, including well-preserved bronze statues and household objects from the 2nd millennium BC. Summer hours vary from year to year. ⊠ *Via Roma 64* ☎ *079/272203* ⊕ *www.museosannasassari. it* ⊠ *€4* ☉ *Tue.–Sun. 9–8; closed Mon.*

## ALGHERO

*34 km (21 miles) southwest of Sassari, 137 km (85 miles) southwest of Olbia.*

A tourist-friendly town of about 45,000 inhabitants with a distinctly Spanish flavor, Alghero is also known as "Barcelonetta" (little Barcelona). Rich wrought-iron scrollwork decorates balconies and screened windows; a Spanish motif appears in stone portals and bell towers. The town was built and inhabited in the 14th century by the Aragonese and Catalans, who constructed seaside ramparts and sturdy towers encompassing an inviting nucleus of narrow, winding streets with whitewashed palazzi. The native language spoken here is a version of Catalan, not Italian, although you probably have to attend one of the Masses conducted in Algherese (or listen in on stories swapped by older fishermen) to hear it. To reach Alghero, head into the Sassari province in the northwestern region of Sardinia. Besides its historic architectural gems such as the Alghero Cathedral and Palazzo d'Albis, the fortified city is well worth a visit to simply stroll and discover local culture on narrow cobblestone streets. The city also has a reputation to serve great food at reasonable prices.

**Capo Caccia.** Head northwest of Alghero for broad sandy beaches and the spectacular heights of an imposing limestone headland. The rugged promontory, blanketed by lush maquis, is close to the Porto Ferro marina, popular Lampianu beach, and remote coves and caves such as the Grotte di Nettuno.

**Fodor's**Choice **Grotta di Nettuno** (*Neptune's Caves*). At the base of a sheer cliff, the
★ pounding sea has carved an entrance to the vast fantastic cavern filled
🜊 with stunning water pools, stalactites, and stalagmites. You must visit with a guide; tours start on the hour. It's possible to reach the caves by boat or by land. Boat trips depart at regular intervals from the port of Alghero for €10 (price of admission to Grotto extra). The dramatic cave and coves, discovered by fishermen in the 18th century, are

considered one of the most popular tourist attractions on the island for their sheer natural beauty. ✉ *13 km (8 miles) west of Alghero* ☎ *079/946540* 💶 *€12* ⏰ *Apr.–Sept., daily 9–7; Oct., daily 9–5; Nov.–Mar., daily 9–4.*

**Escala del Cabirol** (*Mountain Goat's Stairway*). By land, you can reach the entrance to the Grotta di Nettuno by descending the 654 dizzying "goat steps" of the aptly named zigzagging stairway cut into the steep cliff. By public bus, the trip to the top of the stairway takes about 50 minutes. Allow 15 minutes for the descent by foot. ✉ *Via Catalogna* ☎ *079/950179* 💶 *€12 round-trip* ⏰ *From Alghero: 9:15 year-round and 3:10 and 5:10 June–Sept. From Capo Caccia: noon year-round and 4:05 and 6:05 June–Sept.*

**Museo Diocesano d'Arte Sacra** (*Diocesan Museum of Sacred Art*). This cathedral museum is housed in a 13th-century church designed with Catalan Gothic architecture. The usual assortment of religious treasures—paintings, wooden sculptures, and bronze statues—is on display; look for the masterful 16th-century Catalan silverware, intricately forged with ancient motifs. ✉ *Via Maiorca 1* ☎ *079/9733041* ⊕ *www.diocesialghero-bosa.it/* 💶 *€3* ⏰ *Jan.–Mar., Thurs.–Tues. by appointment; Apr., May, and Oct., Thurs.–Tues. 10–1 and 5–8; June and Sept., Thurs.–Tues. 10–1 and 5–9; July and Aug., Thurs.–Tues. 10–1 and 6–11; Dec., Thurs.–Tues. 10–1 by appointment and 4–7; the museum is closed Nov.*

**Torre San Giovanni.** This old stone tower fortress can be climbed for good views from the terrace. Stop at the interesting city history display on the computer terminals inside the tower. There's also a rotating set of exhibits and a miniature model of Alghero's Old Town. ✉ *Via Mateotti 12* ☎ *079/973–1605* 💶 *€2* ⏰ *Apr.–Jun., Tue.–Sun. 10–1 and 5–8; Jul.–Aug., Tue.–Sat., 10–1 and 6:30–10, Sun.–Mon. 6:30–10.*

## CASTELSARDO

*32 km (20 miles) northeast of Sassari.*

The walled seaside citadel of Castelsardo is a delight for craft lovers, with tiny shops crammed with all kinds of souvenirs, particularly woven baskets. The appropriately shaped **Roccia dell'Elefante** (Elephant Rock) on the road into Castelsardo was hollowed out by primitive man to become a *domus de janas* (literally, "fairy house," in fact a Neolithic burial chamber).

# SHOPPING

The Sard are very adept craftsmen and -women. For many generations the people in the mountains had to be self-sufficient and worked with bone, wood, and clay to produce practical yet beautiful items, including fine knives, the must-have tool of the shepherd. The women are traditionally weavers—in wool and straw—or lace-makers. Red coral and filigree jewelry also have a long tradition here. If you are looking for some comestibles to take home, Sardinian wine and honey are highly prized. The narrow streets of Alghero and Castelsardo are the best places to shop for locally made crafts. Porto Cervo has fewer craft shops, but designer names line the shopping streets with top-quality haute couture and jewelry stores plus independent boutiques selling gifts and collectibles.

The walled seaside citadel of **Castelsardo,** 32 km (20 miles) northeast of Sassari, is a delight for basket lovers. Roadside stands and shops in the Old Town sell woven baskets, as well as rugs and wrought iron.

**ISOLA.** ISOLA is state-sponsored cooperative set up to promote Sardinian crafts. Sassari has Sardinia's main craft exhibition center in the public gardens next to Viale Mancini, built specifically as a showcase for handcrafted gifts and souvenirs in wood, precious metal, ceramic, and fabrics. ⊠ *Giardini Pubblici, Sassari* ☏ *079/230101* ⊕ *www.regione. sardegna.it/isola.*

## BEACHES

The beaches around the Costa Smeralda are some of the most exclusive in Europe, but they don't disappoint, with fine golden sand sheltered by red cliffs and fronting azure waters. Most can only be reached by boat, and there are regular small ferries from Porto Cervo. Rentals of sunbeds and towels are reassuringly expensive.

## WHERE TO EAT

**$$$** ╳ **Da Pietro.** The pleasing menu at Da Pietro includes *bucatini*
ITALIAN *all'algherese* (hollow, spaghetti-like pasta with a sauce of clams, capers, tomatoes, and olives) and baked fish with a white-wine sauce keeps this seafood restaurant bustling below its vaulted ceilings. Sample *sebadas*, ravioli stuffed with mascarpone cheese and topped with honey. Look for Da Pietro in the Old Town near Largo San Francesco. ⑤ *Average main: €30* ⊠ *Via Ambrogio Machin 20, Sassari* ☏ *079/979645* ⊘ *Closed Wed. and 2 wks in Dec.*

**$$$** ╳ **L'Assassino.** Get a true taste of great local Sassarese cooking—and
ITALIAN many of the other obscure Sardinian specialties for which you may be searching—in a cozy vaulted room with terra-cotta tiling. Horse, donkey, and roast pig figure prominently on the menu; best of all is a *cena sarda,* a 10-dish tasting menu with *porcetto* (roast suckling pig), also spelled porcheddu. The service is friendly, and the room is warm and cozy. Food is served throughout the afternoon. ⑤ *Average main: €25* ⊠ *Via pettenadu 19, Sassari* ☏ *079/235041* ⊕ *www.trattorialassassino. it* ⊘ *Closed Sun.*

# PORTOFERRAIO, ITALY (ELBA)

Updated
by Bruce
Leimsidor

Elba is the Tuscan archipelago's largest island, but it resembles nearby verdant Corsica more than it does its rocky Italian sisters, thanks to a network of underground springs that keep the island lush and green. It's this combination of semitropical vegetation and dramatic mountain scenery—unusual in the Mediterranean—that has made Elba so prized for so long, and the island's uniqueness continues to draw boatloads of visitors throughout the warm months. Lively Portoferraio, the main port, makes a good base for exploring the island.

## ESSENTIALS

**CURRENCY**

The euro.

**HOURS**

Many shops are open 9–1 and 3:30–7:30 Monday through Saturday. Banks are open weekdays 8:30–1:30 and 2:45–3:45.

**PRIVATE TOURS**

Taxis offer special prices to see the main sights on the island from July through September.

**TELEPHONES**

Tri-band GSM phones work in Italy. You can buy prepaid phone cards at telecom shops, news vendors, and tobacconists in all towns and cities. Phone cards can be used for local or international calls.

## COMING ASHORE

The cruise-ship dock is just a stone's throw from the historic center of Portoferraio, so most passengers just walk to town. If you want to get around the island, public buses operated by ATL (⊕ *www.atl.livorno.it*) stop at most towns several times a day; the tourist office on viale Elba has timetables. Day tickets cost €8.50. There are numerous places to rent bikes, scooters, motorcycles, or cars. Expect to pay around €45 for a compact manual car in low season and €75 in high season.

# EXPLORING ELBA

## PORTOFERRAIO

Especially enjoyable in Portoferraio is a stroll around the *centro storico*, fortified in the 16th century by the Medici grand duke Cosimo I. Most of the pretty, multicolor buildings that line the old harbor date from the 18th and 19th centuries, when the boats in the port were full of mineral exports rather than tourists.

**Marina di Campo.** On the south side of Elba, this small town with a long sandy beach and protected cove is a classic summer vacationer's spot. The laid-back marina is full of bars, boutiques, and restaurants. ⊠ *Elba*.

**Monte Capanne.** The highest point on Elba, Monte Capanna is crossed by a twisting road that provides magnificent vistas at every turn; the tiny towns of **Poggio** and **Marciana** have enchanting little piazzas full of flowers and trees. You can hike to the top of the mountain, or take an unusual open-basket cable car from just above Poggio. ⊠ *Elba*.

**Museo Archeologico.** Exhibits at this museum reconstruct the island's ancient history through a display of Etruscan and Roman artifacts recovered from shipwrecks. ⊠ *Località Linguella, Calata Buccari* ☎ *0565/937111* ⊡ *€2* ⊗ *June 15–Sept. 15, daily 9:30–2:30 and 5–midnight; Sept. 16–June 14, Thurs. 10:30–1:30 and 4–8.*

**Palazzina dei Mulini.** During Napoléon's famous exile on Elba in 1814–15, he built this residence out of two windmills. It still contains furniture from the period and Napoléon's impressive library, with the more than

2,000 volumes that he brought here from France. ✉ *Piazzale Napoleone 1* 🕾 *0565/915846* 🖃 *€7, €13 with admission to Villa San Martino* ⏾ *Mon. and Wed.–Sat. 9–7, Sun. 9–1.*

**Porto Azzurro.** The waters of the port at Elba's eastern end are noticeably *azzurro* (sky-blue). It's worth a stop for a walk and a gelato along the rows of yachts harbored here. ✉ *Elba.*

**Rio Marina.** Elba's quietest town is an old-fashioned port on the northeastern edge of the island. Here you'll find a pebble beach, an old mine, a leafy public park, and ferry service to Piombino. ✉ *Elba.*

**Villa San Martino.** A couple of miles outside Portoferraio, this splendid villa was Napoléon's summer home during his 10-month exile on Elba. Temporary exhibitions are held in a gallery attached to the main building. The Egyptian Room, decorated with idealized scenes of the Egyptian campaign, may have provided Napoléon the consolation of glories past. The villa's classical facade was added by a Russian prince, Anatolia Demidoff, after he bought the house in 1852. ✉ *Località San Martino, Elba* 🕾 *0565/914688* 🖃 *€7, €13 with admission to Palazzina dei Mulini* ⏾ *Tues.–Sat. 9–7 and Sun. 9–1.*

## BEACHES

Elba's most celebrated beaches are the sandy stretches at **Biodola, Procchio,** and **Marina di Campo,** but the entire island—and particularly the westernmost section, encircling Monte Capanne—is ringed with beautiful coastline. Indeed, it seems that every sleepy town has its own perfect tiny beach. Try **Cavoli** and **Fetovaia** anytime but July and August, when all the car-accessible beaches on the island are packed (there are also some accessible only by boat, such as the black-sand beach of **Punta Nera**).

## ACTIVITIES

### WATER SPORTS

**Il Viottolo.** Adventurous types can rent sea kayaks and mountain bikes from this tour operator, or participate in three-day guided excursions on land or by sea. ✉ *Via Fucini 279, Marina di Campo* 🕾 *0565/978005* ⊕ *www.ilviottolo.it.*

**Spaziomare.** If you are hoping to rent a motorboat for a half- or full-day, this is the place. Sailboats to rent by the week are also available. ✉ *Via Vittorio Veneto 13, Porto Azzurro* 🕾 *0565/95112, 348/6017862* ⊕ *www.spaziomare.it.*

**Subnow.** Contact this group of experienced divers for information on diving excursions in the waters of Elba's National Marine Park. ✉ *Via della Foce 89, Località La Foce, Marina di Campo* 🕾 *0565/979051* ⊕ *www.subnow.it.*

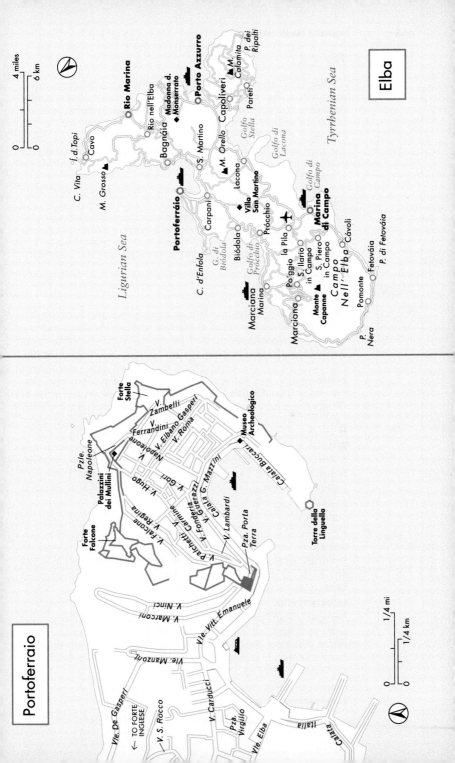

## Portoferraio

Forte Stella

V. Zambelli

Forte Falcone

Pzle. Napoleone

Palazzini dei Mullini

V. Ferrandini

V. Elbano Gasperi

V. Roma

V. Napoleone

V. Gori

V. Hugo

V. Falcone

Carmine

V. Pratchetti

V. Fonderiazzi

V. Guerazzi

Calata G. Mazzini

Museo Archeologico

V. Lambardi

Pza. Porta Terra

Calata Buccari

Torre della Linguella

V. Marconi

V. Ninci

Vle. Vitt. Emanuele

Vle. Manzoni

Vle. De Gasperi

← TO FORTE INGLESE

V. Carducci

V. S. Rocco

Pza. Virgilio

Vle. Elba

Italia

Calata

1/4 mi

1/4 km

## Elba

Ligurian Sea

C. Vita

I. d. Topi

Cavo

M. Grosso

Rio Marina

Rio nell'Elba

Bagnáia

Madonna d. Monserrato

Porto Azzurro

Capoliveri

M. Calamita

P. dei Ripalti

S. Martino

M. Orello

Pareti

Golfo Stella

Golfo di Lacona

Tyrrhenian Sea

Portoferráio

Carpani

Lacona

Golfo di Campo

C. d'Enfola

G. di Biódola

Biódola

Villa San Martino

Prócchio

la Pila

Poggio

S. Ilario

in Campo

S. Piero in Campo

Marina di Campo

Cávoli

Golfo di Prócchio

Marciana

Marciana Marina

Monte Capanne

Campo Nell'Elba

Fetováia

P. di Fetováia

Pomonte

P. Nera

4 miles

6 km

# WHERE TO EAT

$   ✕ **Il Mare.** Homemade pastas and fresh seafood are served here with a
ITALIAN   dash of style. The young chef puts a creative spin on the classics, coming
★   up with such delights as homemade vegetable gnocchi with scampi in a
butter and saffron sauce. The *semifreddi* (literally, "half cold"; frozen
desserts made with ice cream and eggs) are particularly good. Just a
few steps from Rio Marina's pretty port, this is an easy stop on your
way to or from the ferry. ⑤ *Average main: €9* ✉ *Via del Pozzo 16, Rio
Marina* ☎ *0565/962117.*

$$   ✕ **Trattoria da Lido.** Come here for commendable *gnocchetti di pesce*
ITALIAN   (bite-size potato-and-fish dumplings) with a white cream sauce and
fresh *pesce all'elbana* (whitefish baked with vegetables and potatoes).
The bustling, casual trattoria is in the old center of Portoferraio, at the
beginning of the road to the old Medici walls. ⑤ *Average main: €22*
✉ *Salita del Falcone 2* ☎ *0565/914650* ⓧ *Closed mid-Dec.–mid-Feb.*

# PORTOFINO, ITALY

Updated
by Bruce
Leimsidor

Like the family jewels that bedeck its habitual visitors, the Italian Riv-
iera is glamorous, but in an old-fashioned way. The rustic and ele-
gant, the provincial and chic, the cosmopolitan and small-town are
blended together here in a sun-drenched pastiche that defines the Ital-
ian side of the Riviera. Although the region bearing the name Liguria
extends inland, its greatest charms are found on the coast, which has
inspired poets and artists for centuries. One of the most photographed
villages along the Ligurian coast, with a decidedly romantic and afflu-
ent aura, Portofino has long been a popular destination for foreigners.
Once an ancient Roman colony and taken by the Republic of Genoa
in 1229, it has also been ruled by the French, English, Spanish, and
Austrians, as well as by marauding bands of 16th-century pirates. Elite
British tourists first flocked to the lush harbor in the mid-1800s, and
today some of Europe's wealthiest lay anchor in Portofino in summer.

## ESSENTIALS

### CURRENCY
The euro.

### HOURS
Stores are generally open from 9 or 9:30 to 1 and from 3:30 or 4 to 7
or 7:30. Many shops close Sunday. Many national museums are closed
Monday and may have shorter hours on Sunday.

### PRIVATE TOURS
Benvenuto Tours offers full-day tours out of Portofino to the towns
to the east, the Cinque Terre, Lerici, and Portovenere. This is a pricey
option (€450 per person) but an effortless way to see some dramatic
costal scenery and lovely historic villages, including those beloved by
the English romantic poets.

**Contacts Benvenuto Tours.** ☎ *(39)081/007–2114 in Genoa*
⊕ *www.benvenutolimos.com.*

## TELEPHONES

Tri-band GSM phones work in Italy. You can buy prepaid phone cards at telecom shops, news vendors, and tobacconists in all towns and cities. Phone cards can be used for local or international calls.

## COMING ASHORE

Ships must tender passengers ashore in the heart of the picturesque port. There is no train station in Portofino: You must take the bus to Santa Margherita Ligure (€1) and pick up train services from there. An alternative is a ferry, Sirvizio Marittimo di Tigullio, which connects Santa Margherita Ligure to all of the towns along the cost at convenient hours.

A rental car is useful to explore the Ligurian coast, but allow plenty of time to return your rental car as roads become extremely busy during the summer, and journey times may be longer than the distance suggests. Expect to pay about €45 for a compact manual vehicle. Delivery to the portside is an additional cost. Drivers should be warned, however, that while the scenery is spectacular, the drive is very taxing, with constant hairpin turns.

# EXPLORING PORTOFINO AND VICINITY

## PORTOFINO

**Abbazia di San Fruttuoso** (*Abbey of San Fruttuoso*). On the sea at the foot of Monte Portofino, the medieval Abbazia di San Fruttuoso, built by the Benedictines of Monte Cassino, protects a minuscule fishing village that can be reached only on foot or by water—a 20-minute boat ride from Portofino and also reachable from Camogli, Santa Margherita Ligure, and Rapallo. The restored abbey is now the property of a national conservation fund (FAI) and occasionally hosts temporary exhibitions. The church contains the tombs of some illustrious members of the Doria family. The old abbey and its grounds are delightful places to spend a few hours, perhaps lunching at one of the modest beachfront trattorias nearby (open only in summer). Boatloads of visitors can make it very crowded very fast; you might appreciate it most off-season. ⊠ *15-min boat ride or 2-hr walk northwest of Portofino* ☎ *0185/772703* ⊠ *€7 Apr.–Sept., €5 Oct.–Mar.* ⊙ *June–Sept. 15, daily 10–5:45; May & Sept. 16-30, daily 10–4:45; Oct.–Mar., Tues.–Sun. 10–3:45. Last entry 1 hr before closing.*

**Castello Brown.** From the harbor, follow the signs for the climb to Castello Brown—the most worthwhile sight in Portofino—with its medieval relics, impeccable gardens, and sweeping views. The castle was founded in the Middle Ages but restored in the 16th through 18th centuries. In true Portofino form, it was owned by Genoa's English consul from 1870 until it opened to the public in 1961. ⊠ *Above harbor* ☎ *0185/269046* ⊕ *www.castellobrown.it* ⊠ *€3* ⊙ *Apr.–Sept., Wed.–Mon. 10–6; Oct.–Mar., Wed.–Mon. 10–5.*

**Paraggi.** The only sand beach near Portofino is at Paraggi, a cove on the road between Santa Margherita and Portofino. The bus will stop here on request.

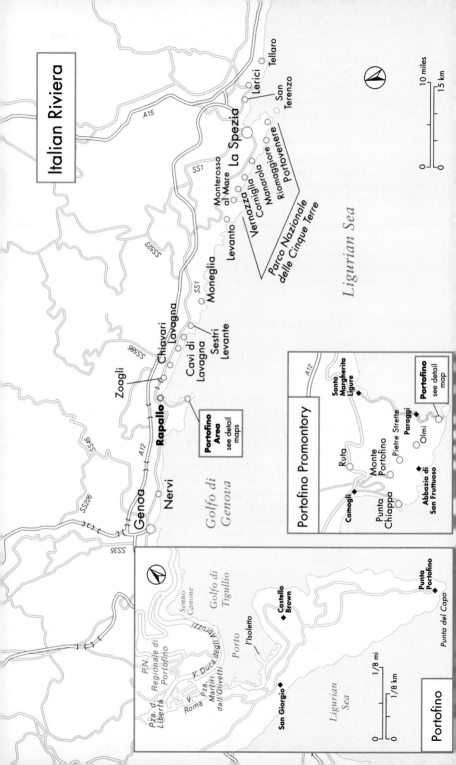

# Italian Riviera

Tellaro
Lerici
San Terenzo
La Spezia

Monterosso al Mare
Vernazza
Corniglia
Manarola
Riomaggiore
Portovenere
Parco Nazionale delle Cinque Terre

Levanto

Moneglia

Chiavari
Lavagna
Cavi di Lavagna
Sestri Levante

Zoagli
Rapallo
Portofino Area see detail maps

Genoa
Nervi

Golfo di Genova

Golfo di Tigullio

Ligurian Sea

A15
SS1
SS523
SS1
SS586
SS225
SS1
SS45
A12
SS225
SS1

10 miles
15 km

## Portofino Promontory

Santa Margherita Ligure
Ruta
Pietre Strette
Monte Portofino
Paraggi
Olmi
Camogli
Punta Chiappa
Abbazia di San Fruttuoso
Portofino see detail map

A12

## Portofino

P.N. Regionale di Portofino
Pza. di Libertà
V. Duca degli Abruzzi
V. Roma
Pza. Martiri dall'Olivetti

Senno Canone
Porto
l'Isoletto
Castello Brown

San Giorgio

Punta Portofino
Punta del Capo

Golfo di Tigullio
Ligurian Sea

1/8 mi
1/8 km

0

**Punta Portofino.** Pristine views can be had from the deteriorating *faro* (lighthouse) at Punta Portofino, a 15-minute walk along the point that begins at the southern end of the port. Along the seaside path you can see numerous impressive, sprawling private residences behind high iron gates.

**San Giorgio.** The small church San Giorgio, sitting on a ridge, was rebuilt four times during World War II. It is said to contain the relics of its namesake, brought back from the Holy Land by the Crusaders. Portofino enthusiastically celebrates Saint George's Day every April 23. ⌧ *Above harbor* ☎ *0185/269337* ☽ *Daily 7–6.*

> **PORTOFINO BEST BETS**
>
> **Linger over an espresso at a waterfront café.** Portofino is a place to see and be seen, so relax and survey your surroundings.
>
> **Walk the hillside paths above the town.** The views along the Riviera are delightful.
>
> **Visit Camogli.** You'll get a touch of gritty reality contrasting with the glitz of Portofino itself.

## SANTA MARGHERITA LIGURE
*5 km (3 miles) from Portofino.*

A beautiful old resort town favored by well-to-do Italians, Santa Margherita Ligure has everything a Riviera playground should have—plenty of palm trees and attractive hotels, cafés, and a marina packed with yachts. Some of the older buildings here are still decorated on the outside with the trompe-l'oeil frescoes typical of this part of the Riviera. This is a pleasant, convenient base, which for many represents a perfect balance on the Italian Riviera: bigger and less Americanized than the Cinque Terre; less glitzy than San Remo; more relaxing than Genoa and environs; and ideally situated for day trips, such as an excursion to Portofino.

## CAMOGLI
*15 km (9 miles) northwest of Portofino, 20 km (12 miles) east of Genoa.*

★ Camogli, at the edge of the large promontory and nature reserve known as the Portofino Peninsula, has always been a town of sailors. By the 19th century it was leasing its ships throughout the continent. Today multicolor houses, remarkably deceptive trompe-l'oeil frescoes, and a massive 17th-century seawall mark this appealing harbor community, perhaps as beautiful as Portofino but without the glamour. When exploring on foot, don't miss the boat-filled second harbor, which is reached by ducking under a narrow archway at the northern end of the first one.

**Acquario** (*Aquarium*). The Castello Dragone, built onto the sheer rock face near the harbor, is home to the Acquario, which has tanks filled with local marine life built into the ramparts. ⌧ *Via Isola* ☎ *0185/773375* ⌫ *€3* ☽ *Summer: 10–12 and 3–7; Winter: 10–11:45 and 2–5:45.*

### RAPALLO

*8 km (5 miles) north of Portofino, 3 km (2 miles) north of Santa Margherita, 28 km (17 miles) east of Genoa.*

Rapallo was once one of Europe's most fashionable resorts, but it passed its heyday before World War II and has suffered from the building boom brought on by tourism. Ezra Pound and D. H. Lawrence lived here, and many other writers, poets, and artists have been drawn to it. Today the town's harbor is filled with yachts. A single-span bridge on the eastern side of the bay is named after Hannibal, who is said to have passed through the area after crossing the Alps.

## SHOPPING

In addition to the fine leather and haute couture for which Italy is known, Liguria is famous for its fine laces, silver-and-gold filigree work, and ceramics. Look for bargains in velvet, macramé, olive wood, and marble. Don't forget the excellent wines, cheeses, dried meats, and olive oils.

Portofino is awash with small boutiques selling fashion and gift items, but it's also one of the most expensive places to shop along the coast, catering to the wealthy yacht owners who call in during the summer. However, all the coastal villages have pretty shops to explore.

The attractive coastal village of Zoagli on the S1, 4 km (2½ miles) east of Rapallo, has been famous for silk, velvet, and damask since the Middle Ages.

## ACTIVITIES

If you have the stamina, you can hike to the **Abbazia di San Fruttuoso** from Portofino. It's a steep climb at first, and the walk takes about 2½ hours one way. Much more modest hikes from Portofino include a 1-hour uphill walk to Cappella delle Gave, a bit inland in the hills, from where you can continue downhill to Santa Margherita Ligure (another 1½ hours) and a gently undulating paved trail leading to the beach at Paraggi (½ hour). Finally, there's a 2½-hour hike from Portofino that heads farther inland to Ruta, through Olmi and Pietre Strette. The trails are well marked, and maps are available at the tourist information offices in Rapallo, Santa Margherita, Portofino, and Camogli.

## BEACHES

The Ligurian coast is known for its rocky vistas, but the Portofino promontory has one sandy beach, on the east side, at **Paraggi.**

## WHERE TO EAT

$ ✕ **Canale.** If the staggering prices of virtually all of Portofino's restau-

BAKERY rants put you off, the long line outside this family-run bakery indicates that you're not alone and that something special is in store. Here all the focaccia Genovese is baked on the spot and served fresh from the oven, along with all kinds of sandwiches, pastries, and other refreshments.

The only problem is there's nowhere to sit—time for a picnic! $\boxed{\$}$ *Average main: €10* ✉ *Via Roma 30* ☏ *0185/269248* ▭ *No credit cards* ☺ *Closed Nov.–Feb.*

**$$$$**
SEAFOOD

✕ **Vento Ariel.** This small, friendly restaurant serves some of the best seafood in town. Dine on the shaded terrace in summer and watch the bustling activity in the nearby port. Only the freshest seafood is served; try the spaghetti *alle vongole* (with clams) or the mixed grilled fish. $\boxed{\$}$ *Average main: €40* ✉ *Calata Porto, Camogli* ☏ *0185/771080* ☺ *Closed Wed., 1st half of Dec., and Jan.*

# ST-TROPEZ, FRANCE

Updated
by Jennifer
Ladonne

Brigitte Bardot kick-started the rush in the early 1960s, and she was followed by the likes of Liz Taylor and Sophia Loren. People still flock to St-Tropez for the sun, the sea, and, the celebrities. The new generation includes Elton, Barbra, Oprah, Jack, and Uma, though they stay hidden in villas, and the people you'll see on the streets are mere mortals, lots of them, many intent on displaying the best—and often the most—of their youth, beauty, and wealth. Still, if you take an early-morning stroll around the pretty port or down the narrow medieval streets with their candied-almond hues, you'll see just how charming St-Tropez can be. There's a weekend's worth of boutiques to explore and many cute cafés where you can sit under colored awnings and watch the spectacle that is St-Trop (*trop* in French means "too much") saunter by. Or head to the beaches, which are some of the most fashionable in Europe.

## ESSENTIALS
### CURRENCY
The euro.

### HOURS
Most stores are open Monday–Saturday 9–7, but many close at lunchtime (usually from noon to 2 or 3), and some open on Sunday during July and August. Museums are generally open 10–5, but most are closed either Monday or Tuesday.

### TELEPHONES
Tri-band GSM phones work in France. You can buy prepaid phone cards at telecom shops, news vendors, and tobacconists in all towns and cities. Phone cards can be used for local or international calls. Orange, SFR, Bouygues Telecom, and Virgin are leading telecom companies. If you have an unlocked GSM phone, LeFrenchMobile (⊕ *www.lefrenchmobile.com*) offers SIM cards (and micro SIM cards) with support in English, unlimited validity of credits, and prepurchase online.

### COMING ASHORE
The port at St-Tropez is too small to accept commercial cruise vessels, so passengers are tendered to a landing dock, which is about a five-minute walk from town. There are no passenger facilities portside. Taxis and tour buses are not allowed into the staging area, which means a walk from the landing stage to transport connections is unavoidable.

Car-rental offices can be found in the town; expect to pay about €75 for an economy manual vehicle. Taxis are available at the port entrance

Golfe de St-Tropez

Port des Pecheurs
Plage de la Fontanette
La Glaye
Mole Jean Réveille
Quartier de la Ponche
r. Cavaillon
av. Antoine de St-Exupéry

Nouveau Port
Vieux Port
r. du Clochet
r. Jean Jaurès
r. de la Citadelle
Monte de la Citadelle
Citadelle

Musée de l'Annonciade
r. François Sibilli
r. de la Citadelle
r. Laugier

q. l'Épi
r. Georges Clémenceau
r. Étienne Berny
r. Gambetta
r. de la Miséricorde
av. Paul Signac

av. de Gén. de Gaulle
av. de 11-Novembre 1918
r. Henri Seillon
r. Gén. Allard
r. des Tisserands
r. des Charrons

blvd. Louis Blanc
Chemin Privé
av. de Gén. Leclerc
blvd. Vasserot
Place des Lices
av. du Maréchal Foch
av. de la Résistance

av. Paul Roussel
Plaza du Quinzième Corps
r. du Temple

TO RAMATUELLE

0    1/8 mi
0    1/8 km

KEY

*i* Tourist information

and can provide tourist itineraries or transfers to the beaches. For single journeys, prices are €3.20 then €0.85 per km (½-mile). Be aware that, especially during the summer, traffic heading into St-Tropez builds up, and you can spend more than an hour just traveling the last two or three miles to the port and town. Always allow plenty of time to return any rental car or make the return taxi journey.

## EXPLORING ST-TROPEZ

**Citadelle.** Head up Rue de la Citadelle to these 16th-century ramparts, which stand in a lovely hilltop park offering a fantastic view of the town and the sea. Amid today's bikini-clad sun worshipers it's hard to imagine St-Tropez as a military outpost, but inside the Citadelle's donjon the **Musée Naval** (Naval Museum) displays ship models, cannons, maps, and pictures of St-Tropez from its days as a naval port (closed for renovation through 2012). ⊠ *Rue de la Citadelle* 🕿 *04–94–97–59–43* 🎟 *Citadelle €2.50* ☽ *Oct.–Mar., daily 10–noon and 1:30–5; Apr.–Sept., daily 10–6:30.*

★ **Musée de l'Annonciade** (*Annunciation Museum*). The legacy of the artists who loved St-Tropez has been lovingly preserved in this extraordinary museum, housed in a 14th-century chapel just inland from the southwest corner of the Vieux Port. Cutting-edge temporary exhibitions keep visitors on their toes while works stretching from pointillists to fauvists to cubists line the walls. Signac, Matisse, Signard, Braque, Dufy, Vuillard, and Rouault are all here, and their work traces the evolution of painting from impressionism to expressionism. The museum also hosts temporary exhibitions every summer, from local talent to up-and-coming international artists. ⊠ *Quai de l'Épi/Pl., Georges Grammont* ☎ *04–94–17–84–10* 🎟 *€5* ⊗ *Jan.–Oct. and Dec., Wed.–Mon. 10–noon and 2–6.*

**Place des Lices.** Enjoy a time-out in the the social center of the Old Town, also called the Place Carnot, just off the Montée Guy Ringrave as you descend from the Citadelle.

> ### ST-TROPEZ BEST BETS
>
> **Stroll around the port.** This is the place to see and be seen; to dress and strut whether you are 17 or 70. Yes, the celebrities flock here, but so do Europe's fashion peacocks.
>
> **Sip an aperitif in the Place des Lices.** Sit in the shade of an ancient plane tree, soak in the Provençal atmosphere, and watch the southern French *joie-de-vivre*.
>
> **Browse the boutiques.** This is stylish shopping at its best, with myriad small and exclusive and upscale shops.

A symmetrical forest of plane trees provides shade to rows of cafés and restaurants, skateboarders, children, and grandfatherly pétanque players. The square becomes a moveable feast (for both eyes and palate) on market days—Tuesday and Saturday—while at night a café seat is as hotly contested as a quayside seat during the day. Just as Deborah Kerr and David Niven once did in *Bonjour Tristesse,* watch the boule players under the glow of hundreds of electric bulbs. Heading back to the Vieux Port area, take in the boutiques lining Rues Sibilli, Clemenceau, or Gambetta to help accessorize your evening look—you never know when that photographer from *Elle* will be snapping away at the trendoisie.

**Quartier de la Ponche.** This Old Town maze of backstreets and ramparts is daubed in shades of gold, pink, ocher, and sky blue. Trellised jasmine and wrought-iron birdcages hang from the shuttered windows, and many of the tiny streets dead-end at the sea. Here you can find the **Port des Pêcheurs** (Fishermen's Port), on whose beach Bardot did a star turn in *And God Created Woman.* Twisting, narrow streets, designed to break the impact of the mistral, open to tiny squares with fountains. The main drag here, Rue de la Ponche, leads into Place l'Hôtel de Ville, landmarked by a *mairie* (town hall) marked out in typical Tropezienne hues of pink and green.

**Vieux Port.** Bordered by Quai de l'Épi, Quai Bouchard, Quai Peri, Quai Suffren, and Quai Jean-Jaurès, Vieux Port is a place for strolling and looking over the shoulders of artists daubing their versions of the view on easels set up along the water's edge. Meanwhile, folding director's chairs at the famous port-side cafés Le Gorille (named for its late exceptionally hirsute manager), Café de Paris, and Sénéquier's are well placed for observing the cast of St-Tropez's living theater play out its colorful roles.

### RAMATUELLE

*12 km (7 miles) southwest of St-Tropez.*

A typical hilltop whorl of red-clay roofs and dense inner streets topped with arches and lined with arcades, this ancient market town was destroyed in the Wars of Religion and rebuilt as a harmonious whole in 1620, complete with venerable archways and vaulted passages. Now its souvenir shops and galleries attract day-trippers out of St-Tropez, who enjoy the pretty drive through the vineyards as much as the village itself. At the top of the village you can visit the Moulin de Paillas, on Route du Moulin de Paillas, a windmill recently restored in the old style with a mechanism made entirely of wood; the site offers a panoramic view of the coastline. Free, guided tours of the windmill are held every Tuesday from 10 to noon. Ramatuelle is also just a heartbeat away from the **Plage de Pamplonne**—a destination location among hippies and starlets alike.

## SHOPPING

Designer boutiques may be spreading like wild mushrooms all over St-Tropez, but the main fashionista strutting platform is along **Rue Gambetta** or **Rue Allard.** For those who balk at spending a small fortune on the latest strappy sandal, **Rue Sibilli,** behind the Quai Suffren, is lined with all kinds of trendy, more affordable boutiques. The **Place des Lices** overflows with produce, regional foods, clothing, and *brocantes* (collectibles) on Tuesday and Saturday mornings. Don't miss the picturesque little fish market that fills up **Place aux Herbes** every morning.

## BEACHES

The famous beaches of St-Tropez lie southeast of the town on a small peninsula.

**Plage de Pamplonne.** A typical hilltop whorl of red-clay roofs and dense inner streets topped with arches and lined with arcades, this ancient market town was destroyed in the Wars of Religion and rebuilt as a harmonious whole in 1620, complete with venerable archways and vaulted passages. Now its souvenir shops and galleries attract day-trippers out of St-Tropez, who enjoy the pretty drive through the vineyards as much as the village itself. Plage de Pamplonne is home to the ever-famous **Club 55**, where the rich and famous are known to play. ⊠ *Plage de Pamplonne* ☎ *04–94–55–55–55* ⊕ *www.leclub55.com.*

## WHERE TO EAT

**$$$**
BISTRO

✕ **La Table du Marché.** This charming bistro, tearoom, and boutique from celebrity chef Christophe Leroy offers up a mouthwatering spread of regional specialties in a surprisingly casual atmosphere. The service is warm, and the homey fare includes cheese and macaroni made chic with lobster, tomato *pistou* tart, and whipped potatoes with truffles. Lunchtime visitors can dive into a nicely balanced set menu or choose from a selection of goods seductively on display. $ *Average main: €30* ⊠ *21* *bis rue Allard, St-Tropez* ☎ *04–94–97–91–91* ⊕ *www.christophe-leroy. com* ⊙ *Nov.–end of Mar.*

**$$** ✕ **Le Café.** The busy terrace here often doubles as a stadium for differ-
BISTRO ent factions cheering on favorite local pétanque players in the Place des
Lices. You, too, can play—borrow some boules from the friendly bar
staff (and get your pastis bottle at the ready: you'll need it to properly
appreciate the full pétanque experience). Hilarious "beginner" pétanque
soirees are on tap Saturday nights in spring and summer. The food is
as good as the setting: Try the Provençal beef stew and traditional fish
soup; there's a well-priced lunch menu. It's always busy, so reservations
are strongly recommended. ⑤ *Average main: €22* ⊠ *5 pl. des Lices, St-
Tropez* ☎ *04–94–97–44–69* ⊕ *www.lecafe.fr.*

# VALENCIA, SPAIN

Updated by
Joanna Styles

Despite its proximity to the Mediterranean, Valencia's history and geography have been defined most significantly by the River Turia and the
fertile floodplain (*huerta*) that surrounds it. Modern Valencia was best
known for its flooding disasters until the River Turia was diverted to the
south in the late 1950s. Since then, the city has been on a steady course
of urban beautification. The lovely *puentes* (bridges) that once spanned
the Turia look equally graceful spanning a wandering municipal park,
and the spectacular futuristic Ciudad de las Artes y de las Sciencias
(City of Arts and Sciences), designed by Valencian-born architect San-
taigo Clalatrava, has at long last created an exciting architectural link
between this river town and the Mediterranean. Valencia's port, and
parts of the city itself, underwent major structural refurbishment for
the America's Cup sailing classic held here in 2007 and 2010. A new
cruise terminal is planned for 2014–15.

## ESSENTIALS
### CURRENCY
The euro.

### HOURS
Museums are generally open from 9 until 7 or 8, but many are closed
on Monday and some close in the afternoon. Most stores are open
Monday–Saturday 9–1:30 and 5–8, but tourist shops may open in the
afternoon and also on Sunday between May and September.

### PRIVATE TOURS
**Valencia Tourist Board.** The Valencia tourist board organizes a number of
guided tours and trips, known as "Experiences," around the city and
further afield. Online discounts are available. ☎ *900/701818* ⊕ *www.
turisvalencia.es.*

### TELEPHONES
Most tri-band and quad-band GSM phones will work in Spain, where
mobile services are 3G-compatible. Public kiosks accept phone cards
that support international calls (cards sold in press shops, bars, and
telecom shops). Major companies include Vodafone.

## COMING ASHORE

Valencia's port area received a face-lift to coincide with the arrival of the America's Cup competition in June 2007. Though the terminal itself has limited facilities, the public interface areas, where the port and waterfront meet the city, have lots of restaurants, cafés, and shops.

It is a long walk from the port to the historic downtown district, but the trip is enjoyable if you want to take the time. You may be interested in the Valencia Cruise Card available from the tourist office in the port. Costing €10, the card includes a shuttle bus from the port stopping at L'Oceanogràphic, Ciudad de las Artes, and the city center, as well as discounts on local attractions and sights. The city has an excellent public transport system (⊕ *www.emtvalencia.es*), so reaching all parts of the city by bus, metro, or tram is a cinch. A single journey is €1.50, and a one-day ticket is €3.90 within the downtown zone, €9.60 for all three zones.

Renting a car won't be an advantage when exploring the city, but it will allow you to head out along the coast or inland to explore the countryside. For an economy manual vehicle, expect to pay about €45 per day.

## EXPLORING VALENCIA

**Casa Museo José Benlliure.** The modern Valencian painter and sculptor José Benlliure is known for his intimate portraits and massive historical and religious paintings, many of which hang in Valencia's Museo de Bellas Artes (Museum of Fine Arts). Here in his elegant house and studio are 50 of his works, including paintings, ceramics, sculptures, and drawings. On display are also works by his son, Pepino, who painted in the small, flower-filled garden in the back of the house, and iconographic sculptures by Benlliure's brother, the well-known sculptor Mariano Benlliure. ⊠ *Calle Blanquerías 23* ☎ *963/919103* ⬚ *€2; free weekends and holidays* ⊙ *Tues.–Sat. 10–2 and 4:30–8:30, Sun. 10–3.*

**Cathedral.** Valencia's 13th- to 15th-century cathedral is the heart of the city. The building has three portals—Romanesque, Gothic, and rococo. Inside, Renaissance and baroque marble was removed to restore the original Gothic style, as is now the trend in Spanish churches. The Capilla del Santo Cáliz (Chapel of the Holy Chalice) displays a purple agate vessel purported to be the Holy Grail (Christ's cup at the Last Supper) and thought to have been brought to Spain in the 4th century. Behind the altar you can see the left arm of **St. Vincent,** who was martyred in Valencia in 304. Stars of the cathedral **museum** are Goya's two famous paintings of St. Francis de Borja, duke of Gandia. To the left of the cathedral entrance is the octagonal tower **El Miguelete,** which you can climb: the roofs of the Old Town create a kaleidoscope of orange and brown terra-cotta, and the sea appears in the background. It's said that you can see 300 belfries from here, including bright-blue cupolas made of ceramic tiles from nearby Manises. The tower was built in 1381 and the final spire added in 1736. ⊠ *Pl. de la Reina* ☎ *963/918127* ⊕ *www.catedraldevalencia.es* ⬚ *Cathedral and museum €4.50, tower €2* ⊙ *Nov.–mid-Mar., Mon.–Sat. 10–5:30; mid-Mar.–Oct., Mon.–Sat. 10–6:30, Sun. 2–6:30.*

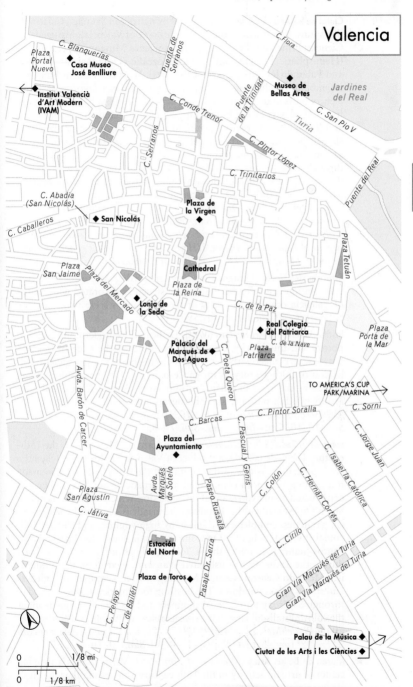

Valencia

C. Blanquerías
Plaza Portal Nuevo
Casa Museo José Benlliure
Puente de Serranos
C. Flora
Museo de Bellas Artes
Jardines del Real
Institut Valencià d'Art Modern (IVAM)
Puente de la Trinidad
C. San Pío V
Turia
C. Conde Trenor
C. Serranos
C. Pintor López
Puente del Real
Plaza Tetuán
C. Trinitarios
C. Abadía (San Nicolás)
Plaza de la Virgen
San Nicolás
C. Caballeros
Cathedral
Plaza San Jaime
Plaza del Mercado
Plaza de la Reina
C. de la Paz
Lonja de la Seda
Real Colegio del Patriarca
Plaza Porta de la Mar
C. de la Nave
Palacio del Marqués de Dos Aguas
Plaza Patriarca
C. Poeta Querol
TO AMERICA'S CUP PARK/MARINA
Avda. Barón de Cárcer
C. Barcas
C. Pintor Sorolla
C. Sorni
C. Pascual y Genis
Plaza del Ayuntamiento
C. Colón
C. Jorge Juan
Avda. Marqués de Sotelo
Paseo Russafa
C. Hernán Cortés
C. Isabella Católica
Plaza San Agustín
C. Játiva
C. Cirilo
Estación del Norte
Pasaje Dr. Serra
Plaza de Toros
C. Pelayo
C. de Bailén
Gran Vía Marqués del Turia
Gran Vía Marqués del Turia
Palau de la Música
Ciutat de les Arts i les Ciències

0    1/8 mi
0    1/8 km

4

**Fodor's Choice** **Ciutat de les Arts i les Ciències.** Designed by native son Santiago Calatrava,
★ this sprawling futuristic complex is the home of Valencia's **Museu de les**
℃ **Ciències Príncipe Felipe** (Prince Philip Science Museum), **L'Hemisfèric**
(Hemispheric Planetarium), **L'Oceanogràfic** (Oceanographic Park),
and **Palau de les Arts** (Palace of the Arts). With resplendent buildings
resembling combs and crustaceans, the Ciutat is a favorite of architecture buffs and curious kids. The Science Museum has soaring platforms filled with lasers, holograms, simulators, hands-on experiments,
and a swell "zero gravity" exhibition on space exploration. The eye-
shaped planetarium projects 3-D virtual voyages on its huge IMAX
screen. At the Oceanographic Park you can take a submarine ride
through a coastal marine habitat. Recent additions include an amphitheater, an indoor theater, and a chamber-music hall. ⊠ *Av. Autovía del
Saler 7* ☎ *902/100031* ⊕ *www.cac.es* ⊠ *Museu de les Ciències €7.70,
L'Hemisfèric €7.70, L'Oceanogràfic €24.50; combination ticket €32.40*
⊙ *Museum mid-Sept.–June, Sun.–Fri. 10–8, Sat. 10–9; July–mid-Sept.,
daily 10–9. L'Oceanogràfic mid-Sept.–June, Sun.–Fri. 10–6, Sat. 10–8;
July–mid-Sept. 10–midnight. L'Hemisfèric daily shows generally every
hr on hr 11–8; Fri. and Sat., additional show at 9.*

**Estación del Norte.** Designed by Demetrio Ribes Mano in 1917, the
train station is a splendid moderniste structure decorated with motifs
of Valencia oranges. The tops of the two towers seem to sprout like
palm trees. ⊠ *Calle Játiva s/n* ☎ *902/240202.*

**Institut Valèncià d'Art Modern (IVAM).** Dedicated to modern and contemporary art, this blocky, uninspired building on the edge of the Old
City—where the riverbed makes a loop—houses a permanent collection of 20th-century avant-garde painting, European Informalism
(including the Spanish artists Antonio Saura, Antoni Tàpies, and Eduardo Chillida), pop art, and photography. ⊠ *Guillem de Castro 118*
☎ *963/863000* ⊕ *www.ivam.es* ⊠ *€2, free Sun.* ⊙ *July and Aug., Tues.–
Sun. 10–10; Sept.–June, Tues.–Sun. 10–8.*

**Lonja de la Seda** (*Silk Exchange*). On the Plaza del Mercado sits the 15th-
century Lonja de la Seda, a product of Valencia's golden age, when the
city's prosperity as one of the capitals of the Corona de Aragón made
it a leading European commercial and artistic center. The Lonja was
constructed as an expression of this splendor. Widely regarded as one of
Spain's finest civil Gothic buildings, its facade is decorated with ghoul-
ish gargoyles, complemented inside by high vaulting and slender heli-
coidal (twisted) columns. Opposite the Lonja stands the **Iglesia de los
Santos Juanes** (Church of the St. Johns), whose interior was destroyed
during the 1936–39 Spanish Civil War, and, next door, the moderniste **Mercado Central** (Central Market), with its wrought-iron girders
and stained-glass windows. The bustling food market is open Monday
through Saturday 8 to 2; local shoppers and visitors alike queue up at
the colorful stalls filled with fruit, vegetables, meat, fish, and confection-
ary. ⊠ *Pl. del Mercado s/n* ☎ *963/917395* ⊕ *www.lonjadevalencia.com*
⊠ *Free* ⊙ *Tues.–Sat. 10–2 and 4:30–8:30, Sun. 10–3.*

★ **Museo de Bellas Artes** (*Museum of Fine Arts*). Valencia was a thriving
center of artistic activity in the 15th century, one reason that the city's

Museum of Fine Arts is among the best in Spain. To get here, cross the old riverbed by the Puente de la Trinidad (Trinity Bridge) to the north bank; the museum is at the edge of the **Jardines del Real** (Royal Gardens), with its fountains, rose gardens, tree-lined avenues, and small zoo. The Royal Gardens are open daily 8–dusk. The permanent collection of the museum, with its lovely palm-shaded cloister, includes many of the finest paintings by Jacomart and Juan Reixach, two of several artists known as the Valencian Primitives, as well as work by Hieronymus Bosch—or El Bosco, as they call him here. The ground floor has a number of the brooding, 17th-century Tenebrist masterpieces of Francisco Ribalta and his pupil José Ribera, a Diego Velázquez self-portrait, and a room devoted to Goya. Upstairs, look for Joaquín Sorolla (Gallery 66), the Valencian painter of everyday Spanish life in the 19th century. ✉ *Calle San Pío V 9* ☎ *963/870300* ⊕ *www.museobellasartesvalencia.gva.es* ✉ *Free* ☉ *Tues.–Sun. 10–8.*

> ### VALENCIA BEST BETS
>
> **Go straight to the top.** The view of Valencia from the Miguelete Tower is magnficient.
>
> **Cast an eye over Ciutat de les Arts i les Ciènces.** One of Spain's most imaginative moderniste developments is in Valencia.
>
> **Leave the bull at home.** Tread carefully in the Museo Nacional de Cerámica, which showcases porcelain, one of the city's most famous exports.

★ **Palacio del Marqués de Dos Aguas** (*Ceramics Museum*). This building near Plaza Patriarca has gone through many additions over the years and now has elements of several architectural styles, including a fascinating baroque alabaster facade. Embellished with carvings of fruits and vegetables, the rococo facade was designed in 1740 by Ignacio Vergara. It centers on the two voluptuous male figures representing the Dos Aguas (Two Waters), a reference to Valencia's two main rivers and the origin of the noble title of the Marqués de Dos Aguas. Since 1954, the palace has housed the **Museo Nacional de Cerámica,** with a magnificent collection of local and artisanal ceramics. Look for the Valencian kitchen on the second floor. ✉ *C. Poeta Querol 2* ☎ *963/516392* ✉ *Palace and museum €3, free Sat. afternoon and Sun. morning* ☉ *Tues.–Sat. 10–2 and 4–8, Sun. 10–2.*

**Palau de la Música** (*Music Palace*). On one of the nicest stretches of the Turia riverbed is this huge glass vault, Valencia's main concert venue. Supported by 10 arcaded pillars, the dome gives the illusion of a greenhouse, both from the street and from within its sun-filled, tree-landscaped interior. Home of the Orquesta de Valencia, the main hall also hosts performers on tour from around the world, including chamber and youth orchestras, opera, and an excellent concert series featuring early, baroque, and classical music. For concert schedules, pick up a Turia guide or one of the local newspapers at any newsstand. To see the building without concert tickets, pop into the **art gallery,** which hosts free changing exhibits. ✉ *Paseo de la Alameda 30* ☎ *963/375020* ⊕ *www.palauvalencia.com* ☉ *Gallery daily 10:30–1:30 and 5:30–9.*

**Plaza del Ayuntamiento.** With the massive baroque facades of the *ayuntamiento* (city hall) and the central post office facing each other across the park, this plaza is the hub of city life. City hall itself houses the municipal tourist office and a museum of paleontology. ⊙ *Ayuntamiento weekdays 8:30–2:30.*

**Plaza de Toros.** Adjacent to the train station is the bullring, one of the oldest in Spain. The best bullfighters are featured during Las Fallas in March, particularly March 18 and 19.

**Museo Taurino** (*Bullfighting Museum*). Down Pasaje Doctor Serra, the Museo Taurino has bullfighting memorabilia, including bulls' heads and matador swords. ⊠ *Pasaje Doctor Serra 10* ☎ *963/883738* 🎫 *Free* ⊙ *Bullring and museum Tues.–Sun. 10–6*

**Real Colegio del Patriarca** (*Royal Seminary of the Patriarch*). This seminary, with its church, cloister, and library, is the crown jewel of Valencia's Renaissance architecture and one of the city's finest sites. Founded by San Juan de Ribera in the 16th century, it has a lovely Renaissance patio and an ornate church, and its museum holds works by Juan de Juanes, Francisco Ribalta, and El Greco. ⊠ *C. de la Nave 1* ☎ *963/514176* 🎫 *€2* ⊙ *Daily 11–1:30.*

**San Nicolás.** A small plaza contains Valencia's oldest church, once the parish of the Borgia Pope Calixtus III. The first portal you come to, with a tacked-on, rococo bas-relief of the Virgin Mary with cherubs, hints at what's inside: every inch of the originally Gothic church is covered with exuberant early-baroque ornamentation. ⊠ *C. Caballeros 35* ☎ *963/913317* 🎫 *Free* ⊙ *Open for mass weekdays 8–9 am and 7–8 pm; Sat. 6:30–8:30 pm; Sun. various masses 8–1:15.*

## SHOPPING

Shoes and leather goods are among Valencia's main products. Both handmade and mass-produced ceramics are created in a range of colors and styles. Fans and silk shawls, along with other traditional Spanish dress, are priced according to quality. Olives and olive oil will make gourmets happy, and olive oil is also used for a range of hair and beauty products. A flea market is held every Sunday morning by the cathedral. Another market takes place on Sunday morning in Plaza Luis Casanova, near Valencia's soccer stadium. If it's great local designer wear you're after, then head straight to the Barrio Carmen.

The town of Manises, 9 km (5 ½ miles) west of Valencia, is a center for Valencian ceramics, known particularly for its azulejos.

## WHERE TO EAT

$ ✕ **La Riuà.** A favorite with Valencia's well connected and well-to-do
SPANISH since 1982, this family-run restaurant a few steps from the Plaza de la Reina specializes in seafood dishes like *anguilas* (eels) prepared with *all i pebre* (garlic and pepper), *pulpitos guisados* (stewed baby octopus), and traditional paellas. Lunch begins at 2 and not a moment before. The walls are covered with decorative ceramics and the gastronomic awards the restaurant has won over the years. 💲 *Average main: €13*

✉ *C. del Mar 27* ☎ *963/914571* ✐ *lariua@lariua.com* ⊕ *www.lariua. com* ⌦ *Reservations essential* ◷ *Closed Sun., Easter wk, and Aug. No dinner Mon.*

**$$** ✕ **El Timonel.** Decorated like the inside of a yacht, this restaurant two
SEAFOOD blocks east of the bullring serves outstanding shellfish. The cooking is simple but makes use of the freshest ingredients; try the grilled *lenguado* (sole) or *lubina* (sea bass). Also top-notch are the eight different kinds of rice dishes, including paella with lobster and *arroz a banda,* with peeled shrimp, prawns, mussels, and clams. For a sweet finale, try the house special *naranjas a la reina,* oranges spiced with rum and topped with *salsa de fresa* (strawberry sauce). Lunch attracts businesspeople, and dinner brings in a crowd of locals and foreigners. ⑤ *Average main: €18* ✉ *Félix Pizcueta 13* ☎ *963/526300* ✐ *restaurante@eltimonel.com* ⊕ *www.eltimonel.com* ◷ *Closed Mon.*

# VALLETTA, MALTA

Updated by Lindsay Bennett

Hulking megalithic temples, ornate baroque churches, narrow old-world streets, and hilltop citadels are Malta's human legacy. Dizzying limestone cliffs, sparkling seas, and charming rural landscapes make up its natural beauty. In its 7,000 years of human habitation, Malta has been overrun by every major Mediterranean power: Phoenicians, Carthaginians, Romans, Byzantines, and Arabs; Normans, Swabians, Angevins, Aragonese, and the Knights of the Order of St. John of Jerusalem; the French, the British, and now tourists. The Germans and Italians tried to take it in World War II—their air raids were devastating—but could not. The islands' history with the Knights of the Order of St. John has given them their lasting character. In 1565, when the forces of Süleyman the Magnificent laid siege here, it was the Knights' turn, with the faithful backing of the Maltese, to send the Turks packing. The handsome limestone buildings and fortifications that the wealthy Knights left behind are all around the islands. Valletta will be the European capital of culture for 2018.

## ESSENTIALS
### CURRENCY
The euro.

### HOURS
Government museums are open daily 10–4 and are closed on Thursday. All sites are closed on January 1, Good Friday, December 24, 25, and 31. Some archaeological sites are open by appointment only. Shops are open Monday–Saturday 9–1 and 4–7.

### TOURS
Darrell Azzopardi is a registered guide who can offer bespoke tours around Malta in English.

Beware of cheap tours: officially licensed guides should wear an identification tag.

**Contacts Darrell Azzopardi** ☎ *9942-2580* ✐ *dazman@onvol.net.*

**TELEPHONES**

Malta's mobile services operate on a single GSM-band system. The system supports text and data but not 3G technology. Public phones operate by means of telecards with smartchip technology. They can be used to make international calls. GO and Vodafone are the main providers.

## COMING ASHORE

Cruise ships dock at the Valletta Waterfront Facility in the heart of the historic Grand Harbour. The facility is extensive, and houses modern, high-quality shops, eight restaurants, and exhibition spaces. Taxi fare to the town of Valetta is €10 and the trip takes only five minutes. It's a steep walk up to the Valletta citadel on foot, but a new elevator (€1) makes the trip much easier. Malta has a well-organized public bus service, but there are also car rentals and taxis. Ferries can also whisk passengers from the port across the Great Harbour to the Three Cities in a few minutes.

Most bus routes across the island start at Valletta Terminal just outside the entrance to the Citadel, and run daily from 5:30 am to 11 pm depending on the route (service ends earlier outside the main towns). Some night routes run in the main tourist areas from midnight until around 4 am. A day ticket is available for €2.60. Bus routes are marked on the maps distributed by the tourist office.

Renting a car would allow you to visit many of Malta's attractions during a day. Prices for a compact manual vehicle are about €35 per day. Driving is on the left. Void of highways, Malta is traversed by country roads with speed limits ranging between 24 and 40 mph. Seatbelt laws are strictly enforced.

Taxis operate on a fixed-fee basis from the port and airport to Valletta and can be extravagantly expensive. Sample fares are (€20) to Marsax-lokk and (€23) to Mdina. Taxi tours can be organized on a per-hour basis; for example, the fare for five hours is about €70. Some taxis have meters, but it is best to ask approximate rates before the ride begins.

## EXPLORING MALTA

### VALLETTA

Malta's capital, the minicity of Valletta, has ornate palaces and museums protected by massive fortifications of honey-color limestone. Houses along the narrow streets have overhanging wooden balconies for people-watching from indoors. The main entrance to town is through the City Gate (where all bus routes end), which leads onto Triq Repubblika (Republic Street), the spine of the grid-pattern city and the main shopping street. Triq Mercante (Merchant Street) parallels Repubblika to the east and is also good for strolling. From these two streets, cross streets descend toward the water; some are stepped. Valletta's compactness makes it ideal to explore on foot. Before setting out along Republic Street, stop at the tourist information office (just inside the city gate) for maps and brochures.

★ **Casa Rocca Piccola.** The exquisitely cultured current owners, Nicolas and Frances de Piro d'Amico Inguanez, host tours of the last of the

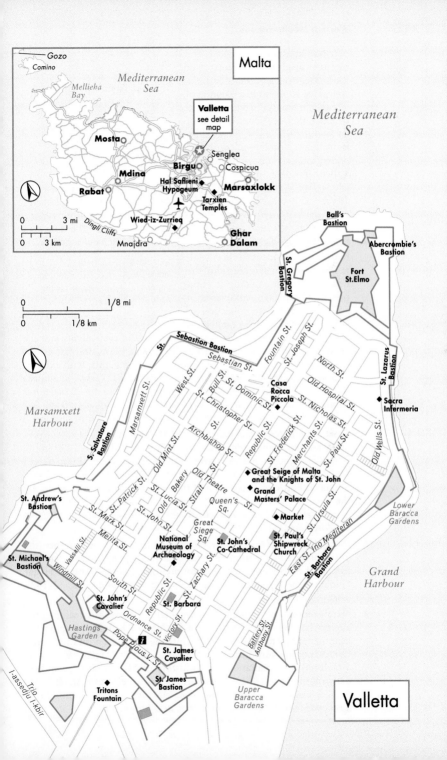

patrician houses still occupied. The treasures inside chart the history of the house, from a portable baroque chapel for baptisms to a painting of "Miss Electricity," commissioned to mark the local contribution of an ambitious ancestor. New exhibits include a costume gallery and an underground bomb shelter, used by Valletta residents during the war. ⊠ *74 Triq Repubblika* ☎ *2122–1499* ⊕ *www.casaroccapiccola.com* ☑ *€9* ⊗ *Guided tours Mon.–Sat. 10–4 on the hour.*

★ **Grand Masters' Palace.** The palace houses the president's office; Malta's Parliament meets here until the new parliament building is completed. The palace, completed in 1574, has a unique collection of Gobelin tapestries; the main hall is

---

**MALTA BEST BETS**

**The Grand Harbour.** Best viewed from the ship when you arrive and depart, the Grand Harbour is one of Europe's finest natural anchorages. Generations of European power brokers have fortified it to create the vista you see today.

**Sacra Infermeria.** The former medieval Hospital of the Knights Hospitallers of St. John, a crusader force, now hosts the "Malta Experience" multimedia presentation.

**St. John's Co-Cathedral.** Caravaggio's masterpiece *The Beheading of St. John the Baptist* is the main attraction here.

---

decorated with frescoes depicting the history of the Knights and the Great Siege. On view are works by Ribera, Van Loo, and Batoni. At the back of the building is the **Armoury of the Knights,** with exhibits of arms and armor through the ages. ⊠ *Palace Sq., Triq Repubblika* ☎ *2124–9349 Palace Armoury* ⊕ *www.heritagemalta.org* ☑ *€10 (joint admission Palace and Armoury), €6 for Palace Armoury* ⊗ *Daily 9–5* ⊗ *The Palace is closed to the public when Parliament is in session.*

**Great Siege of Malta and the Knights of St. John.** A walk-through presentation traces the order's history from its founding in 1099 in the Holy Land and its journeys from Jerusalem to Cyprus, Rhodes, and Malta. Also depicted are epic scenes from the Great Siege of 1565, the naval Battle of Lepanto, and the order's eviction from Malta by the French. ⊠ *Cafe Premier Complex, Treasury St.* ☎ *2124–7300* ⊕ *www.greatsiege.com.mt* ☑ *€7.50* ⊗ *Weekdays 10–4:30, Sat. 10–3* ⊗ *Closed Sun.*

★ **National Museum of Archaeology.** Housed in the Auberge de Provence (the hostel of the Knights from Provence), the museum has an excellent collection of finds from Malta's many prehistoric sites—Tarxien, Ħaġar Qim, and the Hypogeum at Paola. ⊠ *Triq Repubblika* ☎ *2122–1623* ⊕ *www.heritagemalta.org* ☑ *€5* ⊗ *Daily 9–7.*

★ **Sacra Infermeria** (*Hospital of the Knights*). This gracious building, the ancient hospital of the Knights of St. John or Knights Hospillaters, near the seawall has been converted into the Mediterranean Conference Center. For an introduction to the island, see the *Malta Experience,* a multimedia presentation on the history of Malta that is given here daily on the hour. ⊠ *St. Elmo's Bastions, Mediterranean St.* ☎ *2124–3776* ⊕ *www.themaltaexperience.com* ⊗ *Shows weekdays hourly 11–4, weekends hourly 11–2; no show Sun. at 2 July–Sept.*

**Fodor'sChoice**
★ St. John's co-Cathedral. Functional in design but lavishly decorated, the Order of St. John's own church (1578) is Malta's most important treasure. The Knights' colored-marble tombstones on the floor are gorgeous. Each of the side chapels was decorated by a national hostel of the Knights. Many of the paintings and the decoration scheme are by the island's beloved 17th-century painter Mattia Preti (b. 1613). In the Oratory, Caravaggio's only signed work, the dramatic *Beheading of John the Baptist* (1607), is the collection's masterpiece. The cathedral **museum** has illuminated manuscripts and a rich collection of Flemish tapestries. The entrance fee includes an audio guide. Public access (main ticket office) is on Republic Street. ■TIP→ **Narrow heeled shoes such as stilettos are not allowed, but slippers can be purchased at reception.** ⊠ *Pjazza San Gwann, St. John St.* ☎ *2123–9628* ⊕ *www.stjohnscocathedral.com* ☜ *€6* ⊗ *Weekdays 9:30–4:30, Sat. 9:30–12:30 (last admittance 30 min before).*

★ St. Paul's Shipwreck Church. The importance of St. Paul to the Maltese explains the work lavished on this baroque marvel—its raised central vault, oval dome, and marble columns. The *os brachii* (arm bone) relic of the saint is housed in a chapel on the right, a splendid gated chapel is on the left, and a baptismal font stands by the entrance. ⊠ *Triq San Pawl* ☎ *2123–6013* ⊕ *www.maltadiocese.org.*

### THE THREE CITIES

*Birgu is 8 km (5 miles) east of Valletta.*

East across the Grand Harbor from Valletta, the three cities of **Vittoriosa, Senglea,** and **Cospicua** are where the Knights of the Order of St. John first settled—and where crucial fighting took place in the Great Siege of the Turks in 1565. Vittoriosa, also called Birgu, is named for the victory over the Turks. The 5 km (3 miles) of great walls around the cities are the Cottonera Lines, built in the 1670s.

In **Vittoriosa/Birgu** in early October, hundreds of actors stage a Grand Master's crossing of the harbor, and monastery doors on Triq San Lawrenz open to the public for the **Birgu Festa.** On the narrow streets north of the main square you can loop from the Triq La Vallette to the Triq Majjistral on the right. Triq It-Tramuntana takes you past baroque doorways, the Knights' Auberge d'Angleterre (Inn of England), and a Saracen-style house that is thought to date from the 1200s.

**Church of St. Lawrenz.** Below Birgu's main square, the Church of St. Lawrenz is the city's finest church, with the 17th-century painter Mattia Preti's *Martyrdom of San Lawrenz.* ⊠ *Triq San Lawrenz, Birgu* ☎ *2182–7057* ⊕ *www.maltadiocese.org.*

**Gardjola Gardens.** At the tip of Senglea, Gardjola Gardens, once a guard post, has great views across Grand Harbour to Valletta, and a turret carved with a vigilant eye and ear. ⊠ *Triq Portu Salvu, Senglea.*

**Inquisitor's Palace.** The displays in Birgu's Inquisitor's Palace reveal less-discussed aspects of less-tolerant times in Malta. The palace dates from the 1530s and the first Inquistor General and Apostolic delegate to Malta arrived here in 1547. ⊠ *Triq Il-Mina Il Kbira, Birgu* ☎ *2182–7006* ⊕ *www.heritagemalta.org* ☜ *€6* ⊗ *Daily 9–5.*

## PAOLA AND TARXIEN

*Paola is 4.8 km (3 miles) south of Valletta.*

★ **Ħal Saflieni Hypogeum.** This massive labyrinth of underground chambers was used for burials more than 4,000 years ago. Many chambers are decorated with red ocher or fine carvings. ■TIP→ **Book tickets for tours at least a month in advance.** ⊠ *Burial St., on road to Santa Lucija, Paola* ☏ *2180–5018* ⊕ *www.heritagemalta.org* ✇ *€20* ⊙ *Daily 9–4. Tour times must be prebooked.*

**Tarxien Temples.** The three interconnecting Tarxien Temples have curious carvings, oracular chambers, and altars, all dating from about 2800 BC. Nearby are remains of an earlier temple from about 4000 BC. ⊠ *Neolithic Temples St., behind Paola's Church of Christ the King, Tarxien* ☏ *2169–5578* ⊕ *www.heritagemalta.org* ✇ *€6* ⊙ *Daily 9–5.*

## MARSAXLOKK

*8 km (5 miles) southeast of Valletta.*

Malta's main fishing fleet bobs on the water in the wide sheltered bay. The unique colorful fishing boats (luzzu), with their vertical prow and protective "eye of Osiris" symbol, are descendents of Phoenician craft that plied these waters in ancient times. Most afternoons you'll find the fishermen and their families mending nets and preparing for the next sailing. Old honey-colored stone cottages once lived in by these families line the waterfront, though many have now been converted to seafood restaurants and bars. There's a craft market each morning along the waterfront promenade. Sunday hosts a traditional fish market alongside the craft stalls.

## GĦAR DALAM

*9 km (6 miles) southeast of Valletta.*

**cave.** The semifossilized remains of long-extinct species of dwarf elephants and hippopotamuses that roamed the island some 125,000 years ago were found in a cave here. The fossils are now on display in the small **museum.** The earliest evidence of human occupation on Malta dating from 7,000 years ago was found in the excavated upper layer on the cave floor. ⊠ *Zejtun Rd.* ☏ *2165–7419* ⊕ *www.heritagemalta. org* ✇ *€5* ⊙ *Daily 9–5.*

## ZURRIEQ

*11 km (7 miles) south of Valletta.*

On the way to Zurrieq and Qrendi from Valletta you will pass limestone quarries, where orchards are planted, protected from the wind, after the limestone is exhausted.

★ **Blue Grotto.** The turnoff for the Blue Grotto is 1 km (½ mile) beyond the lookout. A steep road takes you to the rocky inlet where noisy boats (€7.50) leave for the grottoes (there are many) and the stained-glass-blue waters that splash their walls. ■TIP→ **Bring a bathing suit in case the water is calm enough for swimming.** ⊠ *Coast Rd.*

**Mnajdra.** From the temple of Mnajdra ("mna-ee-dra"), on the edge of a hill by the sea, views are superb. The temple is encircled by hard coralline limestone walls and has the typical, cloverlike trefoil plan. A visitor center adds useful information about the temple builders and their lifestyle. ⊠ *Triq Ħaġar Qim, Coast Rd., Qrendi* ☎ *2142–4231* ⊕ *www.heritagemalta.org* 🎟 *€9 (combined ticket with Ħaġar Qim)* ☉ *Mid-Oct.–mid-Apr. daily 9–5, mid-Apr.–mid-Oct. daily 9–7.*

**Wied-iz-Zurrieq** (*Zurrieq Valley*). On the far side of town, Zurrieq Valley runs along the road to a lookout over the towering walls of the Blue Grotto's bay. There's a lookout point with parking that offers views of the grotto and surrounding cliffs.

## MDINA

★ *12 km (7 miles) southwest of Valletta.*

In Malta's ancient, walled capital—the longtime stronghold of Malta's nobility—traffic is limited to residents' cars, and the noise of the world outside doesn't penetrate the thick, golden walls. The quiet streets are lined with sometimes block-long, still-occupied noble palaces.

★ **Mdina Cathedral.** The serene, baroque Mdina Cathedral (dedicated to St. Peter and St. Paul) contains Mattia Preti's 17th-century painting *The Shipwreck of St. Paul.* In the cathedral museum are Dürer woodcuts and illuminated manuscripts. ⊠ *Archbishop Sq.* ☎ *2145–4679* ⊕ *www. mdinacathedral.com* 🎟 *€2.50* ☉ *Weekdays 9–4:30, Sat. 9–3:30.*

**Palazzo Falson.** A medieval Patrician stone mansion, dating from between the 13th and 15th centuries, reveals a wealth of original architectural features. The mansion's rooms display more than 45 collections of objects including art works by Anthony Van Dyck, Nicolas Poussin, and Mattia Preti. ⊠ *Villegaignon St.* ☎ *2145–4512* ⊕ *www.palazzofalson. com* 🎟 *€10* ☉ *Tues.–Sun. 10–5.*

## RABAT

The town's name means "suburb"—of Mdina, in this case.

**Catacombs.** Catacombs run under much of Rabat. Up Triq Santa Agatha from Parish Square, the **Catacombs of St. Paul** are clean of bones but full of carved-out burial troughs. Don't forget the way out when you set off to explore. **St. Agatha's Crypt and Catacombs,** farther up the street, were beautifully frescoed between 1200 and 1480, then defaced by Turks in 1551. ⊠ *St. Agatha St.* ☎ *2145–4562* ⊕ *www.heritagemalta. org* 🎟 *€5* ☉ *Daily 9–5.*

**St. Paul's Church.** Completed in 1683, this beautiful church stands above a grotto where St. Paul reputedly took refuge after his shipwreck on Malta. ⊠ *Parish Sq.* ☎ *2145–4467 Parish Office* ⊕ *www.maltadiocese.org.*

## MOSTA

*10 km (6 miles) west of Valletta.*

**Rotunda.** The Rotunda (Church of St. Mary) has the third-largest unsupported dome in Europe, after St. Peter's in Rome and Hagia Sophia in Istanbul. A German bomb fell through the roof during World War II—without detonating. ⊠ *Rotunda Sq.* ☎ *2143–3826* ⊕ *www. maltadiocese.org* ☉ *Daily 9–noon and 3–6.*

## SHOPPING

Most shops in Malta are open from 9 to 7, except in commercial areas where they stay open until 10 pm. Generally stores are closed on Sunday and public holidays. Malta has several crafts that make excellent souvenirs. Blown glass is a modern phenomenon, but is now a signature gift of the island. More traditional are bizzilla (hand-woven lace), silver filigree, globigerina limestone, and coralline limestone. Valletta's main shopping street, **Triq Repubblika,** is lined with touristy shops—pick up postcards and film here, and then venture onto side streets for a look at everyday Maltese wares. At the **open-air market** *(Triq Mercante)*, with some haggling you may snap up a good bargain.

**Joseph Busuttil.** This tiny shop sells a range of quality Maltese crafts including silver and gold filigree jewelry, blown glass, handmade lace, and limestone carvings. ⊠ *222 Merchants St., Valletta* ☎ *2124–3241* ⊗ *Closed Sun.*

## BEACHES

Malta has many lovely beaches, which range from small rock-flanked coves to vast strands. Many beaches see lots of European (mainly British) tourists during the summer season, so they may be busy.

ⓒ **Għajn Tuffieħa Bay.** Malta's prettiest beach, also known as Golden Bay, is also it's wind and kite surfing center, with onshore breezes being particularly advantageous outside the main summer season. Between May and the end of September the beach is very popular with visitors, many of whom stay at the nearby Radisson Blu hotel. Weekends can be crowded with Maltese families who come to spend the day. The soft fine sand is some of the best on an island that has more rocky bays and inlets than sandy beaches. Shade is provided by rented sun umbrellas (summer only). **Best for:** swimming; wind surfing. **Amenities:** food and drink; lifeguards (summer only); parking (no fee); showers; toilets. ⊠ *Southwest of Mellieħa town, Mellieħa.*

## WHERE TO EAT

$ ✕ **Caffe Cordina.** On the ground floor of the original treasury of the
CAFÉ  Knights is Valletta's oldest café. Since 1837, this ornate, vaulted confectionery has produced hot, savory breakfast pastries and *qagħaq ta' l-għasel* (honey rings). The lunch menu also includes sandwiches, salads, and a choice of daily specials. The interior air-conditioned café attracts Valletta movers and shakers, because of its close proximity to Parliament and the law courts. The shaded outside tables in Victoria Square are the city's prime people-watching spots. Enjoy a coffee, beer, or glass of wine and relax. ⑤ *Average main: €7* ⊠ *244–45 Triq Repubblika, Valletta* ☎ *2123–4385* ⊕ *www.caffecordina.com.*

$ ✕ **Guzé.** This young and dynamic team is reinventing the traditional
MODERN  Maltese trattoria with a vibrant contemporary menu using traditional
EUROPEAN  local ingredients. Set in a 400-year-old vaulted stone building, the series
Fodor's Choice  of small simply furnished and elegantly lit dining spaces are intimate.
★  ⚠ **When the restaurant is full, space can be a little tight.** Guzé is known

for its monthly menu—a choice of chef-inspired dishes made with fresh seasonal ingredients—but there's also a good range of staple Maltese dishes on the à la carte menu. $\boxed{\$}$ *Average main: €16* $\boxtimes$ *22 Old Bakery St., Valletta* $\textcircled{\scriptsize\textbf{☎}}$ *2123–9686* $\oplus$ *www.guze.com.mt* $\odot$ *Closed Sun.; no lunch Mon.–Thurs.*

# VENICE, ITALY

Updated
by Bruce
Leimsidor

It's called La Serenissima, "the most serene," a reference to the majesty, wisdom, and immense power of this city that was for centuries the mistress of trade between Europe and the Orient. Built largely on water by men who both defied and loved the sea, Venice is unlike any other town. No matter how many times you've seen it in movies or on TV, the real thing is more startlingly beautiful than you could ever imagine. Its landmarks, the Basilica di San Marco and the Palazzo Ducale, are exotic mixes of Byzantine, Gothic, and Renaissance styles. Shimmering sunlight and silvery mist soften every perspective here, and you understand how the city became renowned in the Renaissance for its artists' rendering of color. It's full of secrets, inexpressibly romantic, and at times given over to pleasure.

## ESSENTIALS
### CURRENCY
The euro.

### HOURS
Shops are generally open 9–1 and 3:30–7:30 and are closed Sunday and Monday morning most of the year, however, tourist shops in the city will remain open throughout the day and into the evening and on Sundays.

### PRIVATE TOURS
Walks inside Venice provides full- and half-day tours by academically trained, English-speaking professional tour guides who will lead you through Venice's dazzling labyrinth. There are several types of small group tours, depending upon your interests, or you can book a tour specially geared to your passions.

**Contacts Walks Inside Venice.** $\textcircled{\scriptsize\textbf{☎}}$ *(39)41/275–0687 for Sara, (39)41/524–1706 for Roberta, (39)41/520–2434 for Cristina* $\oplus$ *www.walksinsidevenice.com.*

### TELEPHONES
Tri-band GSM phones work in Italy. You can buy prepaid phone cards at telecom shops, news vendors, and tobacconists in all towns and cities. Phone cards can be used for local or international calls.

### COMING ASHORE
Venice is a huge port handling vast numbers of cruise ships and much of commercial traffic as well. The cruise terminal sits at the southwestern corner of city, and has two main docking areas, the Marittima area for large ships and the San Basilio for smaller ones.

Marittima has duty-free shops, information desks, and refreshment facilities. From here there is a shuttle bus to Piazzale Roma at the western edge of the city, just outside the port, or you can take Bus 6 from the port entrance. You can also take a boat. Among the seafaring options

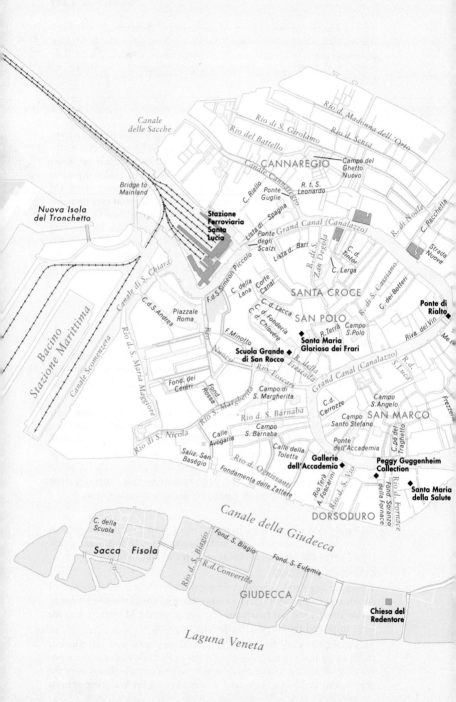

# Venice

**Murano**

*Canale delle Navi*

**San Michele**

*Cimitero San Michele*

*Sacca della Misericordia*

*Canale delle Fondamente Nuove*

◆ **Madonna dell'Orto**

C.po dei Gesuiti

C. d. Gesuiti

Fondamente Nuove

C. d. Squero

R. d. Mendicanti

◆ **Santa Maria dei Miracoli**

*Rio d. S. Marina*

Campo S. Marina

Campo S. Maria

Barbaria delle Tole

Ruga Giuffa

C. Lion

R. d. S. Francesco

R. d. Gorne

Canale di Galeazze

R. d. Greci

**CASTELLO**

*Darsena Grande*

*Rio d. Vergini*

*Rio d. S. Daniele*

*Canale di S. Pietro*

**San Pietro**

Sal. di S. Lio

C. Fiubera

◆ **Basilica di San Marco**

San Zaccaria

◆ **Palazzo Ducale**

◆ **Campanile**

◆ **Piazza San Marco**

Fond. d. Farine

Molo Riva degli Schiavoni

*Rio della Tana*

V. Garibaldi

*Rio d. S. Anna*

R. d. S. Giuseppe

*Bacino di San Marco*

Riva dei Sette Martiri

Riva dei Partigiani

*Rio dei Giardini*

**S. Giorgio Maggiore**

Fond. delle Zitelle

Calle Michelangelo

Viale 24 Maggio

*Darsena di Sant' Elena*

Viale

Fondamenta Piave

**Sant'Elena**

Viale Sant' Elena

Viale quattro Novembre

Viale Vittorio Veneto

Viale Sant' Elena

| 0 | | ]/4 mile |
| 0 | | 400 meters |

are the Alilaguna M Line (Linea M) boat, which travels direct from Marittima to Piazza San Marco. You could also take Linea Blu or Linea Rosso from Tronchetto to San Marco, though this service has more stops enroute. Vaporetto services 41, 42, 51, 52, 61, 62 operate along the same route. The journey takes around 20 minutes.

At San Basilio there are fewer passenger facilities, but the quay has a vaporetto stop, from which services 61, 62, and 82 take you into the heart of Venice. The current fare is €6.50.

Vaporetto services take you right to St. Mark's Square. Cars aren't allowed into Venice proper, so there is no point to renting a car unless you want to explore the Veneto region. Expect to pay about €45 for a compact manual vehicle.

> **VENICE BEST BETS**
>
> **Take a gondola ride along the canals.** Despite the high cost, the views are sublime, and the minor waterways take you to quiet backwaters that are little visited by most tourists.
>
> **Explore Basilica San Marco.** The mother lode of Byzantine treasure and art lies within the walls of this great church.
>
> **Sip an espresso in St. Mark's Square.** From here you can admire the architecture and watch the world go by.

**GETTING TO THE AIRPORT**

If you do not purchase airport transfers from your cruise line, the simplest transfer is to take a vaporetto to Piazzalle Roma and then city bus #5 to Marco Polo Airport, the main airport of Venice. If you are traveling from Treviso airport, there are private buses (€5) from Piazzale Roma that will take to the airport there.

A private *motoscafo* (water taxi) transfer direct from the airport dock to the cruise port will cost around €90 for up to four people but may be a necessary expense for very early departures.

The quickest transfer on public transport is to take the city Bus 5 overland to Piazzale Roma and then transfer from Piazzale Roma to the cruise port. Blue buses run by **ATVO** (☎ *0421/383672* ⊕ *www.atvo.it*) also make a 20-minute trip from the airport to Piazzale Roma (tickets €5). Tickets are sold from machines and at the airport booth in Ground Transportation (open daily 9–7:30), and on the bus when tickets are otherwise unavailable. The ATVO buses are more comfortable, but not any quicker, than the cheaper city busses. A land taxi to Piazzale Roma costs about €30. From Piazzale Roma there are shuttle buses to the cruise terminal.

## EXPLORING VENICE

There's no better introduction to Venice than a trip down the Grand Canal. It is, without a doubt, one of the world's great "avenues." For 4 km (2½ miles) it winds its way in a backward "S," past 12th- to 18th-century palaces built by the city's richest families. There is a definite theatrical quality to the Grand Canal; it's as if each facade had been designed to steal your attention from its rival across the way. The most romantic—albeit expensive—way to see the canal is from a gondola (approximately €60 for up to 4 persons). The next best thing—at a fraction of the cost—is to take in the view from vaporetto Line 1.

## PIAZZA SAN MARCO

One of the world's most evocative squares, Piazza San Marco (St. Mark's Square) is the heart of Venice, a vast open space bordered by an orderly procession of arcades marching toward the fairy-tale cupolas and marble lacework of the Basilica di San Marco.

Piazzetta San Marco, the "little square" leading from Piazza San Marco to the waters of Bacino San Marco (St. Mark's Basin), is a *molo* (landing) that was once the grand entryway to the republic. It's distinguished by two columns towering above the waterfront. One is topped by the winged lion, a traditional emblem of St. Mark that became the symbol of Venice itself; the other supports St. Theodore, the city's first patron, along with his dragon.

Fodor's Choice ★ **Basilica di San Marco.** An opulent synthesis of Byzantine and Romanesque styles, Venice's gem is laid out in a Greek-cross floor plan and topped with five plump domes. It didn't become the cathedral of Venice until 1807, but its original role as the Chiesa Ducale (the doge's private chapel) gave it immense power and wealth. The original church was built in 828 to house the body of Saint Mark the Evangelist. His remains, filched from Alexandria by the doge's agents, were supposedly hidden in a barrel under layers of pickled pork to sneak them past Muslim guards.

A 976 fire destroyed most of the original church. It was rebuilt and reopened in 1094, and for centuries it would serve as a symbol of Venetian wealth and power, endowed with all the riches admirals and merchants could carry off from the Orient, to the point where it earned the nickname "Chiesa d'Oro" (Golden Church). The four bronze horses that prance and snort over the doorway are copies of sculptures that victorious Venetians took from Constantinople in 1204 after the fourth crusade (the originals are upstairs in the Museo di San Marco). The rich, colorful exterior decorations, including the numerous different marble columns, all came from the same source.

The basilica is famous for its 43,055 square feet of mosaics, which run from floor to ceiling thanks to an innovative roof of brick vaulting. Climb the steep stairway to the **Galleria** and the **Museo di San Marco** for the best overview of the basilica's interior. From here you can step outdoors for a sweeping panorama of Piazza San Marco and out over the lagoon to San Giorgio.

Be aware that guards at the basilica door turn away anyone with bare shoulders, midriff, or knees: no shorts, short skirts, or tank tops are allowed. To skip the line at the basilica entrance, reserve your arrival—at no extra cost—on the basilica website. You can also skip the line if you check a bag at the nearby bag-check facility (find it on the map at the basilica entrance)—just show your bag-check ticket to the entrance guard and he'll wave you in. ⊠ *Piazza San Marco, San Marco 328, San Marco* ☎ *041/2708311 basilica, 041/2413817 tour info 10–noon weekdays* ⊕ *www.basilicasanmarco.it* ☟ *Basilica free, Tesoro €2, Santuario and Pala d'Oro €1.50, Galleria and Museo di San Marco €3* ⊙ *May–Sept., Mon.–Sat. 9:45–5, Sun. 2–5; Oct.–Apr., Mon.–Sat. 9:45–5, Sun. 2–4. Last entry 1 hr before closing; interior illuminated Mon.–Sat. 11:30–12:30, Sun. 2–5* Ⓜ *Vallaresso/San Zaccaria.*

**Campanile.** Construction of Venice's famous brick bell tower (325 feet tall, plus the angel) began in the 9th century, and took on its present form in 1514. In 1902, the tower unexpectedly collapsed, taking with it Jacopo Sansovino's 16th-century marble loggia at its base. The largest original bell, called the *marangona,* survived. The crushed loggia was promptly reconstructed, and the new tower, rebuilt to the old plan, reopened in 1912. Today, on a clear day the stunning view includes the Lido, the lagoon, and the mainland as far as the Alps, but, strangely enough, none of the myriad canals that snake through the city. ⊠ *Piazza San Marco* ☎ *041/5224064* 🖃 *€8* ⊙ *Easter–June, Oct., and Nov., daily 9–7; July–Sept., daily 9–9; Nov.–Easter, daily 9–3:45. Last entry 1 hr before closing* Ⓜ *Vaporetto: Vallaresso, San Zaccaria.*

**Fodor's**Choice ★ **Palazzo Ducale** (*Doge's Palace*). Rising above the Piazzetta San Marco, this Gothic fantasia of pink-and-white marble is a majestic expression of Venetian prosperity and power. It served not only as the doge's residence, but also as the central administrative center of the Venetian Republic. The palace's sumptuous chambers have walls and ceilings covered with works by Venice's greatest artists. The ceiling of the **Sala del Senato** (Senate Chamber), featuring *The Triumph of Venice* by Tintoretto, is magnificent, but it's dwarfed by his masterpiece *Paradise* in the **Sala del Maggiore Consiglio** (Great Council Hall). ⊠ *Piazzetta San Marco, Piazza San Marco* ☎ *041/2715911, 041/5209070 Secret Itineraries tour* ⊕ *www.museiciviciveneziani.it* 🖃 *Museums of San Marco Pass €14 (or €16.50 if there is a special exhibition), Musei Civici Pass €18.50.* ⊙ *Apr.–Oct., daily 9–7; Nov.–Mar., daily 9–5. Last entry 1 hr before closing* Ⓜ *Vaporetto: San Zaccaria, Vallaresso.*

## ELSEWHERE IN VENICE

**Fodor's**Choice ★ **Gallerie dell'Accademia.** Napoleon founded these galleries in 1807 on the site of a religious complex he had suppressed. They were carefully and subtly restructured between 1945 and 1959 by the renowned architect Carlo Scarpa. In them you'll find the world's most extensive collection of Venetian paintings. Booking is necessary to see the **Quadreria,** where additional works cover every inch of a wide hallway. A free map notes art and artists, and the bookshop sells a more informative English-language booklet. In the main galleries a €4 audio guide saves reading, but adds little to each room's excellent annotation. ⊠ *Dorsoduro 1050, Campo della Carità just off the Accademia Bridge* ☎ *041/5222247 Quadreria reservations, 041/5200345 reservations* ⊕ *www.gallerieaccademia.org* 🖃 *€6.50, €11 includes Ca' d'Oro and Museo Orientale* ⊙ *Galleria: Tues.–Sun. 8:15 am–7:15 pm, Mon. 8:15–2. Quadreria: Fri. 11 am–1 pm, Sat. 11–noon* Ⓜ *Vaporetto: Accademia.*

**Madonna dell'Orto.** Though built toward the middle of the 14th century, this church takes its character from its beautiful late-Gothic façade, added between 1460 and 1464; it's one of the most beautiful

Gothic churches in Venice. Tintoretto lived nearby, and this, his parish church, contains some of his most powerful work. Lining the chancel are two huge (45 feet by 20 feet) canvases, *Adoration of the Golden Calf* and *Last Judgment*. In glowing contrast to this awesome spectacle is Tintoretto's *Presentation of the Virgin at the Temple* and the simple chapel where he and his children, Marietta and Domenico, are buried. Paintings by Domenico, Cima da Conegliano, Palma il Giovane, Palma il Vecchio, and Titian also hang in the church. A chapel displays a photographic reproduction of a precious *Madonna with Child* by Giovanni Bellini. The original was stolen one night in 1993. ⊠ *Campo della Madonna dell'Orto, Cannaregio* ☎ *041/2750462 Chorus Foundation* ⊕ *www.chorusvenezia.org* ⌦ *€3, Chorus Pass €10* ⊙ *Mon.–Sat. 10–5, Sun. 1–5* Ⓜ *Vaporetto: Orto.*

**4**

🖰 **Peggy Guggenheim Collection.** A small selection of 20th-century painting and sculpture is on display at this gallery in the late heiress Peggy Guggenheim's Grand Canal home. The collection represents the eccentric lady's generally excellent taste. Through wealth and social connections, Guggenheim (1898–1979) became an important art dealer and collector from the 1930s through the 1950s, and her personal collection here in Palazzo Venier dei Leoni includes works by Picasso, Kandinsky, Pollock, Motherwell, and Ernst (at one time her husband). ⊠ *Fondamenta Venier dei Leoni, Dorsoduro 701* ☎ *041/2405411* ⊕ *www.guggenheim-venice. it* ⌦ *€12* ⊙ *Wed.–Mon. 10–6* Ⓜ *Vaporetto: Accademia.*

Fodor'sChoice **Ponte di Rialto** (*Rialto Bridge*). The competition to design a stone bridge
★ across the Grand Canal attracted the best architects of the late 16th century, including Michelangelo, Palladio, and Sansovino, but the job went to the less-famous (but appropriately named) Antonio da Ponte (1512–95). His pragmatic design, completed in 1591, featured shop space and was high enough for galleys to pass beneath. Along the railing you'll enjoy one of the city's most famous views: the Grand Canal vibrant with boat traffic. Ⓜ *Vaporetto: Rialto.*

★ **Santa Maria dei Miracoli.** Tiny yet harmoniously proportioned, this Renaissance gem, built between 1481 and 1489, is sheathed in marble and decorated inside with exquisite marble reliefs. Architect Pietro Lombardo (circa 1435–1515) miraculously compressed the building into its confined space, then created the illusion of greater size by varying the color of the exterior, adding extra pilasters on the building's canal side, and offsetting the arcade windows to make the arches appear deeper. The church was built to house *I Miracoli,* an image of the Virgin Mary by Niccolò di Pietro (1394-1440) that is said to have performed miracles—look for it on the high altar. ⊠ *Campo Santa Maria Nova, Cannaregio* ☎ *041/2750462 Chorus Foundation* ⊕ *www.chorusvenezia.org* ⌦ *€3, Chorus Pass €10* ⊙ *Mon.–Sat. 10–5* Ⓜ *Vaporetto: Rialto.*

★ **Santa Maria della Salute.** En route to becoming Venice's most important baroque architect, 32-year-old Baldassare Longhena won a competition in 1631 to design a shrine honoring the Virgin Mary for saving Venice from a plague that in the space of two years (1629–30) killed 47,000 residents, or one-third of the city's population. It was not completed, however, until 1687—five years after Longhena's death. Outside, this ornate, white Istrian stone octagon is topped by a colossal cupola with snail-like ornamental buttresses and a baroque facade; inside are a polychrome marble floor and six chapels. The Byzantine icon above the main altar has been venerated as the Madonna della Salute (Madonna of Health) since 1670, when Francesco Morosini brought it here from Crete. Do not leave the church without visiting the **Sacrestia Maggiore,** which contains a dozen works by Titian, including his *San Marco Enthroned with Saints* altarpiece. ⊠ *Punta della Dogana, Dorsoduro* ☎ *041/2743928* 🖅 *Church free, sacristy €2* 🕑 *Apr.–Sept., daily 9–noon and 3–6:30; Oct.–Mar., daily 9–noon and 3–5:30* Ⓜ *Vaporetto: Salute.*

**Fodor's**Choice **Santa Maria Gloriosa dei Frari.** This immense Gothic church of russet-★ color brick was completed in 1442 after more than a century of work. *I Frari* (as it's known locally) contains some of the most brilliant paintings in any Venetian church. Inside you'll see works by Giovanni Bellini, Bartolomeo Vivarini, Conatello, and Titian. The Frari also holds a Sansovino sculpture of St. John the Baptist, and Longhena's impressive baroque tomb designed for Doge Giovanni Pesaro. ⊠ *Campo dei Frari, San Polo* ☎ *041/2728618, 041/2750462 Chorus Foundation* ⊕ *www. chorusvenezia.org* 🖅 *€3, Chorus Pass €10* 🕑 *Mon.–Sat. 9–6, Sun. 1–6* Ⓜ *Vaporetto: San Tomà.*

★ **Scuola Grande di San Rocco.** Saint Rocco's popularity stemmed from his miraculous recovery from the plague and his care for fellow sufferers. Throughout the plague-filled Middle Ages, followers and donations abounded, and this elegant example of Venetian Renaissance architecture, built between 1517 and 1560 and including the work of at least four architects, was the result. Although it is bold and dramatic outside, its contents are even more stunning—a series of more than 60 paintings by Tintoretto. ⊠ *Campo San Rocco, San Polo 3052* ☎ *041/5234864* ⊕ *www.scuolagrandesanrocco.it* 🖅 *€8 (includes audio guide)* 🕑 *Daily 9:30–5:30. Last entry ½ hr before closing* Ⓜ *Vaporetto: San Tomà.*

## SHOPPING

Glass, most of it made on the separate island of Murano, is Venice's number-one product, and you'll be confronted by mind-boggling displays of traditional and contemporary glassware, much of it kitsch. Carnival masks also make a unique souvenir. The finest ones are hand-crafted to fit the wearer, but inexpensive alternatives abound. The city also has a long history of supplying lace and luxury materials, though many of the cheaper items on sale are now imported. Don't forget classic Italian design in clothing, shoes, and leather accessories such as purses and belts. All these can be found in the streets radiating out from St Mark's Square.

**Il Merletto.** The best of Burano's renowned lace-making tradition is rarely represented by the examples you'll see on display. However, at Il Merletto, you can ask for the authentic, handmade lace safeguarded in drawers behind the counter. This is the only place in Venice connected with the students of the Scuola del Merletto in Burano, who, officially, do not sell to the public. Hours of operation are daily 10 to 5. ✉ *Sotoportego del Cavalletto under the Procuratie Vecchie, Piazza San Marco 95* ☎ *041/5208406.*

**L'Isola.** L'Isola has chic, contemporary glassware signed by Carlo Moretti. ✉ *Campo San Moisè, San Marco 1468* ☎ *041/5231973* 🌐 *www.carlomoretti.com.*

**Lorenzo Rubelli.** Lorenzo Rubelli, founded in1858, offers the same sumptuous brocades, damasks, and cut velvets used by the world's most prestigious decorators. ✉ *Campiello del Teatro, San Marco 3877* ☎ *041/5236110* 🌐 *www.rubelli.com.*

4

## WHERE TO EAT

$$$$ VENETIAN ✕ **Alla Madonna.** "The Madonna" used to be world-famous as "the" classic Venetian trattoria, but in the past decades, has settled down to middle age. Owned and run by the Rado family since 1954, this Venetian institution looks like one, with its wood-beams, stained glass windows, and panoply of paintings on white walls. Folks still head here to savor the classic Venetian repertoire and, as most dishes are properly prepared (for the stiff prices, they should be), the rooms here are usually bustling so get ready to enjoy a festive and lively meal. $ *Average main: €60* ✉ *Calle della Madonna, San Polo 594* ☎ *041/5223824* 🌐 *www.ristoranteallamadonna.com* ✍ *Reservations essential* ⊙ *Closed Wed., Jan., and 2 wks in Aug.* Ⓜ *Vaporetto: San Silvestro.*

$$$$ VENETIAN ★ ✕ **Vini da Gigio.** Paolo and Laura, a brother-sister team, run this refined trattoria as if they've invited you to dinner in their home, while keeping the service professional. Deservedly popular with Venetians and visitors alike, it's one of the best values in the city. Indulge in pastas such as rigatoni with duck sauce and arugula-stuffed ravioli. Fish is well represented—try the sesame-encrusted tuna—but the meat dishes steal the show. The steak with red-pepper sauce and the *tagliata di agnello* (sautéed lamb fillet with a light, crusty coating) are both superb, and you'll never enjoy a better *fegato alla veneziana* (Venetian-style liver with onions). This is a place for wine connoisseurs, as the cellar is one of the best in the city. Come at lunch or for the second sitting in the evening, to avoid being rushed. $ *Average main: €40* ✉ *Fondamenta San Felice, Cannaregio 3628/A* ☎ *041/5285140* 🌐 *www.vinidagigio.com* ✍ *Reservations essential* ⊙ *Closed Mon. and Tues., 2 wks in Jan., and 3 wks in Aug.* Ⓜ *Vaporetto: Ca' d'Oro.*

## WHERE TO STAY

$ HOTEL Fodor's Choice ★ **Locanda Orseolo.** This cozy, elegant hotel offers a welcome respite from the throngs churning around Piazza San Marco. **Pros:** intimate and romantic; friendly staff; Wi-Fi is free. **Cons:** no elevator; canal-side rooms can be noisy (think singing gondoliers); its reputation and price bracket, mean guests should book as early as possible. $ *Rooms from: €180* ✉ *Corte Zorzi off Campo San Gallo, San Marco 1083* ☎ *041/5204827* 🌐 *www.locandaorseolo.com* *12 rooms* ⊙ *Closed Jan.* 🍽 *Breakfast* Ⓜ *Vaporetto: Rialto or Vallaresso.*

**$$**    🏨 **Palazzo Sant'Angelo sul Canal Grande.** There's a distinguished yet
HOTEL    comfortable feel to this elegant palazzo, which is large enough to
deliver expected facilities and services but small enough to pamper its
guests. **Pros:** convenient to vaporetto stop. **Cons:** modest breakfast;
fee for Wi-Fi, and Internet available only in common areas, not in
rooms. $ *Rooms from: €420* ⊠ *Campo Sant'Angelo, San Marco 3488*
☎ *041/2411452* ⊕ *www.palazzosantangelo.com* ⤵ *14 rooms* ◯ *Breakfast* Ⓜ *Vaporetto: Sant'Angelo.*

**$$**    🏨 **Palazzo Stern.** The gracious terrace that overlooks the Grand Canal
HOTEL    is almost reason alone to stay here. **Pros:** excellent service; lovely views
★    from many rooms; modern renovation retains historic ambience; steps
from vaporetto stop. **Cons:** multiple renovations may turn off some
Venetian architectural purists; rooms with a Grand Canal view are
much more expensive. $ *Rooms from: €340* ⊠ *Calle del Traghetto,
Dorsoduro 2792* ☎ *041/2770869* ⊕ *www.palazzostern.com* ⤵ *18
rooms, 5 junior suites, 1 suite* ◯ *Breakfast* Ⓜ *Vaporetto: Ca' Rezzonico.*

---

# VIGO, SPAIN (FOR SANTIAGO DE COMPOSTELA)

Updated by
Joanna Styles

Spain's most Atlantic region is en route to nowhere, an end in itself.
Northwestern Spain is a series of rainy landscapes, stretching from
your feet to the horizon and the country's wildest mountains, the
Picos de Europa. Ancient granite buildings wear a blanket of moss,
and even the stone *horreos* (granaries) are built on stilts above the
damp ground.

Santiago de Compostela, where a cathedral holds the remains of the
apostle James, has drawn pilgrims over the same roads for 900 years,
leaving northwestern Spain covered with churches, shrines, and former
hospitals. Asturias, north of the main pilgrim trail, has always maintained a separate identity, isolated by the rocky Picos de Europa. This
and the Basque Country are the only parts of Spain never conquered
by the Moors, so regional architecture shows little Moorish influence.

## ESSENTIALS
### CURRENCY
The euro.

### HOURS
Museums generally open from 9 until 7 or 8; many are closed on Mondays and some close in the afternoons. Most stores are open Monday–
Saturday 9–1:30 and 5–8, but tourist shops may open in the afternoon
and also on Sunday between May and September.

### PRIVATE TOURS
**SECCHI.** The company organizes half and full-day tours exploring Galician towns, cities, coastline and countryside. ☎ *981/554176* ⊕ *www.
turismosecchi.com.*

### TELEPHONES

Spain has good land and mobile services. Public kiosks accept phone cards that support international calls (cards sold in press shops, bars, and telecom shops). Mobile services are 3G compatible. Major companies include Vodafone.

### COMING ASHORE

The cruise terminal, which sits on the waterfront directly off the Old Town, was expanded in 2011 to handle larger ships. It's possible to walk from the ship and explore on foot with shops and restaurants close by. Facilities in the terminal include a spa and leisure area within the A Laxe commercial center in the port.

In Vigo a tourist bus operates a continuous hop-on, hop-off service during Easter week and the summer (June 15–Sept. 15) and on cruise-ship days during the rest of the year. Tickets cost €7.50. The bus passes the port when cruise ships are in dock.

> ### SANTIAGO DE CAMPOSTELA BEST BETS
>
> **Santiago's Cathedral.** One of the holiest places in Christendom; the quality of the Romanesque stonework is exquisite.
>
> **The Museo de las Peregrinaciones.** Learn about the triumphs, trials, and tribulations of the medieval pilgrims who journeyed across Europe to worship at the cathedral.
>
> **The atmosphere of Santiago's medieval quarter.** These narrow streets have been serving the needs of travelers since the cathedral was completed in the 12th century.

There is at least one train per hour to Santiago de Compostela. Journey time is around 1½ hours, and tickets cost approximately €10.40 one-way. It's a 30-minute walk from the port to the railway station or a 10-minute taxi trip.

Renting a vehicle would allow you to explore Santiago de Compostela and the rugged countryside of this wild corner of Spain. Rental price for an economy manual vehicle is approximately €45.

## EXPLORING VIGO AND SANTIAGO DE COMPOSTELA

### VIGO

Vigo's formidable port is choked with trawlers and fishing boats and lined with clanging shipbuilding yards. Its sights (or lack thereof) fall far short of its commercial swagger. The city's casual appeal lies a few blocks inland, where the port commotion gives way to the narrow, dilapidated streets of the Old Town. From 8:30 to 3:30 daily on **Rúa Pescadería**, in the barrio called La Piedra, Vigo's famed *ostreras*—a group of rubber-glove fisherwomen who have been peddling fresh oysters to passersby for more than 50 years.

**Parque del Castro.** South of Vigo's Old Town is the hilltop Parque del Castro, a quiet, stately park with sandy paths, palm trees, mossy embankments, and stone benches. Atop a series of steps are the remains of an old fort and a *mirador* (lookout) with fetching views of Vigo's coastline and the Islas Cíes. ⊠ *Between Praza de España and Praza do Rei, beside Av. Marqués de Alcedo.*

## SANTIAGO DE COMPOSTELA

*80 km (50 miles) north of Vigo, 77 km (48 miles) southwest of À Coruña.*

A large, lively university makes Santiago one of the most exciting cities in Spain, but its cathedral makes it one of the most impressive. The building is opulent and awesome, yet its towers create a sense of harmony as a benign St. James, dressed in pilgrim's costume, looks down from his perch.

**Casco Antiguo** (*Old Town*). The best way to spend your time in Santiago de Compostela is to simply to walk around the *casco antiguo*, losing yourself in its maze of stone-paved narrow streets and little plazas. The streets hold many old *pazos* (manor houses), convents, and churches. The most beautiful pedestrian thoroughfares are Rúa do Vilar, Rúa do Franco, and Rúa Nova—portions of which are covered by arcaded walkways called *soportales,* designed to keep walkers out of the rain.

**Cathedral.** From the Praza do Obradoiro, climb the two flights of stairs to the main entrance of Santiago's cathedral. Although the facade is baroque, the interior holds one of the finest Romanesque sculptures in the world, the **Pórtico de la Gloria.** Completed in 1188 by Maestro Mateo, this is the cathedral's original entrance, its three arches carved with figures from the Apocalypse, the Last Judgment, and purgatory. Below Jesus is a serene St. James, poised on a carved column. Look carefully and you can see five smooth grooves, formed by the millions of pilgrims who have placed their hands here over the centuries. On the back of the pillar, people, especially students preparing for exams, lean forward to touch foreheads with the likeness of Maestro Mateo in the hope that his genius can be shared. In his bejeweled cloak, St. James presides over the **high altar.** The stairs behind it are the cathedral's focal point, surrounded by dazzling baroque decoration, sculpture, and drapery. Here, as the grand finale of their spiritual journey, pilgrims embrace St. James and kiss his cloak. In the crypt beneath the altar lie the remains of James and his disciples St. Theodore and St. Athenasius.

A Pilgrims' Mass is celebrated every day at noon. On special, somewhat unpredictable occasions, the *botafumeiro* (huge incense burner) is attached to the thick ropes hanging from the ceiling and prepared for a ritual at the end of the Pilgrims' Mass: as small flames burn inside, eight strong laymen move the ropes to swing the vessel in a massive semicircle across the apse. In earlier centuries, this rite served as an air freshener—by the time pilgrims reached Santiago, they smelled a bit, well, you can imagine. A botafumeiro and other cathedral treasures are on display in the **museums** downstairs and next door. On the right (south) side of the nave is the **Porta das Praterías** (Silversmiths' Door), the only purely Romanesque part of the cathedral's facade. The statues on the portal were cobbled together from parts of the cathedral. The double doorway opens onto the **Praza das Praterías,** named for the silversmiths' shops that used to line it. ⊠ *Praza do Obradoiro* ☎ *981/581155 cathedral, 981/569327 museum* ⊕ *www. catedraldesantiago.es* ✉ *Cathedral free, combined museum ticket €5* ⊙ *Cathedral daily 7 am–9 pm; museums June–Sept., Mon.–Sat. 10–2 and 4–8, Sun. 10–2; Oct.–May, Mon.–Sat. 10–1:30 and 4–8, Sun. 10–1:30.*

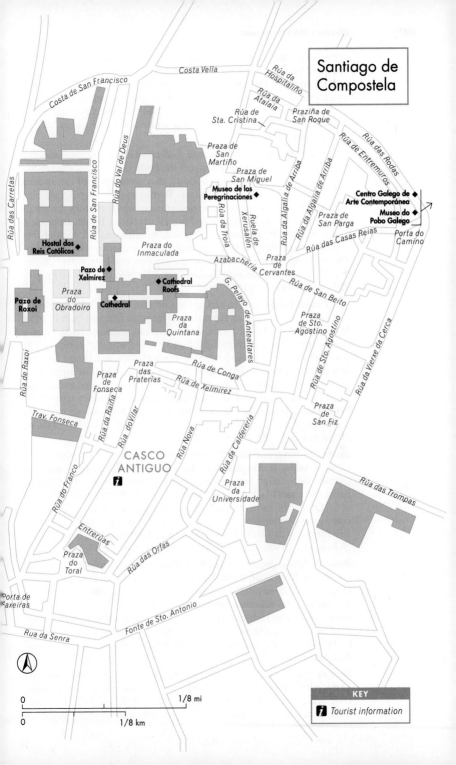

**Cathedral Roofs.** For excellent views of the city, join one of the tours arranged by Xelmírez Palace that takes you across the *cubiertas*, the granite steps of the cathedral roofs. Pilgrims made the same 100-foot climb in medieval times to burn their travel-worn clothes below the Cruz dos Farrapos (Cross of Rags). ⊠ *Pazo de Xelmírez, Praza do Obradoiro* ☎ *981/552985* ⊕ *www.catedraldesantiago.es* ⊡ *€10* ⊙ *Tues.–Sun. 10–2 and 4–8.*

**Centro Galego de Arte Contemporánea** (*Galician Center for Contemporary Art*). On the north side of town, off the Porta do Camino, the CGAC is a stark but elegant modern building that contrasts with the ancient feel of most other places in Santiago. Portuguese designer Álvaro Siza built the museum of smooth, angled granite, which mirrors the medieval convent of San Domingos de Bonaval next door. Inside, a gleaming lobby of white Italian marble gives way to white-walled, high-ceiling exhibition halls flooded with light from massive windows and skylights. The museum has a good permanent collection and even better changing exhibits. ⊠ *Rúa de Valle Inclán s/n* ☎ *981/546619* ⊕ *www.cgac.org* ⊡ *Free* ⊙ *Tues.–Sun. 11–8.*

**Hostal dos Reis Católicos** (*Hostel of the Catholic Monarchs*). The Hostal dos Reis Católicos, facing the cathedral from the left, was built in 1499 by Ferdinand and Isabella to house the pilgrims who slept on Santiago's streets every night. Having lodged and revived travelers for over 500 years, it's the oldest refuge in the world; it was converted from a hospital to a parador in 1954. The facade bears a Castilian coat of arms along with Adam, Eve, and various saints; inside, the four arcaded patios have gargoyle rainspouts said to be caricatures of 16th-century townsfolk. Behind the lobby is the building's focal point, a Renaissance chapel in the shape of a cross. ⊠ *Praza do Obradoiro 1* ☎ *981/582200* ⊕ *www.parador.es* ⊡ *€3* ⊙ *Daily noon–2 and 4–6.*

**Museo das Peregrinacións** (*Pilgrimage Museum*). North of Acibechería (follow Ruela de Xerusalén) is the Museo das Peregrinacións, with Camino de Santiago iconography from sculptures and carvings to *azabache* (compact black coal, or jet) items. For an overview of the history of St. James, the cathedral, and the pilgrimage, as well as the Camino's role in the development of the city itself, this is a key visit. ⊠ *Rúa de San Miguel 4* ☎ *981/581558* ⊕ *www.mdperegrinacions.com* ⊡ *€2.40* ⊙ *Tues.–Fri. 10–8, Sat. 10:30–1:30 and 5–8, Sun. 10:30–1:30.*

**Museo do Pobo Galego** (*Galician Folk Museum*). Next door to the CGAC stands the Museo do Pobo Galego, in the medieval convent of San Domingos de Bonaval. Photos, farm implements, traditional costumes, and other items illustrate aspects of traditional Galician life. The star attraction is the 13th-century self-supporting spiral granite staircase that still connects three floors. ⊠ *C. San Domingos de Bonaval s/n* ☎ *981/583620* ⊕ *www.museodopobo.es* ⊡ *€3* ⊙ *Tues.–Sat. 10–2 and 4–8, Sun. 11–2.*

**Pazo de Xelmírez** (*Palace of Archbishop Xelmírez*). Step into the rich 12th-century Pazo de Xelmírez, an unusual example of Romanesque civic architecture with a cool, clean, vaulted dining hall. The little figures carved on the corbels in this graceful, 100-foot-long space are drinking, eating, and listening to music with great medieval gusto. Each is different, so stroll around for a tableau of mealtime merriment. ⊠ *Praza do Obradoiro* ☎ *981/569327* ⊕ *www.catedraldesantiago.es* 🎫 *Combined ticket for Pazo and cathedral €5* ⊘ *June–Sept., Mon.– Sat. 10–2 and 4–8, Sun. 10–2; Oct.–May, Mon.–Sat. 10–1:30 and 4–8, Sun. 10–1:30.*

## SHOPPING

Souvenirs of Galicia include authentic *zuecos* (hand-painted wooden clogs) still worn in some villages to navigate mud, jewelry and trinkets carved from azabache (jet, or compact black coal), ceramics, and excellent leatherwear of all kinds. Santiago has an excellent selection of religious items in all price ranges.

**Sargadelos.** Galicia is known throughout Spain for its distinctive blue-and-white ceramics with bold modern designs, made in Sargadelos and O Castro. There is a wide selection at Sargadelos. ⊠ *Rúa Nova 16* ☎ *981/581905.*

## WHERE TO EAT

**$$**
SPANISH
✕ **A Barrola.** With polished wooden floors and a lively terrace, this seafood-heavy restaurant is a favorite with the university faculty. The *caldo gallego, santiaguiños* (slipper lobsters), *arroz con bogavante* (rice with lobster), and seafood empanadas are superb, and local delicacies like *angulas* (elvers) and lamprey are served seasonally. If options overwhelm you and you can't decide, you might opt for the *parrillada de pescados* (mixed seafood grill). A Barrola is one of a chain of three restaurants in the area; Casa Elisa and Xantares are both equally popular and within a stone's throw, on Rúa do Franco. $ *Average main: €20* ⊠ *Rúa do Franco 29* ☎ *981/577999* ⊕ *www.restaurantesgrupobarrola. com* ⊘ *Closed Dec.–Apr.; closed Mon. May–Nov.*

**$$**
SEAFOOD
✕ **Carretas.** This casual spot for fresh Galician seafood is around the corner from the Hostal dos Reis Católicos. Fish dishes abound, but the specialty here is shellfish. Start with a plate of melt-in-your-mouth battered mini-scallops, then, for the full experience, order the labor-intensive *variado de mariscos,* a comprehensive platter of langostinos, king prawns, crab, and "goose" barnacles, a white or gray crustacean found in deep waters. *Salpicón de mariscos* presents the same creatures shelled. For dessert, there's the tastier-than-it-sounds fried milk pudding. $ *Average main: €20* ⊠ *Rúa das Carretas 21* ☎ *981/563111* ⊕ *www.restaurantesanclemente.com* ⊘ *Closed Sun. and Mon.*

# VILLEFRANCHE-SUR-MER, FRANCE

Updated by Jennifer Ladonne

Nestled discreetly along the deep scoop of harbor between Nice and Cap Ferrat, this pretty watercolor of a fishing port is a stage set of brightly colored houses—the sort of place where Pagnol's *Fanny* could have been filmed. Genuine fishermen actually skim up to the docks here in weathered blue *barques,* and the streets of the Vieille Ville flow

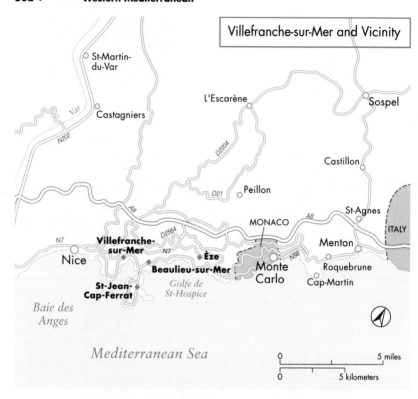

Villefranche-sur-Mer and Vicinity

directly to the waterfront, much as they did in the 13th century. The deep harbor, in the caldera of a volcano, was once preferred by the likes of Onassis and Niarchos and royals on their yachts. The character of Villefranche was subtly shaped by the artists and authors who gathered at the Hôtel Welcome, and above all, Jean Cocteau, who came here to recover from the excesses of Paris life. Villefranche is also the gateway to other treasures along this most select part of the Riviera.

## ESSENTIALS

### CURRENCY
The euro.

### HOURS
Stores open Monday–Saturday 9–7, but many close at lunchtime (usually noon to 2 or 3) and some will open later and on Sunday during July and August. Museums open 10–5, but most are closed on either Monday or Tuesday.

### TELEPHONES
Tri-band GSM phones work in France. You can buy prepaid phone cards at telecom shops, news vendors, and tobacconists in all towns and cities. Phone cards can be used for local or international calls. Orange, SFR, Bouygues Telecom, and Virgin are leading telecom companies. If you have an unlocked GSM phone, LeFrenchMobile (⊕ *www.*

lefrenchmobile.com) offers SIM cards (and micro SIM cards) with support in English, unlimited validity of credits, and prepurchase online.

## COMING ASHORE

Cruise ships dock offshore in the bay of Villefranche-sur-Mer and passengers are tendered to the quayside in the heart of the town. The terminal is small, but has an information center, restrooms, and car-rental kiosks. You can tour Villefranche-sur-Mer itself on foot from here, but to visit surrounding attractions you'll need transport. The train station is a five-minute walk from the cruise port and the service along the coast to Beaulieu and Èze-sur-Mer is frequent (at least two trains per hour), fast (less than 10 minutes travel time), and reliable. Tickets cost around €2 for the short hop between Villefranche-sur-Mer and Beaulieu-sur-Mer. From the train station at Èze-sur-Mer there are frequent shuttle buses to Èze village (15 minutes, Route 83). By train both Nice and Monte Carlo are also within 15-minutes journey time. Frequent bus services by Ligne d'Azur (⊕ *www.lignedazur.com*) link Villefranche-sur-Mer with Beaulieu-sur-Mer, Cap Ferrat, Èze, Nice, and Monte Carlo. One ride is €1.10, and a day pass is €4. Route 81 links Villefranche-sur-Mer with Beaulieu-sur-Mer and St-Jean-Cap-Ferrat (also with Nice). Line 100 links Villefranche-sur-Mer with Nice and Èze-sur-Mer (and on to Monte Carlo).

The cost of car rental is approximately €75 for an economy manual vehicle. However, there are no car-rental options in town so vehicles have to be prebooked and there are fees for delivery and return.

Taxis are plentiful, and can provide tourist itineraries. For a single journey, fares are €3 for pick-up followed by a day fare of €0.90 per km (½-mile) plus a fee for any waiting time. Taxis can be prebooked for return journeys, making them a good option for transfer to local attractions.

## EXPLORING VILLEFRANCHE-SUR-MER AND VICINITY

### VILLEFRANCHE-SUR-MER

**Chapelle St-Pierre.** So enamored was Jean Cocteau of this painterly fishing port that he decorated the 14th-century Chapelle St-Pierre with images from the life of St. Peter and dedicated it to the village's fishermen. ⊠ *Pl. Pollanai Quai Courbet* ☎ *04–93–76–90–70* ⊠ *€2.50* ⊗ *May–mid-Sept., Tues–Sun. 10–noon and 3–7; mid-Sept.–mid-Nov. and mid-Dec.–Apr., Tues.–Sun. 10–noon and 2–6.*

**Citadelle St-Elme.** Open year round, the stalwart 16th-century Citadelle St-Elme, restored to perfect condition, anchors the harbor with its broad, sloping stone walls. Beyond its drawbridge lie the city's administrative offices and a group of minor gallery-museums, with a scattering of works by Picasso and Miró. Whether or not you stop into these private collections of local art (all free of charge), you're welcome to stroll around the inner grounds and to circle the imposing exterior. ⊠ *Harbor* ☒ *Free* ⊗ *Museums: June–Sept., Tues.–Sat. 10–noon and 3–6:30, Sun. 3–6:30; Oct–May, Tues.–Sat. 10–noon and 2–5:30, Sun 2–5:30.*

**Rue Obscure.** Running parallel to the waterfront, the extraordinary 13th-century Rue Obscure (literally, "Dark Street") is entirely covered by vaulted arcades; it sheltered the people of Villefranche when the Germans fired their parting shots—an artillery bombardment—near the end of World War II.

## BEAULIEU-SUR-MER
*4 km (2½ miles) east of Villefranche.*

With its back pressed hard against the cliffs of the corniche and sheltered between the peninsulas of Cap Ferrat and Cap Roux, this once-grand resort basks in a tropical microclimate that earned its central neighborhood the name *Petite Afrique* (little Africa). The town was the pet of 19th-century society, and its grand hotels welcomed Empress Eugénie, the Prince of Wales, and Russian nobility. Today it's still a posh address.

Fodor's Choice   **Villa Kerylos.** One manifestation of Beaulieu's Belle Époque excess is
★   the eye-knocking Villa Kerylos, a mansion built in 1902 in the style of classical Greece (to be exact, of the villas that existed on the island of Delos in the 2nd century BC). It was the dream house of the amateur archaeologist Théodore Reinach, who hailed from a wealthy family from Frankfurt, helped the French in their excavations at Delphi, and became an authority on ancient Greek music. He commissioned an Italian architect from Nice, Emmanuel Pontremoli, to surround him with Grecian delights: cool Carrara marble, rare fruitwoods, and a dining salon where guests reclined to eat *à la grecque*. Don't miss this—it's one of the most unusual houses in the south of France. ⊠ *Rue Gustave-Eiffel* ☎ *04–93–01–01–44* ⊕ *www.villa-kerylos.com* ⊠ *€9; €17 for both villas* ⊙ *Mid-Feb–June and Sept.–Oct., daily 10–6; July and Aug., daily 10–7; Nov.–Feb., weekdays 2–6, weekends 10–6.*

## ST-JEAN-CAP-FERRAT
*2 km (1 mile) south of Beaulieu on D25.*

This luxuriously sited pleasure port moors the peninsula of Cap Ferrat; from its port-side walkways and crescent of beach you can look over the sparkling blue harbor to the graceful green bulk of the corniches. Yachts purr in and out of port, and their passengers scuttle into cafés for take-out drinks to enjoy on their private decks. Unfortunately, Cap Ferrat is a vast peninsula and hides its secrets—except for the Villa Ephrussi, most fabled estates are hidden behind iron gates and towering hedges—particularly well.

★   **Villa Ephrussi de Rothschild.** Between the port and the mainland, the floridly beautiful Villa Ephrussi de Rothschild stands as witness to the wealth and worldly flair of the baroness who had it built. Constructed in 1905 in neo-Venetian style (its flamingo-pink facade was thought not to be in the best of taste by the local gentry), the house was baptized "Ile-de-France" in homage to the Baroness Bétrice de Rothschild's favorite ocean liner (her staff used to wear sailing costumes and her ship travel kit is on view in her bedroom). Precious artworks, tapestries, and furniture adorn the salons—in typical Rothschildian fashion, each room is given over to a different 18th-century "époque." Upstairs are the private apartments of Madame la Baronne, which can only be seen on a guided tour offered around noon. The grounds are landscaped with no fewer than seven theme gardens and topped off with a Temple of Diana; be sure to allow yourself time to wander here, as this is one of the few places on the coast where you'll be allowed to experience the lavish pleasures characteristic of the Belle Époque Côte d'Azur. Tea and light lunches are served in a glassed-in porch overlooking the grounds and spectacular views of the coastline. A combination ticket allows you to also visit Villa Kerylos in nearby Beaulieu in the same week. ⊠ *Av. Ephrussi, St-Jean-Cap-Ferrat* ☎ *04–93–01–33–09* ⊕ *www.villa-ephrussi.com* 💳 *€12; €17 for both villas* ☽ *Mar.–June and Sept.–Oct., daily 10–6; July and Aug., daily 10–7; Nov.–Feb., weekdays 2–6, weekends 10–6.*

### ÈZE

*2 km (1 mile) east of Beaulieu.*

**Fodor'sChoice**
★ Towering like an eagle's nest above the coast and crowned with ram-
parts and the ruins of a medieval château, preposterously beautiful Èze (pronounced *ehz*) is the most accessible of all the perched villages—this means crowds, many of whom head here to shop in the boutique-lined staircase-streets. (Happily, most shops here are quite stylish, and there is a nice preponderance of bric-a-brac and vintage fabric dealers.) But most come here to drink in the views, for no one can deny that this is the most spectacularly sited of all coastal promontories; if you can manage to shake the crowds and duck off to a quiet overlook, the village commands splendid views up and down the coast, one of the draws that once lured fabled visitors—lots of crowned heads, Georges Sand, Friedrich Nietzsche—and residents: Consuelo Vanderbilt, when she was tired of being duchess of Marlborough, traded in Blenheim Palace for a custom-built house here.

**Jardin Exotique** (*Tropical Garden*). From the crest-top Jardin Exotique, full of rare succulents, you can pan your videocam all the way around the hills and waterfront. But if you want a prayer of a chance at enjoying the magnificence of Eze's arched passages, stone alleyways, and ancient fountains, come at dawn or after sunset—or (if you have the means) stay the night—but spend the midday elsewhere. The church of **Notre-Dame,** consecrated in 1772, glitters inside with baroque altarpieces. Èze's tourist office, on Place du Général-de-Gaulle, can direct you to the numerous footpaths—the most famous being the **Sentier Friedrich Nietzsche**—that thread Èze with the coast's three corniche highways. ⊠ *Moyenne Corniche* 💳 *€6* ☽ *Nov.–Jan., daily 9–4:30; Feb. and Mar., daily 9–5; Apr. and May, daily 9–6; June and Sept., daily 9–7; July and Aug., daily 9–7:30; Oct., daily 9–5:30.*

---

## VILLEFRANCHE-SUR-MER BEST BETS

**Èze.** One of the most charming of France's *villages perchés,* or perched villages, is built high on a rocky parapet. Views down the Riviera coast are spectacular.

**Villa Kerylos.** The splendors of ancient Greek art and architecture are beautifully re-created here in the south of France at the home of a wealthy amateur archaeologist.

**Villa Ephrussi de Rothschild.** This magnificent century-old mansion surrounded by glorious gardens is stuffed with the finest furniture and decoration its baroness owner could afford.

4

## SHOPPING

This part of the Riviera coastline has some of the most expensive addresses, and thus some of the finest shopping, with excusive boutiques selling very high-class fashion and decorative goods. In the shops of Cap Ferrat and Beaulieu you'll shop among France's more mature lunching ladies, while Villefranche-sur-Mer has a good selection of characterful boutiques with more down-to-earth prices. The streets of Èze are replete with artists' studios selling excellent art and ceramics, plus cute collectibles. In every town you'll find local Provençal specialties such as excellent olive oil, soaps, dried herbs, colorful fabrics, pottery, and basketwork.

## WHERE TO EAT

**$$$** ✕ **La Grignotière.** Tucked down a narrow side street just a few steps away
FRENCH  from the marketplace, this small and friendly local restaurant offers up generous portions of top-quality, inexpensive dishes. The homemade lasagne is excellent, as is the spaghetti pistou. ⑤ *Average main: €25* ✉ *3 rue du Poilu* ☎ *04–93–76–79–83* ☽ *Closed Wed.*

**$$$** ✕ **Troubadour.** Amid the clutter and clatter of the nearby coast, this is
FRENCH  a wonderful find (and has been for more than 30 years!): comfortably relaxed, this old family house proffers pleasant service and excellent dishes like roasted scallops with chicken broth and squab with citrus zest and beef broth. ⑤ *Average main: €30* ✉ *4 rue du Brec* ☎ *04–93–41–19–03* ☽ *Closed Sun. and Mon., mid-Nov.–mid-Dec., and 1st wk of Mar. and July.*

# Eastern Mediterranean and Aegean

5

PORTS IN CROATIA, CYPRUS, EGYPT, GREECE, ISRAEL, MONTENEGRO, AND TURKEY

Dubrovnik, Croatia

**WORD OF MOUTH**

"Ephesus is probably one of the most incredible sights you will ever see. Even better than Pompeii, IMHO! You will enjoy it more if you're not in a group of 50 or 100. If you stop in Istanbul, you're in for a treat. . . . There is no place like Istanbul."

—zwho

Eastern Mediterranean cruises are especially good for travelers who want to see the archaeological ruins of Europe's two great classical civilizations, Rome and Greece. These ports are rich in history, and some are even rich in natural beauty. There are few ports of call more breathtaking than Santorini or the island of Hvar.

Many Eastern Mediterranean itineraries begin in Piraeus, the seaport of Athens, or Istanbul, and visit ports in Greece and Turkey. Some may cross the Mediterranean to call in Alexandria or Port Said (for an exhausting, daylong visit to Cairo). Other cruises begin in Italy, often in Rome or Venice. These cruises may take in ports in Sicily and southern Italy (if they leave from Rome) or even Malta before heading toward Greece. Cruises beginning in Venice may call at one or more ports along Croatia's breathtaking Adriatic coast, and these port calls are highlights of any voyage.

## ABOUT THE RESTAURANTS

All the restaurants we recommend serve lunch; they may also serve dinner if your cruise ship stays late in port and you choose to dine off the ship. Cuisine in Europe is varied, but Europeans tend to eat a leisurely meal at lunch, but in most ports there are quicker and simpler alternatives for those who just want to grab a quick bite before returning to the ship. Note that several Eastern Mediterranean countries do not use the euro, including Croatia, Cyprus, Egypt, and Turkey. Price categories in those countries are based on the euro-equivalent costs of eating in restaurants. All price categories are based on the average cost of a main course at dinner, so in some cases lunch may be cheaper.

# ALEXANDRIA, EGYPT

Ancient Egypt's gateway to the Mediterranean was founded by Alexander the Great in 331 BC, but its name is inextricably linked with Cleopatra. She inhabited vast palaces and worshipped at monumental temples. The city's great library was also under her control, and her city was protected by one of the Seven Wonders of the Ancient World, the great Pharos of Alexandria, a lighthouse. Sadly, all of these great treasures are lost or buried underneath the modernity. That doesn't mean Alexandria is bereft of history; in a second incarnation it became a decadent, early-20th-century mercantile and colonial enclave with a multicultural mix. It seduced novelist E.M. Forster during World War I and gave birth to Lawrence Durrell's *Alexandria Quartet,* which captivated a generation of American readers in the late 1950s. At the same time, its reputation as an Arabic seat of learning has stayed in the ascendant. With lively streets and graceful cafés, Alexandria is still a great city and remains an utterly charming place to visit.

## ESSENTIALS

### CURRENCY

The Egyptian pound.

### HOURS

Museums are usually open from 9 to 5. Many museums are closed on Monday. Shops open from 8 until 7. During Ramadan (the Muslim month of fasting) opening times vary; during this period shops close during the day but stay open late into the evening.

### TELEPHONES

GSM phones work in Egypt, where mobile systems are single-band and are not 3G-compatible. Telecom Egypt runs the fixed line system. Public phones accept calling cards available from retail outlets; however, connections are not always smooth. Major companies are MobiNil and Vodafone.

### COMING ASHORE

Alexandria's cruise terminal is in the commercial port in the western harbor, and ships dock right alongside busy commercial ships; it's a frenetic environment. The terminal has shopping facilities and a taxi stand.

From the port, it is an easy 20-minute walk along the corniche to the heart of town, but navigating your way to the various attractions can be a challenge, and taxis are the best way to get around. They are inexpensive, and you can flag them down almost anywhere. The driver might try to pick up another passenger en route—it's standard practice, so don't be surprised. Drivers don't use their meters, so you have to guess at the appropriate fare or try to negotiate one in advance. A ride from the cruise port to downtown should be around £E10–£E15. If you look wealthy, expect to pay a bit more.

Though they're picturesque and cheap, trams are likely to take four to five times longer to get where you're going than a taxi would. The main tram station is Raml, near Maydan Sa'd Zaghlul. Buy tickets on board. Horse-drawn *caleches* (carriages) offer an alternative way to tour the town, but agree on a price before you get aboard.

**Contacts Avis** ⊠ *Cecil Hotel, Maydan Sa'd Zaghlul, Raml Station* ☎ *03/485–7400* ⊕ *www.avis.com.*

# EXPLORING ALEXANDRIA

**Abu al-Abbas al-Mursi Mosque.** This attractive mosque was built during World War II over the tomb of a 13th-century holy man, who is the patron saint of the city's fishermen. The area surrounding it has been turned into Egypt's largest and most bizarre religious/retail complex, with a cluster of mosques sharing a terrace that hides an underground shopping center. Intruding on the space is a horrific modernism-on-the-cheap office building (with yet more shops) that is as pointed and angular as the mosques are smooth and curved. If you are dressed modestly and the mosque is open, you should be able to get inside. If so, remove your shoes and refrain from taking photos. ⊠ *Corniche, al-Anfushi, El Anfushi.*

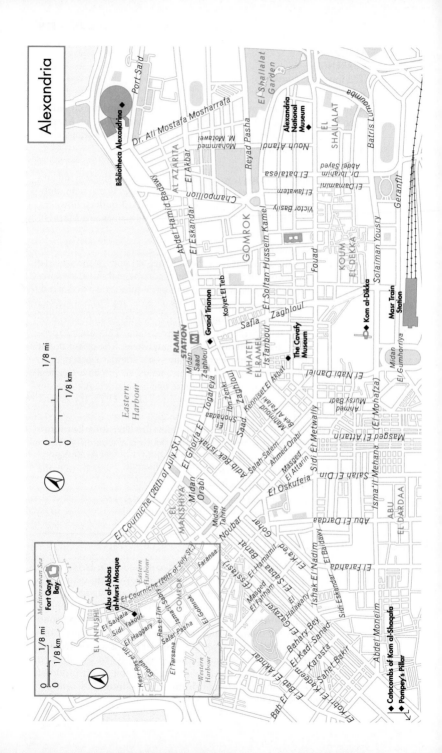

**Alexandria National Museum.** A small but high-quality collection of artifacts includes items found under the waters of the Western Harbor during recent marine archaeological projects. The display galleries cover every era of the city's long history and include Christian pieces, Islamic arts and crafts, and more recent information about Alexandria's colonial era. The early-20th-century Italianate palace that houses the museum, designed by a French architect, is a prime example of this colonial past. ⊠ *110 Shar'a el Horreya, El Shallalat* ☎ *03/483–5519* ⊠ *E30* ☉ *Daily 9–4.*

**Bibliotheca Alexandrina.** This monumental, $190 million, UNESCO-sponsored project began with an instinctively appealing idea: to resurrect the Great Library of ancient

> ### ALEXANDRIA BEST BETS
>
> **Explore the Alexandria National Museum.** A collection of artifacts found under the shallow waters of Alexandria Bay plus galleries explaining the city's different eras help to clarify Egypt's history.
>
> **Fort in Quayt Bay.** The site of Alexandria's famous ancient *Pharos*, or lighthouse, the fort protected Alexandria harbor throughout the Crusader and colonial eras.
>
> **Catacombs of Kom al-Shoqafa.** These Roman catacombs are the most completely excavated ancient site in the city.

Alexandria, once one of the world's major centers of learning. Its location near the Silsileh Peninsula on the edge of the Eastern Harbor has tremendous symbolic resonance, having been the royal quarters in ancient times and one of several possible locations of the original library. The modernist Norwegian-designed building is in the form of an enormous multitiered cylinder tilted to face the sea, with a roof of diamond-shaped windows that allow controlled light into the seven cascading interior floors. The most impressive feature, however, is the curving exterior wall covered in rough-hewn granite blocks from Aswan that have been engraved with letters from ancient languages.

Once you've enjoyed the view of the vast interior from the mezzanine gallery, there's little to hold you in the main hall, but the library has several small museums and exhibitions that are of more interest. The **Manuscripts Museum** has a large collection of rare documents, parchments, and early printed books. The **Impressions of Alexandria** exhibition features paintings and sketches of the city dating from the 15th to the 19th centuries and photographs taken in the late 19th and early 20th centuries. The **Antiquities Museum** on the basement level has a collection of finds from Pharaonic, Roman, and Islamic Alexandria. Examples of monumental Roman statuary include *Huge Forearm Holding a Ball* (nothing else remains of the immense piece), and a finely chiseled bust of the Emperor Octavian (Augustus). Egypto-Roman artifacts include the mummy of Anhk Hor, governor of Upper Egypt, and several 2nd-century funerary masks showing the prevalent cross-styling between the classical Egyptian and Roman Egyptian styles. A planetarium and IMAX theater are the latest additions to the complex. ⊠ *63 Shar'a Soter, Chatby* ☎ *03/483–9999* ⊕ *www.bibalex. org* ⊠ *Library E10, Antiquities Museum E20, Manuscripts Museum E20 Planetarium and IMAX shows E25* ☉ *Sat.–Thurs. 11–7, Fri. 3–7.*

★ **Catacombs of Kom al-Shoqafa.** This is the most impressive of Alexandria's ancient remains, dating from the 2nd century AD. Excavation started in 1892, and the catacombs were discovered accidentally eight years later when a donkey fell through a chamber ceiling. A long spiral staircase leads to the main hall. The stairs run down the outside of a shaft, which excavators used to transport the bodies of the dead. The staircase leads to the rotunda, which, like all but the lowest chamber, is undecorated but striking for the sheer scale of the underground space, supported by giant columns carved out of the bedrock.

A few rooms branch off from the rotunda: the Triclinium was a banquet hall where relatives and friends toasted the deceased, and the Caracalla Hall has four lightly painted tombs and a case of bones. The next level down contains a labyrinth of smaller nooks for storing bodies and leads to the lowest excavated room, which is framed by columns and sculpted snakes. Casts of two statues stand here—the originals are in the Greco-Roman Museum—and three tombs are of interest for their mix of pharaonic and Greek imagery. ⊠ *Shar' El Shenity Abu Mandour, Karmouz* ☎ *03/482–5800* ⌨ *E35* ☉ *Daily 9–4:30.*

**The Cavafy Museum.** The writer Constantine Cavafy was ignored during his lifetime but has received international recognition since his death in 1933. His poetry, which focused on such themes as one's moral dilemmas and uncertainty about the future, spoke to the Greek-speaking community around the Eastern Mediterranean and has been translated into all major languages. The small flat where Cavafy spent the last years of his life has been turned into a museum. Half of it is given over to a re-creation of his home. The other half of the museum houses newspaper clippings about the poet's life and a library of his works. ⊠ *4 Shar'a CP Cavafy(formerly Shar'a Sharm El-Sheikh), Mahatet El Raml* ☎ *03/468–1598* ⌨ *E20* ☉ *Tues.–Sun. 10–3.*

**Fort Qayt Bay.** This sandstone fort lies on the very tip of the Corniche, dominating the view of the Eastern Harbor. It was built on the site of Alexandria's Pharos lighthouse, one of the seven wonders of the ancient world and incorporates its remains—much of which are still visible—into the foundation. A Greek named Sostratus in the 3rd century BC constructed the lighthouse under the Ptolemies. Standing about 400 feet high and capable of projecting a light that could be seen 53 km (35 miles) out to sea, it was one of the most awesome structures created by ancients. The base of the four-tiered Pharos was thought to have contained some 300 rooms, as well as a hydraulic system for lifting fuel to the top of the tower.

In the centuries that followed, the Pharos was damaged and rebuilt several times, until it was finally destroyed in the great earthquake of 1307. It lay in ruins for two centuries until the Mamluk Sultan Qayt Bay had the current fortress constructed in 1479. Recently, a French team found what are thought to be parts of the Pharos in shallow waters just offshore, rekindling local interest in the ancient monument—there is even talk of an underwater museum, although that is unlikely to materialize anytime soon. ⊠ *Corniche (far western end), El Anfushi* ☎ *03/480–9144* ⌨ *E25* ☉ *Daily 9–5:30.*

**Kom al-Dikka** (*Roman Theater*). The focal point of this excavated section of the ancient city is a well-preserved amphitheater—the only one of its kind in Egypt—originally constructed in the 4th century AD, then rebuilt in the 6th century, following an earthquake. At that time a large dome was added (only its supporting columns still stand), and the theater went from being a cultural venue to a forum for public meetings of the City Council—a change deduced from ancient graffiti promoting various political parties. The other half of the site is the ancient baths and living quarters, although much of this area is, in fact, best seen through the fence from the side near Pastroudis Café, where the cisterns and walls are clearly visible. The red bricks mark the location of the heated baths—warmed by an elaborate underground system—which complemented the adjacent cold and steam baths. The whole area fell into disuse after the 7th-century Persian conquest of Egypt. One noteworthy site in the residential section is a Roman house known as the **Villa of the Birds**, so named for its colorful floor mosaics depicting birds in several forms. The colorful and detailed craftsmanship shows a high level of sophistication. The mosaics, now restored, are protected by a modern structure. ⊠ *Off Maydan El Shohada, opposite the Misr train station, Kon al-Dikka* ☎ *03/490–2904* ✉ *E20, E15 for Villa of the Birds* ☉ *Daily 9–4:30.*

**Pompey's Pillar** (*Serapium Oracle*). Despite being Alexandria's most famous tourist sight, Pompey's Pillar is a disappointment. After all, it's just a granite pillar—albeit at 88 feet, a very tall one—placed on a hill surrounded by ruins. Known in Arabic as *al-'Amud al-Sawiri* (Column of the Horseman), the pillar was misnamed after Pompeius (106–48 BC) by the Crusaders. In fact, it dates to the 3rd century AD, when it was erected in honor of the emperor Diocletian on the site of a Ptolemaic temple to Serapis. The late-model sphinxes lying around on pedestals add a little character. The most interesting element, ironically, is that from the hill you can get a glimpse inside the walled cemetery next door, as well as a view of a long and busy market street. ⊠ *Corner of Amoud El Sawary and El Shenity Abou Mandour, Karmouz* ☎ *03/482–5800* ✉ *E20* ☉ *Daily 9–4.*

## SHOPPING

Egyptians are shrewd businessmen and retailers, and Alexandria has long been a trading city. You'll find an amazing array of crafts, but quality varies from first-class to dreadful, so do check items carefully.

Egyptians specialize in worked brass and copper articles, wood inlay on jewelry boxes and chess sets, and leather. The hookah or hubble-bubble pipe is also an interesting remembrance of the country. Egyptian cotton is a byword for quality, and the shops of Alexandria are the place to buy items like bedding and towels. The long flowing *jellabas* worn by the men are cool and comfortable, and there's a never-ending supply of cut-price T-shirts.

If you want to purchase genuine antiques and antiquities, you'll need to have a certificate of approval from the Egyptian authorities to export your purchase, but copies are on sale everywhere. These items needn't be expensive: you can buy a lucky alabaster scarab beetle for a few Egyptian pounds (it's almost a compulsory souvenir of your trip to Egypt).

Whatever you buy, you'll need to haggle. In Egypt very few items have a set price. Some visitors find this stressful, but try to remember that bartering isn't meant to be a argument; it's a discussion to reach a mutually suitable price. Start at around 40% of the first asking price and rise little by little, but walk away if the offer price seems too high. Once you've agreed on a price, it's very bad form to walk away from a transaction.

For cottons, visit the shops on the streets radiating from Sa'd Zaghlul Square. The new cruise terminal promises upmarket shopping opportunities just a short distance from the ship.

**Attarine Market.** This area acquired its reputation in the 1960s as the place where the high-quality antiques sold by fleeing foreigners resurfaced. Those days are long gone. There are now only a few true antiques stores left in the area, but it's fascinating nonetheless to see the tiny workshops where the reproduction French-style furniture so popular in Egypt originates. Almost all the workshops will be happy to sell direct if you find a piece that appeals to you, but consider the challenge of shipping it back home before you give in to temptation. The market actually consists of a series of alleyways, the sum of which feels less established—and far less touristy—than Cairo's Khan al-Khalili. ✛ *To find the market, walk one block west of the Attarine Mosque and cross Shar'a al-Horreya to the alley between the café and the parts store, El Attarine.*

## WHERE TO EAT

★ **Grand Trianon.** One of Alexandria's most stylish institutions since it opened in the 1920s, the Grand Trianon remains a forum for courtship, gossip, and rediscovery. Its most popular area is the café, which has a certain old-world grandeur, despite being the least decorated part of the place. The adjacent restaurant is an extravagant art nouveau jewel, with colorful murals on the wall and a spectacular stained-glass window over the entrance to the kitchen. But the pièce de résistance is in the patisserie around the corner. There, behind elaborately carved wooden cabinets, a series of Venetian wood-panel paintings of sensual water nymphs will take your breath away. The colors are muted, but as your eyes adjust the images will start to shimmer like a Gustav Klimt kiss. The café and restaurant close at midnight, the patisserie at 8 pm. ✉ *Maydan Sa'd Zaghlul, Mahatet El Raml* ☎ *03/486–8539.*

# ASHDOD, ISRAEL

Updated by Jessica Steinberg

Busy Ashdod is not only one of Israel's fastest-growing cities, it's also the country's largest port. Perched on the Mediterranean, it processes more than 60% of the goods imported into Israel. Home to many ancient peoples over the centuries, Ashdod today is a modern, planned city. It's also a convenient jumping-off point for exploring several of Israel's most interesting cities, including Jerusalem, Tel Aviv, and Bethlehem.

## ESSENTIALS

### CURRENCY
The shekel.

### HOURS
Shops are generally open Sunday through Thursday from 9 to 7, though some close in the afternoons. Museums vary in hours, being open Monday through Thursday from around 10 to 6, but most have shorter hours from Friday through Sunday (often open only from 10 to 2 or 3). Some museums close on Fridays.

### PRIVATE TOURS
Several companies can provide private tours for cruise passengers calling Ashdod.

**Contacts Elana Dascal.** ☎ 054/621–6209 ✉ edascal@gmail.com.
**Eshcolot Tours** ☎ 02/566-5555 ✉ advantag@netmedia.net.il. **Ryan Friedland.** ☎ 052/674-7911.
**Philip J. Gordon Lavine.** ☎ 050/812-8842 ✉ philtheguide@gmail.com.

### TELEPHONES
Most multiband mobile phones will work in Israel, and GSM and 3G systems are well established in the urban areas. Major providers are Cellcom Israel, Parner Communication (Orange), and Pelephone.

## COMING ASHORE
Ashdod, 43 miles west of Jerusalem, is Israel's largest port, and is therefore always busy with commercial traffic. The modern passenger terminal has a café, currency-exchange desk, and duty-free shops. Taxi drivers who wait at the terminal building have been security-cleared to work there; reports suggest that they charge a premium above other taxis, about $75. Other taxi drivers may not be allowed access into the port if they have not been approved, so for a cheaper alternative you can try outside the port entrance. Security is tight, so always carry ID and boarding passes.

Route 448 is a direct bus service from Ashdod Central Station to Jerusalem. Buses depart every 30 minutes at peak times, but are less frequent in the middle of the day. The journey takes around 90 minutes, and one-way fare is NIS18. To get to the central station in Ashdod, you'll need to take a taxi from the port if your ship doesn't provide a shuttle bus into town.

Currently it is possible to travel by bus between Jerusalem and Bethlehem, but your journey may be interrupted by security checks, which can be lengthy and may cause havoc with your scheduling. It's probably better to visit Bethlehem on a guided tour if you have limited time.

---

**ASHDOD BEST BETS**

**Dome of the Rock, Jeruslaem.** Holy to both Jews and Muslims, it is here that the lost Jewish Temple constructed by Solomon stood and also the place from where Mohammed was carried up to heaven to receive the wisdom of God.

**Church of the Holy Sepulchre, Jersualem.** The holiest Christian site in Jerusalem is the supposed site of the crucifixion.

**The Dead Sea.** The lowest place on Earth is famous for its salty waters and mud with (supposedly) healing properties.

5

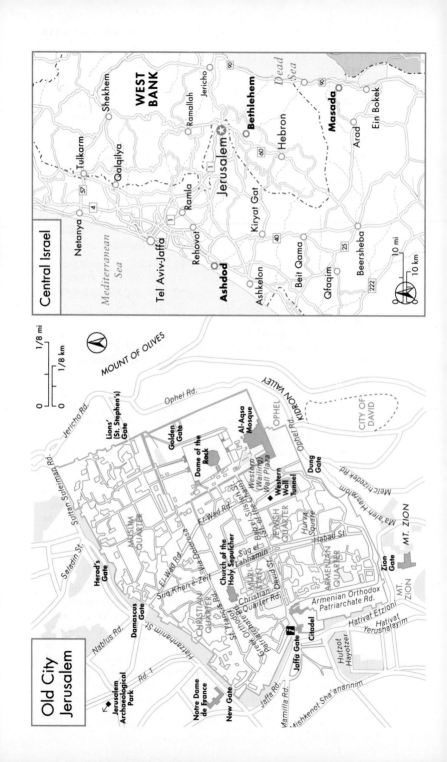

# Old City Jerusalem

| 0 | | 1/8 mi |
| 0 | | 1/8 km |

MOUNT OF OLIVES

Jericho Rd.

Ophel Rd.

Lions' (St. Stephen's) Gate

Golden Gate

Al-Aqsa Mosque

OPHEL

KIDRON VALLEY

Dome of the Rock

Western (Wailing) Wall Plaza

Western Wall Tunnel

Ophel Rd.

CITY OF DAVID

Dung Gate

Ma'aleh Hashalom

Melch Itzedek Rd.

Sultan Suleiman Rd.

MUSLIM QUARTER

El-Wad Rd.

Via Dolorosa

Bab el-Silsileh St.

Bab el-Silsileh St.

JEWISH QUARTER

Hurva Square

Habad St.

Herod's Gate

Saladin St.

Suq Khan e-Zeit

St. Francis Rd.

El-Wad Rd.

Church of the Holy Sepulcher

Suq el-Lahamin

CHRISTIAN QUARTER

MARKET

Christian Quarter Rd.

ARMENIAN QUARTER

Armenian Orthodox Patriarchate Rd.

Zion Gate

MT. ZION

MT. ZION

Damascus Gate

Nablus Rd.

Haitzanamim St.

St. Orthodox

Greek Orthodox Patriarchate Rd.

Quarter David St.

Citadel

Jaffa Gate

Hativat Etzioni

Hativat Yerushalayim

Jerusalem Archaeological Park

Rd. 1

Notre Dame de France

New Gate

Jaffa Rd.

Mamilla Rd.

Hulzot Hayotzer

Mishkenot Sha'ananim

## Central Israel

Mediterranean Sea

WEST BANK

Dead Sea

Netanya

Tel Aviv-Jaffa

Rehovot

Ashdod

Ashkelon

Beit Qama

Qfaqim

Beersheba

Kiryat Gat

Ramla

Tulkarm

Qalqilya

Shekhem

Ramallah

Jericho

Jerusalem

Bethlehem

Hebron

Masada

Arad

Ein Bokek

57

4

1

1

40

25

222

60

1

90

90

10 mi

10 km

There are no car-rental offices at the cruise terminal, so you'll be charged a premium for delivery—or have to take a taxi ride to the rental office. Prices start around $70 for a compact vehicle, but mileage is usually charged on top of that. If you want to combine Jerusalem and Bethlehem with the Dead Sea (doable, albeit as a rather long day of touring), it may be worth engaging a tour company that knows the routes and locations, because this will save you time.

As the security situation in Israel is subject to change, always check whether independent travel is advised before you decide not to book your excursions through your ship, particularly if you wish to visit Bethlehem.

## EXPLORING ISRAEL FROM ASHDOD

### BETHLEHEM

Today the great majority of Bethlehem's residents, as elsewhere in the West Bank, are Muslim. But for Christians the world over, the city is synonymous with the birth of Jesus, and the many shrines that celebrate that event. As well, Bethlehem is the site of the Tomb of Rachel, the only one of the biblical patriarchs and matriarchs not buried in Hebron.

★ **Church of the Nativity.** At this church marking the traditional site of the birth of Jesus, the stone exterior is crowned by the crosses of the three denominations sharing it: the Greek Orthodox, the Latins (Roman Catholic, represented by the Franciscan order), and the Armenian Orthodox. This is the oldest standing church in the country. From the right transept at the front of the church, descend to the **Grotto of the Nativity,** encased in white marble. Long lines can form at the entrance to the grotto, making the suggestion of spending just an hour to see the church an impossibility. Once a cave—precisely the kind of place that might have been used as a barn—the grotto has been reamed, plastered, and decorated beyond recognition. Immediately on the right is a small altar, and on the floor below it is the focal point of the entire site, a 14-point **silver star** with the Latin inscription: *hic de virgine maria jesus christus natus est* ("Here of the Virgin Mary, Jesus Christ was born"). ⊠ *Manger Sq.* ☎ *02/274–1020* 🎟 *Free* 🕙 *Church: Apr.–Sept., daily 6:30 am–7:30 pm; Oct.–Mar., daily 5:30–5:30. Grotto: Apr.–Sept., Mon.–Sat. 9–7:30, Sun. noon–7:30; Oct.–Mar., Mon.–Sat. 9–5:30, Sun. noon–5:30.*

**Church of St. Catherine.** Adjacent to the Church of the Nativity, and accessible by a passage from its Armenian chapel, is Bethlehem's Roman Catholic parish church. From this church, the midnight Catholic Christmas mass is broadcast around the world. Steps descend from within the church to a series of dim grottoes, clearly once used as living quarters. A small wooden door (kept locked) connects the complex with the Grotto of the Nativity. ⊠ *Manger Sq.* ☎ *02/274–2425* 🕙 *Apr.–Sept., daily 6–noon and 2–7; Oct.–Mar., daily 5:30–5:30.*

**Manger Square.** Bethlehem's central plaza and the site of the Church of the Nativity, Manger Square is built over the grotto thought to be the birthplace of Jesus. The end of the square opposite the church is the Mosque of Omar, the city's largest Muslim house of worship. The square occupies the center of Bethlehem's old city. It has a tourist-information office, a few restaurants, and several good souvenir shops.

## CLOSE UP

# Visiting Bethlehem

Although Bethlehem (approximately 70 km [43 miles] from Ashdod) is within the boundaries of the Palestinian Authority, tourists with a foreign passport will have no difficulty visiting; allow 90 minutes for travel. Although security may seem daunting at the heavily fortified border post, you simply show the cover of your passport to be whisked through. Israeli guides are not allowed to take you to the sights, but Israeli tour companies can help arrange for Palestinian guides to meet you at the border. If you're a more independent traveler, you can take one of the Palestinian taxis at the border. If taking a taxi, *sherut* (shared taxi), or bus from East Jerusalem, you must take a local bus or taxi from the Bethlehem side of the terminal to Manger Square. Driving is not recommended. Taxis will offer day-tour services, and this could be a sensible way to link the sites you want to see. Prices run around NIS 200 per hour, but may be inflated by taxi drivers with approval to wait at the cruise pier; you'll have to arrange to have your Israeli taxi driver wait while you visit the sights in Bethlehem and then return you to the pier; be sure to negotiate the price for this waiting time in advance.

**Rachel's Tomb.** This Israeli enclave in a Palestinian area is on the right shortly after passing through the border. The Bible relates that the matriarch Rachel, second and favorite wife of Jacob, died in childbirth on the outskirts of Bethlehem, "and Jacob set up a pillar upon her grave" (Genesis 35:19–20). There is no vestige of Jacob's original pillar, but observant Jews for centuries have hallowed the velvet-draped cenotaph inside the building as the site of Rachel's tomb. Islam as well venerates Rachel. Next to the tomb is a Muslim cemetery, reflecting the Middle Eastern tradition that it is a special privilege to be buried near a great personage. ⊠ *Rte. 60* ⊑ *Free* ☾ *Sun.–Thurs., open 24 hrs.*

**Shepherds' Fields.** As you approach Bethlehem, you'll see the fields of the adjacent town of Beit Sahour, to the east of the city, traditionally identified with the biblical story of Ruth the Moabite, daughter-in-law of Naomi, who "gleaned in the field" (Ruth 2:2) of Boaz, Naomi's kinsman. The same fields are identified by Christian tradition as those where bewildered shepherds "keeping watch over their flock by night" received "tidings of great joy"—word of the birth of Jesus in Bethlehem (Luke 2). Two chapels—the Greek Orthodox Der El Rawat and the Catholic El Ghanem—commemorate the event.

## DEAD SEA

The sudden and startling sight, in this bare landscape, of gleaming, ultramodern hotels surrounded by waving palm trees signals your arrival at the spa-resort area of Ein Bokek, near the southern tip of the Dead Sea. According to the Bible, it was along these shores that the Lord rained fire and brimstone on the people of Sodom and Gomorrah (Genesis 19:24) and turned Lot's wife into a pillar of salt (Genesis 26). Here, at the lowest point on Earth—the bottom of the world: 1,292 feet below sea level—the hot, sulfur-pungent air hangs heavy, and a haze often shimmers over the water. You can float, but you cannot sink, in the warm, salty water.

## MASADA

Fodor'sChoice ★ **Masada.** A symbol of the ancient kingdom of Israel, Masada (Hebrew for "fortress") towers majestically over the western shore of the Dead Sea. Its unusual natural form—a plateau set off on all sides by towering cliffs—attracted Herod the Great, who built an opulent desert palace here. In recognition of its historical significance, this was the first site in Israel to be added to the UNESCO World Heritage List in 2001. To reach the top, most visitors make use of the speedy **cable car.** Starting at 8 am, it runs every half hour, with intermediate runs depending on demand. Maps, a detailed brochure, and a very useful audio guide are available at the top entrance.

The **Northern Palace,** Masada's most impressive structure, is an extraordinary three-tiered structure that seems to hang off the highest and most northerly point of the mountain. The **bathhouse** (upon return from the upper terrace) was a state-of-the-art facility in Herod's time, with its *apodyterium* (changing room), *frigidarium, tepidarium,* and *caldarium* (cold, lukewarm, and hot rooms, respectively). The **synagogue,** one of only four that have been uncovered from the Second Temple period, can be seen in the western casemate. It was likely here, in the community's spiritual center, that the leaders of the revolt against Rome made their fateful decision. In the summer of 2005, the rear genizah was renovated to house a permanent Torah scroll, which is used for bar and bat mitzvah (coming-of-age) ceremonies. Adjoining the lower cable-car station is the **Masada Museum,** with hundreds of artifacts from the site. Especially moving is a set of 12 pottery shards, each bearing a single name. Archeologists believe these might have been lots drawn to decide the order in which the last remaining rebels would die. ⊠ *Off Rte. 3199, Ein Gedi* ☎ *08/658–4207/8* ⊕ *www.parks.org.il* ☞ *Site NIS 27; site and cable car NIS 72* ☉ *Apr.–Sept., Sat.–Thurs. 8–5, Fri. and Jewish holiday eves 8–3; Oct.–Mar., Sat.–Thurs. 8–4, Fri. and Jewish holiday eves 8–2.*

## MOUNT OF OLIVES AND EAST JERUSALEM

The sights in this area are for the most part distinctly Christian. A few are a little off the beaten path, and the best way to explore them is on foot.
**Garden of Gethsemane.** After the Last Supper, the New Testament relates, Jesus and his disciples came to a "place" called Gethsemane. There he agonized and prayed, and there, in the end, he was betrayed and arrested. The **Church of All Nations,** with its brilliantly colorful, landmark mosaic facade, was built in the garden in 1924 on the scanty remains of its Byzantine predecessor. At the altar is the so-called Rock of the Agony, where Jesus is said to have endured his Passion; this is the source of the older name of the church, the **Basilica of the Agony.** ⊠ *Jericho Rd., Kidron Valley, Jerusalem* ☎ *02/626–6444* ☞ *Free* ☉ *Apr.–Sept., daily 8–12 and 2–6; Oct.–Mar., daily 8–12 and 2–5.*

★ **Mt. of Olives Observation Point.** This is the classic panoramic view of the Old City: looking across the Kidron Valley over the gold Dome of the Rock. It's best in the early morning, with the sun at your back, or at sunset on days with some clouds, when the golden glow can compensate for the glare. The Mt. of Olives has been bathed in sanctity for millennia. On the slope beneath you, and off to your left, is the vast **Jewish cemetery**, reputedly the oldest still in use anywhere in the world. Camel and donkey drivers (usually one of each) are always pushing to give you a short ride (not cheap!), and the vendors can be persistent, but a polite "no thank you" is sometimes enough for them to go bother someone else. The frequent police presence has made the locals less aggressive, but still beware of pickpockets here and on the road down to Gethsemane. Fairly good bathrooms are a welcome addition. ✉ *E-Sheikh St., opposite Seven Arches Hotel, Mt. of Olives, Jerusalem.*

## OLD CITY JERUSALEM

Drink in the very essence of Jerusalem as you explore the city's primary religious sites in the Muslim and Christian quarters, and at the Western Wall, and touch the different cultures that share it.

★ **Church of the Holy Sepulcher.** Vast numbers of Christians, especially adherents of the older "mainstream" churches, believe this to be the place where Jesus was crucified by the Romans, was buried, and rose from the dead. On the floor just inside the entrance of the church is the rectangular pink **Stone of Unction**, where, it is said, the body of Jesus was cleansed and prepared for burial. Steep steps take you up to **Golgotha**, or Calvary, meaning "the place of the skull," as the site is described in the New Testament. The tomb itself (**Station XIV**), encased in a pink marble edifice, is in the rotunda to the left of the main entrance of the church, under the great dome that dominates the Christian Quarter. An astonishing peculiarity of the Holy Sepulcher is that it is shared, albeit unequally and uncomfortably, by six Christian denominations (Catholic, Greek Orthodox, Armenian Orthodox, Syrian Orthodox, Egyptian Coptic, and Ethiopian). ✉ *Between Suq Khan e-Zeit and Christian Quarter Rd., Christian Quarter, Jerusalem* ☎ *02/627-3314* 🎫 *Free* ☉ *Apr.–Sept., daily 5 am–9 pm; Oct.–Mar., daily 4 am–7 pm.*

★ **Dome of the Rock and Temple Mount.** The magnificent golden **Dome of the Rock** dominates the vast 35-acre Temple Mount, the area known to Muslims as *Haram esh-Sharif* (the Noble Sanctuary). At its southern end, immediately in front of you as you enter the area from the Western Wall plaza (the only gate for non-Muslims), is the large, black-domed **al-Aqsa Mosque**, the third in holiness for Muslims everywhere. At the center of the plaza stood Herod's splendidly rebuilt Second Temple, the one Jesus knew, renowned as an architectural wonder of its day. The Romans reduced it to smoldering ruins in the summer of AD 70. Jewish tradition identifies the great **rock** at the summit of the hill—now under the gold dome—as the foundation stone of the world, and the place where Abraham bound and almost sacrificed his son Isaac (Genesis 22). Awakened by the archangel Gabriel, Muhammad was taken on the fabulous winged horse el-Burak to the *masjid al-aqsa*, the "farthermost place" (hence the name "al-Aqsa" Mosque). From there he rose to heaven, met God face to face, received the teachings of Islam, and returned to Mecca the same night. Tradition has it that the masjid al-aqsa was none other than Jerusalem, and the great rock the very spot from which the prophet ascended. At the time of this writing, the Muslim shrines were closed to non-Muslims for an indefinite period, leaving the faithful alone to enjoy the wondrous interiors of stained-glass windows, granite columns, green-and-gold mosaics, arabesques, and superb medieval masonry. Security check lines to enter the area are often long; it's best to come early. Note: the Muslim attendants prohibit Bibles in the area. ⊠ *Access between the Western Wall and Dung Gate, Temple Mount, Jerusalem* ☎ *02/622–6250* ☉ *Apr.–Sept., Sun.–Thurs. 7:30 am–11 am and 1:30 pm–2:30 pm; Oct.–Mar., Sun.–Thurs. 7:30 am–10 am and 12:30 pm–1:30 pm, subject to change.*

**Jerusalem Archaeological Park.** Overlooked by many casual visitors, the site still often referred to as the Western and Southern Wall Excavations, or the Ophel, was a historical gold mine for Israeli archaeologists in the 1970s and '80s. Interesting Byzantine and early Arab structures came to light, but by far the most dramatic and monumental finds were from the Herodian period, the late 1st century BC. Exposed to the left of the corner is the white pavement of an impressive main street and commercial area from the Second Temple period. The protrusion left of the corner and high above your head is known as **Robinson's Arch.** Named for a 19th-century American explorer, it is a remnant of a monumental bridge to the Temple Mount which was reached by a staircase from the street where you now stand: look for the ancient steps. ⊠ *Dung Gate, Western Wall, Jerusalem* ☎ *02/627–7550* ⊕ *www.archpark.org.il* 🖃 *NIS 30* ☉ *Sun.–Thurs. 8–5, Fri. and Jewish holiday eves 8–2.*

**Via Dolorosa.** The Way of Suffering—or Way of the Cross, as it's more commonly called in English—is venerated as the route Jesus walked, carrying his cross, from the place of his trial and condemnation by Pontius Pilate to the site of his crucifixion and burial. There are the 14 stations on the Via Dolorosa that mark the route that Jesus took, from trial and condemnation to crucifixion and burial. ⊠ *Muslim and Christian Quarters, Jerusalem.*

★ **Western Wall.** Historically, the Jewish faith has tended to place greater emphasis on the significance of an event than on the place where it may have occurred. Among the exceptions to that rule, the 2,000-year-old Western Wall is in a class of its own. Its status as the most important *existing* Jewish shrine derives from its connection with the ancient Temple, the House of God. It was not itself part of the Temple edifice, but of the massive retaining wall King Herod built to create the vast plaza now known as the Temple Mount. After the destruction of Jerusalem by the Romans in AD 70, and especially after the dedication of a pagan town in its place 65 years later, the city was off-limits to Jews for generations. The memory of the precise location of the Temple—in the vicinity of today's Dome of the Rock—was lost. Even when access was eventually regained, Jews avoided entering the Temple Mount for fear of unwittingly trespassing on the most sacred, and thus forbidden, areas of the ancient sanctuary. With time, the closest remnant of the period took on the aura of the Temple itself, making the Western Wall a kind of holy place by proxy. (Expect a routine check of your bags—smaller is better—by security personnel at the plaza entrance.) ⊠ *Near Dung Gate, Western Wall, Jerusalem* ⊕ *english.thekotel.org* ☉ *Daily 24 hrs.*

**Western Wall Tunnel.** The long tunnel beyond the men's side (north of the plaza) of the Western Wall is not a rediscovered ancient thoroughfare but was deliberately dug in recent years with the purpose of exposing a strip of the Western Wall along its entire length. One course of the massive wall revealed two building stones estimated to weigh an incredible 400 tons and 570 tons, respectively. Local guided tours are available and are recommended—you can visit the site only as part of an organized tour—but the times change from week to week (some include evening hours). The ticket office is under the arches at the northern end of the Western Wall plaza. ⊠ *Western Wall, Jerusalem* 🕾 *02/627–1333* ⊕ *english.thekotel.org* ⌑ *NIS 25* ⊘ *Sun.–Thurs. 7 am–late evening (changing schedules), Fri. and Jewish holiday eves 7–noon. Call ahead for exact times.*

## WEST JERUSALEM

Visitors tend to focus, naturally enough, on the historic and religious sights on the eastern side of town, especially in the Old City; but West Jerusalem houses the nation's institutions, is the repository for its collective memory, and—together with the downtown—gives more insight into contemporary life in Israel's largest city. The world-class Israel Museum and Yad Vashem are located here.

Fodor's Choice **Israel Museum.** In 2010, this eclectic treasure trove and world-class don't-
★ miss museum emerged like a butterfly from a lengthy renewal of its
ⓒ entire main complex. The three main specialties of art, archaeology, and Judaica have been much enhanced by new or rearranged exhibits, fresh ideas, and state-of-the-art presentations. The **Dead Sea Scrolls** are certainly the Israel Museum's most famous—and most important—collection. A Bedouin boy discovered the first of the 2,000-year-old scrolls in 1947 in a Judean Desert cave, overlooking the Dead Sea. All in all, nine main scrolls (one engraved on copper) and bags full of small fragments surfaced over the years: the Israel Museum possesses some of the most important and most complete of these ancient texts. The white dome of the Shrine of the Book, the separate building in which the scrolls are housed, was inspired by the lids of the clay jars in which the first ones were found. ⊠ *Ruppin Rd., Givat Ram, Jerusalem* 🕾 *02/670–8811* ⊕ *www.imj.org.il* ⌑ *NIS 50 (includes audio guide); half price for return visit within 3 months (keep your ticket)* ⊘ *Sun., Mon., Wed., Thurs., Sat., and Jewish holidays 10–5, Tues. 4–9, Fri. and Jewish holiday eves 10–2.*

★ **Yad Vashem.** The experience of the Holocaust—the annihilation of 6 million Jews by the Nazis during World War II—is so deeply seared into the Jewish national psyche that understanding it goes a long way toward understanding Israelis themselves. The institution of Yad Vashem, created in 1953 by an act of the Knesset, was charged with preserving a record of those times. The name *Yad Vashem*—"a memorial and a name (a memory)"—comes from the biblical book of Isaiah (56:5). The Israeli government has made a tradition of bringing almost all high-ranking official foreign guests to visit the place.

The riveting **Holocaust History Museum**—a well-lit, 200-yard-long triangular concrete "prism"—is the centerpiece of the site. Powerful visual and audiovisual techniques in a series of galleries document Jewish life in Europe before the catastrophe and follow the escalation of persecution and internment to the hideous climax of the Nazi's "Final Solution." Video interviews and personal artifacts individualize the experience. ⊠ *Hazikaron St., near Herzl Blvd., Mt. Herzl, Jerusalem* ☎ *02/644–3565* ⊕ *www.yadvashem.org* ✉ *Free* ☉ *Sun.–Wed. 9–5, Thurs. 9–8 (late closing for History Museum only), Fri. and Jewish holiday eves 9–2. Last entrance 1 hr before closing.*

## WHERE TO EAT

$ ✕ **Abu Shukri.** In the heart of the Old City, at Station V on the Via Dolorosa, this place has an extraordinary and well-deserved reputation for the best hummus in town. Don't expect much in the way of decor. This is a neighborhood eatery, and a look at the clientele—Palestinian Arabs and Jewish Israeli insiders—confirms that you have gone local. Enjoy the excellent fresh falafel balls, baba ghanoush, tahini, and *labaneh* (a slightly sour cheese served with olive oil and *za'atar* [spice mixture]); no meat is served. Eat family style, and don't over-order: you can get additional portions on the spot. $ *Average main: $8* ⊠ *63 El-Wad Rd. (Hagai St.), Muslim Quarter, Jerusalem* ☎ *02/627–1538* ⌖ *Reservations not accepted* ⊟ *No credit cards* ☉ *No dinner.*

MIDDLE EASTERN

$ ✕ **Nafoura.** Just inside the Jaffa Gate (up the first street on the left), Nafoura offers a tranquil courtyard for alfresco lunchtime dining. Your table might lean against the Old City's 16th-century wall. The pleasant if unremarkable interior is a comfortable refuge in inclement weather. Start with the traditional meze, an array of salads: the smaller version is enough for two people. Insist on the excellent local dishes only (hummus, eggplant dip, tahini, carrots, and so on) and skip the mushrooms and corn. Ask for the *kibbeh,* delicacies of cracked wheat and ground beef, or the *lahmajun,* the meat-topped "Armenian pizza." From the typical selection of entrées, try the lamb cutlets or the sea bream. The NIS 50 buffet (chicken, kebab, side dishes, and fruit) is an excellent value. $ *Average main: $15* ⊠ *18 Latin Patriarch Rd., Christian Quarter, Jerusalem* ☎ *02/626–0034* ☉ *No dinner.*

MIDDLE EASTERN

# CORFU, GREECE

Updated by
Adrian Vrettos
and Alexia
Amvrazi

Kerkyra (Corfu) is the greenest and, quite possibly, the prettiest of all Greek islands—emerald mountains, ocher-and-pink buildings, shimmering silver olive leaves. The turquoise waters lap rocky coves and bougainvillea, scarlet roses, and wisteria spread over cottages. This northernmost of the major Ionian Islands has, through the centuries, inspired artists, conquerors, royalty, and, of course, tourists. Indeed, when you look at Corfu in total, it's hard to believe that any island so small could generate a history so large. Classical remains vie with architecture from the centuries of Venetian, French, and British rule, leaving Corfu with a pleasant combination of contrasting design elements. The town of Corfu remains one of the loveliest in all of Greece, every nook and cranny tells a story, every street meanders to a myth, even during the busiest summer day. Corfu today is a vivid tapestry of cultures, a sophisticated weave, where charm, history, and natural beauty blend.

### ESSENTIALS

#### CURRENCY
The euro.

#### HOURS
Store hours are typically 9 to 9 on weekdays and 9 to 6 on Saturday. Museums are generally from open 9 to 5, but many are closed on Monday. Some shops, restaurants, and museums close between October and April.

#### TELEPHONES
Tri-band GSM phones work in Greece. You can buy prepaid phone cards at telecom shops, news vendors, and tobacconists in all towns and cities. Phone cards can be used for local or international calls. Vodafone is the leading mobile telecom company. OTE is the national domestic provider. Calls can be made at OTE offices and paid for after completion.

### COMING ASHORE
Boats dock at Corfu's purpose-built cruise port, which has a welcome center with an information desk, car-rental desks, and a taxi stand. A 10-minute ride into the Old Town costs around €17. Alternatively, you can walk along the seafront in about 30 minutes.

You can explore the town on foot, but you need a car to get to some of the island's loveliest places. Prices can range from €35 a day for a compact vehicle (where you pay an additional fee for each km driving) to €80 a day for a four-wheel-drive Jeep with extras. Expect additional charges of around €15 for insurance, delivery, and so forth.

## EXPLORING CORFU

### CORFU TOWN

★ **Byzantine Museum.** Panagia Antivouniotissa, an ornate church dating from the late 15th century, houses an outstanding collection of Byzantine religious art. More than 50 icons from the 13th to the 17th century hang on the walls. Look for works by the celebrated icon painters Tzanes and Damaskinos; they are perhaps the best-known artists of the Cretan style of icon painting, with unusually muscular, active depictions of saints. Their paintings more closely resemble Renaissance art—another Venetian legacy—than traditional, flat orthodox icons. ✉ *3rd Parados Arseniou St.* ☎ *26610/38313* 🎫 *€2* ⊙ *Apr.–Oct., Tues.–Sun. 9–4; Nov.–Mar., Tues.–Sun. 8–3.*

Fodor'sChoice **Campiello.** This medieval quarter, part of a UNESCO-designated World
★ Heritage site, is an atmospheric labyrinth of narrow, winding streets, steep stairways, and secretive little squares. Laundry lines connect balconied Venetian palazzi engraved with the original occupant's coat of arms to neoclassic 19th-century buildings constructed by the British. Small cobbled squares with central wells and watched over by old churches add to the quiet, mysterious, and utterly charming urban space. If you enter, you're almost sure to get lost, but the area is small

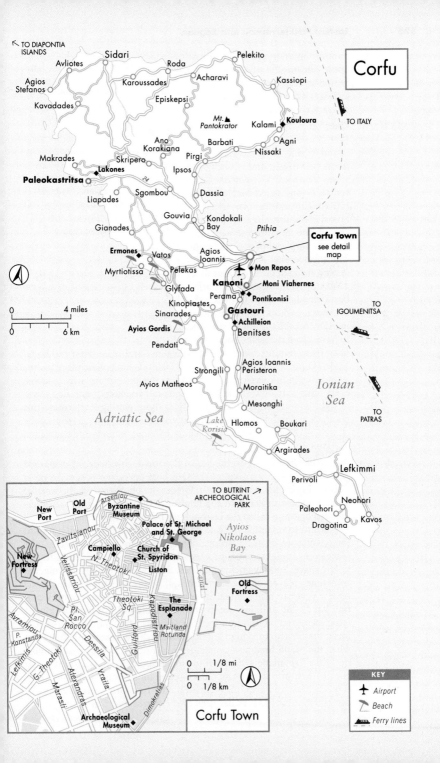

Corfu

← TO DIAPONTIA
ISLANDS

Avliotes
Sidari
Roda
Pelekito
Agios
Stefanos
Karoussades
Acharavi
Kassiopi
Kavadades
Episkepsi
Mt.
Pantokrator
Kalami
Kouloura
TO ITALY
Ano
Korakiana
Barbati
Agni
Makrades
Pirgi
Nissaki
Skripero
Ipsos
Paleokastritsa
Lakones
24
Dassia
Liapades
Sgombou
Gianades
Gouvia
Kondokali
Bay
Ptihia
Ermones
Vatos
Agios
Ioannis
Corfu Town
see detail
map
Myrtiotissa
Pelekas
Mon Repos
Glyfada
Kanoni
Moni Viahernes
Kinopiastes
Perama
Pontikonisi
Sinarades
Gastouri
TO
IGOUMENITSA
Ayios Gordis
Achilleion
Benitses
Pendati
Agios Ioannis
Peristeron
Strongili
Ionian
Sea
Ayios Matheos
Moraitika
TO
PATRAS
Mesonghi
Adriatic Sea
Lake
Korisia
Hlomos
Boukari
Argirades
Lefkimmi
Perivoli
Neohori
Paleohori
Kavos
Dragotina

0      4 miles
0      6 km

New
Port
Old
Port
Arseniou
Byzantine
Museum
TO BUTRINT
ARCHEOLOGICAL
PARK
New
Fortress
Zavitsianou
Palace of St. Michael
and St. George
Ayios
Nikolaos
Bay
Velissariou
Campiello
N. Theotoki
Church of
St. Spyridon
Liston
Avramiou
Pl.
San
Rocco
Theotoki
Sq.
Old
Fortress
P.
Konstanda
Dessila
Kapodistriou
The
Esplanade
Lefkimis
G. Theotoki
Vraila
Gilfordou
Maitland
Rotunda
Marasli
Alexandras
Dimokratias

0      1/8 mi
0      1/8 km

Archaeological
Museum

Corfu Town

KEY
✈ Airport
Beach
Ferry lines

enough so that eventually you'll come out on one of Corfu town's major streets, or on the sea wall. ⊠ *West of the Esplanade, northeast of New Fortress.*

**Fodor'sChoice**
★ **Church of St. Spyridon.** Built in 1596, this church is the tallest on the island, thanks to its distinctive red-dome bell tower, and is filled with silver treasures. The patron saint's remains—smuggled here after the fall of Constantinople—are contained in a silver reliquary in a small chapel; devout Corfiots visit to kiss the reliquary and pray to the saint. The silver casket is carried in procession through the town four times a year. Spyridon was not a Corfiot but a shepherd from Cyprus, who became a bishop before his death in AD 350. His miracles are said to have saved the island four times: once from famine, twice from the plague, and once from the hated Turks. During World War II, a bomb fell on this holiest place on the island but didn't explode. Maybe these events explain why it seems every other man on Corfu is named Spiros. If you keep the church tower in sight you can wander as you wish without getting lost around this fascinating section of town. Agiou Spyridonos, the street in front of the church, is crammed with shops selling religious trinkets and souvenirs. ⊠ *Agiou Spyridonos.*

**CORFU BEST BETS**

**Relax over a coffee at the Liston.** This is a wonderful place to immerse yourself in modern Greek life.

**Take pictures of Pontikonisi.** Mouse Island, as this tiny islet is also known, is one of the iconic Greek landscape views. Shimmering waters and verdant foliage contrast dramatically with the modest whitewashed chapel.

**Explore Paleokastritsa.** A breathtaking landscape of tiny rocky coves, azure waters, and fragrant woodland offers exceptional vistas surrounded by the sound of buzzing cicadas.

**Fodor'sChoice**
★ **The Esplanade.** Central to the life of the town, this huge, open parade ground and park just west of the Old Fortress is, many say, the most beautiful *spianada* (esplanade) in Greece. It is bordered on the west by a street lined with Venetian and English Georgian houses and a famous arcaded building called the **Liston,** built by the French under Napoleon and meant to resemble the Rue du Rivoli in Paris. Cafés spill out onto the passing scene, and Corfiot celebrations, games, and concerts take place here; at night, lovers promenade and children play in this festive public space. Sunday cricket matches, a holdover from British rule, are sometimes played on the northern half of the Esplanade, which was once a Venetian firing range. Standing in the center is an ornate **Victorian bandstand** and, just south of it, the **Maitland Rotunda,** a circular Ionic memorial built in honor of Sir Thomas Maitland, the not-much-loved first British lord high commissioner who was appointed in 1814 when the island became a protectorate of Britain. At the southernmost tip of the Esplanade a **statue of Ioannis Kapodistrias,** a Corfu resident and the first president of modern Greece, looks out over Garitsa bay. Kapodistrias was also, unfortunately, the first Greek president to be assassinated, in 1831. ⊠ *Between Old Fortress and Old Town.*

**New Fortress.** Built in 1577–78 by the Venetians, the New Fortress was constructed to strengthen town defenses—only three decades after the construction of Venetian fortifications on the "Old" Fortress. The French and the British subsequently expanded the complex to protect Corfu town from a possible Turkish invasion. You can wander through the maze of tunnels and fortifications; the dry moat is the site of the town's fish-and-vegetable marketplace. A classic British citadel stands at its heart. At the top, there is an exhibition center. ⊠ *Solomou on promontory overlooking New Port* ☎ 26610–44444 ✉ *€3* ☉ *May–Oct., daily 8:30–8.*

★ **Old Fortress.** Corfu's entire population once lived within the walls of the Old Fortress, or Citadel, built by the Venetians in 1546 on the site of a Byzantine castle. Separated from the rest of the town by a moat, the fort is on a promontory mentioned by Thucydides. Its two heights, or *korypha* ("peaks"), gave the island its name. Standing on the peaks, you have a gorgeous view west over the town and east to the mountainous coast of Albania. A statue of Count Schulenburg, an Austrian mercenary who became a local hero in 1716 when he helped to defeat the invading Turks, stands at the fort's entrance; just inside, there is an exhibition that tells Schulenburg's story. Most of the old Venetian fortifications inside the fortress were destroyed by the British, who replaced them with their own structures. The most notable of these is the **Church of St. George**, built to look like an ancient Doric temple. Near it, overlooking Garitsa bay, there is a shaded café where you can sit and enjoy the splendid view. ⊠ *On eastern point of Corfu town peninsula* ☎ 26610/48310 ✉ *€4* ☉ *Apr.–Oct., Tues.–Sun. 8–4; Nov.–Mar., Tues.–Sun. 7–3.*

Fodor'sChoice ★ **Palace of St. Michael and St. George (Museum of Asian Art).** It may seem a bit incongruous to admire Ming pottery in an ornate British colonial palace as the Ionian Sea shimmers outside the windows. But this elegant, colonnaded, 19th-century Regency structure houses the **Museum of Asian Art**, a notable collection of Asian porcelains, Japanese *ukiyo-e* prints, Indian sculpture, and Tibetan temple art. ⊠ *Palaia Anaktora, at north end of Esplanade* ☎ 26610/30443 ✉ *€3* ☉ *Tues.–Sun. 8:30–4.*

**KANONI**

*5 km (3 miles) southwest of Corfu Town.*

At Kanoni, 5 km (3 miles) south of Corfu town, the site of the ancient capital, you may behold Corfu's most famous view, which looks out over two beautiful islets.

Fodor'sChoice ★ **Mon Repos.** The compact neoclassic palace (really a villa) was built in 1831 by Sir Frederic Adam for his wife, and it was later the summer residence of the British lord high commissioners; the architect, Sir George Whitmore, also designed the Palace of St. Michael and St. George in Corfu town. After Greece won independence from Britain in 1864, Mon Repos was used as a summer palace for the royal family of Greece. Queen Elizabeth II's husband, Prince Philip, was born here in 1921 (he was a royal prince of Greece and Denmark; the Corfiots, who have no love of royalty, call him "the penniless Greek who married a queen"). When King Constantine fled the country in 1967, the

Greek government expropriated Mon Repos. Throughout the 1990s, the estate was entangled in an international legal battle over ownership; the Greek government finally paid Constantine a settlement and opened the fully restored palace as a museum dedicated to the area's archaeological history. After touring the palace, wander around the extensive grounds (entrance is free, so you can do this even if you don't visit the palace), which include the elusive remains of a Doric temple from the 7th and 6th centuries BC and the small but beautiful beach that was once used exclusively by the Greek royal family and is now open to the public. Bring your suit and join the locals on the long pier jutting out into the crystal-clear waters of the Ionian Sea. Opposite Mon Repos are ruins of Ayia Kerkyra, the 5th-century church of the Old City. ✛ *1 km (½ mile) south of Old Fortress, following oceanfront walk* ☎ *26610/41369* 🖾 *€3, gardens free* ☉ *Apr.–Oct., Tues.–Sun. 9–4; Nov.–Mar., Tues.–Sun. 8–3.*

## GASTOURI
*19 km (12 miles) southwest of Corfu Town.*

Fodor'sChoice
★
**Achilleion.** This Teutonic palace, built in the late 19th century for Empress Elizabeth of Austria, is perhaps the most popular tourist attraction in Corfu and remains a monument of 19th-century historicism. The empress used the place as a retreat to escape court life and to ease her heartbreak over husband Franz Josef's numerous affairs and her son Archduke Rudolph's mysterious murder or suicide at Mayerling in 1889. Elizabeth named the palace after her favorite hero, Achilles, whom she inexplicably identified with Rudolph. After Elizabeth was assassinated in 1898, Kaiser Wilhelm II bought the villa and lived in it until the outbreak of World War I, during which time the Achilleion was used by French and Serbian troops as a military hospital. After the armistice, the Greek government received it as a spoil of war. During World War II, it was appropriated and used as a headquarters by the occupying Italian and German forces. In 1962 the palace was restored, leased as a gambling casino, and later used as the set for the casino scene in the James Bond film *For Your Eyes Only.* (The casino has since moved to the Corfu Holiday Palace.)

Today it's a museum, but not a terribly inspiring one. The interior is a series of rather ungainly, uninteresting rooms done in various styles (a pseudo-Byzantine chapel, a pseudo-Pompeian room, a pseudo-Renaissance dining hall), with a smattering of period furniture scattered about; the vulgar fresco called *Achilles in His Chariot,* on the ceiling of the entrance hall, tells you all you need to know about the empress's taste in pseudo-classical art. More appealing is the terrace, laid out like an Ionic peristyle with a number of 19th-century statues, the best of which is *The Dying Achilles.* The gardens, surrounded by olive groves and with a distant view of the sea, are pretty but, all in all, the whole place looks a bit vacuous and forlorn. Still and all, lovers of period style won't want to miss this. For a website on the estate, go to the Wikipedia entry (the easiest way to access it) and then hit the link to the Achilleion site. ✉ *Main street, The Achilleion* ☎ *26610/56210* 🖾 *€6* ☉ *Apr.–Oct., daily 8–7; Nov.–Mar., daily 8:30–3:30.*

## PALEOKASTRITSA
*25 km (16 miles) northwest of Corfu Town.*

This spectacular territory of grottoes, cliffs, and turquoise waters is breathtaking.

**Lakones.** The village of Lakones, built on the steep mountain behind the Paleokastritsa Monastery, looks rather forbidding, but tourists flock there for the view. Kaiser Wilhelm was among many famous people who would make the ascent to enjoy the magnificent panorama of Paleokastritsa's coves from the cafés at Bella Vista, just beyond the village. From nearby Krini you can climb up to the ruins of the 13th-century **Angelokastro**, a fortress built by a despot of Epirus during his brief rule over Corfu. On many occasions during the medieval period the fort sheltered Corfiots from attack by Turkish invaders. Look for the chapel and caves, which served as sanctuaries and hiding places. ⊠ *5 km (3 miles) northeast of Paleokastritsa.*

**Paleokastritsa Monastery.** Paleokastritsa Monastery, a 17th-century structure, is built on the site of an earlier monastery, among terraced gardens overlooking the Ionian sea. Its treasure is a 12th-century icon of the Virgin Mary, and there's a small museum with some other early icons. Note the Tree of Life motif on the ceiling. Be sure to visit the inner courtyard (go through the church), built on the edge of the cliff and looking down a precipitous cliff to the placid green coves and coastline to the south. There's a small gift shop on the premises. ⊠ *On northern headland* ▨ *Donations accepted* ☉ *Daily 7–1 and 3–8.*

5

# SHOPPING

Corfu Town has myriad tiny shops. For traditional goods, head for the narrow streets of the Campiello where olive wood, ceramics, lace, jewelry, and wine shops abound. Kumquat liqueur is a specialty of the island.

**Mironis Olive Wood.** Bowls, sculptures, wooden jewelry, and much more are crammed into two tiny family-run shops. Smaller items are made as you watch. ⊠ *Filarmonikis 27, Corfu Town* ☏ *26610/40621* ▨ *Agiou Spyridon 65, Corfu Town* ☏ *26610/20731.*

**Nikos Sculpture and Jewellery.** Corfu-born Nikos Michalopoulos creates original gold and silver jewelry and sculptures in cast bronze; they're expensive, but worth it. ⊠ *Paleologou 50, Corfu Town* ☏ *26610/31107* ⊕ *www.nikosjewellery.gr* ▨ *N. Theotoki 54, Corfu Town* ☏ *26610/32009.*

**Rolandos.** Visit the talented artist Rolando and watch him at work on his paintings and handmade pottery. ⊠ *N. Theotoki 99, Corfu Town* ☏ *26610/45004.*

# BEACHES

**Glyfada.** The large, golden beaches at Glyfada are the most famous on the island. Though the sands are inevitably packed with sunbathers, it remains one of the hottest hot spots in Corfu. Sun beds, umbrellas, and water-sports equipment is available for rent and there are several tourist resorts. ⊠ *2 km [1 mile] south of Pelekas, Pelekas.*

**Myrtiotissa.** The isolated Myrtiotissa beach, between sheer cliffs, is known for its good snorkeling—and its nude sunbathing. Backed by olive and cypress trees, this sandy stretch was called by Lawrence Durrell in *Prospero's Cell* (with debatable overenthusiasm) "perhaps the loveliest beach in the world." ⊠ *3 km (2 miles) north of Pelekas.*

**Pelekas.** The beach at Pelekas has soft, golden sand and clear water but is developed and tends to be crowded. The huge Aquis Pelekas Beach Hotel resort complex rises up behind it, and Pelekas village is popular with summer tourists. Depending on time of year and demand, there is sometimes a free shuttle service between Pelekas Village and the beach (which is a long and steep walk otherwise).

## WHERE TO EAT

$　✕ **Gerekos.** One of the island's most famous seafood tavernas, Gerekos's

SEAFOOD　raw materials are supplied daily by the family's own fishing boats. The menu varies according to the catch and the season, but the friendly staff will guide your choice. For a light meze, opt for a table on the terrace and try the whitefish *me ladi* (cooked in olive oil, garlic, and pepper) with a salad and some crisp white wine. Too bad this place is located on a dusty resort street with cars going past by diners' toes. ⑤ *Average main: €14* ⊠ *Kontokali bay, 6 km (4 miles) north of Corfu town, Corfu Town* ☎ *26610/91281* ⚖ *Reservations essential.*

$　✕ **Rex.** A friendly Corfiot restaurant in a 19th-century town house, Rex

GREEK　has been a favorite for nearly 100 years, and with good reason. Classic

**Fodor's**Choice　local specialties such as a hearty and meaty *pastitsada* (layers of beef and

★　pasta, called *macaronia* in Greek, cooked in a rich and spicy tomato sauce and topped off with béchamel sauce), *stifado* (meat stewed with sweet onions, white wine, garlic, cinnamon, and spices), and *stamna* (lamb baked with potatoes, rice, beans, and cheese) are reliably delicious. Dishes such as rabbit stewed with fresh figs and chicken with kumquats are successful twists on the regional fare. Look on the menu for the "specials of the day," which might include some other unusual dishes. Outside tables are perfect for people-watching. ⑤ *Average main: €16* ⊠ *Kapodistriou 66, 1 street west of Liston, Corfu Town* ☎ *26610/39649.*

# DUBROVNIK, CROATIA

Updated by
Jane Foster

Commanding a splendid coastal location, Dubrovnik is one of the world's most beautiful fortified cities. Its massive stone ramparts and splendid fortress towers curve around a tiny harbor, enclosing graduated ridges of sun-bleached orange-tiled roofs, copper domes, and elegant bell towers. In the 7th century AD, residents of the Roman city Epidaurum (now Cavtat) fled the Avars and Slavs of the north and founded a new settlement on a small rocky island, which they named Laus, and later Ragusa. On the mainland hillside opposite the island, the Slav settlement called Dubrovnik grew up. In the 12th century the narrow channel separating the two settlements was filled in, and Ragusa and Dubrovnik became one. The city was surrounded by defensive walls during the 13th century, and these were reinforced with towers and bastions during the late 15th century. The city became a UNESCO World Heritage site in 1979. During the war for independence, it came under heavy siege, though thanks to careful restoration work few traces of damage remain. Today Dubrovnik is once again a fashionable, high-class destination; Eva Longoria Parker, Beyoncé, John Malkovich, and Sir Roger Moore have been recent visitors. New in July 2010 is a cable car, which takes visitors up to the top of Mount Srdj for fantastic views down onto the Old Town and out to sea.

---

### DUBROVNIK BEST BETS

**Walk the city walls.** The Old Town's massive Gradske Zidine were begun in the 13th century and reinforced over the years.

**Strolling along the harbor front.** Dubrovnik's picturesque harbor has a promenade perfect for a stroll.

**Relaxing in a café.** All summer long, Dubrovnik's many cafés and restaurants have tables outside (many within the walls of the Old Town), where you can sit under an umbrella and enjoy a seafood lunch or a drink.

---

## ESSENTIALS

### CURRENCY
The Croatian kuna.

### HOURS
Offices are open weekdays from 8:30 to 4. Shops often close for lunch around 1, and may close for as long as three hours; banks also sometimes close for lunch. Post offices are open on Saturday during the main summer season, from June through September.

### TELEPHONES
Most tri- and quad-band GSM phones will work in Croatia. Public phones use calling cards, which can be purchased at the post office, newsstands, and hotels. Major mobile phone companies include TMobile and VIPNet.

## COMING ASHORE
In Dubrovnik almost all ships dock at Gruž Harbor, which is 4 km (2½ miles) from Stari Grad (Old Town). Some ships will provide a free shuttle. The trip to Dubrovnik's Old Town takes about 10 minutes by taxi or 30 to 40 minutes on foot. You can also take a public bus. There's a taxi stand at the harbor.

A few smaller ships might still tender passengers ashore in the Old Town, where you're just steps from everything that Dubrovnik has to offer.

Since the Old Town is compact and pedestrian-friendly, we recommend that you not rent a car in Dubrovnik. It's easy to reach Cavtat by bus or ferry, and unless you want to explore the countryside away from Dubrovnik, a car will not help you. If you choose to rent, expect to pay about €55 for a manual compact vehicle, though you can rent a semiautomatic Smart car at some outlets for about €50. Note, however, that during high season it can be very difficult to find a company that is willing to rent just for one day.

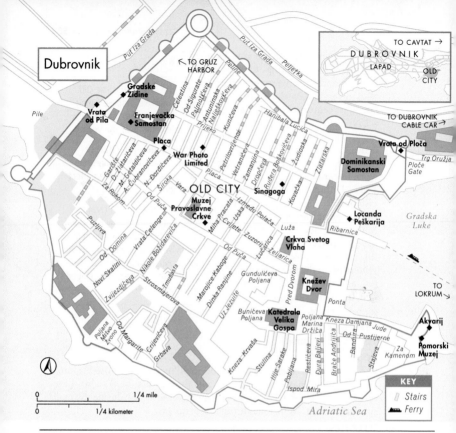

## EXPLORING DUBROVNIK

All the main sites lie in Stari Grad (Old Town) within the city walls, an area that is compact and car-free.

**Akvarij** (*Aquarium*). This dark, cavernous space houses several small pools and 27 well-lit tanks containing a variety of fish from rays to small sharks, as well as other underwater denizens such as sponges and sea urchins. Children will find the octopus in his glass tank either very amusing or horribly scary. ⊠ *Damjana Jude 2, Stari Grad* ☎ *020/323-125* ⊠ *40 Kn* ⊙ *June–Sept., daily 9–9; Apr., May, Oct., and Nov., daily 9–6; Dec.–Mar., Mon.–Sat. 9–1.*

**Crkva Svetog Vlaha** (*Church of St. Blaise*). This 18th-century baroque church replaced an earlier one destroyed by fire. Of particular note is the silver statue on the high altar of St. Blaise holding a model of Dubrovnik, which is paraded around town each year on February 3, the Day of St. Blaise. ⊠ *Luža, Stari Grad* ⊠ *Free* ⊙ *Daily 8–noon and 4:30–7.*

**Dominikanski samostan** (*Dominican monastery*). With a splendid, late-15th-century floral Gothic cloister as its centerpiece, the monastery is best known for its museum, which houses a rich collection of religious paintings by the so-called Dubrovnik School from the 15th and 16th centuries. Look out for works by Božidarević, Hamzić, and Dobričević, as well as gold and silver ecclesiastical artifacts crafted by local gold-smiths. ⊠ *Sv Domina 4, Stari Grad* ☎ *020/321–423* 🎫 *20 Kn* ⊗ *May–Oct., daily 9–6; Nov.–Apr., daily 9–5.*

**Franjevačka samostan** (*Franciscan monastery*). The monastery's chief claim to fame is its pharmacy, which was founded in 1318 and is still in existence today; it's said to be the oldest in Europe. There's also a delightful cloistered garden, framed by Romanesque arcades supported by double columns, each crowned with a set of grotesque figures. In the Treasury a painting shows what Dubrovnik looked like before the disastrous earthquake of 1667. ⊠ *Placa 2, Stari Grad* ☎ *020/321–410* 🎫 *30 Kn* ⊗ *May–Oct., daily 9–6; Nov.–Apr., daily 9–5.*

Fodor's Choice ★ **Gradske Zidine** (*city walls*). Most of the original construction took place during the 13th century, though the walls were further reinforced with towers and bastions over the following 400 years. On average they are 80 feet high and up to 10 feet thick on the seaward side, 20 feet thick on the inland side. ⊠ *Placa, Stari Grad* ☎ *020/324–641* 🎫 *70 Kn* ⊗ *June–July 8 am–7:30 pm; Aug.–mid-Sept. 8 am–7 pm; May and mid-Sept.–Oct. 8 am–6 pm; Nov.–Apr. 10 am–3 pm.*

**Katedrala Velika Gospa** (*Cathedral of Our Lady*). The present struc-ture was built in baroque style after the original was destroyed in the 1667 earthquake. The interior contains a number of notable paintings, including a large polyptych above the main altar depicting the *Assump-tion of Our Lady,* attributed to Titian. The Treasury displays 138 gold and silver reliquaries, including the skull of St. Blaise in the form of a bejeweled Byzantine crown and also an arm and a leg of the saint, likewise encased in decorated gold plating. ⊠ *Držićeva Poljana, Stari Grad* ☎ *020/323–459* 🎫 *Cathedral free, Treasury 15 Kn* ⊗ *May–Oct., Mon.–Sat. 9–5, Sun. 11:30–5; Nov.–Apr., daily 9–noon and 3–5.*

**Knežev Dvor** (*Bishop's Palace*). Originally created in the 15th century but reconstructed several times through the following years, this exquisite building with an arcaded loggia and an internal courtyard shows a combination of late-Gothic and early Renaissance styles. On the ground floor there are large rooms where, in the days of the republic, the Great Council and Senate held their meetings. Over the entrance to the meeting halls a plaque reads: *obliti privatorum publica curate* ("Forget private affairs, and get on with public matters"). Upstairs, the rector's living quarters now accommodate the Gradski Muzej (City Museum), containing exhibits that give a picture of life in Dubrovnik from early days until the fall of the republic. ⊠ *Pred Dvorom 3, Stari Grad* ☎ *020/321–497* 🎫 *40 Kn* ⊗ *May–Oct., daily 9–6; Nov.–Apr., daily 9–4.*

**Muzej Pravoslavne Crkve** (*Orthodox Church Museum*). Next door to the Orthodox church, this small museum displays religious icons from the Balkan region and Russia, as well as several portraits of eminent early-20th-century Dubrovnik personalities by local artist Vlaho Buko-vac. ⊠ *Od Puca 8, Stari Grad* ☎ *020/323–283* 🎫 *10 Kn* ⊗ *May–Oct., Tues.–Sun. 9–2; Nov.–Apr., Mon.–Fri. 9–2.*

**Placa** (*Stradun*). This was once the shallow sea channel separating the island of Laus from the mainland. Although it was filled in during the 12th century, it continued to divide the city socially for several centuries, the nobility living in the area south of Placa and the commoners living on the hillside to the north. Today it forms the venue for the *korzo*, an evening promenade where locals meet to chat, maybe have a drink at one of the numerous open-air cafés, and generally size one another up. ⊠ *Stari Grad.*

**Pomorski Muzej** (*Maritime Museum*). Above the aquarium, on the first floor of St. John's Fortress, this museum's exhibits illustrate how rich and powerful Dubrovnik became one of the world's most important seafaring nations. On display are intricately detailed models of ships as well as engine-room equipment, sailors' uniforms, paintings, and maps. ⊠ *Damjana Jude 2, Stari Grad* 🕿 *020/323–904* 🖃 *40 Kn* ⊙ *May–Oct., Tues.–Sun. 9–6; Nov.–Apr., Tues.–Sun. 9–2.*

**Sinagoga** (*Synagogue*). This tiny 15th-century synagogue, the second-oldest in Europe (after Prague's) bears testament to Dubrovnik's once thriving Jewish community, made up largely of Jews who were expelled from Spain and Italy during the medieval period. ⊠ *Žudioska 5, Stari Grad* 🕿 *020/321–028* 🖃 *20 Kn* ⊙ *May–Sept., daily 10–8; Oct.–Apr., weekdays 10–3.*

**Vrata od Pila** (*Pile Gate*). Built in 1537 and combining a Renaissance arch with a wooden drawbridge on chains, this has always been the main entrance to the city walls. A niche above the portal contains a statue of Sveti Vlah (St. Blaise), the city's patron saint, holding a replica of Dubrovnik in his left hand. From May to October, guards in deep-red period-costume uniforms stand vigilant by the gate through daylight hours, just as they would have done when the city was a republic. ⊠ *Pile, Stari Grad.*

**Vrata od Ploča** (*Ploče Gate*). One of two gates in the town walls, Ploče comprises a stone bridge and wooden drawbridge plus a 15th-century stone arch bearing a statue of Sveti Vlah (St. Blaise). As at Pile Gate, guards in period costume stand vigilant here through the summer season. ⊠ *Ploče, Stari Grad.*

Fodor'sChoice  **War Photo Limited.** Shocking but impressive, this modern gallery devotes
★  two entire floors to war photojournalism. Past exhibitions include images from conflicts in Afghanistan, Iraq, the former Yugoslavia, Israel, Palestine, and Lebanon. Refreshingly impartial by Croatian standards, the message—that war is physically and emotionally destructive whichever side you are on—comes through loudly and clearly. You'll find it in a narrow side street running between Placa and Prijeko. ⊠ *Antuninska 6, Stari Grad* 🕿 *020/322–166* ⊕ *www.warphotoltd.com* 🖃 *30 Kn* ⊙ *May and Oct., Tues.–Sun. 10–4; June–Sept., daily 9–9.*

## BEACHES

**Eastwest Beach.** Eastwest Beach Club is on Banje beach, just a short distance from Ploče Gate, with views across the sea to the tiny island of Lokrum. It's a fashionable spot, with a curving stretch of golden sand, complete with chaise longues and parasols for rent, and a chic bar-restaurant. **Amenities:** food and drink; showers; toilets. **Best for:** partiers; swimming. ⊠ *Frana Supila, Banje Beach* ☎ *020/412–220.*

The more upmarket hotels, such as the Excelsior and Villa Dubrovnik, have their own beaches that are exclusively for the use of hotel guests. The most natural and peaceful beaches lie on the tiny island of **Lokrum,** a short distance south of the Old Town. Through high season, boats leave from the Old Harbor, ferrying visitors back and forth from morning to early evening (9 am to 8 pm, every 30 minutes). Return tickets cost 40 Kn.

## SHOPPING

Despite its role as an important tourist destination, Dubrovnik offers little in the way of shopping or souvenir hunting. If you're in search of gifts, your best bet is a bottle of good Dalmatian wine or *rakija* (a fruit brandy popular throughout much of eastern Europe).

**Croata.** This small boutique close to the Rector's Palace in the Old Town specializes in "original Croatian ties" in presentation boxes. ⊠ *Pred dvorom 2, Stari Grad* ☎ *020/638–330* ⊕ *www.croata.hr.*

**Dubrovačka Kuća.** Tastefully decorated, the wineshop stocks a fine selection of regional Croatian wines, *rakija,* olive oil, and truffle products, plus works of art by contemporary local artists on the upper two levels; it's close to Ploče Gate. ⊠ *Svetog Dominika bb, Stari Grad* ☎ *020/322–092.*

## WHERE TO EAT

**$$$$**
SEAFOOD
Fodor's Choice
★

✕ **Lokanda Peškarija.** Just outside the town walls—and affording unforgettable views over the old harbor—this seafood restaurant is a particularly good value. The seafood on offer is guaranteed fresh each day, not least because the restaurant stands next door to Dubrovnik's covered fish market. It has a beautifully designed, split-level interior with exposed stone walls and wooden beams, plus romantic outdoor candlelit tables by the water. ■ TIP➔ Definitely not only for tourists, locals love eating here as well, so reservations are recommended, especially for dinner. ⑤ *Average main: 90 Kn* ⊠ *Na Ponti, Stari Grad* ☎ *020/324–750* ⊕ *www.mea-culpa.hr* ⊘ *Closed Jan.–Mar.*

**$$$$**
SEAFOOD

✕ **Proto.** A reliable choice for dinner, Proto is on a side street off Stradun, with tables arranged on a vine-covered, upper-level, open-air terrace. The menu features a good selection of traditional Dalmatian seafood dishes—including oysters from nearby Ston—and barbecued meats, notably succulent steaks. The restaurant dates back to 1886. Recent celebrity guests have included actor Richard Gere and Bono. ■ TIP➔ Reservations are recommended. ⑤ *Average main: 140 Kn* ⊠ *Široka 1, Stari Grad* ☎ *020/323–234* ⊕ *www.esculaprestaurants.com.*

# HAIFA, ISRAEL

Updated
by Jessica
Steinberg

Israel's largest port city (and third-largest city overall), Haifa was ruled for four centuries by the Ottomans and gradually grew up the mountainside into a cosmopolitan city whose port served the entire Middle East. In 1902 Theodor Herzl enthusiastically dubbed it "the city of the future." The city is the world center for the Baha'i faith, and the most striking landmark on the city's mountainside is the gleaming golden dome of the Baha'i Shrine, set amid utterly beautiful circular grass terraces that fill the slope from top to bottom.

## ESSENTIALS

### CURRENCY
The shekel.

### HOURS
Shops are generally open Sunday through Thursday from 9 to 7, though some close in the afternoon. Museums vary in hours, but most are open Monday through Thursday from 10 to 6 with shorter hours on Friday through Sunday, often from 10 to 2 or 3. Some museums close on Friday.

### TELEPHONES
Most multiband mobile phones work in Israel, and GSM and 3G systems are well established in the urban areas. Major providers are Cellcom Israel, Parner Communication (Orange), and Pelephone.

## COMING ASHORE
The cruise port sits directly on the Haifa waterfront. The cruise terminal has some shops, a café, currency exchange desk, and a tax-refund kiosk, and the waterfront area is slowly being improved with new restaurants and shops opening their doors. From the port it's an easy walk into downtown, but the city is built on hills, so if you intend to explore on foot, wear comfortable shoes.

The Egged bus cooperative provides regular service from Haifa to Nazareth, and to Tiberias on the Sea of Galilee. To get from Haifa to Tiberias, take the slow Bus 430 (about an hour), which leaves hourly from Merkazit Hamifratz.

Driving is the best way to explore the Lower Galilee, and you can easily link several excursions and take your time enjoying the panoramic views, since Nazareth is only 56 km (35 miles) east of Haifa and the Golan Heights around two hours' drive away. Some newer four-lane highways are excellent, but some secondary roads may be in need of repair. Signposting is clear (and usually in English), with route numbers clearly marked. Prices for a subcompact car are around $80 a day and a compact $100 per day, though many companies charge for mileage.

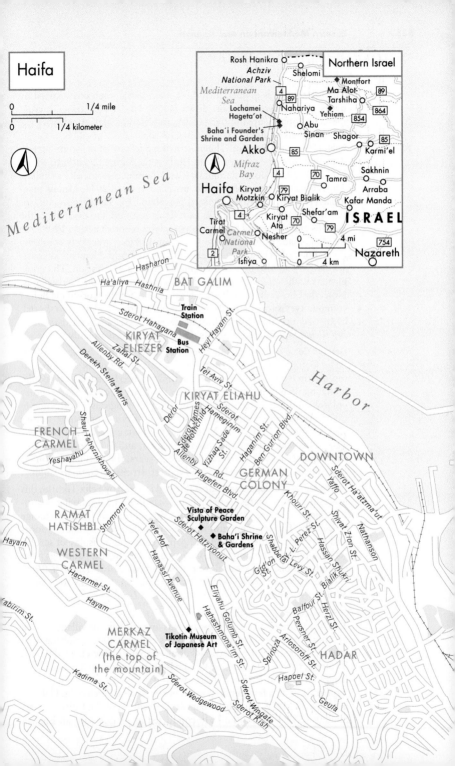

# EXPLORING ISRAEL FROM HAIFA

### HAIFA

The metropolis is divided into three main levels, each crisscrossed by parks and gardens: the port down below; Hadar HaCarmel, a commercial shopping area in the middle; and Merkaz HaCarmel, with the posher hotels and many restaurants, on top.

Fodor'sChoice
★ **Baha'i Shrine and Gardens.** The most striking feature of the stunning gardens that form the centerpiece of Haifa is the Shrine of the Bab, whose brilliantly gilded dome dominates—and illuminates—the city's skyline. The renovated shrine of the Bab, unveiled in April 2011, gleams magnificently with 11,790 gold-glazed porcelain tiles. The Persian authorities martyred Bab in 1850. Baha'u'llah's son and successor built the gardens and shrine and had the Bab's remains reburied here in 1909. The building, made of Italian stone and rising 128 feet, gracefully combines the canons of classical European architecture with elements of Eastern design and also houses the remains of Baha'u'llah's son. The dome glistens with some 12,000 gilded tiles imported from the Netherlands. Note: the Shrine of the Bab is a pilgrimage site for the worldwide Baha'i community; visitors to the shrine are asked to dress modestly (no shorts). ⊠ *16 Golomb St., Merkaz Carmel* ☎ *04/831–3131* ⊕ *www.ganbahai. org.il/en/haifa/* ☒ *Free* ⊗ *Shrine daily 9–noon; gardens daily 9–5.*

Fodor'sChoice
★ **German Colony.** It is only one street—actually a broad boulevard—but "The Colony" packs in history (with explanatory placards), interesting architecture, great restaurants, and wonderful spots for people-watching. Ben Gurion Boulevard was the heart of a late-19th-century colony established by the German Templer religious reform movement. Along either side are robust one- and two-story stone houses with pointed red-tile roofs. Many bear German names, dates from the 1800s, biblical inscriptions above the doors, and old wooden shutters framing narrow windows. Neglected for years, the German Colony is now one of the city's loveliest (and flattest) strolls. ⊠ *German Colony.*

★ **Tikotin Museum of Japanese Art.** Established in 1957 by Felix Tikotin, this graceful venue adheres to the Japanese tradition of displaying beautiful objects that are in harmony with the season, so exhibits change frequently. The Japanese atmosphere, created in part by sliding doors and partitions made of wood and paper, enhances a display of scrolls, screens, pottery and porcelain, lacquer and metalwork, paintings from several schools, and fresh-flower arrangements. ⊠ *88 Hanassi Blvd., Merkaz Carmel* ☎ *04/838–3554* ⊕ *www.tmja.org.il/* ☒ *NIS 50* ⊗ *Sun.– Wed. 10–4, Thurs. 10–7, Fri. 10–1, Sat. and Jewish holidays 10–5.*

### NAZARETH

The Nazareth where Jesus grew up was an insignificant village nestled in a hollow in the Galilean hills. Today's city of 65,000 is pulsing with energy. Apart from the occasional donkey plying traffic-clogged Paulus VI Street, there's little that evokes the Bible in contemporary Nazareth.

**Baptist Church.** Christianity speaks with many voices in Nazareth. The Baptist Church, a few hundred yards north of the Church of St. Gabriel, is affiliated with the Southern Baptist Convention of the United States. Sunday services (10:30 am) are conducted in Arabic with an English translation of the sermon; the Baptist school next door also offers services, with more English speakers, at the same time. The year 2011 marked 100 years of Baptist presence in the Holy Land. ⊠ *Paulus VI St.* ☎ *04/657–6946, 04/657–4370* ⊕ *www.lbc-nazareth.org.*

★ **Basilica of the Annunciation.** Casa Nova Street climbs steeply to the entrance of the Roman Catholic Basilica of the Annunciation, the largest church in the Middle East, consecrated in 1969. It enshrines a small ancient cave dwelling or grotto, identified by many Catholics as the home of Mary. Here, they believe, the angel Gabriel appeared to her and announced (hence, Annunciation) that she would conceive "and bear a son" and "call his name Jesus" (Luke 1). Pilgrim devotions suffuse the site throughout the day. Crusader-era walls and some restored Byzantine mosaics near the grotto bear witness to the antiquity of the tradition. The grotto is in the so-called lower church. Look up through the "well," or opening over the grotto, that connects with the upper church to the grand cupola, soaring 195 feet above you.

**HAIFA BEST BETS**

**Basilica of the Annunciation.** Built on a spot thought to be central to the life of Jesus and his family.

**Baha'i Shrine and Gardens.** A stunning World Heritage site with terraced gardens cascading down a hillside.

**The Golan Heights.** Israel's Little Tuscany has breathtaking countryside.

A spiral staircase leads to the vast upper church, the parish church of Nazareth's Roman Catholic community. The artwork of the site, donated by Catholic communities around the world, is eclectic in the extreme but the more interesting for it. The portico around the courtyard just inside the main gate is decorated with striking contemporary mosaics, many depicting the Madonna and Child in styles and with facial features reflecting the donor nation. The massive main doors leading to the lower church relate, in bronze relief, the central events of Jesus' life; abstract stained-glass windows brilliantly counterpoint the dim lighting here. The large panels on the walls of the upper church, again on the theme of mother and child, include a vivid offering from the United States, a fine Canadian terra-cotta, and mosaics from England and Australia. Particularly interesting are the gifts from Japan (with gold leaf and pearls), Venezuela (a carved-wood statue), and Cameroon (a stylized painting in black, white, and red).

In the exit courtyard, a glass-enclosed baptistery is built over what is thought to have been an ancient mikvah, a Jewish ritual bath. The adjacent small Church of St. Joseph, just past Terra Sancta College, is built over a complex of rock-hewn chambers traditionally identified as the workshop of Joseph the Carpenter. Note that parking is hard to find; try Paulus VI Street or the side streets below it. ⊠ *Casa Nova St.* ☎ *04/657–2501* 🖅 *Free* ☉ *Hours vary by section. Grotto, 6 am–9 pm, Upper Basilica, 8–6, St. Joseph's Church, 7–6. Masses daily at 6:30 am (Italian) and 7:15 am (Arabic), and Sun. at 7, 8:30, 10, 5 pm, and 6 (all Arabic). Programs: Silent Prayer, daily 6–9 am, Nazareth's Rosary, Tues. 8:30 am, Eucharistic Adoration, Thurs. 8:30 am, Candlelight Procession, Sat. 8:30 am.*

**Church of St. Gabriel.** The Greek Orthodox Church of St. Gabriel, about 1 km (¾ mile) north of the junction of Paulus VI and Casa Nova streets, is built over Nazareth's only natural water source, a spring dubbed Mary's Well. The Greek Orthodox, citing the noncanonical Gospel of St. James, believe it to be the place where the angel Gabriel appeared to Mary to announce the coming birth of Jesus. (On Paulus VI Street, at the bottom of the short approach to the church, is a round, white, stone structure marked "Mary's Well," but this is merely a modern outlet.)

The ornate church was built in 1750 and contains a stunning carved-wood pulpit and iconostasis (chancel screen), with painted New Testament scenes and silver-haloed saints. The walls are adorned with frescoes of figures from the Bible and the Greek Orthodox hagiography. A tiny "well" stands over the running water, and a modern aluminum cup gives a satisfying plop as it drops in. (The water is clean; the cup is more suspect.) ⊠ *Off Paulus VI St.* ☎ *04/657–6437* ☜ *Donation expected* ☉ *Mon.–Sat. 8–5, Sun. after services–5.*

☾ **Nazareth Village.** The shepherds, weavers, and other characters in this reconstructed Jesus-era community will delight children and adults alike. Using information gained from archaeological work done in the area, this attraction aims to reconstruct Jewish rural life as Jesus would have known it more than 2,000 years ago. Workshops, farms, and houses have been created with techniques that would have been used at the time. Interpreters in period costume cook and work at winepresses and looms, giving a sense of daily life. The village is geared toward Christian travelers but may also be of interest to others; there is a re-created synagogue and *mikvah* (ritual bath). Guided tours with different themes are offered; check in advance about these, as reservations are required. ⊠ *Nazareth YMCA, 2nd floor, 5105 St., opposite the French hospital* ☎ *04/645–6042* ⊕ *www.nazarethvillage.com* ☜ *NIS 50* ☉ *Mon.–Sat. 9–5 (last tour at 3).*

**Souk.** Full of the aroma of fresh spices, Nazareth's market, in the Old City, has something for everyone, from coffee sets to pastries to T-shirts and antiques. The old lanes are narrow and shops are tiny, with goods spilling into the street, but this souk is more orderly than those in many other Israeli cities. If it does get overwhelming, take a coffee break. ⊠ *Casa Nova St. and vicinity.*

## THE GOLAN HEIGHTS

Considered the most fertile land in Israel, the Golan Heights is known for its many fine wineries. As you drive through these verdant hills, covered with wildflowers in the spring, you'll also see abundant olive groves and apple and cherry orchards. The whole region was once volcanic, and many symmetrical volcanic cones and pronounced reliefs still dominate the landscape, particularly in the upper Golan. The gentle terrain and climate of the rest of the region have historically attracted far more settlement than the less hospitable northern Upper Galilee. Today it's home to Jewish, Druze, and Alawite communities.

★ **Hermon River (Banias) Nature Reserve.** One of the most stunning parts of Israel, this reserve contains gushing waterfalls, dense foliage along riverbanks, and the remains of a temple dedicated to the god Pan. There are two entrances, each with a parking lot: the sign for the first reads Banias Waterfall; the other is 1 km (½ mile) farther along the same road and is marked Banias.

The **Banias Spring** emerges at the foot of mostly limestone Mt. Hermon, just where it meets the basalt layers of the Golan Heights. The most popular short route in the reserve is up to the **Banias Cave,** via the path that crosses the spring. Excavations have revealed the five niches hewed out of the rock to the right of the cave; these are what remain of Hellenistic and Roman temples, depicted in interesting artist's renderings. Three of the niches bear inscriptions in Greek, mentioning Pan, the lover of tunes, Echo, the mountain nymph, and Galerius, one of Pan's priests. ⊠ *Off Rte. 99, Kiryat Shmona* ☎ *04/695–0272* 🖾 *NIS 27* ⊘ *Apr.–Sept., Sat.–Thurs. 8–5, Fri. 8–4; Oct.–Mar., Sat.–Thurs. 8–4, Fri. 8–3; last entrance 1 hr before closing.*

★ **Nimrod's Fortress.** The dramatic views of this towering, burly fortress
☪ perched above Banias, appearing and disappearing behind each curve of the narrow road that leads to it, are part of the treat of a visit to Nimrod's Fortress (Kal'at Namrud). And once you're there, the fortress commands superb vistas, especially through the frames of its arched windows and the narrow archers' slits in its walls. In 1218 the Mameluke warlord al-Malik al-Aziz Othman built this fortress to guard the vital route from Damascus via the Golan and Banias, to Lebanon and to the Mediterranean coast, against a Crusader *reconquista* after their 1187 defeat. Nimrod's Fortress is a highlight for kids, with a ladder down to a vaulted cistern, a shadowy spiral staircase, and unexpected nooks and crannies. A path leads up to the fortress's central tower, or keep, where the feudal lord would have lived. ⊠ *Nimrod's Fortress National Park, Rte. 989, Kiryat Shmona* ☎ *04/694–9277* 🖾 *NIS 21* ⊘ *Apr.–Sept., daily 8–5; Oct.–Mar. 8–4; last entrance 1 hr before closing.*

## SEA OF GALILEE

The Sea of Galilee is, in fact, a freshwater lake, measuring 21 km (13 miles) long from north to south and 11 km (7 miles) wide from east to west. Almost completely ringed by cliffs and steep hills, the lake lies in a hollow about 700 feet below sea level, which accounts for its warm climate and subtropical vegetation. This is Israel's Riviera-on-a-lake, filled with beaches and outdoor recreation facilities. Its shores are also dotted with sites hallowed by Christian tradition (note that several of these sites demand modest dress) as well as some important ancient synagogues. Tiberias itself is one of Judaism's four holy cities, along with Jerusalem, Hebron, and Tzfat (Safed).

# BEACHES

Haifa's coastline is one fine, sandy public beach after another.

**Hof HaShaket.** North of the Leonardo Hotel, Hof HaShaket offers separate gender days: Sunday, Tuesday, and Thursday for women; Monday, Wednesday, and Friday for men; Saturday for whomever. ⊠ *David Elazar St., South Haifa.*

## WHERE TO EAT

**$$** ✕ **Douzan.** Inside this old German Templer building with a pleasant
MEDITERRANEAN outdoor terrace, a huge metal lamp studded with colored glass casts
lacy designs on the walls. The food, much of it prepared by the owner's
mother, is an intriguing combination of French and local Arabic cui-
sines. Her specialty is *kibbeh,* deep-fried torpedoes of cracked wheat
kneaded with minced beef, pine nuts, onions, and exotic spices. A vari-
ation on it is *sfeeha,* puff pastry topped with delicately spiced beef,
onions, and pine nuts. $ *Average main: $17* ✉ *35 Ben Gurion Blvd.,
German Colony* ☎ *04/852-5444* ⊕ *www.rest.co.il.*

**$** ✕ **Nadima Sabithi Eatery.** A somewhat typical one-woman show, Nadima
ISRAELI has been running her home kitchen–style eatery for some 40 years, serv-
ing up the day's offerings on a row of gas burners. There's always a
seasoned rice, *majadera* (rice with lentils), and vegetables stuffed with
meat, while the vegetables themselves are a veritable menu of wild herbs
and roots, including okra, spinach, mallow, and chicory. $ *Average
main: $5* ✉ *35 Yohanan Hakadosh, Wadi Nisnas, Netanya* ⊟ *No credit
cards* ⊘ *Closed Sun. No dinner.*

# HVAR, CROATIA

Updated by
Jane Foster

The island of Hvar bills itself as the "sunniest island in the Adriatic."
Not only does it have the figures to back up this claim—an annual aver-
age of 2,724 hours of sunshine with a maximum of two foggy days a
year—but it also makes visitors a sporting proposition, offering them a
money-back guarantee if there is ever a foggy day. While fog has been
known to happen, hotels don't ordinarily have to give much of their
income back. All this sun is good for the island's fields of lavender,
rosemary, and grapes. Hvar is also probably Croatia's hippest island,
attracting gossip column–worthy celebrities, would-be artists, politi-
cians, and nudists. Visitors have included King Abdullah and Queen
Rania of Jordan, Nicky Hilton (Paris's sister), and local tennis champion
Goran Ivaniševiæ.

### ESSENTIALS

#### CURRENCY
The Croatian kuna. ATMs are easy to find.

#### HOURS
Offices are open weekdays from 8:30 to 4. Shops often close for lunch
around 1 and may close for as long as three hours; banks also sometimes
close for lunch. Post offices are open Saturday during the main summer
season, from June through September.

#### TELEPHONES
Most tri- and quad-band GSM phones will work in Croatia. Public
phones use calling cards, which can be purchased at the post office,
newsstands, and hotels. Major mobile phone companies include TMo-
bile and VIPNet.

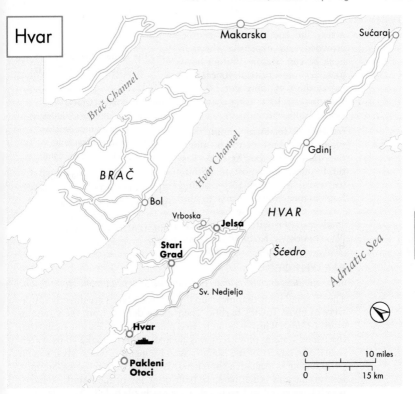

## COMING ASHORE

Ships can't dock in Hvar, so you'll be brought into Hvar Town from the ship by tender, which docks right in town. Most of the town is closed to cars, so the town is best seen on foot, and since many ships make Hvar a short port call (sometimes staying as few as four hours), it doesn't make much sense to set out to do too much. If you are in port long enough, you'll need to rent a car to see more of the island. Expect to pay at least €55 for a manual economy vehicle. The island also has bus service, particularly to Stari Grad and Jelsa, several times a day.

## EXPLORING HVAR

### HVAR TOWN

Hvar is both the name of the island and the name of the capital, near the island's western tip. Little **Hvar Town** rises like an amphitheater from its harbor, backed by a hilltop fortress and protected from the open sea by a scattering of small islands known as Pakleni Otoci. Along the palm-lined quay, a string of cafés and restaurants is shaded by colorful awnings and umbrellas. A few steps away, the magnificent main square, **Trg Sveti Stjepan,** the largest piazza in Dalmatia, is backed by the 16th-century **Katedrala Sveti Stjepan** (Cathedral of St. Stephen). Other notable sights include the *kazalište* (a theater) and the *Franjevački Samostan* (Franciscan monastery). Hvar Town is currently a very "in" spot, so expect it to be crowded and expensive through peak season. Recent visitors have included Tom Cruise, Beyoncé, Italian clothing entrepreneur Luciano Benetton, and local tennis champion Goran Ivanišević.

**Franjevački samostan** (*Franciscan monastery*). East of town, along the quay past the Arsenal, lies the Franjevački samostan. Within its walls, a pretty 15th-century Renaissance cloister leads to the former refectory, now housing a small museum with several notable artworks. ⊠ *Križa bb* ☎ *25 Kn* ☉ *May–Oct., daily 9–1 and 5–7.*

> ### HVAR BEST BETS
>
> **See the Tvrdalj.** This oddly interesting house in Stari Grad is worth a trip.
>
> **Visit the Pakleni Otoci.** The small islands off Hvar's southwest coast have Hvar's best beaches, and are scenic enough to be worth a trip in their own right.
>
> **Wander the pedestrian-only alleys of Hvar Town.** If you have just a few hours in port, spend them wandering the car-free streets of Hvar's picturesque Old Town, stopping at a café or two.

## PAKLENI OTOCI

*Sveti Klement is approximately 20 minutes by boat from Hvar Town.*

The 20 small islets that make up the Pakleni Islands are directly southwest of Hvar Town's harbor. Their name derives from the Croatian word *paklina*, which is what melted pine resin is called (the resin from the island's many pine trees was melted down to make ships watertight). The largest of the islands, Sveti Klement, is where Hvar's main yacht harbor is located; a church here is dedicated to the saint. Summer restaurants and beach bars are built on many of the islands, some of which have excellent beaches that are reachable only by boat. Jerolim, the closest of the islands to Hvar Town, has a famous nude beach.

## JELSA

*10 km (6 miles) east of Stari Grad, 27 km (17 miles) east of Hvar Town.*

In this village on the northern coast of the island you'll see many structures from the Renaissance and baroque periods, though St. Mary's Church dates back to the early 1300s. A tower built by the ancient Greeks overlooks the harbor; it dates to the 3rd or 4th century BC. About 1 km (½ mile) east of the modern town is the older Grad, the original fortified area that was protected by the fortress called Galesink, which now stands in ruins. The small town is an alternative to the busier Hvar Town and is surrounded by swimmable beaches—including the island's most popular nude beaches—and some resorts. It's surrounded by thick forests of pine trees.

## STARI GRAD

*17 km (11 miles) east of Hvar Town.*

**Stari Grad.** The site of the original Greek settlement on Hvar, called Pharos by the Greeks, Stari Grad is a conglomeration of smaller communities; it's also the entry-point to the island for bus transportation from the mainland, as well as passenger ferries. The town is 10 km (6 miles) east of Hvar Town.

**Tvrdalj.** The main sight is the Tvrdalj, the fortified Renaissance villa of the 16th-century poet Petar Hektorović. The home has been renovated twice over the centuries, first in the 18th-century baroque style; a partial restoration was also done in the 19th century. Hektorović attempted to create a "model universe" to be embodied in his home. To that end, a large fishpond is stocked with gray mullet, as they were in the poet's own time, representing the sea; above the fish pond in a tower is a dovecote, representing the air. Ivy was allowed to cover the walls to tie the home to the land. Quotations from his poetry are inscribed on many walls. ✉ *Trg Tvrdalj bb, Stari Grad* ☎ *021/765–068* 🎫 *10 Kn* ⏲ *May, June, Sept., and Oct., daily 10–1; July and Aug. daily 10–1 and 5–8*

## BEACHES

There are several decent beaches within walking distance of town—the best-equipped being the Hotel Amfora's **Bonj les Bains** beach, a pebbled cove rimmed by a 1930s stone colonnade housing private stone cabanas, 10 minutes west of the main square. However, sun worshippers in search of a more back-to-nature experience head for the nearby Pakleni Otoci (Pakleni Islands), which can be reached by taxi boats that depart regularly (in peak season, every hour, from 8 to 8) from in front of the Arsenal in the town harbor. The best-known and best-served are **Sveti Jerolim** (on the island of the same name, predominantly a nudist beach), **Stipanska** (on the island of Marinkovac, home to trendy Carpe Diem Stipanska, complete with a restaurant, lounge-bar, pool, and two beaches with palapas and wooden sun beds for hire), and **Palmižana** (on the island of Sveti Klement, also clothing-optional).

## WHERE TO EAT

**$$** MEDITERRANEAN ✕ **Konoba Menego.** On the steps between the main square and the castle, this authentic stone-walled konoba has candlelit tables and whole *pršut* (prosciutto) hanging from the wooden beamed ceiling. Come here to snack on small platters of locally produced, cold Dalmatian specialties such as *kožji sir* (goat cheese), pršut, *salata od hobotnice* (octopus salad) and *masline* (olives), accompanied by a carafe of homemade wine. Before leaving, round off your meal with *pijane smokve* (figs marinated in brandy), and be sure to check out the world atlas where guests sign on the pages of their hometowns. $ *Average main: 60 Kn* ✉ *Groda bb, Hvar Town* ☎ *021/742–036* 🌐 *www.menego.hr* 💳 *No credit cards* ⏲ *Closed Dec.–Mar.*

**$$$$** SEAFOOD ★ ✕ **Restoran Palmižana.** On the tiny island of Sveti Klement, a 20-minute taxi-boat ride from Hvar Town, this terrace restaurant is backed by a romantic wilderness of Mediterranean flora and offers stunning views over the open sea. The walls are decorated with contemporary Croatian art, and there are classical-music recitals on Sunday morning. Besides fresh seafood, goodies include *kožji sir sa rukolom* (goat cheese with arugula), and *pašticada* (beef stewed in sweet wine and prunes). $ *Average main: 110 Kn* ✉ *Vinogradišće Uvala, Sveti Klement* ☎ *021/717–270* ⏲ *Closed Nov.–Mar.*

# ISTANBUL, TURKEY

Though it is often remarked that Turkey straddles Europe and Asia, it's really the city of Istanbul that does the straddling. European Istanbul is separated from its Asian suburbs by the Bosphorus, the narrow channel of water that connects the Black Sea, north of the city, to the Sea of Marmara in the south. What will strike you more than the meeting of East and West in Istanbul, though, is the juxtaposition of the old and the new, of tradition and modernity. Office towers creep up behind historic old palaces; women in jeans or elegant designer outfits pass others wearing long skirts and head coverings; donkey-drawn carts vie with shiny BMWs for dominance of the streets; and the Grand Bazaar competes with Western-style boutiques and shopping malls. At dawn, when the muezzin's call to prayer rebounds from ancient minarets, there are inevitably a few hearty revelers still making their way home from nightclubs while other residents kneel in prayer.

## ESSENTIALS

### CURRENCY
The Turkish lira.

### HOURS
Shops open daily from 9 to 9, though some will close for an hour or so on Friday lunchtime for prayers. Attractions are usually open daily from 8 until 5 or 6, though some are closed on Monday.

### PRIVATE TOURS
Private tours with a guide are useful and popular. Guides will also help you shop at the Grand Bazaar. The Turkish Tour Guides organization can assure that yours is licensed and knowledgeable.

Contact **Turkish Tour Guides.** ⊕ *www.turkishguides.org.*

### TELEPHONES
If you have a multiband cell phone (some countries use frequencies other than those used in the United States) and your service provider uses the world-standard GSM network (as do T-Mobile, AT&T, and Verizon), you can probably use your phone in Turkey. Roaming fees can be steep, though—99¢ a minute is considered reasonable—and you will probably pay the toll charges for incoming calls. It's almost always cheaper to send a text message than to make a call since text messages have a very low set fee (often less than 5¢). Public phones accept tokens or telephone cards (which can be purchased at newsstands and telecom shops); phones accepting cards will also accept credit cards in payment for calls. Turk Telekom, Turkcell, and Telcim are the major telecom companies.

## COMING ASHORE
Ships dock at Karakoy, in the shadow of the famous Galata Tower. It's possible to walk from the pier to the Sultanahmet (the historic quarter) in about 45 minutes, but the immediate and pervasive bustle of the city might be off-putting (though it's not intrinsically dangerous). Taxis wait at the pier for the 10-minute ride into Sultanahmet.

We strongly advise against renting a car in Istanbul. The public transport system is also quite chaotic, so we recommend you take taxis. Once you reach Sultanahmet, many of the most important sights are all within walking distance of each other.

## GETTING TO THE AIRPORT

If you do not purchase airport transfers from your cruise line, there are several inexpensive possibilities for your transfer from airport to cruise terminal.

Ataturk International Airport is 28 km (17½ miles) outside the city. The light metro line links the airport with downtown at Koça Mustafa Pasha station. Trains run from around 6 am to midnight, but the service is not high-speed and trains can be crowded. From the metro station a 10-minute taxi ride takes you to the cruise quayside.

Airport shuttle buses operated by Havaş leave the arrivals terminal for the Turkish Airlines office in Taksim Square. Departures are every 30 minutes during the day, and prices are currently TL 10 per ticket. A taxi from Taksim Square to the cruise quay takes around 15 minutes.

Taxi fares are about .90 TL for 1 km (about ½ mile); 50% higher between midnight and 6 am. Fares from the airport to downtown are around TL 25–TL 35, and the trip from the airport to the cruise pier takes around 40 minutes depending on traffic (which can be heavy at peak times).

Commercial companies also offer inexpensive door-to-door services. Istanbul Airport Shuttle runs a transfer every couple of hours between 6 am and 9 pm, and prices for airport to cruise port (or downtown hotel) transfers are €10 per person.

**Contacts Istanbul Airport Shuttle.** ☎ *212/518–0354* ⊕ *www.istanbulairportshuttle.com.*

# EXPLORING ISTANBUL

**Fodor's Choice** **Arkeoloji Müzeleri** (*Istanbul Archaeology Museums*). Step into this vast
★ repository of spectacular finds, housed in a three-building complex in
☾ a forecourt of Topkapı Palace, to get a head-spinning look at the civilizations that have thrived for thousands of years in and around Turkey. The most stunning pieces are tombs that include the so-called Alexander Sarcophagus, found in Lebanon, carved with scenes from Alexander the Great's battles, and once believed, wrongly, to be his final resting place. Don't miss a visit to the **Çinili Köşk** (Tiled Pavilion), one of the most visually pleasing sights in all of Istanbul—a bright profusion of colored tiles covers this one-time hunting lodge of Mehmet the Conqueror, built in 1472. The **Eski Şark Eserleri Müzesi** (Museum of the Ancient Orient) transports visitors to even earlier times: The vast majority of the panels, mosaics, obelisks, and other artifacts here, from Anatolia, Mesopotamia, and elsewhere in the Arab world, date from the pre-Christian centuries. One of the most significant pieces in the collection is a 13th-century BC tablet on which is recorded the Treaty of Kadesh, perhaps the world's earliest known peace treaty, an accord between the Hittite king Hattusili III and the Egyptian pharaoh Ramses II. ⊠ *Gülhane Park, next to Topkapı Sarayı* ☎ *212/520–7740* 🖆 *10 TL (total) for*

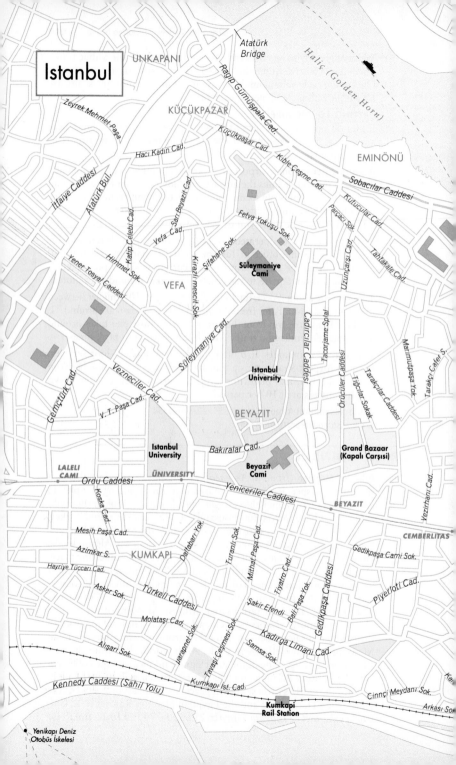

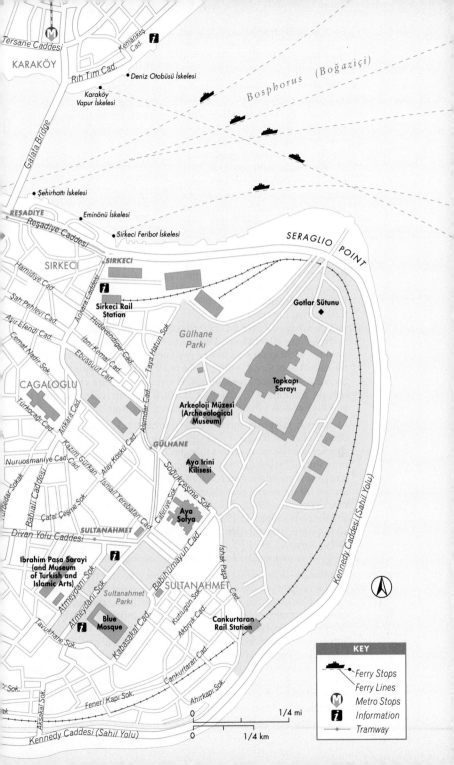

*the 3 museums ☉ Tues.–Sun. 9–7 in summer, 9–5 in winter; ticket sales until an hr before closing.*

**Fodor's Choice ★** **Aya Sofya** (*Hagia Sophia, Church of the Holy Wisdom*). This soaring edifice is perhaps the greatest work of Byzantine architecture and for almost a thousand years, starting from its completion in 537, it was the world's largest and most important religious monument. As Justinian may well have intended, the impression that will stay with you longest, years after a visit, is the sight of the dome. As you enter, the half domes trick you before the great space opens up with the immense dome, almost 18 stories high and more than 30 meters (100 feet) across, towering above—look up into it and you'll see the spectacle of thousands of gold tiles glittering in the light of 40 windows. Only Saint Peter's in Rome, not completed until the 17th century, surpassed Aya Sofya in size and grandeur. It was the cathedral of Constantinople, the heart of the city's spiritual life, and the scene of imperial coronations. It was also the third church on this site: the second, the foundations of which you can see at the entrance, was burned down in the antigovernment Nika riots of 532.

Mehmet II famously sprinkled dirt on his head before entering the church after the conquest as a sign of humility. His first order was for Aya Sofya to be turned into a mosque and, in keeping with the Islamic proscription against figural images, mosaics were plastered over. Successive sultans added the four minarets, *mihrab* (prayer niche), and *minbar* (pulpit for the *imam*) that visitors see today, as well as the large black medallions inscribed in Arabic with the names of Allah, Muhammad, and the early caliphs. In 1935, Atatürk turned Aya Sofya into a museum and a project of restoration, including the uncovering of mosaics, began. ✉ *Aya Sofya Sq.* ☎ *212/522–1750* 🎫 *20 TL* ☉ *Tues.–Sun. 9–7 in summer, 9–5 in winter (last entry 1 hr before closing time).*

**Fodor's Choice ★** **Blue Mosque** (*Sultanahmet Camii*). Only after you enter the Blue Mosque do you understand the name: the inside is covered with 20,000 shimmering blue-green İznik tiles interspersed with 260 stained-glass windows; calligraphy and intricate floral patterns are painted on the ceiling. After the dark corners and stern faces of the Byzantine mosaics in Aya Sofya, this mosque feels gloriously airy and full of light. Indeed, this favorable comparison was the intention of architect Mehmet Ağa (a former student of the famous Ottoman architect Sinan), whose goal was to surpass Justinian's crowning achievement (Aya Sofya). At the behest of Sultan Ahmet I (ruled 1603–17), he created this masterpiece of Ottoman craftsmanship, starting in 1609 and completing it in just eight years, and many believe he indeed succeeded in outdoing the

---

### ISTANBUL BEST BETS

**Aya Sofya.** Once the epicenter of the Christian world, this church constructed in the 6th century is the tour de force of Byzantine architecture.

**Topkapı Sarayı.** This giant palace provides a behind-the-scenes look at daily life, sultan-style, from how a concubine filled her day to where the ruler kept his stash of jewels.

**Shopping at the Grand Bazaar.** Istanbul's giant bazaar has been providing retail therapy since the mid-15th century!

splendor of Aya Sofya. ⊠ *Sultanahmet Sq., Sultanahmet* ۞ *Mosque: Daily 9–6:30 in summer, 9–5 in winter; closed to tourists during prayer times. Mausoleum: Tues.–Sun. 9–4:30.*

★ **Grand Bazaar** (*Kapalı Çarşı*). It's said that this early version of a shopping mall is the largest concentration of stores under one roof anywhere in the world, and that's easy to believe. ⊠ *Yeniçeriler Cad. and Çadırcılar Cad.* ☎ *212/519–1248* ۞ *Mon.–Sat. 8:30–7.*

Fodor'sChoice **Süleymaniye Camii** (*Mosque of Süleyman*). Perched on a hilltop opposite
★ Istanbul University, Süleymaniye Camii is perhaps the most magnificent mosque in Istanbul and is considered one of the architect Sinan's masterpieces. Thanks to a three-year, multimillion-dollar restoration project completed in late 2010, the Süleymaniye can now be seen in its full glory. The tomb of Sinan is just outside the walls, on the northern corner, while those of his patron, Süleyman the Magnificent, and the sultan's wife, Roxelana, are housed in the cemetery adjacent to the mosque. The *külliye*, or mosque complex, still includes a hospital, library, hamam, several schools, and other charitable institutions that mosques traditionally operate, so take a stroll around the beautiful grounds—and don't miss the wonderful views of the Golden Horn. ⊠ *Süleymaniye Cad., near Istanbul University's north gate* ۞ *Daily sunrise–sunset except during prayer times.*

Fodor'sChoice **Topkapı Sarayı** (*Topkapı Palace*). This vast palace on Seraglio Point,
★ above the confluence of the Bosphorus and the Golden Horn, was the residence of sultans and their harems, in addition to being the seat of Ottoman rule from the 1460s until the middle of the 19th century. Few other royal residences match this hilltop compound when it comes to mystery, intrigue, and the lavishly exotic intricacies of court life. Sultan Mehmet II built the original Topkapı Palace, known simply as the New Palace, between 1459 and 1465, shortly after his conquest of Constantinople. Over the centuries, sultan after sultan added ever more elaborate architectural frills and fantasies, until the palace had acquired four courtyards and quarters for some 5,000 full-time residents, including slaves, concubines, and eunuchs.

The main entrance, or Imperial Gate, leads to the **Court of the Janissaries**, also known as the First Courtyard—it is, and has always been, freely accessible to the general public. Today, the courtyard where these members of the sultan's guard once assembled is a tranquil green park full of tourist groups, and there is little to evoke the splendors and tragedies of the palace's extraordinary history. You will begin to experience the grandeur of the palace when you pass through the **Bab-üs Selam** (Gate of Salutation). Süleyman the Magnificent built the gate in 1524 and was the only person allowed to pass through it on horseback; others had to dismount and enter on foot. Prisoners were kept in the towers on either side of the gate before they were executed next to the nearby fountain, a handy arrangement that made it easy for executioners to wash the blood off their hands after carrying out their orders.

The **Second Courtyard**, once the administrative hub of the Ottoman Empire, is planted with rose gardens and ornamental trees, and filled with a series of ornate *köşks*, pavilions once used for the business of state as well as for more mundane matters, like feeding the hordes of servants. The **Harem,** a maze of 400 halls, terraces, rooms, wings, and apartments grouped around the sultan's private quarters, evokes all the exoticism and mysterious ways of the Ottoman Empire. Seeing the 40 or so Harem rooms that have been restored and open to the public, though, brings to mind not just luxury but the regimentation, and even barbarity, of life in this enclosed enclave. A separate ticket must be purchased to visit the Harem.

Beyond the Harem is the **Third Courtyard,** shaded by regal old trees and dotted by some of the most ornate of the palace's pavilions. (From the Harem, you enter to the side of the courtyard, but to see this beautiful space to best advantage, make your way to its main gate, the **Bab-üs Saadet,** or Gate of Felicity, exit and reenter—and consider yourself privileged to do so, because for centuries only the sultan and grand vizier were allowed to pass through the gate.) Foreign ambassadors once groveled in the Arz Odası (Audience Chamber), but access to the courtyard was highly restricted, in part because it housed the **Treasury,** four rooms filled with imperial thrones and lavish gifts bestowed upon generations of sultans, and spoils garnered from centuries of war and invasions. The glittering prizes here are the jewels. The most famous pieces are the 86-carat Spoonmaker's Diamond and the emerald-studded Topkapı Dagger.

The **Fourth Courtyard,** more of an open terrace, was the private realm of the sultan, and the small, elegant pavilions, mosques, fountains, and reflecting pools are scattered amid the gardens that overlook the Golden Horn and Bosphorus. The octagonal **Revan Köşkü,** built by Murat IV in 1636 to commemorate a military victory in eastern Anatolia and the Caucasus, is often referred to in Ottoman histories as the Turban Room (Sarık Odası) because it is where the sultan used to keep his turbans. In the **İftariye** (Golden Cage), also known as the Sofa Köşkü, the closest relatives of the reigning sultan lived in strict confinement under what amounted to house arrest—superseding an older practice of murdering all possible rivals to the throne. Just off the open terrace with the wishing well is the lavishly tiled **Sünnet Odası** (Circumcision Room), where little princes would be taken for ritual circumcision during their ninth or 10th year. ⊠ *Babıhümayun Cad., Gülhane Park, near Sulta-nahmet Sq.* ☎ *212/512–0480* ⊕ *www.topkapisarayi.gov.tr* ☐ *Palace: 20 TL; Harem: 15 TL* ۞ *Palace: Wed.–Mon. 9–7 in summer, 9–5 in winter (last entry 1 hr before closing time). Harem: Wed.–Mon. 9–5 in summer, 9–4 in winter.*

## SHOPPING

Istanbul has been a shopper's town for, well, centuries—the sprawling Grand Bazaar could easily be called the world's oldest shopping mall—but this is not to say that the city is stuck in the past. Along with its colorful bazaars and outdoor markets, Istanbul also has a wide range of modern options. Whether you're looking for trinkets and souvenirs, kilims and carpets, brass and silverware, leather goods, old books, prints and maps, or furnishings and clothes (Turkish textiles are among the best in the world), you can find them here. **Nuruosmaniye Caddesi,** one of the major streets leading to the Grand Bazaar, is lined with some of Istanbul's most stylish shops, with an emphasis on fine carpets, jewelry, and antiques.

**The Arasta Bazaar.** Just behind the Blue Mosque, the Arasta Bazaar is a walkway lined with shops selling items similar to those you'll find at the Grand Bazaar (primarily carpets and ceramics), but often at lower prices. The atmosphere is also considerably calmer and, unlike the Grand Bazaar, the Arasta is open on Sunday. ⊠ *Sultanahmet.*

**The Egyptian Bazaar.** The Egyptian Bazaar is also known as the Spice Market, and has stall after enticing stall filled with mounds of exotic spices and dried fruits. ⊠ *near Yeni Cami Meydanı, Eminönü.*

**Sahaflar Çarşısı.** The Sahaflar Çarşısı, reached through a doorway just outside the western end of the Grand Bazaar, is home to a bustling book market, with both old and new editions. Most are in Turkish, but English and other languages are also represented. The market is open daily, though Sunday has the most vendors. ⊠ *Grand Bazaar.*

## WHERE TO EAT

$ TURKISH ✕ **Doy-Doy.** *Doy-doy* is a Turkish expression for "full" and, unlike many other places in tourist-filled Sultanahmet, you can indeed fill up for a reasonable sum at this no-frills spot frequented by locals. A variety of kebabs and *pide,* a type of Turkish pizza baked in a wood-burning oven, with different toppings are served, and the lunchtime specials, including vegetable stew, meatballs, and eggplant and meat moussaka, are a particularly good deal. The two-level rooftop terrace, open in summer, has fine views of the Blue Mosque and Sea of Marmara—but don't expect to savor the view with a drink in hand, as no alcohol is served. $ *Average main: 12 TL* ⊠ *Şifa Hamamı Sok. 13, Sultanahmet* ☎ *212/517–1588* ⊕ *www.doydoy-restaurant.com.*

$ TURKISH Fodor'sChoice ★ ✕ **Khorasani.** One of Sultanahmet's most popular restaurants emphasizes the Arab- and Kurdish-influenced cuisine of southeastern Turkey, from where the restaurant's owners hail. This translates to delicious mezes like hummus, *muhammara* (hot pepper and walnut spread), and thyme salad, as well as unusual mains that include quail kebab and a pistachio kebab made with both lamb and beef. Diners can sit outdoors on the cobblestoned sidewalk or get a table inside to watch the chefs prepare kebabs over the large charcoal grill. $ *Average main: 26 TL* ⊠ *Ticarethane Sok. 39/41, Sultanahmet* ☎ *212/519–5959* ⊕ *www. khorasanirestaurant.com.*

## WHERE TO STAY

$$$ ⌂ **Ayasofya Konakları.** Nine charming, pastel-color wooden mansions from the late 19th century have been restored by Turkey's Touring and Automobile Club and turned into a row of elegant guest houses, where smallish rooms are furnished in period Ottoman style, with brass beds and chandeliers, wooden floors and furniture, and plush upholstery, and have either half-size tubs or showers. **Pros:** unique, historic buildings;

location adjacent to Aya Sofya. **Cons:** high room rates because of location; some accommodations far from reception and dining area; most rooms lack TV and Wi-Fi. $ *Rooms from: 410 TL* ✉ *Soğukçeşme Sok., Sultanahmet* ☎ *212/513–3660* ⊕ *www.ayasofyakonaklari.com* ⇋ *57 rooms, 10 suites* ⦿ *Breakfast.*

**$$$$**
**Fodor'sChoice**
★

🏨 **Çırağan Palace Kempinski Istanbul.** Once a residence for the Ottoman sultans, the late 19th-century Çırağan Palace (pronounced chi-rahn) is Istanbul's most luxurious hotel, with ornate public spaces that feel absolutely decadent and a breathtaking setting right on the Bosphorus—the outdoor infinity pool seems to hover on the water's edge and most rooms, full of Ottoman-inspired wood furnishings and textiles in warm colors, have balconies overlooking the Bosphorus as well. **Pros:** grand setting in incredible location; over-the-top feeling of luxury; free Wi-Fi. **Cons:** exorbitant price of food and drinks; high rates, especially for rooms that have no Bosphorus view. $ *Rooms from: 1300 TL* ✉ *Çırağan Cad. 32, Beşiktaş* ☎ *212/326–4646* ⊕ *www.kempinski. com/istanbul* ⇋ *282 rooms, 31 suites.*

**$$**
**HOTEL**
**Fodor'sChoice**
★

🏨 **Dersaadet Hotel.** *Dersaadet* means "place of happiness" in Ottoman Turkish and this small, cozy hotel lives up to its name—rooms have an elegant, even plush, feel, with colorful rugs on the floor, antique furniture, and ceilings hand-painted with Ottoman ornamental motifs. **Pros:** extraordinary level of service; lovely terrace; good value. **Cons:** some rooms modest in size; no view from rooms on lower floors. $ *Rooms from: 276 TL* ✉ *Küçükayasofya Cad. Kapıağası Sok. 5, Sultanahmet* ☎ *212/458–0760* ⊕ *www.dersaadethotel.com* ⇋ *14 rooms, 3 suites* ⦿ *Breakfast.*

# KATAKOLON, GREECE (FOR OLYMPIA)

Updated by
Adrian Vrettos
and Alexia
Amvrazi

Katakolon could not seem less of a cruise port if it tried. A tiny enclave clinging to the western Peloponnese coast, it's a sleepy place except when ships dock. But it's a popular cruise destination because of its proximity to Olympia. Ancient Olympia was one of the most important cities in classical Greece. The Sanctuary of Zeus was the city's raison d'être, and attracted pilgrims from around the eastern Mediterranean, and later the city played host to Olympic Games, the original athletic games that were the inspiration for today's modern sporting panplanetary meet. At the foot of the tree-covered Kronion hill, in a valley near two rivers, Katakolon is today one of the most popular ancient sites in Greece. If you don't want to make the trip to Olympia, then Katakolon is an ideal place for a leisurely Greek lunch while you watch the fishermen mend their nets, but there's just not much else to do there.

## ESSENTIALS

### CURRENCY

The euro.

### HOURS

Stores are generally open from 9 to 9 on weekdays and 9 to 6 on Saturday. Museums are generally open from 9 to 5, but many are closed on Monday.

### TELEPHONES

Tri-band GSM phones work in Greece. You can buy prepaid phone cards at telecom shops, news vendors, and tobacconists in all towns and cities. Phone cards can be used for local or international calls. Vodafone is the leading mobile telecom company. OTE is the national domestic provider. Calls can be made at OTE offices and paid for after completion.

### COMING ASHORE

Katakolon is a very small port. Ships dock at the jetty, from where it is a short walk (five minutes) into Katakolon Town. It's a small Greek town with a lot of character; most residents still make their living from fishing; a few restaurants are along the waterfront, as well as shops selling souvenirs to cruise-ship passengers. There are no passenger facilities at the jetty itself. Though there are refreshment stands, telephones, currency exchange offices, and an ATM in the town.

Taxis are available at the dock to meet ships. However, cabs charge an overinflated fixed fare for the journey to Olympia, so it's often better to go on a ship-sponsored excursion.

**Contacts Katakolon Car Rental.** Diplas Dionysios runs this agency, but it has a limited number of vehicles, so it's vital to book in advance if you want to drive yourself to Olympia. Prices for a compact manual vehicle are approx €40 per day. ☎ 26210/41727.

## EXPLORING OLYMPIA

★ **Ancient Olympia.** Located at the foot of the pine-covered Kronion hill, and set in a valley where the Kladeos and Alpheios rivers join, Ancient Olympia is one of the most celebrated archaeological sites in Greece. Home to a sacred sanctuary dedicated to Zeus, Olympia also became famed as the host of the Olympic Games. Just as athletes from city-states throughout ancient Greece made the journey to compete in the ancient Olympics—the first sports competition—visitors from all over the world today make their way to the small modern Arcadian town that appears to have been already been a legend as long ago as the 10th century BC. The Olympic Games, first staged around the 8th century BC, were played here in the stadium, hippodrome, and other venues for some 1,100 years. Today, the venerable ruins of these structures attest to the majesty and importance of the first Olympiads. Modern Olympia, an attractive mountain town surrounded by pleasant hilly countryside, has hotels and tavernas, convenient for visitors to the ancient site.

As famous as the Olympic Games were—and still are—Olympia was first and foremost a sacred place, a sanctuary honoring Zeus, king of the gods, and Hera, his wife and older sister. The sacred quarter was known as the Altis, or the Sacred Grove of Zeus, and was enclosed by a wall on three sides and the Kronion Hill on the other. Inside the Altis were temples, altars, and twelve treasuries of various city-states.

To honor the cult of Zeus established at Olympia as early as the 10th century BC, altars were first constructed outdoors, among the pine forests that encroach upon the site. But around the turn of the 6th century BC, the earliest building at Olympia was constructed, the Temple

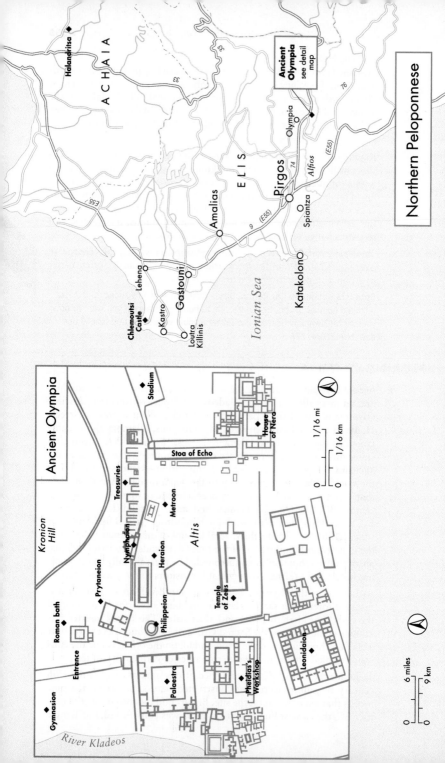

# Ancient Olympia

Kronion Hill

River Kladeos

Gymnasion

Entrance

Roman bath

Prytaneion

Nymphaion

Philippeion

Heraion

Treasuries

Metroon

Stadium

Stoa of Echo

House of Nero

Altis

Temple of Zeus

Pheidias's Workshop

Palaestra

Leonidaion

0       1/16 mi

0       1/16 km

0       6 miles

0       9 km

# Northern Peloponnese

ACHAIA

Halandritsa

ELIS

Olympia

**Ancient Olympia**
see detail map

Pirgos

Amalias

Spiantza

Alfios

Ionian Sea

Katakolon

Gastouni

Lehena

Kastro

Chlemoutsi Castle

Loutra Killinis

33

9 (E55)

74

76

(E55)

of Hera, which originally honored Zeus and Hera jointly, until the Temple of Zeus was constructed around 470 BC. The Temple of Zeus was one of the finest temples in all of Greece. Thirteen columns flanked the sides, and its interior housed the most famous work of ancient Greece—a gold and ivory statue of Zeus. Earthquakes in 551 and 552 finished off the temple.

After the Treasuries, the Bouleu-terion, and the Pelopeion were built, the 5th and 4th centuries BC, the Golden Age of the ancient games, saw a virtual building boom. The monumental Temple of Zeus, the Prytaneion, and the Metroon went up at this time. The enormous Leon-idaion was built around 300 BC, and as the games continued to thrive, the Palaestra and Gymnasion were added to the complex.

> ## OLYMPIA BEST BETS
>
> **The Twelve Labors of Hercules.** This series now in the archaeological museum is regarded as a high point in classical Greek sculpture.
>
> **Statue of Hermes by Praxiteles.** Also in the museum, this is one of the most complete classical statues to have been unearthed.
>
> **Remains of the Temple of Zeus.** The above-mentioned treasures once adorned this vast temple, which was one of the largest and finest in ancient Greece. Today only the platform remains.

The history of the Olympic Games is long and fabled. For almost eleven centuries, freeborn Greeks from the various city-states gathered to participate in the games, held every four years in August or September. These games became so much a part of the culture that the four-year interval between the games became a standard unit of time, an Olympiad. An Olympic truce—the Ekecheiria—allowed safe passage for athletes from the different city-states traveling to the games, and participation in them meant allegiance to a "Panhellenic" ideal of a united Greece. The exact date of the first games is not known, but the first recorded event is a footrace, a *stade,* run in 776 BC. A longer race, a *diaulos,* was added in 724 BC, and wrestling and a pentathlon—consisting of the long jump, the javelin throw, the discus throw, a footrace, and wrestling—in 708 BC. Boxing and chariot racing were 7th-century BC additions, as was the *pankration,* a no-holds-barred match (broken limbs were frequent and strangulation sometimes the end)—Plato, the great philosopher, was a big wrestling fan. By the 5th century BC, the games featured nine events, held over four days, with the fifth day reserved for the ceremonies. Most of the participants were professional athletes, for whom winning a laurel wreath at Olympia ensured wealth and glory from the city-states that sponsored them.

Today's tranquil pine-forested valley at Olympia, set with weathered stones of peaceful dignity, belies the sweaty drama of the first sporting festivals. Stadium foot-races run in the nude; *pankration* wrestling so violent today's Ultimate Fighting matches look tame; week-long bacchanals—serviced by an army of *pornoi* and prostitutes—held in the Olympic Village: Little wonder this ancient event is now called the "Woodstock of its day" by modern scholars (wrestlers, boxers, and discus-throwers being the rock stars of ancient Greece).

For today's sightseer, the ruins of many of Olympia's main structures are still visible. The **Altis** was the sacred quarter was also known as the Sacred Grove of Zeus. In the **Bouleuterion,** the seat of the organizers of the games, the Elean senate, athletes swore an oath of fair play. In the **Gymnasion,** athletes practiced for track and field events in an open field surrounded by porticoes. In the **Hippodrome,** horse and chariot races were run on a vast racecourse. The **House of Nero** was a lavish villa built for the emperor's visit to the games of AD 67, in which he competed. The **Leonidaion** was a luxurious hostel for distinguished visitors to the games; it later housed Roman governors. The **Metroon** was a small Doric temple dedicated to Rhea (also known as Cybele), Mother of the Gods. The **Nymphaion,** a semicircular reservoir, stored water from a spring to the east that was distributed throughout the site by a network of pipes. The **Palaestra** was a section of the gymnasium complex used for athletic training; athletes bathed and socialized in rooms around the square field. The **Pelopeion,** a shrine to Pelops, legendary king of the region now known as the Peloponnese, housed an altar in a sacred grove. **Pheidas's Workshop** was the studio of the great ancient sculptor famed for his enormous statue of Zeus, sculpted for the site's Temple of Zeus. The **Prytaneion** was a banquet room where magistrates feted the winners and a perpetual flame burned in the hearth. The **Stadium** held as many as 50,000 spectators, who crowded onto earthen embankments to watch running events. The starting and finishing lines are still in place. The **Temple of Hera** was one of the earliest monumental Greek temples was built in the 7th century BC. The **Temple of Zeus,** a great temple and fine example of Doric architecture, housed an enormous statue of Zeus that was one of the seven wonders of the ancient world. The famous **Treasuries** were temple-like buildings that housed valuables and equipment of twelve of the most powerful of the city-states competing in the games.

You'll need at least two hours to fully see the ruins and the Archaeological Museum of Olympia (to the north of the ancient site), and three or four hours would be better. ✉ *Off Ethnikos Odos 74, ½ km (¼ mile) outside modern Olympia* ☎ *26240/22517* ⊕ *www.culture.gr* 🎫 *€6, combined ticket with Archaeological Museum €9* ☾ *Sun.–Mon. 9–4; Tues.–Sat. 8–5.*

**Archaeological Museum of Olympia.** Of all the sights in ancient Olympia, some say the modern Archaeological Museum of Olympia gets the gold. Housed in a handsome glass and marble pavilion at the edge of the ancient site, the magnificent collections include the sculptures from the Temple of Zeus and the *Hermes Carrying the Infant Dionysus,* sculpted by the great Praxiteles, which was discovered in the Temple of Hera in the place noted by Pausanias. The central gallery of the museum holds one of the greatest sculptural achievements of classical antiquity: the pedimental sculptures and metopes from the Temple of Zeus, depicting Hercules's Twelve Labors. The *Hermes* was buried under the fallen clay of the temple's upper walls and is one of the best-preserved classical statues. Also on display is the famous *Nike of Paionios.* Other treasures include notable terra-cottas of Zeus and Ganymede; the head of the cult statue of Hera; sculptures of the family and imperial patrons of Herodes

Atticus; and bronzes found at the site, including votive figurines, cauldrons, and armor. Of great historic interest are a helmet dedicated by Miltiades, the Athenian general who defeated the Persians at Marathon, and a cup owned by the sculptor Pheidias, which was found in his workshop on the Olympia grounds. ⊠ *Off Ethnikos Odos 74, ½ km (¼ mile) outside modern Olympia* ☎ *26240/22742* ⊕ *www.culture.gr* ⊠ *€6, combined ticket with Ancient Olympia €9* ☉ *May–Oct., Mon. 11–7:30, Tues.–Sun. 8–7:30; Nov.–Apr., daily 8:30–3.*

## SHOPPING

Lovers of handicrafts will really enjoy shopping in Greece. There's an abundance of ceramics, both traditional and modern, wooden bowls, reproductions of ancient statuary, woven rugs, jewelry, lace, and edibles such as delicious honey and olive oil. Cotton clothing is perfect for the summer temperatures, along with strong handcrafted sandals and leather goods that have always been popular purchases here. Around Olympus other popular souvenirs are reproductions of ancient artifacts found at the ancient site. Shop in modern Olympia or in Katakalon before reboarding your ship. There are just a few shops in Kalakon, but they sell a full range of souvenirs.

★ **Archaeological Museum.** The shop of the Archaeological Museum carries an appealing line of figurines, bronzes, votives, and other replicas of objects found in the ruins. ⊠ *Off Ethnikos Odos 74, north of Ancient Olympia site* ☎ *26240/22742.*

★ **Atelier Exekias.** At Atelier Exekias Sakis Doylas sells exquisite handmade and hand-painted ceramic bowls and urns, fashioned after finds in Ancient Olympia; the glazes and colors are beautiful. ⊠ *Kondoli, Olympia* ☎ *6936/314054 or 26240/23816.*

## WHERE TO EAT

$ ✗ **Aegean.** Don't let the garish signs depicting the menu put you off:
GREEK  the far-ranging offerings are excellent. You can eat lightly—a gyro or pizza—but do venture into some of the more-serious fare, especially such local dishes as the fish that's been oven-baked with onion, garlic, green peppers, and parsley. The house's barrel wine is a nice accompaniment to any meal. ⑤ *Average main: €7* ⊠ *Douma, near Hotel New Olympia, Olympia* ☎ *26240/22540.*

$ ✗ **Taverna Bacchus.** The best restaurants in Greece are often in small villages, and this appealing family-run taverna and inn, a favorite among
GREEK  Olympians, is one such example. Locals start to trek in around 10:30 pm for dishes that include a delicious chicken with oregano. ⑤ *Average main: €8* ⊠ *Ancient Pissa (Mirika), Olympia* ☎ *26240/22298* ☉ *Closed Dec.–Feb.*

# KOPER, SLOVENIA

Updated
by Bruce
Leimsidor

Just half the size of Switzerland, Slovenia is often bypassed in favor of more well-known countries such as Croatia and Italy. The country's relative obscurity owes much to its history. From Roman times to nearly the present day, Slovenian territory was incorporated into far-larger empires, relegating Slovenia through the ages to the role of rustic, if charming, hinterland. Backed by hills planted with olive groves and vineyards, Slovenia's small strip of Adriatic coastline is only 47 km (29 miles) long and dominated by the towns of Koper, Izola, Piran, and Portorož. Following centuries of Venetian rule, the coast remains culturally and spiritually connected to Italy, and Italian is still widely spoken. Koper, Slovenia's largest port, and Izola, its biggest fishery, are workaday towns that nevertheless retain a lot of historical charm. The medieval port of Piran is a gem and a must-see. Its Venetian core is nearly perfectly preserved. The most unspoiled stretch of coast is at the Strunjan Nature Reserve—which also has an area reserved for nudists—between Piran and Izola.

## ESSENTIALS

### CURRENCY

The euro. In major cities banks and ATMs are easy to find, but not all ATMs readily accept international cards.

### HOURS

Most banks are open weekdays 9 to noon and 2 to 4:30, Saturday 9 to 11. The main museums are open Tuesday through Sunday from 10 to 6. Larger shops are open Monday through Saturday from 10 to 6, although smaller ones may open mornings only from 10 to 2. Most stores are closed Sunday. Some restaurants close one day a week—usually Sunday, but sometimes Monday.

### TELEPHONES

The country code for Slovenia is 386. When dialing from outside the country, drop any initial "0" from the area code. Pay phones (although they are becoming rare) take magnetic telephone cards, available from post offices and kiosks. Most tri-band GSM mobile phones will work in Slovenia provided you enable international service.

## COMING ASHORE

Cruise ships dock immediately below Koper's Old Town, at a recently renovated modern passenger terminal. From here, it's 300 meters to Titov trg, the main square, in the pedestrian-only Old Town, where you'll find the city's main sights, plus a useful Tourist Information Center. The Old Town can be explored on foot, so there is no need to rent a car if you decide to stay in Koper. But some people will choose to go into Ljubljana (77 miles [124 km] away, which is about three hours by bus or a little more than two hours by car). Most cruise lines offer tours that include time in Ljubljana. Other popular excursions include the nearby seaside towns of Izola and Piran, the Lipica Stud Farm, and Postojna Cave. There's a taxi stand in the port.

If you choose to rent a car, expect to pay about €55 for a manual compact vehicle, though you can rent a semiautomatic Smart car at some outlets for about €50.

# EXPLORING SLOVENIA FROM KOPER

## KOPER

Today a port town surrounded by industrial suburbs, Koper nevertheless warrants some exploration. The Republic of Venice made Koper the regional capital during the 15th and 16th centuries, and the magnificent architecture of the Old Town bears witness to the spirit of those times. The most important buildings are clustered around **Titov trg,** the central town square. Here stands the **Cathedral,** which can be visited daily from 7 to noon and 3 to 7, with its fine Venetian Gothic facade and bell tower dating back to 1664. Across the square the splendid **Praetor's Palace,** formerly the seat of the Venetian Grand Council, combines Gothic and Renaissance styles. From the west side of Titov trg, the narrow, cobbled **Kidriceva ulica** brings you down to the seafront.

> ### KOPER BEST BETS
>
> **Koper Old Town.** Wander through Koper's lovely medieval car-free streets to arrive on Titov trg, the main square.
>
> **Postojna Cave.** Explore the underground depths of this vast and impressive show cave.
>
> **Ljubljana Castle.** See the Slovenian capital at its best, from the ramparts of the hilltop castle.

## IZOLA

Izola is a normally placid fishing town that lets its hair down in summer. DJs decamp from Ljubljana for parties on the coast, artists set up their studios, and the city adopts the relaxed persona of a shaggy beach town. Less industrial than Koper and less self-consciously pretty than Piran, Izola makes a perfect day outing. It's also a great place to eat. The fish is fresh and the customers—many of them local Slovenians—are demanding.

Like that of its immediate neighbor, Koper, the city's history goes back hundreds of years. Izola rose to prominence in the Middle Ages and then declined in the 16th and 17th centuries with the rise of the port of Trieste in present-day Italy. The name "Izola" comes from the Italian word for "island" and describes a time when the walled city in fact was an island. The city walls were knocked down by the French occupation at the start of the 19th century. The bricks were then used to connect the city to the mainland.

## LIPICA

**Kobilarna Lipica** (*Lipica Stud Farm*). The Kobilarna Lipica was founded in 1580 by the Austrian archduke Karl II. It's where the white Lipizzaners—the majestic horses of the famed Spanish Riding School in Vienna—originated. Today the farm no longer sends its horses to Vienna, but breeds them for its own performances and riding instruction. The impressive stables and grounds are open to the public. Riding classes are available, but lessons are geared toward experienced riders and must be booked in advance. ⊠ *Lipica 5, Sežana* ☎ *05/739–1708* ⊕ *www.lipica.org* ☽ *Dressage performances June–Oct., Tues., Fri., and Sun. at 3. Stable tours July and Aug., daily 9–6; Apr.–June and Sept. and Oct., daily 10–5; Nov.–Mar., daily 11–3.*

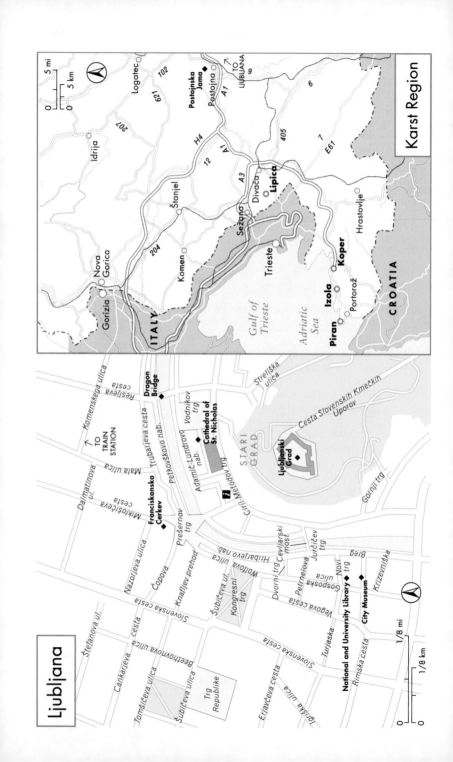

## POSTOJNSKA JAMA

**Postojnska Jama** (*Postojna Cave*). Postojnska Jama conceals one of the largest networks of caves in the world, with 23 km (14 miles) of underground passageways. A miniature train takes you through the first 7 km (4½ miles), to reveal a succession of well-lighted rock formations. This strange underground world is home of the snakelike "human fish" on view in an aquarium in the Great Hall. Eyeless and colorless because of countless millennia of life in total darkness, these amphibians can live for up to 60 years. Temperatures average 8°C (46°F) year-round, so bring a sweater, even in summer. Tours leave every hour on the hour throughout the year. ⊠ *Jamska 30, Postojna* ☎ *05/700–0163* ⊕ *www. postojna-cave.com* ☜ *€22.90* ⊗ *May–Sept., daily 8:30–6; Apr. and Oct., daily 8:30–5; Nov.–Mar., weekdays 9:30–1:30, weekends 9:30–3.*

## LJUBLJANA

Slovenia's small but exceedingly charming capital is enjoying a tourism renaissance. The tiny city center is captivating. Part of the charm is doubtless the emerald green Llubljanica River that winds its way slowly through the Old Town, providing a focal point and the perfect backdrop to the cafés and restaurants that line the banks. Partly, too, it's the aesthetic tension between the stately baroque houses along the river and the white neoclassical, modern, and Secessionist set pieces that dot the streets and bridges everywhere.

**Cathedral of St. Nicholas.** This proud baroque cathedral overlooking the daily market on Vodnikov trg is dedicated to St. Nicholas, the patron saint of fisherman and boatmen who created a powerful guild in medieval Ljubljana. Building took place between 1701 and 1708, under the Italian architect Andrea Pozzo, who modeled it after the church of Il Gesù in Rome. The magnificent frescos on the ceiling of the nave are by the Lombard painter Giulio Qualglio and depict the transfiguration of St. Nicholas and the persecution of Christians under Diocletian and Nero. In 1996, in honor of Pope John Paul II's visit, new bronze doors were added to the church. The main door tells the story of Christianity in Slovenia, whereas the side door shows the history of the Ljubljana diocese. ⊠ *Dolničarjeva 1, Ljubljana* ☎ *01/234–2690* ⊕ *lj-stolnica.rkc. si* ☜ *Free* ⊗ *Daily 7–noon and 3–7.*

**Čevljarski most** (*Cobblers' Bridge*). The most southerly of the historic bridges linking the old and new sides of town, this romantic pedestrian bridge was built in 1931 according to plans by the architect Jože Plečnik. The name (cobbler's bridge) refers to a wooden structure lined with shoemakers' huts that once stood here. ⊠ *Ljubljana.*

★ **City Museum of Ljubljana.** Situated in the grand Auersberg Palace, this museum and its beautifully designed exhibits trace the history of the city from pre-Roman times through the Austrian domination, the World Wars, the Tito years, and finally the establishment of independent Slovenia. In the basement, you can walk on a piece of the ancient Roman road and see a cross-sectioned excavation that shows the burning of Emona by Attila the Hun through a black, charred stratum. If you're interested, you can arrange for a museum guide to take you to other ancient Roman sites around the city. The city museum also houses the world's oldest wooden wheel, dating from 4000 BC. ✉ *Gosposka ulitca 15, Ljubljana* ☏ *01/241 2500* ⊕ *www.mgml.si* 🎫 *€4* ⊙ *Tues.– Sun. 10–6, Thurs. 10–9.*

**Dragon Bridge.** Four fire-breathing winged dragons crown the corners of this locally cherished concrete-and-iron structure. The dragons refer to the mythological origins of the city, when Jason, returning home from winning the Golden Fleece, killed a monster in a swamp on the present site of Ljubljana. ✉ *Ljubljana.*

**Franciskanska cerkev** (*Franciscan Church*). This imposing, pink, high-baroque church was built between 1646 and 1660 for Augustinian priests; the Franciscans took it over in the 18th century and painted it red, the color of their order (although the outside facade has now faded to pink). The main altar, by Francesco Robba (1698–1757), dates from 1736. The three sets of stairs in front are a 19th century addition added after the ground was leveled in the plaza and now serve as a popular meeting place for students. ✉ *Prešernov trg 4, Ljubljana* ☏ *01/4253007* ⊙ *Daily 8–12:30, 1:30–8.*

**Ljubljanski grad** (*Ljubljana Castle*). Ljubljana's hilltop castle affords views over the river and the Old Town's terra-cotta rooftops, spires, and green cupolas. On a clear day, the distant Julian Alps are a dramatic backdrop. The castle walls date from the early 16th century, although the tower was added in the mid-19th century. The surrounding park was landscaped by Plečnik in the 1930s. The castle also houses a virtual museum showcasing Slovenian history through digital technology. ✉ *Studentovska ul, uphill from Vodnikov trg, Grajska planota 1, Ljubljana* ☏ *01/306–4293* ⊕ *www.ljubljanskigrad.si* 🎫 *€8 (including cable car)* ⊙ *Apr.–Oct., daily 9–9; Nov.–Mar., daily 10–7.*

★ **National and University Library.** Built from 1936 to 1941, the National Library is architect Jože Plečnik's secular masterpiece. The external facades present a modernist version of an Italian reanaissance palazzo, using brick, stone, and even archeological remains from excavations around Ljubljana. Inside, there is a beautiful collonaded black marble staircase and a reading room with huge windows at either end to let in light. The austere furniture in the reading room was also designed by Plečnik. Don't miss the beautiful horsehead door handles on the main entrance. ✉ *Turjaška ultica 1, Ljubljana* ☏ *01/2001121* ⊕ *www.nuk. uni-lj.si* ⊙ *Reading Room open weekdays 9–8, Sat. 9–2.*

## SHOPPING

Although you wouldn't come to Slovenia to do much serious shopping, fashionable shoe stores abound in Ljubljana; for the latest selection head to shops on Stari trg in the Old Town.

**Ljubljana Flea Market.** You can pick up antiques and memorabilia at the Ljubljana Flea Market, held on the Breg Embankment each Sunday morning. ✉ *Breg Embankment, Ljubljana.*

**Open-Air Market.** The most interesting shopping experience is undoubtedly a visit to the open-air market, where you can find fresh fruit and vegetables as well as dried herbs and locally produced honey. ✉ *Vodnikov trg, Ljubljana.*

## WHERE TO EAT

**$$$** ✕ **Skipper.** Noted for its vast summer terrace overlooking the marina,
SEAFOOD Skipper is popular with the yachting fraternity. The menu includes
pasta dishes, risottos, grilled meats, and fish. $ *Average main: €30*
✉ *Kopališko nab 3, Koper* ☎ *05/626–1810.*

**$** ✕ **Trta.** In a country filled with pizza joints, this may be Slovenia's best.
PIZZA It offers supersize pies, fresh and inventive ingredients, and a small
garden for warm evenings. Walk south along the river (on the same
side as the Old Town), cross over busy Zoisova cesta, and continue
along Grudnovo nabrežje. $ *Average main: €8* ✉ *Grudnovo nabrezje
21, Ljubljana* ☎ *01/426–5066* ⊕ *www.trta.si* ☾ *Closed Sun.*

# KORČULA, CROATIA

Updated by
Jane Foster

Southern Dalmatia's largest, most sophisticated, and most visited
island, Korčula was known to the ancient Greeks, who named it *Kerkyra Melaina,* or "Black Corfu." Between the 10th and 18th centuries
it spent several periods under Venetian rule. Today most Croatians
know it for its traditional sword dances and its excellent white wines.
Korčula is also the name of the capital, which is near the island's eastern
tip. Eight centuries under Venetian rule bequeathed the town a trove of
Gothic and Renaissance churches, palaces, and piazzas, all built from
fine local stone. Korčula's main claim to fame, though one still disputed
by historians, is that it was the birthplace of Marco Polo (1254–1324).
The approach by sea is breathtaking; if the hour isn't too early, make
sure you're on deck for this one.

### ESSENTIALS

**CURRENCY**
The Croatian kuna. ATMs are easy to find.

**HOURS**
Offices are open weekdays from 8:30 to 4. Shops often close for lunch
around 1, and may close for as long as three hours; banks also sometimes close for lunch. Post offices are open on Saturday during the main
summer season, from June through September.

**TELEPHONES**
Most tri- and quad-band GSM phones will work in Croatia. Public
phones use calling cards, which can be purchased at the post office,
newsstands, and hotels.

### COMING ASHORE

Smaller ships may be able to dock at two cruise-ship docks in Korčula
Town, but larger vessels will have to anchor and tender passengers
ashore at the same dock. The dock area is lined with stores, cafés, and
tourism offices. If you are staying in town, there's no advantage to having a car for your day in port. If you'd like to explore the island, you
can rent a car, scooter, or even a bicycle. Expect to pay about €55 per
day for a compact manual vehicle. Guided tours can also be arranged,
including visits to local vineyards.

5

Korčula Island

Korčula Town

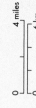

## EXPLORING KORČULA TOWN

At first view, Korčula may seem like a much smaller version of Dubrovnik: the same high walls, the circular corner fortresses, and the church tower projecting from within an expanse of red roofs. The main difference lies in the town plan, as narrow side streets run off the main thoroughfare at odd angles to form a herringbone pattern, preventing cold winter winds from whistling unimpeded through town. The center is small and compact, and can be explored in an hour.

**Katedrala** (*Cathedral*). On the main square, the splendid Gothic-Renaissance cathedral is built from a wheat-colored stone that turns pale gold in sunlight, amber at sunset. Enter through the beautifully carved Romanesque main portal, which is guarded by Adam and Eve standing upon twin lions. Inside, check out the elegant 15th-century ciborium; within, two paintings are attributed to the Venetian master Tintoretto. ⊠ *Trg Sv Marka* 🎫 *15 Kn* 🕑 *May.–Sept., Mon.–Sat. 9 am–7 pm; Nov.–Apr., by appointment.*

**Kopnena Vrata** (*Land Gate*). The main entrance into the Old Town is topped by the 15th-century Revelin Tower, housing an exhibition connected with the *Moreška* sword dance, and offering panoramic views over the Old Town. ⊠ *Kopnena Vrata* 🎫 *15 Kn* 🕑 *July and Aug., daily 9–9; May, June, and Sept., daily 10–2 and 4–8; Nov.–Apr., by appointment only.*

**Kuća Marca Pola** (*Marco Polo House*). A couple of blocks east of the main square is the place where the legendary 13th-century discoverer is said to have been born, when Korčula was part of the Venetian Empire. At present only the tower is open, with a modest exhibition about Polo's life on the first floor and a belvedere up top offering panoramic views. There are plans to restore the entire house and garden to form an educational museum, though this project is unlikely to be realized in the near future. ⊠ *Ul Marka Pola* 🕿 *020/716–529* 🎫 *20 Kn* 🕑 *Apr.–June and Sept.–Oct., daily 9 am–3 pm; July–Aug., daily 9–9* 🕑 *Closed Nov.–Mar.*

**Opatska Riznica** (*Abbot's Treasury*). Next to the cathedral, the treasury museum occupies the 17th-century Renaissance bishop's palace. This collection of sacred art includes Italian and Croatian Renaissance paintings, the most precious being a 15th-centruy triptych, *Our Lady with Saints*, by the Dalmatian master Blaž Jurjev Trogiranin, plus gold and silver ecclesiastical artifacts and ceremonial vestments. ⊠ *Trg Sv Marka* 🎫 *25 Kn* 🕑 *May.–Sept., Mon.–Sat. 9 am–7 pm; Nov.–Apr., by appointment.*

---

### KORČULA BEST BETS

**Search for Marco Polo.** The explorer's purported birthplace is right in the Old Town.

**Sip some wine.** Korčula is a major wine-producing region in Dalmatia; have a glass or buy a bottle of one of the local vintages.

**Watch the Dance of the Moors.** If your ship remains in port on one of the nights the island's famous dance is offered, this is a must-do.

**5**

# SHOPPING

**Cukarin.** This family-run store is renowned for its five different types of delicious handmade biscuits, as well as roasted almonds and home-made *rakija* flavored with local herbs. ✉ *Hrvatska Bratske Zajednice* ☎ *020/711–055* ⊕ *www.cukarin.hr.*

# SPORTS AND ACTIVITIES

### DIVING

**MM Sub.** MM Sub is a diving center based in Lumbarda offering diving instruction and trips for those with some experience. Nearby diving destinations include an underwater archaeological site, as well as several sea caves and shipwrecks. ✉ *Lumbarda* ☎ *020/712–321* ⊕ *www. mm-sub.hr.*

### MOREŠKA DANCES

The Moreška is a colorful sword dance originally performed each year on July 29 (the feast day of the town's protector, St. Theodore). Now it's performed at 9 pm each Monday and Thursday evening from May to October just outside the city walls (tickets 100 Kn), next to the Kopnena Vrata (Land Gate). The word *Moreška* means "Moorish." The dance is said to celebrate the victory of the Christians over the Moors in Spain, but the dance's real roots are conjecture. The dance itself is not native to Croatia, and was performed in many different Mediterranean countries, including Spain, Italy, and Malta. The story of the dance is a clash between the Black (Moorish) king and the White (Christian) king over a young maiden. The dance is done with real swords.

# BEACHES

The closest spot for a quick swim is Banje, a small pebble beach about 10 minutes on foot east of the town walls, close to Hotel Liburnija. For more leisurely bathing, the best beaches lie near the village of **Lumbarda**, which is 6 km (4 miles) southeast of Korčula Town. The most popular of these is the sandy south-facing Przina, 2 km (1 mile) south of Lumbarda, while the smooth-white-stoned Bili Žal lies a short distance east of Lumbarda.

# WHERE TO EAT

**$$$$**
EASTERN
EUROPEAN
**Fodor's** Choice
★

✕ **Adio Mare.** A long-standing favorite with locals and visitors alike, Adio Mare occupies a Gothic-Renaissance building in the Old Town, close to Kuća Marca Pola. There's a high-ceiling dining room, an open-plan kitchen so you can watch the cooks while they work, plus an open-air terrace. The menu has not changed since the restaurant opened in 1974: expect Dalmatian classics such as *pašta-fažol* (beans with pasta) and *pašticada* (beef stewed in wine and prunes), as well as fresh fish and seafood. The local wine, *pošip,* is excellent. ■ TIP➔ **This restaurant is particularly popular, so reservations are strongly recommended, especially in August.** ⑤ *Average main: 120 Kn* ✉ *Sv. Roka 2* ☎ *020/711–253* ⊗ *Closed Nov.–Mar.*

**$$$$**  ╳ **Konoba Mate.** In the courtyard of an old stone cottage in the village of
MEDITERRANEAN  Pupnat (21 miles west of Korčula Town, so you'll need to hire a car or
take a taxi), this welcoming eatery serves gourmet fare prepared from
the family's own farm. The menu changes with the seasons, but look
out for the house specialty, a platter of *pršut* (prosciutto), goat's cheese,
olives, and eggplant pâté, which you might follow with *pašticada* (beef
stewed in sweet wine and prunes, served with gnocchi) as a main.
There's also an excellent wine list, though the house wine, served by
the carafe, is a better value and is extremely palatable. ⑤ *Average main:
110 Kn ⊠ Pupnat bb ☎ 020/717–109 ۩ Closed Sun. lunch.*

# KOTOR, MONTENEGRO

Updated by
Jane Foster

Located in Bokor Kotorska (Kotor Bay), Europe's most southerly fjord,
Kotor lies 50 miles (80 km) west of Podgorica, the capital of Montenegro, from which it is separated by a belt of dramatic, rugged mountains. Listed as a UNESCO World Heritage site, Kotor's medieval Stari
Grad (Old Town) is enclosed within well-preserved defensive walls built
between the 9th and 18th centuries and presided over by a proud hilltop
fortress. In the Middle Ages, as Serbia's chief port, Kotor was an important economic and cultural center with its own highl -regarded schools
of stone-masonry and iconography. Later, it spent periods under the
control of Venice, Austria, and France, though it was undoubtedly the
Venetians who left the strongest impression on the city's architecture.
Since the breakup of Yugoslavia, some 70% of the stone buildings in the
romantic Old Town have been snapped up by foreigners. Fast becoming
a celebrity destination, it's been visited recently by such celebrities as
Catherine Zeta-Jones and Michael Douglas.

### ESSENTIALS
#### CURRENCY
The euro (despite the fact that Montenegro has not yet entered the
European Union).

#### HOURS
Offices are open weekdays from 8 to 4. Shops are generally open weekdays from 9 to 9, Saturday from 8 to 1, though some shut for lunch
around 2 and may close for as long as three hours. Banks stay open
weekdays from 9 to 7, Saturday from 9 to 1.

#### PRIVATE TOURS
Many private travel agencies offer tours, with hiking in the mountains
and rafting on the Tara River being the most popular. Meridian DMC
runs rafting trips on the Tara River as well as sightseeing excursions to
points of interest like Kotor Bay and Dubrovnik.

**Contacts Meridian DMC** ⊠ *Stari Grad 436* ☎ *032/323–448*
⊕ *www.meridiandmc.me.*

#### TELEPHONES
The country code for Montenegro is 382.

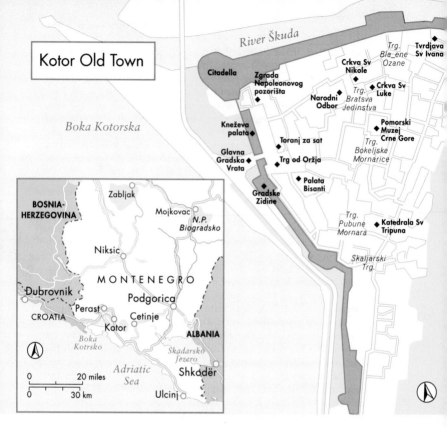

**Kotor Old Town**

River Škuda

Boka Kotorska

Citadella
Zgrada Napoleonovog pozorišta
Crkva Sv Nikole
Trg. Bla_ene Ozane
Tvrdjava Sv Ivana
Narodni Odbor
Trg. Bratsva Jedinstva
Crkva Sv Luke
Kneževa palata
Pomorski Muzej Crne Gore
Toranj za sat
Trg. Bokeljske Mornarice
Glavna Gradska Vrata
Trg od Oržja
Palata Bisanti
Gradske Zidine
Trg. Pubune Mornara
Katedrala Sv Tripuna
Trg. Pubune Mornara
Skaljarski Trg.

BOSNIA-HERZEGOVINA
Zabljak
Mojkovac
N.P. Biogradsko
Niksic
MONTENEGRO
Dubrovnik
Podgorica
Perast
Cetinje
CROATIA
Kotor
Boka Kotrsko
ALBANIA
Skadarsko Jezero
Adriatic Sea
Shkodër
Ulcinj

0    20 miles
0    30 km

## COMING ASHORE

Arriving at Kotor from the water is an impressive experience in itself, so be sure to be up on the deck in advance. Your ship will sail up a 28-km (18-mile) long bay (often referred to as a fjord), with rugged mountains rising in the background. Cruise ships dock on the quay, immediately in front of Kotor's medieval walled Old Town. Since the Old Town is compact and pedestrian-friendly, you do not need to rent a car in Kotor. It's easy to reach nearby Perast by bus or taxi.

## EXPLORING KOTOR

Kotor's Old Town takes approximately half a day to explore. Plan your visit for the morning, when the main sights are open to the public and the afternoon sun has yet to reach peak force.

**Crkva Sveti Luke** (*St. Luke's Church*). Built in 1195, this delightful Romanesque church is the only building in the Old Town to have withstood all five major earthquakes that affected Kotor. Originally a Catholic church, the building later became an Orthodox place of worship. Today there are two altars, one for each faith. ■TIP→ **The church is generally closed but you can ask at the nearby Crkva Sveti Nikole, which is open daily 8–1 and 5–7, and someone will open it for you.** ⊠ *Trg bratstvo i jedinstva.*

**Crkva Sveti Nikole** (*St. Nicholas' Church*). Designed by a Russian architect and built in pseudo-Byzantine style between 1902 and 1909, this is Kotor's most important Orthodox church (the Cathedral, by definition, is Catholic). The gold used to gild the spires was a gift from Russia. ⊠ *Trg bratstvo i jedinstva* ☉ *Daily 8–1 and 5–7.*

**Glavna Gradska Vrata.** The Main Town Gate (also known as the Sea Gate because of its position on the coast), which accesses the Stari Grad (Old Town) via the western facade of the city walls, dates back to the 16th century, and comprises Renaissance and baroque details. Originally, the outer gate bore a relief of the Venetian Lion, but in Tito's time this was replaced by the socialist star and dates recording the liberation of Kotor on November 21, 1944, at the end of WWII. There are two other entrances to the Stari Grad: the Južna Vrata (South Gate) and the Sjeverna Vrata (North Gate). ⊠ *Jadranski put.*

**Gradske Zidine** (*Town Walls*). Especially beautiful at night, when they are illuminated, the well-preserved town walls were built between the 9th and 18th centuries. They measure almost 5 km (3 miles) in length, and reach up to 66 feet in height and 52 feet in width. They form a triangular defense system around the Old Town, then rise up the hill behind it to Tvrdjava Sveti Ivana (St. John's Fortress), 853 feet above sea level. You can walk up to the fortress along the walls. Allow at least one hour to get up and back down. Wear good hiking shoes and don't forget to bring some water. ⊠ *Old Town, Stari Grad.*

**Katedrala Sveti Tripuna** (*St. Tryphon's Cathedral*). Undoubtedly Kotor's finest building, the Romanesque cathedral dates back to 1166, though excavation work shows that there was already a smaller church here in the 9th century. Due to damage caused by a succession of disastrous earthquakes, the cathedral has been rebuilt several times—the twin baroque bell towers were added in the late 17th century. Inside, the most important feature is the 14th-century Romanesque Gothic ciborium above the main altar. Also look out for fragments of 14th-century frescoes, which would once have covered the entire interior. A collection of gold and silver reliquaries, encasing body parts of various saints and crafted by local masters between the 14th and 18th century, is on display in the treasury. ⊠ *Trg Ustanka Mornara* ☎ *032/322–315* ☞ *€1 (treasury)* ☉ *May–Oct., daily 7–7; Nov.–Apr., daily 9–2.*

**Pomorski Muzej Crne Gore** (*Montenegrin Naval Museum*). Housed within the 18th-century baroque Grgurina Palace, this museum traces Montenegro's cultural and economic ties to the sea. In the 18th century, tiny Kotor had some 400 ships sailing the world's oceans. The exhibition

---

**KOTOR'S BEST BETS**

**Kotor Old Town.** Roam the car-free streets of this centuries-old fortified town, now a UNESCO World Heritage site.

**St John's Fortress.** Follow Kotor's medieval walls uphill to arrive at this small fort, affording magnificent views of the Old Town and the bay below.

**Our Lady of the Rock.** Take a boat ride across the bay from Perast to visit a tiny islet, capped by a church.

5

extends over three floors, and includes model ships; paintings of ships, ship owners, and local naval commanders; navigation equipment; and uniforms worn by Montenegrin admirals and captains. ⊠ *Trg Grgurina, Stari Grad* ☎ *032/304–720* ⊕ *www.museummaritimum.com* ⊠ *€4* ☺ *Jul.–Aug., Mon.–Sat. 8 am–11 pm, Sun. 10 am–4 pm; May–June and Sept., Mon.–Sat. 8 am–6 pm, Sun. 9 am–1 pm; Oct.–Apr., weekdays 9 am–5 pm, weekends 9 am–noon.*

**Toranj za sat** (*Clock Tower*). Built in the 17th century and considered a symbol of Kotor, the Clock Tower stands directly opposite the Main City Gate. You'll still find a watchmaker's shop at ground level (locals claim that the same family of watchmakers have worked here since the 17th century). In front of the Clock Tower, the "Pillar of Shame" was used to subject local criminals to public humiliation. ⊠ *Trg od Oržja, Stari Grad.*

**Trg od Oržja** (*Square of Arms*). The Main Town Gate leads directly into the Square of Arms, Kotor's main square, today a large paved space animated by popular open-air cafés. Under Venice, arms were repaired and stored here, hence the name. Notable buildings on the square include the 17th-century **Toranj za Sat** (Clock Tower), the 19th-century **Napoleonovog Pozorišta** (Napoléon Theater), and the 18th-century **Kneževa Palata** (Duke's Palace), the latter two now forming part of the upmarket Hotel Cattaro. ⊠ *Trg od Oržja, Stari Grad.*

★ **Tvrdjava Sveti Ivana** (*St. John's Fortress*). On the hill behind Kotor, 853 feet above sea level, this fortress is approached via a series of serpentines and some 1,300 steps. The fantastic view from the top makes the climb worthwhile: the terra-cotta-tile rooftops of the Old Town, the meandering fjord, and the pine-clad mountains beyond. On the way up, you will pass the tiny Crkva Gospe od Zdravlja (Church of Our Lady of Health), built in the 16th century to protect Kotor against the plague. Be sure to wear good walking shoes and take plenty of water. The route up starts from behind the east side of the city walls. ⊠ *Above Old Town.*

### PERAST

Lying 8 miles (13 km) northwest of Kotor, the peaceful little town of Perast is made up of semiabandoned stone houses built by local sea captains during the 17th and 18th centuries. In the bay in front of Perast lie two charming islets, each with a church.

★ **Gospa od Skrpjela** (*Our Lady of the Rock*). Unlike its sibling island, St. George, this island is man-made. Folklore has it that in 1452, local sailors found an icon depicting the Virgin and Child cast upon a rock jutting up from the water. Taking this as a sign from God, they began placing stones on and around the rock, slowly building an island over it. By 1630 they had erected a church upon the new island. The original icon (which has been attributed to the 15th-century local artist Lovro Dobričević) is displayed on the altar. Over the centuries, locals have paid their respects to it by donating silver votive offerings, some 2,500 of which are now on display. To get here, hop a boat taxi from the waterfront (a five-minute trip). ⊠ *Kotor Bay, Perast* ☎ *032/373–753 for Kotor tourist office information* ⊕ *www.gospa-od-skrpjela.me* ⊠ *€1* ☺ *May–mid-Nov., daily 9–7; mid-Nov.–Apr. by appointment.*

**Muzej Grad Perasta.** In the 17th-century Renaissance-baroque Bujović Palace, on the water's edge, Muzej Grad Perasta (Perast Town Museum) displays paintings of local sea captains and their ships, plus a horde of objects connected to Perast's maritime past. ⊠ *Obala Marka Martinovića bb, Perast* ☎ *032/373–519* ⊕ *www.muzejperast.me* ☒ *€2.50* ⊙ *July–Aug., Mon.–Sat. 9–7, Sun. 9–2; May–June and Sept., Mon.–Sat. 9–5, Sun. 9–2; Oct.–Apr., daily 8–2.*

**Sveti Djordje** (*St. George*). This natural islet is one of Perast's famous pair of islands. It's ringed by a dozen elegant cypress trees and crowned by the Monastery of St. George, dating back to the 12th century and still inhabited by monks. In the 18th century the island became a favorite burial place for local sea captains, whose crypts remain today. ■ **TIP➔ The island is closed to the public, but you can snap photos from shore or neighboring Our Lady of the Rock to your heart's content.** ⊠ *Kotor Bay, Perast.*

## SHOPPING

**Market.** This market that sells fruit and vegetables is just outside the city walls, on the main coastal road, and is filled with colorful, local, seasonal produce: artichokes, asparagus, and cherries in spring; tomatoes, eggplants, and peaches in summer. It takes place every morning but Sunday. ⊠ *E65 runs all the way down the coast. The market is on the road side, immediately outside the old town walls.*

## BEACHES

The small, pebble **town beach,** which is close to the center, is fine for a quick swim; however, for really decent swimming, locals recommend either **Jaz Beach** or **Plavi Horizonti,** both of which are some 14 miles (23 km) south of Kotor, between Tivat and Budva.

## WHERE TO EAT

**$$$$**
SEAFOOD
✗ **Galion.** A five-minute walk along the coast from the Old Town, this sophisticated seafood restaurant occupies an old stone building with a glass-and-steel extension overlooking the bay, offering views of Kotor's medieval walls. Expect funky modern furniture and chill-out music, and a menu featuring favorites such as octopus salad, homemade gnocchi, and barbecued fresh fish. ⑤ *Average main: €24* ⊠ *Šuranj bb* ☎ *032/325–054* ⊕ *www.hotelvardar.com* ⊙ *Closed Nov.–Mar.*

**$**
EASTERN
EUROPEAN
✗ **Kantun.** Locals swear by this friendly, down-to-earth eatery in the Old Town, on a small piazza near the Montenegrin Naval Museum. The menu features a choice of seafood and meat dishes, but ask the waiter to recommend the day's special, which could be anything from *gulaš* (Hungarian goulash) to *sarma* (cabbage leaves stuffed with rice and minced meat). Get a table outside in summer and soak in the Old Town atmosphere, though note that service can be slow when they're busy. The restaurant is open year-round. ⑤ *Average main: €8* ⊠ *Trg od Muzeja bb* ☎ *032/325–757* ▭ *No credit cards.*

5

# KUŞADASI, TURKEY (FOR EPHESUS)

The central and southern Aegean is probably the most developed area of Turkey, and the rolling hills, mountains surrounded by clear blue seas, and glorious white-sand beaches are just a few of the reasons why. Wandering through historic ruins, boating, scuba diving, basking in the Anatolian sun, and eating fresh fish are just some of the ways you can fill your day. Kuşadası itself is the most developed resort along the coast. Surrounding the tiny, atmospheric Old Town, a brash, very touristy development replete with tacky pubs and fish-and-chips restaurants has mushroomed in the last 20 years. On a positive note, Kuşadası is the stepping-stone to some of Turkey's most important ancient sites, including Ephesus and the early Christian site of Meryemana. Kuşadası also offers excellent shopping in high-class goods.

## ESSENTIALS

### CURRENCY
The Turkish lira.

### HOURS
Most shops are open daily from 9 until 9. Attractions are open daily from 8 to 5 or 6, though some are closed on Monday.

### PRIVATE TOURS
Having a private guide in Ephesus can be useful, and there are local companies that can arrange this in advance. Unlicensed guides will be available at the sight, but they may not be very helpful or accurate.

Contacts **Kuşadası Tours.** ✉ *Candan Turhan Bulvarı, 104/1–2* ☎ *256/614–1282, 1–866/921–0299 toll-free from U.S.* ⊕ *www.kusadasitours.com.*

### TELEPHONES
Most tri- and quad-band GSM phones will work in Turkey, but the Turkish mobile system is not 3G-compatible, and handsets are single band. Public phones accept tokens or telephone cards, phones accepting cards will also accept credit cards in payment for calls. Tokens and cards can be purchased at newsstands and telepcom shops. Turk Telekom, Turkcell, and Telcim are the major telecom companies.

## COMING ASHORE

Boats dock at the Ephesus town port. The passenger cruise terminal, Scala Nuova, has international shops such as Body Shop, plus a Starbucks and a Burger King. There is also a duty-free shop for reboarding passengers. From the dock it's a short walk of a few minutes to the port gate and into the town directly beyond, with immediate access to taxis, car rental offices, shops, and restaurants.

The public bus service from Kuşadası to the site at Ephesus and into Selçuk (the town near to Ephesus) is cheap and quick. *Dolmuş* (15-seat minivans) are the bulk of the fleet, and they depart from the bus terminus at Süeyman Demirel Boulevard, a 20-minute walk from the port. There are several services every hour except in mid-afternoon, when services drop to a couple per hour. Journey time is around 15 minutes. Most services stop at the end of the entry road to the archaeological site, leaving passengers with a 10-minute walk to the site entrance.

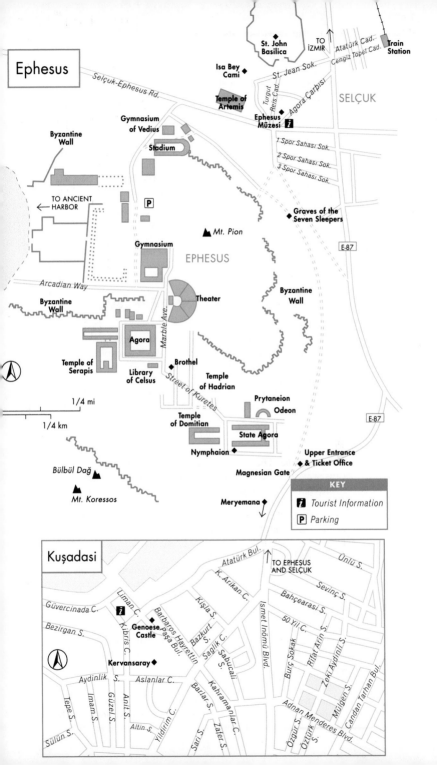

Taxis are plentiful, and they are metered with prices fixed by the municipality. Check that the meter is set to the day (lower) tariff. There are also numerous tour companies that can provide day tours to surrounding attractions. You can make these arrangements in travel agencies in Kuşadası.

Renting a car would allow you to have a full day of sightseeing and to tailor a schedule to your own desires. Car-rental companies are plentiful. Car rental is approximately $70 per day for a compact manual vehicle. You will be quoted a rate in dollars and can pay in dollars.

> **KUŞADASI BEST BETS**
>
> **Kuretes Street, Ephesus.** Follow in the footsteps of millions of Roman citizens and celebrity visitors, including St. Paul of Tarsus.
>
> **The Terrace House, Ephesus.** Venture inside this house to catch a glimpse of high-class interior design, circa the 2nd century AD.
>
> **Ephesus Museum, Selçuk.** Monumental archaeological treasures vie with personal items for prize of best artifact.

## EXPLORING KUŞADASI, SELÇUK, AND EPHESUS

### KUŞADASI

One of the most popular resort towns in the southern Aegean, Kuşadası is an ideal base, geographically, from which to explore the surrounding area. Unfortunately, being popular isn't always easy, and Kuşadası long ago lost its local charm. The huge yacht marina, the largest in the region, has only exacerbated the situation. What was a small fishing village up until the 1970s is now a sprawling, hyperactive town packed with curio shops and a year-round population of around 60,000, which swells several times over in summer with the influx of tourists and Turks with vacation homes.

**Genoese castle.** There aren't many sights in Kuşadası proper, but the causeway off Kadınlar Plajı (Women's Beach), just south of the harbor, connects the town to an old Genoese castle on Güvercin Adası (Pigeon Island). Today the site of a popular disco and several teahouses with gardens and sea views, the fortress was home to three Turkish brothers in the 16th century. These infamous pirates—Barbarossa, Oruc, and Hayrettin—pillaged the coasts of Spain and Italy and sold passengers and crews from captured ships into slavery in Algiers and Constantinople. Rather than fight them, Süleyman the Magnificent (ruled 1520–66) hired Hayrettin as his grand admiral and set him loose on enemies in the Mediterranean. The strategy worked: Hayrettin won victory after victory and was heaped with honors and riches.

**Kervansaray.** Kuşadası's 300-year-old kervansaray, now the Hotel Club Kervansaray, is loaded with Ottoman atmosphere. Its public areas are worth a look even if you're not staying here. ⊠ *Atatürk Bulvarı 1.*

### SELÇUK

*20 km (12 miles) northeast of Kuşadasý on Rte. 515.*

Selçuk, the closest city to the archaelogical site of Ephesus, lies beneath an ancient fortress, and is, unfortunately, often overlooked. The former farming town has interesting sights of its own to offer—St. John the Evangelist was purportedly buried here, and the city has one of the oldest mosques in Turkey.

**İsa Bey Cami** (*İsa Bey Mosque*). İsa Bey Cami is one of the oldest mosques in Turkey, dating from 1375. The jumble of architectural styles suggests a transition between Seljuk and Ottoman design: like later-day Ottoman mosques, this one has a courtyard, not found in Seljuk mosques. The structure is built out of "borrowed" stone: marble blocks with Latin inscriptions, Corinthian columns, black-granite columns from the baths at Ephesus, and pieces from the altar of the Temple of Artemis. ✉ *St. John Sok.* ⊙ *Daily 9–6.*

**St. John Basilica.** The emperor Justinian built the St. John Basilica over a 2nd-century tomb on Ayasoluk Hill, believed by many to have once held the body of St. John the Evangelist. Eleven domes formerly topped the basilica, which rivaled Istanbul's Aya Sofya (Haghia Sophia) in scale. The barrel-vaulted roof collapsed after a long-ago earthquake, but the church is still an incredible sight, with its labyrinth of halls and marble courtyards. It provides beautiful views both of Selçuk's castle and the Plain of Ephesus. ✉ *Entrance off St. John Sok., just east of İsa Bey Cami* ⊙ *Daily 8–5.*

## EPHESUS

**Ephesus Archaeological Site.** The ruins of Ephesus, once the most important Greco-Roman city of the Eastern Mediterranean, is one of the best preserved ancient sites in the world. Today, modern travelers can trace the fault lines of ancient civilization in Ephesus's spectacular landscape of ruined temples, theaters, and colonnaded streets. There are two entrances to the site, which is on a hill, one at the top of the site and one at the bottom. The main avenue is about a mile long but there are a number of intriguing detours, so a minimum visit of two hours can easily stretch to four, not including an hour in the museum in town.

The road leading to the upper entrance of the site passes a 1st-century AD **stadium,** where chariot and horse races were held on a track 712 feet long, and where gladiators and wild beasts met in combat before 70,000 spectators. On the left-hand side after you enter the site from the upper entrance is a 25,000-seat **theater,** backed by the western slope of Mt. Pion. Construction on this huge semicircle, with row upon row of curved benches, was begun by Alexander's general, Lysimachus, and completed by emperors Claudius and Trajan in the 2nd century AD. There is a fine view from the top of the steps. Higher still, near the top of Mt. Pion, are vestiges of the city's Byzantine walls. The theater is used for music and dance performances each May during the Selçuk Ephesus Festival of Culture and Art. Leading away from the theater toward the ancient port, now a marsh, is the **Arcadian Way.** This 1,710-foot-long street was once lined with shops and covered archways. Only a long line of slender marble columns remains.

In front of the theater is Marble Avenue. Follow it to the beautiful, two-story **Library of Celsus.** The courtyard of this much-photographed building is backed by wide steps that climb to the reading room, where you can still see rolls of papyrus. The library is near Marble Avenue's intersection with the **Curetes Street,** a still-impressive thoroughfare named for the college of priests once located there. At this corner is a large house believed to have been a **brothel.** Look for the floor mosaics of three women. To the right along the street are the **terrace houses** the multistoried houses of the nobility, with terraces and courtyards—there is a separate entrance fee to the terrace houses but the elaborate housing complexes of the Ephesian bourgeoisie are very interesting. A block from the brothel is the facade of the **Temple of Hadrian,** with four Corinthian columns and a serpent-headed hydra above the door to keep out evil spirits; beyond is a partially restored fountain dedicated to the emperor Trajan. The street then forks and opens into a central square that once held the **Prytaneion,** or town hall; the Nymphaion, a small temple decked with fountains; and the **Temple of Domitian,** on the south side of the square, which was once a vast sanctuary with a colossal statue of the emperor for whom it was named. All are now a jumble of collapsed walls and columns.

Returning to the Street of Kuretes, turn right to reach the **odeon,** an intimate semicircle with just a few rows of seats, where spectators would listen to poetry readings and music. Columns mark the northern edge of the state agora (market). Beyond, the Magnesian Gate (also known as the Manisa Gate), at the end of the street, was the starting point for a caravan trail and a colonnaded road to the Temple of Artemis. ⊠ *Site entry 4 km (2½ miles) west of Selçuk on Selçuk–Ephesus Rd.* ☎ *232/892–6010* ⊙ *mid-Apr.–mid-Oct., daily 8:30–7; mid-Oct.–mid-Apr., daily 8:30–5:30.*

**Graves of the Seven Sleepers.** According to the legend attached to the Graves of the Seven Sleepers, seven young Christian men hid in a cave to avoid persecution by the Romans in the 3rd century AD. They fell into a sleep that lasted 200 years, waking only after the Byzantine Empire had made Christianity the official state religion. When they died, they were buried here, and a church was built over them. The tombs in the large cemetery are largely from the Byzantine era. ⊠ *South of Sor Sahasi Sok. 3* ⊠ *Free.*

## SHOPPING

The downtown cores of Kuşadası and Selçuk offer excellent shopping opportunities, though prices and quality vary enormously. Generally, Turkey offers an exceptional range of handicrafts in all price ranges, but is most famed for its hand-woven carpets and kilims in a range of sizes and patterns. The finest are made of silk threads, but more common is cotton or wool. Other traditional wares include items with worked brass and copper articles such as large pots and ornate tables, ceramics, marble items, inlaid wooden articles including jewelry boxes and chess sets, or leatherwear fashioned into bags, shoes, or clothing. For a truly exotic gift, take home a genuine *nargile* (hubble-bubble pipe), or a blue glass *boncuk,* a talisman said to ward off the evil eye.

Kuşadası also has several excellent jewelry shops selling gold, precious stones, and modern jewelry and designer watches at competitive prices. Don't forget to haggle over the price of your souvenirs; never pay the first price asked, whatever you want to buy.

## BEACHES

There are many fine beaches around Kuşadası, and these are also served by dolmuş buses.

## WHERE TO EAT

$ ✕ **Ejder Restaurant.** This popular spot overlooking the Selçuk aqueduct
TURKISH is run by Mehmet and his wife, the sole cook. It may sometimes take a while to get your food, but the traditional kebabs and Turkish specialties are well worth the wait. Mehmet takes pride in his guestbook filled with customers' comments, so make sure to add a few lines. $ *Average main: 7 TL* ⊠ *Cengiz Topel Cad. 9/E, Selçuk* ☎ *232/892–3296.*

$ ✕ **Öz Urfa.** The focus at this causal, 50-year-old spot is on kebabs and
TURKISH other Turkish fast food. The modest surroundings, including a pleasant terrace, are just off Barbaros Hayrettin Caddesi, the main thoroughfare. Alcohol is not served. $ *Average main: 10 TL* ⊠ *Cephane Sokak 7/A, Kuşadası* ☎ *256/612–9881* ⊕ *www.ozurfakebabs.com.*

# LIMASSOL, CYPRUS

Updated by
Liz Humphreys

Cyprus, once a center for the cult of the Greek goddess Aphrodite, is a modern island nation that retains an essentially Mediterranean character. Its 3,572 square miles (about the size of Connecticut) encompass citrus and olive groves, pine-forested mountains, and some of Europe's cleanest beaches. Cyprus's strategic position as the easternmost island in the Mediterranean Sea has made it subject to regular invasions by powerful empires. Greeks, Phoenicians, Assyrians, Egyptians, Persians, Romans, Byzantines, the Knights Templar, Venetians, Ottomans and the British—all have either ruled or breezed through here. Vestiges of the diverse cultures that have ruled here dot the island, from remnants of Neolithic settlements and ancient Greek and Roman temple sites, to early Christian basilicas and painted Byzantine churches. But Cyprus isn't limited to its architecture and history; there's also a vibrant lifestyle to be explored.

### ESSENTIALS
#### CURRENCY
The euro.

#### HOURS
Museum hours vary, so it pays to check ahead. Generally, museums tend to close on the early side, around 4 or 5 pm. Most ancient monuments are open from dawn to dusk, which means earlier closing times in the winter months. Many shops close at 2 pm on Wednesdays and Saturdays and are not open at all on Sundays.

#### PRIVATE TOURS
Licensed guides can be hired for half-day or evening (starting at €82.95) and full-day (€130.52) tours, with a 50% surcharge on Sundays; a list of licensed guides is available from the Cyprus Tourist Guides Association.

For more organized guided tours, Argonaftis (based in Limassol) leads day tours including an excursion from Limassol to Kourion, Kolossi

Castle, and Aphrodite's Rock; a "luxury grand tour" that visits the Troodos Mountains, Lefkara, the Kykkos Monastery, and a winery; and a day-trip to Nicosia and Lefkara. The company also offers such specialized tours as an Akamas jeep safari.

For wine lovers, Paphos Wine Tours offers half- or full-day trips in a comfortable air-conditioned van from Limassol to wineries in the Troodos Mountains, with optional stops at the Cyprus Wine Museum, Kolossi Castle, and Omodos; winery tours leaving from Paphos are also available (€50–€60 per person, including morning coffee and picnic lunch, from September to May).

**Contacts Argonaftis Tours** ☎ 25/586333 ⊕ www.argonaftis.com. **Cyprus Tourist Guides Association** ☎ 22/765755 🖶 22766872 ⊕ www.cytouristguides.com. **Paphos Wine Tours** ☎ 99/158312, 99/158324 ⊕ www.paphoswinetours.com.

## TELEPHONES

The country code for Cyprus is 357. GSM-based mobile phones work in Cyprus provided that they can operate at 900 or 1800 MHz. Some public phones accept Telecards, which can be purchased at post offices, banks, souvenir shops, and kiosks; others accept coins.

## COMING ASHORE

Most cruise ships dock at the main port in Limassol, which is about 4 km (2½ miles) southwest of the downtown. This is a vast commercial enterprise, but has dedicated cruise berths and offers a shuttle to the passenger terminal. Here you'll find refreshments, tourist information, currency exchange, and a taxi station. Some cruise ships also call at Larnaca, but at this writing Limassol is the major cruise port.

If you want to explore independently, take a taxi or bus from the port into the downtown. Bus 30 takes about 15 minutes to reach downtown Limassol. Urban taxis have an initial charge of €3.42 (€4.36 at night) and then €0.73 per km in the daytime, €0.85 at night. The waiting time day-rate is €13.66 per hour. Urban taxi drivers are bound by law to run their meter, rural taxis are not, but if you engage a taxi in town it will be classed as an urban taxi.

To travel farther afield, consider taking a service taxi (four- to eight-seat minibus) run by Travel & Express. Service taxis link all major towns for a fixed fee; for instance, Limassol to Larnaca costs €9.90 Monday to Saturday and €11.80 on Sunday. Urban taxis are generally very cheap for local travel, but far more expensive than service taxis between towns. Buses are cheaper, with Limassol to Larnaca a single fare of €3, but they are slower than service taxis.

You can reach many interesting and ancient attractions in the surrounding Cypriot countryside if you rent a vehicle for the day. Car rentals are about €50 for a subcompact manual vehicle. There will be an extra charge for delivery to the port or pick-up in central Limassol.

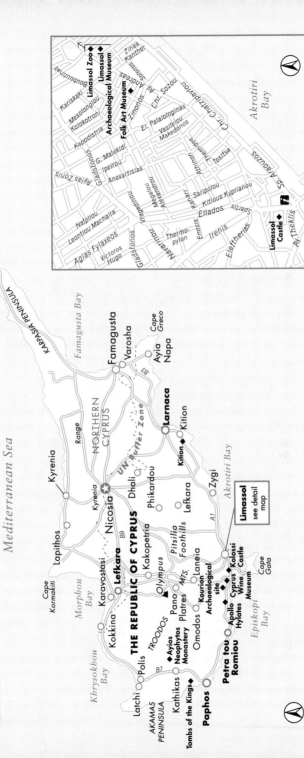

Cyprus

Limassol

Mediterranean Sea

KARPASIA PENINSULA
Cape Andreas

Famagusta Bay
Famagusta
Varosha
Cape Greco
Ayia Napa

Kyrenia
Range
NORTHERN CYPRUS
UN Buffer Zone
Larnaca
Kition
Kition
Zygi
Akrotiri Bay

Kyrenia
Nicosia
Dhali
Phikardou
Lefkara

Lapithos
Kyrenia
B9
THE REPUBLIC OF CYPRUS

Cape Kormakiti
Morphou Bay
Karavostasi
Lefkara
Kakopetria
Olympus
Pano Platres
Pitsilia Foothills
Laneia
Limassol see detail map
Kolossi Castle
Cyprus Wine Museum
Cape Gata

Khrysokhou Bay
Kokkina
TROODOS MTS.
Omodos
Kourion Archaeological site
Apollo Hylates
Episkopi Bay

Latchi
Polis
B7
Ayios Neophytos Monastery
Kathikas
AKAMAS PENINSULA
Tombs of the Kings
Paphos
Petra tou Romiou

20 miles
30 km

Limassol Zoo
Archaeological Museum
Folk Art Museum
Limassol Castle

Zinas Kanther
Chr. Sozou
Ay. Andreas

1/8 mi
1/8 km

Akrotiri Bay

# EXPLORING CYPRUS FROM LIMASSOL

## LIMASSOL AND VICINITY

A major commercial port, cruise-ship port of call, and wine-making center on the south coast, Limassol, 75 km (47 miles) from Nicosia, is a bustling, cosmopolitan town. Luxury hotels, apartments, and guesthouses stretch along 12 km (7 miles) of seafront. In the center, the elegant, modern shops of Makarios Avenue contrast with those of the old part of town, where local handicrafts prevail.

**Apollo Hylates.** The Apollo Hylates (Sanctuary of Apollo of the Woodlands), an impressive archaeological site, stands 3 km (2 miles) west of the Temple of Kourion. It includes a partially restored main sanctuary with enormous Roman columns. ⊠ *Main Paphos Rd.* ☎ *25/991049* 💶 *€1.70* 🕙 *June–Aug., daily 8–7:30; Apr.–May and Sept.–Oct., daily 8–6; Nov.–Mar., daily 8–5.*

**Fodor's** Choice
★

**Cyprus Wine Museum.** Located about 10 minutes west of Limassol in the village of Erimi, this comprehensive museum succeeds at explaining the history of the grape in Cyprus, one of the oldest winemaking regions in the world. You'll get to view ancient wine jugs and vessels on a short guided tour of the museum and watch a film before heading downstairs for a sampling of Cyprus wines, including the island's famous sweet Commandaria, accompanied by tasty halloumi cheese. ⊠ *42 Paphou St., Erimi* ☎ *25/873808* ⊕ *www.cypruswinemuseum.com* 💶 *€7* 🕙 *Daily 9–5.*

★

**Kolossi Castle.** Kolossi Castle, a Crusader fortress of the Knights of St. John, was constructed in the 13th century and rebuilt in the 15th. Though there's not much left of the castle to see, it's worth a visit for the views from the rooftop of the surrounding vineyards, many of which produce Commandaria, the famous sweet wine of Cyprus. ⊠ *11 km (7 miles) west of Limassol, on the road to Paphos* ☎ *25/934907* 💶 *€1.70* 🕙 *June–Aug., daily 8–7:30; Apr.–May and Sept.–Oct., daily 8–6; Nov.–Mar., daily 8–5.*

**Fodor's** Choice
★

**Kourion Archaeological Site.** The Kourion (Curium) Archaeological Site, west of Limassol, has Greek and Roman ruins. Classical and Shakespearean plays are sometimes staged in the impressive amphitheater. Next to the theater is the Villa of Eustolios, a summerhouse built by a wealthy Christian with interesting mosaic floors from the 5th century AD; nearby is the partially rebuilt Roman stadium. ⊠ *19 km (12 miles) west of Limassol, Main Paphos Rd.* ☎ *25/934250* 💶 *€1.70* 🕙 *Jun.–Aug., daily 8–7:30; Apr.–May and Sept.–Oct., daily 8–6; Nov.–Mar., daily 8–5.*

★

**Limassol Castle.** The 14th-century Limassol Castle was built on the site of a Byzantine fortification. Richard the Lionheart married Berengaria of Navarre and crowned her Queen of England here in 1191. The **Cyprus Medieval Museum** in the castle displays medieval armor and relics. ⊠ *Richard and Berengaria Sts.* ☎ *25/305419* ⊕ *www.limassolmunicipal. com.cy* 💶 *€3.40* 🕙 *Tues.–Sat. 9–5, Sun. 10–1.*

**Limassol District Archaeological Museum.** Browse interesting archaeological finds from the Limassol area, including pottery, coins, jewelry, tools, and sculptures, from the Prehistoric period (10,000 BC) up to the Late Roman period (AD 327). The collection also contains many items related to Aphrodite, including ancient terra-cotta figures. ⊠ *5 Anastasi Sioukri & Vyronos* ☎ *25/305157* ⊕ *www. limassolmunicipal.com.cy* 🖅 *€1.70* ⊘ *Mon. 8–2:30; Tues., Wed., Fri. 8–3; Thurs. 8–5; Sat. 9–3.*

**Limassol Zoo.** Reopened in the summer of 2012 after an extensive renovation, the zoo has modern enclosures that use only stone, glass, wood, and rope. Both kids and adults will enjoy the Asian otters, Cyprus oxes, Egyptian geese, and Cuban boa constrictors, among a good variety of other mammals, birds, and reptiles (though no lions, tigers, or elephants here). To see the animals in action, check the website for specific feeding times. ⊠ *Municipal Gardens* ☎ *25/581012* ⊕ *www.limassolzoo.com* 🖅 *€5* ⊘ *Jun.–Aug., daily 9–7; Apr.–May and Sept., daily 9–6; March and Oct., daily 9–5; Nov.–Dec., daily 9–4:30; Jan., daily 9–4.*

**Municipal Folk Art Museum.** For a glimpse of Cypriot folklore, visit the Municipal Folk Art Museum. The collection includes national costumes and fine examples of weaving and other crafts. ⊠ *Agiou Andreou 253* ☎ *25/362303* 🖅 *€2* ⊘ *Weekdays 8:30–3.*

## LARNACA

*51 km (32 miles) southeast of Nicosia, 66 km (41 miles) east of Limassol.*

The seaside resort with its own airport has a flamboyant Whitsuntide celebration, called Cataklysmos, as well as fine beaches, a palm-fringed seaside promenade, and a modern harbor.

Fodor'sChoice **Ayios Lazarus.** In the town center stands one of the island's more impor-
★ tant churches, Ayios Lazarus (Church of Lazarus), resplendent with gold icons and unique woodcarvings. Constructed in AD 890 by Byzantine Emperor Leo VI and restored to its glory in the 17th century, it is a beautiful example of Byzantine architecture. The church includes a fascinating crypt containing the sarcophagus of the Biblical Lazarus mentioned in Luke; Jesus is said to have resurrected Lazarus four days after his death, after which time Lazarus traveled to Kition (Larnaca's ancient city), where he became a bishop for 30 years. ⊠ *Plateia Agiou Lazarou* ☎ *24/652498* 🖅 *Free* ⊘ *Weekdays 8–12:30 and 2:30–5:30; weekends 8–5:30.*

★ **Hala Sultan Tekke.** On the edge of Salt Lake a mosque stands in an oasis of palm trees guarding the Hala Sultan Tekke—burial place of the prophet Muhammad's aunt Umm Haram, and an important Muslim shrine. ⊠ *Salt Lake* 🖅 *Free* ⊘ *Jun.–Aug., daily 8–7:30; Apr.–May and Sept.–Oct., daily 8–6; Nov.–Mar., daily 8–5.*

---

**CYPRUS BEST BETS**

**Visit the mosaics of Paphos.** Some of the finest Roman workmanship yet uncovered, they are an awe-inspiring sight.

**Enjoy the galleries at Larnaca Museum.** The museum is stuffed with ancient Greek and Roman artifacts, from monumental statues to precious jewelry to mundane kitchen utensils.

**Browse for souvenirs at Lefkara.** This whitewashed village has a vibrant Greek heartbeat.

5

**Kition.** Kition, the old Larnaca of biblical times, was one of the most important ancient city-kingdoms. Though most of the ruins are still buried beneath the modern city, you can see architectural remains of temples that date from the 13th century BC. ⊠ *Kyman St., north of Larnaca Museum* ☎ *24/304115* 🖃 *€1.70* ☉ *Mon., Tues., Thurs., and Fri 8–2:30; Wed. 8–5.*

☼ **Larnaca Fort.** The Larnaca Fort was originally built in the late 1300s and then rebuilt in 1625; during British colonial rule, it was used as a prison. Today it's mainly worth visiting for the lovely views of the sea. The small **Medieval Museum** is inside the fort and has finds from Hala Sultan Tekke and Kition. ⊠ *Leoforos Athinon, within sight of marina on seafront* ☎ *24/304576* 🖃 *€1.70* ☉ *Jun.–Aug., weekdays 9–7:30; Sept.–May, weekdays 9–5.*

**Larnaca District Archaeological Museum.** The Larnaca District Archaeological Museum displays treasures, including outstanding sculptures, pottery, and other architectural fragments from prehistoric times through to the Roman period. ⊠ *Plateia Kalograion* ☎ *24/304169* 🖃 *€1.70* ☉ *Mon. 8–2:30; Tue., Thurs., and Fri. 8–3; Wed. 8–5; Sat. 9–3.*

☼ **Municipal Museum of Natural History.** If you'd like to learn more about the natural history of Cyprus, this small museum inside the Municipal Gardens is a must-see. Exhibits on geology, animals, birds, fossils, marine life, insects, plants, and more provide a worthy introduction to the vast array of island life, from the ancient past to the present day. ⊠ *Leoforos Grigori Afxentiou, inside the Municipal Gardens* ☎ *24/652569* 🖃 *€.50* ☉ *Weekdays 9–4, Sat. 10–1.*

★ **Panayia Angeloktistos.** The 11th-century Panayia Angeloktistos church, 11 km (7 miles) south of Larnaca, has extraordinary Byzantine wall mosaics that date from the 6th and 7th centuries. ⊠ *Rte. B4, Kiti* ☎ *24/424646* 🖃 *Free* ☉ *Sept.–May, daily 8–noon and 2–4; Jun.–Aug., daily 2–5:30.*

**Pierides-Marfin Laiki Bank Museum.** The Pierides–Marfin Laiki Bank Museum is a private assemblage of more than 3,000 pieces distinguished by its Bronze Age terra-cotta figures as well as Roman and Byzantine-era art. ⊠ *4 Zinonos Kitieos St., near Lord Byron St.* ☎ *24/814555* ⊕ *www.pieridesfoundation.com.cy* 🖃 *€2* ☉ *Mon.–Thurs. 9–4, weekends 9–1.*

☼ **Salt Lake.** About 7 km (4 miles) southwest of Larnaca, near the airport, is the 6½-square-km (2½-square-mile) Salt Lake. In winter it's a refuge for migrating birds, especially flamingoes, and in summer it dries up with salt deposits. Though you can't walk on the lake itself, there are plenty of nature trails and picnic spots around it. ⊠ *Just off the airport road, 7 km (4 miles).*

**Stavrovouni Monastery.** On a mountain 40 km (25 miles) west of Larnaca stands the Stavrovouni (Mountain of the Cross) Monastery. It was founded by St. Helena in AD 326; the present buildings date from the 19th century. The views from here are splendid. Ideally, you should visit the monastery in a spirit of pilgrimage rather than sightseeing, out of respect for the monks. Only male visitors (no women) are allowed inside the monastery daily. ⊠ *Stavrovouni* ☎ *22/533630* 🖃 *Free* ☉ *Apr.–Aug., 8–noon and 3–6; Sept.–Mar., 7–11 and 2–5.*

## LEFKARA
*40 km (25 miles) northwest of Larnaca, 64 km (40 miles) north of Limassol.*

Some 40 km (25 miles) west of Larnaca, this picturesque village—one of the prettiest in Cyprus—is best known for its lace: Lefkaritika has been woven by hand here for centuries. Much of it is indeed beautiful, and most shopkeepers are willing to bargain. But considerably more evocative is the village itself, clustered on two hills and split between an upper portion, Kato Lefkara, and lower portion, Pano Lefkara. The tiny streets open up to a small plaza in front of the Church of the Holy Cross in Pano Lefkara, with a stupendous view of the surrounding sun-drenched hills.

## TROODOS MOUNTAINS
*20 km (25 miles) north of Limassol.*

North of Limassol, these mountains, which rise to 6,500 feet, have shady cedar and pine forests and cool springs. Small, painted Byzantine churches in the Troodos and Pitsilia foothills are rich examples of a rare indigenous art form. Asinou Church, a UNESCO World Heritage site near the village of Nikitari, and Agios Nikolaos tis Stegis (St. Nicholas of the Roof), south of Kakopetria, are especially noteworthy.

**Kykkos Monastery.** At the Kykkos monastery, founded in 1100, the prized icon of the Virgin is reputed to have been painted by St. Luke; you can view the icon enclosed in a shrine, and the museum also includes other icons, woodcarvings, and embroidery. The monastery has been repeatedly destroyed by fire, and the current structure dates from 1831. ⊠ *20 km west of Pedoulas* ☎ *22/942435* ⊕ *www.kykkos-museum.cy.net* 🎟 *€5* ⊙ *June–Oct., daily 10–6; Nov.–May, daily 10–4.*

## PETRA TOU ROMIOU
*20 km (12 miles) west of Limassol.*

**Fodor's Choice** **Petra tou Romiou.** The legendary birthplace of Aphrodite—Greek god-
★ dess of love and beauty—is a large offshore rock just off the main road between Limassol and Paphos. Swimming around Petra tou Romiou (Aphrodite's Rock) three times is purported to bring you eternal love. Whether or not you believe the legend, it's a dramatic place to stop for a snack or picnic lunch and a look at the unquestionably romantic views. Park in the lot and take the passageway under the highway to the large pebble beach, where you may be tempted to swim or stay for sunset. **Amenities:** food and drink; parking (no fee); toilets; water sports. **Best for:** sunset; swimming. ⊠ *Between Limassol and Paphos.*

## PAPHOS
*68 km (42 miles) west of Limassol.*

In the west of the island and 142 km (88 miles) southwest of Nicosia, Paphos combines a seaside with stellar archaeological sites and a buzzing nightlife. Since the late 1990s it has attracted some of the most lavish resorts on the island (as well as the largest influx of British travelers). It's also the most pedestrian-friendly town in Cyprus, with a long beachside path running alongside most of the hotels all the way down to the pleasant leisure harbor, anchored by a medieval fortress. The surrounding area is one of the most scenic in Cyprus, especially the untrammeled Akamas Peninsula—still accessible only to off-road vehicles. In short, if you want to combine easy accessibility to the beach with interesting historic attractions, this is the place you'll want to make your base.

**Ayios Neophytos Monastery.** The hermit and scholar Neophytos settled at what's now referred to as the Ayios Neophytos Monastery in 1159, carving a home for himself out of the rock. Known in his time as the leading critic of Richard the Lionheart and the Byzantine tax collectors, today he is best known for what became a series of grottoes hewn from the hillside rock and the evocative religious frescoes—some actually painted by Neophytos—they contain. The monastery itself, with no more than a half dozen or so monks, is situated below the grottoes. ⊠ *6 miles north of town* 🎫 *€1.70* ⏱ *Nov.–Mar., daily 9–4; Apr.–Oct., daily 9–1 and 2–6.*

★ **Byzantine Museum.** The Byzantine Museum houses notable mosaics, icons, and sacred books and artifacts collected from churches and monasteries throughout Paphos and dating from the 7th through the 18th centuries. The collection includes one of the oldest icons discovered in Cyprus, the Agia Marina, thought to be from the 8th or 9th century. Though it's on the small side, the museum provides a good introduction to the rich Byzantine history of the Paphos region and is well worth a stop. ⊠ *5 Andrea Ioannou St.* 🕿 *26/931393* 🎫 *€2* ⏱ *Weekdays 9–4, Sat. 9–1.*

**Paphos District Archaeological Museum.** The Paphos District Archaeological Museum displays pottery, jewelry, and statuettes from Cyprus's Roman villas. ⊠ *43 Griva Digheni Ave., Ktima* 🕿 *26/306215* 🎫 *€1.70* ⏱ *Mon. 8–2:30; Tues., Thurs., Fri. 8–3; Wed. 8–5; Sat. 9–3.*

**Paphos Fort.** The squat 16th-century Paphos Fort—a UNESCO World Heritage site—guards the entrance to the harbor; from the rooftop there's a lovely view. ⊠ *Paphos Harbour* 🎫 *€1.70* ⏱ *Daily Nov.–Mar. 8–5; Apr.–May and Sept.–Oct. 8–6; June–Aug. 8–7:30.*

**Fodor's**Choice **Roman Mosaics.** Don't miss the elaborate 3rd- to 5th-century AD Roman
★ mosaics in the Roman Villa of Theseus, the House of Dionysos, and the House of Aion—all part of a UNESCO World Heritage protected site. The impressive mosaics are an easy walk from the harbor. ⊠ *Kato Phaphos, near the habor* 🕿 *26/306217* 🎫 *€3.40* ⏱ *June–Aug., daily 8–7:30; Apr.–May and Sept.–Oct., daily 8–6; Nov.–Mar., daily 8–5.*

**Tombs of the Kings.** The Tombs of the Kings, an early necropolis, date from 300 BC. The coffin niches are empty, but a powerful sense of mystery remains. There are lovely views from here over the Mediterranean Sea. ⊠ *Kato Paphos* 🕿 *26/306295* 🎫 *€1.70* ⏱ *June–Aug., daily 8–7:30; Apr.–May and Sept.–Oct., daily 8–6; Nov.–Mar., daily 8–5.*

## SHOPPING

Cyprus has a great range of handicrafts. Lace and embroidery from Lefkara are still handmade and are widely available. Other items to look for are basketware, ceramics, blown glass, carved wood (the best being olive wood), hand-tied cotton rugs, silverware, and copperware, including beautiful decorative urns. Leather and shoes are excellent value. Museums sell copies of ancient artifacts, and the Orthodox monasteries offer Byzantine icons. Edibles include superb olive oil, honey, and delicious wine.

Shopping in the villages of Lefkara, Omodos, and Laneia is a pleasure, with numerous galleries and shops set along the whitewashed alleyways. In Limassol the main shopping street, Makarios Avenue, has a range of modern boutiques.

## BEACHES

Cyprus has numerous excellent beaches, but they get busy between June and September with vacationers from across Europe.

**Lady's Mile Beach.** The closest beach to Limassol's cruise ship port, Lady's Mile is a 7-km (4-mile) hard sand and pebble beach about a 15-minute drive from the center of town. Its shallow waters are popular with locals, especially on the weekends. Bring your own umbrella if you'd like some shade, as well as insect repellent in the evenings. **Amenities:** food and drink; lifeguards; water sports. **Best for:** swimming. ⊠ *Near New Port, Limassol.*

## WHERE TO EAT

**$$** ✕ **Limanaki.** Chef Sam Kazzaz truly bucks the Cyprus meze trend by
MEDITERRANEAN using touches of Indian and Moroccan flare at his simple yet elegant
**Fodor's Choice** restaurant just a block from the beach in Pissouri (though he also offers
★ Mediterranean fish and meat mezes with eight hours' advance notice); though not located in Limassol proper, it's certainly worth the short drive. He masterfully uses curry in such dishes as Curried Away Calamari and Lamb Jalfrazi, while catering to non-meat eaters with his weekly changing vegetarian special, such as a subtly spiced tagine with chickpeas, eggplant, celery, peppers, and other fresh veggies. Whether you're seated inside surrounded by stone walls or outside on the pleasant terrace, you'll agree this is a Cyprus meal that's different from the rest—and one to remember. ⑤ *Average main: €15* ⊠ *Pissouri Jetty, Pissouri* ☎ *25/221288* ⊕ *www.limanakipissouri.com* ⚞ *Reservations essential* ⊗ *Closed Mon.*

**$** ✕ **Militzis.** This meat-centric restaurant is popular with locals for both
MEDITERRANEAN lunch and dinner; it's well known for its homemade meze and other Cypriot specialties. If you're daring, opt for the liver and intestines of lamb, the salted pork, or the lamb's head. To play it safe, you can't go wrong with the *tavas*—pieces of lamb and beef cooked with potatoes, onions, tomatoes, and spices; the *souvla* (roasted pork in wine); or the moussaka. But best of all for those with hearty appetites is the meze—plate after plate of salad, olives, cheese, seafood, and meats, all for a reasonable fixed price. Sit on the terrace for lovely views of the sea. ⑤ *Average main: €10* ⊠ *42 Piale Pasha St., Larnaca* ☎ *24/655867.*

# MYKONOS, GREECE

Updated by Adrian Vrettos and Alexia Amvrazi

Put firmly on the map by Jackie O, Mykonos has become one of the most popular of the Aegean islands. Although the dry, rugged island is one of the smallest of the Cyclades—16 km (10 miles) by 11 km (7 miles)—travelers from all over the world are drawn to its sandy beaches, its thatched windmills, and its picturesque, whitewashed port town of Mykonos, whose cubical two-story houses and churches have been long celebrated as some of the best examples of classic Cycladic architecture. Here backpackers rub elbows with millionaires, and the atmosphere is decidedly cosmopolitan. Happily, the islanders seem to have been able to fit cosmopolitan New Yorkers or Londoners gracefully into their way of life. For almost 1,000 years, neighboring Delos Island was the religious and political center of the Aegean and host every four years to the Delian games, the region's greatest festival. This is a must-visit site for anyone interested in ancient history.

## ESSENTIALS

### CURRENCY
The euro.

### HOURS
Museums are generally open from 9 to 5, but many are closed on Monday. Shops are open daily in the summer (9 to noon or 1, reopening at 4 or 5 until 9 on weekdays and 9 to 6 on Saturday).

### PRIVATE TOURS
Windmills Travel takes a group every morning for a day tour of Delos. The company also has half-day guided tours of the Mykonos beach towns, with a stop in Ano Mera for the Panayia Tourliani Monastery. Windmills also provides excursions to nearby Tinos; arranges private tours of Delos and Mykonos and off-road jeep trips; charters yachts; and, in fact, handles all tourist services. John van Lerberghe's office, the Mykonos Accommodations Center, is small, but he can plan your trip from soup to nuts.

**Contacts Windmills Travel.** ✉ Fabrica, Mykonos ☎ 22890/26555, 22890/23877 ✎ info@windmills-travel.com ⊕ www.windmillstravel.com.

### TELEPHONES
Tri-band GSM phones work in Greece. You can buy prepaid phone cards at telecom shops, news vendors, and tobacconists in all towns and cities for local or international calls. Vodafone is the leading mobile telecom company. OTE is the national domestic provider. Calls can be made at OTE offices and paid for after completion.

## COMING ASHORE
The main cruise port is about a mile north of Mykonos Town (on the other side of a very steep hill). Shuttle buses transport passengers to town, where you can catch buses or take a taxi to the beaches. If you anchor offshore and are tendered to the island, you'll alight at the old port in the town itself.

Because the island is so small, journey times anywhere are short. There is a cheap (fares between €1.40 and €1.70) and reliable bus service from

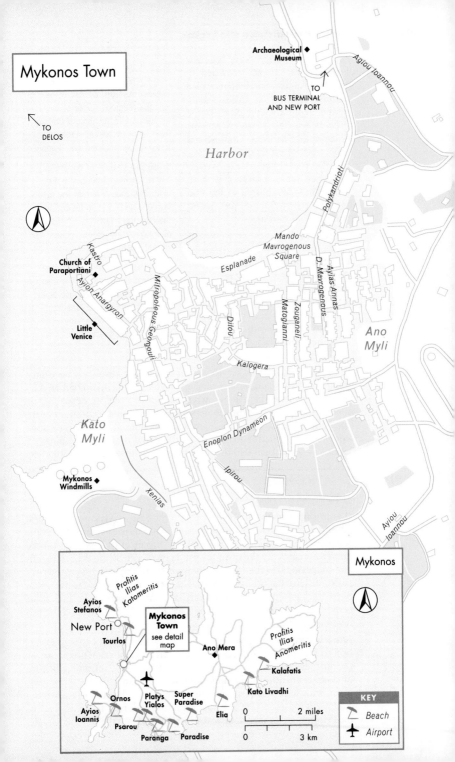

# Mykonos Town

TO DELOS

*Harbor*

Archaeological ◆
Museum

TO
BUS TERMINAL
AND NEW PORT

*Agiou Ioannou*

Polykandrioti

Kastro

Church of
Paraportiani ◆

Ayion Anargyron

Little
Venice ◆

Mitropoleous Georgouli

Esplanade

*Mando
Mavrogenous
Square*

D. Mavrogenous

Ayias Annas

 ◆

*Ano
Myli*

Diiou

Matogianni

Zouganeli

Kalogera

*Kato
Myli*

Enoplon Dynameon

Ipirou

Mykonos
Windmills ◆

Xenias

*Agiou
Ioannou*

---

## Mykonos

Ayios
Stefanos

*Profitis
Ilias
Katomeritis*

New Port ○

Tourlos

**Mykonos
Town**
see detail
map

Ano Mera ◆

*Profitis
Ilias
Anomeritis*

Kalafatis

Kato Livadhi

Ornos

Platys
Yialos

Super
Paradise

Ayios
Ioannis

Psarou

Elia

Paranga

Paradise

| | KEY | |
|---|---|---|
| 〰 | *Beach* | |
| ✈ | *Airport* | |

0 — 2 miles

0 — 3 km

the town to all the main beaches, but services can get crowded in July and August. Small boats called *caïques* also act as taxis, taking people from the old port to the various beaches. These are reliable and popular services. Commercial taxis operate on fixed fare routes, but the taxi system is easily overburdened when a large ship is in port. These are posted at the taxi rank in Mavro Square, just inland from the old harbor.

Most travel offices in Mykonos Town run guided tours to Delos that cost about €40, including boat transportation and entry fee. Alternatively, take one of the caïques that visit Delos daily from the old port: the round-trip costs about €17, and entry to the site (with no guide) is €5. They leave between 8:30 am and 3 pm, and return noon to 4 pm.

> ### MYKONOS BEST BETS
>
> **Explore Ancient Delos.** Delos was the religious center of the Aegean. Large sections of the city have been excavated, revealing treasures magnificent and humble.
>
> **Stroll the streets of Mykonos Town.** Cosmopolitan and bohemian, Mykonos is one of the most fashionable places to be during the European summer, yet the alluring narrow streets retain a vibrant Greek character.
>
> **Spend some time at the beach.** The town sleeps during the heat of the afternoon, so choose one of the island's famous beaches—from fun to hedonism—there's something for every taste.

With reliable transport services, a car rental isn't absolutely necessary, but if you want to do some exploring on your own you can rent an ATV or scooter for two people in town for about €15 to €30, depending on time of the season; motor scooters are not recommended for inexperienced riders (each year people are seriously injured because they don't know how to ride the many hills and narrow roads of Mykonos). A rental car costs about €40 to €50 per day for a subcompact or Smartcar.

## EXPLORING MYKONOS

### MYKONOS TOWN

If your ship remains in port late (often the case in Mykonos), the best time to visit the central harbor is in the cool of the evening, when the islanders promenade along the esplanade to meet friends and visit the numerous cafés. By the open-air fish market, Petros the Pelican preens and cadges eats. In the 1950s a group of migrating pelicans passed over Mykonos, leaving behind a single exhausted bird; Vassilis the fisherman nursed it back to health, and locals say that the pelican in the harbor is the original Petros, though you'll see several lurking around the fish tavernas right off the esplanade.

**Archaeological Museum.** Before setting out on the mandatory boat excursion to the isle of Delos, check out the Archaeological Museum, set at the northern edge of town. It affords insight into the intriguing history of its ancient shrines. The museum houses Delian funerary sculptures, many with scenes of mourning; most were moved to Rhenea when the Athenians cleansed Delos in the 6th century, during the sixth year of the Peloponnesian war, and, under instruction from the Delphic Oracle, the entire island was purged of all dead bodies. The most significant work from Mykonos is a 7th-century BC *pithos* (storage jar), showing the Greeks in the Trojan horse and the sack of the city. ⊠ *Ayios Stefanos, between boat dock and town* ☎ *22890/22325* 🖃 *€3* ☉ *Wed.–Mon. 8:30–2:30.*

**Fodor's**Choice **Church of Paraportiani** (*Our Lady of the Postern Gate*). Mykonians claim
★ that exactly 365 churches and chapels dot their landscape, one for each day of the year. The most famous of these is the Church of Paraportiani. The sloping, whitewashed conglomeration of four chapels, mixing Byzantine and vernacular idioms, looks fantastic. It is solid and ultimately sober, and its position on a promontory facing the sea sets off the unique architecture. ⊠ *Ayion Anargyron, near folk museum.*

★ **Little Venice.** Many of the early ship's captains built distinguished houses directly on the sea here, with wooden balconies overlooking the water. Today this neighborhood, at the southwest end of the port, is called Little Venice. This area, architecturally unique and one of the most attractive in all the islands, is so called because its handsome houses, which once belonged to shipowners and aristocrats, rise from the edge of the sea, and their elaborate buttressed wooden balconies hang over the water—these are no Venetian marble palazzi reflected in still canals. Many of these fine old houses are now elegant bars specializing in sunset drinks, or cabarets, or shops, and crowds head to the cafés and clubs, many found a block inland from Little Venice. These are sometimes soundproofed. ⊠ *Mitropoleos Georgouli.*

**Mando Mavrogenous Square.** Start a tour of Mykonos Town (Hora) on the main square, Mando Mavrogenous Square (sometimes called Taxi Square). Pride of place goes to a bust of Mando Mavrogenous, the island heroine, standing on a pedestal. In the 1821 War of Independence the Mykonians, known for their seafaring skills, volunteered an armada of 24 ships, and in 1822, when the Ottomans landed a force on the island, Mando and her soldiers forced them back to their ships. After independence, a scandalous love affair caused the heroine's exile to Paros, where she died. An aristocratic beauty who becomes a great revolutionary war leader and then dies for love may seem unbelievably Hollywoodish, but it is true.

★ **Mykonos windmills.** Across the water from Little Venice, set on a high hill, are the famous Mykonos windmills, echoes of a time when wind power was used to grind the island's grain. The area from Little Venice to the windmills is called **Alefkandra,** which means "whitening": women once hung their laundry here. A little farther toward the windmills the bars chockablock on shoreside decks are barely above sea level, and when the north wind is up (often) surf splashes the tables. Farther on, the shore spreads into an unprepossessing beach, and tables are placed on sand or pebbles. After dinner (there are plenty of little tavernas here), the bars turn up their music, and knowing the beat thumps into the night, older tourists seek solace elsewhere.

## ANO MERA

*8 km (5 miles) east of Mykonos Town.*

Interesting little tavernas line the central square of Ano Mera, which is the "second city" of Mykonos, in the hills near the center of the island.

**Monastery of the Panayia Tourliani.** Monastery buffs should head to Ano Mera, a village in the central part of the island, where the Monastery of the Panayia Tourliani, founded in 1580 and dedicated to the protectress of Mykonos, stands in the central square. Its massive baroque iconostasis (altar screen), made in 1775 by Florentine artists, has small icons carefully placed amid the wooden structure's painted green, red, and gold-leaf flowers. At the top are carved figures of the apostles and large icons depicting New Testament scenes. The hanging incense holders with silver molded dragons holding red eggs in their mouths show an Eastern influence. In the hall of the monastery, an interesting **museum** displays embroideries, liturgical vestments, and wood carvings. A good taverna is across the street. The monastery's big festival—hundreds attend—is on August 15. ⊠ *On central square* ☎ *22890/71296* ☼ *By appointment only; call in advance.*

## DELOS

Fodor's Choice ★  **Delos.** Arrive at the mythical, magical, and magnificent site of Delos and you might wonder how this barren islet, which has virtually no natural resources, became the religious and political center of the Aegean. One answer is that Dhílos—to use the Modern Greek transliteration—provided the safest anchorage for vessels sailing between the mainland and the shores of Asia; another answer is that it had no other use. A third is provided if you climb Mt. Kynthos to see that the isle is shielded on three sides by other islands. Indeed, this is how the Cyclades—the word means "circling ones"—got their name: they circle around the sacred island.

On the left from the harbor is the **Agora of the Competialists** (circa 150 BC), members of Roman guilds, mostly freedmen and slaves from Sicily who worked for Italian traders. They worshiped the *Lares Competales,* the Roman "crossroads" gods; in Greek they were known as Hermaistai, after the god Hermes, protector of merchants and the crossroads. The **Sacred Way,** east of the agora, was the route, during the holy Delian festival, of the procession to the Sanctuary of Apollo. The **Propylaea,** at the end of the Sacred Way, were once a monumental white marble gateway with three portals framed by four Doric columns. Beyond the Propylaea is the **Sanctuary of Apollo**; though little remains today, when the Propylaea were built in the mid-2nd century BC, the sanctuary was crowded with altars, statues, and temples—three of them to Apollo. Inside the sanctuary and to the right is the **House of the Naxians,** a 7th- to 6th-century BC structure with a central colonnade. Dedications to Apollo were stored in this shrine.

One of the most evocative sights of Delos is the 164-foot-long **avenue of the Lions.** These are replicas; the originals are in the museum. The five Naxian marble beasts crouch on their haunches, their forelegs stiffly upright, vigilant guardians of the Sacred Lake. They are the survivors of a line of at least nine lions, erected in the second half of the 7th century BC by the Naxians. One, removed in the 17th century, now guards the Arsenal of Venice (though with a later head). The **Archaeological Museum** is also on the road south of the gymnasium; it contains most of the antiquities found in excavations on the island: monumental statues of young men and women, stelae, reliefs, masks, and ancient jewelry. Immediately to the right of the museum is a small **Sanctuary of Dionysus**, erected about 300 BC; outside it is one of the more-boggling sights of ancient Greece: several monuments dedicated to Apollo by the winners of the choral competitions of the Delian festivals, each decorated with a huge phallus, emblematic of the orgiastic rites that took place during the Dionysian festivals. Around the base of one of them is carved a lighthearted representation of a bride being carried to her new husband's home.

Beyond the path that leads to the southern part of the island is the **ancient theater,** built in the early 3rd century BC in the elegant residential quarter inhabited by Roman bankers and Egyptian and Phoenician merchants. Their one- and two-story houses were typically built around a central courtyard, sometimes with columns on all sides. Floor mosaics of snakes, panthers, birds, dolphins, and Dionysus channeled rainwater into cisterns below; the best preserved can be seen in the **House of the Dolphins,** the **House of the Masks,** and the **House of the Trident.** A dirt path leads east to the base of Mt. Kynthos, where there are remains from many **Middle Eastern shrines,** including the **Sanctuary of the Syrian Gods,** built in 100 BC. A flight of steps goes up 368 feet to the summit of **Mt. Kynthos** (after which all Cynthias are named), on whose slope Apollo was born. ⊠ *Delos island and historic site, take a small passenger boat from Mykonos Town* ☎ *22890/22259* ⊕ *www. culture.gr* ⊠ *€7* ☉ *Tues.–Sun. 9–3.*

## SHOPPING

Mykonos Town has excellent shopping, with many high-class boutiques aimed at the well-heeled sitting side by side with moderately priced shops selling Greek crafts and fashionable clothing. It's a real pleasure for retail junkies, with a seemingly limitless array of choices. Almost every surface of the narrow alleyways is festooned with cotton clothing or cheerful ceramics, leather shoes, or bars of olive-oil soap. Artists are drawn here as much by the clientele as by the beauty and light of the Aegean, so galleries are numerous. The town is especially famed for its jewelry, from simple strings of colourful beads to precious stones in designer settings. Upscale duty-free jewelry shops also abound.

**White Shop Mykonos.** Anna Gelou's shop, started by her mother 50 years ago, carries authentic copies of traditional handmade embroideries, all using white Greek cotton, in clothing, tablecloths, curtains, and such. ⊠ *Kouzi Gewrgouli 50, Mykonos Town* ☎ *22890/26825.*

★ **Ilias Lalaounis.** Known internationally, Ilias Lalaounis is for fine jewelry based on ancient Greek and other designs, reinterpreted for the modern woman. With many of their earrings and necklaces as lovingly worked as art pieces, the shop is as elegant as a museum. New collections are introduced every year. Stop by at the right hour and you'll get a glass of fine wine. The salespeople all live here and know everything about their island. ✉ *Polykandrioti 14, near taxis, Mykonos Town* ☎ *22890/22444* ⊕ *www.iliaslalaounis.com.*

**Nikoletta.** Mykonos used to be a weaver's island, where 500 looms clacked away. Only Nikoletta remains, where Nikoletta Xidakis sells her skirts, shawls, and bedspreads made of local wool, as she has for 50 years. ✉ *Little Venice, Mykonos Town* ☎ *22890/27503.*

## ACTIVITIES

There's a full range of water sports on offer in Mykonos, and many concessions operate directly on the beach (from May through September). Windsurfing is particularly popular because of the prevailing *meltemi* winds that blow across the island throughout the summer. The windy northern beaches on Ornos Bay are best for this.

**Aphrodite Beach Hotel.** This hotel is known for its water sports facilities. ✉ *Kalafati beach, Mykonos Town* ☎ *28890/71367.*

## BEACHES

There is a beach for every taste in Mykonos. Beaches near Mykonos Town, within walking distance, are **Tourlos** and **Ayios Ioannis. Ayios Stefanos,** about a 45-minute walk from Mykonos Town, has a minigolf course, water sports, restaurants, and umbrellas and lounge chairs for rent. The south coast's **Psarou,** protected from wind by hills and surrounded by restaurants, offers a wide selection of water sports and is often called the finest beach. Nearby **Platys Yialos,** popular with families, is also lined with restaurants and dotted with umbrellas for rent. **Ornos** is also perfect for families.

**Paranga, Paradise, Super Paradise,** and **Elia** are all on the southern coast of the island, and are famously nude, though getting less so. **Super Paradise** is half-gay, half-straight, and swings at night. All have tavernas on the beach. At the easternmost end of the south shores is **Kalafatis,** known for package tours, and between Elia and Kalafatis there's a remote beach at **Kato Livadhi,** which can be reached by road.

## WHERE TO EAT

**$$**  ✕ **Kounelas.** This long-established fresh-fish taverna is where many fish-
GREEK  ermen themselves eat, for solid, no-frills food. The menu depends on the weather—low winds means lots of fish. Note: even in simple places such as Kounelas, fresh fish can be expensive. $ *Average main: €12* ✉ *Off port near Delos boats, Mykonos Town* ☎ *22890/28220.*

**$$$**  ✕ **Sea Satin Market–Caprice.** If the wind is up, the waves sing at this
SEAFOOD  magical spot, set on a far tip of land below the famous windmills of
★  Mykonos. The preferred place for Greek shipowners, Sea Satin Market sprawls out onto a seaside terrace and even onto the sand of the beach bordering Little Venice. When it comes to fish, prices vary according to weight. Shellfish is a specialty, and everything is beautifully presented. In summer, live music and dancing add to the liveliness. $ *Average main: €25* ✉ *On seaside under windmills, Mykonos Town* ☎ *22890/24676.*

# PIRAEUS, GREECE (FOR ATHENS)

Updated by
Adrian Vrettos
and Alexia
Amvrazi

If you come to Athens in search of gleaming white temples, you may be aghast to find that much of the city has melded into what appears to be a viscous concrete mass. Amid the sprawl and squalor, though, the ancient city gives up its treasures. Lift your eyes 200 feet above the city to the Parthenon, and you behold architectural perfection that has not been surpassed in 2,500 years. Today this shrine of classical form, this symbol of Western civilization and political thought, dominates a 21st-century boomtown. To experience Athens fully is to understand the essence of Greece: tradition juxtaposed with a modernity that the ancients would strain to recognize but would heartily endorse. Ancient Athens is certainly the lure for the millions of visitors to the city, but since the late 1990s, inspired by the 2004 Olympics, the people have gone far toward transforming Athens into a sparkling modern metropolis.

## ESSENTIALS

### CURRENCY

The euro.

### HOURS

Most stores are open from 9 to 9 on weekdays, from 9 to 6 on Saturday. Museums are generally open from 9 to 5, but many are closed on Monday.

### TELEPHONES

Tri-band GSM phones work in Greece. You can buy prepaid phone cards at telecom shops, news vendors, and tobacconists in all towns and cities. Phone cards can be used for local or international calls. Vodafone is the leading mobile telecom company. OTE is the national domestic provider. Calls can be made at OTE offices and paid for after completion.

### COMING ASHORE

Piraeus is the port of Athens, 11 km (7 miles) southwest of the city center, and is itself the third-largest city in Greece, with a population of about 500,000. In anticipation of a flood of visitors during the 2004 Olympics, the harbor district was given a general sprucing up. The cruise port has 12 berths, and the terminal has duty-free shops, information, and refreshments.

The fastest and cheapest way to get to Athens from Piraeus is to take the metro. Line 1 (Green Line) reaches the downtown Athens stops most handy to tourists, including Platia Victorias, near the National Archaeological Museum; Omonia Square; Monastiraki, in the old Turkish bazaar; and Thission, near the ancient Agora. The trip takes 25 to 30 minutes. The Piraeus metro station is off Akti Kallimasioti on the main harbor, a 20-minute walk from the cruise port.

A flat fare covering all forms of public transport within central Athens and valid for 1 hour 30 minutes is €1.40. A day pass valid on all buses, trams, metro, and suburban railway is €4. Passes should be validated when first used, and are then valid for 24 hours from that time.

Taxis wait outside the terminal entrance. Taxis into the city are not necessarily quicker than public transport. Taxis rates begin at €1,

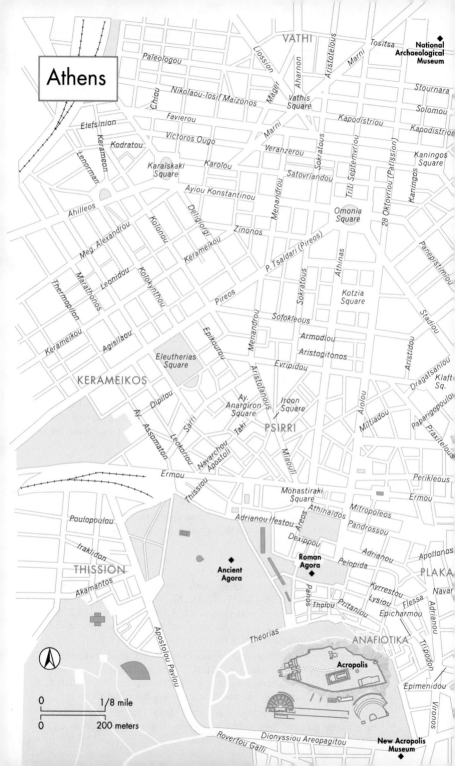

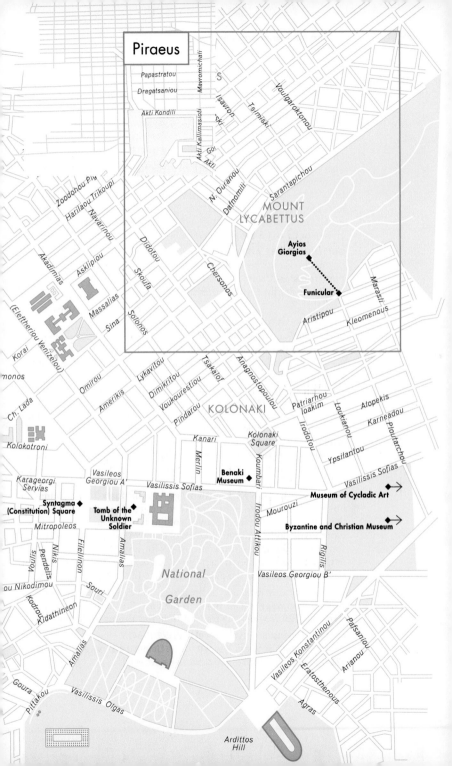

then €0.48 per km (½ miles), and there are numerous surcharges. A taxi takes longer than the metro because of traffic, and costs around €12–€15. Athens taxi drivers have a reputation for overcharging passengers, so make sure the meter is switched on. It is common practice for drivers to pick up other passengers if there is room in the cab. These extra passengers will also pay the full fare for the trip. Radio taxis also have an additional charge of €3 to €5 for the pick-up.

### GETTING TO THE AIRPORT

If you choose not to purchase airport transfers from your cruise line, there are inexpensive options available.

The best way to get to the airport from downtown Athens is by metro or light-rail. Single tickets cost €8, and include transfers within 90 minutes of the ticket's initial validation to bus, trolley, or tram. Combined tickets for two (€14) and three (€20) passengers are also available. Five express buses connect the airport with the metro (Ethniki Amyna and Dafni station), Syntagma Square, Kifissia, Kifissos Bus Station, and Piraeus (from which it is a short taxi ride to the port). Express buses leave the arrivals level of the airport every 10 minutes and operate 24 hours a day. Bus X95 will take you to Syntagma Square (Amalias Avenue); X94 goes to the bus terminus at the Ethniki Amyna metro stop (Line 3), which will get you into Syntagma within 10 minutes. Bus X97 goes to the Dafni metro stop; X93 brings voyagers to the dusty Kifissos intercity bus station. Bus X96 goes directly to Piraeus. The Attiki Odos and the expansion of the city's network of bus lanes has made travel times more predictable, and on a good day the X94 can get you to Ethniki Amyna in 40 minutes. Tickets cost €5 for any of these buses. Once in the city, pick up Metro line 1 for Piraeus and a 20-minute walk or short taxi transfer to the port.

Taxis are readily available at the arrivals level of the Athens airport; it costs an average of €45 to get to the port. Private limousine service starts at €120 for one-way transfer from the airport to the port.

**Contacts Limousine Service Travel** ☎ 210/970–6416 ⊕ www.limousine-service.gr. **Royal Prestige Limousine Service** ☎ 210/988–3221 ☎☎ 210/983–0378 ⊕ www.limousine-services.gr.

---

### ATHENS BEST BETS

**The Parthenon.** Regarded as the pinnacle of ancient architectural achievement, this classical temple has inspired poets, artists, and architects.

**The National Archaeological Museum.** A wide-ranging collection covers Greece's ancient history, from the splendid finds Schliemann excavated at Mycenae to the monumental statues that graced the cities of Attica.

**New Acropolis Museum.** This dazzling new museum at the base of the Acropolis is a welcome development for both Athens and Greece.

# EXPLORING ATHENS

Fodor's Choice ★ **Acropolis.** You don't have to look far in Athens to encounter perfection. Towering above all—both physically and spiritually—is the Acropolis, the ancient city of upper Athens. The Greek term *Akropolis* means "High City," and today's traveler who climbs this table-like hill is paying tribute to the prime source of Western civilization. Most of the notable structures on this flat-top limestone outcrop, 512 feet high, were built from 461 to 429 BC, when the intellectual and artistic life of Athens flowered under the influence of the Athenian statesman Pericles. With most of the major restoration work now completed, a visit to the Acropolis evokes the spirit of the ancient heroes and gods who were once worshiped here. The sight of the Parthenon—the Panathenaic temple at the crest of this *ieros vrachos* (sacred rock) —has the power to stir the heart as few other ancient relics do.

At the loftiest point of the Acropolis stands the **Parthenon,** the architectural masterpiece conceived by Pericles and executed between 447 and 438 BC. It not only raised the bar in terms of sheer size, but also in the perfection of its proportions. Dedicated to the goddess Athena (the name Parthenon comes from the Athena Parthenos, or the virgin Athena), the Parthenon served primarily as the treasury of the Delian League, an ancient alliance of cities formed to defeat the Persian incursion.

Once you pass through the Beulé Gate you will find the **Temple of Athena Nike.** Designed by Kallikrates, the mini-temple was built in 427–424 BC to celebrate peace with Persia. The bas-reliefs on the surrounding parapet depict the Victories leading heifers to be sacrificed. In 1998, Greek archaeologists began dismantling the entire temple for conservation. After laser-cleaning the marble, the team will reconstruct the temple on its original site.

If the Parthenon is the masterpiece of Doric architecture, the **Erechtheion** is undoubtedly the prime exemplar of the more graceful Ionic order. A considerably smaller structure than the Parthenon, it outmatches, for sheer elegance and refinement of design, all other buildings of the Greco-Roman world. For the populace, the Erechtheion, completed in 406 BC, remained Athena's holiest shrine, for legend has it that Poseidon plunged his trident into the rock on this spot, dramatically producing a spring of water, while Athena created a simple olive tree, whose produce remains a main staple of Greek society. A panel of judges declared the goddess the winner, and the city was named Athena.

Most people take the metro to the Acropolis station, where the New Acropolis Museum is just across the main exit. Another entrance is along the rock's northern face via the Peripatos, a paved path from the Plaka district. ⊠ *Dionyssiou Areopagitou, Acropolis* ☎ *210/321–4172, 210/321–0219* ⊕ *www.culture.gr* 🎟 *€12 joint ticket for all Unification of Archaeological Sites* ☉ *Apr.–Oct., daily 8–6:30 (last entry); Nov.– Mar., daily 8–3* Ⓜ *Acropolis.*

**Fodor's**Choice   **Ancient Agora.** The commercial hub of ancient Athens, the Agora was
★   once lined with statues and expensive shops, the favorite strolling
ground of fashionable Athenians as well as a mecca for merchants and
students. The long colonnades offered shade in summer and protection
from rain in winter to the throng of people who transacted the day-
to-day business of the city, and, under their arches, Socrates discussed
matters with Plato and Zeno expounded the philosophy of the Stoics
(whose name comes from the six *stoa,* or colonnades of the Agora).
Besides administrative buildings, it was surrounded by the schools, theaters, workshops, houses, stores, and market stalls of a thriving town.
The foundations of some of the main buildings, which may be most
easily distinguished include the circular Tholos, the principal seat of
executive power in the city; the Mitroon, shrine to Rhea, the mother of
gods, which included the vast state archives and registry office (*mitroon*
is still used today to mean registry); the Bouleterion, where the council
met; the Monument of Eponymous Heroes, the Agora's information
center, where announcements such as the list of military recruits were
hung; and the Sanctuary of the Twelve Gods, a shelter for refugees and
the point from which all distances were measured.

The Agora's showpiece was the **Stoa of Attalos II,** where Socrates once
lectured and incited the youth of Athens to adopt his progressive ideas
on mortality and morality. Today the Museum of Agora Excavations,
this two-story building was first designed as a retail complex and erected
in the 2nd century BC by Attalos, a king of Pergamum. The reconstruction in 1953–56 used Pendelic marble and creamy limestone from
the original structure. On the low hill called Kolonos Agoraios in the
Agora's northwest corner stands the best-preserved Doric temple in all
Greece, the **Hephaistion,** sometimes called the Thission because of its
friezes showing the exploits of Theseus. Like the other monuments, it
is roped off, but you can walk around it to admire its preservation. A
little older than the Parthenon, it is surrounded by 34 columns and is
104 feet in length, and was once filled with sculptures (the only remnant
of which is the mutilated frieze, once brightly colored). ⊠ *3 entrances:
from Monastiraki on Adrianou; from Thission on Apostolou Pav-
lou; and descending from Acropolis on Ayios Apostoloi, Monastiraki*
☎ *210/321–0185* ⊕ *www.culture.gr* 🏛 *€4; €12 joint ticket for holders
of the Acropolis (Unification of Archaeological Sites) ticket* ☉ *Daily
8–3; museum closes ½ hr before site* Ⓜ *Thiseio.*

**Fodor's**Choice   **Benaki Museum.** Just in time for the 2004 Olympics, Greece's oldest
★   private museum received a spectacular face-lift. Established in 1926
by an illustrious Athenian family, the Benaki was one of the first to
place emphasis on Greece's later heritage at a time when many archaeologists were destroying Byzantine artifacts to access ancient objects.
The permanent collection (more than 20,000 items are on display in
36 rooms, and that's only a sample of the holdings) moves chronologically from the ground floor upward, from prehistory to the formation
of the modern Greek state. ⊠ *Koumbari 1, Kolonaki* ☎ *210/367–1000*
⊕ *www.benaki.gr* 🏛 *€7, free Thurs.* ☉ *Wed., Fri., and Sat. 9–5, Thurs.
9 am–midnight, Sun. 9–3* Ⓜ *Syntagma or Evangelismos.*

★ **Byzantine and Christian Museum.** One of the few museums in Europe focusing exclusively on Byzantine art displays an outstanding collection of icons, mosaics, tapestries, and sculptural fragments (the latter provides an excellent introduction to Byzantine architecture). The permanent collection is divided in two main parts: the first is devoted to Byzantium (4th–15th c. AD) and contains 1,200 artifacts while the second is entitled "From Byzantium to the Modern Era" and presents 1,500 artworks dating from the 15th to the 21st century. ✉ *Vasilissis Sofias 22, Kolonaki* ☎ *213/213–9572, 213/723–9511* ⊕ *www.byzantinemuseum.gr* 🎫 *€4* ⊙ *Nov.–Mar., Tues.–Sun. 8; Apr.–Oct., Tues.–Sun. 9–4* Ⓜ *Evangelismos.*

**Fodor's Choice** **Museum of Cycladic Art.** Also known as the Nicholas P. Goulandris Foundation, and funded by one of Greece's richest families, this museum has an outstanding collection of 350 Cycladic artifacts dating from the Bronze Age, including many of the enigmatic marble figurines whose slender shapes fascinated such artists as Picasso, Modigliani, and Brancusi. ✉ *Neofitou Douka 4, Kolonaki* ☎ *210/722–8321 through 210/722–8323* ⊕ *www.cycladic.gr* 🎫 *€7* ⊙ *Mon., Wed., Fri., and Sat. 10–5, Thurs. 10–8, Sun. 11–5* Ⓜ *Evangelismos.*
★ ♲

**Fodor's Choice** **National Archaeological Museum.** Many of the greatest achievements in ancient Greek sculpture and painting are housed here in the most important museum in Greece. Artistic highlights from every period of its ancient civilization, from Neolithic to Roman times, make this a treasure trove beyond compare. With a massive renovation completed, works that have languished in storage for decades are now on view, reorganized displays are accompanied by enriched English-language information, and the panoply of ancient Greek art appears more spectacular than ever.
★

The museum's most celebrated display is the **Mycenaean Antiquities.** Here are the stunning gold treasures from Heinrich Schliemann's 1876 excavations of Mycenae's royal tombs: the funeral mask of a bearded king, once thought to be the image of Agamemnon but now believed to be much older, from about the 15th century BC; a splendid silver bull's-head libation cup; and the 15th-century BC Vaphio Goblets, masterworks in embossed gold.

Withheld from the public since they were damaged in the 1999 earthquakes, but not to be missed, are the beautifully restored **frescoes from Santorini,** delightful murals depicting daily life in Minoan Santorini. Along with the treasures from Mycenae, these wall paintings are part of the museum's Prehistoric Collection.

Other stars of the museum include the works of Geometric and Archaic art (10th to 6th century BC), and kouroi and funerary stelae (8th to 5th century BC), among them the stelae of the warrior Aristion signed by Aristokles, and the unusual *Running Hoplite* (a hoplite was a Greek infantry soldier). The collection of classical art (5th to 3rd century BC) contains some of the most renowned surviving ancient statues: the bareback *Jockey of Artemision,* a 2nd-century BC Hellenistic bronze salvaged from the sea; from the same excavation, the bronze *Artemision Poseidon* (some say Zeus), poised and ready to fling a trident (or thunderbolt?); and the *Varvakios Athena,* a half-size marble version of the gigantic gold-and-ivory cult statue that Pheidias erected in the Parthenon.

Light refreshments are served in a lower ground-floor café, which opens out to a patio and sculpture garden. During the summer months, concerts are often organized in the front garden (check the museum's website). ⊠ *28 Oktovriou (Patission) 44, Exarchia* ☎ *210/821–7717, 210/821–7724* ⊕ *www.namuseum.gr* ✉ *€7* ☺ *Apr.–Oct., Mon. 1:30–8, Tues.–Sun. 9–4; Nov.–Mar., Mon. 1:30–8, Tues.–Sun. 8–3* Ⓜ *Victoria, then 10-min walk.*

Fodor'sChoice  **New Acropolis Museum.** Designed by the celebrated Swiss architect Bernard Tschumi in collaboration with Greek Architect Michalis Fotiadis, the New Acropolis Museum made world headlines when it opened in June 2009. If some buildings define an entire city in a particular era, Athens's newest museum boldly sets the tone of Greece's modern era. Occupying a large plot of the city's most prized real estate, the New Acropolis Museum nods to the fabled ancient hill above it but speaks—thanks to a spectacular building—in a contemporary architectural language.
★

Regal glass walkways, very high ceilings, and panoramic views are all part of the experience. In the five-level museum, every shade of marble is on display and bathed in abundant, UV-safe natural light. Visitors pass into the museum through a broad entrance and move ever upwards. Delicate ancient craftsmanship is contrasted throughout with industrial modern accents (massive columns and symmetrical wall apertures); abundant glass on floors and balcony spaces allow the exhibition levels to gracefully communicate with each other.

The ground floor exhibit, The Acropolis Slopes, features objects found in the sanctuaries and settlements around the Acropolis—a highlight is the collection of theatrical masks and vases from the Sanctuary of the matrimonial deity Nymphe. The next floor is devoted to the Archaic period (650 BC–480 BC), with rows of precious statues mounted for 360-degree viewing. The second floor is devoted to the terrace and small restaurant/bar, which serves mezedes (a more ambitious restaurant is rumored to be in the works). Drifting into the top-floor atrium, the visitor can watch a video on the Parthenon before entering the star gallery devoted to the temple's Pentelic marble decorations, many of which depict a grand procession in the goddess Athena's honor. Frieze pieces (originals and copies), metopes, and pediments are all laid out in their original orientation. With all the ancient and fabled riches now gloriously on view here, a visit of at least two hours to this grand new museum is highly recommended. ⊠ *Dionyssiou Areopagitou 15, Makriyianni, Acropolis* ☎ *210/900–0900* ⊕ *www. theacropolismuseum.gr* ✉ *€5* ☺ *Tues.–Thurs., Sat.–Sun., 8–8; Fri. 8–10; closed Mon.* Ⓜ *Acropolis.*

★  **Roman Agora.** The city's commercial center from the 1st century BC to the 4th century AD, the Roman Market was a large rectangular courtyard with a peristyle that provided shade for the arcades of shops. Its most notable feature is the west entrance's Bazaar Gate, or **Gate of**

**Athena Archegetis,** completed around AD 2; the inscription records that it was erected with funds from Julius Caesar and Augustus. Halfway up one solitary square pillar behind the gate's north side, an edict inscribed by Hadrian regulates the sale of oil, a reminder that this was the site of the annual bazaar where wheat, salt, and oil were sold. On the north side of the Roman Agora stands one of the few remains of the Turkish occupation, the **Fethiye (Victory) Mosque.** The eerily beautiful mosque was built in the late 15th century on the site of a Christian church to celebrate the Turkish conquest of Athens and to honor Mehmet II (the Conqueror). During the few months of Venetian rule in the 17th century, the mosque was converted to a Roman Catholic church; now used as a storehouse, it is closed to the public. Three steps in the right-hand corner of the porch lead to the base of the minaret, the rest of which no longer exists. ✉ *Pelopidas and Aiolou, Plaka* ☎ *210/324–5220* ⊕ *www. culture.gr* ≋ *€2; €12 joint ticket for all Unification of Archaeological Sites* ⊘ *Daily 8–3* Ⓜ *Monastiraki.*

★ **Syntagma (Constitution) Square.** At the top of the city's main square stands the Greek **Parliament,** formerly King Otto's royal palace, completed in 1838 for the new monarchy. It seems a bit austere and heavy for a southern landscape, but it was proof of progress, the symbol of the new ruling power. The building's saving grace is the stone's magical change of color from off-white to gold to rosy mauve as the day progresses. In recent years the square has become the new frontline of mass protests against harsh austerity measures and the ongoing economic crisis in Greece, as well as the base for the citizen movement of the "Indignants." ✉ *Vasilissis Amalias and Vasilissis Sofias, Syntagma Sq.* Ⓜ *Syntagma.*

---

## SHOPPING

Athens has great gifts, particularly handmade crafts. Shops stock copies of traditional Greek jewelry, silver filigree, Skyrian pottery, onyx ashtrays and dishes, woven bags, attractive rugs (including *flokati,* or shaggy goat-wool rugs), wool sweaters, and little blue-and-white pendants designed as amulets to ward off the *mati* (evil eye). Greece is also known for its well-made shoes (most shops are clustered around the Ermou pedestrian zone and in Kolonaki), its furs (Mitropoleos near Syntagma), and its durable leather items (Pandrossou in Monastiraki).

Shops on Pandrossou sell small antiques and icons, but keep in mind that many of these are fakes. You must have government permission to export genuine objects from the ancient Greek, Roman, and Byzantine periods. Many museums sell good-quality reproductions or miniatures of their best pieces.

**Fodor's Choice** ★ **Center of Hellenic Tradition.** The Center is an outlet for quality handicrafts—ceramics, weavings, sheep bells, wood carvings, prints, and old paintings. Take a break from shopping in the center's quiet and quaint I Oraia Ellas café, to enjoy a salad or mezedes in clear view of the Parthenon. Upstairs is an art gallery hosting temporary exhibitions of Greek art. ✉ *Mitropoleos 59 and Pandrossou 36, Monastiraki* ☎ *210/321–3023, 210/321–0517.*

**FodorśChoice**  **Korres.** Natural beauty products blended in traditional recipes using
★ Greek herbs and flowers have graced the bathroom shelves of celebrities like Rihanna and Angelina Jolie but in Athens they are available at most pharmacies for regular-folk prices. For the largest selection of basil-lemon shower gel, coriander body lotion, olive-stone face scrub, and wild-rose eye cream, go to the original Korres pharmacy (behind the Panathenaic Stadium). Not surprisingly, Korres also maintains a traditional laboratory for herbal preparations such as tinctures, oils, capsules, and teas. ⊠ *Eratosthenous 8 and Ivikou, Pangrati* ☎ *210/722–2744* ⊕ *www.korres.com.*

**Thiamis.** Iconographer Aristides Makos creates beautiful hand-painted, gold-leaf icons on wood and stone. His slightly cluttered shop also sells beautiful handmade model ships and made-to-order items. ⊠ *Asklipiou 71, Kolonaki* ☎ *210/363–7993* ⊕ *www.thiamis.com.*

## WHERE TO EAT

On Mitropoleos off Monastiraki Square are a handful of counter-front places selling *souvlaki*—grilled meat rolled in a pita with onions, *tzatziki* (yogurt-garlic dip), and tomatoes—the best bargain in Athens. Make sure you specify whether you want a souvlaki sandwich or a souvlaki plate, which is an entire meal.

**$$$$**  ✕ **Daphne's.** Discreet service and refined Mediterranean and Greek
GREEK dishes (such as pork with celery and egg lemon sauce, fricassee of melt-
**FodorśChoice** off-the-bone lamb with greens, beef with olives, rabbit in mavrodaphne
★ wine sauce and the traditional *moussaka*) help make Daphne's one of the most exclusive (and at times pricey) destinations in Plaka. The Pompeian frescoes on the walls, the fragments of an ancient Greek building in the garden, and the tasteful restoration of the neoclassic building in terra-cotta and ochre hues also contribute to a pleasant and romantic evening. ⑤ *Average main: €40* ⊠ *Lysikratous 4, Plaka* ☎ *210/322–7971* ⊕ *www.daphnesrestaurant.gr.*

**$**  ✕ **O Platanos.** Set on a picturesque pedestrianized square, this is one
GREEK of the oldest tavernas in Plaka (established 1932)—a welcome sight
**FodorśChoice** compared with the many overpriced tourist traps in the area. A district
★ landmark—it is set midway between the Tower of the Winds and the Museum of Greek Popular Musical Instruments—it warms the eye with its pink-hue house, nicely color-coordinated with the bougainvillea-covered courtyard. Although the rooms here are cozily adorned with old paintings and photos, most of the crowd opts to relax under the courtyard's plane trees (which give the place its name). Platanos is packed with locals, who flock here because the food is good Greek home cooking and the waiters fast and polite. Don't miss the oven-baked potatoes, lamp or veal casserole with spinach or eggplant, fresh green beans in savory olive oil, fresh grilled fish, and the exceptionally cheap but delicious barrel retsina. Open for lunch. ⑤ *Average main: €15* ⊠ *Diogenous 4, Plaka* ☎ *210/322–0666* ▭ *No credit cards* ☉ *Closed June–Aug.*

## WHERE TO STAY

**$**
**HOTEL**
**Fodor'sChoice**
★

Acropolis Select. For only €10 more than many basic budget options, you get to stay in a slick-looking hotel with a lobby full of designer furniture in the residential neighborhood of Koukaki, south of Filopappou Hill, a 15-minute walk from the Acropolis, so not quite in the center of things. **Pros:** comfortable rooms; friendly staff; located in a pretty, low-key neighborhood; great value for money. **Cons:** no free Wi-Fi; small elevator. ⑨ *Rooms from: €75* ✉ *Falirou 37–39, Koukaki* ☎ *210/921–1610* ⊕ *www.acropoliselect.gr* ↗ *72 rooms.*

**$$$$**
**Fodor'sChoice**
★

Electra Palace. If you want simple elegance, excellent service, and a great location, this is the hotel for you—rooms from the fifth floor up have a view of the Acropolis and in summer you can bask in the sunshine at the outdoor swimming pool as you take in the view of Athens's greatest monument or catch the sunset from the rooftop garden. **Pros:** gorgeous rooms; great location; outstanding service: early check-in available. **Cons:** pricey! ⑨ *Rooms from: €330* ✉ *Nikodimou 18–20, Plaka* ☎ *210/337–0000* ⊕ *www.electrahotels.gr* ↗ *135 rooms, 20 suites* ⑨ *Breakfast.*

# PORT SAID, EGYPT (FOR CAIRO)

One of the world's great cosmopolitan cities for well over a thousand years, Cairo is infinite and inexhaustible. Different religions, different cultures—sometimes, it seems, even different eras—coexist amid the jostling crowds and aging monuments gathered here at the start of the Nile delta. But if you come expecting a city frozen in time, you're in for a shock: Cairo's current vitality is as seductive as its rich past. Like so much else in Egypt, Cairo's charm is a product of its history, the physical remains of a thousand years of being conquered and reconquered by different groups. Cairo gradually reveals its treasures, not with pizzazz and bells and whistles, but with a self-assured understatement. On a one-day visit you'll only be able to take in the tip of a vast iceberg of treasures here.

### ESSENTIALS

#### CURRENCY

The Egyptian pound. U.S. currency is accepted for high-value items in shops but not in restaurants and markets. ATMs are not common. You'll need small local bills for tips in Egypt, particularly to use the restroom.

#### HOURS

Museums are usually open from 9 to 5. Many museums are closed on Monday. Shops are open from 8 am until 7 pm. During Ramadan (the Muslim month of fasting), opening times vary; shops close during the day but stay open late into the evening.

#### TELEPHONES

Mobile phone coverage is limited to Cairo, the Nile Valley and delta, and the Red Sea coast. The mobile system in Egypt is 3G-supportive. Vodafone, Etisalat Egypt, and Mobinil are the major providers in the country.

5

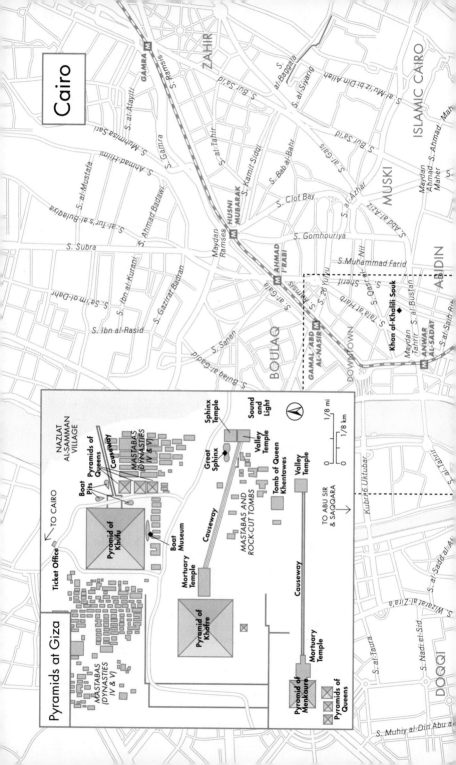

# Cairo

**Pyramids at Giza**

ZAHIR

S. Ramsis
S. al-Alayili
S. Mumtisa Sari
S. Ahmad Badawi
S. Ahmad-Hilmi
S. al-Mustafa
GAMRA
S. Gamra
S. al-Tahir

HUSNI MUBARAK
S. al-Tahir
Maydan Ramses
S. Kamil Sidqi
S. Bab al-Bahr
S. Bur Said
S. al-Gais
S. al-Baggala
S. al-Siyarig
S. al-Mu'izz bi Din Allah
ISLAMIC CAIRO

S. Clot Bay
S. al-Azhar
MUSKI
Maydan Ahmad S. Ahmad. Mah
Maher
S. Abd al-'Aziz

AHMAD I'RABI
S. Gomhouriya
S. Muhammad Farid
Sherif
S. 26 Yulyu
S.Nil
ABIDIN

S. al-Bulaqiya
S. al-Tur S. al-Bulaqiya
S. Subra
S. Gazirat Badran
S. Ibn-al-Kuranti
S. Sa'im al-Dahr
S. Ibn al-Rasid

GAMAL 'ABD AL-NASIR
Tala'at Harb
S. Qasr
S. al-Bustan
Khan al-Khalili Sook
Maydan Tahrir
ANWAR AL-SADAT
S. al-Saih Rih

BOULAQ
S. Bulaq al-Gadid
S. Sanan
DOWNTOWN

NAZLAT AL-SAMMAN VILLAGE
Causeway
Pyramids of Queens
MASTABAS (DYNASTIES IV & V)
Boat Pits
Pyramid of Khufu
Boat Museum
TO CAIRO
Ticket Office
MASTABAS (DYNASTIES IV & V)

Sphinx Temple
Sound and Light
Great Sphinx
Valley Temple
Tomb of Queen Khentawes
MASTABAS AND ROCK-CUT TOMBS
Mortuary Temple
Causeway
Valley Temple
TO ABU SIR & SAQQARA

Pyramid of Khafre
Causeway
Mortuary Temple
Pyramid of Menkaure
Pyramids of Queens

1/8 mi
1/8 km
0

Kubri 6 Uktubar
DOQQI
S. al-Tahir
S. Wizarat al-Zira'a
S. Nadi-el-Sid
S. al-Sadd al-'Al
S. al-Taura
S. Muhiy al-Din Abu a

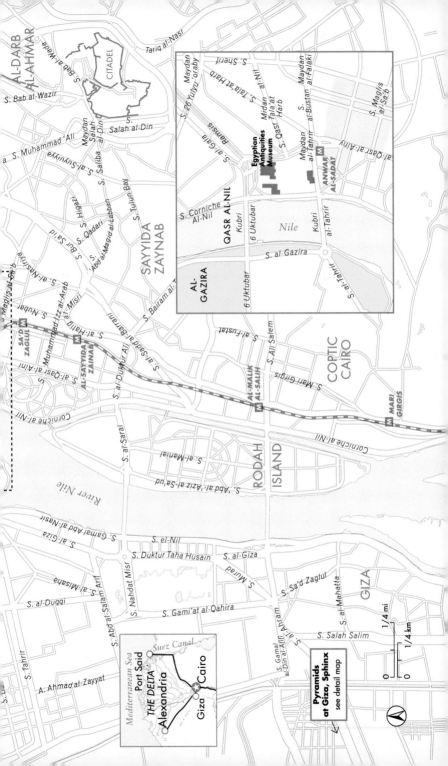

AL-DARB AL-AHMAR

CITADEL

Tariq al-Nasr

S. Bab al-Wazir

S. Bab al-Wazir

S. Salah al-Din

Maydan Salah al-Din

Salah al-Din

S. Muhammad 'Ali

S. Suyufiyya

S. Saliba

S. al-Magid al-Labban

S. Qadari

S. Bur Sa'id

S. Tulun Bay

Maydan Ahmad 'oraby

S. 26 Yulyu 'oraby

S. Tala'at Harb

S. Sherif

Maydan al-Falaki

S. Maglis al-Sa'b

Maydan al-Nil

Midan al-Tahrir

S. Qasr al-Nil

Maydan al-Bustan

S. al-Gala

S. Ramsis

Egyptian Antiquities Museum

Maydan al-Tahrir

ANWAR AL-SADAT

S. Qasr al-Ainy

S. Corniche Al-Nil

QASR AL-NIL

Kubri 6 Uktubar

Nile

Kubri al-Tahrir

S. al-Gazira

AL-GAZIRA

6 Uktubar

S. al-Tahrir

SAYYIDA ZAYNAB

S. Khairat

S. 'Abd al-Magid al-Labban

S. Bairam al-Tunsi

S. al-Fustat

S. Ali Salem

COPTIC CAIRO

S. Maglis al-Sa'b

SA'D ZAGLUL

S. Nubar

S. Muhammad Izz al-Arab

S. al-Nasriya

S. al-Khalig

AL-SAYYIDA ZAINAB

S. al-Sadd al-Barrani

S. al-Qasr al-Aini

S. al-Saida al-Barrani

S. al-Duktur Ali

AL-MALIK AL-SALIH

S. Mari Girgis

MARI GIRGIS

Corniche al-Nil

Corniche al-Nil

S. al-Saral

S. el-Manial

RODAH ISLAND

S. 'Abd al-'Aziz al-Sa'ud

River Nile

S. al-Giza

S. Gamal Abd al-Nasir

S. Nahdat Misr

S. el-Nil

S. Duktur Taha Husain

S. al-Giza

S. Murad

S. Sa'd Zaglul

S. al-Mahatta

GIZA

S. al-Duqqi

S. al-Misaha

S. 'Abd al-Salam Arif

S. Gami'at al-Qahira

S. Gamal al-Din al-Afifi al-Ahram

S. Salah Salim

S. Tahrir

A. Ahmad al-Zayyat

Mediterranean Sea

Suez Canal

Port Said

THE DELTA

Alexandria

Giza Cairo

Pyramids at Giza, Sphinx
see detail map

1/4 mi

1/4 km

0

## COMING ASHORE

Ships with passengers bound for Cairo generally dock at Port Said, Egypt's premier commercial port. The town was founded at the southern outlet of the Suez Canal as a camp for engineers and workers building the waterway in the mid-19th century. From the port it is a short walk into this unprepossessing town, but there is little to hold the visitor. Most passengers will choose to take a ship-sponsored shore excursion into Cairo.

Taxis wait at the dock entrance, and can offer transfers to Cairo for a day rate, but this is a port where we strongly recommend a ship-sponsored excursion because of the distance and schedule issues. If you decide to travel independently, it's important to agree on a price and to assess the condition of the vehicle first. The journey is long, and a breakdown would be a major inconvenience. We caution strongly against trying to rent a car to visit Cairo. There are too many security issues, and driving in Cairo traffic is not an experience the average cruise passenger is prepared for.

### CAIRO BEST BETS

**The Cairo Museum.** The most comprehensive collection of ancient Egyptian artifacts in the world, this museum is a must for serious history buffs or curious amateurs keen to catch sight of a mummy.

**The Pyramids.** When you view the Pyramids (and the Sphinx), you are sure to be awed. The mystery of their origin remains, and that's part of the allure.

**Khan al-Khalili souk.** One of the world's oldest and most authentic markets, Khan al-Khalili is a cornucopia of crafts ranging from the mundane to the magnificent.

## EXPLORING CAIRO

Fodor'sChoice
★

**The Egyptian Antiquities Museum.** On the north end of Maydan Tahrir, this huge neoclassical building is home to the world's largest collection of ancient Egyptian artifacts. With more than 100,000 items in total, it is said that if you were to spend just one minute on each item, it would take over nine months to complete the tour. Needless to say, you need to be selective here.

Some of the museum's finest pieces are in the center of the ground floor, below the atrium and rotunda. The area makes a good place to start, acting as a preview for the rest of the museum. Among the prized possessions here are three colossi of the legendary New Kingdom pharaoh Ramses II (1290–1224 BC); a limestone statue of Djoser (around 2600 BC), the 2nd Dynasty pharaoh who built the Step Pyramid in Saqqara; several sarcophagi; and a floor from the destroyed palace of Akhenaton (1353–1335 BC), the heretic monotheist king. The Narmer Palette, a piece from about 3000 BC, is thought to document the first unification of northern and southern Egypt.

On the museum's upper floor is the famous Tutankhamun collection. Look for its beautiful gold funerary mask and sarcophagus (Room 3), ancient trumpet (Room 30), thrones (rooms 20 and 25), the four huge gilded boxes that fit one inside the other (exhibits 7 and 8, located in the hallway just outside Room 30), and a royal toilet seat to boot (outside Room 30); it is one of the few air-conditioned rooms in the museum. (The collection is scheduled to be relocated to the new Grand Egyptian Museum in Giza as early as 2010.) Also upstairs is the royal Mummy Room, which houses 11 pharaonic dignitaries, including the body of Ramses II (Room 52). If you are discouraged by the Mummy Room's steep entrance fee, don't miss the assortment of mummified animals and birds in the adjacent room (Room 53), which has no additional charge. Also on the upper floor is a series of specialized exhibits, including a collection of papyri and Middle Kingdom wooden models of daily life (rooms 24 and 27).

In 2003, the museum unveiled Hidden Treasures of the Egyptian Museum, more than 150 of the best objects that form part of the museum's vast stock of artifacts kept in storage. Fittingly, the new galleries sit in the museum basement, where the catalogued items used to lie on dark dusty shelves. In 2009, a permanent Children's Museum was opened and aimed specifically at younger visitors. These galleries combine authentic artifacts with Lego models (donated by the Danish State) to explain aspects of life and customs in ancient Egypt. Children are free to use Lego bricks to construct their own models. ⊠ *al-Mathaf al-Masri, Maydan Tahrir, Downtown* ☎ *02/2579–6948* 🖙 *Museum £E80, Mummy Room £E100* ☉ *Daily 9–6:30.*

## GIZA
*12 km (8 miles) southwest of Cairo.*

The three pyramids of Khufu (Greek name: Cheops), Khafre (Chephren), and Menkaure (Mycerinus) dominate the Giza Plateau. Surrounding the father-son-grandson trio are smaller pyramids belonging to their female dependents, and the *mastabas* (large, trapezoid-shape tombs) of their courtiers and relatives. The word *mastaba* comes from the Arabic word for bench, which these tombs resemble in shape, if not in scale, and the mastabas were often painted and/or decorated with reliefs inside, with the actual burial sites placed in shafts cut into the bedrock. The great Sphinx crouches at the eastern edge of the plateau, guarding the necropolis. A museum south of the Great Pyramid contains one of the most extraordinary artifacts from ancient Egypt, Khufu's own royal boat. The pyramids, Sphinx, and some of the mastabas date from the Fourth Dynasty, while other mastabas date to the Fifth and Sixth Dynasties. South of the Sphinx and its adjacent temples, archaeologists have recently found the living and eating areas of the workmen who built the pyramids, as well as the cemeteries where they were buried.

**Great Sphinx.** Carved from the living rock of the pyramids plateau during the 4th Dynasty, the enigmatic limestone Sphinx is attached Pharaoh Khafre's funerary complex. The figure of a recumbent lion with a man's face wearing a *nemes* (traditional headdress of the pharaoh) was thought to be Khafre in the guise of Ra-Harakhte, a manifestation of the Sun God. The role of the Sphinx was to guard the vast royal necropolis that incorporated the pyramids and *mastabas* (large trapezoidal tombs) on the Giza plateau, and it's visited as part of the longer visit incorporating these other monuments at the site. It's possible to get close to the Sphinx along a wide viewing platform that has been built around it, but climbing is forbidden and there's no entry into the small interior chambers (most of the Sphinx, however, is solid rock). ⊠ *Fayyum Rd.* ☒ *Sphinx £E60 (includes both Pyramids and Sphinx), Sound & Light Show £E75* ⊙ *Daily 8–6:30; Sound & Light Show (in English) Oct.–Apr., Mon.–Wed. and Fri.–Sat. 6:30 pm, Thurs. 7:30 pm, Sun. 9:30 pm; May–Sept., Mon.–Wed. and Fri.–Sat. 8:30 pm, Thurs. 9:30 pm, Sun. 11:30 pm.*

Fodor's Choice ★ **Pyramid Plateau.** Three 4th-Dynasty pyramids dominate the skyline of the desert plateau to the southwest of Cairo. The largest is that of Pharaoh Khufu (Greek name: Cheops) also known as "The Great Pyramid." The second was built by his son Khafre (Greek name: Chephren). The smallest of pyramids was built by Menkaure (Greek name: Mycerinus), the grandson of Khufu who reigned from 2490 to 2472 BC. These are surrounded by smaller pyramids belonging to their respective female dependents, as well as numerous *mastabas* (large trapezoidal tombs) of their lesser relatives and courtiers. The site is "guarded" by the monumental carved-limestone Sphinx. A small museum in the shadow of Khufu's Pyramid contains the Pharaoh's Royal Solar Boat, by tradition the boat used to transport the Pharaoh on his final journey to the afterlife after his mummy was entombed. The pyramid interiors are open on a rotating basis, and ticket numbers are limited to 150 per morning and another 150 per afternoon. A range of *mastabas* will be open to view on any given day. The ticket office will give you current information when you buy your ticket. Buses and cars are no longer allowed on the plateau; electric trams link the ticket office with the plateau, from where you'll be able to explore the site on foot. ⊠ *Pyramids Rd.* ☒ *General admission £E60 (includes both Pyramids and Sphinx), Great Pyramid £E100, Khafre's Pyramid £E30, Mankaure's Pyramid £E25, Solar Boat Museum £E50* ⊙ *Site daily 8–6:30, pyramid and tomb interiors daily 9–4 (but the openings are staggered, so not all pyramid interiors are open every day).*

## SHOPPING

Cairo has always been a mercantile and trading town. The hundreds of magnificent mosques and palaces scattered around the city are a testament to Cairo's highly skilled craftspeople. The artisans of Egypt continue this tradition of detailed workmanship, offering a tremendous array of handmade items.

Egyptians specialize in worked brass and copper articles, wood inlay on jewelry boxes and chess sets, and leatherwear. The hookah is also an interesting regional specialty. Egyptian cotton is a byword for quality, and the shops of Cairo are a great place to buy items like bedding and towels. If you want to purchase genuine antiques and antiquities you'll need to have a certificate of approval from the Egyptian authorities to export your purchase, but reproductions are on sale everywhere. These items needn't be expensive: you can buy a lucky alabaster scarab beetle for a few Egyptian pounds—in fact, this small item is almost a compulsory souvenir of your trip to Egypt.

**Fodor's Choice** ★ **Khan al-Khalili.** Cairo shopping starts at this great medieval souk. Although it has been on every tourist's itinerary for centuries, and some of its more visible wares can seem awfully tacky, the Khan is where everyone—newcomer and age-old Cairene alike—goes to find traditional items: jewelry, lamps, spices, clothes, textiles, handicrafts, water pipes, metalwork, you name it. Whatever it is, you can find it somewhere in this skein of alleys or the streets around them. Every Khan veteran has the shops he or she swears by—usually because of the fact (or illusion) she or he is known there personally and is thus less likely to be overcharged. Go, browse, and bargain hard. Once you buy something, don't ask how much it costs at the next shop; you'll be happier that way. Many shops close Sunday. ⊠ *Islamic Cairo North, Cairo.*

> **GRAND EGYPTIAN MUSEUM**
>
> The Grand Egyptian Museum will be a fitting home for the mother lode of ancient artifacts excavated in the country in the last 150 years. When opened it will be the world's biggest museum dedicated to ancient Egypt, covering 123 acres (50 hectares) on the Giza Plateau less than 2 miles from the Pyramids. The foundation stone of the museum was laid in 2002, and at this writing only the research labs of the complex are complete. Current estimates are that the museum will open to the public in 2013.

## WHERE TO EAT

**$$**
SEAFOOD
✕ **The Fish Market.** On the upper deck of a boat permanently moored on the west bank of the Nile, the scene here is decidedly simple: there's no menu, just a display of unbelievably fresh fish, shrimp, crabs, calamari, and shellfish on ice. Pick what appeals, pay by weight, and the kitchen will prepare it however you like, with a slew of Middle Eastern salads on the side. The delicious bread is baked on the premises in a *baladi* (country) oven. ⑤ *Average main: £E330* ⊠ *26 Shar'a al-Nil, Giza, Cairo* ☎ *02/3570–9694* ⟁ *Reservations essential.*

**$$**
MIDDLE EASTERN
✕ **Naguib Mahfouz Café.** Named after Egypt's most famous novelist and run by the Oberoi Hotel Group, this is a haven of air-conditioned tranquility in the midst of the sometimes-chaotic Khan al-Khalili. The restaurant serves variations on the usual Egyptian dishes, dressed up in historically resonant names to justify what, by the standards of the area, constitute exorbitant prices. That being said, the food and service are also of higher quality than you'll find in most of the nearby restaurants. The adjoining café serves lighter fare, consisting mostly of sandwiches, at a fraction of the price of the main dishes. ⑤ *Average main: £E330* ⊠ *5 al-Badestan La., Khan al-Khalili, Islamic Cairo North, Cairo* ☎ *02/2590–3788.*

# RHODES, GREECE

Updated by
Adrian Vrettos
and Alexia
Amvrazi

The island of Rhodes (1,400 square km [540 square miles]) is one of the great islands of the Mediterranean. It was long considered a bridge between Europe and the East, and has seen many waves of settlement throughout recorded history. Ancient Rhodes was a powerful city and its political organization became the model for the city of Alexandria in Egypt. When Rome took the city in 42 BC, it was fabled for its beauty and for the sanctuary of Lindos, which drew pilgrims from around the region. Rhodes was a crucial stop on the road to the Holy Land during the Crusades. It came briefly under Venetian influence, then Byzantine, then Genoese, but in 1309, when the Knights of St. John took the city from its Genoese masters, its most glorious modern era began. Today Rhodes is a popular holiday island for Europeans who come for the sun and the beaches.

## ESSENTIALS

### CURRENCY
The euro.

### HOURS
Shops are open from 9 to 9 on weekdays and from 9 to 6 on Saturday. Museums are generally open from 9 to 5, but many are closed on Monday.

### TELEPHONES
Tri-band GSM phones work in Greece. You can buy prepaid phone cards at telecom shops, news vendors, and tobacconists in all towns and cities. Phone cards can be used for local or international calls. Vodafone is the leading mobile telecom company. OTE is the national domestic provider. Calls can be made at OTE offices and paid for after completion.

## COMING ASHORE

Ships dock at the commercial port directly outside the city walls of Rhodes Town. It is a short walk from the port to all the attractions of the walled citadel. For this reason, there are few facilities in the port itself.

The bus station for services down the east coast is found by turning right outside the port and walking for 10 minutes to Rimini Square. There are several services to Lindos each day. Journey time is about one hour, and ticket prices are €5.

Taxis wait outside the port gates but can also be found at Rimini Square. For a journey to Lindos, prices are fixed at a fare of €35 one-way. Journey time is approximately 30 minutes. You could enjoy a full day touring Rhodes island if you rent a car, though both Rhodes's Old Town and Lindos are pedestrian-only or have very limited vehicular access. Costs are €45 per day for a subcompact vehicle, and the major companies can bring a car to the port for you.

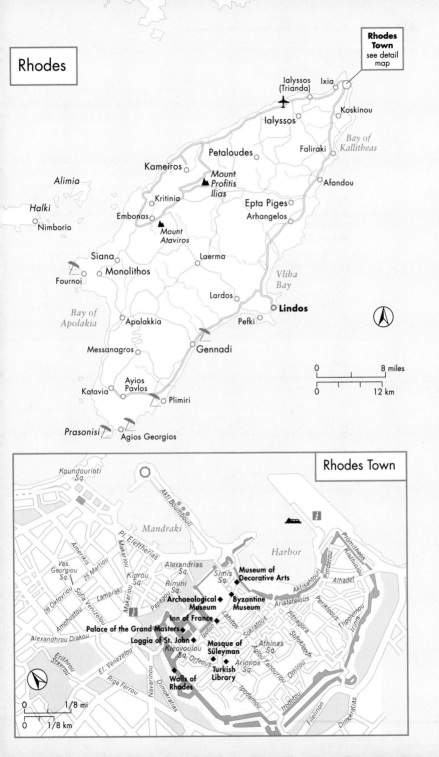

## EXPLORING RHODES

### RHODES TOWN

Rhodes Town is still a city of two parts: the Old Town, a UNESCO World Heritage site, contains exceptional medieval architecture, Orthodox and Catholic churches, and an alluring old Turkish quarter. Spreading away from the walls that encircle the Old Town is the modern metropolis, or new town.

**Archaeological Museum.** The Hospital of the Knights, completed in 1489, houses the town's Archaeological Museum. In the courtyard just beyond the imposing facade are cannonballs from the Ottoman siege of 1522, and, in surrounding halls, are two well-known representations of Aphrodite: the *Aphrodite of Rhodes,* who, while bathing, pushes aside her hair as if she's listening; and a standing figure, known as *Aphrodite Thalassia,* or "of the sea," as she was discovered in the water off the northern city beach. Other important works include two 6th-century BC *kouros* (statues of idealized male youth) found in the nearby ancient city of Kameiros, and the beautiful 5th-century BC funerary stela of Timarista bidding farewell to her mother, Crito. ⊠ *Mouseou Sq.* ☎ 22413/65200 🖾 €6 ⊙ *Apr.–Oct., daily 8–8; Nov.–Mar., Tues.–Sun. 9–4.*

**Byzantine Museum.** Icons and frescoes from churches throughout Rhodes Town (most of them long since destroyed) are displayed within the 11th-century Lady of the Castle church, once the Byzantine cathedral and, under the Turks, a mosque. ⊠ *Off Mouseou Sq.* ☎ 22413/65200 🖾 €6 ⊙ *Apr.–Oct., daily 8–8; Nov.–Mar., Tues.–Sun. 9–4.*

**Inn of France.** The Inn of France, the most elaborate of the striking inns on this famously historic street, today houses a French language institute (appropriately enough). The facade is ornately carved with the fleur-de-lis and heraldic patterns and bears an inscription that dates the building between 1492 and 1509. ⊠ *About halfway down street of Knights from Loggia of St. John.*

**Loggia of St. John.** Before the court of the Palace of the Grand Masters is the Loggia of St. John. This 19th-century neo-Gothic structure stands on the site of the 14th-century church of St. John, patron of the Knights of St. John and the final resting place of many members of the order. Used as an ammunition storehouse during Turkish occupation, the church was reduced to rubble in an explosion sparked by lightning in 1856.

**Mosque of Süleyman.** The Mosque of Süleyman was built circa 1522 to commemorate Sultan Süleyman's conquest of Rhodes and rebuilt in 1808, with a graceful minaret and distinctive pink and white stripes. ⊠ *At top of Sokratous* ☎ 22413/65200 🖾 *Closed for renovation.*

**Museum of Decorative Arts.** Housed in a stone-vaulted warehouse of the Knights, the town's museum of decorative arts, which is closed for a renovation through much of 2013, exhibits finely made ceramics, wooden tools and utensils, and costumes and textiles from the various regions of the Dodecanese. ⊠ *Argyrokastrou Sq.* ☎ 22413/65200 🖾 €3 ⊙ *Apr.–Oct., Tues.–Sun. 8:30–7; Nov.–Mar., Tues.–Sun. 8:30–3.*

**Fodor's Choice**
★ **Palace of the Grand Masters.** The Knights of St. John built most of their monuments along a street known as the **Street of the Knights** (Ippoton), which descends from the Palace of the Grand Masters, at the highest spot of the medieval city, toward the commercial port. This cobbled lane is a little more than a third of a mile long and follows the route that once connected the ancient acropolis to the harbor. This medieval assemblage is bordered on both sides by the **Inns of the Tongues**, where the Knights supped and held their meetings. **The Palace of the Grand Masters of the Knights of Rhodes** (to use its official name) is a massive affair with fairy-tale towers, crenellated ramparts, and more than 150 rooms. Situated at the top of

> ### RHODES BEST BETS
>
> **Walk down the Street of the Knights.** This medieval street is one of the most complete of its kind in the world. Imagine the Crusader knights going about their business here.
>
> **Explore the Turkish Quarter.** These narrow alleyways now play host to boutiques and cafés, but it's still a living district with real Aegean character.
>
> **Survey Lindos Town from the Acropolis above.** The splendid vista includes a tangle of narrow streets, whitewashed walls, and terra-cotta roofs down to the horseshoe bay with azure waters.

the Street of the Knights, it is the place to begin a tour. Unscathed during the Turkish siege of Rhodes in 1522, the palace was destroyed in 1856 by an explosion of ammunition stored nearby in the cellars of the Church of St. John; the present structure—a Mussolini-era Italian reconstruction—was rebuilt in a storybook, pseudo-medieval style then all the rage in the early 20th century and was later used as a holiday abode for King Vittorio Emmanuele III of Italy. Today, the palace's collection of antiques and antiquities includes Hellenistic and Roman mosaic floors from Italian excavations in Kos, and in the permanent exhibition downstairs, extensive displays, maps, and plans showing the layout of the city will help you get oriented before wandering through the labyrinthine Old Town. ✉ *Ippoton, Old Town* ☎ *22413/65270* 🎟 *€6* ◷ *May–Oct., Mon. 9–4, Tues.–Sun. 8–8; Nov.–Apr., Tues.–Sun. 9–4.*

★ **Turkish Library.** The Turkish Library dates to the late 18th century and houses a rare collection of Turkish, Persian, and Arab manuscripts, including many rare Korans. Striking reminders of the Ottoman presence, the library and the Mosque of Suleyman are still used by those members of Rhodes's Turkish community who stayed in Rhodes after the 1923 population exchange, a mass repatriation of Greek and Turkish migrants. ✉ *Sokratous, opposite Mosque of Süleyman* ☎ *2241/7400* 🎟 *Free* ◷ *Mon.–Sat. 9:30–3.*

**Walls of Rhodes.** One of the great medieval monuments in the Mediterranean, the walls of Rhodes are wonderfully restored and illustrate the engineering capabilities as well as the financial and human resources available to the Knights of St. John. For 200 years the Knights strengthened the walls by thickening them, up to 40 feet in places, and curving them so as to deflect cannonballs. The moat between the inner and outer walls never contained water; it was a device to prevent invaders from constructing siege towers. You can also get a sense of the enclosed city's massive scale by walking inside the moat. ⊠ *Old Town* ☎ *22413/65270* 🎟 *Moat free; tours €2* ⊙ *Tours Tues. and Sat. 8–noon (arrive at least 15 min. early).*

## LINDOS

*19 km (12 miles) southwest of Epta Piges, 48 km (30 miles) southwest of Rhodes Town.*

Lindos, cradled between two harbors, had a particular importance in antiquity. It had a revered sanctuary, consecrated to Athena, whose cult probably succeeded that of a pre-Hellenic divinity named Lindia, and the sanctuary was dedicated to Athena Lindia. Lindos prospered during the Middle Ages, and under the Knights of St. John. Only at the beginning of the 19th century did the age-old shipping activity cease. The population decreased radically, reviving only with the 20th-century influx of foreigners.

Lindos is enchanting and remarkably well preserved. Many 15th-century houses are still in use. Everywhere are examples of Crusader architecture: substantial houses of finely cut Lindos limestone, with windows crowned by elaborate arches. Intermixed with these Crusader buildings are whitewashed, geometric, Cycladic-style houses. Many floors are paved with black-and-white pebble mosaics. The narrow alleyways can get crowded in summer.

Fodor's Choice ★ ☾ **Acropolis of Lindos.** For about €5, you can hire a donkey for the 15-minute climb from the modern town up to the Acropolis of Lindos. The winding path leads past a gauntlet of Lindian women who spread out their lace and embroidery like fresh laundry over the rocks. The final approach ascends a steep flight of stairs, past a marvelous 2nd-century BC **relief of the prow of a Lindian ship,** carved into the rock.

The entrance to the Acropolis takes you through the **Medieval Castle** built by the Knights of St. John, then to the Byzantine **Chapel of St. John** on the next level. The Romans, too, left their mark on the acropolis, with a temple dedicated to Diocletian. On the **upper terraces,** begun by classical Greeks around 300 BC, are the remains of elaborate **porticoes** and **stoas,** commanding an immense sweep of sea and making a powerful statement on behalf of Athena and the Lydians (who dedicated the monuments on the Acropolis to her); the lofty white columns of the temple and stoa on the summit must have presented a magnificent picture. The main portico of the stoa had 42 Doric columns, at the center of which an opening led to the staircase up to the **Propylaia** (or sanctuary). The **Temple of Athena Lindia** at the very top is surprisingly modest, given the drama of the approach. As was common in the 4th century BC, both the front and the rear are flanked by four Doric columns. Numerous inscribed statue bases were found all over the summit, attesting in many cases to the work of Lindian sculptors, who were clearly second to none. ⊠ *Above New Town* ☎ *22440/31258* ⊕ *www.culture.gr* 🎟 *€6* ⊙ *May–Oct., Tues.–Sun. 8–5:40, Mon. 8–2:40; Nov.–Apr., Tues.–Sun. 8–2:40.*

**Church of the Panayia.** A graceful building with a beautiful bell tower, the Church of the Panayia probably antedates the Knights, though the bell tower bears the arms of Grand Master d'Aubusson with the dates 1484–90. Frescoes in the elaborate interior were painted in 1779 by Gregory of Symi, and the black-and-white pebble floor is a popular Byzantine design. ⊠ *Off main square* ⊙ *May–Oct., daily 9–2 and 5–9; Nov.–Apr., call number posted on church to have door unlocked.*

## SHOPPING

Lovers of handicrafts will really enjoy shopping in Rhodes. There's an abundance of ceramics, both traditional and modern, wooden bowls, reproductions of ancient statuary, woven rugs, jewelry, lace, and edibles such as delicious honey, olive oil, and of course, olives themselves. Cotton clothing is perfect for the summer temperatures. Strong handcrafted sandals and leather goods are also excellent choices.

Souvenir shopping in Rhodes Town is concentrated on Sokratous Street and the labyrinth of narrow alleyways in the old Turkish Quarter. You'll find the same merchandise in the alleyways of Lindos, where every inch of wall space is used for display—sometimes to the detriment of pedestrian traffic flow. Rhodes Town has a number of high-class jewelers and camera shops, whereas Lindos has more art galleries. The winding path that leads up to the citadel of Lindos is traditionally where Lindian women spread out their lace and embroidery over the rocks like fresh laundry.

**Astero Antiques.** Mahalis Hatziz, owner of Astero Antiques, travels throughout Greece each winter to fill his shop with some of the most enticing goods on offer on the island. ⊠ *Ayiou Fanouriou 4, off Sokratous, Rhodes Town* ☎ *22410/34753.*

## BEACHES

Rhodes is a popular island with European vacationers, and the beaches all around the island have well-developed facilities.

**Lachania.** Stretching uninterrupted for several miles, Lachania beach begins a mile north of Gennadi; drive alongside until you come to a secluded spot.

## WHERE TO EAT

**$$$** ✕ **Dinoris.** The great hall that holds Dinoris was built in AD 310 as a
SEAFOOD hospital and then converted into a stable for the Knights in 1530. The
★ fish specialties and the spacious, classy setting lure appreciative and demanding clients, from visiting celebs to Middle Eastern sheikhs. For appetizers, try the variety platter, which includes *psarokeftedakia* (fish balls made from a secret recipe) as well as mussels, shrimp, and lobster. Other special dishes are sea urchin salad and grilled calamari stuffed with cheese. In warm months, cool sea air drifts through the outdoor garden area enclosed by part of the city's walls. ⑤ *Average main: €25* ⊠ *Mouseou Sq. 14a, Rhodes Town* ☎ *22410/25824* ⌕ *Reservations essential* ⊙ *Closed Jan.*

**$$**   **GREEK**   **Fodor's Choice**   **★**   ✕ **Mavrikos.** The secret of this longtime favorite, one of the finest restaurants on Rhodes, is an elegant, perfect simplicity. Seemingly straightforward dishes, such as sea-urchin salad, fried *manouri* cheese with basil and pine nuts, swordfish in caper sauce, and lobster risotto, become transcendent with the magic touch of third-generation chef Dimitris Mavrikos, who now owns this 75-year-old family-run institution with his brother, Michalis. He combines the freshest ingredients with classical training and an abiding love for the best of Greek village cuisine. The meat dishes, including oven-baked lamb, are also sublime. ⑤ *Average main: €20* ⊠ *Main square, Lindos* ☎ *22440/31232* ⊘ *Closed Nov.–Mar.*

# SANTORINI, GREECE

Updated by Adrian Vrettos and Alexia Amvrazi

Undoubtedly the most extraordinary island in the Aegean, crescent-shape Santorini remains a mandatory stop on the Cycladic tourist route—even if it's necessary to enjoy the sensational sunsets from Ia, the fascinating excavations, and the dazzling white towns with a million other travelers. Arriving by boat, you are met by one of the world's truly breathtaking sights, the caldera: a crescent of cliffs, striated in black, pink, brown, white, and pale green, rising 1,100 feet, with the white clusters of the towns of Fira and Ia perched along the top. The encircling cliffs are the ancient rim of a still-active volcano, and you are sailing east across its flooded caldera. Victims of their own success, the main towns of Santorini can at peak times seem overburdened by an unrelenting mass of backpackers and tour groups. Even so, if you look beneath the layers of gimcrack tourism, you'll find that Santorini is still a beautiful place.

## ESSENTIALS

### CURRENCY
The euro.

### HOURS
Museums are generally open from 9 to 5, but many are closed on Monday. Shops are open daily in the summer, from 9 to noon or 1, reopening from 4 or 5 until 9 on Monday through Saturday; and from 9 to 6 on Sunday. Many shops and restaurants are closed between October and April.

### TELEPHONES
Tri-band GSM phones work in Greece. You can buy prepaid phone cards at telecom shops, news vendors, and tobacconists in all towns and cities. Phone cards can be used for local or international calls. Vodafone is the leading mobile telecom company. OTE is the national domestic provider. Calls can be made at OTE offices and paid for after completion.

### COMING ASHORE
Cruise ships anchor in the spectacular caldera, and in almost all cases passengers are tendered to the small port of Skala Fira, a sheer 1,000 feet below the capital, Fira. You can either take the funicular to the top or take a donkey ride up the steep winding path that claws its way

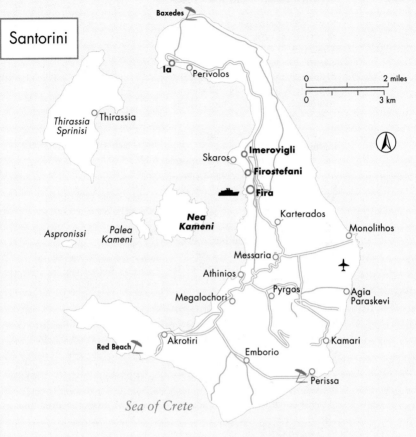

# Santorini

Baxedes

Ia
Perivolos

*Thirassia Sprinisi*
Thirassia

Skaros
**Imerovigli**
**Firostefani**
**Fira**

Karterados

Monolithos

*Aspronissi*
*Palea Kameni*
**Nea Kameni**

Messaria

Athinios

Megalochori
Pyrgos
Agia Paraskevi

Red Beach
Akrotiri
Emborio
Kamari

Perissa

*Sea of Crete*

0 — 2 miles
0 — 3 km

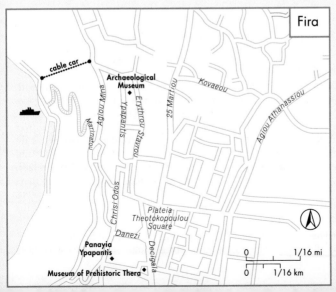

# Fira

cable car

**Archaeological Museum**

*Kovaeou*

*25 Martiou*

*Agiou Mina*

*Marinatou*

*Ypapantis*

*Erythrou Stavrou*

*Agiou Athanassiou*

*Christ Odos*

*Danezi*

*Plateia Theotokopoulou Square*

*Decigala*

**Panayia Ypapantis**

**Museum of Prehistoric Thera**

0 — 1/16 mi
0 — 1/16 km

to the top; regardless of your mode of travel, the cost is the same (€5). The donkey drivers are very persistent, but be aware that donkey droppings make the path slippery and smelly (especially relevant if you decide to go up on foot, which is also possible).

Regular bus services (approximately every 30 minutes in summer, dropping to every 1½ hours in winter with shoulder seasons) travel from Thira to Ia and Akrotiri. Schedules are posted in the station. Ticket prices range from €1.40 to €3. The main taxi stand sits next to the bus station in the main town square. Fares are reasonable, with a trip from Fira to Ia costing approximately €15.

If you rented a car for the day, you could probably see most of what Santorini has to offer. The island is compact, and it's difficult to get lost. Prices are €50 per day for a subcompact manual vehicle, but you can get an ATV for around €25 or a motorbike or scooter with prices starting at about €10 a day, including third-party liability coverage. If you rent a quad, bike, or scooter don't wear shorts or sandals, insist on the helmet (which the law requires), and get a phone number, in case of breakdown. Don't rent a scooter if you aren't an experienced rider.

> ### SANTORINI BEST BETS
>
> **The view of Santorini from the ship.** The panoramic vista of the immense volcano with white-washed settlements tumbling over the caldera edge is unique and quite unforgettable.
>
> **The remains of ancient Akrotiri.** A city frozen in time by volcanic ash, ancient Akrotiri tells a fascinating story of a rich Aegean civilization that seems to have escaped before disaster struck.
>
> **Strolling the streets of Ia.** Santorini's most beautiful village has foliage-draped Cycladic houses, boutiques, and eateries. The views are best at sunset.

## EXPLORING SANTORINI

### FIRA

Tourism, the island's major industry, adds more than 1 million visitors per year to a population of 7,000. As a result, Fira, the capital, midway along the west coast of the east rim, is no longer only a picturesque village but a major tourist center, overflowing with discos, shops, and restaurants. It soon becomes clear what brings the tourist here: with its white, cubical white houses clinging to the cliff hundreds of feet above the caldera, Fira is a beautiful place. The blocked-off Ypapantis Street (west of Panayia Ypapantis cathedral) leads to Kato Fira (Lower Fira), built into the cliff-side overlooking the caldera, where prices are higher and the vista wonderful. For centuries, the people of the island have been digging themselves rooms with a view right in the cliff face. Along Eikostis Pemptis Martiou (25th March Street), you'll find inexpensive restaurants and accommodations—many bars and hotel rooms now occupy the caves. The farther away from the caldera you get, the cheaper the restaurants.

**Archaeological Museum.** This fascinating squint into the island's millenia of history offers displays of pottery, statues, and grave artifacts found at excavations mostly from ancient Thira and Akrotiri, from the Minoan through the Byzantine periods. ⊠ *Stavrou and Nomikos, Mitropoleos, behind big church* ☎ *22860/22217* 🎟 *€3, including Museum of Prehistoric Thera* ☉ *Apr.–Oct., Tues.–Sun. 9–4; Nov.–Mar., Tues.–Sun. 8:30–3.*

★ **Museum of Prehistoric Thera.** This is the treasure house that displays pots and frescoes from the famed excavations at Akrotiri. Note the fresco fragments with the painted swallows (who flocked here

> **ANCIENT AKROTIRI**
>
> The best archaeological site on Santorini is near the tip of the southern horn of the island. Unfortunately, at this writing the site is closed (and has been for some time) for structural repairs. There was some hope that it might reopen, but such hopes have become commonplace for the past few years, so check ahead before you plan a visit.

because they loved the cliffs) and the women in Minoan dresses. The swallows, which still come in spring, remain the island's favorite design motif. The fossilized olive leaves from 60,000 BC prove the olive to be indigenous. ⊠ *Mitropoleos, behind big church* ☎ *22860/23217* ⊕ *www.culture.gr* 🎟 *€3, including Archaeological Museum* ☉ *Summer, Tues.–Sun. 8–7:30; winter, 8:30–3.*

**Panayia Ypapantis.** The modern Greek Orthodox cathedral of Panayia Ypapantis is a major landmark; you'll quickly note how the local priests, with somber faces, long beards, and black robes, look strangely out of place in summertime, tourist-jammed Fira. ⊠ *Southern part of town.*

## FIROSTEFANI

Firostefani used to be a separate village, but now it is an elegant suburb north of Fira. The 10-minute walk between it and Fira, along the caldera, is one of Santorini's highlights. From Firostefani's single white cliff-side street, walkways descend to traditional vaulted cave houses, which are fast becoming pensions. Though close to the action, Firostefani feels calm and quiet.

## IMEROVIGLI

Imerovigli, on the highest point of the caldera's rim, is what Firostefani was like a decade and a half ago. It is now being developed, and for good reasons: it is quiet, traditional, and less expensive. The 25-minute walk from Fira, with incredible views, should be on everyone's itinerary. The lodgments, some of them traditional cave houses, are mostly down stairways from the cliff-side walkway. The big rock backing the village was once crowned by Skaros castle, where Venetial the conqueror raised his flag in 1207; it housed the island's administrative offices. It collapsed in an earthquake, leaving only the rock.

## IA

Fodor's Choice ★ At the tip of the northern horn of the island sits Ia (or Oia), Santorini's second-largest town and the Aegean's most-photographed village. Ia is more tasteful than Fira (for one thing, no establishment here is allowed to play music that can be heard on the street), and the town's cubical white houses (some vaulted against earthquakes) stand out against the green-, brown-, and rust-color layers of rock, earth, and solid volcanic ash that rise from the sea. Every summer evening, travelers from all over the world congregate at the caldera's rim—sitting on whitewashed fences, staircases, beneath the town's windmill, on the old **Kastro**—each looking out to sea in anticipation of the performance: the Ia sunset. The three-hour rim-edge walk from Ia to Fira at this hour is unforgettable.

Ia is set up like the other three towns—Fira, Firostefani, and Imerovigli—that adorn the caldera's sinuous rim. There is a car road, which is new, and a cliff-side walkway (Nikolaos Nomikou), which is old. Shops and restaurants are all on the walkway, and hotel entrances mostly descend from it—something to check carefully if you cannot negotiate stairs easily. In Ia there is a lower cliff-side walkway writhing with stone steps, and a long stairway to the tiny blue bay with its dock below. Short streets leading from the car road to the walkway have cheaper eateries and shops. There is a parking lot at either end, and the northern one marks the end of the road and the rim. Nothing is very far from anything else.

The main walkway of Ia can be thought of as a straight river, with a delta at the northern end, where the better shops and restaurants are. The most-luxurious cave-house hotels are at the southern end, and a stroll by them is part of the extended evening promenade. Although it is not as crowded as Fira, where the tour boats deposit their thousands of hasty shoppers, relentless publicity about Ia's beauty and tastefulness, accurate enough, are making it impassable in August. The sunset in Ia may not really be much more spectacular than in Fira, and certainly not better than in higher Imerovigli, but there is something tribally satisfying at the sight of so many people gathering in one spot to celebrate pure beauty. Happily, the night scene isn't as frantic as Fira's—most shop owners are content to sit out front and don't cotton to the few revelers' bars in operation. In winter Ia feels pretty uninhabited.

**Fodor's Choice**
★
**Naval Museum of Thera.** Set in an old neoclassic mansion, once destroyed in the big earthquake, the Naval Museum of Thera has now risen like a phoenix from the ashes. The collection displays ships' figureheads, seamen's chests, maritime equipment, and models—all revealing the extensive nautical history of the island, Santorini's main trade until tourism took over. ⊠ *Near telephone office* ☎ *22860/71156* ✉ *€3* ☉ *Apr.–Oct., Wed.–Mon. 10–2 and 5–8.*

### NEA KAMENI

**Nea Kameni.** To peer into a live, sometimes smoldering volcano, join one of the popular excursions to Nea Kameni, the larger of the two Burnt Isles. After disembarking, you hike 430 feet to the top and walk around the edge of the crater, wondering if the volcano is ready for its fifth eruption during the last hundred years—after all, the last was in 1956. Some tours continue on to Therassia, where there is a village. Tours (about €20) are scheduled regularly.

## SHOPPING

The dramatic landscapes and light of Santorini are an inspiration to the creative—the archipelago is home to artists working in many genres. There are many galleries selling exquisite one-of-a-kind jewelry and hundreds of others selling artistic accessories for the home.

The locals say that in Santorini there is more wine than water, and it may be true: Santorini produces more wine than any two other Cyclades. Thirty-six varieties of grape thrive here. Farmers twist the vines into a basketlike shape, in which the grapes grow, protected from the wind.

**Fodor's** Choice ★ **Bead Shop.** Marina Tsiagkouri's shop has expanded, but beads are still the main reason to go. Who can resist her unique beads made from Santorini's volcanic rock? ⊠ *Opposite entrance to Museum of Prehistoric Thera, Fira* ☎ *22860/25176.*

**Costas Dimitrokalis.** With purchases that can be mailed anywhere, Costas Dimitrokalis and Matthew Dimitrokalis sell locally made embroideries of Greek linen and Egyptian cotton, rugs, pillowcases in hand-crocheted wool with local designs, and more. ⊠ *1 block from cable car, Fira* ☎🖂 *22860/22957.*

**Kostas Antoniou Jewelry.** Many of Kostas's pieces were inspired by ancient Thera. Master jeweler Gerry Kafieris sells his Triton jewelry collection here, including delicate minautre mosaics. ⊠ *In Spiliotica shopping area, near Archaeological Museum, Fira* ☎ *22860/22633.*

★ **Phenomenon.** Christoforos Asimis studied painting at Athens University, and has had many exhibitions there and abroad. The nearby cathedral's murals are his. His paintings specialize in the light and landscape of his home island. His wife, Eleni, who also studied in Athens, creates some of Santorini's most elegant jewelry. ⊠ *Ypapantis walkway, Palia Fabrika, Fira* ☎ *22860/23041* ⊕ *www.santorini.info/paliafabrika/index.html.*

## BEACHES

Santorini's volcanic rocks have produced unusual beaches of black and red sand that make for dramatic vistas. One thing to note is that this sand absorbs the suns rays and gets much hotter than golden sand. The black-sand beaches of **Kamari** (and of Perissa) are popular and consequently overdeveloped. Deck chairs and umbrellas can be rented, and tavernas and refreshment stands abound.

**Red Beach.** This comes up a winner on several fronts: it is quiet, has a taverna, and is covered with red-hued sands (have your Nikon handy). ⊠ *On southwest shore below Akrotiri, Akrotiri.*

## WHERE TO EAT

**$$**
GREEK
★
✕ **Kastro.** Spyros Dimitroulis's restaurant is primarily patronized for its view of the famous Ia sunset, and at the magical hour it is always filled. Happily, the food makes a fitting accompaniment. A good starter is olives stuffed with cream cheese, dipped in beer dough, and fried,

served on arugula with a balsamic sauce. For a main dish try mussels with oil-pepper sauce. Lunch is popular. $ *Average main: €20* ⊠ *Near Venetian castle, Ia* ☎ *22860/71045.*

$ ✕ **Lithos.** Dimitris Anastopoulos's restaurant deftly proves you can eat
GREEK well, inexpensively, and have a caldera view. Start with steamed mussels with ouzo and masticha liqueur or pastry flutes with Edam, sundried tomatoes, capers, and yogurt. For a main dish, try chicken with artichokes and capers in lemon cream sauce, or Lithos pork tenderloin, with mushrooms and kefalotiri cheese in red-wine sauce. Desserts are a specialty, and cheesecake with wild blackberries tastes as good as it looks. The oil and wine are from Dimitris's farm in the Peloponnese, and the fish is local. From the high caldera street, walk down to the lower until you see the sign. This neighborhood jumps at night. $ *Average main: €13* ⊠ *Caldera, Fira* ☎ *22860/24421* ⊕ *www.lithossantorini. com* ☯ *Closed Nov.–Mar.*

$ ✕ **Skaros Fish Taverna.** This rustic open-air taverna, one of the few res-
GREEK taurants in Imerovigli, has spectacular caldera views. It serves fresh fish and Santorini specialties, such as octopus in onion sauce, and mussels with rice and raisins. $ *Average main: €14* ⊠ *On cliff-side walkway, Imerovigli* ☎ *22860/23616* ☯ *Closed Nov.–Mar.*

# SPLIT, CROATIA

Updated by
Jane Foster

The heart of Split lies within the walls of Roman emperor Diocletian's retirement palace, which was built in the 3rd century AD. Born in the nearby Roman settlement of Salona in AD 245, Diocletian achieved a brilliant career as a soldier and became emperor at the age of 40. In 295 he ordered this vast palace to be built in his native Dalmatia, and when it was completed he stepped down from the throne and retired to his beloved homeland. In 615, when Salona was sacked by barbarian tribes, refugees took shelter within the stout palace walls and divided up the vast imperial apartments into more modest living quarters. Thus, the palace developed into an urban center. Under the rule of Venice (1420–1797), Split became one of the Adriatic's main trading ports. When the Habsburgs took control during the 19th century, an overland connection to Central Europe was established by the construction of the Split–Zagreb–Vienna railway line. The Tito years saw a period of rapid urban expansion: industrialization accelerated.

## ESSENTIALS

### CURRENCY
The Croatian kuna.

### HOURS
Offices are open weekdays from 8:30 to 4. Shops often close for lunch around 1 and may close for as long as three hours; banks also sometimes close for lunch. Post offices are open on Saturday during the main summer season, from June through September.

### TELEPHONES
Most tri- and quad-band GSM phones will work in Croatia. Public phones use calling cards, which can be purchased at the post office, newsstands, and hotels. Major mobile phone companies include TMobile and VIPNet.

## COMING ASHORE

Cruise ships dock in the city port, which is a 10-minute walk from Split's charming Old Town, which itself lies within the walls of Diocletian's Palace overlooking the sea. In the Old Town, you will find a useful tourist information office. Immediately opposite the port lie the train station and bus station, and there's also a taxi stand at the port.

Since the Old Town is compact and pedestrian-friendly, we recommend that you not rent a car in Split. However, if you do choose to rent, to explore further afield, expect to pay about €55 for a manual compact vehicle, though you can rent a semiautomatic Smart car at some outlets for about €50.

### SPLIT BEST BETS

**Diocletian's Palace.** Explore this vast ancient palace, which now hosts the heart of Split's magnificent Old Town, a UNESCO World Heritage site.

**Meštroviæ Gallery.** See the works of Croatia's finest 20th-century sculptor—pieces in wood, marble, and bronze, displayed in his former summer villa.

**Green retreat.** Stroll across Marjan Peninsula, planted with pine trees and fragrant Mediterranean herbs, for superb views down onto the Old Town and out to sea.

5

---

## EXPLORING SPLIT

The Old Town (often referred to as the Grad), where most of the architectural monuments are found, lies within the walls of Diocletian's Palace, which fronts on the seafront promenade, known to locals as the Riva. West of the center, Varoš is a conglomeration of stone fishermen's cottages built into a hillside, behind which rises Marjan, a 3½-km-long (2-mile-long) peninsula covered with pinewoods.

★ **Dioklecijanova Palača** (*Diocletian's Palace*). The original palace was a combination of a luxurious villa and a Roman garrison, based on the ground plan of an irregular rectangle. Each of the four walls bore a main gate, the largest and most important being the northern *Zlatna Vrata* (Golden Gate), opening onto the road to the Roman settlement of Salona. The entrance from the western wall was the *Željezna Vrata* (Iron Gate), and the entrance through the east wall was the *Srebrena Vrata* (Silver Gate). The *Mjedna Vrata* (Bronze Gate) in the south wall faced directly onto the sea, and during Roman times boats would have docked here. The city celebrated the palace's 1,700th birthday in 2005. ✉ *Obala Hrvatskog Narodnog Preporoda, Grad.*

★ **Galerija Meštrović** (*Meštrović Gallery*). A modern villa surrounded by extensive gardens, this building designed by Ivan Meštrović was his summer residence during the 1920s and '30s. Some 200 of his sculptural works in wood, marble, stone, and bronze are on display, both indoors and out. There is a small open-air cafe in the garden with a lovely sea view. ✉ *Šetalište Ivana Meštrovicá 46, Meje* ☎ *021/340–800* ⊕ *www.mdc.hr* 🎟 *30 Kn* ☉ *May–Sept., Tues.–Sun. 9–7; Oct.–Apr., Tues.–Sat. 9–4, Sun. 10–3.*

**Kaštelet.** Entrance to the Galerija Meštrović is also valid for the nearby Kaštelet, housing a chapel containing a cycle of New Testament

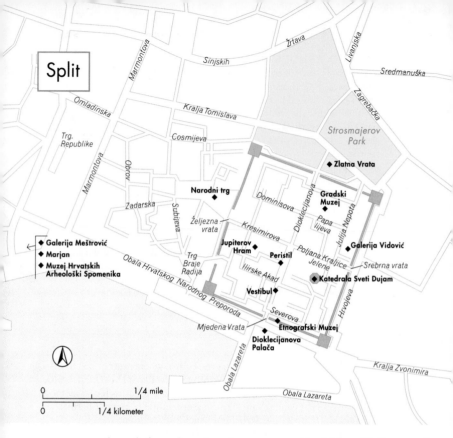

bas-relief wood carvings that many consider Meštrović's finest work. ⊠ *Šetalište Ivana Meštrovicá 39, Meje.*

**Galerija Vidović** (*Vidović Gallery*). Emanuel Vidović (1870–1953) is acknowledged as Split's greatest painter. Here you can see 74 of his works, donated to the city by his family. Large, bold canvasses depict local landmarks cast in hazy light, while the sketches done outdoors before returning to his studio to paint are more playful and colorful. ⊠ *Poljana Kraljice Jelene bb, Grad* ☎ *021/360–155* ⊕ *www.galerija-vidovic.com* 🗓 *10 Kn* ⊗ *June–Sept., Tues.–Fri. 9–9, weekends 9–4; Oct.–May, Tues.–Fri. 10–5, Sat. 9–1, Sun. 10–1.*

**Gradski Muzej** (*City Museum*). Split's city museum is worth a quick look both to marvel at the collection of medieval weaponry and to see the interior of this splendid 15th-century town house. The dining room, on the first floor, is furnished just as it would have been when the Papalić family owned the house, giving some idea of how the aristocracy of that time lived. ⊠ *Papaličeva 1, Grad* ☎ *021/360–171* ⊕ *www.mgst.net* 🗓 *10 Kn* ⊗ *May.–Sep, Tues.–Fri. 9–9, Sat.–Mon. 10–4; Oct.–Apr., Tues.–Fri. 10–5, Sat.–Mon. 9–1.*

**Jupiterov Hram** (*Jupiter's Temple*). This Roman temple was converted into a baptistery during the Middle Ages. The entrance is guarded by the mate (unfortunately damaged) of the black-granite sphinx that stands in front of the cathedral. Inside, beneath the coffered barrel vault and ornamented cornice, the 11th-century baptismal font is adorned with a stone relief showing a medieval Croatian king on his throne. Directly behind it, the bronze statue of St. John the Baptist is the work of Meštrović. ⊠ *Kraj Sv Ivana, Grad* 🖃 *5 Kn* ⊙ *May–Oct., daily 8–7.*

**Katedrala Sveti Dujam** (*Cathedral of St. Dominius*). The main body of the cathedral is the 3rd-century octagonal mausoleum designed as a shrine to Emperor Diocletian. During the 7th century, refugees from Salona converted it into an early Christian church, ironically dedicating it to Sv Duje (St. Domnius), after Bishop Domnius of Salona, one of the many Christians martyred during the late emperor's persecution campaign. The cathedral's monumental main door is ornamented with magnificent carved wooden reliefs, the work of Andrija Buvina of Split. Inside, the hexagonal Romanesque stone pulpit, with richly carved decoration, is from the 13th century. The high altar, surmounted by a late-Gothic canopy, was executed by Bonino of Milan in 1427. ⊠ *Peristil, Grad* 🖃 *Cathedral free, bell tower 10 Kn* ⊙ *Nov.–Apr, daily 8–6; May–Oct., daily 8–7.*

**Marjan** (*Marjan Hill*). Situated on a hilly peninsula, this much-loved park is planted with pine trees and Mediterranean shrubs and has been a protected nature reserve since 1964. A network of paths crisscrosses the grounds, offering stunning views over the sea and islands. ⊠ *Marjan.*

**Muzej Hrvatskih Arheološki Spomenika** (*Museum of Croatian Archaeological Monuments*). This modern building displays early Croatian religious art from the 7th through the 12th centuries. The most interesting exhibits are fine stone carvings decorated with plaitwork designs, surprisingly similar to the geometric patterns typical of Celtic art. In the garden you can see several stećci, monolithic stone tombs dating back to the cult of the Bogomils (an anti-imperial sect that developed in the Balkans during the 10th century). ⊠ *Šetalište Ivana Meštrovića 18, Meje* 🕿 *021/323–901* ⊕ *www.mhas-split.hr* 🖃 *10 Kn* ⊙ *Mon.–Fri. 9–1 and 5–8, Sat. 9–2.*

**Narodni trg** (*People's Square*). A pedestrianized expanse paved with gleaming white marble, and rimmed by open-air cafés, this is contemporary Split's main square. Although religious activity has to this day centered on Peristil, Narodni trg became the focus of civic life during the 14th century. In the 15th century the Venetians constructed several important public buildings here: the Town Hall (housing a contemporary art gallery, with erratic opening hours), plus the Rector's Palace and a theater, the latter two sadly demolished by the Habsburgs in the 19th century. The Austrians, for their part, added a Secessionist building at the west end of the square. ⊠ *Grad.*

**Peristil** (*Peristyle*). From Roman times up to the present day, the main public meeting place within the palace walls, this spacious central courtyard is flanked by marble columns topped with Corinthian capitals and richly ornamented cornices linked by arches. There are six columns on both the east and west sides, and four more at the south end, which mark the monumental entrance to the Vestibul. During summer, occasional live concerts are held here. ⊠ *Grad.*

**Vestibul.** The cupola of this domed space would once have been decorated with marble and mosaics. Today there's only a round hole in the top of the dome, but it produces a stunning effect: the dark interior, the blue sky above, and the tip of the cathedral's bell tower framed in the opening. ⊠ *Peristil, Grad.*

**Zlatna Vrata** (*Golden Gate*). Formerly the main entrance into the palace, Zlatna Vrata, on the north side of the palace, is the most monumental of the four gates. Just outside the Zlatna Vrata stands Meštrović's gigantic bronze **statue of Grgur Ninski** (Bishop Gregory of Nin). During the 9th century, the bishop campaigned for the use of the Slav language in the Croatian Church, as opposed to Latin, thus infuriating Rome. This statue was created in 1929 and placed on Peristil to mark the 1,000th anniversary of the Split Synod, then moved here in 1957. Note the big toe on the left foot, which is considered by locals to be a good luck charm and has been worn gold through constant touching. ⊠ *Dioklecijanova, Grad.*

## SHOPPING

Dalmatian women—and those from Split in particular—are renowned for their elegant sense of style. Despite a poor local economy, you'll find countless exclusive little boutiques selling women's clothes, some representing the new generation of young Croatian designers, and shoes imported from Italy. However, the city's most memorable shopping venue remains the *pazar,* the colorful open-air market held each morning just outside the palace walls. When looking for gifts, bear in mind that Dalmatia produces some excellent wines, which you can buy either in Split or while visiting the islands.

**Croata.** Overlooking Trg Brace Radića, close to the seafront, Croata specializes in "original Croatian ties" in presentation boxes. ⊠ *Mihovilova Širina 7, Grad* ☎ *021/346–336.*

**Vinoteka Terra.** Vinoteka Terra is a stone cellar close to Bačvice Bay, where you can taste Croatian regional wines, accompanied by savory appetizers, before purchasing bottles. It also stocks truffle products and olive oils. ⊠ *Prilaz Braće Kaliterna 6, Bačvice* ☎ *021/314–800* ⊕ *vinoteka.hr.*

## BEACHES

**Uvala Bačvica** (*Bačvice Bay*). This is the area's best beach and it's a 10-minute walk east of the Old Town. It does get very busy in summer, but if you don't mind the crowds, you can rent beach chairs and umbrellas, and there's a string of cafés and bars along this stretch of coast. **Amenities:** food and drink; showers. **Best for:** partiers; swimming. ⊠ *Šetalište Petra Preradovića, Bačvica.*

## WHERE TO EAT

**$$$$** ✕**Kod Jose.** This typical Dalmatian *konoba* is relaxed and romantic,
EASTERN with exposed stone walls and heavy wooden furniture set off by candle-
EUROPEAN light. The waiters are wonderfully discreet, and the *rižot frutta di mare*
(seafood risotto) delicious. You'll find it just outside the palace walls,
a five-minute walk from Zlatna Vrata (Golden Gate)—it's slightly hidden away, so many tourists miss it. There are also tabels outside on a
small open-air terrace if you come here in summer. ⑤ *Average main:
€90* ✉ *Sredmanuška 4, Manuš* ☎ *021/347–397.*

**$$** ✕**Pizzeria Galija.** The best pizzas in town, as well as delicious pasta
PIZZA dishes and a range of colorful salads, good draft beer and wine sold
by the glass, are to be found in this centrally located pizzeria, which
is close to the fish market. A favorite with locals, its dining room is
bustling and informal, with heavy wooden tables and benches. There's
also a terrace for open-air dining out front. The owner, Željko Jerkov,
is a retired Olympic gold medal–winning basketball player. ⑤ *Average
main: €60* ✉ *Tončićeva 12, Grad* ☎ *021/347–932* ▭ *No credit cards.*

5

# The North Sea

## PORTS IN BELGIUM, GREAT BRITAIN, IRELAND, AND THE NETHERLANDS

Bruges, Belgium

## WORD OF MOUTH

"Amsterdam is so walkable and safe, you can easily just 'follow your nose' without needing a walking plan. We loved wandering around that lovely city, at all hours of the day and night."

—MaureenB

"In Edinburgh we walked the Royal Mile (more than once), visited Holyrood Palace, the Britannia, Mary King's Close."

—d1carter

Ports in the United Kingdom have long been the starting points for many transatlantic crossings, but these days your ship is more likely to begin its journey in Harwich than Southampton, and may cruise around the North Sea and British Isles or continue to the Baltic or even around the Mediterranean.

Some ships by U.S.-based cruise lines are even based year-round or part of the year in England to facilitate easier cruising in Europe. These increasingly busy ports sometimes include more exotic destinations such as the Canary Islands on their itineraries.

## ABOUT THE RESTAURANTS

All the restaurants we recommend serve lunch; they may also serve dinner if your cruise ship stays late in port and you choose to dine off the ship. Europeans tend to eat a leisurely meal at lunch, but in most ports there are quicker and simpler alternatives for those who just want to grab a quick bite before returning to the ship. You'll be able to pay in euros only in Belgium, Ireland, and the Netherlands; prices in England and Scotland are in British pounds. All restaurant prices are based on the average cost of a main course at dinner. Price categories in the United Kingdom are based on the euro-equivalent costs of eating in restaurants.

# AMSTERDAM, NETHERLANDS

Updated by
Liz Humphreys

Amsterdam has as many facets as a 40-carat diamond polished by one of the city's gem cutters: the capital, and spiritual "downtown," of a nation ingrained with the principles of tolerance; a veritable Babylon of old-world charm; a font for homegrown geniuses such as Rembrandt and Van Gogh; a cornucopia bursting with parrot tulips and other greener—more potent—blooms; and a unified social zone that takes in cozy bars, archetypal "brown" cafés, and outdoor markets. Although impressive gabled houses bear witness to the Golden Age of the 17th century, their upside-down images reflected in the waters of the city's canals symbolize and magnify the contradictions within the broader Dutch society. With a mere 768,000 friendly souls and with almost everything a scant 10-minute bike ride away, Amsterdam is actually like a village that happens to pack the cultural wallop of a megalopolis.

## ESSENTIALS

### CURRENCY

The euro. ATMs are common and credit cards are widely accepted in all but restaurants, where only European cards with PIN are accepted widely.

## HOURS

Shops open Tuesday, Wednesday, Friday, and Saturday from 9 or 10 until 6; they are open later on Thursday. Most stores are closed on Sunday and some on Monday. Museums open from 9 until 6, with one late-opening night during the week.

## PRIVATE TOURS

If you want a private chauffeured tour around Amsterdam or other parts of Holland (including such options as the flower market at Aalsmeer, Delft, the fishing villages of Vollendam and Marken, and more), Amsterdam City Tours offers private cars or minibuses starting at €225 and provides tours lasting from three to eight hours. They also offer Amsterdam group city tours by bus (1 hour, 45 min., €13) or bus and boat (3 hours, €29).

Contacts **Amsterdam City Tours.** ☏ *31/299411111* ⊕ *www.amsterdamcitytours.*

## TELEPHONES

Most tri- and quad-band GSM mobile phones should work in the Netherlands, which operates a 3G mobile system with dual-band handsets. Most public phones take phone cards (available at numerous shops) and some take credit cards, and will connect international calls. Major telecom companies are Vodafone and Orange.

## COMING ASHORE

Ships dock at the cruise terminal on the IJ River, a 15-minute walk (one tram stop) from the main train station, the transport hub of the city. The terminal, constructed of glass in the shape of a wave, is attached to the Mövenpick Hotel and the Muziekgebouw concert hall. It has tourist information, shopping facilities, a Subway restaurant, an ATM (available from 7–7 daily), luggage lockers, and free Internet access on dedicated consoles. Passengers can walk directly from the terminal into the town or rent a bike (or a Segway, also available at the terminal) and take to the cycle tracks that crisscross the city. For trips to other locations around the Netherlands, take Tram 26 to reach the main train station (Centraal Station) or Tram 25 to the bus station on the southeast side of Centraal Station.

The so-called Canal Bus (which is actually a boat) picks up passengers from the cruise terminal and makes nine stops around Amsterdam, including some of Amsterdam's major museums, traveling around on the water. A day-ticket for the Canal Bus is €22; save 10% if you buy your ticket in advance online. The bus makes a stop just outside the central train station. Public bus and tram services are also useful for visiting the attractions; single tickets cost €2.60 for a maximum one-hour journey, while a day ticket is €7.50. In Amsterdam, most transit tickets have been replaced with reusable plastic chipcards, which you can purchase at Centraal Station; you can also buy one-hour and one-day disposable chipcards on board the bus or tram.

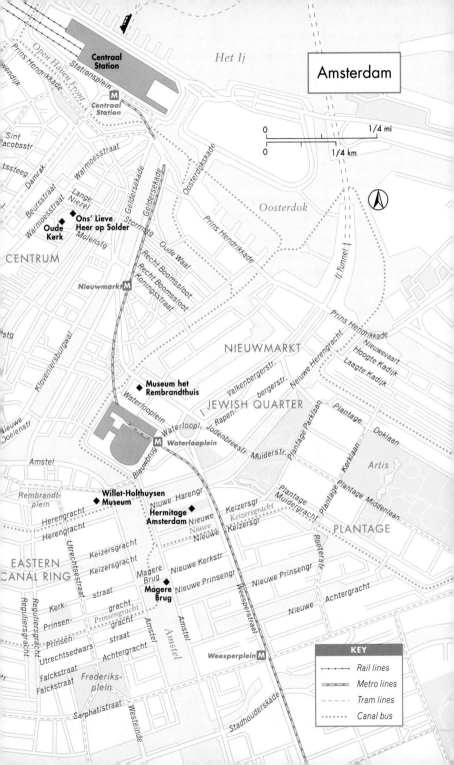

# EXPLORING AMSTERDAM

**Fodor's** Choice ★ ☺ **Amsterdam Museum** (*Amsterdam Historical Museum*). Any city that began in the 13th century as a boggy swamp to become the trading powerhouse of the world in the 17th century has a fascinating story to tell, and this museum does it superbly. It's housed in a rambling amalgamation of buildings, once a convent, which was used as Amsterdam's Civic Orphanage. Before visiting the actual museum, walk past the entrance and check out the glassed Schuttersgalerij (Civil Guards Gallery) lined with huge portraits of city militias—though not in the same league as *The Night Watch*, you can see them for free. Recently, 21st-century renditions of civil guard paintings have been added to the collection, notably one featuring the "Maid of Amsterdam," with a joint in one hand and Rembrandt's face tattooed on her chest. ⊠ *Kalverstraat 92 and Sint Luciënsteeg 27, Centrum* ☎ *020/523–1822* ⊕ *www.amsterdammuseum.nl* ⊠ *€10* ⊗ *Daily 10–5.*

**Fodor's** Choice ★ **Anne Frankhuis** (*Anne Frank House*). Anne Frank, one of the most famous authors of the 20th century, wrote the inspiring diary of a Jewish girl who was forced to hide with her family here in a hidden apartment from the Nazis. In the pages of *The Diary of Anne Frank* (published posthumously in 1947 as *The Annex* by her father—the title she chose) the young Anne recorded two increasingly fraught years living in secret in a warren of rooms at the back of this 1635 canal house with her family, the Van Pels family, and the dentist Fritz Pfeffer, a total of five adults and three children. The entrance to the flat was hidden behind a hinged bookcase. Here, like many *onderduikers* ("people in hiding") throughout Amsterdam, Anne dreamed her dreams, wrote her diary, and pinned up movie-star pictures to her wall (still on view). It's hard to imagine how the group lived and tried to avoid capture and attention. All but Otto Frank were ultimately killed during the war. Miep Gies, one of the friends who helped with the hiding, found Anne's diary after the raid and kept it through the war. ■ **TIP→ The line to get into the Anne Frank House is extremely long, especially in the summer. It moves (sort of) quickly, but it's best to arrive early or book tickets online to avoid the worst crowds.** ⊠ *Prinsengracht 263-267, Centrum* ☎ *020/556–7105* ⊕ *www.annefrank.nl* ⊠ *€9* ⊗ *Mar.–Sept., daily 9–9 (Sat. until 10); July–Aug., daily 9–10; Sept.–Mar., daily 9–7 (Sat. until 9).*

**Fodor's** Choice ★ **Brouwersgracht** (*Brewers' Canal*). Regularly voted Amsterdam's most beautiful street, this wonderful canal at the northern border of the Jordaan is lined by residences and former warehouses for brewers, fish processors, and tanneries that traded here in the 17th century when Amsterdam was the "warehouse of the world." Without sacrificing the ancient vibe, most of the buildings have been converted into luxury apartments. Of particular note are Nos. 204–212 and their trapezium gables. At No. 162, there are two dried fish above the door. This decoration on a metal screen was the forerunner of the gable stone denoting occupation. The canal provides long views down the grand canals that are perfect for photo ops. The Brouwersgracht runs westward from the end of the Singel (a short walk along Prins Hendrikkade from Centraal Station) and forms a cap to the western end of the Grachtengordel.

On top of the old canal mansions dotting the Brouwersgracht are symbols referring to the breweries that used this waterway to transport their goods to thirsty drinkers hundreds of years ago. ⊠ *Jordaan.*

**Dam** (*Dam Square*). Home to the Koninklijk Paleis (Royal Palace) and the Nieuwe Kerk, Dam Square (or just Dam), is Amsterdam's main square. It traces its roots to the 12th century and the dam built over the Amstel (hence the city's name). The waters of the Damrak (the continuation of the Amstel) once reached right up to the Dam, with ships and barges sailing to the weigh house. Folks came here to trade, talk, protest, and be executed. In the 17th century it was hemmed in by houses and packed with markets. Behind the Nieuwe Kerk there's an atmospheric warren of alleys with *proeflokaal* (liquor tasting house) *De Drie Fleschjes* (the Three Small Bottles) on Gravenstraat dating from 1650. In the 19th century the Damrak was filled in to form the street leading to Centraal Station, and King Louis, Napoléon's brother, demolished the weigh house in 1808 because it spoiled the view from his bedroom window in the Royal Palace. Today the Dam is a bustling meeting point with street performers and fairs on high days and holidays. ⊠ *Amsterdam.*

> ## AMSTERDAM BEST BETS
>
> **Canal-boat trip.** It may seem kitschy, but this is the best way to get a feel for the canal ring historic area and to take in the wonderful architecture of the Old City.
>
> **Vincent van Gogh.** The world's richest repository of the tragic artist's work has been transferred from the Van Gogh Museum to the grand Hermitage Amsterdam museum while the Van Gogh undergoes renovations; it's expected to reopen in April 2013.
>
> **Rijksmuseum.** This grand gallery reopened in April 2013; it's a must-see.

**Fodor's Choice**
★ **Magere Brug** (*Skinny Bridge*). Of Amsterdam's 60-plus drawbridges, the Magere Brug is the most famous and provides gorgeous views of the Amstel and surrounding area. It was purportedly first built in 1672 by two sisters living on opposite sides of the Amstel who wanted an efficient way of sharing that grandest of Dutch traditions: the *gezellige* (socially cozy) midmorning coffee break. Walk by at night when it's spectacularly lit. Many replacements to the original bridge have come and gone, and this, dating from 1969, is just the latest. ⊠ *Between Kerkstraat and Nieuwe Kerkstraat, Centrum.*

**Fodor's Choice**
★ **Museum het Rembrandthuis** (*Rembrandt House Museum*). This is the house that Rembrandt bought, flush with success, for 13,000 guilders (a princely sum) in 1639, and where he lived and worked until 1656 when declared bankrupt. The inside is a remarkable reconstruction job, as the contents have been assembled based on inventories made when Rembrandt was forced to sell everything, including an extravagant collection of art and antiquities (a contributing factor in his money troubles). He originally chose this house on what was then the main street of the Jewish Quarter, to experience firsthand the faces he would use in his Old Testament religious paintings. The house interior has been restored with contemporaneous elegant furnishings and artwork in the

reception rooms, a collection of rarities that match as closely as possible the descriptions in the inventory, and the main studio, occasionally used by guest artists, which is kept fully stocked with paints and canvases. But it doesn't convey much of the humanity of Rembrandt himself. The little etching studio is perhaps the most atmospheric. Littered with tools of the trade, a printing press, and a line hung with drying prints (there are demonstrations), it's easy to imagine Rembrandt finding respite here, experimenting with form and technique, away from uncomfortable schmoozing for commissions (and loans) in the grander salon. The museum owns a huge collection of etchings with 260 of the 290 he made represented, and a changing selection is on permanent display. ⊠ *Jodenbreestraat 4–6, Centrum* ☎ *020/520–0400* ⊕ *www.rembrandthuis.nl* ⊠ *€10* ☉ *Daily, 10–5.*

**Fodor's Choice**  **Ons' Lieve Heer op Solder** (*Our Lord in the Attic Museum*). With its
★  elegant gray-and-white facade and spout gable, this appears to be just another lovely 17th-century canal house, and on the lower floors it is. But tucked away in the attic is a clandestine place of Catholic worship, a *schuilkerk* (hidden church), one of the very few to survive more or less in its original state. Catholic Masses were officially forbidden from 1578, but the Protestant authorities in Amsterdam turned a blind eye provided the churches were not recognizable as such from the outside. The Oude Kerk was de-Catholicized and stripped of its patron, St. Nicholas, so this little church, consecrated in 1663, was dedicated to him until the St. Nicolaaskerk opened in 1887. The chapel itself is a triumph of Dutch classicist taste, with magnificent marble columns, gilded capitals, a colored-marble altar, and the *Baptism of Christ in the Jordan* (1716) painting by Jacob de Wit presiding over all.

The grandeur continues through the house, which was renovated by merchant Jan Hartan between 1661 and 1663. Even the kitchen and chaplain bedroom remain furnished in the style of the age, and the drawing room, or *sael*, looks as if it were plucked from a Vermeer painting. Besides boasting canvases by Thomas de Keyser, Jan Wynants, and Abraham de Vries, the house also displays impressive collections of church silver and sculptures. The new part of the museum, on the other side of the alley, hosts temporary exhibitions. ⊠ *Oudezijds Voorburgwal 40, Centrum* ☎ *020/624–6604* ⊕ *www.opsolder.nl* ⊠ *€8* ☉ *Mon.–Sat. 10–5, Sun. 1–5.*

★  **Oude Kerk** (*Old Church*). Amsterdam's oldest church has evolved over three centuries to look as it does today. What began as a wooden chapel in 1306 was built up to a hall church and then a cross basilica between 1366 and 1566 (and fully restored between 1955 and 1979). It was violently looted during the Reformation and stripped of its altars and images of saints—though the looters did leave the 14th-century paintings still visible on its wooden roof, as well as the Virgin Mary stained-glass windows that had been set in place in 1550. The famed Vater-Müller organ was installed in 1726. Don't miss the carved choir stalls that illustrate proverbs relating to cardinal sins, among other things. Within this open, atmospheric space, there's a gravestone for Rembrandt's wife Saskia van Uylenburgh and also for Kiliaen van Rensselaer, one of the Dutch founders of what is now New York, and by the door, a bronzed hand cupping a naked breast. This is one of a series of sculptures placed throughout Amsterdam in 1982 by an anonymous artist. The Oude Kerk is as much exhibition space as a place of worship, hosting the annual World Press Photography competition and top-notch modern-art shows. Its carillon is played every Tuesday at 2 and every Saturday at 4—the best place to listen is the bridge in front of the church. ⊠ *Oudekerksplein 23, Centrum* ☎ *020/625–8284* ⊕ *www. oudekerk.nl* 🖾 *€5* ☉ *Mon.–Sat. 11–5, Sun. 1–5:30.*

**Fodor'sChoice**
★ **Rijksmuseum** (*State Museum*). Rembrandt's *The Night Watch*, Vermeer's *The Love Letter,* Frans Hals's *Portrait of a Young Couple . . .* you get the picture. The Netherlands' greatest museum, the famed Rijksmuseum is home to a near infinite selection of masterpieces by these top masters along with Steen, Ruisdael, Hobbema, Cuyp, and the rest of their Golden Age ilk. As of Spring 2013 the revamped museum will finally open its doors after a massive renovation both indoors and out.

While the collection encompasses both the West and Asia, and ranges from the 9th through the 19th centuries, the bulk is of 15th- to 17th-century paintings, mostly Dutch. But if your time is limited, head directly for Rembrandt's *The Night Watch,* with its central figure, the "stupidest man in Amsterdam," Frans Banningh Cocq. Other unmissable masterpieces include Vermeer's *The Little Street*—a magical sliver of 17th-century Delft life—and his incomparable *The Love Letter,* in which a well-appointed interior reveals a mistress and her maid caught in the emotional eddies of a recently opened and read billet-doux. Ostensibly, a more sedate missive is being read in Vermeer's *Woman in Blue Reading a Letter,* on view nearby.

For an institution dedicated to antiquity and art history, the Rijksmuseum has shown a remarkable technical savvy in making its vast collection more accessible via its incredible website. On the sub-site Rijksstudio you can see, download, share, and do basically anything else you like with images of 125,000 works from the museum's collection. ■TIP➔ **Don't leave the country without visiting the mini-museum at Schiphol Airport** (⊠ *Holland Boulevard between piers E and F behind passport control* ☎ *020/653–5036* ☉ *Daily 6 am–8 pm*). ⊠ *Stadhouderskade 42, Museum District* ☎ *020/674–7000* ⊕ *www.rijksmuseum. nl* 🖾 *€14 (subject to change after the reopening)* ☉ *Daily 9–6. Library, Print Room, and Reading Room (ID required): Tues.–Sat. 10–5.*

**Fodor'sChoice**
★ **Stedelijk Museum of Modern Art.** Amsterdam's celebrated treasure house of modern art, the Stedelijk finally reopened (in September 2012) following a massive refurbishment of this wedding-cake Neo-Renaissance structure built in 1895. In true Amsterdam fashion, the locals were quick to nickname the futuristic addition by globally acclaimed local architects Benthem/Crouwel the *Badkuip* (Bathtub); it incorporates a glass-walled restaurant (which you can visit, along with the museum shop, without a museum ticket). The new Stedelijk boasts twice the exhibition space compared to the old, thanks, in part, to the new Bathub, which will now host temporary shows (watch out for Suprematist Malevich in 2013 and the noted South-African-Dutch painter Marlene Dumas in 2014).

As for the Stedelijk's old building, it is now home to the museum's own fabled collection of modern and contemporary art. While this collection harbors many works by such ancients of modernism as Chagall, Cézanne, Picasso, Monet, Mondriaan, and Malevich, there is a definite emphasis on the post-World War II period: with such local CoBrA boys as Appel and Corneille; American pop artists as Warhol, Johns, Oldenburg, and Liechtenstein; abstract expressionists as de Kooning and Pollock; and contemporary German expressionists as Polke, Richter, and Baselitz; and displays of Dutch essentials like De Stijl school, including the game-changing *Red Blue Chair* that Gerrit Rietveld designed in 1918 and Mondriaan's 1920 trail-blazing *Composition in Red, Black, Yellow, Blue, and Grey.* ⊠ *Paulus Potterstraat 13, Museum District* ☎ *020/573–2911* ⊕ *www.stedelijk.nl* ☒ *€15* ☉ *Tues. and Wed. 11–5; Thurs. 11–10; Sat. and Sun. 10–6; closed Mon.*

**Fodor's** Choice
★

**Willet-Holthuysen Museum.** Here's a rare chance to experience what it was like to live in a gracious mansion on the Herengracht in the 18th century. In 1895, widow Sandrina Louisa Willet-Holthuysen bequeathed this house to the city, along with all of its contents. It was actually built in 1687 but has been renovated several times and is now under the management of the Amsterdam Museum. Take an hour or so to discover its interiors and artwork, including a sumptuous ballroom and a rarities cabinet. Complete the Dutch luxury experience by lounging in the French-style garden in the back. ⊠ *Herengracht 605, Centrum* ☎ *020/523–1822* ⊕ *www.willetholthuysen.nl* ☒ *€8* ☉ *Weekdays 10–5, weekends 11–5.*

## SHOPPING

Souvenir shops are filled with wooden clogs and ceramics bearing windmill or tulip motifs, but Amsterdam offers more than just cheap and cheerful items. There's a major market in diamonds and also in antiques. At the lower end of the price scale, there's a market in collectibles and one-of-a-kind items, plus cutting-edge design for the home.

**Kalverstraat,** the city's main pedestrians-only shopping street, is where much of Amsterdam does its day-to-day shopping. Running parallel to Kalverstraat is the **Rokin,** a main tram route lined with shops offering high-priced trendy fashion, jewelry, accessories, antiques, and even an old master painting or two. Shoppers will love to explore the **Negen Straatjes** (Nine Streets), nine charming, tiny streets that radiate from behind the Royal Palace. Here, in a sector bordered by Raadhuisstraat and Leidsestraat, specialty and fashion shops are delightfully one-of-a-kind. Heading even farther to the west, you enter the chic and funky sector of the **Jordaan,** where generation after generation of experimental designers have set up shop to show their imaginative creations. Though adventurous collectors are increasingly looking to the Jordaan district for unique finds, the more expensive **Spiegelkwartier** is the city's mainstay for high-end antiques. The **De Baarsjes** neighborhood in the western part of the city is progressively attracting small galleries that showcase exciting works of art.

★ Whether hunting for treasures or trash, you could get lucky at one of Amsterdam's flea markets. The best is **Waterlooplein** flea market (Monday–Saturday 9–5), which surrounds the perimeter of the Stopera (Muziektheater/Town Hall complex) building. The **Bloemenmarkt** (along the Singel canal, between Koningsplein and Muntplein), is another of Amsterdam's must-see markets, where flowers and plants are sold from permanently moored barges (Monday–Saturday 9–5).

## WHERE TO EAT

$ ✕ **Bakkerswinkel.** This genteel yet unpretentious bakery and tearoom EUROPEAN evokes an English country kitchen, one that lovingly prepares and serves **Fodor's**Choice breakfasts, high tea, hearty-breaded sandwiches, soups, and divine slabs ★ of quiche. The closely clustered wooden tables don't make for much privacy, but this place is a true oasis if you want to indulge in a healthful breakfast or lunch. The convenient location on busy Zeedijk will only be open until 2014, when the original Bakkerswinkel reopens at Warmoesstraat 69 after renovations. There are several other locations: such as one complete with a garden patio in the Museum District and another at Westergasfabriek, plus a takeout-only counter at Warmoesstraat 133. ⑤ *Average main: €8* ⊠ *Zeedijk 37, Red Light District* ☎ *020/489–8000* ⊕ *www.debakkerswinkel.com* ☉ *No dinner.*

$ ✕ **Pancake Bakery.** It's hard to go wrong when going out for Dutch pan- DUTCH cakes in Amsterdam. But the quaint Pancake Bakery rises above the ★ pack of similar eateries with its medieval vibe, canal-side patio near the ☉ Anne Frank House, and a mammoth menu with more than 75 choices of sweet and savory toppings. There are also omelets, and a convincing take on the folk dish of *erwtensoep* (a superthick, smoked sausage–imbued pea soup—only available from Oct. to April). But don't rise too early for your pancakes—the bakery doesn't open till noon—and be prepared to wait: reservations are only taken for groups of six or more. ⑤ *Average main: €11* ⊠ *Prinsengracht 191, Western Canal Ring* ☎ *020/625–1333* ⊕ *www.pancake.nl* ⚱ *Reservations not accepted.*

## WHERE TO STAY

$$$$ ▦ **Conservatorium Hotel.** An impressive early 20th-century bank turned HOTEL music school is a visual feast, with a glass-roofed, tree-filled courtyard **Fodor's**Choice lobby and dramatically modern guest rooms, many of them duplexes, ★ with huge windows, muted tones, and splashes of color. **Pros:** stunning contemporary surroundings; spacious and beautiful accommodations; spa with lap pool; near museums. **Cons:** quite expensive; a bit removed from city center. ⑤ *Rooms from: €325* ⊠ *Van Baerlestraat 27, Museum District and Environs* ☎ *020/570–0000* ⊕ *www.conservatoriumhotel. com* ⇆ *129 rooms, 42 suites* ⎮○⎮ *No meals.*

$$$$ ▦ **Dylan Amsterdam.** Lacquered trunks, mahogany screens, modernist HOTEL hardwood tables, and luxurious upholstery all lend design flair to these lovely quarters on the site of the historic Municipal Theater, which burned down in the 17th century (an arched entryway remains). **Pros:** a taste of old Amsterdam; good for celebrity spotting; updated business facilities. **Cons:** some parts of the hotel feel overdesigned; few

**6**

rooms have canal views. ⑤ *Rooms from: €275* ⊠ *Keizersgracht 384, Western Canal Ring* ☎ *020/530–2010* ⊕ *www.dylanamsterdam.com* ➥ *40 rooms, 8 suites* ⭕ *No meals.*

$$$
HOTEL
Fodor$Choice
★
☺

⑤ **Mövenpick.** Most of the business-like rooms in this striking glass skyscraper built on an island within the blossoming docks area offer stunning views of the Amsterdam skyline and beyond. **Pros:** upper-floor suites offer the best views in town; the terrace is a great waterfront spot for refreshments; atmosphere is casual and welcoming. **Cons:** lacks Dutch character; a bit off the beaten path. ⑤ *Rooms from: €229* ⊠ *Piet Heinkade 11, Eastern Docklands, Station and Docklands* ☎ *020/519–1200* ⊕ *www.moevenpick-amsterdam.com* ➥ *408 rooms, 31 suites* ⭕ *No meals.*

**TAX-FREE SHOPPING**

Since 2007, the minimum amount spent by non-EU cruise passengers to become eligible for a tax refund dropped from €136 to €50. Participating shops display the Duty-Free Shopping sticker.

# ANTWERP, BELGIUM

Updated by Liz Humphreys

In its heyday, Antwerp (*Antwerpen* in Flemish, *Anvers* in French) played second fiddle only to Paris. It became Europe's most important commercial center in the 16th century, and this wealth funded many architectural and artistic projects. Masters such as Rubens and Van Dyck established the city as one of Europe's leading art centers, and its innovative printing presses produced missals for the farthest reaches of the continent. It also became, and has remained, the diamond capital of the world. Antwerp is today Europe's second-largest port, and has much of the zest often associated with a harbor town. The historic Oude Stad, the heart of the city, distills the essence of Antwerp. The narrow, winding streets, many of them restricted to pedestrian traffic, are wonderful for strolling, the squares are full of charm, and the museums and churches are the pride of the city.

## ESSENTIALS

### CURRENCY
The euro. ATMs are common.

### HOURS
Museums and attractions are usually open from 9:30 to 5; many are closed on Monday. Most shops are open Monday–Saturday 9–6.

### PRIVATE TOURS
You can arrange for a personal English-speaking guide through the *Toerisme Antwerpen* (the city tourist office). However, this requires two days' to three weeks' notice, depending on the season. You can ask your guide to show you any part of the city that interests you, either by neighborhood or by theme (fashion, history, architecture, etc.). The tourism bureau also sells booklets that sketch out walks through the city focusing on fashion and architecture.

Contacts **Toerisme Antwerpen.** ⊕ *www.visitantwerpen.be.*

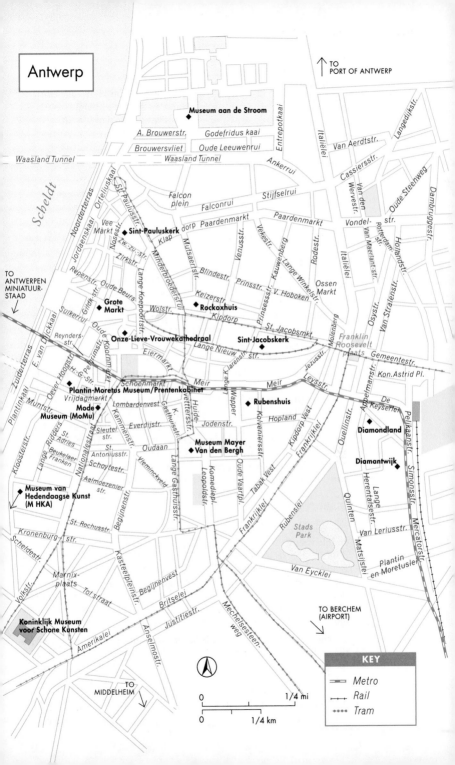

**TELEPHONES**

Tri-band GSM phones work in Belgium. You can buy prepaid phone cards at telecom shops, news vendors, and tobacconists in all towns and cities. Phone cards can be used for local or international calls. Proximus, Mobistar, and BASE are the leading telecom companies.

**COMING ASHORE**

The cruise port couldn't be better placed for passengers, as vessels dock directly at the heart of the city. All the major attractions and museums of the historic center are within walking distance of the dock. The commercial port has no facilities for disembarking passengers, but a wealth of shopping options and restaurants lies just outside the gates. Antwerp's tram and metro public transit system is extensive and reliable. A €1.20 ticket is good for one hour on all forms of public transport, including buses. You'll pay €2 if you buy your ticket on the bus, so prepay at a ticket machine at a bus stop, at the station, at the tourist office, or at news vendors in the city; a day pass buys unlimited travel for one full day. Passes are €5 if you prepay, €6 if you buy on the bus or tram. Car-rental offices are in Antwerp (and are quite expensive at around €100 per day for a compact manual vehicle). Travel by taxi has a per-km charge of around €1.90 on top of an initial pick-up price of €2.95, which makes it expensive for day tours but acceptable for short trips. Rates are higher at night.

> **ANTWERP BEST BETS**
>
> **Museum Aan de Stroom.** Don't miss this comprehensive new museum that strives to showcase Antwerp's history and relations with the world through often-fascinating and highly detailed exhibits.
>
> **Sint-Pauluskerk.** This late-Gothic church features outstanding religious art by a range of Flemish masters including Rubens and Van Dyck.
>
> **Onze-Lieve-Vrouwekathedraal.** A triumph of the Gothic architectural style, decorated by some of Peter Paul Rubens' finest religious works.

## EXPLORING ANTWERP

**Diamondland.** A spectacular showroom, Diamondland was created to enable visitors to get a sense of the activity that goes on behind closed doors in the security-conscious Diamantwijk. All explanations are in English and you can watch several diamond cutters at work. Many of the hundreds of jewelry pieces on display (and for sale) are specially designed by an in-house jeweler. ⊠ *Appelmansstraat 33A, Diamantwijk* ☎ *03/229–2990* ⊕ *www.diamondland.be* ☉ *Mon.–Sat. 9:30–5:30, by appointment only* Ⓜ *Trams 2, 6, 9, or 15.*

**Diamantwijk.** The diamond trade has its own quarter in Antwerp, where the skills of cutting and polishing the gems have been handed down for generations by a tightly knit community. Multimillion-dollar deals are agreed upon with a handshake, and the Antwerp Diamond High Council was established in 1975 to further the industry. Some 85% of the world's uncut diamonds pass through Antwerp. Twenty-five million carats are cut and traded here every year, more than anywhere else in the world. The district occupies a few nondescript city blocks west of Centraal Station. A large part of the community is Jewish, so you'll see shop signs in Hebrew and Hasidic men with traditional dark clothing and side curls. Below the elevated railway tracks, a long row of stalls and shops gleams with jewelry and gems.

Diamond cutting began in Brugge but moved to Antwerp in the late 15th century when a new technique for polishing and cutting gems evolved here. When a flood of rough diamonds from South Africa hit the markets in the 19th century, Antwerp rose to the top of the field. Today the industry employs some 8,000 workers, including expert polishers and cutters, serving 1,800 dealers. Jewish establishments close on Saturday for the Sabbath, but there are still enough shops open in the neighborhood to have a good browse. ⊠ *Bounded by De Keyserlei, Pelikaanstraat, Lange Herentalsestraat, and Lange Kievitstraat, Diamantwijk* Ⓜ *Tram 2 or 15.*

**Grote Markt.** The heart of the Oude Stad, the Grote Markt is dominated by a huge fountain splashing water onto the paving stones. Atop the fountain stands the figure of the legendary Silvius Brabo, who has been poised to fling the hand of the giant Druon Antigon into the river Scheldt since the 19th century. Another famous monster slayer, St. George, is perched on top of a 16th-century guild house at Grote Markt 5, while the dragon appears to be falling off the pediment. ⊠ *Grote Markt, Oude Stad.*

**Stadhuis.** The triangular square is lined on two sides by guild houses and on the third by the Renaissance Stadhuis. Antwerp's town hall was built in the 1560s during the city's Golden Age, when Paris and Antwerp were the only European cities with more than 100,000 inhabitants. In its facade, the fanciful fretwork of the late-Gothic style has given way to the discipline and order of the Renaissance. The public rooms are suitably impressive, though the heavy hand of 19th-century restoration work is much in evidence. You can see the interior with guided tour. Tours take place (in English) on Sundays at 2 pm (tickets are 8 euros and can be purchased from the tourist office). ⊠ *Grote Markt, Oude Stad* ☎ *03/232–0103* Ⓜ *Metro 2, 3, or 5.*

**Mode Museum (MoMu).** To get up to speed on the latest clothing designers, head to MoMu for a fashion crash course. Housed within ModeNatie, an early 19th-century building with a 20th-century makeover, you'll find comprehensive exhibits, some highlighting the avant-garde work of contemporary Flemish designers such as the renowned Antwerp Six. Rotating exhibits also make the most of the museum's collections of clothing, accessories, and textiles dating back to the 18th century; you can ponder the workmanship of delicate antique lace alongside deconstructed blouses from the late 1990s. Also in the museum's complex are the Flanders Fashion Institute, the fashion academy of the Royal Academy of Fine Arts (the designer wellspring), a brasserie, library, reading room, and a boutique. You can pick up a brochure with information in English. ⊠ *Nationalestraat 28, Sint-Andrieskwartier* ☎ *03/470–2770* ⊕ *www.momu.be* 🖅 *€8* 🕙 *Tues.–Sun. 10–6; every first Thurs. of the month 10–9* Ⓜ *Tram 4, 8, or 15.*

**Fodor's Choice**
★
**Museum aan de Stroom** (*MAS*). This ambitious museum in a striking red sandstone and glass building next to Antwerp's old dock area aims to place Antwerp's history into a world context. Five floors of exhibits explore themes such as trade and shipping, men and gods, here and elsewhere, and prestige and symbols, showcasing everything from pre-Columbian artifacts to gas masks from World War II. It's all capped off with a panoramic rooftop view and a Michelin 2-star restaurant, 't Zilte. Note that most of the museum's documentation is not in English; for a translation, use your Smartphone to read the QR codes placed next to many exhibits, or borrow a MAS Smartphone from the information desk. ⊠ *Hanzestedenplaats 1, Oude Stad* ☎ *03/338–4434* ⊕ *www. mas.be* ⊡ *€10* ⊙ *Tues.–Fri. 10–5, Sat.–Sun. 10–6; last tickets sold one hour before closing.*

**Fodor's Choice**
★
**Museum Mayer Van den Bergh.** Pieter Bruegel the Elder's arguably greatest and most enigmatic painting, *Dulle Griet,* is the showpiece here (room 9). Often referred to in English as "Mad Meg," it portrays an irate woman wearing helmet and breastplate—a sword in one hand, and food and cooking utensils in the other—striding across a field strewn with the ravages and insanity of war. There is no consensus on how to read this painting. Some consider it one of the most powerful antiwar statements ever made. Others claim that it denounces the Inquisition. Either way, nothing could be further from the Bruegelian villages than this nightmare world. In 1894, Mayer Van den Bergh bought *Dulle Griet* for 480 Belgian francs. Today it is priceless. The museum also has a set of Bruegel's witty, miniature illustrations of *Twelve Proverbs,* based on popular Flemish sayings.

Mayer Van den Bergh was a passionate art connoisseur who amassed a private collection of almost 4,000 works in the 19th century. The collection includes treasures such as a life-size polychrome statue from about 1300 of St. John resting his head on Christ's chest (room 6). It is, however, the Bruegels that make this small museum a must. There's an English-language pamphlet included with admission that reviews part of the collection. ⊠ *Lange Gasthuisstraat 19, Kruidtuin* ☎ *03/338–8188* ⊕ *www.mayervandenbergh.be* ⊡ *€8 (€10 in combination with Rubenshuis)* ⊙ *Tues.–Sun. 10–5; free last Wed. of the month.* Ⓜ *Tram 7 or 8.*

**Museum van Hedendaagse Kunst (M HKA).** One of Belgium's most important contemporary art venues; here you'll find paintings, installations, video art, and experimental architecture from international artists, including works by the mysterious Flemish theater director/choreographer/artist Jan Fabre, whose sculptures and installations, often based on or involving insects, have established him as a leading figure in the Belgian art world. The museum, which also contains an art house cinema and library, is housed in a renovated grain silo. There's also a roof terrace café. ⊠ *Leuvenstraat 32, Het Zuid* ☎ *03/260–9999* ⊕ *www. muhka.be* ⊡ *€8* ⊙ *Tues.–Wed. and Fri.–Sun. 11–6; Thurs. 11–9* Ⓜ *Bus 6 or 23, or Tram 8.*

**Fodor's Choice**
★
**Onze-Lieve-Vrouwekathedraal.** A miracle of soaring Gothic lightness, the Cathedral of Our Lady contains some of Rubens' greatest paintings and is topped by its 404-foot-high north spire—now restored to its original

gleaming white and serving as a beacon that can be seen from far away. Work began in 1352 and continued in fits and starts until 1521. Despite this, it is a homogeneous monument, thanks to a succession of remarkable architects, including Peter Appelmans, Herman and Domien de Waghemakere, and Rombout Keldermans the Younger. The tower holds a 49-bell carillon played at various times throughout the year.

The cathedral's art treasures were twice vandalized, first by Calvinists in 1566 and again by the French revolutionary army at the end of the 18th century. The French even broke up the floor so that their horses would not slip on it. The masterpieces were either sold at auction or carried off to Paris. Some, but by no means all, have subsequently been returned. Other works, either donated or purchased, make up an outstanding collection of 17th-century religious art, including four Rubens altarpieces, glowing with his marvelous red, allegedly fortified by pigeon's blood. The panels of *De Kruisafneming* (*The Descent from the Cross*) triptych—Mary's visit to Elizabeth (with the painter's wife as Mary) and the presentation of Jesus in the temple—are among the most delicate and tender biblical scenes ever painted. *De Hemelvaart van de Maagd Maria* (*The Assumption of the Virgin Mary*), painted for the high altar, shows the Virgin being carried upward by massed ranks of cherubs toward the angel waiting to crown her Queen of the Angels. *De Hemelvaart* (*The Assumption*) is skillfully displayed so that the rays of the sun illuminate it exactly at noon. ⊠ *Handschoenmarkt, Oude Stad* ☎ *03/213–9951* ⊕ *www.dekathedraal.be* ⊡ *€5* ☉ *Weekdays 10–5, Sat. 10–3, Sun. 1–4* Ⓜ *Tram 2, 3, 4, 5, 8, 9, 10, 11, or 15.*

★ **Plantin-Moretus Museum/Prentenkabinet.** This was the home and printing plant of an extraordinary publishing dynasty. For three centuries, beginning in 1576, the family printed innumerable Bibles, breviaries, and missals; Christophe Plantin's greatest technical achievement was the *Biblia Regia* (in room 16): eight large volumes containing the Bible in Latin, Greek, Hebrew, Syriac, and Aramaic, complete with notes, glossaries, and grammars.

The first three rooms were the family quarters, furnished in 16th-century luxury and containing several portraits by Rubens. Others remain as they were when occupied by accountants, editors, and proofreaders, while many contain Bibles and religious manuscripts dating back to the 9th century, including one owned by King Wenceslas of Bohemia. The workshops are filled with Plantin's 16 printing presses. Two typefaces designed here, Plantin and Garamond, are still in use. The presses are in working order—you can even purchase a copy of Plantin's sonnet, *Le Bonheur de ce monde* ("An Ode to Contentment"), in any of seven European languages, printed on an original press. There's a free information brochure available in English. ⊠ *Vrijdagmarkt 22–23, Sint-Andrieskwartier* ☎ *03/221–1450* ⊕ *www.museumplantinmoretus. be* ⊡ *€8; free last Wed. of the month* ☉ *Tues.–Sun. 10–5; last ticket sold at 4:30* Ⓜ *Tram 3, 9, or 15; bus 22, 25, or 26.*

**Rockoxhuis.** This was the splendid Renaissance home of Rubens' friend and patron Nicolaas Rockox (1560-1640), seven times mayor of Antwerp. A humanist and art collector, Rockox moved here in 1603. The art on display includes two of Rubens' works. One is *Madonna en Kind* (*Madonna and Child*), a delicate portrait of Rubens' first wife, Isabella, and their son, Nicolaas; the other is a sketch for the *Kruisiging* (*Crucifixion*). The collection also includes works by Van Dyck, Frans Snijders, Joachim Patinier, Jordaens, and David Teniers the Younger. The setting makes visiting this collection an exceptional experience. Rather than being displayed on museum walls, the paintings are shown in the context of an upper-class baroque home, furnished in the style of the period. A documentary slide show in English describes Antwerp at that time. ⊠ *Keizerstraat 10–12, Stadswaag* ☎ *03/201–9250* ⊕ *www. rockoxhuis.be* ☒ *€2.50* ☉ *Tues.–Sun. 10–5; free on the last Wednesday of the month* Ⓜ *Tram 2, 3, 10, 11, or 15.*

★ **Rubenshuis.** A fabulous picture of Rubens as painter and patrician is presented here at his own house. Only the elaborate portico and temple, designed by Rubens in Italian baroque style, were still standing three centuries after the house was built. Most of what's here is a reconstruction (completed in 1946) from the master's own design. It represents Rubens at the pinnacle of his fame, a period during which he was appointed court painter to Archduke Albrecht and, with his wife, was sent on a diplomatic mission to Madrid, where he also painted some 40 portraits. He conducted delicate peace negotiations in London on behalf of Philip IV of Spain, and while in London he painted the ceiling of the Whitehall Banqueting Hall and was knighted by Charles I of Great Britain. The most evocative room in Rubens House is the huge studio, where drawings by Rubens and his pupils, as well as old prints, help to re-create the original atmosphere. In Rubens' day, visitors could view completed paintings and watch from the mezzanine while Rubens and his students worked. Rubens completed about 2,500 paintings, nearly all characterized by the energy and exuberance that were his hallmark. A few Rubens works hang in the house, including a touching sketch in the studio of the Annunciation and a self-portrait in the dining room. Unfortunately, his young widow promptly sold off some 300 pieces after his death in 1640. ⊠ *Wapper 9, Meir* ☎ *03/201–1555* ⊕ *www. rubenshuis.be* ☒ *€8 (€10 in combination with Museum Mayer Van den Bergh); free last Wed. of the month* ☉ *Tues.–Sun. 10–5; last ticket at 4:30* Ⓜ *Tram 2, 3, 5, or 15; bus 22, 25, or 26.*

**Sint-Jacobskerk.** Peter Paul Rubens is buried in the white sandstone St. Jacob's Church. A painting depicting him as St. George posed between his two wives, Isabella Brant and Helena Fourment, hangs above his tomb. The three-aisle church blends late-Gothic and baroque styles; the tombs are a who's who of prominent 17th-century Antwerp families. A notable visitor (W. A. Mozart) allegedly played the organ here during his 1727 stay in the city. ⊠ *Lange Nieuwstraat 73–75, Meir* ☎ *03/225–0414* ⊕ *www.mkaweb.be* ☒ *€2* ☉ *Apr.–Oct., Mon.–Fri. 2–5* Ⓜ *Tram 10 or 11.*

**Sint-Pauluskerk.** The late-Gothic St. Paul's Church, built 1530–71, is a repository of more than 50 outstanding paintings, including a series known as the 15 mysteries of the Rosary by Antwerp's finest painters of the time. There are three by Rubens, including a visceral depiction of Jesus's flagellation, as well as early works by Jordaens and Van

Dyck. The church is further enriched by more than 200 17th- and 18th-century sculptures, including the ten baroque confessionals attributed to Peeter Verbruggen the Elder. A baroque altar completed in 1639 towers over the more somber Gothic nave. Sint-Pauluskerk was restored in 1968 after damage from a major fire. ⊠ *Veemarkt 14, Oude Stad* ☎ *03/231–3321* ⊕ *www.mkaweb.be* ⊠ *Free* ☉ *Apr. 1–Oct. 14, daily 2–5* Ⓜ *Tram 4 or 7; Bus 6 or 34.*

## SHOPPING

Antwerp has a reputation for edgy chic, due in large part to its clothing designers; followers of fashion consider the city in a league with Milan and Paris. Credit for this development goes to the so-called Antwerp Six (students of Linda Loppa from the class of 1981 at Antwerp's Fashion Academy) and in equal measure to the new wave of talent that has more recently stormed the catwalks. Ready-to-wear by stalwarts Ann Demeulemeester, Dirk Bikkembergs, Dries Van Noten, Martin Margiela, and relative newcomers Raf Simons, Véronique Branquinho, and Wim Neels command high prices. However, in the shopping area south of Groenplaats, prices are less astronomical. And, of course, the Diamantwijk is prime territory for glittering precious stones.

The elegant **Meir**, together with its extension to the east, **De Keyserlei**, and at the opposite end, **Huidevettersstraat**, is where you will find high-street standbys and long-established names. Shopping galleries branch off all three streets. The area in and around the glamorous **Horta Complex**, on Hopland, is also a popular shopping hub. For avant-garde tastes, the best-known area is **De Wilde Zee**, which straddles the Meir and Oude Stad. The nearby Schuttershofstraat, Kammenstraat, and Nationalestraat are also fizzing with new spots. Another pedestrian area for general shopping is **Hoogstraat**.

**Ann Demeulemeester.** Ann Demeulemeester sells her clothes in an elegant corner store not far from the M HKA (Museum van Hedendaagse Kunst). ⊠ *Leopold de Waelplaats, Het Zuid* ☎ *03/216–0133* ⊕ *www. anndemeulemeester.be.*

**Diamondland.** The largest diamond showroom is Diamondland, where tours of polishers, goldsmiths, and setters at work can be arranged before you settle down to business. Loose diamonds can be set while you wait. The store is open by appointment only, Mon.–Sat., 9:30–5:30. ⊠ *Appelmansstraat 33a, Diamantwijk* ☎ *03/229–2990* ⊕ *www. diamondland.be.*

**Het Modepaleis.** Dries Van Noten collections for men and women can be found in the splendid Modepaleis, a five-story Belle Époque building that he bought in 1989. ⊠ *Nationalestraat 16, Sint-Andrieskwartier* ☎ *03/470–2510* ⊕ *www.driesvannoten.be.*

## WHERE TO EAT

**$$$**
BELGIAN ✕ **Zuiderterras.** A stark, glass-and-black-metal construction, this riverside café and restaurant was designed by avant-garde architect bOb (his spelling) Van Reeth; it resembles a docked cruise ship. You're

virtually assured a good view, since large windows stretch on all sides. You'll have the river traffic on one side and, on the other, a view of the cathedral and the Oude Stad. The food is as modern as the surroundings, with dishes such as ravioli with fennel, parmesan, and pistachio crumble. $ *Average main: €25* ✉ *Ernest Van Dijckkaai 37, Oude Stad* ☎ *03/234–1275* ⊕ *www.zuiderterras.be.*

**$$**    ✕ **'t Hofke.** It's worth visiting here for the location alone, in the Vlaeykens-
**BELGIAN**    gang alley, where time seems to have stood still. The cozy dining room has the look and feel of a private home. The lunch menu includes a large selection of salads and omelets, as well as more substantial fare in the evening. Try for a table in the courtyard. $ *Average main: €17* ✉ *Vlaeykensgang, Oude Koornmarkt 16, Oude Stad* ☎ *03/233–8606* ⊕ *www.thofke.com* Ⓜ *Tram 2, 3, 4, 5, 8, or 15.*

# COBH, IRELAND (FOR CORK)

The major metropolis of the South, Cork is Ireland's second-largest city—but it runs a distant second, with a population of 119,400, roughly a tenth the size of Dublin. Cork is a spirited place, with a formidable pub culture, a lively traditional music scene, a respected and progressive university, attractive art galleries, and offbeat cafés. The city received a major boost in 2005 when it was named a Capital of Culture by the EU—the smallest city ever to receive the designation. The result was a burst in development; one of the lasting legacies is a striking but controversial redesign of the city center (Patrick Street and Grand Parade) by Barcelona-based architect Beth Gali. Outside the city, the rolling countryside gives way to rugged coastline hosting tiny villages, each with their own piece of history. Many set sail for the New World from here; some were destined not to arrive.

## ESSENTIALS

### CURRENCY
The euro. ATMs are common.

### HOURS
Shops and businesses are generally open Monday through Saturday from 9:30 to 5:30 or 6; some open later and some open on Sunday. Most museums are open Monday–Saturday 9–5 and may have shorter hours on Sunday.

### PRIVATE TOURS
Adams & Butler conducts special-interest tours; topics include gardens, architecture, ghosts, and golf.

**Contacts Adams & Butler** ✉ *58 Foster Ave., the Carriage House, Mount Merrion, Co. Dublin* ☎ *01/288-9355* ⊕ *www.adamsandbutler.com.*

### TELEPHONES
Most tri- and quad-band GSM phones will work in Ireland, and the country's mobile system is 3G compatible with excellent coverage. Public phones accept prepaid call cards (available in shops and telecom offices) and credit cards. Eircom, BT Ireland, and Vodafone are the major telecom suppliers.

# Cork City

MONTENOTTE

TO TIROLI

Lwr. Glanmire Rd.

Penrose's Quay

Alfred St.

Summer Hill

Wellington Rd.

Brian Boru Bridge

Anderson's Quay

Custom House Quay

Victoria Quay

Victoria Rd.

Albert Rd.

Merchant's Quay

Bus Station

Albert St.

SOUTH DOCKLANDS

Parnell Pl.

Lapp's Quay

Lee

Anglesea St.

Richmond Hill

St. Patrick's Hill

Mac Curtain St.

St. Patrick's Quay

Merchant St.

Oliver Plunkett St.

Albert Quay

Union Quay

CITY CENTRE SOUTH

Leitrim St.

Coburg St.

Camden Pl.

Patrick's Bridge

Street

Maylor St.

Morgan St.

Mall

Fr. Mathew Quay

George's Quay

Mary St.

John St.

Pine St.

Lavitt's Quay

Winthrop St.

Robert St.

Cook St.

CITY CENTRE NORTH

Upper St.

Emmet Pl.

Crawford Art Gallery

Academy St.

Paul Street

Marlborough St.

English Market

Princes St.

Cove St.

Sullivan's Quay

St. Anne's Church

John Redmond

Church St.

Christy Ring Br.

Pope's Quay

Kyrl's Quay

River Lee

Corn Market St.

Grand Parade

Bishop Lucey Park

Tuckey St.

South

Tourist Information Office

SHANDON

Dominick St.

Shandon St.

Castle St.

Kyle St.

S. Main St.

South Gate Br.

Proby's Quay

Fort St.

St. Shandon Br.

N. Main St.

Liberty St.

WASHINGTON VILLAGE

Hanover St.

Wandesford Quay

Bishop St.

Old Market Pl.

Adelaide St.

Grattan St.

Peter's St.

Washington St.

S. Crawford St.

St. Fin Barre's Cathedral

Dean St.

Blarney St.

Bachelor's Quay

North Mall

Henry St.

Sheares St.

Court House

WESTERN ROAD

Gill Abbey St.

Boyce's St.

Grenville St.

Dyke Pde.

Lancaster Quay

South Channel

College Rd.

1/8 mi

1/8 km

0

0

SUNDAY'S WELL

Sunday's Well Rd.

Cork City Gaol

River Lee (North Channel)

The Mardyke

Western Rd.

River Lee (S. Channel)

Connaught Ave.

Donovan's Rd.

Fitzgerald's Park

Fitzgerald's Park

University College Cork

N

**Inset map:**

N22

WATERFORD

N25

Youghal Bay

Youghal

CORK

Fota

Midleton

Great Island

St. Georges Channel

Cork City see detail map

Cobh

Power Head

Cork Harbour

Kinsale

Blarney

N22

R. Lee

N20

10 mi

15 km

0

0

## COMING ASHORE

Large ships dock at Cobh's dedicated cruise terminal adjacent to the Cobh Heritage Centre. There are basic facilities for passengers, including restrooms, taxis, and tourist information, but no cafés, restaurants, or shops.

There is a rail link between Cobh and Cork. It runs once or twice an hour throughout the day, so it would be possible to explore Cork and Cobh in the same day by public transport. Smaller vessels dock at the City Quays in the heart of Cork City; from here you can tour the town on foot.

Renting a car would be an advantage for touring the Kerry countryside around the town and the associated attractions. The cost for a compact manual vehicle is approx €50. Taxis can be engaged to run tour itineraries, although charges are complicated, and the costs are fairly expensive, best shared among four people. Drivers can choose to charge by the minute rather than per kilometer.

---

### CORK BEST BETS

**Strolling along Patrick Street.** The historic storefronts along this famous thoroughfare have graced a thousand tourist brochures—it's an atmospheric place to browse for a souvenir or two.

**Kissing the Blarney Stone.** The "magic" stone at Blarney Castle is said to give you the gift of gab to get what you want.

**Visiting the Queenstown Story at Cobh Heritage Centre.** This site tells the story of the millions of emigrants who set sail to the United States, and of the tragic last voyage of the *Lusitania.*

---

# EXPLORING COUNTY CORK

## COBH

*24 km (15 miles) southeast of Cork City.*

Many of the people who left Ireland on immigrant ships for the New World departed from Cobh, a pretty fishing port and seaside resort 24 km (15 miles) southeast of Cork City on R624.

Fodor's Choice    **Cobh Heritage Centre.** Many of the people who left Ireland on immigrant
★    ships for the New World departed from Cobh, which was formerly known as Queenstown. The center's Queenstown Story exhibit, in the old Cobh railway station, re-creates the experience of the 2.5 million emigrants who left from here between 1848 and 1950. It also tells the stories of great transatlantic liners, including the *Titanic,* whose last port of call was Cobh, and the *Lusitania,* which was sunk by a German submarine off this coast on May 7, 1915. Many of the *Lusitania*'s 1,198 victims are buried in Cobh, which has a memorial to them on the local quay. ⊠ *Old Railway Building, Lower Rd.* ☎ *021/481–3591* ⊕ *www.cobhheritage.com* ☜ €7.50 ۞ *Nov.–Mar., Mon.–Sat. 9:30–5, Sun. 11–5; Apr.–Sept., daily 9:30–6.*

**St. Colman's Cathedral.** The best view of Cobh, well worth the uphill stroll, is from St. Colman's Cathedral, an exuberant neo-Gothic granite church designed by the eminent British architect E. W. Pugin in 1869, and completed in 1919. Inside, granite niches portray scenes of the

Roman Catholic Church's history in Ireland, beginning with the arrival of St. Patrick. ☎ *021/481–3222* ⊕ *www.cobhcathedralparish.ie.*

## CORK CITY

**Bishop Lucey Park.** This tiny green park in the heart of the city opened in 1985 in celebration of the 800th anniversary of Cork's Norman charter. During its excavation, workers unearthed portions of the city's original fortified walls, now preserved just inside the arched entrance. Sculptures by contemporary Cork artists are found throughout the park. ⊠ *Grand Parade, Washington Village.*

☺ **Cork City Gaol.** This castle-like building contains an austere, 19th-century prison. Life-size wax figures occupy the cells, and sound effects illustrate the appalling conditions that prevailed into the 20th century. Also here, in the Governor's House, the **Radio Museum Experience** exhibits genuine artifacts from the 1923 radio station, 6CK, and tells the story of radio broadcasting in Cork. ⊠ *Sunday's Well Rd., Sunday's Well* ☎ *021/430–5022* ⊕ *www.corkcitygaol.com* ☜€8 ☉ *Nov.–Feb., daily 10–4; Mar.–Oct., daily 9:30–5.*

**Court House.** A landmark in the very center of Cork, this magnificent classical building has an imposing Corinthian portico and is still used as the district's main courthouse. The exterior has been cleaned and fully restored and looks every bit as good as it did when it was built in 1835. ⊠ *Washington St., Washington Village* ☎ *021/427–2706* ☉ *Weekdays 9–5.*

★ **Crawford Art Gallery.** The large redbrick building was built in 1724 as the customs house and is now home to Ireland's leading provincial art gallery. An imaginative expansion has added gallery space for visiting exhibitions and adventurous shows of modern Irish artists. The permanent collection includes landscape paintings depicting Cork in the 18th and 19th centuries. Take special note of works by Irish painters William Leech (1881–1968), Daniel Maclise (1806–70), James Barry (1741–1806), and Nathaniel Grogan (1740–1807). The café, run by the Allen family of Ballymaloe, is a good place for a light lunch or a homemade sweet. ⊠ *Emmet Pl., City Center South* ☎ *021/490–7855* ⊕ *www. crawfordartgallery.ie* ☜ *Free* ☉ *Mon.–Sat. 10–5; Thurs. 10–8 pm.*

★ **English Market.** Food lovers (and, who, pray, isn't?): be sure to make a beeline for one of the misleadingly small entrances to this large and famous mecca for foodies. Fetchingly housed in an elaborate, brick-and-cast-iron Victorian building, it bears the official name of the Princes Street Market, but it's also known locally as the Covered Market along with its general nickname. Among the 140 stalls, keep an eye out for the Alternative Bread Co., which produces more than 40 varieties of handmade bread every day. Iago, Sean Calder-Potts's deli, has fresh pasta, lots of cheeses, and charcuterie. The Olive Stall sells olive oil, olive-oil soap, and olives from Greece, Spain, France, and Italy. Kay O'Connell's Fish Stall, in the legendary fresh-fish alley, purveys local smoked salmon. O'Reilly's Tripe and Drisheen is the last existing retailer of a Cork specialty, tripe (cow's stomach), and *drisheen* (blood sausage). Upstairs is the Farmgate, an excellent café. ⊠ *Entrances on Grand Parade and Princes St., City Center South* ⊕ *www.corkenglishmarket.ie* ☉ *Mon.–Sat. 9:30–5:30.*

**Fitzgerald's Park.** This small, well-tended park is beside the River Lee's north channel in the west of the city. The park contains the **Cork Public Museum**, a Georgian mansion that houses a well-planned exhibit about Cork's history since ancient times, with a strong emphasis on the city's Republican history. ⊠ *Western Rd., Western Road* ☎ *021/427–0679* ⊕ *www.corkcity.ie/services/recreationamenityculture/museum* ⊠ *Free* ⊙ *Mon.–Sat. 11–1 and 2:15–5, Sun. 3–5; closed Sun. Oct.–Mar.*

**Patrick's Bridge.** From here you can look along the curve of Patrick Street and north across the River Lee to St. Patrick's Hill, with its tall Georgian houses. The hill is so steep that steps are cut into the pavement. Tall ships that served the butter trade used to load up beside the bridge at Merchant's Quay before heading downstream to the sea. The design of the large, redbrick shopping center on the site evokes the warehouses of old. ⊠ *Patrick St., City Center South.*

**Paul Street.** A narrow stretch between the River Lee and Patrick Street and parallel to both, Paul Street is the backbone of the trendy shopping district that now occupies Cork's old French Quarter. The area was first settled by Huguenots fleeing religious persecution in France. Musicians and other street performers often entertain passersby in the Rory Gallagher Piazza, named for the late rock guitarist, whose family was from Cork. The shops here offer the best in modern Irish design—from local fashions to hand-blown glass. ⊠ *City Center South.*

**St. Anne's Church.** The church's pepper-pot Shandon steeple, which has a four-sided clock and is topped with a golden, salmon-shaped weather vane, is visible from throughout the city and is the chief reason why St. Anne's is so frequently visited. The Bells of Shandon were immortalized in an atrocious but popular 19th-century ballad of that name. Your reward for climbing the 120-foot-tall tower is the chance to ring the bells, with the assistance of sheet tune cards, out over Cork. Beside the church, **Firkin Crane,** Cork's 18th-century butter market, houses two small performing spaces. Adjacent is the **Shandon Craft Market.** ⊠ *Church St., Shandon* ☎ *021/450–5906* ⊠ *€6* ⊙ *Easter–Oct., Mon.– Sat. 10–4; Nov.–Easter, Mon.–Sat. 11–3.*

**St. Fin Barre's Cathedral.** On the site that was the entrance to medieval Cork, this compact, three-spire Gothic cathedral, which was completed in 1879, belongs to the Church of Ireland and houses a 3,000-pipe organ. According to tradition, St. Fin Barre established a monastery on this site around AD 650 and is credited as being the founder of Cork. ⊠ *Bishop St., Washington Village* ☎ *021/496–3387* ⊕ *cathedral.cork. anglican.org* ⊙ *Weekdays 9:30–5, Sat. 10–5.*

★ **University College Cork.** The Doric, porticoed gates of UCC stand about 2 km (1 mile) from the city center. The college, which has a student body of roughly 10,000, is a constituent of the National University of Ireland. The main quadrangle is a fine example of 19th-century university architecture in the Tudor-Gothic style, reminiscent of many Oxford and Cambridge colleges. Several ancient ogham stones are on display in the North Quadrangle (near the visitor center), and the renovated Crawford Observatory's 1860 telescope can be visited. The Honan Collegiate Chapel, east of the quadrangle, was built in 1916 and modeled on the 12th-century, Hiberno-Romanesque style, best exemplified by the remains of Cormac's Chapel at Cashel. The UCC chapel's stained-glass windows, as well as its collection of art and crafts, altar furnishings, and textiles in the Celtic Revival style, are noteworthy. Three large, modern buildings have been successfully integrated with the old, including the Boole Library, named for mathematician George Boole (1815–64), who was a professor at the college. Both indoors and out the campus is enhanced by works of contemporary Irish art. The **Lewis Glucksman Gallery,** in a striking new building astride the college's entrance gates, displays works from the college's outstanding collection and hosts cutting-edge contemporary-art exhibitions. ✉ *College Rd., Western Road* ☎ *021/490–1876* ⊕ *www.ucc.ie* ✍ *Free* ☉ *Visitor center weekdays 9–5; call for hrs Easter wk, July, Aug., and mid-Dec.–mid-Jan.; guided tours by arrangement.*

## BLARNEY
*10 km (6 miles) northwest of Cork City.*

★ **Blarney Castle.** In the center of Blarney is Blarney Castle, or what remains of it: the ruined central keep is all that's left of this mid-15th-century stronghold. The castle contains the famed **Blarney Stone**; kissing the stone, it's said, endows the kisser with the fabled "gift of gab." It's 127 steep steps to the battlements. To kiss the stone, you must lie down on the battlements, hold on to a guardrail, and lean your head way back. It's good fun and not at all dangerous. Expect a line from mid-June to early September; while you wait, you can admire the views of the wooded River Lee valley and chuckle over how the word "blarney" came to mean what it does. As the story goes, Queen Elizabeth I wanted Cormac MacCarthy, Lord of Blarney, to will his castle to the Crown, but he refused her requests with eloquent excuses and soothing compliments. Exhausted by his comments, the queen reportedly exclaimed, "This is all Blarney. What he says he rarely means."

You can take pleasant walks around the castle grounds; Rock Close contains oddly shaped limestone rocks landscaped in the 18th century, and a grove of ancient yew trees that is said to have been a site of Druid worship. In early March there's a wonderful display of naturalized daffodils. ☎ *021/438–5252* ⊕ *www.blarneycastle.ie* ✍ *€10* ☉ *May and Sept., Mon.–Sat. 9–6:30, Sun. 9–5:30; June–Aug., Mon.–Sat. 9–7, Sun. 9–5:30; Oct.–Apr., Mon.–Sat. 9–sunset Sun. 9–5 or sunset.*

## KINSALE
*29 km (18 miles) southwest of Cork City on R600.*

Foodies flock to Kinsale, a picturesque port that pioneered the Irish small-town tradition of fine dining in unbelievably small restaurants. In the town center, at the tip of the wide, fjord-like harbor that opens out from the River Bandon, upscale shops and eateries with brightly painted facades line small streets. Kinsale is also a center for sailing.

★ **Charles Fort.** The British built Charles Fort on the east side of the Bandon River estuary in the late 17th century, after their defeat of the Spanish and Irish forces. One of Europe's best-preserved "star forts" encloses some 12 cliff-top acres and is similar to Fort Ticonderoga in New York State. If the sun is shining, take the footpath signposted Scilly Walk; it winds along the harbor's edge under tall trees and then through the village of Summer Cove. ⊠ *3 km (2 miles) east of town* ☎ *021/477–2263* ⊕ *www.heritageireland.ie* ⊠ *€4* ☼ *Mid-Mar.–Oct., daily 10–6; Nov.–mid-Mar., daily 10–5.*

**Desmond Castle and the International Museum of Wine.** This museum occupies a 15th-century fortified town house—originally a custom house—that has a dark history. It was used as a prison for French and American seamen in the 1700s, and was subsequently a jail and then a workhouse. Now it contains displays that tell the story of the wine trade and its importance to the Irish diaspora in France, America, Australia, and New Zealand. ⊠ *Cork St.* ☎ *021/477–4855* ⊕ *www.winegeese.ie* ⊠ *€3* ☼ *Mid-Apr.–mid-Oct., daily 10–6.*

## SHOPPING

Ireland is *the* place to buy linen and wool products, but the Waterford crystal factory is no longer operating (the name lives on, but no crystal is currently produced in Ireland). The area is still good for ceramics and antiques. Celtic motifs are found on everything from jewelry to coffee cups. In Cork, Paul Street is the backbone of the trendy shopping scene, while Patrick Street has high-end names mixed with antique and souvenir shops. Blarney and Kinsale both have a range of shops selling arts and crafts from around the country.

**Blarney Woollen Mills.** With the largest stock and the highest turnover of Blarney's crafts shops, this noted emporium sells everything from Irish-made high fashion to Aran hand-knit items to leprechaun key rings. ☎ *021/451–6111* ⊕ *www.blarney.com.*

**Quills.** A good selection of Irish-made apparel for women and men is always available at Quills. ⊠ *107 Patrick St., City Center South, Cork City* ☎ *021/427–1717.*

## WHERE TO EAT

**$**
IRISH
✕ **Farmgate Café.** One of the best—and busiest—informal lunch spots in town is on a terraced gallery above the fountain at the Princes Street entrance to the atmospheric English Market. All ingredients used at the café are purchased in the market below. One side of the gallery opens onto the market and is self-service; the other side is glassed in and has table service (reservations advised). Tripe and *drisheen* (blood sausage) is one dish that is always on the menu; daily specials include less challenging but no less traditional dishes, such as corned beef with *colcannon* (potatoes and cabbage mashed with butter and seasonings) and loin of smoked bacon with *champ* (potatoes mashed with scallions or leeks). ⑤ *Average main: €14* ⊠ *English Market, City Center South, Cork City* ☎ *021/427–8134* ⊕ *www.corkenglishmarket.ie* ☼ *Closed Sun. No dinner.*

**$$$**
EUROPEAN
★
✕ **Jim Edwards.** One of Ireland's original bar-restaurants, this is a famous Kinsale institution known for its generous portions of local steak, lamb, and duck, and fresh seafood, all prepared under the careful eye of the owner and his wife, Paula. Choose from the inexpensive daily specials in the busy bar ($), or have a more leisurely meal among the

mahogany tables and dark-red decor of the somewhat baronial restaurant. With seafood this fresh, the preparation is kept simple: Kinsale oysters au naturel or crab claws tossed in garlic butter to start, followed by 10 ounces of prime fillet steak or medallions of monkfish (caught this morning) in a spring onion, ginger, and lime sauce. Fresh lobster from the tank is always available. The classic homemade desserts (profiteroles, crème brûlée) are substantial, and the Irish coffee is renowned. ⑤ *Average main: €26* ⊠ *Market Quay* ☎ *021/477–2541* ⊕ *www.jimedwardskinsale.com.*

# DOVER, UNITED KINGDOM

Updated by
Ellin Stein

Although the southeast of England is the most densely populated part of Britain, once you escape London's sprawling suburbs, you will find hundreds of small farms set in a gentle landscape. Kent, the most southeasterly county, is known as the garden of England, famous for its apples, hops (used for brewing beer), and, increasingly, excellent vineyards. The Kent landscape is dotted with oast houses, small round towers with tilted pointed roofs originally used for drying hops, although most have now been converted into desirable homes. The area is rich in history, notably the cathedral in Canterbury, the center of the Anglican Church and the site of the murder of St. Thomas á Becket. On the coast you'll find both seaside resorts and Britain's busiest port, Dover, historically the gateway to continental Europe.

## ESSENTIALS

### CURRENCY
The British pound sterling. ATMs are common and credit cards are widely accepted.

### HOURS
Museums are open daily during normal business hours and some evenings, while shops usually open from 9 until 5:30 or 6. Many are open on Sunday.

### TELEPHONES
Dual-band GSM phones work in the United Kingdom. You can buy prepaid phone cards at telecom shops and news vendors in all towns and cities. Phone cards can be used for local or international calls. Vodafone, T-Mobile, Virgin, and Orange are the leading telecom companies.

## COMING ASHORE
Ships dock at the Western Docks in Dover. There are two passenger terminals. Terminal 1 is in a converted Victorian railway station, while Terminal 2 is a purpose-built passenger facility opened in 2000. The terminals have currency-exchange facilities, car-rental kiosks, and cafés, plus a taxi stand.

There are direct trains to London Victoria and London Charing Cross (about two hours) from Dover Priory Station (take a taxi to the station). Ticket prices start at £21 round-trip but vary depending on the time of the train. There is also a faster but less frequent service to London St. Pancras. The train journey to Canterbury is around 30 minutes, with several trains per hour. Tickets are around £8 per single journey.

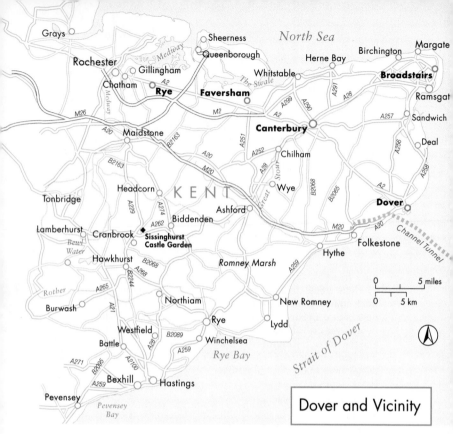

**Dover and Vicinity**

London Victoria Coach Station (⇨ *see Harwich, below*) can also be reached in 2½ hours by bus. There are also bus departures from the Eastern Docks (a taxi ride or a 15-minute walk along the seafront) and, occasionally, directly from the cruise terminal.

A car rental is recommended for exploring the Kent countryside but not for a visit to London, where traffic, congestion charges, and parking difficulties abound. Rental rates begin at £32 per day for an economy manual vehicle. But given the distance, this is a good opportunity to see the beauty of Kent rather than trek all the way into central London.

### GETTING TO THE AIRPORT

If you choose not to purchase aiport transfers from your cruise line, the easiest way to get to the airport from the cruise port to Heathrow airport is to contract a private taxi or transfer company. Several companies offer the services with prices of a one-way transfer of around €185 for vehicles carrying a maximum of three people. For other transport options, including bus and train, it's necessary to connect through central London, which may be tiring depending how much luggage you are carrying and may not be a money-saving option depending on how many travelers are in your party.

**Contacts Prompt Airport Cars.** ☎ 020/3384–4659 ⊕ www.promptexecutivehire. co.uk. **Road Express.** ☎ 0844/822–2616 ⊕ www.road-express.co.uk.

# EXPLORING DOVER AND VICINITY

## DOVER

*122 km (76 miles) southeast of London.*

The busy passenger port of Dover has for centuries been Britain's gateway to Europe. Its chalk **White Cliffs** are a famous and inspirational sight, though you may find the town itself a bit disappointing; the savage bombardments of World War II and the shortsightedness of postwar developers left the city center an unattractive place. However, there are still some historic legacies, notably the castle, as well the ruins of a Roman lighthouse and a late Saxon church on its grounds, and a well-preserved Roman residence.

★ **Dover Castle.** Spectacular and with plenty to explore, Dover Castle, towering high above the ramparts of the white cliffs, is a mighty medieval castle that has served as an important strategic center over the centuries, even in World War II. Most of the castle, including the keep, dates to Norman times. It was begun by Henry II in 1181 but incorporates additions from almost every succeeding century. There's a lot to see besides the castle rooms, and many of the exhibits will appeal to kids, including the Siege of 1216, the Princess of Wales Regimental Museum, and Castle Fit for a King. ■**TIP→ Tour the secret wartime tunnels, a medieval and Napoleonic-era system that was used again during World War II.** ☒ *Castle Rd.* ☎ *01304/211067* ⊕ *www.english-heritage.org.uk* 🎟 *£16.50* ☉ *Apr.–July and Sept., daily 10–6; Aug., daily 9:30–6; Oct.–early Nov., daily 10–5; mid-Nov.–Mar., weekends 10–4.*

**Roman Painted House.** Believed to have been a hotel, this structure includes some Roman wall paintings, along with the remnants of an ingenious heating system. ☒ *New St.* ☎ *01304/203279* ⊕ *www.theromanpaintedhouse.co.uk* 🎟 *£3* ☉ *Early–mid-Apr., daily 10–5; late Apr.–May, Tues. and Sat. 10–5; Jun.–mid-Sept, Tues.–Sun. 10–5; last admission 30 min before closing.*

## CANTERBURY

*28 km (17 miles) northwest of Dover.*

A bustling medieval cathedral town, charming Canterbury has good shopping, plenty of history, and just enough to see in a day. Thousands flocked to the city's magnificent cathedral, the Church of England's equivalent to the Vatican, in the 12th century, a pilgrimage immortalized in Geoffrey Chaucer's *Canterbury Tales*, and it remains well worth a visit. They flocked here to see the shrine of the murdered archbishop St. Thomas á Becket, and buildings that served as pilgrims' inns (and survived the World War II bombing of the city) still dominate the city center. Going back even further, there's evidence of a prosperous society in the Canterbury area as early as the Bronze Age (around 1000 BC), and it was an important Roman city, as well as a center of Anglo-Saxon culture in the Kingdom of Kent.

Fodor'sChoice **Canterbury Cathedral.** The focal point of the city was the first of
★ England's great Norman cathedrals. Nucleus of worldwide Anglicanism, the Cathedral Church of Christ Canterbury (its formal name) is a living textbook of medieval architecture. The building was begun

in 1070, demolished, begun anew in 1096, and then systematically expanded over the next three centuries. When the original choir section burned to the ground in 1174, another replaced it, designed in the new Gothic style, with tall, pointed arches. The cathedral is popular, so arrive early or late in the day to avoid the crowds. You can just walk around, or you can buy a guidebook with an overview of the building's history, use an audio guide for the most detail, or take a tour.

The cathedral was only a century old, and still relatively small, when Thomas à Becket, the archbishop of Canterbury, was murdered here in 1170. Becket, a defender of ecclesiastical interests, had angered his friend Henry II, who was supposedly heard to exclaim, "Will no one rid me of this troublesome priest?" Thinking they were carrying out the king's wishes, four knights burst in on Becket in one of the side chapels and killed him. Two years later Becket was canonized, and Henry II's subsequent penitence and submission to the authority of the Church helped establish the cathedral as the center of English Christianity.

Becket's tomb, destroyed by Henry VIII in 1538 as part of his campaign to reduce the power of the Church and confiscate its treasures, was one of the most extravagant shrines in Christendom. In **Trinity Chapel,** which held the shrine, you can still see a series of 13th-century stained-glass windows illustrating Becket's miracles. So hallowed was this spot that in 1376, Edward, the Black Prince, warrior son of Edward III and a national hero, was buried near it. The actual site of Becket's murder is down a flight of steps just to the left of the nave. In the corner, a second flight of steps leads down to the enormous Norman **undercroft,** or vaulted cellarage, built in the early 12th century. A row of squat pillars whose capitals dance with animals and monsters supports the roof.

If time permits, explore the **cloisters** and the small monastic buildings to the north of the cathedral. The 12th-century octagonal water tower is still part of the cathedral's water supply. The Norman staircase in the northwest corner of the Green Court dates from 1167 and is a unique example of the architecture of the times. ⊠ *Cathedral Precincts* ☎ *01227/762862* ⊕ *www.canterbury-cathedral.org* 🖃 *£9, free for services and ½ hr before closing; £5 for tour; £3.50 for audio guide* ☉ *Easter–Sept., Mon.–Sat. 9–5:30, Sun. 12:30–2:30; Oct.–Easter, Mon.–Sat. 9–5, Sun. 12:30–2:30. Last entry ½ hr before closing. Restricted access during services.*

---

### DOVER BEST BETS

**Canterbury Cathedral.** One of Britain's greatest churches, this was an important place of pilgrimage and the scene of one of the country's darkest crimes.

**The White Cliffs of Dover.** Best seen from the water, these iconic cliffs are part of the national psyche and, on a sunny day, an exceptionally breathtaking vista.

**Rye.** Though there are no attractions as such here, the sheer quaintness and "Englishness" of Rye makes it a great place to relax, soak in the atmosphere, and shop for souvenirs.

**Canterbury Roman Museum.** Belowground, at the level of the remnants of Roman Canterbury, this museum features colorful mosaic Roman pavement and a hypocaust—the Roman version of central heating. Displays of excavated objects (some of which you can hold in the Touch the Past area) and computer-generated reconstructions of Roman buildings and the marketplace help re-create the past. ■**TIP➜ Up to four kids get in free with an adult.** ⊠ *Butchery La.* ☎ *01227/785575* ⊕ *www.canterbury. co.uk* ⌲ *£6; combined ticket with Canterbury Heritage Museum £10* ⊙ *Daily 10–5; last admission at 4. Closed last wk in Dec.*

**The Canterbury Tales.** It's a kitschy audiovisual (and occasionally olfactory) dramatization of 14th-century English life—touristy but popular. You'll "meet" Chaucer's pilgrims and view tableaus illustrating five tales. In summer, actors in period costume play out scenes from the town's history. ⊠ *St. Margaret's St.* ☎ *01227/479227* ⊕ *www. canterburytales.org.uk* ⌲ *£8.25* ⊙ *Nov.–Feb., daily 10–4:30; Mar.–June, Sept., and Oct., daily 10–5; July and Aug., daily 9:30–5.*

**Medieval city walls.** For an essential Canterbury experience, follow the circuit of the 13th- and 14th-century walls, built on the line of the Roman walls. Those to the east survive intact, towering some 20 feet high and offering a sweeping view of the town. You can access these from a number of places, including Castle Street and Broad Street.

## FAVERSHAM
*45 km (28 miles) northwest of Dover.*

In Roman times, Faversham was a thriving seaport. Today the port is hidden from sight, and you could pass through this market town without knowing it was there. Still, Faversham is a worthwhile stop for those in search of Ye Quaint Olde Englande: The town center, with its Tudor houses grouped around the 1574 Guildhall and covered market, looks like a perfect stage set. There are no actual sights here, as such, but it's a lovely place to take a break and have a stroll.

## BROADSTAIRS
*36 km (22 miles) north of Dover.*

Like other Victorian seaside towns on this stretch of coast, Broadstairs was once the playground of vacationing Londoners. Charles Dickens spent many summers here between 1837 and 1851 and wrote glowingly of its bracing freshness. Today grand 19th-century houses line the waterfront. In the off-season Broadstairs is a peaceful retreat, but day-trippers pack the town in July and August.

**Dickens House Museum.** This house was originally the home of Mary Pearson Strong, on whom Dickens based the character of Betsey Trotwood, David Copperfield's aunt. Dickens lived here from 1837 to 1839 while writing *The Pickwick Papers* and *Oliver Twist*. Some rooms have been decorated to look as they would have in Dickens's day, and there's a reconstruction of Miss Trotwood's room as described by Dickens. ⊠ *2 Victoria Parade* ☎ *01843/861232* ⊕ *www.dickensfellowship.org* ⌲ *£3.50* ⊙ *Apr.–Oct., daily 2–5.*

### RYE

★ *64 km (40 miles) south of Dover.*

With cobbled streets and ancient timbered dwellings, Rye is an artist's dream. Once a port (the water retreated, and the harbor is now 2 miles away), the town starts where the sea once lapped at its ankles and then winds its way to the top of a low hill that overlooks the Romney Marshes. Virtually every building in the little town center is intriguingly old; some places were smugglers' retreats. This place can be easily walked without a map, but if you prefer guidance, the local tourist office has an interesting audio tour of the town, as well as maps.

## SHOPPING

The little towns of Kent are great places to browse for collectibles, china, silver, and secondhand books. The streets of Canterbury have an excellent selection of souvenirs, some of them decidedly kitsch. Rye has great antiques shops, perfect for an afternoon of rummaging, with the biggest cluster at the foot of the hill near the tourist information center. The English can find bargains; it's harder for Americans, given the exchange rate. The town still has a number of potteries.

**Black Sheep Antiques.** This shop has a superior selection of antique crystal and silver. ⊠ *72 The Mint* ☎ *01797/224508.*

**Collectors Corner.** A good mix of furniture, art, and silver is found at Collectors Corner. ⊠ *2 Market Rd.* ☎ *01797/225796.*

**David Sharp Pottery.** Like the ceramic name plaques that are a feature of the town? They are on offer at this tidy shop. ⊠ *55 The Mint* ☎ *01797/222620.*

## WHERE TO EAT

$    ✕ **City Fish Bar.** Long lines and lots of satisfied finger licking attest to the
BRITISH    deserved popularity of this excellent fish-and-chips outlet in the center of town. Everything is freshly fried, the batter crisp and the fish tasty; the fried mushrooms are also surprisingly good. There's no seating, so your fish is wrapped up in paper, and you eat it where you want, perhaps in the park. This place closes at 7. ⑤ *Average main: £6* ⊠ *30 St. Margaret's St., Canterbury* ☎ *01227/760873* ▭ *No credit cards.*

$$    ✕ **Webbes at the Fish Café.** One of Rye's most popular restaurants occu-
SEAFOOD    pies a brick building that dates to 1907, but the interior has been
Fodor's Choice    redone in a sleek, modern style. The ground-floor café has a relaxed
★    atmosphere, and upstairs is a more formal dining room. Most of the seafood here is caught nearby, so it's very fresh. Sample the shellfish platter with oysters, whelks, winkles, shrimp, and crab claws, or try the grilled squid with bok choy. Reservations are recommended for dinner. ⑤ *Average main: £15* ⊠ *17 Tower St., Rye* ☎ *01797/222226* ⊕ *www. webbesrestaurants.co.uk* ☉ *Closed Mon. Oct.–Apr. No dinner Sun.*

## WHERE TO STAY

$$ **Abode Canterbury.** This glossy boutique hotel inside the Old City
HOTEL walls offers an up-to-date style in traditional Canterbury. **Pros:** central
location; luxurious handmade beds; great restaurants and bars. **Cons:**
one of the priciest hotels in town; bar gets quite crowded. $ *Rooms
from: £135* ✉ *30–33 High St., Canterbury* ☎ *01227/766266* ⊕ *www.
abodehotels.co.uk* 🛏 *73 rooms.*

# DUBLIN, IRELAND

In his inimitable, irresistible way, James Joyce immortalized the city
of Dublin in works like *Ulysses* and *Dubliners.* He claimed to have
chosen Dublin as the setting for his work because it was a "center of
paralysis" where nothing much ever changed. What would he make
of Temple Bar—the city's erstwhile down-at-the-heels neighborhood,
now crammed with restaurants and hotels? Or of the city's newfound
status as a bustling hub of the European economy? Yet despite all
these advances, traditional Dublin is far from buried. The fundamen-
tals—the Georgian elegance of Merrion Square, the Norman drama of
Christ Church Cathedral, the foamy pint at an atmospheric pub—are
still on hand to gratify. Most of all, there are the locals themselves:
the nod and grin when you catch their eye on the street, the eager-
ness to share a tale or two, and their paradoxically dark but warm
sense of humor.

### ESSENTIALS

**CURRENCY**

The euro. ATMs are common.

**HOURS**

Shops and businesses are generally open Monday through Saturday
from 9:30 to 5:30 or 6; some open later and some open on Sunday.
Most museums open daily Monday through Saturday from 9 until 5;
museums may have shorter hours on Sunday.

**TELEPHONES**

Most tri- and quad-band GSM phones will work in Ireland, and the
country's mobile system is 3G compatible with excellent coverage. Pub-
lic phones accept prepaid call cards (available in shops and telecom
offices) and credit crads. Eircom, BT Ireland, and Vodafone are the
major telecom suppliers.

### COMING ASHORE

Small ships dock at the quayside of the River Liffey, close to the
downtown area. Larger ships berth at Alexandra Quay, 1.2 miles
from downtown. Alexandra Quay is part of the great Dublin Port,
with a range of visitor facilities including cafés, shops, information
desks, and restrooms. Buses 53 and 53A run from the port into the
city. Ticket prices are set according to the number of zones traveled,
beginning at €1.40.

Taxis can be hired to run tour itineraries, although charges are compli-
cated. Initial charges are a maximum of €4.10, then €1.03 per km (½

6

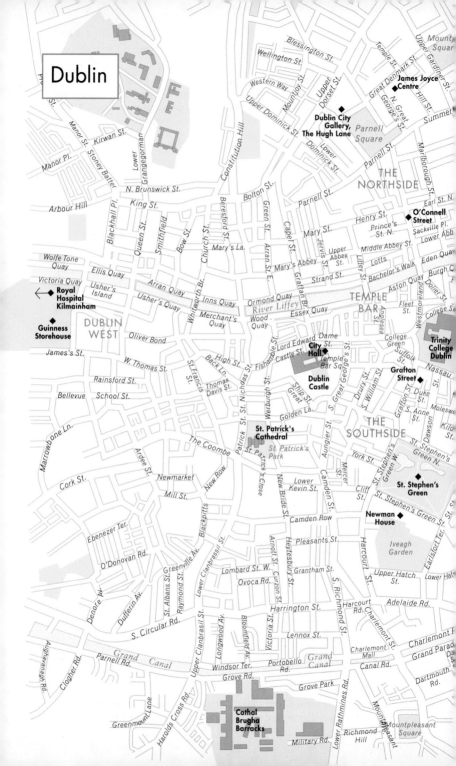

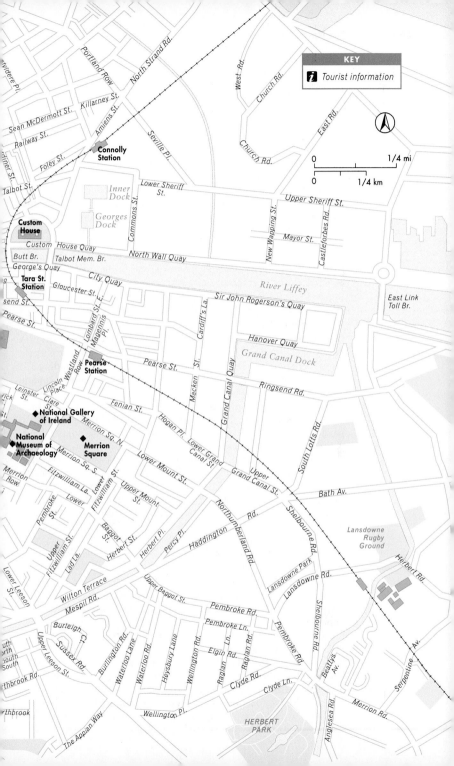

**KEY**

*i* Tourist information

0                    1/4 mi

0                    1/4 km

Portland Row

Sean McDermott St.

Killarney St.

North Strand Rd.

Railway St.

Amiens St.

Seville Pl.

Foley St.

Talbot St.

West. Rd.

Church St.

East Rd.

Church Rd.

**Connolly Station**

Inner Dock

Lower Sheriff St.

Upper Sheriff St.

Georges Dock

Commons St.

New Wapping St.

Mayor St.

Castleforbes Rd.

**Custom House**

Custom House Quay

Butt Br.

Talbot Mem. Br.

North Wall Quay

George's Quay

City Quay

*River Liffey*

East Link Toll Br.

**Tara St. Station**

Gloucester St. E.

Lombard St. E.

Magennis Pl.

Cardiff's La.

Sir John Rogerson's Quay

Pearse St.

Hanover Quay

send St.

Pearse St.

*Grand Canal Dock*

**Pearse Station**

Westland Row

Lincoln Place

Pearse St.

Macken St.

Grand Canal Quay

Ringsend Rd.

Leinster St.

Clare St.

Fenian St.

Hogan Pl.

Lower Grand Canal St.

Upper Grand Canal St.

South Lotts Rd.

♦ **National Gallery of Ireland**

Merrion Sq. N.

♦ **National Museum of Archaeology**

Merrion Sq. S.

♦ **Merrion Square**

Lower Mount St.

Bath Av.

Merrion Row

Fitzwilliam La.

Lower Fitzwilliam St.

Upper Fitzwilliam St.

Upper Mount St.

Northumberland Rd.

Shelbourne Rd.

*Lansdowne Rugby Ground*

Herbert Rd.

Pembroke St. Lower

Baggot St.

Herbert St.

Herbert Pl.

Percy Pl.

Haddington Rd.

Upper Fitzwilliam St.

Lad La.

Herbert St.

Lansdowne Park

Lansdowne Rd.

Wilton Terrace

Upper Baggot St.

Shelbourne Rd.

Lower Leeson St.

Mespil Rd.

Pembroke Rd.

Pembroke Rd.

Burleigh Ct.

Pembroke Ln.

Sussex Rd.

Burlington Rd.

Waterloo Lane

Waterloo Rd.

Heytsbury Lane

Wellington Rd.

Elgin Rd.

Raglan Ln.

Raglan Rd.

Pembroke Rd.

Beattys Av.

Serpentine Av.

Upper Leeson St.

th rth South

South Rd.

thbrook Rd.

thbrook

Raglan Rd.

Clyde Rd.

Clyde Ln.

Anglesea Rd.

Merrion Rd.

Wellington Pl.

The Appian Way

*HERBERT PARK*

mile). Drivers can choose to charge by the minute rather than per km. Don't rent a car if you are planning to tour Dublin, but a rental car does offer freedom to explore the countryside and coast around the city. The cost per day for a compact manual vehicle begins at €60.

## EXPLORING DUBLIN

**City Hall.** Facing the Liffey from Cork Hill at the top of Parliament Street, this grand Georgian municipal building (1769–79), once the Royal Exchange, marks the southwest corner of Temple Bar. Today it's the seat of the Dublin Corporation, the elected body that governs the city. Thomas Cooley designed the building with 12 columns that encircle the domed central rotunda, which has a fine mosaic floor and 12 frescoes depicting Dublin legends and ancient Irish historical scenes. The 20-foot-high sculpture to the right is of Daniel O'Connell, "The Liberator." He looks like he's about to begin the famous speech he gave here in 1800. The building houses a multimedia exhibition—with artifacts, kiosks, graphics, and audiovisual presentations—tracing the evolution of Ireland's 1,000-year-old capital. ⊠ *Dame St., Dublin West* ☎ *01/222–2204* ⊕ *www.dublincity.ie/RecreationandCulture* ⊠ *€4* ☼ *Mon.–Sat. 10–5:15.*

**Custom House.** Seen at its best when reflected in the waters of the Liffey during the short interval when the high tide is on the turn, the Custom House is the city's most spectacular Georgian building. Extending 375 feet on the north side of the river, this is the work of James Gandon, an English architect who arrived in Ireland in 1781, when the building's construction commenced (it continued for 10 years). Crafted from gleaming Portland stone, the central portico is linked by arcades to pavilions at either end. A statue of Commerce tops the copper dome, whose puny circumference, unfortunately, is out of proportion to the rest of the building. Statues on the main facade are based on allegorical themes. Note the exquisitely carved lions and unicorns supporting the arms of Ireland at the far ends of the facade. After Republicans set fire to the building in 1921, it was completely restored and reconstructed to house government offices. A visitor center traces the building's history and significance, and the life of Gandon. ⊠ *Custom House Quay, Northside* ☎ *01/888–2538* ⊕ *www.visitdublin.com* ⊠ *Free* ☼ *Mid-Mar.–Oct., weekdays 10–12:30, weekends 2–5; Nov.–mid-Mar., Wed.–Fri. 10–12:30, Sun. 2–5.*

★ **Dublin City Gallery, The Hugh Lane.** The Francis Bacon studio, reconstructed here exactly as the artist left it on his death (including his diary, books, walls, floors, ceiling, and even dust!), makes this already impressive gallery a must-see for art lovers and fans of the renowned British artist. Built as a town house for the Earl of Charlemont in 1762, this residence was so grand that the Parnell Square street on which it sits was nicknamed "Palace Row" in its honor. Sir William Chambers, who also built the Marino Casino for Charlemont, designed the structure in the best Palladian manner. Its delicate and rigidly correct facade, extended by two demilune (half-moon) arcades, was fashioned from the "new" white Ardmulcan stone (now seasoned to gray). Charlemont was one of the cultural locomotives of 18th-century Dublin—his walls were hung with Titians and Hogarths, and he frequently dined with Oliver Goldsmith and Sir Joshua Reynolds—so he would undoubtedly be delighted that his home is now a gallery, named after Sir Hugh Lane, a nephew of Lady Gregory (W. B. Yeats's aristocratic patron). Lane collected both impressionist paintings and 19th-century Irish and Anglo-Irish works. A complicated agreement with the National Gallery in London (reached after heated diplomatic dispute) stipulates that a portion of the 39 French paintings amassed by Lane shuttle between London and here. Time it right and you'll be able to see Pissarro's *Printemps,* Manet's *Eva Gonzales,* Morisot's *Jour d'Été,* and, the jewel of the collection, Renoir's *Les Parapluies.*

> ## DUBLIN BEST BETS
>
> **Admire the Georgian architecture.** The magnificent neoclassical buildings form an impressive framework on which the life of the 21st-century city hangs.
>
> **Have a pint of Guinness.** The people of Dublin have a reputation for friendliness and a love of life that's infectious, so find a seat in a pub and enjoy.
>
> **Wander through St. Stephen's Green.** This park offers recreation as well as history—scattered throughout are memorials to the city's literary giants.

Irish artists represented include Roderic O'Conor, well known for his views of the west of Ireland; William Leech, including his *Girl with a Tinsel Scarf* and *The Cigarette*; and the most famous of the group, Jack B. Yeats (W. B.'s brother). The museum has a dozen of his paintings, including *Ball Alley* and *There is No Night.* The mystically serene Sean Scully Gallery displays seven giant canvasses by Ireland's renowned abstract modernist. ⊠ *Parnell Sq. N, Northside* ☎ *01/222–5550* ⊕ *www. hughlane.ie* ▣ *Free* ⊗ *Tues.–Thurs. 10–6, Fri. and Sat. 10–5, Sun. 11–5.*

**Grafton Street.** It's no more than 200 yards long and about 20 feet wide, but brick-lined Grafton Street, open only to pedestrians, can claim to be the most humming street in the city, if not in all of Ireland. It's one of Dublin's vital spines: the most direct route between the front door of Trinity College and St. Stephen's Green, and the city's premier shopping street, with Dublin's most distinguished department store, Brown Thomas, as well as tried and trusted Marks & Spencer. Grafton Street and the smaller alleyways that radiate off it offer dozens of independent stores, a dozen or so colorful flower sellers, and some of the Southside's most popular watering holes. In summer, buskers from all over the world line both sides of the street, pouring out the sounds of drum, whistle, pipe, and string.

**Fodor's**Choice **Guinness Storehouse.** Ireland's all-dominating brewery—founded by
★ Arthur Guinness in 1759 and at one time the largest stout-producing brewery in the world—spans a 60-acre spread west of Christ Church Cathedral. Not surprisingly, it's the most popular tourist destination in town—after all, the Irish national drink is Guinness stout, a dark brew made with roasted malt. The brewery itself is closed to the public, but the Guinness Storehouse is a spectacular attraction, designed to woo— some might say brainwash—you with the wonders of the "dark stuff."

In a 1904 cast-iron-and-brick warehouse, the museum display covers six floors built around a huge, central glass atrium, which is shaped like a giant pint glass. Beneath the glass floor of the lobby you can see Arthur Guinness's original lease on the site, for a whopping 9,000 years. The exhibition elucidates the brewing process and its history, with antique presses and vats, a look at bottle and can design through the ages, a history of the Guinness family, a fascinating archive of Guinness advertisements, and a chance to pull your own perfect pint. The star attraction is undoubtedly the top-floor **Gravity Bar,** with 360-degree floor-to-ceiling glass walls that offer a nonpareil view out over the city at sunset while you sip your free pint. One of the bar's first clients was one William Jefferson Clinton. You'll find the Guinness logo on everything from piggy banks to underpants in the Guinness Store on the ground floor. ⊠ *St. James' Gate, Dublin West* ☏ *01/408–4800* ⊕ *www.guinness-storehouse.com* ⊑ *€14.40* ⊘ *July and Aug., daily 9:30–7; Sept.–June, daily 9:30–5.*

**James Joyce Centre.** Few may have read him, but everyone in Ireland has at least heard of James Joyce (1882–1941)—especially since owning a copy of his censored and suppressed *Ulysses* was one of the top status symbols of the early 20th century. Joyce is of course now acknowledged as one of the greatest modern authors, and his *Dubliners, Finnegan's Wake,* and *A Portrait of the Artist as a Young Man* can even be read as quirky "travel guides" to Dublin. Open to the public, this restored 18th-century Georgian town house, once the dancing academy of Professor Denis J. Maginni (which many will recognize from a reading of *Ulysses*), is a center for Joycean studies and events related to the author. It has an extensive library and archives, exhibition rooms, a bookstore, and a café. The collection includes letters from Beckett, Joyce's guitar and cane, and a celebrated edition of *Ulysses* illustrated by Matisse. The interactive "James Joyce and Ulysses" exhibition allows you to delve into the mysteries and controversies of the novel. The center is the main organizer of "Bloomstime," which marks the week leading up to the Bloomsday celebrations. (Bloomsday, June 16, is the single day *Ulysses* chronicles, as Leopold Bloom winds his way around Dublin in 1904.) ⊠ *35 N. Great George's St., Northside* ☏ *01/878–8547* ⊕ *www.jamesjoyce.ie* ⊑ *€5, guided tour €10* ⊘ *Tues.–Sat. 10–5, Sun. noon–5.*

Fodor'sChoice ★ **Merrion Square.** Created between 1762 and 1764, this tranquil square a few blocks east of St. Stephen's Green is lined on three sides by some of Dublin's best-preserved Georgian town houses, many of which have brightly painted front doors crowned by intricate fanlights. Leinster House, the National Museum of Natural History, and the National Gallery line the west side of the square. It's on the other sides, however, that the Georgian terrace streetscape comes into its own—the finest houses are on the north border. Even when the flower gardens here are not in bloom, the vibrant, mostly evergreen grounds, dotted with sculpture and threaded with meandering paths, are worth strolling through. Several distinguished Dubliners have lived on the square, including Oscar Wilde's parents, Sir William and "Speranza" Wilde (No. 1); Irish national leader Daniel O'Connell (No. 58); and authors W. B. Yeats (Nos. 52 and 82) and Sheridan LeFanu (No. 70). Until 50 years ago the square was a fashionable residential area, but today most of the houses serve as offices. At the south end of Merrion Square, on Upper Mount Street, stands the Church of Ireland St. Stephen's Church. Known locally as the "pepper canister" church because of its cupola, the structure was inspired in part by Wren's churches in London. An open-air art gallery featuring the works of local artists is held on the square on Sundays. ⊠ *Southeast Dublin* ⊕ *www.merrionsquareart.com* ⊙ *Daily sunrise–sunset.*

**Fodor's Choice** **National Gallery of Ireland.** Caravaggio's *The Taking of Christ* (1602), ★ Van Gogh's *Rooftops of Paris* (1886), Vermeer's *Lady Writing a Letter with Her Maid* (circa 1670) . . . you get the picture, or rather, you'll *find* the picture here. Established in 1864 and designed by Francis Fowke (who also designed London's Victoria & Albert Museum), the National Gallery of Ireland is one of Europe's finest smaller art museums, with "smaller" being a relative term: the collection holds more than 2,500 paintings and some 10,000 other works. But unlike Europe's largest art museums, the National Gallery can be thoroughly covered in a morning or afternoon without inducing exhaustion.

A highlight of the museum is the major collection of paintings by Irish artists from the 17th through 20th centuries, including works by Roderic O'Conor (1860–1940), Sir William Orpen (1878–1931), and William Leech (1881–1968). The Yeats Museum section contains works by members of the Yeats family, including Jack B. Yeats (1871–1957), the brother of writer W. B. Yeats, and by far the best-known Irish painter of the 20th century.

The collection also claims exceptional paintings from the 17th-century French, Dutch, Italian, and Spanish schools, and works by French impressionists Monet, Sisley, and Renoir. The amply stocked gift shop is a good place to pick up books on Irish artists. Free, guided tours are available on Saturday at 2 and on Sunday at 1 and 2. ⊠ *Merrion Sq. W, Southeast Dublin* ☎ *01/661–5133* ⊕ *www.nationalgallery.ie* ☑ *Free; special exhibits €10* ⊙ *Mon.–Wed., Fri., and Sat. 9:30–5:30, Thurs. 9:30–8:30, Sun. noon–5:30.*

★ **National Museum of Archaeology.** Just south of Leinster House is Ireland's National Museum of Archaeology, one of four branches of the National Museum of Ireland, and home to a fabled collection of Irish artifacts dating from 7000 BC to the present. Organized around a grand rotunda, the museum is elaborately decorated, with mosaic floors, marble columns, balustrades, and fancy ironwork. It has the largest collection of Celtic antiquities in the world, including gold jewelry, carved stones, bronze tools, and weapons.

The Treasury collection, including some of the museum's most renowned pieces, is open on a permanent basis. Among the priceless relics on display are the 8th-century Ardagh Chalice, a two-handled silver cup with gold filigree ornamentation; the bronze-coated iron St. Patrick's Bell, the oldest surviving example (5th–8th century) of Irish metalwork; the 8th-century Tara Brooch, an intricately decorated piece made of white bronze, amber, and glass; and the 12th-century bejeweled oak Cross of Cong, covered with silver and bronze panels.

The *Or: Ireland's Gold* exhibition gathers together the most impressive pieces of surprisingly delicate and intricate prehistoric gold work—including sun disks and the late Bronze Age gold collar known as the Gleninsheen Gorget—that range in dates from 2200 to 500 BC. Upstairs, Viking Ireland is a permanent exhibit on the Norsemen, featuring a full-size Viking skeleton, swords, leatherworks recovered in Dublin and surrounding areas, and a replica of a small Viking boat. The newest attraction is an exhibition entitled *Kinship and Sacrifice*, centering on a number of Iron Age "bog bodies" found along with other objects in Ireland's peat bogs.

The 18th-century Collins Barracks, near Phoenix Park (⇨ *see Phoenix Park*), houses the National Museum of Decorative Arts and History, a collection of glass, silver, furniture, and other decorative arts. ⊠ *Kildare St. Annex, 7–9 Merrion Row, Southeast Dublin* ☏ *01/677–7444* ⊕ *www.museum.ie* ⊡ *Free* ☉ *Tues.–Sat. 10–5, Sun. 2–5.*

**Newman House.** One of the finest examples of Georgian Dublin, Newman House is actually two imposing town houses joined together. The earlier of the two, No. 85 St. Stephen's Green (1738), has two landmarks of Irish Georgian style: the Apollo Room, decorated with stuccowork depicting the sun god and his muses; and the magnificent Saloon, crowned with an exuberant ceiling aswirl with cupids and gods, created by the Brothers Lafranchini–the finest *stuccadores* (plaster workers) of 18th-century Dublin. Next door at No. 86 (1765), the staircase, set against pastel walls, is one of the city's most beautiful rococo examples—with floral swags and musical instruments picked out in cake-frosting white. To explore the rich history and architecture of the houses you must join a guided tour. At the back of Newman House hides Dublin's "secret garden" (⇨ *see Iveagh Gardens*). ⊠ *85–86 St. Stephen's Green, Southside* ☏ *01/475–7255* ⊕ *www.ucd.ie/campusdevelopment/developmentprojects* ⊡ *House and garden €5* ☉ *Tours June–Aug., Tues.–Fri. at 2, 3, and 4.*

**O'Connell Street.** Dublin's most famous thoroughfare, which is 150 feet wide, was previously known as Sackville Street, but its name was changed in 1924, two years after the founding of the Irish Free State. After the devastation of the 1916 Easter Uprising, the Northside street had to be almost entirely reconstructed, a task that took until the end of the 1920s. At one time the main attraction of the street was Nelson's Pillar, a Doric column towering over the city center and a marvelous vantage point, but it was blown up in 1966, on the 50th anniversary of the Easter Uprising. A major cleanup and repaving have returned the street to some of its old glory. The large monument at the south end of the street is dedicated to Daniel O'Connell (1775–1847), "The Liberator," and was erected in 1854 as a tribute to the orator's achievement in securing Catholic Emancipation in 1829. Look closely and you'll notice that O'Connell is wearing a glove on one hand, as he did for much of his adult life, a self-imposed penance for shooting a man in a duel. But even the great man himself is dwarfed by the newest addition to O'Connell Street: the 395-foot-high spire was built in Nelson's Pillar's place in 2003, and today this gigantic, stainless-steel monument dominates the street.

★ **Royal Hospital Kilmainham.** This replica of Les Invalides in Paris is regarded as the most important 17th-century building in Ireland. Commissioned as a hospice for disabled and veteran soldiers by James Butler—the Duke of Ormonde and viceroy to King Charles II—it was completed in 1684, making it the first building erected in Dublin's golden age. It survived into the 1920s as a hospital, but after the founding of the Irish Free State in 1922, the building fell into disrepair. The entire edifice has since been restored. The architectural highlight is the hospital's baroque chapel, distinguished by its extraordinary plasterwork ceiling and fine wood carvings. ⊕ *www.rhk.ie.*

**Irish Museum of Modern Art.** The Royal Hospital also houses the Irish Museum of Modern Art, which concentrates on the work of contemporary Irish artists such as Richard Deacon, Richard Gorman, Dorothy Cross, Sean Scully, Matt Mullican, Louis Le Brocquy, and James Coleman. The museum also displays works by some non-Irish 20th-century greats, including Picasso and Miró, plus recent hotshots like Damien Hirst, and regularly hosts touring shows from major European museums. The Grass Roots Café serves light fare such as soups and sandwiches. The hospital is a short ride by taxi or bus from the city center. ⊠ *Kilmainham La., Dublin West* ☎ *01/612–9900* ⊕ *www.imma. ie* ⊠ *Free* ☉ *Royal Hospital: Mon, Tues., and Thurs.–Sat. 10–5:30, Wed. 10:30–5:30, Sun. noon–5:30. Museum: Tues. and Thurs.–Sat. 10–5:30, Wed. 10:30–5:30, Sun. noon–5:30; tours Wed. and Fri. at 2:30, Sat. at 11:30*

**Fodor's**Choice **St. Stephen's Green.** Dubliners call it simply Stephen's Green, and green
★ it is (year-round)—a verdant, 27-acre Southside square that was used for the public punishment of criminals until 1664. After a long period of decline, it became a private park in 1814—the first time in its history that it was closed to the public. Its fortunes changed again in 1880, when Sir Arthur Guinness paid for it to be laid out anew. Flower gardens, formal lawns, a Victorian bandstand, and an ornamental lake with lots of waterfowl are all within the park's borders, connected by paths guaranteeing that strolling here or just passing through will offer up unexpected delights (such as palm trees). Among the park's many statues are a memorial to W. B. Yeats and another to Joyce by Henry Moore. In the 18th century, the walk on the north side of the green was referred to as the Beaux Walk because most of Dublin's gentlemen's clubs were in town houses here. Today it's dominated by the legendary Shelbourne hotel. On the south side is the alluring Georgian Newman House. ⊠ *Southside* ⊠ *Free* ☉ *Daily sunrise–sunset.*

**Fodor's**Choice **Trinity College Dublin.** Founded in 1592 by Queen Elizabeth I to "civi-
★ lize" (Her Majesty's word) Dublin, Trinity is Ireland's oldest and most famous college. The memorably atmospheric campus is a must; here you can track the shadows of some of the noted alumni, such as Jonathan Swift (1667–1745), Oscar Wilde (1854–1900), Bram Stoker (1847–1912), and Samuel Beckett (1906–89). Trinity College, Dublin (familiarly known as TCD), was founded on the site of the confiscated Priory of All Hallows. For centuries Trinity was the preserve of the Protestant Church; a free education was offered to Catholics—provided that they accepted the Protestant faith. As a legacy of this condition, until 1966

6

Catholics who wished to study at Trinity had to obtain a dispensation from their bishop or face excommunication.

Trinity's grounds cover 40 acres. Most of its buildings were constructed in the 18th and early 19th centuries. The extensive **West Front,** with a classical pedimented portico in the Corinthian style, faces College Green and is directly across from the Bank of Ireland; it was built between 1755 and 1759, and is possibly the work of Theodore Jacobsen, architect of London's Foundling Hospital. The design is repeated on the interior, so the view is the same from outside the gates and from the quadrangle inside. On the lawn in front of the inner facade stand statues of two alumni, orator Edmund Burke (1729–97) and dramatist Oliver Goldsmith (1730–74). On the right side of the cobblestone quadrangle of **Parliament Square** (commonly known as Front Square) is Sir William Chambers's theater, or Examination Hall, dating from the mid-1780s, which contains the college's most splendid Adamesque interior, designed by Michael Stapleton. The hall houses an impressive organ retrieved from an 18th-century Spanish ship and a gilded oak chandelier from the old House of Commons; concerts are sometimes held here. The chapel, left of the quadrangle, has stucco ceilings and fine woodwork. The looming campanile, or bell tower, is the symbolic heart of the college; erected in 1853, it dominates the center of the square. ☎ *01/896–1000* ⊕ *www.tcd.ie.*

## SHOPPING

There's a tremendous variety of stores in Dublin, many of which are quite sophisticated. Department stores stock internationally known fashion designer goods and housewares, and small boutiques sell Irish crafts and other merchandise. If you're at all interested in modern and contemporary literature, be sure to leave yourself time to browse through the bookstores. Don't forget a bottle of Irish whiskey or a bottle or two of Guinness.

**Francis Street** is the hub of Dublin's antiques trade. **Grafton Street** has mainly chain stores. The smaller streets off Grafton Street have worthwhile crafts, clothing, and designer houseware shops. **Nassau Street,** Dublin's main tourist-oriented thoroughfare, has some of the best-known stores selling Irish goods. **Temple Bar** is dotted with small boutiques—mainly intimate, quirky shops that traffic in a selection of trendy goods, from vintage clothes to some of the most avant-garde Irish garb anywhere in the city. Note that many museums have excellent gift shops selling crafts, books, and prints, among other items.

Fodor's Choice
★
**Cathach Books.** Head here for a fine array of first editions of Irish literature and many other books of Irish interest, plus old maps of Dublin and Ireland. ⊠ *10 Duke St., Southside* ☎ *01/671–8676* ⊕ *www.rarebooks.ie.*

## WHERE TO EAT

$
CAFÉ
⨯ **Busyfeet & Coco Café.** This bustling, quirky bohemian café emphasizes good, wholesome food. Organic ingredients play a prominent role on a menu that's laden with delicious salads and sandwiches. Try the grilled

goat-cheese salad served with walnut-and-raisin toast and sun-dried-tomato tapenade on a bed of arugula. The delicious Mediterranean quesadilla wrap—with roasted vegetables, napolitana sauce, and mature cheddar—is a must. It's also one of the city center's best-situated spots for a bit of people-watching, as Dublin's young and hip stroll by all day long. Live music every Saturday night. $ *Average main: €8* ⊠ *41–42 S. William St., Southside* ☎ *01/671–9514* ⌦ *Reservations not accepted.*

# GREENOCK, SCOTLAND (FOR GLASGOW)

Updated by Mike Gonzalez

In the days when Britain still ruled over an empire, Glasgow pronounced itself the Second City of the Empire. The term "Clyde-built" (from Glasgow's River Clyde) became synonymous with good workmanship and lasting quality. Glasgow had fallen into a severely depressed state by the mid-20th century, but during the century's last two decades the city cleaned up and started looking forward. Modern Glasgow has undergone an urban renaissance: A booming cultural life, stylish restaurants, and an air of confidence make it Scotland's most exciting city. Glasgow is particularly remarkable for its architecture, from the unique Victorian cityscapes of Alexander "Greek" Thomson (1817–75) to the cutting-edge art nouveau vision of Charles Rennie Mackintosh (1868–1928). The city also has some of the most exciting museum collections outside London.

6

## ESSENTIALS

### CURRENCY
The British pound sterling. ATMs are common and credit cards are widely accepted.

### HOURS
Museums are open from 9 until 5, while shops usually open from 9 until 5:30 or 6. Shops are open on Sunday.

### PRIVATE TOURS
Private tours can be arranged through Glasgow Taxis or Little's Chauffeur Drive.

**Contacts Glasgow Taxis.** ☎ *0141/429–7070* ⊕ *glasgowtaxisltd.co.uk.* **Little's Chauffeur Drive.** ☎ *0141/883–2111* ⊕ *www.littles.co.uk.*

### TELEPHONES
Dual-band GSM phones work in the United Kingdom. You can buy prepaid phone cards at telecom shops and news vendors in all towns and cities. Phone cards can be used for local or international calls. Vodafone, T-Mobile, Virgin and Orange are the leading telecom companies.

### COMING ASHORE
Vessels dock at Greenock's Ocean Terminal in the main port. Passengers walk the few yards to the terminal building, which has tourist information, refreshments, currency exchange, car-rental kiosks, and a taxi stand. A new waterfront walkway leads into the town of Greenock, where there are shops, restaurants, and some fine Victorian architecture dating from the time when the town was an important transatlantic port. However, there's little to hold visitors here.

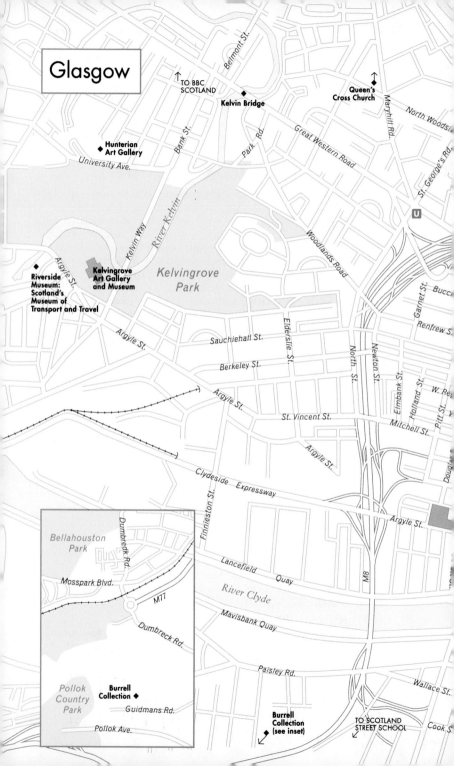

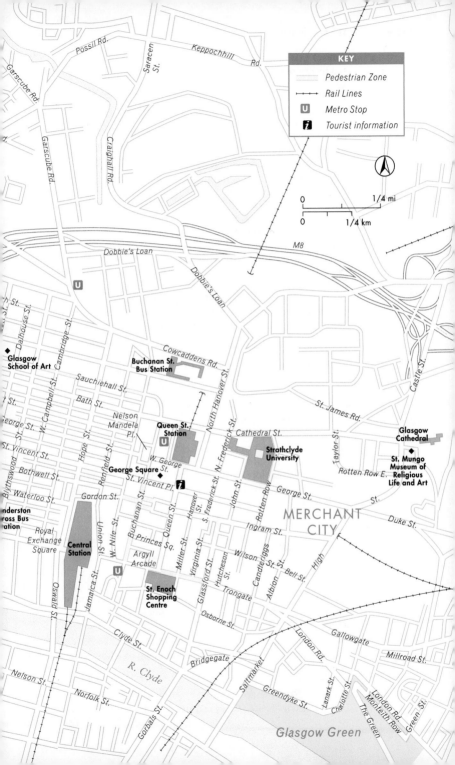

**KEY**

Pedestrian Zone
Rail Lines
**U** Metro Stop
**ℹ** Tourist information

0      1/4 mi
0      1/4 km

Possil Rd.

Saracen St.

Keppochhill Rd.

Garscube Rd.

Craighall Rd.

Garscube Rd.

*M8*

*Dobbie's Loan*

*Dobbie's Loan*

**U**

Cowcaddens Rd.

◆ **Glasgow School of Art**

Dalhouse St.

Cambridge St.

**Buchanan St. Bus Station**

North Hanover St.

St. James Rd.

Castle St.

Sauchiehall St.

W. Campbell St.

Bath St.

Hope St.

Renfield St.

Nelson Mandela Pl.

**Queen St. Station**

**U**

Cathedral St.

N. Frederick St.

Taylor St.

**Glasgow Cathedral** ◆

**Strathclyde University**

◆ **St. Mungo Museum of Religious Life and Art**

George St.

St. Vincent St.

Bothwell St.

W. George St.

**George Square** ◆

St. Vincent Pl. **ℹ**

Hanover St.

S. Frederick St.

John St.

Rotten Row

George St.

Rotten Row E.

St.

Duke St.

**MERCHANT CITY**

Buthswood

Waterloo St.

Gordon St.

Union St.

Buchanan St.

Queen St.

Ingram St.

**enderston ross Bus ation**

*Royal Exchange Square*

**Central Station**

Oswald St.

Jamaica St.

W. Nile St.

Princes Sq.

Miller St.

Virginia St.

Glassford St.

Hutcheson St.

Wilson St.

Candleriggs

St.

Bell St.

High

**U**

**Argyll Arcade**

**St. Enoch Shopping Centre**

Trongate

Albion St.

Osborne St.

London Rd.

Gallowgate

Millroad St.

Clyde St.

Bridgegate

Saltmarket

Greendyke St.

London Rd.

Monteith Row

The Green

Green St.

Charlotte St.

Lanark St.

Nelson St.

Norfolk St.

Gorbals St.

*R. Clyde*

*Glasgow Green*

A black taxi to downtown Glasgow is a fixed-price of £45 one-way. Private hire firms operate to and from Greenock but must be booked in advance. They are significantly cheaper. In Glasgow, Network Cars (which will also pick up from Greenock if booked) and Inverclyde Taxis in Greenock) are the best choices. From the station in Greenock (Greenock West), regular train services run into Glasgow city. From the port to the railway station it's a £4 taxi trip. The journey to Glasgow takes 30 to 40 minutes; trains run three or more times per hour, and tickets start at £6.80 round trip (off-peak is the cheapest ticket, after 9:30 am and not between 4:30 and 6:30 pm). You can also take Buses 901, 906, and 907 into Glasgow from the Greenock bus station. A Daytripper ticket, which covers transport to and from Glasgow and within the city for a day, costs £19 for 2 adults and up to 4 children or £10.70 for 1 adult and 2 children.

---

### GLASGOW BEST BETS

**Kelvingrove Art Gallery and Museum.** A fantastic collection of European art, featuring such luminaries as Rembrandt and Monet, set in a stunning neo-Renaissance edifice.

**Glasgow School of Art.** Designed by Charles Rennie Mackintosh, this building is a tour de force of British art nouveau and one of the finest architectural statements in a city full of fine civic buildings. Tickets for the Mackintosh Trail are £16 and entry to all Mackintosh sites in the city and transport between them. Purchase at the tourist office in Glasgow.

**Hunterian Art Gallery.** This gallery features works by Tintoretto, Sir Joshua Reynolds, and Auguste Rodin—all donated by a private collector.

---

Once in Glasgow, Subway (tickets £1.40 a single trip or £3.80 for a whole day Discovery ticket, use after 9.30 a.m.) and bus services (tickets £1.85) can get you around easily. There are also numerous metered taxis. If you want to explore the majestic landscapes of southwestern Scotland independently, it pays to rent a vehicle (approximately £50–£70 per day for a manual economy vehicle) or take a custom guided tour.

**Contacts Network Cars.** ☎ 01415/571110. **Inverclyde Taxis.** ☎ 01475/734563.

## EXPLORING GLASGOW

The Greater Glasgow and Clyde Valley Tourist Board, at 11 George Square, provides information on all services available in and around the city, as well as details of tours within and around the city. Most tours begin from here, too, and can be booked in advance. It also has a well-stocked shop.

Fodor's Choice
★

**Burrell Collection.** An elegant, ultramodern building of pink sandstone and stainless steel houses thousands of items of all descriptions, from ancient Egyptian, Greek, and Roman artifacts to Chinese ceramics, bronzes, and jade. You can also find medieval tapestries, stained-glass windows, Rodin sculptures, and exquisite French-impressionist paintings—Degas's *The Rehearsal* and Sir Henry Raeburn's *Miss Macartney,* to name two. Eccentric millionaire Sir William Burrell (1861–1958) donated this collection of some 8,000 pieces to the city in 1944. The 1983 building was designed with large glass walls so that the items on display could relate to their surroundings in Pollok Country Park: art and nature, supposedly in perfect harmony. You can get here via Buses 45, 48, and 57 from Union Street, or it's a leisurely 15-minute walk from the Pollokshaws West rail station. ⊠ *2060 Pollokshaws Rd., South Side* ☎ *0141/287–2550* ⊕ *www.glasgowmuseums.com* ✉ *Free* ☉ *Mon.–Thurs. and Sat. 10–5, Fri. and Sun. 11–5.*

**George Square.** The focal point of Glasgow is lined with an impressive collection of statues of worthies: Queen Victoria; Scotland's national poet, Robert Burns (1759–96); the inventor and developer of the steam engine, James Watt (1736–1819); Prime Minister William Gladstone (1809–98); and towering above them all, Scotland's great historical novelist, Sir Walter Scott (1771–1832). The column was intended for George III (1738–1820), after whom the square is named, but when he was found to be insane toward the end of his reign, his statue was never erected. On the square's east side stands the magnificent Italian Renaissance–style **City Chambers**; the handsome **Merchants' House** fills the corner of West George Street, crowned by a globe and a sailing ship. ⊠ *Between St. Vincent and Argyle Sts., City Center* Ⓜ *Buchanan St.*

**Fodor's Choice** ★ **Glasgow Cathedral.** The most complete of Scotland's cathedrals (it would have been more complete had 19th-century vandals not pulled down its two rugged towers), this is an unusual double church, one above the other, dedicated to Glasgow's patron saint, St. Mungo. Consecrated in 1136 and completed about 300 years later, it was spared the ravages of the Reformation—which destroyed so many of Scotland's medieval churches—mainly because Glasgow's trade guilds defended it. A late-medieval open-timber roof in the nave and lovely 20th-century stained glass are notable features. In the lower church is the splendid crypt of St. Mungo, who was originally known as St. Kentigern (*kentigern* means "chief word"), but who was nicknamed St. Mungo (meaning "dear one") by his early followers in Glasgow. The site of the tomb has been revered since the 6th century, when St. Mungo founded a church here. Mungo features prominently in local legends; one such legend is about a pet bird that he nursed back to life, and another tells of a bush or tree, the branches of which he used to miraculously relight a fire. The bird, the tree, and the salmon with a ring in its mouth (from another story about him) are all to be found on the city of Glasgow's coat of arms, together with a bell that Mungo brought from Rome. ⊠ *Cathedral St., City Center* ☎ *0141/552–8198* ⊕ *www.glasgow-cathedral.com* ✉ *Free* ☉ *Apr.–Sept., Mon.–Sat. 9:30–5:30, Sun. 1–5; Oct.–Mar., Mon.–Sat. 9:30–4:30, Sun. 1–4:30* Ⓜ *Buchanan St.*

★ **Glasgow School of Art.** The exterior and interior, structure, furnishings, and decoration of this art nouveau building, built between 1897 and 1909, form a unified whole, reflecting the inventive genius of Charles Rennie Mackintosh, who was only 28 years old when he won the competition for its design. Architects and designers from all over the world come to admire it. Book ahead for daily guided tours, which cost £8.75 and begin at 11 and 3 (sometimes more frequently in the summer). Otherwise, you can visit four galleries that host frequently changing exhibitions. A visitor center has a small Mackintosh exhibition and sells a good selection of prints, postcards, and books. ⊠ *11 Dalhousie St., City Center* ☎ *0141/353–4526* ⊕ *www.gsa.ac.uk/tours* ⊠ *£8.75* ⊗ *Building: daily 10:30–5. Exhibitions: Mon.–Sat. 10:30–4:30, Sat. 10–2.* Ⓜ *Cowcaddens.*

★　**Hunterian Art Gallery.** Opposite Glasgow University's main gate, this gallery houses William Hunter's (1718–83) collection of paintings (his antiquarian collection is housed in the nearby Hunterian Museum). You'll also find prints, drawings, and sculptures by Tintoretto, Rembrandt, and Auguste Rodin, as well as a major collection of paintings by James McNeill Whistler, who had a great affection for the city that bought one of his earliest paintings. Also in the gallery is a replica of **Charles Rennie Mackintosh's town house,** which once stood nearby. The rooms contain Mackintosh's distinctive art nouveau chairs, tables, beds, and cupboards, and the walls are decorated in the equally distinctive style devised by him and his artist wife, Margaret. The gallery is free, but the Mackintosh House and occasional special exhibitions are £5. ⊠ *Hillhead St., West End* ☎ *0141/330–5431* ⊕ *www.hunterian.gla.ac.uk* ⊠ *Free, Mackintosh house £5* ⊗ *Tues.–Sat. 10–5, Sun. 11–4* Ⓜ *Hillhead.*

**Fodor's Choice**　**Kelvingrove Art Gallery and Museum.** Worthy of its world-class reputation,
★　the Kelvingrive Art Gallery and Museum attracts local families as well
⊗　as international visitors. This combination of cathedral and castle was designed in the Renaissance style and built between 1891 and 1901. The stunning red-sandstone edifice is an appropriate home for works by Botticelli, Rembrandt, Monet, and others; the museum has been hailed as "one of the greatest civic collections in Europe." The Glasgow Room houses extraordinary works by local artists. There's a Mackintosh and the Glasgow Style room, a picture promenade, and a natural-history exhibit on creatures of the past. Whether the subject is Scottish culture, design, or storytelling, every wall and room begs you to look deeper; labels are thought provoking and sometimes witty. You could spend a weekend here, but in a pinch three hours would do one level justice—there are three. Leave time to visit the gift shop and the attractive basement restaurant. ⊠ *Argyle St., West End* ☎ *0141/276–9599* ⊕ *www. glasgowmuseums.com* ⊠ *Free* ⊗ *Mon.–Thurs. and Sat. 10–5, Fri. and Sun. 11–5* Ⓜ *Kelvinhall.*

**Queen's Cross Church.** Head for the Charles Rennie Mackintosh Society Headquarters, housed in the only church Mackintosh designed, to learn more about the famous Glasgow-born architect and designer. Although one of the leading lights in the art nouveau movement, Mackintosh died in relative obscurity in 1928. Today he's widely accepted as a brilliant innovator. The church has beautiful stained-glass windows and a light-enhancing, carved-wood interior. The center's library and shop provide further insight into Glasgow's other Mackintosh-designed buildings, which include Scotland Street School, the Martyrs Public School, and the Glasgow School of Art. The church sits on the corner of Springbank Street at the junction of Garscube Road with Maryhill Road; a cab ride can get you here, or take a bus toward Queen's Cross from stops along Hope Street. ⊠ *870 Garscube Rd., West End* ☎ *0141/946–6600* ⊕ *www.crmsociety.com* ⊠ *£4* ⊗ *Apr.–Oct., Mon., Wed., and Fri. 10–5; Nov.–Mar., Mon., Wed., and Fri. 10–4.*

Fodor's Choice
★
♺
**Riverside Museum: Scotland's Museum of Transport and Travel.** An extraordinary new riverside museum designed by Zaha Hadid celebrates the area's industrial heritage with flair. Its huge metal structure with curving walls echoes the covered yards where ships were built on the Clyde. Glasgow's history of shipbuilding is celebrated in the world-famous collection of Clyde-built ship models. Some of the locomotives built at the nearby St. Rollox yards are also on display. There are cars from every age and many countries suspended on a kind of flying roadway above the main museum. You can wander down Main Street, circa 1930, without leaving the building: the pawnbroker and the Italian café, the subway train and the funeral parlor are frozen in time. Relax with a coffee in the café, wander out onto the expansive riverside walk, or board the tall ship that is moored permanently behind the museum. Bus 100 from George Square brings you here, or you can walk from the Partick subway station in 10 minutes. ✉ *100 Poundhouse Pl., West End* ☎ *0141/287–2720* ⊕ *www.glasgowlife.org.uk/museums* ✆ *Free* ⊙ *Mon.–Thurs. and Sat. 10–5, Fri. and Sun. 11–5* Ⓜ *Partick.*

**St. Mungo Museum of Religious Life and Art.** An outstanding collection of artifacts, including Celtic crosses and statuettes of Hindu gods, reflects the many religious groups that have settled throughout the centuries in Glasgow and the west of Scotland. This rich history is depicted in the stunning Sharing of Faiths Banner, which celebrates the city's many different faiths. A Zen garden creates a peaceful setting for rest and contemplation, and elsewhere stained-glass windows include a depiction of St. Mungo himself. ✉ *2 Castle St., City Center* ☎ *0141/276–1625* ⊕ *www.glasgowmuseums.com* ✆ *Free* ⊙ *Tues.–Thurs. and Sat. 10–5, Fri. and Sun. 11–5* Ⓜ *Buchanan St.*

## SHOPPING

Glasgow is a shopper's dream, with its large department stores, designer outlets, quirky boutiques, and unique markets. Choice items include such traditional Scottish crafts as tartans, kilts, knitwear, and of course, whisky. Join the throngs of style-conscious and unseasonably tan locals along Argyle, Buchanan, and Sauchiehall streets. Should the weather turn *dreich,* you can avoid getting *drookit* by sheltering in one of the many covered arcades in the city center. For more unusual items, head to the West End's Byres Road and Great Western Road.

Many of Glasgow's young and upwardly mobile make their home in **Merchant City,** on the edge of the city center. Shopping here is expensive, but the area is worth visiting if you're seeking the youthful Glasgow style. If you're an antiques connoisseur and art lover, a walk along **West Regent Street,** particularly its **Victorian Village,** is highly recommended, as there are various galleries and shops, some specializing in Scottish antiques and paintings.

**Glasgow School of Art.** The Glasgow School of Art sells books, cards, jewelry, and ceramics. Students often display their work during the degree shows in June. ✉ *167 Renfrew St., City Center* ☎ *0141/353–4526.*

**Hector Russell Kiltmakers.** Hector Russell Kiltmakers specializes in Highland outfits, wool and cashmere clothing, and women's fashions. ⊠ *110 Buchanan St., City Center* ☎ *0141/221–0217.*

Fodor's Choice **Princes Square.** By far the best shopping center is the art nouveau Princes
★ Square, with high-quality shops alongside pleasant cafés and restaurants. Look for the Scottish Craft Centre, which carries an outstanding collection of work created by some of the nation's best craftspeople. ⊠ *48 Buchanan St., City Center* ☎ *0141/221–0324.*

## ACTIVITIES

**Royal Troon.** Founded in 1878, Royal Troon has two 18-hole courses: the Old, or Championship, Course and the Portland Course. The views are magnificent, but the courses can get windy. Access for non-members is limited between May and mid-October to Monday, Tuesday, and Thursday only; day tickets cost £220 and include two rounds, morning coffee, and a buffet lunch, but there are cheaper options. ⊠ *Craigend Rd., Troon* ☎ *01292/311555* ⊕ *www.royaltroon.co.uk* ⚲ *Old Course: 18 holes, 7,150 yds, SSS 74. Portland Course: 18 holes, 6,289 yds, SSS 70.*

## WHERE TO EAT

$    ✕ **Café Gandolfi.** Occupying what was once the tea market, this trendy
BRITISH café draws the style-conscious crowd. Wooden tables and chairs crafted by Scottish artist Tim Stead are so fluidly shaped it's hard to believe they're inanimate. The café opens early for breakfast, serving croissants, eggs *en cocotte* (casserole-style), and strong espresso. Don't miss the smoked venison or the finnan haddie (smoked haddock). The bar on the second floor is more intimate and much less busy—and lets you order from the same menu. ⓢ *Average main: £13* ⊠ *64 Albion St., Merchant City* ☎ *0141/552–6813* ⊕ *www.cafegandolfi.com.*

$    ✕ **Willow Tearoom.** This Sauchiehall Street eatery takes up part of a
BRITISH department store originally designed by Charles Rennie Mackintosh. The original tearoom is now reduced to a gallery at the back of a Mackintosh-themed jewelry and gift shop, but it retains his trademark furnishings, including high-back chairs with elegant lines and subtle curves. The St. Andrew's Platter is an exquisite selection of trout, salmon, and prawns. Scottish and Continental breakfasts are available throughout the day, and the scrambled eggs with salmon is traditional Scots food at its finest. The in-house baker guarantees fresh scones, cakes, and pastries. ⓢ *Average main: £8* ⊠ *217 Sauchiehall St., City Center* ☎ *0141/332–0521* ⊕ *www.willowtearooms.co.uk* ⊙ *No dinner.*

# HARWICH, UNITED KINGDOM (FOR LONDON)

Updated by
Ellin Stein

An urban center since Roman times, London combines streets redolent with history with the vibrant modernity of a world city. If London offered only famous landmarks like the Tower, Big Ben, and St. Paul's Cathedral, it would nevertheless be a top international destination. But it is so much more: the green oases of the parks and squares; a dining scene that encompasses both superstar chefs and affordable restaurants serving cuisines from around the world; and shops and galleries that reflect the city's status as a hotbed of trailblazing style and art. At the same time, London's traditional character remains. Double-decker red buses still trundle around, soldiers in tall bearskin hats still guard Buckingham Palace, the theaters still offer some of the world's best productions, and there is still an abundance of museums containing incomparable collections. Far from being a monument to the past, London is constantly growing and changing. Harwich is now commonly used as the point of embarkation for many ships that use "London" as a base.

## ESSENTIALS

### CURRENCY

The British pound sterling. ATMs are common and credit cards are widely accepted.

### HOURS

Museums are open daily during normal business hours and some evenings, while shops usually open from 9 until 5:30 or 6. Many are open on Sunday.

### TELEPHONES

Dual-band GSM phones work in the United Kingdom. You can buy prepaid phone cards at telecom shops and news vendors in all towns and cities. Phone cards can be used for local or international calls. Vodafone, T-Mobile, Virgin, and Orange are the leading telecom companies.

### COMING ASHORE

Vessels dock in the commercial port at Harwich, which is small but busy with commercial and ferry traffic. Port amenities include a mainline train station for transfers into London, a café, bar, ATMs, and an exchange bureau.

When larger cruise ships dock, the port schedules extra trains between Harwich International station (*not* Harwich Town) and Liverpool Street station in London. The journey time for these and normal weekday trains is 80 minutes. On weekends, one change is required, and the journey is one hour 45 minutes. Ticket prices are around £19 roundtrip. Taxi (private hire or minicab) transfer to London is prohibitively expensive at around £160 or more.

### GETTING TO THE AIRPORT

If you do not purchase airport transfers from your cruise line there are several ways to reach the Heathrow airport from the cruise port. The easiest but costliest way would be to book a private direct tranfer by taxi or private hire company. Costs are around £170, but this covers from one to three people traveling in the same vehicle. Depending on traffic conditions, the transfer should be around one hour.

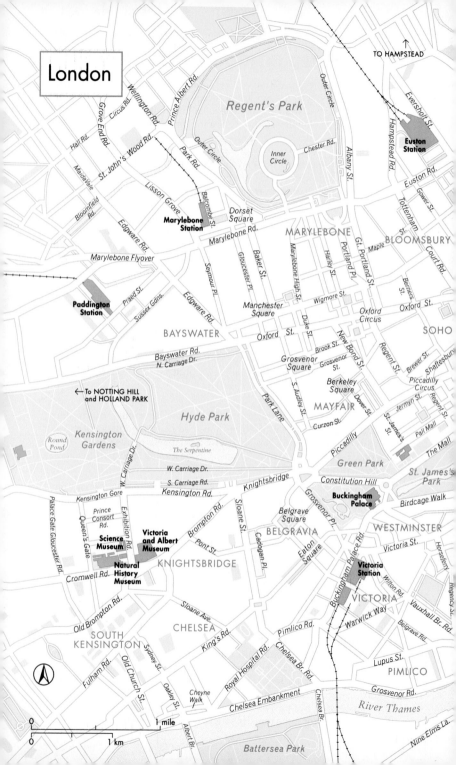

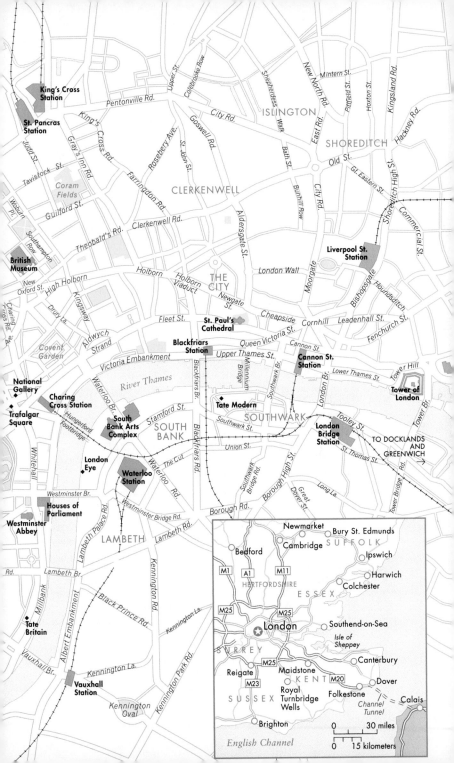

There are several public transport options, but each of these involves a transfer between rail and Underground stations within London, which may not be practical if you have bulky luggage. Once at Liverpool Street station, it's generally best to transfer to your chosen mode of transport to take you from central London to Heathrow airport unless you take a transfer offered by your cruise line direct to the airport.

The least expensive option is the London Underground, but carraiges can be busy with little luggage space. From Liverpool Street take the Hammersmith and City line to King's Cross. From King's Cross the Piccadily line takes you directly to Heathrow. The time for the journey is around 1:20 hours and costs £5.30.

Aimed more at travelers than commuters, Heathrow Express offers a much quicker journey, 15 minutes from Paddington Station to Heathrow. To reach Paddington, take the Hammersmith and City line from Liverpool Street. Heathrow Express tickets cost £18 one-way.

The Heathrow Connect train links Paddington with Heathrow airport, stopping at selected minor stations along the 30-minute route. Prices are £8.50 one-way.

Contacts **Cruise Transfer.com.** ☎ *0800/043–2752, 888/556–8616 from U.S.* ⊕ *www.cruisetransfer.com.* **Prompt Airport Cars.** ☎ *020/3384–4659* ⊕ *www.promptexecutivehire.co.uk.* **Airport Express.** ☎ *0800/783–7899, 07702/787–600 from U.S.* ⊕ *www.aidg.co.uk.*

---

## LONDON BEST BETS

**Buckingham Palace.** A prime chance to catch sight of British royalty.

**The British Museum.** One of the world's richest historical and archaeological collections, and it's completely free.

**The Tower of London.** Experience the city's rich history, from dirty deeds to the dazzling Crown Jewels.

---

## EXPLORING LONDON

Fodor's Choice
★

**British Museum.** With a facade like a great temple, this celebrated treasure house, filled with plunder of incalculable value and beauty from around the globe, occupies an immense Greco-Victorian building that makes a suitably grand impression. Inside are some of the greatest relics of humankind: the Parthenon Sculptures (Elgin Marbles), the Rosetta Stone, the Sutton Hoo Treasure—almost everything, it seems, but the Ark of the Covenant. The three rooms that comprise the **Sainsbury African Galleries** are a must-see in the Lower Gallery—together they present 200,000 objects, highlighting such ancient kingdoms as the Benin and Asante. The museum's focal point is the **Great Court**, a brilliant modern design with a vast glass roof that reveals the museum's covered courtyard. The revered **Reading Room** has a blue-and-gold dome and hosts temporary exhibitions. If you want to navigate the highlights of the almost 100 galleries, join the free **eyeOpener** 30- to 40-minute tours by museum guides (details at the information desk).

The collection's greatest hits include the **Rosetta Stone,** found by French soldiers in 1799, and carved in 196 BC by decree of Ptolemy V in Egyptian hieroglyphics, demotic (a cursive script developed in Egypt), and Greek. Maybe the **Parthenon Sculptures** should be back in Greece, but while the debate rages on, you can steal your own moment with the Elgin Marbles. Also in the West Wing is one of the Seven Wonders of the Ancient World—in fragment form: the **Mausoleum of Halikarnassos.** Upstairs are some of the most popular galleries, especially beloved by children, are the **Egyptian mummies.** Nearby are the glittering 4th-century **Mildenhall Treasure** and the equally splendid 8th-century Anglo-Saxon **Sutton Hoo Treasure** (with magnificent helmets and jewelry). ⊠ *Great Russell St., Bloomsbury* ☎ *020/7323–8000* ⊕ *www.britishmuseum.org* ✉ *Free; donations encouraged* ⊙ *Galleries Sat.–Thurs. 10–5:30, Fri. 10–8:30. Great Court Sat.–Thurs. 9–6, Fri. 9 – 8.30* Ⓜ *Russell Square, Holborn, Tottenham Court Rd.*

**Fodor's Choice** ★ **Buckingham Palace.** It's rare to get a chance to see how the other half—well, other minute fraction—lives and works. But when the Queen heads off to Scotland on her annual summer holiday (you can tell because the Union Jack flies above the palace instead of the Royal Standard), the palace's 19 State Rooms open up to visitors (although the north wing's private apartments remain behind closed doors). With fabulous gilt moldings and walls adorned with masterpieces by Rembrandt, Rubens, and other old masters, the State Rooms are the grandest of the palace's 775 rooms. The **Changing the Guard,** also known as **Guard Mounting,** remains one of London's best free shows and culminates in front of the palace. ⊠ *Buckingham Palace Rd., St. James* ☎ *020/7766–7300* ⊕ *www.royalcollection.org.uk* ✉ *£18* ⊙ *Aug.–late Sept., daily 9:45–6 (last admission 3:45); times subject to change; book ahead for disabled access; check website before visiting* Ⓜ *Victoria, St. James's Park, Green Park.*

**Houses of Parliament.** If you want to understand some of the centuries-old traditions and arcane idiosyncrasies that make up constitution-less British parliamentary democracy, the Palace of Westminster, as the complex is still properly called, is the place to come. The architecture in this 1,100-room labyrinth impresses, but the real excitement lies in stalking the corridors of power. A palace was first established on this site by Edward the Confessor in the 11th century. William II started building a new palace in 1087, and this gradually became the seat of English administrative power. However, fire destroyed most of the palace in 1834, and the current complex dates largely from the middle of the 19th century.

Visitors aren't allowed to snoop too much, but the **Visitors' Galleries** of the House of Commons do afford a view of democracy in process when the banks of green-leather benches are filled by opposing MPs (members of Parliament). When they speak, it's not directly to each other but through the Speaker, who also decides who will get time on the floor. After the 1834 fire, the **Clock Tower** was completed in 1858, and contains the 13-ton bell known as **Big Ben.** At the southwest end of the main Parliament building is the 323-foot-high Victoria Tower. ⊠ *St. Stephen's Entrance, St. Margaret St., Westminster*

☎ *020/7219–4272, 0844/847–1672* ⊕ *www.parliament.uk/visiting*
🎫 *Free; £15 tours (must book ahead)* ☉ *Call to confirm hrs for Visitors Galleries. Tours: Aug., Mon., Tues., Fri., Sat. 9.15–4.30, Wed. and Thurs. 1.15–4.30; Sept., Mon., Fri., Sat. 9.15–4.30, Tues., Wed., Thurs. 1.15–4.30* Ⓜ *Westminster.*

★
☾ **London Eye.** To mark the start of the new millennium, architects David Marks and Julia Barfield conceived a beautiful and celebratory structure that would allow people to see this great city from a completely new perspective. They came up with a giant Ferris wheel, which, as well as representing the turn of the century, would also be a symbol of regeneration. The London Eye is the largest cantilevered observation wheel ever built and among the tallest structures in London. The 25-minute slow-motion ride inside one of the enclosed passenger capsules is so smooth you'd hardly know you were suspended over the Thames. On a clear day you can see for up to 25 miles, with a bird's-eye view over London's most famous landmarks as you circle through 360 degrees. If you're looking for a special place to celebrate, champagne and canapés can be arranged ahead of time. ■ TIP→ **Buy your ticket online to avoid the long lines and get a 10% discount. For an extra £10, you can save even more time with a Fast Track flight for which you check in 15 minutes before your "departure."** You can buy a combination ticket for the Eye and other London attractions—check online for details—or board the London Eye River Cruise here for a 40-minute sightseeing voyage on the Thames. ⊠ *Riverside Building, County Hall, Westminster Bridge Rd., South Bank* ☎ *0870/990–8883* ⊕ *www.londoneye.com* 🎫 *£18.60; cruise £12* ☉ *June and Sept., daily 10–9; July and Aug., daily 10–9:30; Oct.–Mar., daily 10–8:30* Ⓜ *Waterloo.*

Fodor's Choice
★
☾ **National Gallery.** Standing proudly on the north side of Trafalgar Square is one of the world's supreme art collections, with more than 2,300 masterpieces on show. Picasso, van Gogh, Michelangelo, Leonardo, Monet, Turner, and more—all for free. Watch our special temporary exhibitions as well.

This brief selection is your jumping-off point, but there are hundreds of other paintings to see, enough to fill a full day. In chronological order: (1) **Van Eyck** (circa 1395–1441), *The Arnolfini Portrait*—a solemn couple holds hands, the fish-eye mirror behind them mysteriously illuminating what can't be seen from the front view. (2) **Holbein** (1497–1543), *The Ambassadors*—two wealthy visitors from France stand surrounded by what were considered luxury goods at the time. Note the elongated skull at the bottom of the painting, which takes shape when viewed from an angle. (3) **Leonardo da Vinci** (1452–1519), *The Virgin and Child*—this exquisite black-chalk "Burlington Cartoon" depicts the master's most haunting Mary. (4) **Velazquez** (1599–1660), *Christ in the House of Martha and Mary*—in this enigmatic masterpiece the Spaniard plays with perspective and the role of the viewer. (5) **Turner** (1775–1851), *Rain, Steam and Speed: The Great Western Railway*, the whirl of rain, mist, steam, and locomotion is nothing short of astonishing (spot the hare). (6) **Caravaggio** (1573–1610), *The Supper at Emmaus* —a cinematically lightened, freshly resurrected Christ blesses bread in an astonishingly domestic vision from the master of chiaroscuro. (7) **Van Gogh** (1853–1890), *Sunflowers* — painted during his sojourn with Gauguin in Arles, this is quintessential Van Gogh. (8) **Seurat** (1859–91), *Bathers at Asnières*—this static summer day's idyll is one of the pointillist extraordinaire's best-known works. ⊠ *Trafalgar Square, Westminster* ☎ *020/7747–2885* ⊕ *www.nationalgallery.org.uk* ✉ *Free; charge for special exhibitions; audio guide £3.50* ⊗ *Sun.–Thurs. 10–6, Fri. 10–9* Ⓜ *Charing Cross, Embankment, Leicester Square.*

**Fodor's Choice** ★ **St. Paul's Cathedral.** St. Paul's is simply breathtaking. The structure is Sir Christopher Wren's masterpiece, completed in 1710 after 35 years of building, and, much later, miraculously spared (mostly) by World War II bombs. Wren's first plan, known as the New Model, did not make it past the drawing board. The second, known as the Great Model, got as far as the 20-foot oak rendering before it also was rejected. You can see it displayed in the Trophy Room. The third plan was accepted, with the fortunate proviso that the architect be allowed to make changes as he saw fit. Without that, there would be no dome, because the approved design had a steeple—and St. Paul's simply would not be St. Paul's as we know it without the dome, the third largest in the world and easily recognizable on the skyline from many an angle around London. Up 163 spiral steps is the **Whispering Gallery,** an acoustic phenomenon; you whisper something to the wall on one side, and a second later it transmits clearly to the other side, 107 feet away. Behind the high altar is the **American Memorial Chapel,** dedicated to the 28,000 GIs stationed in the United Kingdom who lost their lives in World War II. Among the famous figures whose remains lie in the **Crypt** are the Duke of Wellington and Admiral Lord Nelson. The Crypt also has a gift shop and a café. ⊠ *St. Paul's Churchyard, The City* ☎ *020/7236–4128* ⊕ *www.stpauls.co.uk* ✉ *£15 (includes multimedia guides and guided tours)* ⊗ *Cathedral Mon.–Sat. 8:30–4; Shop Mon.–Sat. 9–5, Sun. 10–5; Crypt Café Mon.–Sat. 9–5, Sun. noon–4* Ⓜ *St. Paul's.*

**Fodor's Choice** ★ ☾ **Tate Britain.** The stately neoclassical institution may not be as ambitious as its sibling Tate Modern on the South Bank, but Tate Britain's bright galleries lure only a fraction of the Modern's crowds and are a great place to explore British art from 1500 to the present. First opened in 1897, funded by the sugar magnate Sir Henry Tate, the museum includes the Linbury Galleries on the lower floors, which stage temporary (and often popular) exhibitions, whereas the upper floors show the permanent collection. Pictures are regularly re-hung and whatever is on view, you can find classic works by John Constable, Thomas Gainsborough, George Stubbs, David Wilkie, Francis Bacon, Duncan Grant, Barbara Hepworth, and Ben Nicholson and an outstanding display from J.M.W. Turner in the Clore Gallery, including many later vaporous and light-infused works such as *Sunrise with Sea Monsters*. Sumptuous Pre-Raphaelite pieces are a major drawcard while the Contemporary British Art galleries bring you face to face with Damien Hirst's *Away from the Flock* and other recent conceptions. The Tate Britain also hosts the annual Turner Prize exhibition, with its accompanying furor over the state of contemporary art, from about October to January each year. ⊠ *Millbank, Westminster* ☎ *020/7887–8888* ⊕ *www.tate.org.uk/britain*

6

⊡ *Free, special exhibitions £9–£15; Tate-to-Tate shuttle £5 each way; River Roamer ticket £12.60* ⊘ *Sat.–Thurs. 10–6 (last entry at 5.15), Fri. 10–10 (last entry at 9:15)* Ⓜ *Pimlico (signposted 5-min walk).*

**Fodor's Choice**
★
Ⓒ
**Tate Modern.** This spectacular renovation of a mid-20th-century power station is the most-visited museum of modern art in the world. Its great permanent collection, which starts in 1900 and ranges from modern masters like Matisse to the most cutting-edge contemporary artists, is arranged thematically—Landscape, Still Life, and the Nude. Its block-buster temporary exhibitions showcase the work of individual artists like Gaugin, Warhol, and Gerhard Richter. The vast **Turbine Hall** is a dramatic entrance point used to showcase big, audacious installations that tend to generate a lot of publicity. Past highlights include Olafur Eliasson's massive glowing sun and Carsten Holler's huge metal slides. ⊠ *Bankside, South Bank* ☎ *020/7887–8888* ⊕ *www.tate.org.uk/modern* ⊡ *Free, charge for special exhibitions* ⊘ *Sun.–Thurs. 10–6, Fri. and Sat. 10–10 (last admission to exhibitions 45 min before close)* Ⓜ *Southwark, Mansion House, St. Paul's.*

**Fodor's Choice**
★
**Tower of London.** Nowhere else does London's history come to life so vividly as it does in this minicity of 20 towers filled with heraldry and treasure, the intimate details of lords and dukes and princes and sovereigns etched in the walls (literally, in some places), and quite a few pints of royal blood spilled on the stones. This is one of Britain's most popular sights—the Crown Jewels are here—and you can avoid lines by buying a ticket in advance on the website, by phone, at any tube station, or from the automatic kiosks on arrival. The visitor center provides an introduction to the Tower. Allow at least three hours for exploring, and take time to stroll along the battlements for a wonderful overview. The Crown Jewels are worth the wait, the White Tower is essential, and the Medieval Palace and Bloody Tower should at least be breezed through. ⊠ *H. M. Tower of London, Tower Hill, The City* ☎ *0844/482–7777, 0844/482–7799* ⊕ *www.hrp.org.uk* ⊡ *£19* ⊘ *Mar.–Oct., Tues.–Sat. 9–5:30, Sun. and Mon. 10–5:30; last admission at 5. Nov.–Feb., Tues.–Sat. 9–4:30, Sun. and Mon. 10–4:30; last admission at 4* Ⓜ *Tower Hill.*

**Trafalgar Square.** This is literally the center of London: a plaque on the corner of the Strand and Charing Cross Road marks the spot from which distances on U.K. signposts are measured. **Nelson's Column** stands at the heart of the square (which is named after the great admiral's most important victory), guarded by haughty lions designed by Sir Edwin Landseer and flanked by statues of two generals who helped establish the British Empire in India, **Charles Napier** and **Henry Havelock**. The fourth plinth is given over to rotating works by contemporary sculptors. Great events, such as New Year's Eve celebrations, political protests, and sporting triumphs always see the crowds gathering in the city's most famous square. Although Trafalgar Square is known to Chinese tourists as Pigeon Square, feeding the birds is now banned and the gray flocks have flown. ⊠ *Trafalgar Sq., Westminster* Ⓜ *Charing Cross.*

**Fodor's Choice** **Westminster Abbey.** A monument to the nation's rich—and often bloody
★ and scandalous—history, the abbey rises on the Thames skyline as
one of London's most iconic sites. The mysterious gloom of the lofty
medieval interior is home to more than 600 statues, tombs, and com-
memorative tablets. About 3,300 people, from kings to composers to
wordsmiths, are buried in the abbey. It has been the scene of 16 royal
weddings and no fewer than 38 coronations—the first in 1066, when
William the Conqueror was made king here.

There's only one way around the abbey, and as there will almost certainly be a long stream of shuffling tourists at your heels, you'll need
to be alert to catch the highlights. Enter by the north door then turn
around and look up to see the **painted-glass rose window,** the largest
of its kind. Step into the small Chapel of St. Michael, where a tomb
effigy of Joseph Gascoigne Nightingale fights off a sheet-draped figure
of death. Next enter the adjacent Tomb of St. John the Baptist past a
lovely statue of the Virgin Mary and child.

As you walk east toward the apse you'll see the **Coronation Chair,** at
the foot of the Henry VII Chapel, which has been briefly graced by
nearly every regal posterior since Edward I ordered it in 1301. Continue
through the South Ambulatory to the **Chapel of St. Edward the Confessor,** which contains the shrine to the pre-Norman king. Because of its
great age, you must join one of the vergers' tours to be admitted to the
chapel (details available at the admission desk; there is a small charge),
or attend Holy Communion within the shrine on Tuesdays at 8 am). To
the left, you'll find **Poets' Corner.** Geoffrey Chaucer was the first poet to
be buried here in 1400, and other statues and memorials include those
to William Shakespeare, D.H. Lawrence, T.S. Eliot, and Dylan Thomas
as well as non-poets, Laurence Olivier and George Frederick Handel
among them; look out for the 700-year old frescoes. ⊠ *Broad Sanctuary,
Westminster* ☎ *020/7222–5152* ⊕ *www.westminster-abbey.org* ✉ *Abbey and museum, £15 adults; children under 11 free if accompanied by
adult; free audio tour* ⊙ *Abbey, weekdays 9:30–3:30; closes 1 hr after
last admission. Museum, daily 10:30–4; Cloisters, daily 8–6; College
Garde, Apr.–Sept., Tues.–Thurs. 10–6; Oct.–Mar., Tues.–Thurs. 10–4.
Chapter House, daily 10–4; services may cause changes to hrs, so call
ahead* Ⓜ *Westminster.*

6

## SHOPPING

Napoléon was being scornful when he called Britain a nation of shopkeepers, but Londoners have had the last laugh, as the city has become
a leading international shopping destination. You can shop like royalty
at the Duchess of Cambridge's favorite boutique, discover unusual silver spoons in an antiques shop, or find an early edition of Wuthering
Heights on Charing Cross Road. If your time is limited, head for one of
the city's grand department stores, such as Selfridges or Liberty, where
you can find enough booty for your entire gift list.

The main shopping drags are Regent Street (upscale) and Oxford Street
(mass-market). Knightsbridge and Bond Street are for top international
designers, Hoxton and Shoreditch for young edgy ones. Chelsea has

fashionable boutiques plus home furnishings stores, Covent Garden quirky shoe stores.

Fodor'sChoice  **Fortnum & Mason.** Although popularly known as the Queen's grocer,
★  and the impeccably mannered staff wear traditional tailcoats, F&M's food hall stocks gifts for all budgets, such as loads of irresistibly packaged luxury foods stamped with the gold "By Appointment" crest for less than £5. Try the teas, preserves (unusual products include rose-petal jelly), condiments, chocolate, tins of pâté, or Gentleman's Relish (anchovy paste). The store's famous hampers are always a welcome gift. The gleaming food hall spans two floors and includes a sleek wine bar designed by David Collins, with the rest of the store devoted to upscale homewares, men and women's gifts, toiletries, and accessories, women's jewelry and cosmetics, and clothing and toys for children. If you start to flag, break for afternoon tea at one of the four other restaurants (one's an indulgent ice-cream parlor)—or a treatment in the Beauty Rooms. ⊠ *181 Piccadilly, St. James's* ☎ *020/7734–8040* ⊕ *www. fortnumandmason.com* Ⓜ *Green Park.*

★  **Harrods.** With an encyclopedic assortment of luxury brands, this Knightsbridge institution has more than 300 departments and 20 restaurants, all spread over 1 million square feet on a 5-acre site. If you approach Harrods as a tourist attraction rather than as a fashion hunting ground, you won't be disappointed. Focus on the spectacular food halls, the huge ground-floor perfumery, the marble-lined accessory rooms, the excellent Urban Retreat spa, and the Vegas-like Egyptian Room. At the bottom of the nearby Egyptian escalator, there's a bronze statue depicting the late Princess Diana and Dodi Fayed, son of the former owner, dancing beneath the wings of an albatross. Nevertheless, standards of taste are enforced with a customer dress code (no shorts, ripped jeans, or flip-flops). ■ TIP→ **Be prepared to brave the crowds (avoid visiting on a Saturday if you can), and be prepared to pay if you want to use the bathroom on some floors(!).** ⊠ *87–135 Brompton Rd., Knightsbridge* ☎ *020/7730–1234* ⊕ *www.harrods.com* Ⓜ *Knightsbridge.*

## WHERE TO EAT

$$$  ✕ **Medlar.** What's there *not* to like about Medlar? Sensationally assured
MODERN  Modern European cuisine, effortless service and elegant oak-wood
EUROPEAN  floors, mirrored walls, and a luxe gray/lime-green stenciled color scheme make for a complete neighborhood package at the quieter World's End stretch of the King's Road. Set lunch is a steal at £25, where you'll find such winners as crab ravioli with fondant leeks and samphire, rabbit with red onion marmalade, or fillet steak with snails and triple-cooked chips. Desserts—like pear and frangipane tart and clotted cream—couldn't be more delicious. ⑤ *Average main: £22* ⊠ *438 King's Rd., Chelsea* ☎ *020/7349–1900* ⊕ *www.medlarrestaurant.co.uk* ⚇ *Reservations essential* Ⓜ *Fulham Broadway, Sloane Sq.*

$$  ✕ **The Riding House Café.** Stuffed squirrel lamp holders peer down on
BURGER  trendy diners at this groovy New York–style small-plates-and-deluxe-burgers all-dayer just north of Oxford Circus. Everything's reclaimed, salvaged, or bespoke, so you'll find stuffed birds and taxidermy dotted

around, reclaimed blue theater seats at the counter bar, bright orange leather banquettes, or old snooker table legs holding up your dining table. Opt for a £5 small plate of sea bass ceviche with lime and chili, and head straight for the poached-egg chorizo hash browns or a mighty decadent foie gras hamburger, with gherkin and chips—a bargain at £13.90. $ *Average main: £14* ✉ *43 Great Titchfield St., Noho* ☎ *020/7927* ⊕ *www.ridinghousecafe.co.uk* ⊸ *Reservations essential* Ⓜ *Oxford Circus.*

## WHERE TO STAY

**$$**
B&B/INN
🏠 **B&B Belgravia.** At this modern guesthouse near Victoria Station, a clean, chic white color scheme, simple modern furniture, and a lounge where a fire crackles away in the winter are all geared to stylish comfort. **Pros:** nice extras like free use of a laptop in the hotel lounge; coffee and tea always available. **Cons:** bathrooms and rooms are small; unimaginative breakfasts; can be noisy, especially on lower floors. $ *Rooms from: £135* ✉ *64–66 Ebury St., Victoria* ☎ *020/7259–8570* ⊕ *www. bb-belgravia.com* ⊸ *17 rooms* ¶◎¶ *Breakfast* Ⓜ *Knightsbridge.*

**$$$**
HOTEL
🏠 **Charlotte Street Hotel.** Modern flair and the traditional are fused with real style in public spaces and bedrooms beautifully decorated with unique printed fabrics from designer Kit Kemp; bathrooms are truly impressive, lined with gleaming granite and oak—with walk-in showers and flat-screen TVs, so you can catch up on the news while you soak in the deep baths. **Pros:** elegant, luxurious; great attention to detail. **Cons:** the popular bar can be noisy; reservations are necessary for the restaurant. $ *Rooms from: £288* ✉ *15 Charlotte St., Bloomsbury* ☎ *020/7806–2000, 800/553–6674 in U.S.* ⊕ *www.charlottestreethotel. com* ⊸ *46 rooms, 6 suites* Ⓜ *Goodge St.*

**$$$**
HOTEL
🏠 **Millennium Gloucester.** Although the sleek lobby, with polished wood columns, a warming fireplace, and glittering chandeliers, is quite opulent, guest rooms have a traditionally masculine look, done in neutral creams and earth tones and furnished with blond-wood desks and leather chairs. **Pros:** good deals available if you book in advance. **Cons:** lighting in some bedrooms is a bit too subtle; bathrooms are relatively small but have all you need; public areas and restaurant can get crowded. $ *Rooms from: £145* ✉ *4–18 Harrington Gardens, Kensington* ☎ *020/7373–6030* ⊕ *www.millenniumhotels.co.uk/ millenniumgloucester* ⊸ *143 rooms* ¶◎¶ *Breakfast* Ⓜ *Gloucester Rd.*

6

# INVERGORDON, SCOTLAND

Updated by Mike Gonzalez

The port of Invergordon is your gateway to the Great Glen, an area of Scotland that includes Loch Ness and the city of Inverness. Inverness, the capital of the Highlands, has the flavor of a Lowland town, its winds blowing in a sea-salt air from the Moray Firth. The Great Glen is also home to one of the world's most famous monster myths: in 1933, during a quiet news week, the editor of a local paper decided to run a story about a strange sighting of something splashing about in Loch Ness. But there's more to look for here besides Nessie, including

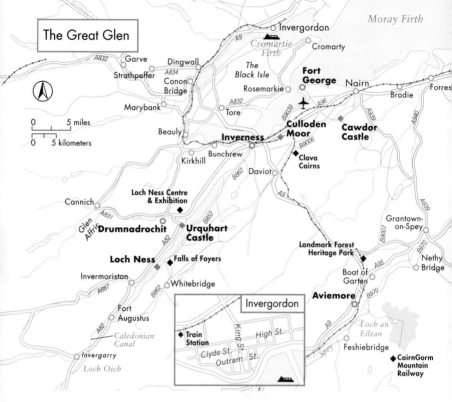

inland lochs, craggy and steep-sided mountains, rugged promontories, deep inlets, brilliant purple and emerald moorland, and forests filled with astonishingly varied wildlife, including mountain hares, red deer, golden eagles, and ospreys.

## ESSENTIALS

### CURRENCY

The British pound sterling. ATMs are common and credit cards are widely accepted.

### HOURS

Museums are open from 9 until 5, while shops usually open from 9 until 5:30 or 6. Shops are open on Sunday.

### PRIVATE TOURS

Around Lochness (⊕ *www.aroundlochness.com* ☎ *01456/486675*) and Montains to Sea (⊕ *www.mountains2sea.co.uk* ☎ *07826/688871*) arrange tours of the area from Invergordon. From Inverness, tours run regularly to and around Loch Ness. They are run by the Jacobite Experience (⊕ *www.jacobite.co.uk* ☎ *01463/233999*). They have their own bus services to collect you from Inverness. Prices vary according to the length of tour. It is advisable to book these tours ahead. Jacobite also runs a combined tour of Inverness and Loch Ness.

There are hop on/hop off bus tours of Inverness (tickets £10) and a bus tour combining the city tour with Loch Ness (tickets £21). You can get information from the visitor center.

**Contacts Around Lochness.** ☎ *01456/486675* ⊕ *www.aroundlochness.com.* **Montains To Sea.** ☎ *07826/688871* ⊕ *www.mountains2sea.co.uk.* **The Jacobite Experience.** ☎ *01463/233999* ⊕ *www.jacobite.co.uk.*

### TELEPHONES

Dual-band GSM phones work in the United Kingdom. You can buy prepaid phone cards at telecom shops and news vendors in all towns and cities. Phone cards can be used for local or international calls. Vodafone, T-Mobile, Virgin, and Orange are the leading telecom companies.

> ### GREAT GLEN BEST BETS
>
> **Monster hunting at Loch Ness.** Even though numerous scientific studies have failed to prove the existence of Scotland's most famous monster, you're sure to be on the lookout, just in case he makes an appearance.
>
> **Urquhart Castle.** A sublime setting on the banks of Loch Ness makes Urquhart one of the world's most romantic and wistful fortresses.
>
> **Aviemore.** The rugged landscapes of the Cairngorm Mountains contrast sharply with the verdant lowland glens; a mountain train takes the strain, so you don't need to work up a sweat.

### COMING ASHORE

There is no dedicated cruise terminal at Invergordon. Ships dock at one of the town quays—usually Admiralty Quay, the closest to the town. At the pier there is a tourist information kiosk manned only when ships are in dock.

Passengers can walk into the center of Invergordon for public transportation to surrounding sights. The X99 bus goes directly to Inverness. Scotrail trains connect with Inverness to the south and Dornoch to the north. The Invergordon railway station is 1 km (½ mile) from the port.

A car is a great asset for exploring the Great Glen, especially since the best of the area is away from the main roads. You can use the main A82 from Inverness to Fort William, or use the smaller B862/B852 roads (former military roads) to explore the much quieter east side of Loch Ness.

Taxis do not meet the ships as a matter of course.

## EXPLORING INVERGORDON AND THE GREAT GLEN

### INVERNESS

Inverness seems designed for the tourist, with its banks, souvenirs, high-quality woolens, and well-equipped visitor center. Compared with other Scottish towns, however, Inverness has less to offer visitors who have a keen interest in Scottish history. Throughout its past, Inverness was burned and ravaged by the restive Highland clans competing for dominance in the region. Thus, a decorative wall panel here and a fragment of tower there are all that remain amid the modern shopping facilities and 19th-century downtown developments. The town does make a good base, however, for exploring the northern end of the Great Glen.

**Inverness Castle.** One of Inverness's few historic landmarks is reddish sandstone Inverness Castle (now the local Sheriff Court), nestled above the river off Castle Road on Castle Hill. The current structure is Victorian, built after a former fort was blown up by the Jacobites in the 1745 campaign.

Ⓒ **Inverness Museum and Art Gallery.** The excellent, although small, Inverness Museum and Art Gallery covers archaeology, art, local history, and the natural environment in its lively displays. ⊠ *Castle Wynd* ☎ *01463/237114* ⊕ *www.invernessmuseum.com* ☒ *Free* ☉ *Tues.–Sat. 10–5.*

## CULLODEN MOOR

★ **Culloden Moor.** Culloden was the scene of the last major battle fought on British soil—to this day considered one of the most infamous and tragic of all. Here, on a cold April day in 1746, the outnumbered, fatigued Jacobite forces of Bonnie Prince Charlie were destroyed by the superior firepower of George II's army. The victorious commander, the duke of Cumberland (George II's son), earned the name of the "Butcher" of Cumberland for the bloody reprisals carried out by his men on Highland families, Jacobite or not, caught in the vicinity. In the battle itself, the duke's army—greatly outnumbering the Scots— killed more than 1,000 soldiers. The National Trust for Scotland has re-created a slightly eerie version of the battlefield as it looked in 1746 that you can explore with a guided audio tour. An innovative visitor center enables you to get closer to the sights and sounds of the battle and to interact with the characters involved. Academic research and technology have helped re-create the Gaelic dialect, song, and music of the time. The excellent on-site café serves homemade soups, sandwiches, and cakes. ⊠ *B9006, Culloden* ☎ *0844/4932159* ⊕ *www.nts. org.uk/Culloden* ☒ *£10* ☉ *Nov–Mar, daily 10–4; Apr.–Oct., daily 9–6; last entry half hr before closing.*

## FORT GEORGE

★ **Fort George.** As a direct result of the battle at Culloden, the nervous government in London ordered the construction of a large fort on a promontory reaching into the Moray Firth: Fort George was started in 1748 and completed some 20 years later. It's perhaps the best-preserved 18th-century military fortification in Europe. A visitor center and tableaux at the fort portray the 18th-century Scottish soldier's way of life. The fort is 14 miles northeast of Iverness. ⊠ *Off B9006, Ardersier* ☎ *01667/460232* ⊕ *www.historic-scotland.gov.uk* ☒ *£6.90* ☉ *Apr.– Sept., daily 9:30–5; Oct.–Mar., daily 10–4; last admission 45 mins before closing.*

## CAWDOR CASTLE

Fodor'sChoice **Cawdor Castle.** Shakespeare's (1564–1616) *Macbeth* was Thane of Caw-
★ dor, but the sense of history that exists within the turreted walls of
Ⓒ Cawdor Castle is more than fictional. Cawdor is a lived-in castle, not an abandoned, decaying structure. The earliest part of the castle is the 14th-century central tower; the rooms contain family portraits,

tapestries, fine furniture, and paraphernalia reflecting 600 years of history. Outside the castle walls are sheltered gardens and woodland walks. Children will have a ball exploring the lush and mysterious Big Wood, with its wildflowers and varied wildlife. There are lots of creepy stories and fantastic tales amid the dank dungeons and drawbridges. If you like it here, the estate has cottages to rent. ⊠ *B9090, 5 miles southwest of Nairn, Cawdor* ☎ *01667/404401* ⊕ *www.cawdorcastle.com* ⊠ *Grounds £5.50; castle £9.50* ⊙ *May–mid-Oct., daily 10–5.*

## LOCH NESS EXHIBITION CENTRE

☺ **Loch Ness Centre & Exhibition.** If you're in search of the infamous beast Nessie, head to the Loch Ness Centre & Exhibition, which explores the facts and the fakes, the photographs, the unexplained sonar contacts, and the sincere testimony of eyewitnesses. You'll have to make up your own mind on Nessie. All that's really known is that Loch Ness's huge volume of water has a warming effect on the local weather, making the loch conducive to mirages in still, warm conditions. Whether or not the *bestia aquatilis* lurks in the depths is more than ever in doubt since 1994, when the man who took one of the most convincing photos of Nessie confessed on his deathbed that it was a fake. You can take a cruise of the loch from the center, too. ⊠ *A82, Drumnadrochit* ☎ *01456/450573* ⊕ *www.lochness.com* ⊠ *£6.50* ⊙ *Easter–May, Sept., and Oct., daily 9:30–5; June, 9–5:30; July and Aug., daily 9–6; Nov.–Easter, daily 10–3:30; last admission ½ hr before closing.*

## URQUHART CASTLE

**Urquhart Castle.** About 2 miles southeast of Drumnadrochit, this castle is a favorite Loch Ness monster–watching spot. This romantically broken-down fortress stands on a promontory overlooking the loch, as it has since the Middle Ages. Because of its central and strategic position in the Great Glen line of communication, the castle has a complex history involving military offense and defense, as well as its own destruction and renovation. The castle was begun in the 13th century and was destroyed before the end of the 17th century to prevent its use by the Jacobites. The ruins of what was one of the largest castles in Scotland were then plundered for building material. A visitor center relates these events and gives an idea of what life was like here in medieval times. ⊠ *A82, Drumnadrochit* ☎ *01456/450551* ⊕ *www.historic-scotland. gov.uk/places* ⊠ *£7.20* ⊙ *Apr.–Sept., daily 9:30–6; Oct., 9:30–5; Nov.–Mar., daily 9:30–4:30; last admission 45 mins before closing.*

## LOCH NESS

**Loch Ness.** From the A82 you get many views of the formidable and famous Loch Ness, which has a greater volume of water than any other Scottish loch, a maximum depth of more than 800 feet, and its own monster—at least according to popular myth. Early travelers who passed this way included English lexicographer Dr. Samuel Johnson (1709–84) and his guide and biographer, James Boswell (1740–95), who were on their way to the Hebrides in 1783. They remarked at the time about the poor condition of the population and the squalor of their homes. Another early travel writer and naturalist, Thomas Pennant (1726–98), noted that the loch kept the locality frost-free in winter. Even General Wade came here, his troops blasting and digging a road up much of the eastern shore. None of these observant early travelers ever made mention of a monster. Clearly, they had not read the local guidebooks.

### AVIEMORE

Once a quiet junction on the Highland Railway, Aviemore now has all the brashness and concrete boxiness of a year-round holiday resort. The Aviemore area is a versatile walking base, but you must be dressed properly and carry emergency safety gear for high-level excursions onto the near-arctic plateau.

★ **Cairngorms National Park.** A rugged wilderness of mountains, moorlands, glens, and lochs, Cairngorms National Park is the country's second-oldest national park. Past Loch Morlich at the high parking lot on the exposed shoulders of the Cairngorm Mountains are dozens of trails for hiking and cycling. The park is especially popular with birding enthusiasts, as it's the best place to see the Scottish crossbill, the only bird unique to Britain. Weather conditions in the park change abruptly, so be sure to have the proper gear or seek out many of the guided options. This is a massive park, but a good place to start exploring is the visitor center in Aviemore. ☎ 01479/873535 ⊕ www.cairngorms.co.uk.

**CairnGorm Mountain Railway.** A funicular railway to the top of Cairn Gorm (the mountain that gives its name to the region), the CairnGorm Mountain Railway operates both during and after the ski season and affords extensive views across the Cairngorms and the broad valley of the Spey. At the top is a visitor center and restaurant. Prebooking is recommended. ✉ B970 ☎ 01479/861261 ⊕ www.cairngormmountain. co.uk ⌨ £9.95 ⊙ Daily 10–4:30.

## SHOPPING

All things "Highland" make the best souvenirs. Tartans and kilts, tweed clothing, and woolen and cashmere knits are made here in the glens. Modern breathable outdoor clothing is also in great abundance. The beauty of the landscape inspires artists and craftspeople, and you'll find their paintings, ceramics, and wooden carved items in markets and specialty shops. Foodies will love the natural smoked salmon.

### INVERNESS

★ **Riverside Gallery.** The Riverside Gallery sells paintings, etchings, and prints of Highland landscapes, as well as abstract and representational contemporary work by Highland artists. ✉ 11 Bank St., Inverness ☎ 01463/224781 ⊕ www.riverside-gallery.co.uk.

**Victorian Market.** Don't miss the atmospheric indoor Victorian Market, built in 1870. It houses more than 40 privately owned specialty shops. ✉ Academy St., Inverness.

## WHERE TO EAT

**$$** ✕ **Riva.** Facing Inverness Castle, Riva has views over the River Ness from
ITALIAN  its window seats. The dining room has subtly lighted deep-red walls lined
with black-and-white photographs of Italian cityscapes. Tasty Italian
dishes include pasta carbonara (with eggs, cream, and bacon), as well as
more unusual concoctions like ravioli *alla granchio* (crab-and–tiger prawn
ravioli on arugula). The service can be inconsistent. $ *Average main: £16*
✉ *4–6 Ness Walk, Inverness* ☎ *01463/237377* ⊘ *No lunch Sun.*

**$$** ✕ **Rocpool Restaurant.** Highly recommended by locals, the Rocpool has
BRASSERIE  a calming mix of dark and light woods and cream and pale mint fur-
nishings. The frequently changing menu may include such favorites
as sweet-pea-and-spinach risotto for lunch and loin of venison with
creamed parsnips and wild mushrooms for dinner. $ *Average main: £18*
✉ *1 Ness Walk, Inverness* ☎ *01463/717274* ⊘ *Closed Sun.*

# LEITH, SCOTLAND (FOR EDINBURGH)

Updated
by Mike
Gonzalez

One of the world's stateliest cities and proudest capitals, Edinburgh is
built—like Rome—on seven hills, making it a striking backdrop for the
ancient pageant of history. In a skyline of sheer drama, Edinburgh Castle
watches over the capital city, frowning down on Princes Street as if disap-
proving of its modern razzmatazz. Nearly everywhere in Edinburgh (the
"-burgh" is always pronounced *burra* in Scotland) there are spectacular
buildings, whose Doric, Ionic, and Corinthian pillars add touches of neoclassical grandeur to the largely Presbyterian backdrop. The city is justly
proud of its gardens, green lungs that bring a sense of release to frenetic
modern life. Conspicuous from Princes Street is Arthur's Seat, a child-size
mountain with steep slopes and little crags, like a miniature Highlands
set down in the middle of the busy city. Appropriately, these theatrical
elements match Edinburgh's character—after all, the city has been a stage
that has seen its fair share of romance, violence, tragedy, and triumph.

6

### ESSENTIALS

#### CURRENCY
The British pound sterling. ATMs are common and credit cards are
widely accepted.

#### HOURS
Museums are open from 9 until 5, while shops usually open from 9
until 5:30 or 6. Shops are open on Sunday.

#### PRIVATE TOURS
Private tours may be difficult to arrange, but there are a number of
city sightseeing tours departing from the street outside Waverley station. There is no need to book these in advance. Tickets are £12. Uncle
Bob's Audio Walking Tours provide downloadableAudio tours for those
wanting to walk the city on their own. Rabbie's Trail Burners run tours
to the area around the city, including a day trip to the Rosslyn Chapel
made famous by Dan Brown.

**Contacts Rabbie's Trail Burners.** ☎ *0131/2263133* ⊕ *www.robbies.com.*
**Uncle Bob's Audio Walking Tours.** ⊕ *www.edinburghtour.com.*

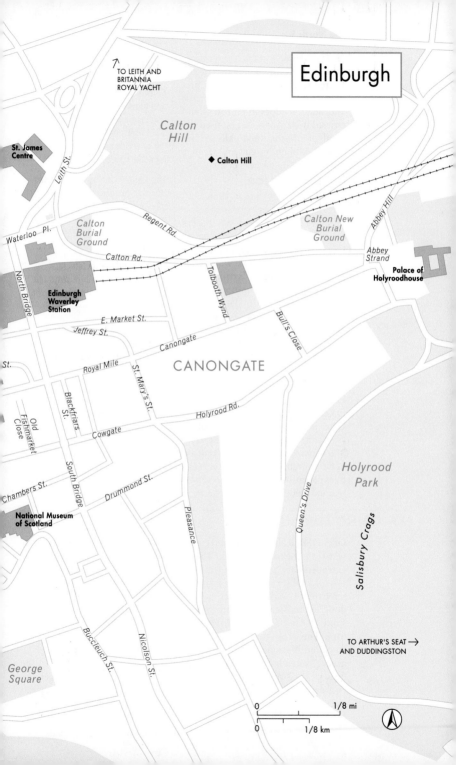

**TELEPHONES**

Dual-band GSM phones work in the United Kingdom. You can buy pre-paid phone cards at telecom shops and news vendors in all towns and cities. Phone cards can be used for local or international calls. Vodafone, T-Mobile, Virgin, and Orange are the leading telecom companies.

## COMING ASHORE

Currently ships larger than 220 meters (720 feet) must anchor offshore at Leith and passengers must be tendered ashore. Smaller ships can dock at the quayside in Leith Town. The whole waterfront area, named Ocean Terminal, has received a multimillion-pound redevelopment since the late 1990s, and significantly more is due to be invested in the years up to 2019; a tram system to link the Leith waterfront to central Edinburgh should be open sometime in 2013. There are few facilities at the passenger terminal itself, but a huge complex of shopping, eating, and entertainment venues sits right outside the door.

From Leith, Buses 11, 22, 34, 35 and 36 make the 15-minute trip to the Princes Street stop in central Edinburgh; one-way fare is £1.20, and a day ticket £3. Taxis are plentiful and wait at the Ocean Terminal taxi line. Costs include an initial charge of £2.50, then £0.25 for every 225 meters (758 feet) until 2 km (1½ miles), after which charges climb to £0.25 per 210 meters (688 feet). Don't rent a car if you plan to spend your port day in Edinburgh, but a car will open up much of the surrounding countryside to exploration if you want to venture further. Rental rates for a compact manual vehicle are approximately £55 per day.

---

> ### EDINBURGH BEST BETS
>
> **Edinburgh Castle.** The twists and turns of Scottish history have unfolded in this true bastion atop a volcanic peak. Stay for the firing of the one o'clock gun, but remember to cover your ears!
>
> **The Palace of Holyroodhouse.** Home to Scottish and English monarchs throughout the ages, Holyroodhouse has many stories to tell—including one of the most vile deeds in Edinburgh's history.
>
> **Calton Hill.** The architectural panorama of Edinburgh plays out before your eyes from this height.

## EXPLORING EDINBURGH

**Calton Hill.** Robert Louis Stevenson's favorite view of his beloved city was from the top of this hill. The architectural styles represented by the extraordinary collection of monuments here include mock Gothic—the Old Observatory, for example—and neoclassical. Under the latter category falls the monument by William Playfair (1789–1857) designed to honor his talented uncle, the geologist and mathematician John Playfair (1748–1819), as well as his cruciform **New Observatory.** The piece that commands the most attention, however, is the so-called **National Monument,** often referred to as "Scotland's Disgrace." Intended to mimic Athens's Parthenon, this monument to the dead of the Napoleonic Wars was started in 1822 to the specifications of a design by Playfair. But in 1830, only 12 columns later, money ran out, and the facade became a monument to high aspirations and poor fund-raising. The tallest monument on Calton Hill is the 100-foot-high

**Nelson Monument,** completed in 1815 in honor of Britain's naval hero Horatio Nelson (1758–1805); you can climb its 143 steps for sweeping city views. The **Burns Monument** is the circular Corinthian temple below Regent Road. Devotees of Robert Burns may want to visit one other grave—that of Mrs. Agnes McLehose, or "Clarinda," in the Canongate Graveyard. ⊠ *Bounded by Leith St. to the west and Regent Rd. to the south, New Town* ☎ *0131/556–2716* ⊕ *www.cac.org.uk* ✉ *Nelson Monument £3* ⊙ *Nelson Monument Oct.–Mar., Mon.–Sat. 10–3; Apr.–Sept., daily 10–6.*

**Charlotte Square.** At the west end of George Street is the New Town's centerpiece—an 18th-century square with one of the proudest achievements of Robert Adam, Scotland's noted neoclassical architect. On the north side, Adam designed a palatial facade to unite three separate town houses of such sublime simplicity and perfect proportions that architects come from all over the world to study it. Happily, the Age of Enlightenment grace notes continue within, as the center town house is now occupied by the **Georgian House** museum, and to the west stands **West Register House.** ⊠ *West end of George St., New Town.*

**Fodor's**Choice  **Edinburgh Castle.** The crowning glory of the Scottish capital, Edin-
★  burgh Castle is popular not only because it's the symbolic heart of
☾  Scotland but also because of the views from its battlements: on a clear day the vistas—stretching to the "kingdom" of Fife—are breathtaking. ■TIP➔ There's so much to see that you need at least three hours to do the site justice, especially if you're interested in military sites.

You enter across the **Esplanade,** the huge forecourt built in the 18th century as a parade ground. The area comes alive with color and music each August when it's used for the Military Tattoo, a festival of magnificently outfitted marching bands and regiments. Heading over the drawbridge and through the gatehouse, past the guards, you can find the rough stone walls of the **Half-Moon Battery,** where the one-o'clock gun is fired every day in an impressively anachronistic ceremony; these curving ramparts give Edinburgh Castle its distinctive appearance from miles away. Climb up through a second gateway and you come to the oldest surviving building in the complex, the tiny 11th-century **St. Margaret's Chapel,** named in honor of Saxon queen Margaret (1046–93), who had persuaded her husband, King Malcolm III (circa 1031–93), to move his court from Dunfermline to Edinburgh. Edinburgh's environs—the Lothians—were occupied by Anglian settlers with whom the queen felt more at home, or so the story goes (Dunfermline was surrounded by Celts). The **Crown Room,** a must-see, contains the "Honours of Scotland"—the crown, scepter, and sword that once graced the Scottish monarch. Upon the **Stone of Scone,** also in the Crown Room, Scottish monarchs once sat to be crowned. In the section now called **Queen Mary's Apartments,** Mary, Queen of Scots, gave birth to James VI of Scotland. The **Great Hall** displays arms and armor under an impressive vaulted, beamed ceiling. Scottish parliament meetings were conducted here until 1840.

Military features of interest include the **Scottish National War Memorial,** the **Scottish United Services Museum,** and the famous 15th-century Belgian-made cannon *Mons Meg.* This enormous piece of artillery has

**6**

been silent since 1682, when it exploded while firing a salute for the duke of York; it now stands in an ancient hall behind the Half-Moon Battery. Contrary to what you may hear from locals, it's not *Mons Meg* but the battery's gun that goes off with a bang every weekday at 1 pm, frightening visitors and reminding Edinburghers to check their watches. ✉ *Castle Esplanade and Castlehill, Old Town* 🕾 *0131/225–9846 Edinburgh Castle, 0131/226–7393 War Memorial* ⊕ *www.edinburghcastle. gov.uk* 🎟 *£14* ⊘ *Apr.–Sept., daily 9:30–6; Oct.–Mar., daily 9:30–5; last entry 45 mins before closing.*

**High Kirk of St. Giles.** Sometimes called St. Giles's Cathedral, this is one of the city's principal churches. However, anyone expecting a rival to Paris's Notre Dame or London's Westminster Abbey will be disappointed: St. Giles is more like a large parish church than a great European cathedral. There has been a church here since AD 854, although most of the present structure dates from either 1120 or 1829, when the church was restored. The tower, with its stone crown towering 161 feet above the ground, was completed between 1495 and 1500. The most elaborate feature is the **Chapel of the Order of the Thistle,** built onto the southeast corner of the church in 1911 for the exclusive use of Scotland's only chivalric order, the Most Ancient and Noble Order of the Thistle. It bears the belligerent national motto "nemo me impune lacessit" ("No one provokes me with impunity"). Inside the church stands a life-size statue of the Scot whose spirit still dominates the place—the great religious reformer and preacher John Knox, before whose zeal all of Scotland once trembled. The church lies about one-third of the way along the Royal Mile from Edinburgh Castle. ✉ *High St., Old Town* 🕾 *0131/225–9442* ⊕ *www.stgilescathedral.org.uk* 🎟 *£3 suggested donation* ⊘ *May–Sept., weekdays 9–7, Sat. 9–5, Sun. 1–5; Oct.–Apr., Mon.–Sat. 9–5, Sun. 1–5.*

Fodor'sChoice ★ **National Gallery of Scotland.** Opened to the public in 1859, the National Gallery presents a wide selection of paintings from the Renaissance to the postimpressionist period within a grand neoclassical building designed by William Playfair. Most famous are the old master paintings bequeathed by the Duke of Sutherland, including Titian's *Three Ages of Man.* Many masters are here; works by Velázquez, El Greco, Rembrandt, Goya, Poussin, Turner, Degas, Monet, and Van Gogh, among others, complement a fine collection of Scottish art, including Sir Henry Raeburn's *Reverend Robert Walker Skating on Duddingston Loch* and other works by Ramsay, Raeburn, and Wilkie. The Weston Link connects the National Gallery of Scotland to the Royal Scottish Academy and provides expanded gallery space as well as a restaurant, bar, café, shop, and information center. ✉ *The Mound, New Town* 🕾 *0131/624–6336* ⊕ *www.nationalgalleries. org* 🎟 *Free* ⊘ *Fri.–Wed. 10–5, Thurs. 10–7.*

Fodor'sChoice ★ ☺ **National Museum of Scotland.** This museum traces the country's fascinating story from the oldest fossils to the most recent popular culture, making it a must-see for first-time visitors to Scotland or anyone interested in history. One of the most famous treasures is the Lewis Chessmen, 11 intricately carved ivory chess pieces found in the 19th century on one of Scotland's Western Isles: other pieces are in London's British Museum. An extensive renovation in 2011 freed up space in the basement, creating a dramatic, crypt-like entrance. Visitors now rise to the light-filled, birdcage wonders of the Victorian grand hall and the upper galleries in glass elevators. Highlights include the hanging hippo and sea creatures of the Wildlife Panorama, a life-size skeleton cast of a *Tyrannosaurus rex*, Viking brooches, Pictish stones, Jacobite relics, the Stevenson family's inventions, including lighthouse optics, and Queen Mary's *clarsach* (harp). All this is free, but donations are welcomed to help renovate 11 other galleries. ⊠ *Chambers St., Old Town* ☎ *0131/225–7534* ⊕ *www.nms.ac.uk* ⌨ *Free* ☉ *Daily 10–5.*

★ **Palace of Holyroodhouse.** Once the haunt of Mary, Queen of Scots, and the setting for high drama—including at least one notorious murder, several major fires, and centuries of the colorful lifestyles of larger-than-life, power-hungry personalities—this is now Queen Elizabeth's official residence in Scotland. A doughty and impressive palace standing at the foot of the Royal Mile in a hilly public park, it's built around a graceful, lawned central court at the end of Canongate. When the queen or royal family is not in residence, you can take a tour. The free audio guide is excellent. ■TIP➜ **There's plenty to see here, so make sure you have at least two hours to tour the palace, gardens (in summer), and the ruins of the 12th-century abbey.** The **King James Tower** is the oldest surviving section, containing the rooms of Mary, Queen of Scots, on the second floor, and Lord Darnley's rooms below. Though much has been altered, there are fine fireplaces, paneling, plasterwork, tapestries, and 18th- and 19th-century furnishings throughout. **The Queen's Gallery,** in a former church and school at the entrance to the palace, holds rotating exhibits from the Royal Collection. There is a separate admission charge.

Behind the palace lie the open grounds and looming crags of Holyrood Park, the hunting ground of early Scottish kings. From the top of Edinburgh's mini mountain, **Arthur's Seat** (822 feet), views are breathtaking. ⊠ *Abbey Strand, Old Town* ☎ *0131/556–5100* ⊕ *www.royalcollection. org.uk* ⌨ *£10.75, £6 Queen's Gallery, £15.10 joint ticket* ☉ *Apr.–Oct., daily 9:30–6; Nov.–Mar., daily 9:30–4:30; last admission 1 hr before closing. Closed during royal visits.*

**Royal Scottish Academy.** The William Playfair–designed academy hosts temporary art exhibitions (Monet paintings, for example), but is also worth visiting for a look at the imposing, neoclassic architecture. The underground Weston Link connects the museum to the National Gallery of Scotland. ⊠ *The Mound, New Town* ☎ *0131/225–6671* ⊕ *www. royalscottishacademy.org* ⌨ *Free* ☉ *Mon.–Sat. 10–5, Sun. noon–5.*

**Scottish National Portrait Gallery.** A magnificent red-sandstone Gothic building dating from 1889 houses this must-see institution. Conceived as a gift to the people of Scotland, the recently revamped gallery is organized under five broad themes: Reformation, Enlightenment, Empire, Modernity, and Contemporary. The refurbished complex features a photography gallery, a gallery for contemporary art, and a fancy glass elevator. New spaces hold exhibits on various aspects of Scots history and life, including *The Visual Culture of the Jacobite Cause* and *Playing for Scotland: The Making of Modern Sport.* ⊠ *1 Queen St., New Town* ☎ *0131/624–6200* ⊕ *www. nationalgalleries.org* ⌨ *Free* ☉ *Fri.–Wed. 10–5, Thurs. 10–7.*

6

## SHOPPING

Despite its renown as a shopping street, **Princes Street** in the New Town disappoints some visitors with its dull, anonymous modern architecture, average chain stores, and fast-food outlets. It is, however, one of the best spots to shop for tartans, tweeds, and knitwear, especially if your time is limited. One block north of Princes Street, **Rose Street** has many smaller specialty shops; part of the street is a pedestrian zone, so it's a pleasant place to browse.

The streets crossing George Street—Hanover, Frederick, and Castle—are also worth exploring. **Dundas Street,** the northern extension of Hanover Street, beyond Queen Street Gardens, has several antiques shops. **Thistle Street,** originally George Street's "back lane," or service area, has several boutiques and more antiques shops. **Stafford and William streets** form a small, upscale shopping area in a Georgian setting.

As may be expected, many shops along the **Royal Mile** sell what may be politely or euphemistically described as tourist ware—whiskies, tartans, and tweeds. Careful exploration, however, will uncover some worthwhile establishments. Shops here also cater to highly specialized interests and hobbies. Close to the castle end of the Royal Mile, just off George IV Bridge, is **Victoria Street,** with specialty shops grouped in a small area. Follow the tiny West Bow to **Grassmarket** for more specialty stores.

**Ocean Terminal.** The Ocean Terminal houses a large collection of shops, as well as bars and eateries. Here you can also visit the former royal yacht *Britannia.* ⊠ *Ocean Dr., Leith.*

## WHERE TO EAT

**$**
BRITISH
✕ **The King's Wark.** Along the shoreline at Leith is a gastropub with a pleasant atmosphere and quality food that continues to win plaudits. At lunchtime, the dark-wood bar does a roaring trade in simple fare such as gourmet burgers and fish cakes, but in the evening the kitchen ups the ante with such dishes as sea trout stuffed with smoked mackerel risotto. Old stone walls attest to the building's 15th-century origins. Book early to sample the legendary breakfast. ⑤ *Average main: £14* ⊠ *36 The Shore, Leith* ☎ *0131/554–9260.*

**$$**
ITALIAN
✕ **Valvona & Crolla VinCaffe.** Every Scot with a passion for food knows Valvona & Crolla, the country's first Italian delicatessen and wine merchant. This eatery of the same name may lack the old-world feel of the original on Elm Row, but the menu created by food writer and cook Mary Contini is as wonderful as you would expect. The fare is relatively simple, but the quality of the ingredients ensure that treats such as the white pizza with cured bacon, fried calamari, and linguine with crab meat do nothing to tarnish the brand's reputation. Watch for tastings and cultural events staged here. ⑤ *Average main: £15* ⊠ *11 Multrees Walk, New Town* ☎ *0131/557–0088* ⊕ *www.vincaffe.com.*

# ROTTERDAM, NETHERLANDS

Rotterdam is the industrial center of Holland and the world's largest port. When Rotterdam's city center and harbor were completely destroyed in World War II, the authorities decided to start afresh rather than try to reconstruct its former maze of canals. The imposing, futuristic skyline along the banks of the Maas River has been developing since then, thanks in large part to the efforts of major figures such as Rem Koolhaas, Eric van Egeraat, and UN Studio. Elsewhere in the region you can step back in time: wander through the ancient cobbled streets in Leiden and buy china in Delft that once colored the world with its unique blue. Many other colors are on view in Holland's fabled tulip fields. Every spring, green thumbs everywhere make a pilgrimage to Lisse to view the noted tulip gardens at Keukenhof and to drive the Bollenstreek Route, which takes them through miles of countryside glowing with gorgeous hues and blooms.

## ESSENTIALS

### CURRENCY

The euro. ATMs are common and credit cards are widely accepted in all but restaurants, where only European cards with PIN are accepted widely.

### HOURS

Shops open Tuesday, Wednesday, Friday, and Saturday from 9 or 10 until 6; they are open later on Thursday. Most stores are closed on Sunday and some on Monday. Museums open from 9 until 6 with one late opening night during the week.

### PRIVATE GUIDES

Private tour guides are available from Gilde-Rotterdam for walking, bus, or bicycle tours within the city. Tours start at €4 and run on weekdays. Spido offers a 75-minute guided Rotterdam Harbour boat tour several times daily at a cost of €10.50.

**Contacts Gilde-Rotterdam.** ☎ *31/104362844* ⊕ *www.gilderotterdam.nl.* **Spido.** ☎ *31/102759988* ⊕ *spido.nl/en/rotterdam-harbour-tour.*

### TELEPHONES

Most tri- and quad-band GSM mobile phones should work in the Netherlands, which operates a 3G mobile system with dual-band handsets. Most public phones take phone cards (available at numerous shops) and some take credit cards, and will connect international calls. Major telecom companies are Vodafone and Orange.

### COMING ASHORE

Ships dock at the historic terminal building in the city dock, once the headquarters of the Holland America Line. The terminal offers handicraft displays, shopping facilities, and an information desk. A hotel including restaurants, a café, a theater, and a shopping center is currently being built next to the terminal and is expected to open in 2013. A shuttle service operates between the terminal and the town. Each bus has an English-speaking host who can answer any questions that you have. A water-taxi service also operates from the port across the River Maas into the heart of the Old Town. A 15-minute round-trip costs approximately €30.

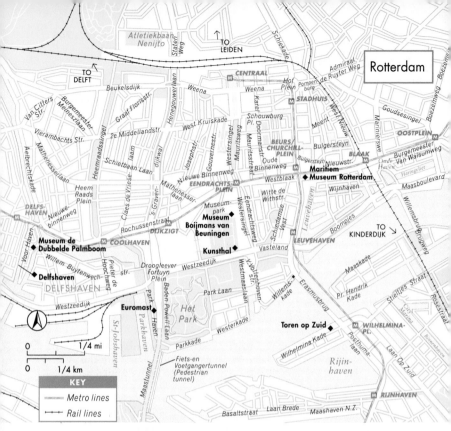

The terminal has a taxi service desk where you can arrange for trips at fixed prices. It is also possible to book journeys and trips ahead of time. All drivers speak English. Public transport is efficient and modern. Tram routes Erasmus, 20, 23, and 25 link the port with Rotterdam Central Station (this station area is currently undergoing a comprehensive renovation program). All public transport is now paid for with an electronic chip card which deducts the amount of the journey from the amount registered on the card. The easiest option for cruise passengers is to purchase a disposable chip card that can be loaded with a single one-hour travel pass good for the tram, bus, and metro (equivalent to a single ticket); a two-journey travel pass; or a one-, two-, or three-day travel card. If you intend to use public transport throughout the day, the one-day travel card would be simplest; it costs €7. While the one-hour travel card can be purchased from personnel aboard trams and buses, the other passes must be purchased from machines at stations. Rotterdam is bicycle-friendly. Bikes can be rented at the central train station at a cost of €6.50 per day.

The train journey from Rotterdam to Delft takes 15 minutes, and there are several services per hour; ticket prices are €10.20 round-trip for first-class and €6 round-trip for second-class. The train journey from Rotterdam to Leiden takes 34 minutes, with several services every hour;

ticket prices are €22.80 round-trip for first-class and €13.40 round-trip for second-class. The journey to Amsterdam takes one hour, or 40 minutes on the faster Fyra train, with several services every hour; round-trip tickets are €46.20 in first-class and €27.20 in second-class.

# EXPLORING ROTTERDAM AND VICINITY

## ROTTERDAM

Cobbled streets, gabled houses, narrow canals overhung with lime trees, and antiques shops give the historic center a tangible feeling of history, and Leiden's university's academic buildings, the historic Waag (Weigh House) and the Burcht fortress, the stately mansions lining the Rapenburg—the most elegant canal in the town—and no fewer than 35 hofjes (groups of houses surrounding little courtyards) make it a rewarding place for a stroll. As you walk about, keep a watch for verses painted on lofty gables, a project started some 10 years ago. The proverbs, sayings, and poems now number more than 70, and are in a multitude of languages.

**Delfshaven.** The last remaining nook of old Rotterdam is the old port area, reconstructed to appear just as it was when originally built—an open-air museum with rows of gabled houses lining the historic waterfront, trendy galleries, cafés, and restaurants. Walk along the Voorhaven, Achterhaven, and neighboring Piet Heynplein and marvel at the many historic buildings. For historic sights in the environs, check out the working mill of **Korenmolen de Distilleerketel** (open Wednesday and Saturday only), the fascinating **Museum de Dubbelde Palmboom** on Rotterdam city history, and the **Oudekerk/Pilgrimvaders Kerk.** Tram No. 4 connects Delfshaven with the rest of the city, as does the nearby Delfshaven metro station. ⊠ *Achterhaven and Voorhaven, Delfshaven.*

**Euromast.** For a bird's-eye view of the contrast between Delfshaven and the majority of the city, as well as a spectacular panorama of city and harbor, visit the 600-foot-high Euromast. Designed by Rotterdam architect Huig Maaskant in 1960, this was the Netherland's tallest building for many years; when a new medical facility for the Erasmus University usurped the honor in 1970, an additional 25 feet were added to the tower in six days, restoring Euromast to its premier position. On a clear day, you can just about see the coast. The main observation deck is at 315 feet, but the **Euroscoop** is a rotating panoramic elevator that will carry you another 300 feet from there to the top of the mast. For the thrill seekers among us, on weekends from May to September you can skip the elevator and rappel down from the observation deck, or shoot down the rope slide in about 10 seconds on Europe's fastest "zip wire" (make reservations via the Web at ⊕ *www.abseilen.nl*). There's also a restaurant at the top. You can even stay up the tower overnight in one of two special suites, but be warned the prices are as high as the experience. Down below, the park at the base of the Euromast is where many Rotterdammers spend time when the weather is good. ⊠ *Parkhaven 20, Delfshaven* ☎ *010/436–4811* ⊕ *www.euromast.nl* ☒ *€9.25; rappel or rope slide €49.50* ☽ *Apr.–Sept., daily 9:30 am–11 pm; Oct.–Mar., daily 10 am–11 pm.*

6

**Kunsthal.** This "art house" sits at one end of the visitor-friendly museum quarter and hosts major temporary exhibitions. There is no permanent collection, other than the massive, multistory boxlike center itself, designed by architect-prophet Rem Koolhaas. Opinions about the building are sharply divided: some say the design bridging the gap between the Museumpark and the dike is a clever spatial creation; others consider it an ugly mix of facades (part glass, part brick, and part corrugated iron) that has led to rusted iron, stained concrete, and cracks in the central walkway. The biggest complaint is the lack of elevator, compounded by the hazards of the central ramp, whose steep angle makes this a potential ski slope for wheelchair users. Fortunately, the eclectic exhibitions, usually three or four at any one time, are always fascinating, regardless of the setting. ⊠ *Westzeedijk 341, Museumpark* ☎ *010/440–0301* ⊕ *www.kunsthal.nl* 🎫 *€11* ☉ *Tues.– Sat. 10–5, Sun. 11–5.*

> **ROTTERDAM BEST BETS**
>
> **Modernist architecture.** Rotterdam eschewed rebuilding the city after the destruction of WWII and instead strode resolutely into modernism.
>
> **The Kinderdijk Windmills.** This archetypal Dutch landscape isn't a theme park—the windmills were grouped to pump water out of the polders. Today the vista is picture-perfect.
>
> **Old Delft.** This tangle of canals and medieval streets, with its array of ornate decoration and flower-bedecked windows, offers some of the prettiest views in Holland.

Fodor's Choice
★
☯ **Maritiem Museum Rotterdam.** A sea lover's delight, the Maritime Museum is Rotterdam's noted nautical collection. Appropriately perched at the head of the Leuvehaven harbor, it was founded by Prince Hendrik in 1874. Set against the background of modern and historical maritime objects, the seafaring ways of old Rotterdammers make more sense. Star attraction of the ground floor is a large model of the Europoort, which shows how the Rotterdam area has developed over the centuries into the major seaport of today. The upper floors are mainly given over to rotating exhibitions on seafaring themes. Children have half a floor dedicated to them, called "Professor Plons" (Professor Plunge), where museum staff are on hand to help with looking through a real periscope, donning a hard hat and taking to the driving seat of a scaled-down crane, and engaging in many other activities dealing with the themes of water and ships. Kids will also love the museum's prize exhibit, the warship *De Buffel*, moored in the harbor outside, dating back to 1868. The ship has been perfectly restored and is fitted out sumptuously, as can be seen in the mahogany-deck captain's cabin. ⊠ *Leuvehaven 1, Witte de With* ☎ *010/413–2680* ⊕ *www. maritiemmuseum.nl* 🎫 *€7.50* ☉ *July and Aug., Mon.–Sat. 10–5, Sun. 11–5; Sept.–June, Tues.–Sat. 10–5, Sun. 11–5.*

Fodor's Choice
★ **Museum Boijmans van Beuningen.** Rotterdam's finest shrine to art, with treasures ranging from Pieter Bruegel the Elder's 16th-century *Tower of Babel* to Mondriaan's extraordinary *Composition in Yellow and Blue*, ranks among the greatest art galleries in Europe. The top attraction

here is the collection of old masters, which covers West European art from the 14th to the 19th century. In particular 15th- to 17th-century Dutch and Flemish art are well represented, including painters such as Van Eyck, Rubens, Hieronymous Bosch, and Rembrandt. The modern art section runs the gamut from Monet to Warhol and beyond, picking up Kandinsky, Magritte, and Dalí in between. In the Decorative Art and Design collection, both precious ornamental objects and everyday utensils dating from medieval times are displayed. In the museum café, note the fantastic collection of chairs, each by a different designer. More artworks embellish the museum gardens. ⊠ *Museumpark 18–20, Museumpark* ☎ *010/441–9400* ⊕ *www.boijmans. nl* ⊠ *€12.50* ۞ *Tues.–Sun. 11–5.*

**Museum de Dubbelde Palmboom** (*Double Palm Tree Museum*). Devoted to the history of Rotterdam and its role as an international nexus, this museum traces the city's history from prehistoric times to the current day. The focus is on how exotic wares imported by the East India Company affected the city. The building itself is redolent of history: not only do its heavy beams and brick floors waft you back to yesteryear, but there even seems to be a faint smell of grains, recalling the many years the building spent as a warehouse. Ask for the informative guide in English, as all labeling is in Dutch. The first floor has some fascinating archaeological finds: one of the spouted ancient jugs has been traced to a town near Cologne, providing proof that traveling merchants were apparently very active in trading ceramics. ⊠ *Voorhaven 12, Delfshaven* ☎ *010/476–1533* ⊕ *www.museumrotterdam.nl* ⊠ *€6, ticket also valid for a same-day visit to the Schielandshuis* ۞ *Tues.–Sun. 11–5.*

**Toren op Zuid.** An office complex by celebrated modern architect Renzo Piano, this structure houses the head offices of KPN Telecom. Its eye-catching billboard facade glitters with 1,000-odd green lamps flashing on and off, creating images provided by the city of Rotterdam, in addition to images provided by KPN and an art academy. The facade fronting the Erasmus Bridge leans forward by 6 degrees, which is the same as the angle of the bridge's pylon. It is also said that Piano could have been making a humorous reference to his homeland, as the Tower of Pisa leans at the same angle. ⊠ *Wilhelminakade 123, Kop van Zuid.*

## DELFT

*15 km (9 miles) northwest of Rotterdam.*

Fodor'sChoice ★ With time-burnished canals and streets, Delft radiates a peaceful calm that recalls the quieter pace of the Golden Age of the 17th century. Back then the town counted among its citizens the artist Johannes Vermeer, who decided one spring day to paint the city gates and landscape across the Kolk harbor from a house's window on the Schieweg (now the Hooikade). The result was the 1660 *View of Delft* (now the star of the Mauritshuis Museum in The Hague), famously called by Marcel Proust "the most beautiful painting in the world." Spending a few hours in certain parts of Delft, in fact, puts you in the company of Vermeer. Imagine a tiny Amsterdam, canals reduced to dollhouse proportions, narrower bridges, merchants' houses less grand, and you have the essence of Old

6

Delft. But even though the city has one foot firmly planted in the past, another is planted in the present: Delft teems with hip cafés, jazz festivals, and revelers spilling out of bars.

Fodor's Choice
★
**Museum Het Prinsenhof.** A former dignitary-hosting convent of St. Agatha, the Prinsenhof Museum is celebrated as the residence of Prince William the Silent, beloved as *Vader des Vaderlands* (Father of the Nation) for his role in the Spanish Revolt and a hero whose tragic end here gave this structure the sobriquet "cradle of Dutch liberty." The complex of buildings was taken over by the government of the new Dutch Republic in 1572 and given to William of Orange for his use as a residence. On July 10, 1584, fevered by monies offered by Philip II of Spain, Bathasar Gerard, a Catholic fanatic, gained admittance to the mansion and succeeded in shooting the prince on the staircase hall, since known as Moordhal (Murder Hall). The fatal bullet holes—the *teykenen der koogelen*—are still visible in the stairwell. Today, the imposing structure is a museum, with a 15th-century chapel, a quaint courtyard, and a bevy of elegantly furnished 17th-century rooms filled with antique pottery, silver, tapestries, and House of Orange portraits, along with exhibits on Dutch history. ⊠ *Sint Agathaplein 1* ☎ *015/260–2358* ⊕ *www.prinsenhof-delft.nl* ☜ *€7.50; combined ticket to Het Prinsenhof and Nusantara museums €10* ⊘ *Tues.–Sun. 11–5.*

Fodor's Choice
★
**Vermeer Centrum** (*Vermeer Center*). Housed in the former St. Lucas Guild, where Delft's favorite son was dean for many years, the Center takes visitors on a multimedia journey through the life and work of Johannes Vermeer. Touch screens, projections, and other interactive features are interspersed with giant reproductions of the master's work, weaving a tale of 17th-century Delft and drawing you into the mind of the painter. ☎ *015/213–8588* ⊕ *www.vermeerdelft.nl* ☜ *€7* ⊘ *Daily 10–5.*

## KINDERDIJK

Fodor's Choice
★
**Kinderdijk.** The sight of the 19 windmills at Kinderdijk under sail is magnificently and romantically impressive. Not surprisingly, this landmark sight (so valued it is found on the UNESCO World Heritage list) is one of the most visited places in the Netherlands. These are water-pumping mills whose job was to drain water from the Alblasserwaard polder enclosed by the rivers Noord and Lek—a function now performed by the 1950 pumping station with its humongously sized water screws, which you pass on the way to the site. The somewhat chocolate-boxy name (which means "child's dyke") comes from a legend involving a baby who washed up here in a cradle after the great floods of 1421, with a cat sitting on its tummy to keep them both from tumbling out.

Rarer than ever, these windmills date all the way back to 1740. Just 150 years ago 10,000 windmills were in operation across the country, but today only 1,000 remain. These have been saved from the wrecking ball thanks to the help of heritage organizations. The windmills are open in rotation, so there is always one interior to visit. A walk through a working windmill gives fascinating insight into how the millers and their families lived. The mills can be seen in full action (wind permitting) from 1 pm to 5 pm on Saturdays in July and August, as well as on National

Windmill Day (second Saturday of May) and National Monument Day (second weekend of September). Throughout the first week following the first Monday of September the mills are illuminated at night, really pulling out the tourist stops. You can walk around the mills area whenever you like, so it's a great way to spend a leisurely afternoon. There are a couple of cafés for snacks, but if the weather is good bring a picnic. ⊠ *Molenkade, Kinderdijk* ☎ *078/691–2830* ⊕ *www.molenskinderdijk. nl* ⊡ *Interior of mill: €6.00 (incl. film at visitor's center)* ⊙ *Interior of mill: Apr.–Oct., daily 9:30–5:30.*

## SHOPPING

Rotterdam is the number-one shopping city in the south of Holland, and it offers some excellent interior design galleries. Its famous **Lijnbaan** and **Beurstraverse** shopping centers, as well as the surrounding areas, offer a dazzling variety of shops. The archways and fountains of the Beurstraverse—at the bottom of the Coolsingel, near the Stadhuis—make this newer, pedestrianized area more pleasing to walk around. **Van Oldenbarneveldtstraat** and **Nieuwe Binnenweg** are the places to be if you want something different; there is a huge variety of alternative fashion to be found here. Exclusive shops and boutiques can be found in the Entrepotgebied, Delfshaven, Witte de Withstraat, Nieuwe and Oude Binnenweg, and Van Oldenbarneveldtstraat. **West Kruiskade** and its vicinity offers a wide assortment of multicultural products in the many Chinese, Suriname, Mediterranean, and Arabic shops. You should also walk through the **Entrepot Harbor design district,** alongside the city marina at Kop van Zuid, where there are several interior-design stores.

**De Bijenkorf.** De Bijenkorf is a favorite department store, the best in Rotterdam, designed by Marcel Breuer (the great Bauhaus architect) with an exterior that looks like its name, a beehive. There's a good range of clothing and shoes from both designers and the store's own label, plus a selection of cosmetics and perfume on the ground floor, with a Chill Out department on the same floor geared toward street- and club-wear; here, on some Saturdays a DJ keeps it mellow, and you can even get a haircut at in-store Kinki Kappers. De Bijenkorf is well known for its excellent household-goods line, ranging from lights and furniture to sumptuous fabrics and rugs. Check out the second-floor restaurant with its view out over the Coolsingel and Naum Gabo's sculpture *Constructie.* ⊠ *Coolsingel 105, Centrum* ☎ *0800/0918* ⊕ *www.debijenkorf.nl.*

**De Porceleyne Fles.** It's corny, even sometimes a little tacky (miniature clogs, anyone?), but no visit to Delft would be complete without stopping at a Delft porcelain factory to see plates and tulip vases being painted by hand and perhaps picking up a souvenir or two. De Porceleyne Fles is the original and most famous home to the popular blue-and-white pottery. Regular demonstrations of molding and painting pottery are given by the artisans. On the bottom of each object is a triple signature: a plump vase topped by a straight line, the stylized letter "F" below it, and the word "Delft." Blue is no longer the only official color. In 1948, a rich red cracked glaze was premiered depicting profuse flowers, graceful birds, and leaping gazelles. There is New Delft, a range of green, gold, and black hues, whose exquisite minuscule figures are drawn to resemble an old Persian tapestry; the Pynacker Delft, borrowing Japanese motifs in rich oranges and golds; and the brighter Polychrome Delft, which can strike a brilliant sunflower-yellow effect. ⊠ *Royal Delftware Factory, Rotterdamseweg 196* ☎ *015/251–2030* ⊕ *www.royaldelft.com* 🖃 *museum €12* ⊗ *mid-Mar.–Oct., daily 9–5; Nov.–mid-Mar., Mon.–Sat. 9–5.*

## WHERE TO EAT

$    ✕ **Café Dudok.** Lofty ceilings, a cavernous former-warehouse interior,
CAFÉ    long reading tables stacked with international magazines and papers—little wonder this place attracts an artsy crowd. At its most mellow, the spot is perfect for a lazy afternoon treat of delicious homemade pastries, but you can come here for breakfast, lunch, high tea, dinner, or even a snack after midnight. They offer a small selection for vegetarians. The brasserie, on a mezzanine above the open kitchen at the back, looks out over the Rotte River. Since it's terribly crowded at times, you should get here unfashionably early to avoid disappointment—there's nowhere else like it in Rotterdam. ⑤ *Average main: €10* ⊠ *Meent 88, Centrum* ☎ *010/433–3102* ⊕ *www.dudok.nl.*

$    ✕ **Café Floor.** Adjacent to the Stadsschouwburg (Municipal Theater),
CONTEMPORARY    this popular spot doesn't look too inviting from the outside, but the interior is modern, light, and airy; the staff are friendly; and the kitchen produces excellent food. Try the lamb brochette, so tender the meat practically dissolves on your tongue. There's also a good selection of tapas available and a delicious passion-fruit cheesecake. The beautiful garden at the back, and accompanying birdsong from the local fauna, make this a restful stop. This place is a favorite with local and international regulars, so be prepared to be patient if you go late-ish on a Saturday. ⑤ *Average main: €12* ⊠ *Schouwburgplein 28, Centrum* ☎ *010/404–5288* ⊕ *www.cafefloor.nl.*

# SOUTHAMPTON, UNITED KINGDOM

Updated by    Southampton, in the county of Hampshire, may not be in every tourist
Ellin Stein    brochure, but this city and its environs hold all kinds of attractions—and not a few quiet pleasures. Close to London, the green fields of Hampshire divide the cliffs and coves of the West Country from the hustle and bustle of the big city. Two important cathedrals, Winchester and Salisbury (pronounced *sawls*-bree), are nearby, as are stately homes, intriguing market towns and hundreds of haunting prehistoric remains; Stonehenge, the most famous of these, should not be missed. These, however, are just the highlights. Anyone spending time in the region should rent a car and set out to discover the quiet back-road villages that were home to numerous literary greats lived—such as Chawton, where Jane Austen lived—or the semiwilderness of the New Forest.

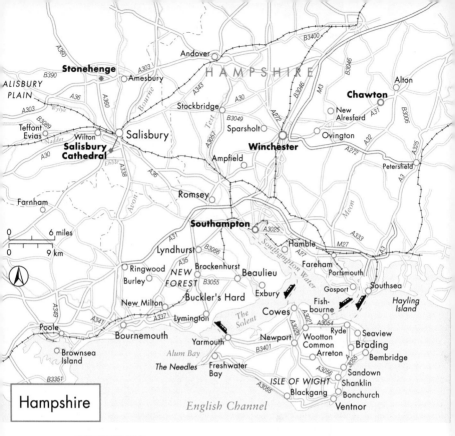

## ESSENTIALS

### CURRENCY
The British pound sterling. ATMs are common and credit cards are widely accepted.

### HOURS
Museums are open from 9 until 5, while shops usually open from 9 until 5:30 or 6. Some shops are open on Sunday.

### TELEPHONES
Dual-band GSM phones work in the United Kingdom. You can buy prepaid phone cards at telecom shops and news vendors in all towns and cities. Phone cards can be used for local or international calls. Vodafone, T-Mobile, Virgin, and Orange are the leading telecom companies.

### COMING ASHORE
Southampton is a busy cruise port, and has four separate cruise terminals, each with its own dock, refreshment facilities, and dedicated taxi rank. City Cruise Terminal and Mayflower Terminal are situated in the Western Docks closest to the city (5 minutes by car), while Ocean Terminal and Queen Elizabeth II Terminal are in the Eastern Docks, a couple of minutes farther away from the downtown. Taxi fares to downtown/railway station are around £6. The Eastern Docks have a public bus link (routes U1 and U6) that runs to downtown.

There are four or five train services every hour, and fares start at £39.40 round-trip. By bus, the journey takes around 2½ hours; prices start at £14 round-trip. The rail journey from Southampton to Salisbury takes 40 minutes and starts at £16.80 round-trip; there are trains every half hour. Bus services take around 40 minutes with return ticket prices around £6.40. The rail journey from Southampton to Winchester takes around 20 minutes; fares start at £11.60 round-trip. Bus services take around 30 minutes, with return ticket prices around £4.80.

Renting a car for the day would allow you to explore towns and attractions in the surrounding area more easily. Rental prices are approximately £35 for an economy manual vehicle.

| HAMPSHIRE BEST BETS |
|---|
| **Stonehenge.** This world-famous megalithic monument has captured the popular imagination. Although we're sure of its age, its origins and exact purpose remain a mystery. |
| **Winchester.** Once the capital of England, this diminutive city has many architectural treasures on show, including one of the finest cathedrals in Britain. |
| **Chawton.** Jane Austen lived here for many years; devotees can be inspired by the atmosphere in the very room where she wrote her greatest works. |

### GETTING TO THE AIRPORT

If you do not purchase airport transfers from your cruise line, the simplest way to reach Heathrow Airport is by private transfer company or hire cab. The journey time is around two hours from terminal to terminal, but prices for a vehicle for one to three people are expensive, at around £116.

Aside from bespoke transfer, the easiest other option is by bus. National Express runs direct services between Southampton Bus Station and Heathrow departing once every 1 hour, 45 minutes or so. Journey time is just over 2 hours. Single journey price is £12.50.

Trains from Southampton terminate at Waterloo Station in London. The journey time is about 90 minutes. There are four or five train services every hour, and fares start at £39.40 round-trip. To reach Heathrow, the least expensive option is the London Underground, but carriages can be busy with little luggage space. From Waterloo Station take the Bakerloo Line to Piccadilly Circus, from where the Piccadilly line will take you directly to Heathrow. The time for the journey is around 1:20 hours and costs £5.30.

Aimed more at travelers than commuters, the Heathrow Express offers a much quicker, direct journey, 15 minutes from Paddington Station to Heathrow. To reach Paddington, take the Bakerloo Underground line from Waterloo Station. Heathrow Express tickets cost £18 one-way.

The Heathrow Connect train runs every half-hour from Paddington to Heathrow, stopping at local stations along the 30-minute route. Prices are £8.50 one-way.

From the cruise terminal to downtown Southampton (bus or train station) the taxi fare should be around £7 to £10. If you are traveling from airport to cruise terminal, be sure to note the name of the terminal your ship is docked at, because the four terminals are a couple of miles apart.

# EXPLORING HAMPSHIRE

## SOUTHAMPTON

*Central Southampton is about 2 km (1 mile) from the cruise-ship docks.*

Seafaring Saxons and Romans used Southampton's outer harbor as a commercial trading port for centuries, allowing the city to become one of England's wealthiest. Though still home to England's second-largest container terminal, it is now primarily used for passenger traffic. As the home port of many great ocean liners of the 20th century, including the *Queen Mary* and the ill-fated *Titanic,* as well as being the departure point for Henry V's fleet bound for Agincourt and the *Mayflower,* Southampton has one of the richest maritime traditions in England. Much of the city center is unremarkable, having been hastily rebuilt after World War II bombing, but bits of the city's history peek out from between modern buildings. The Old Town retains its medieval air, and considerable parts of Southampton's castellated town walls remain. Other attractions include an art gallery, extensive parks, and a couple of good museums. The Southampton International Boat Show, a 10-day event in mid-September, draws huge

**Mayflower Park and the Pilgrim Fathers' Memorial.** This memorial was built to commemorate the departure of 102 passengers on the North America–bound *Mayflower* from Southampton on August 15, 1620. A plaque also honors the 2 million U.S. troops who embarked from Southampton during World War II. ⊠ *Western Esplanade.*

**SeaCity Museum.** This new £15 million museum is devoted to Southampton's storied maritime history. The Gateway to the World gallery brings together artifacts from Roman, Saxon, and medieval times with models, mementos, and pieces of furniture from the age of the great clippers and cruise ships. The *Titanic* gallery displays a wealth of memorabilia relating to one of the most famous of the cruise ships that sailed from the city—footage, photos, crew lists, and so on. Boat buffs will relish plenty of vital statistics dealing with the history of commercial shipping. ⊠ *Havelock Rd.* ☎ *023/8083–3007* ⊕ *www.seacitymuseum.co.uk* ⊠ *£8.50* ☉ *Daily 10–5.*

## WINCHESTER

*25 km (16 miles) northeast of Southampton.*

One of the region's most compelling and historically rich destinations, and still a thriving market town, Winchester is among the most historic of English cities. For more than four centuries it served first as the capital of the ancient kingdom of Wessex and then of England. Alfred the Great, whose court was here, laid out the street plan. Its imposing cathedral, the final resting place of notables ranging from Saxon kings to Jane Austen, still dominates the skyline.

**Great Hall.** A short walk west of the cathedral, this hall is all that remains of the city's Norman castle, and it's still used today for events and ceremonies. Here the English Parliament met for the first time in 1246; Sir Walter Raleigh was tried for conspiracy against King James I in 1603; and Dame Alice Lisle was sentenced to death by the brutal Judge Jeffreys for sheltering fugitives, after Monmouth's Rebellion in 1685. The

**6**

hall's greatest relic hangs on its west wall: King Arthur's Round Table has places for 24 knights and a portrait of Arthur bearing a remarkable resemblance to King Henry VIII. In fact, the animal skin–covered table dates back only to the 13th century and was repainted by order of Henry on the occasion of a visit by the Holy Roman Emperor Charles V; the real Arthur was probably a Celtic chieftain who held off the invading Saxons after the fall of the Roman Empire in the 5th or 6th century. The Tudor monarchs revived the Arthurian legend for political purposes. Take time to wander through the garden named for the two Queen Eleanors—a re-creation of a medieval shady retreat. ✉ *Castle Hill* ☎ *01962/846476* ⊕ *www.hants.gov.uk/greathall* 🎫 *Free* ⊙ *Daily 10–5.*

★ **Winchester Cathedral.** The city's greatest monument, begun in 1079 and consecrated in 1093, presents a sturdy, chunky appearance in keeping with its Norman construction, so that the Gothic lightness within is even more breathtaking. Its tower, transepts, and crypt, and the inside core of the great Perpendicular nave, reveal some of the world's best surviving examples of Norman architecture. Other features, such as the arcades, the presbytery (behind the quire, holding the high altar), and the windows, are Gothic alterations carried out between the 12th and 14th century. Little of the original stained glass has survived, however, thanks to Cromwell's Puritan troops, who ransacked the cathedral in the 17th century during the English Civil War, but you can still see the sumptuously illuminated 12th-century Winchester Bible in the Library and Triforium Gallery.

Among the many well-known people buried in the cathedral are William the Conqueror's son, William II ("Rufus"), mysteriously murdered in the New Forest in 1100; Izaak Walton (1593–1683), author of *The Compleat Angler,* whose memorial window in Silkestede's Chapel was paid for by "the fishermen of England and America"; and Jane Austen, whose grave lies in the north aisle of the nave. The tombstone makes no mention of Austen's literary status, though a brass plaque in the wall, dating from 80 years after her death, celebrates her achievements, and modern panels provide an overview of her life and work. Firmly in the 20th century, Antony Gormley's evocative statue *Sound II* (1986) looms in the crypt, as often as not standing in water (as it was designed to do), because of seasonal flooding. You can also explore the bell tower—with far-reaching views in fair weather—and other recesses of the building on a tour. Special services or ceremonies may mean the cathedral is closed to visits, so call ahead. Outside the cathedral, explore the Close, the area that nearly envelopes the cathedral and contains neat lawns and the Deanery, Dome Alley, and Cheyney Court. ✉ *The Close, Cathedral Precincts* ☎ *01962/857200* ⊕ *www.winchester-cathedral.org.uk* 🎫 *Cathedral £4.80; bell tower £6; cathedral and bell tower £9.50* ⊙ *Cathedral Mon.–Sat. 10–4 (last admission 3), Sun. 12:30–2:30. Library and Triforium Gallery Apr.–Oct., Mon. 2–4, Tues.–Sat. and national holidays 10:30–4; Nov.–Mar., Sat. 10:30–3:30. Free tours on the hr Mon.–Sat. 10–3, bell tower tours June–Aug., Mon., Wed., and Fri. 2:15; Sat. 11:30 and 2:15; Sept.–late May, Wed. 2:15, Sat. 11:30 and 2:15.*

## CHAWTON

*49 km (30 miles) northeast of Southampton.*

In this tiny Hampshire village you'll find the elegant but understated house where Jane Austen (1775–1817) lived the last eight years of her life and wrote three of her novels. Now a museum, it effectively evokes her life there.

★ **Jane Austen's House.** Here, in an unassuming redbrick house, Jane Austen wrote *Emma, Persuasion,* and *Mansfield Park,* and revised *Sense and Sensibility, Northanger Abbey,* and *Pride and Prejudice.* Now a museum, the house retains the modest but genteel atmosphere suitable to the unmarried daughter of a clergyman. In the left-hand parlor, there's a piano similar to the one Jane would play every morning before repairing to a small writing table in the family dining parlor—leaving her sister, Cassandra, to do the household chores ("I find composition impossible with my head full of joints of mutton and doses of rhubarb," Jane wrote). In the early 19th century the road near the house was a bustling thoroughfare, and one traveler reported that a window view proved that the Misses Austen were "looking very comfortable at breakfast." Jane was famous for working through interruptions, but one protection against the outside world was the famous door that creaked. She asked that its hinges remain unattended to because they gave her warning that someone was coming. The museum often schedules readings and other special events, so call ahead. ⊠ *Signed off A31/A32 roundabout* ☎ *01420/83262* ⊕ *www.jane-austens-house-museum.org. uk* ☐ *£7.50* ⊗ *Jan.–mid-Feb., weekends 10:30–4:30; mid-Feb.–May and Sept.–Dec., daily 10:30–4:30; June–Aug., daily 10–5; last admission 30 mins before closing.*

## SALISBURY CATHEDRAL

Fodor's Choice **Salisbury Cathedral.** Salisbury is dominated by the towering cathedral,
★ a soaring hymn in stone. It is unique among cathedrals in that it was conceived and built as a whole in the amazingly short span of 38 years (1220–58). The spire, added in 1320, is the tallest in England and a miraculous feat of medieval engineering—even though the point, 404 feet above the ground, is 2½ feet off vertical. For a fictional, keenly imaginative reconstruction of the drama underlying such an achievement, read William Golding's novel *The Spire.* The excellent model of the cathedral in the north transept, the "arm" of the church to your left as you look toward the altar, shows the building about 20 years into construction, and makes clear the ambition of Salisbury's medieval builders. For all their sophistication, the height and immense weight of the great spire have always posed structural problems. In the late 17th century Sir Christopher Wren was summoned from London to strengthen the spire, and in the mid-19th century Sir George Gilbert Scott, a leading Victorian Gothicist, undertook a major program of restoration. He also initiated a clearing out of the interior and removed some less-than-sympathetic 18th-century alterations, returning a more authentically Gothic feel. Despite this, the interior seems spartan and a little gloomy, but check out the remarkable lancet windows and sculpted tombs of crusaders and other medieval notables. The clock in

6

the north aisle—probably the oldest working mechanism in Europe, if not the world—was made in 1386.

The **cloisters** are the largest in England, and the octagonal **Chapter House** contains a marvelous 13th-century frieze showing scenes from the Old Testament. Here you can also see one of the four original copies of the **Magna Carta**, the charter of rights the English barons forced King John to accept in 1215; it was sent here for safekeeping in the 13th century. ■TIP→ **Join a free 45-minute tour of the church, leaving two or more times a day. There are also daily tours of the roof and spire (except on Sunday from October through April).** For a peaceful break, the café in the cloister offers freshly baked cakes and pastries. ⌧ *Cathedral Close, Salisbury* ☎ *01722/555120* ⊕ *www.salisburycathedral.org.uk* ⌧ *Cathedral and Chapter House free; suggested donation £6.50; tower tour £10* ⊙ *Cathedral Mon.–Sat. 10–5, Sun. 12–4. Chapter House Mon.–Sat. 9:30–4:30, Sun. 12:45–3:45.*

## STONEHENGE

Fodor's Choice
★

**Stonehenge.** Mysterious and ancient, Stonehenge has baffled archaeologists for centuries. One of England's most visited monuments, the circle of giant stones standing starkly against the wide sweep of Salisbury Plain still has the capacity to fascinate and move those who view it. This World Heritage site is now enclosed by barriers due to incidents of vandalism and growing fears that its popularity could threaten its existence, and visitors are kept on a paved path a short distance away from the stones. But if you visit in the early morning before the crowds have arrived, or in the evening, when the sky is heavy with scudding clouds, you can experience Stonehenge as it once was: a mystical, awe-inspiring place. Stonehenge was begun about 3000 BC, and it continued being changed and in use until around 1600 BC. It was made up of an outer circle of 30 sarsen stones, huge sandstone blocks weighing up to 25 tons, which are believed to have originated from the Marlborough Downs, and an earlier inner circle of bluestones that was constructed around 2500 BC. Within these circles was a horseshoe-shape group of sarsen trilithons (two large vertical stones supporting a third stone laid horizontally across it) and within that another horseshoe-shape grouping of bluestones. The sarsens used in the trilithons averaged 45 tons. Many of the huge stones were brought here from great distances before the invention of the wheel, and it's not certain what ancient form of transportation was used to move them. The bluestones, for example, are thought to have come from the Preseli Hills on the Atlantic coast of Wales, and may have been moved by raft over sea and river, and then dragged on rollers across country despite weighing as much as 4 tons each—a total journey of 149 miles as the crow flies. However, every time a reconstruction of the journey has been attempted, it has failed. The labor involved in quarrying, transporting, and carving these stones is astonishing, all the more so when you realize that it was accomplished about the same time as the construction of Egypt's major pyramids. Stonehenge (the name derives from the Saxon term for "hanging stones") has been excavated several times over the centuries, although some of the site's mysteries have been solved, the primary reason for its erection remains unknown. It's fairly certain that it was a religious site, and that worship here involved the cycles of the sun; the alignment of the stones on the axis of the midsummer sunrise and midwinter sunset makes this clear. The Druids certainly had nothing to do with the construction: the monument had already been in existence for nearly 2,000 years by the time they appeared. Some historians have maintained that Stonehenge was a kind of Neolithic computer, with a sophisticated astronomical purpose—an observatory of sorts—though evidence from excavations in the early 20th century shows that it had once been used as a burial ground. Excavations at Durrington Walls, another archaeological site a couple of miles northeast (off A345), have unearthed a seasonally occupied settlement dating from around 2500 BC, which may have been built and occupied by those who constructed Stonehenge. Another possibility is that this Neolithic village was home to those who performed the religious rites at Stonehenge, where people gathered from far and wide to feast and worship. The finds show Stonehenge not to be an isolated monument, but part of a much larger complex of ceremonial structures. Since it's no longer possible to closely examine the prehistoric carvings, some of which show axes and daggers, bring a pair of binoculars to help make out the details on the monoliths. To fully engage your imagination, or to get that magical photo, it's worth exploring all aspects of the site, both near and far. It has a particularly romantic aspect at dawn and dusk, or by a full moon. Your ticket entitles you to an informative audio tour, but in general, visitor amenities at Stonehenge are limited, especially for such a major tourist attraction. A new visitor center was under construction at the time of this writing, and this may cause some travel disruption. ■ TIP→ **English Heritage arranges access to the stone circle outside of normal hours. These tours require a payment of £15.30 well in advance.** ✉ *Junction of A303 and A344/A360, Amesbury* ☎ *0870/333–1181, 01722/343830 for private tours* ⊕ *www.english-heritage.org.uk* ✍ *£7.80* ⊗ *Mid-Mar.–May and Sept.–mid-Oct., daily 9:30–6; June–Aug., daily 9–7; mid-Oct.–mid-Mar., daily 9:30–4. Last admission 30 mins before closing.*

## SHOPPING

Almost every town in this part of England has a tempting array of shops selling antiques, collectibles, and one-of-a-kind items. English china makes a fitting souvenir, as do copies of the various Austen novels set in the region. For a post-tour pick-me-up, try English blended teas in presentation sets.

**King's Walk,** off Friarsgate in Winchester, has a number of stalls selling antiques, crafts, gift items, and bric-a-brac.

## WHERE TO EAT

$$
MODERN BRITISH

✕ **Chesil Rectory.** The timbered and gabled building may be Old English–it dates back to the mid-15th century–but the cuisine is modern British, using locally sourced ingredients. Dishes might include venison carpaccio for a starter, followed by slow-cooked pork rib eye or oven-roasted halibut. Good-value fixed-price lunches and early-evening dinners are available. Service and the heritage charm of the surroundings enhance the quality of the food. ⑤ *Average main: £17* ✉ *1 Chesil St., Winchester* ☎ *01962/851555* ⊕ *www.chesilrectory.co.uk.*

**$$**
MODERN BRITISH
× **The Pig.** Funkier sister of glamorous Lime Wood hotel, this New Forest "restaurant with rooms" puts the emphasis on localism and seasonality and is a local favorite. Lunch and dinner are served in a large conservatory overlooking lawns, and 95% of the ingredients are sourced within 15 miles. The frequently changing menu may include dishes like Lymington pollock with Dorset clams or Lyme Bay scallops with bacon. As the name suggests, porcine dishes feature prominently. You can overnight in one of the 26 comfortable rooms in the main building (an 18th-century former royal hunting lodge) or the converted stable block. All combine a slightly retro, shabby-chic style with modern bathrooms. Guests may accompany the "staff forager" on expeditions to find edible fauna such as wild garlic. ⑤ *Average main: £16* ✉ *Beaulieu Rd., Brockenhurst* ☎ *01590/622354* ⊕ *www.thepighotel.com.*

# ZEEBRUGGE, BELGIUM (FOR BRUGES)

Updated by
Liz Humphreys

Long thought of as a Sleeping Beauty reawakened, Bruges is an ancient town where the rhythm of medieval life resonates from every street corner. The city thrived during the 13th century as a member of the Hanseatic League, and an era of unprecedented wealth began under such Burgundian rulers as Philip the Good and Charles the Bold in the 15th century. At this time, Hans Memling and Jan van Eyck took art in a new direction with the famed Flemish Primitive style of painting, while fine civil and domestic buildings advertised the wealth generated by trade. When the city fell into poverty as its rivers silted in the 16th century, this architecture was preserved as if in aspic. Today Bruges is a compact and atmospheric maze of tangled streets, narrow canals, handsome squares, and gabled buildings. The town has not only awakened from its slumbers, but is also bright-eyed with spruced-up shops, restaurants, and cafés.

## ESSENTIALS

### CURRENCY
The euro. ATMs are common and credit cards are widely accepted.

### HOURS
Shops open Tuesday, Wednesday, Friday, and Saturday from 9 or 10 until 6; they are open later on Thursday. Most stores are closed on Sunday and some on Monday. Museums open from 9 until 6 with one late opening night during the week.

### PRIVATE TOURS
Though there are no guided tours that leave from Zeebrugge itself, you can take a variety of tours once you get to Bruges. And if you book in advance with Toerisme Brugge, you can hire a guide for a two-hour private tour for €60 (€30 for each additional hour).

**Contacts Toerisme Brugge.** ☎ *32/50444646* ⊕ *www.brugge.be.*

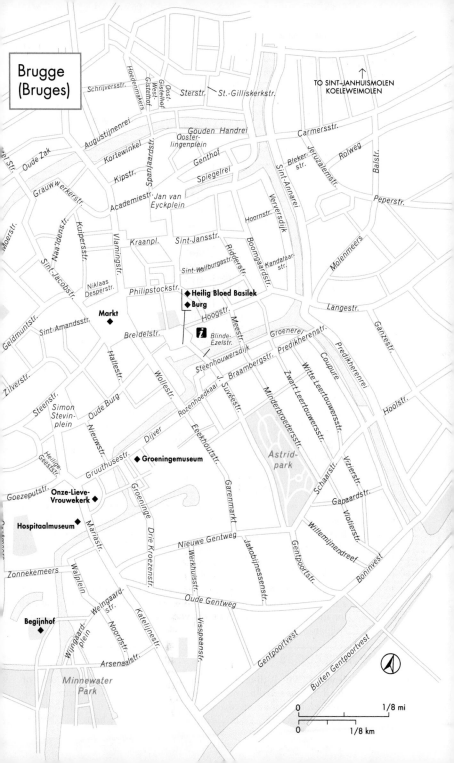

# Brugge (Bruges)

Schrijversstr.

Hoedenmakers

Oost-Gistelhof
West-Gistelhof

Sterstr.    St.-Gilliskerkstr.

TO SINT-JANHUISMOLEN
KOELEWEIMOLEN

Gouden Handrei

Carmersstr.

Augustijnenrei

Kortewinkel

Oosterlingenplein

Oude Zak

J. Str.

Kipstr.

Genthof

Spiegelrei

Bleker-str.

Jeruzalemstr.

Rolweg

Balstr.

Grauwwerkersstr.

Academiestr.

Jan van Eyckplein

Sint-Annarei

Peperstr.

Moerstr.

Naaldenstr.

Kuipersstr.

Vlamingstr.

Kraanpl.

Sint-Jansstr.

Hoornstr.

Ververschdijk

Boomgaardstr.

Kandelaar-str.

Molenmeers

Sint-Jacobstr.

Niklaas Desperstr.

Philipstockstr.

Sint-Wallburgastr.

Ridderstr.

♦ **Heilig Bloed Basilek**

♦ **Burg**

Geldmuntstr.

Sint-Amandsstr.

♦ **Markt**

Breidelstr.

Hoogstr.

Meestr.

Groenerei

Predikherenstr.

Langestr.

Ganzestr.

Zilverstr.

Steenstr.

Simon Stevin-plein

Hallestr.

Oude Burg

Wollestr.

*Blinde-Ezelstr.*

Steenhouwersdijk

J. Suvéestr.

Braambergstr.

Predikherenstr.

Witte Leertouwersstr.

Coupure

Predikherenrei

Hoolstr.

Heilige Geeststr.

Nieuwstr.

Dijver

Rozenhoedkaai

Eekhoutstr.

Zwart Leertouwersstr.

Minderbroedersstr.

Gruuthusestr.

♦ **Groeningemuseum**

*Astrid-park*

Schaarstr.

Vizierstr.

Goezeputstr.

**Onze-Lieve-Vrouwekerk** ♦

Groeninge

Garenmarkt

Gapaardstr.

Violierstr.

**Hospitaalmuseum** ♦

Mariastr.

Drie Kroezenstr.

Nieuwe Gentweg

Werkhuisstr.

Jakobijnessenstr.

Gentpoortstr.

Willemijnendreef

Boninvest

Zonnekemeers

Walplein

Oude Gentweg

Weingaard-str.

Gentpoortvest

**Begijnhof** ♦

Wijngaard-plein

Noordstr.

Katelijnestr.

Arsenaalstr.

Visspaanstr.

Buiten Gentpoortvest

*Minnewater Park*

0            1/8 mi

0            1/8 km

**TELEPHONES**

Tri-band GSM phones work in Belgium. You can buy prepaid phone cards at telecom shops, news vendors, and tobacconists in all towns and cities. Phone cards can be used for local or international calls. Proximus, Mobistar, and BASE are the leading telecom companies.

## COMING ASHORE

Cruise ships dock at Zeebrugge—14 km (9 miles) from the city of Bruges—at the King Leopold II dam or at Zweedse Kaai (Swedish Quay). From Zweedse Kaai, the Zeebrugge port authority provides a free shuttle to the exit of the cruise terminal. These locations are 2 km (1½ miles) from Zeebrugge train station. There are no passenger facilities within the port itself. The reliable and modern rail system ensures swift and efficient transfer from the station to a range of Belgian cities, including Ghent, Antwerp, and Brussels. The dock is within walking distance of the seafront of Zeebrugge Town, with its seafront promenade, Russian submarine exhibit, and historic fishing district.

Taxis wait at the dockside to transfer passengers not booked on organized trips into Zeebrugge, or you can walk to the train stations, though the roads are rather industrial. There are two stations, Zeebrugge Dorp, nearest to the Swedish Quay and open on weekdays from September to June, and Zeebrugge Strand, nearest to King Leopold II and open on weekends from September to June and daily in July and August. By rail from the center of Zeebrugge it is a 20-minute journey to Bruges at a current cost of €4.40 one-way for first-class and €2.90 one-way for second-class; the rail journey to Antwerp takes about two hours, at a cost of €24.60 one-way for first-class and €16 one-way for second-class. It is 15 minutes by road from the Zeebrugge docks to Bruges. You can also take a taxi into Bruges for a fixed rate of €50. Travel by taxi has a per-km (per-½ mile) charge of around €2.50, which makes it expensive for day tours but acceptable for short trips.

Vehicle-rental offices are located in Bruges (around €100 per day for a compact manual shift vehicle), but rail transport is most practical for independent travelers unless you really want to see more of the Belgian countryside.

---

> ### BRUGES BEST BETS
>
> **Boat trip on the canals.** The lifeblood of medieval Bruges, the canals now offer some of the finest views of the city's delightful architecture and distinctive streets and alleyways.
>
> **Belfort.** Climb the medieval tower for exceptional views across the tiled rooftops and ornate gables of this tiny enclave.
>
> **Groeningemusem.** The art of the Flemish Primitives and their successors form the core of this gallery, one of the finest of its kind in the world.

## EXPLORING BRUGES

**Begijnhof.** This 13th-century béguinage is a pretty and serene cluster of small whitewashed houses, a pigeon tower, and a church surrounding a pleasant green at the edge of a canal. The Begijnhof was founded in 1245 by Margaret, Countess of Constantinople, to bring together the

Beguines—girls and widows from all social backgrounds who devoted themselves to charitable work but who were not bound by religious vows. The last of the Beguines died about 50 years ago; today the site is occupied by the Benedictine nuns, who still wear the Beguine habit. Although most of the present-day houses are from the 16th and 17th centuries, they have maintained the architectural style of the houses that preceded them. One house (No.1) has been set aside as a small museum. Visitors are asked to respect the order's vow of silence. The horse-and-carriage rides around the town have a 10-minute stop outside the béguinage—long enough for a quick look round. ⊠ *Oude Begijnhof, off Wijngaardstraat* ☎ *050/33–00–11* 💲 *Free, No. 1 house visit €2* ♡ *Begijnhof daily 6:30–6:30; house Mon.–Sat. 10–5, Sun. 2:30–5* Ⓜ *Bus 12.*

> **THE NAME GAME**
>
> You'll find two spellings of the town name. That's because Belgium has two languages, Flemish and French. In French the spelling is Bruges; in Flemish it's Brugge. Since the city sits in the mainly Flemish-speaking region of Flanders, Brugge is more technically correct—though you won't have a problem if you call the city Bruges, as most tourists do.

**Fodor'sChoice** ★ **Burg.** A popular daytime meeting place and an enchanting, floodlighted scene after dark, the Burg is flanked by striking, centuries-old civic buildings. Named for the fortress built by Baldwin of the Iron Arm, the Burg was also the former site of the 10th-century Carolingian Cathedral of St. Donaas, which was destroyed by French Republicans in 1799. You can wander through the handsome, 18th-century law court, the Oude Gerechtshof, the Voormalige Civiele Griffie with its 15th-century front gable, the Stadhuis, and the Heilig Bloed Basiliek. The Burg is not all historic splendor, though—in sharp contrast to these buildings stands a modern construction by Japanese artist Toyo Ito, added in 2002. Public opinion is sharply divided over Ito's pavilion; you'll either love it or hate it. ⊠ *Hoogstraat and Breidelstraat* Ⓜ *Bus 1 or 12.*

**Fodor'sChoice** ★ **Groeningemuseum.** The tremendous holdings of this gallery give you the makings for a crash course in the Flemish Primitives and their successors. Petrus Christus, Hugo Van der Goes, Hieronymus Bosch, Rogier van der Weyden, Gerard David, Pieter Bruegel (both Elder and Younger), Pieter Pourbus—all the greats are represented here. Here you can see Jan van Eyck's wonderfully realistic *Madonna with Canon Van der Paele,* in which van Eyck achieved texture and depth through multiple layers of oil and varnish. There's also one of Hans Memling's greatest works, the *Moreel Triptych.* As if this weren't enough, the museum also encompasses a strong display of 15th- to 21st-century Dutch and Belgian works, sweeping through to Surrealist and contemporary art. The Groeninge is set back from the street in a pocket-size park behind a medieval gate. ⊠ *Dijver 12* ☎ *050/44–87–11* 💲 *€8* ♡ *Tues.–Sun. 9:30–5* Ⓜ *Bus 1 or 12.*

**Heilig Bloed Basiliek.** The Basilica of the Holy Blood manages to include both the austere and the ornate under one roof—not to mention one of Europe's most precious relics. The 12th-century Lower Chapel retains a stern, Romanesque character. From this sober space, an elaborate, external Gothic stairway leads to the stunningly lavish Upper Chapel, which was twice destroyed—by Protestant iconoclasts in the 16th century and by French Republicans in the 18th—but both times rebuilt. (Note that the Upper Chapel is closed to visitors during Eucharistic Mass on Sunday 11 to noon.) The original stained-glass windows were replaced in 1845, and then again after an explosion in 1967, when they were restored by the Brugge painter De Loddere. The basilica's namesake treasure is a vial thought to contain a few drops of the blood of Christ, brought from Jerusalem to Brugge in 1149 by Derick of Alsace when he returned from the Second Crusade. It is exposed here every Friday in the Lower Chapel 8:30 to 10 and in the Upper Chapel 10 to 11 and 3 to 4, and on other apparently random occasions for veneration: queue up to place your right hand on the vial and take a moment for quiet reflection. The small museum next to the basilica is the usual home of the basilica's name-sake reliquary. ⊠ *Burg 13* ⊕ *www.holyblood.com* 🖾 *Museum, €2* ☉ *Apr.–Sept., daily 9:30–noon and 2–5; Oct.–Mar., daily 10–noon and 2–4* Ⓜ *Bus 1 or 12.*

Fodor'sChoice ★ **Hospitaalmuseum.** Home to the greatest collection of Hans Memling paintings in the world, the **Oud Sint-Janshospitaal** is one of the oldest surviving medieval hospitals in Europe. It was founded in the 12th century and remained in use until the early 20th century. Furniture, paintings, and hospital-related items are attractively displayed; the 13th-century middle ward, the oldest of three, was built in Romanesque style. Other fascinating 18th-century paintings show patients arriving by sedan chair and being fed and ministered to by sisters and clerics. Some of the actual sedan chairs that were used are also on display. But the highlights of the collection are the six major works (and plenty of minor ones) by Hans Memling (1440–94) that are of breathtaking quality and rank among the greatest—and certainly the most spiritual—of the Flemish Primitive school. Memling was born in Germany, but spent the greater part of his life in Brugge. ⊠ *Mariastraat 38* 🕾 *050/44–87–11* 🖾 *€8* ☉ *Tues.–Sun. 9:30–5* Ⓜ *Bus 1 or 12.*

Fodor'sChoice ★ **Markt.** Used as a marketplace since 958, this square is still one of the liveliest places in Brugge. In the center stands a memorial to the city's medieval heroes, Jan Breydel and Pieter De Coninck, who led the commoners of Flanders to their short-lived victory over the aristocrats of France. On the east side of the Markt stand the provincial government house and the post office, an excellent pastiche of Burgundian Gothic. Old guild houses line the west and north sides of the square, their step-gabled facades overlooking the cafés spilling out onto the sidewalk. These buildings aren't always as old as they seem, though—often they're 19th-century reconstructions. The medieval **Belfort** (Belfry) on the south side of the Markt, however, is the genuine article. The tower dates to the 13th century, its crowning octagonal lantern to the 15th century. The valuables of Brugge were once kept in the second-floor treasury; now the Belfort's riches are in its remarkable 47-bell carillon, which rings even truer thanks to the new bells it was given in 2010. (Impressing Belgians with a carillon is no mean feat, as Belgium has some of the best in the world.) If you haven't walked enough, you can climb 366 winding steps to the clock mechanism, and from the carillon enjoy a gorgeous panoramic view. Back in the square, you may be tempted by the **horse-drawn carriages** that congregate here; a half-hour ride for up to five people, with a short stop at the Begijnhof, costs €39 plus "something for the horse." ✉ *Intersection of Steenstraat, St-Amandstraat, Vlamingstraat, Philipstockstraat, Breidelstraat, and Wollestraat* ☎ *050/44–87–11* ✉ *Belfort €8* ✆ *Belfort daily 9:30–5.*

**Onze-Lieve-Vrouwekerk.** The towering spire of the plain Gothic Church of Our Lady, begun about 1220, rivals the Belfry as Brugge's symbol. It is 381 feet high, the tallest brick construction in the world. While brick can be built high, it cannot be sculpted like stone; hence the tower's somewhat severe look. The art history highlight here is the *Madonna and Child* statue carved by Michelangelo, an early work. The great sculptor sold it to a merchant from Brugge when the original client failed to pay. It was stolen by Napoléon, and during World War II by Nazi leader Hermann Göring; now the white-marble figure sits in a black-marble niche behind an altar at the end of the south aisle. The choir museum contains many 13th- and 14th-century polychrome tombs, as well as two mausoleums: that of Mary of Burgundy, who died in 1482 at the age of 25 after a fall from her horse; and that of her father, Charles the Bold, killed in 1477 while laying siege to Nancy in France. Note that while you can enter the church for free, you'll need a ticket to see most of the major artworks, including the Michelangelo statue. ✉ *Dijver and Mariastraat* ✉ *Church free; choir museum €4* ✆ *Tues.–Fri. 9:30–5, Sat. 9:30–4:45, Sun. 1:30–5* Ⓜ *Bus 1 or 12.*

## SHOPPING

Bruges has many trendy boutiques and shops, especially along Nordzandstraat, as well as Steenstraat and Vlamingstraat, both of which branch off from the Markt. Ter Steeghere mall, which links the Burg with Wollestraat, deftly integrates a modern development into the historic center. The largest and most pleasant mall is the Zilverpand off Zilverstraat, where 30-odd shops cluster in Flemish gable houses. Souvenir shops crowd around the Markt, Wollestraat, Breidelstraat, and Minnewater. Bruges has been a center for lace-making since the 15th century. Handmade lace in intricate patterns, however, takes a long time to produce, and this is reflected in the price. For work of this type, you should be prepared to part with €250 or more. Art and antiques abound, with furniture and decorative objects from the surrounding Flanders region. You also can't go far in the city center without seeing a tempting window display of handmade chocolates, truffles, and pralines. These are delicious to enjoy while you stroll.

## ACTIVITIES

### CYCLING
The city is easy to explore on two wheels, and many Bruges city dwellers use bicycles daily. Cyclists can go in both directions along more than 50 one-way streets, marked on the tarmac with an image of a bicycle circled in blue. The Bruges tourist office sells a cycling brochure outlining five different routes around the city. The Green Bike Tour provides bike

rental and a guided tour (leaving 10 am daily from the Concertgebouw at 't Zand 34 from April to October) for €15. Tours return in the early afternoon. You can rent bicycles in several places.

Contacts **The Green Bike Tour.** ✉ *St. Kwintensstraat 12, Bruges* ☎ *32/50612667.*

## WHERE TO EAT

**$$$** ✕ **Chez Olivier.** Set above a quiet canal, with white swans gliding below,
FRENCH   this French charmer is purely romantic. Chef Olivier Foucad uses impeccably fresh ingredients for "light food," such as scallops in ginger and herbs, duck in rosemary honey, and lightly marbled Charolais beef. Lunches are a bargain and the staff is flexible—if you want one main course or two starters instead of the full prix fixe menu, just ask. For the best views, request a window seat next to the water. ⑤ *Average main: €28* ✉ *Meestraat 9* ☎ *050/33–36–59* ⊕ *www.chezolivier.be* ۞ *Closed Thurs. and Sun. and 2 wks in July. No lunch Sat.* Ⓜ *Bus 1.*

**$** ✕ **De Torre.** For traditional Belgian food at honest prices, this is the
BELGIAN   place. From noon until 10 pm, Flemish stew, tomato with shrimp, mussels, or fillet of sole are served as they are in many Flemish homes. The 18th-century house is decorated in art deco style, and the sunny terrace has a lovely view of the Reien. ⑤ *Average main: €15* ✉ *Langestraat 8* ☎ *050/34–29–46* ⊕ *www.de-torre.com* ۞ *Apr.–Sept, closed Tues.; Oct.– Mar., closed Tues., Wed.* Ⓜ *Bus 6 or 16.*

# The Baltic

## PORTS IN DENMARK, ESTONIA, FINLAND, GERMANY, LATVIA, POLAND, RUSSIA, AND SWEDEN

Vegetable and flower vendor, Helsinki

**WORD OF MOUTH**

"We did the Baltic in June, and St. Petersburg was the highlight of the trip. . . . The sights are amazing . . . . For us, we disembarked in every port except St. Petersburg on our own, so we did not have to wait in lines for a tour to assemble and begin."

— jacketwatch

Northern European itineraries are increasingly popular. You may depart from Stockholm or Copenhagen and visit several of the Baltic's top ports. A special treat for Baltic cruisers is often a stop in St. Petersburg, Russia, and this is why many people take these cruises.

Some Baltic itineraries begin in a U.K. port or even in Amsterdam (⇨ *"The North Sea" for more information about these ports*). Some may include stops in Norway (⇨ *"Norway" for Norwegian ports*). These cruises may be longer than the typical Mediterranean cruise and may cost more, which is one reason why they aren't as popular with first-timers to European cruising. But the number of ships doing Baltic itineraries continues to expand, and there are now some one-week cruises in these northern waters during the summer.

### ABOUT THE RESTAURANTS

All the restaurants we recommend serve lunch; they may also serve dinner if your cruise ship stays late in port and you choose to dine off the ship. Cuisine in Europe is varied, but Europeans tend to eat a leisurely meal at lunch; in most ports there are quicker and simpler alternatives for those who just want to grab a quick bite before returning to the ship. Note that several Baltic countries do not use the euro, including Denmark, Estonia, Finland, Latvia, Poland, Russia, and Sweden. Price categories in those countries are based on the euro-equivalent costs of eating in restaurants.

---

# COPENHAGEN, DENMARK

Updated by
Gelu Sulugiuc

Copenhagen—"København" in Danish—has no glittering skylines, few killer views, and only a handful of meager skyscrapers. Bicycles glide alongside manageable traffic at a pace that's utterly human. The early-morning air in the pedestrian streets of the city's core, Strøget, is redolent of freshly baked bread and soap-scrubbed storefronts. If there's such a thing as a cozy city, this is it. Filled with museums, restaurants, cafés, and lively nightlife, the city has its greatest resource in its spirited inhabitants. The imaginative, unconventional, and affable Copenhageners exude an egalitarian philosophy that embraces nearly all lifestyles and leanings. Despite a tumultuous history, Copenhagen survives as the liveliest Scandinavian capital, with some excellent galleries and museums. With its backdrop of copper towers and crooked rooftops, the venerable city is amused by playful street musicians and performers, soothed by one of the highest standards of living in the world, and spangled by the thousand lights and gardens of Tivoli.

## ESSENTIALS

### CURRENCY

The monetary unit in Denmark is the krone (DKr), divided into 100 øre. Even though Denmark hasn't adopted the euro, the Danish krone is firmly bound to it at about DKr 7.5 to 1€, with only minimal fluctuations in exchange rates.

### HOURS

Museum hours vary, though the major collections are open Tuesday through Sunday from 10 to 5. Stores are open weekdays from 9:30 to 5:30 (or sometimes 7).

### TELEPHONES

Tri-band GSM phones work in Denmark. You can buy prepaid phone cards at telecom shops, news vendors, and tobacconists in all towns and cities. Phone cards can be used for local or international calls.

## COMING ASHORE

The city's main cruise port at Langelinie Pier is one of the best in Europe. Although it's a 10-minute drive or 30-minute walk from the downtown core, the port is within walking distance of the Little Mermaid and the attractions of the seafront. Taxis wait outside the cruise terminal. The on-site Copenhagen Cruise Information Center is run by the city tourist office, and there is a selection of shops housed in the renovated old wharf warehouses selling typical souvenirs.

Some ships dock at the Freeport Terminal, which is a further 30 minutes on foot from the downtown core (i.e., a full hour's walk from the center). Taxis wait outside the terminal, and the cost is around DKr 125 for the trip into town. A small number of ships (primarily smaller vessels) dock at the quayside at Nordre Toldbod, which sits beside the Little Mermaid and is a 10-minute walk from the city center; however, there are no passenger facilities here.

City Bikes is a citywide project offering free bike rental. There's a City Bike rack at Langelinie Pier, so you can pick up a bike here and cycle along the waterfront to the center or take a bike from a rack in the center to cycle back to the ship at the end of your day.

A water-taxi service to the city center leaves from the end of Langelinie Pier hourly. The boat stops at various parts of the city, and you can hop on and hop off as you wish. A one-day ticket costs DKr 40. A taxi direct to downtown (10 to 15 minutes) costs around DKr 70–DKr 90 from Langelinie.

There is a dedicated cruise lounge at the Illum department store on Strøget in the city center, where you can wait for transfers, leave purchases for later collection, have a free coffee, or rest during your day ashore.

Car rentals cost around DKr 1,185 per day for an economy manual vehicle; however, public transport is much more convenient for a short city visit. The metro and bus services are clean and efficient, with tickets costing DKr 24 for a single-ride two-zone ticket for one hour of unlimited travel; stamp your ticket as you board the bus or before boarding the train.

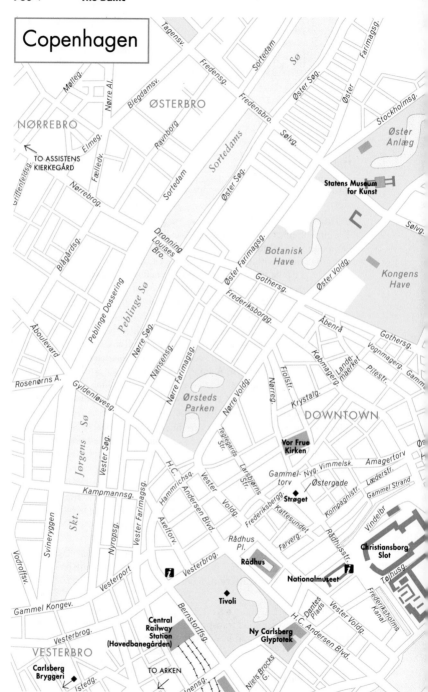

# Copenhagen

NØRREBRO

ØSTERBRO

TO ASSISTENS KIERKEGÅRD

Statens Museum for Kunst

Øster Anlæg

Botanisk Have

Kongens Have

Ørsteds Parken

DOWNTOWN

Vor Frue Kirken

Strøget

Christiansborg Slot

Rådhus

Nationalmuseet

Tivoli

VESTERBRO

Central Railway Station (Hovedbanegården)

Ny Carlsberg Glyptotek

Carlsberg Bryggeri

TO ARKEN

Jorgens Sø

Peblinge Sø

**GETTING TO THE AIRPORT**

If you do not purchase airport transfers from your cruise line, there are easy and inexpensive options for travel between the cruise terminals and the airport.

For Langelinie Pier, take the metro (DKr 28.50) upstairs in the airport train station at Terminal 3. Trains depart every 4 minutes during the day and every 15 minutes during night hours. There are two possible routes to and from the airport to Langelinie Pier: Either get off at Copenhagen Central Station and then take a taxi to the cruise terminal, or get off at Østerport Station (three more minutes of travel) and take Bus 26 (DKr 25), which stops at the cruise terminal. The 20-minute taxi ride between airport and pier costs around DKr 250.

For Freeport Terminal, take the metro to Copenhagen Central Station (DKr 28.50); a taxi from the station to the terminal will cost around DKr 75. A taxi direct from the airport to Freeport Terminal will cost around DKr 300.

> **COPENHAGEN BEST BETS**
>
> **Tivoli Gardens.** One of Europe's finest and most famous planned green spaces, Tivoli is part formal garden, part woodland, part theme park.
>
> **Amalienborg Palace.** These rococo palaces, built by the Royal Family at the height of Danish influence, are architectural delights filled with artistic treasures gathered from around Europe.
>
> **The Little Mermaid.** This diminutive statue is the city's most famous landmark, and though she's a little disappointing in real life, you haven't been to Copenhagen if you don't say hello to her.

## EXPLORING COPENHAGEN

★ **Amalienborg.** The four identical rococo buildings occupying this square have housed royals since 1784. It's still the queen's winter residence. The Christian VIII palace across from the royal's wing houses the Amalienborg Museum, which displays the second part of the Royal Collection (the first is at Rosenborg Slot) and chronicles royal lifestyles between 1863 and 1947. Here you can view the study of King Christian IX (1818–1906) and the drawing room of his wife, Queen Louise. Rooms are packed with royal heirlooms and treasures.

In the square's center is a magnificent equestrian statue of King Frederik V by the French sculptor Jacques François Joseph Saly. It reputedly cost as much as all the buildings combined. Every day at noon, the Royal Guard and band march from Rosenborg Slot through the city for the changing of the guard. At noon on Queen Margrethe's birthday, April 16, crowds of Danes gather to cheer their monarch, who stands and waves from her balcony. On Amalienborg's harbor side is the garden of Amaliehaven, at the foot of which the queen's ship often docks. ⊠ *Christian VIII's Palace, Amalienborg Pl., Frederiksstaden* ☎ *33/12–21–86* ⊕ *dkks.dk/amalienborgmuseet* ☞ *Museum: DKr 65* ☾ *Museum: May–Oct. daily 10–4, Nov.–Dec. Tues.–Sun. 11–4.*

**Carlsberg Bryggeri** (*Carlsberg Brewery*). A large, ornate chimney makes this mid-19th-century brewery visible from a distance. J. C. Jacobson, one of Denmark's most important historical figures, named the brewery after his son Carl; "berg," or mountain, signifies the brewery's location on Valby Hill. The four giant granite elephants that guard the main entrance illustrate that Jacobsen was a well-traveled man who adored art. The elephants are in fact inspired by Bernini's famous obelisk in Rome. In the visitor center, new interactive displays, also in English, take you step by step through the brewing process. At the end of your visit, you're rewarded with a complimentary beer sampling. The Carlsberg Museum, also on the grounds, tells the story of the Jacobsen family, their beer empire, and Carlsberg's extensive philanthropy, which still greatly benefits Danish culture. Large-scale beer production has now moved outside of the city and the old brewery complex is being transformed into a combined neighborhood for arts, culture, and living. ⊠ *Gamle Carlsberg Vej 11, Vesterbro* ☎ *33/27–12–82* ⊕ *www.visitcarlsberg.com* ✉ *DKr 70 (includes 2 beers or soft drinks)* ☉ *Tues.–Sun. 10–5.*

**Fodor's** Choice
★
**Christiansborg Slot.** Surrounded by canals on three sides, the massive granite Christiansborg Castle is where the queen officially receives guests. From 1441 until the fire of 1795, it was used as the royal residence. Even though the first two castles on the site were burned, Christiansborg remains an impressive neobaroque and neoclassical compound. It now houses parliament and the prime minister's office. ⊠ *Slotsholmen, (area around Christiansborg; bordered by Boørsgade, Vindebrogade, and Frederiksholms Kanal), Centrum.*

**Kongelige Repræsantationslokaler** (*Royal Reception Chambers*). At the Kongelige Repræsantationslokaler, you're asked to don slippers to protect the floors in this impossibly grand space. ⊠ *Christiansborg Slot, Slotsholmen* ☎ *33/92–64–92* ✉ *DKr 70* ☉ *Tours: May–Sept., daily at 3, Oct.–Apr., Tues.–Sun., 3.*

**Ruins of Bishop Absalon's castle.** While Christiansborg was being rebuilt around 1900, the national museum excavated the ruins of Bishop Absalon's castle beneath it. The resulting dark, subterranean maze contains fascinating models and architectural relics. ⊠ *Christiansborg Slot, Slotsholmen* ☎ *33/92–64–92* ✉ *DKr 40* ☉ *May–Sept., daily 10–5; Oct.–Apr., Tues.–Sun., 10–5.*

**Christianshavn.** Cobbled avenues, antique street lamps, and Left Bank charm make up one of the oldest neighborhoods in the city. Today the area harbors restaurants, cafés, and shops, and its ramparts are edged with green areas and walking paths, making it the perfect neighborhood for an afternoon amble.

**Den Lille Havfrue** (*The Little Mermaid*). Somewhat overhyped, this 1913 statue commemorates Hans Christian Andersen's lovelorn Little Mermaid. (You may want to read the original Hans Christian Andersen tale in advance; it's a heart-wrenching story that's a far cry from the Disney animated movie.) Donated to the city by Carl Jacobsen, the son of the founder of Carlsberg Breweries, the innocent waif has also been the subject of some cruel practical jokes, including decapitation and the loss of an arm, but she's currently in one piece. The Langelinie promenade is thronged with Danes and visitors making their pilgrimage to the statue, especially on sunny Sundays. Although the statue itself is modest, the views of the surrounding harbor are not. ⊠ *Langelinie promenade, Østerbro.*

Fodor's Choice
★
ⓒ
**Nationalmuseet** (*National Museum*). One of the best museums of its kind in Europe, the Nationalmuseet is inside an 18th-century royal residence that's peaked by massive overhead windows. Extensive permanent exhibits chronicle Danish cultural history from prehistoric to modern times. The museum has one of the largest collections of Stone Age tools in the world, as well as Egyptian, Greek, and Roman antiquities. The exhibit on Danish prehistory features a great section on Viking times. The children's museum, with replicas of period clothing and a scalable copy of a real Viking ship, makes history fun for those under 12. Displays have English labels, and the do-it-yourself walking tour, History of Denmark in 60 Minutes, offers a good introduction to Denmark; the guide is free at the information desk. ⊠ *Frederiksholms Kanal 12, Centrum* ☎ *33/13–44–11* ⊕ *www.natmus.dk* ⊡ *Free* ☉ *Tues.–Sun. 10–5.*

★ **Ny Carlsberg Glyptotek.** The exquisite antiquities and a world-class collection of impressionist masterpieces make this one of Copenhagen's most important museums. The neoclassical building was donated in 1888 by Carl Jacobsen, son of the founder of the Carlsberg Brewery. Surrounding its lush indoor garden, a series of rooms house works by Pissarro, Degas, Monet, Sisley, Rodin, and Gauguin. The museum is also renowned for its extensive assemblage of Egyptian and Greek pieces, not to mention Europe's finest collection of Roman portraits and the best collection of Etruscan art outside Italy. A modern wing, designed by the acclaimed Danish architect Henning Larsen, provides a luminous entry to the French painting section. From June to September, guided English-language tours start at 2. The café overlooking the winter garden is well known among Copenhageners for its Sunday brunch. ⊠ *Dantes Pl. 7, Centrum* ☎ *33/41–81–41* ⊕ *www.glyptoteket. dk* ⊡ *DKr 50; free Sun.* ☉ *Tues.–Sun. 11–5.*

★
ⓒ
**Statens Museum for Kunst.** Old-master paintings—including works by Rubens, Rembrandt, Titian, El Greco, and Fragonard—as well as a comprehensive array of antique and 20th-century Danish art make up the National Art Gallery collection. Also notable is the modern art, which includes pieces by Henri Matisse, Edvard Munch, Henri Laurens, Emil Nolde, and Georges Braque. The space also contains a children's museum, which puts on shows for different age groups at kids' eye-level. Wall texts are in English. The bookstore and café are also worth a visit. ⊠ *Sølvgade 48–50, Østerbro* ☎ *33/74–84–94* ⊕ *www.smk.dk* ⊡ *Museum: Free. Special exhibitions: DKr 95* ☉ *Tues. and Thurs.–Sun. 10–5, Wed. 10–8.*

★ **Strøget.** Though it is referred to by one name, the city's pedestrian spine, pronounced *Stroy*-et, is actually a series of five streets: Frederiksberggade, Nygade, Vimmelskaftet, Amagertorv, and Østergade. By midmorning, particularly on Saturday, it is congested with people, baby strollers, and street performers. Past the swank and trendy—and sometimes flashy and trashy—boutiques of **Frederiksberggade** is the double square of **Gammeltorv** (Old Square) and **Nytorv** (New Square). In addition to shopping, you can enjoy Strøget for strolling, as hundreds do. In summer the sidewalks have a festive street-fair atmosphere.

Fodor'sChoice
★
☾
**Tivoli.** Copenhagen's best-known attraction, conveniently next to its main train station, attracts an astounding 4 million people from mid-April to mid-September. Tivoli is more than just an amusement park: among its attractions are a pantomime theater, an open-air stage, 38 restaurants (some of them very elegant), and frequent concerts, which cover the spectrum from classical to rock to jazz. Fantastic flower exhibits color the lush gardens and float on the swan-filled ponds.

The park was established in the 1840s, when Danish architect George Carstensen persuaded a worried King Christian VIII to let him build an amusement park on the edge of the city's fortifications, rationalizing that "when people amuse themselves, they forget politics." The Tivoli Guard, a youth version of the Queen's Royal Guard, performs every day. Try to see Tivoli at least once by night, when 100,000 colored lanterns illuminate the Chinese pagoda and the main fountain. Some evenings there are also fireworks displays. Call to check the season's opening and closing dates as well as family discounts. Tivoli is also open select hours around Halloween and from mid-November until late December. ⊠ *Vesterbrog. 3(on border of Vesterbro district), Centrum* ☎ *33/15–10–01* ⊕ *www.tivoli.dk* ⊠ *Grounds: DKr 95. Unlimited ride pass: DKr 199* ☾ *Apr.–Sept., Sun.–Thurs. 11 am to 10 or 11 pm, Fri. 11 am–12:30 am, Sat. 11–midnight.*

Fodor'sChoice
★
**Trapholt Museum for Moderne Kunst** (*Trapholt Museum of Modern Art*). Just east of town is the Trapholt Museum for Moderne Kunst, one of Denmark's largest—and most highly acclaimed—modern-art museums. Rising over the banks of the Kolding Fjord, this sprawling white complex has been artfully incorporated into its surroundings, affording lovely water and parkland views from its floor-to-ceiling windows. A collection of 20th-century Danish paintings is displayed in the light-filled galleries; it includes works by Anna Ancher, Ejler Bille, Egill Jakobsen, J. A. Jerichau, Jais Nielsen, Richard Mortensen, Aksel Jørgensen, and Franciska Clausen. A true highlight is the Danish Furniture Museum, housed in a specially designed annex that is accessed via a circular ramp topped by a skylight. The superbly displayed collection includes the world's largest assemblage of Danish-designed chairs, offering a unique historical overview of the birth and popularization of the nation's furniture design. The museum keeps its furniture storage room open to the public, so you can peruse the entire collection even when it's not officially on display.

The Danish ceramics collection, one of the largest in Denmark, is also well worth a look, featuring works by Thorvald Bindesbøll and one-of-a-kind ceramics by Axel Salto, whose pieces often resemble living organisms. Famous designer Arne Jacobsen's summer cottage was moved to Trapholt and opened on its grounds. Café Trapholt serves coffee, beverages, and light meals. The gift shop sells local and international art and design-related gifts. ⊠ *Æblehaven 23, Kolding* ☎ *76/30–05–30* ⊕ *www. trapholt.dk* ⊠ *DKr 65* ☾ *Tues.–Sun. 10–5, Wed. 10–8.*

7

## SHOPPING

A showcase for world-famous Danish design and craftsmanship, Copenhagen seems to have been set up with shoppers in mind. In fact, its very name (København in Danish), means the "merchant's harbor," because it was once a major center of trade. The spirit of those days remains, with countless specialty shops in almost every corner of the city. The best buys are such luxury items as amber, crystal, porcelain, silver, and furs. Danish clothing design is now coming into fashion and is considered one of the nation's most important exports.

Look for offers and sales (*tilbud* or *udsalg* in Danish) and check antiques and secondhand shops for classics at cut-rate prices. Although prices are inflated by a hefty 25% Value-Added Tax (Danes call it *moms*), non–European Union citizens can receive about an 18% refund if they are willing to do the paperwork. For more details and a list of all tax-free shops, ask at the tourist office for a copy of the *Tax-Free Shopping Guide, or visit the website Global Blue* (⊕ *www.global-blue.com*).

**Georg Jensen.** This elegant, austere shop is aglitter with sterling, which is what you'd expect from one of the most recognized names in international silver. Jensen has its own museum next door. ⊠ *Amagertorv 4, Centrum* ☎ *33/11–40–80* ⊕ *www.georgjensen.com.*

**Illums Bolighus.** Part gallery and part department store, Illums Bolighus will surround you with cutting-edge Danish and international design—art glass, porcelain, silverware, carpets, and loads of grown-up toys. Staff will help you file your value-added tax refund on site—don't forget to get some documents stamped at customs upon leaving Denmark and mail them back. ⊠ *Amagertorv 10, Downtown* ☎ *33/14–19–41* ⊕ *www.illumsbolighus.dk.*

**Information Center for Danish Crafts and Design.** The Information Center for Danish Crafts and Design provides helpful information on galleries, shops, and workshops specializing in Danish crafts and design, including jewelry, ceramics, wooden toys, and furniture. Its website has listings and reviews of the city's best crafts shops. ⊠ *Kongens Nytorv 1E, 1., Centrum* ☎ *33/12–61–62* ⊕ *www.danishcrafts.dk.*

**Royal Copenhagen Factory Outlet.** The Royal Copenhagen Factory Outlet has a good deal of stock, often at reduced prices. You can also buy Holmegaard Glass at the Royal Copenhagen store in Centrum and this factory outlet. ⊠ *Søndre Fasanvej 9, Frederiksberg* ☎ *38/34–10–04* ⊕ *www.royalcopenhagen.com* ⊙ *Weekdays 10–6, Sat. 10–2.*

## WHERE TO EAT

$

SCANDINAVIAN

★

✕ **Ida Davidsen.** This five-generations-old, world-renowned lunch spot is synonymous with smørrebrød, the Danish open-face sandwich. The often-packed dining area is dimly lighted, with worn wooden tables and news clippings of famous visitors on the walls. Creative sandwiches include the H. C. Andersen, with liver pâté, bacon, and tomatoes. The terrific duck is smoked by Ida's husband, Adam, and served alongside a horseradish-spiked cabbage salad. ⑤ *Average main: Dkr 200* ⊠ *Store Kongensgade 70, Centrum* ☎ *33/91–36–55* ⊕ *www.idadavidsen.dk* ⌖ *Reservations essential* ⊙ *No dinner. Closed weekends and July.*

$$   ✕ **Søren K.** Occupying a bright corner of the Royal Library's mod-
EUROPEAN  ern Black Diamond extension, this cool-toned restaurant, with clean lines, blond-wood furnishings, and recessed lighting, serves French-Scandinavian concoctions. For waterfront views, choose a table inside up against the glass walls or outside. Signature dishes include dried Danish ham with thyme and *beurre noir* or scallops, corn purée, and watercress. The menu always has vegetarian dishes and a fish of the day. It's the perfect lunchtime spot, with a two-course menu for about DKr 200. ⑤ *Average main: Dkr 205* ⊠ *Søren Kierkegaards Pl. 1, Centrum* ☎ *33/47–49–49* ⊕ *www.soerenk.dk* ⊘ *Closed Sun.*

## WHERE TO STAY

$$   ⬚ **Copenhagen Marriott Hotel.** This large Marriott on the waterfront is a
HOTEL  well-oiled machine. **Pros:** all rooms have both tub and shower combo and either city or canal-side views. **Cons:** no restaurants nearby; small windows in the rooms; slightly generic. ⑤ *Rooms from: Dkr 1899* ⊠ *Kalvebod Brygge 5, Centrum* ☎ *88/33–99–00* ⊕ *www.marriott.com/cphdk* ⇆ *401 rooms, 10 suites* ⦿ *No meals.*

$$$$   ⬚ **Copenhagen Strand.** You can't stay closer to the harbor than here.
HOTEL  **Pros:** close to city attractions, most bathrooms have both a tub and shower. **Cons:** restaurant only serves breakfast; tight quarters; morning street noise; very expensive. ⑤ *Rooms from: Dkr 4000* ⊠ *Havneg. 37, Centrum* ☎ *33/48–99–00* ⊕ *www.copenhagenstrand.dk* ⇆ *174 rooms, 2 suites* ⦿ *Breakfast.*

$$   ⬚ **Radisson Blu Scandinavia Hotel.** South across the Stadsgraven from
HOTEL  Christianshavn stands one of Denmark's largest hotels, as well as Copenhagen's only casino. **Pros:** good-size rooms with great city views; several on-site restaurants. **Cons:** it's about a mile to Centrum; feels like the business hotel it is, which isn't to everyone's taste. ⑤ *Rooms from: Dkr 1605* ⊠ *Amager Blvd. 70, Amager* ☎ *33/96–50–00* ⊕ *www.radissonblu.dk/scandinaviahotel-koebenhavn* ⇆ *542 rooms, 42 suites* ⦿ *No meals.*

# GDAŃSK, POLAND

Updated by
Dorota Wąsik

Gdańsk is special to Poles—and to Scandinavians and Germans, who visit the region in great numbers. From 1308 to 1945 Gdańsk was an independent city-state called Danzig. In 1997 Gdańsk celebrated its 1,000th year as a Baltic city. It remains well known as the cradle of the anti-Communist workers' movement that came to be known as *Solidarność* (Solidarity)—after the collapse of the Soviet bloc in 1989, Solidarity leader Lech Wałęsa became president of Poland in the nation's first free elections since World War II. Although Gdańsk was almost entirely destroyed during World War II, the streets of its Główne Miasto (Main Town) have been lovingly restored and still retain their historical and cultural richness. The Stare Miasto (Old Town) contains several churches and the beautifully reconstructed Ratusz Główny (Old Town Hall). At the north end of the Old Town sit the shipyards that captivated world attention during the 1970s and '80s but have since undergone a difficult restructuring process. It might be tempting to see its lot as a metaphor to the last few decades of Polish history. Gdańsk is part of the so-called Tri-city—the other two of the triplets being Sopot, a fashionable 19th-century resort, and Gdynia, a 1920s, modernist-style port town, where most cruise ships arrive. The three components of the Tri-city are not very far apart, and they are conveniently linked by a suburban rail system (SKM).

## ESSENTIALS

### CURRENCY
The Złoty. U.S. currency is not accepted, and credit cards are not universally accepted, especially in smaller shops and eateries. ATMs are widespread.

### HOURS
Shopping hours are generally weekdays from 7 am until 6 or 7 pm, with shorter hours on the weekend. Museums are typically open Tuesday through Sunday from 10 am until 4 pm.

### TELEPHONES
Most international mobile phones (3G included) work in Poland, but do check your roaming charges in advance. Major local telecom companies are Era, Plus, and Orange. It is easy to get a prepaid phone and recharge it as you need it (you can get the cards at mobile operators' shops, newsagents, gas stations, even supermarkets). Due to the fast growth of the mobile network, there are fewer public phones now, but you will still find them. They operate with phone cards, which can be bought at newsstands. Public phones support international calls.

## COMING ASHORE
Most cruise ships arrive at Gdynia, either at the Francuskie (French) or Pomorskie (Pomeranian) Quay. The port is within a 20-minute walk (about 1 km) of the SKM (suburban rail) stop, which is right next to the main railway station in Gdynia. This train is the easiest and most economical means of transportation within the Tri-city, and the ride into Gdańsk city center takes about 30 minutes. Taxis are readily available, but a ride between Gdańsk to Gdynia will cost you about zł 100 .

A few ships arrive in Gdańsk itself. These will dock at two sites in the outer harbor of the city: Oliwskie Quay on the east bank and Westerplatte Quay on the west bank. Both lie 6 km (3.7 miles) from the downtown center. Facilities at Oliwskie Quay, the bigger of the two, include shops and taxi kiosks. It is 1 km (½ mile) to the Oliwa train station for the journey into downtown Gdańsk, or 300 meters to a tram stop (Routes 2, 5, 10, 14, and 15 head into the city). Westerplatte Quay has almost no facilities, with only restrooms and a taxi kiosk. Bus route 106 travels into the city. The downtown core can be easily explored on foot.

Car rentals are not useful for exploring the city, but would allow you to visit the surrounding Pomeranian region. An economy manual vehicle is approximately €63 per day. Companies will pick you up at the port but may add an extra charge. Taxis or limousines can be hired for touring. Taxi rates are zł 5–zł 7 at pickup then zł 3 per km.

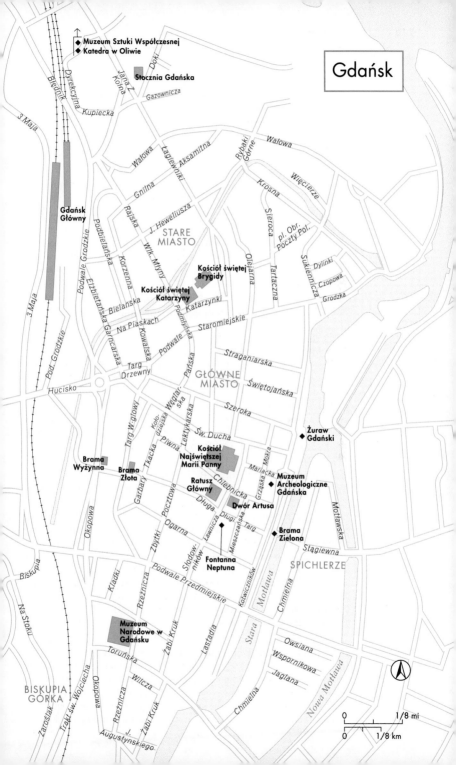

## EXPLORING GDAŃSK

★ **Brama Wyżynna** (*High Gate*). The historic entrance to the Old Town of Gdańsk is marked by this magnificent Renaissance gate, which marks the beginning of the so-called Royal Route, along which the king passed through the city on his annual visit. The gate is adorned with the flags of Poland, Gdańsk, and the Prussian kingdom. Its builder, Hans Kramer of Dresden, erected it as a link in the chain of modern fortifications put up to frame the western city borders between 1574 and 1576. The brick gate was renovated and decorated in 1588 by Flemish sculptor Willem van den Blocke, whose decorations you can still see today. ⊠ *Off Wały Jagiellońskie, at ul. Długa, Stare Miasto.*

**Brama Zielona** (*Green Gate*). The eastern entrance to the medieval city of Gdańsk is at the water's edge. Construction, supervised by Regnier of Amsterdam and Hans Kramer of Dresden, lasted from 1568 to 1571. This 16th-century gate also doubled as a royal residence. Unfortunately, the name no longer fits: the gate is now painted brown. ⊠ *At eastern end of Długi Targ, Stare Miasto.*

**Brama Złota** (*Golden Gate*). Brama Złota Just behind the Brama Wyżynna, the Golden Gate was the second through which the king passed on the Royal Route. This structure dates from 1614, and combines characteristics of both the Italian and Dutch Renaissance. It was built to the design of Abraham van den Blocke. The stone figures (by Pieter Ringering) along the parapet (on the Wały Jagiellońskie facade) represent allegories of the city's citizen's virtues: Prudence, Justice, Piety, and Concord. On the Długa street facade there are allegories of Peace, Freedom, Fortune, and Fame—the pursuits of Gdańsk city over the centuries. Next to the Golden Gate squats the house of the **St George's Brotherhood,** erected by Glotau between 1487 and 1494 in the late-Gothic style. ⊠ *Off Wały Jagiellońskie, at western end of ul. Długa, Stare Miasto.*

★ **Dwór Artusa** (*Artus Mansion*). Behind the Fontanna Neptuna on Długi Targ, one of the more significant of the grand houses was constructed over a period from the 15th through the 17th centuries and is now a museum. The mansion was named for mythical English King Arthur, who otherwise has no affiliation with the place. This and the other stately mansions on the Długi Targ are reminders of the traders and aristocrats who once resided in this posh district. The court's elegant interior houses a huge, 40-foot-high Renaissance tiled stove, possibly the world's largest, a mid-16th-century masterpiece by George Stelzener. The mansion's collection also includes Renaissance furnishings, paintings, and holy figures. The building was the meeting place of the Gdańsk city nobles. ⊠ *Długi Targ 43, Stare Miasto* ☎ *058/346–33–58* 🖃 *zł 10* ☉ *Mon. 11–3, Tues.–Sat. 10–6, Sun. 11–6.*

Fodor'sChoice
★
☾
**Fontanna Neptuna** (*Neptune Fountain*). One of the city's most distinctive landmarks is the elaborately gilded, 17th-century fountain at the western end of Długi Targ. The fountain itself is perhaps the best-known symbol of Gdańsk, emphasizing its bond with the sea. It was sculpted by Peter Husen and Johann Rogge. The general conceptual design was developed by Abraham van den Blocke. The magnificent surrounding fencing was

added in 1634. Between 1757 and 1761 Johann Karl Stender remade the fountain chalice and plinth in the rococo style and added a whole array of sea creatures. ⊠ *ul. Długa, east of Wały Jagiellońskie, Stare Miasto.*

**Fodor's Choice** ★ **Katedra w Oliwie** (*Oliwa Cathedral*). The district of Oliwa, northwest of the Old Town, is worth visiting if only for its magnificent cathedral complex. Originally part of a Cistercian monastery, the church was erected during the 13th century. Like most other structures in Poland, it has been rebuilt many times, resulting in a hodgepodge of styles from Gothic to Renaissance to rococo. The cathedral houses a **museum** as well as one of the most impressive rococo organs you're ever likely to hear—and see. It has more than 6,000 pipes, and when a special mechanism is activated, wooden angels ring bells and a wooden star climbs up a wooden sky. Demonstrations of the organ and a brief narrated church history are given almost hourly on weekdays in summer (May through September), less frequently on weekends and the rest of the year. ⊠ *ul. Cystersów 10, Oliwa* ⊕ *www.archikatedraoliwa.pl* ⊙ *Church daily; museum June–mid-Sept., weekdays 10–5, Sat. 10–3.*

**Fodor's Choice** ★ **Kościół Najświetszej Marii Panny** (*St. Mary's Church*). The largest brick church in the world—and the largest church of any kind in Poland—St. Mary's is on the north side of ulica Piwna. The sanctuary can accommodate 25,000 people. This enormous 14th-century church underwent major restoration after World War II. Although it originally held 22 altars, 15 of them have been relocated to museums in Gdańsk and Warsaw. The highlight of a visit is the climb up the hundreds of steps to the top of the church tower. The church also contains a 500-year-old, 25-foot-high astronomical clock that has only recently been restored to working order after years of neglect. It keeps track of solar and lunar progressions, and it displays the signs of the zodiac, something of an anomaly in a Catholic church. ⊠ *Podkramarska 5, at ul. Piwna, Stare Miasto* ⊕ *www.bazylikamariacka.pl* ⊠ *zł 4 (church); zł 5 (tower)* ⊙ *Church Mon.–Sat. 9–5, Sun. 1–5; tower Apr.–Oct. only.*

**Kościół świetej Brygidy** (*St. Brigitte's Church*). This church, a few blocks north of the shipyards, is a prime example of the fundamental link in the Polish consciousness between Catholicism and political dissent. After the Communist government declared martial law in 1981 in an attempt to force Solidarity to disband, the union's members began meeting here secretly during celebrations of mass. A statue of Pope John Paul II can be seen in front of the church. ⊠ *ul. Profesorska 17, near Ratusz Główny (Old Town Hall), Stare Miasto* ⊕ *www.brygida.gdansk.pl.*

---

**GDAŃSK BEST BETS**

**Stocznia Gdańska.** This shipyard was the seat of the social movement that began the downfall of Communism in Eastern Europe, so the site resonates with living history.

**Stroll the lanes and alleyways of the Old Town.** This district is a triumph of Renaissance architecture and a riot of ornate gables, cornices and lintels.

**Kościół Najświetszej Marii Panny.** This is the largest brick-built church in the world and the largest church of any kind in Poland.

7

**Kościół świetej Katarzyny** (*St. Catherine's Church*). The former parish church in Gdańsk's Old Town is supposedly the oldest church in the city: its construction was begun in the 1220s; the tower was constructed in the 1480s; the carillon of 37 bells was added in 1634. The 17th-century astronomer Jan Hevelius is buried in the presbytery of the church, below which lies what's left of the town's oldest Christian cemetery (which dates from the 10th century). At this writing, the church is undergoing renovation but can still be visited. ⊠ *Wielki Młyn, Stare Miasto* ☎ *058/301–15–95* ⊕ *www.gdansk.karmelici.pl.*

**Muzeum Archeologiczne Gdańska** (*Gdańsk Archaeological Museum*). Gdańsk's small archaeological museum displays Slavic tribal artifacts, including jewelry, pottery, boats, and bones. ⊠ *ul. Mariacka 25–26, Stare Miasto* ☎ *058/322–21–00* ⊕ *www.archeologia.pl* ⌦ *Zł 6* ⊘ *Tues.–Sun. 10–4.*

★ **Muzeum Narodowe w Gdańsku** (*National Museum in Gdańsk*). The former Franciscan monastery, just south of the old walls of the Main Town, exhibits 14th- to 20th-century art and ethnographic collections. Hans Memling's triptych *Last Judgment* is the jewel of the collection. ⊠ *ul. Toruńska 1, off ul. Okopowa, Stare Miasto* ☎ *058/301–70–61* ⊕ *www.muzeum.narodowe.gda.pl* ⌦ *zł 10 (free Sun.)* ⊘ *Oct.–April, Tue.–Fri. 9–4, Sat. and Sun. 10–5; May–Sept. Tues.–Sun. 10–5; June–Aug., Thurs. 12–7.*

**Muzeum Sztuki Współczesnej** (*Modern Art Museum*). Two museums can be found in a beautiful park surrounding the cathedral in Oliwa in the former Abbots' Palace. The Modern Art Museum has a large collection of works by Polish artists from the inter-war period onward. The Ethnographic Museum has the same hours and contact information but a separate admission fee. ⊠ *Pałac Opatów, Cystersów 18, Oliwa* ☎ *058/552–12–71* ⊕ *www.muzeum.narodowe.gda.pl* ⌦ *Zł 10* ⊘ *Tues.–Sun. 9–4.*

**Muzeum Etnograficzne** (*Ethnographic Museum*). Connected to the Modern Art Museum, administratively and physically, is the Muzeum Etnograficzne, in the former Abbots' Granary. The museum display has fine examples of local crafts from the 19th century and also has an interesting display of amber folk jewelry. It has a separate entrance from the Modern Art Museum and a separate admission fee, but the hours and other contact information are the same for both museums. ⊠ *ul. Cystersów 19, Oliwa* ☎ *058/552–12–71* ⊕ *www.muzeum.narodowe. gda.pl* ⌦ *zł 8* ⊘ *Tues.–Sun. 9–4.*

★ **Ratusz Główny** (*Old Town Hall*). Although Gdańsk's original town hall was completely destroyed during World War II, a careful reconstruction of the exterior and interior now recreates the glory of Gdańsk's medieval past. During the summer season the tower is accessible to visitors and well worth climbing for the view. Inside, the **Muzeum Historii Miasta Gdańska** (Gdańsk Historical Museum) covers more than five centuries of Gdańsk's history in exhibits that include paintings, sculptures, and weapons. ⊠ *ul. Długa 47, Stare Miasto* ☎ *058/301–48–72* ⌦ *Museum zł 10 (free Tues.)* ⊘ *Tues. 10–3, Wed.–Sat. 10–4, Sun. 11–4.*

Fodor'sChoice **Stocznia Gdańska** (*Gdańsk Shipyard*). Stocznia Gdańska Three huge ★ and somber crosses perpetually draped with flowers stand outside the gates of the former Lenin Shipyards, which gave birth to the Solidarity movement. The crosses outside the entrance to the shipyards are the **Pomnik Poległych Stoczniowców** (Monument to Fallen Shipyard Workers) There are also plaques that commemorate the struggle, and a quotation by Pope John Paul II inspired by his visit to the monument in 1987: "The Grace of God could not have created anything better; in this place, silence is a scream." Formerly inside the shipyard gates (and now a bit further away), the **Roads to Freedom** exhibition once consisted of a number of symbolic gates, which until recently led to a multimedia exhibition in the historic BPH room on Plac Solidarności, where the Gdańsk Agreements were signed. The BPH room, which has been renovated, reopened in 2007 in a new location at Wały Piastowskie Street (a short walk from the shipyard itself, halfway between the shipyards and the Main Railway Station). The exhibition traces the beginning and development of the Solidarity movement, taking you on a virtual tour through 1980s Poland. ✉ *Wały Piastowskie 24, Stare Miasto* ☎ *058/308–44–28* ⊕ *www.ecs.gda.pl* 🎫 *Zł 6* ⊙ *Oct.–Apr., Tues.–Sun. 10–5; May–Sept., Tues.–Sun. 10–6.*

**Żuraw Gdański** (*Harbor Crane*). Żuraw Gdański, built in 1444, Gdańsk's crane was medieval Europe's largest—and today it's also Europe's oldest. It used to play the double role of a port crane and city gate. The structure was given its present shape between 1442 and 1444. Today it houses the **Muzeum Morskie** (Maritime Museum), with a collection of models of the ships constructed in the Gdańsk Shipyards since 1945. At the museum ticket office, inquire about tickets for tours of the *Sołdek*, a World War II battleship moored nearby on the canal. ✉ *Szeroka 67, Stare Miasto* ☎ *058/301–69–38* ⊕ *www.cmm.pl* 🎫 *Zł 8* ⊙ *Oct.–June, Tues.–Sun. 10–3; July–Sept., Tues.–Sun. 10–4.*

## SHOPPING

The Tri-city is not a shopping destination. Nevertheless, Gdańsk and Sopot are good places to look for amber jewelry. You'll find souvenir shops and stores specializing in amber everywhere in town. In fact, they can't be missed they are so ubiquitous.

## WHERE TO EAT

**$$**
POLISH
✗ **Czerwone Drzwi.** "Behind the red door" (that's what *Czerwone Drzwi* means in Polish) is an elegant café-cum-restaurant, a favorite with Gdańsk's fashionable people (with well-stocked wallets). The menu changes with the seasons. 💲 *Average main: zł 50* ✉ *ul. Piwna 52/53, Stare Miasto* ☎ *058/301–57–64* ⊕ *www.reddoor.gd.pl.*

**$$$**
SEAFOOD
Fodor'sChoice
★
✗ **Pod łososiem.** "The Salmon" is certainly the most famous restaurant in Gdańsk, with a long-standing reputation. It is memorable for its elegant baroque-era dining rooms, well-oiled maître d', attentive service, and excellent seafood (the menu also extends to game and fowl dishes). Try the salmon or smoked eel to start, followed by flounder or grilled trout. You may want to try the famous Goldwasser vodka—after all, this is its original source. 💲 *Average main: zł 75* ✉ *ul. Szeroka 52/53* ☎ *058/301–76–52* ⊕ *www.podlososiem.com.pl.*

# HAMBURG, GERMANY

Updated by
Giulia Pines

Water—in the form of the Alster Lakes and the Elbe River—is Hamburg's defining feature and the key to the city's success. A harbor city with an international past, Hamburg is the most tolerant and open-minded of German cities. The media have made Hamburg their capital. Add to that the slick world of advertising and you have a populace of worldly and fashionable professionals. Not surprisingly, the city of movers and shakers is also the city with most of Germany's millionaires. Hamburg has been a major port for more than 1,000 years, but it reached the crest of its power during the 19th century. What you see today is the "new" Hamburg. World War II bombing raids destroyed more than half of the city. In spite of the 1940–44 raids, Hamburg now stands as a remarkably faithful replica of that glittering prewar city—a place of enormous style, verve, and elegance, with considerable architectural diversity, including turn-of-the-20th-century art nouveau buildings.

## ESSENTIALS

### CURRENCY
The euro. ATMs are common if you need cash.

### HOURS
Stores are open Monday through Saturday from 8 am until 8 pm. Museum hours vary, but core hours are 10 am until 5 pm, with shorter opening on Sundays. Some state museums are closed on Monday.

### TELEPHONES
Tri- and quad-band GSM phones should work in Germany, where the mobile system supports 3G technology. Phone cards for public phones are available at newsagents and will allow international calls. Major companies include Vodafone, T2, and T-Mobile.

## COMING ASHORE
Hamburg has constructed a state-of-the-art cruise port and terminal as part of the regeneration of the Überseequartier district and surrounding HafenCity (a totally new city district). The main terminal, called HafnCity 2012, will have a hotel, restaurants, and direct metro access to downtown. The port is already accepting cruise ships, but not all facilities are open at this writing.

The older Hafn City Terminal is currently the main welcome terminal for cruise passenegers. It has a Welcome Center and a café. Public bus access is a short stroll through the terminal exit gate. Altona Terminal is a modern structure that provides facilities including shops and an information desk, but at present there are no cafés or restaurants. There is a bus stop for public transport into downtown Hamburg. Although city attractions are not far from the terminals, it would be sensible to take transportation to the attractions rather than walking, due to the heavy construction going on in the area.

Passengers exploring the city will find no benefit in renting a car; in fact, many major attractions are within walking distance of each other. But if you want to explore the area by car, a car rental costs €51 for a compact manual vehicle. Taxi meters start at €2.90, and the fare is €2 per km (½ miles) for the first 5 km, €1.90 for between 5 and 10 km and €1.40 for each km thereafter. Waiting time is €25 per hour. You can hail taxis on the street or at stands, or order one by phone.

The HVV, Hamburg's public transportation system, includes the U-bahn (subway), the S-bahn (suburban train), and buses. At this writing, a one-way fare starts at €2.85 for a one-zone ticket covers *one* unlimited ride in the Hamburg inner-city area. Tickets are available on all buses and at automatic machines in all stations and at most bus stops. A *Single-Tageskarte* (all-day ticket) for the inner-city districts, valid until 6 am the next day, costs €6.95. If you're traveling with family or friends, a *Partner Day Ticket* (group or family ticket) is a good value—a group of up to five adults (children count as half an adult) can travel for the entire day for €9.90–€19.30 (depending on the number of fare zones the ticket covers).

## EXPLORING HAMBURG

**Fodor's Choice**
★ **Alster** (*Alster lakes*). These twin lakes provide downtown Hamburg with one of its most memorable vistas. The two lakes meet at the Lombardsbrücke and Kennedybrücke (Lombard and Kennedy bridges). The boat landing at the Jungfernstieg, below the Alsterpavillon, is the starting point for lake and canal cruises. Small sailboats and rowboats, hired from yards on the shores of the Alster, are very much a part of the summer scene. Every Hamburger dreams of living within sight of the Alster, but only the wealthiest can afford it. Some lucky millionaires own the magnificent garden properties around the Alster's perimeter, known as the Millionaire's Coast. But you don't have to be a guest on one of these estates to enjoy the waterfront—the Alster shoreline has 6 km (4 miles) of tree-lined public pathways. The Aussenalster 50-minute lake tour costs €12; the Fleet-Fahrt costs €19. The Dämmertour costs €19 and includes one drink. ■**TIP**➜ **Popular among joggers, these trails are a lovely place for a stroll.** Ⓜ *Jungfernstieg (U-bahn).*

★ **Deichstrasse.** The oldest residential area in the Old Town of Hamburg, which dates from the 14th century, now consists of lavishly restored houses from the 17th through the 19th century. Many of the original houses on Deichstrasse were destroyed in the Great Fire of 1842, which broke out in No. 38 and left approximately 20,000 people homeless; only a few of the early dwellings escaped its ravages. Today Deichstrasse and nearby Peterstrasse, which is steps away from the site of the former city wall, are of great historical interest. At No. 35–39 Peterstrasse, for example, is the replica of the baroque facade of the Beylingstift complex, built in 1751. Today, the Johannes Brahms Museum sits in No. 39, the composer's former home. All the buildings in the area have been painstakingly designed to look like the original buildings, thanks largely to nonprofit foundations. ⊠ *Altstadt* Ⓜ *Rödingsmarkt (U-bahn).*

★ **Tierpark Hagenbeck** (*Hagenbeck Zoo*). One of the country's oldest and
☼ most popular zoos is family-owned. Founded in 1907, it was the world's first zoo to let wild animals such as lions, elephants, chimpanzees, and others roam freely in vast, open-air corrals. In summer, you can ride a

Tierpark
Hagenbeck

Verbindungsb. Str.
Tiergartenstr.
E-Siem

Planten
un
Blomen

Juliusstr.
Lagerstr.
Jungiusstr.
Marseillerstr.

Alter
Botanischer
Garten

Schulterblatt
Schanzenstr.
Karolinenstr.
B.D. Kirchhöfen
Jungiusstr.
Gorch-Fock-Wall
Caffamacherreihe

Wohlwillstr.
Neuer Kamp
Feldstr.
Holstenglacis
Dammtorwall

**U** FELDSTR.

Kaiser-Wilhelmstr.
Backer breiterg
Fuhlentwiete

Budapesterstr.
Karl-Muck-
Platz

Paulinen-
pl.
Heiligengeistfeld
Neustädtstr.

ST. PAULI
Glacischaussee
Grosse
Wallenlagen
Holstenwall
Hütten Pilatuspool
Wexstr.
Stadthausbr.

Dettlev Bremerstr.
Holstenwall
Neander str.
Ater Steinweg
Düsternstr.

ST. PAUL **U**
Hütten
Neuer Steinweg

Spielbudenpl.
Millerntorpl.
Ludwig-Erhard-Str.
STADTHAUS
BRÜCKE

Zirkusweg
Heligoländer Allee
Gerstackerstr.
St. Michaelis Kirche ◆
RÖDINGSMARKT **U**

Hopfenstr.
Elb
Park
Rothesoodstr.
Böhmkenstr.
Herrengraben
Admiralitat Str.
Rödings-Markt

Bernhard-Nocht-Str.
**S**
Seewartenstr.
Venusberg
Martin-Lutherstr.
Kajen

LANDUNGS-
BRÜCKEN **U**
Ditmar Koelstr.
Schaar
Steinweg
Stubbenhuk
SteinHof
BAUMWALL **U**

**i**
Neust Neuerweg
Welkenstr.

Johannis Bollwerk
Vorsetzen
Baumwall

Elbe

KEY

**S** S-Bahn

**U** U-Bahn

**i** Tourist information

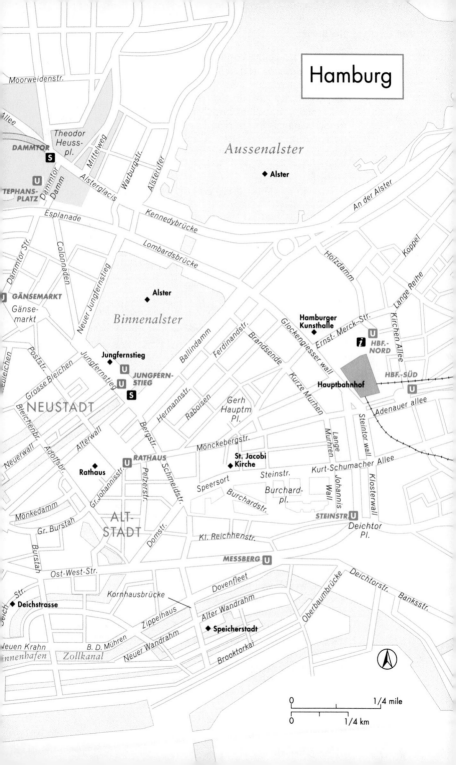

pony. The Tropen-Aquarium sits on the same property as the zoo and a tour through it is like a trip around the world. Sea life, insects, curious reptiles, marvelous birds, and exotic mammals live in replicas of their natural habitat. Detailed recreations of deserts, oceans, rain forests, and jungles are home to birds, fish, mammals, insects, and reptiles from almost every continent, including a "Madagascar" village with black-tailed lemurs. ⊠ *2 Lokstedter Grenzstr. at Hamburg-Stellingen, Stellingen* ☎ *040/530–0330* ⊕ *www.hagenbeck.de* 🖾 *€20 for zoo, €14 for aquarium, €30 for zoo and aquarium* ☉ *Zoo: Mar.–June, Sept., and Oct., daily 9–6; July and Aug., daily 9–7; Nov.–Feb., daily 9–4:30. Aquarium: daily 9–6* Ⓜ *Hagenbecks Tierpark (U-bahn).*

**HAMBURG BEST BETS**

**Enjoy the art in the Kunsthalle.** With works ranging from the Renaissance to the modern era, the gallery offers a visual timeline of European art.

**Tour the Rathaus.** The sumptuous decor of the Town Hall epitomizes the power and confidence of the 19th-century city.

**Tour the Alster Lakes.** Wonderful vistas of the city pass by at a genteel pace when you take a boat cruise here.

★ **Jungfernstieg.** This wide promenade looking out over the Alster lakes is the beginning of the city's premier shopping district. Laid out in 1665, it used to be part of a muddy millrace that channeled water into the Elbe. Hidden from view behind the sedate facade of Jungfernstieg is a network of several small shopping centers that together account for almost a mile of shops selling everything from souvenirs to haute couture. Many of these passages have sprung up in the past two decades, but some have been here since the 19th century; the first glass-covered arcade, called Sillem's Bazaar, was built in 1845. ⊠ *Neustadt* Ⓜ *Jungfernstieg (U-bahn).*

★ **Hamburger Kunsthalle** (*Art Gallery*). One of the most important art museums in Germany, the Kunsthalle has 3,500 paintings, 650 sculptures, and a coin and medal collection that dates from the ancient Roman era. In the postmodern, cube-shaped building designed by Berlin architect O. M. Ungers, the **Galerie der Gegenwart** has housed a collection of international modern art since 1960, including works by Andy Warhol, Joseph Beuys, Georg Baselitz, and David Hockney. With 1,200 drawings and other visuals, graphic art is well represented, including works by Pablo Picasso and Horst Janssen, a Hamburg artist famous for his satirical worldview. In the other areas of the museum, you can view works by local artists dating from the 16th century. The outstanding collection of German Romantic paintings includes pieces by Caspar David Friedrich. Paintings by Holbein, Rembrandt, Van Dyck, Tiepolo, and Canaletto are also on view, while late-19th-century impressionism is represented by works by Leibl, Liebermann, Manet, Monet, and Renoir. ⊠ *Glockengiesserwall, Altstadt* ☎ *040/4281–31200* ⊕ *www.hamburger-kunsthalle.de* 🖾 *Permanent exhibition €8.50* ☉ *Tues., Wed., and Fri.–Sun. 10–6, Thurs. 10–9* Ⓜ *Hauptbahnhof (U-bahn and S-bahn).*

**Fodor's**Choice ★ **Rathaus** (*Town Hall*). To most Hamburgers this large building is the symbolic heart of the city. As a city-state—an independent city and simultaneously one of the 16 federal states of Germany—Hamburg maintains city and state governments, both of which have their administrative headquarters in the Rathaus. An ostentatious neo-Renaissance affair, the building dictates political decorum in the city. To this day, the mayor of Hamburg never welcomes VIPs at the foot of its staircase, but always awaits them at the very top—whether it's a president or the queen of England. The immense neo-Renaissance building, with its 647 rooms and imposing central clock tower, is not the most graceful structure in the city, but the sheer opulence of its interior is astonishing. A 40-minute tour begins in the ground-floor Rathausdiele, a vast pillared hall. Although you can only view the state rooms, their tapestries, huge staircases, glittering chandeliers, coffered ceilings, and grand portraits give you a sense of the city's great wealth in the 19th century and its understandable civic pride. ✉ *Rathausmarkt, Altstadt* ☎ *040/42831–2470* ⊕ *www.hamburgische-buergerschaft.de* 🖃 *Tours €3* ⊙ *Tours weekdays, half-hourly 10:15–3:15; Sat., half-hourly 10:15–5:15; Sun., half-hourly 10:15–6:15; English tours weekdays 11:15, 1:15, and 3:15; Sat. 11:15, 1:15, 3:15, and 5:15; Sun. 11:15, 1:15, 3:15, and, if there is demand, 4:15* Ⓜ *Rathaus (U-bahn), Jungfernstieg (U-bahn/S-bahn).*

★ **St. Jacobi Kirche** (*St. James's Church*). This 15th-century church was almost completely destroyed during World War II. Only the interiors survived, and reconstruction was completed in 1963. The interior is not to be missed—it houses such treasures as a massive baroque organ and three Gothic altars from the 15th and 16th centuries. ✉ *Jacobikirchhof 22, at Steinstr., Altstadt* ☎ *040/303–7370* 🖉 *info@jacobus.de* ⊕ *www.jacobus.de* ⊙ *Apr.–Sept., Mon.–Sat. 10–5, Sun. after 11 am; Oct.–Mar., Mon.–Sat. 11–5, Sun. after 11 am. English guided tours available on request at info@jacobus.de* Ⓜ *Rathaus (U-bahn), Jungfernstieg (U-bahn/S-bahn).*

**Fodor's**Choice ★ **St. Michaelis Kirche** (*St. Michael's Church*). The Michel, as it's called locally, is Hamburg's principal church and northern Germany's finest baroque-style ecclesiastical building. Constructed between 1649 and 1661 (the tower followed in 1669), it was razed after lightning struck almost a century later. It was rebuilt between 1750 and 1786 in the decorative Nordic baroque style, but was gutted by a terrible fire in 1906. The replica, completed in 1912, was demolished during World War II. The present church is a reconstruction.

The distinctive 436-foot brick-and-iron tower bears the largest tower clock in Germany, 26 feet in diameter. Just above the clock is a viewing platform (accessible by elevator or stairs) that affords a magnificent panorama of the city, the Elbe River, and the Alster lakes. ■ TIP→ **Twice a day, at 10 am and 9 pm (Sunday at noon), a watchman plays a trumpet solo from the tower platform.** In the crypt a 30-minute movie about the 1,000-year history of Hamburg and its churches is shown.

For a great view of Hamburg's skyline, head to the clock tower at night. In the evenings you can sip a complimentary soft drink while

7

listening to classical music in a room just below the tower, usually held from 5:30 pm to 11:00 pm. Check ⊕ *www.nachtmichel.de* or call ☎ *040/2851–5791* to confirm times. ⊠ *Englische Planke 1, Neustadt* ☎ *040/376–780* ⊕ *www.st-michaelis.de* ☎ *Tower €4; show, tower, and crypt €6* ☉ *May–Oct., daily 9–8; Nov.–Apr., daily 10–5:30* Ⓜ *Rödingsmarkt (U-bahn), Stadthausbrücke (S-bahn).*

Fodor'sChoice
★
☾
**Speicherstadt** (*Warehouse District*). This imposing cluster of massive brick buildings sits along canals near the Elbe and reveals yet another aspect of Hamburg's extraordinary architectural diversity. Once home to tons of cargo imported by Hamburg, today the area is a mix of offices, restaurants, amusements, and warehouses. These warehouses are still used to store and process every conceivable commodity, from coffee and spices to raw silks and hand-woven Oriental carpets. An entire residential area was torn down (including many Renaissance and baroque buildings) to store the wares. Today, the area is home to Hamburg Dungeon, a haunted-house attraction; the Miniatur Wunderland, the site of the largest model railway in the world; and a few museums celebrating the area's shipping past.

**Speicherstadtmuseum.** Although you won't be able to tour the storage spaces, the nonstop comings and goings will give you a good sense of a port at work. If you want to learn about the history and architecture of the old warehouses, detour to the Speicherstadtmuseum. ⊠ *Am Sandtorkai 30, Speicherstadt* ☎ *040/321–191* ⊕ *www.speicherstadtmuseum. de* ☎ *€3.50* ☉ *Apr.–Oct., weekdays 10–5, weekends 10–6; Nov.–Mar., Tues.–Sun. 10–5* Ⓜ *Baumwall (U-bahn)* ⊠ *Speicherstadt is bounded by Am Sandtorkai and Brooktorkai and the Elbe River., Speicherstadt* ☎ *040/3690–1799* ⊕ *www.hafencity.com* ☎ *Free* ☉ *Visitor center: May–Sept., Tues., Wed., and Fri.–Sun. 10–6, Thurs. 10–8* Ⓜ *Messberg (U-bahn).*

## SHOPPING

Hamburg's shopping districts are among the most elegant on the continent, and the city has Europe's largest expanse of covered shopping arcades, most of them packed with small, exclusive boutiques. The streets **Grosse Bleichen** and **Neuer Wall,** which lead off Jungfernstieg, are a high-price-tag zone. The Grosse Bleichen leads to six of the city's most important covered (or indoor) malls, many of which are connected. The marble-clad **Galleria** is modeled after London's Burlington Arcade. Daylight streams through the immense glass ceilings of the **Hanse-Viertel,** an otherwise ordinary reddish-brown brick building. The **Kaufmannshaus,** also known as the Commercie, and the upscale (and former first-class hotel) **Hamburger Hof** are two of the oldest and most fashionable indoor malls. There are also the **Alte Post** and the **Bleichenhof,** while over-the-top, stunningly designed **Europa Passage** is the city's latest arrival on the luxury shopping mall scene.

Some of the country's premier designers, such as Karl Lagerfeld, Jil Sander, and Wolfgang Joop, are native Hamburgers, or at least worked here for quite some time, so high-class fashion is well in evidence. For souvenirs, the most famous must-buys are *Buddelschiffe* (ships in bottles) and other maritime memorabilia.

**Alsterhaus.** Alsterhaus is Hamburg's famous and high-end department store. A favorite with locals, it's a large and elegant landmark. For a treat, check out the gourmet food hall and the champagne bar. ⊠ *Jungfernstieg 16–20, Neustadt* ☎ *040/3590–1218.*

**Antik-Center Hamburg.** The Antik-Center Hamburg has a treasure trove of "antiques" from the '50s, '60s, and '70s. The staff ships purchases anywhere in the world. ⊠ *Gertigstrasse 67, Altstadt* ☎ *0172/400–4011* ⊕ *www.wirtschaftswunder-welt.de.*

## WHERE TO EAT

$$ ✕ **Rive.** This harborside oyster bar is known for both its German nouvelle cuisine and its classic local dishes. Choose between such dishes as hearty *Matjes mit dreierlei Saucen* (herring with three sauces) or *Dorade in der Salzkruste* (dorado cooked in salt crust). Media types come to this shiplike building for the fresh oysters, clams, and spectacular view. ⊠ *Van-der-Smissen Str. 1, Kreuzfahrt-Center, Altona* ☎ *040/380–5919* ⊕ *www.rive.de* ⌖ *Reservations essential* Ⓜ *Königstrasse (S-bahn).*

GERMAN

$ ✕ **River-Kasematten.** There is no other restaurant in town that better embodies Hamburg's international spirit and its lust for style, entertainment, and good seafood. Once a legendary jazz club with performances by Ella Fitzgerald and the like, it now hosts a fascinating mix of hip guests. Sushi, spiced-up regional fish dishes, and exotic soups are the order of the day. The lunch buffet (weekdays noon–3) for just €9.90 is a steal; it's even better on the outside terrace. The ambience— black oak floors, leather seats, and redbrick walls—is elegant yet casual. ⊠ *St. Pauli Fischmarkt 28–32, St. Pauli* ☎ *040/300–60190* ⊕ *www. river-kasematten.de* ⌖ *Reservations essential* Ⓜ *Fischmarkt (Bus 112), Reeperbahn (S-bahn).*

ECLECTIC
★

# HELSINKI, FINLAND

Updated by
David Dunne

A city of the sea, Helsinki was built along a series of oddly shaped peninsulas and islands jutting into the Gulf of Finland. Nature dictates life in this Nordic land, where winter brings perpetual darkness, and summer perpetual light. A disastrous fire in the early 1800s destroyed many of Helsinki's traditional wooden structures, and as a result, Helsinki has some of the purest neoclassical architecture in the world. Add to this foundation the influence of Stockholm and St. Petersburg sprinkled with the local inspiration of 20th-century Finnish design, and the result is a European capital city that is as architecturally eye-catching as it is distinct. Today Helsinki is still a meeting point of eastern and western Europe, a fact reflected in its cosmopolitan image, its influx of Russians and Estonians, and its generally multilingual population. Outdoor summer bars (*terrassit,* as the locals call them) and cafés in the city center are perfect for people-watching on a summer afternoon.

## ESSENTIALS

### CURRENCY

The euro. Local banks and Forex offices usually give the best rates and charge a minimal commission. ATMs are common and credit cards are widely accepted.

### HOURS

Smaller stores are generally open weekdays from 9 am to 6 pm and Saturday from 9 am to 1 pm; larger department stores are open until 9 pm weekdays and until 6 pm on Saturday. Stores are often open on Sunday from June through August and during December. The majority of museums are closed on Monday.

### TELEPHONES

Most tri-band and quad-band GSM phones work in Finland, but the Finnish mobile system is not 3G-compatible. You can buy prepaid phone cards at telecom shops, news vendors and tobacconists in all towns and cities. Phone cards can be used for local or international calls. Major companies include Elisa and Finnish 2G.

## COMING ASHORE

Helsinki is a busy cruise destination and sees many ships throughout the season. Ships dock at one of three distinct areas.

Katajanokka Quay has a terminal with souvenir shop, toilets, and taxi station. From Katajanokka Terminal, local Bus 13 or Tram T4 will take you to Helsinki city center, but this is also reachable on foot. If you want to ride, Trams 4 and 4T stop here.

South Harbour has a terminal at Olympia Quay with shopping, information, a taxi rank, currency exchange, and Internet access and a second quay called Makasiini Quay. It's a 15-minute walk into downtown from the South Harbour port entrance. Trams 1A, 3B, and 3T run from the port into town.

Hernasaari Harbour has two quays with access to the dedicated cruise terminal with shops, information desk, taxi rank, and Internet access. It's a longer walk into Helsinki from here, but the terminal is served by Bus routes 14B and 16.

Taxis wait at all terminals to take visitors downtown, and this may be the most convenient way to travel if you don't want to take the cruise shuttle service. Journey times are short from all the terminals, the longest being around 15 minutes. Taxis are plentiful (albeit expensive) and make a convenient way to link attractions. Taxis take credit cards. A 5-km (3-mile) trip is currently €10.30, while a 10-km (6-mile) trip is €16.10. A car rental is not a sensible option if you intend to explore the city, as parking is difficult. Expect to pay €76 per day for a compact manual vehicle.

Tickets for the Helsinki public transport system cost €2.50 from the driver, or €2 from a ticket machine. Day tickets are €6.80—these are valid on trams, buses, the metro and the ferry to Soumenlinna. Ticket machines sell one-day tickets. Tram services 3B and 3T link many of the most important city attractions so in conjunction with a day ticket could be used as hop-on hop-off services.

## EXPLORING HELSINKI

★ **Ateneumin Taidemuseo** (*Ateneum Art Museum of the Finnish National Gallery*). The best traditional Finnish art is housed in this splendid neo-classical complex, one of three museums organized under the Finnish National Gallery umbrella. The gallery holds major European works, but the outstanding attraction is the Finnish art, particularly the works of Akseli Gallen-Kallela, inspired by the national epic *Kalevala*. The rustic portraits by Albert Edelfelt are enchanting, and many contemporary Finnish artists are well represented. The two other museums that make up the National Gallery are **Kiasma** and **Synebrychoff.** ⊠ *Kaivok. 2, Keskusta* ☎ *09/6122–5510 information* ⊕ *www.fng.fi; www.ateneum. fi* ⊠ *€8, extra charge for special exhibits* ⊙ *Tues. and Fri. 10–6, Wed. and Thurs. 10–8, weekends 11–5.*

**Cygnaeuksen Galleria** (*Cygnaeus Gallery*). This diminutive gallery, in a cottage with a tower overlooking the harbor, is the perfect setting for works by various Finnish painters, sculptors, and folk artists. This was once the summer home of Fredrik Cygnaeus (1807–1881), a poet and historian who generously left his cottage and all the art inside to the Finnish public. ⊠ *Kalliolinnantie 8, Kaivopuisto* ☎ *09/4050–9628* ⊕ *www.nba.fi/en/gygnaeusgallery* ⊠ *€6.50* ⊙ *May–Sept., daily 11–5* Ⓜ *Trams 3B and 3T, Kaivopuisto.*

**Fodor'sChoice**
★ **Designmuseo** (*Design Museum*). The best of Finnish design can be seen here in displays of furnishings, jewelry, ceramics, and more. ⊠ *Korkeavuorenk. 23, Keskusta* ☎ *09/622–0540* ⊕ *www.designmuseum.fi* ⊠ *€8* ⊙ *Sept.–May, Tues. 11–8, Wed.–Sun. 11–6; June–Aug., daily 11–6* Ⓜ *Bus 16, Tram 10.*

**Finlandiatalo** (*Finlandia Hall*). This white, winged concert hall was one of Alvar Aalto's last creations. It's especially impressive on foggy days or at night. If you can't make it to a concert here, try to take a guided tour. ⊠ *Mannerheimintie 13e, Keskusta* ☎ *09/402–41* ⊕ *www.finlandiatalo.fi* ⊠ *€11.50 for guided tours on Wed. 2pm* ⊙ *Symphony concerts usually held Wed. and Thurs. nights* Ⓜ *Trams 4, 7 and 10 stop at Mannerheimintie next to Finlandia Hall (National Museum's stop).*

**Gulf of Finland Archipelago.** In winter, Finns walk across the frozen sea with dogs and even baby buggies to the nearby islands. On the land side, the facades of the Eira and Kaivopuisto districts' grandest buildings form a parade of architectural splendor. One tradition that remains, even in this upscale neighborhood, is rug washing in the sea—an incredibly arduous task. You may be surprised to see people leave their rugs to dry in the sea air without fear of theft. ⊠ *South of Merisatamaranta, Merisatama.*

**Havis Amanda.** This fountain's brass centerpiece, a young woman perched on rocks surrounded by dolphins, was commissioned by the city fathers to embody Helsinki. Sculptor Ville Vallgren completed her in 1908 using a Parisian girl as his model. Partying university students annually crown the Havis Amanda with their white caps on the eve of Vappu, the May 1 holiday. ⊠ *Eteläespl. and Eteläranta, Keskusta/ Kauppatori.*

7

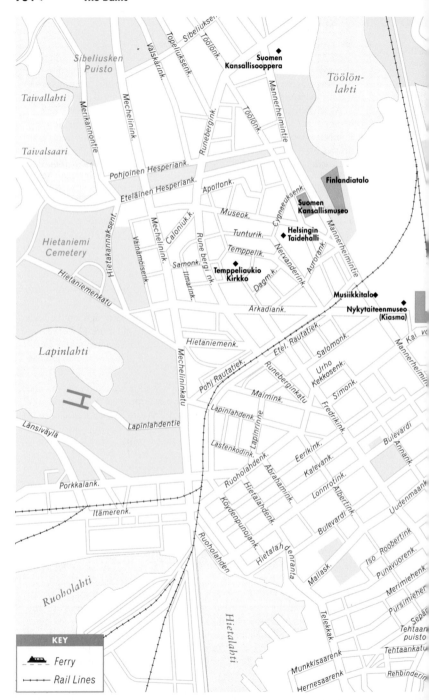

Sibeliusken Puisto

Taivallahti

Taivalsaari

Merikannontie

Topeliuksenk.

Väiskärink.

Sibeliuksen.

Töölönk.

Runeberginek.

Töölönk.

Mannerheimintie

Suomen Kansallisooppera

Töölön-lahti

Pohjoinen Hesperiank.

Eteläinen Hesperiank.

Apollonk.

Mecheliink.

Finlandiatalo

Museok.

Cygneuksenk.

Suomen Kansallismuseo

Hietaniemi Cemetery

Hietakannaksent.

Väinämöisenk.

Mechelinink.

Caloniuk.k.

Rune bergi nk.

Tunturik.

Tunturik.

Temppelik.

Helsingin Taidehalli

Mannerheimintie

Samonk.

Itmärink.

Temppeliaukio Kirkko

Dagm k.

Nervanderink.

Aurorank.

Hietaniemenkatu

Musiikkitalo

Arkadiank.

Nykytaiteenmuseo (Kiasma)

Lapinlahti

Hietaniemenk.

Etel. Rautatiek.

Salomonk.

Kai

Mannerheimin

Mechelininkatu

Pohj Rautatiek.

Runeberginkatu

Urho Kekkosenk.

Simonk.

Malmink.

Fredrikink.

Lapinlahdenk.

Lapinrinne

Länsiväylä

Lapinlahdentie

Lastenkodink.

Eerikink.

Kalevank.

Bulevardi

Annank.

Ruoholahdenk.

Abrahamink.

Lonnrotink.

Albertink.

Porkkalank.

Hietalahdenk.

Bulevardi

Uudenmaank.

Itämerenk.

Köydenpunojank.

Hietalah denranta

Iso Roobertink.

Punavuorenk.

Malласк.

Merimiehenk.

Pursimieher.

Ruoholahden

Ruoholahti

Hietalahti

Telekkak.

Tehtaan puisto

Separ

Tehtaankatu

Munkkisaarenk.

Hernesaarenk.

Rehbinderin

**KEY**

🚢 Ferry

+—+ Rail Lines

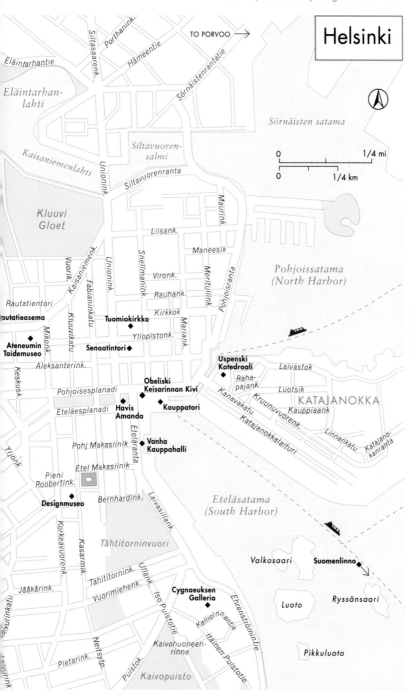

**Helsinki**

TO PORVOO →

Eläintarhantie

Siltasaarenk.

Porthanink.

Hämeentie

Sörnäistenrantatie

Eläintarhan-lahti

Siltavuoren-salmi

*Sörnäisten satama*

Kaisaniemenlahti

Unionink.

Siltavuorenranta

0        1/4 mi

0        1/4 km

Kluuvi
Gloet

Liisank.

Maneesik.

Maurink.

Merituliink.

Pohjoisranta

*Pohjoissatama
(North Harbor)*

Vuorik.

Kaisaniemenk.

Unionink.

Snellmaninк.

Vironk.

Rauhank.

Kirkkok.

Fabianinkatu

Rautatientori

autatieasema

Mikonk.

Kluuvikatu

Tuomiokirkko

Yliopistonk.

Marlank.

**Ateneumin
Taidemuseo**

Senaatintori ◆

Keskusk.

Aleksanterink.

Uspenski
Katedraali
◆

Raha-
pajank.

Laivastok.

Luotsik.

**KATAJANOKKA**

Pohjoisesplanadi

**Obeliski
Keisarinnan Kivi**

Kanavakatu

Kruunuvuorenk.

Kauppiaank.

Etelä esplanadi

**Havis
Amanda**

◆ **Kauppatori**

Katajanokkalaituri

Linnankatu

Katajano-
kanranta

Yrjönk.

Pohj Makasiinik.

Eteläranta

**Vanha
Kauppahalli**

Etel Makasiinik.

Pieni
Roobertink.

Bernhardink.

Laivasillank.

*Eteläsatama
(South Harbor)*

**Designmuseo** ◆

Korkeavuorenk.

Kasarmik.

**Tähtitorninvuori**

Valkosaari

**Suomenlinna** ●

Jääkärink.

Tähtitorink.

Vuorimiehenk.

Ullank.

Iso Puistotie

Ehrenströmintie

Itäinen Puistotie

Luoto

*Ryssänsaari*

Pietärink.

Neitsytp.

Puistok.

**Cygnaeuksen
Galleria** ◆

Kalliolinnantie

Kaivohuoneen-
rinne

*Kaivopuisto*

*Pikkuluoto*

**Helsingin Taidehalli** (*Helsinki Art Gallery*). Here you'll see the best of contemporary Finnish art, including painting, sculpture, architecture, and industrial art and design. ✉ *Nervanderink. 3, Keskusta* ☏ *09/454–2060 office, 40/450–7211 tickets* ⊕ *www.taidehalli.fi* 🖂 *€8, can vary for special exhibitions* ⊗ *Tues., Thurs., and Fri. 11–6; Wed. 11–8; weekends 11–6* Ⓜ *Kamppi stop.*

★ **Kauppatori** (*Market Square*). At this Helsinki institution, open year-round, wooden stands with orange and gold awnings bustle in the mornings when everyone—tourists and locals alike—comes to shop, browse, or sit and enjoy coffee and conversation. You can buy a freshly caught perch for the evening's dinner, a bouquet of bright flowers for a friend, or a fur pelt. In summer, the fruit and vegetable stalls are supplemented by an evening arts-and-crafts market. The crepes, made-to-order by one of the tented vendors, are excellent. ✉ *Eteläranta and Pohjoisespl., Keskusta/Kauppatori* ⊗ *Weekdays 6:30–6, Sat. 6:30–4, and in the summer Sun. 10–5.*

**Musiikkitalo** (*Helsinki Music Center*). Since it opened in 2011, the Helsinki Music Center has been praised for its acoustics and daring design. It's home to the Sibelius Academy and two symphony orchestras. Guided tours are available, but most are in Finnish—check the website for details. The one-hour guided walking tour introduces participants to what happens here, as well as to the architecture, main audience, and the concert hall. ✉ *Mannerheimintie 13 a, Töölö* ☏ *0600/900–900 tour tickets, 020/707–0421 service desk* ⊕ *www.musiikkitalo.fi.*

★ **Nykytaiteenmuseo (Kiasma)** (*Museum of Contemporary Art*). Praised for the boldness of its curved steel shell but condemned for its encroachment on the territory of the Mannerheim statue, this striking museum displays a wealth of Finnish and foreign art from the 1960s to the present. Look for the "butterfly" windows, and don't miss the view of Töölönlahti from the north side of the fifth-floor gallery. ✉ *Mannerheiminaukio 2, Keskusta/Pääposti* ☏ *09/1733–6501 information and theater tickets* ⊕ *www.kiasma.fi* 🖂 *€8* ⊗ *Tues. 10–5; Wed. and Thurs. 10–8.30; Fri: 10–10; weekends 10–5.*

**Obeliski Keisarinnan Kivi** (*Czarina's Stone*). This obelisk with a double-headed golden eagle, used by Imperial Russia, was erected in 1835, toppled during the Russian Revolution in 1917, and fully restored in 1972. ✉ *Kauppatori along Pohjoisespl., Keskusta/Kauppatori.*

**Rautatieasema** (*Central Train Station*). This outdoor square and the adjoining train station are the city's bustling commuter hub. The station's huge granite figures are by Emil Wikström; the solid building they adorn was designed by Eliel Saarinen, one of the founders of the early-20th-century National Romantic style. ✉ *Kaivok. 1, Rautatientori, Keskusta*

---

**HELSINKI BEST BETS**

**Temppeliaukio Kirkko.** This church, seemingly rising out of living rock, pushes the boundaries of architecture.

**Senaatintori.** The symmetry of this neoclassical city square is a joy to the eye.

**Kauppatori.** Enjoy a steaming cup of coffee while browsing in the market or immersing yourself in daily life.

☎ *0600/41–902 information in English (€1 for answered call plus local network charge)* ⊕ *www.vr.fi/en* ⊙ *Information, daily 7–10 pm.*

★ **Senaatintori** (*Senate Square*). The harmony of the three buildings flanking Senaatintori exemplifies one of the purest styles of European architecture, as envisioned and designed by German architect Carl Ludvig Engel. This is the heart of neoclassical Helsinki. On the square's west side is one of the main buildings of Helsingin Yliopisto (Helsinki University), and up the hill is the university library. On the east side is the pale yellow Valtionneuvosto (Council of State), completed in 1822 and once the seat of the Autonomous Grand Duchy of Finland's Imperial Senate. At the lower end of the square, stores, and restaurants now occupy former merchants' homes. ⊠ *Bounded by Aleksanterink. to south and Yliopistonk. to north, Senaatintori* ⊙ *Cathedral on Senate Square: daily 9–6.*

**Suomen Kansallismuseo** (*National Museum of Finland*). Architect Eliel Saarinen and his partners combined the language of Finnish medieval church architecture with elements of art nouveau to create this vintage example of the National Romantic style. The museum's collection of archaeological, cultural, and ethnological artifacts gives you insight into Finland's past. ⊠ *Mannerheimintie 34, Keskusta* ☎ *09/40–501, 09/4050–9544 ticket office, 09/4050–9552 guided tours* ⊕ *www.nba. fi/en/nationalmuseum* 🎫 *€8* ⊙ *Tue. 11–8; Wed.–Sun. 11–6* Ⓜ *Trams 7A, 7B, 4, 4T and 10 stop at Kansallismuse/Nationalmuseum (National Museum of Finland).*

Fodor'sChoice **Suomen Kansallisooppera** (*Finnish National Opera*). Grand gilded operas,
★ classical ballets, and booming concerts all take place in Helsinki's splendid opera house, a striking example of modern Scandinavian architecture. All events at the opera house draw crowds, so buy your tickets early. ⊠ *Helsinginkatu 58, Keskusta* ☎ *09/4030–2210 house tours, 09/4030–2211 box office* ⊕ *www.opera.fi/en* ⊙ *Box office Tues.–Fri. 10–5; house tours, in English, in summer Tues. and Thurs. at 3, or by appointment* Ⓜ *Trams 3T, 4, 7A/7B, 8 and 10.*

Fodor'sChoice **Suomenlinna** (*Finland's Castle*). A former island fortress, Suomenlinna is
★ a perennially popular collection of museums, parks, and gardens, and has been designated a UNESCO World Heritage site. In 1748 the Finnish army helped build the impregnable fortress, long referred to as the Gibraltar of the North; since then it has expanded into a series of interlinked islands. Although Suomenlinna has never been taken by assault, its occupants surrendered once to the Russians in 1808 and came under fire from British ships in 1855 during the Crimean War. Today Suomenlinna makes a lovely excursion from Helsinki, particularly in early summer when the island is engulfed in a mauve-and-purple mist of lilacs, introduced from Versailles by the Finnish architect Ehrensvärd.

Suomenlinna is easily reached by public ferry (€2.50 one-way, €3.60 round-trip) or private boat (€3.50 one-way, €5.50 round-trip), both of which leave from Helsinki's Kauppatori. The ferry ride from South Harbor to Suomenlinna takes about 15 minutes. Plan to spend an afternoon on the islands; you'll need about four hours to explore the fortress and museums. Note that the days open and the hours of sites are limited off-season.

Although its fortification occupied six islands, its main attractions are now concentrated on three: Iso Mustasaari, Susisaari, and Kustaanmiekka. There are no street names on the island, so get a map for about €2 from the Helsinki City Tourist Office before you go, or buy one at the visitor center on the island. ☎ *029/53–38410* ⊕ *www.suomenlinna.fi/en.*

**Suomenlinna Visitor Centre.** From June through August, guided English-language tours leave daily at 11 am and 2 pm from the Suomenlinna Visitor Centre; call to arrange tours at other times. The center, which is in the same building as the Suomenlinna Museum, is on the shore of Tykistölahti Bay, about 400 yards south of the main ferry terminal ⊠ *Suomenlinna C 74, Suomenlinna* ☎ *029/53–38410, 029/53–38410 tours* ⊕ *www. suomenlinna.fi* ☉ *Oct.–Apr., daily 10:30–4:30; May–Sept., daily 10–6.*

**Suomenlinna Museo** (*Suomenlinna Museum*). The Suomenlinna Museo is housed in the same building as the visitor center. Exhibits cover the building of the fortress and the fleet and early life on islands; the ticket price includes the *Suomenlinna Experience* multimedia show. ⊠ *Suomenlinna museum, Suomenlinna C 74, Suomenlinna* ☎ *09/684– 1850* ⊕ *www.nba.fi/fi/suomenlinna_museo* ⊠ *€6.50* ☉ *May–Sept., daily 10–6; Oct.–Apr., daily 10:30–4:30.*

★ **Temppeliaukio Kirkko** (*Temple Square Church*). Topped with a copper dome, the church looks like a half-buried spaceship from the outside. It's really a modern Lutheran church carved into the rock outcrops below. The sun shines in from above, illuminating a stunning interior with birch pews, modern pipe organ, and cavernous walls. Ecumenical and Lutheran services in various languages are held throughout the week. ⊠ *Lutherinkatu 3, Töölö* ☎ *09/2340–5940* ⊕ *www. helsinginseurakunnat.fi* ☉ *Mon.–Thurs. 10–8; Fri. and Sat. 10–5:45; Sun. 11:45–5:45; closed during weddings, concerts, and services.*

Fodor'sChoice **Tuomiokirkko** (*Lutheran Cathedral of Finland*). The steep steps and green
★ domes of the church dominate Senaatintori. Completed in 1852, it is the work of famous architect Carl Ludvig Engel, who also designed parts of Tallinn and St. Petersburg. Wander through the tasteful blue-gray interior, with its white moldings and the statues of German reformers Martin Luther and Philipp Melanchthon, as well as the famous Finnish bishop Mikael Agricola. Concerts are frequently held inside the church. The crypt at the rear is the site of frequent historic and architectural exhibitions and bazaars. ⊠ *Unioninkatu 29, Senaatintori* ☎ *09/2340–6120* ⊕ *www.helsinginseurakunnat.fi* ☉ *Sept.–May, daily 9–6; June–Aug., 9–midnight.*

★ **Uspenski Katedraali** (*Uspenski Orthodox Cathedral*). Perched atop a small rocky cliff over the North Harbor in Katajanokka is the main cathedral of the Orthodox Church in Finland. Its brilliant gold onion domes are its hallmark, but its imposing redbrick edifice, decorated by 19th-century Russian artists, is no less distinctive. The cathedral was built and dedicated in 1868 in the Byzantine-Slavonic style and remains the biggest Orthodox church in Scandinavia. ⊠ *Kanavak. 1, Katajanokka* ☎ *0207/220–683* ⊕ *www.ort.fi* ☉ *Oct.–Apr., Tue.–Fri. 9:30–4, Sat. 9.30–2, Sun. noon–3; May–Sept., weekdays 9:30–4, Sat. 9:30–2, Sun. noon–3; closed for weddings and other special events.*

★ **Vanha Kauppahalli** (*Old Market Hall*). Piles of colorful fish roe, marinated Greek olives, and much more—the old brick market hall on the waterfront is a treasury of delicacies. The vendors set up permanent stalls with decorative carved woodwork. ⊠ *Eteläranta, along South Harbor, Kauppatori* ⊙ *Weekdays 8–6, Sat. 8–4.*

## SHOPPING

From large, well-organized malls to closet-size boutiques, Helsinki has shopping for every taste. Most sales staff in the main shopping areas speak English and are helpful. Smaller stores are generally open weekdays 9–6 and Saturday 9–1. Small grocery stores are often open on Sunday year-round; other stores are often open on Sunday from June through August and December. The Forum and Kamppi complexes and Stockmann's department store are open weekdays 9–9, Saturday 9–6, and (in summer and Christmastime) Sunday noon–6. An ever-expanding network of pedestrian tunnels connects the Forum, Stockmann's, and the train-station tunnel.

The area south and west of Mannerheimintie has been branded Design District Helsinki. It includes roughly 170 venues, most of them smaller boutiques and designer-run shops selling handmade everything from jewelry to clothing to housewares. The majority are located on Fredrikinkatu and Annankatu; look for a black Design District Helsinki sticker in the window. You can pick up a map detailing the shops in the district at most participating stores. Kiosks remain open late and on weekends; they sell such basics as milk, juice, camera film, and tissues. Stores in Asematunneli, the train-station tunnel, are open weekdays 10–10 and on weekends noon–10.

**Design Forum Finland.** This shop sells items from many of the nearby stores as well as items by designers without places of their own. It also puts on exhibitions featuring particular artists and it has a café. ⊠ *Erottajank. 7, Punavouri* ☎ *09/6220–8130* ⊕ *www.designforum.fi.*

**Hietalahden Tori.** At the outdoor flea market (open weekdays 8–7, Saturday 8–4) that's held here, you can get an ever-changing assortment of used items; the indoor market brims with food, flowers, fish, and more. ⊠ *Bulevardi and Hietalahdenkatu* ☎ *09/3107–1396* ⊙ *Weekdays 6:30–6, Sat. 6:30–4 (with extended summer hours).*

**Marimekko.** Since the 1950s Marimekko has been selling bright, unusual clothes for men, women, and children in quality fabrics. Though the products are expensive, they're worth a look even if you don't plan to buy. There are four locations in central Helsinki. ⊠ *Pohjoisespl. 2, Esplanadi* ☎ *09/686–0240* ⊕ *www.marimekko.com* ⊠ *Pohjoisespl. 33, Kämp Galleria, Esplanadi* ☎ *09/686–0240* ⊕ *www.marimekko. com* ⊠ *Kamppi shopping center, Urho Kekkosen Katu 1, Keskusta* ☎ *010/344–3300.*

## ACTIVITIES

Taking a sauna is the big Finnish pastime. It's a place to get cleansed and do some socializing.

## WHERE TO EAT

**$$$**
SCANDINAVIAN
**Fodor's**Choice
★

✕**Kosmos.** Just a short walk from Stockmann's department store, this cozy restaurant has become a lunchtime favorite among businesspeople working nearby. Come evening, it's given over to artists and journalists. Its high ceilings and understated interior give it a Scandinavian air of simplicity and efficiency. Menu highlights include reindeer fillet in a sauce of spruce shoots and rosemary that's served with roasted potatoes, and *vorschmack*, a ground meat and anchovy dish, which is served here with *Duchesse* potatoes (a rich version of mashed), pickles, and beets. ⑤ *Average main: €25* ✉ *Kalevank. 3, Keskusta* ☎ *09/647–255* ⊕ *www. kosmos.fi* ☺ *Closed Sun. and in July. No lunch Sat.* Ⓜ *Trams 3B, 6, 9, 10: Student House stop.*

**$$**
SCANDINAVIAN

✕**Salutorget Scandinavian Bistro.** Right beside City Hall, this building retains Doric columns and deep wood panels that harken back to the days when it was a bank rather than an elegant restaurant. Toast skagen, a Nordic classic, is a good bet for a starter—it's shrimp, mayo, and chives on toasted bread, topped with a generous dollop of whitefish roe. Moose Wallenbergare, served with potato purée, game sauce, and cranberry jam, is definitely worth trying as a main course. Salutorget has adopted with gusto the very British concept of afternoon tea. Two Sunday brunch sittings are available, at noon and 3. ⑤ *Average main: €21* ✉ *Pohjoisesplanadi 15, Esplanadi, Helsinki* ☎ *09/6128–5950* ⊕ *www. salutorget.fi/en.*

# RĪGA, LATVIA

Updated by
Dorota Wąsik

Rīga has an upscale, big-city feel unmatched in the region. The capital (almost as large as Tallinn and Vilnius combined) is the business center of the area while original, high-quality restaurants and hotels have earned Rīga some bragging rights among its Western European counterparts. The city also doesn't lack for beauty—Rīga's Old Town (now a UNESCO World Heritage site) is one of Europe's most striking examples of the art nouveau architectural style. Long avenues of complex and sometimes whimsical Jugendstil facades hint at Rīga's grand past. Many were designed by Mikhail Eisenstein, the father of Soviet director Sergei. This style dominates the city center; you can see the finest examples at Alberta 2, 2a, 4, 6, 8, and 13; Elizabetes 10b; and Strēlnieku 4a.

### ESSENTIALS

#### CURRENCY

The monetary unit in Latvia is the lat. In addition to banks, which change cash and traveler's checks, there are numerous currency-exchange booths and ATMs. Credit cards are accepted in major hotels, restaurants, and shops (mostly Visa and MasterCard, with American Express accepted occasionally).

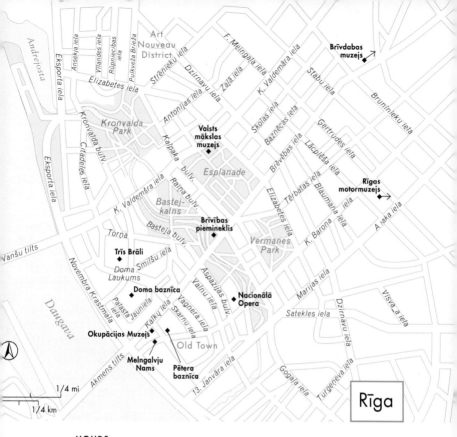

## HOURS

Banks are open weekdays 9–4, but some open as early as 8 and close as late as 7. Most are closed on Saturday, but some stay open 9–3. Museums are generally open Wednesday–Sunday 11–5. Some stay open until 6. Shops open between 10 and 11 and close between 5 and 7, with shorter hours on Saturday. Most shops are closed on Sunday; however, convenience stores are open 7 days a week.

## TELEPHONES

The Latvian mobile phone system is 3G-compatible, Tele2, and Latvijas Mobilias Telefons being the main providers. Public phones support international calls. Some kiosks accept credit cards. Phone cards are available at tobacconists/newspaper shops.

## COMING ASHORE

In addition to larger cruise ships, ferries connect Rīga with Kiel and Lübeck (in Germany) and Stockholm (in Sweden). The cruise port is in the main port, close to the historic downtown core. The walk from port to the downtown core is 15 minutes along the waterfront. The passenger welcome center has good facilities, including restaurants, restrooms, currency-exchange facilities, and ATMs.

To reach the Old Town you can take an inexpensive shuttle transfer or taxi. Taxis are more expensive from the port than within the city center. Drivers must display an operating license and a meter. Stick to the state cabs with orange and black markings. Insist that the meter be turned on; if there is no meter, choose another taxi or decide on a price beforehand. Public transportation can be paid for by the ride, or you can get a 24-hour pass. Services run from 5:30 am to midnight. Some routes have 24-hour service. Trams 6 and 11 connect the Old Town with the Esplanāde area and run regularly throughout the day. Buy tickets at numerous outlets and validate them in the machine on board.

## EXPLORING RĪGA

In many ways, the wonder of Rīga resides less in its individual attractions and more in the fabric of the town itself. In the medieval **Old Town,** an ornate gable or architrave catches the eye at every turn. The somber and the flamboyant are both represented in this quarter's 1,000 years of architectural history. Don't hesitate to just follow where your desire leads—the Old Town is compact and bounded by canals, so it's difficult to get totally lost.

When the Old Town eventually became too crowded, the city burst out into the newer inner suburbs. The rich could afford to leave and build themselves fine fashionable mansions in the style of the day; consequently, city planners created a whole new Rīga. Across the narrow canal, you'll find the **Esplanāde,** a vast expanse of parkland with formal gardens and period mansions where the well-heeled stroll and play. Surrounding this is the **art nouveau district.** Encompassing avenues of splendid family homes (now spruced up in the postcommunist era), the collection has been praised by UNESCO as Europe's finest in the art nouveau style. The best examples are at Alberta 2, 2a, 4, 6, 8, and 13; Elizabetes 10b; and Strēlnieku 4a.

If the weather permits, eschew public transport and stroll between the two districts, taking in the varied skylines and multifaceted facades, and perhaps stopping at a café or two as you go. The city has churches in five Christian denominations and more than 50 museums, many of which cater to eclectic or specialist tastes.

☺ **Brīvdabas muzejs.** The Open-Air Ethnographic Museum is well worth the 9-km (5-mile) trek from downtown. At this countryside living museum, farmsteads and villages have been crafted to look like those in 18th- and 19th-century Latvia, and costumed workers engage in traditional activities (beekeeping, smithing, and so on). ⊠ *Brīvibas 440* ☎ *6799–4515* ⊕ *www.brivdabasmuzejs.lv* ⊠ *Ls 2.50* ☺ *Daily 10–5.*

★ **Brīvības piemineklis.** The central Freedom Monument, a 1935 statue whose upheld stars represent Latvia's united peoples (the Kurzeme, Vidzeme, and Latgale), was the rallying point for many nationalist protests during the late 1980s and early 1990s. Watch the changing of the guard every hour on the hour between 9 and 6. ⊠ *Brīvibas and Raina.*

**Doma baznīca** (*Dome Cathedral*). In Doma laukums (Dome Square), the nerve center of the Old Town, the stately 1210 cathedral dominates.

Reconstructed over the years with Romanesque, Gothic, and baroque elements, this place of worship is astounding as much for its architecture as for its size. The massive 6,768-pipe organ is among the largest in Europe, and it is played nearly every evening at 7 pm. Check at the cathedral for schedules and tickets. ⊠ *Doma laukums* ☎ *6/722–7573* ⊕ *www.doms.lv* ⊗ *Tues.–Fri. 1–5, Sat. 10–2.*

**Melngalvju Nams.** The fiercely Gothic Blackheads House was built in 1344 as a hotel for wayfaring merchants (who wore black hats). Partially destroyed during World War II and leveled by the Soviets in 1948, the extravagant, ornate building was renovated and reopened in 2000 for Rīga's 800th anniversary. The facade is a treasured example of Dutch Renaissance work. ⊠ *Ratslaukums 7* ☎ *6/7043678* ⊕ *www.melngalvjunams.lv* ⊗ *Tues.–Sun. 10–5.*

> ### RĪGA BEST BETS
>
> **Elizabetes Street.** The heart of art nouveau Rīga has some exceptional period architecture and is a testament to the wealth generated here by shipping and trade in the early 20th century.
>
> **Old Town.** The fabric of this medieval core remains remarkably intact, with Gothic spires sheltering church naves and winding cobbled streets revealing sturdy gables.
>
> **The Esplanāde.** The green lung of the city, this huge park has fine formal gardens and planned woodlands. Enjoy a picnic here in warm weather.

**Nacionālā Opera.** Latvia's restored 18th-century National Opera House, where Richard Wagner once conducted, is worthy of a night out. ⊠ *Aspazijas 3* ☎ *6/707–3777* ⊕ *www.opera.lv* ⊗ *Mon.–Sat. 10–7, Sun. 11–7.*

★ **Okupācijas muzejs.** The Latvian Occupation Museum details the devastation of Latvia at the hands of the Nazis and Soviets during World War II, as well as the Latvians' struggle for independence in September 1991. In front of the museum is a monument to the Latvian sharpshooters who protected Lenin during the 1917 revolution. ⊠ *Strēlnieku laukums 1* ☎ *6/721–2715* ⊕ *www.okupacijasmuzejs.lv/en* ✍ *Donations accepted* ⊗ *May–Sept., daily 11–6; Oct.–Apr., Tues.–Sun. 11–5.*

**Pētera baznīca.** Towering St. Peter's Church, originally built in 1209, had a long history of annihilation and conflagration before being destroyed most recently in 1941. Rebuilt by the Soviets, it lacks authenticity but has a good observation deck on the 200-foot spire. ⊠ *Skārņu 19* ☎ *6/722–9426* ⊕ *www.peterbaznica.lv* ⊗ *Tues.–Sun. 10–7.*

**Rīgas motormuzejs.** At the Motor Museum, the Western cars on display can impress, but the Soviet models—including Stalin's iron-plated limo and a Rolls-Royce totaled by Brezhnev himself—are the most fun. ⊠ *Eizensteina 6* ☎ *6/7025888* ⊕ *www.motormuzejs.lv* ✍ *Ls 2* ⊗ *Daily 10–6.*

**Trīs Brāli.** The Three Brothers—a trio of houses on Mazā Pils—show what the city looked like before the 20th century. The three oldest stone houses in the capital (No. 17 is the oldest, dating from the 15th century) span several styles, from the medieval to the baroque. The building at No. 19 is the city's **architecture museum.** ⊠ *Mazā Pils 17, 19, 21* ☎ *6/722–0779* ⊕ *www.archmuseum.lv* ⊗ *Mon. 9–6, Tues.–Thurs. 9–5, Fri. 9–4.*

**Valsts mākslas muzejs.** The National Art Museum has a gorgeous interior, with imposing marble staircases linking several large halls of 19th- and 20th-century Latvian paintings. ⊠ *K. Valdemāra 10a* ☎ *6732–4461* ⊕ *www.lnmm.lv* ✉ *Ls 3* ☉ *Mon., Wed., Thurs, and weekends 11–5, Fri. 11–8.* ☉ *Closed Tues.*

## SHOPPING

You'll find many souvenir and gift shops in the streets of the Old Town, many of which specifically cater to visitors. Latvia is famed for its linen, which is fashioned into clothes and household items such as tea towels and table runners. Woolen sweaters, mittens, and socks with traditional patterns have been worn by generations of locals during the winter. Amber items are everywhere, although their quality can vary, so shop around. Also popular are jewelry, carved ornaments, and Rīga Black Balsam, a liqueur made from an ancient recipe incorporating herbs and medicinal roots.

## WHERE TO EAT

$    ✕ **Cydonia.** One of Rīga's premier dining establishments, Cydonia gas-
MEDITERRANEAN    tropub serves outstanding Mediterranean cuisine, with an emphasis on seafood, as well as light soups and salads. The dining room is furnished in a fashionable Scandinavian style—simple yet cozy, with an abundance of natural materials like wood and stone. There's also a lovely kids' corner with toys and crayons. ⑤ *Average main: Ls7* ⊠ *Berga Bazārs, Dzirnavu 84/1* ☎ *6/7282055* ⊕ *www.cydonia.lv.*

$    ✕ **Staburags.** Found in the the art nouveau Hotel Viktorija in downtown
EASTERN    Rīga, this may be the capital's best place to sample Latvian national cui-
EUROPEAN    sine, with such offerings as roast leg of pork, sauerkraut, an assortment of potato dishes, and smoked chicken. ⑤ *Average main: Ls5* ⊠ *Caka 55* ☎ *6729–9787* ⊕ *www.hotelviktorija.lv.*

# ST. PETERSBURG, RUSSIAN FEDERATION

Commissioned by Peter the Great as "a window looking into Europe," St. Petersburg is a planned city built on more than 100 islands in the Neva Delta linked by canals and arched bridges. It was first called the "Venice of the North" by Goethe. Little wonder it's the darling of today's fashion photographers. With its strict geometric lines and perfectly planned architecture, so unlike the Russian cities that came before it, St. Petersburg is almost too European to be Russian. And yet it's too Russian to be European. Memories of revolutionary zeal and one of the worst ordeals of World War II, when the city—then known as Leningrad—withstood a 900-day siege and blockade by Nazi forces, are still fresh in the minds of citizens. Nevertheless, St. Petersburg is filled with pleasures and tantalizing treasures, from golden spires and gilded domes to pastel palaces and candlelit cathedrals.

## ESSENTIALS

### CURRENCY

The ruble. There are ATMs in the city, but exchange bureaus are more plentiful. Credit cards are increasingly accepted, but ask first to be sure.

### HOURS

Stores have recently extended their opening hours considerably—many stay open until 8 or 9 pm, or on Sunday.

### PRIVATE TOURS

Cruise passengers who do not wish to take expensive and crowded tours offered by their ships but who still do not wish to deal with the bureaucracy and cost of getting a Russian visa can still visit St. Petersburg on a private tour with an accredited company. These tours must be arranged in advance, but they offer the opportunity to get fast entry to major museums without having to stand in long lines and include the services of a knowledgeable guide. While privately arranged tours are often cheaper than the ones offered by ships, this is not the case in St. Petersburg, where a private tour might even be more expensive if you are just, say, a couple. However, you get superior service and more personal attention on these tours and do not have to travel in a large bus with dozens of other passengers. For many people, this is worth the cost.

**Contacts Alla Tours.** ☏ *(7)812/312–5355* ⊕ *www.alla-tour.com.* **SPb Tours.** ☏ *(7)812/331–5383* ⊕ *www.spb-tours.com.*

### TELEPHONES

Some tri- and quad-band mobile phones may work in St. Petersburg, but mobile service on the whole is patchy. The network does not yet support 3G services, and handsets are single-band. Public phones take phone cards, which can be bought at newsstands. Note that public phones in Metro stations work on a different system and require a different card.

### COMING ASHORE

Independent travel is not as easy in St. Petersburg as in other destinations, as you need to obtain a tourist visa prior to the cruise departure to explore without a certified guide; for the vast majority of travelers, it is simply not a practical matter to get a separate visa for a typical two-night cruise visit. It is also worth considering that independent travelers need to line up for tickets at museums and attractions, while guided groups do not. This can cut down your sightseeing time considerably. Whether you travel independently or with an accredited small tour company, it is approximately 20 minutes on foot to the port entrance, from where you will be able to take a taxi.

# EXPLORING ST. PETERSBURG

★ **Dvortsovaya Ploshchad** (*Palace Square*). One of the world's most magnificent plazas, the square is a stunning ensemble of buildings and open space, a combination of several seemingly incongruous architectural styles in perfect harmony. It's where the city's imperial past has been preserved in all its glorious splendor, but it also resonates with the

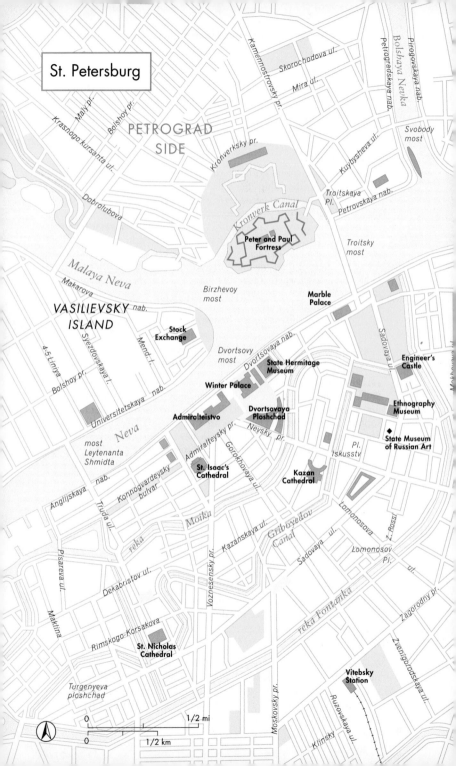

history of the revolution that followed. Here, the fate of the last Russian tsar was effectively sealed, on Bloody Sunday in 1905, when palace troops opened fire on peaceful demonstrators, killing scores of women and children. It was across Palace Square in October 1917 that Bolshevik revolutionaries stormed the Winter Palace and overthrew Kerensky's Provisional Government, an event that led to the birth of the Soviet Union. Almost 75 years later, during tense days, huge crowds rallied on Palace Square in support of perestroika and democracy. Today, the beautiful square is a bustling hubbub of tourist and

> ## ST. PETERSBURG BEST BETS
>
> **The State Hermitage Museum.** This immense and ornate royal palace is one of the finest art repositories in the world.
>
> **Dvortsovaya Ploshchad.** The seeds of the revolution were sown in this historic and architecturally stunning square.
>
> **The downtown core.** Known by the epithet "Venice of the North," St. Petersburg offers marvelous vistas at every turn.

marketing activity, lively yet seemingly imperturbable as ever. Horseback and carriage rides are available for hire here. A carriage ride around the square costs about 200R per person. A 20-minute tour of the city in the direction of your choosing costs about 2,000R, for up to six people. ⊠ *City Center* Ⓜ *Nevsky Prospekt.*

**Kazan Cathedral** (*Kazansky Sobor*). After a visit to Rome, Tsar Paul I (1754–1801) commissioned this magnificent cathedral, wishing to copy—and perhaps present the Orthodox rival to—that city's St. Peter's. It was erected between 1801 and 1811 from a design by Andrei Voronikhin. Inside and out, the church abounds with sculpture and decoration. On the prospect side the frontage holds statues of St. John the Baptist and the apostle Andrew as well as such sanctified Russian heroes as Grand Prince Vladimir (who advanced the Christianization of Russia) and Alexander Nevsky. Note the enormous bronze front doors— exact copies of Ghiberti's Gates of Heaven at Florence's Baptistery. ⊠ *2 Kazanskaya Pl., City Center* ☎ *812/314–4663* ⊘ *Open daily 8:30–8; services weekdays at 10 am and 6 pm, weekends at 7 and 10 am and 6 pm* Ⓜ *Nevsky Prospekt.*

**Fodor's**Choice
★

**Peter and Paul Fortress** (*Petropavlovskaya Krepost*). The first building in Sankt-Piter-Burkh, as the city was then called, the fortress was erected in just one year, between 1703 and 1704. The date on which construction began on the fortress is celebrated as the birth of St. Petersburg.

The fortifications display several gates, along with arsenal buildings and the **Engineer's House** (*Inzhenerny Dom*), which is now a branch of the Museum of the History of St. Petersburg (as are all exhibits in the fortress) and presents displays about the city's pre-revolutionary history.

The main attraction of the fortress, however, is the **Cathedral of Sts. Peter and Paul** (*Petropavlovsky Sobor*). Constructed between 1712 and 1733 on the site of an earlier wooden church, it's highly unusual for a Russian Orthodox church. Instead of the characteristic bulbous domes, it's adorned by a single, slender, gilded spire whose height (400 feet)

7

made the church the city's tallest building for more than two centuries. Starting with Peter the Great, the cathedral served as the burial place of the tsars.

Several of the fortress's bastions were put to use over the years mainly as political prisons. One of them, **Trubetskoi Bastion,** is open to the public as a museum. Famous prisoners include some of the People's Will terrorists, who killed Alexander II in 1881; plus revolutionaries Leon Trotsky and Maxim Gorky. ⊠ *3 Petropavlovskaya Krepost, Petrograd Side* ☎ *812/230–6431; 812/232–9454 excursions* 🖾 *Cathedral 140R, cathedral and other sights and exhibitions 250R, audio guide in English, French, German, Spanish, or Italian 250R (purchase guide at the Fortress's Information Center, at Ioanovsky Ravelin; the deposit of 2,000R or a document, such as a passport or driver's license, is required)* ⊙ *Thurs.–Tues. 11–6, kassa open until 5 Thurs.–Mon., until 4 on Tues. Cathedral of Sts. Peter and Paul closed Wed., fortress closed last Tues. of month* Ⓜ *Gorkovskaya.*

Fodor'sChoice
★
**St. Isaac's Cathedral** (*Isaakievsky Sobor*). St. Isaac's is the world's third-largest domed cathedral, and the first monument you see of the city if you arrive by ship. Tsar Alexander I commissioned the construction of the cathedral in 1818 to celebrate his victory over Napoléon.

The interior of the cathedral is lavishly decorated with malachite, lazulite, marble, and other precious stones and minerals. Gilding the dome required 220 pounds of gold. When the city was blockaded during World War II, the gilded dome was painted black to avoid its being targeted by enemy fire. Despite efforts to protect it, the cathedral nevertheless suffered heavy damage, as bullet holes on the columns on the south side attest. ⊠ *1 Isaakievskaya Pl., Admiralteisky* ☎ *812/315–9732* 🖾 *Cathedral 200R, colonnade 100R* ⊙ *Cathedral May–Sept., Thurs.–Tues. 10 am–7 pm and 8 pm–10:30 pm; Oct.–Apr., Thurs.–Tues. 11–6 and 7 pm–9:30 pm* Ⓜ *Sennaya Ploshchad.*

Fodor'sChoice
★
**State Hermitage Museum** (*Gosudarstvenny Ermitazh Muzey*). Leonardo's *Benois Madonna* . . . Rembrandt's *Danaë* . . . Matisse's *The Dance* . . . you get the picture. As the former private art collection of the tsars, this is one of the world's most famous museums, virtually wallpapered with celebrated paintings. In addition, the walls are works of art themselves, for this collection is housed in the lavish Winter Palace, one of the most outstanding examples of Russian baroque magnificence. The museum takes its name from Catherine the Great (1729–96), who used it for her private apartments. Between 1764 and 1775 the empress undertook to acquire some of the world's finest works of art.

A wealth of Russian and European art is on show: Florentine, Venetian, and other Italian art through the 18th century, including Leonardos and Michelangelos, two Raphaels, eight Titians, and works by Tintoretto, Lippi, Caravaggio, and Canaletto. The Hermitage also houses a superb collection of Spanish art, of which works by El Greco, Velázquez, Murillo, and Goya are on display. Its spectacular presentation of Flemish and Dutch art contains roomfuls of Van Dycks. Also here are more than 40 canvasses by Rubens and an equally impressive number of Rembrandts. There is a smattering of excellent British paintings including works by Joshua Reynolds, Thomas Gainsborough, and George Morland.

Reflecting the Francophilia of the empresses Elizabeth and Catherine, the museum is second only to the Louvre in its assortment of French art. Along with earlier masterpieces by Lorrain, Watteau, and Poussin, the collection runs the whole gamut of 19th-century genius, with Delacroix, Ingres, Corot, and Courbet. There is also a stunning collection of impressionists and postimpressionists, including works by Monet, Degas, Sisley, Pissarro, and Renoir. Sculptures by Auguste Rodin and a host of pictures by Cézanne, Gauguin, and van Gogh are followed by Picasso and a lovely room of Matisse.

Possibly the most-prized section of the Hermitage is the first-floor's **Treasure Gallery,** also referred to as the *Zolotaya Kladovaya* (Golden Room). This spectacular collection of gold, silver, and royal jewels includes ancient Scythian gold and silver treasures, plus precious stones, jewelry, and jewel-encrusted items from the 16th through the 20th centuries. ⊠ *2 Dvortsovaya Pl., City Center* ☎ *812/710–9625 recorded information in Russian; 812/710–9079 information desk; 812/571–8446 tours* ⊕ *www.hermitagemuseum.org* ✉ *State Hermitage Museum 400R (free 1st Thurs. of month), two-day combined-entrance ticket 780R (this can only be purchased through the website), personal excursion guide 7,000R for groups up to seven people, Treasure Gallery 300R in addition to the entrance ticket price (check the schedule for the tours to the gallery a day before your visit by calling the tour service phone)* ⊗ *Tues.–Sat. 10:30–6, Sun. 10:30–5; kassa (ticket window) open Tues.–Sat. until 5, Sun. until 4* Ⓜ *Nevsky Prospekt.*

Fodor'sChoice ★ **State Museum of Russian Art** (*Gosudarstvenny Russky Muzey*). In 1898 Nicholas II turned the stupendously majestic neoclassical Mikhailovsky Palace (Mikhailovsky Dvorets) into a museum that has become one of the country's most important art galleries. The collection at the museum, which is sometimes just referred to as the Russian Museum, has scores of masterpieces on display, from outstanding icons to mainstream art of all eras. For many years much of this work was unknown in the West, and it's fascinating to see the stylistic parallels and the incorporation of outside influences into a Russian framework. Painters of the World of Art movement—Bakst, Benois, and Somov—are also here. There are several examples of 20th-century art, with works by Kandinsky and Kazimir Malevich. ⊠ *4/2 Inzhenernaya ul., City Center* ☎ *812/595–4248* ⊕ *www.rusmuseum.ru* ✉ *350R* ⊗ *Mon. 10–5, Wed.–Sun. 10–6, kassa open until 1 hr before closing* Ⓜ *Nevsky Prospekt.*

Fodor'sChoice ★ **Winter Palace** (*Zimny Dvorets*). With its 1,001 rooms swathed in malachite, jasper, agate, and gilded mirrors, this famous palace—the residence of Russia's rulers from Catherine the Great (1762) to Nicholas II (1917)—is the focal point of Palace Square. The palace, now the site of the State Hermitage Museum, is the grandest monument of that strange hybrid: the Russian rococo, in itself an eye-popping mix of the old-fashioned 17th-century baroque and the newfangled 18th-century neoclassical style. Now "Russianized," the palace's neoclassic ornament lost its early gracefulness and Greek sense of proportion and evolved toward the heavier, more monumental, imperial style. Still, the exterior is particularly successful and pleasing.

The palace, which was created by the Italian architect Bartolomeo Francesco Rastrelli, stretches from Palace Square to the Neva River embankment. It was the fourth royal residence on this site, commissioned in 1754 by Peter the Great's daughter Elizabeth. By the time it was completed, in 1762, Elizabeth had died and the craze for the Russian rococo style had waned. Catherine the Great left the exterior unaltered but had the interiors redesigned in the neoclassical style of her day. In 1837, after the palace was gutted by fire, the interiors were revamped once again. Three of the palace's most celebrated rooms are the **Gallery of the 1812 War,** where portraits of Russian commanders who served against Napoléon are on display; the **Great Throne Room,** richly decorated in marble and bronze; and the **Malachite Room,** designed by the architect Alexander Bryullov. ⊠ *34 Dvortsovaya Pl., City Center* ☎ *812/710–9625 recorded information in Russian or 812/710–9079 directory service in Russian and English* ⊕ *www.hermitagemuseum.org* ▦ *400R; 2-day combined-entrance ticket 780R (this can only be purchased through the website* ⊘ *Tues.–Sat. 10:30–6, Sun. 10:30–5 kassa open Tues.–Sat. until 5, on Sun. until 4* Ⓜ *Nevsky Prospekt.*

## SHOPPING

Pick up a copy of Russian *Vogue* and you may be surprised to see that it nearly outdoes its Parisian and American counterparts for sheer glitz and trendy garb. And all those nifty threads that the models are wearing are fully stocked in the international boutiques around the city.

A two-tiered system of stores exists in St. Petersburg. Western-style shops taking credit-card payment have replaced the old *Beriozkas* (Birch Trees) emporiums, which were stocked only for foreigners. State-run shops are also better stocked now than before. Only rubles (as opposed to credit cards) are accepted in the state-run shops, however, and you'll have a tough time maneuvering through the cashiers if you don't speak some Russian.

The central shopping district is Nevsky prospekt and the streets running off it. Don't expect too many bargains beyond the bootlegged CDs and videos (which could be confiscated at customs in the United States), however, because prices for items such as clothes and electronic goods are just as high as in the West, and in the chic stores in hotels they are even higher.

For true souvenirs of the city, think quality crafts just like the tsars did. Ceramic painted eggs, á la Fabergé, and almost anything ornate and gilded are typical of the "imperial" style. Look also for good quality linens. Furs may not be to everybody's taste, but wealthy locals still prefer them during the freezing winters. For kitsch, what better than a set of Russian dolls? These vary in quality and in price.

## WHERE TO EAT

$    ✕**Teremok**. Don't be intimidated by the café's spartan setting. Teremok's
CAFÉ    owners penny-pinch only on furnishings and presentation. Cooked
in front of your eyes, their famous blini—priced at 40R–300R—are
deservedly rated the best in town. Stuffed with mushrooms, ham, pork,
grilled chicken, cream, honey, and a dozen other fillings, the blini, rich
in flavor and never over- or underdone, taste as if a Russian mom
cooked them. A single blini is so rich and hefty, it may leave you stuffed.
Be conservative when you order unless you are absolutely starving. In
addition to this café, Teremok also runs a chain of 15 street stands. ⊠ *60
Nevsky pr., City Center* 🕾 *No phone* Ⓜ *Nevsky Prospekt.*

$$   ✕**Tinkoff**. The crowded, loftlike Tinkoff was St. Petersburg's first micro-
AMERICAN    brewery. Trendy people come to enjoy beer and tasty comfort food in
a relaxed, club-like dining room. Frequent Western jazz, lounge, and
cool pop acts appear at Tinkoff, but when they're here the cover price
gets very high, usually around 1,500R. There's a sushi bar, with combos
starting from 250R, but you're better off sticking with the beer and
burgers. ⊠ *7 Kazanskaya ul., City Center* 🕾 *812/718–5566* ⊕ *www.
tinkof.ru* Ⓜ *Nevsky Prospekt.*

# STOCKHOLM, SWEDEN

Updated
by Lola
Akinmade-
Åkerström

Stockholm is a city in the flush of its second youth. In the last 10 years
Sweden's capital has emerged from its cold, Nordic shadow to take the
stage as a truly international city. The streets are flowing with a young
and confident population keen to drink in everything the city has to
offer. The glittering feeling of optimism, success, and living in the "here
and now" is rampant in Stockholm. Of course, not everyone is looking
to live so much in the present; luckily, Stockholm also has plenty of his-
tory. Stockholm boasts a glorious medieval Old Town, grand palaces,
ancient churches, sturdy edifices, public parks, and 19th-century muse-
ums—its history is soaked into the very fabric of its airy boulevards,
built as a public display of the city's trading glory.

### ESSENTIALS

#### CURRENCY

The unit of currency is the krona (plural kronor). Sweden is not in the
euro zone.

#### HOURS

Banks are open weekdays 9:30–3; larger branches until 5 and 6 on
Thursday. The bank at Arlanda International Airport is open every day
with extended hours, and the Forex and X-Change currency-exchange
offices also have extended hours. Take a queue-number ticket from
near the door and wait your turn. It's not uncommon to come across
cashless bank branches in some smaller towns so it's worth checking
before traveling.

#### TELEPHONES

Most tri- or quad-band GSM phones work in Sweden, though handsets
are single-band, where the system is 3G-compatible. Public phones in
Sweden take phone cards or credit cards. Phone cards can be bought

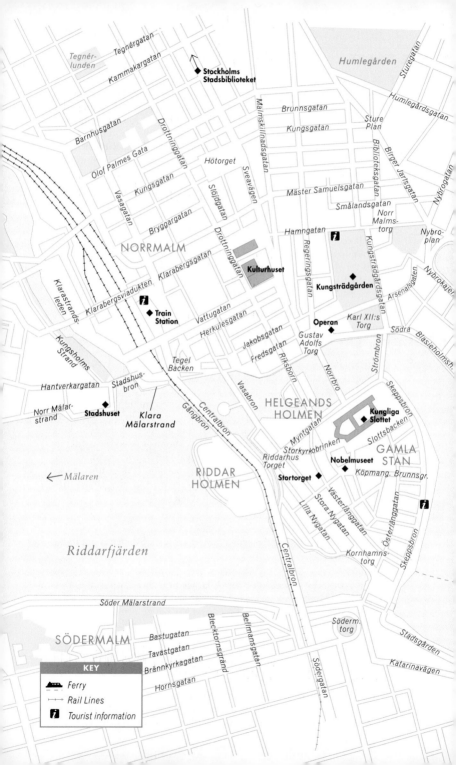

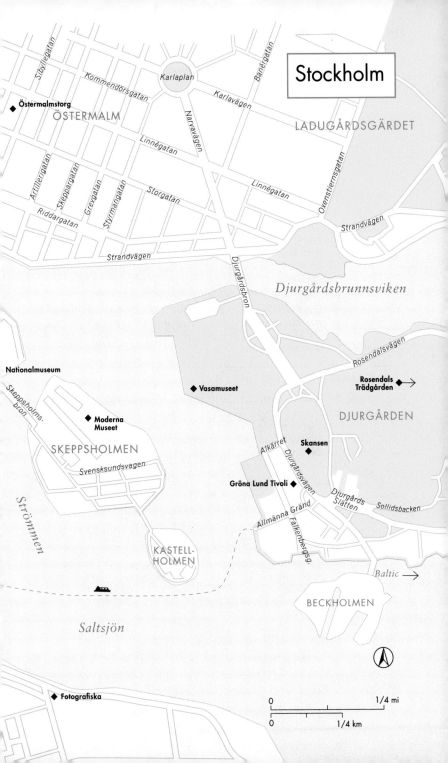

at telecom shops, newsstands, and tobacconists. Public phones support international calls. Main providers include Telia, Tele2, Comviq, Vodafone, and T-Mobile.

### COMING ASHORE

Most vessels dock at various quays in the heart of the Gamla Stan (Old Town). How far you have to walk to the attractions depends on which quay you are moored at. This is one port where you'll want to be out on deck as the ship arrives and the city comes within camera distance. If all berths are full (eight of them), there is a mooring buoy in the harbor, and passengers will be tendered ashore. You can reach everything in the city (museums, shops, restaurants, and cafés) from the quays on foot.

Alternatively, some vessels dock at Nynasham outside the city. It is a 15-minute walk from the port at Nynasham to the railway station for the one-hour journey into central Stockholm. A one-day travel card covers this journey and all other public transport trips within the city. SL (Stockholm Transport) runs a modern and reliable public transit system. Tickets are valid for one hour from validation and cost SKr 30 per journey within Zone 1 (central Stockholm). A one-day card is SKr 100.

Taxis are plentiful but expensive, and most drivers speak some English. Current rates are SKr 45 for pick-up, then around SKr 9 per km depending on the company. So expect to pay SKr100 (over US$14) for about a five-minute taxi ride.

## EXPLORING STOCKHOLM

**Fodor's Choice** ★ **Fotografiska.** Opened in 2010, this contemporary photography museum housed in a 1906 redbrick art nouveau building along Stockholm's waterfront spotlights edgy fine art photography and past exhibitions have included celebrity photographer Annie Leibovitz and director Anton Corbijn. ⊠ *Stadsgårdsleden 22, Södermalm* ☎ *08/50900500* ⊕ *www.fotografiska.eu* ⊠ *Skr 110* ☉ *Daily 10–9.*

☺ **Gröna Lund Tivoli.** Smaller than Copenhagen's Tivoli or Göteborg's Liseberg, this amusement park has managed to retain much of its historical charm, while making room for some modern, hair-raising rides among the pleasure gardens, amusement arcades, and restaurants. If you're feeling especially daring, try the Power Tower. At 350 feet, it's one of Europe's tallest free-fall amusement-park rides and one of the best ways to see Stockholm, albeit for about three seconds, before you plummet. There isn't an adult who grew up in Stockholm who can't remember the annual excitement of Gröna Lund's April opening. Go and you will see why. ⊠ *Allmänna Gränd 9, Djurgården* ☎ *08/58750100* ⊕ *www.gronalund.com* ⊠ *SKr 95, not including tickets or passes for rides* ☉ *Late Apr.–mid-Sept., daily. Hrs vary but are generally noon-11pm. Call ahead for specific information.*

☺ **Kulturhuset** (*Culture House*). Since it opened in 1974, architect Peter Celsing's cultural center, a glass-and-stone monolith on the south side of Sergels Torg, has become a symbol of modernism in Sweden. Stockholmers are divided on the aesthetics of this building—most either love it or hate it. Here there are exhibitions for children and adults, a library, a theater, a youth center, an exhibition center, and a restaurant. Head to Café Panorama, on the top floor, to savor traditional Swedish cuisine and a great view of Sergels Torg down below. ⊠ *Sergels torg 3, City* ☎ *08/50831508* ⊕ *www.kulturhuset.stockholm.se* ⊗ *Weekdays 9–7, weekends 11–5.*

**Fodor'sChoice**
★
**Kungliga Slottet** (*Royal Palace*). Designed by Nicodemus Tessin, the Royal Palace was completed in 1760 and replaced the previous palace that had burned down at the location in 1697. The four facades of the palace each have a distinct style: the west is the king's, the east the queen's, the south belongs to the nation, and the north represents royalty in general. Watch the changing of the guard in the curved terrace entrance, and view the palace's fine furnishings and Gobelin tapestries on a tour of the Representationsvän (State Apartments). To survey the crown jewels, which are no longer used in this self-consciously egalitarian country, head to the Skattkammaren (Treasury). The Livrustkammaren (Royal Armory) has an outstanding collection of weaponry, coaches, and royal regalia. Entrances to the Treasury and Armory are on the Slottsbacken side of the palace. ⊠ *Slottsbacken 1, Gamla Stan* ☎ *08/4026130* ⊕ *www.royalcourt.se* ⊡ *SKr 150* ⊗ *Mid-May–mid-Sept., daily 10–5; mid-Sept.–mid-May, daily noon-4.*

**Kungsträdgården.** Once the royal kitchen garden, this is now Stockholm's smallest but most central park. It is often used to host festivals and events, but is best seen in its everyday guise: as a pleasant sanctuary from the pulse of downtown. Several neat little glass-cube cafés sell light lunches, coffee, and snacks. ⊠ *Kungsträdgården* ☎ *08/55510090* ⊕ *www.kungstradgarden.se.*

**Moderna Museet** (*Museum of Modern Art*). The museum's excellent collection includes works by Picasso, Kandinsky, Dalí, Brancusi, and other international artists. You can also view examples of significant Swedish painters and sculptors and an extensive section on photography. The building itself is striking. Designed by the well-regarded Spanish architect Rafael Moneo, it has seemingly endless hallways of blond wood and walls of glass. ⊠ *Skeppsholmen, Exercisplan, City* ☎ *08/51955200* ⊕ *www.modernamuseet.se* ⊡ *SKr 120* ⊗ *Tues. 10–8, Wed.–Sun. 10–6.*

**Fodor'sChoice**
★
**Nationalmuseum.** Allow at least an hour if you want to see most of the paintings and sculptures on display at this impressive museum. The emphasis is on Swedish and Nordic art, but other areas are well represented. Look especially for some fine works by Rembrandt. The print and drawing department is also impressive, with a nearly complete collection of Edouard Manet prints. ■TIP➜ **From summer 2013, the Nationalmuseum will be undergoing major renovations. Many of its works will be temporararily relocated to the Royal Swedish Academy of Fine Arts at Fredsgatan 12, with different hours likely.** ⊠ *Södra Blasieholmshamnen, City* ☎ *08/51954410* ⊕ *www.nationalmuseum.se* ⊡ *SKr 100* ⊗ *Jan.–Aug., Tues. 11–8, Wed.–Sun. 11–5; Sept.–Dec., Tues. and Thurs. 11–8, Wed., Fri., and weekends 11–5.*

**Nobelmuseet.** The Swedish Academy meets at Börshuset (the Stock Exchange) every year to decide the winner of the Nobel Prize for literature. The building is also the home of the Nobel Museum. Along with exhibits on creativity's many forms, the museum displays scientific models, shows films, and has a full explanation of the process of choosing prizewinners. The museum does a good job covering the controversial selections made over the years. It's a must for Nobel Prize hopefuls and others. ⊠ *Börshuset, Stortorget 2, Gamla Stan* ☎ *08/53481800* ⊕ *www.nobelmuseum.se* ⌧ *SKr 70* ⊙ *Mid-May–mid-Sept., Wed., Thurs., and Sat.–Mon., 10–6, Tues. and Fri. 10–8; mid-Sept.–mid-May, Tues. 11–8, Wed.–Sun. 11–5.*

**Operan** (*Opera House*). Stockholm's baroque Opera House is almost more famous for its restaurants and bars than for its opera and ballet productions, but that doesn't mean an evening performance should be missed. There's not a bad seat in the house. For between just SKr 50 to 100 you can even get a listening-only seat (with no view). Still, its food and drink status can't be denied. It has been one of Stockholm's artistic and literary watering holes since the first Operakällaren restaurant opened on the site in 1787. ⊠ *Gustav Adolfs Torg, City* ☎ *08/7914400* ⊕ *www.operan.se.*

**Östermalmstorg.** The market square and its neighboring streets represent old, established Stockholm. **Saluhall** looks more like a collection of boutiques than the indoor food market it is; the fish displays can be especially intriguing. At the other end of the square, **Hedvig Eleonora Kyrka,** a church with characteristically Swedish faux-marble painting throughout its wooden interior, is the site of frequent lunchtime concerts in spring and summer. ⊠ *Nybrog. at Humlegårdsg., Östermalm* ⊕ *www.ostermalmshallen.se.*

Fodor's Choice
★
**Rosendals Trädgården** (*Rosendal's Garden*). This gorgeous slice of greenery is a perfect place to spend a few hours on a late summer afternoon. When the weather's nice, people flock to the garden café, which is in one of the greenhouses, to enjoy tasty pastries and salads made from the locally grown vegetables. Pick your own flowers from the vast flower beds (paying by weight), stroll through the creative garden displays, or take away produce from the farm shop. ⊠ *Rosendalsterrassen 12, Djurgården* ☎ *08/54581270* ⊕ *www.rosendalstradgard.se* ⌧ *Free* ⊙ *May–Sept., weekdays 11–5, weekends 11–6; Oct.–Apr. call ahead for specific information.*

★
♺
**Skansen.** The world's first open-air museum, Skansen was founded in 1891 by philologist and ethnographer Artur Hazelius, who is buried here. Drawing from all parts of the country, he preserved examples of traditional Swedish architecture, including farmhouses, windmills, barns, a working glassblower's hut, and churches. Not only is Skansen

## STOCKHOLM BEST BETS

**Stroll the streets of Gamla Stan.** Stockholm's Old Town is replete with architectural treasures and teeming with street life.

**Immerse yourself in Nordic tradition at Skansen.** The world's first open-air museum recreates 19th- and early 20th-century rural life.

**Unfurl the sails at Vasamuseet.** This spectacular 17th-century warship was raised from the ocean floor and painstakingly renovated in the 1960s.

a delightful trip out of time in the center of a modern city, but it also provides insight into the life and culture of Sweden's various regions. In addition, the park has a zoo, carnival area, aquarium, theater, and cafés. ⊠ *Djurgårdsslätten 49–51, Djurgården* ☎ *08/4428000* ⊕ *www. skansen.se* ⊠ *Park and zoo: Jan.–Apr. SKr 70, May and Sept. SKr 90, June–Aug. SKr 110. Aquarium: SKr 100.* ⊙ *Nov.–Feb., weekdays 10–3, weekends 10-4; Mar., Apr., and Oct., daily 10–4; May–June 19, daily 10–8; June 20–Aug. 10–8; Sept., daily 10–8.*

**Fodor's** Choice
★ **Stadshuset** (*City Hall*). The architect Ragnar Östberg, one of the founders of the National Romantic movement, completed Stockholm's city hall in 1923. The headquarters of the city council, the building is functional but ornate: its immense **Blå Hallen** (Blue Hall) is the venue for the annual Nobel Prize dinner, Stockholm's main social event. You must take a tour to visit City Hall. You can also take a trip to the top of the 348-foot tower, most of which can be achieved by elevator, to enjoy a breathtaking panorama of the city and Riddarfjärden. ⊠ *Hantverkarg. 1, Kungsholmen* ☎ *08/50829058* ⊕ *www.stockholm.se* ⊠ *SKr 90, tower Skr 40* ⊙ *Tours of City Hall in English, Sept.–May, daily on the hour 10–3; June–Aug., daily every 30 min. 9:30–4. Tower open May–Sept., daily 9:15–4:30.*

**Stockholms Stadsbiblioteket** (*Stockholm City Library*). The Stockholm City Library is among the most captivating buildings in town. Designed by the famous Swedish architect E. G. Asplund and completed in 1928, the building's cylindrical, galleried main hall gives it the appearance of a large birthday cake. Inside is an excellent "information technology" center with free Internet access—and lots of books, too. ⊠ *Sveav. 73, Vasastan* ☎ *08/50830900* ⊕ *www.biblioteket.se* ⊙ *Mon.–Thurs. 9–9, Fri. 9–7, weekends noon–4.*

**Stortorget** (*Great Square*). Here in 1520 the Danish king Christian II ordered a massacre of Swedish noblemen. The slaughter paved the way for a national revolt against foreign rule and the founding of Sweden as a sovereign state under King Gustav Vasa, who ruled from 1523 to 1560. One legend holds that if it rains heavily enough on the anniversary of the massacre, the old stones still run red. ⊠ *Near Kungliga Slottet, Gamla Stan.*

**Vasamuseet** (*Vasa Museum*). The warship *Vasa* sank 10 minutes into its maiden voyage in 1628, consigned to a watery grave until it was raised from the seabed in 1961. Its hull was preserved by the Baltic mud, free of the shipworms (really clams) that can eat through timbers. Now largely restored to her former glory (however short-lived it may have been), the man-of-war resides in a handsome museum. The sheer size of this cannon-laden hulk inspires awe and fear in equal measure. The political history of the world may have been different had she made it out of harbor. Daily tours are available year-round. ⊠ *Galärvarvsv. 14, Djurgården* ☎ *08/51954800* ⊕ *www.vasamuseet.se* ⊠ *SKr 110* ⊙ *June–Aug., daily 8.30–6; Sept.–May, Thurs.–Tues. 10–5, Wed. 10–8.*

## SHOPPING

If you like to shop till you drop, then charge on down to MOOD, PUB, NK, and Gallerian, the four main department stores and malls in the central city area. All of them carry top-name brands for both men and women. For souvenirs and crafts peruse the boutiques and galleries in Västerlånggatan, the main street of Gamla Stan. For jewelry, crafts, and fine art, hit the shops that line the raised sidewalk at the start of Hornsgatan on Södermalm. Drottninggatan, Birger Jarlsgatan, Biblioteksgatan, Götgatan, and Hamngatan also offer some of the city's best shopping.

**Gallerian.** Just down the road from Sergels Torg, this large indoor mall has designer chic to spare, selling toys to fashion in beautiful surroundings. ⊠ *Hamng. 37, City* ☎ *08/53337300* ⊕ *www.gallerian.se.*

Fodor's Choice ★ **Hötorgshallen.** For a good indoor market hit Hötorgshallen, directly under the Filmstaden movie theater. The market is filled with butcher shops, coffee and tea shops, and fresh-fish markets. It's closed on Sunday. ⊠ *Hötorget, City* ☎ *08/230001* ⊕ *www.hotorgshallen.se.*

**MOOD.** Stockholm's newest destination for high-end shopping spans an entire city block. ⊠ *Jakobsbergsg. 15, Norrmalm* ⊕ *www. moodstockholm.com.*

Fodor's Choice ★ **NK.** Sweden's leading department store is the unmissable NK; the initials, pronounced enn-*koh*, stand for Nordiska Kompaniet. You pay for the high quality here. ⊠ *Hamng. 18–20, across street from Kungsträdgården, City* ☎ *08/7628000* ⊕ *www.nk.se.*

**PUB.** Before becoming a famous actress, Greta Garbo used to work at PUB, which has 42 independent boutiques. Garbo fans will appreciate the small exhibit on level H2—a collection of photographs begins with her employee ID card. ⊠ *Drottningg. 63 and Hötorget, City* ☎ *08/7891930* ⊕ *www.pub.se.*

## WHERE TO EAT

Most Stockholm restaurants specialize in the preparation of perennially popular, Swedish-style fish and shellfish. Innovative and traditional herring assortments and locally sourced roe are especially popular as starters. These starters are often large enough for a light, affordable lunch. Note that many restaurants are closed on Sunday.

**$$**
VEGETARIAN
Fodor's Choice ★
✕ **Hermans.** Hermans is a haven for vegetarians out to get the most bang for their kronor. The glassed-in back deck and open garden both provide breathtaking vistas across the water of Stockholm harbor, Gamla Stan, and the island of Djurgården. The food, served buffet style, includes various vegetable and pasta salads, warm casseroles, and such entrées as Indonesian stew with peanut sauce and vegetarian lasagna. The fruit pies, chocolate cakes, and cookies are delicious. ⑤ *Average main: SKr 155* ⊠ *Fjällg. 23B* ☎ *08/6439480* ⊕ *www.hermans.se.*

**$$$$**
SCANDINAVIAN
Fodor's Choice ★
✕ **Mathias Dahlgren.** From the elegant modern dining room to what's on the plate—simple, artistically rendered local food that its eponymous chef has dubbed "natural cuisine"—this place doesn't disappoint. And for his trouble Dahlgren has picked up two Michelin stars since opening in late 2007. Don't miss this place—and keep in mind that prices in

the bar, where lunch is served on weekdays, are much lower than in the dining room. $ *Average main: SKr 1,650* ⊠ *Grand Hotel, S Blasieholm-shamen 6* ☎ *08/6793584* ⊕ *www.mathiasdahlgren.com* ⌘ *Reservations essential* ⊙ *No lunch weekends. Closed Sun.*

$$ ✕**Pelikan.** Beer, beer, and more beer is the order of the day at this tra-
SCANDINAVIAN ditional drinking hall, a relic of the days when Södermalm was the
Fodor'sChoice dwelling place of the city's blue-collar brigade. Today's more bohemian
★ residents find it just as enticing, with the unvarnished wood-paneled walls, faded murals, and glass globe lights fulfilling all their down-at-the-heel pretensions. The food here is some of the best traditional Swedish fare in the city. The herring, meatballs, and salted bacon with onion sauce are all great choices. $ *Average main: SKr 216* ⊠ *Blekingeg. 40* ☎ *08/55609090* ⊕ *www.pelikan.se* ⊙ *No lunch Fri.–Sun.*

$$$ ✕**Prinsen.** Still in the same location as when it opened in 1897, the
SCANDINAVIAN Prince serves both traditional and modern Swedish cuisine, but it's the
★ traditional that brings most people here. The interior is rich with mellow, warm lighting; dark-wood paneling; and leather chairs and booths. The restaurant is rightly known for its scampi salad and *Wallenbergare*, a classic dish of veal, cream, and peas. Downstairs you'll find a bar and a space for larger parties. $ *Average main: SKr 295* ⊠ *Mäster Samuelsg. 4, Norrmalm* ☎ *08/6111331* ⊕ *www.restaurangprinsen.eu* ⌘ *Reservations essential.*

## WHERE TO STAY

Stockholm can be a relatively stagnant town when it comes to hotel development, with few new openings each year. But while the hotel choices here are often not trendily brand-new, they're still plentiful and include everything from grand five-star properties down to basic, affordable hostel accommodation.

$$$$ 🏨**Grand Hotel.** At first glance the Grand seems like any other world-class
HOTEL international hotel, and in many ways it is. **Pros:** unadulterated luxury;
Fodor'sChoice world-class service; great bar. **Cons:** some rooms are small; faded in
★ parts; very expensive. $ *Rooms from: SKr 3,000* ⊠ *Södra Blasieholm-shamnen 8, City* ☎ *08/6793500* ⊕ *www.grandhotel.se* ⇆ *269 rooms, 31 suites* ⦿| *Breakfast.*

$$ 🏨**Radisson Blue Strand Hotel.** An art nouveau monolith, built in 1912
HOTEL for the Stockholm Olympics, this hotel has been completely and tastefully modernized. **Pros:** central location; elegant rooms; energized public areas. **Cons:** has a slight chain-hotel feel; beds too soft for some. $ *Rooms from: SKr 1,895* ⊠ *Nybrokajen 9, City* ☎ *08/50664000* ⊕ *www.radissonblu.com* ⇆ *149 rooms, 3 suites* ⦿| *Breakfast.*

$$ 🏨**Scandic Grand Central.** The eco-friendly Scandic Grand Central is in an
HOTEL impressive 130-year-old building, just steps away from the city's main
Fodor'sChoice train station, right in the heart of Stockholm's business district. **Pros:**
★ central to everything; everything's new (hotel opened in late 2011). **Cons:** noisy location. $ *Rooms from: SKr 1650* ⊠ *Kungsg. 70, City* ☎ *08/51252000* ⊕ *www.scandichotels.com* ⇆ *391 rooms* ⦿| *Breakfast.*

$$ 🏨**Sheraton Hotel.** Popular with businesspeople, the Sheraton is also an
HOTEL ideal hotel for the tourist on a generous budget looking for comfort

and luxury. **Pros:** great location; big rooms; extremely comfortable beds. **Cons:** lower-floor rooms can be noisy; terrible view from courtyard rooms. $ *Rooms from: SKr 1,995* ⊠ *Tegelbacken 6, City* ☎ *08/4123400* ⊕ *www.sheratonstockholm.com* ⤳ *436 rooms, 29 suites* ❙❂❙ *Breakfast.*

# TALLINN, ESTONIA

Updated by
Dorota Wąsik

Tallinn's tiny gem of an Old Town, the most impressive in the region, is an ideal cruise destination. It has romantic towers, ankle-wrenching cobblestone streets, cozy nooks, city-wall cafés, and a dozen other attractions–all within 1 square km. In many ways still the same town as during the medieval era, it is compact enough to reveal itself on a short visit. In this eminently walkable city it is possible to see the main sights and venture into intimate corners during your trip and feel that you've found your own personal Tallinn. The city has blossomed in the post-Communist era and revels in its resurgent popularity, but it hasn't forgotten its roots. It's still charming and distinctive, despite having strode headlong into the 21st century.

## ESSENTIALS

### CURRENCY

Since 2011, Estonia has used the euro. National banks, with branches in all major and most minor cities, change cash and traveler's checks at fair commissions. There is a good network of ATMs, and credit cards are widely accepted in Estonia, although Visa and MasterCard are more common than American Express.

### HOURS

Banks are open weekdays 9–4, but some open as early as 8 and close as late as 7. Most are closed on Saturday, but some stay open 9–3. Museums are generally open Wednesday–Sunday 11–5. Some stay open until 6. Shops open between 10 and 11 and close between 5 and 7, with shorter hours on Saturday. Most shops are closed on Sunday, except for shopping centers and malls, which stay open 7 days a week, until late.

### TELEPHONES

Most tri- and quad-band mobile phones should work in Estonia. The mobile service is dual-band and supports text and data services. Pay phones take phone cards. Buy cards at any kiosk. You can use these to make international calls.

### COMING ASHORE

The Old City Harbor Port sits in the very heart of modern Tallinn and is half a mile from the city center. Terminal facilities are comprehensive, and include a restaurant, bank–exchange facilities, tourist information shops, and restrooms. Taxis wait outside the terminal building for journeys into the Old Town; otherwise, it's only a short walk from the port.

Taxi drivers are bound by law to display an operating license and a meter. There is no need to rent a car while in Tallinn, as all the major attractions are in the Old Town, which is very close to the cruise pier.

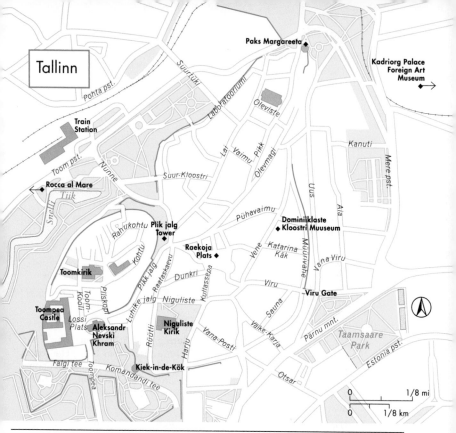

## EXPLORING TALLINN

Tallinn's tiny Old Town, the most impressive in the region, has romantic towers, ankle-wrenching cobblestone streets, cozy nooks, city-wall cafés, and a dozen other attractions—all within 1 square km (½ square mile). In the 1990s, Vanalinn (the lower Old Town)—historically the domain of traders, artisans, and ordinary citizens—sprouted glitzy neon signs in otherwise charming alleys and sights. The stately, sedate Toompea (Upper Town), a hillock that was the site of the original Estonian settlement, is on the burial mound of Kalev, the epic hero of Estonia. Toompea Castle, crowning the hill, is now the seat of the country's parliament and is not open to visitors. Summer visitors can experience the unforgettable white nights, when the sun never completely sets.

**Aleksandr Nevski Khram.** The 19th-century Russian Orthodox Alexander Nevsky Cathedral, with the country's largest bell, is a symbol of the centuries of Russification endured by Estonia. ⊠ *Lossi pl. 10, Toompea* ☎ *644-3484* ☉ *Daily 8–7.*

**Dominiiklaste Kloostri Muuseum.** Wander through the ages in the ancient stone galleries and narrow hallways of the Dominican Monastery Museum, founded in 1246 and now displaying 15th- and 16th-century stone carvings. At 5 pm enjoy a half-hour baroque music concert. ⊠ *Vene 16, Vanalinn* ☎ *644-4606* ⊕ *kloostri.ee* ☉ *Daily 10–6.*

**Kadriorg Palace Foreign Art Museum.** The baroque palace, built for Catherine I by her husband Peter the Great in 1721, merits a visit not just for its impressive and thorough exhibition of 16th- to 20th-century art, but also for the palace's architectural beauty and manicured gardens. Kadriorg Palace offers a glimpse into history, from Russian imperial splendor to Soviet Socialist Realist art, with Estonian and European masterpieces along the way. ✉ *Weizenbergi 37* ☎ *606–6400* ⊕ *www.kadriorumuuseum.ee/en* ✍ *€4.80* ⊙ *May–Sept., Tues.–Sun. 10–5; Oct.–Apr., Wed.–Sun. 10–5.*

★ **Kiek-in-de-Kök.** At the southern end of the Old Town looms this magnificent, six-story tower church (the name is Low German for "peep in the kitchen"), so called because during the 15th century one could peer into the kitchens of lower town houses from here. The tower has a museum of contemporary art and ancient maps and weapons. ✉ *Komandandi 2, Vanalinn* ☎ *644–6686* ⊕ *www.linnamuuseum.ee/kok* ✍ *€4.50* ⊙ *Mar.–Oct., Tues.–Sun. 10:30–6; Nov.–Feb., Tues.–Sun. 10:30–5.*

**Niguliste Kirik.** The 15th-century Church of St. Nicholas, part of the Estonian Art Museum, is famed for its fragment of a treasured frieze, Bernt Notke's (1440–1509) *Danse Macabre*, a haunting depiction of death. ✉ *Niguliste 3, Vanalinn* ☎ *631–4330* ⊕ *www.nigulistemuuseum.ee/en* ✍ *€3.50* ⊙ *Wed.–Sun. 10–5.*

**Paks Margareeta.** The stocky guardian of the northernmost point of the Old Town, Fat Margaret, is a 16th-century fortification named for a particularly hefty cannon it contained. Now it houses the Maritime Museum and a roof with a view of Old Town. ✉ *Pikk 70, Vanalinn* ☎ *641–1408* ⊕ *www.meremuuseum.ee* ✍ *€4* ⊙ *Wed.–Sun. 10–6.*

Fodor's Choice ★ **Raekoja Plats.** Tallinn's Town Hall Square has a long history of intrigue, executions, and salt (Tallinn's main export in the Middle Ages). You can tour the only surviving Gothic **town hall** in northern Europe. Old Thomas, its weather vane, has been atop the town hall since 1530. Near the center of the square, an L-shaped stone marks the site of a 17th-century execution, where a priest was beheaded for killing a waitress who had offered him a rock-hard omelet. Across the square stands the town **apothecary,** which dates from 1422. ✉ *Raekoja plats 11* ☎ *645–7900 for town hall, 631–4860 for apothecary* ✍ *Town Hall: €4* ⊙ *Town Hall: Mon.–Sat. 10–4.*

☾ **Rocca al Mare.** A 15-minute taxi ride from the center, the 207-acre Open-Air Ethnographic Museum provides a breath of fresh air and

---

**TALINN BEST BETS**

**Shopping in Vanalinn.** These alleyways have been a bustling commercial center for more than 500 years. History practically oozes from every stone and the galleries are a shopper's delight.

**Raekoja Plats.** One of the finest city squares in the Baltic, Raekoja Plats is the social center of the city, hosting markets, concerts, and parades.

**Aleksandr Nevski Khram.** This Orthodox church is a wonderfully ornate example of its type, with onion domes and an interior full of votives and icons.

an informative look into Estonia's past, from farm architecture to World War II–era deportations. ✉ *Vabaõhumuuseumi 12* ☎ *654–9101* ⊕ *www.evm.ee/keel/eng* 💶 *€3* ⊗ *Late Apr.–late Sept., daily 10–8; late Sept.–late Apr., daily 10–5.*

**Toomkirik.** The Lutheran Dome Church (Cathedral of Saint Mary the Virgin) is the oldest church in the country, founded by the occupying Danes in the 13th century and rebuilt in 1686. ✉ *Toom-kooli 6, Toompea* ☎ *644–4140* ⊕ *www.eelk.ee/tallinna.toom* ⊗ *Tues.–Sun. 9–5.*

## SHOPPING

Tallinn has a wide range of crafts on sale. Fragrant juniper wood is carved into bowls and dolomite stone is fashioned into candlesticks and coasters. A whole range of handblown glass, ceramics, delicate wrought iron, and art is sold in tiny galleries. Hand-knitted sweaters, gloves, and socks keep the locals snug in winter and are signature souvenirs here. Warming quilts are also available, as well as a good range of leather goods. Sweet tooths will love the chocolates made by Kalev and the hand-painted marzipan that's sold in presentation boxes. The Old Town is the place to browse, with some excellent shops around Katerina kälk (Catherine Passage).

## WHERE TO EAT

**$$$**
ECLECTIC

✕ **Gloria.** The art nouveau interior compliments the French-influenced menu of highbrow European food like beef Stroganoff or tournedos Rossini. To maintain its tradition of decadence, Gloria offers a *tabacalera* (tobacco shop) complete with Cuban cigars and an extensive wine cellar. ⑤ *Average main: €25* ✉ *Müürivahe 2* ☎ *640–6800* ⊕ *www.gloria.ee* ⌚ *Reservations essential Jacket and tie* ⊗ *Closed Sun. No lunch Sat.*

**$**
EASTERN
EUROPEAN
Fodor'sChoice
★

✕ **Olde Hansa.** In a 15th-century building in the Old Town, this restaurant recreates medieval times with waiters in period costume, candlelit tables, and historic Eastern European recipes for such dishes as nobleman's smoked filet mignon in mushroom sauce and wild boar with game sauce and forest berries. The honey beer is out of this world, and the old-fashioned food is always fresh and tasty. ⑤ *Average main: €15* ✉ *Vanaturg 1* ☎ *627–9020* ⊕ *www.oldehansa.ee.*

# VISBY, SWEDEN

Updated
by Lola
Akinmade-
Åkerström

Gotland is Sweden's main holiday island, a place of ancient history, a relaxed summer-party vibe, wide sandy beaches, and wild cliff formations called *raukar* (the remnants of reefs formed more than 400 million years ago). Measuring 125 km (78 miles) long and 52 km (32 miles) at its widest point, Gotland is where Swedish sheep farming has its home. In its charming glades, 35 varieties of wild orchids thrive, attracting botanists from all over the world. Gotland's capital, Visby, reflects this full and fascinating history, and the architecture of its downtown core is classified as a World Heritage site.

## ESSENTIALS

### CURRENCY

The unit of currency is the krona (plural kronor). Sweden is not in the euro zone.

### HOURS

Banks are open weekdays 9:30–3; larger branches until 5 and 6 on Thursday. The bank at Arlanda International Airport is open every day with extended hours, and the Forex and X-Change currency-exchange offices also have extended hours. Take a queue-number ticket from near the door and wait your turn. It's not uncommon to come across cashless bank branches in some smaller towns so it's worth checking before traveling.

### TELEPHONES

Most tri- or quad-band GSM phones work in Sweden, though handsets are single-band, where the system is 3G-compatible. Public phones in Sweden take phone cards or credit cards. Phone cards can be bought at telecom shops, newsstands, and tobacconists. Public phones support international calls. Main providers include Telia, Tele2, Comviq, Vodafone, and T-Mobile.

### COMING ASHORE

Vessels dock in the town port; from here it is a 5- to 10-minute walk into the center of town. The port has only the most basic facilities, but shops and restaurants are on hand in town.

You don't need public transport to explore Visby. However, if you want to discover all that Gotland has to offer independently, you'll need transportation. Renting a car would free you up to explore at your own pace. An economy manual vehicle starts at SKr 800 per day.

## EXPLORING GOTLAND

### VISBY

Gotland's capital, Visby, is a delightful hilly town of about 22,000 people. Medieval houses, ruined fortifications, churches, and cottage-lined cobbled lanes make Visby look like it's from a fairy tale. Thanks to a very gentle climate, the roses that grow along many of the town's facades bloom even in November. In its heyday Visby was protected by a wall, of which 3 km (2 miles) survive today, along with 44 towers and numerous gateways. It is considered the best-preserved medieval city wall in Europe after that of Carcassonne, in southern France. Take a stroll to the north gate for an unsurpassed view of the wall.

Fodor'sChoice

★

☾

**Fårö.** It takes a five-minute ferry crossing to reach tiny, secluded Fårö from Gotland, to the south. A popular summer retreat for Scandinavians, the island has just 600 year-round residents. Legendary Swedish filmmaker Ingmar Bergman once called this island home; every June, film fanatics head over to celebrate Bergman Week. And in September, the island celebrates Fårönatta—a night when its shops, restaurants, and attractions stay open all night and the church holds a midnight mass. Head to the Digerhuvud area to find some impressive natural "sea stacks," weather rock formations that are known as *raukar*. They often take on human

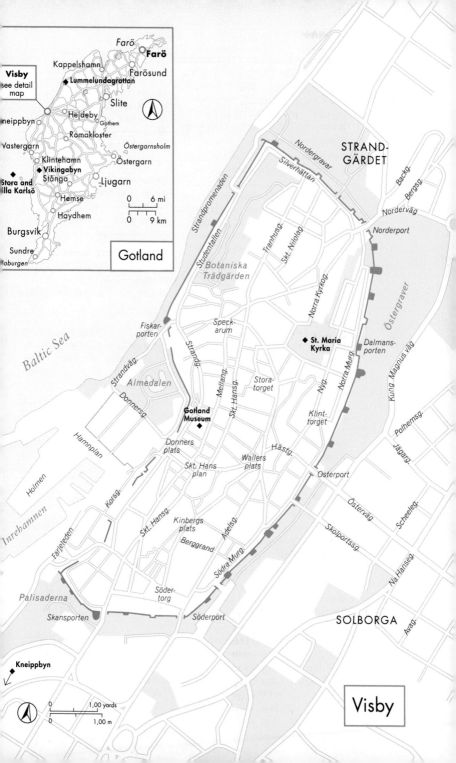

Gotland

**Visby**
see detail
map

Farö
**Farö**
Kappelshamn
**Lummelundagrottan**
Farösund
Slite
neippbyn
Hejdeby
Gothem
Romakloster
Vastergarn
Östergarnsholm
Klintehamn
Östergarn
**Vikingabyn**
Stånga
**Stora and**
**illa Karlsö**
Ljugarn
Hemse
Haydhem
0        6 mi
0        9 km
Burgsvik
Sundre
oburgen

STRAND-
GÄRDET

Nordergravar
Backg.
Silverhättan
Bergsg.
Strandpromenaden
Tranhusg.
Skt. Nikolaig.
Norderväg
Norderport
Studentallen
Botaniska
Trädgården
Norra Kyrkog.
Östergraver
Baltic Sea
Fiskar-
porten
Speck-
arum
St. Maria
Kyrka
Dalmans-
porten
Kung  Magnus väg
Strandväg.
Strandg.
Almedalen
Mellang.
Skt. Hansg.
Norra Murg.
Nyg.
Donnersg.
Stora-
torget
Polhernsg.
Jägarg.
Hamnplan
Gotland
Museum
Klint-
torget
Holmen
Donners
plats
Hästg.
Wallers
plats
Osterport
Skt. Hans
plan
Österväg
Scheeleg.
Inrehamnen
Korsg.
Skolportssg.
Kinbergs
plats
Adelsg.
Skt. Hansg.
Berggrand
Na Hanseg.
Södra Murg.
Palisaderna
SOLBORGA
Avag.
Söder-
torg
Skansporten
Söderport

**Kneippbyn**

0        1,00 yards
0        1,00 m

Visby

profiles, fueling local myths and legends. Note that basic services, including police, medical services, and banks, are virtually nonexistent on Fårö itself. If you really want to retreat from the world, Fårö is it. ⊕ *www.gotland.info.*

**Gotland Museum.** The Länsmuseet på Gotland, Gotland's county museum, contains examples of medieval artwork, prehistoric gravestones and skeletons, and silver hoards from Viking times. Be sure to also check out the ornate "picture stones" from AD 400–600, which depict ships, people, houses, and animals. ⊠ *Strandg. 14* ☎ *0498/292700* ⊕ *www.gotlandsmuseum.se* ⊠ *SKr 100* ⊘ *Daily 11–6.*

### VISBY BEST BETS

**Follow your whim along the streets of Visby.** The wealth of architectural splendor funded by Hanseatic trade means there's a wonderful vista on almost every corner.

**Explore the dramatic and wind-swept countryside beyond the city walls.** Wild orchids, rocky coastal precipices, and grassy meadows abound.

**Church-hopping.** Gotland has about 100 old churches that are still in use (Visby itself has 13); exploring them is a major pastime.

**Kneippbyn.** This resort with a water park and amusement park brings droves of families in summer; there are over 600 rooms, cabins, apartments, and camping sites. Locations from the Pippi Longstocking TV show, including her house, Villa Villekulla, are here. ⊠ *3 km south of Visby, Gotland* ⊕ *www.kneippbyn.se* ⊠ *Skr 135–245* ⊘ *Parks open May–Aug.*

**St. Maria Kyrka.** Visby's cathedral is the only one of the town's 13 medieval churches that is still intact and in use. Built between 1190 and 1225 as a place of worship for the town's German parishioners, the church has few of its original fittings because of the extensive and sometimes clumsy restoration work done over the years. That said, the sandstone font and the unusually ugly angels decorating the pulpit are both original features worth a look. ⊠ *Västra kyrkog., Visby* ☎ *0498/206800* ⊕ *www.svenskakyrkan.se* ⊘ *Daily 10–5.*

### GOTLAND

There's a lot to see out on the island, so if you want to spend the day exploring, you can see a fair amount in your day in port. Definitely get out of Visby itself if you want to see some of the island's churches.

**Lummelundagrottan.** The 4 km (2½ miles) of stalactite caves at Lummelunda, about 18 km (11 miles) north of Visby on the coastal road, are unique in this part of the world and well worth a visit. ⊠ *Lummelunds Bruk* ☎ *0498/273050* ⊕ *www.lummelundagrottan.se* ⊠ *SKr 130* ⊘ *May–Sept., daily 10–5.*

**Stora and Lilla Karlsö.** These two bird sanctuaries are off the coast south of Visby. The bird population consists mainly of guillemots, which look like penguins. Visits to these sanctuaries are permitted only in the company of a recognized guide. Contact each sanctuary for its tour times. ☎ *0498/240450 for Stora, 0498/241139 for Lilla* ⊕ *www.storakarlso.se; www.lillakarlso.org* ⊠ *SKr 325 for Stora, SKr 300 for Lilla* ⊘ *May–Aug., daily.*

CLOSE UP

## Gotland's Churches

The island has about 100 old churches dating from Gotland's great commercial era that are still in use today. **Barlingbo**, from the 13th century, has vault paintings, stained-glass windows, and a remarkable 12th-century font. The exquisite **Dalhem** was constructed around 1200. **Gothem**, built during the 13th century, has a notable series of paintings of that period. **Grötlingbo** is a 14th-century church with stone sculptures and stained glass (note the 12th-century reliefs on the facade). **Öja**, a medieval church decorated with paintings, houses a famous holy rood from the late-13th century. The massive ruins of a Cistercian monastery founded in 1164 are now called the **Roma Kloster Kyrka** (Roma Cloister Church). **Tingstäde** is a mix of six buildings dating from 1169 to 1300.

○ **Vikingabyn** (*Viking Village*). Be a Viking for a day at this 10th-century village re-creation. Kids and adults can try their hands at baking Viking bread, axe throwing, archery, and other activities. There are also performances along with guided tours and lectures. ⊠ *Tofta Strand, Gotland* ☎ *0498/297100* ⊕ *www.vikingabyn.se* ⊠ *Skr 120* ⊙ *June–Aug., Mon.–Sat. 10–5.*

## SHOPPING

Gotlanders are self-sufficient and resourceful people and have developed many handicrafts, so there is a range of handcrafted souvenirs to choose from, including blown glass, metal objects, sculptures, woven items, and ceramics. Sheepskin and wool items are a particular specialty.

## ACTIVITIES

The unspoiled countryside and onshore waters are a perfect playground if you want to get active. Many visitors simply rent a bike and take to the safe open roads, or try kayaking or windsurfing on the water.

Fodor's Choice ★ **Gotland Active Store.** Adventure tours and packages that cover Gotland and nearby islands are available from this company. ⊠ *Hamng. 4, Visby* ☎ *0772/070400* ⊕ *www.gotlandactive.se.*

**Gotlands Cykeluthyrning.** Bicycles, tents, and camping equipment can be rented from Gotlands Cykeluthyrning. ⊠ *Skeppsbron 2, Visby* ☎ *0498/214133* ⊕ *www.gotlandscykeluthyrning.com.*

**Gotlands Upplevelser.** For an aquatic adventure, Gotlands Upplevelser will rent you a canoe and a life jacket or windsurfing equipment. They also offer rock-climbing courses. ⊠ *Getsvältans väg 8, Högklint* ☎ *0730/751678* ⊕ *www.gotlandsupplevelser.se.*

7

## WHERE TO EAT

**$$**
SWEDISH

✕ **Bakfickan.** It may have one of the best locations in town—right in Stora Torget next to medieval ruins of St. Karin—but this restaurant is decorated in what could be called Fisherman's Shack Rustic, with wood benches, shellfish and seafood displays, details from fishing boats, small metal buckets resting on shelves, and menus scribbled on chalkboards. Expect a tight squeeze—there isn't much space to maneuver inside. Try the fried Baltic herring with mashed potatoes, or on a brisk day, warm up with its hearty fish stew with a dollop of aioli. ⑤ *Average main: SKr 185* ⊠ *Stora Torget 1, Visby* ☎ *0498/271807* ⊕ *www. bakfickan-visby.nu.*

**$$$**
SCANDINAVIAN
Fodor's Choice
★

✕ **Donners Brunn.** Bo Nilsson, the chef proprietor of this atmospheric restaurant, was once chef at the renowned Operakällaren in Stockholm. Now, in a beautiful orange-brick house on a small square in Visby, he cooks for a mix of locals and visitors, who dine in cellar-like halls surrounded by white stone walls. The menu uses excellent local ingredients to make French-influenced dishes that are reasonably priced, given their quality. Its house specialty of Gotland lamb shanks with sweetbread and turnips is absolutely delicious; you may want to finish with a rich and sticky-sweet crème brûlée topped with a mixed-berry compote. ⑤ *Average main: SKr 285* ⊠ *Donners Plats 3* ☎ *0498/271090* ⊕ *www. donnersbrunn.se* ⌲ *Reservations essential* ☉ *No lunch. Closed Sun.*

# WARNEMÜNDE, GERMANY (FOR BERLIN)

Updated by
Giulia Pines

Since the fall of the Iron Curtain, no city in Europe has seen more development and change. Two Berlins that had been separated for 40 years struggled to meld into one, and in the scar of barren borderland between them sprang government and commercial centers that have become the glossy spreads of travel guides and architecture journals. But even as the capital moves forward, history is always tugging at its sleeve. Between the wealth of neoclassical and 21st-century buildings, there are constant reminders, both subtle and stark, of the events of the 20th century. For every relocated corporate headquarters, a church stands half ruined, a synagogue is under 24-hour guard, and an empty lot remains where a building either crumbled in World War II or went up in dynamite as East Germany cleared a path for its wall. There are few other cities where the past and the present collide with such energy.

### ESSENTIALS
#### CURRENCY
The euro. ATMs are common and credit cards are widely accepted.

#### HOURS
Stores are open Monday through Saturday from 8 am to 8 pm. Museum hours vary, but core hours are from 10 am to 5 pm, with shorter hours on Sunday. Some state museums are closed on Monday.

## TELEPHONES

Most tri- and quad-band GSM phones will work in Germany, where the mobile system supports 3G technology. Phone cards for public phones are available at newsagents and will allow international calls. Major companies include Vodafone, T2, and T-Mobile.

## COMING ASHORE

A state-of-the-art Warnemünde cruise terminal opened in 2005, but it has limited passenger facilities. The best thing about the terminal is that it is within 300 yards of a railway station for easy onward connections through the town of Rostock. Travel time into Rostock is 20 minutes, with train journeys to Berlin taking 2 hours 45 minutes. Prices to Berlin are €39 round-trip. Trains from Rostock to Berlin run approximately three times per hour depending on time of day.

Once in Berlin, you'll find an integrated network of subway (U-bahn) and suburban (S-bahn) train lines, buses, and trams (in eastern Berlin only). Most visitor destinations are in the broad reach of the fare zones A and B. At this writing, both the €2.40 ticket (fare zones A and B) and the €3.10 ticket (fare zones A, B, and C) allow you to make a one-way trip with an unlimited number of changes between trains, buses, and trams.

Buy a Kurzstreckentarif ticket (€1.40) for short rides of up to six bus or tram stops or three U-bahn or S-bahn stops. The best deal if you plan to travel around the city extensively is the Tageskarte (day card for zones A and B), for €6.50, good on all transportation (€7 for A, B, C zones).

There is a Hertz rental office at the port. Alternatively, you can easily travel by train into nearby Rostock and pick up a vehicle there. If you want to visit Berlin, public transport is more practical than a car rental. However, renting a vehicle would allow you to explore the other towns along the Baltic coastline and enjoy the countryside and beaches. The cost for a compact manual vehicle is approximately €80 per day.

## EXPLORING BERLIN

🕐 **Berliner Fernsehturm** (*Berlin TV Tower*). Finding Alexanderplatz is no problem: just head toward the 1,207-foot-high tower piercing the sky. Built in 1969 as a signal to the West (clearly visible over the wall, no less) that the East German economy was thriving, it is deliberately higher than both western Berlin's broadcasting tower and the Eiffel Tower in Paris. You can get the best view of Berlin from within the tower's disco ball–like observation level; on a clear day you can see for 40 km (25 miles). One floor above, the city's highest restaurant rotates for your panoramic pleasure. ■ TIP→ **During the summer season, order VIP tickets online to avoid a long wait.** ⊠ *Panoramastr. 1a, Mitte* ☎ *030/247–5750* ⊕ *www.tr-turm.de* ☎ *€12* ☉ *Nov.–Feb., daily 10 am–midnight; Mar.–Oct., daily 9 am–midnight; last admission ½ hr before closing* Ⓜ *Alexanderplatz (U-bahn and S-bahn).*

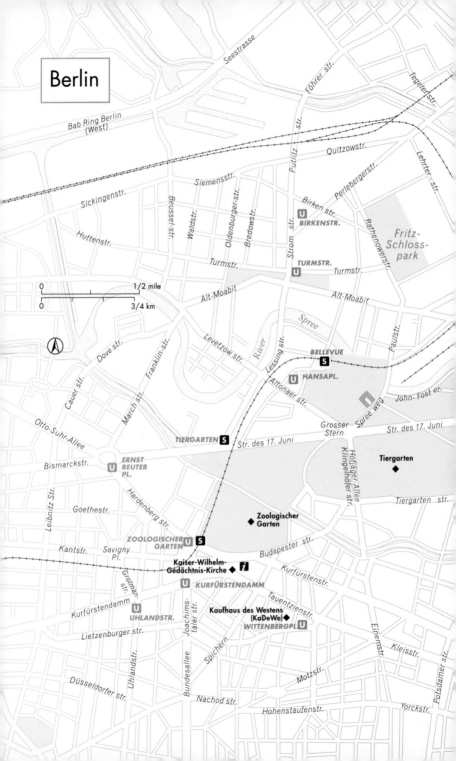

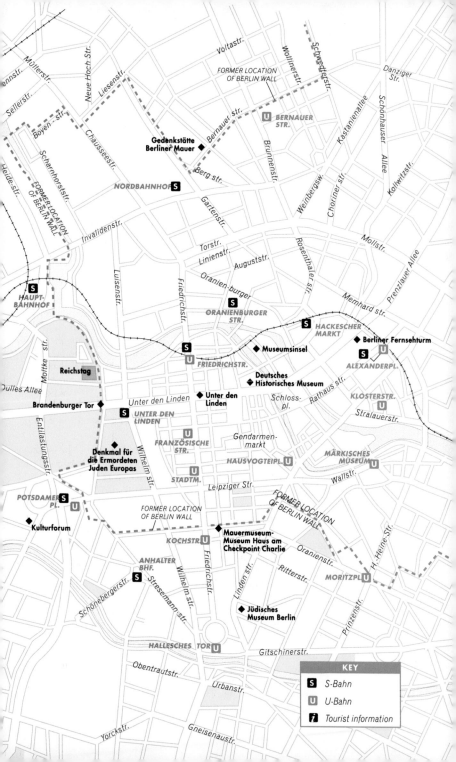

Fodor'sChoice   **Brandenburger Tor** (*Brandenburg Gate*). Once the pride of Prussian
★   Berlin and the city's premier landmark, the Brandenburger Tor was
left in a desolate no-man's-land when the wall was built. Since the
wall's dismantling, the sandstone gateway has become the scene of
the city's Unification Day and New Year's Eve parties. This is the sole
remaining gate of 14 built by Carl Langhans in 1788–91, designed
as a triumphal arch for King Frederick Wilhelm II. Its virile classical
style pays tribute to Athens's Acropolis. The quadriga, a chariot drawn
by four horses and driven by the Goddess of Victory, was added in
1794. Troops paraded through the gate after successful campaigns—
the last time in 1945, when victorious Red Army troops took Berlin.
The upper part of the gate, together with its chariot and Goddess of
Victory, was destroyed in the war. In 1957 the original molds were
discovered in West Berlin, and a new quadriga was cast in copper and
presented as a gift to the people of East Berlin. A tourist-information
center is in the south part of the gate. ⊠ *Pariser Pl., Mitte* Ⓜ *Unter
den Linden (S-bahn).*

**Denkmal für die Ermordeten Juden Europas** (*Memorial to the Murdered
Jews of Europe*). An expansive and unusual memorial dedicated to the
6 million Jews who were killed in the Holocaust, the monument was
designed by American architect Peter Eisenman. The stunning place
of remembrance consists of a grid of more than 2,700 concrete stelae,
planted into undulating ground. The abstract memorial can be entered
from all sides and offers no prescribed path. ■TIP➡ **An information
center that goes into specifics about the Holocaust lies underground at
the southeast corner.** ⊠ *Cora-Berliner-Str. 1, Mitte* ☎ *030/2639–4336*
⊕ *www.stiftung-denkmal.de* ☑ *Free* ⊗ *Daily 24 hrs; information center: Oct.–Mar., Tues.–Sun. 10–7; Apr.–Sept., Tues.–Sun. 10–8* Ⓜ *Unter
den Linden (S-bahn).*

**Deutsches Historisches Museum** (*German History Museum*). The museum
is composed of two buildings. The magnificent pink, baroque Prussian arsenal (Zeughaus) was constructed between 1695 and 1730, and
is the oldest building on Unter den Linden. It also houses a theater,
the Zeughaus Kino, which regularly presents a variety of films, both
German and international, historic and modern. The new permanent
exhibits, reopened after much debate in mid-2006, offer a modern and
fascinating view of German history since the early Middle Ages. Behind
the arsenal, the granite-and-glass Pei-Bau building by I. M. Pei holds
often stunning and politically controversial changing exhibits, such as
2010's unprecedented blockbuster, *Hitler und die Deutschen* (*Hitler
and the Germans*), which explored the methods of propaganda used
by Hitler and the Nazis to gain power. ⊠ *Unter den Linden 2, Mitte*
☎ *030/203–040* ⊕ *www.dhm.de* ☑ *€8* ⊗ *Daily 10–6.*

**Gedenkstätte Berliner Mauer** (*Berlin Wall Memorial Site*). This site combines memorials and a museum and research center on the Berlin Wall.
The division of Berlin was particularly heart wrenching on Bernauer
Strasse, where neighbors and families on opposite sides of the street
were separated overnight. The Reconciliation Chapel, completed in
2000, replaced the community church dynamited by the Communists
in 1985. The church had been walled into the "death strip," and was

seen as a hindrance to patrolling it. A portion of the wall remains on Bernauer Strasse, and an installation meant to serve as a memorial unfortunately only confuses those wondering what the border once looked like. For a wealth of images and information, head into the museum, where German-speakers can even hear radio broadcasts from the time the wall was erected. ⊠ *Bernauer Str. 111, Wedding* ☎ *030/464–1030* ⊕ *www.berliner-mauer-gedenkstaette.de* ⊠ *Free, tours €3* ☉ *Apr.–Oct., Tues.–Sun. 9:30–7; Nov.–Mar., Tues.–Sun. 9:30–6* Ⓜ *Bernauer Strasse (U-bahn), Nordbahnhof (S-bahn).*

> ## BERLIN BEST BETS
>
> **Brandenburger Tor.** The gate is the symbolic heart of the city, and one of the few survivors of the WWII era.
>
> **Museumsinsel.** Berlin's most famous museums are all here, including the Neuesmuseum and its Egyptian collection, as well as the grand altar of Pergamon.
>
> **Reichstag.** The historic seat of Germany's federal parliament, the Reichstag is also remarkable for its synthesis of architectural styles.

**Jüdisches Museum Berlin** (*Jewish Museum*). The history of Germany's Jews from the Middle Ages through today is chronicled here, from prominent historical figures to the evolution of laws regarding Jews' participation in civil society. A few of the exhibits document the Holocaust itself, but this museum celebrates Jewish life and history far more than it focuses on the atrocities committed during WWII. An attraction in itself is the highly conceptual building, designed by Daniel Libeskind, who will also direct the construction of a new adjacent building holding a library and temporary exhibitions. Various physical "voids" in the oddly constructed and intensely personal modern wing of the building represent the idea that some things can and should never be exhibited when it comes to the Holocaust. ∎**TIP➔ Reserve at least three hours for the museum and devote more time to the second floor if you're already familiar with basic aspects of Judaica, which are the focus of the third floor.** ⊠ *Lindenstr. 9–14, Kreuzberg* ☎ *030/2599–3300* ⊕ *www.jmberlin.de* ⊠ *€5* ☉ *Mon. 10–10, Tues.–Sun. 10–8* Ⓜ *Hallesches Tor (U-bahn).*

**Kaiser-Wilhelm-Gedächtnis-Kirche** (*Kaiser Wilhelm Memorial Church*). A dramatic reminder of World War II's destruction, the ruined bell tower is all that remains of this once massive church, which was completed in 1895 and dedicated to the emperor, Kaiser Wilhelm I. The Hohenzollern dynasty is depicted inside in a gilded mosaic, whose damage, like that of the building, will not be repaired. The exhibition revisits World War II's devastation throughout Europe. On the hour, the tower chimes out a melody composed by the last emperor's great-grandson, the late Prince Louis Ferdinand von Hohenzollern. ⊠ *Breitscheidpl., Western Downtown* ☎ *030/218–5023* ⊕ *www.gedaechtniskirche-berlin.de* ⊠ *Free* ☉ *Memorial Church daily 9–7; old tower Mon.–Fri. 10–6, Sat. 10–5:30, Sun. 12–5:30.* Ⓜ *Zoologischer Garten (U-bahn and S-bahn).*

★ **Kulturforum** (*Cultural Forum*). This unique ensemble of museums, galleries, and the Philharmonic Hall was long in the making. The first designs were submitted in the 1960s and the last building completed in 1998. Now it forms a welcome modern counterpoint to the thoroughly restored Prussian splendor of Museum Island.

**Gemäldegalerie** (*Paintings Gallery*). The Gemäldegalerie reunites formerly separated collections from East and West Berlin. It's one of Germany's finest art galleries, and has an extensive selection of European paintings from the 13th to 18th century. Seven rooms are reserved for paintings by German masters, among them Dürer, Cranach the Elder, and Holbein. A special collection has works of the Italian masters—Botticelli, Titian, Giotto, Lippi, and Raphael—as well as paintings by Dutch and Flemish masters of the 15th and 16th centuries: Van Eyck, Bosch, Brueghel the Elder, and van der Weyden. The museum also holds the world's second-largest Rembrandt collection. ✉ *Matthäikirchpl. 4, Tiergarten* ☎ *030/266–424242* ⊕ *www.smb.museum* 🎟 *€8* ⊙ *Tues., Wed., and Fri.–Sun. 10–6; Thurs. 10–10* Ⓜ *Potsdamer Platz (U-bahn and S-bahn).*

**Mauermuseum-Museum Haus am Checkpoint Charlie.** Just steps from the famous crossing point between the two Berlins, the Wall Museum–House at Checkpoint Charlie presents visitors with the story of the wall and, even more riveting, the stories of those who escaped through, under, and over it. The homespun museum reviews the events leading up to the wall's construction and, with original tools and devices, plus recordings and photographs, shows how East Germans escaped to the West (one ingenious contraption was a miniature submarine). Exhibits about human rights and paintings interpreting the wall round out the experience. ■**TIP**➔ **Come early or late in the day to avoid the multitudes dropped off by tour buses.** (Monday can be particularly crowded.) ✉ *Friedrichstr. 43–45, Kreuzberg* ☎ *030/253–7250* ⊕ *www.mauermuseum.com* 🎟 *€12.50* ⊙ *Daily 9 am–10 pm* Ⓜ *Kochstrasse (U-bahn).*

Fodor'sChoice **Museumsinsel** (*Museum Island*). On the site of one of Berlin's two origi-
★ nal settlements, this unique complex of five state museums, a UNESCO World Heritage site, is an absolute must.

The **Alte Nationalgalerie** (Old National Gallery, entrance on Bodestrasse) houses an outstanding collection of 18th-, 19th-, and early-20th-century paintings and sculptures. Works by Cézanne, Rodin, Degas, and one of Germany's most famous portrait artists, Max Liebermann, are part of the permanent exhibition. Its Galerie der Romantik (Gallery of Romanticism) collection has masterpieces from such 19th-century German painters as Karl Friedrich Schinkel and Caspar David Friedrich, the leading members of the German Romantic school. The **Altes Museum** (Old Museum), a red-marble, neoclassical building abutting the green Lustgarten, was Prussia's first building purpose-built to serve as a museum. Designed by Karl Friedrich Schinkel, it was completed in 1830. The permanent collection of the Altes Museum consists of everyday utensils from ancient Greece as well as vases and sculptures from the 6th to 4th century BC. Etruscan art is its highlight, and there are a few examples of Roman art. Antique sculptures, clay figurines, and bronze art of the Antikensammlung (Antiquities Collection) are also housed here; the other part of the collection is in the Pergamonmuseum. At the northern tip of Museum Island is the **Bode-Museum,** a somber-looking gray edifice graced with elegant columns. The museum presents the state museums' stunning collection of German and Italian sculptures since the Middle Ages, the Museum of Byzantine Art, and a huge coin collection. Museum Island's new shining star, however, is the **Neues Museum** (New Museum), which reopened in 2009. Originally designed by Friedrich August Stüler in 1843–55, the building was badly damaged in World War II and only now has been elaborately redeveloped by British star architect David Chipperfield, who has been overseeing the complete restoration of Museum Island. Instead of completely restoring the Neues Museum, the architect decided to integrate modern elements into the historic landmark, while leaving many of its heavily bombed and dilapidated areas untouched. The result is a stunning experience. Home to the Egyptian Museum, including the famous bust of Nefertiti (who, after some 70 years, has returned to her first museum location in Berlin), it also features the Papyrus Collection and the Museum of Prehistory and Early History. Even if you think you aren't interested in the ancient world, make an exception for the **Pergamonmuseum** (entrance on Am Kupfergraben). The museum's name is derived from its principal display, the Pergamon Altar, a monumental Greek temple discovered in what is now Turkey and dating from 180 BC. The altar was shipped to Berlin in the late 19th century. Equally impressive are the gateway to the Roman town of Miletus and the Babylonian processional way. If you get tired of antiques and paintings, drop by any of the museums' cafés. ⊠ *Entrance to Museumsinsel: Am Kupfergraben, Mitte* ☎ *030/2664–24242* ⊕ *www.smb.museum* ⊠ *All Museum Island museums: €14; individual museum admissions €8–€10* ⊙ *Pergamon-museum: Fri.–Wed. 10–6, Thurs. 10–10. Alte Nationalgalerie: Tues., Wed., and Fri.–Sun. 10–6; Thurs. 10–10. Altes Museum: Fri.–Wed. 10–6, Thurs. 10–10. Neues Museum: Sun.–Wed. 10–6, Thurs.–Sat. 10–8. Bode-Museum: Tues., Wed., and Fri.–Sun. 10–6; Thurs. 10–10* Ⓜ *Hackescher Markt (S-bahn).*

★ **Reichstag** (*Parliament Building*). After last meeting here in 1933, the Bundestag, Germany's federal parliament, returned to its traditional seat in the spring of 1999. British architect Sir Norman Foster lightened up the gray monolith with a glass dome, which quickly became a main attraction: you can circle up a gently rising ramp while taking in the rooftops of Berlin and the parliamentary chamber below. At the base of the dome is an exhibit on the Reichstag's history, in German and English. ■**TIP**→ **After terrorism warnings at the end of 2010, the Reichstag tightened its door policy, asking all visitors to register their names and birthdates in advance either for regular admission or to reserve a place on a guided tour.** A riverwalk with great views of the government buildings begins behind the Reichstag. ⊠ *Pl. der Republik 1, Tiergarten* ⊠ *Bundeskanzleramt, Besucherdienst* ☎ *030/2273–2152, 030/2273–5908 Reichstag* ⊟ *030/2273–0027 Reichstag, 030/4000–1881 Bundes-*

*kanzleramt* ⊕ *www.bundestag.de* ▧ *Free* ☉ *Daily at 10:30, 1:30, 3:30, 6:30* Ⓜ *Brandenburger Tor (S-bahn), Bundestag (U-bahn).*

**Tiergarten** (*Animal Garden*). The quiet greenery of the 630-acre Tiergarten is a beloved oasis, with some 23 km (14 miles) of footpaths, meadows, and two beer gardens. The inner park's 6½ acres of lakes and ponds were landscaped by garden architect Joseph Peter Lenné in the mid-1800s.

**Unter den Linden.** The name of this historic Berlin thoroughfare, between the Brandenburg Gate and Schlossplatz, means "under the linden trees," and it was indeed lined with fragrant and beloved lindens until the 1930's. Imagine Berliners' shock when Hitler decided to fell the trees in order to make the street more parade-friendly. The grand boulevard began as a riding path that the royals used to get from their palace to their hunting grounds (now the central Berlin park called Tiergarten). It is once again lined with linden trees planted after World War II.

★   **Zoologischer Garten** (*Zoological Gardens*). Even though Knut, the polar
Ↄ   bear cub who captured the heart of the city, is sadly no longer with us, there are 14,000 other animals to see here, many of whom may be happy to have their time in the spotlight once again. There are 1,500 different species (more than any other zoo in Europe), including those rare and endangered, which the zoo has been successful at breeding. New arrivals in the past years include a baby rhinoceros. ■**TIP**➔ Check the feeding times posted to watch creatures such as seals, apes, hippos, crocodiles, and pelicans during their favorite time of day. The animals' enclosures are designed to resemble their natural habitats, though some structures are ornate, such as the 1910 Arabian-style Zebra House. Pythons, frogs, turtles, invertebrates, Komodo dragons, and an amazing array of strange and colorful fish are part of the three-floor aquarium. ✉ *Hardenbergpl. 8 and Budapester Str. 32, Western Downtown* ☎ *030/254–010* ⊕ *www.zoo-berlin.de* ▧ *Zoo or aquarium €13, combined ticket €20* ☉ *Zoo: Oct.–mid-Mar., daily 9–5; mid-Mar.–Oct., daily 9–7. Aquarium: daily 9–6* Ⓜ *Zoologischer Garten (U-bahn and S-bahn).*

## SHOPPING

Although Ku'damm is still touted as the shopping mile of Berlin, many shops are ho-hum retailers. The best stretch for exclusive fashions are the three blocks between Leibnizstrasse and Bleibtreustrasse. For gift items and unusual clothing boutiques, follow this route off Ku'damm: Leibnizstrasse to Mommsenstrasse to Bleibtreustrasse, then on to the ring around Savignyplatz. Fasanenstrasse, Knesebeckstrasse, Schlüterstrasse, and Uhlandstrasse are also fun places to browse.

The finest shops in Mitte (historic Berlin) are along Friedrichstrasse. Nearby, Unter den Linden has just a few souvenir shops and a Meissen ceramic showroom. Smaller clothing and specialty stores populate the Scheunenviertel. The area between Hackescher Markt, Weinmeister Strasse, and Rosa-Luxemburg-Platz alternates pricey independent designers with groovy secondhand shops. Neue Schönhauser Strasse curves into Alte Schönhauser Strasse, and both streets are full of stylish casual wear. Galleries along Gipsstrasse and Sophienstrasse round out the mix.

**Kaufhaus des Westens** (*KaDeWe*). The largest department store in continental Europe, classy Kaufhaus des Westens (KaDeWe) has a grand selection of goods on seven floors, as well as food and deli counters, champagne bars, beer bars, and a winter garden on its top floor. Its wealth of services includes fixing umbrellas and repairing leather and furs. ⊠ *Tauentzienstr. 21–24, Western Downtown* ☎ *030/21210* ⊕ *www.kadewe.de* ☉ *Mon.–Thurs. 10–8, Sat. 10–9, Sun. 9:30–8.*

## WHERE TO EAT

**$$**  ✕ **Café Einstein Stammhaus.** The Einstein is a Berlin landmark and a leading coffeehouse in town. Set in the historic grand villa of silent movie star Henny Porten, it charmingly recalls the elegant days of the Austrian-Hungarian empire, complete with slightly snobbish waiters gliding across squeaking parquet floors. The Einstein's very own roasting facility produces some of Germany's best coffee, and the cakes are fabulous, particularly the fresh strawberry cake best enjoyed in the shady garden behind the villa in summer. The café also excels in preparing solid Austrian fare such as schnitzel or goulash for an artsy, highbrow clientele. ⊠ *Kurfürstenstr. 58, Schoeneberg* ☎ *030/2639–1918* ⊕ *www.cafeeinstein.com* Ⓜ *Kurfürstenstrasse (U-bahn).*

AUSTRIAN
Fodor'sChoice
★

**$$$**  ✕ **Lutter & Wegner.** One of the city's oldest vintners (*Sekt,* German champagne, was first conceived here in 1811 by actor Ludwig Devrient), Lutter & Wegner has returned to its historic location across from Gendarmenmarkt. The dark-wood-panel walls, parquet floor, and multitude of rooms take you back to 19th-century Vienna. The cuisine is mostly Austrian, with superb game dishes in winter and, of course, a Wiener schnitzel with lukewarm potato salad. The sauerbraten (marinated pot roast) with red cabbage has been a national prizewinner. ■ TIP➜ **In the Weinstube, meat and cheese plates are served until 3 am.** ⊠ *Charlottenstr. 56, Mitte* ☎ *030/2029–5417* ⊕ *www.l-w-berlin.de* Ⓜ *Französische Strasse and Stadtmitte (U-bahn).*

GERMAN

7

# Norway

## ÅLESUND, BERGEN, FLÅM, GEIRANGER, HAMMERFEST, HONNINGSVAG, KRISTÌANSAND, OSLO, TROMSØ, TRONDHEIM

Bergen harbour, Norway

## WORD OF MOUTH

"We sailed from Bergen to Kirkenes in late July. It never did get dark, just a very long twilight. By October, say, the days would be quite short. Some ports—Aalesund, for example—were visited for several hours. Others, only minutes. It's a wonderful, scenic voyage, so free of hassles."

—USNR

Updated by
Anne-Sophie
Redisch

Norway's most renowned cruise itinerary is the *Hurtigruten*, which literally means "Rapid Route." Ships that follow this route, which were historically known as coastal steamers, depart from Bergen and stop at 34 ports along the coast in a week, ending in Kirkenes, near the Russian border, before turning back.

Ships may stop in one port for just a few minutes to load and unload passengers who use the scenic route for transportation, so these steamers are more than just pleasure cruises for the people who choose to live in the isolated coastal villages in Norway's northern reaches. But many passengers on these routes are Americans, here to enjoy the dramatically beautiful Norwegian scenery.

Many of these ships, which are operated primarily by Hurtigruten (the Norwegian cruise line, which was once known in the United States as Norwegian Coastal Voyage), are more than just ferries. They do have some cruise ship–style amenities, though not "big-ship" amenities. So you can expect to find a sauna on board some of the ships but not a full-fledged spa, a restaurant but not a choice of restaurants. And while food is included in your cruise fare (unless you book a transportation-only passage, as some backpackers and short-haul travelers do), you pay extra (and dearly) for alcohol; luckily, the ships allow you to carry your own alcohol on board.

Norway is also a popular destination among major cruise lines—both luxury and mainstream—and many northern European cruises in the summer include some stops in Norway, though they may also include Århus or Copenhagen in Denmark or stops in Sweden, *which are covered in "The Baltic."*

## ABOUT THE RESTAURANTS
Most of the restaurants we recommend serve lunch; they also serve dinner if your cruise ship stays late in port and you choose to dine off the ship. Cuisine in Europe is varied, though you should expect restaurants in Norway to focus primarily on Norwegian specialties; you'll have more choices in larger cities like Oslo and Bergen. Europeans tend to eat a leisurely meal at lunch, but in most ports there are quicker and simpler alternatives for those who just want to grab a quick bite before returning to the ship.

# ÅLESUND, NORWAY

On three islands and between two bright blue fjords is Ålesund, home to 45,000 inhabitants and one of Norway's largest harbors for exporting dried and fresh fish. About two-thirds of its 1,040 wooden houses were destroyed by a fire in 1904. In the rush to shelter the 10,000 homeless victims, Germany's Kaiser Wilhelm II, who often vacationed here, led a swift rebuilding that married German art nouveau (*Jugendstil*) with Viking flourishes. Winding streets are crammed with buildings topped

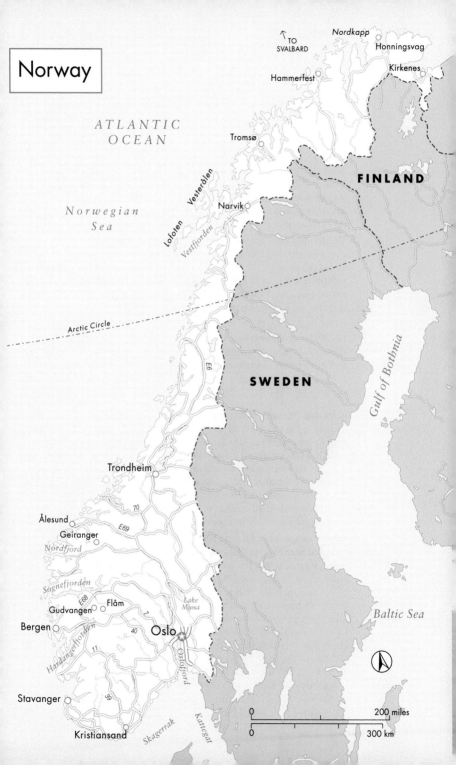

with turrets, spires, gables, dragons' heads, and curlicues. Today Åle-sund is considered one of the few art nouveau cities in the world. Inquire at the tourism office for one of the insightful guided walking tours.

### ESSENTIALS

### CURRENCY
Norway is a non-EU country and has opted to keep its currency, the Norwegian krone. ATMs are readily available.

### HOURS
Banks are generally open weekdays 9 to 3. Many offices and embassies close at 3 from June to August. Stores are generally open weekdays 9 to 5 or 6 and Saturday 9 to 1 or 2. Some grocery stores are open until 11 pm on weekdays and Saturdays. All stores are closed Sunday.

### TELEPHONES
The country code for Norway is 47. There are no area codes—you must dial all eight digits of any phone number wherever you are. Most tri- and quad-band GSM phones work in Norway, so if your service pro-vider offers service in Europe, you will likely be able to use your mobile phone along the Norwegian coast, even while hugging the shoreline on ship. Public telephones are relatively rare.

### COMING ASHORE
Ålesund is at the entrance to the world-famous Geirangerfjord. Turrets, spires, and medieval ornaments rise above the skyline of the colorful town and its charming architecture. Cruise ships dock in the center of town.

## EXPLORING ÅLESUND

**Aalesunds Museum.** This gem of a museum highlights the city's past, including the great fire of 1904 and the escape route that the Norwe-gian Resistance established in World War II—its goal was the Shetland Islands. Handicrafts on display are done in the folk-art style of the area. You can also see the art nouveau room and learn more about the town's unique architecture. ⊠ *Rasmus Rønnebergsgt. 16* ☎ *70–12–31–70* ⊕ *www.aalesunds.museum.no* 🖾 *NKr 50* ☉ *Mid-Sept.–Apr., weekdays 9–3; May–mid-Aug., weekdays 9–4, weekends noon–4; mid-Aug.–mid-Sept., weekdays 9–3, Sun. noon–4.*

☾ **Atlanterhavsparken** (*Atlantic Sea Park*). Teeming with aquatic life, this is one of Scandinavia's largest aquariums. Right on the ocean, 3 km (2 miles) west of town, the park emphasizes aquatic animals of the North Atlantic, including anglers, octopus, and lobster. See the daily diving show at which the fish are fed. The divers actually enter a feeding frenzy of huge, and sometimes aggressive, halibut and wolffish. The Humbodt penguins are also popular with children. After your visit, have a picnic, hike, or take a refreshing swim at the adjoining Tueneset Park. The bus that leaves from St. Olavs Plass makes the 15-minute journey to the park once every hour during the day, Monday through Saturday. There's also a shuttle bus from the cruise terminal (NKr 200 round-trip). ⊠ *Tueneset* ☎ *70–10–70–60* ⊕ *www.atlanterhavsparken. no* 🖾 *NKr 140* ☉ *June–Aug., Sun.–Fri. 10–7, Sat. 10–4; Sept.–May, Mon.–Sat. 11–4, Sun. 11–6.*

**Kniven.** You can drive or take a bus up the nearby mountain Aksla to this vantage point, "the knife," for a splendid view of the city, which absolutely glitters at night.

**Runde.** Norway's southernmost major "bird rock"—one of the largest in Europe—is the breeding ground for some 200 species, including puffins, gannets, and cormorants. The region's wildlife managers maintain many observation posts here. In summer, straying into the bird's nesting areas is strictly forbidden. Contact the local tourist office for more information. ☎ *70–15–76–00* ⊕ *www.visitalesund-geiranger.com/en/ The-bird-island-Runde.*

## SHOPPING

The first Saturday of each month is known as "Town Saturday," when shops in the city center are open later than usual.

## WHERE TO EAT

$

NORWEGIAN

✕ **Fjellstua.** This mountaintop restaurant has tremendous views over the surrounding peaks, islands, and fjords. There is also a terrace that's open when the weather allows. On the menu might be Norwegian salt cod, baked salmon, or homemade rissoles (similar to croquettes). ⑤ *Average main: NKr 175* ⊠ *Top of Aksla Mountain* ☎ *70–10–74–00* ⊕ *www.fjellstua.no* ⊗ *Closed Dec. and Jan.*

# BERGEN, NORWAY

8

Many visitors fall in love with Bergen, Norway's second-largest city, at first sight. Seven rounded lush mountains, pastel wood houses, the historic wharf, winding cobblestone streets, and Hanseatic relics all make it a place of enchantment. Surrounded by forested mountains and fjords, it's only natural that most Bergensers feel at home either on the mountains (skiing, hiking, walking, or at their cabins) or at sea (fishing and boating). As for the rainy weather, most visitors quickly learn the necessity of rain jackets and umbrellas. The surviving Hanseatic wooden buildings on Bryggen (the quay, or wharf) are topped with triangular cookie-cutter roofs and painted in red, blue, yellow, and green. Monuments in themselves (they are on the UNESCO World Heritage List), the buildings tempt travelers and locals to the shops, restaurants, and museums inside.

### COMING ASHORE

Cruise ships dock at Skoltegrunnskaien and Jekteviken/Dokkeskjærskaien. Both are within a 15-minute walk of the city center. Free shuttle buses are available from Jekteviken/Dokkeskjærskaien. From Skoltegrunnskaien, buses stop near the docks. The trip to the city center costs NKr 27 on the public bus. Once in the city center, nearly all of the attractions are within walking distance.

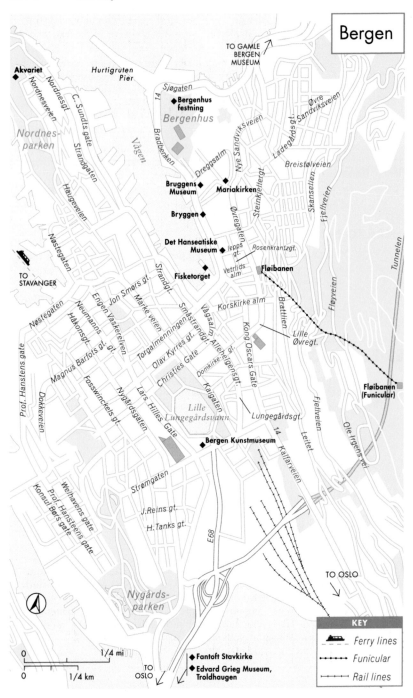

# Bergen

TO GAMLE
BERGEN
MUSEUM

Hurtigruten
Pier

Akvariet ◆

Sjøgaten

Bergenhus ◆
festning

Bergenhus

Nordnesparken

Nordnesveien

Nordnesgt.

C. Sundts gate

Strandgaten

Haugeveien

Vågen

Bradbenken

Dreggsalm

Nye Sandviksveien

Øvre
Sandviksveien

Ladegårds gt.

Breistølveien

Bruggens ◆
Museum

Mariakirken ◆

Steinkjellergt.

Skanselien

Fjellveien

Bryggen ◆

Øvregaten

Tunnelen

Det Hanseatiske ◆
Museum

Jepps
gt.

Rosenkrantzgt.

Nøstegaten

Nøstegaten

TO
STAVANGER

Fisketorget ◆

Vetrlids
alm

Fløibanen ■

Fløyveien

Prof. Hanstens gate

Dokkeveien

Strandgt.

Jon Smørs gt.

Marke veien

Engen Vaskerelven

Neumanns
gt.

Håkonsgt.

Magnus Barfots gt.

Fosswinckels gt.

Nygårdsgaten

Lars Hilles Gate

Torgalmenningen

Småstrandgt.

Olav Kyrres gt.

Christies Gate

Domkirke gt.

Vågsalm

Allehelgensgt.

Kaigaten

Korskirke alm

Kong Oscars Gate

Brattlien

Lille
Øvregt.

Fløibanen ■
(Funicular)

Lille
Lungegårdsvann

Lungegårdsgt.

Fjellveien

Leitet

Ole Irgensvei

Bergen Kunstmuseum ◆

Strømgaten

14

Kalfarveien

J.Reins gt.

H.Tanks gt.

E68

Welhavens gate

Prof. Hansteens gate

Konsul Børs gate

TO OSLO

Nygårdsparken

◆ | 0 ——— 1/4 mi

0 ——— 1/4 km

TO
OSLO

◆ Fantoft Stavkirke
◆ Edvard Grieg Museum,
   Troldhaugen

**KEY**

⛴ *Ferry lines*

•••••• *Funicular*

—⊢⊢⊢— *Rail lines*

# EXPLORING BERGEN

🔄 **Akvariet.** The Bergen Aquarium is one of the largest collections of North Sea fish and invertebrates in Europe. It has 60 tanks and two outdoor pools with seals and penguins. Tanks inside are filled with schools of colorful tropical fish as well as Norwegian salmon and common eels, which tend to wrap around each other. There is also a section with alligators from different parts of the world on display. *The Aquarium: Bergen and the Local Coastline*—a 360-degree video directed by one of Norway's most beloved animators, the late Ivo Caprino—is shown every hour, as is the 3D-film *SOS Planet*. The aquarium is on Nordnes Peninsula, a 20-minute walk from the fish market. You can also take Bus 11 or the ferry from the fish market. ⊠ *Nordnesbakken 4, Nordnes* ☎ *55–55–71–71* ⊕ *akvariet.no* 🖅 *NKr 200, NKr 150 in winter* ⊙ *May–Aug., daily 9–7; Sept.–Apr., daily 10–6.*

**Bergenhus festning** (*Bergenhus Fortress*). The major buildings at the medieval Bergenhus are Håkonshallen (Haakon's Hall) and Rosenkrantztårnet (Rosenkrantz Tower). Both are open to visitors. **Håkonshallen** is a royal ceremonial hall erected during the reign of Håkon Håkonsson in the mid-1200s. It was badly damaged by the explosion of a German ammunition ship in 1944, but was restored by 1961. Erected in the 1560s by the governor of Bergenhus, Erik Rosenkrantz, **Rosenkrantztårnet** served as a combined residence and fortified tower. ⊠ *Bryggen* ☎ *81–57–04–00 Bergenhus festning, 55–31–60–67 Håkonshallen* ⊕ *www.bymuseet.no* ⊙ *Grounds open daily 6:30 am–11 pm. Late Sept.–mid-May: Håkonshallen, Thurs. 3–6, Fri.–Wed. noon–3; Rosenkrantztårnet, Sun noon–3. Mid-May–late Sept.: both open daily 10–4.*

**Fodor's**Choice ★ **Bergen Kunstmuseum** (*Bergen Art Museum*). An important Bergen institution and one of the largest museums in Norway, the Bergen Art Museum is housed in several buildings along Lake Lille Lungeårdsvann. Works by Max Ernst, Paul Klee, Vassily Kandinsky, Pablo Picasso, Joan Miró, and the Dutch Renaissance masters are all on display. Norwegian artists include Edvard Munch, J.C. Dahl, Adolph Tidemand, Hans Gude, Harriet Backer, and Per Krogh. ⊠ *Rasmus Meyers allé 3, Downtown* ☎ *55–56–80–00* ⊕ *www.kunstmuseene.no/Default. asp?enhet=kunstmuseum&sp=2* 🖅 *NKr 100* ⊙ *Mid-May–mid-Sept., daily 11–5; mid-Sept.–mid-May, Tues.–Sun. 11–5.*

**Fodor's**Choice ★ **Bryggen** (*The Wharf*). A trip to this merchant city is incomplete without a trip to the historic Hanseatic harborside, Bryggen. A row of mostly reconstructed 14th-century wooden buildings that face the harbor makes this one of the most charming walkways in Europe, especially on a sunny day. Several fires, the latest in 1955, destroyed some of the original structures. Today the old houses hold boutiques and restaurants. Bryggen has been a UNESCO World Heritage site since 1979. ⊠ *Bryggen.*

★ **Det Hanseatiske Museum.** One of the best-preserved buildings in Bergen, the Hanseatic Museum was the 16th-century office and home of an affluent German merchant. The apprentices lived upstairs, in boxed-in beds with windows cut into the wall. Although claustrophobic, the snug rooms had the benefit of being relatively warm—a blessing in the unheated building. In summer, there are daily guided tours in Norwegian,

8

German, French, and English. ⊠ *Finnegården 1A, Bryggen* ☎ *55-54-46-90* ⊕ *www.museumvest. no/?action=static&id=8* ✉ *NKr 60* ◷ *Mid-May–mid-Sept., daily 9–5; mid-Sept.–mid-May, Tues.–Sat. 11–2, Sun. 11–4.*

**Edvard Grieg Museum, Troldhaugen.** Built in 1885, Troldhaugen was the home of Norway's most famous composer, Edvard Grieg. He composed many of his best-known works in a garden cottage by the lakeshore. In 1867 he married his cousin Nina, a Danish soprano. They lived in the white clapboard house with green gingerbread trim for 22 years. A salon and gathering place for many Scandinavian artists then, it now houses mementos—a piano, paintings, prints—of the composer's life. The interior has been kept as it was during Grieg's time here. Concerts are held both at Troldhaugen and at Troldsalen next door. ⊠ *Troldhaugsveien 65, Paradis* ☎ *55–92–29–92* ⊕ *www. kunstmuseene.no/troldhaugen* ✉ *NKr 80* ◷ *Oct.–Apr., daily 10-4; May-Sept., daily 9–6.*

Fodor's Choice ★ **Fantoft Stavkirke** (*Fantoft Stave Church*). During the Middle Ages, when European cathedrals were built in stone, Norway used wood to create unique stave churches. These cultural symbols stand out for their dragons' heads, carved doorways, and walls of staves (vertical planks). Though as many as 750 stave churches may have once existed, only 30 remain standing. The original stave church here, built in Fortun in Sogn in 1150 and moved to Fantoft in 1883, burned down in 1992. Since then, the church has been reconstructed to resemble the original structure. From the main bus station next to the railway station, take any bus leaving from Platform 19, 20, or 21. ⊠ *Fantoftvn. 38* ☎ *55–28–07–10* ⊕ *fantoftstavkirke.com* ✉ *NKr 44* ◷ *Mid-May–mid-Sept., daily 10:30–6.*

**Fisketorget** (*Bergen Fish Market*). The busy fish market is one of Bergen's most popular attractions. Turn-of-the-20th-century photographs of this pungent square show fishermen in Wellington boots and raincoats and women in long aprons. Now the fishmongers wear bright-orange rubber overalls as they look over the day's catch. In 2012, some of the market moved indoors, to a brand-new food hall. Fruits, vegetables, and flowers are on offer, as are handicrafts and souvenirs. Try a classic Bergen lunch of shrimp or salmon on a baguette with mayonnaise and cucumber. ⊠ *Bryggen* ☎ *55–55-20-00* ⊕ *www.torgetibergen.no/english. asp* ◷ *June–Aug., daily 7–7; Sept.–May, Mon.–Sat. 7–4.*

---

### BERGEN BEST BETS

**Bryggen.** Bergen's historic seafront promenade, which dates from the 11th century, is the city's most atmospheric street.

**Mariakirken.** This Romanesque church is the oldest structure in Bergen still used for its original purpose.

**Rasmus Meyer Collection.** The prescient collector purchased most of the works here while the artists were still unknown. His collection is now on display at the Bergen Art Museum. The collection of Munch paintings is the best in Norway outside of Oslo.

## NIGHTLIFE

Bergen is a university town, and the thousands of students who live and study here year-round contribute to making the city's nightlife livelier than you might expect in a small town. Most nightspots center on Ole Bulls Plass, the plaza at one end of Torgallmenningen. Within a stone's throw of the plaza you can find dozens of relaxing bars, bustling pubs, dancing, live music, and trendy cafés.

**Altona vinbar.** For a quiet glass of wine in intimate and historic surroundings, try Altona, a hotel bar in a 400-year-old wine cellar. The food is good, too. ⊠ *Augustin Hotel, Strandgaten 81, Nordnes* ☎ *55–30–40–00.*

**Café Opera.** A classic—both sumptuous and stylish. It's often crowded on Friday and Saturday nights, when there are DJs. There's also a quiz night on Monday, readings, and more. ⊠ *Engen 18, Downtown* ☎ *55–23–03–15* ⊕ *www.cafeopera.org.*

**Kafe Kippers.** Head to this large outdoor café at sunset for cozy wool blankets and a spectacular view of the water. ⊠ *Georgernes Verft 12, Nordnes* ☎ *55–30–40–80.*

**Logen Teater.** If you prefer conversation over dancing, try Logen Teater, a popular meeting place with live acoustic music every Sunday. Edvard Grieg has performed here, and so have Sergei Rachmaninoff and Rickie Lee Jones. ⊠ *Øvre Ole Bulls pl. 6, Downtown* ☎ *55–23–20–15* ⊕ *www.logen-teater.no.*

## SHOPPING

Bergen has several cobblestoned pedestrian shopping streets, including Gamle Strandgaten, (Gågaten), Torgallmenningen, Hollendergaten, and Marken. Stores selling Norwegian handicrafts are concentrated along the Bryggen boardwalk. Near the cathedral, the tiny Skostredet has become popular with young shoppers. The small, independent specialty stores here sell everything from army surplus gear to tailored suits and designer trinkets. Most Bergen shops are open Monday–Wednesday and Friday from 9 to 5; Thursday from 9 to 7; and Saturday from 10 to 3. Bergen's shopping centers—Galleriet, Kløverhuset, and Bergen Storsenter—are open weekdays from 9 to 9 and Saturday from 9 to 6.

**Galleriet.** This is the best of the downtown shopping malls, with over 70 shops, including GlasMagasinet and more exclusive small shops along with all the chains. ⊠ *Torgallmenningen 8, Downtown* ☎ *55–30–05–00* ⊕ *www.galleriet.com.*

**Hjertholm.** At this gift shop, most everything is of Scandinavian design. The pottery and glassware are of the highest quality—much of it is made by local artisans. ⊠ *Galleriet Shopping Center, Torgallmenningen 8, 5th fl., Downtown* ☎ *55–31–70–27* ⊕ *www.hjertholm.no.*

**Norsk Flid.** Established in 1895, the Bergen branch of this famous handicraft store sells national costumes and other Norwegian crafts, clothes, blankets and gift items. ⊠ *Vågsallmenningen 3, Downtown* ☎ *55–54–47–40* ⊕ *www.norskflid.no/bergen.*

# ACTIVITIES

Bergen is literally wedged between the mountains and the sea, and there are plenty of opportunities to enjoy the outdoors. Bergensers are quick to do so on sunny days. In summer, don't be surprised to see many Bergensers leaving work early to enjoy sports and other outdoor activities, or to just relax in the parks.

### HIKING

Like most Norwegians, Bergensers love to go hiking, especially on one of the seven mountains that surround the city.

**Bergen Turlag (DNT).** The Bergen Trekking Association arranges hikes and maintains cabins for hikers. You can pick up maps of many self-guided walking tours from the office, as well as from local bookstores. ✉ *Tverrgt. 4–6, Downtown* ☎ *55–33–58–10* ⊕ *www.bergen-turlag.no.*

**Mt. Fløyen.** Take the funicular up Mt. Fløyen, and minutes later you'll be in the midst of a forest. From the nearby shop and restaurant, well-marked paths fan out over the mountains. Follow Fløysvingene Road down for an easy stroll, with great views of the city and harbor. ✉ *Vetrlidsallmenningen 21, Bryggen* ☎ *55–33–68–00* ⊕ *www.floibanen.no.*

**Mt. Ulriken.** Mt. Ulriken is popular with walkers and hikers of all levels. The easiest way to reach the summit is via the cable car from Haukeland University Hospital. (To get there, take the double-decker bus that leaves from Torget.) Once you get off the cable car, you'll find trails leading across the mountain plateau, Vidden, which is above the tree line. The plateau connects the Fløyen and Ulriken mountains, and you can hike between them in four to six hours. Views from the alpine trail are spectacular. Be advised that foggy and rainy weather, even in the summer months, can make hiking here dangerous. Consult the tourist information center or Bergen Turlag for maps and general advice. ☎ *53–64–36–43* ⊕ *www.ulriken643.no.*

# WHERE TO EAT

**$$$**
NORWEGIAN
★

✕ **Bølgen & Moi.** In late 2012, this branch of the trendy Bølgen & Moi chain moved to grand and majestic quarters, with marble walls, tall columns, chandeliers, fabulous ceiling details, and a new champagne and seafood bar. What hasn't changed is its very good-value lunch menu, which includes their famous fish soup and a crayfish sandwich. Dinner might include turbot with asparagus and a citrus hollandaise, a modern take on a Norwegian classic. $ *Average main: NKr 290* ✉ *Vågsalmenningen 16* ☎ *55–59–77–00* ⊕ *www.bolgenogmoi.no.*

**$$$**
NORWEGIAN

✕ **Wesselstuen.** Housed in an 18th-century wine cellar, this distinctive restaurant is known for its convivial atmosphere and unpretentious, authentic Norwegian fare. This is a good place to try reindeer steak or salt cod. Light meals and more international options are also available. Note that the restaurant doesn't open until 2 pm on Sunday. $ *Average main: NKr 270* ✉ *Øvre Ole Bulls pl. 6, Downtown* ☎ *55–55–49–49* ⊕ *www.wesselstuen.no.*

# FLÅM

Flåm is on an arm of the world's longest (at 204 km [127 miles]) and deepest (at 1,308 meters [4,291 feet]) fjord. The village of only 500 inhabitants is set against a backdrop of steep mountains, thundering waterfalls, narrow valleys, and deep canyons. Cruise ships—bringing primarily British and German passengers—began transiting the majestic Sognefjord to Flåm in the late 19th century. Today, it's Norway's fourth most popular port of call, a fact that can be attributed not only to the beauty of the fjord but also to the popularity of the Flåm Railway, considered to be one of Europe's most dramatic rail excursions.

## COMING ASHORE

Ships dock directly in the harbor of Flåm. Sights are easily accessible from the dock. The train station is a five-minute walk from the pier.

## EXPLORING FLÅM

**Flåmsbana** (*Flåm Railway*). This trip is only 20 km (12 miles) long, but it takes 40 to 55 minutes (one-way) to travel the 2,850 feet up the steep mountain gorge. The line includes 20 tunnels and a bridge. A masterpiece of Norwegian engineering, it took 20 years to complete, and is today one of Norway's prime tourist attractions, with more than 600,000 visiting each year. ⊠ *Flåm train station* ☎ *57–63–21–00* ⊕ *www.visitflam.no/flaamsbana.*

**Flåmsbana Museet.** If you have time to kill before the train departs, make sure you visit the Flåm Railway Museum. Building the Flåm Railway was a remarkable feat in engineering, and this museum illustrates the challenges the builders faced in detail. You'll find it in the old station building, 300 feet from the present one. ⊠ *Flåm train station* ☎ *57–63–23–10* ⊕ *www.visitflam.no/flaamsbana-museet* ☒ *Free* ☯ *May–Sept., daily 9–5; Oct.–Apr., daily 1:30–3.*

**Fretheim Hotell.** One of western Norway's most beautiful hotels, the Fretheim has a classic, timeless look and is worth your time if you want to drop in to see the lobby. ⊠ *Flåm Harbor* ☎ *57–63–63–00* ⊕ *www. fretheim-hotel.no.*

# GEIRANGER, NORWAY

*85 km (52½ miles) southwest of Åndalsnes.*

★ The Geirangerfjord, which made the UNESCO World Heritage List in 2005, is Norway's most spectacular and perhaps best-known fjord. The 16-km-long (10-mile-long), 960-foot-deep Geirangerfjord's most stunning attractions are its roaring waterfalls—the Seven Sisters, the Bridal Veil, and the Suitor. Perched on mountain ledges along the fjord, deserted farms at Skageflå and Knivsflå are being restored and maintained by local enthusiasts.

## EXPLORING GEIRANGER

The village of Geiranger, at the end of the fjord, is home to only 250 year-round residents, but in spring and summer its population swells to 5,000 due to visitors traveling from Hellesylt to the east. In winter, snow on the mountain roads means that the village is often isolated.

★ **Trollstigen.** The most scenic route to Geiranger from Åndalsnes is the two-hour drive along Route 63 over Trollstigen (the Troll's Ladder). After that, the Ørneveien (Eagles' Road) to Geiranger, which has 11 hairpin turns and was completed in 1952, leads to the fjord.

## SHOPPING

The handful of shops in Geiranger emphasize traditional Norwegian cottage crafts such as wood carvings and woven and knitted goods, like Norwegian sweaters. All the shops are along the main street.

## ACTIVITIES

### HIKING

Trekking through fjord country can occupy a few hours or several days. Trails and paths are marked by signs or cairns with a red "T" on them. Area tourist offices and bookshops have maps, and you can always ask residents for directions or destinations.

# GUDVANGEN, NORWAY

On an arm of Sognefjord, Gudvangen is at the foot of steep cliffs soaring 5,500 feet above the water's surface and plunging deep to form one of the region's deepest fjord basins. Snow-capped mountains, green cliffs, and veils of tumbling waterfalls characterize the vertical landscape on the approach to Gudvangen. The fjord is so narrow in places that during winter the sun can't reach the valley floor. Mystical Gudvangen is the site of white caves and medieval stave churches. Standing sentinel over the ornate entrances to the venerable wooden sanctuaries are visages of fierce trolls and dragons, carved by long-dead Viking craftsman from the region.

### COMING ASHORE

Cruise passengers are brought ashore by tender at one of two small piers, which are both in the center of town.

## EXPLORING GUDVANGEN

**Stalheim Hotel.** In the spectacular Nærøyfjorden, a UNESCO World Heritage site of steep mountains and waterfalls that form a beautiful valley, drivers must navigate 13 hairpin turns on Stalheimskleiva, a section of road not quite a mile in length, to reach this hotel. An inspiration to painters and other artists, Stalheim Hotel is furnished with a spectacular collection of Scandinavian furniture and antiques, and it also has a large collection of buildings dating back from the 16th and 17th centuries. ✉ *Stalheimsvegen 131, Stalheim* ⊕ *stalheim.dnn.gasta.no.*

**Tvindefossen.** From Stalheim it's not a long drive to Tvinde, a name derived from the Norwegian word for two. En route, you'll pass the villages of Oppheim and Vinje, as well as Oppheim Lake. But the best waterfall of this area is Tvindefossen, which has a 152-meter (500-ft) drop down steep stone cliffs. Nearby is the town of Voss, the bottling source of one of the world's most expensive waters.

**Undredal stavkirke** (*Stave Church*). The village of Undredal, home to 80 humans and 500 goats, also has Norway's smallest stave church, which was probably built in 1147. ✉ *Undredal* ⊕ *naroyfjorden.no/ verdsarvbygdene/undredal?lang=en.*

**White Caves** (*De hvite grottene i Gudvangen*). These impressive caves are composed of anorthosite, a type of marble that contains both gold and aluminum. A stone bar-and-restaurant serves refreshments. The caves are just off the E16 to Voss, about 6 km from Gudvangen. Only pre-booked groups can visit. ✉ *Gudvangen* ☎ *48–07–55–55* ⊕ *gudvangen. com/magical-white-caves.*

## SHOPPING

Gudvangen Fjordtell, which is right at the port, has two souvenir shops that are open daily during the cruising season. Look for Viking souvenirs, Dale sweaters, and accessories made of seal, fox, reindeer, and moose.

## ACTIVITIES

### FISHING

The Nærøy River is one of 20 salmon rivers that receive special protection from the Norwegian government.

### HIKING AND WALKING

**Heritage Adventures.** This outfitter offers multiday hikes, and leisurely day-hikes (5 or 10 km) in pristine forests and pastures along the shores of the breathtaking Nærøyfjord, a UNESCO World Heritage site. A picnic lunch and a short scenic fjord cruise are also included. All hikes must be booked in advance. ☎ *56–52–95–90* ⊕ *www. heritageadventures.no.*

### RAFTING

Because of the different grades of the rivers, ranging from two to five, rafting in Gudvangen is suitable for beginners as well as experienced rafters. Strandaelva and Raundalselva (the Stranda and Raundal rivers) have been rated between three and five for experienced rafters. The Vosso is a grade two, recommended for families with children.

### WATERFALL ABSEILING

This waterborne experience allows you to rappel down Skjervefossen, a waterfall that plunges 100 meters (330 feet).

8

*Sørøysundet*

The Royal and Ancient
Polar Bear Society

Storelv-
bakken

Bratt-
bakken

Morenveien

Ballast-
bakken

Idrettsveien

Strandgata

Nybakken

Hammegata

Parggata

Batteriet

Storgata

Sjøgata

Rådhus-
plassen

Mellomgata

Sørøygata

Corn Moes gate

Sjøgata

Kirkegata

Salsgata

Museum of Post-War
Reconstruction

Nedre Hauen

Turistveien

Øvre Hauen

| 0 | | 1/8 mi |
| 0 | | 1/8 km |

# HAMMERFEST, NORWAY

More than 600 miles north of the Arctic Circle, the world's northernmost town is also one of the most widely visited and oldest places in Northern Norway. *Hammerfest* means "mooring place" and refers to the natural harbor (remarkably free of ice year-round thanks to the Gulf Stream) that is formed by the crags in the mountain. Hammerfest is the gateway to the Barents Sea and the Arctic Ocean, a jumping-off point for Arctic expeditions. Once a hunting town, Hammerfest's town emblem features the polar bear. In 1891 the residents of Hammerfest, tired of the months of darkness that winter always brought, decided to brighten their nights: they purchased a generator from Thomas Edison, and Hammerfest thus became the first city in Europe to have electric street lamps.

## COMING ASHORE

Ships dock either at quay number 1 or 2 in the city center, or at quay number 9 at Fuglenes, about a mile away. If you'd rather not walk, there are buses and taxis to take you the short distance to the city center. Ships sometimes anchor and tender passengers ashore to the dock in the town center. There is no terminal in the port area and only limited facilities, but the town center is only a few steps away, and it has everything you might need.

## EXPLORING HAMMERFEST

In addition to two museums, there are several shops within Hammerfest's small city center. There is also a market selling souvenirs and other goods outside the town hall.

**Museum of Post-War Reconstruction** (*Gjenreisningsmusee*). Although it covers the county of Finnmark's history since the Stone Age, this museum primarily focuses on World War II, when the German army forced Finnmark's population to evacuate, and the county was burned to the ground as part of a scorched-earth policy. Through photographs, videos, and sound effects, the museum recounts the residents' struggle to rebuild their lives. The exhibition includes authentic rooms that were built in caves after the evacuation, as well as huts and postwar houses. ⊠ *Kirkegt. 21* ☎ *78–40–29–30* ⊕ *www.gjenreisningsmuseet.no* ☒ *Nkr 50* ☉ *June–mid-Aug., daily 10-4; mid-Aug.–May, daily 11–2.*

**The Royal and Ancient Polar Bear Society.** Isbjørnklubben was founded by two businessmen whose goal was to share the town's history as a center of hunting and commerce. Exhibits depict aspects of Arctic hunts, including preserved and stuffed polar bears, seals, lynx, puffins, and wolves. You can only become a member by visiting in person, so it's a very exclusive club open only to those who have actually visited the world's northernmost city. Members get a membership card and diploma, and a sought-after silver-and-enamel polar bear pin. Part of the fee is donated to the World Wildlife Foundation. ⊠ *Havnegata 3* ☎ *78–41–31–00* ⊕ *www.isbjornklubben.no* ☒ *Membership NKr 180* ☉ *June and July, weekdays 6–6, weekends 6–4; Aug.–May, weekdays 9–4, weekends 10–2.*

## ACTIVITIES

**Hammerfest Turist** (*Tourist information*). Stop at the tourist office to learn about activities in the region, including golf, walking tours, birdwatching trips, and boating. A popular activity is coast sightseeing, in which a catamaran takes you to small fishing villages on Sørøya Island. Also popular are city tours; highlights include a ride up Salen Mountain for spectacular views of the city, and a visit to the Meridian Column, erected in 1854 to mark the first international measurement of the earth's circumference and shape. ⊠ *Havnegata 3* ☎ *78–41–21–85* ⊕ *www.hammerfest-turist.no.*

### HIKING AND WALKING

Hammerfest is a paradise for those who enjoy long ambles. The tourist office organizes a four-hour scenic walking excursion to reach Kjøttvikvarden, a landmark built in 1850 to help fishermen become oriented on long journeys. They also provide suggested walking routes such as the Gammelveien trail, a 30-minute walk that starts from the town church and heads up an old road. ⊠ *Havnegt. 3* ☎ *78–41–31–00* ⊕ *www.hammerfest-turist.no.*

8

# HONNINGSVÅG, NORWAY

Searching in 1553 for a northeast passage to India, British navigator Richard Chancellor came upon a crag 307 yards above the Barents Sea. He named the jut of rock North Cape, or *Nordkapp*. Today Europe's northernmost point is a rite-of-passage journey for nearly all Scandinavians and many others. Most cruise passengers visit Nordkapp from Honningsvåg, a fishing village on Magerøya Island. The journey from Honningsvåg to Nordkapp covers about 35 km (22 miles) across a landscape characterized by rocky tundra and grazing reindeer, which are rounded up each spring by Sami herdsmen in boats. The herdsmen herd the reindeer across a mile-wide channel from their winter home on the mainland. Honningvåg's northerly location makes for long, dark winter nights and perpetually sun-filled summer days. The village serves as the gateway to Arctic exploration and the beautiful Nordkapp Plateau, a destination that calls to all visitors of this region.

Most of those who journey to Nordkapp, the northernmost tip of Europe, are in it for a taste of this unique, otherworldly, rugged yet delicate landscape. You'll see an incredible treeless tundra, with crumbling mountains and sparse dwarf plants. The subarctic environment is very vulnerable; so don't disturb the plants. Walk only on marked trails and don't remove stones, leave car marks, or make campfires. Because the roads are closed in winter, the only access is from the tiny fishing village of Skarsvåg via Sno-Cat, a thump-and-bump ride that's as unforgettable as the desolate view.

## COMING ASHORE

One of Northern Norway's largest ports welcomes about 100 cruise ships annually during the summer season. The port itself has no services, but within 100 yards are shops, museums, tourist information, post office, banks, restaurants, and an ice bar.

## EXPLORING HONNINGSVÅG AND NORDKAPP

### HONNINGSVÅG

**Nordkappmuseet** (*North Cape Museum*). On the third floor of Nordkapphuset (North Cape House), this museum documents the history of the Arctic fishing industry and the history of tourism at North Cape. You can learn how the trail of humanity stretches back 10,000 years, and about the development of society and culture in this region. ⊠ *Fiskerivn. 4, Honningsvåg* ☎ *78–47–72–00* ⊕ *www.nordkappmuseet.no* ✉ *Nkr 50* ⊙ *June–mid-Aug., Mon.–Sat. 10–7, Sun. noon–7; mid-Aug.–May, weekdays noon–4.*

### NORDKAPP

*34 km (21 miles) north of Honningsvåg.*

On your journey to Nordkapp you'll see an incredible expanse of treeless tundra, with crumbling mountains and sparse, dwarf plants. The subarctic environment is very vulnerable; so don't disturb the plants. Walk only on marked trails and don't remove stones, leave car marks, or make campfires. The roads are open for buses through most of winter.

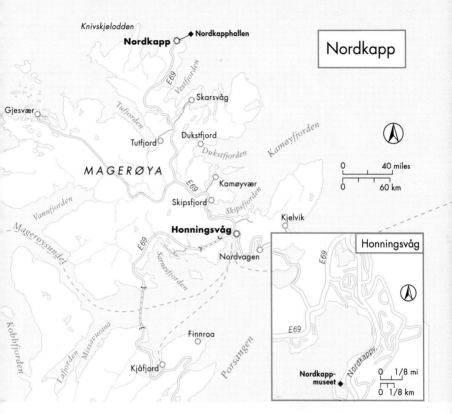

**Nordkapphallen** (*North Cape Hall*). The contrast between the near-barren territory outside and this tourist center is striking. Blasted into the interior of the plateau, the building is housed in a cave and includes an ecumenical chapel, a souvenir shop, and a post office. Exhibits trace the history of the cape, from Richard Chancellor, an Englishman who drifted around it and named it in 1533, to Oscar II, king of Norway and Sweden, who climbed to the top of the plateau in 1873. Celebrate your pilgrimage to 71° North at one of the cafés. The hefty admission covers the exhibits, parking, other facilities, and entrance to the plateau itself. ☎ 78–47–68–60 ⊕ *www.rica-hotels.com/special-offers/tilbud/nordkapphallen* ✉ NKr 235. Ticket is valid for 48 hrs ⊗ Mid-May–mid-Aug., daily 11 am–1 am; mid- to late Aug., daily 11 am–10 pm; Sept.–mid-May, daily 11–3.

## SHOPPING

Honningsvåg has several shops selling Norwegian souvenirs and handicrafts.

**Arctic Suvenirs.** This shop, in the same building as the tourist center, stays open until late at night, when cruise ships call. The shop features a range of Norwegian souvenirs, T-shirts, books, knitting products, and pewter—all tax-free. ✉ *Nordkapphallen, Fiskeriveien 4, Honningsvåg* ☎ 78–47–37–12.

## WHERE TO EAT

**$**
SCANDINAVIAN

**×Corner.** The daily catch often dictates the menu here, though pasta is always available—and so is crispy cod tongue. $ *Average main: NKr 190* ⊠ *Fiskeriveien 2A, Honningsvåg* ☎ *78–47–63–41* ⊕ *www.corner.no.*

# KRISTIANSAND, NORWAY

*326 km (202 miles) southwest of Oslo and 232 km (144 miles) southeast of Stavanger.*

Nicknamed "Sommerbyen" ("Summer City"), Norway's fifth-largest city has 78,000 inhabitants. Norwegians come here for its sun-soaked beaches and beautiful harbor.

According to legend, in 1641 King Christian IV marked the four corners of Kristiansand with his walking stick, and within that framework the grid of wide streets was laid down. The center of town, called Kvadraturen, still retains the grid, even after numerous fires. In the northeast corner is Posebyen, one of northern Europe's largest collections of low, connected wooden house settlements. There's a market here every Saturday in summer. *Fisketorvet* (the fish market) is near the south corner of the town's grid, right on the sea.

### COMING ASHORE

Cruise ships dock directly at Kristiansand's cruise-ship terminal. The town's main sights are a 1/3-mile or 10-minute walk from the terminal.

## EXPLORING KRISTIANSAND

**Agder naturmuseum og botaniske hage** (*Agder Natural History Museum and Botanical Garden*). The area's natural history from the Ice Age to the present is on display here, starting with the coast and moving on to the high mountains. There's a rainbow of minerals on display, as well as a rose garden with varieties from 1850. There's even the country's largest collection of cacti. ⊠ *Gimle gård, Gimlevn. 23* ☎ *38–05–86–20* ⊕ *www.naturmuseum.no* 🖾 *NKr 50* ☉ *Mid-June–mid-Aug., daily 11–5; mid-Aug.–mid-June, Tues.–Fri. 10–3, Sun. noon–4; closed Mon. and Sat.*

**Christiansholm Festning** (*Christiansholm Fortress*). This circular fortress with 16-foot-thick walls, on a promontory opposite Festningsgata, was completed in 1674. Its role has been much more decorative than defensive; it was used once, in 1807 during the Napoleonic Wars, to defend the city against British invasion. Now it contains art exhibits. However, the best part is walking around the grounds—the gates open early in the morning. ⊠ *Østre Strandgt 52B* ☎ *38–07–51–50 number is for Kristiansand municipality* ⊕ *www.kristiansand.kommune.no/Anlegg-lokaler-og-utstyr-til-leie/Leie-av-arealer-til-utendors-arrangement1/Christiansholm-festning* ☉ *Mid-May–Sept., daily 9–9.*

★
☾
**Dyreparken Kristiansand** (*Kristiansand Zoo and Amusement Park*). One of Norway's most popular attractions, Dyreparken Kristiansand is actually five separate parks, including a water park (bring bathing suits and

towels); a forested park; an entertainment park; a theme park; and a zoo, which contains an enclosure for Scandinavian animals such as wolves, snow foxes, lynxes, and elks. The theme park, Kardemomme By (Cardamom Town), is named for a book by the Norwegian illustrator and writer Thorbjørn Egner. In the zoo, the *My Africa* exhibition allows you to move along a bridge observing native savanna animals such as giraffes and zebras. The park is 11 km (6 miles) east of town. ✉ *Kardemomme By* ☎ *97–05–97–00* ⊕ *www.dyreparken.no* 🖃 *NKr 399, includes admission to all parks and rides; discounts offered off-season, reduced fee for kids* ☾ *June–Aug., daily 10–7; Sept.–May, weekdays 10–3, weekends 10–5.*

☾ **Kristiansand Kanonmuseum** (*Cannon Museum*). At the Kristiansand Kanonmuseum you can see the cannon that the occupying Germans rigged up during World War II. With a caliber of 15 inches, the cannon was said to be capable of shooting a projectile halfway to Denmark. In the bunkers, related military materials are on display. This little museum is a gem. Kids love running around the grounds, but keep an eye on them, since there aren't railings everywhere. ✉ *Kroodden* ☎ *38–08–50–90* ⊕ *www.kanonmuseet.no* 🖃 *NKr 65* ☾ *Mid-May–mid-June and mid-Aug.–late Sept., Mon.–Wed. 11–3, Thurs.–Sun. 11–5; mid-June–mid-Aug., daily 11–6; late Sept.–late Nov. and Feb.–mid-May, Sun. noon–4.*

**Oddernes kirke** (*Oddernes Church*). The striking rune stone in the cemetery of Oddernes kirke says that Øyvind, godson of Saint Olav, built this church in 1040 on property he inherited from his father. One of the oldest churches in Norway, it has a baroque pulpit from 1704 and is dedicated to Saint Olav. ✉ *Jegersbergvn. 2* ☎ *38–19–68–60* ⊕ *www.visitkrs.no/en/TellusView/?&TLl=en&TLp=431420* 🖃 *Free* ☾ *July–mid-Aug., weekdays 11–2.*

**Fodor's** Choice **Ravnedalen** (*Raven Valley*). A favorite with hikers and strolling nannies,
★ Ravnedalen is a lush park that's filled with flowers in springtime. Wear comfortable shoes to hike the narrow, winding paths up the hills and climb the 200 steps up to a 304-foot lookout. There is a café on-site, and open-air concerts in summer. ⊕ *ravnedalen.no.*

☾ **Vest-Agder-museet Kristiansand** (*County Museum*). The region's largest cultural museum has more than 40 old buildings on display. The structures, transported from other locations in the area, include two *tun*—farm buildings traditionally set in clusters around a common area—which suited extended families. If you have children with you, check out the old-fashioned toys, which can still be played with. The museum is 4 km (2½ miles) east of Kristiansand on Route E18. ✉ *Vigevn. 22B, Kongsgård* ☎ *38–10–26–80* ⊕ *www.vestagdermuseet.no* 🖃 *NKr 50* ☾ *Mid-June–Aug., weekdays 10–5, weekends noon–5; Sept.–mid-June, weekdays 9–3, Sun. noon–5.*

**8**

## ACTIVITIES

**Samsen Kulturhus.** Whether you're an experienced pro or just a gung-ho beginner, you can rent climbing equipment or learn more about the sport from Samsen Kulturhus. ⊠ *Vestervn. 2, Kristiansand* ☎ *38–00–64–00* ⊕ *www.samsen.com.*

**Troll Mountain.** Troll Mountain, about one hour's drive from Kristiansand, organizes many activities. Be it mountain climbing, sailing, biking, rafting, paintball, or even beaver or deer safaris, this is the place for outdoorsy types. ⊠ *Setesdal Rafting og Aktivitetssenter, Rte. 9, Evje* ☎ *37–93–11–77* ⊕ *www.troll-mountain.no.*

### FISHING

**Lillesand Tourist Office.** You can get a permit at any sports store or at the Lillesand Tourist Office. ☎ *37–40–19–10, 93–01–17–81* ⊕ *www.lillesand.com.*

### HIKING

**Baneheia Skog** (*Baneheia Forest*). In addition to the gardens and steep hills of Ravnedalen, the Baneheia Skog is full of evergreens, small lakes, and paths that are ideal for a lazy walk or a challenging run. It's just a 15-minute walk north from the city center.

### HORSEBACK RIDING

**Islandshestsenteret** (*The Icelandic Horse Center*). If you're at home in the saddle, then head to Islandshestsenteret. Specializing in the Icelandic horse breed, this center offers courses, trips, and camping for children and adults. ⊠ *Søgne, Kristiansand* ☎ *38–16–98–82* ⊕ *www.islandshestsenteret.no.*

## SHOPPING

There are many shops next to Dyreparken in Kristiansand.

**Kvadraturen.** You'll find 300 stores and eating spots in this part of the Old Town, which was commissioned by King Christian IV in the mid-1600s. ⊕ *www.kvadraturen.no.*

**Sørlandssenteret.** One of the region's larger shopping centers, Sørlandssenteret contains 130 stores, a pharmacy, and a post office. ⊠ *Barstølveien 31–35* ☎ *38–04–91–00* ⊕ *www.sorlandssenteret.no.*

# OSLO, NORWAY

What sets Oslo apart from other European cities is not so much its cultural traditions or its internationally renowned museums as its simply stunning natural beauty. How many world capitals have subway service to the forest, or lakes and hiking trails within the city limits? But Norwegians will be quick to remind you that Oslo is a cosmopolitan metropolis with prosperous businesses and a thriving nightlife. During the mid-19th century, Norway and Sweden were ruled as one kingdom, under King Karl Johan. It was then that the grand main street that is his namesake was built, and Karl Johans Gate has been at the center of city life ever since. In 1905 the country separated from

Sweden, and in 1925 an act of Parliament finally changed the city's name back to Oslo from Kristiania, its Swedish name. Today Oslo is Norway's political, economic, industrial, and cultural capital. The Norwegian royal family lives in Oslo, and it is also where the Nobel Peace Prize is awarded.

### COMING ASHORE

Cruise ships navigate beautiful Oslofjord en route to Oslo and dock in the compact city center. Many of Oslo's attractions can be explored on foot from the docks, but Oslo has a good subway system, as well as plentiful buses and taxis.

Taxis are radio dispatched from a central office, and it can take up to 30 minutes to get one during peak hours. Taxi stands are all over town. It is possible to hail a cab on the street, but cabs are not allowed to pick up passengers within 100 yards of a stand. Never take pirate taxis; all registered taxis should have their roof lights on when they're available. Rates start at around NKr 109 for hailed or rank cabs, and NKr 91 for ordered taxis, depending on the time of day and the company.

## EXPLORING OSLO

Fodor'sChoice **Aker Brygge.** This area was the site of a disused shipbuilding yard
★ until redevelopment saw the addition of residential town houses and a commercial sector. Postmodern steel and glass buildings dominate the skyline now. The area has more than 60 shops and 35 restaurants, including upmarket fashion boutiques, pubs, cinemas, a theater, a comedy club, and a shopping mall. There is an open boulevard for strolling. Service facilities include banks, drugstores, and a parking garage for 1,600. ⊠ *Aker Brygge* ☎ *22–83–26–80* ⊕ *www.akerbrygge.no* ⌨ *Free* ⊗ *Shopping hrs weekdays 10–8, Sat. 10–6; grocery store and restaurants are open later.*

**Akershus Festning og Slott** (*Akershus Fortress and Castle*). Dating to 1299, this stone medieval castle and royal residence was developed into a fortress armed with cannons by 1592. After that time, it withstood a number of sieges and then fell into decay. It was finally restored in 1899. Summer tours take you through its magnificent halls, the castle church, the royal mausoleum, reception rooms, and banqueting halls. Explore Akershus Fortress on your own with the Fortress Trail Map, which you can pick up at the visitor center. Note that the castle is closed during official visits, which happen a couple weekends a year. ⊠ *Akershus festning, Sentrum* ☎ *23–09–35–53* ⊕ *www.forsvarsbygg.no/festningene/ Festningene/Akershus-festning* ⌨ *Fortress grounds and concerts: free. Castle: NKr 70, including audio guide* ⊗ *Sept.–Apr., weekends noon–5; May–Aug., Mon.–Sat. 10–4, Sun. noon–4.*

★ **Fram-Museet.** This was the ship used by the legendary Polar explorer
ⵛ Roald Amundsen when be became the first man to reach the South Pole, in December 1911. Once known as the strongest vessel in the world, this enormous Norwegian polar ship has advanced farther north and south than any other surface vessel. Built in 1892, it made three voyages to the Arctic (they were conducted by Fridtjof Nansen and Otto Sverdrup, in addition to Amundsen). Climb on board and peer

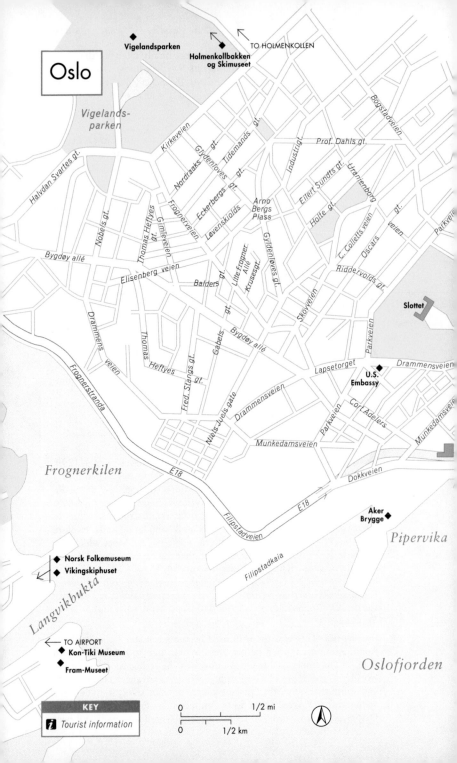

# Oslo

Vigelands-
parken

◆ Vigelandsparken

◆ Holmenkollbakken
og Skimuseet

TO HOLMENKOLLEN

Kirkeveien
Gydenløves gt.
Tidemands gt.
Prof. Dahls gt.
Bogstadveien
Nordraaks gt.
Eckerbergs gt.
Frognerveien
Gimleveien
Løvenskiolds
Industrig.
Ellert Sundts gt.
Holte gt.
Uranienborg
gt.
Parkv
Arno
Bergs
Plass
Nobels gt.
Thomas Heftyes gt.
Halvdan Svartes gt.
Bygdøy allé
Elisenberg veien
Gydenløves gt.
C. Colletts veien
Oscars
veien
Riddervolds gt.
Skoveien
Balders gt.
Litle Frogner
Allé
Krusesgt.
Parkveien
Slottet
Drammens veien
Thomas Heftyes
Gabels gt.
Bygdøy allé
Lapsetorget
Drammensveien
◆ U.S.
Embassy
Frognerstranda
Fred. Stangs gt.
Niels Juels gate
Drammensveien
Parkveien
Cort Adelers
Munkedamsveien
Munkedamsveien
E18
Frognerkilen
Filipstadveien
Dokkveien
E18
◆ Aker
Brygge
Pipervika
◆ Norsk Folkemuseum
◆ Vikingskiphuset
Filipstadkaia
Langvikbukta
TO AIRPORT
◆ Kon-Tiki Museum
◆ Fram-Museet
Oslofjorden

| KEY |
| --- |
| 𝒊 Tourist information |

0 — 1/2 mi
0 — 1/2 km

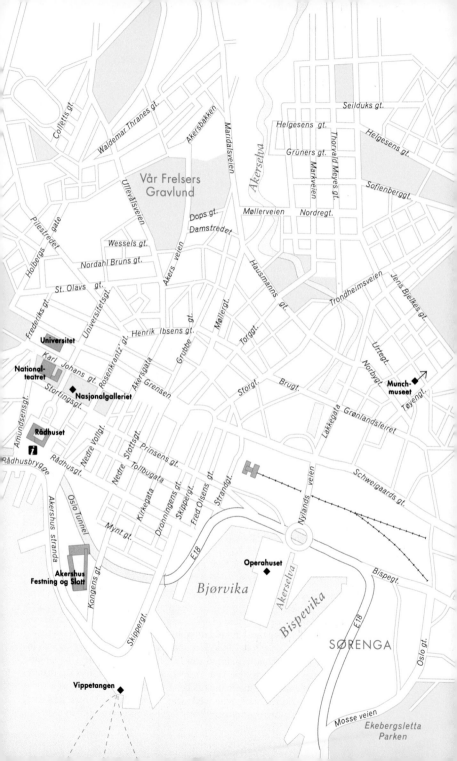

inside the captain's quarters, which has explorers' sealskin jackets and other relics on display. Surrounding the ship are many artifacts from expeditions. ⊠ *Bygdøynesvn. 36, Bygdøy* 🕾 *23–28–29–50* ⊕ *www.frammuseum.no* 🔄 *NKr 80* ⊗ *June–Aug., daily 9–6; Sept. and May, daily 10–5; Oct. and Mar.–Apr., daily 10–4; Nov.–Feb., weekdays 10–3, weekends 10–4.*

**Fodor's Choice**
★ **Holmenkollbakken og skimuseet** (*Holmenkollen Ski Jump and Ski Museum*). A feat of world-class engineering, this beloved ski jump was first constructed in 1892 and has been rebuilt numerous times, remaining a distinctive part of Oslo's skyline. The cool, futuristic-looking jump you see today was finished in 2010. It offers spectacular views and some repose from Oslo's

**OSLO BEST BETS**

**Aker Brygge.** Once a dilapidated shipyard, this is now an upscale residential and commercial district.

**Munch Museet.** Munch is Norway's most famous artist. You can see a version of *The Scream* here; there's another version in the Nasjonalgalleriet if you want a broader introduction to Norwegian art.

**Vigelandsparken.** The 212 bronze, granite, and wrought-iron sculptures by Gustav Vigeland skillfully and artistically detail his life, thoughts, and interpretations of his childhood.

urbanity, and it still hosts international competitions. The ski-jump simulator puts you in the skis of real jumpers, and the world's oldest ski museum presents 4,000 years of ski history. Check on hours before visiting; they're subject to change, particularly in the fall through spring months. Guided tours of the museum and jump tower are both available. ⊠ *Kongevn. 5, Holmenkollen* 🕾 *22–92–32–00* ⊕ *holmenkollen.com* 🔄 *Jump tower and museum (joint ticket): NKr 110* ⊗ *Oct.–Apr., daily 10–4; May and Sept., daily 10–5; June–Aug, daily 9–8.*

★ **Kon-Tiki Museum.** The museum celebrates Norway's most famous 20th-ⓒ century explorer. Thor Heyerdahl made a voyage in 1947 from Peru to Polynesia on the *Kon-Tiki,* a balsa raft, to lend weight to his theory that the first Polynesians came from the Americas. His second craft, the *Ra II,* was used to test his theory that this sort of boat could have reached the West Indies before Columbus. The museum also has a film room and artifacts from Peru, Polynesia, and the Easter Islands. ⊠ *Bygdøynesvn. 36, Bygdøy* 🕾 *23–08–67–67 press 4 for English* ⊕ *www.kon-tiki.no* 🔄 *NKr 80* ⊗ *Mar.–May, Sept., and Oct. daily 10–5; June–Aug, daily 9:30–6; Nov.–Feb. daily 10–4.*

**Fodor's Choice**
★ **Munchmuseet** (*Munch Museum*). Edvard Munch, Norway's most famous artist, bequeathed his enormous collection of works (about 1,100 paintings, 3,000 drawings, and 18,000 graphic works) to the city when he died in 1944. The museum is a monument to his artistic genius, housing the largest collection of his works and also mounting changing exhibitions. Munch actually painted four different versions of *The Scream,* the image for which he's best known, and one of them is on display here. While most of the Munch legend focuses on the artist as a troubled, angst-ridden man, he moved away from that pessimistic and dark approach to more optimistic themes later in his career. ⊠ *Tøyengt. 53,*

*Tøyen* ☎ *23–49–35–00* ⊕ *www.munch.museum.no* ✉ *NKr 95* ⊙ *Sept.–May, Tues.–Sat. 10–4, Sun. 10–5; June–Aug., daily 10–5.*

★ **Nasjonalgalleriet** (*National Gallery*). The gallery, part of the National Museum of Art, Architecture and Design, houses Norway's largest collection of art created before 1945. The deep-red Edvard Munch room holds such major paintings as *The Dance of Life,* one of two existing oil versions of *The Scream,* and several self-portraits. Classic landscapes by Hans Gude and Adolph Tidemand—including *Bridal Voyage on the Hardangerfjord*—share space in galleries with other works by major Norwegian artists. The museum also has works by Monet, Renoir, Van Gogh, and Gauguin, as well as contemporary works by 20th-century Nordic artists. ✉ *Universitetsgt. 13, Sentrum* ☎ *21–98–20–00* ⊕ *www.nasjonalmuseet.no* ✉ *NKr 50; free on Sun.* ⊙ *Tues., Wed., and Fri. 10–6, Thurs. 10–7, weekends 11–5.*

Fodor'sChoice
★
⏱ **Norsk Folkemuseum** (*The Norwegian Museum of Cultural History*). One of the largest open-air museums in Europe, this is a perfect way to see Norway in a day. From the stoic stave church (built in AD 1200) to farmers' houses made of sod, the old buildings here span Norway's regions and most of its recorded history. Indoors, there's a fascinating display of folk costumes. The displays of richly embroidered, colorful *bunader* (national costumes) from every region include one set at a Telemark country wedding. The museum also has stunning dragon-style wood carvings from 1550 and some beautiful *rosemaling,* or decorative painted floral patterns. The traditional costumes of the Sami (Lapp) people of Northern Norway are exhibited around one of their tents. If you're visiting in summer, ask about Norwegian Evening, a summer program of folk dancing, guided tours, and food tastings. On Sundays in December, the museum holds Oslo's largest Christmas market. ✉ *Museumsvn. 10, Bygdøy* ☎ *22–12–37–00* ⊕ *www.norskfolkemuseum.no* ✉ *NKr 110* ⊙ *Mid–Sept.–mid-May, weekdays 11–3, weekends 11–4; mid-May–mid-Sept., daily 10–6.*

Fodor'sChoice
★ **Operahuset.** Oslo's opera house opened in 2008 with a fanfare that included the presence of the Norwegian king and a host of celebrities. The white marble and glass building, designed by renowned Norwegian architect firm Snøhetta, is a stunning addition to the Oslo waterfront, and the pride of Norwegians. It doesn't just look good; acoustics inside the dark oak auditorium are excellent, too. The program includes ballet, orchestra concerts, rock, and opera. Locals and tourists alike enjoy visiting at off hours, eating in the venue's restaurants, and walking on the building's roof. ✉ *Kirsten Flagstads pl. 1* ☎ *21–42–21–00* ⊕ *www.operaen.no* ✉ *Free entrance; guided tours NKr 100* ⊙ *Tours in English in summer.*

**Rådhuset** (*City Hall*). This redbrick building is best known today for the awarding of the Nobel Peace Prize, which takes place here every December. Inside, many museum-quality masterpieces are on the walls. After viewing the frescoes in the main hall, walk upstairs to the banquet hall to see the royal portraits. Free drop-in guided tours are available. Meet in the main hall for the 45-minute tour at the noted times. To visit the City Hall Gallery, enter harborside. Special exhibits

8

are hung throughout the year. On festive occasions, the central hall is illuminated from outside by 60 large spotlights that simulate daylight. ✉ *Fridtjof Nansens Plass, Sentrum* ☎ *02180* ⊕ *www.radhusets-forvaltningstjeneste.oslo.kommune.no/english* ✉ *Free* ⊙ *Drop-in guided tours of City Hall: Sept.–May, Wed. at 10, noon, and 2; June–Aug., daily at 10, noon, and 2.*

**Slottet** (*The Royal Palace*). At one end of Karl Johans Gate, the vanilla-and-cream-color neoclassical palace was completed in 1848. The equestrian statue out in front is of Karl Johan, King of Sweden and Norway from 1818 to 1844. The palace is only open to the public in summer, when there are guided tours (in English). ■TIP→ **Kids of all ages will love the Royal Palace's changing of the guard ceremony, accompanied by the Norwegian Military Band, that takes place daily, rain or shine, at 1:30.** ✉ *Slottsplassen* ☎ *81–53–31–33 Billettservice, for tickets* ⊕ *www. kongehuset.no* ✉ *Tours: NKr 95* ⊙ *Tours: Mid-June–mid-Aug., Mon.– Thurs. and Sat. at noon, 2, and 2:20; Fri. and Sun. 2, 2:20, and 4.*

**Fodor'sChoice**
★
☾
**Vigelandsparken** (*Vigeland Sculpture Park*). A vast green lung and a favorite hangout for locals, Vigelandsparken has 212 bronze, granite, and wrought-iron sculptures by Gustav Vigeland (1869–1943) as well as ample park space. The 56-foot-high granite *Monolith* is a column of 121 upward-striving nudes surrounded by 36 groups on circular stairs. The *Angry Boy*, a bronze of an enraged cherubic child stamping his foot, draws legions of visitors and has been filmed, parodied, painted red, and even stolen. Kids love to climb on the statues. There's also a museum on-site for those wishing to delve deeper into the artist's work. ✉ *Frognerparken, Frogner* ☎ *23–49–37–00* ⊕ *www.vigeland.museum. no* ✉ *Park: free. Museum: NKr 50* ⊙ *Park: year-round, dawn–dusk. Museum: May–Aug.: Tues.–Sun. 10–5, Sept.–Apr.: Tues.–Sun. noon–4.*

**Fodor'sChoice**
★
☾
**Vikingskipshuset** (*Viking Ship Museum*). The Viking legacy in all its glory lives on at this classic Oslo museum. Chances are you'll come away fascinated by the *Gokstad, Oseberg,* and *Tune,* three blackened wooden Viking ships that date to AD 800. Discovered in Viking tombs around the Oslo fjords between 1860 and 1904, the boats are the best-preserved Viking ships ever found; they have been on display since the museum's 1957 opening. In Viking times, it was customary to bury the dead with food, drink, useful and decorative objects, and even their horses and dogs. Many of the well-preserved tapestries, household utensils, dragon-style wood carvings, and sledges were found aboard ships. The museum's rounded white walls give the feeling of a burial mound. Avoid summertime crowds by visiting at lunchtime. ✉ *Huk Aveny 35, Byg-døy* ☎ *22–13–52–80* ⊕ *www.ukm.uio.no/vikingskipshuset* ✉ *NKr 60* ⊙ *May–Sept., daily 9–6; Oct.–Apr., daily 10–4.*

## SHOPPING

Oslo is the best place in the country for buying anything Norwegian. Popular souvenirs include knitwear, wood and ceramic trolls, cheese slicers, boxes with rosemaling, gold and silver jewelry, items made from pewter, smoked salmon, caviar, akvavit, chocolate, and geitost, the sweet brown goat cheese that can be found in just about every Norwegian kitchen.

Established Norwegian brands include Porsgrund porcelain, Hadeland and Magnor glass, David Andersen jewelry, and Husfliden handicrafts (most of which are sold in branches of the Norsk flid crafts chain). You may also want to look for popular, classical, or folk music CDs; English translations of Norwegian books; or clothing by Norwegian designers, such as Moods of Norway.

Prices in Norway, as in all of Scandinavia, are generally much higher than in other European countries. Prices of handmade articles, such as knitwear, are controlled, making comparison shopping pointless. Otherwise, shops have both sales and specials—look for the words *salg* and *tilbud*. In addition, if you are a resident of a country other than Norway, Sweden, Finland, or Denmark, you can have the Norwegian value-added tax (MVA) refunded at the airport when you leave the country. When you make a purchase, you must clearly state your country of residence in order to have the necessary export document filled in by store staff.

**Basarhallene,** the arcade behind Oslo *domkirke* (cathedral), is worth a browse for glass and crystal and handicrafts made in Norway. Walk 15 minutes west of the city center and you can wander up the tree-lined Bygdøy Allé and browse the fashionable **Frogner** and **Bygdøy** areas, which are brimming with modern- and antique-furniture stores, interior design shops, food shops, art galleries, haute couture, and Oslo's beautiful people. The streets downtown around **Karl Johans Gate** draw many of Oslo's shoppers. The concentration of department stores is especially high in this part of town. **Majorstuen** starts at the *T-bane* (subway) station with the same name and proceeds down Bogstadveien to the Royal Palace. Oslo is not famed for its markets, but there's a small flower market on Stortorget in front of the cathedral, and a few stalls selling souvenirs and secondhand records on Youngstorget. Every Saturday, a flea market is open at **Vestkanttorget,** at Amaldus Nilsens Plass near Frognerparken. **Grünerløkka,** a 15-minute walk north of the center, is blooming with trendy new and bohemian fashion boutiques, vintage stores, and many other quirky little shops.

**Aker Brygge.** More than a shopping center, essentially a waterside pedestrian paradise, this renovated shipyard is where Oslo hangs out. Open late, it has 60 shops and 35 restaurants. ☎ *22–83–26–80* ⊕ *www.akerbrygge.no.*

**GlasMagasinet.** More an amalgam of shops under one roof than a true department store, GlasMagasinet has stores selling handcrafted items made with glass, silver, and pewter. It's opposite the cathedral. ✉ *Stortorvet 9, Sentrum* ☎ *22–82–23–00* ⊕ *www.glasmagasinet.no.*

**Paleet.** The elegant Paleet opens up into a grand, marbled atrium and has many high-end clothing, accessories, and food stores—and there's a food court in the basement. ✉ *Karl Johans gt. 37–43, Sentrum* ☎ *23–08–08–11* ⊕ *www.paleet.no.*

## ACTIVITIES

Oslo's natural surroundings and climate make it ideally suited to outdoor pursuits. The Oslofjord and its islands, the forested woodlands called the *marka,* and as many as 18 hours of daylight in summer all make the Norwegian capital an irresistible place for outdoor activities.

## NIGHTLIFE

Oslo's cafés, restaurant-bars, and jazz clubs are laid-back and mellow. But if you're ready to party, there are many pulsating, live-rock and dance clubs to choose from. Day or night, people are usually out on Karl Johans Gate, and many clubs and restaurants in the central area stay open until the early hours. Aker Brygge, the wharf area, has many bars and some nightclubs, attracting mostly tourists, couples on first dates, and other people willing to spend extra for the waterfront location. Grünerløkka and Grønland have even more bars, pubs, and cafés catering to a younger crowd. An older crowd ventures out to the less-busy west side of Oslo, to Frogner and Bygdøy.

Drinking out is very expensive, starting at around NKr 70 for a beer or a mixed drink. Many Norwegians save money by having a *vorspiel*—a "pre-party" at friends' houses before heading out on the town. Some bars in town remain quiet until 11 pm or midnight when the first groups of vorspiel partiers arrive.

**Bibliotekbaren og Vinterhaven.** If you're more partial to lounging than drinking, the Bibliotekbaren og Vinterhaven (Library Bar and Winter Garden) is a stylish hangout with old-fashioned leather armchairs, huge marble columns, and live piano music. Politicians, actors, musicians, journalists, and locals have come here for nearly 100 years for informal meetings, quiet chats, or just to enjoy the tempting sandwich and cake buffet. ⊠ *Hotel Bristol, Kristian IVs gt. 7, Sentrum* ☎ *22–82–60–00.*

**Blå.** This is one of the most important Nordic clubs for jazz, electronica, hip-hop, and related sounds. The patio, along the Akerselva River, is popular in summer. ⊠ *Brennerivn. 9C, Grünerløkka* ☎ *98–25–63–86* ⊕ *www.blaaoslo.no.*

**Herr Nilsen.** At Herr Nilsen, some of Norway's most celebrated jazz artists perform in a stylish space. There's live music several nights a week and jazz on Saturday at 4 pm. ⊠ *C.J. Hambros pl. 5, Sentrum* ☎ *22–33–54–05* ⊕ *www.herrnilsen.no.*

## WHERE TO EAT

**$**
NORWEGIAN
☺ ✕ **Asylet.** This popular pub right by Grønland Torg serves homemade traditional Norwegian food in an atmospheric setting. The building, which dates from the 1730s, was once an orphanage. The big lunch menu features a good selection of *smørbrød* (open-faced sandwiches) as well as smoked-salmon salad and the traditional *karbonade* (a sort of open-faced hamburger, served with fried onions). There is a fireplace inside, and a beer garden for enjoying the sun in summer. $ *Average main: NKr 180* ⊠ *Grønland 28* ☎ *22–17–09–39* ⊕ *www.asylet.no.*

$ **✕Beach Club.** This diner, its American origins "adjusted to a Norwegian
AMERICAN way of life," has been drawing the crowds since it opened in 1989.
The classics burgers are all there, but for something a bit different try
the "Favourite," with cheese, bacon and chili con carne; or the Zorba
(chicken burger with tzatziki); and then a Beach Lime Pie for dessert.
Full American-style breakfasts are also available, and there's also a
small kids' menu. The original Keith Haring on the walls and the big terrace for sunny days are two more pluses here. $ *Average main: NKr 150*
✉ *Bryggetorget 14, Aker Brygge* ☎ *22–83–83–82* ⊕ *www.beachclub.no.*

$$$ **✕Det Gamle Rådhus.** If you're in Oslo for just one night and want an
NORWEGIAN authentic dining experience, head to the city's oldest restaurant—
**Fodor's**Choice housed in Oslo's first town hall, a building that dates from 1641. It's
★ known for its traditional fish and game dishes such as the moose entre-
cote or the Røros reindeer. An absolute must, if you're lucky enough
to be visiting at the right time, is the house specialty, the pre-Christmas
lutefisk platter. The backyard has a charming outdoor area for dining
in summer. $ *Average main: NKr 270* ✉ *Nedre Slottsgt. 1, Sentrum*
☎ *22–42–01–07* ⊕ *www.gamleraadhus.no* ☾ *Closed Sun.*

$ **✕Fru Hagen.** The classic chandeliers and velvet sofas here make it look
BISTRO like a vintage neighborhood hangout. Locals gather here for fresh, well-
executed comfort food—burgers, pasta, sandwiches, and salads—or the
spicy chicken salad, a house specialty. At night, Fru Hagen lets its hair
down further, becoming a disco/bar that's open until 3 am. $ *Average
main: NKr 150* ✉ *Thorvald Meyers gt. 40, Grünerløkka* ☎ *45–49–19–
04* ⊕ *www.fruhagen.no.*

## WHERE TO STAY

8

$$ **Grand Hotel.** This very central hotel is the choice of visiting heads
HOTEL of state, rock musicians, and Nobel Peace Prize winners. **Pros:** period
**Fodor's**Choice features have been preserved throughout; Ladies Floor, with 13 unique
★ rooms designed for women travelers; beautiful pool and spa. **Cons:** gets
busy during festivals and in December, during Nobel Peace Prize week.
$ *Rooms from: NKr 1440* ✉ *Karl Johans gt. 31, Sentrum* ☎ *23–21–
20–00* ⊕ *www.grand.no* ↪ *292 rooms, incl. 54 suites* ⦿*Breakfast.*

$$$$ **Hotel Continental.** History meets modernity at this landmark—it's a
HOTEL sophisticated stay with stylish guest rooms and posh common areas.
**Fodor's**Choice **Pros:** exemplary service; beautiful, well-appointed rooms; great gym.
★ **Cons:** restaurant and bars are very busy with locals as well as guests;
very expensive. $ *Rooms from: NKr 3300* ✉ *Stortingsgt. 24–26, Sen-
trum* ☎ *22–82–40–00* ⊕ *www.hotelcontinental.no* ↪*155 rooms, 23
suites* ⦿*No meals.*

$$ **Radisson Blu Plaza Hotel.** The understated elegance helps keep the
HOTEL rooms filled at this business hotel. **Pros:** great top floor bar; very good
★ breakfast buffet; luxuriously grand bathtubs; excellent location. **Cons:**
this is northern Europe's tallest hotel, so it's not very intimate; the
breakfast room can get crowded. $ *Rooms from: NKr 1495* ✉ *Sonja
Henies pl. 3* ☎ *22–05–80–00* ⊕ *www.radissonblu.com/plazahotel-oslo*
↪ *676 rooms, 20 suites* ⦿*Breakfast.*

# TROMSØ, NORWAY

Tromsø surprised visitors in the 1800s: they thought it very sophisticated and cultured for being so close to the North Pole—hence its nickname, the Paris of the North. It looks the way a polar town should—with ice-capped mountain ridges and jagged architecture that is an echo of the peaks. The midnight sun shines from May 21 to July 21, and it is said that the northern lights decorate the night skies over Tromsø more than over any other city in Norway. Tromsø is home to only 69,000 people, but it's very spread out—the city's total area, 2,558 square km (987 square miles), is the most expansive in Norway. The downtown area is on a small, hilly island connected to the mainland by a slender bridge. The 13,000 students at the world's northernmost university are one reason the nightlife here is uncommonly busy.

## COMING ASHORE

Cruise ships dock either in the city center at Prostneset or 4 km (2½ miles) north of the city center at Breivika. Step off the ship in Prostneset, and you're in the city center. A shuttle is offered between Breivika and the city center.

## EXPLORING TROMSØ

☺ **Fjellheisen.** To get a sense of Tromsø's immensity and solitude, take this cable car from the mainland, just across the bridge and behind the cathedral, up to the island's mountains. *Storsteinen* (Big Rock), 1,386 feet above sea level, has a great city view. In summer a restaurant is open at the top of the lift. ⊠ *Sollivn. 12, Tromsdalen* ☎ *77–63–87–37* ⊕ *www.fjellheisen.no* ✉ *NKr 120* ⊙ *Mid-May–July, daily 10 am–1 am; Aug., daily 10–10; Sept., daily 10–5; Oct.–Dec., daily 11–4; Feb.–Mar., 10–4; Apr.–mid-May, daily 10–5.*

**Ishavskatedralen** (*Arctic Cathedral*). Tromsø's signature structure was designed by Jan Inge Hovig to evoke the shape of a Sami tent as well as the iciness of a glacier. Opened in 1964, it represents northern Norwegian nature, culture, and faith. The immense stained-glass window depicts the Second Coming. There are midnight sun concerts in summer, starting at 11:30 pm. ⊠ *Hans Nilsens v. 41, Tromsdalen* ☎ *47–68–06–68* ⊕ *www.ishavskatedralen.no* ✉ *NKr 35; midnight sun concerts NKr 130* ⊙ *June–mid-Aug., Mon.–Sat. 9–7, Sun. 1–7; mid-Aug.–mid-Sept., daily 3–6; mid-Sept.–mid-May, daily 4–6; mid-May through end of May, daily 3-6.*

☺ **Polaria.** Housed in a striking modern building by the harbor, the adventure center Polaria examines life in and around the polar and Barents regions. Explore the exhibits on polar travel and arctic research, then check out two panoramic films, *Svalbard—Arctic Wilderness* and *Northern Lights in Arctic Norway.* The aquarium has sea mammals, including bearded seals. ⊠ *Hjalmar Johansens gt. 12* ☎ *77–75–01–00* ⊕ *www.polaria.no* ✉ *NKr 105* ⊙ *Mid-May–mid-Aug., daily 10–7; mid-Aug.–mid-May, daily 11–5.*

**Polarmuseet** (*Polar Museum*). Inside a customs warehouse from 1830, Polarmuseet documents the history of the polar regions. There are exhibitions on wintering in the Arctic, trapping, Arctic seal hunting,

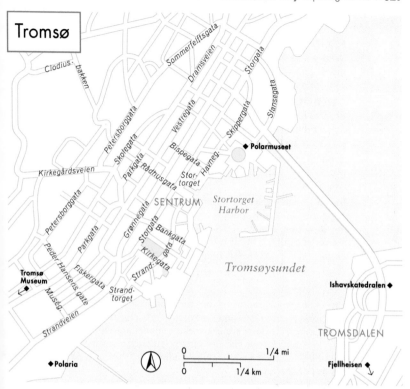

and on famous Norwegian polar explorers like Fridtjof Nansen and Roald Amundsen. Part of the University of Tromsø, the museum opened in 1978, on the 50th anniversary of Amundsen leaving Tromsø for the last time, in search of his explorer colleague Umberto Nobile. ⊠ *Søndre Tollbodgt. 11B* ☎ *77–62–33–60* ⊕ *www.polarmuseum.no* ⊡ *NKr 50* ☉ *Mid-Aug.–mid-June daily 11–5; mid-June–mid-Aug. daily 10–7.*

☋ **Tromsø Museum** (*Tromsø University Museum*). Dating from 1872, Northern Norway's oldest scientific institution is dedicated to the nature and culture of the region. Learn about the northern lights, wildlife, fossils and dinosaurs, minerals and rocks, and church art from 1300 to 1800. Outdoors you can visit a Sami *gamme* (turf hut), and a replica of a Viking longhouse. The pretty Arctic-Alpine Botanical Garden is the most northern in the world, at roughly the same latitude as Alaska's north coast. ⊠ *Lars Thørings v. 10* ☎ *77–64–50–00* ⊕ *uit.no/tmu* ⊡ *NKr 50* ☉ *June–Aug., daily 9–6; Sept.–May, weekdays 10–4:30, Sat. noon–3, Sun. 11–4.*

## ACTIVITIES

### HIKING AND WALKING

With wilderness at its doorstep, Tromsø has more than 100 km (62 miles) of walking and hiking trails in the mountains above the city. They're reachable by funicular.

### OUTDOOR ACTIVITY OUTFITTERS

Tromsø has more than 100 km (62 miles) of walking and hiking trails in the mountains above the city. They're reachable by funicular.

**Lyngsfjord Adventure.** This tour company offers dog sledding, reindeer sledding, snowmobile safaris, snowshoeing, northern lights viewing, and the chance to sleep in Sami tents. ☎ 77–71–55-88 ⊕ *www. lyngsfjord.com.*

**Tromsø Villmarkssenter.** This outfitter, located a half hour outside the city, organizes winter dogsledding trips, northern lights safaris, glacier walking, kayaking, summit tours, and Sami-style dinners, which take place around a campfire inside a *lavvu* (a Sami tent). ⊠ *Straumsvegen 603, Kvaløya* ☎ 77–69–60–02 ⊕ *www.villmarkssenter.no.*

## SHOPPING

One of Norway's leading regions for handmade arts and crafts, Tromsø is a treasure trove of shops, particularly along the main pedestrian street Storgata, where a market sells regional and international products. Pick up art from the city's many galleries or craft shops (such as glass-blowing and candle-making studios), or score such Arctic delicacies as reindeer sausages.

## WHERE TO EAT

**$$** ✕ **Vertshuset Skarven.** The several restaurants and bars here mostly

SEAFOOD emphasize seafood, but there's also a steak house. The menu in this Arctic pantry might include soup of Kamchatka crab, delicious halibut and coalfish, Arctic reindeer, or whale carpaccio. The fish lunch at Skarven is a good value. The pleasant terrace is usually packed in summer. ⑤ *Average main: NKr 255* ⊠ *Strandtorget 1* ☎ 77–60–07–20 ⊕ *www.skarven.no.*

# TRONDHEIM, NORWAY

One of Scandinavia's oldest cities, Trondheim was the first capital of Norway, from AD 997 to 1380. Founded in 997 by Viking king Olav Tryggvason, it was first named Nidaros (still the name of the cathedral), a composite word referring to the city's location at the mouth of the Nidelva River. Today, it's Central Norway's largest (and Norway's third-largest) city, with a population of 150,000. The wide streets of the historic city center remain lined with brightly painted wood houses and striking warehouses. But it's no historic relic: it's also the home to NTNU (Norwegian University of Science and Technology) and is Norway's technological capital.

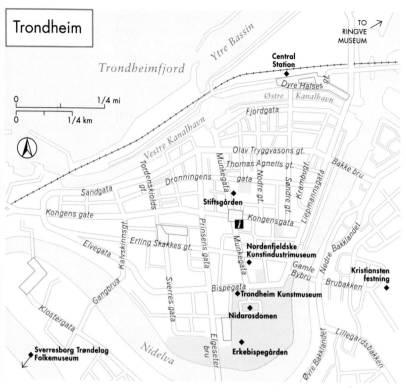

**COMING ASHORE**

Cruise ships dock at one of two piers. Both of these are within easy walking distance of the city center. There are no facilities at the piers, but you'll find everything you need—from banks to tourist offices—in the city.

## EXPLORING TRONDHEIM

Trondheim is home to some wonderful historical buildings and sites. Take in the cathedral where Norway's kings are blessed (they're no longer crowned), visit some of the oldest buildings in the country, and marvel at the country's largest entirely wooden palace. If that's not your thing, stop in at a museum, or just enjoy the relatively mild climate as you walk along Nidelva River, admiring the view.

**Erkebispegården** (*Archbishop's Palace*). Erkebispegården is the oldest secular building in Scandinavia, dating from around 1160. It was the residence of the archbishop until the Reformation in 1537. The Archbishop's Palace Museum has original sculptures from Nidaros Cathedral and archaeological pieces from throughout its history. Within Erkebispegården's inner palace is the Rustkammeret/Resistance Museum, which traces military development from Viking times to the present through displays of uniforms, swords, and daggers. The dramatic events of World War II get a special emphasis. ■**TIP**➔ **Opening times for the various museums and wings in the Erkebispegården and for the cathedral vary greatly by season.** ⊠ *Kongsgårdsgt. 1* ☎ *73-89-08-00* ⊕ *www. nidarosdomen.no* ⊠ *NKr 120 (includes entry to Nidaros Cathedral)* ⊙ *Hrs. vary greatly.*

**Kristiansten festning.** Built by J. C. Cicignon after the great fire of 1681, the Kristiansten Fort saved the city from conquest by Sweden in 1718. During World War II, the German occupying forces executed members of the Norwegian Resistance here; there's a plaque in their honor. The fort has spectacular views of the city, the fjord, and the mountains. ☎ *81–57–04–00* ⊕ *www.forsvarsbygg.no/festningene/Festningene/ Kristiansten-festning* ⊠ *Free* ⊙ *Grounds open daily 8 am–1 am.*

**Nidarosdomen** (*Nidaros Cathedral*). Trondheim's cathedral was built on the grave of King Olav, who formulated a Christian religious code for Norway in 1024. The town quickly became a pilgrimage site for Christians from all over Northern Europe, and Olav was canonized in 1164. Construction of Nidarosdomen began in 1070, but the oldest existing parts of the cathedral date from around 1150. It has been ravaged on several occasions by fire and rebuilt each time, generally in a Gothic style. Since the Middle Ages, Norway's kings have been crowned and blessed in the cathedral. The crown jewels are on display here. Forty-five-minute guided tours are offered in English from mid-June to mid-August. ⊠ *Kongsgårdsgt. 2* ☎ *73–89–08–00* ⊕ *www. nidarosdomen.no* ⊠ *NKr 120 with Erkebispegården, otherwise NKr 60* ⊙ *Hrs. vary greatly with seasons.*

★ **Nordenfjeldske Kunstindustrimuseum.** The Tiffany windows are magnificent at this museum of decorative arts, which houses an impressive collection of furniture, silver, and textiles. The Scandinavian Design section features a room interior designed by the Danish architect Finn Juhl in 1952. The 1690 bridal crown by Adrian Bogarth is also memorable. *Three Women–Three Artists* features tapestries by Hannah Ryggen and Synnøve Anker Aurdal, and glass creations by Benny Motzfeldt. ⊠ *Munkegt. 5* ☎ *73–80–89–50* ⊕ *www.nkim.no* ⊠ *NKr 80* ⊙ *June–late Aug., Mon.–Sat. 10–5, Sun. noon–5; late Aug.–May, Tues.–Sat. 10–3, Sun. noon–4.*

**Fodor'sChoice** **Stiftsgården.** Built in the 1770s, Stiftsgården is now the official royal residence in Trondheim; Princess Märtha Louise held her wedding reception here in 2002. The architecture and interior are late baroque and highly representative of 18th-century high society's taste. Tours offer insight into the festivities marking the coronations and blessings of the kings in the cathedral. ⊠ *Munkegt. 23* ☎ *73–84–28–80 guided tour information* ⊕ *www.nkim.no/stiftsgarden* ⊠ *NKr 80* ⊙ *June–mid-Aug., Mon.–Sat. 10–4, Sun. noon–4. Tours on the hr.*

Ⓒ **Sverresborg, Trøndelag Folkemuseum.** Near the ruins of King Sverre's medieval castle is this open-air historical museum that depicts everyday life in Trøndelag during the 18th and 19th centuries. The stave church here, built in the 1170s, is the northernmost preserved church of its type in Norway. In the Old Town you can visit a 1900s dentist's office and an old-fashioned grocery store that sells sweets. In the summer there are farm animals on-site, and a range of activities for children. ✉ *Sverresborg allé 13* ☎ *73–89–01–10* ⊕ *www.sverresborg.no* 🎫 *NKr 100 in summer; NKr 55 the rest of the year* ☉ *June–Aug., daily 11–6; Sept.–May, weekdays 11–3, weekends noon–4.*

**Trondheim Kunstmuseum** (*Trondheim Art Museum*). The town's art museum houses some 4,000 works of art, including many by regional artists. ✉ *Bispegt. 7B* ☎ *73–53–81–80* ⊕ *www.tkm.museum.no* 🎫 *NKr 60* ☉ *Tues and Thurs.–Sun. 11–3, Wed. 11–9.*

## SHOPPING

**Arne Ronning.** Sweaters by Dale of Norway and other designers are available here. ✉ *Nordregt. 10* ☎ *73–53–13–30* ⊕ *www.arneronning.no.*

**Gullsmed Møller.** Founded in 1770, this is Northern Europe's oldest goldsmith. It sells versions of the Trondheim Rose, the city symbol since the 1700s. ✉ *Munkegt. 3* ☎ *73–52–04–39* ⊕ *www.gullsmedmoller.no.*

**Jens Hoff Garn & Ide.** For knitted clothes and blankets, try this shop. ✉ *Sirkus Shopping, Solsiden* ☎ *90–26–31–40* ⊕ *www.jenshoff.no.*

**Norsk Flid.** Trondheim's branch of the popular handicraft store. ✉ *Olav Tryggvasongt. 18* ☎ *73–83–32–30* ⊕ *www.norskflid.no/trondheim.*

## ACTIVITIES

### CYCLING

**Trondheim Bysykkel.** Some 125 city bikes can be borrowed in the city center. Parked in easy-to-see stands at central locations, the distinctive red-and-white bikes come with shopping baskets. To rent a bicycle, you need to buy a subscription—ask at the tourist office for more information. ⊕ *www.bysykler.no/trondheim_bysykkel.asp.*

### HIKING AND WALKING

**Bymarka.** This wooded area on Trondheim's outskirts has a varied and well-developed network of trails—60 km (37 miles) of gravel paths, 80 km (50 miles) of ordinary paths, 250 km (155 miles) of ski tracks.

**Ladestien** (*Lade Trail*). This 8-km trail along the edge of Lade Peninsula has great views of Trondheimsfjord. It's a nice hike whatever your fitness level. ⊕ *www.trondheim.kommune.no/content/1094810105/Ladestien.*

**Nidelvstien Trail.** This trail runs along the river from Tempe to the Leirfossene waterfalls. ⊕ *www.trondheim.kommune.no/content.ap?thisId=1094810136.*

## WHERE TO EAT

Trondheim is known for the traditional dish *surlaks* (marinated salmon served with sour cream). A sweet specialty is *tekake* (tea cake), which looks like a thick-crust pizza topped with a lattice pattern of cinnamon and sugar.

8

**$$$**  ✕ **Havfruen.** The long-running "Mermaid" is Trondheim's foremost and
SEAFOOD   most stylish fish restaurant. Taking its cues from France, the restaurant
★   excels at bouillabaisse as well as many other fish dishes, which change
seasonally. The warm decor uses orange, greens, and reds accented by
wood. The wine list includes a wide range of whites, highlighting dry
French varieties. ⑤ *Average main: NKr 299* ✉ *Kjøpmannsgt. 7* ☎ *73–
87–40–70* ⊕ *www.havfruen.no* ☾ *Closed Sun. No lunch.*

**$$**  ✕ **Vertshuset Tavern.** Housed in what was once a 1739 tavern in down-
NORWEGIAN   town Trondheim, this restaurant is now part of the Sverresborg folk
museum. The traditional menu includes homemade fish cakes and
meatballs; *rømmegrøt* (sour-cream porridge); creamed fish soup and
*spekemat* (cured meat). On weekends, the restaurant opens at 2 pm.
⑤ *Average main: NKr 200* ✉ *Sverresborg allé 11* ☎ *73–87–80–70*
⊕ *www.tavern.no* ☾ *No lunch weekdays.*

# Atlantic Islands

## PORTS IN THE CANARY ISLANDS, ICELAND, AND MADEIRA

**WORD OF MOUTH**

"As I started reading more about all the various islands (especially in the Canaries), it struck my mind that cruises might be more efficient at [letting you see] everything. I checked online, and sure enough, there are a ton of them."

—mistadobalina

Though not in the Mediterranean proper, a few islands in the Atlantic are commonly included on many so-called Mediterranean-cruise itineraries. The Canary Islands and Iceland are sometimes included on transatlantic crossings, but the Canary Islands or Madeira may also be included on longer western Mediterranean cruises, while Iceland is included in some summer Scandinavia cruises. All of these islands offer dramatically beautiful scenery, and although their respective influences are vastly different, they each offer something unique. All are popular summer vacation destinations for Europeans.

# FUNCHAL, MADEIRA

Updated by
Joanna Styles

Wine connoisseurs through the ages have savored Madeira's eponymous export, but a sip of this heady elixir provides only a taste of the island's many delights. The natural beauty of this island is like no other, from the cliffs that plummet seaward to mountain summits cloaked in silent fog. The magic has captivated travelers for centuries. Multiple microclimates, exotic topography and vegetation, and designated nature reserves create an amazing ecodestination. The Laurissilva Forest that occupies a lofty coastal strip above the sea has been classified as part of the Madeira Nature Reserve and a UNESCO World Natural Heritage site. The island is the only region in the world where ancient forest dating back before the Ice Age can be found. Flora and fauna in the four nature reserves are still being discovered to this day. With this awesome heritage, Madeira has the power to keep its core a sanctuary for centuries to come.

## ESSENTIALS

### CURRENCY
The euro. ATMs are common and credit cards are widely accepted.

### HOURS
Most shops are open weekdays from 9 to 1 and 3 to 7, Saturday from 9 to 1; malls and supermarkets often remain open until at least 10, and some stores are also open on Sunday. Most museums are closed Monday, and churches generally close for a couple of hours in the middle of the day.

### TOUR OPERATOR
Madeira Explorers run guided walks and tours around the island's most spectacular sights. Half- and full-day trips are available.

Contacts **Madeira Explorers.** ☎ 291/763701 ⊕ www.madeira-levada-walks.com.

### TELEPHONES
Most tri- and quad-band GSM phones will work in Madeira, and Portugal has a well-organized 3G-compatible mobile network, which extends to Madeira. You can buy prepaid phone cards at telecom shops, news vendors, and tobacconists in all towns and cities. Phone cards can be used for local or international calls. Major companies include Vodafone and Optimus.

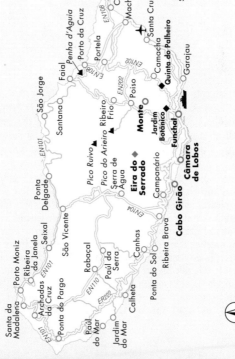

## COMING ASHORE

Funchal's cruise port is close to the town center, but ships dock away from the entrance. There may be a shuttle into Funchal; otherwise, there are cabs at the port entrance, or it is a pleasant half-mile walk. There are few tourist facilities at the port itself, though a few souvenir kiosks open when the boats are in dock.

Taxis are numerous, and the prices are government-controlled. There's a base of €2 (€2.60 on weekends), then €0.63 per km. Fares for public buses begin at €1.90 for your initial journey including the price of a rechargeable electronic Giro card, and €1.25 thereafter provided you have sufficient funds on the card. A full-day Giro card is €4.40, and this may be the most practical and easy solution if you intend to use public transport to get around. You'll need to pass this card over an electronic reader as you enter and leave the bus to register your fare.

Funchal is the center of a good network of bus routes to the major sights of the island, but check on the frequency and times of return to Funchal before you set out.

If you plan to spend your day ashore in Funchal, you should not rent a car; however, a vehicle would enable you to explore other areas of the island during your day. A manual economy vehicle is approximately €45 per day.

> ### MADEIRA BEST BETS
>
> **Take a trip down the toboggan run at Serra do Monte.** This unique and exhilarating experience is a must, but hold onto your hat!
>
> **View the *poios* (terraces).** An ancient method of growing crops in mountainous areas, terraces are rare in Europe, yet there are thousands here on Madeira.

## EXPLORING MADEIRA

### FUNCHAL

When colonists arrived in Madeira in July 1419, the valley they settled was a mass of bright yellow fennel (*funchal* in Portuguese). Today the bucolic fields are gone, and the community that replaced them is the self-governing island's bustling business and political center.

**Adegas de São Francisco.** The St. Francis Wine Lodge takes its original name from the convent that once stood on this site. Today the operation is owned by the island's famous winemaking Blandy family and is also known as the Old Blandy Wine Lodge. Here you can see how the wine and wine barrels are made, visit cellars where the wine is stored, and hear tales about Madeira wine. One legend has it that when the Duke of Clarence was sentenced to death in 1478 for plotting against his brother, King Edward IV, he was given his choice of execution methods. He decided to be drowned in a "vat of Malmsey," a barrel of the drink. There's plenty of time for tasting at the end of the visit and a shop for purchasing the wine. ⊠ *Av. Arriaga 28* ☎ *291/740110* ⊕ *www. madeirawinecompany.com* 🎟 *€5* ⊙ *Tours weekdays at 10:30, 2:30, 3:30, and 4:30, Sat. at 11. Wine shop weekdays 10–6:30, Sat. 10–1.*

**Antiga Alfândega.** The stately Old Customs House is home to Madeira's parliament (closed to the public). From here deputies govern the island, which is part of Portugal but enjoys greater autonomy than the mainland provinces. The building's original 16th-century Manueline style was given baroque touches during renovations that followed the devastating 18th-century earthquake that almost leveled faraway Lisbon. ⊠ *Av. do Mar and Av. das Comunidades Madeirenses* ☎ *291/210500.*

**Casa Museu Frederico de Freitas.** This delightful museum has been renovated in the style of a 19th-century quinta, inside the attractive 18th-century Casa Calçada. Inside you can find antique furniture, oriental carpets, and paintings collected by the 20th-century lawyer and veteran traveler, Dr. Frederico de Freitas. Don't miss the adjacent Casa dos Azulejos, a museum dedicated to decorative tiles from Spain, Persia, Turkey, Holland, and Syria that date from medieval times to the nineteenth century as well as Portuguese tiles rescued from demolished buildings on the island. ⊠ *Calçada de Santa Clara 7* ☎ *291/202570* 🎟 *€2.50* ☼ *Tues.–Sat. 10–5:30.*

**Convento de Santa Clara.** Inside the working 17th-century Santa Clara Convent (ring for entry), the painted wood walls and the ceiling are lined with ceramic tiles, giving the sanctuary an Arabic look. There are two beautiful internal cloisters; one is filled with orange trees. The adjacent church contains the tomb of Zarco, the discoverer of Madeira. ⊠ *Calçada de Santa Clara 15* ☎ *291/742602* ☼ *Mon.–Sat. 10–noon and 3–5.*

**Fortaleza do Pico.** The Fort of the Peak was built in 1611 to protect the settlement against pirate attacks. It's a steep walk to get here, but worth the effort for the dazzling views of the city. The fortress has been in the possession of the navy since 1933, but you can view parts of the ramparts, and there's a small room that has prints of the building over the years on display. ⊠ *Calçada do Pico* ☎ *No phone* 🎟 *Free* ☼ *Daily 9–6.*

**Fortaleza de São Tiago.** This robust construction was started by 1614, if not earlier, when French corsairs began to threaten Funchal's coveted deepwater harbor. Thanks to continuous use—by British troops when their nation was allied with Portugal against Napoléon, and during the visit of the Portuguese king Dom Carlos in 1901—much of the military stronghold has been preserved. You can wander around the ramparts, which offer interesting views over the Old Town and sea below. A former governor's house inside it is now the **Museu de Arte Contemporânea,** which has changing exhibitions of works from the 1960s and later, most by local artists. ⊠ *Rua do Portão de São Tiago* ☎ *291/213340* 🎟 *€2.50 for exhibitions, free at other times* ☼ *Mon.–Sat. 10–12:30 and 2:30–5:30.*

**Fodor's**Choice **Jardim Botânico.** The Botanical Garden is on the grounds of an old ★ plantation 3 km (2 miles) northeast of Funchal. Its well-labeled plants—including anthuriums, bird-of-paradise flowers, and a large cactus collection—come from four continents. Savor wonderful views of Funchal, and check out the petrified trunk of a 10-million-year-old heather tree. There's also a natural-history museum, and a small exotic-birds garden. You can get here on Bus 29, 30, or 31, which stop across the street from the market in front of Madeira's Electric Company. You can also take another cable car from the top of the gardens to Monte (⊙ *Daily 9:30–6* ⊟*€8.25 single, €12.75 return*). ⊠ *Caminho do Meio* ☎ *291/211200* ⊕ *www.madeirabotanicalgarden. com* ⊟ *€3* ⊙ *Gardens daily 9–6.*

⟳ **Madeira Story Centre.** Fun for children, this museum is a great introduction to Madeira for first-time visitors. It's not high-tech, but a series of models, paintings, archive TV footage and multimedia displays explain the history and culture of the island, from the days of pirates to the flying boats that brought the first plane passengers to Funchal. There's a roof terrace with fine views over town, a souvenir shop, and daily activities for kids. ⊠ *Rua Dom Carlos I 27–29* ☎ *291/100770* ⊕ *www. storycentre.com* ⊟ *€10* ⊙ *Daily 10–6, shop until 7.*

Fodor'sChoice  **Mercado dos Lavradores** (*Farmers' Market*). In the center patio of the
★  Farmers' Market, women—sometimes in Madeira's native costume of a full, homespun skirt with yellow, red, and black vertical stripes and an embroidered white blouse—sell orchids, bird-of-paradise flowers (the emblem of Madeira), anthuriums, and other blooms. The lower-level seafood market displays the day's catch. Note the rows of fierce-looking espada. Their huge, bulging eyes are caused by the fatal change in pressure between their deepwater habitat and sea level. ⊠ *Largo dos Lavradores* ⊙ *Weekdays 7 am–8 pm, Sat. 7 am–2 pm.*

**Museu de Arte Sacra.** Funchal's Museum of Sacred Art has Flemish paintings, polychrome wood statues, and other treasures displayed in a former bishop's palace. Most of the priceless paintings were commissioned by the first merchants of Madeira, who traded sugar for Flemish art so they could decorate their private chapels. The *Adoration of the Magi* was painted in 1518 for a wealthy trader from Machico and was paid for not in gold, but in sugar. You can tell how important this commodity was to the island by examining Funchal's coat of arms: it depicts five loaves of sugar in the shape of a cross. ⊠ *Rua do Bispo 21* ☎ *291/228900* ⊕ *www.museuartesacrafunchal.org* ⊟ *€3* ⊙ *Tues.–Sun. 10–12:30 and 2:30–6, Sun. 10–1.*

⟳ **Museu Municipal.** Animals found on Madeira and in its seas—including a ferocious-looking collection of stuffed sharks—are on display in the city museum. Attached is a small aquarium, where you can watch the graceful movements of an octopus and view a family of sea turtles. ⊠ *Rua Mouraria 31* ☎ *291/229761* ⊟ *€3.60* ⊙ *Tues.–Fri. 10–6, weekends noon–6.*

**Museu da Quinta das Cruzes** (*Crosses Manor Museum*). Once the home of a Genoese wine-shipping family, the 17th-century building and grounds of this museum are as impressive as its collection of antique furniture. Of special interest are the palanquins—lounge chairs once used to carry the grand ladies of colonial Madeira around town. Don't miss the small garden filled with ancient stone columns, window frames, arches, and tombstone fragments rescued from buildings that have been demolished around the island. It also has an alluring café. ⊠ *Calçada do Pico 1* ☎ *291/740670* ⊟ *€2.50* ⊙ *Tues.–Sun. 10–12:30 and 2–5:30.*

**Palácio de São Lourenço.** Built in the 17th century as Madeira's first fortress, the St. Lawrence Palace is still used as a military headquarters. At certain times its grand rooms are open to visitors and you can see the grand Ballroom and other state rooms filled with sumptuous works of art and antique furniture. ⊠ *Entrance on Av. Zarco* ☎ *291/202530* ⊡ *Free* ⊗ *Wed. 10 am, Fri. 3 pm, Sat. 11 am.*

**Parque Santa Catarina.** Abloom with flowers all year-round, St. Catarina Park covers an area of around 43,000 square yards with fantastic views over Funchal and its bay up to the Ponta do Garajau. In the center of the park rests the tiny **Capela de Santa Catarina** (St. Catherine's Chapel), built by Madeira's discoverer João Gonçalves Zarco in 1425. It's one of the island's oldest buildings. Just above the park is a pink mansion called **Quinta Vigia,** the residence of the president of Madeira—it's closed to the public but you can visit its eighteenth-century chapel, lined with beautiful tiles. ⊠ *Between Av. do Infante and Av. Sá Carneiro, overlooking the harbor.*

**Quinta do Palheiro.** Also known as the Blandy Gardens, this 30-acre estate 5 km (3 miles) northeast of Funchal is owned by the Blandy wine family. The formal gardens have flowering perennials. You can stroll the gardens and the grounds, where camellia trees bloom between December and April, but you can't tour the family's house. To get here, head out of town on N101, the road to the airport. At the fork make a left onto N102 and follow the signs toward Camacha. Also, bus 36A departs weekday mornings at 9:45 from in front of the Palácio de São Lourenço, on Avenida das Comunidades Madeirenses (next to the marina). It returns at 12:35. ⊠ *Caminho Quinta do Palheiro 32* ☎ *291/793 044* ⊕ *www.palheiroestate.com* ⊡ *€10.50* ⊗ *Weekdays 9:30–4:30 pm.*

**Sé.** Renowned for its ceiling with intricate geometric designs of inlaid ivory, Funchal's cathedral dates from 1514 and reveals an Arabic influence throughout. Don't miss the carved, gilded choir stalls in the side entrance and in the chancel (they depict the prophets and the apostles), or the intricate tile work at the side entrance and in the belfry. ⊠ *Largo da Sé* ☎ *No phone* ⊗ *Daily 8–6.*

**Fodor's**Choice ★ **Teleférico da Madeira.** The sleek, Austrian-engineered cable-car service has more than 40 cars that travel from Funchal's Old Town waterfront up to Monte at 1,804 feet above sea level. The trip takes 15 minutes one way, and there are great views to enjoy as you float silently up and over the city. ⊠ *Caminho das Barbosas 8* ☎ *291/780280* ⊕ *www. madeiracablecar.com* ⊡ *€10 one-way, €15 round-trip* ⊗ *Daily 9:30–6 (last round-trip 5:30, last uphill trip 5:45).*

## MONTE

*6 km (4 miles) northeast of Funchal.*

**Madeira Cable Car.** The most enjoyable approach to Monte is on the cable car that departs from Funchal's Old Town. A second cable car departs from Monte down to the Jardim Botânico ⊠ *Caminho das Barbosas 8* ☎ *291/780280* ⊕ *www.madeiracablecar.com* ⊡ *€10 one-way, €15 round-trip* ⊗ *Daily 9:30–6 (last round-trip 5:30, last uphill trip 5:45).*

★ **Tábuas de Madeira.** The village of Monte is home to one of Madeira's oddest attractions: *tábuas de Madeira* or *carrinhos do Monte* (the snowless sled ride). The sleds were first created to carry supplies from Monte to Funchal; later, passenger sleighs hauled as many as 10 people at a time and required six drivers. Nowadays the rides are just for fun, and no one in Madeira should miss this experience that will take 10 years off your life and stay with you forever. Dressed in white and wearing goatskin boots with soles made of rubber tires, drivers line up on the street below the Nossa Senhora do Monte church. The sleds, which have cushioned seats, look like big wicker baskets; their wooden runners are greased with lard. Two drivers run alongside the sled, controlling it with ropes as it races downhill on a 10-minute trip nearly back to Funchal (you will have to walk about 1 km (½ mile) to reach Funchal or take one of the many taxis that line up at the end of the ride). If the sled starts going too fast, the drivers jump on the back to slow it down. ✉ *Serra do Monte* 📞 *€20 for 1 person, €25 for 2, €37.50 for 3 people* ⊙ *Mon.–Sat. 9–6, Sun. 9–1.*

## CÂMARA DE LOBOS

*20 km (12 miles) west of Funchal.*

On coastal route N101 you'll pass many banana plantations on the way to Câmara de Lobos—a fishing village made famous by Winston Churchill, who came here (in a borrowed Rolls-Royce equipped with a bar) to paint pictures of the multicolored boats and the fishermen's tiny homes. A plaque marks the spot where he set up his easel. The promenade that protrudes from the main plaza offers magnificent views west to Cabo Girão.

## CABO GIRÃO

*16 km (10 miles) west of Câmara de Lobos.*

At 1,900 feet, Cabo Girão is on one of the highest sea cliffs in the world. Totally uninhabited, it offers unimpeded views of ribbons of terraces carved out of even the steepest slopes and farmers daringly cultivating grapes or garden vegetables. Through centuries, thousands upon thousands of *poios* (terraces) have been built in Madeira.

## EIRA DO SERRADO

*16 km (10 miles) northwest of Funchal.*

The *miradouro* (viewpoint) at Eira do Serrado overlooks the Grande Curral—the crater of a long-extinct volcano in the center of the island, sometimes referred to as Madeira's belly button. From here Pico Ruivo and the craggy central summits look like a granite city.

## SHOPPING

Madeira has many thriving forms of handicraft, including lots of basketwork and rattan furniture. Embroidery was introduced to the island at the start of the 20th century. Tropical flowers are perfectly packaged for onward transportation. (It's legal to bring flowers into the United States from Madeira as long as they're inspected at the U.S. airport upon arrival.)

Fortified Madeira wine served as an aperitif or with dessert, depending on its sweetness, is the island's most famous product. The four varieties, from driest to sweetest, are Sercial, Verdelho, Boal, and Malmsey. Unlike other wines, Madeira is heated to produce its distinctive mellow flavor—a process that supposedly developed after thirsty sailors sampled the Madeira that had been shipped through equatorial heat and discovered its improved taste.

**Bordal.** This store specializes in traditional Madeiran embroidery and produces beautifully handcrafted linen, pillowcases, table cloths, towels, and baby clothes. ⊠ *Rua Doutor Fernão Ornelas 77* ☎ *291/222965* ⊕ *www.bordal.pt* ⊙ *Weekdays 9–1 and 2–7, Sat. 9:30–1.*

**Casa do Turista.** This store sells museum-quality Madeiran crafts of all types. Prices are reasonable, if not the cheapest in town. ⊠ *José S. Ribeiro 2, on corner with seafront* ☎ *291/224907.*

**Madeira Wine Company.** This company sells an exhaustive selection of the local tipple, covering virtually every vintage produced on the island for the past 35-odd years. ⊠ *Av. Arriaga 28* ☎ *291/740100* ⊕ *www. madeirawinecompany.com.*

## WHERE TO EAT

$ ✕ **Gavião Novo.** It's best to make reservations or to arrive early to bag a
PORTUGUESE table at this cozy, traditional restaurant in the heart of the Old Town. The family-run restaurant offers simple local food such as grilled limpets, tuna with fried cornmeal, fish stews, and delicious kebabs. ⊠ *Rua de Santa Maria 131* ☎ *291/229238.*

$ ✕ **Golden Gate Grand Café.** Just across from the tourist office in the heart
CAFÉ of Funchal, this restaurant-café has been open for business off and on since 1814. Sit in the airy interior, capture one of the tables that flank the sidewalk, or—even better—bag a seat on the balcony. You can pop in for coffee, light local dishes, or British-style afternoon tea, or you can settle in for a feast of creative Portuguese and international dishes. Don't miss the delicious desserts such as *sorvete de banana e maracujá* (banana and passion-fruit sorbet). ⊠ *Av. Arriaga 29* ☎ *291/234383.*

# GRAN CANARIA, CANARY ISLANDS (LAS PALMAS)

Updated by
Joanna Styles

The circular island of Gran Canaria has three distinct identities. Its capital, Las Palmas, population 382,000, is a thriving business center and shipping port; the white-sand beaches of the south coast are tourist magnets; the interior is rural. Las Palmas, the largest city in the Canary Islands, is for the most part a dirty port city, overrun by sailors, tourists, traffic jams, diesel-spewing buses, and hordes of shoppers. One side of the city is lined with docks for huge container ships, while the other oddly harbors Europe's famous 7-km (4½-mile) Canteras beach. A quaint historic quarter redeems the city's mismatched commercial buildings. The south coast, a boxy 1960s development along wide avenues, is a family resort. At the southern tip of the island, the popular Playa del Inglés gives way to the empty dunes of Maspalomas, the most spectacular sight of the island. The isle's more pristine interior is a steep highland that reaches 6,435 feet at Pozo de las Nieves. Although it's green in winter, Gran Canaria does not have the luxurious tropical foliage of the archipelago's western islands.

## ESSENTIALS

### CURRENCY

The euro. ATMs are common and credit cards are widely accepted.

### HOURS

Shops are generally open Monday to Saturday from 9 to 1 and again from 4 to 8 or 9. Most places close for siesta, but some resort shops may stay open throughout the day and may also be open on Sunday. Museums are usually open from 10 until noon, but have varied afternoon opening hours.

### TELEPHONES

Most tri- and quad-band GSM phones will work in the Canary Islands, where mobile services are 3G-compatible. Public kiosks accept phone cards that support international calls (cards sold in press shops, bars, and telecom shops).

## COMING ASHORE

Ships dock at the busy Santa Catalina terminal in the Las Palmas port. There are toilets, ATMs, bus stops, and a taxi stand at the terminal itself, while the huge El Muelle shopping center beckons directly across from the port gates. The terminal is a 10-minute walk from the north end of the city center. The southern end, where most sights are located, is a mile on foot (about 5 minutes by taxi).

Because Gran Canaria is quite large—1,560 sq km (602 sq miles)—renting a car will not get you to all of the island's far corners during your short stay; however, a car will surely aid in island exploration. (We recommend that you go no farther than Maspalomas.) An economy manual vehicle costs approximately €30 to €40 per day. There are numerous car-rental offices in Las Palmas, but the easiest option is to prebook a car online using Cicar (⊕ *www.cicar.com*), though Gran Canaria has several other rental agencies. Taxis also wait outside the terminal building, and they can be contracted for tourist itineraries, at €0.51 per km (½ mile), with waiting rate of €12.75 per hour. They can also be negotiated off the meter for around €25 per hour.

---

## GRAN CANARIA BEST BETS

■ **Casa de Colón**. Gran Canaria was supposedly the last landfall for Christopher Columbus before his arrival in the New World; the museum contains various artifacts of early transatlantic voyages.

■ **Dunas de Maspalomas**. Trek down south to witness the grand reminder that the Canaries share their latitude with the Sahara.

■ **La Vegueta and Triana**. Stroll the historic quarters of Las Palmas.

## EXPLORING GRAN CANARIA

### LAS PALMAS

Las Palmas is a long, sprawling city, strung out for 10 km (6 miles) along two waterfronts of a peninsula. Though most of the action centers on the peninsula's northern end along the lovely Las Canteras beach, the sights are clustered around the city's southern edge. Begin in the old quarter, La Vegueta, at the **Plaza Santa Ana** (don't miss the bronze dog statues), for a tour of interesting colonial architecture. Then make your way into the neighboring quarter of Triana, a treasure trove of small shops and cafés and restaurants. It's quite a walk from one end of town to the other, so at any point you may want to hop one of the many canary-yellow buses. Buses 1, 2 and 3 run the length of the city.

**Casa Museo Colón** (*Columbus Museum*). The Casa Museo Colón is in a palace where Christopher Columbus may have stayed when he stopped to repair the *Pinta*'s rudder. Nautical instruments, copies of early navigational maps, and models of Columbus's three ships are on display in the palace, which retains many original features. Two rooms hold pre-Columbian artifacts, and one floor is dedicated to paintings from the 16th to the 19th century. There's a focus on self-portraits. ⊠ *Colón 1, Vegueta* ☎ *928/311255* ☞ *Free* ☉ *Weekdays 9–7, Sat. 9–6, Sun. 9–3.*

**Catedral Santa Ana.** St. Anne's Cathedral took four centuries to complete, so the neoclassical Roman columns of the 19th-century exterior contrast sharply with the Gothic ceiling vaulting of the interior. Baroque statues are displayed in the cathedral's **Museo de Arte Sacro** (Museum of Religious Art), arranged around a peaceful cloister. Ask the curator to open the *sala capitular* (chapter house) to see the 16th-century Valencian tile floor. Be sure to check out the black stone dog sculptures outside the cathedral's main entrance—these are four examples of the Gran Canaria hounds that gave the island its name. ⊠ *Espíritu Santo 20, facing Plaza Santa Ana, Vegueta* ☎ *928/314989* ☞ *€3* ☉ *Weekdays 10–4:30, Sat. 10–1:30.*

**Centro Atlántico de Arte Moderno** (*Atlantic Center for Modern Art*). The Centro Atlántico de Arte Moderno has earned a name for curating some of the best avant-garde shows in Spain, with a year-round calendar of exhibitions. The excellent permanent collection includes Canarian art from the 1930s and 1940s and works by the well-known Lanzarote artist César Manrique. The center also has a fine collection of contemporary African art. ⊠ *Los Balcones 11, Vegueta* ☎ *928/311800* ⊕ *www. caam.net* ☞ *Free* ☉ *Tues.–Sat. 10–9, Sun. 10–2.*

**Ermita de San Telmo.** Destroyed by Dutch attackers in 1599, this chapel was rebuilt in the 17th century. Inside is a fine baroque altarpiece with rich gold leaf and wooden details. ⊠ *Plaza de San Telmo, Triana.*

**Parque Santa Catalina.** Ride a *guagua* (bus) to Parque Santa Catalina, or get off at the neighboring Parque Doramas (stops are listed on big yellow signs; the 2, 3, and 30 generally cover the entire city), to peek at the elegant Santa Catalina Hotel. Next to the Parque Doramas is the **Pueblo Canario,** a model village with typical Canarian architecture. ⊠ *Las Palmas.*

9

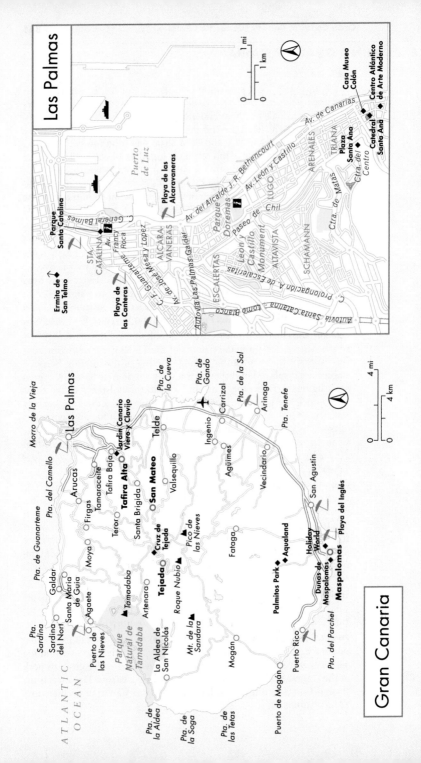

## MASPALOMAS AND THE SOUTHERN COAST

*60 km (36 miles) southwest of Las Palmas.*

One of the first places in Spain to welcome international tourists (starting in 1962), Maspalomas remains a beach resort with all the trappings. It's somewhat incongruously backed by empty sand dunes that resemble the Sahara—despite beachfront overdevelopment in the town, it retains appealing stretches of isolated beach on the outskirts, as well as a bird sanctuary. Much of the area around the dunes is a protected nature reserve.

**Aqualand Maspalomas.** The largest water park in the Canary Islands has wave pools, slides, and just about everything else splash-related. ⊠ *Ctra. Palmitos Park, Km 3* ☎ *928/140525* ⊕ *www.aqualand.es* 🎫 *€25* ☉ *July–Aug., daily 10–6; Sept.–June, daily 10–5.*

**Holiday World.** This amusement park has bumper cars and other carnival rides, including a Ferris wheel visible from miles away. ⊠ *Av. Touroperator Tui 18* ☎ *928/730498* ⊕ *www.holidayworld-maspalomas.com* 🎫 *Admission free; rides vary; unlimited rides €30* ☉ *Apr.–Sept., daily 6 pm–midnight; Oct.–March, Sun.–Thurs. 5 pm–11 pm, Fri.–Sat. 5 pm–midnight.*

**Palmitos Park.** One of the main attractions in this part of the island, this part–botanical garden and part-zoo has 1,500 tropical birds, a butterfly sanctuary, an orchid house, 160 species of tropical fish, many crocodiles, and parrot shows. ⊠ *Ctra. Palmitos, 6 km, inland from Maspalomas* ☎ *928/797070* ⊕ *www.palmitospark.es* 🎫 *€28.50* ☉ *Daily 10–6.*

## TEJEDA

*About 34 km (21 miles) southwest of Las Palmas, on the rustic 811 local road.*

At the village of Tejeda, the road begins to ascend through a pine forest dotted with picnic spots to the **Parador Cruz de Tejeda.** From the parador, continue uphill about 21 km (13 miles) to the **Mirador Pico de las Nieves,** the highest lookout on Gran Canaria. Here, too, is the **Pozo de la Nieve,** a well built by clergymen in 1699 to store snow.

## SAN MATEO

*17 km (11 miles) southwest of Las Palmas, en route to Tejeda.*

From Tejeda, the road winds down to San Mateo, whose local cheese is famous throughout the island. You can find it at the weekend market. Pass **Santa Brigida** and turn right toward the golf club on the rim of the Bandama crater. Continue to the village of Atalaya, where there are cave houses and pottery workshops.

## TAFIRA ALTA

*7 km (4½ miles) southwest of Las Palmas.*

Along the main road leading into Las Palmas from San Mateo is Tafira Alta, an exclusive suburb where many of the city's wealthiest families live.

**Jardín Canario Viero y Clavijo.** In Tafira Alta (just north of Las Palmas) is one of Spain's largest botanical gardens, with plants from all the islands grouped in their natural habitats. ⊠ *Ctra. de Centro, Km 7* ☎ *928/219580* ⊕ *www.jardincanario.org* ☉ *Daily 8–6:30.*

# BEACHES

The beaches along Gran Canaria's eastern and southern coasts are the island's major attractions.

### LAS PALMAS

**Las Canteras.** One of the best urban beaches in Spain is found at the northwest end of the city. Its perfect yellow sands are flanked by a pleasant promenade, which goes for just over 3 km (nearly 2 miles), from the Alfredo Kraus Auditorium, in the south, where surfers congregate, to the Playa del Confital, in the north. The beach is protected by a natural volcanic reef, La Barra, which runs parallel to most of the beach and makes for safe swimming. Lounge chairs and sunshades can be rented year-round. This is a very popular beach that can be extremely crowded in summer. **Amenities:** food and drink; lifeguards; showers; toilets; water sports. **Best for:** sunset; surfing (at southern end); swimming; walking. ⊠ *Las Canteras.*

### MASPALOMAS AND THE SOUTHERN COAST

All of these beaches abut one another, and you can walk them in sequence (hindered only by a pair of rocky dividers) along the shore. A boardwalk links Playa de Tarajalillo to the rest of the beaches until the dunes separate the boardwalk from the Maspalomas beach and Playa de la Mujer.

Fodor's Choice ★ **Maspalomas.** The island's most emblematic beach and one of the most beautiful, Maspaloma has golden sand that stretches for 2.7 km (1.7 miles) along the southern tip of Gran Canaria. Behind this beach are the famous Maspalomas dunes as well as palm groves and a saltwater lagoon, which lend an air of isolation and refuge to the beach. Bathing is safe everywhere except at La Punta de Maspalomas, where currents converge. Topless bathing is acceptable and there's a nudist area at La Cañada de la Penca. This beach is busy year-round. **Amenities:** food and drink; lifeguards; showers; toilets. **Best for:** nudists; sunrise; sunset; swimming; walking. ⊠ *Maspalomas.*

**Playa de Tarajalillo.** To the east of San Agustín, this black-sand and gravel beach is quieter than many of the others in the area. It's a popular spot with fishermen and windsurfers. The almost permanent strong breeze and waves mean bathers should be careful. **Amenities:** none. **Best for:** solitude; sunrise; windsurfing. ⊠ *San Agustín.*

**Playa de San Agustín.** To the east of Maspalomas, this smaller beach consists of golden sands and some rocks. The promenade has lush vegetation nearby, making it one of the most picturesque on the island. This is a quieter beach than Maspalomas and Playa del Inglés. Bathing is safe in calm conditions, but watch out for strong currents when the waves get up. Lounge chairs and sunshades line the beach. **Amenities:** food and drink; lifeguards; showers; toilets; water sports. **Best for:** sunrise; walking. ⊠ *San Agustín.*

**Playa de las Burras.** Sandwiched between Playa del Inglés and Playa de San Agustín, this little sandy beach is protected by a breakwall, making it a favorite with families. Small fishing boats are moored in the bay and the seafront promenade connects the neighboring resorts. Swimming's safe. There are plenty of lounge chairs and sunshades. **Amenities:** food and drink; lifeguards; showers; toilets. **Best for:** sunrise; swimming. ✉ *San Agustín.*

★ **Playa del Inglés.** Rivaling Maspalomas for popularity, Playa del Inglés has a lot going, including partying at the beach bars, sports, competitions, and concerts. There's nearly 3 km (1.9 miles) of golden sands, flanked by a pleasant seafront promenade that's great for early morning and evening strolls. Swimming is generally safe, although windy conditions can create waves—it's a favorite spot with surfers. Lounge chairs and sunshades are available along the beach, and there's also a nudist area, which is signposted. **Amenities:** food and drink; lifeguards; showers; toilets; water sports. **Best for:** partiers, nudists, sunrise; swimming; walking; windsurfing. ✉ *Playa del Inglés.*

**Playa de las Mujeres.** "The Women's Beach" is around the corner from the Maspalomas lighthouse in Meloneras. Consisting of gray shingles and small rocks, this quiet beach currently has no amenities, although the expansion of Meloneras, along with the construction of several high-end hotels, may change that in the future. Swimming is generally safe. **Amenities:** none. **Best for:** solitude; sunset. ✉ *Urb Meloneras, Maspalomas.*

## BOATING AND SAILING

**Escuela de Vela de Puerto Rico sailing school.** Some of Spain's best sailors have trained and taught here. It's about 13 km (8 miles) west of Maspalomas. ✉ *Playa de Puerto Rico, Puerto Rico* ☎ *928/291567.*

**Multiacuatic.** Two-hour whale- and dolphin-watching trips leave from Puerto Rico, about 13 km (8 miles) west of Maspalomas. ✉ *Muelle Puerto Base, Puerto Rico* ☎ *928/153747* ⊕ *www.dolphinwhales.es* 🖃 *€25* 🕑 *Departures Mon.–Sat. at 10:30 and 1.*

## GOLF

**Lopesan Meloneras Golf.** Half of the 18 holes at this par-71 course face the mountains, and the other half face the sea. Several are practically on the beach. ✉ *Autopista GC 500, s/n, Meloneras* ☎ *928/145309* ⊕ *www.lopesan.com.*

**Maspalomas Golf.** Surrounded by the famous Maspalomas dunes, this 18-hole, par-73 course has ocean views from many of its long, wide greens. The course was designed by Mackenzie Ross. ✉ *Av. T.O. Neckerman s/n, Maspalomas* ☎ *928/762581* ⊕ *www.maspalomasgolf.net.*

**Oasis Golf.** Just ten minutes outside Las Palmas, this 18-hole, par-54 course, designed by Blake Stirling, is one of the best places to play on the island; some golfers think it's one of the best courses in the world. It's the only course on the island that allows night play. ✉ *Autopista del Sur, km 6.4, Telde* ☎ *928/684890.*

## WINDSURFING

**Club Mistral.** Rent windsurfing gear, kayaks, and boogie boards from Club Mistral. Classes are also available. ✉ *Playa del Tarajalillo, Ctra. del Sur, Km 44, Maspalomas* ☎ *928/157158* ⊕ *www.club-mistral.com.*

# SHOPPING

Las Palmas has easily the best shopping on the islands. The main commercial areas are located around Calle Mesa y López (south of the port) and Triana in the old quarter. Here you'll find all the major international and Spanish fashion stores, duty-free stores, and shops selling local crafts, hats and clothes, Russian caviar, tackle for fishing and catching crabs, and lots more.

**Centro Comercial El Muelle.** This modern shopping mall opposite the Santa Catalina Park has stores selling all the major Spanish fashion brands, several sports shops, and a movie theater. ⊠ *Muelle de Santa Catalina s/n, Las Canteras, Las Palmas* 🕾 *928/327527* ⊕ *www.ccelmuelle.es* 🕙 *Mon.–Sat. 10 am–10 pm.*

**El Corte Inglés.** If you want to one-stop-shop for souvenirs, try the department store El Corte Inglés, in Las Canteras. ⊠ *Mesa y Lopez 18, Las Canteras, Las Palmas* 🕾 *928/263600* ⊕ *www.elcorteingles.es* 🕙 *Mon.–Sat., 9:30–9:30.*

**FEDAC.** As the official artisan shop, FEDAC carries a selection of genuine Gran Canaria crafts and handiwork. ⊠ *Domingo J. Navarro, Triana, Las Palmas* 🕾 *928/369661* 🕙 *Weekdays 9:30–1:30 and 4:30–8.*

**La Despensa del Sur.** Canary cheese, wine, and mojo are all available at this store; the adjoining restaurant serves traditional fare and snacks. ⊠ *Cano 33, Triana, Las Palmas* 🕾 *928/360195* ⊕ *www.ladespensadelsur.com* 🕙 *Weekdays 9–9, Sat. 10–4.*

# WHERE TO EAT

**$$**
SPANISH
★

✕ **Casa Montesdeoca.** The hallways of this 14th-century mansion in the historic quarter are stone labyrinths. During the Inquisition, the Jewish Montesdeoca family escaped from their pursuers through hidden doors and secret tunnels. Today the mansion only conceals a romantic restaurant with an outdoor patio draped with bougainvillea. Fresh fish—including *cherne* (sea bass) and *rape* (monkfish)—is prepared on an outdoor grill steps from your table. The wine list has the best bottles from each island. 💲 *Average main: €16* ⊠ *Montesdeoca 10, Vegueta, Las Palmas* 🕾🕾 *928/333466* 🕙 *Closed Sun. and Aug.*

**$**
INTERNATIONAL

✕ **Te lo dije Pérez.** Just below the cathedral square is one of the island's best bars for having a beer—there's a huge selection—along with some tapas. The bar feels a bit like a French café, with high ceilings and black and red furnishings. Some unusual tapas plates include nachos with eggplant and ginger sauce and a genuine German sausage as well as spinach and walnut croquettes. There are inside and outside tables, but you may have to stand at this very busy venue. 💲 *Average main: €8* ⊠ *Obispo Codina 6, Vegueta, Las Palmas* 🕾🕾 *928/249087* ⊕ *www.telodijeperez.com* 🕙 *Closed Sun.*

# LANZAROTE, CANARY ISLANDS

The most easterly Canary, Lanzarote, is right out of a science-fiction film, with solidified lava and dark, disconcerting dunes in its interior. The entire island has been declared a UNESCO Biosphere Reserve with its unique moonlike landscapes. It was named for the Italian explorer Lancelotto Alocello. The founder of modern-day Lanzarote, however, was artist and architect César Manrique, the unofficial artistic guru of the Canary Islands. He designed most of the esoteric tourist attractions and gave the island its distinctive low-rise whitewashed buildings. Overall, Lanzarote has avoided the high-rise destruction that mars its western counterparts, though an abundance of budget resorts on the east side of the island are less than attractive. Outside of the port and touristy beaches, Lanzarote's austere and barren land-scape is strangely breathtaking, with the greatest scenery within Parque Nacional Timafaya.

## ESSENTIALS

### CURRENCY
The euro. ATMs are common and credit cards are widely accepted.

### HOURS
Shops are generally open Monday through Saturday from 9 to 1 and again from 4 until 8 or 9. Most places close for siesta, but some resort shops may stay open throughout the day and also stay open on Sunday. Museums are usually open from 10 until noon, but have varied afternoon opening hours.

### TELEPHONES
Most tri- and quad-band GSM phones will work in the Canary Islands, where mobile services are 3G-compatible. Public kiosks accept phone cards that support international calls (cards sold in press shops, bars, and telecom shops).

## COMING ASHORE
Cruise ships dock at Puerto Mármoles, about 3 km (2 miles) west of the capital. A walkway goes along the shoreline from the port to the center of town. Although it takes you away from the busy main road, it's a long and not very attractive walk, so it's best to take either a shuttle bus or a taxi from just outside the cruise terminal into Arre-cife proper.

**Lanzarote Vision Tour Bus.** Take in the whole island via these distinc-tive tours on yellow hop-on, hop-off buses. The Green Route visits the north of the island, including Costa Teguise, Arrecife, the Fun-dación César Manrique, and the Cueva de los Verdes; the Red Route heads south, to Playa Blanca, Puerto del Carmen, two bodegas, and the Parque Nacional de Timanfaya. Tickets, which are valid for a single day, can be bought online, at official Lanzarote Vision sales points throughout the island, and through hotels and travel agencies. ⊠ *Av. de las Playas, Puerto del Carmen* ☎ *928/511089* ⊕ *www.lanzarotevision. es* ☒ *€19.50.*

9

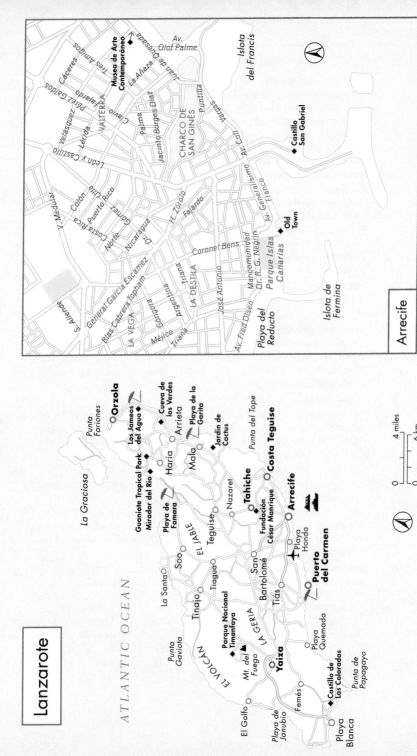

# Lanzarote

ATLANTIC OCEAN

La Graciosa

Punta Fariones

**Orzola**

Punta Gaviota

**Guinate Tropical Park**
**Mirador del Río**

**Los Jameos
del Agua**

**Cueva de
los Verdes**

Playa de Famara

Haria

Arrieta

**Playa de la
Garita**

Mala

**Jardín de
Cactus**

EL JABLE

Teguise

Nazaret

**Tahiche**

**Costa Teguise**

Punta del Tope

La Santa

Soo

Tiagua

Tinajo

San
Bartolomé

**Fundación
César Manrique**

**Arrecife**

**Parque Nacional
Timanfaya**

EL VOLCAN

Tías

LA GERIA

Playa Honda

**Puerto
del Carmen**

**Mt. del
Fuego**

El Golfo

Playa de
Janubio

**Yaiza**

Playa
Quemada

Femés

**Castillo de
Las Coloradas**

Punta de
Papagayo

Playa
Blanca

0 —— 4 miles
0 —— 6 km

## Arrecife

V. Medular

S. Alfonso

Cáceres

Tres Amigos

Perez Galdós

Clavio Iepanda

VAITERRA

**Museo de Arte
Contemporáneo**

Av.
Otof Palme

Velásquez

Lérida

Palma

Av. La Añaza

Islota
del Francis

León y Castillo

Colón

Gómez Rica
Puerto Rico

Quita Rico

Costa Rica

Jacinto Borges Díaz

Norte

Nicaragua

CHARCO DE
SAN GINÉS

Puntilla

Vargas

Av. Coll

**Castillo
San Gabriel**

General García Escámez

Blas Cabrera Topham

Góngora

LA VEGA

Argentina

Triana

LA DESTILA

H. Zerolo

Fajardo

Coronel Bens

José Antonio

Mancomunidad
Dr. R. G. Negrín

Av. Generalísimo
Franco

**Old
Town**

Méjico

Triana

Av. Fred Olsen

Parque Islas
Canarias

Playa del
Reducto

Islota de
Fermina

## EXPLORING LANZAROTE

### ARRECIFE

Although Arrecife has fully 50,000 of the 130,000 people that live on Lanzarote, this small city remains a place where life moves at a more sedate pace than it does in bustling Santa Cruz or Las Palmas. The coastline here is strung with line after line of rocky reefs (in fact, "reef" is what *arrecife* means in Spanish). A stroll around the back streets near the lagoon gives you an idea of the old Arrecife. The local Playa del Reducto is a good place to get in some beach time if you're spending the day here.

**Castillo San Gabriel.** The Castillo San Gabriel is a double-wall fortress once used to keep pirates at bay. A museum, due to open in 2013, will cover important events in the city's past. ⊠ *Arrecife.*

**Museo de Arte Contemporáneo** (*Museum of Contemporary Art*). The old, waterfront fortress **Castillo San José** was turned into this stunning museum by the architect César Manrique. One of his paintings is on display, along with other modern Spanish works. ⊠ *Av. de Naos s/n* ☎ *928/812321* ⊡ *Free* ☉ *Daily 11–9.*

**Old Town.** Arrecife isn't the most attractive part of Lanzarote, but the Old Town is interesting, particularly the area around the Charco de San Ginés (lagoon). The **tourist office,** housed in the original bandstand in the municipal park, has detailed maps and information about local points of interest. ⊠ *Parque Municipal* ☎ *928/816174* ☉ *Office open Weekdays 10–7; Sat., 10–1.*

### COSTA TEGUISE

*7 km (4½ miles) northeast of Arrecife.*

Costa Teguise is a green-and-white complex of apartments and several large hotels. It's a typical '80s resort and past its heyday, although it still draws thousands of visitors every year. King Juan Carlos owns a villa here, near the Meliá Salinas hotel.

**9**

☾ **Guinate Tropical Park.** In the northern part of the island, Guinate Tropical Park has 1,300 species of exotic birds and animals, and amazing views of La Graciosa Island and the ocean. ⊠ *Costa Teguise* ☎ *928/835500* ⊕ *www.guinatepark.com* ⊡ *€14* ☉ *Daily 10–5.*

**Jardín de Cactus** (*Cactus Garden*). The Jardín de Cactus, north of Costa Teguise between Guatiza and Mala, was César Manrique's last creation for Lanzarote. The giant metal cactus that marks the entrance comes close to tacky, but the gardens artfully display nearly 10,000 cacti of more than 1,500 varieties from all over the world. ⊠ *Costa Teguise* ☎ *928/529397* ⊡ *€5* ☉ *Daily 10–5:45.*

★ **Los Jameos del Agua.** These water caverns, 15 km (9 miles) north of the Costa Teguise, were created when molten lava streamed through an underground tunnel and hissed into the sea. Look for the tiny albino crabs on the rocks in the underground lake—this species, which is blind, is found nowhere else in the world. There are bars and restaurants around the lake, and the **Casa de los Volcanes** is a good museum of volcanic science. Night visits are possible on Tuesdays and Saturdays. ⊠ *Costa Teguise* ☎ *928/848020* ⊡ *Days €8, nights €78* ☉ *Daily 10–6:30; night visits Tues. and Sat. 7 pm–midnight.*

**Cueva de los Verdes** (*Green Caves*). If the Jameos del Agua caverns weren't enough for you, then head to this cave, just across the highway. Guided walks take you through a 1-km (½-mile) section of underground volcanic passageway. It's one of the best tours on the island. ✉ *Costa Teguise* ☎ *928/848484* 🎫 *€8* ⊗ *June–Sept., daily 10–7; Oct.–May, daily 10–6.*

**Mirador del Río.** Designed by César Manrique, this lookout in the most northern point of the island lets you see the islet of **La Graciosa** from at altitude of 474 meters (1,550 feet). From the lookout you can also see smaller protected isles—Montaña Clara, Alegranza (the Canary closest to Europe), and Roque del Este. ✉ *Costa Teguise* 🎫 *€4.50* ⊗ *Daily 10–5:45.*

**LAZNAROTE BEST BETS**

**Parque Nacional Timanfaya.** The vast volcanic, otherworldly landscape will ambush your senses. The volcano-grilled barbecue lunch at Restaurante del Diablo is unforgettable.

**Cesar Manrique's Landmarks.** Lanzarote's architectural hero made his mark across the island, most notably at the Cactus Garden and Fundaion Cesar Manrique.

**Teguise.** Wander the street of Lanzarote's charming former capital, circa 1852.

**Orzola.** The little fishing village of Orzola is 9 km (5½ miles) north of Jameo del Agua. Small boat excursions leave here each day for the neighboring islet of La Graciosa, where there are fewer than 500 residents and plenty of quiet beaches. ✉ *Costa Teguise.*

## PUERTO DEL CARMEN

*11 km (7 miles) southwest of Arrecife.*

Most beach-bound travelers to Lanzarote head to the sandy strands of the Puerto del Carmen area, the island's busiest resort. The small fishing port and marina are surrounded by numerous cafés and restaurants, with the main commercial center behind them. Puerto Carlero, nearby, is a newer addition to the resort; this attractive marina makes a quieter base for a holiday.

## TAHÍCHE

*6 km (3½ miles) north of Arrecife.*

★ **Fundación César Manrique.** The former home of this accomplished artist and architect is now a museum and foundation displaying a collection of his paintings and sculptures, as well as works by other 20th-century artists. The real attraction is the house itself, designed by Manrique to blend with the volcanic landscape. Built into a series of lower-level caves, with palm trees ascending into the upper floor, are a series of unusual, whitewashed living rooms. The maze of spaces invites you to walk from room to room through indoor tunnels and outdoor courtyards. ✉ *Ctra. Tahíche–San Bartolomé, 2 km (1 mile) west of Tahíche* ☎ *928/843138* ⊕ *www.fcmanrique.org* 🎫 *€8* ⊗ *July–Oct., daily 10–7; Nov.–June, Mon.–Sat. 10–6, Sun. 10–3.*

## YAIZA

*18 km (11 miles) west of Arrecife.*

Yaiza is a quiet, whitewashed village with good restaurants. Largely destroyed by a river of lava in the 1700s, it's best known as the gateway to the volcanic national park.

Fodor'sChoice **Parque Nacional Timanfaya** (*Timanfaya National Park*). The Parque
★ Nacional Timanfaya, popularly known as "the Fire Mountains," takes up much of southern Lanzarote. As you enter the park from Yaiza, the first thing you'll see is the staging area for the Canaries' best-known **camel rides**. A bumpy camel trek lasts about 20 minutes. The volcanic landscape inside Timanfaya is a violent jumble of exploded craters, cinder cones, lava formations, and heat fissures. The park is protected, and you can visit only on a bus tour or a camel ride. A taped English commentary explains how the parish priest of Yaiza took notes during the 1730 eruption that buried two villages. He had plenty of time—the eruption lasted six years, making it the longest known eruption in volcanic history. By the time it was over, more than 75% of Lanzarote was covered in lava. Throughout the park, on signs and road markers, you'll see a little devil with a pitchfork; this *diablito* was designed by Manrique.

The **Ruta de los Volcanes** bus tour takes you around the central volcanic area on a 14-km (9-mile) circuit that was designed to have minimal impact on this natural park. Tickets can be bought at the stand at the entrance to the National Park. ■TIP➜ **During summer, visit in late afternoon to avoid the crowds.** ⊠ *Centro de Visitantes Mancha Blancha, Ctra. de Yaiza a Tinajo, Km 11.5, Tinajo* ☎ 928/118042 ⊠ *Ruta de los Volcanes €8* ⊗ *Visitor center weekdays 9–3. Ruta de los Volcanes July–Sept., daily 9–7; Oct.–June, daily 9–5:45.*

## SHOPPING

9

The Canary Islands are known for lacy, hand-embroidered tablecloths and placemats, plus locally made ceramics and *timples* (typical musical instrument). Vegetation is scarce on Lanzarote, but the grapes grown by farmers in volcanic ash produce a distinctive Canarian wine. Locals also take great pride in the island's tiny potatoes, which you will on most menus as *papas canarias,* accompanied by fresh mojo sauces. The Canary Islands are free ports—no value-added tax is charged on luxury goods—but while the streets are packed with shops selling jewelry, cameras, and electronics, prices are still fairly high, so don't expect any phenomenal bargains.

Shopping is low-key in Arrecife. The main shops are on and around the pedestrian-only Calle León y Castilla. For island crafts and produce, go to the open market in the village of **Teguise** on Sunday between 9 and 2. Some vendors set up stalls in the plaza; others just lay out a blanket in the street and sell embroidered tablecloths, leather goods, costume jewelry, African masks, and other items.

## ACTIVITIES

Due to its climate and popularity with European vacationers, Lanzarote is well equipped for a range of sports and activities throughout the year, from water sports and diving to golf. Staff speak good English.

### BIKING

**Lanzarote Freeride.** Biking is a popular and practical way to tour the island, as Lanzarote is not particularly hilly. Lanzarote Freeride's bike rentals start at €22 a day. ☎ 696/972982 ⊕ *www.lanzarotefreeride.eu.*

### DIVING

One of the island's official diving centers is near Las Cucharas beach.

**Calipso Diving Lanzarote.** A well-established dive school with PADI Resort Center status. ⊠ *CC Calipso, local 3, Av. Islas Canarias, Costa Teguise* ☎ 928/590879 ⊕ *www.calipso-diving.com.*

### GOLF

**Costa Teguise Golf.** These 18 holes, which are outside the Costa Teguise development, have unusual sand traps filled with black-lava cinders. The course is par 72. ⊠ *Av. del Golf s/n, Costa Teguise* ☎ 928/590512 ⊕ *www.lanzarote-golf.com.*

## BEACHES

**Playa de Famara.** Directly opposite Costa Teguise on the north coast of Lanzarote is one of the island's most attractive beaches. Set in a natural cove, its 6 km (3.7 miles) of sand are flanked by spectacular cliffs. The riptide here makes for excellent surfing and windsurfing, and Playa de Famara is regularly used for world championships for those sports. That said, the strong currents mean swimming can be dangerous. **Amenities:** food and drink; lifeguards; showers; toilets; water sports. **Best for:** sunset; surfing; walking; windsurfing. ⊠ *Teguise.*

🐣 **Playa de la Garita.** Not far from the Jardín de Cactus, Playa de la Garita is a wide bay of crystalline water favored by surfers in winter and snorkelers in summer. The 850 meters (½ mile) of golden sands are safe for swimming, making this a popular spot for families. The beach does get busy in the summer, but is reasonably quiet the rest of the year. Lounge chairs and umbrellas are available for rent. **Amenities:** food and drink; lifeguards; showers; toilets; water sports. **Best for:** snorkeling; surfing; swimming. ⊠ *Haria.*

**Playa de las Cucharas.** This is the best of Costa Teguise's several small beaches. The sands are protected from high wind and waves by the natural bay formed in the coastline. A pleasant seafront promenade takes you around the beach and into the southern stretches of the resort. Getting a spot for your towel in the summer can be a challenge, especially at weekends. **Amenities:** food and drink; lifeguards; showers; toilets; water sports. **Best for:** sunrise; swimming. ⊠ *Costa Teguise.*

**Playa del Reducto.** It may not be in the same league as some of the beaches in the south, but Playa del Reducto is still an attractive urban beach, ideal for relaxing after you've looked around Arrecife. It's well maintained and protected by natural reefs, so swimming is usually like swimming in a warm lake (though do watch out for rocky outcrops at low tide). The beach is backed by a pleasant promenade that goes all the way to Puerto del Carmen. **Amenities:** food and drink; showers; toilets. **Best for:** sunrise; walking. ⊠ *Arrecife.*

**Playa de los Pocillos.** Slightly north of Puerto del Carmen, this beach is near most of the area's development; hotels and apartments are restricted, however, to the other side of the highway, leaving the 2-km (1-mile) yellow-sand beach surprisingly pristine. Finding a spot to place your towel can be difficult in summer. Lounge chairs and umbrellas are available. **Amenities:** food and drink; lifeguards; showers; toilets; water sports. **Best for:** sunrise; swimming; walking. ⊠ *Tías.*

**Playa Grande.** Puerto del Carmen's main beach is a busy strip of yellow sand that's as close as you can get to an urban beach on Lanzarote outside Arrecife. Lounge chairs and umbrellas are available for rent. Backing the beach is a seafront promenade with plenty of souvenir shops and restaurants. You can take the promenade all the way to Arrecife. **Amenities:** food and drink; lifeguards; showers; toilets; water sports. **Best for:** swimming. ⊠ *Puerto del Carmen.*

**Playa Matagorda.** On this northern extension of Playa de los Pocillos, there are alternating sections of gravel and gray sand. A perpetually windy spot, this busy beach has gentle waves that are perfect for those learning to surf. Lounge chairs and beach umbrellas are available. **Amenities:** food and drink; lifeguards; showers; toilets; water sports. **Best for:** surfing; swimming; walking. ⊠ *Tías.*

**Playa Mujeres.** Facing west across to Fuerteventura and the Isla de Lobos, this is a very popular beach. The sandy bay provides safe swimming conditions, and the beach is cleaned regularly. Amenities are limited to a few small bars. On the way to the beach, look out for the ruins of some bunkers from World War II. **Amenities:** food and drink. **Best for:** snorkeling; sunset; swimming. ⊠ *Playa Blanca.*

**Playa Papagayo.** The rugged coastline to the east of Playa Blanca has several stunning beaches, but most people think that Playa Papagayo is the island's most beautiful. This small bay with fine white sand is perfect for sunbathing, as it's protected from the wind by cliffs at both ends. You have to walk along a dirt path to get here, so take suitable footwear as well as plenty of drinking water. Despite its remoteness, this is a busy beach, particularly in summer. **Amenities:** none. **Best for:** snorkeling; sunrise; swimming. ⊠ *Playa Blanca.*

## WHERE TO EAT

**$$**
SPANISH
★

✕ **Lilium.** Creative cooking with Canarian roots is the philosophy behind the dishes at this modern restaurant that's just around the corner from the beach. Although there are a few tables outdoors, the dining mainly takes place inside, where copper and chocolate tones accompany floral touches. Standout dishes here include plantain croquettes and a slow-cooked suckling pig, served with a fruit reduction. Reservations are a good idea on weekends. $ *Average main: €16* ⊠ *Primo de Rivera 103, Arrecife* ☎ *928/524978* ⊕ *restaurantelilium.com* ☉ *Closed Sun.*

9

**$$**  ✕ **El Diablo.** This must be one of the world's most unusual restaurants.
SPANISH  Here, in the middle of Timanfaya National Park, chicken, steaks,
★  and spicy sausages are cooked over a volcanic crater using the earth's
natural heat. You have to be on the Ruta de los Volcanes bus tour
to get here. $ *Average main: €15* ⊠ *Timanfaya National Park, Yaiza*
☎ *928/840057.*

# REYKJAVÍK, ICELAND

Iceland is an epic land. It tempts with epithets like "The Land of Fire
and Ice," but these just hint at the delights this island has in store. It
is a land of dazzling white glaciers and black sands, blue hot springs,
rugged lava fields, and green, green valleys. This North Atlantic island
offers insight into the ferocious powers of nature, ranging from the
still-warm lava volcanic eruptions to the chilling splendor of the Vat-
najökull Glacier. Ice caps cover 11% of the country, more than 50% is
barren, 6% consists of lakes and rivers, and less than 2% of the land
is cultivated. There's hardly a tree to be seen, making the wildflowers
and delicate vegetation all the more lovely. Sprawling Reykjavík, the
nation's nerve center and government seat, is home to half the island's
population. On a bay overlooked by proud Mt. Esja (pronounced *eh-
shyuh*), with its ever-changing hues, Reykjavík presents a colorful sight,
its concrete houses painted in light colors and topped by vibrant red,
blue, and green roofs. In contrast to the almost treeless countryside,
Reykjavík has many tall, native birches, rowans, and willows, as well
as imported aspens, pines, and spruces.

## ESSENTIALS
### CURRENCY
The Icelandic krona has experienced a dramatic drop in value relative to
foreign currencies; although prices have been adjusted upward in some
cases (particularly for exported goods), prices still favor Americans and
Europeans at this writing.

### HOURS
Most businesses close early on weekdays and are closed on Sunday.
Some museums are open only in summer. Shops are typically open
weekdays from 9 to 6, but a growing number of stores—especially
food stores—are open on weekends with shorter hours. Souvenir shops
(along with bakeries and kiosks) are open daily.

### TELEPHONES
Iceland has no area codes; within the country, simply dial the seven-
digit number. Non-800 numbers starting with 8 often indicate cellular
phones. Most tri- and quad-band GSM phones work in Iceland. You
can also buy prepaid phone cards at telecom shops and newsstands.

## COMING ASHORE
Ships dock at Skarfabakki Quay in Reykjavik, which sits 4 km (2½ miles)
from the city center. The Cruise Visitor Welcome Centre has a range of
facilities, including currency exchange, V.A.T. refunds, car rental, a shop,
Internet access (including Wi-Fi), and toilets. Free shuttle buses transfer
passengers downtown, but taxis also generally wait to meet the ship. If

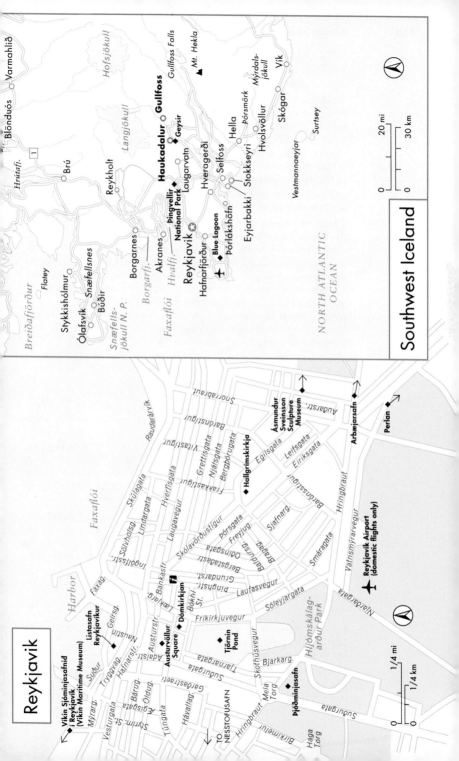

# Reykjavik

**Vikin Sjóminjasafnið í Reykjavík (Vikin Maritime Museum)**

**Listasafn Reykjavíkur**

Harbor

Faxaflói

**Dómkirkjan**

**Austurvöllur Square**

**Tjörnin Pond**

**Þjóðminjasafn**

Hallgrímskirkja

**Ásmundur Sveinsson Sculpture Museum**

**Arbæjarsafn**

**Perlan**

✈ **Reykjavik Airport (domestic flights only)**

Hljómskálag-arður Park

TO NESSTOFUSAFN

Haga Torg

Mela Torg

## Southwest Iceland

Varmahlíð
Blönduós
Hrútafj.
Brú
Reykholt
Langjökull
Hofsjökull
Gullfoss Falls
**Gullfoss**
Mt. Hekla ▲
Geysir
**Haukadalur**
Laugarvatn
Þórsmörk
Mýrdals-jökull
Vík
Skógar
Hvolsvöllur
Hella
Selfoss
Hveragerði
**Þingvellir National Park**
Stokkseyri
Eyjarbakki
**Reykjavík**
Þorlákshöfn
**Blue Lagoon**
Hafnarfjörður
Akranes
Borgarnes
Hvalfj.
Borgarfj.
Breiðafjörður
Flatey
Stykkishólmur
Ólafsvík
Búðir
Snæfellsnes
Snæfells-jökull N. P.
Faxaflói
Vestmannaeyjar
Surtsey
NORTH ATLANTIC OCEAN

0   20 mi
0   30 km

you want to walk, it is an easy stroll into town, but you can never be sure of the weather.

A car rental is expensive in summertime per day for a compact manual vehicle. All the international companies have offices in the city. Many roads outside the capital are hard surface but not asphalt, so a car is necessary if you want to explore on your own. Driving can be difficult in snow and ice.

There are many companies in Reykjavík offering group or individual tours, but the costs for these activities can be high. Tourist information centers in Reykjavík have many brochures for day tours. Taxis can also perform tour services. Prices may be fixed or, for shorter journeys, metered, and taxis accept credit cards.

---

**ICELAND BEST BETS**

**The "Golden Triangle."** Iceland in miniature, Strukkur, Gullfoss, and Þingvellir epitomize the raw and vital beauty of Iceland's landscapes.

**The National Museum.** A fascinating treasure trove of Viking artifacts is beautifully displayed in this museum that charts the history of Iceland from the first settlers to today.

**Blue Lagoon.** Luxuriate in the earth's gift of volcanically heated water gushing to the surface. The luxury pool and spa let you simply surrender to the bliss.

---

## EXPLORING SOUTHWESTERN ICELAND

### REYKJAVÍK

**Árbæjarsafn.** At the Open-Air Municipal Museum, 19th- and 20th-century houses furnished in old-fashioned style display authentic household utensils and tools for cottage industries and farming. During the summer you can see demonstrations of farm activities and taste piping-hot *lummur* (chewy pancakes) cooked over an old farmhouse stove. To get to the museum, take Bus 12 or 19. ⊠ *Ártúnsblettur, Kistuhyl 4* ☎ *411–6300* ⊕ *www.minjasafnreykjavikur.is* ⬛ *ISK 1,100* ☉ *June–Aug., daily 10–5; Sept.–May, guided tours daily 1 pm.*

**Ásmundur Sveinsson Sculpture Museum.** Some of Ásmundur Sveinsson's original sculptures, depicting ordinary working people, myths, and folktale episodes, are exhibited in the museum's gallery and studio and in the surrounding garden. It's on the southwest edge of Laugardalur Park, opposite the traffic circle at its entrance. Take Bus 15 or 17 from Hlemmur station (a 5-minute ride). ⊠ *Sigtún 105* ☎ *553–2155* ⊕ *www.artmuseum.is* ⬛ *ISK 1,100* ☉ *Daily May–Sept., 10–5; Oct.–Apr., 1–5.*

**Austurvöllur Square.** East Field is a peculiar name for a west-central square. The reason: it's just east of the presumed spot where first settler Ingólfur Arnarson built his farm, today near the corner of Aðalstræti.

★ **Dómkirkjan** (*Lutheran Cathedral*). A place of worship has existed on this site since AD 1200. The small, charming church, built 1788–96, represents the state religion, Lutheranism. It was here that sovereignty and independence were first blessed and endorsed by the church. It's also where Iceland's national anthem, actually a hymn, was first sung in 1874. Since 1845, members and cabinet ministers of every Alþing parliament have gathered here for a service before the annual session. Among the treasured items inside is a baptismal font carved and donated by the famous 19th-century master sculptor Bertel Thorvaldsen, who was half Icelandic. ⊠ *Austurvöllur* 🕾 *520–9700* ⊕ *www.domkirkjan.is/enska.html* ☉ *Mon.–Fri. 10–4:30, unless in use for services.*

★ **Hallgrímskirkja** (*Hallgrímur's Church*). Completed in 1986 after more than 40 years of construction, the church is named for the 17th-century hymn writer Hallgrímur Pétursson. It has a stylized concrete facade recalling both organ pipes and the distinctive columnar basalt formations you can see around Iceland. You may luck into hearing a performance or practice on the church's huge pipe organ. In front of Hallgrímskirkja is a statue of Leifur Eiríksson, the Icelander who discovered America 500 years before Columbus. (Leif's father was Eric the Red, who discovered Greenland.) The statue, by American sculptor Alexander Calder, was presented to Iceland by the United States in 1930 to mark the millennium of the Alþing parliament. ⊠ *At the top of Skólavörðustígur* 🕾 *510–1000* ⊕ *www.hallgrimskirkja.is* 🎫 *Tower ISK 600* ☉ *Daily 9–5.*

**Listasafn Reykjavíkur** (*Reykjavík Art Museum*). Also known as Hafnarhús, this former warehouse of the Port of Reykjavík now houses the city's art museum. The six galleries occupy two floors, and there's a courtyard and multipurpose space. The museum's permanent collection includes a large number of works donated by the contemporary Icelandic artist, Erró. There are also regular temporary exhibitions. ⊠ *Tryggvagata 17* 🕾 *590–1200* ⊕ *www.artmuseum.is* 🎫 *ISK 1,100* ☉ *Fri.–Wed. 10–5, Thurs. 10–8.*

**Perlan.** On top of Öskjuhlíð, the hill overlooking Reykjavík Airport, Perlan (the Pearl) was opened in 1991 as a monument to Iceland's invaluable geothermal water supplies. Among the indoor and outdoor spectacles are art exhibits, musical performances, markets, a permanent Viking history exhibit, and fountains that spurt water like geysers. Above the six vast tanks, which once held 24 million liters of hot water, the panoramic viewing platform offers telescopes and a cafeteria complete with ice cream parlor. The crowning glory is a revolving restaurant under the glass dome; it's pricey, but the view is second to none ⊠ *Öskjuhlíð Hill* 🕾 *562–0200* ⊕ *www.perlan.is* ☉ *Daily 10–9.*

**Þjóðminjasafn** (*National Museum*). Viking treasures and artifacts, silver work, wood carvings, and some unusual whalebone carvings are on display here, as well as maritime objects, historical textiles, jewelry, and crafts. There is also a coffee shop. ⊠ *Suðurgata 41* 🕾 *530–2200* ⊕ *www.natmus.is* 🎫 *ISK 1,200* ☉ *May 1–Sept. 15, daily 10–5; Sept. 16–Apr. 30, Tues.–Sun. 11–5.*

☺ **Tjörnin Pond.** This natural pond by the city hall attracts birds—and bird lovers—year-round and is also popular among ice-skaters in winter. Children love feeding bread to the many varieties of swans and ducks in the pond. ⊠ *Next to the Raðhús* 🎫 *Free.*

**Víkin Sjóminjasafnið í Reykjavík (Víkin Maritime Museum).** Housed in an old fish factory with great views of the harbor, the maritime museum features an exhibition on Icelandic fisheries, trading vessels, and displays a whole Costal Guard vessel that can be explored. ⊠ *Grandargarði 8* ☎ *517–9400* ⊕ *www.maritimemuseum.is* ⊠ *ISK 1,200* ⊙ *June 1–Sept. 15, daily 10–5; Sept. 16–May 31, Tues–Sun. 11–5.*

## BLUE LAGOON

*15 km (9 miles) from Keflavík Airport and 50 km (31 miles) from Reykjavík (turn off toward the village of Grindavík).*

**Fodor's Choice** **Blue Lagoon.** This world-renowned therapeutic wonder is now in a shel-
★ tered site where man-made structures blend with geologic formations. A reception area includes food concessions and boutiques where you can buy health products made from the lagoon's mineral-rich ingredients. Bathing suits are available to rent, and futuristic bracelets keep track of your locker code, any other purchases, and the length of your visit (all of which no doubt make useful marketing statistics). Buses run from the BSÍ bus terminal in Reykjavík to the Blue Lagoon twice daily and three times a day in July and August, or you can get to the airport on your own by taking a special FlyBus. ⊠ *Bláalónið, Grindavík* ☎ *420–8800* ⊕ *www.bluelagoon. com* ⊠ *ISK 4,800* ⊙ *Sept.1–May 31, 10–8; June 1–Aug. 31, 9–9pm.*

## ÞINGVELLIR

*About 50 km (31 miles) northeast of Reykjavík. Take Ring Rd. about 9 km (5½ miles) just past the town of Mosfellsbær; turn right on Rte. 36.*

This has been the nation's most hallowed place since AD 930, when the settler Grímur Geitskór chose it as the first site for what is often called the world's oldest parliament, the Icelandic Alþingi (General Assembly). In July of each year delegates from all over the country camped at Þingvellir, meeting to pass laws and render judicial sentences. Iceland remained a nation-state, ruled solely by the people without a central government, until 1262, when it came under the Norwegian crown; even then, the Alþingi continued to meet at Þingvellir until 1798, but it had long lost its lawmaking powers.

**Þingvellir National Park.** Þingvellir National Park, at the northern end of Þingvallavatn—Iceland's largest lake—is a potent symbol of Icelandic heritage. Many national celebrations are held here, and it was named a UNESCO World Heritage Site in 2004. Besides its historic interest, Þingvellir holds a special appeal for naturalists: it is the geologic meeting point of two continents. At Almannagjá, on the west side of the plain, is the easternmost edge of the North American tectonic plate, otherwise submerged in the Atlantic Ocean. Over on the plain's east side, at the Heiðargjá Gorge, you are at the westernmost edge of the Eurasian plate.

A path down into Almannagjá from the top of the gorge overlooking Þingvellir leads straight to the high rock wall of **Lögberg** (Law Rock), where the person chosen as guardian of the laws would recite them from memory. At the far end of the gorge is the **Öxarárfoss** (Öxará Waterfall). Beautiful, peaceful picnic spots are a bit beyond it. Just behind Lögberg, the river cascades down and forms the forbidding **Drekkingarhylur** pool, where women were drowned during the late middle ages. ⊠ *Þingvellir* ⊕ *www.thingvellir.is.*

**Þingvallabær.** Across the plain from Lögberg stand the church and the gabled manor house of Þingvallabær, where the government of Iceland often hosts visiting heads of state. Free, one-hour tours are offered on weekdays in the summer leaving at 10 am from the church. ⊠ *Þingvellir* ☎ *482–2660* ⊕ *www.thingvellir.is* ☉ *Church May–Sept., daily 9–5:30; Information center summer daily 9–5, winter Sat.–Sun. 9–5.*

**Nikulásargjá Gorge.** The Nikulásargjá Gorge, reached by a footbridge, is better known these days as Peningagjá (Money Gorge) because it's customary to fling a coin into the gorge's icy-cold water and make a wish. Don't even dream about climbing down to wade here—it might look shallow, but it's more than 30 feet deep. ⚠ **The water is ice cold.** ⊠ *Þingvellir* ⊕ *www.thingvellir.is.*

### HAUKADALUR
*About 35 km (22 miles) northeast of Laugarvatn via Rte. 37 and then Rte. 35.*

**Fodor's** Choice ★  The geothermal field in Haukadalur, home of the Geysir and Strokkur geysers, is one of Iceland's classic tourist spots.

The famous **Geysir** hot spring (the literal origin of the term, geyser) only erupts a few times a year, but the more reliable **Strokkur** spouts up boiling water as high as 100 feet at five-minute intervals. In the same area there are small natural vents from which steam rises, as well as beautiful, exotic-colored pools. Don't crowd Strokkur, and always be careful when approaching hot springs or mud pots—the ground may be treacherous, suddenly giving way beneath you. Stay on formal paths or established tracks.

To get here from Laugarvatn, take Route 37 (from Lake Laugarvatn you can take the short spur, Route 364, southwest to Route 37) northeast for 25 km (16 miles) to the junction with Route 35. Take Route 35 about 10 km (6 miles) northeast to Hótel Geysir, which is next to the springs.

### GULLFOSS
*About 6 km (4 miles) east of Geysir along Rte. 35.*

**Gullfoss.** Measuring 105 feet high, thundering Gullfoss (Golden Falls) is a double cascade in the Hvítá River, turning at right angles in mid-drop. Gullfoss enters a dramatic chasm, which nonetheless has its gentle sides. The modest visitor center is named in memory of Sigríður Tómasdóttir, who fought against flooding the falls for a hydroelectric reservoir scheme in the early 20th century. She is said to have threatened to throw herself into the falls; a trailside plaque further honors her.

## SHOPPING

Reykjavík is a happening and fun shopping town. The main shopping downtown is on and around Austurstræti, Aðalstræti, Hafnarstræti, Hverfisgata, Bankastræti, Laugavegur, and Skólavörðustígur. There are also two large American-style shopping malls. Both Kringlan and Smáralind make great places to shop when the weather turns inclement.

Sheepskin rugs and Viking-inspired jewelry are popular souvenirs. An amble along **Skólavörðustígur** from Laugavegur to Hallgrímskirkja church takes you past many tempting woolen, jewelry, and crafts shops, as well as art galleries. Laugavegur and Skólavörðustígur streets are both filled with jewelry stores that craft unique pieces, often incorporating gold or silver with materials found in Iceland, like lava rock, creating a very eye-catching effect.

| ICELAND VAT REFUNDS |
| --- |
| A 25.5% *virðisaukaskattur* (value-added tax, or V.A.T.), commonly called VSK, applies to most goods and services. V.A.T. is almost always included in a price; if not, that fact must be stated explicitly. Foreign visitors who purchase ISK 4,000 or more on one receipt can claim a partial refund on the V.A.T. |

**Anna María design.** Founded in 1986, this workshop and store sells a variety of jewelry for both men and women, made from a variety of materials that encompass silver, gold, and Icelandic stones. ⊠ *Skólavörðustígur 3* ☎ *551–0036* ⊕ *www.annamariadesign.is*.

**Handprjónasambandið.** The Handknitting Association of Iceland, Handprjónasambandið, has its own outlet, selling, of course, only hand-knit items of various kinds. ⊠ *Skólavörðurstígur 19* ☎ *552–1890* ⊕ *www.handknit.is* ⊙ *Mon.–Sat. 9–6; Sun. 11–5.*

## ACTIVITIES

If you are looking for a more active adventure, there are numerous opportunities for adventure sports, including ATV Tours, quad biking, Jeep safaris, and glacier tours. You can also explore the countryside on horseback, and whale-watching is a growth activity.

**Iceland Tour Guide Association** ⊠ *Mörkin 6* ☎ *588–8670* ⊕ *www.touristguide.is.* **Reykjavík Excursions** ⊠ *BSÍ Bus Terminal, Vatnsmýrarvegi 10* ☎ *580–5040* ⊕ *www.re.is* ⊙ *Daily 4 am–11 pm.*

## WHERE TO EAT

$
FAST FOOD
★

**✗ Bæjarins beztu.** Facing the harbor in a parking lot, this tiny but well-known fast-food hut is famous for serving the original Icelandic hot dog; one person serves about a thousand hot dogs a day from the window. Ask for *AYN-ah-med-UTL-lou,* which will get you "one with everything": mustard, tomato sauce, *rémoulade* (mayonnaise with finely chopped pickles), and chopped raw and fried onions. $ *Average main: IKr 320* ⊠ *Tryggvagata and Pósthússtræti* ☎ *894–4515* ⊕ *www.bbp.is/* ⊙ *Sun.–Thurs., 10 am–12:30 am; Fri.–Sat., 10 am–4:30 am.*

$$$$
EUROPEAN
Fodor's Choice
★

**✗ Grillmarket.** A collaborative project by well-known culinary innovators Hrefna Rós Sætran (founder/owner of the Fish Market) and Guðlaugur P. Frímannsson, Grillmarkaðurinn emphasizes seasonal, organic, locally grown ingredients in a beautifully designed interior that's heavy on natural materials such as wood and stone. The menu is equally "earthy" featuring lots of smoked, grilled, and barbecued meat dishes. For something classic, try the grilled chicken wings or grilled pork ribs; for something more unique, order the Minke whale steak. ⑤ *Average main: IKr 4,495* ⊠ *Lækjargata 2a, Reykjavík* ☎ *571–7777* ⊕ *www.grillmarkadurinn.is.*

# TENERIFE, CANARY ISLANDS (SANTA CRUZ DE TENERIFE)

Updated by
Joanna Styles

Tenerife is the largest of the Canary Islands but actually 112 km (70 miles) off the coast of southern Morocco. It is towered over by the volcanic peak of Mt. Teide, which at 12,198 feet is Spain's highest mountain. The slopes leading up to Teide are covered with pines in the north and with barren lava fields in the south. Popular with vacationing Europeans, the resort towns of Tenerife win no prizes for beauty, but the natural attractions and kind islanders more than compensate for the late-20th-century high-rise hotels and apartment blocks.

## ESSENTIALS

### CURRENCY
The euro. ATMs are common and credit cards are widely accepted.

### HOURS
Shops are generally open Monday to Saturday between 9 and 1 and again from 4 until 8 or 9. Most places close for siesta, but some resort shops may stay open throughout the day and also open on Sunday. Museums are usually open from 10 until noon, but have varied afternoon opening hours.

### TELEPHONES
Most tri- and quad-band GSM phones will work in the Canary Islands, where mobile services are 3G-compatible. Public kiosks accept phone cards that support international calls (cards sold in press shops, bars, and telecom shops).

### COMING ASHORE
Vessels dock at the port of Santa Cruz, on the island's northeast side. If your ship docks at the berth farthest from the terminal, it is a 15-minute walk to the port exit. Once you reach the gates, the city of Santa Cruz is accessible on foot. There are few passenger facilities in the port, but the shopping district is close and taxis are readily available.

Renting a car would allow you to explore much of the island during your stopover. An economy manual vehicle begins at €40 per day. There are car-rental offices in Santa Cruz de Tenerife, but the easiest option is to prebook a car online for pick-up at Muelle Ribera (Ribera dock) using Cicar (⊕ *www.cicar.com*). Taxis also wait outside the terminal building, and they can be contracted for tourist itineraries, but on the meter these trips can be expensive; try to negotiate an hourly rate. Having private transport (rental car or taxi) would be more practical with only a day in port.

9

# EXPLORING TENERIFE

## SANTA CRUZ DE TENERIFE

**Auditorio de Tenerife.** A magnificent white shell of an auditorium dominates the west end of the city. Built by the architect Santiago Calatrava in 2003, the auditorium has a year-round program of concerts and opera. If you want a guided tour, it's best to book one ahead of time. ☒ *Av. de la Constitución 1, Santa Cruz* ☎ *922/568625* ⊕ *www.auditoriodetenerife.com* ☒ *Tours €5* ☉ *Tours in English: Oct.–June, Mon.–Sat. 12:30; July–Sept., weekdays 12:30 and 5:30, Sat. 12:30.*

**Castillo San Cristóbal** (*Saint Christopher's Castle*). The walls of the city castle were uncovered when the car park under the Plaza de España was built. The site is now a museum that includes an 18th-century cannon, a shot from which reputedly cost Britain's Admiral Nelson his right arm in an attack he led in 1794. Entrance to the museum is via a stairway opposite the lake. ☒ *Pl. de España, Santa Cruz* ☒ *Free* ☉ *Mon.–Sat. 10–6.*

**Iglesia de Nuestra Señora de la Concepción** (*Church of Our Lady of the Conception*). The Iglesia de Nuestra Señora de la Concepción has a six-story Moorish bell tower. The church was renovated as part of an urban-renewal project that razed blocks of slums in this area. Church opening times vary, but you can generally visit before and after Mass. ☒ *Pl. de la Iglesia, Santa Cruz* ☎ *922/242387* ☒ *Free.*

**Mercado de Nuestra Señora de Africa** (*Market of Our Lady of Africa*). This colorful city market is part bazaar and part food emporium. Stalls outside sell household goods; inside, stands displaying everything from flowers to canaries are arranged around a patio. Downstairs, a stroll through the seafood section will acquaint you with the local fish. A flea market with antiques and secondhand goods is held here on Sunday. ☒ *Av. de San Sebastián, Santa Cruz* ☉ *Daily 6:30–3.*

**Museo de Bellas Artes** (*Museum of Fine Arts*). Old masters and modern works are in the two-story Museo de Bellas Artes, including canvases by Breughel and Ribera. Many works depict local events. The museum is on the Plaza Príncipe de Asturias. ☒ *José Murphy 12, Santa Cruz* ☎ *922/274786* ☒ *Free* ☉ *Tues.–Fri. 10–8, weekends 10–3.*

**Museo de la Naturaleza y el Hombre** (*Museum of Nature and Man*). Primitive ceramics and mummies are on display at the Museo de la Naturaleza y el Hombre. The ancient Guanches mummified their dead by rubbing the bodies with pine resin and salt and leaving them in the sun to dry for two weeks. ☒ *Fuentes Morales s/n, Santa Cruz* ☎ *922/535816* ⊕ *www.museosdetenerife.org* ☒ *€3, free Sun.* ☉ *Tues.–Sun. 9–7.*

**Parque Marítimo César Manrique.** Just west of the auditorium, this maritime park with its three saltwater pools and tropical gardens is a favorite with locals. Designed by the Lanzarote architect César Manrique, the park combines volcanic rock with palms and local flora. ☒ *Av. de la Constitución 5, Santa Cruz* ☎ *922/229368* ⊕ *www.parquemaritimo.com* ☒ *€2.50* ☉ *Daily 10–6.*

**Plaza de España.** The heart of Santa Cruz de Tenerife is the Plaza de España. The cross in the plaza is a monument to those who died in the

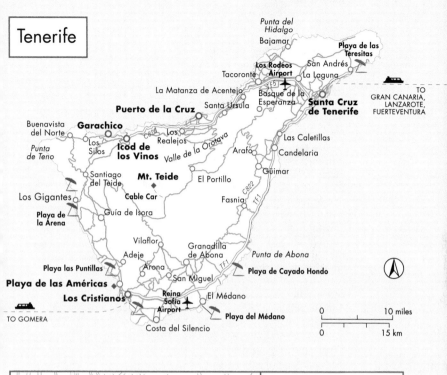

# Tenerife

Punta del Hidalgo
Bajamar
**Playa de las Teresitas**
San Andrés
Tacoronte
**Los Rodeos Airport**
La Laguna
TO GRAN CANARIA, LANZAROTE, FUERTEVENTURA
La Matanza de Acentejo
Bosque de la Esperanza
**Santa Cruz de Tenerife**
Santa Ursula
**Puerto de la Cruz**
Buenavista del Norte
**Garachico**
Los Realejos
Las Caletillas
Punta de Teno
Los Silos
**Icod de los Vinos**
Valle de la Orotava
Arafo
Candelaria
Santiago del Teide
**Mt. Teide**
El Portillo
Güimar
Los Gigantes
**Cable Car**
Fasnia
**Playa de la Arena**
Guía de Isora
Los Cristianos
Vilaflor
Granadilla de Abona
Punta de Abona
Adeje
**Playa las Puntillas**
Arona
**Playa de Cayado Hondo**
**Playa de las Américas**
San Miguel
**Los Cristianos**
**Reina Sofía Airport**
El Médano
TO GOMERA
Costa del Silencio
**Playa del Médano**

0   10 miles
0   15 km

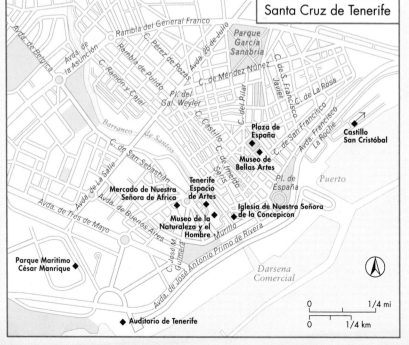

# Santa Cruz de Tenerife

Avda. de Bélgica
Rambla del General Franco
Avda. de la Asunción
C. Pérez de Rozas
Avda. 25 de Julio
Parque García Sanabria
Avda. de la Asunción
Rambla de Pulido
C. de Méndez Núñez
C. de S. Francisco Javier
C. de La Rosa
C. Ramón y Cajal
Pl. del Gal. Weyler
C. del Pilar
Barranco de Santos
C. Castillo
C. de San Francisco
Avda. Francisco La Roche
C. de San Sebastián
C. de Imelda
Seris
**Plaza de España**
**Castillo San Cristóbal**
Avda. de La Salle
**Museo de Bellas Artes**
Pl. de España
Puerto
Avda. de Buenos Aires
**Mercado de Nuestra Señora de Africa**
**Tenerife Espacio de Artes**
**Iglesia de Nuestra Señora de la Concepción**
Avda. de Tres de Mayo
**Museo de la Naturaleza y el Hombre**
C. José M. Guimerá
Murillo
Avda. de José Antonio Primo de Rivera
**Parque Marítimo César Manrique**
Darsena Comercial
0   1/4 mi
0   1/4 km
**Auditorio de Tenerife**

Spanish civil war, which was actually launched from Tenerife by General Franco during his exile here. For two weeks before Lent each year, during Carnaval, Santa Cruz throbs to a Latin beat emanating from this plaza. Castillo San Cristóbal and the tourist office are both here. ⊠ *Pl. de España, Santa Cruz.*

**Tenerife Espacio de Artes.** Soon after it opened in 2008, this art museum quickly became the main landmark for contemporary art on the islands due to its sleek low-rise design as well as its avant-garde exhibitions. Designed by the Swiss architects Herzog & Meuron, it's next to the Museo de la Naturaleza. The emphasis is on the 20th and 21st centuries, and art incorporating or commenting on modern technology. A major permanent exhibition is dedicated to the Tenerife surrealist artist, Oscar Domínguez. ⊠ *Av. San Sebastián 8, Santa Cruz* ☎ 922/849057 ⊕ *www.teatenerife.es* ☞ €5 ☼ *Tues.–Sun. 10–8.*

**TENERIFE BEST BETS**

**Venture to the summit of Mt. Teide.** Snow-capped for much of the year, this ancient volcano is the tallest in the Canaries and the highlight of any trip to Tenerife.

**Explore the village of La Orotava.** Home to nobility in the 17th and 18th centuries, this village teems with elegant squares, streets, and churches renowned for their facades. But everything is closed on weekends.

**Stroll the ramblas and cobbled streets of Santa Cruz.** Here the atmosphere of medieval Spain couldn't be more palpable.

## PUERTO DE LA CRUZ
*36 km (22 miles) west of Santa Cruz.*

Puerto de la Cruz is the oldest resort in the Canaries. Despite mass tourism, it has retained some of its Spanish charm and island character. The old sections of town have colonial plazas and *paseos* (promenades) for evening strolls.

**Casa de Vino La Baranda.** Wine and food lovers will want to head to this winery, which is about halfway between Puerto de la Cruz and Los Rodeos Airport, at the El Sauzal exit on the main highway. Opened by the Canary Islands' government to promote local vintners, it includes a wine museum, shop, and tasting room, where for a small fee you can sample some of Tenerife's best wines. The complex also has a tapas bar and a restaurant with nouvelle Canarian fare. Also here is a **honey museum**, with exhibits as well as tasting sessions. ⊠ *Simón 49, Autopista General del Norte, Km 21, El Sauzal* ☎ 922/572535 ⊕ *www.tenerife.es/casa-vino* ☼ *Oct.–June, Tues. 10:30–6:30, Wed.–Sat. 9–9, Sun. 11–6; July–Sept., Tues. 10:30–6:30, Wed.–Sat., 10–7:30, Sun. 11–6.*

**Jardín Botánico** *(Botanical Garden).* Filled with over 4,000 varieties of tropical trees and plants, and sonorous birds, the Jardín Botánico was founded in 1788, on the orders of King Carlos III, to propagate warm-climate species brought back to Spain from the Americas. The gardens are closed during stormy weather or when the wind speed exceeds 40 kph (25 mph). ⊠ *Retama 2* ☎ 922/383572 ☞ €3 ☼ *Oct.–Mar., daily 9–6; Apr.–Sept., daily 9–7.*

☺ **Lago Martiánez.** Because Puerto de la Cruz has uninviting black-sand beaches, the town commissioned Lanzarote artist César Manrique in 1965 to build Lago Martiánez, a forerunner of today's water parks. It's an immense, and immensely fun, public pool on the waterfront, with landscaped islands, bridges, and a volcano-like fountain that sprays sky-high. The complex also includes several smaller pools and a restaurant-nightclub. ⊠ *Av. de Colón s/n* ☎ *922/385955* 🎫 *€4.50* ⊙ *Sept. 16–May, daily 10–6; June–Sept. 15, daily 10–7.*

☺ **Loro Parque.** This huge subtropical garden and zoo holds 1,300 parrots, many of which are trained to ride bicycles and perform other tricks. The garden also has the world's largest penguin zoo. The dapper Antarctic birds receive round-the-clock care from marine biologists and other veterinary specialists in a climate-controlled environment. Also here is one of Europe's largest aquariums, with an underwater tunnel, a dolphin-and killer-whale show, and some gorillas. Free trains leave for the park from the Plaza Reyes Católicos. ⊠ *Av. Loro Parque s/n* ☎ *922/373841* ⊕ *www.loroparque.com* 🎫 *€33 (combined ticket with Siam Park €56)* ⊙ *Daily 8:30–6:45.*

**Plaza del Charco.** It's a two-minute walk from the Plaza de la Iglesia to this plaza, one of the prettiest and liveliest in town. ⊠ *Pl. del Charco, Puerto de la Cruz.*

**Puerto de la Cruz.** The tourist office's building, a royal customhouse from the 17th century, is one of the best examples of a typical Canary house on the island. It's outfitted with balconies, an interior patio, and intricate wood carvings. ⊠ *Casa de la Aduana, Las Lonjas s/n* ☎ *922/386000* ⊕ *turismo.puertodelacruz.es* ⊙ *Weekdays 9–8, weekends 9–5*

### ICOD DE LOS VINOS
*26 km (16 miles) west of Puerto de la Cruz.*

Attractive plazas rimmed by unspoiled colonial architecture and pine balconies form the heart of Tenerife's most historic wine district. A 3,000-year-old **dragon tree** towers 57 feet above the coastal highway, C820. The Guanches worshiped these trees as symbols of fertility and knowledge; the sap, which turns red upon contact with air, was used in healing rituals.

### GARACHICO
*5 km (3 miles) west of Icod de los Vinos.*

Garachico is one of the most idyllic and best-preserved towns on the islands, and it's well worth a quick visit. It was the main port of Tenerife until May 5, 1706, when Mt. Teide blew its top, sending twin rivers of lava downhill. One filled Garachico's harbor, and the other destroyed most of the town. Legend has it that the eruption was unleashed by an evil monk. One of the buildings that withstood the eruption was the **Castillo San Miguel,** a tiny 16th-century fortress on the waterfront. Island crafts, such as embroidery and basket making, are demonstrated inside. From the roof you can see the two rivers of lava, now solidified on the mountainside. You can also visit the **Convento de San Francisco,** which was unscathed, and the 18th-century parish church of **Santa Ana.**

9

## MT. TEIDE

*60 km (36 miles) southwest of Puerto de la Cruz, 63 km (39 miles) north of Playa de las Américas.*

**Parque Nacional del Teide** (*Teide National Park*). This park includes the volcano itself and the **Cañadas del Teide,** a violent jumble of volcanic leftovers from El Teide and the neighboring Pico Viejo. Within this area you can find blue hills (the result of a process called hydrothermal alteration); spiky, knobby rock protrusions; and lava in varied colors and textures. The bizarre, photogenic rock formations known as the **Roques de García** are especially memorable; a two-hour trail around these rocks—one of 21 well-marked hikes inside the park—is recommended.

You enter the Parque Nacional del Teide at El Portillo. Exhibits at the visitor center explain the region's natural history; a garden outside labels the flora found within the park. The center also offers trail maps, video presentations, guided hikes, and bus tours. A second park information center, near Los Roques de García and next to the Parador Nacional Cañadas del Teide, has details and trail maps. ⊠ *Parque Nacional del Teide, Orotava* ☏ *922/922371* ⊙ *Daily 9–4.*

**Cable Car.** On its way to the top of Mt. Teide, the cable car passes sulfur steam vents. You can get a good view of southern Tenerife and Gran Canaria from the top, although you'll be confined to the tiny terrace of a bar. The station also has a restaurant. ☏ *922/010440* ⊕ *www. telefericoteide.com* 🎟 *€20* ⊙ *Ascent: daily 9–4; descent: daily 9–5.*

**Climbing the Teide Crater.** If you're planning on hiking in the park, plan ahead. Take warm clothing even in summer, suitable footwear, sun protection, and plenty of drinking water. The trail to the top (No. 10) of the volcano is closed when it's snowy, usually about four months of the year. The difficult final 656 feet to the volcano crater itself takes about 40 minutes to climb, and you need a special free pass to do so—bring a photocopy of your passport's information page to the visitor center, or book online. If you stay at the refuge and access the crater before 8 am, you don't need a pass. ⊕ *www.reservasparquesnacionales.es.*

## LOS CRISTIANOS AND PLAYA DE LAS AMÉRICAS

*74 km (44 miles) southwest of Santa Cruz, 10 km (6 miles) west of Reina Sofía Airport.*

The sunniest (and probably tackiest) tourist area on Tenerife is the southwestern shore, where high-rise hotels are built chockablock above the beaches. Sun, beaches, and nightlife constitute the attractions here for millions of northern Europeans desperate for a dose of warm sunshine. These loud and brash resorts aren't to everyone's taste. If you're looking for peace and quiet, you'll probably want to give this area a wide berth.

**Siam Park.** This giant water park covers just about all the aquatic bases, from sleepy, restful pools to the heart-stopping Tower of Power, which drops you 28 meters (90 feet) into a "shark-infested" aquarium. ⊠ *Autopista del Sur, take exit 28 or 29, San Eugenio bajo* ☏ *922/373841* ⊕ *www.siampark.net* 🎟 *€33 (combined ticket with Loro Parque €56)* ⊙ *May–Oct., daily 10–6; Nov.–Apr., 10–5.*

# SHOPPING

The Canary Islands are free ports—no value-added tax is charged on luxury goods. The streets are packed with shops, but not all offer much in the way of savings. Choose a reputable store to buy electronic goods: make sure the boxed item is the one you want to purchase, and check your bill and credit card receipt carefully. The islands are also known for lacy, hand-embroidered tablecloths and place mats. If you're looking for the real thing, be prepared to pay for it, and watch out for cheap Asian imitations. Cuban-style cigars are also renowned, and many connoisseurs claim that Canary cigars are of better quality and cheaper than their Caribbean equivalents.

By Canary Island standards, Santa Cruz de Tenerife is a major shopping center, although it doesn't have the variety and number of stores found in Las Palmas. Calle Castillo, the main pedestrian street through the center of town, is lined with souvenir shops, trendy boutiques, and electronics stores. Calle del Pilar has higher-end fashions and the department stores Marks & Spencer and El Corte Inglés (another branch is next to the bus terminal).

**Artenerife.** Artenerife sells traditional crafts made by local artisans and guaranteed by the island's government as *productos artesanos*. The selection includes Tenerifan *calado*—exquisitely embroidered linen tablecloths and place mats—and clay pottery made using the same methods as those used by the island's aboriginal settlers. (The aborigines didn't use potter's wheels; rather, they rolled the clay into *churros,* or cylindrical strips, and hand-kneaded these into bowls. Pebbles, branches, and shells were used to buff the results.) ⊠ *Pl. de España, near tourist office, Santa Cruz* ☎ *922/291523* ⊕ *www.artenerife.com* ☉ *Weekdays 10–5, Sat. 11–2.*

**La Casa de Los Balcones.** Near Plaza España, this shop stocks colorful Canarian blankets, embroideries, jars of mojo sauce, and hefty bags of gofio. ⊠ *Castillo 30, Santa Cruz* ☎ *922/245734* ⊕ *www.casa-balcones. com* ☉ *Mon.–Sat. 9:30–8:30.*

**La Cava La Cubana.** Local and foreign cigars are available at this tobacco shop. ⊠ *Edif. Olimpo, Candelaria 28, Santa Cruz* ☉ *Weekdays 10–2 and 4–6, Sat. 11–2.*

# BEACHES

Tenerife's beaches are sandy but not extensive, and crowded with vacationers at all times of year. The newest and sunniest tourist area on Tenerife is the southwestern shore, where high-rise hotels are built chockablock above the beaches.

**El Médano.** More than 2 km (1 mile) long, this is the longest beach on the island and also one of the most distinctive—the conical top of Montaña Roja (Red Mountain) lies at its southern tip. The golden sands and exemplary facilities earn it the country's "Blue Flag" rating, and the gentle waves make for safe swimming. It's a good beach for those who want to try their hand at windsurfing. **Amenities:** food and drink; lifeguards; showers; toilets; water sports. **Best for:** sunset; swimming; walking; windsurfing. ⊠ *Arona.*

**Las Vistas.** Part of the eight beaches making up the sands in Playa de las Américas and Los Cristianos, Las Vistas has clean yellow sand and perfect bathing conditions thanks to a series of breakwalls that protect the beaches from high waves. Lounge chairs and parasols are available for rent. After sunbathing on this Blue Flag beach, take a stroll along the seafront promenade, one of the longest pedestrian stretches in Europe. **Amenities:** food and drink; lifeguards; showers; toilets; water sports. **Best for:** sunset; swimming; walking. ⊠ *Los Cristianos.*

**Playa de las Teresitas.** Santa Cruz's beach, Las Teresitas, is about 7 km (4½ miles) northeast of the city, near the town of San Andrés. The 1½ km (1 mile) of beach was created using white sand imported from the Sahara and planted with palms. A man-made barrier runs parallel to the sands and ensures safe bathing. Busy in the summer and on weekends, this beach is especially popular with local families. The 910 TITSA bus route connects the beach with Santa Cruz. There's a good choice of bars and restaurants, and plenty of lounge chairs for rent. **Amenities:** food and drink; lifeguards; showers; toilets. **Good for:** sunset; swimming; walking. ⊠ *San Andrés, Santa Cruz.*

## ACTIVITIES

Due to its climate and popularity with European vacationers, Tenerife is well equipped for a range of sports and activities. There are 21 marked hiking trails around Mt. Teide. Maps are kept at the park visitor's center. Tenerife has six golf courses, and the climate means that you'll be able to get a round in most days of the year.

### GOLF

Tenerife's noteworthy golf courses are all in the south of the island.

**Amarilla Golf Club.** In San Miguel, not far from Campo Golf, is this 18-hole course, where the greens front the ocean. ⊠ *Urb. Amarilla Golf, San Miguel, Los Cristianos* ☎ *922/730319* ⊕ *www.amarillagolf.es.*

**Golf Abama.** This course boasts over 22 lakes and more than 90,000 palms along its 18 holes. ⊠ *Ctra. Gral TF-47, km 9, Playa de San Juan, Guía de Isora, Los Cristianos* ☎ *922/126000* ⊕ *www.abamahotelresort.com.*

**Golf Las Américas.** Adjacent to Playa de las Américas, Golf Las Américas has an 18-hole course with views of the ocean and La Gomera Island. ⊠ *Playa de las Américas, Arona, Los Cristianos* ☎ *922/752005* ⊕ *www.golf-tenerife.com.*

**Golf Costa Adeje.** There's a 27-hole course and views of the sea at this club. ⊠ *Fince de los Olivos, Adeje, Los Cristianos* ☎ *922/710000* ⊕ *www.golfcostaadeje.com.*

## WHERE TO EAT

**$$**
SPANISH
✕ **El Lateral 27.** This restaurant's key position in the main shopping street makes it a handy place to stop for a meal after sightseeing, especially since the kitchen is open from 11 am to midnight. If there are free tables, sit outside on the pleasant terrace in the leafy pedestrian street—inside is

less pretty. Specialties include a wide range of salads such as *ensalada de bacalao confitado con pimientos asados* (slow-cooked cod with baked peppers) and fresh fish. $ *Average main: €13* ✉ *Bethencourt Alfonso 27, Santa Cruz* ☎ *922/287774* ⊙ *Closed Sun.*

$ ✗ **Tasca Tagoror.** Opposite the Mencey Hotel, this tiny bar serves Canary
SPANISH cooking in abundant portions at reasonable prices. Tasca Tagoror (it means "meeting place" in Guanche) has a low, beamed ceiling with white walls dashed with gray rock. Seating is on wooden benches or stools around barrels, which doesn't exactly encourage lingering. Food is simple and unpretentious—daily specials might include fried fresh sardines with black potatoes or chicken breast with garlic and mushrooms. The wine list is surprisingly comprehensive. $ *Average main: €8* ✉ *Doctor José Naveiras 9, Santa Cruz* ☎ *922/274163* ⊙ *Closed Sun. June–Oct.*

# INDEX

## PHOTO CREDITS

9 (left), Windstar Cruises. 9 (right), Norwegian Cruise Line. 11 (left), Royal Caribbean International. 11 (right), Princess Cruises. 13 (left), SeaDream Yacht Club. 13 (right), Cunard Line. 14, Juan Manuel Silva/age fotostock. Chapter 1: Planning a European Cruise: 17, Pawel Wysocki/age fotostock. Chapter 2: Cruise Lines & Cruise Ships: 63, Costa Cruises. 68 (top), Michel Verdure/Azamara Cruises. 68 (bottom), Azamara Cruises. 70-73, Azamara Cruises. 74-81, Carnival Cruise Lines. 82-85, Celebrity Cruises. 90 (top) and 90 (bottom), Mike Louagie. 91 (top), Philip Plisson. 91 (bottom) and 92 (top and center), François Lefebvre. 92 (bottom), Eric Laignel. 94-107, Costa Cruises. 108-15, Crystal Cruises. 116-25, Cunard Line. 126-30, Disney Cruise Line. 132-45, Holland America Line. 146-48, Hurtigruten. 150-52, Lindblad Expeditions. 154-65, Louis Cruises. 166-75, MSC Cruises. 176-87, Norwegian Cruise Line. 188-95, Oceania Cruises. 196-200, Paul Gauguin Cruises. 202-11, Princess Cruises. 212-17, Regent Seven Seas. 218-29, Royal Caribbean International. 230-37, Seabourn Cruise Line. 238-43, SeaDream Yacht Club. 244-55, Silversea Cruises. 256-63, Star Clippers. 264-71, Windstar Cruises. Chapter 3: River and Specialty Cruises: 273, Abercrombie & Kent Picture Library. Chapter 4: Western Mediterranea: 299, Glen Allison/age fotostock. Chapter 5: Eastern Mediterranean & Aegean: 507, Peter Adams/age fotostock. Chapter 6: The North Sea: 631, Javier Larrea/age fotostock. Chapter 7: The Baltic: 727, SuperStock/age fotostock. Chapter 8: Norway: 799, Sylvain Grandadam/age fotostock. Chapter 9: Atlantic Islands: 835, Gonzalo Azumendi / age fotostock.

# ABOUT OUR WRITERS

Linda Coffman is a freelance travel writer and the originator of CruiseDiva.com, her Web site, which has been dishing out cruise-travel advice and information since 2000. Before that, she was the cruise guide for About.com. Her columns and articles have appeared in *Cruise Travel, Porthole, Consumers Digest,* and other regional and national magazines; the *Chicago Sun-Times, Denver Post;* and on numerous Web sites, including those for *USA Today,* Fodors.com, and the Travel Channel. She's an avid cruiser, who enjoys sailing on ships of every size to any port worldwide but spends most of her time cruising the Caribbean. Linda thinks cruising is in her Norwegian blood and credits her heritage for a love of all things nautical. When not at sea, she makes her home in Augusta, Georgia, with her husband, Mel. Linda is the primary cruise correspondent for Fodor's and updated all the cruise line and cruise ship sections for this edition.

Although photographer and writer Victoria Tang currently calls Paris home, she has lived and traveled internationally since childhood. She's the author of two guidebooks translated into Dutch, Spanish, and Estonian and has written for numerous publications. Victoria covered river and barge cruising for this edition, as well as many of the Europe-based cruise lines, and she updated our coverage of Corsica and Sardinia.

The following writers updated coverage and contributed valuable insights for the European cruise ports of call: Lola Akinmade-Åkerström (Sweden), Alexia Amvrazi and Adrian Vrettos (Greece), Lindsay Bennett (Malta), David Dunne (Finland), Jane Foster (Croatia, Montenegro), Mike Gonzalez (Scotland), Liz Humphreys (Belgium, Cyprus, the Netherlands), Jennifer Ladonne (France), Bruce Leimsidor (Italy, Slovenia), Giulia Pines (Germany), Anne-Sophie Redisch (Norway), Ellin Stein (England), Jessica Steinberg (Israel), Paul Sullivan (Iceland), Joanna Styles (Portugal, Spain), Gelu Sulugiuc (Denmark), Dorota Wąsik (Estonia, Latvia, Lithuania, Poland, and Ukraine).